CÔTE D'OR

CÔTE D'OR

A Celebration of the Great Wines of Burgundy

BY

CLIVE COATES M.W.

University of California Press
Berkeley   Los Angeles

University of California Press
Berkeley and Los Angeles, California

Published by arrangement with George Weidenfeld & Nicolson Ltd
A division of the Orion Publishing Group

ISBN 0-520-21251-7

Typeset by CST, Eastbourne
Maps by Jenny Dooge
Printed by Butler & Tanner, Frome and London

Printed in the United Kingdom
9 8 7 6 5 4 3 2

By the same author

Claret
The Wines of France
Grands Vins: the Finest Châteaux of Bordeaux and their Wines

CONTENTS

Dedication

To Becky and Russell
And all my friends, the top wine growers in Burgundy

PREFACE

Côte d'Or, A Celebration of the Great Wines of Burgundy: the title says it all. This is not a general guide to the whole of Burgundy from Chablis to the Beaujolais. Nor will you find all the growers in the Hautes-Côtes. It is a celebration of the great wines, the great vineyards and the great growers of the Golden Slope itself, for it is here that the finest expressions of Pinot Noir and Chardonnay in the world are produced.

I have loved red Burgundy for decades, ever since the first really great Pinot Noir passed my lips. Who could fail to be entranced? Here is a wine which can sing like a nightingale, shine forth like a sapphire, intrigue like the most complex of chess problems, and seduce like the first kiss of someone you are just about to fall in love with. Moreover great Burgundy can inspire like a great orator, satisfy like the most subtle of three-star meals, and leave you at peace at the end like the slow movement of a Mozart piano concerto. At its best the wine is complex but not puzzling, profound but not didactic, perfect but not intimidating, and magnificent but never other than friendly.

Chardonnay, too, is a majestic grape variety. There is more competition here from outside Burgundy. There are also more disappointing Chardonnay cellars and wines within Burgundy than for Pinot Noir. Nevertheless the great Pulignys, Meursaults and Chassagnes make the most complete statement white wine is capable of uttering: as 'serious' as their counterparts in red. Great white Burgundy is ripe but dry, austere in the best sense, rich without a suggestion of residual sugar, nutty, honeyed and gently oaky; subtle, profoundly elegant and persistent on the finish. It can age almost as well as the red wine.

Burgundy is the most fascinating, the most complex and the most intractable fine-wine region in the world. It is also the most personal and the most individual. Nowhere is fine wine – occasionally great wine, but also, sadly, frequently disappointing wine - made in such small quantities, in so many different ways, by so many characters, each convinced that only he or she has the magic recipe for success. Nowhere else is wine made which demonstrates quite such an expression of the soil the vines lie in and the particular way they are tended and the wines made and reared. Nowhere else is the personality and the expertise, the passion and the sweat of the wine-maker so closely paralleled by the wine in the glass. This is wine-making at its most committed, yet most humble and most artisanal. But this is where - just from time to time, enough to fill your heart with joy, but sufficiently rarely to be a continued source of exasperation - something so sublimely correct and so breathtakingly individual is created that to experience it is to experience life itself.

Burgundy, says Hugh Johnson, is easier to judge, taste and understand than Bordeaux. Here I must take issue. Appreciate and enjoy: yes. Understand: no. Burgundy is an enigma. I have spent more than thirty years as a wine professional, first as merchant, now as writer. I feel I understand Bordeaux. I doubt I will ever fully comprehend Burgundy. Yet I visit perhaps 250 growers in the Côte d'Or every year. I spend at least three weeks in the summer (mainly sampling whites) and three weeks in the winter (mainly sampling reds) each year, just within the Côte d'Or. Visit Bordeaux, and you can sample with relative ease the wares (usually one single *grand vin*) of the top 150 châteaux. You will have tasted all the best, all made more or less the same way, and you can form your judgement over the vintage and the wines which stand out or fail to sing. To do justice to the Côte d'Or in the same way would entail not only visiting twice as many addresses and sampling perhaps six or ten wines at each, but the time and curiosity to learn the different approaches of each wine-maker. Moreover, while the main wines of Bordeaux can be amassed together to be reviewed subsequently in bottle, to locate all the Burgundies even once several years later is a daunting task. One can only be familiar with the tip of the iceberg.

Everyone who is honest will therefore commence writing a book on Burgundy with not only due humility but a faint sense of futility. Can anyone do justice to such an impossible task? On the other hand, such has been the improvement in quality in the region over the last decade, such has been the reasonableness with prices - in French franc terms no more in 1996 than they were in 1986 - and such has been the emergence of dozens and dozens of unsung Burgundian heroines and heroes producing such very good wine it is unfair not to give them their due recognition and exposure, to aid their commercial success. If my first justification for writing this book is that I have probably covered more ground more regularly in the Côte d'Or than any other writer in the last decade and a half, the second must be the quality and the value of the wines today.

Wine people are generous people. In England, the USA and mainland Europe there are groups of Burgundy-lovers, amateurs and professionals, who have helped me set up tastings, invited me to share bottles and generally given me immeasurable opportunities to increase my experience of Burgundy. In Burgundy itself I have not only sampled at most of the top domaines every year and most of the rest one year in two or three, not only isolated a commune on most visits to pay a call on absolutely everybody in the appellation, but invited those I know best to an annual party to examine the vintage that is ten years old. This is held at the Bouilland farmhouse of Becky Wasserman and her husband Russell Hone. I arrive with a few cases of champagne, some sides of smoked salmon and large quantities of fine mature unpasteurised English cheese (so much better for wine than the French counterparts!). The growers come with their bottles. It is fun as well as instructive.

What I have also done, as you will see in the second section, is to make an in-depth study of some sixty-one of the top domaines. This has involved the best part of a day going round each *climat* that the estate exploits, discussing the *terroir* and the viticulture, moving to the winery to talk about wine-making, making a vertical tasting of one of their wines, and then remaining to uncover the history, the philosophy and everything else under the sun at an extended lunch afterwards. Understand the man or woman behind the wine and all the background that goes with it, and you will better comprehend the wines that are made. To these estates and the persons responsible - and to their ancestors - I owe a particular word of thanks.

INTRODUCTION

Today's Côte d'Or is the most exciting wine region in the world. There has been an explosion of quality over the last decade and a half. The villages are vibrant with a new generation of qualified, talented, committed men and women, infinitely curious about all the wines of the world, willing and able to share their experience and expertise with their neighbours and to taste their wines one with another, and continually seeking to fine-tune their techniques of viticulture, vinification and *élevage* in order further to increase the quality of the bottles they are producing. There is one goal: perfection.

Moreover, while no-one would call Burgundy cheap – for all sorts of reasons: not least the price of land, the pitifully small scale of the operations and the impossibility of making top-quality wine without reducing yields to a minimum, the wine cannot be inexpensive – prices have remained remarkably stable over the last ten years. A glance at ex-cellars lists will show a significant rise between 1982 and 1985, since when (rising in 1989 but falling thereafter) they have remained at a par. Though the short but excellent 1995 vintage has naturally caused an increase over 1994 levels, the wines in real terms are better value today than they were a decade ago. It is only sad that in English-speaking countries the rate of exchange has sunk against the French franc and we foreigners have not been able to benefit from this generosity.

And there has been a further cause for celebration. Since 1985 Burgundy has enjoyed a twelve-year (as I write this introduction) and perhaps continuing run of good to very fine vintages. Though one could argue that the average vintage standard for white wines has been not as high as for the reds, these reds have not produced a less than 'good' vintage year since 1984 – and the best 1984s, though ageing now – are by no means to be decried. God seems to be smiling on the resurgence of modern Burgundy. In 1985, again in 1988 and 1989, triumphantly so in 1990, again in 1991, 1993 and 1995 we have red-wine vintages which are very good if not very fine. Even in the softer and less consistent vintages such as 1992 and 1994 there is much to enjoy, and wines which can be enjoyed soon, preventing the infanticide of the greater years. 1996 is yet again a very successful vintage.

Burgundy has evolved considerably since the early 1980s. Growers now act like *négociants*, bottling and commercialising their wares as well as tending the vines and making the wine. Increasingly, perhaps to make up for land they have lost as estates get split up in the natural process of being passed down from one generation to another, or as leases and share-cropping arrangements come to an end, some growers have set up in a small way as merchants, and buy in others' fruit, must or finished wine.

Merchants, for their part, are increasingly acting as growers. Most now prefer not to buy finished wine but to contract for the fruit and vinify it themselves alongside the produce of their own estates, these estates having themselves been enlarged by acquisition over the years. In their dealing with their suppliers *négociants* are more and more taking an active role in the vineyards, a partnership which hitherto did not exist.

Unlike their fathers and grandfathers – and unlike today in previous generations it would have been unheard of for a female to take an active role in the wine-making – today's Burgundian wine-maker has been to wine-school. While not all you are taught at the *Viti* in Beaune or the University of Dijon is entirely compatible with the role of a producer of serious *premier* or *grand cru*, growers today have the technical background to help comprehend why it is that they do what they do, and what would be the result if they modified their approach. Today they have the knowledge and the confidence to help them experiment in their search for improvement, and what could be the greater impetus towards higher standards than the fact that it is your name that is eventually going to be on the bottle?

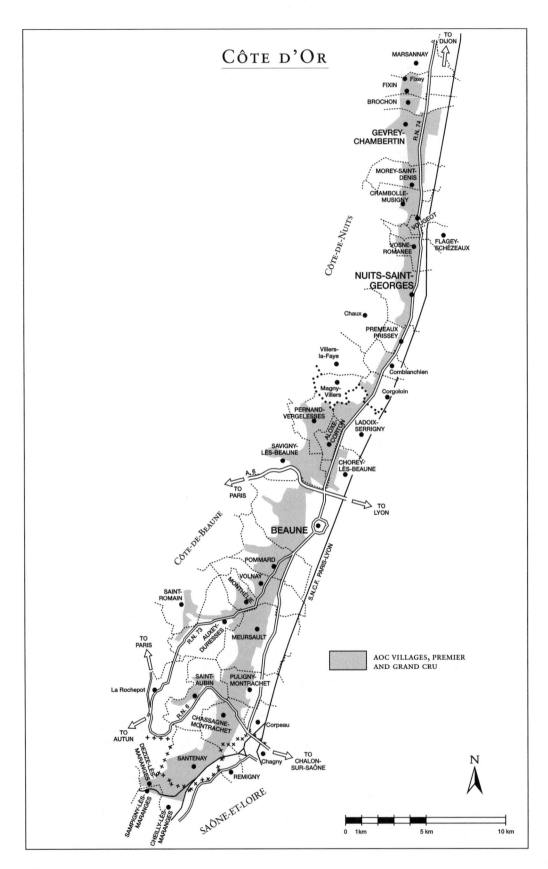

CÔTE D'OR

TO DIJON

MARSANNAY

FIXIN • Fixey

BROCHON

GEVREY-CHAMBERTIN

R.N. 74

MOREY-SAINT-DENIS

CHAMBOLLE-MUSIGNY

CÔTE-DE-NUITS

VOUGEOT

VOSNE-ROMANÉE

FLAGEY-ECHÉZEAUX

NUITS-SAINT-GEORGES

Chaux •

PREMEAUX PRISSEY

Villers-la-Faye •

Comblanchien •

Magny-Villers

Corgoloin

PERNAND-VERGELESSES

LADOIX-SERRIGNY

ALOXE-CORTON

SAVIGNY-LÈS-BEAUNE

CHOREY-LÈS-BEAUNE

A. 6

TO PARIS

TO LYON

CÔTE-DE-BEAUNE

BEAUNE

S.N.C.F. PARIS-LYON

POMMARD

VOLNAY

MONTHÉLIE

SAINT-ROMAIN

R.N. 73

AUXEY-DURESSES

MEURSAULT

TO PARIS

AOC VILLAGES, PREMIER AND GRAND CRU

SAINT-AUBIN

PULIGNY-MONTRACHET

La Rochepot •

R.N. 6

CHASSAGNE-MONTRACHET

Corpeau •

TO AUTUN

DEZIZE-LÈS-MARANGES

SANTENAY

Chagny •

TO CHALON-SUR-SAÔNE

REMIGNY

SAMPIGNY-LÈS-MARANGES

CHEILLY-LÈS-MARANGES

SAÔNE-ET-LOIRE

N

0   1km   5 km   10 km

A generation or more ago Burgundy was on its knees. Over-fertilisation in the 1960s and 1970s, the introduction of high-yield, low-quality clones and the clamp-down on bolster wines from the south of France and Algeria led to wine which was thin, pallid, fruitless and short-lived. The vineyard is still weak in this respect, for it takes time and money to replant and Burgundy's reputation has taken a long time to recover. But at least the problems are being faced. Good husbandry, *biologique* if not *biodynamique* is the order of the day. Growers understand the crucial importance of low yields. Today's clones are judged by quality rather than quantity. Action can be taken to reduce erosion, sterilise the vineyard against viral diseases, improve the drainage, counteract the effects of past fertilisation mistakes, space out the fruit to reduce depredation, protect it against rot, increase the efficiency of the ripening process, mitigate against the effects of last-minute rain, eliminate all but the very best fruit before vinification begins, concentrate the must by equalising the solid-liquid ratio, control the fermentations, improve the wine's ability to settle out its impurities naturally, and prevent it from contamination and deterioration during the process of *élevage*: in short to translate as purely as possible the very best fruit into the very best wine.

Together with a new understanding, a new mind-set and new techniques, is new equipment. Cellars are temperature-controlled where necessary, and so are the fermentation vats. There are all sorts of new machines to help the wine-maker in his task, to reduce his physical labour in the vineyard and in the cellar, and to enable him to control the wine-making process in exactly the way he wishes to proceed. Moreover today's winery is increasingly spotlessly clean. The old, bug-infested barrels have been taken out and burnt, and if there is sometimes a little too much new oak, this problem is not as bad as it was a few years ago.

Wine-making, at least for great Burgundy, is, however, not so much a creative approach as most outsiders think. Wine-makers can destroy, you will be told, through incompetence or ignorance, but they cannot make any better wine than the potential quality of the fruit, the *matière première* in the first place. The wine-maker's role is one of preventive medicine. And increasingly the move is towards a hands-off approach. The more you manipulate the wine the more you risk reducing what is good and individual about it. The greater the quality of the fruit at the time of the harvest the better the possibility of the wine. The last twenty years have seen a revolution in the cellar and in the understanding of wine-making. We are now in the middle of as important a revolution out there in the vineyard.

BURGUNDY: THE ARCANE AND THE FRAGMENTED

Burgundy is considered complicated, difficult and confusing. It is certainly complex, with an extraordinary variety of individual vineyards, estates and wine-making styles and techniques crammed into a very small region.

In the Côte d'Or there are some 5,500 hectares producing some 245,500 hectolitres (2.7 million cases) of wine a year (all figures exclude generics), of which 78.5 per cent is red wine from the Pinot Noir and 21.5 per cent is white wine from the Chardonnay. There are two village-overlapping appellations (Côte-de-Beaune-Villages and Côte-de-Nuits-Villages), and twenty-five village appellations, most of which can produce both red and white wine (plus Côte-de-Beaune, not to be confused with the above and described on page 198). Within the villages there are a total of 476 *premiers crus*, probably an equal number of *lieux-dits* which are not *premiers crus*, and thirty-two *grands crus*. Moreover there are quite a number of special wine place-names individual to particular growers - such as Bouchard Père et Fils' Vigne-de-l'Enfant-Jésus, from Beaune's *premier cru* Les Grèves, or Louis Latour's Château Corton-Grancey.

With the exception of the latter there are very few monopolies, whole appellations or vineyards within the fief of a single owner. Most vineyards - or *climats*, to use the Burgundian expression - are divided up among a number of individual owners. The most commonly cited example of this is the 50 ha Clos-de-Vougeot: 100 plots and 80 owners, an average of 62 ares each.

It is this fragmentation which causes the confusion. Unlike Bordeaux, an area of large estates producing (usually) a single *grand vin*, Burgundy is a region of small domaines spread over a number of different *climats*, producing everything from various generics to, if they are lucky, *grand cru*. And of course the quantities of each wine produced will be in Bordeaux terms minuscule. Château Lafite produces 21,000 cases a year of *grand vin* and 15,000 cases of Carruades. Romanée-Conti, the vineyard, yields 540 cases, and Romanée-Conti, the domaine, 8,310. A typical top Burgundian domaine, today marketing most of its produce in bottle - a little may be sold off in bulk at the outset to help with the cash flow - would probably be one like that of Michel Lafarge in Volnay: 10 ha, but commercialising ten different wines.

Burgundy seems perplexing because of its nomenclature. During the eighty or so years after 1848 - Gevrey was the first, Morey the last - the Côte d'Or villages complicated matters by tagging on the name of their best vineyard on to that of the village, in order to raise the prestige of these lesser wines. Thus Gevrey became Gevrey-Chambertin, Aloxe Aloxe-Corton, while both Puligny and Chassagne chose Montrachet, whose *climat* straddles their borders, as a suffix. Meanwhile in Gevrey, but thankfully only in that commune, certain *climats*, later to be confirmed as *grands crus*, claimed Chambertin, to which they were contiguous, also as a suffix. Thus Gevrey-Chambertin is a village, Charmes-Chambertin a *grand cru*. The only solution to these complications is knowledge.

There is another tradition, now a legal rule, which needs appreciation. The thirty-two *grands crus* exist in their own right. No further geographical clarification is necessary. A name such as Le Musigny says it all. The *premier cru* and *lieu-dit* designations, on the other hand, need to be preceded and qualified by the name of the village. Thus, a wine from Les Amoureuses is described as Chambolle-Musigny, Les Amoureuses, with or without (this is optional) the mention that the *climat* is a *premier cru*. Each *premier cru* is an appellation in its own right.

So if Burgundy seems on the face of it difficult to comprehend at first, a little perseverance will soon clarify matters. And the solution to the fact that on the face of it a number of people seem to be offering the same wine is to understand that even more than the geographical origin it is the name of the domaine which made the wine that is important. Bordeaux châteaux names are brand names, and the top ones have a classification, which is a help to the consumer - even if that of 1855 is somewhat out of date. It is the land in Burgundy, not the wine-maker or his estate, which is classified. The classification is based on geographical possibility, not on the quality in the bottle. And there are good wine-makers and bad. One grower's Chambertin can be sublime, another's beneath contempt. In the pages that follow you will see a personal classification of these wine-makers, something which will never be attempted officially. I hope it helps clarify the level of individual estate quality today.

How Burgundy Works

Once upon a time, back before the French Revolution, the vineyards of the Côte d'Or were owned by the church and the aristocracy. Even then they were fragmented and leased out, and often at second, third or even fourth hand, the ultimate owners letting to the local *bourgeoisie* who then sub-let to tenant farmers who actually did the work.

Essentially there were, and still are, two forms of leasing arrangement. The first (*fermage*) was a simple rental arrangement, the tenant paying in cash, after which he was a free man, but responsible for all expenses. The second (*métayage*) was a share-cropping agreement, the landlord usually continuing to pay the capital costs (replanting and so on) and being recompensed by a portion, normally half, of the fruit. The tenant could render his share in grapes, or go as far as making the wine and selling it (in bulk or in bottle) on his landlord's behalf. But the principle was a share of the crop to each side.

Employees, too, were recompensed in different ways. One would be the usual so much per hour or month, under the direct supervision of the *patron*. The second was a looser arrangement: *à la tâche*. Here the worker was paid by the job, for example for looking after a plot of land for the whole year. When and how the job was done – and how time-consuming the task – then lay in the worker's hands.

These arrangements still continue. It is impossible to assess what proportion of the Côte d'Or vineyard is leased rather than exploited by the owner (for very many leasing arrangements are between close members of the same family and are in practice owner-occupier, so to speak, rather than rented off), but my guess is a good third.

These leases normally run on an on-going nine-year basis until the *vigneron* reaches retirement age. Landlords are not allowed, even at the end of the nine years, to rescind the lease unless they are prepared to work the land themselves. A fortunate incompetent, therefore, can be in for life. In the past decade two great domaines, Lafon and Méo-Camuzet, have taken back their *métayers'* – highly competent, it has to be underlined – vines as the leases came to their end. Others though, even when the father has reached sixty, have been prepared to sign a new lease with the son.

Ownership of the Côte d'Or vineyard, operationally already largely split up into family exploitable portions, was totally transformed by the French Revolution. The lands of the church were very quickly seized, and sold off in 1791. Those of the nobility followed a couple of years later. It was not, however, the peasant farmer who benefited. He did not have the means. It was the *bourgeoisie*, in many cases those who had been around before 1789. The *Code Napoléon* abolished primogeniture, however, and thus began the fragmentation of ownership which has led inexorably to the morcellation of Burgundy today.

The grower, then, can be an owner in his own right, an exploiter on behalf of his parents or the rest of his family, or he can be a *fermier* or a *métayer*, or indeed a combination of the lot! While today almost everybody keeps a little back for bottling for selling at the garden gate or home consumption, the next great divide is between those who sell the bulk of their domaine off either as fruit, must or young wine, and those who keep the majority back for eventual sale in bottle. The last fifteen years have seen amazing changes here. In the early 1970s hardly 15 per cent of Côte d'Or wine was domaine-bottled. Today the proportion is well over 50 per cent, and the more prestigious the origin the more likely it will be to leave Burgundy with the owner's, not a *négociant*'s, name on it. What this means, of course, is that fine Burgundy can today only really come direct from the domaines.

Merchant or grower, the next step after the wine is made is to sell it. The bigger firms will have their own team of salesmen and agents within metropolitan France. The smaller growers will tend to go direct, hoping to place their wines in the top Michelin-starred restaurants, a sure way to fame and fortune. Both will do extensive mail-order business within France.

Exporting can be a nightmare, certainly outside the EC where different rules and regulations apply. For instance capacity within the Community is expressed in centilitres, e.g. 75 cl. Officially this won't do for the US, whose authorities insist on 750 ml on the label, though it means exactly the same thing. For the larger *négociant* this is a small problem. The small grower can be forgiven if he decides it is not worth the bother.

The established merchants will tend to export directly to an agent, the smaller will deal through a broker, who can be established either in Burgundy or in the exporting country. Sales, naturally, are almost by allocation, especially for the limited stock of the better wines. Only a small amount of retail outlets will eventually get hold of some stock, for no one domaine can deal with everybody. Moreover, in order to keep their place in the queue, the bad must be bought with the good, the Bourgogne *rouge* together with the Richebourg, the badly quoted vintage together with the triumphant successes.

The implications of this on the consumer who wishes to buy top Burgundy are discussed on page 000.

THE ROLE OF THE *NÉGOCIANT*

As mentioned above, until very recently the vast majority of Burgundy was sold under a *négociant* or merchant label. Individual land-holdings were, and continue to be, tiny, prices were low, and the growers simply did not have the wherewithal or the space, as well as the experience, which would enable them to look after the wine, bottle it, and subsequently market it. It was simpler and more economic to divide the process: the grower tended the vines and made the wine, the merchant – or brokers on his behalf – would tour the area soon after, buy up the stock, blend parcels of the same wine together into a more economic unit, and see to its sale. The advantage to the grower was payment sooner rather than later, and no need for any investment in a maturation cellar or bottling plant. Indeed his responsibilities ceased after the malos had finished and the wine was collected. For the merchant the attraction was the availability of the pick of the crop, without the capital expense of the ownership of land, and the benefits of scale: the creation of a brand image, and so on.

As I have said, the position has radically changed since the early 1980s. Yet the role of the *négociant*, particularly at the bottom end of the hierarchical scale – and, it must be said, at the lower end of the quality scale too – is still important. These wines are now rarely seen on the export market, in Britain and the USA. But a walk through a French supermarket is instructive.

THE ROLE OF THE MEDIA

Of increasing importance over the last fifteen years – an influence which is both beneficial and malign – is the wine-writer. Wine-writers can range from journalists who know nothing whatsoever about wine to those who wear another hat, that of wine professional, most of the time. Here I must declare an interest. Today I am a writer; yesterday (that is, up to 1984) I was a wine-merchant. I still consider myself a 'professional' whatever that may precisely mean, and I have a certificate, having passed the Master of Wine examination, to prove at least some competence in this respect.

Prior to the media-isation of the world of wine, reputations took time to expand, particularly in a region of reduced quantity as the Côte d'Or. About the only way to by-pass the slow progress was to get your wine into a three-star restaurant. Equally it was years before a decline in quality was recognised. Today, a newcomer like Dominique Laurent, who produced his first vintage in 1992, achieves fame almost overnight. And the under-achievers, either permanently or temporarily, can be fingered from the outset. The consumer is advised before he or she even receives his or her opening offer. This, surely, is on the face of it to be welcomed: good honest up-to-date opinion, informed and unprejudiced, guiding the private customer to spend his money in the best way possible.

But . . . life sadly is not perfect. Wine critics are often mis-informed, or just plain pig-ignorant. They *are* prejudiced. They set about doing the job of sampling Burgundy in the wrong way and at the wrong time. They try to imply that there is only one way to judge a wine, i.e. according to the personal taste of that critic, forgetting how subjective and temperamental taste can be, and also ignoring that most wine is made for being consumed and judged mature with food and friends and not immature alongside numerous other bottles. The bad critics look at Pinot through Cabernet-tinted spectacles and so criticise it for being what it never set out to be. And generally they cause anger in the Côte d'Or and confusion at home. Moreover, and this is a situation which is almost universal in the USA, though thankfully largely absent in Britain, the trade has allowed itself to be emasculated. Instead of continuing to buy and sell on their own professional judgement, they have consigned themselves into the role of mere purveyors. They buy what the *Wine Spectator* and the *Wine Advocate* score highly and they sell their wares by proclaiming the magazines' marks. It is totally crazy.

The only way to become a competent judge of young Burgundy is to spend many years at the coal-face: to go down there as often as possible, to listen a lot, to say little, and to learn much. This is what I do. Sadly I seem to be largely alone. There are many growers I visit who have never seen another writer; many cellars who would dearly love to welcome others to explain what they are trying to do. Let us not forget the hundreds of different ways Burgundy can be made. All you have to do is to permute zero to 100 per cent stems, zero to 100 per cent new wood, fermenting at 25° all the way up to 35°C and above, cold soaking or no. All of these *can* make great Burgundy. But you need to understand what the grower is doing, and the person him or herself, in order to understand and be able to judge the wine.

Burgundy is a wine which suffers more from manipulations such as racking, fining and bottling than more tannic wines. It is therefore advisable to descend when the majority of the wines are in good form. June is a good time for whites, provided the malos are not late to complete; November a good time for last year's reds. It is necessary not only to understand where the wine is in its development, but also, for instance, whether the *cuvée* is from young vines, and whether what you are being given to sample is the finished blend: in short how close is what you are tasting to the finished article? If what you are given to taste is a sample from the single new oak cask (out of six) of a wine which was racked the previous week and to which is to be added half as much again of a separate *cuvée* of young-vine wine, you are wasting your time (and that of your reader). If, further, you are doing your sampling in a hotel or another cellar among a hundred other samples in a great rush, you risk missing the fragrance, delicacy and complexity - which is what Pinot Noir and Chardonnay in Burgundy are all about - in favour of extreme colour and quantities of tannin, alcohol and new oak. And you are falling into the trap of judging Burgundy by its immediacy rather than by its true potential.

Burgundy has been much maligned - more so than any other region - by certain elements of the media. Robert Parker proclaimed that the region was a dinosaur of poor quality and high prices: totally the opposite of the truth. The *Wine Spectator* has criticised the increasing bunch of estates who refuse to play ball with its *modus operandi* and submit samples for mammoth tastings. Both arrive in the region only a few months after the wines have been bottled, before they have had a chance to recover, and attempt to rate every wine in percentage points out of 100. The time for accurate ratings such as this is much later, a year or two after bottling and shipment, dispassionately in groups of twenty-five or so. At the outset it is sufficient merely to note how successful the estate has been, given its reputation and the standing in the hierarchy of each of its wines.

Moreover the British media has been accused, if not of being corrupt, of having vested interests. It so happens that most of us who write seriously about Burgundy are, or were, professionals. The majority are Masters of Wine. In my view this is nothing but a good thing, we have years of experience behind us to back up our judgements, qualifications to prove our competence. The three best recent books on Burgundy have been written by Anthony Hanson, a merchant who has been scrupulously meticulous about pointing out where he has a personal and commercial involvement; by Remington Norman, who used to be a full-time merchant but is no longer; and by Serena Sutcliffe, who used to represent a couple of houses in Burgundy together with David Peppercorn her husband, but is now the director of the wine department of Sotheby's. All three are Masters of Wine. To those who accuse these professionals or ex-professionals of pulling punches, over-praising or whatever, I say where is your proof? What is perhaps also noteworthy is that while there are many MWs who have crossed over to become writers, there has so far, and not for want of trying, been only one journalist or writer who has successfully sat the Master of Wine exam. Give me a professional approach every time!

How Top Burgundy is Made

Geology and the Concept of *Terroir*

Of all the various factors which influence a wine's character and flavour - the variety, the viticultural, vinification and maturation methods, and of course the climate - the most fundamental, the one least open to radical alteration or change, is the land in which the grower has planted his or her vines. The land is *there*. It faces in a particular direction, it drains so, it is protected so, its physical, chemical and biological make-up is such and such. One can tinker at the edges, but one cannot really modify the basic structure.

It is here, literally on the bedrock, that the difference between great wine and merely good wine lies. Some vineyards can produce great wine, others never will. The Côte d'Or consists of a 40-kilometre, south-east-facing slope where in the middle of the incline all the physical characteristics of the 'right place' lie on a soil and sub-soil of the 'right type' and great wine can be produced.

Moreover such is the complexity, within a basic geological formula, and such is the multiplicity of different aspects, micro-climates and other elements within the concept of the word *terroir*, that you only have to move a matter of a few dozen metres up, down or sideways and while the wine is fundamentally the same, it will be, yes, just that little bit different: sufficiently separate to merit being called by another name and to be bottled apart. It is for this reason that we can accept that as many as 476 *premiers crus* and thirty-two *grands crus*, some of them very small, others impossibly tiny, *are* justified. Find a grower who can offer you several adjoining *climats*, all of the same age and clone, all made in exactly the same way, and you will notice the differences. These are real; and they will be the same whatever the vintage, whatever the climate.

There are limited places in the world - more than we realise today, for some are still to be discovered - but few and far between nonetheless, where the right choice of grape complements great *terroir* and can produce great wine. The Côte d'Or is manifestly one of them. With modern technology good wine can be produced anywhere, with the obvious climatic limits, even on the quasi-hydroponic sands of the Salins du Midi in the south of France. Great wine is rare because the great *terroirs* are rare.

This conveys by implication an important duty on the Burgundian wine-maker. If he possesses great land and is unable or unwilling to do his utmost to produce as great a wine as he can from it, then, quite simply, he should be taken out and shot and the vines given to one of the other small domaines where the proprietor *does* take his or her responsibilities seriously. Otherwise humanity is being deprived of its just deserts, and that is too important a matter to be left unattended.

The geology of the Côte d'Or is complex but not inexplicable. During the time of the dinosaurs, the Jurassic period some 195 to 135 million years ago, what is now Burgundy was underwater. In this sea lived, died and were deposited on the bottom countless small animals such as oysters, molluscs of various types, sea urchins, chrinoids and brachiopods. The soil that has resulted is rich in these fossils. Clay, sand and gravel, formed out of the decomposition and erosion of other soils, combined with the calcium carbonate in the water to deposit marl and other variations of mudstone. Elsewhere a third type of rock was formed by the precipitation of carbonate of lime from sea-water and its subsequent settling out to form oolitic limestone.

Somewhat later, beginning about 35 million years ago in the Oligocene period and continuing into the Miocene (from 26 million years ago onwards), as the Alps and other European mountain ranges were being formed, a rift began to form the flatland and lagoons of the Bresse, the Saône and the Doubs. Where, abruptly, the Morvan came to its easterly end and fell into the plain, there was exposed for all to see, and facing precisely in the direction where it would be bathed in sun from the first rays of the morning, a golden slope. Later it would be found to be an ideal site for the grape.

The Côte d'Or, then, is largely limestone, but limestone of a number of different types, thicknesses, permeability, hardnesses, colour and percentage of clay therein. There are faults. There are valleys formed by rivers tumbling out of the higher ground from the west. There are places where there are a number of different surface soils within the space of 50 metres. On most slopes the age and character of the rock changes abruptly as you descend from the trees above to the road below.

In essence the oldest of the limestones, the fossil rich Bajocian, on top of which can be found Bathonian, and between which is a softer marly limestone, will be found in the northern Côte-de-Nuits. A sub-variety of the Bathonian limestone is the pink marble of Prémeaux and the more creamy marble of Comblanchien, and this will be found in Nuits-Saint-Georges.

Once you move into the Côte-de-Beaune these older limestones sink beneath the ground, to surface again in Chassagne, and the surface limestone rock is the later Callovian, Argovian, or, most recent of all, Rauracian, containing fossilised sea-urchins. These limestones are in general more prone to erosion. There are parts where they have degenerated into what the Burgundian call *lave*, and can be easily broken up manually.

As important as the bedrock is the surface soil. Up-slope there is little of this, erosion being a perennial problem in the Côte d'Or, particularly in the Côte-de-Nuits. The earth can consist of any blend of decomposed limestone debris, harder stones such as flints and even larger rocks, gravels of various sizes, sands and accumulations of clay. In general there is more clay and more nitrogenous matter, and of course worse drainage, at the foot of the slope; the least clay and the most 'pure' limestone, hence providing an auspicious home for the Chardonnay, at the top.

The golden slope is divided into two halves. In the north, the Côte-de-Nuits, the aspect is in principle to the east, the slope is in general steeper, and the width of vineyard area narrower, hardly a couple of hundred metres at Prémeaux. Beyond the hill of Corton the orientation of the Côte-de-Beaune turns towards the south-east, there are more valleys into the hillsides, the slope is more gentle and the east-west extent of vines is wider: at Savigny and Chorey almost 4 kilometres.

CLIMATE

Less so than in Alsace, more so than in Bordeaux, Burgundy enjoys a continental climate. What this means is that the climate is more uneven than at the coast. Yet if you take all four climatic parameters together (rainfall, relative humidity, temperature and hours of sunshine), the climates in Bordeaux and Burgundy are really very similar.

The Côte d'Or is drier, particularly in July and August, than both the Côtes Chalonnaise and Mâconnais and the Hautes-Côtes. Overall precipitation corresponds very closely to that of Bordeaux, but is less even; there being more very heavy storms - often accompanied by hail - and more periods of drought. Early spring (February, March and April) are dry months, as is July, but May and June can be wet, which does not help the flowering. Luckily September and October tend to be dry as well, which helps prevent rot.

Relative humidity, as a result of the proximity of the ocean, is greater in Bordeaux than Burgundy at the beginning of the day, but is lower by the end of it. Overall the figures are very close. Burgundy, though, is both cooler and more sunny than Bordeaux, not so much because it is less hot in the summer as because it is colder in winter and the days are longer. It is warmer, however, in Dijon than it is in the Côte Chalonnaise, but warmer still in Beaune, and being marginally further to the north, as well as inland, late summer days are longer and sunnier than in Bordeaux, helping maturity. The Côte-de-Beaune starts picking around the time the Merlots are collected in the Gironde. The Côte-de-Nuits on the same sort of day the Cabernets are attacked, a week later.

Burgundy, however, has a great advantage over Bordeaux. In the Gironde there are in general larger estates and more grape varieties. Hence a harvest which can extend over three weeks. In the Côte d'Or a week is usually maximum, and a glance at the projected weather forecast can ensure that the growers' best sites are reserved for collection during the best periods, if the weather seems inclement.

GRAPE VARIETIES

Pinot Noir

There are a very large number of Pinots, both beyond the simple Pinot Noir and within the aegis of this single variety. A gypsy of a grape, it has been called. And if by gypsy you think of the temperamental Carmen, then you have got it in one. The variety is sensitive to cold, both during the winter and during the flowering. It buds early, making spring frost a potential hazard, and ripens early. The Pinot Noir produces a small cylindrical-conical cluster of densely packed, slightly oval berries. As a result of their being close together, and the Pinot Noir skin being thin, grey rot can be a serious problem if the weather turns humid towards harvest time.

As important are two other traits. Wine made from Pinot Noir is much more susceptible than other varieties to over-production. The concentration and character dissolve rapidly if the yield is excessive. And this point of diminishing returns starts at a much lower level than with other varieties. A Cabernet or a Merlot can yield satisfactory wine at 55 even 60 hl/ha. The limit for Pinot Noir is 45, and apart from exceptional years such as 1990, anything over 35 for *grand cru* and 40 for *premier cru* is an admission that the grower has not set his sights as high as he should.

Moreover Pinot Noir is very susceptible to temperature as it reaches the end of its ripening cycle. As with other varieties the wine can be mean and unripe if the sun fails to shine, but if the weather is too hot and roasted a Pinot Noir wine is also prone to being coarse and leaden-footed.

It is said to be an old variety, close to wild *Vitis vinifera*. There are a number of legends as to how it arrived in the region. One concerns the Celtic tribe, the Aedui, ancestors of today's Burgundians, who were seduced by the delicious wines of Lombardy, invaded Italy to enjoy them further, and stayed there until they were forced out by the emerging Roman empire a couple of hundred years later in about 200 BC. They brought the Pinot Noir back with them. A nice story, until you start looking for Pinots in northern Italy.

Other historians like to suggest the Pinot is indigenous, and only needed to be adapted from the wild - by the Aedui or anyone else. A third, following on from the generally accepted origin of French viticulture lying with the establishment of a Phoacean Greek colony in what is now Marseilles in around 600 BC, and the gradual dissemination of the science of vine farming up the Rhône and beyond, cite the origin of the Pinot Noir and other local grapes in the Middle East. What is not explained by any of these theories, but is clear from Roman records, is that wine was not definitely *made* in Burgundy (as opposed to being consumed) until about AD 200. And the first recorded mention of the Pinot Noir dates from as late as 1375.

A Pinot Noir wine is rarely a blockbuster. Fragrance, finesse and delicacy are the keynotes, not size, muscle and overwhelming tannins. Because of the thickness of the skins being less than, say, the Cabernet Sauvignon or the Syrah, there is less colour, less tannin and less body. Nevertheless there should be no lack of intensity, grip, depth and complexity.

The flavour of a young Pinot Noir is of slightly sweet, freshly crushed, soft summer fruits: a fragrant, silky, multi-faceted and delicately elegant combination of raspberries, strawberries, cherries, mulberries and currants of different types. Concentrated young Burgundy often offers up a hint of coffee. From the oak – and this element should not be excessive – there can come vanilla and fondant, mocha and cigar-box. The character of Pinot Noir is fragile and elusive though, and it should not be swamped, either by too much oak, or excessive maceration.

As a Pinot Noir evolves it takes on a totally different character. As with all wines the spice elements of the flavours of maturity begin to emerge. The oak changes into cedar or sandalwood. An animal, gamey, almost vegetal character begins to emerge. The fruit flavours deepen, incorporating hints of damson and blackberry. The whole thing becomes more sensuous. The residual flavours are sweet, but naturally sweet, ethereal, multi-faceted, totally magical.

Sadly, few of us get the chance to consume magical old Burgundy. Some wines are just not made for this sort of long-term keeping. Others come from less illustrious vintages, less auspicious *terroirs*. Most are consumed far in advance of their prime, for the simple reason that there is nothing else to buy within our budgets. Some authorities misleadingly believe Burgundy doesn't keep. (Nonsense: all properly balanced wine will keep much longer than we think it will. Hence tasting notes of vigorous 1945s, 1947s and 1949s further on in these pages.)

There is a fashion, encouraged if not insisted upon by certain American writers, for Burgundies to be reared, whatever their provenance, in 100 per cent new oak, for the wine to have the deepest colour possible – or the reverse, to be marked down if the colour is light – to be big and tannic, and generally the sort of wine a Pinot Noir is impossible of being. I shall discuss these 'misnomers' in the pages that follow. Suffice it to say here that these wines do not age and will not make the lovely fragrant old Burgundies that, every now and then, we are lucky enough to encounter: Burgundy which sets our hearts afire.

Chardonnay

Though in the past called Pinot-Chardonnay, Chardonnay in fact has no close connection with the Pinot family. The variety is fairly vigorous. It starts and finishes its growing season just a little after the Pinot Noir but is nevertheless also susceptible to spring frost. *Coulure* is also a problem. It forms a small, relatively compact winged-cylindrical cluster of small berries, not so densely closed as that of the Pinot Noir, and so is less prone to grey rot. Over-maturity is much more of a problem. At this stage, somewhere between full ripeness and the onset of *pourriture noble*, the acidity of the grape is at its lowest, and the wines therefrom will attenuate quickly. In vineyards where the vines are over-cropped – and Chardonnay too has its low limits if the objective is truly *premier* and *grand cru* wine: say 38 hl/ha for *grand cru*, 43 for *premier cru* and 48 for village wine – the fruit can pass from only-just-ripe to over-ripe without ever having become properly concentrated and will never have sufficient acidity to produce a balanced and stylish wine.

Chardonnay grows well on soils with more limestone and less clay. If the latter is too preponderant the wine will be leaden-footed, heavy and four-square. Hence, in general, up at the top of the slope is where it will thrive best. Moreover, requiring less sun-hours to ripen, and in any case not being vinified with its stems, the Chardonnay can make good wine where the red results would be a bit weak and thin. Hence the preference for Chardonnay up in the valleys at higher altitudes and west-facing slopes.

The best Côte d'Or white Burgundies are, of course, vinified in wood, a percentage of which will be new. If the vineyard has not been over-cropped, Chardonnay, with its blend of ripe, subtle, opulent peachy or nutty-buttery fruit and oak, and with its round, rich, mouth-feel is one of the great wine flavours in the world. And it can age exceptionally well in bottle.

VITICULTURE

Back from the Brain-dead: Movements Towards a Living Soil

It is alarming to see how much damage could have been be done so rapidly. Through a combination of ignorance, negligence, cynicism and a regard for solely short-term profit (and damn the consequences), the Burgundian vineyard was reduced to the status almost of a desert, in terms of its natural nutrient and micro-flora and fauna content, in little over thirty years. The misuse of fertilisers, chemical weedkillers and heavier and heavier tractors had the effect not only of neutralising and homogenising the soil, of compacting it, so rendering it less permeable (and more prone to erosion), and of increasing the amounts of nitrogen and potassium therein, so reducing the acidity, but, by evading the need to plough encouraged the vine to be lazy and only extend its roots on the surface where the artificial nutrient was, rather than deep into the bed rock, where it would find whatever was special and unique about its particular *climat*.

It has taken a mere thirty years to go downhill. It may take more than that to climb up. There are some vineyards today, not fertilised since the end of the 1970s, which *still* have too high a potassium content. There are others which because there are important root systems close to the surface cannot now be ploughed, or the vine would be decapacitated. We will have to wait until the vineyard is replanted. There are still vines belonging to that infamous strain, the Pinot Droit, planted for quantity and not quality in the 1960s. Vineyard husbandry is a long-term process.

Happily, almost at the brink, and helped by agricultural engineers such as Claude Bourguignon and other experts, the Burgundian *vigneron* began to realise he was not only ruining his soil but taking out the very individuality which lies at the heart of the word *terroir*. Today everybody is at least *biologique* - which I would term merely common-sensical logic - or *biodynamique*.

Biologique

This starts with the principle that what is unique about a particular *terroir* must at all costs be preserved. Not only is this *terroir* an expression of the chemical composition of the surface soil and the sub-soil beneath it, but it is represented by the micro-flora and -fauna within it. Those who are proponents of natural yeasts will point out that each individual site will or should have its own family of natural yeasts. The soil must be able to breathe. Hence it must be ploughed. One of the beneficial side-effects of traditional ploughing is that the earth can be banked up against the vine in the autumn, so protecting it against cold. To avoid compacting the soil too much, a new lighter breed of tractors with balloon wheels is being evolved.

It has been discovered that a return to traditional methods has a number of beneficial side-effects. Not only does the elimination of all fertilisation apart from a delicate composting one year in three encourage the vine to send its roots deep down into the sub-soil in search of its nutrient, which gives these vines a more distinctive, better balanced wine, but the plant itself is more healthy. It will suffer less from cryptogamic disease (mildew, oidium), it will react better to cold, as well as heat and drought, and it will be more efficient in turning sun-hours into sugar in the grape.

La lutte biologique (organic viticulture) follows naturally on from this logical approach to the *terroir*. Instead of spraying against insect depredation as a matter of rote, cultivate predators and release them just the next generation of spider or grape-worm is due to appear. Instead of using synthetic or systematic sprays against mildew and oidium, and in enormous quantities, use just the exact amount of sulphur and copper sulphate, perfectly natural chemicals. Moreover, in today's world where keeping the yield under control, not letting it get too high, is as important as encouraging a harvest in the first place, is it so bad if your vines *do* naturally lose a little of their fruit during the summer?

Biodynamique

Bio-dynamism is so far practised by few in Burgundy. However those few include such big names as Lalou Bize at the Domaine Leroy and Auvenay and the Domaines Leflaive, Lafon and Comte Armand, at least partly, as well as Jean-Claude Rateau in Beaune, Thierry Guyot in Saint-Romain and others. Moreover there are many illustrious domaines outside the Côte d'Or who have 'gone bio-dynamic' recently.

The principle behind bio-dynamism is cosmic: that not only the moon, but the position of the planets in the Zodiac should govern when we should plant, when we should plough, when we should treat and when we should harvest: that the planets, not just the moon, exert an influence on agriculture on the earth.

There are four elements in any plant: the root, the leaf, the flower and the fruit. Indeed there are four types of plant: those cultivated for their root, such as a carrot; their leaf, such as a lettuce; their flower, such as a sunflower; and their fruit, such as the vine. These correspond to the four elements of Earth, Water, Air and Fire as follows:

Earth	Root	Taurus, Virgo, Capricorn
Water	Leaf	Cancer, Scorpio, Pisces
Air	Flower	Gemini, Libra, Aquarius
Fire	Fruit	Aries, Leo, Sagittarius

Every nine days the moon passes in front of one of these constellations, the force of which will be greater or lesser depending on the wax and wane of the moon itself and the position of the planets.

What all this boils down to is that there are certain dates where the efficiency of a treatment can be much greater than on others, certain dates which are appropriate and others which are not. A friend in Burgundy, no mean gardener, planted three rows of new potatoes at ten-day intervals in 1995. The first and the third, she later found out, happened to coincide with a bio-dynamically recommended day. These thrived. The second, on a bad day, produced a meagre harvest.

Bio-dynamic treatments are homoeopathic. Sulphur and copper sulphate, against oidium and mildew are allowed. Against other depredations preparations based on silica and infused with plants as varied as nettle, dandelion, bracken, camomile, arsenic and valerian are used. Home-made compost, based on cattle dung, is recommended. In some cases the treatment is placed inside a cow horn, buried in the earth on one special date and dug up on another before being diluted by 10 million parts and applied.

Sometimes the extremes of bio-dynamism sound like black magic. But the point is: it works. We should learn not to scoff.

Preparation of the Soil

A virgin, or a least cleared piece of land, presents the farmer with what in the case of a Côte d'Or vineyard can be a once-in-a-lifetime opportunity. Now is the time, before replanting, to have the soil analysed and remedy any defects, to inject it against viral and other diseases, to install an efficient drainage system, to break up the land to crush or eliminate really large rocks, to renew all the stakes and wires and to renew the surface soil at the top with the earth that has been washed down to the bottom.

Clones or Sélection Massale?

What is a clone? A clone is a population of vines all deriving from the same mother plant. Each vine will be genetically the same as its neighbour.

The advantage of clonal selection is that clones, by and large, are more resistant to disease and crop more uniformly. Their disadvantages? Uniformity, a lack of variety. Conversely *sélection massale*, propagation from a number of the vineyard's own most successful plants, will bring with it all the defects of these plants, but will also give diversity.

Clonal selection is becoming more popular, but this pace is hindered by the very time-scale of producing and testing the clones in the first place. It *is* a slow process, and it is only relatively recently - since 1980 or so - that clones which will be useful to the *grand cru* owner in Vosne-Romanée, as opposed to the bulk grower in the Mâconnais, have been evolved. We are only now into the second generation of these clones.

The ideal, of course, is a combination of the two, the availability of a dozen or more high-quality, relatively low-yielding, disease-resistant clones. Clones of clones: this is the future.

Selection of Rootstock
As important as the fruit-bearing end of the piece of wood to be propagated is the end that will produce the root system. As a result of a nasty little aphid called *phylloxera,* a *Vitis vinifera* variety such as a Pinot Noir or a Chardonnay will not thrive in the soils of nearly all the vineyard areas of Europe, including Burgundy. As a consequence a graft is required: Pinot Noir on to a non-*vinifera* root such as *vupestris* or *berlandieri*, these having a more aphid-resistant, and harder bark. Once again progress here is only just beginning: the task being to adapt precisely not only the rootstock with the clonal or *massale* selection of the grape variety but to the land on which it is to be planted. Here the pH of the soil, its physical condition (exposure, drainage) and the type of surface soil (how much clay, sand, gravel) on top of the basic limestone needs to be calculated and the rootstock chosen accordingly. Moreover, some are more vigorous than others. Some race towards over-maturity in September. The SO4 is notorious in both respects. Is this a good or bad thing? It is up to the *vigneron* to decide. Favoured rootstocks - they mostly seem to be branded with complicated numbers - by quality Burgundy domaines include 161/49 or Fercal for the Pinot Noir, and 3309c and 101–14mg for Chardonnay.

Spacing
The Côte d'Or is a densely populated vineyard. As opposed to the New World it is felt that the greater the population the better the wine, for there will be more competition among the root systems and these will have to dig deeper and thus become more complex, and further, that the vigour of each vine, and so its tendency to over-produce, will be reduced. Densities of up to 12,500 vines per hectare (less than one metre between vines and rows) are commonplace. 10,000 (1 metre by 1 metre) is the norm.

Ray-grass and Other Methods of Combating Erosion
Côte d'Or vineyards, generally inclining east to south-east, are usually planted up and down the slope. This does not maximise the vines' ability to take the maximum from the sun - that would be a north-south planting - but it aids the flow of water away from the vines when it rains.

Unfortunately, on the Côte d'Or's steep slopes and with its sometimes violent thunderstorms, erosion can be a problem. One solution to this is the planting of a special grass between the rows. This has been pioneered by the Gouges family in Nuits-Saint-Georges (see page 454). The addition of the grass has a minor disadvantage: the rate of frost damage is increased. But as well as combating erosion there are a number of positive advantages caused by the competition between the grass and the root-system, which latter then has to seek lower down for its nutrient. The result is an increase in concentration and character in the wine, and not only that, but its potential alcohol and acidity too. Not surprisingly, other Burgundians, cautious at first, are following suit.

Pruning and Training Systems

Having got this far, the Côte d'Or *vigneron* will be aware of two things. His, not the wine-maker's (for all that they may be the same individual) is the creative role. This role is to produce, at the time of harvest, fruit which is in as ripe and healthy a condition as possible, and at a yield per hectare which is compatible with the production of high-quality, concentrated wine. As any Burgundian wine-maker will tell you: 90 per cent of the potential quality lies in the quality of the fruit in the first place. The wine-maker's task is (merely?) to translate this into the finest possible wine. He will not be able to *add* quality. His role is (merely, again) not to screw it up.

Viticultural tasks therefore have two objectives. To keep the plant and its fruit healthy, and to keep the yield within acceptable limits. The way the vine is pruned and trained is vital to both of these pursuits. Pruning must be severe, to six or so buds per vine. And there are essentially two systems of training the adult vine: Guyot or Cordon du Royat.

The first, Guyot, though recent in Burgundy, having only been introduced in the 1930s, is the most widespread. This is a single Guyot, one cane extending horizontally from the mother trunk, on which are the six buds, plus a short spur near the trunk on which there is one bud, which will usually produce next year's cane.

The Cordon system involves spur, not cane pruning. The lateral, horizontal branch will be old wood, not a cane from last year, and at intervals along it will be spurs of one or two buds.

For Chardonnay most growers prefer the single Guyot system. Increasingly for Pinot Noir, because the bunches can be spaced out, reducing the risk of rot, and because the harvest can be more easily controlled, growers in the Côte d'Or are opting for the Cordon method.

High-training and the Importance of the Leaf Canopy

There are always those who have quite other ideas. One such is Henri Latour in Auxey-Duresses. He has developed his own Lyre system, high-trained, the canopy divided at the top to let in the sun. The Burgundians being fuddy-duddies, this is only 'tolerated' by the authorities. Latour's wines, however, are very good. And that should be enough justification.

The leaf canopy, of course, is the engine-room of the vine. It is here the vital process of photosynthesis is taking place. Train the vines a bit higher, maximise the leaf space and you will gain sugar, say people such as Christophe Roumier and Jacques Seysses: so a higher hedge in their vineyards.

Later on, of course, surplus leaves and shoots will be removed. This will encourage the vine to concentrate its energies on the fruit, and will protect that fruit by aiding air circulation, reducing the risk of rot. Moreover, fruit exposed to the direct rays of the sun in the last few weeks of the growing season will produce wine with a better and more stable natural colour.

Keeping the Harvest Down. Is Green Harvesting Effective?

The earlier steps are taken to keep the harvest within limits the better. Techniques such as green harvesting pale into inefficient insignificance when compared with the pruning itself and subsequent debudding even before the flowering takes place.

What is the objective? Six bunches per vine for Pinot Noir, eight for Chardonnay. So prune to six or eight in the first place. Some buds will be double-yolkers, so to speak, so one embryonic bunch must be rubbed out, one embryonic flower removed. Moreover, to eliminate the second generation, once the danger of frost has gone, nip out this bud, on the opposite side of the cane to the first, as well. Drastic action perhaps, and if the flowering is unsuccessful, perhaps unnecessary. But best done at this time than later. Obviously you *can* reduce the harvest immediately after flowering, or just before the *véraison*, this latter being what is generally known as green harvesting, but what will probably happen, say opponents, is merely that the remaining bunches will expand to compensate, and your juice/solid ratio will be worse than it would have been in the first place. In my view green harvesting should be a last resort, and needs to be as drastic as one in two bunches eliminated to have any material effect.

Old Vines and Low Yields

Vines, like people, decline in vigour as they age. Like some people, what they produce gets better. As the root system gets more impressive, the more complex becomes the fruit. When this gets concentrated by a lower production – and a yield which is naturally rather than artificially small – the resultant wine will be richer and creamier in mouth-feel: the taste of old vines. Naturally growers will boast about the venerable age of certain of their plots. Let's hope they are not encouraged to exaggerate.

With old vines, of course, come low yields. But beware the sort of low yield which comes from a vineyard where half the vines are dead or long since ripped out. Beware irregularity. There are many vineyards where old vines, as they have given up the ghost, have been replaced with young ones (this process is known as *repiquage*). In this case you could have a row which goes: young vine (thirteen bunches), old vine (one bunch), young vine (sixteen bunches), old vine (two bunches), and so on. An average of eight bunches per vine: probably 35-40 hl/ha. But you will get no low-*rendement* feel in the resultant wine nor, of course, any old-vine flavour.

Where a Large (–ish) Harvest Can Be an Advantage

Have you ever wondered why 1973, 1979 and 1982 were all surprisingly good white wine Côte d'Or vintages? So did I, until suddenly a bit of lateral thinking gave me the explanation.

As we all know, in Champagne the first pressing gives the best wine. Subsequent pressings provide lesser quality, and it is beneath the dignity of the top *grande marque* houses to allow them house-room.

What would be the effect on the wine, in what promised to be an abundant harvest, if a first gentle pressing of Côte d'Or Chardonnay produced sufficient wine to fill the allowed *rendement* and the juice from any subsequent pressings was spirited away separately to provide *vin ordinaire* for the workers? Would this not produce a *grand vin* of above average quality, above expectation for the vintage? Was this the explanation for the white-wine success of 1973, 1979 and 1982? Is there a lesson to be learned today?

Where the AC Laws Need to Be Rewritten

Politicians rarely have the courage of their own convictions. Prior to 1974 there was the Cascade System. Effectively there was no limit to what the Burgundian *vigneron* could produce: only to what he was allowed to label. Thus if the wine in question was a *grand cru* where the maximum *rendement* was 30 hl/ha, and the production was in fact 60 hl/ha, the first 30 hl would be labelled as *grand cru*, the next 5 as village or *premier cru* (where the maximum was 35 hl/ha), the next 15 hl as *Bourgogne* (the limit being 50 hl/ha) and the remainder as *vin ordinaire*. Yet all the wine was the same.

This was obviously an unsatisfactory state of affairs, open to abuse; foreigners shipping the *vin ordinaire* – or another wine perhaps – in bulk and labelling it *grand cru*, for example.

Instead of merely limiting the grower to a simple maximum, implying that if he/she overproduced, AC would be withheld, the INAO (*Institut National des Appellations d'Origine*) not only increased the *rendement de base* (from 30 hl to 35 hl for *grand cru rouge* and from 35 hl to 42 hl for *premier cru* and village red wine), but allowed, indeed encouraged, the grower to overproduce by advancing the possibility of an extra 20 per cent above the maximum, subject to tasting. This is called PLC (*Plafond Limite de Classement*).

There are three fundamental flaws here. Firstly, except in exceptional vintages such as 1990, diminishing returns, as I have already pointed out, in at 35, 40 and 45 hl/ha for *grand cru*, *premier cru* and village red wines respectively. You simply cannot produce *grand cru* worthy of the name at 42 hl/ha and *premier cru* at 48. Secondly, the *rendement annuel* (as opposed to the *rendement de base*) and the percentage of PLC were supposed to be varied according to the nature of the vintage, i.e. if there was frost or hail damage it would be reduced. In fact it rarely varies. Thirdly, this so-called tasting inspection: it takes place once, long before bottling (why not judge the finished article as well), and the judges are the local trade, growers, brokers and *négociants*. You can be faulted on typicity: rarely if ever on a lack of basic quality or concentration.

What needs to be done? Eliminate the concept of PLC for a start. Differentiate between *premier cru* and village wine but raise the *rendement de base* for village *rouge* from 40 to 45 hl. And set these as absolute limits. Anyone who continually (not just a one-off unfortunate experience with rain) overproduces should be heavily fined, and the whole *cuvée* confiscated (this could make an interesting third auction sale, to add to the Hospices de Beaune and Hospices de Nuits). Moreover, bottled wine should be sampled, and the judging be somewhat less of a formality.

Combating Cryptogamic Diseases, Insect Depredation and Grey Rot

In Burgundy's marginal climate, and with at least one sensitive grape (though I believe the Chardonnay is not as hardy as some people think), keeping pests and diseases at bay is a continual problem. In fact the most effective way of reducing contamination happens to be precisely what any grower should be looking for, a healthy plant in a living soil with a deep and complex root system, bearing only a modicum of fruit.

From the word go, at the beginning of the season, you will see the curious, insect-like, vineyard tractors travelling up and down the vine rows pumping out clouds of moist insect-repellent combined with sulphur and/or copper sulphate against the diseases and pests which threaten the vine. In the main these are now under control, and have been for some time, though the incidence of grape-worm seems to be on the increase.

Grey rot is a more serious problem. It is the same fungus as that of noble rot, yet is rarely noble in Burgundy, and always disastrous in Pinot Noir. Any seriously lengthy outbreak of rain will encourage rot, if the temperature remains high. The thinner the skin of the fruit the quicker it will set in. And rotten grapes give rotten wine, wine without colour, which will tend to be high in volatile acidity, and which will not clarify well.

Spacing out of the bunches, removal of some or all of the covering leaves to aid aeration can help. There are also anti-rot sprays, which harden the skin (as does the application of copper sulphate). The long-term solution, I believe, is clonal: the eventual production of a Pinot Noir with a thicker skin. In the meanwhile it makes the necessity to *trier* (sort through the fruit to eliminate what is substandard at the time of the harvest) all the more acute.

Machine Harvesting?

We arrive at the date of the harvest. The winery has had its annual spring-clean. The fermentation vats have been scrubbed and sterilised. The pipes have been washed and sterilised. The crusher-destemmer is back from servicing. The new barrels have been broken in with a mixture of hot water, salt and something abrasive like gravel, to leach out their green tannins. Space has been cleared. Everyone is keeping a nervous eye on the weather forecast but otherwise raring to go. Finally sugar readings in the vineyards indicate the fruit is ripe. A plan of campaign - what order the vineyards are to be attacked - is drawn up. So does the quality Côte d'Or *vigneron* climb up on to his harvesting machine and gallop off to battle? The answer is no. These are useful, indeed today essential, tools in the production of merely good wine. In the Côte d'Or they are out of place. For a start they prevent *triage* in the vineyard - and it is in the vineyard that *triage* should commence, for the contact between mouldy and clean fruit, and the intermingling of their juices can make the effort pointless. Secondly they separate the fruit from its stem too early, encouraging oxidation. Thirdly they do not differentiate between the ripe fruit and the *verjus*, that of the second generation. And fourthly there is a direct relation between slightly unripe fruit and a herbaceous taint in the wine if the fruit is machine-harvested.

You will see plenty of machines in Chablis and in the Mâconnais. There are some in the Hautes-Côtes. But they are out of place in the Côte d'Or.

VINICULTURE

A few general axioms to start off with:

• The grander the *terroir* the more hands-off and anonymous must be the thumb-print of the wine-maker. The public wants to taste the character of Chambertin, not the wine-making signature of M. Machin.
• Some 90 per cent of the quality of the wine derives from the fruit in the first place (I have said this before but it cannot be emphasised enough).
• The art of wine-making is disaster-preventive, not creative. You cannot make a silk purse out of a sow's ear. (I have also said this before.) On the other hand the wine-maker is no mere cypher. He or she can exert a lot of influence over the character of the wine, which is why one Chambertin is different from another. A great wine-maker needs flair, imagination and the inspiration of divine discontent.
• There are numerous different ways to produce high-quality Burgundy. No one magic recipe. And Burgundy for this reason is the most individualistic wine-growing area in the world.
• Every vintage poses its own problems and solutions. Above all, wine-makers must be flexible.

Triage
In order to maximise the quality of the fruit, the first thing to do once the harvest reaches the winery is to perform another *triage* (why doesn't Burgundian law, like that in Châteauneuf-du-Pape, make this compulsory?). The fruit is poured out on to a conveyor belt and picked over by a team who reject anything unripe, bruised or rotten. The belt can have a light underneath (which helps eliminate unripe berries or bunches) as *chez* Philippe Charlopin. It can have a device which riddles it from side to side (which helps shake off raindrops) as at the Domaine de Courcel. There can even be a wind tunnel (to dry the fruit) as *chez* Faiveley.

Then comes the moment of segregation. Is the fruit Pinot Noir or Chardonnay? Are we producing Chambertin or Montrachet?

RED WINE

Saignée, and Other Methods of Concentrating the Must
Saigner means to bleed. Some of the free-run juice is allowed to seep away (it can make a very pleasant rosé) with the object of equalising the solid-liquid ratio in the must. Increasingly used since the early 1970s, this is a useful technique. Sadly there are one or two disadvantages. Firstly, this free-run juice is very aromatic, and a wine without these aromas risks being a little humdrum, lacking high tones. Secondly, the eventual result can be a bit four-square. It is difficult to anticipate at the outset quite what is the optimum percentage of juice which needs to be tapped off. For obvious reasons you cannot do a trial run. If too much is run off the wine can be a little too dense and solid.

Today, various people in Burgundy are experimenting with machines which can concentrate the must by eliminating merely the water, not the esters which make up the flavour. Naturally the machines are costly. But the results, with the water being removed by a sort of reverse osmosis at normal temperatures and pressures, are very promising.

Once again, however, the moral of the story is not to overproduce in the first place. If your vines are old and the pruning severe, the berries will be small and concentrated in all but the most depressingly rainy harvests.

Chaptalisation and Acidification

Chaptalisation is permitted up to a level which would increase the alcohol content of the wine by 2°. At long last it is up to the wine-maker how and when he adds his sugar. Officially he used to have to do this all at once, and at the beginning of fermentation. Most wine-makers would rather do this in stages, and at the end, for this keeps the temperature high, resulting in a better extract of flavour and structural elements from the fruit. Two degrees, i.e. increasing the alcohol level of an 11° wine by 18 per cent, seems already quite enough, but many Burgundians are lobbying to have the level raised to 2.5°. I consider this would only be an excuse for greater overproduction and worse husbandry. I trust this lobby is resisted.

You are not allowed both to chaptalise and acidify. Does this seem churlish? If so, imagine a wine which needed both to make it palatable. Should it be allowed to be anything but *vin ordinaire*? Is it going to taste any better than that, even after it has been concocted?

Some wine-makers will argue - and it affects whites more than reds - that acidified wines never integrate properly, the acidity always appears to be 'separate' from the fruit. I have found this less of a problem with reds, and I can understand those who turn a blind eye in the direction of the law, and de-acidify a little, at the same time as chaptalising a little. The answer, of course, is to keep the *rendement* down. This will reduce the need to do either.

While we are on the subject, what is the optimum alcoholic level for red Burgundy? I would suggest for *grand* and *premier cru* somewhere between 12.5° and 13.5°, the more concentrated and full-bodied the wine the nearer to this upper limit. Bearing in mind a loss of about half a degree during fermentation, this means chaptalising up to 14°. But a wine which was only at 12° naturally would not be 'concentrated and full bodied' for it is only after reaching 11.5° that the wine begins to develop the higher alcohols and double sugars that give the rich, full-mouth feel we call concentrated, and if it were to be chaptalised to the limit it would be unbalanced, giving a 'hot' effect on the after-taste. This is another argument for keeping the rules unchanged. Leave the job to photosynthesis, not to the sugar bags! Too much Burgundy is still today, sadly, over-chaptalised.

The Stems

In the past top red Burgundy was rarely destemmed. Today, with the exception of some - but these some include illustrious names such as the Domaine de la Romanée-Conti and Dujac - most Côte d'Or reds come from destemmed fruit. What are the arguments for and against?

The arguments for the stems are as follows: that they add tannin and structure, and also acidity; that they help to produce a more even fermentation because they will absorb some of the heat (fermentation is an exo-thermic reaction); that some at least of the fermentation can begin within the unbroken grape, so producing more complex flavours; that they add to the solid matter of the fermenting environment; and that they physically aid the fermentation, furthering aeration, helping the drainage of the juice and so on. Many growers retain 10 or 15 per cent just for this purpose. But it would appear from my discussions with growers that the main reason for not eliminating the stems is that this is the way that domaine has always made its red Burgundy.

Critics will argue that, first, while the fruit may be ripe the wood may not be, and the presence of the stems may impart a harsh green twiggy taste; that even if ripe the flavours mask the finesse of the crushed-soft-red fruit of the Pinot Noir; that the colour of the wine is reduced; that (conversely to the argument that the stems *add* acidity) they may bring potassium with them (if that is still in excess in the soil) and so *reduce* the acidity of the wine. Vinifying with no stems results in a slightly higher alcohol level - for the fermentation is more efficient, and produces a more mellow wine with a richer, fatter, mouth-feel, especially in the poorer vintages. Again, as with all Burgundy, it boils down to personal taste. I personally find, lover of La Tâche as I am, that I usually prefer wine from destemmed or largely destemmed fruit, and so does most of the new generation of Côte d'Or wine-makers. The wine seems smoother and richer; the fruit more intense. But then the diversity of Burgundy is one of its compelling charms. It would be tragic if the wine-making became standardised.

Cold Soaking and the '*Méthode* Accad'

The theory behind cold soaking, the maceration before fermentation, i.e. without alcohol, of the grape skins in their own juice, is that a better colour is fixed, more sophisticated tannins result and more vibrant fruit flavours are extracted.

In most years, in fact, Burgundy usually being quite cool at the time of the harvest, and therefore unless artificially heated, fermentations taking three or four days to get going, most wines will undergo a brief period of cold soaking. What is meant by the Accad method is where this is deliberately prolonged - to a week or more.

Accad is of Lebanese origin, and is an agricultural engineer as well as an oenologist. He was one of the first to point out the damage twenty years of over-fertilisation had done to the Burgundian vineyard. He has preached the gospel of biological viticulture for years, and has been a viticultural consultant to many leading estates. It is only on the vinification side that his views are controversial. Sadly he has been his own worst enemy, preferring to let myth and exaggeration circulate rather than coming out and explaining his methods, their rationale and their results. He has also been a poor communicator with his own clients, and consequently is no longer employed by many of them.

There are two main criticisms of the *méthode* Accad. Firstly that unless you are equipped with a cooling unit the must has to be very heavily sulphured in order to inhibit the fermentation from commencing; that this sulphur takes months if not years to dissipate and combines with and degrades the flavour elements of the wine. The second and most important bone of contention is that the wine which results will taste untypical anyway. I myself have confused young Accad Burgundy with Côte-Rôtie.

Accadiens will answer that firstly, on the sulphur side, the amount at bottling is no higher than that at non-Accad domaines, and anyway more and more people are now equipped to keep the temperature down (to 16-18°C) by cooling, thus eliminating the necessity to over-sulphur in the first place. They will retort to the accusation of non-typicity that firstly a young Accad wine in fact tastes like young Burgundy used to taste like forty or fifty years ago, and that after a decade, when the wine is mature, it *will* be typical (and, moreover, that what it tastes like in the meanwhile is immaterial).

I have listened to both sides carefully. There are many Accadiens (though they dislike the term) whom I admire, whose intelligence I respect, who would be the last people to abandon all in search of some crackpot magic path to great wine. So I am prepared to give them the benefit of the doubt. I am also prepared to give the wines time to mature properly - for many who pursue this path only started in 1987 or 1988. And I have sampled their wines *in situ*. These 1987s, a year which in the main has not aged gracefully, are among the best, certainly among the freshest and with the most sophisticated tannins. On their own the wines seem to be not too untypical and very good. Moreover, after several years' experience, most Accad followers have now adapted his principles to their own vines and cellar practices and have gone their own independent way. As a result the cold soaked wines are better in vintages today than they were at the outset.

But blind, among a host of non-Accad wines, they do not show well at least in their youth.

At a 1988 tasting, held three-and-a-bit years after the vintage, all the tasters (a group of top British professionals) marked the cold soaked wines low, as they did three years further on when we completed a similar survey of the 1991s. At this stage, therefore, while sympathetic, I remain agnostic.

Accad-inspired domaines in the Côte d'Or up to early 1995 included the following:

Philippe Battachi, Domaine de Clos-Noir, Gevrey-Chambertin
Château de la Tour, Vougeot
Jacky Confuron-Cotetidot, Vosne-Romanée
Jean Grivot, Vosne-Romanée
Manière-Noirot, Vosne-Romanée
Pernin-Rossin, Vosne-Romanée
Georges Chicotot, Nuits-Saint-Georges
Comte Senard, Aloxe-Corton

NB: Many of these no longer employ M. Accad. By 1995 many too (such as Grivot) had so modified the principles that they could no longer be called 'Accad-inspired'.

Yeasts: Cultured or not

The arguments for or against cultured yeasts flow along similar lines to those of clones versus *sélection massale*: in effect either employing that little bit of control mankind has already achieved over nature, or letting Mother Nature go rampant, with all the danger, but also with all the possibility for excitement, that might be involved.

Up to very recently, fermentations have traditionally been enabled to take place by the presence in the vineyards and wineries of native wild yeasts. And the big positive argument for continuing to use them is that they are specific and individual to each particular *climat* and wine-maker. Alter the yeast and you change the flavour of the wine. Use the same yeast for several wines and you risk standardising their flavours. So keep to the natural yeasts and preserve the diversity.

There are, unfortunately, a number of down sides. Firstly there needs to be a certain quantity of them in the first place, which quantity can be reduced if there is rain at the time of the harvest. Secondly their efficiency is variable, particularly at the beginning and at the end of fermentation. At the beginning is not too much of a problem, but at the end, when there is only the barest element of non-fermented sugar left, and when the level of alcohol will be such as to inhibit yeast activity, a prolonged finish to the process can leave the wine open to oxidation or volatile acidity contamination.

Moreover there are good yeasts as well as bad yeasts. Some wild yeasts can give very barnyardy flavours. One, *brettanomyces*, is very often cited as a cause of some unusual and rustic flavour in many a red wine.

In fact there is not just one yeast out there in the wild, but a whole family of them, some useful at the start of fermentation, others at the end; some which will produce one flavour, others which will produce another; some which will suit one grape variety, others which will adapt to a different *cépage*. There are even yeasts which promote colour extraction, or longevity, or increase the richness and creaminess of the mouth-feel. And there is no reason in theory why producing artificial strains of them, to suit the particular sort of wine you want to make, should not be warmly welcomed, as they are, for instance at the Domaine Georges Mugneret (Mugneret-Gibourg) in Vosne-Romanée. Other domaines start off using the natural yeasts and then add artificial strains later. The danger with cultured yeasts, particularly with white wines, is that all the resulting wines will taste the same. As with clones, this is a part of wine-making which is still very much in its infancy.

Temperatures of Fermentation

Here again, as with attitudes to the amount of stems and the amount of new oak, Burgundy shows a greater diversity of attitude than almost any other wine-making region in the world. There are those who insist on fermenting at a maximum of 28°C, others who choose to maintain the temperature within a very narrow band of 30-32°, and wine-makers who have no qualms about letting the thermometer rise to 35° and above. François Faiveley likes low temperatures: his argument being that the flavour elements are volatile and will be lost if the fermentation is too hot. Above 32°C, with a fragile variety such as the Pinot Noir, the nose of the wine disappears. Patrice Rion and the Domaine Daniel Rion like to ferment at exactly 32°. Too low, in his view, leads to wines which lack body and structure; any higher, and the wine risks being coarse. Jacques Lardière, at Jadot, on the other hand, vinifies at 35° plus. The wine doesn't suffer, he says, and he extracts more of the individuality of the *terroir* this way.

The point is that different elements in the wine get extracted at different temperatures: the fruit at cooler temperatures, the best of the tannins at a higher degree. Once again the wine-maker must be prepared to adapt. He or she must pay regard to the quality of the fruit in the first place and adapt accordingly. Flexibility should be the keynote.

Length of Maceration

The duration of the *cuvaison*, after which the wine, having finished its fermentation, is drawn off its lees, is also of profound importance, and is closely allied with the temperature at which that maceration has taken place.

From the start, even before the fermentation – which lasts only a few days – begins, the effect of the skins macerating with the juice is to extract colouring matter, flavour and structure from the fruit. The colour comes from the phenolic compounds: anthocyanins and tannins. The former are extracted quickly (and break down in the wine over the next five years). The tannins, which preserve the colour and give the possibility of long ageing, leach out at an even rate. Too short a maceration and the wine is consequently light and ephemeral. Too long and it will be coarse and dense. There will be an optimum moment, which will also depend on the temperature, which will be a desirable compromise between structure and fruit: indeed when the balance of the wine will be at its best. Once again today's wine-maker will adjust to the quality of the harvested fruit. If there is a danger of rot, or of hail taint, then *cuvaison* must be reduced. But perhaps the temperature raised higher to maximise extraction quicker.

WHITE WINE

A number of the subjects discussed in the previous pages – chaptalisation, acidification, cultured yeasts or not – apply equally to the production of white and red wine. I refer readers to those paragraphs above.

Where white wine-making differs most fundamentally from red is that it takes place without the skins and stems, in (we are speaking here about the Côte d'Or's better wines) small wood rather than in tank or *foudre* (large wooden vats) and at much lower temperatures.

Skin Contact

The flavour elements within a ripe grape are not distributed evenly. They are congregated towards the outside, within or very near the skin, not in the middle. The idea behind skin contact, before pressing and fermentation – usually for six to twenty-four hours in a cool place – is to take advantage of the fruit's breakdown after picking and to leach out flavours from the skin into the juice. Otherwise they would largely be lost. Obviously if the skin is bruised or in any other way contaminated this exercise would be inappropriate. But, say the adherents, if not, why not allow your fruit to rest overnight after picking in order to extract a bit more flavour this way?

Experience has shown, however, that skin-contacted wines - if I can describe them as such - do not age well. They are very upfront and aromatic when young, but they thin out, becoming vegetal and attenuated quite rapidly thereafter. Appropriate for regional wines such as Mâcon Blanc, but not for fine Meursault.

Pressing
Most white Burgundy is therefore pressed as soon as possible after its entry into the winery. Of the various types of press the most preferred is today the pneumatic horizontal type, within which is an inflatable cylindrical balloon the expansion of which presses the fruit gently against the outside. Today's machines are very sensitive, producing much more elegant musts than hitherto, and the wine-maker can, if he or she so desires, make a number of different pressings of the same load of fruit. The first, obviously, will produce the best wine.

Fermentation in Wood
In most cases (Ramonet is an exception) the growers then allow the pressed juice to settle out its gross lees (this is called *débourbage*) after which it is decanted into oak barrels and allowed to ferment. In some cases fermentation may be encouraged to begin in bulk, and, once it is under way, then continue in wood. But always, the principle that it takes place in wood is paramount. Only this way will a proper oak and wine mix of flavour be achieved. A wine which has been fermented in bulk and then matured in oak will never balance these elements correctly.

Temperatures of Fermentation
Fermentation is an exo-thermic chemical reaction. It produces heat. But usually cellars are cool or environments are temperature-controlled and the heat can conveniently escape easily from the barrel. The result is that white Burgundy ferments at about 20-24°C. Higher temperatures (than the 16-18° for most white wines) are desirable. They produce wines with richness, concentration and fat.

ÉLEVAGE
The third part of wine-making, *élevage*, does not, I feel, receive the importance it deserves. Even if we might today take Henri Jayer's 1985 pronouncement - that 80 per cent of Burgundy was good at the outset, but only 20 per cent by the time it got into the bottle - with a pinch of salt, those of us who are used to tasting new wine out of cask are only too well aware of the pitfalls that can lie ahead of it and the ease with which it can deteriorate through incompetence and neglect.

Once again there is a cardinal rule which should underlie every aspect of *élevage*. Just as the object of viticulture is to produce as superb fruit as possible, and that of viniculture to translate that superb fruit into superb young wine, so the principle behind the *élevage* of this wine is to look after it until it is time for it to be bottled, and to prepare it for bottling so that it will mature thereafter into a great mature wine. And that means manipulating it as little as possible. The more you muck about with it, the more you risk taking out of it just those elements, for they are more fragile, that make one wine different from, and better than another. What is required is a hands-off, preventative approach.

The Malo-lactic Fermentation
Subsequent to the sugar-alcohol fermentation is the malo-lactic fermentation - from malic acid into lactic acid. Similarly carbon dioxide is formed, which (see below) can help to protect the wine from oxidation, if not allowed to escape. The effect is to round off the wine, to reduce its acidity.

This fermentation is caused, not by yeasts secreting enzymes, as in the case of alcoholic fermentation, but by bacterial action, and if it is slow to commence (for some reason it occurs much more tardily in Burgundy than in Bordeaux), it can be encouraged, both by warming up the cellar to 18°C or so, and by inoculation. Most Burgundians, though, prefer to let nature take its course. Warming up the cellar excessively - Michelot in Meursault used to be guilty of this, and the combination of the heat and the natural dampness of his cellar made you feel you were going into a Turkish bath - can result in rather four-square wines with a lack of zip.

For red wines an efficient malo is essential. The wine is rendered more supple, and it needs fully to complete rather than to continue in bottle, which would upset the balance and cause off-flavours.

As far as white wines are concerned, some establishments such as Jadot or Sauzet prefer to stop the malos of certain wines at some stage in order to preserve their natural acidities. This is far preferable to acidification. Critics, however, aver that it produces rather hard, unyielding wines.

With white wines, of course, malos take place in cask. While there is now a movement in Bordeaux which sponsors the achievement of red-wine malos also in cask, rather than, as hitherto, in bulk before the wine is racked into small wood, red Burgundies have always undergone malo in cask in the top estates. These red wines are deemed to be richer and better integrated as a result.

Advantages and Disadvantages of New Oak

There is no subject in Burgundian wine-making today which is more controversial, which causes more heated argument, than the amount of new oak which is applicable to the Pinot Noir and Chardonnays of differing qualities and pretensions produced up and down the Côte d'Or. As with all the other bones of contention - stems, temperatures of fermentation, etc. - the response you will get at the growers' end is as diverse as can be.

The public sees the flavour of new oak as a plus point, as an indication of quality. And indeed the judicious marriage of wine and oak produces something with a more enhanced complex flavour than wine on its own. The moot point is, of course, what percentage of new oak is 'judicious'? Where do you draw the line and say this wine has too much? And, often forgotten, how do very oaky young wines develop?

There are entrenched positions on both sides. And increasingly, and I view this with sorrow, growers who are preparing two *cuvées* of the same wine: one very oaky for the American market, one less so for Europe and the rest of the world. Surely the producer him or herself should decide what is best for his or her wine, rather than let the market (or more simply, one broker's, or critic's, assessment of what will get high marks) dictate?

Wine in a new oak cask, because the wood is more porous, will evolve faster, because it is more exposed to oxygen. (For this reason, as Thierry Matrot points out, it is a disaster in white-wine vintages where, like in 1986, there has been some *pourriture*. The extra oxygenation only makes the wines even more coarse and unbalanced as they evolve.) The newer the cask, the faster the malo will complete, the sooner it will need racking, and the earlier it will need to be bottled. (Of course, what usually happens is that the wine-maker will equalise the wine at each racking so that the new oak element is the same in each cask.)

Moreover, and this is crucial, the tannins imparted by an oak cask are different from those the wine acquires during its maceration. Wine tannins slowly break down as the wine ages. Wood tannins are more rigid. When young, the 'puppy fat' and primary fruit of the wine may seem sufficient to balance up with the new wood. But this may not be the case at five or ten years old. If the wine is noticeably oaky at the time of bottling it will be even more so down the road later on.

The flavours of Pinot Noir and Chardonnay, I submit, are delicate. These are wines of fragrance and complexity: wines of elegance. Unless they are very powerful and concentrated, *grands crus* of a great vintage, they will be overwhelmed by any more than a hint of new wood. Charles Rousseau gets it right, I think: 100 per cent for Chambertin and Clos-de-Bèze going down to 50 to 33 per cent for the rest of his top wines, hardly any at all for the village Gevrey-Chambertin. And that is just until the first racking in September: six months at most. Others such as Ponsot and Gouges believe in very much less, barely one-tenth. Most growers steer a path somewhere in between these approaches.

But there are some who believe in 100 per cent new oak for all their wines. Some in 200 per cent (by which we mean racking from new into *new* wood after twelve months or so). Among these are the wines of Dominique Laurent, some of the American *cuvées* imported by Bobby Kacher, and those made by Henri Jayer. Jayer is regarded by many as a god. I have had many a spectacular bottle from his range. But I have also had mature wines (the 1985 Cros-Parentoux, for example) which were spoiled by too much oak. And the effect gets worse and worse as the wine gets exposed to air in the glass.

You can argue, as does my friend Mel Knox, who imports French barrels into California, that there is no such thing as over-oaked wine, just under-wined oak. And we mustn't forget that there are well-made oak barrels and poorly made oak barrels; nor the potentially deleterious effect of mouldy, bug-infested, far too *old* barrels. Nevertheless, in my view, Burgundy risks offering us today more wines which are over-oaked than under-oaked. As Robert Drouhin said to me once: 'We are wine-makers, not carpenters.' Personally, I want to taste the fruit.

Keeping the Wine on its Lees

The lees of a wine, the deposit which settles out at the bottom of the cask, consists of dead yeast cells, tartrate crystals, colouring matter and a number of other things. If these are 'clean' they do nothing but good. The wine can gain richness and nutrients from them and increase in complexity and character. They also help protect the wine from oxidation. For this reason rackings are never so drastic that a little turbid juice is not left in the cask, and the wines, both red and white, are kept as long as possible on their lees between rackings.

After the malo, the first racking, in order to allow most of the carbon dioxide to escape (but not all, for its presence also helps preserve the wine) and in order to admit a little oxygen in to aid the wine's development, tends to be aerobic. Further rackings, and there should usually only be the need for one in Burgundy before preparation for bottling - too many would risk the wine drying up and losing its fruit - will be anaerobic, without the presence of air.

Bâtonnage

Bâtonnage is the periodic stirring up of the lees of a very young wine. This is a technique which is applied to white wines, but only rarely to reds. The object is to release into the liquid flavours presently locked up and to enable a more efficient extraction of the feeding matter in these lees. It is appropriate in the case of wines to be drunk young, which sadly is the case for even the most illustrious white Burgundies. It should not, in my view, be considered for *grands crus*. These should be allowed to release their flavours more gently and over a longer time scale. I don't mind *bâtonnage* in ephemeral village Meursault, delicious after two years in bottle. But not Le Montrachet!

Care of the Wine in Cask

Wine is at its most vulnerable during the period of its *élevage* in barrel. At the beginning the carbon dioxide produced by the fermentations will protect it, as will, to a certain extent, the fine lees. But after a while the CO_2 will have more or less escaped and the lees after the midsummer/September racking will be less rich.

It is vital, therefore that the barrels are kept topped up, that the ambient temperature and humidity are correct, and that the wine is protected from bacterial contamination as well as oxygenation. Wines in cask, especially when they approach the time when they need a racking, often exhibit reductive flavours - H$_2$S, and so on. These can be cleaned up by an aeration. A wine which has just been racked may appear temporarily a bit oxidised. This again will go. But once serious oxidation or other off-flavours set in, there is little one can do except pour the wine down the drain.

The wine-maker should therefore not continually attack the same cask when offering tasting samples. After being regularly exposed to aeration and then refurbished it will not be representative of the lot as a whole. This was so *chez* Gouges, with all the casks *bande à côté* (bung to the side) except one, the tasting barrel. Once when I found the sample puzzling I asked to taste another cask. This involved a certain amount of heaving and rolling barrels about. But the result was a totally different wine. Today all the barrels *chez* Gouges are *bande dessus* (bung upright) and, as elsewhere, I can choose which cask I want to sample.

What does one use for topping up? A bit of *vin de presse*? Some of the generic wine? Bottles left over after a tasting session? Obviously it *should* be exactly the same wine. In the Burgundian situation it is very unlikely that every single cask is topped up with the identical wine. But let's hope that today's serious growers realise that there is a problem here, and that they do not abuse it.

Clarification: Enzymes, Fining and Filtration

Wines are fined and filtered not just to annoy Robert Parker, who has made somewhat of a fetish about the subject, but because there are or may be elements within them which have not settled out naturally, and which need to be removed to avoid them contaminating the wine after it has been bottled. Today the addition of certain enzymes at the time of fermentation aids the natural clarification process, so making fining and filtration less necessary. Moreover, a wine can be filtered using *Kieselguhr* - a diatomaceous earth which has an electrostatic cleaning effect, like most fining agents - earlier in its career in cask.

Excessive fining and filtration, as well as the pumping of the wine which goes with it, is of course just as disastrous as excessive anything else. The process *can* strip a wine of all its beauty if not carried out properly. And here the strictures of Robert Parker, Kermit Lynch and others have done the wine world a great service. But, I believe, and I have taken part in a number of tastings to test this theory out, both that 'filtration properly carried out does not strip or attenuate a wine', to quote Professor Emile Peynaud, and also that after five or ten years you cannot tell the difference.

The answer is simple. If a detailed analysis indicates that there is no need to fine or filter, then don't. Subject the wine to as few manipulations as possible is after all the cardinal rule. But if one or other or both of these processes *are* necessary, then do it but of course do it gently. No consumer ten years on, with a contaminated bottle in his hand, is going to thank you for your policy of 'no filtration'.

When to Bottle

I strongly believe that the length of time the wine is allowed to rest in cask before bottling has a profound effect on its quality. A little too early may not be too bad a thing. Rather too late is a significant error. Here once again the *éleveur* has to exercise discretion, imagination and flexibility. The humidity and ambient temperature of the cellar play as crucial a role as does the wine itself.

Most white wine is bottled after a year, early in September just before the vintage for a wine like a village Meursault. This has the decided advantage of releasing the cask for the next year's wine. *Grands crus* may be held until November. Some growers - Lafon, Coche-Dury, Pierre Morey, Leflaive - bottle later. They may have deep, cold, humid cellars, like Lafon, and/or have produced more concentrated wine in the first place. They may, like Leflaive, leave the wine until September in cask but then give it six months more in stainless-steel tanks. It is easy to point out that the best growers seem to bottle later. But that is putting the cart before the horse. It is because, being the best growers, they produce the best, most concentrated wine, that the wine can keep eighteen months in cask.

Quite a lot of red wine, for reasons more of cellar space than personal conviction, apart from releasing the barrels, is also bottled after a little under a year. Here I am unconvinced this is a good thing. Red wine - serious red wine anyway - needs a year and a half or so to gain in depth in cask. Few of the twelve-month red-wine growers rank up with the stars of the Burgundian firmament.

On the other hand, keeping wine, unless excessively tannic and concentrated (and even 1990 did not produce many of these) up to two years in wood is in my view a grave error. The resulting wine will be dry and astringent. Even Lalou Bize-Leroy, with her 13 hl/ha concentrated 1993s, did not leave them more than fifteen months in cask. Most top red Burgundy is bottled between February and May on its second year: earlier if the vintage is a bit weak, and also earlier if a lot of new wood has been used in its *élevage*.

Bottling, Particularly Hand-bottling and Contract-bottling

On the principle that great wines should be handled with personal care, a number of larger concerns, as well as the tiny domaines which have always done it, have reverted to hand-bottling by gravity rather than machine. It is the gentlest way to approach what is probably the greatest shock the wine has yet to experience in its brief career. François Faiveley is one of these. It is an approach to be commended.

On the other hand, most of the small bottling lines you see in Burgundian cellars, if sensitively used, will not do the wine any long-term harm. The main thing to remember is that the bottling process is upsetting, and together with the subsequent transport all the way into the cellar of those who have bought *en primeur* will render a fragile wine like Burgundy unfit for judgement for maybe as much as a year.

An unquantifiable statistic (I forgot to include the question in my growers' questionnaire) is the amount of domaines who use contract-bottlers. Contract-bottling *can* be perfectly good. But the danger is both that in order to protect himself the bottler will do a belt and braces job (fine and filter to excess) and also that the speed the wine is bottled will further strip out flavours from it.

Notes for the Consumer

Has the Style of Burgundy Evolved Over the Years?

Burgundy of the 1940s and 1950s was a sturdier animal than it is today. There are a number of reasons for this. Firstly the average age of the vineyards was high, being essentially still the first generation of grafted vines planted after phylloxera. Secondly the yield was lower. And thirdly, lest we forget, the 1945-1959 period offered a regular series of very good vintages.

How genuine the wines were, i.e. whether - and I am talking about the serious *négociants* and the few domaine-bottlers of the period - what was in the bottle was 100 per cent Pinot Noir, is difficult now to tell. Old wines exhibit all sorts of spice and other elements in their flavour, some to such an extent that it becomes very difficult to guess their variety and therefore origin. Judging by the wines which have come my way over the last six years, during which I have made a particular point of buying up all the small lots of old wine I could afford, I would say that the vast majority of *these were* totally pure and unadulterated. (But this, it should be noted, is the *crème de la crème*. I am not talking about second-division merchants' Burgundy.)

In the 1960s and 1970s (though we should not forget 1964 and 1966, even 1962 and 1969, as very good vintages), as a result of increased but unregulated production thanks to the new clones and new fertilisers, the wines in general became lighter and weaker. Burgundy became wishy-washy and expensive. At the top domaine level, however, this deterioration was less apparent.

Which brings us to the 1980s, and the emergence as sellers in bottle rather than in cask, of perhaps three-quarters of the domaines discussed in the subsequent pages in this book. Here we can definitely talk about an evolution, and an on-going one. Wines have clearly improved in quality. The tannins are more sophisticated, the wines have a better acidity, the fruit flavours are purer and there is more site specificity. Moreover, and just as important, the quality in the lesser years has improved in tandem. So far there has been more progress in red wine than in white. But the lover of red Burgundy is now in the happy position of having a large number of quality estates to chose from.

How Does Burgundy Age?

The abiding principle here is that, provided the balance is correct, any wine will last much better than you think. The most important factor is the acidity in the wine. Acidity preserves the freshness and the fruit, and hence the balance and the elegance. Too many wines today, sadly - and the yield has a lot to do with this - lack the grip, this combination of youthful vigour and acidity, which will ensure that they can last.

I cite an example: yesterday I opened two 1991 white wines, a Meursault, Clos-du-Cromin from Patrick Javillier and a Puligny-Montrachet, Les Folatières from Jean Pascal. Nineteen ninety-one is not the greatest vintage for white Burgundy, but at four and a half years old I expected there to be reasonable vigour if no great depth and concentration. The result? The Javillier was all it should be, because it had a nice fresh acidity. The Pascal, which should have been a lot better (it probably cost half as much again at the outset) was old and tired. On the other hand I have had many a wine - usually, it has to be said, red rather than white - which has been quite delicious, though way beyond even the most ambitious originally suggested drink-by date.

When to Drink Your Wine

As a general rule, assuming a better-than-usual vintage of normal proportions, a well balanced wine will be at its peak as follows:

Red Wines

Mainstream village Côte-de-Beaune	4-10 years (after the vintage)
Mainstream village Côte-de-Nuits *Premier cru* Côte-de-Beaune	6-12 years
Lighter *grand cru* *Premier cru* Côte-de-Nuits	8-15 years
Grand cru	10-25 years

White Wines

Lighter village wines	2-5 years
Better village wines	4-8 years

Premier cru	6-12 years
Grand cru	8 or more to 15 or more years

Make allowances, obviously, for different types of vintages. A lighter red wine year such as 1992 or 1994 will obviously come on stream earlier than 1993 or 1995. And conversely for very rich, tannic vintages.

Naturally the wine will change, becoming mellow but less fresh, during this period of 'Optimum Drinking'. Here your own personal taste comes into it. Make regular notes. You will soon figure out where your own optimum is.

Above all, please, I implore you, do not commit infanticide. One of the *raisons d'être* of magazines like *The Vine* is to review vintages periodically, on their way to maturity, so that you, the reader, do not have to waste your precious bottles.

How to Judge Young Wine

Judging young wine needs time and concentration, a lack of interruption – and ideally, a certain amount of physical comfort, in order to be as relaxed as possible. Moreover, one should be hungry and not tired, and the taste-buds should not already be saturated by dozens of other samples. Manifestly, there is a finite limit to the amount of wine which can be assessed in one session or one day, and while the professional, because he or she does it regularly, can absorb more before the perception decreases, even he or she, in my experience, should limit themselves. Arrogantly we always think we can attempt more than we in fact can.

Plenty of time is essential, as one cannot do the job properly if rushed. It is on and by the finish that a young wine is properly judged. The nose is a good clue, but it can be funky, the palate may be overloaded with tannin, but on the finish and the after-taste one can assess if all the elements – fruit, tannin, acidity, oak, fat, elegance and complexity – are there, and whether in balance. The length is a vital clue.

Do not forget, also, that – if you are in a Burgundian cellar – you will have someone with you – your host – who not only knows a great deal more about it than you do but who will probably be only too happy to explain; and in Burgundy this will be the person responsible for making the wine. Use the opportunity; ask questions; say what you think, and if corrected re-taste; compare and contrast. In short listen and learn.

How to Judge a Good Grower

Imagine the following scenario. You are in, say, Gevrey-Chambertin, and the vintage is good, and you have enjoyed what you have been given to taste. Do you trust your judgement? Do you get out your credit card and start filling up your boot? Putting aside the fact that you can always refer to a book such as this for a second opinion, one final tip is to ask to taste a lesser wine of a lesser vintage. Anyone can or should produce fine wine from fine land in a fine vintage (otherwise they should change their *métier*: go and sell sausages, as one grower put it to me once). But only the good growers produce good wine from lesser *climats* in lesser vintages. So if you want to be sure you can rely on M. Machin's Lavaux-Saint-Jacques 1995, ask to see his Marsannay 1994 as well.

How to Buy Good Burgundy

It is important to be fully informed, which is why I have written this book. And I here refer readers to Appendices One, Two and Three: Rating the Vintages, Rating the Vineyards, Rating the Domaines and *Négociants*. You may assume that each of these is of equal importance. Not so. The name of the grower on the label is paramount. The *climat* is of marginally less precedence and the vintage very much the least.

Burgundy is not a tannic wine. So the poorer vintages will not be dominated by rather unripe tannins as they are in Bordeaux. Even if the wine may be rather lean at the outset, provided the fruit was not rotten, it will eventually mellow, indeed if from a top grower and a good site, be remarkably pleasant.

For a number of years, until my stock ran out, I used to amuse myself by serving a perfectly respectable village Gevrey-Chambertin, 1985 vintage, alongside a Clos-Saint-Jacques 1984 from Charles Rousseau. They had cost me the same amount of money. Which did my guests prefer? Inevitably the 1984. Not a rich, concentrated wine, but a wine of individuality, complexity and elegance.

SHOULD YOU BUY BURGUNDY *EN PRIMEUR*?

Buying futures, taking advantage of your retailer's opening offer is, as far as Burgundy is concerned, sometimes the only way to get hold of the top wines. In Bordeaux, normally, and with the exception of a handful of *recherché* Pomerols, the wines can be bought several years down the road at the equivalent price in real terms. In Burgundy the majority – certainly the *crème de la crème* – disappears out of sight the moment they are offered and are rarely seen again. So buying futures is the only way to get them.

However, unlike Bordeaux, the 'campaign' is extended all the way through the second year and into the third. Some growers and *négociants* fix a price, based on their costs, in the spring or summer following the vintage. Others wait until the next year's wine is in the cellar, so that they can take its quality and quantity into account. Yet more do not commercialise the wine until it is in bottle the following summer. This complicates life for the *en primeur* buyer. How can he or she compare prices? It is a nuisance which just has to be endured.

GETTING HOLD OF IT

This is the difficult bit. You have earmarked what you want. Then you find you can't get hold of it.

In order to avoid future frustration I think every wine-consumer, every Burgundy-lover certainly, however rich, must accept a certain vinous statute of limitation. Not one of time but one of availability. Great Burgundy is made in tiny quantities. There is never enough to go round. Each grower can only deal with a limited number of retailers. Those retailers are obviously going to favour their best customers, people like them who are prepared to take the rough with the smooth, the lesser *cuvées* and vintages as well as the fine and grand.

Naturally you as buyer want to cherry-pick. But don't be surprised if sometimes you can't.

GETTING THE MOST OUT OF YOUR BOTTLES

The correct storage and the eventual service of the wine at the right temperature and in the right environment is as vital as the choice of the best wine in the first place. The role of the owner does not stop at the moment he writes out his cheque.

Bottles should be stored on their side, away from light, heat and movement. They should be allowed to rest undisturbed at an ideal temperature of 11°C (52°F). Temperatures up to 14°C (59°F) can be tolerated, provided there are no sudden jumps. The wine will only mature sooner. The temperature can also fall to 8°C (45°F) without any harm being caused to the wine. Moreover the atmosphere must be humid, a minimum of 70 per cent. This is good for wine but bad for labels. If your home environment cannot provide all this it is a waste of money not to go to the expense of leasing suitable space outside. Why pay £200 a dozen and then skimp on an extra £5 a year for proper storage?

Most red wines are served too warm; most white wines too cold. White Burgundy is a rich wine, and to serve it straight from the depth of the refrigerator is only to stun its flavours: 10–11°C (50-52°F) is optimum.

At least the too-cold glass of Montrachet can be left to gently warm up. If the Musigny is too warm it is irreparably ruined. When we used to talk about room temperature we were referring to the times before universal central heating. What was meant was 16°C (63°F) not 20°C plus (70°F plus). If the red wine is served at too high a temperature its freshness and fragrance are lost. If stored at this level, as sadly happens in restaurants, it very quickly becomes stewed.

Decant both red and white Burgundy if you wish, but at the last minute. Most Burgundians object, preferring the wine to evolve totally in the glass. I find decanting improves the wine. It also makes the service of it easier.

The Art of Good Living

The Art of Good Living, in the gastronomic sense, is the service of good mature wine alongside the appropriate food in the company of good friends. If you have a really great wine to offer, precede it with something similar but lower down the scale. It will set it off better. It will taste even grander.

And then, forget about pecking orders and 90 plus or 19-point scores. And forget also about what it is worth, or what it would cost you to replace it. Just enjoy it!

SPELLING IDIOSYNCRASIES

Burgundy is notoriously haphazard over spelling. Vineyard names can be singular or plural (Griotte or Griottes); hyphenated or not (Beaux-Monts or Beaumonts); can incorporate the definite article or not; and can even use prepositions such as *Aux* or *En* rather than *Le* or *Les*. Moreover no-one is quite sure whether and when to hyphenate. It is Nuits-Saint-Georges, but should it be Clos de la Roche or Clos-de-la-Roche?

By and large I have tried to follow what the growers themselves put on their labels, except where I know them to be in error, i.e. Clos-Vougeot instead of Clos-de-Vougeot. But sometimes I have never seen, or forgotten, what was on the label.

You will notice therefore a number of alternating spellings in the pages that follow. But this is one of the charms of Burgundy.

A NOTE ON THE STAR-RATING SYSTEM

In Part Three of this book the reader will find a multitude of tasting notes on individual wines. It is also necessary to rate the domaines as a whole, and that I have done in Part One.

I have chosen a system which is analogous to that used in the *Michelin* guide. Anyone who has used *Michelin* will be familiar with this, and with its rigorous - even mean - approach. In vinous terms this can be translated as follows:

*** **The best.** A domaine which will not only have significant holdings in *grand cru* vineyards but which will consistently make very high quality wines from them. Naturally they will ask high prices. These domaines are rare.

** **A fine domaine.** Again it will have fine vineyard holdings. High results can be expected and will be priced accordingly.

* **A very good domaine.** The customer can safely buy wines with confidence here.

PART ONE

THE VILLAGES,
THE VINEYARDS,
THE DOMAINES

THE CÔTE DIJONNAISE

The term Côte Dijonnaise applies to such vineyards as exist north of Marsannay in what are now the Dijon suburbs. There have never been a great number of vines here, and of course there are now even fewer, as the city has expanded. But, stubbornly, a few still exist.

Anthony Hanson (*Burgundy*, 1995) has uncovered a grower called Jean Dubris, at the Domaine de la Gras in Plombières-lès-Dijon, which is north of the River Ouche. A couple of kilometres further on, in Daix, the Mortet family of Gevrey own land, and both Denis and his brother Thierry cultivate a couple of hectares.

Further south, in Larrey, there is a vineyard called Montre-Cul whose main owner is Charles Quillardet, now part of Patriarche, and nearby, at Fontaine d'Ouche, there is a vineyard called Les Marcs d'Or which is *en métayage* to the Derey family of Couchey (see page 50).

It is the area round Daix, Hauteville-lès-Dijon and Ahuy, according to Denis Mortet, which is the most interesting. The aspect is right, the geology promising, and there is no reason why one shouldn't produce neat, correct examples of Bourgogne, Pinot Noir or Chardonnay which would have more finesse than the generics from the plain on the east side of the Nuits-Dijon highway. But the locals are not interested, unfortunately. Mortet and his brother seem to be the only ones prepared to bother. It is a sad state of affairs, an opportunity being missed.

MARSANNAY

In 1987, the wines of Marsannay, hitherto simple Bourgogne, but able to be specially differentiated as Bourgogne de Marsannay or Bourgogne de Marsannay-la-Côte, were elevated to village *Appellation Contrôlée*.

This is the closest appellation to the city of Dijon, indeed Marsannay and its neighbours Chenôve and Couchey, over which the vineyard overflows, are more or less suburbs of the city itself. For some years, since 'invented' in the 1920s by the Domaine Clair-Daü, one of the leading local estates, the area has been famous for its *rosé*, and good Pinot Noir *rosé* can be a delicious drink, perhaps the best *rosé* of all; but strangely, since the elevation to village level, the production of *rosé* has declined.

This, at least, is what the locals say. In fact, as *rosé* statistics are usually incorporated into the figure for *rouge*, any trend is difficult to substantiate. Today the *Union Générale de Syndicats*, though not the BIVB (*Bureau Interprofessionel des Vins de Bourgogne*), do publish separate figures. In 1993 96 hectares produced 3,750 hectolitres (495,000 bottles) of *rouge* (where the maximum production allowed, including PLC, is 48 hl/ha), 20 ha produced 765 hl (100,980 bottles) of white (max. 54 hl/ha), while 58 ha yielded 2,931 hl (386,992 bottles) of *rosé* (where the production maximum is 60 hl/ha). Is this less than it used to be?

Marsannay-la-Côte and Couchey

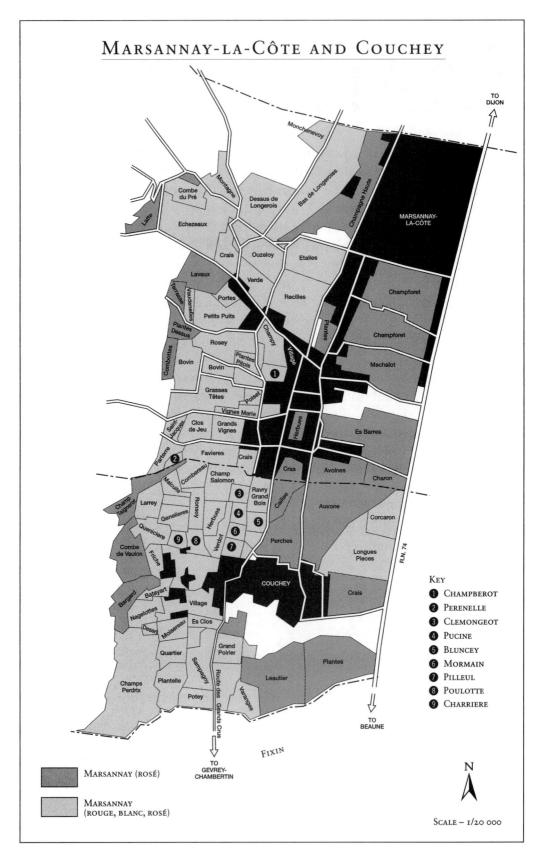

TO DIJON

Monchenevoy

Combe du Pré

Montagne

Dessus de Longerois

Bas de Longerois

Champagne Haute

MARSANNAY-LA-CÔTE

Latre

Echezeaux

Crais

Ouzeloy

Etalles

Lavaux

Verde

Champforet

Terrassenellas

Nauderellas

Portes

Recilles

Plantes

Champforet

Petits Puits

Plantes Dessus

Rosey

Champy

Mechalot

Combottes

Bovin

Plantes Pitois

Bovin

❶

Village

Grasses Têtes

Poise

Es Barres

Vignes Marie

Saint-Jacques

Clos de Jeu

Grands Vignes

Herbues

Partenre

❷

Favieres

Crais

Combereau

Champ Salomon

Cras

Avolnes

Charon

Malcuite

Ravry Grand Bois

❸

Champ Taignerot

Larrey

Ronsoy

❹

Coûtes

Auvone

Corcaron

Genelieres

Herbues

❺

Queniciere

❾

❽

❻

Perches

Longues Pieces

R.N. 74

Combe de Vaulon

Verdot

❼

Friche

COUCHEY

Crais

Bargard

Batayart

Village

Nagelottes

Desen

Moisereau

Es Clos

Grand Poirier

Plantes

Quartier

Stampagny

Leautier

Champs Perdrix

Plantelle

Potey

Route des Grands Crus

Varanges

TO BEAUNE

FIXIN

TO GEVREY-CHAMBERTIN

KEY

❶ CHAMPBEROT
❷ PERENELLE
❸ CLEMONGEOT
❹ PUCINE
❺ BLUNCEY
❻ MORMAIN
❼ PILLEUL
❽ POULOTTE
❾ CHARRIERE

N

▢ MARSANNAY (ROSÉ)

▢ MARSANNAY (ROUGE, BLANC, ROSÉ)

SCALE — 1/20 000

THE VINEYARD

While there are no first growths, let alone *grands crus*, in Marsannay, there are a number of officially recognised *lieux-dits*. These are as follows: Le Boivin; Les Champs-Perdrix; Les Champs-Salomon; Les Echézeaux; Les Favières; Les Finottes; Les Grasses-Têtes; Les Longeroies; Dessus-des-Longeroies; En la Montagne; En Montchevenoy; Les Recilles; Les Roseys; Clos-du-Roi; Saint-Jacques; Les Vaudenelles; Les Vignes-Maries.

These occupy the land above (i.e. westward of) the *Route des Grands Crus* which runs along the middle of the village. Below this road the vines can produce Marsannay *rosé*, but if the wine is red or white it can only be called Bourgogne.

The geology of the Marsannay slopes is complex. Essentially it is good Bathonian or Bajocian limestone, but there are parts where this is replaced by loess or an argilo-siliceous silt, parts which are very clayey indeed, parts with an abundance of stone and gravel, parts where the soil resembles a black grit. Some of these are more propitious for the vine than others.

Of equal importance is the shelter afforded by the Côte itself. Above Marsannay an important valley winds up into the hills. The soil is very clayey here, and the vines very exposed, leading to an abruptly cooler micro-climate. This land will never make good wine, and it ought to be declassified. Yet on some of the lower, more sheltered land on the wrong side of the village, there are some gravel soils which could and do in fact make a very nice little wine.

THE WINE

When the elevation to full village status occurred, leaving the northern part of Brochon as Côte-de-Nuits-Villages, an appellation which can also be applied to the wines of Fixin if the growers so wish, I remember wondering why it hadn't been decided merely to raise the status of Marsannay to this halfway house. Why full village status, which seems to be a higher level? I cannot speak for the authority's reasoning, but now that I know the wines better, I can view this separate village status as quite logical. The wines in fact are different.

The Brochon-Fixin red wines are bigger, quite sturdy, with that robustness the French call *sauvage*. Marsannay reds are, or should be, rather lighter, though they gain in strength as one travels from north to south. It is a mistake to give them too much backbone and muscle. There should only be medium body - there should not be an excess of oak either - and the fruit, as much red fruit flavours as black, should be allowed to sing out. Marsannay is not serious Burgundy: it is the Côte-de-Nuits' version of a Chorey-lès-Beaune or a good Bouzeron. But that is no reason for it not to be a very agreeable, stylish, fruity wine for reasonably early drinking.

While there is this big difference between Marsannay and Fixin *rouge*, there is less of a difference between the white wines, and indeed the resemblance continues into the white wines of Morey-Saint-Denis. When they are well made, such as in the cellar of Bruno Clair where you can taste them side by side, all three - though the Marsannay is the lightest - have a crisp, fruity leanness (but lean in the best sense, which recalls a combination of apple, melon, greengage and peach). This is a long way from the honeyed butteriness of Meursault. They are best quite young, while still fresh. Incidentally vintage years follow the quality of the local reds, which is logical, rather than the relative success of the white wine communes of the Côte-de-Beaune.

And so to the *rosé*. The *rosé* sells for less than the red and the white, which is good from the consumer's point of view, for I'm sure in the best cellars the *rendement* is not excessively higher. It can be commercial, confected and a bit sweet, if you find the wrong source; but it can be poised, racy and delightfully fruity and elegant if you stick to the best such as those from Hugenot, Régis Bouvier and the aforementioned Bruno Clair. *Rosé* suffers from not being considered serious. But why do we have to be 'serious' all the time? And surely it is no more or less serious than the red and the white. It deserves to be more popular. I would suggest that there are all manner of occasions and dishes, especially during the summer, when a Marsannay *rosé* would be just as appropriate as anything else. And twice as delicious.

THE GROWERS OF CHENOVE, MARSANNAY AND COUCHEY

(all in Marsannay unless otherwise stated)

BART

19 ha: owned and *en fermage*. Chambertin, Clos-de-Bèze (41 a); Bonnes-Mares (1.03 ha); Fixin *premier cru* Les Hervelets; village Chambolle-Musigny; village Santenay *rouge et blanc*; village Marsannay *rouge, blanc et rosé*; Côte-de-Nuits-Villages.

The youthful Martin Bart's grandfather was a Clair of Clair-Daü, and it is from the dismemberment of this domaine in the early 1980s that much of the estate derives: the Clos-de-Bèze, for instance, and the Bonnes-Mares, whose vines were planted in 1935.

The wines are made in a large modern cellar constructed in 1987. There is total de-stemming and an average of 25 per cent new oak. The results are full, rich and with good intensity.

RÉGIS BOUVIER

12.50 ha: owned and *en fermage*. Marsannay *rouge, blanc et rosé*, including the *lieux-dits* Clos-du-Roi and Les Longeroies; village Morey-Saint-Denis, including the *lieu-dit* En La Rue de Vergy; village Gevrey-Chambertin; village Fixin.

Régis Bouvier struck out on his own - there is a separate Domaine René et Bernard Bouvier run by his father and brother - in 1981. He had 3 ha then, which he has since extended, the Gevrey being the latest addition. This is a neat, efficient set-up, with epoxy-resin-lined cement vats and automatic *pigeage* in a cellar constructed in 1987. Good wines.

MARC BROCOT

5 ha: owned and *en fermage*. Village Gevrey-Chambertin; Marsannay, Les Echézeaux (*rouge*); Marsannay *blanc*.

Marc Brocot is a large dark-haired man in his early forties who up to 1988 sold nearly everything he produced in bulk. But since then he's been keeping back more and more for selling in bottle. The grapes are totally destemmed, matured using one-third new oak and bottled just before the subsequent vintage. These are attractively plump fruity wines for the medium term.

*BRUNO CLAIR

20 ha: owned and *en fermage*. Chambertin, Clos-de-Bèze (1 ha); Corton-Charlemagne (34 a); Gevrey-Chambertin *premier cru* in Clos-Saint-Jacques, Les Cazetiers and Clos-du-Fonteny (*monopole*); Savigny-lès-Beaune *premier cru* La Dominode; village Morey-Saint-Denis in the *lieu-dit* En La Rue de Vergy (*rouge*); village Morey-Saint-Denis (*blanc*); village Chambolle-Musigny in the *lieu-dit* Les Veroilles; village Vosne-Romanée in the *lieu-dit* Les Champs-Perdrix; village Aloxe-Corton; Marsannay, including the *lieux-dits* Les Grasses-Têtes, Les Longeroies, Les Vaudenelles (all *rouge*); Marsannay *blanc et rosé*.

This is the most important property in the village. Its origins, like those of the Domaine Bart (see above) lie in the old Clair-Daü estate, broken up in the early 1980s. Bruno Clair has expanded since, notably by rescuing land above Clos-de-Tart and Bonnes-Mares. Some of the vines in Savigny-lès-Beaune, La Dominode date from 1902.

Clair is a meticulous wine-maker, anxious above all for purity and elegance. These are not for those who like their Burgundies sweet, syrupy and fat. He works alongside André Geoffroy, who has vines in Fixin (see below), and oenologist Philippe Brun out of a splendidly cavernous cellar behind his house. The quality here, from perfectly respectable beginnings in 1986, has improved enormously. This is now one of the top domaines in Burgundy.

See Profile, page 385.

DEREY FRÈRES, DOMAINE DE LA CROIX-SAINT-GERMAIN, COUCHEY

19 ha: owned and *en fermage/métayage*. Marsannay, *rouge, blanc et rosé* including the *lieux-dits* Vignes-Maries and Les Champs-Perdrix; Fixin *premier cru* Les Hervelets; village Fixin; village Gevrey-Chambertin; Côte-de-Nuits-Villages.

The Derey domaine has been passed down from father to son since 1650, and is currently, despite the current title, run by Albert Derey and his son Hervé. One-third new wood here, but in my experience somewhat lack-lustre wines. A curiosity in the portfolio is the Clos-des-Marcs-d'Or, half a hectare of Chardonnay in Fontaine d'Ouche belonging to the City of Dijon, which the Dereys farm on a *métayage* basis.

FOUGERAY DE BEAUCLAIR

21.68 ha: owned and *en fermage*. Bonnes-Mares (1.61 ha); village Savigny-lès-Beaune *rouge et blanc* in the *lieu-dit* Les Gollardes; village Vosne-Romanée in the *lieu-dit* Les Damodes; village Gevrey-Chambertin in the *lieu-dit* Les Sauvrées; village Fixin, including the 'Clos Marion'; Marsannay, *rouge, rosé et blanc*, including the *lieux-dits* Les Favières, Les Saint-Jacques, Les Grasses-Têtes, Le Dessus-des-Longeroies; Côte-de-Nuits-Villages.

There have been improvements in the last few years: a new cellar, and the arrival of son-in-law Patrice Ollivier. The domaine came into existence in 1986 when Bernard Clair, father of Bruno, leased to Jean-Louis Fougeray his Bonnes-Mares. This parcel is the totality of that part of the *grand cru* which lies in Morey-Saint-Denis. From 1994 they have taken on the lease of the Domaine Marion's Fixin.

JEAN FOURNIER

14.23 ha: owned and *en fermage*. Marsannay *rouge, blanc et rosé*, including the *lieux-dits* Les Longeroies, Clos-du-Roi, Les Echézeaux; village Gevrey-Chambertin.

No immediate relation to other Fourniers (there are two Fournier domaines in neighbouring Couchey), Jean Fournier, bluff, middle-aged, ages his wines for eight months in barrel and then a further twelve in tank before bottling. The wines are clean, not rustic, but could do with an extra zip of personality.

ANDRÉ GEOFFROY

3.50 ha: owned. Village Fixin, *rouge et blanc*.

André Geoffroy works alongside Bruno Clair (see above) and makes elegant, fruity, 'modern' wines from his Fixin estate. The white wine is particularly good, and he supplies this to Jadot who make a splendid wine with it, with twice the volume and depth of a Marsannay *blanc*.

ALAIN GUYARD

9 ha: owned. Village Vosne-Romanée in the *lieu-dit* Aux Réas; village Gevrey-Chambertin; village Fixin; Côte-de-Nuits-Villages; Marsannay *rouge, rosé et blanc*.

Alain Guyard has now taken over from his father Lucien at this friendly domaine next to the one-star restaurant Les Gourmets. No startling *climats* but competently-made wines. 'I find I become more and more anti new wood,' says Guyard *père*. 'If the wine is good it needs no more than a touch.' A touch here is one-fifth.

HUGUENOT

20 ha: owned and *en fermage*. Charmes-Chambertin (22a); Gevrey-Chambertin *premier cru* Les Fontenys; village Gevrey-Chambertin; village Fixin, including the *lieu-dit* Les Petits-Crais; Marsannay *rouge, blanc et rosé* including the *lieux-dits* La Montagne, Les Echézeaux, Les Champs-Perdrix, Clos-du-Roi, Champs-Salomon; Côte-de-Nuits-Villages.

The big, bearded Jean-Louis Huguenot runs one of the best domaines in the village, vinifying in epoxy-resin-lined concrete vats and stainless steel in a modern cellar, retaining 10 per cent of the stems and using 15 per cent new oak. Good clean-cut Marsannays. The Champs-Perdrix, adjoining the vineyards of Fixin, is a recent addition to the range, and full and plummy. The Echézeaux is less fat and rich, but a stylish example for medium-term drinking.

CHÂTEAU DE MARSANNAY

45 ha: owned. Clos-de-Vougeot (21 ha); Vosne-Romanée *premier cru* Les Orveaux; Gevrey-Chambertin *premier cru*; village Fixin; Marsannay *rouge* in the *lieu-dit* Les Echézeaux; Marsannay *rouge, rosé et blanc*.

This pretentious tourist-trap was bought by Patriarche in 1990 when they acquired Charles Quillardet to become a sort of red counterpoint to the Château de Meursault. I am sure it is very successful. Sadly the wines, sold under such pretentious names as Cuvée Anne de Sault, Cuvée Charles le Téméraire and Cuvée Pierre de Baufremont, are very commercial. The reds are soulless, the *rosés* flat and suspiciously sweet.

★PHILIPPE NADDEF, COUCHEY

5 ha: owned and *en fermage/métayage*. Mazis-Chambertin (40 a); Gevrey-Chambertin *premier cru* in Les Cazetiers, Les Champeaux; village Gevrey-Chambertin, including a *vieilles vignes cuvée*; village Fixin; Marsannay *rouge*.

This is the only grower I know in Couchey, but a very good one he is! Philippe Naddef is lean, dark, intense and perfectionistic. He has been on his own since 1983, working mainly with the vines from his maternal grandfather.

The recipe is 100 per cent destalking, fifteen to eighteen days' maceration at temperatures up to 32°C with lots of *pigeages*, and 100 per cent new oak for all except the Marsannay. The results are full, rich, vibrant and long-lasting.

CÔTE-DE-NUITS-
VILLAGES

This is a useful local appellation encompassing peripheral minor villages of the Côte. Though not so well known as its equivalent, Côte-de-Beaune-Villages, Côte-de-Nuits-Villages provides an inexpensive introduction to the great wines of the Côte, and is often as good as a lesser grower's village wine at half the price.

The villages entitled to the appellation Côte-de-Nuits-Villages are Fixin (which can also sell off wine as Fixin) and Brochon, which are both to the north; at the southern end of the Côte are Prissey, Comblanchien and Corgoloin.

According to Sylvain Pitiot and Pierre Poupon (*Atlas des Grands Vignobles de Bourgogne*), there are 310 ha of land entitled to this appellation (this includes all of Fixin's village AC). In 1993 the declaration, from 157 ha under Pinot Noir and 3 ha under white grapes, was 6,902 hl (911,000 bottles) of red wine and 129 hl (17,000 bottles) of white wine.

Depending on where it comes from - for in practice there is little blending of the wines of the northern sector with those of the south - the wine can be either a lesser sort of Nuits-Saint-Georges or a Fixin look-alike. In general it will have medium to full body (more than a Marsannay or an Hautes-Côtes), be robust, fruity and a little four-square. I find the wines of Fixin and Brochon origins more interesting - more elegant - than those of the south.

There is a little white, as noted above. I have rarely tasted it.

Recommended Sources: Denis Bachelet, Michel Esmonin et Fille; Philippe Rossignol (all Gevrey-Chambertin); Chopin et Fils; Daniel Chopin-Groffier (both Comblanchien); Domaine de l'Arlot, Jean-Jacques Confuron; Philippe Gavignet; Daniel Rion (all Nuits-Saint-Georges); Robert Jayer-Gilles (Magny-lès-Villers in the Hautes-Côtes).

FIXIN

Fixin, pronounced Fissin, is the next commune south on the Côte d'Or. It is in fact an amalgamation of two communes, Fixey and Fixin. The two villages are now part of the same sprawl, originally being a few hundred metres apart, with Fixey being further up the slope and to the north.

Fixin's best-known estate, the Clos-de-la-Perrière, lies underneath the trees above the village on the southern side. As its name suggests it was once the site of a quarry. The Dukes of Burgundy used the *manoir* as a hunting lodge, but donated it to the monks of Citeaux - who used it as a convalescent home - in 1142.

Two of the main vineyards of the village, Clos-du-Chapitre and Les Arvelets, came under the jurisdiction of another ecclesiastical establishment, Saint-Mammès-de-Langres, associated with the Abbey of Bèze.

The village also has Napoleonic connections. Some 160 years ago Claude Noisot, a local aristocrat who had fought alongside the Emperor in many a battle, and who had even accompanied him in exile to Elba, arrived back in the village. He proceeded to re-christen one of his vineyards Clos-Napoléon (prior to that it had been called Aux Cleusots or Les Echézeaux), instal a small museum of memorabilia and commission a statue from the Dijon sculptor Rudé for the local village square. All this did much to help the esteem of the local wine.

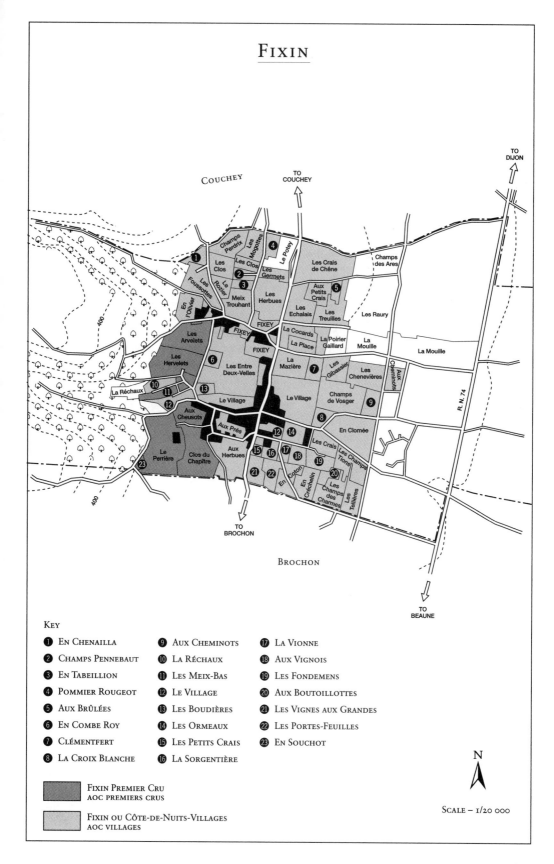

LOCATION

The appellation is roughly square, with the *premiers crus* (there are no *grands crus*) huddled together up-slope at the southern end. The decree for village AC extends halfway down between the *Route des Grands Crus* and the main road, while in Gevrey-Chambertin, a kilometre or so to the south, village land extends across the Dijon-Nuits highway and beyond.

The soil structure is based on a hard Bajocian limestone, capable of taking a fine marble polish, and is a mixture of marl and limestone debris. It is more stony as one mounts the slope, and steeper to the south (Clos-de-la-Perrière, Clos-du-Chapitre) than to the north in Les Hervelets and Les Arvelets). Only in the Clos-du-Chapitre itself is the brown-coloured limestone of Bathonian origin, and here the soil is the most stony of all.

THE VINEYARD

Premiers Crus: There are eight, in whole or in part: Les Arvelets; Clos-de-la-Perrière (*monopole*); Clos-du-Chapitre (*monopole*); Clos-Napoléon (*monopole*); Les Hervelets; Les Meix-Bas; Queue-de-Hareng (which lies adjacent to the Clos-de-la-Perrière but is in the neighbouring commune of Brochon); and En Suchot. In practice only five of these are ever seen (see below).

The appellation Fixin *premier cru* exists for both red and white wine. Philippe Joliet at the Clos-de-la-Perrière - he made 10 hl from half a hectare of young vines in 1993 - is the only producer of *premier cru* white wine that I know of. Altogether these *premiers crus* cover 22.38 ha (1.62 of which is in Brochon) and produce around 700 hl (92,400 bottles) per annum.

Village Wine: Village Fixin can be sold as such or under the name Côte-de-Nuits-Villages (see page 000). This makes the precise area delimited as village wine in the commune difficult to establish. The list of *lieux-dits* enumerated in Pitiot and Poupon's *Atlas des Grands Vignobles de Bourgogne* add up to 107.35 ha. Against this must be compared the actual declaration in 1993 of 77.51 ha (of which 1.08 ha was white) and a production figure of 3,347 hl (44,180 bottles of red wine) and 36 hl (4,752 bottles of white wine).

The word perennially used to describe the wines of Fixin is *sauvage*, a connotation equally applied to the wines of Brochon and to some extent to those vineyards in the northern part of Gevrey which lie on the same line of slope.

'*Sauvage*' wines, at their worst, can be merely lumpy and artisanal: size without grace. At their best, a richness as well as a power is indicated, a hardness in youth, but an ability to age to produce something which while always a little austere, is nevertheless of interest and depth when the wine softens up. Clos-du-Chapitre and Clos-Napoléon have this, and so do some of the village wines, though obviously to a lesser degree of distinction. The Fixin from Les Arvelets and Les Hervelets, however, are lighter and softer: feminine, if one is still permitted to use the term.

THE PREMIERS CRUS
LES ARVELETS (3.36 HA) • LES HERVELETS (4.32 HA)

As it is permitted to declare the produce from the Les Meix-Bas as Les Hervelets, that is what everyone does and Les Meix-Bas is never seen. To complicate matters further, Les Arvelets can be declared as Les Hervelets, but not, for some reason, vice versa. These two *premiers crus* are the only ones in Fixin not to be monopolies. They lie north of the three others on a slope which is more gentle and less stony. The wine is not as strong and manly here as in the *premiers crus* below. The volume is that of Morey rather than Gevrey, but in good hands there can be plenty of elegance. Dr Lavalle was even prepared to compare the wine with that of Clos-Saint-Jacques in Gevrey-Chambertin. But that, I fear, is going a little too far.

Recommended Sources: Pierre Gelin (Les Hervelets); Vincent et Denis Berthaut (Les Arvelets).

CLOS-DE-LA-PERRIÈRE (6.80 HA)

This *premier cru* incorporates En Suchot and Queue-de-Hareng and is the monopoly of Philippe Joliet (see below).

CLOS-DU-CHAPITRE (4.79 HA) • CLOS-NAPOLÉON (1.83 HA)

These two *premiers crus* lie alongside each other underneath the Clos-de-la-Perrière. Both are monopolies. The Domaine Gelin owns the latter and farmed the former up to the 1984 vintage on behalf of the Domaine Marion. Marion has since sold this to Guy Dufouleur (see below).

THE GROWERS

BERNARD, DOMAINE DU CLOS-SAINT-LOUIS

7.66 ha: owned. Fixin *premier cru* Les Hervelets; village Fixin including the *lieu-dit* L'Olivier; village Gevrey-Chambertin; Marsannay *blanc et rosé*; Côte-de-Nuits-Villages.

Philippe Bernard has now taken over from his father Charles at this long-established family domaine, situated at the north end of the village under the Fixey church. Part of the carefully restored old building houses a museum of old viticultural and vinicultural implements. With land mainly at the Couchey side of the village, these are only medium-weight wines. Sometimes they can be too slight, but they do not lack style.

VINCENT AND DENIS BERTHAUT

13 ha: *en fermage/métayage*. Fixin *premier cru* Les Arvelets; village Fixin including the *lieux-dits* Les Clos, Les Crais; Gevrey-Chambertin *premier cru*; village Gevrey-Chambertin; Côte-de-Nuits-Villages.

Vincent, bald, around fifty, and his younger, taller, bespectacled and also balding brother Denis, run this domaine, much of which is rented or share-cropped. One of the Gevrey owners is the Domaine Chézeaux, the rest of whose land is *en métayage* to the Domaine Ponsot in Morey-Saint-Denis. The Gevrey-Chambertin *premier cru* comes from Cazetiers and Lavaux-Saint-Jacques, but there is not a lot of it, and in short vintages it is incorporated into the village *cuvée*. Well-made, rich wines here, bottled two years after the vintage; the Arvelets showing much more sophisticated tannins than the village Fixins. The domaine is cautious about new oak, preferring the barrels to be 'run in' by the Gerbet domaine in Vosne-Romanée - Denis Berthaut being married to one of the Gerbet sisters.

PIERRE GELIN
(formerly Gelin et Molin)

11.0 ha: owned and *en fermage*. Chambertin, Clos-de-Bèze (60 a); Mazis-Chambertin (38 a) until 1994; village Gevrey-Chambertin in the *lieu-dit* of Clos-Prieur; Fixin *premier cru* Clos-du-Chapitre (*monopole*), Clos-Napoléon (*monopole*), Les Hervelets; village Fixin.

The year 1995 saw the end of an era at this domaine. André Molin, brother-in-law of Stéphane Gelin, retired, and the estate was then split between the two families. Jean-Michel Morin now has charge of the Mazis and the Hervelets. Moreover, with the changes that have happened in the Marion family, the Gelins no longer exploit the Clos-du-Chapitre (see above).

Gelin believes in a long *cuvaison* at 30–32°C, without stalks, and uses about 25 per cent new oak for his top wines. These are rich, substantial wines, the Clos-Napoléon a little fatter and more masculine than the Hervelets but not as muscular or as long-lasting as the Clos-du-Chapitre.

MANOIR DE LA PERRIÈRE

6.80 ha: owned. Fixin, Clos-de-la-Perrière (*monopole*).

Dominating the village, as it has done for nearly nine centuries, the Manoir de la Perrière dates in part from before the donation of the vineyard by Duke Eudes of Burgundy to his brother Henri of the Abbey of Citeaux, in 1102 or 1142, depending on the source of your information. Essentially, however, its construction can be placed in the thirteenth to fifteenth centuries. The cavernous, vaulted, earth-floored cellar contains a large and impressive medieval press.

The building and its splendidly situated vineyard have belonged to the Joliet family since 1853. Philippe Joliet, the current proprietor, angry, bearded and unkempt, rules over his domaine like a medieval lord. There is but one *cuvée* of wine, which is a pity, given the potential economies of scale, and more often than not it is a bit rustic, though the 1990 is good. On the basis of the 1990 I would suggest that the vineyard *could* certainly live up to its past reputation as the best in the commune, and would produce a more feminine, less *sauvage* wine than the Clos-du-Chapitre and Clos-Napoléon further down the slope.

From the 1994 vintage there is a little young-vine white wine. So far I have not sampled it. And in this year Joliet's son Benigne joined his father in the cellar.

GILBERT MONIOT-DEFRANCE

3 ha: owned. Village Fixin, including the *lieux-dits* La Mazière, Les Champs-Perdrix.

This is a small, somewhat artisanal set-up, run by the vigorous, seventy-something Gilbert Moniot. There is no new wood, and bottling takes place when sales demand. Some of the 1993 was still in cask more than two and a half years after the vintage. The Champs-Perdrix is a fuller wine than the Mazière.

GEVREY-CHAMBERTIN

With Gevrey we arrive at the beginning of the finest sector of the Burgundian vineyards. Gevrey-Chambertin is the largest of the great communes of the Côte-de-Nuits and can boast nine out of the twenty-four Côte-de-Nuits *grands crus*. It therefore vies with Vosne - which has six - as being the most important commune of them all: the apogee of Burgundy, the pinnacle of the Pinot Noir.

The wines are indeed - or should be - sumptuous. At the summit are Chambertin and Chambertin, Clos-de-Bèze: immaculate and full, firm and rich, concentrated and masculine, similar but subtly different from one another. Ruchottes and Mazis are less structured, but pure and intense. Chapelle and Griottes show a hint of red fruit, cherries or raspberries, according to taste, and the velvet changes discreetly to silk. Charmes and Mazoyères are softer and more feminine, Latricières coarser and more spicy. But all can inspire. And the brilliance and poise of Clos-Saint-Jacques, denied *grand cru* status, forever points a finger at the errors of the *Appellation Contrôlée* ratings.

Gevrey is not only a large commune but a large village, with some eighty families making a living out of wine. A great many of these now bottle their own produce, and have set up in competition with larger, earlier established domaines. As two or three of these senior exploitations are sadly currently under-achieving, these new enterprises are not without customers. The village is today a happy hunting-ground for those seeking out good wine.

Gevrey-Chambertin is a full and sturdy wine, rich and masculine, but with a touch of the fleshy and the exotic. Sensual and vigorous, it is more flamboyant than Vosne and more substantial than Chambolle. Musigny can be said to be the queen, the epitome of delicacy and finesse, but Le Chambertin is king, simply the complete Burgundy. '*Tout le Grand Bourgogne possible*,' to quote the poet Gaston Rompnel.

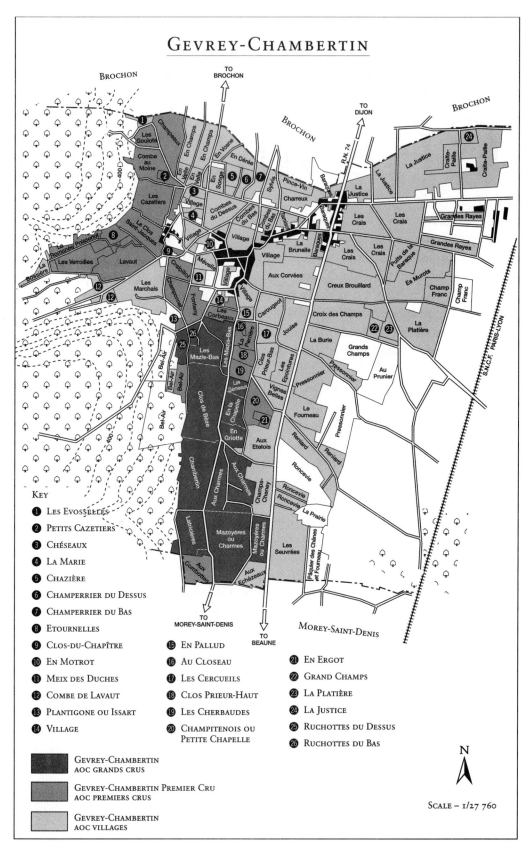

GEVREY-CHAMBERTIN

BROCHON

TO BROCHON

BROCHON

TO DIJON

BROCHON

Les Goulots

Champeaux

En Champs

En Champs

En Vosne

En Dérée

Sylvie

Pince-Vin

La Justice

Craite-Paille

La Justice

Craite-Paille

Combe au Moine

En Mêle

En Pallud

En Songe

Charreux

La Justice

Les Cazetiers

Village

Combes du Dessus

Combes du Bas

Combe du Bas

Les Crais

Les Crais

Grandes Rayes

Le Clos Saint-Jacques

Village

Village

Fontenys

Barques

Grandes Rayes

Romanée Poissenot

Les Verroilles

Lavaut

Créspillot

Mévelle

La Brunelle

Barques

Les Crais

Les Crais

Puits de la Barque

Bossière

Les Marchais

Champonnet

Fontany

Village

Aux Corvées

Creux Brouillard

Es Murots

Champ Franc

Champ Franc

Les Corbeaux

Village

Carougeot

Croix des Champs

La Platière

Plantigone ou Issart

La Perrière

Joulise

La Burie

Grands Champs

Les Mazis-Bas

Les Mazis-Bas

Clos Prieur-Bas

Les Epointures

Pressonnier

Au Prunier

Pressonnier

Bel-Air

Les Cimeaux

Vignes Belles

Pressonnier

Bel-Air

Clos de Bèze

En la Chapelle

Le Fourneau

Bel-Air

En Griotte

Aux Etelois

Renard

Renard

Chambertin

Aux Charmes

Aux Charmes

Champs-Cheney

Roncevie

Roncevie

La Prairie

Roncevie

Latricières

Mazoyères ou Charmes

Mazoyères ou Charmes

Les Seuvrées

Paquier des Chênes et Fourneau

Aux Combottes

Aux Echézeaux

S.N.C.F. PARIS-LYON

KEY

1 LES EVOSSELLES
2 PETITS CAZETIERS
3 CHÉSEAUX
4 LA MARIE
5 CHAZIÈRE
6 CHAMPERRIER DU DESSUS
7 CHAMPERRIER DU BAS
8 ETOURNELLES
9 CLOS-DU-CHAPÎTRE
10 EN MOTROT
11 MEIX DES DUCHES
12 COMBE DE LAVAUT
13 PLANTIGONE OU ISSART
14 VILLAGE

15 EN PALLUD
16 AU CLOSEAU
17 LES CERCUEILS
18 CLOS PRIEUR-HAUT
19 LES CHERBAUDES
20 CHAMPITENOIS OU PETITE CHAPELLE

21 EN ERGOT
22 GRAND CHAMPS
23 LA PLATIÈRE
24 LA JUSTICE
25 RUCHOTTES DU DESSUS
26 RUCHOTTES DU BAS

TO MOREY-SAINT-DENIS

TO BEAUNE

MOREY-SAINT-DENIS

TO MOREY-SAINT-DENIS

GEVREY-CHAMBERTIN
AOC GRANDS CRUS

GEVREY-CHAMBERTIN PREMIER CRU
AOC PREMIERS CRUS

GEVREY-CHAMBERTIN
AOC VILLAGES

N

SCALE – 1/27 760

HISTORY

The name Gevrey comes from Gabriacus, a name dating from Gallo-Roman times and first recorded in AD 640. About this time, the Abbey of Bèze was given land by Duke Amalgaire of Burgundy which the monks planted with vines. Shortly afterwards, so legend has it, a peasant named Bertin decided that he, too, would plant vines on his neighbouring plot. From the *campus* or *champ* Bertin comes the title of Gevrey's greatest vineyard.

In 894, the Abbey of Sainte-Benigne was donated land by another Burgundian Duke, Richard Le Justicier. This abbey soon came under the jurisdiction of the great ecclesiastical establishment at Cluny. The castle, built at the behest of the abbot, still stands. In the Middle Ages the Abbey of Bèze sold their vineyards to the Cathedral Chapter of Saint-Mammès at Langres, who remained the nominal proprietors until the French Revolution. During the seventeenth century the Chapter leased out Clos-de-Bèze and other vineyards in their possession, as did other ecclesiastical establishments such as the closer abbey at Citeaux. Clos-Saint-Jacques passed to the Morizot family. Claude Jomard, a local parliamentarian, took a twenty-year lease over Clos-de-Bèze, and, it is said, had to make some significant reparations to the state of the vineyard. It must originally have been a walled enclosure, but little of this stands today.

Meanwhile, alongside, we find an Act dated 1276 signed by Guillaume de Grancey and the Abbey at Cluny, referring to vines in the Champ Bertin. At the end of the fifteenth century there is a similar deed between the Sire de Thénissey and the *Chapitre* at Langres.

Chambertin, perhaps because it was earlier to be leased into secular hands, seems always to have had the edge in terms of reputation over Clos-de-Bèze. Claude Arnoux, an *emigré* Beaunois priest, published one of the first accounts of the wines of Burgundy in London in 1728. Chambertin, in Arnoux's opinion, is 'the most considerable wine in all Burgundy . . . . It has all the qualities and none of the defects of the other wines.' It sold for twice that of the wines of Volnay, Pommard and Beaune, at 40–42 pounds sterling the *queue*. A century later, André Jullien placed Chambertin second only to the Romanée-Conti of all the red wines of Burgundy. Clos-de-Bèze is not mentioned at all. Perhaps the explanation is that the wine from either *climat* was sold as Chambertin, *tout court*, as is permitted today.

Much of the renown of Chambertin is due to the forceful promotion of the *négociant* Claude Jobert. Jobert arrived in Gevrey in 1731, started dealing with the successors to Claude Jomard, and by 1750 was in control of over half of Chambertin and Clos-de-Bèze. In all he built up a domaine of over 500 *ouvrées* (more than 20 ha) in Gevrey, Morey and Chambolle. He even succeeded in changing his name to Claude Jobert de Chambertin! By the time of his death in 1761 Chambertin was fetching 400 *livres* the *queue*, ten times the price it had commanded in the previous century.

Clos-de-Bèze and Chambertin were auctioned off as *biens nationaux* on 29 January and 26 October 1791, the price of the Chambertin achieving 777 *livres* an *ouvrée* (Clos-de-Vougeot had fetched 606 *livres*), a record price. A certain Claude Antoine Gelquin soon found himself with 2 ha of Chambertin, one of the Clos-de-Bèze, three of Clos-Saint-Jacques, Cazetiers, Charmes, Chapelle, Ruchottes, etc. Fairly soon the inevitable further parcellation was to begin.

Napoléon's predilection for the wines of Chambertin is well known. He is reputed to have drunk little else. It would seem that the Emperor drank his Chambertin - five or six years bottled with an embossed 'N' - much diluted with water. On the retreat from Moscow, though, his cellar was stolen by Cossacks, or so his stewards alleged. The French market was soon flooded with fake Chambertin 'returned from Russia', enough to have been the production of a number of vintages!

The wine of Chambertin and Clos-de-Bèze, not least because of this Napoleonic patronage, has a great reputation. Understandably the neighbouring wines have sought to share its glory. If Chambertin and Clos-de-Bèze were undisputed first growths, then any contiguous vineyard should be a sort of lesser first growth as well, and entitled to the name, so went the argument. Moreover, thanks to some astute lobbying by the local mayor, by decree of Louis-Philippe in 1847, the village of Gevrey (and hence the wines too) was allowed to suffix its name with that of Chambertin. This established a trend which was soon followed by most of the other villages on the Côte.

In 1855 Dr Lavalle (*Histoire et Statistique de la Vigne et des Grands Vins de la Côte d'Or*) decreed one single *tête de cuvée* in Gevrey-Chambertin, by which he meant Chambertin and Chambertin, Clos-de-Bèze. As *premières cuvées* he listed Clos-Saint-Jacques in first place, followed by 'Fouchère', Chapelle (*haute*), Mazis (*haute*), Ruchottes (*du dessus*), Charmes (*haute*), Griottes (*haute*), Veroilles (*vieille*), Estournelles and Cazetiers (*haute*). Latricières and Mazoyères were included among the *deuxièmes cuvées*.

As the nineteenth century progressed, little by little, discreetly and stealthily, a number of the *climats* surrounding Chambertin and Clos-de-Bèze began to tag the magic word on to their names, just as the Napoleonic decree had permitted the village itself to do. Mazis became Mazis-Chambertin; Griottes, Griottes-Chambertin, and so on. This proved useful when it came to the official codification of the concept of *grand cru* in the 1930s. At the same time many *climats* were absorbed into superior neighbours, notably Les Gemeaux into Chapelle and Fouchère (see above) into Chambertin itself.

The AOC laws of 1936 confirmed a number of historical practices. Firstly that Clos-de-Bèze could be prefixed with the name Chambertin, but that the six or seven other *grands crus* could only hyphenate it on as a suffix. Secondly that Clos-de-Bèze could be sold as Chambertin *tout court*, but not vice versa. An allowance was given to the producers of Mazoyères-Chambertin to call their wine Charmes-Chambertin, as had been their practice up until then. Moreover the village appellation overlaps into the next commune to the north. Some 50 hectares of Brochon can make wine which can be labelled village Gevrey-Chambertin.

Unlike nearly all the other villages of the Côte d'Or, Gevrey-Chambertin possesses a substantial amount of village AC land on the 'wrong', i.e. eastern, side of the road. Morey has a little; Nuits-Saint-Georges a scrap (but including a *premier cru*); but the only other commune with a large amount east of the N74 is Chorey-lès-Beaune. The explanation is similar: the action of rivers rushing out of the Hautes-Côtes has pushed alluvial limestone debris and gravel - good land for the vine - further into the flatlands of the Saône.

LOCATION

The village of Gevrey-Chambertin, south of Brochon, north of Morey-Saint-Denis, lies on the same level as its *grands crus* at the point where the Combe de Lavaux opens out into the valley. It sprawls all the way down to the main road and then beyond towards the railway line, which side, with several *zones industriels*, is the newest part.

At the top of the village is its château, constructed in the late thirteenth century by Yves de Chazan, Abbot of Cluny. Only two of the four original towers still remain. The cellars are impressive, as are the fortifications. Once inside, you were well and truly protected! Nearby is the church of Saint Aignan, a bit of an architectural muddle, but externally medieval. More impressive is the restored Cellier des Dîmes, once a chapter house, later the place where tenants of the church would come to pay their rent in kind. The ground floor - and the loft above - were used for storing the cereals; the cellar for wine. One local *vigneron*, the excellent Claude Dugat, rents the cellars today.

Having spent the past 100 years taking up the cobbles in the main part of Gevrey, to replace them with tarmac, the last decade has seen those cobbles replaced, as the local authorities attempt to make the village pedestrian-friendly. As a result the poor motorist has to drive around the houses to get from A to B. The *Route des Grands Crus* is interrupted, and those who live on the periphery now get the noise which plagued those who were in the centre. Gevrey is nevertheless a friendly, bustling place, with several good restaurants of varying degrees of pretension and expense. Every September it hosts Le Roi Chambertin, a combination of blind-tasting competition, similar to the Clos-de-Vougeot *tastevinage*, general open house and grand dinners.

THE VINEYARD

Grands Crus: There are eight or nine *grands crus*: Chambertin; Chambertin, Clos-de-Bèze; Chapelle-Chambertin; Charmes-Chambertin (incorporating Mazoyères-Chambertin); Griottes-Chambertin; Latricières-Chambertin; Mazis-Chambertin; and Ruchottes-Chambertin.

These comprise some 87 ha and produce an average of 2,600 hl (343,000 bottles) per annum. Charmes and Mazoyères together contribute over a third of this.

They lie in one contiguous mass on the south side of the village, either above the *Route des Grands Crus* (Mazis, Ruchottes, Clos-de-Bèze, Chambertin, Latricières), or below it (Chapelle, Griottes, Charmes) on the way to Morey-Saint-Denis.

Premiers Crus: There are twenty-six *premiers crus* in Gevrey-Chambertin, in whole or in part. Altogether they cover some 86 ha and produce 3,500 hl (460,000 bottles) a year. In alphabetical order they are as follows: Bel-Air (part); La Boissière (part); Les Cazetiers; Les Champeaux; Les Champitonnois (more commonly known as La Petite-Chapelle); Les Champonnets; Les Cherbaudes; Clos-du-Chapitre; Clos-Prieur (part); Clos-Saint-Jacques; Clos-des-Varoilles; Au Closeau; La Combe-aux-Moines; Aux Combottes; Les Corbeaux (part); Le Craipillot; Les Ergots; Les Estournelles (-Saint-Jacques); Le Fonteny; Les Goulots; Les Issarts; Lavaux-Saint-Jacques; Les Petits-Cazetiers; La Perrière; Le Poissenot; La Romanée (part).

Village Wine: Including the 50 ha in the commune of Brochon, but entitled to the Gevrey-Chambertin AC, there are 369 ha of village vineyard. The average production is 135,000 hl (18.3 million bottles). The appellation Gevrey-Chambertin, like that of Vosne-Romanéee, but not that of Morey-Saint-Denis, applies to red wine only.

The village wines come from three distinct sections: the north, Brochon side of the village; the south, underneath the *grands crus*; and from across the main Nuits-Saint-Georges to Dijon highway.

The wines from the northern sector are full, rich, muscular, sometimes a bit burly. Those from the south are lighter, more fragrant, more feminine. While those from the 'wrong' side of the road have less definition and elegance and tend also to be on the lighter side. A judicious blend, agree most of the locals, makes the best of all possible worlds, though many growers produce village wines from single vineyards.

THE GRANDS CRUS
CHAMBERTIN

Surface Area: 12.90 ha • **Average Production:** 390 hl (51,000 bottles)

Principal Proprietors: *Armand Rousseau (2.20 ha); Jean and Jean-Louis Trapet (1.90 ha); Rossignol-Trapet (1.70 ha); Camus (1.69 ha); Jacques Prieur (83 a); *Mme Michèle Rolland (Héritiers Latour) (61 a); *Leroy (50 a); *(from 1992) Pierre Damoy (47 a); Rebourseau (46 a); Adrien Belland (41 a): Gabriel Tortochot (40 a); Louis Remy (32 a); Jean Raphet (21 a); *Philippe Charlopin (Madame Baron) (21 a); *Joseph Drouhin (20 a); Bertagna (20 a); Clos-Frantin (Bichot) (17 a); Bouchard Père et Fils (15 a); *Denis Mortet (Mme Quillardet) (15a); Domaine de Chézeaux (Ponsot) (14 a).

(NB Some of these figures include land in Clos-de-Bèze.)

There are some fifty-five separate parcels of land in the Chambertin *cadastre*, some as little as 50 square metres in size, yet four domaines – and it was not so long ago that it was three, the Trapet estate being divided as recently as 1990 – own over half this *grand cru*. There were twelve proprietors in 1829, fifteen in 1910 and around twenty-five today, if one groups together several members of the same family where the wine is made in common, but ownership split for tax and inheritance reasons.

Chambertin lies above the *Route des Grands Crus* between Latricières and Clos-de-Bèze, sheltered under the Montagne de la Combe-Grisard, at an altitude of between 275 and 300 metres. Up-slope, where it and Clos-de-Bèze meet, there is what looks like a quarry. It is merely the rock formation.

The soil is a limestone of Bajocian origin, and the incline is gentle: a little more so than Latricières, which is almost flat except just under the trees, but less so than Clos-de-Bèze. In parts, particularly to the south, and up-slope, the vines are on white oolite *marnes blanches*. Elsewhere the earth is browner, mixed with clay and pebbles. The proportion of fine earth to rock and pebbles (68 per cent to 32 per cent) is identical to that at Montrachet. Purely a coincidence?

What is the difference between Chambertin and Clos-de-Bèze? Charles Rousseau, who produces plenty of each at a high level of quality, says of Chambertin: 'It is male, and sturdy. It lacks a bit of finesse in its youth, but then it rounds off. Clos-de-Bèze is more complex, *plus racé* [more racy], more delicate.'

These are virile wines. The tannins are more obvious than in the top wines of Vosne-Romanée. Chambertins are full, firm and austere at the outset; structured and fleshy, with a flavour of black fruit, liquorice and coffee beans initially; mellowing into something rich, concentrated, generous and warm-hearted when they mature. The Clos-de-Bèze is more perfumed in its youth; the Chambertin more severe, perhaps the bigger of the two. Both are true *vins de garde*, needing a decade at least to soften up. Perhaps neither is ever as subtle as the top wines of Vosne-Romanée, but both can be magnificent.

CLOS-DE-BÈZE
Surface Area: 15.40 ha • **Average Production:** 464 hl (61,000 bottles)

Principal Proprietors: ★(since 1992) Pierre Damoy (5.36 ha); ★Armand Rousseau (1.50 ha); Drouhin-Laroze (1.47 ha); ★Joseph Faiveley (1.29 ha); Marion (1.00 ha formerly sold by Bouchard Aîné, leased to Henri Roch of Nuits-Saint-Georges from 1994); ★Bruno Clair (98 a); Gelin (60 a); ★Louis Jadot (42 a); ★Robert Groffier (41 a); André Bart (41 a); Rebourseau (33 a); ★Thomas-Moillard (29 a); Duroché (25 a); Jacques Prieur (15 a); ★Joseph Drouhin (12 a). (NB Clos-de-Bèze can be bottled as Chambertin, but not vice versa.)

In all there are some forty separate parcels in Clos-de-Bèze, but despite it being larger, there is a lower number of different proprietors. As can be seen, one domaine, sadly for long an under-achiever, but now happily under new and determinedly perfectionist management, has no less than 34.8 per cent of the *climat*. Like Chambertin itself, the majority of the proprietors are Gibriacois (as the adjective of Gevrey is rendered).

Clos-de-Bèze lies due north of Chambertin, between it and Mazis, on the same altitude of between 275 and 300 metres. The incline is a little steeper, particularly at the top of the slope, and the soil, brown in colour, is a little less deep. In parts the Bajocian bedrock shows through. Again in parts there are plenty of small stones and pebbles. If there is one difference compared with Chambertin it is the absence of *marnes blanches*, the white oolite which is apparent in some of the upper sections of the more southerly *climat*.

Gaston Roupnel said of Chambertin and Clos-de-Bèze: 'The wine blends grace and vigour. It combines austerity and power with finesse and delicacy. Together there is all that is necessary for a synthesis that is generosity and perfection itself.'

At their best these two wines are certainly not just among the top wines of Burgundy but among the top red wines of the world. And, good as the next rung may be, be it Mazis or Ruchottes or Clos-Saint-Jacques, there is a considerable margin between the two.

CHAPELLE-CHAMBERTIN

Surface Area: 5.49 ha • **Average Production:** 165 hl (22,000 bottles)

Principal Proprietors: *(since 1992) Pierre Damoy (2.22 ha); Jean and Jean-Louis Trapet (60 a); Rossignol-Trapet (55 a); Drouhin-Laroze (51 a); *Louis Jadot (39 a); Ponsot (30 a).

Chapelle-Chambertin lies immediately underneath Clos-de-Bèze, with Griottes to the south and the *premier cru* Les Cherbaudes to the north. It takes its name from the chapel of Notre-Dame-de-Bèze, originally built in 1155, reconstructed by Philippe de Beaujeu in 1547 (and reconsecrated by the Bishop of Bethlehem), but subsequently deliberately burnt to the ground in order to increase the land by 2 *ouvrées* in 1830. Originally Chapelle was just the southerly section, but this *grand cru* absorbed the *climat* of Les Gemeaux (1.75 ha) during the course of the nineteenth century.

The slope is modest here. The shallow pebbly soil, based on hard rock, which sticks out in places, is a little richer than in neighbouring Griottes. Of all the *grands crus* down-slope from the *Route des Grands Crus* – which are lighter and more 'feminine' than those above - this is the sturdiest wine, though not as full (or as fine) as Chambertin itself. It is rich and plummy, and can resemble Clos-de-Bèze, but in the final analysis it doesn't have quite the volume, nor the concentration, nor the flair.

CHARMES-CHAMBERTIN AND MAZOYÈRES-CHAMBERTIN

Surface Area: 30.83 ha • **Average Production:** 980 hl (130,000 bottles)

Principal Proprietors: Camus (6.90 ha); *Perrot-Minot (1.56 ha); *Armand Rousseau (1.50 ha); Taupenot-Merme (1.44 ha); Jean Raphet (1.38 ha); Rebourseau (1.32 ha); Hervé Arlaud (1.13 ha); Jean Bastien-Richard (1.11 ha); Dupont-Tisserandot (1.00 ha); Naigeon/Domaine les Varoilles (75 a); Domaine Ponnelle (74 a); *Dujac (70 a); Truchot-Martin (65 a); Pierre Bourée (65 a); Gabriel Tortochot (57 a); Seguin (57 a); *Denis Bachelet (43 a); *Claude Dugat (42 a); Duroché (41 a); *Jacky Confuron-Cotétidot (39a); *Geantet-Ponsiot (38 a); Coquard-Loison (32 a); *Christian Serafin (31 a); *Dominique Gallois (29 a); *Christophe Roumier (27 a); *Bernard Dugat (24 a); Pierre Amiot (23 a); Huguenot (21 a); Humbert (20 a); *Philippe Charlopin-Parizot (18 a); *Bernard Maume (17 a); *Joseph Roty (16 a).

For 150 years, growers in Mazoyères have been able to sell their wine under the more user-friendly label of Charmes, and there is now hardly a Mazoyères to be seen, except *chez* Camus, who has over 3 ha in each, and makes two separate *cuvées*. Mazoyères lies under Latricières, and in part stretches down to the main road - the only other *grand cru* in Burgundy apart from Clos-de-Vougeot to do this. Charmes adjoins it to the north, under Chambertin. The etymology of Mazoyères is obscure. Could it, like Mazis, have something to do with *maisons* (houses)? But Charmes, though the wine is indeed charming, comes from *chaume*, a piece of vineyard abandoned at one time (*en friche*) and then replanted.

Once again the slope is gentle. The surface soil is meagre, made up of decayed limestone (*lave*) with an abundance of gravel and stones at the lower levels. In the Charmes the rock is less decomposed. In the old days lumps of iron ore would be dug up in the course of ploughing the vineyard, and these would be sent off to a foundry in Langres to be worked into metal.

The wine of the Mazoyères section is firmer, fuller and gamier, but less fine, less pure and fragrant, than that of the Charmes - certainly the Charmes-du-Haut, which is round and less sturdy, but can have plenty of finesse. All in all this is the least exciting of the Gevrey *grands crus*, and the most forward. Yet in good hands, like the wines of Denis Bachelet, for example, it can nevertheless be very exciting, with a violet and raspberry perfume, a texture which can be velvety, even silky-smooth, and no lack of intensity: if not quite the Musigny of Gevrey, then perhaps its Amoureuses. As always, it depends on the grower.

GRIOTTES-CHAMBERTIN

Surface Area: 2.73 ha • **Average Production:** 90 hl (12,000 bottles)

Principal Proprietors: ★Ponsot/Domaine des Chézeaux (89 a); Suzanne Thomas-Collignon (68 a) (*en métayage* to ★André Esmonin, some sold to ★Louis Jadot); ★Joseph Drouhin (53 a); Jean-Claude Fourrier (26 a); ★Claude Dugat (16 a); ★Joseph Roty (8 a).

This is the smallest of the Gevrey *grands crus*, and lies squeezed in between Charmes and Chapelle, just under the point where Chambertin meets Clos-de-Bèze. As every book on Burgundy will tell you, *griotte* is a type of cherry, used for jam-making, and that is what the wine tastes like. Yes, it can have a flavour of cherries, if you are looking for them - I find more of a cornucopia of all sorts of red and black small fruits, plus liquorice and violets - but the name has more mundane origins. As so often, it is the soil - *criotte* or *crai*: chalk - as in Criots-Bâtard-Montrachet.

There is little surface soil here. The roots delve straight into broken-up rock impacted with pebbles and fossils. The wine, however, can be sublime. Is it just that most of the people able to show you a Griottes are fine producers, or is it coincidence, but I find a major difference between Griottes and Chapelle, particularly in terms of intensity and finesse? Moreover, it has a poise and individuality which raises it above all but the very best Charmes. Griottes is never a blockbuster - the tannins are always soft, the acidity is usually gentle, and the wine is perfumed, harmonious and seductive - but oh, it is ever so seductive!

LATRICIERES-CHAMBERTIN

Surface Area: 7.35 ha • **Average Production:** 255 hl (33,660 bottles)

Principal Proprietors: Camus (1.5 ha); ★Joseph Faiveley (1.21 ha); Rossignol-Trapet (76 a); Jean and Jean-Louis Trapet (75 a); Drouhin-Laroze (67 a); Louis Remy (58 a); ★Leroy (57 a); Vadey-Castagnier/Newman (53 a); Ponsot (up to 1994), Bize (from 1995) (32 a); Duroché (28 a).

Latricières - the word means poor in the sense of infertile - lies directly to the south of Chambertin. It shares much of the same soil and subsoil, a white oolitic marl on a solid rock base, with very little surface earth, but the land is flatter. There is almost no slope except at the upper end just under the trees.

Dr Morelot (1831) ignores it - probably the wine was passed off as Chambertin in those days - and Lavalle (1855) classed it as a *deuxième cuvée*. 150 years ago there were three proprietors (Gournot, Ouvrard and Marion); today there are ten.

Latricières is a sturdy wine, robust in its youth, spicy and gamey in its maturity, and it lacks both the distinction of Chambertin and Clos-de-Bèze and the finesse of Mazis and Griottes. In good hands though (Leroy and Faiveley for example) we can find a thoroughly satisfactory, warm-hearted bottle. But a Latricières is a second division *grand cru* nonetheless.

MAZIS-CHAMBERTIN

Surface Area: 9.10 ha • **Average Production:** 320 hl (42,250 bottles)

Principal Proprietors: ★Hospices de Beaune (1.75 ha); ★Joseph Faiveley (1.20 ha); Rebourseau

(96 a); *Bernard Maume (67 a); Vachet-Rousseau (54 a); *Armand Rousseau (50 a); Suzanne Thomas-Collignon (50 a) (*en métayage* to *André Esmonin); Gabriel Tortochot (42 a); *Philippe Naddef (42 a); Gelin (38 a); Camus (37 a); Dupont-Tisserandot (36 a); *D'Auvenay (Mme Bize-Leroy) (26 a); *Vadey-Castagnier/Newman (19 a); *Joseph Roty (12 a); *Philippe Charlopin-Parizot (12 a).

Mazis, often spelt with a 'y', and with or without the final 's', has the same etymological origin, it is suggested, as Mazoyères, and indeed various Maizières: the word means hamlet. It lies under Ruchottes, between Clos-de-Bèze and the village of Gevrey, above the *Route des Grands Crus* and is divided into the Mazis *hauts* and the Mazis *bas*, the former being the choicer parcel. Since 1855 it has absorbed part of Les Corbeaux, increasing its surface area by about 60 ares.

The soil is similar to that of Clos-de-Bèze, shallow, especially in the *hauts*, the Bajocian bedrock poking out in places, and the wine, at its best, comes the closest in quality, both in volume and in distinction, to the two great *grands crus*. Mazis is well-coloured, rich in tannin, has good grip, and a most attractive, even opulent fruit: blackberry and black cherry to add to the *petits fruits rouges*. Madame Lalou Bize of Maison Leroy has for long produced a Mazis to conjure with: indisputably *grand vin*. Now she owns a parcel in her own right - and it is the same vines whose wine she bought in the first place.

RUCHOTTES-CHAMBERTIN

Surface Area: 3.30 ha • **Average Production:** 115 hl (15,000 bottles)

Principal Proprietors: *Armand Rousseau (Clos-des-Ruchottes) (1.10 ha); *Mugneret-Gibourg (67 a); *Christophe Roumier (54 a); Suzanne Thomas-Collignon (50 a) (*en métayage* to *André Esmonin, often bought by *Jadot); François Trapet (21 a); Henri Magnien (16 a); Château de Marsannay (10 a); Marchand-Grillot (8 a).

Ruchottes - the word comes from *rochers* (rocks) - is always plural, while Griottes and Mazis can be either. The *climat*, small, steep, much parcellated, lies above Mazis and beneath a little road which disappears into the mountains on its way to Curley. Across the road is the *premier cru* Le Fonteny.

As in the top part of Chambertin and Latricières, there is oolitic *marnes blanches* here, and once again very little surface soil. The result is a wine of the same size as Mazis, but with more of the structure showing, less lush, more mineral. A *vin de garde*, and a very satisfactory one. Give it time. There is plenty of depth, a mulberry-type fruit and a suggestion of gameyness.

All three principal proprietors owe their land to the break-up of the Thomas-Bassot domaine. Thomas-Bassot was founded in 1852, and soon became the proprietor of the lion's share of Ruchottes. In 1976, after a succession of family problems and personal tragedies, the firm was sold to Jean-Claude Boisset and the domaine was put on the market. Christophe Roumier farms the Ruchottes of Michel Bonnefond, a wine-lover who lives near Rouen.

THE *PREMIERS CRUS*

The twenty-six *premiers crus* of Gevrey can be conveniently grouped into three sections:

(a) Up-slope from the village itself, on the south-east facing slope of the extension of the Combe-de-Lavaux.

Here you will find La Boissière (part *premier cru*: *monopole* of Domaine Harmand-Geoffroy), La Romanée (part), Clos-des-Varoilles (*monopole* of the Domaine les Varoilles), Le Poissenot, Lavaux-Saint-Jacques, Estournelles (-Saint-Jacques), Clos-Saint-Jacques, Clos-du-Chapitre (which lies down-slope from Clos-Saint-Jacques), Les Cazetiers, Les Petits-Cazetiers, La

Combe-aux-Moines, Les Champeaux and Les Goulots. This is the best area for *premier cru* Gevrey-Chambertin.

CLOS-SAINT-JACQUES (6.70 HA)

When they came to decree what was *grand cru* and what was not in the 1930s, it was decided that only *climats* contiguous with Chambertin and Clos-de-Bèze would be considered for top rank. Ruchottes and Mazoyères scraped in, for a finger of each touches the magic core. Clos-Saint-Jacques, on its own, but perfectly poised on the Combe-de-Lavaux flank, was excluded. No one who owns a part of this vineyard (there are only five, and four of them produce excellent wine) would agree with this judgement. Neither would more dispassionate outsiders.

In the Armand Rousseau cellar you are given the Saint-Jacques to taste *after* the Clos-de-la-Roche, Ruchottes and Mazis, and the Saint-Jacques is awarded a higher percentage of new oak. It is always the better wine.

The vineyard, which until 1954 belonged exclusively to the Comte de Moucheron, is on the same elevation as Chambertin, and the soil is a white marl similar in constitution, though the incline is marginally greater. The fruit ripens just a little later, owing to a fresh wind which can flow out of the Combe. But the wine can be exquisite: rich, ample, full-bodied and distinctive. This is a wine of real depth and dimension, slightly lusher and plumper than the two greatest Gevrey wines, but no less classy, no less inspiring. It is clearly head and shoulders above all the other Gevrey *premiers crus*.

Recommended Sources: Bruno Clair (Marsannay); Louis Jadot (Beaune); Michel Esmonin et Fille; Armand Rousseau (both Gevrey-Chambertin). The fifth grower is Jean-Claude Fourrier (Gevrey-Chambertin).

LAVAUX-SAINT-JACQUES (9.53 HA)
ESTOURNELLES-SAINT-JACQUES (2.09 HA)

Lavaux-Saint-Jacques lies immediately south of Clos-Saint-Jacques, with the smaller Estournelles above it. Here it is not so much soil structure or exposition which precludes the wines from pretension to *grand cru* status but the sheltering and cooling effect of the valley into which the road at the bottom of the slope rapidly disappears. Walk from the Clos-Saint-Jacques boundary on the north side across to where Lavaux meets Varoilles and Poissenot on the other side – a distance of less than 400 metres – and you will notice a drop in temperature. In the winter, when frost or snow hits the ground, you can also see the micro-climatic difference, as the ground warms up each morning.

Nevertheless the wines from these two *climats* can be excellent *premier cru* examples: fullish, rich, plump, ample and meaty without hard edges or rusticity, and with plenty of fruit.

Recommended Sources:
Lavaux-Saint-Jacques: Bernard Dugat; Claude Dugat; André Esmonin; Bernard Maume; Denis Mortet; Vachet-Rousseau (all Gevrey-Chambertin); Jacky Confuron-Cotétidot (Vosne-Romanée); Louis Jadot (Beaune).
Estournelles-Saint-Jacques: André Esmonin (who has 1 ha, the lion's share) (Gevrey-Chambertin); Louis Jadot (Beaune).

LE POISSENOT (2.20 HA)

Further into the valley you will find Le Poissenot (note the wines of Geantet-Ponsiot in Gevrey-Chambertin and Louis Jadot in Beaune).

LA ROMANÉE (1.06 HA)

(see the Domaine les Varoilles)

CLOS-DES-VAROILLES (5.97 HA)

(monopoly of the Domaine les Varoilles)

LA BOISSIÈRE

Part of which (0.45 ha) is *premier cru*, and is the monopoly of Domaine Harmand-Geoffroy.

The wines get progressively leaner as one retreats into the valley. Sometimes the tannins can be a little unsophisticated.

LES CAZETIERS (8.43 HA) • LES PETITS-CAZETIERS (0.45 HA)
LA COMBE-AUX-MOINES (4.77 HA) • LES GOULOTS (1.81 HA)
LES CHAMPEAUX (6.68 HA)

These *climats* lie on the other side of Clos-Saint-Jacques and have an exposure which is more to the east, even, the case of La Combe-aux-Moines, marginally to the north.

Les Cazetiers is almost as well exposed as Clos-Saint-Jacques, and the wine can approach it in quality, though it never seems to really equal it. (You can taste the two alongside each other *chez* Bruno Clair, Rousseau and Jadot.) It is an equally sizeable wine, just a little more to the sturdy, robust side, but can be splendidly rich and satisfying.

Beyond Les Cazetiers, which is a wide, extensive vineyard, are Les Petits-Cazetiers, La Combe-aux-Moines and Les Goulots, with Les Champeaux lying underneath. This is rocky, stony territory, the vineyard broken up into terraces. With the exception of one or two Combe-aux-Moines, this is second-division territory; the micro-climate is cooler, and the wines, though they can be quite substantial, do not have the proper definition and finesse.

Recommended Sources:

Les Cazetiers: Bruno Clair (Marsannay); Philippe Naddef (Couchey); Armand Rousseau; Christian Serafin (both Gevrey-Chambertin); Joseph Faiveley (Nuits-Saint-Georges); Louis Jadot (Beaune).
La Combe-aux-Moines: Joseph Faiveley (Nuits-Saint-Georges); Dominique Gallois (Gevrey-Chambertin); Louis Jadot (Beaune).
Les Champeaux: Philippe Naddef (Couchey); Denis Mortet (Gevrey-Chambertin).

(b) The second sector lies between the *grands crus* of Ruchottes and Mazis and the village itself. Lowest down, marching with Mazis *bas*, is Les Corbeaux, a section of which is plain village AC. Just above is Le Fonteny (singular or plural) and above that Les Champonnets, the obscure (I have never seen an example) Craipillot, and the tiny Issarts.

Only the first three are of importance, in that you are likely to see them on a label. They produce wines of a medium weight, with good fruit and often charming balance; but without the weight or concentration of a good Lavaux-Saint-Jacques or Cazetiers.

LES CORBEAUX (3.21 HA) • LE FONTENY (3.73 HA)
LES CHAMPONNETS (3.32 HA) • LE CRAIPILLOT (2.76 HA)

(usually declared as plain *premier cru*)

LES ISSARTS (0.62 HA)

(usually declared as plain *premier cru*)

Recommended Sources:

Les Corbeaux: Denis Bachelet (Gevrey-Chambertin); Bruno Clavelier (Vosne-Romanée)
Le Fonteny: Bruno Clair (Marsannay); Christian Serafin; Joseph Roty (Gevrey-Chambertin).
Les Champonnets: André Esmonin (Gevrey-Chambertin).

(c) Down-slope from Mazis and Chapelle-Chambertin lies the third sector of Gevrey-Chambertin *premiers crus*. Running from north to south these are Au Closeau (which I have never been offered), La Perrière, Clos-Prieur *haut* (not to be confused with Clos-Prieur *bas*, merely village AC), Les Cherbaudes, Les Champitonnois (usually declared as La Petite-Chapelle) and En Ergot (which has also failed to come my way).

AU CLOSEAU (0.53 HA)
(usually declared as *premier cru tout court*)

LA PERRIÈRE (2.47 HA) • CLOS-PRIEUR (*HAUT*) (1.98 HA)

LES CHERBAUDES (2.18 HA)

LA PETITE-CHAPELLE (LES CHAMPITONNOIS) (4.00 HA)

EN ERGOT (1.16 HA)
(usually declared as *premier cru tout court*)

These are the most 'feminine' of the Gevrey-Chambertin *premiers crus*: medium in body, soft-centred, aromatically *petits fruits rouges*, and when good, extremely charming. When not good, or in poor vintages, they can be weedy and will attenuate rapidly.

Recommended Sources:
Les Cherbaudes and *La Perrière:* Bernard Maume makes a good *premier cru* blend of his two parcels (Gevrey-Chambertin).
La Petite-Chapelle: Bernard Dugat (Gevrey-Chambertin).

This leaves Bel-Air, which lies above Clos-de-Bèze, part of which (2.65 ha) is *premier cru*, and Aux Combottes (4.57 ha). I have rarely seen the former, but I have often been seduced by wines from this latter *climat*.

AUX COMBOTTES (4.57 HA) • BEL-AIR (2.65 HA)

If you look at the map, you may be puzzled by the standing of Aux Combottes, for it lies directly between Latricières and Clos-de-la-Roche, on the same line as Chambertin itself. Why is this not *grand cru*? The answer lies in the micro-climate. Combottes is in the faintest of hollows, so drains marginally less well. Above it, there is a break in the hill where the Combe Grisard disappears into the Hautes-Côtes, and this lets a breeze flow over the Combottes vines. It's a small thing, but the result is the grapes do not ripen as well as they do either in Clos-de-la-Roche or in Latricières. The wine is never as full or as concentrated.

But it can be delicious: elegant, supple, intense and full of cherry, raspberry, red currant fruit. It is a sort of Gevrey-Chambolle cross, but in a unique way: I find no Morey parallel.

Recommended Sources:
Aux Combottes: Dujac, Hubert Lignier (Morey-Saint-Denis); Leroy (Vosne-Romanée).

THE GROWERS
*DENIS BACHELET

3 ha: owned. Charmes-Chambertin (43 a); Gevrey-Chambertin *premier cru* Les Corbeaux; village Gevrey-Chambertin; Côte-de-Nuits-Villages.

Denis Bachelet took over his small family domaine in 1983 when he was in his early twenties, and has since augmented it a little, but this is still essentially a one-man band. Happily it is a perfectionist and excellent one. Low yields are critical, in Bachelet's view. The fruit is completely destemmed, macerated *à froid* for three or four days, given a *cuvaison* of medium length (seven to eleven days) and 100 per cent new oak is used for the Charmes. The wines are kept in their lees as long as possible, and hand-bottled without filtration.

The Denis Bachelet style is for wines of intensity, great elegance and subtlety: feminine in the best sense. They are concentrated, harmonious, pure and understated. Bachelet's Charmes is a ravishing example – a wine which really sings. Except for his 1991s, which are marginally unimpressive, this domaine has not put a foot wrong.

PHILIPPE BATTACHI, DOMAINE DE CLOS-NOIR

6 ha: owned and *en fermage*. Clos-de-la-Roche (20 a); Morey-Saint-Denis *premier cru* in Les Millandes, Les Charrières; village Morey-Saint-Denis; village Gevrey-Chambertin including the *lieux-dits* Les Jeunes Rois (*vieilles vignes*) and Les Evocelles; village Fixin; Côte-de-Nuits-Villages.

Battachi is a handsome somewhat academic-looking man in his late forties, who lives in a fine old house secreted away in the middle of the village, with a cellar under the Casino supermarket nearby. In 1986 he branched out on his own and has since been selling progressively less and less to the *négoce*.

Battachi is a follower of the cold pre-fermentation-maceration principle of Guy Accad. The bunches are destemmed, fermented at low temperature, and no new oak is used. As with other followers of cool maceration techniques, some of the mid-1980 vintages – and here in particular the 1990s – took far too long to finish their malos. But, like many, he has adapted the principle to his own wine and *terroir*. Recent results have shown a lot of promise.

LUCIEN BOILLOT ET FILS

13.81 ha. Côte-de-Nuits owned and *en fermage*. Côte-de-Beaune nearly all owned (the Angles and the Croix-Noires remain *en fermage* from other members of the family).

Gevrey-Chambertin *premier cru* in Les Champonnets, Les Corbeaux, Les Cherbaudes; village Gevrey-Chambertin including the *lieu-dit* Les Evocelles; Nuits-Saint-Georges *premier cru* Les Pruliers; village Fixin; Côte-de-Nuits-Villages; village Beaune in the *lieu-dit* Les Epenottes; Pommard *premier cru* in Les Croix-Noires and Fremiers; village Pommard; Volnay *premier cru* in Les Angles, Les Brouillards, Les Caillerets; village Volnay.

Pierre and Louis Boillot, sons of Lucien, have been running this domaine for a decade or more, and are now themselves the proprietors of most of it. They are cousins of the Boillots in Volnay and Pommard, which explains the range on offer here. The Gevrey-Chambertin wines, and others in the locality, have been taken on since 1978.

The wines are vinified in a large modern cellar in the middle of the village. The grapes are entirely destemmed, given a few days' cold maceration and then fermented at 32-33°C. Some 30 per cent new oak is used overall.

These are usually nicely substantial wines, rich and concentrated, meaty and with a touch of the robust. Occasionally, as in 1992, and with one or two of the 1993s, I have encountered disappointments. But a good, even very good, source.

PIERRE BOURÉE ET FILS

4 ha: owned. Charmes-Chambertin (65 a); Gevrey-Chambertin *premier cru* Les Champeaux; village Gevrey-Chambertin including the *lieu-dit* Clos-de-la-Justice (*monopole*); Beaune *premier cru* Les Epenottes.

Bourée is as much a *négociant* as a domaine, and a very traditional one at that. Owned by Louis Vallet, a slight and somewhat shy man in his sixties, and his sons Jean-Christophe and Bernard – they are direct descendants of the original Bourée who founded the firm in 1864 – this is an affair which is almost defiant in its insistence in not moving with the times. There is no temperature control, no destemming, some new oak but a great deal more oak which looks incredibly aged, and no bottling before at least two years or more.

I have had good Bourée wines in the past, and remember a couple of 1969s bought by the Wine Society in my time there. But of late I find myself unimpressed. The wines lack succulence and grip. All too often I find them attenuated. Vallet Frères is a subsidiary name for the *négociant* business.

★ALAIN BURGUET

5.35 ha: owned and *en fermage*. Gevrey-Chambertin *premier cru* Les Champeaux; village Gevrey-Chambertin including a *vieilles vignes cuvée* and the *lieux-dits* Les Billards, Les Regnards.

Alain Burguet is an example of how it is still possible to build up a domaine from scratch, without ample resources or having to make a 'sensible' marriage , even with today's high prices of land. He is in his forties, short, solid, quietly determined, even grim. And so is the wine, full and masculine, uncompromising, sturdy, concentrated and long-lasting.

The grapes are almost entirely destemmed, and vinified at a high temperature. *Cuvaisons* are long. There is no fining and minimum filtration. Burguet is not seeking wines which are *flatteur* in their youth. These are deliberate *vins de garde*.

Of late there have been two changes in Burguet vinification technique. Somewhat reluctantly, at least at first, he has started to augment the amount of new oak. And now he has a new cellar at the top of the village, he is able to keep the wine longer in cask. Hitherto it was bottled after fourteen months.

Burguet's village *vieilles vignes* is at least the equal of most growers' *premiers crus*. If I was to pick one village wine as a yardstick, this would be it. The Champeaux was from eight-year-old vines in 1993, and is a recent addition.

See Profile, page 357.

CAMUS PÈRE ET FILS

18 ha: owned. Chambertin (1.69 ha); Charmes-Chambertin (3.03 ha); Latricières-Chambertin (1.51 ha); Mazis-Chambertin (37 a); Mazoyères-Chambertin (3.87 ha); village Gevrey-Chambertin.

What a magnificent line-up! But what a disappointment when you taste the wines today.

The domaine was built up by Joseph Camus in the crisis years of the 1930s, and even then was selling no inconsiderable percentage directly to private customers. Joseph was succeeded by his son Léon, and Léon by Hubert, today a handsome man in his late fifties. The unselfish Hubert spends most of his time on the committees of a large number of organisations which govern and promote what goes on in Burgundy: at the expense, I fear, of the wines. There is 100 per cent destemming, a three-week *cuvaison*, and two-thirds new oak. But then the wine is kept two and a half years in cask. Sadly even after a year or so the wine seems to lack freshness and concentration.

This is one of the few domaines to bottle Mazoyères under its real name. I have had plenty of fine old Camus wines from the 1960s and 1950s.

PHILIPPE CHARLOPIN-PARIZOT

12 ha: owned and *en fermage/métayage*. Chambertin (21 a) (owned by Mme Baron, but made and bottled by Charlopin); Mazis-Chambertin (12 a); Charmes-Chambertin (18 a); village Gevrey-Chambertin; village Morey-Saint-Denis; village Chambolle-Musigny; village Vosne-Romanée; village Fixin.

Philippe Charlopin, a short, chubby man in his forties with an abundant mane of curly hair, inherited 1.8 ha from his father in 1976 and has been gradually building up his domaine ever since. Originally from Gevrey, he moved to Marsannay in 1987, but has now returned, and occupies part of the old Charles Quillardet cellars on the main road to Dijon.

The grapes are destemmed, given a deliberate pre-fermentation maceration (up to eight days in 1988), and fermented at a maximum of 30°C, with the *cuvaison* varying from twelve days to twenty, depending on the vintage. Unusually, there is no racking, the wine being kept in its lees until bottling a year later.

Quality has improved greatly here in the last five years, promoting the domaine firmly into the 'very good' class. The wines are plump and plummy, well-coloured and fullish without being too sturdy. A domaine to watch.

See Profile, page 375.

Pierre Damoy

10.37 ha: owned. Chambertin (47 a); Chambertin Clos-de-Bèze (5.36 ha); Chapelle-Chambertin (2.22 ha); village Gevrey-Chambertin including the *lieu-dit* Clos-Tamisot (*monopole*).

What a rapid difference a new broom can make! After many years in the wilderness, this potentially magnificent domaine, with its lion's share of both Clos-de-Bèze and Chapelle-Chambertin, built up in the 1930s, has been taken in hand. The young Pierre Damoy, grandson of the eponymous Pierre and nephew of Jacques, the current proprietor, arrived during the summer of 1992. What has he changed? 'Almost everything. Even the label!' The yield has been severely reduced. There is much more new oak, and, more importantly, the old oak has been taken out and burnt. There is, if possible, no longer any fining or filtering. The first results have been extremely promising. From being a perpetual under-achiever this domaine is now an emerging super-star. About time too! But better late than never. One just wishes one could say the same about Camus, about Drouhin-Laroze, about Fourrier, about Rebourseau . . .

Drouhin-Laroze

12 ha: owned. Chambertin, Clos-de-Bèze (1.47 ha); Latricières-Chambertin (67 a); Chapelle-Chambertin (51 a); Bonnes-Mares (1.49 ha); Clos-de-Vougeot (1.02 ha); Gevrey-Chambertin *premier cru* in Lavaux-Saint-Jacques, Clos-Prieur; village Gevrey-Chambertin.

Founded by Jean-Baptiste Laroze around 1850, the domaine is today run by his descendants Bernard and Philippe Drouhin, father and son. The relationship with Robert Drouhin of the Beaune *négociants* Joseph Drouhin is distant.

While the wines can be found in many of France's three-star restaurants they are little seen in Britain or the USA, and, I feel, with justification. On the face of it there seems nothing wrong with the way they are made (100 per cent destemming, plenty of new oak, and no old barrels, no delayed bottling, a tidy and extensive - not to say impressive - cellar), but something is missing somewhere. The wines are fruity, often a little sweet, but they lack real depth and concentration. Too often they are merely facile and pretty. Given the impressive array of top *climats* the judgement must be: should do better.

★Claude Dugat

4 ha: owned. Charmes-Chambertin (42 a); Griottes-Chambertin (16 a); Gevrey-Chambertin *premier cru* in Lavaux-Saint-Jacques; village Gevrey-Chambertin.

Claude Dugat, born in 1956, elder and balding cousin of Bernard, is now in charge here, and keeps his wine in the cellars of the beautifully restored Cellier des Dîmes, once a chapter house, next to Gevrey's church. Up to the 1991 vintage the Lavaux-Saint-Jacques bore the label of his father Maurice, a familiar figure as one of the Cadets de Bourgogne who sing, clap and interrupt at the dinners at the Clos-de-Vougeot. The Griottes is bottled under the name of Françoise, Claude's sister.

This Dugat makes his wine slightly differently from his cousin, retaining more of the stems, but the wines are arguably even better: very rich and concentrated, with marvellous classy fruit and very good grip. Another fine source.

★BERNARD DUGAT-PY

4.30 ha: owned and *en fermage*. Charmes-Chambertin (31 a); Gevrey-Chambertin *premier cru* in Lavaux-Saint-Jacques, Petite-Chapelle; village Gevrey-Chambertin, including a *vieilles vignes cuvée*.

This is a small domaine whose marvellous vaulted cellar was once the crypt of the church of a leprosarium. Bernard Dugat has now taken over completely from his father Pierre, under whose label old bottles can still be found, and is now selling less and less *en vrac*. A small amount of the stems is retained, the wine vinified at a maximum of 32°C, and the top wines are reared in 50–100 per cent new oak. There is minimal racking, no fining and no filtration.

The wines have an old-vine, minimum-yield concentration, are abundantly fruity and very stylish and well balanced. A high-class establishment presided over by a charming couple.

DUPONT-TISSERANDOT

11 ha: owned. Charmes-Chambertin (67 a); Mazis-Chambertin (21 a); Corton (33 a); Gevrey-Chambertin *premier cru* in Les Cazetiers, Lavaux-Saint-Jacques, Bel-Air; village Gevrey-Chambertin; village Savigny-lès-Beaune; village Fixin.
11.50 ha: *en fermage/métayage*. Charmes-Chambertin (32 a); Mazis-Chambertin (15 a); Gevrey-Chambertin *premier cru*; Les Cazetiers; village Gevrey-Chambertin; Marsannay.

With a total of 22 ha this is a vast exploitation, and it still sells most of its produce off in bulk to the *négoce*. Bernard Dupont, who started the whole thing off in 1954 when he married Gisèle Tisserandot - he was a grocer before, and somewhat thrown in the deep end - is now *en retraite*. Responsibility has been ceded to his daughters and sons-in-law: Patricia and Didier Chevillon and Françoise and Jean-Louis Guillard.

My experience of Dupont-Tisserandot, in bottle, is not extensive. But what I have seen has not impressed me. Moreover the cellar seems a bit of a shambles. There is rather too much old oak.

GILLES DUROCHÉ

8.26 ha. Owned and *en fermage*. Clos-de-Bèze (25 a); Charmes-Chambertin (37 a); Latricières-Chambertin (28 a); Gevrey-Chambertin *premier cru* in Lavaux-Saint-Jacques, Les Champeaux, Les Estournelles; village Gevrey-Chambertin.

Philippe Duroché started off with 3 ha in 1954 on the death of his father, and slowly built up this domaine to the present size before handing over the reins to his son Gilles at the end of the 1980s.

This is a very efficient set-up, with a spotlessly tidy cellar in the centre of the village. There is total destemming, a few days' pre-fermentation maceration, a twelve to fifteen day *cuvaison*, and no fining. The vines in the Champeaux are still young, and those in the Latricières and the Estournelles only fifteen years or so, though in the Clos-de-Bèze they are venerable. They could use a bit more new oak here (only one-third for the Clos-de-Bèze), but the quality is good, and the wines are rich and succulent. My hunch is that they can only get better.

★ANDRÉ ESMONIN, DOMAINE DES ESTOURNELLES

7 ha: owned, *en métayage*. Griottes-Chambertin (59 a); Mazis-Chambertin (42 a); Ruchottes-Chambertin (42 a); Gevrey-Chambertin *premier cru* in Les Champonnets, Les Estournelles-Saint-Jacques, Lavaux-Saint-Jacques; village Gevrey-Chambertin.

The domaine also looks after the Hospices de Beaune's holdings in Mazis-Chambertin and Clos-de-la-Roche.

There are at least three noteworthy aspects to this fine domaine. Firstly it farms for the Hospices de Beaune (see above), and also for the Thomas family, donors of the Hospices Mazis. Secondly it owns the lion's share of Estournelles, and probably makes the best example of it to be found in Burgundy. Lastly it is the one domaine where you can sample Griottes, Mazis and Ruchottes, the three best *grands crus* outside the big two in my view, alongside each other. Every year I seem to prefer a different one, I see from my notes. The home team prefers the Ruchottes, which are the oldest vines.

The recipe is 100 per cent destemming, fermentation at a high temperature after four days' cold maceration, and 25 per cent new oak. The wines are rich in colour, virile, profound and concentrated. As recently as 1990 Esmonin sold just over 50 per cent of his produce in bottle. Today he sells all. A fine source.

★MICHEL ESMONIN ET FILLE

6.63 ha: owned and *en fermage/métayage*. Gevrey-Chambertin *premier cru* Clos-Saint-Jacques; village Gevrey-Chambertin; Côte-de-Nuits-Villages.

The *fille* is the attractive, capable, thirty-something Sylvie, qualified both as an *ingénieur agronome* and an *oenologue*, and it is she who is in charge at the domaine. It is only since her arrival in 1987 that a serious amount has been sold in bottle. Today hardly 10 per cent is disposed of in bulk.

There is 100 per cent destemming, two to five days' cold maceration, fermentation at a maximum of 30-32°C, with a long *cuvaison*, and 50 per cent new wood for the Clos-Saint-Jacques. The atmosphere is tidy, competent and quietly confident; the wines suitably more feminine and more elegant when they are young than those of the cousins down the road.

See Profile, page 000.

JEAN-CLAUDE FOURRIER

9 ha: owned. Griottes-Chambertin (26 a); Gevrey-Chambertin *premier cru* in Clos-Saint-Jacques, La Combe-aux-Moines, Les Cherbaudes, Les Champeaux (the last two currently blended together as *premier cru tout court*); village Gevrey-Chambertin including the *lieu-dit* Aux Echézeaux; village Morey-Saint-Denis; village Chambolle-Musigny; Vougeot *premier cru* in Les Petits-Vougeots.

This is another formerly prestigious domaine which seems to have given up the ghost in recent years. This is doubly sad, for the holdings are impressive and the ages of the vines especially venerable.

A few handfuls of unstemmed bunches are left in the vats, the rest destalked, and after three to five days' cold maceration the fermentation is allowed to rise to 34°C and the *cuvaison* prolonged 'to extract the *matière*'. This domaine dislikes new oak, and believes in bottling after twenty-two months in cask.

I see glimmers of hope here. Some of the better 1993s, in cask at fourteen months old, showed promise. More importantly, perhaps, I get the distinct impression that Jean-Claude's son Jean-Marie, who has done *stages* with Henri Jayer and Domaine Drouhin in Oregon, is aware of the property's current reputation, and intends to do something about it.

DOMINIQUE GALLOIS

3.5 ha: owned. Charmes-Chambertin (29 a); Gevrey-Chambertin *premier cru* in La Combe-aux-Moines, Les Petits-Cazetiers, Les Goulots; village Gevrey-Chambertin.

The dark-haired Dominique Gallois took over from his father in 1989, and it is only since then that we have seen these wines on the market. The vines are encouragingly old, the grapes 80 per cent destemmed, and macerated for a fortnight or so. There is no system for heating or cooling the must in the large, empty, deep, dark cellar. These wines have depth, and are slow to develop, but are a little rigid at first. A cellar to watch.

VINCENT GEANTET-PONSIOT

13 ha: owned and *en fermage*. Charmes-Chambertin (50 a); Gevrey-Chambertin *premier cru* Le Poissenot; village Gevrey-Chambertin including the *lieu-dit* Les Jeunes-Rois and a *vieilles vignes cuvée*; Chambolle-Musigny *premier cru*; village Chambolle-Musigny; Marsannay.

Vincent Geantet took charge here in 1982, when his father Edmond handed over control, and things have gently been improving ever since. The quality since 1990 is especially commendable.

No stems are used. Following a deliberate cooling down of the fruit for five days, the temperature is then allowed to rise to as much as 36°C during a twelve to fifteen day *cuvaison*. One-third new wood is employed for the *élevage*.

These are intensely flavoured wines, but not blockbusters. There is succulent perfumed fruit, and good balance: no solidity, no hard edges. A very good source.

LAURENT GOILLOT-BERNOLLIN

8 ha: owned and *en fermage*. Village Gevrey-Chambertin, including a *vieilles vignes cuvée*; village Marsannay.

Laurent Goillot lives in the last house in Gevrey on the main road towards Dijon, and has been in charge of this domaine since the death of his father-in-law, Pierre Bernollin, in 1985. My experience of these wines is limited. They seem good and sturdy, occasionally a bit tough.

MICHEL GUILLARD

3.70 ha: owned. Gevrey-Chambertin *premier cru* in Lavaux-Saint-Jacques, Les Poissenots, Les Corbeaux; village Gevrey-Chambertin including a *vieilles vignes cuvée*.

Michel Guillard is yet another member of the improving, forty-something-year-old Gevrey *vignerons*. His vineyard approach is emphatically *biologique*. In the past, he told me, his wine was too hard, so in 1990 he bought a heat exchanger. Now he doesn't macerate so long, but if necessary he can raise the temperature. The result is more sophisticated tannins. The wines he has produced since then are stylish, concentrated and complex. The cellars, in the middle of the village, are rather cramped, but they are well worth a visit.

JEAN-MICHEL GUILLON

8.50 ha: owned and *en fermage*. Gevrey-Chambertin *premier cru* in La Petite-Chapelle, Clos-Prieur and Les Champonnets; village Gevrey-Chambertin.

Jean-Michel Guillon was in aeronautics. He lived for a while in Tahiti. Then, for some reason – for he has no family connections with Burgundy – he got the wine bug. Fifteen years ago he installed himself in Gevrey-Chambertin. And he has since built up this domaine from scratch.

He leaves a quarter of the bunches with their stems intact, macerates *à froid* for six to seven days, then lets the temperature rise up to 36°C, even 37°. Some 30 per cent new oak is used; there is pre-filtration using *Kieselguhr*, and after that the wine is left until bottling fourteen to sixteen months after the vintage.

The set-up is clean and looks efficient. The man himself is a tall, handsome, vigorous and youthful forty-five or fifty, and his wines are well made. But do they all taste a little too like each other?

GÉRARD HARMAND-GEOFFROY
(formerly Louis Geoffroy et Fils)

5.93 ha: owned. Mazis-Chambertin (17 a); Gevrey-Chambertin *premier cru* in Les Champeaux, La Perrière, La Boissière (*monopole*); village Gevrey-Chambertin including the *lieu-dit* Clos-Prieur.

This is a domaine on the up and up, and it has recently taken over some of the land of Gérard Vachet-Rousseau on a *métayage* basis (see page 83). It sailed under the banner of Lucien Geoffroy until 1990, though son-in-law Gerard Harmand has been in charge for some years.

The viticultural approach is seriously *biologique*, encouraging the vine to produce its own defences to any depredatory attack, and the pruning is very short. When the fruit arrives in the modern winery in Gevrey's Place de Lois it is 100 per cent destemmed, there is a *cuvaison* of ten to twelve days, and 25–30 per cent new oak is employed during the *élevage*. Bottling takes place early in order to preserve the fruit.

The wines are concentrated and intense, full without being too structured, and are crammed with summer-pudding fruit. A very good source. Currently the Clos-Prieur, not from the *premier cru*, section, is to be preferred to the Boissière, which is young vines.

HERESZTYN

11 ha: owned. Clos-Saint-Denis (23 a); Gevrey-Chambertin *premier cru* in Les Goulots, Les Corbeaux, Les Champonnets, La Perrière; village Gevrey-Chambertin; Morey-Saint-Denis *premier cru* Les Millandes.

The original Heresztyn, Jean, arrived from Poland in 1932, worked in the Gelin domaine in Fixin and for Jean Trapet in Gevrey-Chambertin, and slowly but surely built up a domaine for himself. Now it is the third generation, an extended family of five brothers and sisters, husbands and wives, who run things, guarded by a noisy Alsatian, from premises in the centre of the village.

Some 30 per cent of the stems are retained. There is a long *cuvaison* at a maximum temperature of 33°C, and 50 per cent new oak is employed for the *élevage*. They do not filter.

Things are improving here, and there seems to be a bit more new wood for the lesser *cuvées*. Nevertheless these are proportionately not as good as the wines from better sited vineyards. But the Millandes is a consistent success.

Christian Serafin (see page 82) is a cousin.

HUMBERT ET FILS

5 ha: owned. Charmes-Chambertin (20 a); Gevrey-Chambertin *premier cru* in Les Estournelles-Saint-Jacques, Lavaux-Saint-Jacques, La Petite-Chapelle, Le Poissenot; village Gevrey-Chambertin.

The Humbert brothers - I always wonder whether they are twins - are large, dark, and solid. Until recently one was cellar manager for the Domaine Damoy. The family possesses some good land, but they don't make the best out of it. The wines lack concentration and flair.

PHILIPPE LECLERC

7.84 ha: owned. Gevrey-Chambertin *premier cru* in Les Cazetiers, Les Champeaux, La Combe-aux-Moines; village Gevrey-Chambertin in the *lieu-dit* La Platière; village Chambolle-Musigny.

The Leclerc domaine was split between Philippe (born in 1951), and his elder brother René (see below) in 1974, and they have since gone entirely separate ways. Philippe, with his neat beard and elegant clothes, gives one the impression that he has just got off the set of some swashbuckling movie. He believes in picking late, macerating slowly at less than 30°C with 20 per cent of the stems, and then giving the wines a good two years in new wood with a very high toast, delaying the malo, and bottling without either fining or filtration.

This results in big, spicy, almost brutally tannic and oaky wines. They can certainly be rich, but I find a lack of grace. Their olde-worlde presentation is uncompromisingly rustic, but this for some reason does not put off the tourists who flock to his boutique in the centre of the village.

RENÉ LECLERC

9.50 ha: owned. Gevrey-Chambertin *premier cru* in La Combe-aux-Moines, Lavaux-Saint-Jacques, Les Champeaux; village Gevrey-Chambertin including the *lieu-dit* Clos-Prieur.

The curly-headed, greying René, a decade or so older than Philippe, makes his wine in a modern cellar down by the main road. Recently he too has opened a shop in the middle of the village itself.

Again there is a long *cuvaison* and the wines are given two years in wood. But only 10 per cent of the stems are retained, and temperatures allowed to rise to 32°C. Here, however, there is little new oak, and too much old wood. As a result, for the wines are never very concentrated in the first place, they tend to dry out and lose their focus and elegance.

ANDRÉ LUCOT-JAVELIER

5 ha: owned and *en fermage*. Charmes-Chambertin (9 a); Gevrey-Chambertin *premier cru* in Les Cazetiers, plus a number of parcels blended together to make a *premier cru tout court*; village Gevrey-Chambertin.

The stocky, bespectacled Hervé Moineau, son-in-law of André and Suzanne Lucot – the vines came from her, Javelier, side – has been in charge here since 1990, since when the domaine has sold more and more in bottle. Moineau has increased the quantity of new wood, and recently extended his cellar in order to facilitate bottle storage.

The wine is vinified using 90 per cent of the stems and given a fortnight-long *cuvaison*. There is 50 per cent new wood for the top two wines.

The domaine is still learning, as far as the *élevage* is concerned, but things are improving. I enjoyed the top 1993s in cask.

HENRI MAGNIEN ET FILS
GFA DU MEIX-COQUEBRIQUE

4 ha: owned and *en fermage*. Ruchottes-Chambertin (16 a); Gevrey-Chambertin *premier cru* in Les Cazetiers, Les Estournelles-Saint-Jacques, Les Champeaux, Lavaux-Saint-Jacques (the last two blended together); village Gevrey-Chambertin.

François Magnien succeeded his father Henri at this estate, whose winery nestles under the Cazetiers vineyard at the top of the village, in 1987. His wife is a painter, and the office has a secondary function as a gallery to show off her wares.

Henri vinifies with 10-15 per cent of the stems, keeping the temperature below 30°C. He then warms up the *cave* to promote an early malo, uses a maximum of 25 per cent new oak (he doesn't like over-oaky wines, he says), and bottles a year or so after the vintage, without filtration.

These are supple, fruity wines for the medium rather than the long term: good but without the depth and concentration for great.

JEAN-PHILIPPE MARCHAND

4 ha: owned. Charmes-Chambertin (20 a); Gevrey-Chambertin *premier cru* Les Combottes; village Gevrey-Chambertin; Morey-Saint-Denis *premier cru* Clos-des-Ormes; village Morey-Saint-Denis; Chambolle-Musigny *premier cru* Les Sentiers.

Jean-Philippe is the eldest son of the Morey-based Charles Marchand, and set up on his own in 1983. He also operates as a *négociant* and a producer of liqueurs such as *Crème de Cassis*.

All the stems are retained, the temperature of the fermentation allowed to rise to 30°C, and 30 per cent new oak is utilised. The style of the house is one of femininity and elegance rather than undue weight and muscle. Good to very good: but could be better.

MARCHAND-GRILLOT ET FILS

9 ha: owned and *en fermage/métayage*. Ruchottes-Chambertin (8 a); Gevrey-Chambertin *premier cru* in La Petite-Chapelle, Les Perrières; village Gevrey-Chambertin; village Morey-Saint-Denis; village Chambolle-Musigny.

Michel Marchand and his son Jacques run this domaine, and are cousins of Claude and Jean-Philippe (see above). They have two separate cellars underneath the rear of their adjoining houses in the quaintly named Rue Aquatique, and muse occasionally about joining them up, which would save a lot of manhandling. The trouble is they are not exactly on the same level. Some 25 per cent of the stems are retained. There are a few days' cold maceration before the fermentation unleashes itself, and a *cuvaison* of ten to twelve days at temperatures up to 32°C. These Marchands are not great fans of new oak, and tend to bottle lighter vintages quite early, before the Christmas of the following year.

The wines used to be good here – stylish, balanced and fruity, and on the feminine side – but in recent years the domaine seems to have lost its way.

BERNARD MAUME

4.33 ha: owned. Mazis-Chambertin (67 a); Charmes-Chambertin (17 a); Gevrey-Chambertin *premier cru* in Lavaux-Saint-Jacques, Les Champeaux, Les Cherbaudes, La Perrière (the last two blended together); village Gevrey-Chambertin, including the *lieu-dit* En Pallud.

Bernard Maume leads a double life. His days are spent as a lecturer at the University of Dijon, or undergoing research into yeasts and starches, and his spare time running his small estate, inherited from an uncle, with his son Bertrand. He is an amiable man, thoughtful enough to provide a few warmed-up *gougères* for the travelling wine-writer to munch through as he samples the wines.

Naturally, much thought has gone into the wine-making process. Maume destems entirely, macerates at cooler temperatures for four or five days, believes in a long (three or four weeks) *cuvaison*, at a maximum of 30°C, and lodges his wine in a selection of different oak origins, depending on the *cuvée*, a quarter of which, overall, is new. Racking is kept to a minimum, and the wines are not filtered.

What I like about Maume's wines is their rampant individuality. The Mazis is sexy and exotic, wanton and dangerous. The Charmes is more refined. I described the 1989s in *The Vine* as Eliza Doolittle and Professor Higgins. They are full, rich and concentrated, but sometimes they lack a little grace. Nevertheless this is a very good source.

The vines in Les Champeaux are relatively young: twelve years old in 1994.

★★DENIS MORTET

10 ha: owned and *en fermage*. Chambertin (15 a); Clos-de-Vougeot (31 a); Gevrey-Chambertin *premier cru* in Lavaux-Saint-Jacques, Les Champeaux; village Gevrey-Chambertin including the *lieux-dits* En Champs *vieilles vignes*, Au Velle and En Motrot (*monopole*); Chambolle-Musigny *premier cru* Aux Beaux-Bruns; Marsannay.

What was formerly the domaine Charles Mortet et Fils was divided after the 1991 harvest, Denis Mortet (born in 1956) and his younger brother Thierry having decided to go their separate ways. Denis was then lucky enough to be approached by a neighbour about to retire, and has since taken over this man's 4.5 ha domaine *en fermage*. This includes a large parcel of Lavaux-Saint-Jacques.

The results here have been fine for some time. Today they are brilliant. Total destemming, four to six days of pre-fermentation maceration, a thirteen to fifteen day *cuvaison*, at a maximum temperature of 32°C, and a percentage of new oak which varies from 25–80 per cent, depending on the *cuvée*. Moreover there is a change in the origin of the wood as well: a mixture for the lesser wines, solely Vosges for the best. No filtration: sometimes no fining either.

But of course great wine-making cannot be encapsulated in a single paragraph. It is about a meticulous attention to detail from the vineyard onward, a very low yield, a very severe selection of fruit, and, above all, flair and imagination. Our man has got this in spades. The wines are full-bodied, concentrated, harmonious, intensely flavoured, and splendidly elegant. The 1993s, the first vintage with the additional parcels of land, were particularly exciting.

See Profile, page 000.

THIERRY MORTET

4.50 ha: owned and *en fermage*. Chambolle-Musigny *premier cru* Aux Beaux-Bruns; village Gevrey-Chambertin including the *lieu-dit* Clos-Prieur.

Thierry Mortet's first vintage was 1992 (see above). He makes the wine in the same way as his brother, and so far the results are very encouraging. If there was more of a track record of wines in bottle and a more prestigious line-up he would perhaps merit a star.

HENRI REBOURSEAU

13.62 ha: owned and *en métayage*. Chambertin (46 a); Chambertin, Clos-de-Bèze (33 a) (these are blended together); Clos-de-Vougeot (2.21 ha); Mazis-Chambertin (96 a); Charmes-Chambertin (1.32 ha); Gevrey-Chambertin *premier cru* Le Fonteny; village Gevrey-Chambertin.

The imperative that if you possess great land you have a duty to mankind to produce great wine applies with more force the greater the cornucopia of richness: as here. Sadly one can only report disappointment, though there have been one or two occasions in the last decade when I thought that things might have turned the corner.

The grapes are destemmed, vinified at up to 34°C after a few days *maceration à froid*, the *cuvaison* lasting a fortnight, and there is 100 per cent new oak for the Chambertin. The wines are both fined and filtered. But even in oak they lack intensity and definition.

HENRI RICHARD

3.20 ha: owned. Charmes- and Mazoyères-Chambertin (1.11 ha); village Gevrey-Chambertin.

From headquarters on the main road - one of the last houses on the Beaune side - this small domaine is one of the few which offer you both Charmes- and Mazoyères-Chambertin, their large parcel overlapping the boundary between the two. The Charmes is preferred, and given a little more new oak. As a result, perhaps, I find the Mazoyères a little more robust.

Today run by Madame Richard (Henri died in 1985), her daughter Margaret Bastien-Richard and a young *caviste*, this domaine produces neat, fresh, fruity wines which evolve in the medium term. Bottling is by gravity, without filtration.

PHILIPPE ROSSIGNOL

5.60 ha: owned and *en fermage/métayage*. Gevrey-Chambertin *premier cru* Les Corbeaux; village Gevrey-Chambertin, including a *vieilles vignes cuvée*; village Fixin; Côte-de-Nuits-Villages.

Philippe Rossignol, born in 1956, in Burgundy but not *dans les vignes*, as he puts it, has built up his domaine from scratch since the mid-1970s. It was only in 1993 he was proudly able to offer some *premier cru* wine. He's one of the few *vignerons* with premises below the main road on the way to the railway station.

The grapes are entirely destemmed, and vinified after five or six days' cold maceration at a maximum temperature of 34°C. He only employs some 15 per cent new oak, but the rest is new-ish. and the results are very good, though sometimes a little hard and austere at the outset. I look forward to the time when he has a larger range of *premiers crus* to offer.

ROSSIGNOL-TRAPET

13 ha: owned. Chambertin (1.7 ha); Chapelle-Chambertin (55 a); Latricières-Chambertin (76 a); Gevrey-Chambertin *premier cru* in La Petite-Chapelle, Clos-Prieur; village Gevrey-Chambertin; Beaune *premier cru* Les Teurons; village Beaune in the *lieu-dit* Les Mariages; village Morey-Saint-Denis; village Savigny-lès-Beaune.

The well-known Trapet domaine was divided in 1990, at which time both Jean Trapet and his brother-in-law, Jacques Rossignol, officially retired. Jacques' half is today administered by his sons David and Nicolas.

Some 30 per cent or so – it depends on the vintage – of the stems are retained. Fermentation is controlled at a maximum of 32°C, the percentage of new oak varies from a quarter to one-half, and bottling takes place early, about fourteen months after the vintage.

The result, just like over the road at what is now Jean and Jean-Louis Trapet, is good: round, medium-full wines, plump and fruity; but rarely mind-blowing: so far a mere echo of the great Trapet wines of the 1950s and 1960s. I'd like to see a bit more concentration, a bit more excitement here.

★JOSEPH ROTY

7.80 ha: owned and *en fermage*, Charmes-Chambertin (16 a), Griottes-Chambertin (8 a); Mazis-Chambertin (12 a); Gevrey-Chambertin *premier cru* Le Fonteny; village Gevrey-Chambertin including the *lieux-dits* Les Champs-Chenys, Clos-Prieur and Brunelle; Marsannay.

Joseph Roty is one of Burgundy's *enfants terribles* – arrogant, voluble, excitable, quick to take offence (even when none was intended), impossible to pin down, infuriating but again at the same time lovable. It is difficult to get into his cellar, but once in it is almost impossible to get out. I think I hold the world record for the shortest visit: one and a half hours. I should long ago have given up on this difficult, touchy and exasperating man. But he does make very good wine.

Viticulture is *biologique*, old vines are preserved, and the yields cut to the minimum. He vinifies with some of the stems, for a long time, at a very cold temperature, never more than 28°C (and preferably at 25°C). The wine then goes into well-charred new wood: 100 per cent for the *grands crus*. Minimal racking, no filtration and no fining.

Roty's wines are very distinctive. They are full, very intense, very perfumed and very harmonious. They are certainly immensely seductive. Sometimes, though, I find them just a touch sweet, just a shade over-oaky. Roty only started in 1968, his father having died when he was a child, and my experience of old mature Rotys is scant. I look forward to seeing the vintages of the late 1980s when they are fully mature. Perhaps then I'll award him 2 stars.

★★★ARMAND ROUSSEAU

14 ha: owned. Chambertin (2.20 ha); Chambertin, Clos-de-Bèze (1.50 ha); Charmes-Chambertin (1.36 ha); Mazis-Chambertin (53 a); Ruchottes-Chambertin, Clos-des-Ruchottes (1.06 ha); Clos-de-la-Roche (1.48 ha); Gevrey-Chambertin *premier cru* in Clos-Saint-Jacques, Les Cazetiers, Lavaux-Saint-Jacques; village Gevrey-Chambertin.

A visit to taste in Charles Rousseau's cellar is one of the delights of every Burgundy visit. This is a domaine with a proven record of producing fine wine which dates back to the 1930s, when Charles' father Armand was one of the very first to start putting his own wine into bottle. Armand died in 1959 at the age of seventy-five, and the mantle passed to Charles, born in 1932, a short man with a large head, a voluble expansive presence and a lush squeaky laugh. Waiting in the wings, so to speak, for Charles is still firmly in charge, is his son Nicolas.

Some 15 per cent of the stems are retained, to aid the efficiency of the fermentation as much as anything else. The *cuvaison* lasts fifteen days, at a maximum temperature of 31°C, and the top three wines, the third being the Clos-Saint-Jacques (not the Mazis or the Ruchottes) get 100 per cent new wood. But it all starts in the vineyard, says Charles, with a low yield which is established early in the season, by hard pruning and debudding. He is contemptuous of the current fashion for green harvesting.

Rousseau's wines are rich in colour, pure in texture, never over-oaked, always concentrated, balanced, vigorous and very classy. Moreover they are all quite distinctive, each an expression of its own *terroir*. This is superb wine-making, from one of the gentlemen of Burgundy.

See Profile, page 621.

SCE Sedovi • De la Tassée • Les Perrières

12.5 ha: owned and *en métayage*. Gevrey-Chambertin *premier cru* La Petite-Chapelle; Chambolle-Musigny *premier cru* in Les Charmes, Les Baudes; village Gevrey-Chambertin including the *lieu-dit* Champerrier; village Chambolle-Musigny; village Savigny-lès-Beaune; Marsannay.

François Perrot runs these two domaines, the Perrières exploiting the Gevrey wines and La Tassée those in Chambolle. There is a modern ugly winery up against the slope above the Champonnet *climat*. But the results I find thin and disappointing.

★Christian Serafin

4.70 ha: owned and *en fermage*. Charmes-Chambertin (31 a); Gevrey-Chambertin *premier cru* in Les Cazetiers, Le Fonteny; village Gevrey-Chambertin including the *lieu-dit* Les Corbeaux and a *vieilles vignes cuvée*.

Stanislaus Serafin arrived from Poland before the war (the family are cousins of the Heresztyns), worked first as a mason, but in 1947 bought a piece of land and set himself up as a *vigneron*. He gradually built up an estate, which his son Christian inherited in 1988, though the latter had been responsible for the wine for a decade or more.

One would have agreed then: a good domaine, but not an exciting one. The last five years, however, have seen a distinct improvement, as if Christian had been somewhat constrained in the past. This is today an excellent source.

The vineyard is organically cultivated, great attention being paid to restricting the yield, and, when it comes to the harvest, to a *triage* of the fruit. Some of the stalks are left in - it depends on the vintage and the *cuvée* - and after several days' cold maceration, the fermentation is allowed to progress up to a maximum temperature of 35°C. *Cuvaisons* are long. There is 70-80 per cent new wood, much more than hitherto. And no longer any filtration.

Serafin's wines are full-bodied, meaty, and abundantly rich, with a good touch of spice. His *vieilles vignes* village Gevrey-Chambertin is usually better than his Fonteny.

Denis Thibault

9 ha: owned and *en fermage/métayage*. Village Gevrey-Chambertin; village Morey-Saint-Denis; village Vosne-Romanée.

Denis Thibault deserves to be better recognised, but he is almost too self-effacing . . . so it is we who will have to make the effort. Only village wines, but only the old-vine elements of such (the rest is sold off in bulk); the grapes mostly destemmed, cold-soaked for six days or so, then fermented up to 35°C, matured with a third new wood and bottled in the early spring sixteen months or so after the vintage. These are very clean, pure wines: admirable Pinot Noir.

Gabriel Tortochot

11 ha: owned. Chambertin (40 a); Charmes-Chambertin (53 a); Mazis-Chambertin (42 a); Clos-de-Vougeot (21 a); Gevrey-Chambertin *premier cru* in Lavaux-Saint-Jacques, Les Champeaux; village Gevrey-Chambertin; village Morey-Saint-Denis.

What will happen when the seventy-plus Gabriel Tortochot finally passes into the Great Tasting Room in the Sky? He and his wife Jacqueline have two daughters, but they and their husbands have other careers. This would be a splendid estate for some young Burgundian tiger to take on *en fermage*! Gabriel is a fine man, and an influential figure, having served on the national INAO Committee, and having been president of the *Union Générale des Grands Vins de Bourgogne* and the local *Syndicat des Vignerons* for over twenty years.

The grapes are completely destemmed, vinified at 30-34°C, and the top wines get 100 per cent new oak. The other wines get old wood, of which there is too much in this cellar. Currently the Tortochot wines do not excite me.

FRANÇOIS TRAPET

5.40 ha: owned and *en fermage/métayage*. Ruchottes-Chambertin (21 a); Gevrey-Chambertin *premier cru* La Petite-Chapelle; village Gevrey-Chambertin including the *lieu-dit* Les Cargeots.

For some years I have been watching a new cellar being constructed at the Mazis end of the village. It will eventually provide a new modern home for the eccentric, bearded François Trapet's estate. Meanwhile he uses his father's damp, old, cramped premises round the corner.

The wine is currently kept in a mixture of new and what looks like very old casks, usually bottled before the Christmas of the second year (the 1993s being late to finish their malos being an exception) after a light *Kieselguhr* filtration. These are somewhat sturdy, old-fashioned wines, but of good concentrated quality.

JEAN AND JEAN-LOUIS TRAPET

12 ha: owned. Chambertin (1.90 ha); Chapelle-Chambertin (60 a); Latricières-Chambertin (75 a); Gevrey-Chambertin *premier cru* in La Petite-Chapelle, Clos-Prieur; village Gevrey-Chambertin; Marsannay.

This is the other half of the Trapet domaine (see Rossignol-Trapet) divided in 1990, and today it is Jean-Louis, son of the ebullient Jean, who is in charge.

Some 15–20 per cent of the fruit is destemmed. There is a five to eight days' cold maceration, and then a long (three to four week) *cuvaison* at a maximum temperature of 32°C. Plenty of new oak is employed for the top wines, with an overall three-year rotation. Bottling can be quite early, with most of the wines in bottle by Christmas of the second year in most vintages, without filtration and by gravity.

Techniques, therefore, are similar to those over the road at Rossignol-Trapet, and the results are the same: good but not great. Jean-Louis is at pains to point out the benefits of the pre-fermentation cold maceration, which he has extended, and the work he has done in the vineyard to persuade the roots to dig deeper. I suspect things may be better here than at Rossignol-Trapet - and there is certainly some healthy competition going on, which is to everyone's advantage - but I have yet to see it in bottle.

VACHET-ROUSSEAU PÈRE ET FILS

7 ha: owned. Mazis-Chambertin (54 a); Gevrey-Chambertin *premier cru* Lavaux-Saint-Jacques; village Gevrey-Chambertin including a *vieilles vignes cuvée*.

The tall, handsome, black-bearded Gérard Vachet - his mother Lucette was *née* Rousseau, but there is no immediate connection with the famous Rousseau domaine - presides over a tidy cellar, an efficient establishment which gives you confidence in his wines the moment you enter the door.

Total destemming, five to six days' cold maceration, temperatures up to maximum of 32°C, and one-third new oak is the recipe here, and the results are excellent: clean, vibrantly poised wines, succulent and stylish. A very good source.

Sadly in 1995 Gérard Vachet decided to give up. Some of the land was sold. The rest was leased out on *métayage* basis to Gérard Harmand (see page 76).

VAROILLES

13.5 ha: owned. Charmes-Chambertin (78 a); Bonnes-Mares (Domaine Paul Misset) (50 a); Clos-de-Vougeot (Domaine Paul Misset) (60 a); Gevrey-Chambertin *premier cru* in Clos-des-Varoilles (*monopole*), Les Champonnets, La Romanée (*monopole*); village Gevrey-Chambertin including *lieux-dits* of Clos-de-Meix-des-Ouches (*monopole*), Clos-du-Convent (*monopole*), Clos-Saint-Pierre and Clos-Prieur.

The Domaine les Varoilles now belongs to the Swiss company Hamel having previously belonged to Jean-Pierre Naigeon of the *négociants* Naigeon-Chauveau, through which the wines continue to be distributed. Naigeon continues, however, as a consultant, and it is his son Patrice who is responsible for the wines.

Complete destemming is practised here, but, instead of the more traditional *pigeage*, an automatic device to break up the cap and submerge it in the must is used. The *cuvaison* lasts ten to twelve days, the wines are given only a modicum of new oak, and bottling takes place after a little over a year.

The results are good here, sometimes very good, but I find the style of the Varoilles wines, though elegant, a little lean. I'd like a bit of fat. It would give the wines more generosity and sex-appeal.

ALAIN VOEGELI

2.50 ha: *en fermage*. Village Gevrey-Chambertin.

Alain Voegeli exploits the land of Madame Suzanne Servoz, what was once part of the Domaine Etienne Grey (of Grey-Poupon Mustard). He makes one wine - the young-vine wine is sold off in bulk - and it is plump, elegant and generous. It comes forward in the medium term.

MOREY-SAINT-DENIS

Morey-Saint-Denis leads a schizophrenic existence, and has never achieved the reputation of either Gevrey to the north or Chambolle to the south, despite being the possessor of four and a bit *grands crus* – the bit being a small part of Bonnes-Mares, most of which lies across the border in Chambolle.

The reason for this is simple: for generations the local growers, abetted by the *négoce*, passed off their wines as Gevrey-Chambertin. And for generations wine-writers have tended to dismiss Morey as a sort of inferior halfway house, neither Gevrey nor Chambolle, and not as good as either.

Admittedly the village possesses an impossibly large number of tiny *premiers crus* – only three out of twenty are larger than 3 ha (and one of these, Monts-Luisants, is planted with white grapes as well as red) – and consequently these lack definition in the minds of all but the most experienced locals. But, despite this and the fact that the area of village appellation has been extended across the main road to the east – a deleterious step in my view – the wines of Morey *do* have character and a distinct personality, and they *can* be just as fine (and sadly sometimes just as miserable) as all but the very, very best of either Chambolle or Gevrey-Chambertin. What is holding Morey back is that by and large the average standard of quality of the domaines is lower than in the neighbouring villages. But that is a problem only the locals can solve.

MOREY-SAINT-DENIS

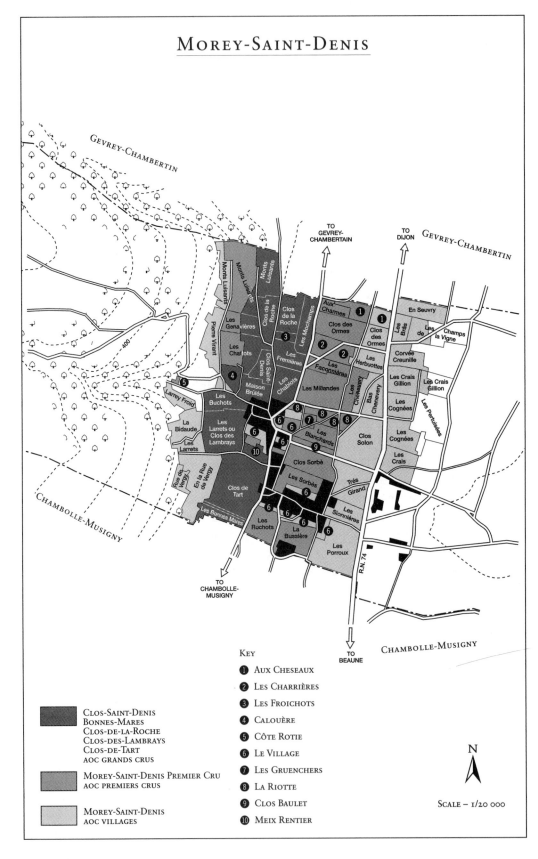

KEY

1. AUX CHESEAUX
2. LES CHARRIÈRES
3. LES FROICHOTS
4. CALOUÈRE
5. CÔTE ROTIE
6. LE VILLAGE
7. LES GRUENCHERS
8. LA RIOTTE
9. CLOS BAULET
10. MEIX RENTIER

CLOS-SAINT-DENIS
BONNES-MARES
CLOS-DE-LA-ROCHE
CLOS-DES-LAMBRAYS
CLOS-DE-TART
AOC GRANDS CRUS

MOREY-SAINT-DENIS PREMIER CRU
AOC PREMIERS CRUS

MOREY-SAINT-DENIS
AOC VILLAGES

N

SCALE – 1/20 000

HISTORY

The origins of Morey-Saint Denis, known as Mirriacum in 1120 according to Dangay et Aubertin, are closely connected with the Cistercian Abbey of Citeaux and its benefactors, the *seigneurs* of Vergy (though there is much archaeological evidence of a Gallo-Roman settlement centuries before the arrival of the monks). This heritage is illustrated by the survival of the word 'Clos' in a number of *climats*.

It was in that year, 1120, that Savaric de Vergy ceded to Citeaux much of the land in the village. In 1300 responsibility passed to the Abbey of Saint-Germain-des-Près, when they bought the priory of Gilly, to which the lands at Morey were tied. A century later, when the local Cistercians acquired the château at Gilly - now a splendidly renovated but expensive hotel - the village came back into local hands, and until the revolution the land was owned either by the Abbaye de Citeaux or the descendants of the Vergys and the other grand families of Burgundy such as the Saulx-Tavannes and the Croonembourgs, owners at one time of La Romanée-Conti itself.

The first important vineyard settlement seems to have been that of the Clos-de-Tart. It was originally Tart-le-Haut, to distinguish it from the village in the plain beyond Dijon, and was exploited by the nuns of the newly created Notre-Dame-de-Tart almost from the foundation of their establishment in 1125 until the Revolution. Notably it has remained, once it regained its present size in 1251, both unaltered and a monopoly.

Clos-Saint-Denis, which was originally a mere 2.14 ha instead of today's 6.62 ha, takes its name from a college of canons installed in 1023 up in the hill beyond Vergy. They owned a number of parcels of land, including part of Les Saint-Georges in Nuits. Like the Clos-de-Tart the land passed after the Revolution into the Marey-Monge family.

Clos-des-Lambrays, elevated to *grand cru* in 1981, seems never to have enjoyed ecclesiastical ownership, indeed its origins are somewhat enshrouded in mist, though references to it date back to the fourteenth century. After the Revolution it was split among as many as seventy-four proprietors. Subsequently, under the Joly, Rodier and Cosson families, it was reassembled, and is now to all extents and purposes a monopoly.

Clos-de-la-Roche, as Henri Cannard says, is an enigma. The vineyard dates from much later and has never been enclosed. Some writers have suggested - for why La Roche rather than Les Roches? - that it was originally the site of some Druidic religious ritual. Originally it covered a mere 4.57 ha. Now, having absorbed several *premiers crus*, lastly in 1971, it occupies 16.90 ha.

A number of other *climats* have clear religious origins: the Clos-de-la-Bussière, for example, which belonged to the Cistercian abbey of Bussières-sur-Ouche. There is the Clos-des-Ormes, today sadly without a single elm tree (*orme*) in sight, the Clos-Baulet and the Clos-Sorbé.

Probably more so than in the rest of the Côte-de-Nuits, a consequence of its lack of reputation perhaps, the village continued to plant a large quantity of Gamay until well into the last half of the nineteenth century. Only in the plum vineyards, suggests Dr Lavalle, will you find solely the Pinot. In 1855 a mere 70 ha out of 160 was planted with the noble grape.

In Lavalle's opinion, the wine of Clos-de-Tart was supreme: a *tête de cuvée*. Bonnes-Mares, that small part within the confines of the villages, Les Lambrays (not a Clos in those days!) and Clos-de-Laroche (*sic*) were regarded as *premières cuvées*, while Clos-Saint-Denis was among half a dozen *deuxièmes*.

Morey was late to adopt the usual practice of tagging on the name of the most important *cru* to the village name. This did not happen until 1927.

For the locals had found themselves in a dilemma. Which name? Morey-Tart did not sing, as neither did Morey-la-Roche. The anti-clerical lobby would disapprove of Morey-Saint-

Denis. Some suggested Morey-Chambertin, but the neighbours would not hear of it. Morey-les-Ormes was even put forward. But it wasn't vinous enough. The discussion went on for years. In the end, despite a certain opposition, Morey-Saint-Denis it became, for who would dare to criticise a saint with his head under his arm?

But as everyone has hitherto pointed out Clos-Saint-Denis is not Morey's best wine . . . it's Clos-de-la-Roche.

LOCATION

Only the excellent Gevrey-Chambertin *premier cru* Les Combottes separates Latricières-Chambertin from Clos-de-la-Roche, after which the rest of Morey's *grands crus* follow in a line above the *Route des Grands Crus* which runs through the village until the *climat* of Bonnes-Mares overlaps into Chambolle-Musigny. With the exception of the Monts-Luisants, Les Challots and Les Genavrières (spelt with an a), which lie up-slope from Clos-de-la-Roche and Clos-Saint-Denis, the Morey-Saint-Denis *premiers crus* lie beneath the *Route des Grands Crus* on either side of the *Grande Rue* which runs from the church opposite the entrance to the Clos-de-Tart down to the main road.

Morey is a compact village, with the *Grande Rue* as its main road, off which is many an imposing mansion fronted by a large courtyard, these being the headquarters of many of its leading growers. Above the village, and its Place du Monument, a road disappears into the hills behind the Domaine Ponsot, but only goes as far as a farm and an old marble quarry. Across the main road, where you will find Morey's wine-making co-operative, a rare foundation in the Côte d'Or, vines on the Gevrey side were elevated to *Appellation Contrôlée* status in the early 1980s.

The appellation is only about a kilometre wide, from north to south, and forms a square, rising to 350 metres in the Monts-Luisants, from which you can see the snows of Mont Blanc (but if you can, it means it's going to rain tomorrow). Up at the top of the slope above the *grands crus* white grape varieties, entitled to village AC (and indeed *premier cru* in Monts-Luisants) are planted on light Bathonian limestone. Further down the slope the soil is more of Bajocian origin, brown and calcareous. The Clos-de-Tart and the Bonnes-Mares are marked by their stones. There is more sand in the Clos-des-Lambrays. In the Clos-Saint-Denis and the Clos-de-la-Roche there is marl, and it is less stony.

THE VINEYARD

Grands Crus: Morey has four *grands crus* in its own right. From north to south they are Clos-de-la-Roche, Clos-Saint-Denis, Clos-des-Lambrays and Clos-de-Tart. Part of Bonnes-Mares lies in the commune. Ignoring this, the *grands crus* cover fractionally under 40 ha and produce an average of 1,325 hl (175,000 bottles) per year.

Premiers Crus: Today there are twenty *premiers crus* in Morey-Saint-Denis, a number having been absorbed into Clos-Saint-Denis and Clos-de-la-Roche over the years. Altogether they comprise some 33 ha and produce 1,760 hl (232,000 bottles) per annum. In alphabetical order they are as follows: Les Blanchards; Les Chaffots; Aux Charmes; Les Charrières; Les Chenevery; Aux Cheseaux; Clos-Baulet; Clos-de-la-Bussière; Clos-des-Ormes; Clos-Sorbé; Côte-Rôtie; Les Façonnières; Les Genavrières; Les Gruenchers; Les Millandes; Les Monts-Luisants; La Riotte; Les Ruchots; Les Sorbès; Le Village.

In 1995 the local growers' syndicate lodged an application with the INAO for the re-classification as *premier cru* of part (2.5 ha) of En la Rue de Vergy. The *climat* lies up-slope from Clos-de-Tart.

Village Wine: There are some 64 ha of village wine. This produces an average of 2,800 hl (370,000 bottles) a year.

The Morey-Saint-Denis appellation, unlike that of Gevrey-Chambertin or Chambolle-Musigny, applies to white wines as well as red. But the production is tiny, less than 3 ha producing 80 hl in 1993.

The red wine of Morey is said to be a cross between Gevrey and Chambolle, more structured but with less fragrance than the latter; suppler and less sturdy than the former. This is simple and it is true. There is a frank, lush fruitiness about a good Morey which makes it very appealing. Logic would also suggest that the wines to the north would be more Gevrey-like, those to the south more Chambolle-like. This is less easy to agree with. Remember that the vines to the south lie under Bonnes-Mares, itself a fuller, more tight-knit wine than Clos-Saint-Denis and Clos-de-la-Roche. Moreover, on this side we have the Roumier domaine's monopoly of the Clos-de-la-Bussière: no Chambolle touches here! Happily - for glib simplification is boring - the commune does not generalise easily.

THE GRANDS CRUS
CLOS-DE-LA-ROCHE

Surface Area: 16.90 ha • **Average Production:** 565 hl (74,000 bottles)

Principal Proprietors: *Ponsot (3.31 ha); *Dujac (1.95 ha); *Armand Rousseau (1.48 ha); Pierre Amiot (1.20 ha); Coquard-Loison-Fleurot (1.17 ha); Georges Lignier (1.05 ha); Peirazeau (80 a); Morey Co-operative (79 a); Louis Remy (67 a); *Leroy (67 a); Hervé Arlaud (66 a); Guy Castagnier (59 a); *Hospices de Beaune (44 a); Truchot-Martin (43 a); Jean Raphet (38 a); Michel Magnien (37a); Maurice (Hubert) Lignier (31 a); Philippe Battachi (20 a).

Clos-de-la-Roche has grown from 4.57 ha in 1861 to 16.90 ha today, absorbing the *lieux-dits* of Chabiots, Fremières, Froichots, Mauchamps and the bottom of Monts-Luisants in the process. (Who's to say it wouldn't have gobbled up Gevrey-Chambertin, Les Combottes if it hadn't been over the boundary?) If that sounds greedy, a glance at the map, or a wander along between the vines will show that there is nothing unnatural here. The extra territory is at the same altitude (270-300 metres), and of the same geological mixture - on a Bajocian limestone base, brown in colour, mixed gently with clay and limestone rock scree, and in places barely 30 centimetres deep. At least this *grand cru* has not extended itself below the *Route des Grands Crus*.

There is a gentle incline, more so than across the border in Latricières and Chambertin itself, which aids the drainage, and the aspect is firmly to the east, while in the Clos-Saint-Denis next door there is a faint suggestion of a few degrees further to the north.

It is the biggest and the classiest of the Morey *grands crus*. But the structure has an inherent lushness to it. There is none of the austerity of Chambertin, nor the muscular density of Bonnes-Mares. The fruit has an element of the exotic, with a splendidly seductive perfume of *myrtille* (bilberry, huckleberry), sometimes black cherry, or violets, or truffles. Ample and classy it certainly is. But dignified? I think not. It definitely doesn't stand on its dignity.

CLOS-SAINT-DENIS

Surface Area: 6.62 ha • **Average Production:** 230 hl (30,000 bottles)

Principal Proprietors: Georges Lignier (1.49 ha); *Dujac (1.47 ha); Bertagna (53 a); *Ponsot (38a); Jouan (36a); Jean-Paul Magnien (32 a); Heresztyn (23 a); Peirazeau (20 a); Pierre Amiot (18 a); Coquard-Loison-Fleurot (17 a); *Charlopin (17 a); * Louis Jadot (17 a).

If the extent of this Clos, prior to the Revolution, was a mere 2.12 ha, there are, to quote Danguy et Aubertin, 'no natural limits in Morey', and the *climat* has expanded to fill all the space between Clos-de-la-Roche and the road up into the hills, absorbing part of Les Chaffots and La Calouère and all of Maison-Brûlée in the meanwhile.

Clos-Saint-Denis does not reach all the way down to the *Routes des Grands Crus*, for what was Les Chabiots is now Clos-de-la-Roche. But otherwise it is on the same level and much the same soil structure – a brown Bajocian marl – mixed more with rock than pebbles, high in phosphorus, with perhaps just a little more clay than in the Clos-de-la-Roche.

This is the most Chambolle-like of the Morey *grands crus* despite its position. The words supple and delicate spring to mind, as do fragrant and 'feminine'. There is a purity and class here, when the wine is at its best, which is quite different from that in the Clos-de-la-Roche, and though it is less structured it is no less intense. The fruit flavours are of raspberries and red currants, and the structure gentle and quietly dignified. In Jacques Seysses' cellar at the Domaine Dujac you can see the two side by side. On its own you might find each hard to place, but put together the different origins are inescapable.

CLOS-DES-LAMBRAYS

Surface Area: 8.84 ha • **Average Production:** 295 hl (39,000 bottles)

Principal Proprietor: Domaine des Lambrays (Saier). Jean Taupenot-Merme owns 420 square metres.

It was not until 1981 that this *climat* was finally promoted to *grand cru*. Judging by the bottles it produced in the late 1940s this was indisputably fully merited. But by then the Domaine des Lambrays, in the hands of the Cosson family, had fallen on hard times. Having failed to take up the cudgels to get the land classed as *grand cru* in 1936, the widow Renée Cosson allowed the vineyard to decline, failing to replace dead vines. By the 1970s the wine-making had deteriorated too, and when it finally changed hands after her death in 1977 – being bought in 1979 – a major project of replantation and rehabilitation was necessary, and inevitably, with a low average age of vineyard, the wines that followed under the new regime were somewhat thin and uninspiring.

The new owner was a consortium whose shareholders were the Saier family, owners of an existing domaine in Mercurey and Aloxe-Corton, together with Roland Pelletier de Chambure. The latter died prematurely in 1988 and the Saier brothers bought up his share, at the top of the market. Currently, as this book goes to press, the Domaine des Lambrays is once more for sale, ironically just as the vineyard is beginning to reach an acceptable age of maturity.

The Clos-des-Lambrays reaches furthest up the hill of all the Morey *grands crus*, and inclines gently to the north as well as east. The soil is less marly, more pure limestone than in the other *climats*, and there is also sand.

Charles Quittanson, who has written a monograph on the Clos, speaks of iron hands in velvet gloves, and others remark on the substance that this *climat* can produce. ('*Très corsé*,' says Henri Cannard, while Clos-de-Tart and Clos-de-la-Roche are merely '*corsé*'.)

The 1993, I wrote, when I sampled it in cask, was 'definitely Morey (rather than Gevrey or Bonnes-Mares) in its structure and texture': rich and plummy, balanced and classy: not a block-buster. But not (?yet) unmistakably of proper *grand cru* quality.

Nevertheless the Saiers and their resident manager, Thierry Brouhin, have been unstinting in their efforts both in equipment and in attention to detail to promote the quality of this wine, and the château, park and its outbuildings have been largely restored. Success, in the sense of the fabulous Clos-des-Lambrays of the past, will surely come. I shall never forget a 1949 Alexis Lichine was once kind enough to open for me at the Prieuré; nor the 1947; nor the 1945 . . .

CLOS-DE-TART

Surface Area: 7.53 ha • **Average Production:** 230 hl (30,000 bottles)

Monopoly of Mommessin, SA
Directly up-slope from the village itself is the Clos-de-Tart. The large, impressive, two-level, deep cellar is nineteenth century, but the buildings opposite, comprising the offices and lodging for some of the vineyard workers, are medieval, once a monastic *dortoir*.

Sequestered by the Revolutionary State, the Clos was sold at auction early in 1791, between the disposal of Romanée-Saint-Vivant and that of Chambertin, and acquired by Charles Dumaine of Nuits-Saint-Georges for F 68,200. Dumaine and Nicholas-Joseph Marey often acted in tandem, and perhaps on this occasion Dumaine was acting on behalf of the Marey (later Marey-Monge) family, for it was into their hands that the Clos-de-Tart was to pass. In the crisis of the 1930s, having been first exploited by the *négociants* Champy of Beaune and then by Chauvenet of Nuits-Saint-Georges, descendants of the Marey-Monge dynasty sold the Clos-de-Tart to Mommessin of Macon. Other holdings in the Morey-Saint-Denis area passed to the Groffier family. Since 1932 the Clos-de-Tart has remained with Mommessin. The resident manager is Sylvain Pitiot, who has recently taken over from Henri Perrault.

The vines, unlike most of the Côte, are planted north–south rather than up and down the slope, a neat compromise between the need to protect against erosion and the requisite of efficient drainage. The vineyard here is very stony, resting on a Bathonian calcareous base at the top of the slope, evolving into Bajocian, with a little more clay, and a little more depth of surface soil at the foot. Renewal of the vineyard is by *sélection massale* on a regular basis to ensure a thirty-five-year average age.

Full-bodied but 'feminine' is how Clos-de-Tart is described. '*Une grande dame,*' says Bazin. I must demur. The flavour of Clos-de-Tart betrays the fact that it is vinified with 80 per cent of the stems, and this *sous bois*, earthy texture I do not find feminine. The wine is robust and tannic, with rich cherry fruit and a certain spice. Older vintages have been excellent, but currently I find it lacks elegance.

In 1992 an experiment using prolonged cold maceration techniques was essayed. It was found not to be a success, and in 1993 production reverted to traditional methods.

THE PREMIERS CRUS

There are currently twenty *premiers crus* in Morey-Saint-Denis, and few are of a size significant enough to give them a distinct personality of their own. It is convenient to discuss them under four separate headings:

(a) Those which lie up-slope from Clos-Saint-Denis and Clos-de-la-Roche:

LES CHAFFOTS (2.62 HA) • CÔTE-RÔTIE (1.23 HA)
LES GENAVRIÈRES (1.19 HA)
(with an a, please note)
LES MONTS-LUISANTS (5.39 HA)

Hitherto a terrain given over to white wine, this sector has been gradually taken over by the Pinot Noir since 1960. Ponsot (see below) are one of the few who have not replanted all their land in black grapes. The land is poor and rocky, with very little surface soil, and up here at above 300 metres it is marginally cooler. The result is wine with a good acidity, so it keeps well, but with a certain leanness. The fruit flavours combine red currants and cherries, with a hint of damsons in some years.

Recommended Sources:
Les Monts-Luisants blanc: Ponsot (Morey-Saint-Denis).

(b) Underneath Clos-de-la-Roche, at the Gevrey-Chambertin end, you will find in a line from north to south:

AUX CHARMES (1.17 HA) • **AUX CHESEAUX** (PART) (1.49 HA)

CLOS-DES-ORMES (3.15 HA) • **LES CHARRIÈRES** (2.27 HA)

LES FAÇONNIÈRES (1.67 HA) • **LES MILLANDES** (4.2 HA)

(one of the larger *climats*)

Underneath the latter, part of Les Chenevery (1.90 ha) is also graded *premier cru*.

Premier cru reaches down to within a couple of hundred metres of the main road, roughly on a line with the last houses of the village and the hotel-restaurant Castel de Très Girard.

This is where you will find the best of Morey's *premiers crus*. A good Clos-des-Ormes or Millandes, the two most commonly seen, is a rich, ample wine with good backbone and plenty of ripe black cherry and blackberry fruit: very much a lesser - but by no means ignoble - Clos-de-la-Roche.

From the Chenevery the Polish Georges Bryczek produces, with permission granted at an audience in 1979, a *Cuvée du Pape Jean-Paul II*.

Recommended Sources:
Clos-des-Ormes: Georges Lignier (Morey-Saint-Denis).
Les Façonnières: Michel (Hubert) Lignier (Morey-Saint-Denis).
Les Millandes: Pierre Amiot (Morey-Saint-Denis); Heresztyn (Gevrey-Chambertin).

(c) Moving south towards the village of Morey we find:

LES GRUENCHERS (51 A) • **LA RIOTTE** (2.45 HA)

LES BLANCHARDS (1.97 HA) • **LE VILLAGE** (PART) (90 A)

CLOS-BAULET (87 A) • **CLOS-SORBÉ** (3.55 HA) • **LES SORBÈS** (2.68 HA)

Here the wines are similar, but they have less definition and less finesse: good worthy Moreys but rarely exciting.

Recommended Sources:
La Riotte: Perrot-Minot (Morey-Saint-Denis).
Les Sorbès: Bernard Serveau (Morey-Saint-Denis).

(d) On the southern side of the village, underneath Clos-de-Tart and Bonnes-Mares, lie the two last *premiers crus*:

LES RUCHOTS (2.58 HA)

CLOS-DE-LA-BUSSIÈRE (2.59 HA)

(monopoly of the Domaine Georges Roumier of Chambolle-Musigny)

If you stand on the *Route des Grands Crus* with your back to the Clos-de-Tart and look down-slope, you will see the land sink into a little hollow in the Ruchots, and then rise again. This keeps the Bussière - which is the land on the rise - very well drained, and in the hands of Christophe Roumier it makes a very good wine, not a bit like the rest of his range: fullish, meaty, robust and animal, but rich and succulent after a goodly period of maturity.

Recommended Sources:
Les Ruchots: Pierre Amiot (Morey-Saint-Denis).
Clos-de-la-Bussière: Georges Roumier (Chambolle-Musigny).

THE GROWERS
PIERRE AMIOT ET FILS

10 ha: owned and *en métayage*. Clos-de-la-Roche (1.20 ha); Clos-Saint-Denis (18 a);
Charmes-Chambertin (23 a); Gevrey-Chambertin *premier cru* Chenevery Les Combottes;
Morey-Saint-Denis *premier cru* in Aux Charmes, Les Chenevery, Les Millandes, Les Ruchots;
Chambolle-Musigny *premier cru* Les Baudes; village Morey-Saint-Denis; village Gevrey-Chambertin.

Pierre Amiot is a short, fat, rotund man in his late fifties with a luxuriant moustache. He
couldn't look more French if he tried! Now he is approaching retirement, and the reins are
gradually being taken up by two of his sons, Jean-Louis and Didier. A third, Christian, is
responsible for the vines of the late Jean Servelle in Chambertin-Musigny.

Destemming is total here, and the top wines receive one-third new oak. In good vintages
the results can be very good, but they are proportionately less exciting in worse years,
especially if the crop has been abundant. Perhaps the new generation will take things in hand.
The first step would be to reduce the yield.

GEORGES AND EDWARD BRYCZEK

5 ha: owned and *en fermage*. Morey-Saint-Denis *premier cru* Les Chenevery (*Cuvée du Pape Jean-Paul II*); village Morey-Saint-Denis; village Gevrey-Chambertin; village Chambolle-Musigny.

Georges Bryczek was born in Poland in 1912 and came to France in 1938, working after the
war for a number of local *vignerons* before setting up on his own in the early 1950s. In 1979
he made a pilgrimage to Rome where he had an audience with his compatriot and presented
him with some of his best wine. His Holiness blessed the wine and the estate, signed Bryczek's
livre d'or and gave him permission to name the wine *Cuvée du Pape Jean-Paul II*.

Bryczek's cellar is now a shrine, every nook and cranny stuffed with fairy lights, religious
kitsch and his own rather naive paintings and sculpture.

The wine, sadly, is unexceptional. But a new generation is now in charge, and we may
therefore expect an improvement.

GUY CASTAGNIER-VADEY/GILBERT VADEY-RAMEAU
CHRISTOPHER NEWMAN

Castagnier-Vadey: 4 ha: *en fermage*. Clos-de-Vougeot (50 a); Clos-de-la-Roche (59 a); Clos-Saint-Denis (35 a); Charmes-Chambertin (40 a); village Morey-Saint-Denis; village Gevrey-Chambertin; village Chambolle-Musigny.

Newman: 1.25 ha: owned. Latricières-Chambertin (53 a); Mazis-Chambertin (19 a);
Bonnes-Mares (33 a).

One domaine: three labels. Firstly we have the estate which has come down the female line
from Odette Rameau, wife of Gilbert Vadey, which is now administered by their son-in-law
Guy Castagnier; secondly we have Castagnier's own estate; and thirdly the small domaine
Christopher Newman inherited from his father Robert. Robert Newman's original intention
had been to set up a joint venture with Alexis Lichine, Lichine to be responsible for making
and selling the wine, and being allowed to buy a half share in due course. It never worked out,
Lichine neglecting his side of the bargain, and so Newman kept everything for himself but
entrusted the care of the land, on a *métayage* basis, to one of Lichine's favourite growers, Gilbert
Vadey. This Castagnier has inherited.

The wine is made at the top of the village, off the Place du Monument, but is now matured
in Castagnier's new cellars below his house down in the plain. The grapes are usually totally
destemmed, vinified classically after a day's cold maceration, and given one-half new wood.

Large sales are made to France's mail-order Savour Club.

The Vadey wines had a high reputation in the 1970s, but when I first came to call on Guy Castagnier I found even the 1990s a bit dilute and vintages of the Newman wines of the 1980s have not impressed. The 1993s, however, were better.

**DUJAC

11.50 ha: owned and (Vosne-Romanée only) *en fermage*. Clos-de-la-Roche (1.95 ha); Clos-Saint-Denis (1.47 ha); Charmes-Chambertin (70 a); Bonnes-Mares (43 a); Echézeaux (69 a); Gevrey-Chambertin *premier cru* Les Combottes; Morey-Saint-Denis *premier cru*; Chambolle-Musigny *premier cru* Les Gruenchers; Vosne-Romanée *premier cru* Les Beaumonts; village Morey-Saint-Denis (including *blanc*); village Chambolle-Musigny.

A splendid and perfectionist domaine which has only been in existence for little over twenty-five years, when Jacques Seysses' father bought the Domaine Marcel Graillet for his son. Traditional in some ways (100 per cent of stems retained), ultra modern in others (cloned selection, cultured yeasts, low-temperature fermentation, enzymes to clarify the wine) and with a healthily biological approach to viticulture under vineyard manager Christophe Morin, the Dujac wines, almost entirely matured in new oak, are strikingly individual. Never very deep in colour - because of the stems - yet intense, perfumed, silky-smooth and impeccably balanced.

There is a small associate *négociant* company, Druid Wine, which specialises in Meursault. See Profile, page 418.

ROBERT GIBOURG

8 ha: owned and *en métayage*. Clos-de-la-Roche (7 a); Corton, Les Renardes (17 a); village Gevrey-Chambertin; village Morey-Saint-Denis, including the *lieu-dit* Clos-de-la-Bidaude; village Chambolle-Musigny; Aloxe-Corton *premier cru* Les Valozières; village Ladoix.

For years I used to wonder who was clearing and replanting some derelict land above the *grand cru* Clos-des-Lambrays. The answer came when I first visited the vigorous, stocky Robert Gibourg, in his early fifties, owner and creator of this domaine. The first vintage of this resurrected land, the Clos-de-la-Bidaude - the top planted with Chardonnay, the lower slopes with Pinot Noir - will be in 1996.

There are good, sturdy wines here, kept one year in cask, and then returned to vat before the bottling. And M. Gibourg also operates as a *négociant*.

*ROBERT GROFFIER PÈRE ET FILS

8 ha: owned. Chambertin, Clos-de-Bèze (41 a); Bonnes-Mares (98 a); Chambolle-Musigny *premier cru* in Les Amoureuses, Les Hauts-Doix, Les Sentiers; village Gevrey-Chambertin.

This Morey-based domaine is singular in that it owns not one wine in the commune. What it does possess is good-sized plots in all the *climats* it is present in, including the largest single slice of Chambolle-Musigny, Les Amoureuses (1.09 ha). As you drive up the hill from Vougeot to Chambolle you will see Robert Groffier's large hoarding.

In all other ways Robert Groffier, who works alongside his forty-year-old son Serge, is self-effacing, somewhat shy and gentle, and the wines are like the man himself: not rugged blockbusters, but pure, intense, understated and elegant.

He leaves about a third of the fruit un-destemmed, vinifies at 30-32°C after five days' cold maceration, and the amount of new oak varies from 30–70 per cent. The results are fine. See Profile, page 468.

CLOS DES LAMBRAYS
See page 90.

GEORGES LIGNIER ET FILS

15 ha: *en fermage*. Clos-de-la-Roche (1.05 ha); Clos-Saint-Denis (1.49 ha); Bonnes-Mares (29 a); Gevrey-Chambertin *premier cru* Les Combottes; Morey-Saint-Denis *premier cru* Clos-des-Ormes; village Morey-Saint-Denis; village Gevrey-Chambertin; village Chambolle-Musigny.

This is in many ways an exasperating domaine. Sometimes, as in 1990, the results are fine. Frequently, though, they are rather a disappointment. With just over 2 ha in the Clos-des-Ormes, the lion's share, this Lignier is the main supplier of this wine to the *négoce*, and it is often better under their bottlings than under his.

The man himself, Georges, grandson of Georges, a notable Morey figure, was born in 1952, and lost his father early. Lean, fair, thinning on top, and with piercing blue eyes, he appears thoughtful, somewhat inscrutable.

The grapes are almost entirely destemmed, vinified at up to 34°C after a few days' cold maceration, and the top wines given 50 per cent new oak. The cellar is a rabbit warren, somewhat cramped, but extensive. Why is the wine so irregular? It is a puzzle.

HUBERT LIGNIER

7.70 ha: owned and *en métayage*. Clos-de-la-Roche (80 a); Charmes-Chambertin (10 a); Morey-Saint-Denis *premier cru* in Les Chaffots, Les Façonnières, Les Chenevery; Gevrey-Chambertin *premier cru* Les Combottes; Chambolle-Musigny *premier cru* Les Baudes; village Morey-Saint-Denis; village Gevrey-Chambertin; village Chambolle-Musigny.

Born in 1936, and elder cousin of the above, Hubert Lignier exploits some vines on a *métayage* basis for a family in Fixin. These are sold to the co-operative, of which he is president.

His own wines have a higher reputation than those of cousin Georges, especially in America, and with this judgement I would generally agree, though I do not rate him as highly as some writers. There is little difference in the bald wine-making details, but Hubert's wines come over as richer and more obviously oaky, as well as being more consistent.

JEAN-PAUL MAGNIEN

4.50 ha: owned and *en fermage/métayage*. Clos-Saint-Denis (32 a); Charmes-Chambertin (20 a); Morey-Saint-Denis *premier cru* in Les Monts-Luisants, Les Gruenchers, Les Façonnières, Clos-Baulet; Chambolle-Musigny *premier cru* Les Sentiers; village Morey-Saint-Denis; village Chambolle-Musigny.

Jean-Paul's family were restaurateurs. This didn't interest him so he set up as a *vigneron*. He destems entirely, ferments at a maximum of 30°C after a few days' cold maceration, and gives the wine one-fifth new oak during the first year. Thereafter the wine goes into wood which I fear is a little too old, and this detracts from the elegance of the wines. The man himself is *sympa*, and also, I believe, *sérieux*. So I am sure my assessment will prove to be an underestimate in the years to come.

MICHEL MAGNIEN

9.75 ha: owned and *en fermage*. Charmes-Chambertin (28 a); Clos-de-la-Roche (37 a); Clos-Saint-Denis (12 a); Gevrey-Chambertin *premier cru* Les Cazetiers; Morey-Saint-Denis *premier cru* in Les Chaffots, Les Millandes, Les Monts-Luisants; village Gevrey-Chambertin including the *lieu-dit* Les Seuvrées; village Morey-Saint-Denis.

There is another Magnien in the village and a third in Gevrey but Michel, smallish, greying and in his late forties, who operates from a modern house and cellar on the 'wrong' side of the road, is related to neither of them. The wine-making is flexible here, and the use of the stems and the amount of the new oak varies with the vintage. But the results are unexciting.

CLAUDE MARCHAND

5 ha: owned. Griottes-Chambertin (15 a); Clos-de-la-Roche (12 a); Morey-Saint-Denis *premier cru* in Les Millandes, Les Façonnières, Clos-des-Ormes; Gevrey-Chambertin *premier cru* Les Combottes; Chambolle-Musigny *premier cru* Les Sentiers; village Morey-Saint-Denis; village Chambolle-Musigny; village Gevrey-Chambertin.

Father of Jean-Philippe of Gevrey (see page 78), Claude Marchand lives in one of the imposing mansions in Morey's *Grande Rue*, between the Ligniers on one side and Serveau and Amiot on the other. He is now approaching retirement, and much of the above will increasingly be exploited by Jean-Philippe in the future.

Unlike the son, who retains most of the stems, Claude Marchand now destems completely. Much of the Morey *premier cru* is sold as such, without a vineyard name, or as *premier cru vieilles vignes*.

★HENRI PERROT-MINOT

9 ha: owned. Charmes-Chambertin (1.56 ha); Morey-Saint-Denis *premier cru* La Riotte; Chambolle-Musigny *premier cru* La Combe-d'Orveau; village Morey-Saint-Denis in the *lieu-dit* En la Rue de Vergy; village Gevrey-Chambertin; village Chambolle-Musigny.

Henri Perrot-Minot, brother-in-law of Jean Taupenot, who lives opposite, has now been joined by his son Christophe. This has brought with it a distinct improvement in the wines, and they have stopped selling in bulk. Some 20–30 per cent of the stems are retained, the fermentation temperature allowed to rise to 32°C, after four to five days' cold maceration, and 30-40 per cent new wood is utilised. The wines are nicely rich, individual and stylish. This is the best source for that elusive Chambolle *premier cru* La Combe-d'Orveau: the vines lie above and adjacent to Le Musigny itself.

★PONSOT

8.73 ha: owned and *en métayage*. Owned: Clos-de-la-Roche (3.31 ha); Chapelle-Chambertin (47 a); Morey-Saint-Denis *premier cru* Les Monts-Luisants (*rouge et blanc*); village Gevrey-Chambertin; village Morey-Saint-Denis.

En métayage to the Mercier family (Domaine Chézeaux): Griottes-Chambertin (89 a); Clos-Saint-Denis (32 a); Chambolle-Musigny *premier cru* Les Charmes (58 a).

Formerly *en métayage* elsewhere, but no longer exploited: Latricières-Chambertin (32 a); Chambolle-Musigny *premier cru* Les Charmes.

Quality has blown hot and cold here in the past decade, but at its best it can be glorious, and now that Laurent Ponsot, son of Jean-Marie (mayor of Morey and member of numerous committees) is more and more able to take the decisions, I hope for fewer disappointments in the years to come.

The domaine has pioneered clonal selection, the mother plants being its own finest old vines. There are, you will be firmly told, 'no rules' in the wine-making here. Destemming is optional, there is a maximum temperature of 30°C during the *cuvaison*, very little new oak, and neither fining nor filtration.

The resulting wines are very individual: rich, exotic and spicy. Sometimes they work, sometimes they don't. Beware also of other wines under the Chézeaux label. Not all are the Ponsots' creation.

See Profile, page 573.

JEAN RAPHET ET FILS

12 ha: owned and (part of Charmes-Chambertin) *en métayage*. Chambertin, Clos-de-Bèze (21 a); Charmes-Chambertin (1.10 ha); Clos-de-la-Roche (38 a); Clos-de-Vougeot (1.47 ha); Gevrey-Chambertin *premier cru* in Lavaux-Saint-Jacques and Les Combottes; village Gevrey-

Chambertin; village Morey-Saint-Denis; village Chambolle-Musigny.

Jean Raphet and his son Gérard are in charge at this important domaine. Some 10 per cent of the stems are retained; the wine is fermented for twelve days at a maximum temperature of 32-34°C and bottled after eighteen months. Only 5 per cent of new wood is used, but the remainder of the barrels are recent enough. Half the crop is sold off in bulk.

The line-up is impressive, the atmosphere efficient, and the results can be very good: rich, full, plummy and succulent. More attention to the quantities produced, i.e. a reduction in the *rendement*, and a little more new oak, would easily bring this domaine up to star level.

LOUIS REMY

2.60 ha: owned. Chambertin (32 a); Latricières-Chambertin (58 a); Clos-de-la-Roche (66 a); Morey-Saint-Denis *premier cru* Aux Cheseaux; Chambolle-Musigny *premier cru* Derrière-la-Grange; village Chambolle-Musigny in the *lieu-dit* Les Fremières.

Madame Marie-Louise Remy and her daughter Chantal Remy-Rosier are the surviving Remys in the wine business, the Gevrey-based domaine of Madame Remy's brother-in-law, Philippe, having been sold to the Domaine Leroy in 1989.

At the top of the village, under Clos-des-Lambrays and facing on to the Place du Monument, Madame Remy occupies a substantial and attractive mansion, opposite which is a splendid two-level deep-vaulted cellar, somewhat too extensive, it would appear, for their rather small domaine.

I have had some splendid old Louis Remy wines from the 1940s, 1950s and 1960s, but of late - Louis died during the vintage in 1982 - quality has dipped. Chantal Remy-Rosier is a qualified oenologist, however, and there is no reason why the ancient reputation should not be recaptured. A small percentage of stems are retained, the *cuvaison* lasts fifteen days, at temperatures up to 30-32°C, and some 10 per cent of the barrels are renewed annually.

BERNARD SERVEAU ET FILS

7 ha: owned. Morey-Saint-Denis *premier cru* Les Sorbès; Chambolle-Musigny *premier cru* in Les Amoureuses, Les Sentiers, Les Chabiots; Nuits-Saint-Georges *premier cru* Les Chaines-Carteaux; village Chambolle-Musigny.

Bernard Serveau's son Jean-Louis is now in charge here, and quality is beginning to improve. When I first visited the estate in the mid-1980s neither the appearance of the cellar, nor the wines in cask gave me much confidence for the end product, and bottling took place two years after the vintage. Things have been tightened up since. The wines of the 1990s show promise and finesse.

CLOS-DE-TART

See page 90.

JEAN TAUPENOT-MERME

9 ha: owned. Charmes-Chambertin (1.44 ha); Morey-Saint-Denis *premier cru* La Riotte; Gevrey-Chambertin *premier cru* Bel-Air; village Morey-Saint-Denis; village Gevrey-Chambertin; village Chambolle-Musigny. Plus a few rows of Clos-des-Lambrays, hardly enough to make one barrel of wine.

Jean Taupenot hails from Saint Romain, where his twin brother Pierre continues to run the family domaine. He married the vivacious and attractive Denise Merme, sister of Madame Perrot-Minot (*q.v.*), and has since built on her inheritance.

He vinifies with a variable amount of the stems, prefers a long three-week *cuvaison*, and employs one-quarter new wood. The wines can be good, but lack flair and real concentration.

JACKY TRUCHOT-MARTIN

7 ha: owned and *en fermage/métayage*. Clos-de-la-Roche (45 a); Charmes-Chambertin (65 a); Morey-Saint-Denis *premier cru* Clos-Sorbès; Gevrey-Chambertin *premier cru* Les Combottes; Chambolle-Musigny *premier cru* Les Sentiers; village Morey-Saint-Denis; village Gevrey-Chambertin; village Chambolle-Musigny.

Jacky Truchot arrived in Morey in 1961 to take over the vines of his cousins, M. and Mme Henri Mauffre, who had no children. He has preserved their splendid old-style label.

The grapes are destemmed, fermented for ten to twelve days, the top wines given one-third new oak, and bottled without filtration. Since 1990 he has stopped selling to the *négoce*.

The wines are on the light side, even in 1990, and the quality is variable.

CHAMBOLLE-MUSIGNY

'In the opinion of many,' says Dr Lavalle in 1855 – and he has been echoed by just about every other writer on the subject since – 'this commune produces the most delicate wines of the Côte-de-Nuits.'

Delicate, yes. But feeble, no. Chambolle-Musigny's wines may be lighter in structure than those of Vosne or Gevrey, but they can and should be every bit as intense. Being less dense they will show the perfume of the Pinot Noir, not to mention this variety's inherent elegance, more radiantly. Gaston Roupnel talks of silk and lace, Anthony Hanson of 'subtle nobility', Remington Norman writes of the epitome of the finesse of which Burgundy is capable. I too find myself irresistibly seduced, particularly as recent vintages seem to have favoured the commune, and this has been put to good use by an increasing quantity of very good local domaines.

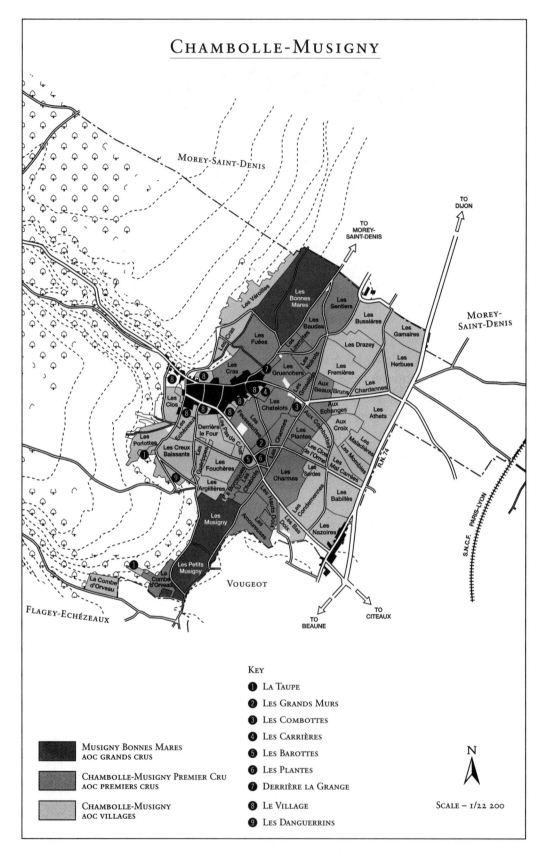

CHAMBOLLE-MUSIGNY

MOREY-SAINT-DENIS

TO DIJON

TO MOREY-SAINT-DENIS

MOREY-SAINT-DENIS

Les Véroilles
Les Bonnes Mares
Les Sentiers
Les Baudes
Les Bussières
Les Gamaires
Les Cras
Les Fuées
Les Lavrottes
Les Drazey
Les Herbues
Les Cras
Les Gruenchers
Les Groseilles
Les Noirots
Les Fremières
Les Chardannes
Aux Beaux Bruns
Les Chatelots
Aux Echanges
Les Athets
Les Clos
Derrière le Four
Les Pas de Chat
Les Fousselottes
Les Charmes
Aux Combottes
Aux Croix
Maladières
Les Mombies
Les Portottes
Les Echézeaux
Les Cras
Les Creux Baissants
Les Guéripes
Les Fouchères
Les Plantes
Les Clos de l'Orme
Les Carrées
Les Mal Carrées
Les Argillières
Les Barottes
Les Chabiots
Les Charmes
Les Serdes
Les Babillès
Les Musigny
Les Hauts Doix
Les Condemennes
Les Nazoires
Les Petits Musigny
Les Bas Doix
Les Amoureuses
La Combe d'Orveau
La Combe d'Orveau

R.N. 74

S.N.C.F. PARIS-LYON

VOUGEOT

FLAGEY-ECHÉZEAUX

TO BEAUNE

TO CITEAUX

KEY

1. LA TAUPE
2. LES GRANDS MURS
3. LES COMBOTTES
4. LES CARRIÈRES
5. LES BAROTTES
6. LES PLANTES
7. DERRIÈRE LA GRANGE
8. LE VILLAGE
9. LES DANGUERRINS

MUSIGNY BONNES MARES
AOC GRANDS CRUS

CHAMBOLLE-MUSIGNY PREMIER CRU
AOC PREMIERS CRUS

CHAMBOLLE-MUSIGNY
AOC VILLAGES

N

SCALE – 1/22 200

HISTORY

Chambolle takes its name from the rushing action of the stream or little river Grône which comes tumbling out of the Combe-de-Chamboeuf above the village. When there was a severe thunderstorm a fresh flood would bubble like boiling water through the vines below: hence 'Campus Ebulliens' or *champ bouillant*. The village was known as Cambola in 1110, and was dependent on the nearby Gilly-lès-Citeaux until 1500, the date authorisation was given to the inhabitants to build a local church. This was completed six years later under the orders of Jean Moisson, an ancestor of the De Vogüé family, and is one of the richest of the Côte, with wall paintings in the choir, classed as a *monument historique*. It is well worth a visit. Opposite the church is a venerable lime tree, said to have been planted during the time of Henri IV.

Like Morey-Saint-Denis, much of the land was under the direct control of the monks of Citeaux until sequestered at the time of the French Revolution. Pierre Gros, the Canon of Saint-Denis-de-Vergy, donated the *Champ de Musigné* to the Cistercian monks in 1110, at the same time that they were establishing the Clos-de-Vougeot. It has been suggested that the origin of the name is Gallo-Roman: a certain Musinus, perhaps.

The origin of Bonnes-Mares, Chambolle's second *grand cru*, lies in the word *marer*, to cultivate, though it has been suggested that there is a second, more felicitous connection with the *bonnes mères*, the Bernardine nuns of Notre-Dame-de-Tart.

Dr Lavalle, in 1855, decreed but one *tête de cuvée*, Musigny itself. Bonnes-Mares and the *climats* of Véroilles, Fuées, Cras and Amoureuses were *première cuvée*. Véroilles lies above Bonnes-Mares and has since lost status, being only partly *premier cru* today, while Fuées and Cras are the extension of this same slope as it turns round to face the south above the village itself. The Amoureuses lies directly below Le Musigny.

Lavalle goes on to say that, while the main road must be considered the lower limit for *bons crus*, one can nevertheless find good wine from the other side of the road, a truth which still holds good today. Two examples are the Bourgogne Bons-Bâtons of Ghislaine Barthod and Michelle and Patrice Rion. He also points out that the soil of the commune in general is not as fertile and therefore does not produce as much wine as in Morey or Vougeot, indeed only 5 *pièces* per hectare in Musigny though 7 or 8 elsewhere, he says. This premise seems to hold good now only in years of hail damage. The Combe-de-Chamboeuf affords an entrance into the Côte for a swathe of hail, and Chambolle, like parts of Nuits, tends to suffer more than most.

LOCATION

The commune of Chambolle-Musigny is roughly square in shape, with the addition of a tongue which flicks out to the south over the vineyards of Musigny and up into the Combe-d'Orveau.

Divided into two by the river Grône and the valley at the foot of the Combe-de-Chamboeuf, part of the land immediately south of the village is on slopes which face north, and these provide village wines. Below the *grand cru* of Bonnes-Mares, which overlaps into Morey-Saint-Denis to the north, below the village itself, and below Le Musigny, stretching down halfway towards the main road, lie the *premiers crus*.

The *terroir* of Chambolle-Musigny is marked by its high percentage of active limestone and its lack of clay. There is also less magnesium in the soil. Only in the northern section of Le Musigny, where it touches a *lieu-dit* suitably called Les Argillières, and on the Morey side of Bonnes-Mares is there a marked percentage of clay - *marnes blanches* in the case of the latter. Elsewhere the soil is a light, very pebbly, limestone debris, meagre in depth, lying on the base rock of Bathonian and Bajocian limestone. Erosion is a problem, particularly in Musigny itself.

THE VINEYARD

Grands Crus: Chambolle-Musigny possesses two *grands crus*: Bonnes-Mares of which 1.6 ha out of 15 lies in the neighbouring commune of Morey-Saint-Denis, and Le Musigny. Including the Morey segment these two comprise just under 26 ha and produce an average of 760 hl (100,300 bottles) per year.

Premiers Crus: There are twenty-three *premiers crus*, in whole or in part. Altogether they cover some 60 ha and produce 2,050 hl (270,000 bottles) per year. In alphabetical order these are as follows: Les Amoureuses, Les Baudes, Aux Beaux-Bruns (part), Les Borniques, Les Carrières, Les Chabiots, Les Châtelots, La Combe-d'Orveau (part), Aux (or Les) Combottes (part), Les Cras (part), Aux Echanges, Les Feusselottes, Les Fuées, Les Grands-Murs, Derrière-la-Grange, Les Groseilles, Les Gruenchers, Les Hauts-Doix, Les Lavrottes, Les Noirots, Les Plantes, Les Sentiers, Les Véroilles (part).

Village wine: There are some 94 ha of village land. This produces an average of 4,060 hl (536,000 bottles) per year.

Like Gevrey and Vosne, but unlike Morey and Vougeot, the appellation Chambolle-Musigny, village or *premier cru*, covers red wine only. There is, however, a little Le Musigny *blanc*.

In general, and as you would expect, the wines of Chambolle-Musigny are at their most sturdy to the north, on the border with Morey-Saint-Denis, and at their most ethereal where the land abuts Vougeot to the south. Nevertheless, however, I find an immediate difference between, say, the Morey of the Roumier's Clos-de-la-Bussière, and Robert Groffier's Chambolle-Musigny, Les Sentiers from the adjacent vineyard, a difference which is more than just a question of different wine-making. And I find less of a difference between Groffier's Sentiers and his Hauts-Doix, or between Freddy Mugnier's Fuées and his Amoureuses. Wherever they come from, all these four wines are archetypal Chambolles: ballerinas, not shot-putters.

THE GRANDS CRUS
LE MUSIGNY

Surface Area: 10.86 ha • **Average Production:** 300 hl (39,600 bottles)

Principal Proprietors: ★De Vogüé (7.14 ha); ★Mugnier (1.14 ha); Jacques Prieur (77 a); ★Joseph Drouhin (67 a); ★Leroy (27 a); Deschamps/Ponnelle (21 a); ★Louis Jadot (17 a); Moine-Hudelot (12 a). Also Georges Roumier (10 a); ★Joseph Faiveley (3 a).

Le Musigny is one of the very greatest *climats* in the whole of the Côte d'Or, one of a handful which includes Chambertin and Clos-de-Bèze, La Tâche and Romanée-Conti. This is more than a prince of the blood in the royal house of Burgundy, as Pierre Léon-Gauthier would have it. This is majesty itself. And if one is thinking of its texture and character, the queen rather than the king. The other four can fight among themselves for the role of consort.

The vineyard has always consisted of two sections, divided by a path. The northern part, slightly the larger, is Grand-Musigny, or simply Musigny. The southern, in the plural, is Les Petits-Musignys. This might make you expect the latter was the more morcellated, but no. This part is the monopoly of the Domaine Comte Georges de Vogüé.

In Dr Lavalle's day, the two comprised 10.05 ha. In 1929, part of the Chambolle *premier cru* La Combe-d'Orveau, further to the south, and across another path, was incorporated, adding 61 a. In 1989 4 *ouvrées* (15.3 a) belonging to the Domaine Jacques Prieur, were added on the Grand-Musigny side.

The *climat* lies between 260 and 300 metres in altitude, the slope varying between 8 and 14 per cent. The soil is middle Bathonian oolite up-slope, but more exposed Comblanchien limestone debris further down. It is quite different from the *grands crus* of Morey and Gevrey, and indeed of Bonnes-Mares and the rest of Chambolle. There is a red clay you do not find elsewhere. There is also a less high level of active limestone.

Having remained in ecclesiastical hands during the Middle Ages, but always apart from the Clos-de-Vougeot, and indeed never having been enclosed, the vineyard began to be divided in the seventeenth and eighteenth centuries, and among its owners are to be found the Fathers of the Oratory in Dijon, the Grand Prior of Champagne, and local parliamentary families such as the Bouhiers and the De Berbuseys. From the Bouhiers, today's principal owners, the De Vogüé family are descended. They can trace their ownership in the best vines of the Côte back longer than most.

As well as their lion's share of Musigny *en rouge*, the De Vogüé domaine has persisted with planting a small parcel of Chardonnay. Until recent times it was common to mix between 5 and 10 per cent of the Chardonnay in among the Pinots Noirs in order to give the wine an extra zip of acidity, and to soften it up. Today the De Vogüé domaine keeps its Chardonnay apart, in a little parcel of one-third of a hectare, and would normally make about three casks of it - but currently part of this parcel is very young vines. It is a full wine, with its own peculiar flavour, nothing like a Corton-Charlemagne or a Montrachet. Musigny, consequently, is the only *grand cru* with the exception of Corton which can be white as well as red.

At its best the red wine can be quite simply the most delicious wine to be found in Burgundy. Speaking personally, and I'm not the only one, it is *the* summit of achievement. With its vibrant colour, exquisitely harmonious, complex, profound bouquet, the blissful balance between tannin, acidity and the most intensely flavoured fruit - all the *petits fruits rouges* you could reasonably imagine - and its incomparable breed, depth, originality and purity on the finish, a great Musigny is heaven in a glass. Would that one could afford to drink it more often.

LES BONNES-MARES
Surface Area: 15.06 ha • Average Production: 466 hl
(13.54 in Chambolle; 1.52 in Morey) (615,000 bottles)

Principal Proprietors: ★De Vogüé (2.67 ha); Bernard Clair/Domaine Fougeray de Beauclair (1.60 ha); ★Georges Roumier (1.50 ha); Drouhin-Laroze (1.49 ha); ★Louis Jadot (1.11 ha); Bart (1.03 ha); ★Robert Groffier (97 a); Deschamps-Ponnelle (63 a); Varoilles (50 a); ★Dujac (43 a); Peirazeau (39 a); ★Mugnier (36 a); ★Pierre Bertheau (34 a); Newman/Castagnier (33 a); Moine-Hudelot (32 a); Georges Lignier (29 a); Hervé Roumier (27 a); ★D'Auvenay (26 a); Bouchard Père et Fils (24 a); ★Joseph Drouhin (23 a); Hervé Arlaud (21 a).

Bonnes-Mares is rare among *grands crus* in that it has shrunk rather than grown over the last century. Curiously part of the land within the nineteenth-century wall of the Clos-de-Tart used to be Bonnes-Mares. This anomaly was rectified in 1965.

This left 1.52 ha within Morey, the rest in the commune of Chambolle. All of the former, and a little else besides, belongs to Bernard Clair and is leased to Domaine Fougeray de Beauclair. The rest of this *grand cru* is divided among some thirty-five proprietors, according to Bazin. Some of these must be the members of the same family who vinify together. Twenty-five declared a harvest in 1993. Bonnes-Mares seems always to have been divided. Some 140 years ago there were already at least seventeen proprietors.

The *climat* lies between 265 and 300 metres and south of Clos-de-Tart, and is geologically cut in two diagonally across the slope from the top at the Morey end towards the bottom in the middle of the vineyard. North of this the soil is heavier and contains more clay, a marl known as *terres rouges*. South towards Chambolle the soil is lighter in colour and texture and there are fossilised oysters. This is the *terres blanches*. All over the vineyard the stone and pebble content is high. At the top of the slope there is little but broken-up limestone on top of the limestone rock. Further down the surface soil may be as much as 70 cm thick. Erosion, however, seems to be less of a problem than in Musigny, though the incline of the slope is similar.

The geological division helps explain the generally held view that the Bonnes-Mares which come from the Morey-Saint-Denis end are bigger and more vigorous than those of the Chambolle proximity. I find that many Bonnes-Mares, when you taste them alongside Clos-Saint-Denis and Clos-de-la-Roche in the same cellar, are more muscular, somewhat more dense, four-square and closed-in: masculine wines indeed. There is also often an element of spice, which I find in Clos-de-Tart but not the other Morey *grands crus*.

To compare Bonnes-Mares and Le Musigny in the same cellar - at De Vogüé or *chez* Freddy Mugnier for example - is equally illuminating. Here the difference is enormous. One can hardly believe that the wines come from the same commune.

Bonnes-Mares, then, is scarcely Chambolle-Musigny. The texture is velvet, even worsted, rather than silk and lace. The wine is full, firm and sturdy, needing its time. There is depth and richness, but not the nuance and breed of one of the really top *grands crus*. The tannic power can be almost too much.

THE *PREMIERS* CRUS

Some of the twenty-four *premiers crus* in Chambolle-Musigny are very small, and so insignificant that they are rarely vinified and declared separately. In the 1993 harvest report there is no mention of Les Borniques, Les Carrières, Aux Echanges and Les Grands-Murs (this latter vineyard, however, can be called Les Feusselottes). And in this vintage, in terms of declaration, nine of the rest are smaller than 1 ha in size. Some, however, merit an entry in their own right.

LES AMOUREUSES (5.40 HA)

The *climat* lies down-slope from Le Grand-Musigny on several levels as the land descends abruptly in a series of small cliffs towards Vougeot. A large board on the left, as one takes the little road up to Chambolle, announces 'Robert Groffier et Fils - Les Amoureuses'. Groffier, with over a hectare, is the largest owner.

This is a vineyard which, like Clos-Saint-Jacques in Gevrey-Chambertin, is regarded by most - and priced accordingly - as the equal of a *grand cru*. In Robert Groffier's cellar, and elsewhere, I regularly prefer it to the Bonnes-Mares. But Bonnes-Mares it is not. Les Amoureuses is really a sort of younger brother to Musigny itself: perfumed, silky-smooth, intense and soft rather than brutal and muscular, and with real finesse.

Recommended Sources:
Robert Groffier (Morey-Saint-Denis); De Vogüé, Mugnier, Georges Roumier, Pierre Bertheau, Amiot-Servelle, Moine-Hudelot (all Chambolle-Musigny); Joseph Drouhin, Louis Jadot (Beaune).

The wines of Les Hauts-Doix (1.75 ha), adjacent but lower down, and facing a little towards the north, are less fine, but similar. Robert Groffier's is a good example.

LES CHARMES (9.53 HA)

Across the road up to Chambolle is the large *climat* of Les Charmes. This is the most familiar *premier cru*, but the vineyard is more morcellated. The number of owners runs into the dozens.

At its best this is yardstick Chambolle, fresh in expression, ripe, juicy and elegant in its fruit, medium-bodied, and simply delicious. It doesn't have the intensity of Amoureuses, nor the hidden depth of Les Cras or Les Fuées, nor the slight spice and roasted quality of Sentiers or Baudes. It is simply itself: classic Chambolle-Musigny.

Recommended Sources:
Amiot-Servelle; Ghislaine Barthod; Pierre Bertheau (Chambolle); Leroy (Vosne); Daniel Rion (Nuits); Ponsot (Morey); Alain Hudelot-Noëllat (Vougeot).

LES FEUSSELOTTES (4.40 HA) • LES PLANTES (2.57 HA)
LES COMBOTTES (1.55 HA) • LES CHÂTELOTS (2.96 HA)

Further up the slope, towards the village lies Les Feusselottes; on either side are two separate parcels called Les Plantes and to the north you will find Les Combottes, some of which is not *premier cru*. Above Les Charmes lies Les Châtelots. All these produce similar wines.

Recommended Sources:
Les Feusselottes: Dr Georges Mugneret (Vosne-Romanée).
Les Plantes: Jacques-Frédéric Mugnier (Chambolle-Musigny).
Les Châtelots: Ghislaine Barthod (Chambolle-Musigny).

LES SENTIERS (4.89 HA) • LES BAUDES (3.42 HA)
LES LAVROTTES (0.92 HA) • DERRIÈRE-LA-GRANGE (0.47 HA)
LES NOIROTS (2.85 HA) • LES GRUENCHERS (2.82 HA)
LES GROSEILLES (1.34 HA) • AUX BEAUX-BRUNS (1.54 HA IN *PREMIER CRU*)

These are the *premiers crus* which lie under Bonnes-Mares. There is a little bit more muscle here, despite which they are true Chambolles. In addition there is a touch of spice, and in hot summers more of an element of cooked fruit, than elsewhere in the commune: a fertile hunting ground for the Chambolle lover.

Recommended Sources:
Les Sentiers: Robert Groffier (Morey-Saint-Denis).
Les Baudes: Ghislaine Barthod (Chambolle-Musigny).
Derrière-la-Grange: Amiot-Servelle (Chambolle-Musigny).
Les Gruenchers: Dujac (Morey); Armelle et Bernard Rion (Vosne-Romanée).
Aux Beaux-Bruns: Ghislaine Barthod (Chambolle-Musigny); Denis Mortet, Thierry Mortet (Gevrey-Chambertin).

LES FUÉES (4.38 HA) • LES CRAS (3.45 HA) • LES VÉROILLES (0.37 HA)

Véroilles lies above the southern end of Bonnes-Mares, and only recently has part of it been promoted to *premier cru*. Fuées and Cras end the extension southwards of the Bonnes-Mares slope.

This is an area of *premier cru* wine second only to that of Amoureuses. The wines are nicely firm, with a certain backbone and a cool dignity: poised wines with very good fruit and no lack of elegance. I like them very much indeed.

Recommended Sources:
Les Fuées: Mugnier, Ghislaine Barthod (Chambolle-Musigny), Joseph Faiveley (Nuits-Saint-Georges).
Les Cras: Ghislaine Barthod, Georges Roumier (Chambolle-Musigny).
Les Véroilles: Ghislaine Barthod (Chambolle-Musigny).

LES CHABIOTS (1.50 HA) • LES BORNIQUES (1.43 HA)

Above Les Amoureuses and in the same line as Le Musigny, if inching just to the north, you would expect something worth a second sip from here. Sadly, much of the area looks more or less derelict and I know of no good examples of these two *climats*.

LA COMBE D'ORVEAU (2.38 HA)

South of the Petits-Musignys, but in the same line with it, and overlooking the vineyards of Echézeaux on the south-facing side of the Combe, this *premier cru climat* (there is also a bit of village AC under this name, from which the Domaine Jean Grivot of Vosne-Romanée produce a very good wine) is little known but can produce some extremely good wine. It is more Echézeaux than Amoureuses however, with a satisfying core of concentration and depth. But no lack of elegance either.

Recommended Sources:

Bruno Clavelier (Vosne-Romanée); Joseph Faiveley (Nuits-Saint-Georges); Perrot-Minot (Morey-Saint-Denis).

THE GROWERS
BERNARD AMIOT

5.50 ha: owned and *en fermage*. Chambolle-Musigny *premier cru* in Les Charmes, Les Châtelots; village Chambolle-Musigny including the *lieu-dit* Aux Echézeaux.

Chambolle and Morey are villages rich in Amiots, but not all are closely related to each other, and this Amiot is no close cousin of Pierre in Morey (see page 93). Bernard Amiot exploits his domaine, built up since 1962, with his son Frédéric, and makes soft, harmonious, ample wines. Sometimes, though, they are a little *too* soft. A small percentage of the stems are retained, maceration lasts about ten to twelve days at temperatures up to 32°C, and the first growths go into new wood until the first racking.

AMIOT-SERVELLE

6.77 ha: owned. Clos-de-Vougeot (41 a); Chambolle-Musigny *premier cru* in Les Amoureuses, Derrière-la-Grange, Les Charmes; village Chambolle-Musigny.

Christian Amiot, one of the sons of Pierre of Morey-Saint-Denis, married Elizabeth, daughter of the late Jean Servelle, in the late 1980s, and, since the 1990 vintage, what used to be Servelle-Tachot has sailed under new colours.

Quality has improved too. Christian Amiot is a sensitive wine-maker, fully prepared to adapt the recipe according to the nature of the ingredients: no stems, a few days' cold maceration, controlled fermentations and no excess of new oak.

★GHISLAINE BARTHOD-NOËLLAT

6.64 ha: owned and *en fermage*. Chambolle-Musigny *premier cru* in Les Charmes, Les Cras, Les Fuées, Les Véroilles, Aux Beaux-Bruns, Les Baudes, Les Châtelots; village Chambolle-Musigny.

Ghislaine Berthod took over wine-making responsibility from her father Gaston in 1987, and from the 1992 vintage onwards the labels bear her name and not her father's. What has happened here since 1987 is exemplary of modern-day Burgundy. Ghislaine went to wine school. Gaston, though, once a soldier, had no theoretical qualifications. The yield is now much less than it used to be. There is a *table de trie*. There is more control over vinification temperatures, more *pigeage* and less *remontage*; self-bottling rather than contract bottling; fining and filtering only when absolutely necessary; and so on.

The result has been a leap in quality from the merely good to the definitely fine, making this cellar a splendid place to compare the nuances between different Chambolle first growths. In addition to the above there is some young-vine Combottes and a splendid Bourgogne *rouge* from a *lieu-dit* called Les Bons-Bâtons on the other side of the main road.

See Profile, page 336.

7.16 ha: owned and *en fermage*. Bonnes-Mares (38 a); Chambolle-Musigny *premier cru* in Les Amoureuses, Les Charmes; village Chambolle-Musigny.

I am very tempted to give Pierre Bertheau a star for I am always impressed by what I sample in cask here. But Pierre and his son François sell 40 per cent of their harvest off in bulk, and ship little to Britain, so my experience of their wines in bottle is more limited.

The *cuvaison* lasts ten to twelve days, at a maximum temperature of 30°C, and the new oak element is limited to 10 per cent. The wines are succulent, elegant and very classic examples of Chambolle. In addition to the specific *premier cru* listed above there is a *premier cru tout court* from vines in Les Baudes, Les Noirots and Les Groseilles.

HENRI FELLETIG

7.00 ha: owned and *en fermage*. Chambolle-Musigny *premier cru* (from Les Fuées, Les Noirots, Les Borniques and Les Chabiots); village Chambolle-Musigny.

The tall, bearded, jovial Henri Felletig, whose ancestors hailed from Romania, makes two separate *premiers crus cuvées* initially, and does not always blend them together. I find his wines fruity, but neither particularly concentrated nor sufficiently elegant. There is also, I gather, a Gevrey-Chambertin *premier cru* sold under his wife's name, René Bobant-Felletig. But I have never sampled it.

JOËL HUDELOT-BAILLET

14.40 ha: owned and *en fermage*. Bonnes-Mares (12 a); Chambolle-Musigny *premier cru* Les Charmes; village Chambolle-Musigny.

Joël Hudelot took over his parents' estate in the early 1980s, changed the wine-making to produce more of a *vin de garde* and has built up a good private clientele, both domestically and in Belgium and Switzerland. He does not seem very interested in exporting to Britain and the USA though - a question of once bitten, twice shy perhaps. My experience of his wines is largely confined to what I have consumed in the local restaurants. They are nicely cool and firm, but perhaps they lack a little generosity. A bit like his neighbour Michel Modot, in fact.

MICHEL MODOT

6.70 ha: owned and *en fermage*. Chambolle-Musigny *premier cru* in Les Charmes, Les Lavrottes; village Chambolle-Musigny.

In Michel Modot's cellar there are photographs of four generations of Modots in military uniform: great-grandfather during the Franco-Prussian War, grandfather during the First World War, father during the Second, and Michel himself doing his military service. Modot retains 20 per cent of the stems, macerates for twelve days at a maximum of 28°C and uses one-quarter new wood. The wines have colour and substance, but lack a little flair. Modot still sells 40 per cent or so of his production to the *négoce*.

DANIEL MOINE-HUDELOT

6.80 ha: owned and *en fermage*. Le Musigny (12 a); Bonnes-Mares (32 a); Clos-de-Vougeot (15 a); Chambolle-Musigny *premier cru* in Les Amoureuses, Les Charmes and *premier cru tout court*; village Chambolle-Musigny.

Daniel Moine, mayor of Chambolle, lives in a house on the edge of the village overlooking the *climat* of Feusselottes. He used to exploit, on behalf of several aged aunts, a larger piece of Musigny, but the family sold out to Madame Bize of Leroy in 1990, and Moine could not match her price. The vines in the Charmes are still quite young, being planted in 1980, and part of Clos-de-Vougeot was replaced after the 1985 frosts. Moine likes plenty of new wood

- from 20 per cent upwards for the Charmes - and produces round, fragrant elegant wines, at the top levels of high quality.

★★Jacques-Frédéric Mugnier

4 ha: owned. Le Musigny (1.15 ha); Bonnes-Mares (0.35 ha); Chambolle-Musigny *premier cru* in Les Amoureuses, Les Fuées, Les Plantes; village Chambolle-Musigny.

The Mugnier domaine occupies the Château de Chambolle-Musigny, a rather gaunt pile built in 1709 with a splendid, if rather sparsely filled, cellar in the basement. The vines used to be farmed by outsiders, but in 1984 Freddy Mugnier returned to take over. He supplements his living by working as an airline pilot three days a week.

Quality has improved dramatically here, and now more than matches the impressive landholdings. The wines are very pure, and have excellent intensity and finesse.

See Profile, page 568.

★★Georges Roumier et Fils

14.2 ha: owned and *en fermage* (and *en métayage* under the label of Christophe Roumier: wines asterisked). Le Musigny (10 a); Bonnes-Mares (1.50 a); Clos-de-Vougeot (32 a); Corton-Charlemagne (20 a); Chambolle-Musigny *premier cru* in Les Amoureuses, Les Cras; Morey-Saint-Denis *premier cru monopole* Clos-de-la-Bussière; village Chambolle-Musigny. ★Ruchottes-Chambertin (two-thirds of 0.54 ha), ★Charmes-Chambertin (half of 0.27 ha).

This is one of Burgundy's most important domaines, today run by Jean-Marie Roumier and his son Christophe, who has been making the wine since 1982. The style of wine they produce is atypical for Chambolle: substantial, quite sturdy. They need time. Catch them in their adolescence and they can be a bit heavy, a bit four-square. Let them mature properly and you are in for a treat.

See Profile, page 614.

Hervé Roumier

9.50 ha: owned and *en fermage*. Bonnes-Mares (27 a); Echézeaux (36 a); Clos-de-Vougeot (27 a); Chambolle-Musigny *premier cru* in Les Amoureuses, Les Fuées; village Chambolle-Musigny.

Hervé Roumier, son of Alain who was for a long time *régisseur* of the Domaine Comte Georges de Vogüé, has inherited part of his father's estate, and farms the rest, as he does the vines of the Roblot family. I have visited this cellar from time to time over the last decade but never been particularly impressed. Some 40 per cent of the crop is sold off in bulk.

Hervé Sigaut

6.50 ha: owned and *en fermage*. Chambolle-Musigny *premier cru* in Les Sentiers, Les Fuées, Les Charmes, Les Châtelots; Morey-Saint-Denis *premier cru* in Les Carrières, Les Millandes; village Chambolle-Musigny; village Pommard.

When I first made the acquaintance of this domaine it was Maurice Sigaut who was in charge, but he is now *en retraite* and responsibility has passed to his son Hervé. Total destalking here, controlled temperatures - not above 31°C - during the fermentation, a maceration which can last ten days to twenty, depending on the vintage, and a judicious 30 per cent of new oak for the better wines. My experience of mature wines from this cellar is limited.

★★★ Comte Georges de Vogüé

12 ha: owned. Le Musigny (7.14 ha); Bonnes-Mares (2.67 ha); Chambolle-Musigny *premier cru* Les Amoureuses (also Les Baudes and Les Fuées, but this goes into the village wine); village Chambolle-Musigny.

This famous domaine can trace its ancestry back to the Middle Ages, and occupies a Renaissance courtyard - the château is no longer inhabited - in the middle of the village. The cellars are substantial and impressive.

Having been through a long period when the wine was not up to standard, things were taken in hand in the late 1980s, and from 1989 the team of François Millet in the cellar, Jean-Luc Pépin in the office and Elizabeth de Ladoucette, daughter of the late Comte, have not put a foot wrong. The 1990 Musigny is one of the truly great Burgundies it has been my privilege to drink young.

See Profile, page 651.

LÉNI VOLPATO

3 ha: owned and *en fermage*. Chambolle-Musigny *premier cru* in Chabiots, Les Feusselottes; village Chambolle-Musigny.

Léni Volpato is most renowned for a Passetoutgrains made from very old vines: one of the first successful examples of this blend of Gamay and Pinot Noir that I have ever tasted. He farms land belonging to the local Prudhon family. These vines have recently been acquired by Labouré-Roi.

VOUGEOT

The commune of Vougeot is so dominated by its famous Clos that one tends to forget that there is both village and *premier cru* wine as well as *grand cru*: not much - only 15½ hectares - but enough to note. I have to say though, that just as the magic name of Clos-de-Vougeot is more likely than not to lead to disappointment, this being for the most part a second division *grand cru* rather than a first division one such as Le Musigny, Richebourg or Romanée-Saint-Vivant, so I find the *premier cru* wines of the commune of minor importance. This is not, as it might be, say, in Fixin, for a want of good growers. So it must be the *terroir*. I feel the authorities, having been saddled with the inescapable fact of decreeing the whole of the Clos as *grand cru*, bent rather too far backwards to be kind to the rest of the commune.

Vougeot

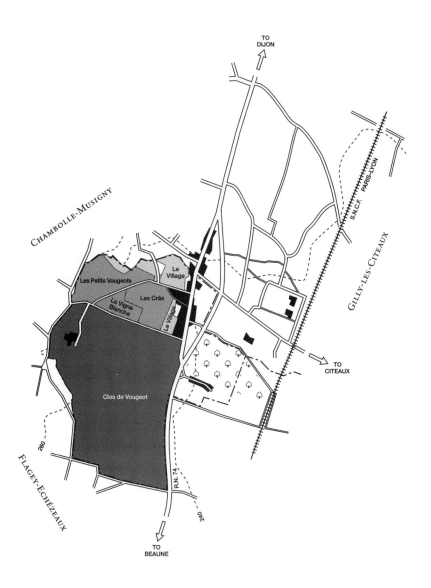

TO
DIJON

S.N.C.F. PARIS-LYON

GILLY-LES-CITEAUX

CHAMBOLLE-MUSIGNY

Le
Village

Les Petits Vougeots

Les Crâs

La Vigne
Blanche

Le Village

TO
CITEAUX

Clos de Vougeot

260

FLAGEY-ECHÉZEAUX

R.N. 74

240

TO
BEAUNE

Clos-de-Vougeot
AOC GRANDS CRUS

Vougeot Premier Crus
AOC PREMIERS CRUS

Vougeot
AOC VILLAGES

N

Scale – 1/20 000

LOCATION

Just as the Clos itself is notorious for occupying lower land - all the way down to the main road - than any of the other *grands crus*, so the *premiers crus*, immediately to the north, very nearly run down to the backs of the houses in the village, now thankfully for its inhabitants, by-passed. There is a fault in the land here, a series of small cliffs descending like a giant staircase. Above lie the vines of Le Musigny and Les Amoureuses. At the bottom is a small lake, fed by the source of the Vouge river and the Grône which flows down from the combe above Chambolle-Musigny. The adjacent village Vougeot vines almost seem to be planted in a hole in the ground. Wherever you are you seem to be looking down on them.

The soil here is very light, a fragile mixture of limestone scree and debris, but mixed with rather more alluvial soil than most. Drainage can be a problem.

THE VINEYARD

Grand Cru: The Clos-de-Vougeot accounts for more than 80 per cent of the land in the commune. There are 50.59 ha which produce around 1,800 hl (240,000 bottles) of wine a year. The wine can only be red.

Premiers Crus: There are four: Les Cras, La Vigne-Blanche (Le Clos-Blanc), Clos-de-la-Perrière and Les Petits-Vougeots (in part). The appellation allows both red and white wine. The surface area comprises 11.68 ha and produces about 350 hl (46,200 bottles) of red and 100 hl (13,200 bottles) of white wine a year.

Village Wine: There are 4.83 ha of village wine producing about 90 hl (12,000 bottles) of red and 36 hl (4,750 bottles) of white wine a year.

Village and *premier cru* Vougeot *rouge* is a light wine, superficially similar in structure to Chambolle-Musigny. But it lacks both the intensity and the class of a typical Chambolle. Too often, frankly, it's a bit weak.

There are only two white Vougeots regularly seen on the market; that of L'Héritier-Guyot, rather gross and over-oaked; and that of Bertagna, youngish vines, but pleasantly fragrant. Neither is really serious. The growers in Meursault have nothing to fear.

THE GRAND CRU
CLOS-DE-VOUGEOT

Surface Area: 50.59 ha • **Average Production:** 1,800 hl (240,000 bottles)

Principal Proprietors: ★Château de la Tour (5.48 ha); ★Méo-Camuzet (3.03 ha); Rebourseau (2.21 ha); ★Louis Jadot (2.15 ha); ★Leroy (2.07 ha); Paul Misset (2.06 ha) - worked until 1995 by both Armelle et Bernard Rion and Daniel Rion, and by the Domaine les Varoilles; ★Jean Grivot (1.85 ha); Gros Frère et Soeur (1.56 ha); Jean Raphet (1.47 ha); ★ René Engel (1.37 ha); François Lamarche (1.35 ha); ★Faiveley (1.29 ha); Jacques Prieur (1.28 ha); ★Alain Hudelot-Noëllat (1.05 ha); Pierre André (1.07 ha); L'Héritier-Guyot (1.05 ha); Drouhin-Laroze (1.02 ha).

A further forty proprietors/*exploitants* work over 20 ares of vines including: Bouchard Père et Fils, ★Daniel Chopin, ★Jacky Confuron-Cotétidot, ★Thomas-Moillard, ★Georges Roumier, ★Dr Georges Mugneret, ★Amiot-Servelle, ★Denis Mortet, ★Alfred Haegelen, ★Joseph Drouhin, ★Mongeard-Mugneret, ★Jean-Jacques Confuron, ★Robert Arnoux, ★Anne Gros, ★Michel Gros, ★Gros Frère et Soeur.

This is not the largest *grand cru* in Burgundy - Corton and Corton-Charlemagne are quite a bit more substantial - but it is the largest in the Côte-de-Nuits. Of the twenty-four *grands crus* here, only Clos-de-Vougeot and Echézeaux could be said to be sizeable.

Like Echézeaux, like most of Burgundy, the Clos is split up. Today there are some eighty proprietors and 100 different parcels, some of which are detailed and recommended above.

The history of the Clos-de-Vougeot is exemplary of the history of vinous Burgundy. At the beginning of the twelfth century, the centre of the western world was neither London, nor Paris, nor even Rome, but the Abbey of Cluny in the southern Mâconnais. Founded by the followers of Saint Benedict in AD 910, Cluny was the wealthiest and most powerful religious settlement in Christendom.

Elsewhere in France, however, there were Benedictines who felt that with such power had come a relaxation in the strict monastic virtues laid down by their founder saint. Humility, obedience, silence, even chastity, had been forgotten, replaced by rich living, sumptuous eating and drinking, and a worldliness far removed from the original objective. One such was Robert, Abbot of Molesmes, a monastery north of Dijon between Langres and Les Riceys. Robert had attempted unsuccessfully to reform the way of life at Molesmes but he found that only a few of his fellow monks wished to return to the simple life. In 1098, with some twenty companions, he left Molesmes and established a new monastery, a reformed commune, on the flat plains of eastern Burgundy, in a clearing within a forest of oaks and marshy reedlands. From the ancient French word for reed, *cistel*, the name evolved to the Latin *cistercium*. The new order became known as the Cistercians and the new abbey was named Citeaux.

But at Citeaux the land was unsuitable for the vine. No matter how hard they tried, the monks could not persuade the vine to thrive in the marshy bogs surrounding the abbey. Following the Vouge river upstream, the monks explored the higher ground to the west. Eventually they settled on some uncultivated slopes, bartered with some Burgundian landowners and acquired a few hectares of land. This was the nucleus of the Clos-de-Vougeot.

The monastery soon started receiving gifts of adjoining land suitable for the vine. The poverty, industry, austerity and saintliness of the Cistercians contrasted well with the opulent high life of the other religious orders. Donors shrewdly decided that the appropriate gesture in this world would be recompensed when it might be needed later, and the vineyard grew. Around 1160, a press house was constructed but it was not until 1336 that the vineyard took the form we know today and, later still, that the famous wall, forming the Clos, was eventually completed. Finally, in Renaissance times, the château was constructed, affording guest rooms for the abbot and distinguished visitors. The château has been modified several times since, being completed in 1891 and restored after the Second World War. It is now the headquarters of the Chevaliers de Tastevin, Burgundy's leading wine promotion fraternity.

Clos-de-Vougeot, by now a vineyard of some 50 ha, remained in the ownership of the Cistercians until the French Revolution in 1789 when it was sequestered and put up for sale as a *bien national*. It was decided to sell the Clos as one lot and, on 17 January 1791, ahead of six adversaries, it was acquired by a Parisian banker, one Jean Foquard, for the huge sum of 1,140,600 *livres*, payable in *assignats* (paper money). Foquard, it appears, never settled his debt and the authorities turned to Lambert Goblet, the monk cellarist or *magister celarii*, to continue to administer the estate. A year later the vineyard passed to the brothers Ravel but after the Restoration in 1815, the Clos-de-Vougeot changed hands yet again, the Ravels and their associates having been continually in dispute over their relative shares and responsibilities over a period of twenty-five years.

This time the Clos-de-Vougeot's proprietor was a man of financial substance. Jules Ouvrard took the ownership of this important vineyard with the seriousness that it deserved. He was the local *député* (Member of Parliament) for much of his career. He was a conscientious proprietor, with land in Corton, Chambertin and Volnay as well as being the owner of La Romanée-Conti which he vinified at Clos-de-Vougeot.

After Ouvrard's death in 1860, there was the usual difficulty about inheritance and this was not finally resolved until the Clos was sold - for F 600,000 - in 1889. For the first time the land was divided. Originally there were six purchasers, five Burgundian wine-merchants and one other; but these six soon became fifteen and now there are eighty: an average of 0.6 hectares or 250 cases per proprietor.

The Clos-de-Vougeot is not only one of the largest *grands crus* in Burgundy but the only one whose land runs from the slope right down to the main road running between Nuits-Saint-Georges and Dijon. Not surprisingly over such a large area, the soil structure is complex and there are differences in aspect and drainage. Add to these the many different owners, each making an individual wine, and you can see why there are variations from one grower's Clos-de-Vougeot to another's.

At the top and best part of the Clos, where the vineyard borders the *grands crus* of Grands-Echézeaux to the south and Le Musigny to the north, the soil is a pebbly, oolitic limestone of Bathonian origin. There is little clay. Here there are two unofficial *lieux-dits* (unofficial in the sense that they are not legally recognised as parts of the Clos as are, for instance, the sub-divisions of Corton), Le Grand Maupertuis and Le Musigni (*sic*). Halfway down the slope, the soil becomes marl, that is a mixture of limestone and clay, but limestone of a different origin - Bajocian; however, there are still pebbles here so the land drains well. Further down the slope still the soil is less good; it becomes more alluvial and drains less well.

Understandably, Clos-de-Vougeot wines from this lower part of the vineyard are criticised. The critics argue that this land is not worthy of its *grand cru* status, pointing out that over the wall to the south the vineyards are only entitled to the plain Vosne-Romanée appellation. If the Clos had not been one large vineyard, contained within its retaining walls, it would never have been decreed *grand cru* in its entirety.

Tradition has it that the original ecclesiastical proprietors produced three wines: from the top or best land came the *Cuvée des Papes*; from the middle the *Cuvée des Rois*; and from the lower slopes the *Cuvée des Moines*, and only this one was sold commercially. Some people suggest the division was, in fact, vertical, as you face up the slope, not horizontal. Is the wine from the lower, flatter, slope inferior? In practice as well as in principle, yes: but it nevertheless remains more important to choose your grower rather than the geography within the vineyard. Jean and Etienne Grivot own a large area of Clos-de-Vougeot, by which I mean almost 2 hectares; but on the lower levels of the *climat*. Yet with old vines - at least half date from 1920 - and with meticulous vinification, this is by no means one of the lesser Clos-de-Vougeot wines. In fact, I would certainly place it in the top ten. Jean Grivot explains that in dry vintages the upper slopes can become a little parched though he fairly admits that the lower land can get somewhat humid if the weather turns wet.

At its best, Clos-de-Vougeot can rank among the greatest Burgundies, alongside Chambertin and the best of Vosne-Romanée. But it rarely does so. Normally I would consider it in the second division of *grands crus*, comparable with those of Morey and Corton, or indeed its neighbours Echézeaux and Grands-Echézeaux. In style, the wine is plumper, lusher and spicier than Chambertin or La Tâche; less firm, less intensely flavoured and with less definition. It also does not possess the cumulative complexity and fragrance of Musigny. Yet when rich, fullish and generous, with a fruit which is half redolent of soft red, summer berries and half that of blackberries and chocolate, plus undertones of liquorice, burnt nuts and even coffee (a promising sign in a young Burgundy), the wine can be immensely enjoyable. Sadly, because of the vineyard's size and renown and the multiplicity of owners, it is one of the most abused names in the area.

THE *PREMIERS CRUS*

LE CLOS-BLANC (3.05 HA)

This *climat*, producing white wine as the name suggests, is the monopoly of L'Héritier-Guyot, suppliers of *cassis* and other liqueurs (see below).

CLOS-DE-LA-PERRIÈRE (2.16 HA)

Part of Les Petits-Vougeots and a monopoly of Bertagna (see below).

LES PETITS-VOUGEOTS (3.49 HA) • LES CRAS (2.99 HA)

Les Petits-Vougeots lies up-slope, under Musigny, though several metres lower, while Les Cras lies the other side of Le Clos-Blanc, about two-thirds of the way down the slope towards the road.

At the Bertagna domaine, which is the only cellar I know where one can compare different *premiers crus* Vougeots of the same colour, I found the Cras a little fuller but also a bit coarser than the Petits-Vougeots, while their Clos-de-la-Perrière, which has more new oak, has the most richness and definition of all. But that is a very small statistical sample. Alain Hudelot-Noëllat, the Domaine Clerget, Jean Mongeard-Mugneret, as well as L'Héritier-Guyot, are the only other sources for Vougeot in bottle that I know of.

Recommended Source: Bertagna.

THE GROWERS

BERTAGNA

14 ha: owned. Chambertin (20 a); Clos-Saint-Denis (30 a); Clos-de-Vougeot (50 a); Corton (25 a); Corton-Charlemagne (27 a); Vougeot *premier cru* in Clos-de-la-Perrière (*monopole*), Les Cras, Les Petits-Vougeots; Nuits-Saint-Georges *premier cru* Les Murgers; Vosne-Romanée *premier cru* Les Beaux-Monts; Chambolle-Musigny *premier cru* Les Plantes; village Vougeot (Clos Bertagna); village Chambolle-Musigny.

The Domaine Bertagna was acquired by the Reh family of Germany (owners of the excellent Trier-based Reichsgraf von Kesselslatt estate) in 1982. But it was not until 1988 that the wine was anything other than uninspiring. Since then there has been a distinct improvement. Between 10 and 30 per cent of the stems are retained. There is automatic temperature control of the fermentation, keeping the maximum below 32°C, and an overall three-year cycle of new oak. These are well-coloured, plump, fleshy wines. The Vougeot *blanc* vines date from 1985. Having recently ventured into Corton, the domaine is still seeking to expand.

CHRISTIAN CLERGET

5.35 ha: owned and *en fermage*. Echézeaux (1.10 ha); Chambolle-Musigny *premier cru* Les Charmes; Vougeot *premier cru*; village Vosne-Romanée; village Chambolle-Musigny; village Morey-Saint-Denis.

Christian Clerget is now in charge here, his father Georges and uncle Michel being *en retraite*. But the wine is still marketed under all three labels.

The wine-making takes place in a jumble of houses and *caves* in the village of Vougeot, and produces something sturdy, but which can be artisanal. There is a wide disparity between the village wines, kept in old oak (*too* old), and the Echézeaux and Chambolle-Musigny, Les Charmes, stored in new oak. But even here, the wines miss the nuance of the best.

L'HÉRITIER-GUYOT

11.53 ha: owned. Clos-de-Vougeot (1.05 ha); Vougeot *premier cru* (*blanc*) Le Clos-Blanc; Vougeot *premier cru* (*rouge*) Les Cras; Chambolle-Musigny *premier cru* Les Baudes.

Some 75 per cent of L'Héritier-Guyot's turnover comes from liqueurs such as *Crème de Cassis*, and 60 per cent of the rest is *négociant* wine. It was in 1982 that Marie-José Mermod took over the wine side but only since 1990 or so that proper quality became the prime objective. 'We have changed everything since then,' you are told. The wines *have* improved, but there is still a way to go.

*★ALAIN HUDELOT-NOËLLAT

10 ha: owned and *en fermage*. Richebourg (28 a); Romanée-Saint-Vivant (48 a); Clos-de-Vougeot (1.05 ha); Vosne-Romanée *premier cru* in Les Suchots, Les Beaumonts, Les Malconsorts; Nuits-Saint-Georges *premier cru* Les Murgers; Chambolle-Musigny *premier cru* Les Charmes; village Vosne-Romanée; village Chambolle-Musigny; village Vougeot (Les Petits-Vougeots).

Despite occasional inconsistency in the past – but since 1989 things have been more regular here – this is definitely one of the top domaines in Burgundy, for when Alain Hudelot's top wines are singing they are truly magnificent. The vines are old and the cellar tidy and efficient. Hudelot retains about 10 per cent of the stems, believes in a long maceration at up to 32°C, and gives his *grands crus* 100 per cent new oak. He neither fines nor filters.

These are wines of great flair and concentration: full, opulent and multi-dimensional. The only weak point is the Vougeot. But that is the soil, not the wine-making of Alain Hudelot.

See Profile, page 480.

PIERRE LABET

5 ha: owned. Beaune *premier cru* in Les Couchérias; village Beaune (Clos-des-Monsnières) *rouge et blanc*; Savigny-lès-Beaune *premier cru blanc* in Les Vergelesses.

The wines of François Labet's father Pierre are also made at the Château de la Tour. The Chardonnay vines are young, but both the red and white wines are plump, balanced and attractive.

CHÂTEAU DE LA TOUR

5.48 ha: owned. Clos-de-Vougeot (5.48 ha).

The château, a nineteenth-century folly which makes a curious contrast with the medieval bastion further up the slope, is the second building within the Clos of Vougeot, and is the headquarters of the largest owner of the *grand cru*. The joint proprietors are the sisters Jacqueline Labet and Nicole Déchelette, and it is François, Jacqueline's son, who is responsible for the wine.

Since 1987 vinification methods have been inspired by the oenologist Guy Accad, and one's reaction to the wine will therefore be somewhat conditioned by one's attitude to Accad wines in general. I find this Clos-de-Vougeot usually very good – the economies of scale give Labet the opportunity to vinify several *cuvées* of vines of different ages, and to make a *vieilles vignes* bottling – but not outstanding.

See Profile, page 646.

VOSNE-ROMANÉE AND FLAGEY-ECHÉZEAUX

Vosne-Romanée is the greatest Pinot Noir village on earth. It is the last of the *hors concours* communes of the Côte-de-Nuits - in the sense that it contains *grand cru climats* - as one travels south towards Nuits-Saint-Georges. It possesses six of the twenty-four great-growth vineyards of this part of the Côte. There are a further two in Flagey-Echézeaux.

This may not be as many as Gevrey-Chambertin which has eight; nor may their combined harvest be as much as that of Corton. But in the eyes of wine connoisseurs - or in their hearts and minds - the wines of Vosne are wines to conjure with: La Romanée-Conti, incomparably the most expensive Burgundy money can buy; La Tâche, often its peer, occasionally its superior; sumptuous Richebourg; silky-smooth Romanée-Saint-Vivant; not to mention a host of delicious *premiers crus*, some, like Cros-Parentoux after Henri Jayer has breathed magic life into it, which are every bit as good as a *grand cru*, and a first division *grand cru* at that.

But not only are there fine *climats* and great *terroirs* in Vosne-Romanée, today's village contains a very large number of estates, from the large and majestic to the discreet and modest, which produce excellent wine. Some are long established. Others have only begun to bottle seriously in the last decade or so. But today, given a successful vintage, the consumer can hardly go wrong.

The Vosne-Romanée style is for wines which are rich, austere, sensual, masculine and aristocratic. The Abbé Courtépée, writing before the French Revolution, said of Vosne-Romanée: '*Il n'y a pas de vins communs*' (There are no common wines in the village). The same could be said today.

FLAGEY-ECHÉZEAUX AND VOSNE-ROMANÉE

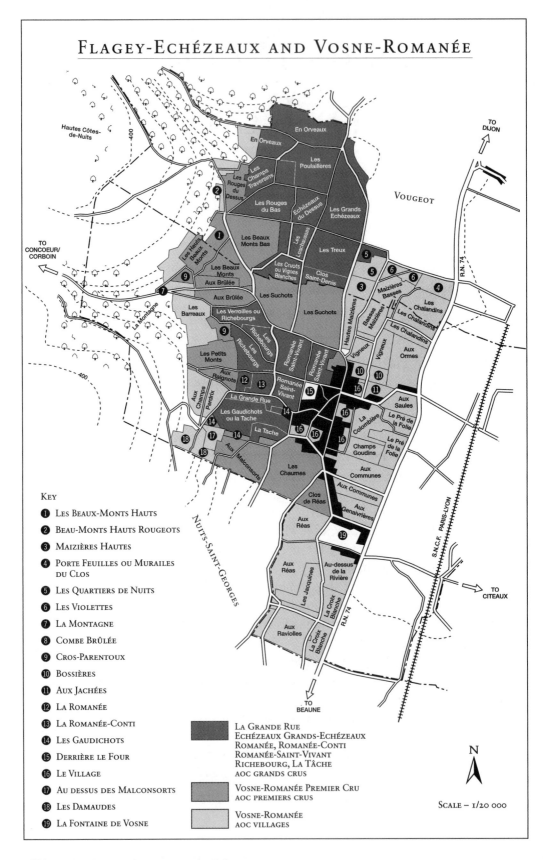

KEY

1. LES BEAUX-MONTS HAUTS
2. BEAU-MONTS HAUTS ROUGEOTS
3. MAIZIÈRES HAUTES
4. PORTE FEUILLES OU MURAILES DU CLOS
5. LES QUARTIERS DE NUITS
6. LES VIOLETTES
7. LA MONTAGNE
8. COMBE BRÛLÉE
9. CROS-PARENTOUX
10. BOSSIÈRES
11. AUX JACHÉES
12. LA ROMANÉE
13. LA ROMANÉE-CONTI
14. LES GAUDICHOTS
15. DERRIÈRE LE FOUR
16. LE VILLAGE
17. AU DESSUS DES MALCONSORTS
18. LES DAMAUDES
19. LA FONTAINE DE VOSNE

LA GRANDE RUE
ECHÉZEAUX GRANDS-ECHÉZEAUX
ROMANÉE, ROMANÉE-CONTI
ROMANÉE-SAINT-VIVANT
RICHEBOURG, LA TÂCHE
AOC GRANDS CRUS

VOSNE-ROMANÉE PREMIER CRU
AOC PREMIERS CRUS

VOSNE-ROMANÉE
AOC VILLAGES

N

SCALE – 1/20 000

HISTORY

Vosne-Romanée is mentioned in documents as early as the sixth century, successively as Vaona, Vadona, Vanona and Voone: the word means forest. In AD 890 the priory of Saint-Vivant was founded there by Manasses the First, and this soon attracted gifts of vineyards, notably from Alix de Vergy in 1232. Most of the best vineyards originally belonged either to this establishment, a Clunaic order, or to the Cistercian abbey in nearby Citeaux.

By the time of the mid eighteenth century much of the land had been secularised. The Croonembourgs had sold Romanée to the Prince de Conti. La Tâche and a section of Romanée-Saint-Vivant were in private hands. Much of Richebourg, though, still belonged to the church.

The Revolution changed everything. Almost immediately the church landholdings were sequestered. Rather later the vineyards belonging to the lords of the *ancien régime* were to follow suit. The aristocratically owned Romanée-Conti and La Tâche were sold off as *biens nationaux* on the same day (21 April 1794), while the ecclesiastical holdings of Richebourg had been auctioned off three years earlier, together with the Clos-de-Vougeot, on 17 January 1791. As with the rest of Burgundy, the next century saw most of the *climats* becoming increasingly sub-divided. Only the very greatest, as much by luck as anything else, were able to preserve their unity.

Dr Lavalle in 1855 divided the vineyards of Vosne-Romanée and Flagey into five levels of quality. Romanée-Conti, Richebourg, La Tâche and La Romanée, along with Grands-Echézeaux, were decreed *têtes de cuvées*, Romanée-Saint-Vivant and La Grande-Rue as *premières cuvées* along with Malconsorts, Beaux-Monts, Brûlées and Suchots.

In advance of the disciplines of *Appellation Contrôlée* in the mid-1930s, both Richebourg and La Tâche were enlarged, the former incorporated Les Varoilles (or Véroilles), the latter part of Les Gaudichots, the proprietors having been able to prove that the wines were of equal standing, and a 'local, loyal and constant' precedent had been set. Similarly the southern section of Romanée-Saint-Vivant was absorbed. More recently, La Grande-Rue has been upgraded to *grand cru*.

LOCATION

The two communes of Vosne-Romanée and Flagey-Echézeaux lie adjacent to each other between that of Vougeot, to the north, and Nuits-Saint-Georges, to the south. While the village of Flagey, anomalously for Burgundy, lies down beyond the railway line, definitely on the wrong side of the tracks, the sleepy village of Vosne lies in the middle of its vineyards, on the line where *premier cru* gives way to village wine, set well away from the main road. Vosne-Romanée is not a village of much architectural interest. It is small and tranquil. At one end is a square and the village church, at the other a more imposing *mairie*. Between the two is the Château de Vosne-Romanée, property of the Liger-Belair family. This dates in part from the mid seventeenth century, mainly from the end of the eighteenth. The second storey was constructed in the 1850s. The village suffered badly both at the hands of Austrian troops in Napoleonic times and German soldiers in 1870. Little remains of the original medieval village. Chambolle, with its steep streets and narrow *culs de sac* has more charm. Morey, with its wide main street off which there are many substantial medieval and late Renaissance courtyards, is more imposing.

THE VINEYARD

It is convenient to take these two *communes* together. Flagey possesses solely its two *grands crus*: Grands-Echézeaux and Echézeaux. All its other wines are labelled as Vosne-Romanée.

Grands Crus: There are eight *grands crus*: Echézeaux, Grands-Echézeaux, La Grande-Rue, La Romanée-Saint-Vivant, Richebourg, La Tâche, La Romanée and La Romanée-Conti.

These comprise 75 ha and produce an average of 2,240 hl (300,000 bottles) per annum. Of this, one *climat*, Echézeaux, provides over half. Four of these *grands crus* are the monopoly of a single owner.

Premiers Crus: There are eleven in Vosne-Romanée. From south to north they are: Aux Malconsorts, Les Chaumes, Clos-de-Réas, Les Gaudichots, Aux Reignots, Cros-Parentoux, Les Petits-Monts, Aux Brûlées, Les Beaux-Monts, Les Suchots and La Croix-Rameau. There are a further two in Echézeaux, sold as Vosne-Romanée: Les Rouges and En Orveaux.

These total 58 ha and produce an average of 2,400 hl (316,800 bottles) per annum.

Village Wine: There are a total of 105 ha of village vineyard. The average production is 4,700 hl (500,000 bottles).

The appellation Vosne-Romanée covers red wine only.

THE GRANDS CRUS
ROMANÉE-CONTI

Surface Area: 1.81 ha • **Average Production:** 45hl (5,940 bottles)

Monopoly of the Domaine de la Romanée-Conti, Vosne-Romanée

This most celebrated *grand cru* in Burgundy is surrounded by La Grande-Rue to the south, Richebourg to the north, and Romanée-Saint-Vivant to the east. On these three sides it is bounded by a small stone wall. Merely a path separates Romanée-Conti from La Romanée, its neighbour further up the slope.

Roughly square in shape – a mere 150 metres by 150 – and lying precisely in mid-slope at an altitude of between 260 and 275 metres – the incline of about 6 degrees ensures a perfect drainage without any grave danger of erosion, and the aspect marvellous exposure from early morning until dusk.

The soil is *limono-argileux*, a fine sandy-clay mixture, in this case feeble in the sand content, brown in colour and mixed with pebbles and limestone scree. For most of the *climat* this is based on a subsoil of Prémeaux limestone of the lower Bathonian period. At the foot the subsoil is a marl formed by the deposits of small fossilised oysters (*marnes à ostrea acuminate*). There is a depth of barely 50 cm of surface soil before one encounters the bare rock. Since 1985, along with the other DRC vineyards, the land has been cultivated biologically.

(For a history of this *climat* and a description of the wine see Domaine de la Romanée-Conti, page 000.)

LA ROMANÉE

Surface Area: 0.85 ha • **Average Production:** 31 hl (4,092 bottles)

Monopoly of the Château de Vosne-Romanée, M. Le Comte Liger-Belair

The *climat* is managed by Régis Forey, Vosne-Romanée, who makes the wine. The *élevage*, bottling and marketing of the wine is by Maison Bouchard Père et Fils, Beaune.

The tiny La Romanée, the smallest *Appellation Contrôlée* in France, lies directly up-slope from Romanée-Conti, and is separated from it by a path. The altitude ranges from 275 to 300 metres, and the incline is a little steeper at from 9 degrees upwards. Further up-slope is the *premier cru* Aux Reignots.

The soil structure, however, is similar: again *limono-argileux,* feeble in the sand fraction, mixed with pebbles, based on a friable Prémeaux limestone. The depth of surface soil, however, is much less.

Opinions are divided as to whether this was ever part of the Romanée now known as Romanée-Conti. The consensus seems to agree that it was not, the *climat* being grouped together from parcels called Aux Echanges and Au-Dessus-de-la-Romanée, some of which belonged to the Domaine Lamy de Samerey before the Revolution, by the Liger-Belair family in the first thirty years of the nineteenth century. The Liger-Belairs have owned it ever since.

How does it differ from Romanée-Conti itself? Or indeed from Richebourg, its neighbour to the north, the closest vines of which belong to the DRC? At its best it is equally perfumed, but it doesn't have quite the aristocratic intensity of Romanée-Conti or the sumptuousness of Richebourg. It is an austere wine in its youth, and there is an element of reserve even when it is fully mature. But it is unmistakably of *grand cru* lineage.

LA TÂCHE
Surface Area: 6.06 ha • **Average Production:** 151 hl (20,000 bottles)

Monopoly of the Domaine de la Romanée-Conti, Vosne-Romanée
La Tâche is made up of two *lieux-dits*: La Tâche and La Tâche-Gaudichots. It lies to the south of Romanée-Conti and La Romanée, and runs parallel with these two *climats*, being separated from them only by the newest Côte d'Or *grand cru*, La Grande-Rue. Lying between 255 and 300 metres in altitude, steeper at the top, flatter at the bottom, but well-drained nevertheless, La Tâche encompasses a number of different soil structures: decomposed limestone of the lower Bathonian period at the top, thinly covered by pebbles and limestone debris; deeper, richer, more clayey soil at the bottom of the slope, in parts mixed with fossilised oyster deposits.

Since 1985, as with the other DRC vineyards, La Tâche has been cultivated biologically.

(For a history of this *climat* and a description of the wine, see the profile on the Domaine de la Romanée-Conti, page 596.)

RICHEBOURG
Surface Area: 8.03 ha • **Average Production:** 228 hl (30,000 bottles)

Principal Proprietors: ★Domaine de la Romanée-Conti (3.51 ha); ★Leroy (0.78 ha); Gros Frère et Soeur (0.69 ha); ★A.F. Gros (0.69 ha); ★Anne Gros (0.60 ha); Liger-Belair (0.52 ha) - *en métayage* to Denis Mugneret; ★Méo-Camuzet (0.35 ha); ★Grivot (0.32 ha); Mongeard-Mugneret (0.31 ha); ★Hudelot-Noëllat (0.28 ha).

Richebourg lies immediatly to the north of La Romanée and Romanée-Conti and up-slope from Romanée-Saint-Vivant. It is made up of two *lieux-dits*: Les Richebourgs and Les Véroilles-sous-Richebourg. While the aspect of Romanée-Conti faces due east, that of Richebourg inclines just a little towards the north at its upper end.

Lying between 280 and 260 metres of altitude, the gradient is similar to that of Romanée-Conti, as is the soil structure, a pebbly clay-sand mixture with a low sand content, mixed with limestone debris, lying on the rosy Prémeaux rock of the lower Bathonian period.

Originally owned by the monastery of Citeaux, the majority of Richebourg was sold off as a *bien national* in 1790. By 1855 the owners included M. Frantin (who owned the bulk of Les Véroilles), M. Marey (already a proprietor before the Revolution), M. Duvault-Blochet (ancestor of the Villaines of the DRC), M. Liger-Belair, M. Lausseure, and M. Marillier. As with La Tâche and Gaudichots, the proprietors of Les Véroilles were able to prove to the Court of Appeal in Dijon in the 1920s that their wine had been sold as Richebourg and at the same price for long enough to warrant this section being officially included within the *grand cru*.

Richebourg is undisputably the best of the non-monopoly *grands crus* of Vosne. It is fuller, fatter, richer, more intense and generous, but more masculine and long-lasting than Romanée-Saint-Vivant. At its best it can offer an explosion of flavours: coffee and chocolate when young, violets when mature; all within a velvet-textured cornucopia of small black and red fruits. I count some Richebourgs among the greatest Burgundies I have ever tasted. 'Sumptuous,' said Camille Rodier more than sixty years ago. How I agree!

ROMANÉE-SAINT-VIVANT
Surface Area: 9.44 ha • Average Production: 233 hl (30,800 bottles)

Principal Proprietors: *Domaine de la Romanée-Conti (5.29 ha); *Leroy (0.99 ha); *Domaine de Corton-Grancey (Louis Latour) (0.76 ha); *Jean-Jacques Confuron (0.50 ha); Christophe and France Poisot (0.49 ha) - vines looked after by Dominique Mugneret, the fruit being sold to *Maison Joseph Drouhin; *Hudelot-Noëllat (0.48 ha); *Robert Arnoux (0.35 ha); *Domaine de l'Arlot (0.25 ha); *Clos-de-Thorey (Moillard-Grivot and Thomas-Moillard) (0.17 ha); *Sylvain Cathiard (0.17 ha).

Romanée-Saint-Vivant is the closest *grand cru* to the village of Vosne-Romanée, the vines running down behind the church at the northern end of the village to the courtyard of the old abbey of Saint-Vivant, now (having been the property of the Marey-Monge family) belonging to the Domaine de la Romanée-Conti.

The incline here is gentle, the altitude between 265 and 250 metres, and the exposure to the east. The soil is heavier than it is further up the slope, and there is more of it: a brown clay-limestone mixture mixed with pebbles on a Bajocian marl base.

For 650 years the land was the property of the local abbey, a Clunaic dependency. In the sixteenth century the bottom end of the parcel known as the Clos-des-Quatre-Journaux was detached. This is the section now owned by Thomas-Moillard, Arnoux, Poisot, Arlot and Cathiard. During the Revolution the rest was acquired by Nicolas-Joseph Marey of Nuits-Saint-Georges, known as Marey the younger, for F 91,000. The Marey-Monge family (as they were to become) sold off part of their inheritance in 1898 to Louis Latour and Charles Noëllat. They retained the rest until 1966 when a lease was granted to the Domaine de la Romanée-Conti. The Neyrand family, heirs of Mlle Geneviève Marey-Monge, last of her line, sold this to the DRC after her death in September 1988, for, it is understood, about 60 million francs.

Romanée-Saint-Vivant is the lightest, the most delicate and the most feminine of the Vosne *grands crus*. For me there is a distinct resemblance to Musigny. At its best it is an exquisitely perfumed wine, silk where Richebourg is velvet, but no less intense, no less beautiful. While in the DRC line-up the Richebourg is usually the superior, elsewhere, at Leroy or Hudelot-Noëllat, this is not always the case. It is a question of personal taste.

LA GRANDE-RUE
Surface Area: 1.65 ha • Average Production: 60 hl (8,000 bottles)

Monopoly of the Domaine François Lamarche, Vosne-Romanée
By official decree of 8 July, 1992 La Grande-Rue, sandwiched between La Tâche and La Romanée/Romanée-Conti, became the thirty-first *grand cru* of the Côte d'Or.

It shares the same geology and aspect, it occupies the same position on the slope, and prior to the mid-1930s, when the rest became officially *grands crus*, it sold without difficulty at high prices as Romanée-Grande-Rue. Dr Lavalle, in 1855, considered the wine as good as Romanée-Saint-Vivant and Les Véroilles-sous-Richebourg, if not the equal of Richebourg, La Tâche or Romanée-Conti itself. Why then was La Grande-Rue not appointed *grand cru* in the first place? Apparently the Lamarche family, proprietors since 1933, were not sufficiently concerned to insist on it.

The more recent elevation, fifty-six years later, clearly demonstrates the INAO's attitude to classification in Burgundy. It is the land and not the quality of the wine which is classified. The vines no doubt *can* produce *grand cru* quality. In the 1940s and 1950s they did. But they have not done so for more than twenty years. If you compare the average production with that of Romanée-Conti next door you can see one of the explanations why not. If you visit the region in the autumn just before the harvest and walk along the road that separates the two *climats* another will be apparent: the DRC vines in immaculate condition, all excess foliage pruned back, all excess bunches of grapes eliminated; the Lamarche vines all over the place, groaning with fruit. François Lamarche's wine-making is also suspect.

It is a sad state of affairs. Let us hope for an improvement

GRANDS-ECHÉZEAUX
Surface Area: 9.14 ha • **Average Production:** 290 hl (34,000 bottles)

Principal Proprietors: ★Domaine de la Romanée-Conti (3.53 ha); Mongeard-Mugneret (1.84 ha) (some of which is leased off); Domaine Baron Thénard/Bordeaux-Montrieux (1.15 ha) (sold through ★Remoissenet Père et Fils); ★Engel (0.50 ha); ★Joseph Drouhin (0.47 ha); Henri de Villamont (0.43 ha); Gros Frère et Soeur (0.37 ha); Lamarche (0.30 ha); Georges Noëllat (0.30 ha); Domaine du Clos-Frantin (0.25 ha). In total there are twenty-one proprietors.

Grands-Echézeaux forms a roughly triangular piece which fits into and squares off the south-west corner of Clos-de-Vougeot. On the other two sides it is bounded by the much more extensive Echézeaux. Originally it belonged to the Abbey of Citeaux, but, unlike the Clos-de-Vougeot itself, seems to have led a secular existence since at least the seventeenth century, one of the pre-Revolutionary proprietors being the influential Marey family.

Relatively flat, at 260 metres, the brown soil is quite deep, a chalky limestone mixed with clay and pebbles on a Bajocian limestone base.

Generally regarded, and priced accordingly, as superior to Echézeaux, Grands-Echézeaux is a richer, more structured wine with greater intensity and definition, and a black fruit, gamey flavour: rustic in the best sense. It can be firm, even hard in its youth, less obviously generous than either Echézeaux or the more refined *grands crus* of Vosne-Romanée. It needs time. But the best are clearly as good as the best Clos-de-Vougeot. And a lot more interesting than the least good.

ECHÉZEAUX
Surface Area: 37.69 ha • **Average Production:** 1,200 hl (158,000 bottles)

Principal Proprietors: ★Domaine de la Romanée-Conti (4.67 ha); Mongeard-Mugneret (3.80 ha) (some leased off); ★Emmanuel Rouget (2.00 ha) (exploiting the land of Georges, ★Henri and Lucien Jayer); ★Mugneret-Gibourg (1.24 ha); Lamarche (1.10 ha); Domaine du Clos-Frantin (1.00 ha); ★Joseph Faiveley (0.87 ha); ★Dujac (0.69 ha); ★Grivot (0.57 ha); ★Engel (0.55 ha); ★Jayer-Gilles (0.54 ha); ★Joseph Drouhin (0.53 ha); ★Jacky Confuron-Cotétidot (0.48 ha); Thierry Vigot-Battault (0.40 ha); ★Jadot (0.35 ha); Jacques Prieur (from 1996) (0.34 ha). In total there are eighty-four proprietors.

Echézeaux is one of the largest *grands crus* in Burgundy. It lies up-slope and to the south of Grands-Echézeaux and the Clos-de-Vougeot. However, unlike the Clos, it does not run down all the way to the *Nationale*. The lower slopes are merely village wine, sold as Vosne-Romanée *tout court*. The Vosne-Romanée *premiers crus* of Beaux-Monts, Brûlées and Suchots separate Echézeaux from Richebourg and Romanée-Saint-Vivant.

Within Echézeaux there are a number of *lieux-dits*, not seen on labels, but important locally to locate a grower's vines. Above Grands-Echézeaux are Les Poulaillères, where the Domaine de la Romanée-Conti's vines are situated, and Echézeaux-du-Dessus. On the Chambolle-Musigny border lies En Orveaux. At the top of the slope are Les Champs-Traversins and Les Rouges-du-Bas. Below the *premier cru* of Les Beaux-Monts (*bas*) are Les Loachausses, and Les

Criots-en-Vignes-Blanches. Lower down, next to Les Suchots, are Clos-Saint-Denis and Les Treux. While lowest still, outside the wall of Clos-de-Vougeot, lies Les Quartiers-de-Nuits.

Naturally in such a large vineyard the *terroir* varies considerably. At its highest point the *grand cru* reaches 300 metres, at its lowest 250. Up-slope the incline is steep (up to 13 degrees) and the surface soil thin with the underlying rock often visible. The stone here is Bajocian, friable in parts, hard in others, sometimes pure, sometimes with an important clay content. Lower down the incline is flatter, the soil richer and deeper and the drainage less efficient.

Is there then, as in Clos-de-Vougeot, a difference in quality between the different sections? The answer is certainly yes, but to a lesser degree, for the very bottom of the slope is not *grand cru*. As always in Burgundy, the degree of competence of the wine-maker is paramount. Moreover, many of the land-holders possess a number of different parcels within the conglomerate *climat*.

Echézeaux is in general a second-division *grand cru*, without the concentration and finesse of the best. In many cases the customer would be better off with a top *premier cru* wine, though he may not find it any cheaper. The wine is looser-knit than Grands-Echézeaux, with the same aspect of the rustic, but suppler tannins. It can be very good indeed, but is rarely fine.

THE PREMIERS CRUS

With the recent elevation of La Grande-Rue to *grand cru*, there are now thirteen *premiers crus* in Vosne-Romanée (and Echézeaux). To the south, between the village and the Nuits-Saint-Georges boundary, lie Aux Malconsorts, Les Chaumes and Clos-de-Réas (the latter the monopoly of the Domaine Jean Gros). Above La Tâche, La Romanée and Richebourg you will find Les Gaudichots, Aux Reignots, Les Petits-Monts and Cros-Parentoux. While further north are Aux Brûlées, Les Beaux-Monts, Les Suchots and La Croix-Rameau. Part of Beaux-Monts is technically in Flagey-Echézeaux, as are En Orveaux and Les Rouges.

From south to north, then.

AUX MALCONSORTS (5.86 HA)

The *climat* lies on the Nuits-Saint-Georges border, indeed marches with Les Boudots across the boundary. Nevertheless there is little of Nuits-Saint-Georges about the wine. It is more true to say that Boudots is much more of a Vosne than a Nuits. Lying as it does next to La Tâche, and it would seem, on identical land, Malconsorts can be a bargain. The wine is less intense, and less structured than the *premiers crus* which lie on the northern side of the village. But it can have both flair, fat, finesse and a fine perfume.

Recommended Sources: Alain Hudelot-Noëllat (Vougeot); Sylvain Cathiard (Vosne-Romanée); Thomas-Moillard (Nuits-Saint-Georges). The latter have the lion's share of this *climat*. The other main proprietor is the Domaine du Clos-Frantin. Their wines do not excite me. Nor do those of Lamarche.

LES CHAUMES (6.46 HA)

Downslope from Les Malconsorts lies Les Chaumes. The slope is more gentle, the surface soil deeper and richer, and there is more clay and alluvial soil in its composition. The result is wine of a little less depth and personality, a little less style. While I rate Malconsorts in its own way the equal of Beaux-Monts, Brûlées and the other top *premiers crus* on the other side of the village, that cannot be said of Les Chaumes. Properties such as Méo-Camuzet, in their pricing structure, seem to agree.

Recommended Sources: Méo-Camuzet; Jean Tardy (both Vosne-Romanée); Daniel Rion (Nuits-Saint-Georges). Méo-Camuzet are the principal owners of this *climat*. The Domaine Arnoux is another, and their wines are improving. Lamarche also have vines in this *climat*.

CLOS-DE-RÉAS (2.12 HA)

This walled triangular vineyard is the monopoly of the Domaine Michel Gros. Though further down towards the valley than all the other *premiers crus*, few would deny that the wine fully merits the title of first growth, and is a very good one at that. The wine is not a heavyweight, but has the pure fragrance of Pinot Noir at its most elegant.

Recommended Source: Michel Gros (Vosne-Romanée).

LES GAUDICHOTS (1.03 HA)

Lamarche have got some Gaudichots - it lies above La Grande-Rue and La Tâche - and so have the Domaine de la Romanée-Conti, Thomas-Moillard and Arnaud Machard de Gramont of Prémeaux-Prissey (but these are young vines). But the only wines I have ever seen are those of Régis Forey, of Vosne-Romanée, and Thierry Vigot-Battault, who lives up in the Hautes-Côtes at Messanges. In their hands we have a sturdy beast, not without depth and richness, even concentration, but *sauvage*. It needs time.

Recommended Sources: Forey Père et Fils (Vosne-Romanée); Thierry Vigot (Messanges).

AUX REIGNOTS (1.62 HA)

The main grower here is the Château de Vosne-Romanée, whose wines are made by Régis Forey and then turned over to Bouchard Père et Fils. Sylvain Cathiard and Robert Arnoux are the other major participants. Like the Gaudichots, which it adjoins - here we are above La Romanée - the wine has a touch of the rustic. But it is full, rich and substantial nevertheless.

Recommended Sources: Sylvain Cathiard (Vosne-Romanée); Maison Bouchard Père et Fils (Beaune).

LES PETITS-MONTS (3.67 HA)

There are not many who produce this wine in bottle. Yet the *climat*, though small, is split between as many as twenty growers. One is the Domaine de la Romanée-Conti, who sell their wine off in bulk. Véronique Drouhin is another: I have had some fine recent vintages from her. Denis Mugneret is a third. The Gerbet sisters exploit 40 ares; Jean Mongeard 30. Another grower is Robert Sirugue, who also bottles his, but whose wine has not impressed me. The *climat* lies above Richebourg.

Recommended Source: Véronique Drouhin - sold under the Joseph Drouhin label - (Beaune).

CROS-PARENTOUX (1.01 HA)

This is a small *premier cru* which lies above Richebourg and alongside that bit of Richebourg known as Les Véroilles. The site is cool, the soil very shallow, containing particles of gritty sand. I only know of two owners: Méo-Camuzet and Henri Jayer, the latter, of course, being for so long the *métayer* and subsequently avuncular *éminence grise* for the former. Under both labels (and you will now see the name of Emmanuel Rouget as well - see below) this is a wine of *grand cru* standard, and first-division *grand cru* at that: full, powerful, rich, oaky and splendidly concentrated. An essence of a wine: brutal when young, velvety, mellow and exotic when mature.

Recommended Sources: Méo-Camuzet; Emmanuel Rouget (who now exploits the Henri Jayer vines) (both Vosne-Romanée).

AUX BRÛLÉES (4.53 HA)

Divided by the road which goes up to Concoeur, Aux Brûlées marches with Les Beaumonts on one side, facing south-east, and Richebourg on the other, inclining to the north-east. From these schizophrenic origins there is nevertheless plenty of wine of quality: one with backbone, richness and depth in a particularly masculine sort of way.

Recommended Sources: Engel; Grivot; Leroy; Méo-Camuzet (all Vosne-Romanée).

LES BEAUX-MONTS (11.39 HA)

Sometimes contracted to Beaumonts this is one of the largest of the Vosne-Romanée *premiers crus*. Though it lies up-slope and adjacent to Echézeaux, and is only separated from Richebourg by the smaller Aux Brûlées, it has a distinct personality of its own, which comes in part from its exposure which inclines partly towards the south, and partly from its soil which contains marl and clay. It is a nice big wine, but perfumed, full of finesse, even lush.

Recommended Sources: Alain Hudelot-Noëllat (Vougeot); Grivot; Leroy; Rouget/Jayer (all Vosne-Romanée); Jean-Jacques Confuron; Moillard-Grivot; Daniel Rion (Nuits-Saint-Georges); Louis Jadot (Beaune).

LES SUCHOTS (13.07 HA)

This is another large *premier cru*, the largest in the commune. It lies on the same level as Romanée-Saint-Vivant, on flatter, richer, deeper soil than the Beaux-Monts. Nevertheless it is less structured than the above. At its best it can, like Romanée-Saint-Vivant, produce wine with a considerable flair and perfume, but there is usually a slightly gamey, rustic touch which betrays the fact that its northern neighbour is Echézeaux.

Recommended Sources: Alain Hudelot-Noëllat (Vougeot); Robert Arnoux; Grivot (both Vosne-Romanée); Domaine de l'Arlot (Nuits-Saint-Georges); Louis Jadot (Beaune). Other owners include Jacky Confuron-Cotétidot, the Cacheux-Blée family and Manière-Noirot. The Domaine de la Romanée-Conti owns a hectare of vines, which is farmed by Henri Roch of the Domaine Prieuré-Roch.

LA CROIX-RAMEAU (0.60 HA)

This small *climat* is an enclave within Romanée-Saint-Vivant which the four joint owners have tried - unsuccessfully so far - to get incorporated into the *grand cru*. Lamarche are one of these. But the only wine I have ever seen was that of Jacques Cacheux. These vines were planted in 1986. I was not impressed.

EN ORVEAUX (1.79 HA)

Sylvain Cathiard has a plot in this small *climat* up-slope from Echézeaux on the Chambolle side. One can see the proximity: elegance, medium body, intensity.

Recommended Source: Sylvain Cathiard (Vosne-Romanée).

LES ROUGES (2.62 HA)

We are almost up in the hills here, at 320 metres and above the central part of Echézeaux. One of the few proprietors whose wines I know is the Grivot family - this parcel coming from their aunt Jacqueline Jayer. It is a more pedestrian wine than their better *premiers crus*: less succulent, a little four-square.

THE GROWERS
*ROBERT ARNOUX

12 ha: owned and *en fermage/métayage*. Romanée-Saint-Vivant (35 a); Echézeaux (79 a); Clos-de-Vougeot (43 a) (top); Vosne-Romanée *premier cru* in Les Suchots, Les Chaumes; Nuits-Saint-Georges *premier cru* in Les Corvées-Pagets, Les Procès; village Vosne-Romanée including the *lieu-dit* Les Maizières; village Nuits-Saint-Georges including the *lieu-dit* Les Poisets.

Robert Arnoux, who died in 1995 aged sixty-four, was a large and somewhat intimidating man on first acquaintance. He had doubled his exploitation since he took over from his father in the 1950s, and this has necessitated frequent extensions to the cellar underneath his house, set back from the main Nuits-Dijon highway. He has been succeeded by his son-in-law, Pascal Lachaux (born in 1962).

I have had fine quality from this domaine in the past, particularly from its Romanée-Saint-Vivant and its Suchots, old vines at the top of the vineyard. The wines are rich, sturdy and tannic, mixed with a good dollop of new oak (50 per cent for the *grands crus*), perhaps a little on the robust side, and need time to mature. Good but not great would be an apt summary of the wines of the 1980s, but since then there has been a distinct improvement. The 1993s are definitely fine.

In 1994 the vines in the Chaumes were young.

PATRICE CACHEUX-SIRUGUE
(formerly, Jacques Cacheux-Blée)

5 ha: owned and *en fermage*. Echézeaux (66 a); Vosne-Romanée *premier cru* in Les Suchots, La Croix-Rameau; village Vosne-Romanée; village Nuits-Saint-Georges.

In 1994 there was a change of generation and a change of name. Jacques Cacheux (medium height, shy, gentle, greying, bespectacled), who had arrived in the village from Cambrai and married the local Lucette Blée in the 1950s, so becoming a *vigneron*, took his retirement. His much taller and darker son Patrice (born in 1958) is now in charge. Patrice's wife is Patricia, née Sirugue.

Patrice has already changed the vinification techniques employed by his father. The grapes are now totally destemmed, macerated for a shorter period - a week or so - and bottled without fining or filtering. The object is supple wines for drinking in the medium term. Jacques wines were fuller and more tannic. The 1990s were full and sturdy if not *that* elegant. The 1992s - even given the vintage - I found disappointing. The vines in La Croix-Rameau were six years old in 1992.

*SYLVAIN CATHIARD

5.5 ha: owned and *en fermage/métayage*. Romanée-Saint-Vivant (17 a); Clos-de-Vougeot (20 a); Vosne-Romanée *premier cru* in Les Suchots, Les Reignots, Les Malconsorts, En Orveaux; Nuits-Saint-Georges *premier cru* Les Murgers; village Vosne-Romanée; village Chambolle-Musigny; village Nuits-Saint-Georges.

Sylvain Cathiard, a quiet, serious man with a slight stutter, in his early forties, now exploits almost the entirety of the land formerly controlled by his father André. He is also a *métayer* for the Moillard holdings in Les Malconsorts, Nuits-Saint-Georges Clos-de-Thorey and in Romanée-Saint-Vivant. But all the fruit here is rendered to Moillard for vinification.

The grapes are entirely destemmed, macerated for a fortnight at temperatures of up to 33°C, and the *premiers crus* are given 30–40 per cent new wood. These are wines of concentration and elegance. They will keep. A good source, especially for that *rara avis*, the En Orveaux.

*BRUNO CLAVELIER

6 ha: owned and *en fermage/métayage*. Vosne-Romanée *premier cru* in Les Beaux-Monts, Les Brûlées; Nuits-Saint-Georges *premier cru* Aux Cras; Chambolle-Musigny *premier cru* La Combe-d'Orveau; Gevrey-Chambertin *premier cru* Les Corbeaux; village Vosne-Romanée including the *lieux-dits* La Montagne (*monopole*) and Les Hautes-Maizières.

Bruno Clavelier (born in 1964), a qualified *oenologue*, took over the vines of his parents and maternal grandparents (Brosson) in 1987 and has since enlarged this domaine by extending it into Nuits-Saint-Georges and Gevrey-Chambertin, and augmented the percentage of the wine sold in bottle.

The average age of the vines is old here. The fruit is 90 per cent destemmed, the wine vinified classically at 28-30°C and matured using a maximum of 30 per cent new oak. The wines are not filtered. Full, rich and perfumed, this is quality produce from a rising star.

★JACKY CONFURON-COTÉTIDOT

11 ha: owned and *en fermage/métayage*. Charmes-Chambertin (39.30 a); Mazis-Chambertin (9.50 a); Clos-de-Vougeot (25.39 a); Echézeaux (47.52 a); Gevrey-Chambertin *premier cru* in Craipillot, Lavaux-Saint-Jacques; Vosne-Romanée *premier cru* Les Suchots; Nuits-Saint-Georges *premier cru* in Les Murgers, Vignes-Rondes; village Vosne-Romanée; village Chambolle-Musigny; village Nuits-Saint-Georges; village Gevrey-Chambertin.

The irrepressible and engaging Jacky Confuron, born in 1936, and married to Bernadette (she didn't bring any vines with her as dowry, but nevertheless Jacky has added her maiden name in order to avoid confusion with other Confurons) claims that he is not so much a disciple of the so-called Accad method of cold pre-fermentation maceration as Accad's mentor. He was cold macerating long before Accad came on the scene!

Confuron has attracted a lot of attention, particularly when his 1986s were refused the 'label', being considered atypical (his father's were accepted: the samples were identical). He thrives on this, and likes to play the eccentric. Underneath there is a slight chip on his shoulder, but a serious passion for old vines, low yields, long *cuvaisons* and no filtration.

Late in 1994 the Confuron family took over an estate in Gevrey-Chambertin.

★★PHILIPPE ENGEL, DOMAINE RENÉ ENGEL

7 ha: owned. Clos-de-Vougeot (1.37 ha); Grands-Echézeaux (50 a); Echézeaux (55 a); Vosne-Romanée *premier cru* Les Brûlées; village Vosne-Romanée.

In the decade and a half since he took over after his father's early death in 1981, Philippe Engel (born in 1955) has transformed this domaine from the very good, selling much of its produce in bulk, to the very serious indeed, now bottling everything.

The fruit is completely destemmed and given a couple of days to macerate before the fermentation starts. Maceration lasts up to three weeks, and maturation employs 30–50 per cent new oak. The result is wine of great intensity, splendid style and individuality, and real power to last. A fine source. His 1992s, harvested at 32 hl/ha in an otherwise abundant vintage, were with those of Leroy the best range I sampled in a three-week visit in November 1993.

See Profile, page 425.

★RÉGIS FOREY, DOMAINE FOREY PÈRE ET FILS

4.5 ha: owned and *en métayage*. Echézeaux (38 a); Vosne-Romanée *premier cru* Les Gaudichots; Nuits-Saint-Georges *premier cru* in Les Saint-Georges, Les Perrières; village Vosne-Romanée; village Nuits-Saint-Georges.

Forey is also responsible for the vines and wine-making for the Château de Vosne-Romanée in La Romanée and Les Gaudichots. The *élevage* and bottling of these wines is by Bouchard Père et Fils.

The tall, dark Régis Forey (born in 1960) is married to Chantal Jacob of the Jacob domaine in Echevronne. But the two exploitations are kept separate. Forey makes his wine in the old cellar of the Château de Vosne-Romanée. There is partial destemming here, some pre-fermentation maceration, and long *cuvaisons*, resulting in full, rich concentrated wines which keep well. I find the Gaudichots better than the Echézeaux, as well as being more individual. The vines touch those of La Tâche. A good source.

DOMAINE DU CLOS-FRANTIN

5.8 ha: owned. Richebourg (8 a); Grands-Echézeaux (25 a); Echézeaux (1 ha); Clos-de-Vougeot (63 a); Chambertin (17 a); Corton-Charlemagne (1.10 ha); Aloxe-Corton; Vosne-Romanée *premier cru* Les Malconsorts.

The Domaine du Clos-Frantin was acquired by Maison Albert Bichot of Beaune in 1964. *Inter alia* this company also owns Lupe-Cholet in Nuits-Saint-Georges and the Long-Depaquit and Moutonne domaines in Chablis. The fruit is destemmed and vinified for fifteen days. There is 100 per cent new oak for the *grands crus*.

I have never been enthused by the wines of Bichot, but, fortified by flattering remarks emanating from the other side of the Atlantic, I called in November of 1992 to sample the 1991s. This confirmed my long-held view: third-division stuff.

DOMAINE FRANÇOIS GERBET

15.7 ha: owned. Clos-de-Vougeot (31 a); Echézeaux (19 a); Vosne-Romanée *premier cru* Les Petits-Monts; village Vosne-Romanée including the *lieu-dit* Aux Réas. Two-thirds of the exploitation is in the Hautes-Côtes-de-Nuits at Concoeur.

The Gerbet sisters - Marie-Andrée, tall and blonde, Chantal, petite and brunette - are additionally Mesdames Vincent Berthaut (*viticulteur* in Fixin) and Denis Berin (airline pilot). There is a third sister who lives in Paris. François, their father, who arrived and fell in love with a local girl during the war, retired in 1983.

The recipe here is for destalking in most vintages, a *cuvaison* of about a fortnight, and 75 per cent new wood for the top three wines and the separately bottled village Aux Réas. The vines are old in this domaine. The wines have good style and keep well. But sometimes I find them over-oaked.

★★ÉTIENNE GRIVOT, DOMAINE JEAN GRIVOT

14.5 ha: owned (the domaine is *fermier* for the Grivot family vineyard). Richebourg (31 a); Clos-de-Vougeot (1.86 ha); Echézeaux (61 a); Vosne-Romanée *premier cru* in Les Beaux-Monts, Les Brûlées; Les Chaumes, Les Suchots and Les Rouges; Nuits-Saint-Georges *premier cru* in Les Boudots, Les Pruliers, Les Roncières; village Vosne-Romanée including the *lieu-dit* Les Bossières; village Nuits-Saint-Georges including the *lieux-dits* Les Lavières and Les Charmois; village Chambolle-Musigny in the *lieu-dit* La Combe-d'Orveau.

The lean, somewhat serious Etienne Grivot (born in 1959) and his ascetic bearded father Jean have been producing excellent wine at this domaine for many years, and a change in vinification methods in 1987, when Etienne adopted the cold, pre-fermentation maceration technique, has not affected the quality. Up to 1988 some of the wines (Echézeaux, Vosne-Romanée *premier cru* Les Rouges) were labelled Jacqueline Jayer: Mlle Jayer being Madame Jean Grivot's aunt.

Almost entirely destemmed, the must is cold macerated for a few days, the length depending on the vintage, vinified at 28–32°C, and kept in a maximum of one-quarter new wood (10 per cent for lesser wines) until the first racking. These elegant, perfumed, distinctive wines are proof, if such were still required, of the efficacy of the so-called Accad method. A fine source.

See Profile, page 461.

★ANNE (ET FRANÇOIS) GROS

5 ha: owned and *en fermage*. Richebourg (60 a); Clos-de-Vougeot (93 a); village Vosne-Romanée; village Chambolle-Musigny.

The petite, charming and attractive Anne Gros (born in 1966) has been in charge here since

1988, this estate having been detached from the old Louis Gros domaine in 1963. Prior to her arrival it disposed of half of its wine in bulk. Anne is now selling everything in bottle and from 1985 the label bears solely her name.

Some 20 per cent of the stems are retained; the fermentation temperatures allowed to climb up to 32°C; and 90 per cent new wood is used for the *grands crus*. There has been a considerable improvement in a short space of time, and we can now see a sure touch here, producing fragrant wines whose characteristic is intensity and finesse rather than power. A good source.

See Profile, page 473.

GROS FRÈRE ET SOEUR

18.4 ha: owned and *en fermage*. Richebourg (69 a); Grands-Echézeaux (34 a); Clos-de-Vougeot (1.56 ha); village Vosne-Romanée. There is a large exploitation at Concoeur in the Hautes-Côtes-de-Nuits.

Bernard Gros, stocky, dark, moustached (born in 1958) is the younger brother of Michel Gros (see Jean Gros) and started work at the domaine of his uncle Gustave and aunt Colette in 1980, taking over on Gustave's death in 1984.

Apart from an insistence on cultured yeasts, the wine-making techniques do not differ very much from that of his brother. The higher toast in the oak, though, makes its presence felt in the wines. They seem chunkier, and as well, like the man itself, they are more exuberant. But perhaps they have less finesse. Currently the vines are young in this domaine, major replantation having taken place since 1984.

See Profile, page 473.

*JEAN ET MICHEL GROS

Jean Gros: 7.9 ha: owned and *en fermage*. Richebourg (22 a); Clos-de-Vougeot (21 a); Vosne-Romanée *premier cru* Clos-de-Réas (2.12 ha) (*monopole*); village Vosne-Romanée; village Nuits-Saint-Georges; village Chambolle-Musigny.

Michel Gros: 9.9 ha: owned and *en fermage*. Richebourg (18 a); village Vosne-Romanée including the *lieu-dit* Clos-de-la-Fontaine; village Chambolle-Musigny.

Both domaines include significant holdings in the Hautes-Côtes-de-Nuits. The above figures are prior to the 1996 vintage.

This is yet another part of the old Louis Gros domaine, first split in 1963, and now further divided between father Jean and son Michel (born in 1956), tall, a little shy, and his pretty, dark-haired sister Anne-Françoise (married to François Parent of Pommard).

Effectively, however, Jean et Michel Gros is one domaine, the differentiation occurring at the time of labelling. A small percentage of the stems are retained; the *cuvaison* prolonged to ten to fourteen days at a maximum of 33°C; and the *grands crus*, and sometimes the Clos-de-Réas, matured in 100 per cent new wood.

I have had great Gros wines in the past. They are very pure, very intense and have a breed which I find wholly admirable. Just recently, however (since the 1991 vintage) I have noticed a slight lack of real concentration, as if the wines had been over-cropped.

Currently the Clos-de-Vougeot is young vines, planted in 1986.

From the 1996 vintage, further inheritance changes have taken place. The label Jean Gros has ceased. All the Richebourg will now pass into the hands of A.F. Gros in Pommard (in order to avoid splitting the Clos-de-Réas) and other minor alterations have been made.

See Profile, page 473.

ALFRED HAEGELEN-JAYER

4.2 ha: owned and *en fermage*. Clos-de-Vougeot (80 a); Echézeaux (26 a); Nuits-Saint-Georges *premier cru* Les Damodes; village Vosne-Romanée; village Chambolle-Musigny; village Nuits-Saint-Georges.

The charming, diminutive Alfred Haegelen (born in 1939) hails from Alsace, arrived in Burgundy in 1969, and married Madeleine, a niece of the great Henri Jayer.

One-third of the stems are left; the *cuvaison* lasts eighteen days; and one-third new oak is used. I like the style of Haegelen's wines. They are full without being robust, and rich and concentrated: indeed extremely succulent, nicely long-tasting Pinot Noir. A good source.

★★HENRI JAYER
GEORGES JAYER
LUCIEN JAYER
EMMANUEL ROUGET

7 ha: owned and *en fermage/métayage*. Echézeaux (1.43 ha); Vosne-Romanée *premier cru* in Les Beaumonts, Cros-Parentoux; village Vosne-Romanée; village Nuits-Saint-Georges.

It was only by accident that the genial, bullet-headed Henri Jayer (born in 1922) became a wine-maker and hence a guru. Youngest of three, he was approached during the war by M. Camuzet, mayor of Vosne: 'Would you like to look after my vines for me?' So a share-cropping lease was drawn up which was to last until the late 1980s. In the meanwhile he made the wines of his elder brothers: Georges and Lucien.

Henri has now retired, and the family vines are tended by his nephew Emmanuel Rouget, who lives in the old Gouroux premises in Flagey. A little wine, for friends and some of France's three-star restaurants, still goes out under Jayer's name. Despite the change, the wines remain the same.

Jayer's reputation, so high today, dates from the time he altered his vinification methods towards the end of the 1970s. Total destemming, a week-long maceration *à froid* before fermentation, lots of new oak, no filtration and hand bottling. And in addition, a meticulous attention to cleanliness, keeping the wine topped up regularly in cask, and so on.

The result: wines rich in colour and aroma, opulently oaky, full but not aggressively tannic, and vibrantly intense in flavour. The Cros-Parentoux is the real star, even better than the Echézeaux, of which there are three individual bottlings corresponding to the brothers' three holdings.

See Profile, page 495.

FRANÇOIS LAMARCHE

8.2 ha: owned and *en fermage*. La Grande-Rue (1.65 ha) (*monopole*); Clos-de-Vougeot (1.36 ha); Grands-Echézeaux (30 a); Echézeaux (1.10 ha); Vosne-Romanée *premier cru* in Les Suchots, Les Chaumes, Les Malconsorts; village Vosne-Romanée.

François Lamarche (born in 1944), his sister Geneviève and his wife Marie-Blanche have recently been rewarded in their efforts to persuade the authorities to elevate La Grande-Rue to *grand cru* status, a task neglected by the older generation in the 1930s.

François has modified the wine-making methods since he has been in charge. The fruit is now entirely destemmed, the percentage of new oak has been raised - to 40 per cent overall - and the wine is bottled sooner, after eighteen months. All this is as it should be. Quality, nevertheless, once very fine at this domaine, today still leaves something to be desired. I find the wines lack breed and definition. And even in 1990 some were far too weedy. The 1993s, however, suggest this domaine may have turned the corner.

***LEROY

22.4 ha: owned. Chambertin (50 a); Latricières-Chambertin (57 a); Clos-de-la-Roche (67 a); Musigny (27 a); Clos-de-Vougeot (1.91 ha); Richebourg (78 a); Romanée-Saint-Vivant (99 a); Corton-Renardes (50 a); Corton-Charlemagne (43 a); Gevrey-Chambertin *premier cru* Les Combottes; Chambolle-Musigny *premier cru* Les Charmes; Vosne-Romanée *premier cru* in Les Beaux-Monts, Les Brûlées; Nuits-Saint-Georges *premier cru* in Les Boudots, Les Vignerondes; Savigny-lès-Beaune *premier cru* Les Narbantons; Volnay *premier cru* Santenots; village Gevrey-Chambertin; village Chambolle-Musigny in the *lieu-dit* Les Fremières; village Vosne-Romanée in the *lieu-dit* Les Genevrières; village Nuits-Saint-Georges in the *lieux-dits* Les Lavières, Aux Allots, Au Bas-de-Combe; village Pommard in the *lieux-dits* Les Vignots, Les Trois Follots; Auxey-Duresses *blanc*. In addition Madame Bize-Leroy's other estate, the personally-owned Domaine d'Auvenay, has important holdings in Mazis-Chambertin, Bonnes-Mares, Chevalier-Montrachet, Criots-Bâtard-Montrachet, Puligny-Montrachet *premier cru* Les Folatières and Meursault (see page 244).

This is the greatest estate in Burgundy. It is also, at 1,000 francs per bottle for Chambertin in 1993, almost certainly the most expensive.

Lalou Bize, part owner, and until 1993 joint manager with Aubert de Villaine of the Domaine de la Romanée-Conti, bought the moribund 12 ha Domaine Charles Noëllat in Vosne-Romanée for 65 million francs in 1988. Part of the finance came from the sale of one-third of Leroy SA to her Japanese agents Takashimaya. The next year there was a further acquisition: 19 million francs for the 2.5 ha Domaine Philippe Remy in Gevrey-Chambertin. More land in Musigny and elsewhere followed the year after, altogether creating one of the most impressive ranges of wine to be seen anywhere in one cellar.

The wines are magnificently impressive too. The old vines have been jealously preserved. The yields are cut to the quick, and reduced even further by the domaine's insistence on cultivation according to bio-dynamic principles. There is no destemming, a long *cuvaison* and plenty of new oak. The results are breathtakingly intense, pure and concentrated, and curiously quite different in style from those at the Domaine de la Romanée-Conti, despite the approach being superficially similar.

See Profile, page 527.

MANIÈRE-NOIROT

9 ha: owned and *en fermage/métayage*. Echézeaux (25 a); Vosne-Romanée *premier cru* Les Suchots; Nuits-Saint-Georges *premier cru* in Les Damodes, Les Boudots; village Vosne-Romanée.

Marc and Thérèse Manière have been running this family domaine since 1972, and today make their wine by Accad methods: total destemming, and a week-long *macération à froid* before fermentation. After that the wine is matured using a goodly proportion of new oak. In recent years they have ceased selling off any of the produce in bulk. There are good things here, but my experience is limited.

**MÉO-CAMUZET

15 ha: owned and *en fermage*. Richebourg (35 a); Clos-de-Vougeot (3.03 ha) (2.20 ha exploited); Corton (45 a); Vosne-Romanée *premier cru* in Cros-Parentoux, Aux Brûlées, Les Chaumes; Nuits-Saint-Georges *premier cru* in Aux Boudots and Aux Murgers; village Vosne-Romanée; village Nuits-Saint-Georges.

This is a fine domaine, but one which only recently has been selling all its produce in bottle. The urbane, silver-haired Jean Méo, civil servant and politician, and great-nephew of Étienne Camuzet, inherited a domaine which was largely leased out *en métayage* to Henri Jayer, the Faurois family, Jean Tardy and others. Up to 1983 his own share was sold in bulk to the *négoce*.

From the 1988 vintage onward the *métayage* arrangements began to come to an end and Jean-Nicolas Méo (born in 1964), son of Jean, arrived to take charge, helped by the avuncular genius of Henri Jayer.

The wine is made in the Jayer way, not unnaturally: total destemming, several days' cold maceration, long *cuvaisons* and lots of new oak. And the results are exciting. It is only with the Clos-de-Vougeot in recent years (the 1991 and the 1992) that I have had any qualms. And this is curious, for the domaine has a huge holding, ideally placed adjacent to the château: no young vines, and all the economies of scale one would wish.

See Profile, page 000.

MONGEARD-MUGNERET

20 ha: owned and *en fermage*. Richebourg (31 a); Clos-de-Vougeot (79 a); Grands-Echézeaux (1.84 ha); Echézeaux (2.73 ha) (owns 3.50 ha); Vosne-Romanée *premier cru* in En Orveaux, Les Suchots, Les Petits-Monts; Nuits-Saint-Georges *premier cru* Les Boudots; Vougeot *premier cru* Les Cras; Savigny-lès-Beaune *premier cru* Les Narbantons; village Vosne-Romanée; village Nuits-Saint-Georges; village Fixin; village Savigny-lès-Beaune; village Puligny-Montrachet.

The bluff, rotund Jean Mongeard (born in 1929), madly busy on this committee and that, has now conceded responsibility for the wine-making to his tall, bespectacled son Vincent (born in 1956).

The grapes are now largely destemmed, allowed to cold macerate for a few days, vinified at a high temperature and matured using up to 60 per cent new oak for the *grands crus*, 40-50 per cent for the village wines. The barrels have quite a high toast. All this leads to full, sturdy well-coloured wines, with plenty of concentration. They seem to me to have become more elegant over the last decade.

Mongeard was one of the first to experiment with a new machine which removes excess water from the must by heat-induced evaporation: a technique which is destined to avoid both the need to chaptalise and to *saigner*. He has also recently swapped some of his Echézeaux on a *fermage* basis with some of Bernard Clerc's Puligny-Montrachet. A good source.

DENIS MUGNERET PÈRE ET FILS

8 ha: owned and *en fermage/métayage*. Richebourg (52 a); Clos-de-Vougeot (73 a); Vosne-Romanée *premier cru* Les Petits-Monts; Nuits-Saint-Georges *premier cru* in Les Saint-Georges, Aux Boudots; village Vosne-Romanée; village Nuits-Saint-Georges; village Gevrey-Chambertin.

Denis (born in 1936) and his son Dominique (born in 1961) farm land *en métayage* for the Liger-Belair family in Richebourg, Clos-de-Vougeot and Nuits-Saint-Georges, Les Saint-Georges.

The grapes are almost completely destemmed, given a few days' cold maceration, vinified at temperatures up to 32°C and matured in 30–75 per cent new oak. Half the produce is sold off in bulk.

The quality is inconsistent here, but is improving. The range is impressive. Let's hope the wine will be equally so!

*GÉRARD MUGNERET

8.50 ha: owned and *en fermage/métayage*. Echézeaux (65 a); Vosne-Romanée *premier cru* in Les Brûlées, Les Suchots; Nuits-Saint-Georges *premier cru* Les Chaignots, Les Boudots; Chambolle-Musigny *premier cru* Les Charmes; Savigny-lès-Beaune *premier cru* Les Gravins; village Vosne-Romanée; village Gevrey-Chambertin.

Gérard Mugneret, a vigorous, welcoming man in his forties, is one of the *métayers* of his late uncle Dr Georges Mugneret's estate (see below). The fruit is totally destemmed, given a few days' cold maceration before fermentation (up to 34°C), a long maceration, and the wine matured in an average of one-third new oak.

The results are impressive: pure, focused, rich and stylish. Sadly the wine is rarely found on the export market.

**DR GEORGES MUGNERET
MUGNERET-GIBOURG

8.9 ha: owned. Clos-de-Vougeot (34 a); Ruchottes-Chambertin (0.64 a); Echézeaux (1.25 a); Chambolle-Musigny, *premier cru* Les Feusselottes; Nuits-Saint-Georges *premier cru* Les Vignes-Rondes, Les Chaignots; village Vosne-Romanée.

The charming, hospitable and elegant Mugneret ladies, Jacqueline and her daughters Marie-Christine and Marie-Andrée, produce meticulously crafted wines from the yield of their estate, most of which is tended either *en métayage* or *à la tâche* by other *vignerons*.

The fruit is entirely destemmed, cold macerated for two or three days, and fermented using cultured yeasts at a temperature of up to 33°C. There is a healthy percentage of new oak: from 20 per cent up to 80 per cent for the top wines. These wines are fullish, concentrated, very stylish and extremely well balanced: delicious examples of pure Pinot Noir. A fine domaine.

See Profile, page 563.

PERNIN-ROSSIN

7.8 ha: owned and *en fermage/métayage*. Clos-de-la-Roche (4 a) (a quarter of a barrel!); Vosne-Romanée *premier cru* in Les Beaumonts, Les Reignots; Nuits-Saint-Georges *premier cru* in La Richemone (jointly owned with Gérard Depardieu); Morey-Saint-Denis *premier cru* in Les Monts-Luisants; Chambolle-Musigny *premier cru*; village Vosne-Romanée; village Morey-Saint-Denis.

André Pernin and Monique Rossin were among the first to associate themselves with Guy Accad (separating later as a result of what they felt was neglect on his part) but continue to make wine by his methods. In the mid-1980s I found their wines very good: surprisingly good 1986s for instance. But in the vintages of the 1990s I have been less impressed. While other followers of the cold maceration technique adapted the idea to suit their own wines, thus letting the *terroir* unmistakably sing out, the Pernin-Rossins' examples continued to taste distinctly odd: too un-Burgundian. This is nevertheless a domaine which practises careful, conscientious wine-making and believes in low yields. Good, but could do better.

ARMELLE ET BERNARD RION
(formerly Rion Père et Fils)

8 ha: owned and *en fermage/métayage*. Clos-de-Vougeot (72 a); Vosne-Romanée *premier cru* Les Chaumes; Nuits-Saint-Georges *premier cru* Les Damodes, Les Chaignots, Les Murgers; Chambolle-Musigny *premier cru* Les Lavrottes, Les Gruenchers; village Vosne-Romanée; village Nuits-Saint-Georges; village Chambolle-Musigny in the *lieu-dit* Les Echézeaux.

Bernard Rion (born in 1955) is a cousin of the Rions of Prémeaux. The grapes are entirely destemmed, fermented at a high temperature, given long *cuvaisons*, and matured using a high percentage of new oak (50 per cent for the village and *premiers crus*, the totality for the Clos-de-Vougeot).

These are quite structured wines which take time to show their full glory. But sometimes I feel they lack flair and elegance.

Bernard and his wife are additionally breeders of bearded collies and other dogs, as well as being professional truffle hunters

***ROMANÉE-CONTI

25.6 ha: owned and *en fermage*. La Romanée-Conti (1.81 ha) (*monopole*); La Tâche (6.06 ha) (*monopole*); Richebourg (3.51 ha); Romanée-Saint-Vivant (5.29 ha); Grands-Echézeaux (3.53 ha); Echézeaux (4.67 ha); Le Montrachet (68 a). Plus other land in Vosne-Romanée, the produce of which is sold off in bulk/or farmed by others.

This is the most famous name in Burgundy, and one of its largest domaines: certainly probably the largest in terms of *grand cru* ownership. Jointly owned by the De Villaine and Leroy/Bize/Roch families and today administered by the scholarly Aubert de Villaine (born in 1939) and Henri-Frédérick Roch (born in 1962), the DRC (or Domaine de la Romanée-Conti), at an unapologetically high price, produces some of the most sought-after wines in the world.

There is never any destemming here. After a careful *triage* (sorting out of the sub-standard fruit) the must is left for five or six days at a low temperature, then fermented at up to 33°C, now with mechanical *pigeage* two or three times a day, before being matured entirely in new oak.

Are the wines worth these high prices? For the sublimely individual, poised and intensely flavoured Romanée-Conti itself, and the lusher but equally magical La Tâche, the answer is indisputably yes. For the other wines, where there is competition at less greedy levels, the response is moot. You can often do better elsewhere. And then there is a question of style. The 100 per cent stems sometimes leave an unmistakable taste. This is not to the taste of the more modern school of Burgundian wine-makers who have adopted Henri Jayer as their guru. But the beauty of Burgundy is its diversity. There is plenty of room for both. And the DRC at its best produces prodigiously fine wine.

See Profile, page 596.

*EMMANUEL ROUGET

(see Henri Jayer)

ROBERT SIRUGUE

11 ha: owned and *en fermage/métayage*. Echézeaux (13 a); Vosne-Romanée *premier cru* Les Petits-Monts; village Vosne-Romanée; village Chambolle-Musigny.

Robert Sirugue (born in 1934) runs this domaine with his son Jean-Louis and daughter Marie-France out of a large airy *cave* which connects underneath two of the family houses. The fruit is destemmed, vinified for ten to twelve days at temperatures of 30-32°C, and there is from 15–50 per cent new oak utilised. Some of the harvest is sold off in bulk.

This is a domaine which used to have a high reputation. Sadly the results today do not excite me.

JEAN TARDY

5 ha: owned and *en métayage*. Clos-de-Vougeot (13a); Vosne-Romanée *premier cru* Les Chaumes; Nuits-Saint-Georges *premier cru* Les Boudots; village Nuits-Saint-Georges in the *lieu-dit* Le Bas-de-Combe; village Chambolle-Musigny in the *lieu-dit* Les Athets.

Jean Tardy and his son Olivier are the last remaining *métayers* for the Méo-Camuzet domaine in their three best *climats*. The fruit is destemmed, allowed to ferment at its own pace, at up to 32°C, and matured using a goodly percentage of new oak, up to 100 per cent for the top *climats*. They are not kept too long in cask. I like the style here: rich, balanced and pure, plump and intensely flavoured. The Nuits-Saint-Georges Les Boudots is possibly the best example of this *climat*.

See Profile, page 638.

FABRICE VIGOT

5.30 ha: owned and *en fermage/métayage*. Echézeaux (60 a); village Vosne-Romanée; village Nuits-Saint-Georges.

Fabrice Vigot is the younger brother of Thierry, who lives up in the Hautes-Côtes in Messanges. Until 1988 they worked together, but then Fabrice, who wanted to produce somewhat more supple wines, decided to go his own way.

He adopts a *biologique* approach in the vineyards, macerates at up to 32°C and uses from 20–50 per cent new oak. Good Echézeaux in 1993 and 1991, but the results with other wines and in other vintages are more uneven.

CHÂTEAU DE VOSNE-ROMANÉE

3.2 ha: owned. La Romanée (83 a); Vosne-Romanée *premiers crus* in Aux Reignots, Les Chaumes; village Vosne-Romanée.

There are two Liger-Belair exploitations in Vosne-Romanée. The château is the property of General Henry Liger-Belair, and these wines are made by Régis Forey (*q.v.*) and bottled and sold by Bouchard Père et Fils.

The family of Xavier Liger-Belair own a separate estate. These vines are looked after by Denis Mugneret (see page 133) and others.

NUITS-SAINT-GEORGES

Situated roughly halfway between Beaune and Dijon, Nuits-Saint-Georges effectively marks the start (or the end, depending which direction you are going in) of the Côte-de-Nuits, the greatest fiefdom of the Pinot Noir in the world. Nuits-Saint-Georges is a large commune, second in size in this part of the world to Gevrey-Chambertin, and the name Nuits-Saint-Georges, easy to recognise, easy to pronounce - and sadly, still, easy to abuse - is familiar to wine-lovers all over the world.

The town itself is an industrial conglomeration rather than a viticultural village and is the commercial centre of the Côte-de-Nuits. Here are the *négociants*, the *tonneleries*, the transport agents, the schools, the banks and the markets. It is a bustling, busy, friendly place, less self-conscious than Beaune, with one good hotel-restaurant, the Côte d'Or, bang in the middle of a dog-leg in the main road. The vineyards stretch on either side of a gap in the Côte, out of which from Arcenats and L'Etang-Vergy, two villages in the Hautes-Côtes, flows a stream called the Meuzin. On the southern side the vines continue into the commune of Prémeaux, whose wines are entitled to the Nuits-Saint-Georges appellation. Beyond Clos-de-la-Maréchale, Nuits' southernmost *premier cru*, the land is Côte-de-Nuits-Villages, not village wine, and one is soon across the border into the Côte-de-Beaune.

The original Nuits was a Gallo-Roman villa further out into the plain. The name, though, has no nocturnal connections. It is more likely to be a corruption of the Celtic *un win*, a stream in a valley, or otherwise to have something to do with nuts. In the early Middle Ages the area was the domaine of Hugues, *sire* of Vergy, who donated much of the land to the local monastery of Saint-Denis and the prior of Saint-Vivant. Slowly a village began to expand further up the valley of the river Meuzin in the site it occupies today. Though it was originally fortified, it lost its strategic importance when the Duchy of Franche-Comté was absorbed into the Kingdom of France in 1678. Nuits-Saint-Georges was no longer a frontier outpost and the wall surrounding it was slowly dismantled over the succeeding couple of hundred years. As a result of this, and the fact that the main road thunders right though the centre, Nuits has little of the medieval attraction of, say, Beaune.

Like Beaune, though, it has its own Hospices, a charitable foundation dating from 1692, and similarly endowed with vines. The wines are also sold by auction, and this takes place on the Sunday preceding Palm Sunday, following a tasting at the Clos-de-Vougeot. The Hospices de Nuits possesses 10 hectares, and all the *cuvées* sold at auction come from *premiers crus*.

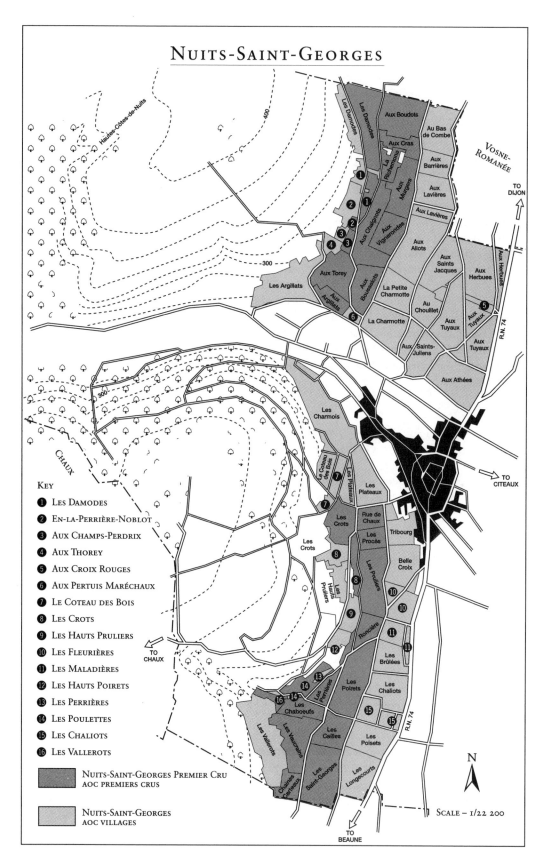

NUITS-SAINT-GEORGES

Hautes-Côtes-de-Nuits

Les Damodes

Aux Boudots

Au Bas
de Combe

Aux Cras

La Richemone

Aux Mugeats

Aux
Barrières

Aux
Lavières

Aux Chaignots

Aux Lavières

Aux
Vignerondes

Aux
Allots

Aux
Saints
Jacques

Aux
Herbues

Aux Torey

Les Argillats

Aux
Bousselots

La Petite
Charmotte

Au
Chouillet

Aux
Tuyaux

Aux
Argillas

La Charmotte

Aux Tuyaux

Aux
Saints-
Juliens

Aux
Tuyaux

Aux Athées

Les
Charmois

CHAUX

Le Coteau
des Bois

Les Plateaux

Les
Plateaux

Les
Crots

Rue de
Chaux

Les Crots

Les
Procès

Tribourg

Les Hauts Pruliers

Les Pruliers

Belle
Croix

Roncière

Les
Brûlées

Les Hauts Poirets

Les
Perrières

Les
Poirets

Les
Chaliots

Les Poulettes

Les
Chaboeufs

Les Vallerots

Les Veaucrains

Les Cailles

Les Poisets

Champs
Perdaux

Les
Saint-Georges

Les
Longecourts

VOSNE-
ROMANÉE

TO
DIJON

Aux Herbues

R.N. 74

TO
CITEAUX

TO
CHAUX

R.N. 74

TO
BEAUNE

N

KEY

1. LES DAMODES
2. EN-LA-PERRIÈRE-NOBLOT
3. AUX CHAMPS-PERDRIX
4. AUX THOREY
5. AUX CROIX ROUGES
6. AUX PERTUIS MARÉCHAUX
7. LE COTEAU DES BOIS
8. LES CROTS
9. LES HAUTS PRULIERS
10. LES FLEURIÈRES
11. LES MALADIÈRES
12. LES HAUTS POIRETS
13. LES PERRIÈRES
14. LES POULETTES
15. LES CHALIOTS
16. LES VALLEROTS

NUITS-SAINT-GEORGES PREMIER CRU
AOC PREMIERS CRUS

NUITS-SAINT-GEORGES
AOC VILLAGES

SCALE – 1/22 200

HISTORY

As early as 1023, the date it featured in a donation made to the Chapitre de Saint-Denis-de-Vergy, the Clos-Saint-Georges, as it was then, was established as the commune's senior vineyard. This was the sole wine of the area regarded as a *tête de cuvée* – and therefore the equal of the Romanées, Richebourg and La Tâche, and only these, in Vosne-Romanée – by Dr Morelot in 1831. By the time of Dr Lavalle, writing in 1855, its reputation had slipped to that of what I might call the second division of *grands crus*: Clos-des-Lambrays and Corton, and is classed as a *tête de cuvée* alongside Vaucrains, Cailles, Porrets, Pruliers, Boudots, Cras, Murgers and Thorey (the wines of Prémeaux being assessed separately), but at the head of them, a position it continued to occupy in *Le Vin de Bourgogne* by Camille Rodier in 1920. By that time the town, as it had become by then, like most of the other villages of the Côte, had appropriated Saint-Georges to tag on as a suffix to its name, in an effort to raise the visibility of the rest of the wines.

One further element of Nuits' glory must not be forgotten. In 1698 Louis XIV, the Sun King, was suffering from what in some versions of the legend is described as a fistula, but what Richard Olney, in his *Romanée-Conti* prosaically insists was gout (the king was fifty at the time). Guy-Crescent Fagon, the king's doctor prescribed *vieux bourgogne*, in place of the then fashionable, but more acidic, champagne. Nuitons will tell you that this Burgundy was a Nuits from the Abbey of Saint-Vivant. Who would be so uncharitable as to ask them for proof? Anyway the 'cure' seems to have done the trick, and the resultant publicity didn't do Burgundy any harm.

LOCATION

Nuits-Saint-Georges has no *grands crus* but an impressive list of twenty-seven *premiers crus* plus another nine in Prémeaux. On the Vosne side the *vignoble* is wide, the slope gentle except right at the top under the trees, which is where you will find the first growths. The best known include Boudots, Richemone, Murgers, Damodes and Chaignots.

South of the village the vineyards begin again and the slope is narrower, with the main road climbing up at a slant as it continues south towards the village of Prémeaux. Here lie Pruliers, Roncières, Poirets (or Porrets), Vaucrains, Cailles, and, the most southerly, Les Saint-Georges itself. I call this section middle Nuits-Saint-Georges.

Across the border into Prémeaux the incline is at first steeper and the vineyard more confined. This is the narrowest section, east to west, of the entire Côte d'Or. Here you will find Les Forêts, Perdrix, Corvées, Argillières and two *monopoles*, both *clos*: Arlot and Maréchale. The aspect of the Clos-de-la-Maréchale is distinctly south-east rather than east, and the slope is once again quite gentle.

The soil structure of the Nuits-Saint-Georges *vignoble* is no less complex than the rest of Burgundy – indeed more so, for it is 6 kilometres as the crow flies from Les Boudots on the Vosne boundary to the end of the Clos-de-la-Maréchale. To aid us, some major studies of the land have been attempted recently. Over a couple of years at the beginning of the 1990s a team of geologists and geographers led by M. Lenouf of the University of Dijon analysed the soil in each *premier cru*. Following this a team of professional testers, including Georges Pertuiset, president of the *sommeliers* of the region, Jean Siegrist of the local INRA, René Naudin, expert in the effects of maturation in oak, local brokers Becky Wasserman and Russell Hone, and others, including the Nuits-Saint-Georges proprietors themselves and even myself, if I occasioned to be in the region, participated in some extensive tastings, *climat* by *climat*, to see if we could isolate in words the effects of these *terroir* differences in the character of each *cru*. Sadly the result of this latter undertaking was less successful than that provided by the geologists.

North of the town the subsoil underneath the *premier cru*, like that of Vosne-Romanée, is essentially a Bathonian limestone in origin, covered with a mixture of pebbles, silt, limestone debris and clay. Further down the slope, in the area of the village vines, there is marl of Oligocene origin, covered by clay-sand mixtures, *limons* of different types, together with pebbles and alluvial matter brought down by the river Meuzin from the Hautes-Côtes. At first the wines have a lot in common with those from neighbouring vineyards across the commune boundary, but the incidence of clay increases as one travels south. The soil becomes richer and the wines as a result have a tendency to be four-square.

In middle Nuits-Saint-Georges the limestone is Bathonian or the harder Comblanchien. Here and there in the *premiers crus* the surface soil will contain sand or gravel, moderating the effect of the clay. Erosion is more of a problem here, one solution to which, pioneered by the Gouges family, is to plant a special ray-grass between the rows of vines. In the village wine areas of this section the soil is less alluvial than the other side of the village, and the *limons* are higher in their percentage of clay and mixed with Bathonian and Bajocian debris. This is the best part of the commune. In a line beginning with Les Saint-Georges, and continuing at 245-260 metres above sea level successively through Les Cailles, Les Poirets (or Porrets), Les Roncières and finally Les Pruliers, not forgetting Les Vaucrains which is directly above Saint-Georges, run the greatest wines of Nuits, and true Nuits-Saint-Georges (which arguably Boudots is not).

Across into Prémeaux the soil is very thin on the higher slopes, the structures very complicated – that of the Clos-de-l'Arlot being quite different from its neighbours north and south. Most of the vineyard here is on rock. Lower down on the flatter land – there is in fact one *premier cru* vineyard, part of Les Grandes-Vignes, which lies on the 'wrong' side of the main road – the soil is deeper and there is more clay and marl. In general the wines here are more sinewy, slightly hard and robust (Clos-de-l'Arlot being an exception), with less breed, less concentration and less definition.

The authorities were quite correct to deny any vineyard in Nuits-Saint-Georges the status of *grand cru*. At their best they can have depth and finesse as well as richness and structure, but at *premier cru* rather than *grand cru* level. Moreover there is always a certain minerally, gamey hint of the rustic (country rather than sophisticated charm, to borrow Anthony Hanson's description of the wines of a grower in Fixin, equally applicable here) and a certain leaden-footedness that detracts from the real class, definition and flair. In mitigation it is fair to point out that as a consequence of the huge popularity of the name, there has been much abuse, and to judge by some of today's *négociant* wines (not the *négociants* mentioned between these covers, I hasten to add) this abuse continues, Côte-de-Nuits-Villages being passed off as Nuits-Saint-Georges. More sin has been committed in this name than in the name of all the other villages in Burgundy put together. Not everything is the fault of the wines themselves, least of all of the growing number of good individual properties.

THE VINEYARD

Premiers Crus: There are thirty-seven *premiers crus* in Nuits-Saint-Georges and Prémeaux, in whole or in part. For convenience I divide these into the three sub-areas I have already outlined.

Northern Nuits-Saint-Georges: Aux Argillas (*Les* Argillas is village Nuits); Aux Boudots; Aux Boisselots; Aux Chaignots; Aux Champs-Perdrix (part); Aux Cras; Les Damodes (part); Aux Murgers; En-la-Perrière-Noblot (part); La Richemone; Aux Thorey (part); Aux Vignes-Rondes.

Middle Nuits-Saint-Georges: Les Cailles; Les Chaboeufs; Chaines-Carteaux; Les Crots (part); Les Perrières; Les Poirets (or Porrets); Les Poulettes (part); Les Procès; Les Pruliers; Les

Hauts-Pruliers (part); Les Roncières; Rue de Chaux; Les Saint-Georges; Les Vallerots (part); Les Vaucrains.

Prémeaux: Les Argillières; Clos-des-Argillières; Clos-de-l'Arlot (*monopole*); Clos-de-la-Maréchale (*monopole*); Les Didiers; Les Forêts; Les Grandes-Vignes (part); Aux Corvées; Les Corvées-Pagets; Aux Perdrix; Les Terres-Blanches (part).

Within these, a number of growers boast monopolies over a particular sub-section or *clos*. Others are sold under other main names. Among these latter wines can be numbered: the Château Gris of Lupe-Cholet, a 2.80 ha enclosure within Les Crots; the Clos-Saint-Marc, which lies within the Corvées and is an exclusivity of Maison Bouchard Père et Fils of Beaune; and another part of the Corvées known as the Clos-des-Corvées which is owned by the Thomas family, was hitherto a monopoly of Maison Jadot and is now operated by the Domaine Prieuré-Roch. Moreover, a couple of vineyards close to Les Saint-Georges itself have slyly, like the town of Nuits, added Saint-Georges to their title as if it were some magic road to everlasting success. Thus Les Poirets or Porrets (despite being separated from it by Les Cailles) and Les Forêts (despite being separated from it by Les Didiers) are more often than not suffixed '-Saint-Georges'. It's amazing what you can get away with!

These *premiers crus* cover 142.79 ha, of which 42.25 ha lie in Prémeaux, and produce some 5,700 hl (753,000 bottles) of red wine a year.

Village Wine: There are 175.32 ha of village wine in Nuits-Saint-Georges, of which a mere 11.79 lie in Prémeaux. Production averages 7,000 hl (929,000) bottles a year.

White Wine: Like Morey-Saint-Denis, but unlike most of the other villages on the Côte-de-Nuits, Nuits-Saint-Georges produces some white wine, both village and *premier cru*. While the separate bottling of white wine is relatively new, and the quantities are certainly rare (*confidentiel* is a nice French translation) it must be remembered that it has always been the practice until the last generation or so to plant a few white grape vines among the reds in order to soften the wine and lend it a bit of vivacity.

The main impetus behind Nuits *blanc*, however, comes from another angle. As recounted more fully on page 454, Henri Gouges discovered some mutated Pinot Noir, producing white grapes, before the war, took cuttings and propagated them, and in 1947 had enough to produce some wine. Others have borrowed cuttings from him. I call this mutation Pinot Gouges. Others make white wine from Chardonnay or Pinot Beurot, or a mixture of all three. There is not much: 2.54 ha at the last count, and 102 hl (135,000 bottles). You have to know your merchant well to be able to get hold of some. But the wine is intriguing. Meursault it isn't, nor Corton either, and it comes in different styles. In most cases it is best at four to eight years rather than ten plus. But it is worth investigating.

THE PREMIERS CRUS

These are dealt with roughly in a north-south order:

AUX BOUDOTS (6.30 HA)

This *climat*, perfectly sited at 250-290 metres above sea level, marches with the Vosne-Romanée *premier cru* Les Malconsorts. The soil is a brown limestone mixed with a fine gravel, just a touch of clay and fragments of white oolitic rock, resting on the pink limestone of Comblanchien, here rather more eroded and crumbly than further south.

The wine is altogether more Vosne in character than Nuits. Indeed the vineyards further down the slope, on the other side of the excellent village *climat* Au Bas de Combe, produce village Vosne-Romanée rather than Nuits-Saint-Georges. There is an elegant, potential silkiness here which is alien to Nuits, and while by no means light, the wine is neither as full and gutsy as middle Nuits nor as full and firmly concentrated as a Vosne from, say, Suchots or Beaumonts.

Some years ago, having bought a Boudots and a Malconsorts from the same source, I much amused myself by offering blind samples to professional friends. Find the commune, I would demand. Or: one is Vosne and the other Nuits. Which is which? We came to the conclusion I have outlined above.

Recommended Sources: Jean Grivot; Leroy; Méo-Camuzet; Denis Mugneret; Gérard Mugneret; Jean Tardy (all Vosne-Romanée). Jean-Jacques Confuron (Nuits-Saint-Georges). Louis Jadot (Beaune) – this being from the Domaine André Gagey.

LES DAMODES (8.55 HA) • AUX CRAS (3.00 HA)
LA RICHEMONE (1.92 HA) • AUX MURGERS (4.89 HA)

Cras, Richemone and Murgers are the next three *climats* on the same level of slope as Les Boudots, while Les Damodes runs along the top of all four. The soil structure is similar, based on the same Comblanchien pink limestone rock, but there is more gravel, especially in Murgers, and less soil and more broken-up rock in the upper slopes of Les Damodes, where the incline is steeper and there is some sand.

Damodes can be lighter, Murgers quite meaty, but otherwise these form a sort of halfway house between Boudots and the yardstick flavours of the northern section of Nuits-Saints-Georges one finds in Aux Chaignots and Aux Vignes-Rondes. While there is a bit of Vosne about them, and therefore an innate elegance, none would be confused with a Malconsorts.

Recommended Sources:
Les Damodes: Alfred Haegelen (Vosne-Romanée); Jean Chauvenet; Joseph Faiveley; Fernand Lechenaut; Gilles Remoriquet (all Nuits-Saint-Georges). Robert Jayer-Gilles (Magny-lès-Villers in the Hautes-Côtes).
Aux Cras: Bruno Clavelier (Vosne-Romanée).
La Richemone: Alain Michelot (Nuits-Saint-Georges).
Aux Murgers: Bertagna; Alain Hudelot-Noëllat (both Vougeot). Sylvain Cathiard; Jacky Confuron-Cotétidot; Méo-Camuzet (all Vosne-Romanée).

AUX CHAIGNOTS (5.86 HA) • AUX VIGNES-RONDES (3.84 HA)
AUX BOUSSELOTS (4.24 HA) • AUX THOREY (5.00 HA)
EN-LA-PERRIÈRE-NOBLOT (0.30 HA) • AUX CHAMPS-PERDRIX (0.73 HA)
AUX ARGILLAS (1.89 HA)

The first four *climats* above provide exemplars of northern Nuits-Saint-Georges. Only small parts of Champs-Perdrix and En-la-Perrière-Noblot, both being at the top of the slope, are classed as *premier cru*. The bottom of Argillas (Aux Argillas) is *premier cru*, while the land above, as here the land curves round to disappear into the Hautes-Côtes, is merely village (Les Argillats). The best part of Thorey, under the title Clos-de-Thorey, is a monopoly of the Domaine Thomas-Moillard.

Once again the base rock is Comblanchien limestone but there is Bajocian *ostrea acuminata* containing fossilised oysters in Les Vignes-Rondes, Les Bousselots and Aux Argillas and in the lower part of those vineyards the base rock, still pink, is the Bathonian *calcaire* de Prémeaux. There is rather more gravel and pebbles than further north mixed up with broken white oolite rock; and rather more clay and marl.

The wines here are rich, full, elegant but nonetheless quite sturdy; not as muscular as they are south of Nuits-Saint-Georges, but not quite as concentrated as the best of that section can provide either.

Recommended Sources:

Aux Chaignots: Henri Gouges, Gérard Mugneret, Dr Georges Mugneret (both Vosne-Romanée); Robert Chevillon, Joseph Faiveley, Alain Michelot (all Nuits-Saint-Georges).

Aux Vignes-Rondes: Jacky Confuron-Cotétidot, Leroy, Dr Georges Mugneret (all Vosne-Romanée); Joseph Faiveley, Daniel Rion (both Nuits-Saint-Georges).

Aux Bousselots: Jean Chauvenet, Robert Chevillon, Philippe Gavignet, François Legros, Gilles Remoriquet (all Nuits-Saint-Georges).

Aux Thorey: Thomas-Moillard (Clos-de-Thorey *monopole*) (Nuits-Saint-Georges).

En-la-Perrière-Noblot: Machard de Gramont (Nuits-Saint-Georges).

Aux Champs-Perdrix: Alain Michelot (Nuits-Saints-Georges).

Aux Argillas: Philippe Gavignet (Nuits-Saint-Georges).

I now turn to the middle part of the Nuits-Saints-Georges *vignoble*.

<h2 style="text-align:center">Les Crots (1.16 ha) • Rue de Chaux (2.12 ha)</h2>

<h2 style="text-align:center">Les Procès (1.34 ha) • Les Hauts-Pruliers (0.40 ha)</h2>

These small and relatively little-known *climats* lie immediately south of the town of Nuits-Saint-Georges and the road which winds up to the village of Chaux in the Hautes-Côtes (half-way up is a very good vantage point from which to get a panoramic view of the southern Côte-de-Nuits).

Les Crots, most of which is taken up with the vineyards of the Château Gris, is on a steep escarpment, necessitating terracing for the vines. The soil is superficial and very stony, on a pink Comblanchien bedrock. Underneath, in the Rue de Chaux and Procès there is more surface soil, more clay, and the Bathonian rock is of two types, white oolite as well as the pink Prémeaux limestone. Les Procès and Les Hauts-Pruliers are more stony.

The wines here have neither the elegance nor the definition of either the best of the northern sector nor the top *climats* just a little further down the line. They have colour and weight, but an absence of real grace and flair. Sometimes the tannins can be a bit brutal. There is a lot of difference between a Pruliers and even the best of the Hauts-Pruliers above. Good honest bottles from the best sources nonetheless.

Recommended Sources:

Rue de Chaux: Bertrand Ambroise, Jean Chauvenet, Gilles Remoriquet (all Nuits-Saint-Georges).

Les Procès: Robert Arnoux (Vosne-Romanée).

Les Hauts-Pruliers: Daniel Rion (Nuits-Saint-Georges).

<h2 style="text-align:center">Les Pruliers (7.11 ha) • Les Roncières (0.97 ha)</h2>

<h2 style="text-align:center">Les Porrets or Poirets or Porrets-Saint-Georges (7.35 ha)</h2>

At 250-270 metres above sea level, at an incline which varies between 8 and 12 per cent, these three vineyards are ideally placed, and their wine is second only to Les Saint-Georges itself. With the exception of Les Poirets there is less clay, however, than in this most famous vineyard or in Les Procès to the north, but there are plenty of stones: more gravel in Les Poirets and the southern part of Les Pruliers, mixed in with limestone earth of various colours - yellower in the Roncières where the rock is white oolite, browner in the other two *climats* on either side of it where the oolite mixes with pink Prémeaux limestone.

These three wines, and it may be the fruity suggestions of the name of Les Pruliers (and Porrets could come from *poirier*, a pear tree), seem to me to have an impressive, often somewhat cooked fruit flavour: plums mixed with the general soft-fruit aspects of the Pinot Noir. The wines are full, profound, meaty, rich, sinewy and backward, rather tougher in their youth than those from the northern sector. But be patient! They gain a lot in generosity as they soften up. Of the three, Porrets is the most approachable, the most obviously elegant right from the beginning.

Recommended Sources:

Les Pruliers: Jean Grivot (Vosne-Romanée); Robert Chevillon, Henri Gouges (both Nuits-Saint-Georges).

Les Roncières: Jean Grivot (Vosne-Romanée); Robert Chevillon, François Legros (both Nuits-Saint-Georges).

Les Porrets: Joseph Faiveley, Henri Gouges (Clos des Porrets-Saint-Georges), Alain Michelot, Thomas-Moillard (all Nuits-Saint-Georges).

LES PERRIÈRES (2.47 HA) • LES POULETTES (2.13 HA)
LES CHABOEUFS (2.80 HA) • LES VALLEROTS (0.87 HA)
CHAINES-CARTEAUX (2.53 HA)

Above Les Porrets, Les Cailles and Les Saint-Georges, there is a little gap in the line of the hills, a suspicion of a valley. This means that the steep Chaines-Carteaux is moved around to face just a little to the north, as does the *climat* of Les Vallerots, only the lowest elements of which are designated *premier cru*. Chaboeufs lies in the middle, down which flows an air current, marginally lowering the micro-climate. Poulettes and Perrières are on the other side, the former above the latter, on quite a steep slope.

The Perrières vineyard, as the name suggests (*perrière* being synonymous with *carrière*, a quarry) is very rocky and stony. There are a number of faults here in the rock, exposing both white oolite and pink Prémeaux limestone. Above, in the Poulettes, the vines are on terraces and the oolite comes to the fore. In the Chaboeufs there is more clay and more sand, as there is in the Chaines-Carteaux.

With the exception of Les Perrières, which produces a somewhat atypical Nuits-Saint-Georges - lighter, minerally but elegant - this is not great terrain. That lies further down the slope. Chaboeufs is the best, but again, as in Procès, for instance, the size can overwhelm the fruit, and the tannins can be a bit unsophisticated.

It is in Les Perrières that Henri Gouges has collected his mutated Pinot and produces white wine.

Recommended Sources:

Les Perrières: Jean Chauvenet, Robert Chevillon, François Legros (all Nuits-Saint-Georges); Régis Forey (Vosne-Romanée).

Les Chaboeufs: Jean-Jacques Confuron, Philippe Gavignet (both Nuits-Saint-Georges).

LES SAINT-GEORGES (7.52 HA) • LES CAILLES (7.11 HA)
LES VAUCRAINS (6.20 HA)

Here, just as the commune, if not the wine, is about to overflow into neighbouring Prémeaux, we have the greatest *climat* in Nuits-Saint-Georges, and two worthy princes of the blood. The three are large vineyards: Vaucrains lies up-slope at 260-280 metres; Les Cailles is directly north of Les Saint-Georges at 245-260 metres.

One of the clues to Les Saint-Georges' supremacy is perhaps the complexity of its soil structure. The Bathonian rock is of all three neighbouring types (Prémeaux, white oolite and Comblanchien). The earth is very stony, so it drains well, though the slope at 7-8 degrees is quite gentle, and the clay is mixed with a little more soil than elsewhere. Across in Les Cailles things are similar, except that there is no Prémeaux stone. There is also more sand. Up above, in the Vaucrains, the soil is not so much gravelly or pebbly as rocky, and with quite large stones at that, but it is quite heavy. Again there is clay and sand. But the rock is mainly oolite.

What this means in terms of wine is that we have two elements in Cailles and Vaucrains which are then blended together in Les Saint-Georges to produce something greater than the sum of its parts. Les Cailles, in Nuits-Saint-Georges terms, is subtle and feminine, with very seductive, composed, soft fruit flavours. Vaucrains is vigorous, rich and full-bodied; sturdy but not too wild and untameable.

And Les Saint-Georges is the synthesis of the lot. In my experience it definitely *is* the best wine of the commune. It is simply the most complete, the most complex, and the most profound. When you get the richness of a fine year, and the balance you can find in a top grower's Les Saints-Georges, you *can*, yes, easily get tempted into arguing for its elevation to *grand cru*.

Recommended Sources:

Les Saint-Georges: Régis Forey, Denis Mugneret (for Ligier-Belair) (both Vosne-Romanée); Robert Chevillon, Joseph Faiveley, Henri Gouges, Alain Michelot, Gilles Remoriquet (all Nuits-Saint-Georges).

Les Cailles: Robert Chevillon, Fernand Lechenaut, Alain Michelot (all Nuits-Saint-Georges).

Les Vaucrains: Bertrand Ambroise, Jean Chauvenet, Robert Chevillon, Henri Gouges, Alain Michelot (all Nuits-Saint-Georges).

We now cross into the commune of Prémeaux.

LES DIDIERS (2.45 HA)
(monopole of the Hospices de Nuits-Saint-Georges)

LES FORÊTS OR CLOS-DES-FORÊTS-SAINT-GEORGES (7.11 HA)
(monopole of the Domaine de l'Arlot)

AUX CORVÉES OR CLOS-DES-CORVÉES (5.13 HA)
(monopole, up to 1994, of Louis Jadot; for 1995, of Prieuré-Roch)

AUX CORVÉES (CLOS-SAINT-MARC) (0.93 HA)
(monopole of Bouchard Père et Fils)

LES CORVÉES-PAGETS (1.48 HA) • AUX PERDRIX (3.49 HA)

LES ARGILLIÈRES (0.22 HA) • CLOS-DES-ARGILLIÈRES (4.22 HA)

LES GRANDES-VIGNES OR CLOS-DES-GRANDES-VIGNES (2.21 HA)
(monopole of Domaine Thomas-Moillard)

CLOS-DE-L'ARLOT (5.45 HA)
(monopole of the Domaine de l'Arlot)

CLOS-DE-LA-MARÉCHALE (9.55 HA)
(monopole of Maison Joseph Faiveley)

LES TERRES-BLANCHES (0.91 HA)

Here we come to the narrowest, and in part, the steepest section of the Côte. The road from Nuits-Saint-Georges runs at an angle up the slope towards Prémeaux, descends within the village, but then climbs up again so that as you get to the end of the Clos-de-la-Maréchale you are well above 240 metres. It is therefore a bit surprising that the vineyards opposite should be only Côte-de-Nuits-Villages, not village AC, while on the Nuits side of the village again on the east side of the road, part of Les Grandes-Vignes has been decreed *premier cru*.

Among these twelve *premiers crus* the soil varies significantly. To the north - in Didiers, Forêts, Corvées, Perdrix, and Argillières - it is relatively deep in mid-slope, brown or yellow-brown mixed with sand and clay and stones of various origins, mainly oolitic, on a Comblanchien base.

The wines here are sturdy, muscular and masculine. They can have plenty of richness, but they can lack refinement. Didiers perhaps represents a halfway house down from Les Saint-

Georges (my experience is naturally with the Hospices de Nuits *cuvée* but this can have different *éleveurs*) but otherwise we are quite a step away from the finesse and nuance of Nuits-Saint-Georges' greatest *climat*.

The soil in Les Grandes-Vignes is similar, but there is a little less clay, the active limestone is higher, and the Bathonian base rock is more complex. My experience comes both from the Thomas-Moillard wine and that of Domaine Daniel Rion, whose vines are village AC. The Clos-des-Corvées, until 1994 a Jadot monopoly (the land is owned by a member of the Thomas family), is similarly sturdy: size without much grace. Like most of the above it is a little obvious.

Many of these *climats* are *monopoles*. The Clos-de-la-Maréchale repeats the soil structure of Forêts and Corvées, but the angle of the slope is flatter and the orientation more towards the south. There is no denying a suggestion of the rustic in the full, robust character of the wine. It ages well, though.

At the Clos-de-l'Arlot there is a distinct fault in the rock. Behind the garden of this estate there is plenty of evidence of quarrying. In front, the vineyard itself is on several levels, with a slope of 35 per cent.

All this produces a light wine, notwithstanding Jean Paul de Smet's particular style of wine-making (all the stems and whole grape maceration). For from the Clos-des-Forêts he produces something rather more sturdy. Clos-de-l'Arlot is feminine, the fruit flavours cherry and redcurrant-like. But quite how much this is the Domaine de l'Arlot thumbprint, and how much is the signature of the *climat*, it is difficult to tell.

Recommended Sources:
Les Didiers: Hospices de Nuits (but depends on who does the *élevage*).
Clos-des-Forêts: Arlot (Nuits-Saint-Georges).
Clos-des-Corvées: Louis Jadot (Beaune) up to 1994.
Les Corvées-Pagets: Robert Arnoux (Vosne-Romanée).
Les Argillières: Daniel Rion (Nuits-Saint-Georges).
Clos-des-Grandes-Vignes: Thomas-Moillard (Nuits-Saints-Georges).
Clos-de-l'Arlot: Arlot (Nuits-Saints-Georges).
Clos-de-la-Maréchale: Joseph Faiveley (Nuits-Saints-Georges).

NUITS-SAINTS-GEORGES:
GROWERS AND *NEGOCIANTS*
HERVÉ ARLAUD

11.19 ha: owned and *en fermage/métayage*. Bonnes-Mares (21 a); Clos-Saint-Denis (13 a); Clos-de-la-Roche (40 a); Charmes-Chambertin (19 a) (plus 1.13 ha *en métayage*); Gevrey-Chambertin *premier cru* Les Combottes; Morey-Saint-Denis *premier cru* in Les Millandes, Les Cheseaux, Les Ruchots; Nuits-Saint-Georges *premier cru* Les Procès; village Gevrey-Chambertin; village Morey-Saint-Denis; village Chambolle-Musigny.

In the books you will find the Arlaud domaine listed under Morey-Saint-Denis. Indeed that is where Joseph, Hervé's father, continues to live. Hervé, though, born in 1953, vinifies and operates from a cellar in the back streets of Nuits-Saint-Georges, hard by the church. He vinifies for twelve to fourteen days, having destemmed 90 per cent, uses 10 per cent new wood, continues to sell quite a lot off in bulk, and bottles the rest after fourteen to sixteen months. I have tasted some fine wines at the top levels here, but lower down the scale I have found them a little slight.

DANIEL BOCQUENET
4.5 ha: owned. Village Nuits-Saint-Georges.

Daniel Bocquenet works out of a new cellar under Mont Charmois and makes a single wine, much of which he sells off in bulk. It is rich, concentrated and quite marked by new wood.

★JEAN CHAUVENET

9.50 ha: owned and *en fermage/métayage*. Nuits-Saint-Georges *premier cru* in Rue de Chaux, Les Damodes, Les Bousselots, Les Perrières, Les Vaucrains; village Nuits-Saint-Georges; village Vosne-Romanée.

Jean Chauvenet's wines are made by his handsome son-in-law, Christophe Drag. Since 1990 the destemming has been total. After a few days' cold soaking the fermentation takes place, controlled at 28-34°C. Thereafter maturation takes place in from 10–25 per cent new oak. Chauvenet continues to sell 60 per cent of his village Nuits (of which he owns 7.20 ha) in bulk.

Things have much improved here in recent years. The tannins are more sophisticated, the fruit expression richer and more classy, the flavours more complex: all because there is more attention to detail, more control and no stems. This is a very good place to study the differences between Nuits *premiers crus*.

HUBERT CHAUVENET-CHOPIN

10 ha: owned and *en fermage/métayage*. Nuits-Saint-Georges *premier cru* in Les Murgers, Aux Argillas, Aux Thorey; village Nuits-Saint-Georges; village Chambolle-Musigny; Côte-de-Nuits-Villages.

Hubert Chauvenet is gradually taking over the wines of his father-in-law Daniel Chopin of Comblanchien (*q.v.*), but nevertheless operates a sizeable property in his own right, Almost total destemming, a few days' cold maceration, fermentations at 30-32°C and from 30–50 per cent new oak. Good but variable things here in my (admittedly limited) experience. But worth watching.

PASCAL CHEVIGNY

5 ha: *en fermage*. Nuits-Saint-Georges *premier cru* Hauts-Pruliers; Vosne-Romanée *premier cru* Les Petits-Monts; village Nuits-Saint-Georges; village Vosne-Romanée including the *lieu-dit* Les Champs-Perdrix.

Pascal Chevigny, tall, handsome and curly-haired, a little *sérieux*, took charge of his family exploitation in 1988/1989. He destems completely, practises a *saignée* if necessary (up to 40 per cent in 1994), ferments up to 32°C and uses 25–50 per cent new wood. Some of his 1993s were held almost two years before bottling, but the 1994s were bottled after little more than a year. Things have improved considerably since 1992. Worth keeping an eye on.

MICHEL CHEVILLON

8.2 ha: owned and *en fermage/métayage*. Nuits-Saint-Georges *premier cru* in Les Saint-Georges, Les Forêts, Les Champs-Perdrix, Les Crots (the last two blended together); village Nuits-Saints-Georges; village Vosne-Romanée.

Michel Chevillon is a first cousin of Robert (see below) but his wine is rather more rustic. Not only is there no new wood, more importantly, there is too much old wood. He vinifies with a goodly proportion of the stems.

★ROBERT CHEVILLON

13 ha: owned and *en fermage/métayage*. Nuits-Saints-Georges *premier cru* in Les Saint-Georges, Les Cailles, Les Vaucrains, Les Roncières; Les Pruliers; Les Perrières; Les Chaignots; Les Bousselots; village Nuits-Saint-Georges, *blanc et rouge*.

This is a splendid domaine with a marvellous palette of *premiers crus* and very old vines - seventy-five years in the case of the first three above. A small percentage of stems is retained, there is no cold maceration, the fermentation temperatures are held between 30° and 33°C and one-third new wood is utilised in the maturation. Nothing special about the recipe, but the results are rich, opulent, classy and individual. And there is that *rara avis*, Nuits-Saint-Georges *blanc*.

See Profile, page 379.

GEORGES CHICOTOT

6.40 ha: owned and *en fermage/métayage*. Nuits-Saint-Georges *premier cru* in Les Saint-Georges, Les Vaucrains, Les Pruliers, La Rue-de-Chaux; village Nuits-Saint-Georges.

'Jojo' Chicotot is a slight, balding, dark-haired, intense man in his forties; he looks like a jockey. His cellars lie in the middle of town next to the hairdressers. The wines are made by Accad methods, protected by not disengaging the CO_2 and bottled late without either fining or filtration. I have found an absence of fat and generosity in his wines.

COTTIN FRÈRES
LABOURÉ ROI

This is a large, thriving *négociant* which has the marketing exclusivity of four important domaines in Burgundy, including that of Chantal Lescure in Nuits-Saint-Georges and René Manuel in Meursault (the other two are Chablis and Pouilly-Fuissé), and works very closely with a number of growers who continue to sell the majority of their wines off in bulk. More recently, it has entered partnerships with the 30 ha Domaine Ropiteau-Mignon in Meursault and the 44 ha domaine Michel Pont of Volnay and Savigny-lès-Beaune. Late in 1996 the Lescure domaine decided to go it alone, and Bouchard Père et Fils took over the responsibility of the Ropiteau-Mignon wines.

Chantal Lescure: 16.26 ha. Clos-de-Vougeot (31 a); Vosne-Romanée *premier cru* Les Suchots; Nuits-Saint-Georges *premier cru* Les Damodes; Pommard *premier cru* Les Bertins; Beaune *premier cru* Les Chouacheux; village Chambolle-Musigny; village Pommard; village Volnay.

René Manuel: 5 ha. Meursault *premier cru* in Clos-des-Bouches-Chères (*monopole*), Les Poruzots; village Meursault *blanc et rouge*.

Vinification is state-of-the-art in a modern factory close to the motorway. You will not be disappointed. But I don't think you will be excited either. The Cottin brothers are urbane and welcoming. The atmosphere is efficient and businesslike. What they need is a super-star wine-maker with the flair of Jacques Lardière of Maison Jadot.

★★JOSEPH FAIVELEY

115 ha: owned and *en fermage*. Chambertin, Clos-de-Bèze (1.29 ha); Latricières-Chambertin (1.21 ha); Mazis-Chambertin (1.20 ha); Le Musigny (3 a); Clos-de-Vougeot (1.28 ha); Echézeaux (87 a); Corton, Clos-des-Cortons-Faiveley (*monopole*) (2.97 ha); Corton-Charlemagne (53 a); Gevrey-Chambertin *premier cru* in Les Cazetiers, La Combe-aux-Moines; Chambertin-Musigny *premier cru* in Les Fuées, La Combe-d'Orveau; Nuits-Saint-Georges *premier cru* in Les Saint-Georges, Les Porrets-Saint-Georges, Les Damodes, Clos-de-la-Maréchale (*monopole*); Aux Vignes-Rondes; village Gevrey-Chambertin including the *lieu-dit* Les Marchais; village Nuits-Saint-Georges including the *lieux-dits* Les Argillats, Les Lavières, Les Athées. Plus a large domaine in the Côte Chalonnaise, based in Mercurey, some of the produce of which is sold under the name of Domaine de la Croix-Jacquelet.

While Maison Faiveley is a *négociant* François Faiveley is in the fortunate position of being able to supply most of his requirements - certainly at the top end of the scale - from his own family domaine. And he intends to keep it that way. He has no wish to expand beyond a point where he feels he cannot personally supervise and guarantee the evolution and quality of every bottle that leaves his cellar door.

This is one of the greatest sources of quality wine in the whole of Burgundy. The wines are outstandingly clean, rich, balanced and concentrated, and the best are hand-bottled without filtration, and say so on the label.

See Profile, page 434.

CHRISTIAN GAVIGNET-BETHANIE ET FILLES

12 ha: owned and *en fermage*. Nuits-Saint-Georges *premier cru* in Les Poulettes, Aux Damodes, Les Chaignots; village Nuits-Saint-Georges including the *lieu-dit* Les Athées; Côte-de-Nuits-Villages.

The *filles*, Christine and Claire, are as much involved as the parents here, especially on the sales and marketing side, the family being an assiduous attender of food and wine fairs throughout the country. All the stems are used, the wine ferments at a maximum temperature of 25°C. Only 5 per cent of the barrels are renewed each year. I have found most of the wines rustic here. And I was not altogether surprised to find that one of the daughters had absolutely not the faintest idea what a *saignée* is.

PHILIPPE GAVIGNET

9.80 ha: owned and *en fermage*. Nuits-Saint-Georges *premier cru* in Les Chaboeufs, Les Bousselots; village Nuits-Saint-Georges including the *lieu-dit* Les Argillats, and a tiny bit of Nuits-Saint-Georges *blanc*; Côte-de-Nuits-Villages.

There are a number of Gavignets in Nuits-Saint-Georges. This is the best. Philippe, born in 1961, took over from his father Michel in 1992. He leaves 25 per cent of the stems in his *premier cru* vinifications, cold macerates for five days, holds the temperature at 30-32°C and uses between a quarter and a third new wood. Good, substantial, vigorous wines here. In 1994, for the first time, he produced a barrel of white Nuits-Saint-Georges, from Gouges clones planted in the Argillas.

★★HENRI GOUGES

14.50 ha: *en fermage* (family owned). Nuits-Saint-Georges *premier cru* in Les Saint-Georges, Les Vaucrains, Chaines-Carteaux, Clos-des-Porrets-Saint-Georges (*monopole*); Les Pruliers, Les Chaignots; Les Perrières (*blanc*); village Nuits-Saint-Georges.

If domaines could be doyens, this would be the doyen of the commune, having bottled and sold its wine direct since the 1920s. Today the two cousins - Pierre, who looks after the vines, and Christian, the wine - are in charge, grandsons of the late Henri, who died in 1967. After a blip in the early 1980s quality is back on song here, and the results are magnificent, but not for those who expect plump, vibrant, oaky wines. The Gouges style is for austerity, compactness and a minimum of new oak. Patience is required, and expected.

See Profile, page 454.

HOSPICES DE NUITS-SAINT-GEORGES

8.10 ha: owned. Nuits-Saint-Georges *premier cru* in Les Saint-Georges, Les Didiers (*monopole*), Les Forêts, La Rue de Chaux, Les Boudots, Les Murgers, Les Corvées-Pagets, Aux Vignes-Rondes; village Nuits-Saint-Georges.

Smaller and less well-known than the Hospices de Beaune, but with a rather better track-record of quality wine-making in recent years, this is a fine estate. The *premiers crus*, under the names of their donators, are sold by auction on the Sunday prior to Palm Sunday, after a tasting at the Clos-de-Vougeot. The quality in the final bottle depends, of course, on who does the subsequent *élevage*. As with its Beaune counterpart, there is a danger of over-oaking.

DOMINIQUE LAURENT

Dominique Laurent – his notice board slyly says Dom. Laurent, leading the innocent to believe he is a domaine – is a new star in the Côte d'Or firmament. Formerly a pastry chef, and with the girth to prove it, he was bitten by the wine bug, moved to Nuits, and set about buying up the odd cask here and there from some of the leading growers in the Côte-de-Nuits. Quantities are minuscule, the approach is determinedly 'hands off', and the wines are for those who like lots of oak (Laurent often racks from new to new, i.e. to give his wines, as he puts it, '200 per cent' new oak). It is early days, for his first vintage was 1992 – hence the lack of star-rating – but the results are undeniably pure, concentrated and of high quality. We'll see how they develop in bottle.

FERNAND LECHENAUT ET FILS

9.0 ha: owned and *en fermage/métayage*. Clos-de-la-Roche (8 a); Nuits-Saint-Georges *premier cru* in Les Damodes, Les Cailles, Les Bousselots; Chambolle-Musigny *premier cru* (Les Plantes, Les Borniques); village Nuits-Saint-Georges; village Vosne-Romanée; village Chambolle-Musigny; village Morey-Saint-Denis.

Following the death of Fernand Lechenaut in 1986, his sons Vincent and Philippe have made a major shift towards domaine-bottling. Total destemming, three to six days' maceration *à froid*, fermentation temperatures up to 35°C and from one-third to one-half (100 per cent for the Clos-de-la-Roche) new oak. Good succulent wines with plenty of dimension.

FRANÇOIS LEGROS

4.8 ha: owned and *en fermage/métayage*. Nuits-Saint-Georges *premier cru* in Les Bousselots, Les Perrières, Les Roncières; Chambolle-Musigny *premier cru* Les Noirots; Vougeot *premier cru* Les Cras; Morey-Saint-Denis *premier cru* in Clos-Sorbé, Les Millandes, La Riotte; village Nuits-Saint-Georges; village Chambolle-Musigny.

This is an impressive roll-call, which even if does not add up to much, at least affords a reasonable quantity in each appellation: for none of the parcels is less than a quarter of a hectare. François Legros, born in 1958, started to exploit the family domaine in 1988, having been *régisseur* for the Domaine Ponnelle for a decade after his studies at the Beaune *Viti*.

He retains 10–20 per cent of the stems, macerates at 18°C for four to five days, ferments at a maximum temperature of 33°C and uses 10–20 per cent new oak. The results so far are variable.

COMTESSE MICHEL DE LOISY

3 ha: owned and *en fermage*. Clos-de-Vougeot (67 a); Vougeot *premier cru* Les Cras; village Nuits-Saint-Georges.

The family of Françoise de Loisy-Loquin, an attractive woman in her early forties, were once big movers in the Crémant de Bourgogne market, owners of the brands Moingeon-Guéneau and Labouré-Goutard. All this has gone, leaving only the Clos-de-Vougeot (the Vougeot, Les Cras is a recent addition) and some village Nuits-Saint-Georges. But this Françoise de Loisy now bottles herself, in a deep, dark cellar in an alley towards the southern end of the village.

The wines, to quote Anthony Hanson, are not for the faint-hearted, though destemmed totally, they are given a long maceration, and come out black, tannic and inky, obstinately old-fashioned. But there is richness underneath.

In 1995 part of the Clos-de-Vougeot (48 of 65 a) was sold off.

BERTRAND MACHARD DE GRAMONT

4 ha: owned and *en fermage*. Village Nuits-Saint-Georges, including the *lieux-dits* Les Hauts-Pruliers and Les Allots; village Vosne-Romanée in the *lieu-dit* Les Réas.

Bertrand Machard de Gramont is the brother of Arnaud, who has his headquarters in Prissey and operates a much larger domaine (see page 154), and ex-husband of Chantal Lescure, whose equally sizeable domaine is now marketed by the Cottin brothers of Labouré-Roi. For the full history concerning this family and its somewhat scandalous past I refer readers to Remington Norman's *Great Domaines of Burgundy.*

There is careful wine-making here, and hand-bottling without filtration: all the benefits of a lack of economies of scale when you have a perfectionist at hand. But my experience of the wines in bottle is limited.

ALAIN MICHELOT

7.66 ha: owned and *en fermage/métayage.* Nuits-Saints-Georges *premier cru* in Les Saint-Georges, Les Vaucrains, Les Cailles, Les Fôrets, Les Chaignots, La Richemone, Les Champs-Perdrix; Morey-Saint-Denis *premier cru* Les Charrières; village Nuits-Saint-Georges; village Morey-Saint-Denis.

Alain Michelot is a large, bluff, friendly individual in his early fifties, his ginger hair and beard now greying, and has his headquarters in a recently extended cellar off the main road which runs through the middle of Nuits. No stems, four to five days' maceration, vinification at a maximum temperature of 30°C and 30 per cent new oak is the recipe. And the results are usually good (the Saint-Georges and Vaucrains vines are currently quite young). They'd be even better if Michelot didn't crop *'une bonne cinquante'* (50hl/ha) and reduced his harvest to 40 or so. But a good *cave* in which to compare a *gamme* of *premiers crus.*

PRIEURÉ-ROCH

11 ha: owned and *en fermage.* Clos-de-Vougeot (62 a); Chambertin, Clos-de-Bèze (1 ha) (owned by the Domaine Marion); Vosne-Romanée *premier cru* Les Suchots; village Vosne-Romanée including the *lieux-dits* Clos-Goilotte (*monopole*) and Les Hautes-Maizières; Nuits-Saint-Georges *premier cru* Clos-des-Corvées (*monopole*).

Henri-Frédéric Roch, *co-gérant* of the Domaine de la Romanée-Conti, and his wine-maker, Philippe Pacalet, operate out of a converted garage, almost opposite the Hotel La Côte d'Or in the middle of Nuits. He took on the *fermage* of the Domaine Marion's Clos-de-Bèze in 1994.

Prices are very high here, the single-vineyard village Vosnes being even more expensive than many growers' *premiers crus.* But I find the wines slight and uninteresting.

HENRI ET GILLES REMORIQUET

8 ha: owned and *en fermage/métayage.* Nuits-Saint-Georges *premier cru* in Les Saint-Georges, Les Damodes, Les Bousselots, La Rue de Chaux; village Nuits-Saint-Georges including the *lieu-dit* Les Allots.

Father Henri is now *en retraite* and it is the tall, *sympa*, bespectacled Gilles Remoriquet who is in charge here: up to 15 per cent of the stems, a brief cold maceration, fermentations up to 32°C at the start and then prolonged at 28-30°, and 10-20 per cent new oak. These are good, rich, meaty wines, typical Nuits-Saint-Georges. They need time.

*THOMAS-MOILLARD

32.74 ha: almost entirely owned (only some Hautes-Côtes is farmed). Chambertin (5 a); Chambertin Clos-de-Bèze (24 a); Romanée-Saint-Vivant (17 a); Bonnes-Mares (15 a); Clos-de-Vougeot (60 a); Corton, Clos-du-Roi (84 a); Corton-Charlemagne (23 a); Vosne-Romanée *premier cru* in Les Malconsorts, Les Beaux-Monts; Nuits-Saint-Georges *premier cru* in Clos-de-Thorey (*monopole*), Clos-des-Grandes-Vignes (*monopole*), Les Forêts, Les

Richemones, Les Murgers; Beaune *premier cru* Les Grèves; village Nuits-Saint-Georges; village Savigny-lès-Beaune, *rouge et blanc*.

An impressive line-up, and very impressive quality, curiously unrecognised in the outside world. The wines here are intensely coloured, pure, backward and very concentrated, with a sort of cool aloofness which comes from relatively lowish fermentation temperatures (below rather than above 30°C), no stems and long *cuvaisons*. About 30 per cent new oak is used, so this element does not get exaggerated either.

Most of the domaine is cultivated by outsiders on a *métayage* basis, but Thomas-Moillard, the domaine end of *négociants* Moillard-Grivot, have arranged things so that they buy in the *métayer*'s share of the fruit and vinify it all themselves.

See Profile, page 641.

PRÉMEAUX: GROWERS AND *NÉGOCIANTS*

BERTRAND AMBROISE

14 ha: owned and *en fermage/métayage*. Clos-de-Vougeot (17 a), Corton, Le Rognet (50 a), Corton-Charlemagne (20 a); Nuits-Saint-Georges *premier cru* in Les Vaucrains, La Rue de Chaux; Pommard *premier cru* Les Saussilles; village Vosne-Romanée in the *lieu-dit* Les Damodes; village Nuits-Saint-Georges; village Pommard; village Saint-Aubin *blanc*; Côte-de-Nuits-Villages.

Bernard Ambroise's growing domaine - the Clos-de-Vougeot and the Vosne-Romanée were new in 1993, the Gevrey and the Pommard in 1991 - has its origins in the vines of his father-in-law Michel Dupasquier, under whose name, up to 1990, much of the wine appeared. These are big wines, with plenty of fruit and guts, but I find they lack grace.

*DOMAINE DE L'ARLOT

14 ha: owned. Romanée-Saint-Vivant (25 a); Vosne-Romanée *premier cru* Les Suchots; Nuits-Saint-Georges *premier cru* in Clos-des-Forêts-Saint-Georges (*monopole*), Clos-de-l'Arlot (*monopole*) *rouge et blanc*; Côte-de-Nuits-Villages in the *monopole* Clos-du-Chapeau; Beaune *premier cru* Les Grèves.

In 1987 the insurance group AXA, owners of Bordeaux's Château Pichon-Longueville-Baron and other estates, bought the moribund Clos-de-l'Arlot, and installed Jean-Pierre de Smet, a disciple of Jacques Seysses of the Domaine Dujac, to run it.

The cellar is splendid (so too is the newly renovated château) and Smet's wine-making is meticulous, closely following his master's methods. This is an address for those who wish to be seduced by Nuits on the light side (especially the Clos-de-l'Arlot itself), not for those who seek hand-to-hand combat. There is also - and in reasonable quantity, for a whole hectare is under vine - a white Nuits-Saint-Georges.

See Profile, page 326.

**JEAN-JACQUES CONFURON

7 ha: owned. Romanée-Saint-Vivant (50 a); Clos-de-Vougeot (50 a); Vosne-Romanée *premier cru* Les Beaux-Monts; Chambolle-Musigny *premier cru* (from Les Châtelots and Les Feusselottes); Nuits-Saint-Georges *premier cru* in Les Boudots, Les Chaboeufs; village Chambolle-Musigny; village Nuits-Saint-Georges in the *lieu-dit* Les Fleuriers; Côte-de-Nuits-Villages.

The origins of this domaine lie with the Noëllat estate in Vosne-Romanée, and the vines have passed through the female side for a couple of generations since. The owners are now Alain and Sophie Meunier, Sophie being *née* Confuron. Quality has improved considerably here in recent years, helped by a new *cuverie* and extended cellar constructed in the late 1980s, and is now of the very highest order, with low harvests and a firmly *biologique* approach to the viticulture. A small percentage of stems is left, the wine cold macerated for five days, fermentation temperatures are maintained at 30°C and up to 100 per cent (especially for the American customers) new oak is used. Sometimes I find the American *cuvées* a bit exaggerated in this last respect, but the quality of the wine is classy, poised and very fine. Alain Meunier's wine deserves greater recognition. He also has a *négociant's* licence (Féry-Meunier) and a separate cellar in Savigny-lès-Beaune for the Côte-de-Beaune he buys in.

See Profile, page 403.

DUBOIS ET FILS

20 ha: owned and *en fermage*. Nuits-Saints-Georges *premier cru* in Les Forêts-Saint-Georges, Clos des Argillières; Savigny-lès-Beaune *premier cru* Les Narbantons; village Chambolle-Musigny in the *lieu-dit* Les Combottes; village Vosne-Romanée in the *lieu-dit* Les Chalandins; village Nuits-Saint-Georges including the *lieu-dit* Les Longecourts; village Savigny-lès-Beaune in the *lieu-dit* Les Gollardes; village Beaune in the *lieu-dit* Blanche Fleur; Côte-de-Nuits-Villages.

This is a large family domaine, all the members of three generations seemingly actively involved, and the welcome is warm. The wine is made without the stems, vinified at 28-34°C after a few days' cold soaking, and 20 per cent new oak is used. During the *élevage* the wines are aged partly in tank, partly in wood, the receptacles being interchanged when the wines are racked. I find them quite structured, but somewhat lean and unstylish.

MACHARD DE GRAMONT

23 ha: owned and *en fermage*. Vosne-Romanée *premier cru* Les Gaudichots; Nuits-Saint-Georges *premier cru* in Les Damodes, Les Vallerots; Savigny-lès-Beaune *premier cru* in Les Guettes, Les Vergelesses (*blanc*); Beaune *premier cru* in Les Choucheux, Les Coucherias; Pommard *premier cru* Le Clos-Blanc; village Chambolle-Musigny in the *lieu-dit* Les Nazoires; village Nuits-Saint-Georges including the *lieux-dits* En-La-Perrière-Noblot, Les Hauts-Poirets; village Aloxe-Corton; village Chorey-lès-Beaune; village Savigny-lès-Beaune; village Beaune in the *lieu-dit* Les Epenottes; village Pommard; village Puligny-Montrachet in the *lieu-dit* Les Houillères.

Most of this domaine, run by Arnaud Machard de Gramont, has been built up since the family split in 1983. The headquarters, a cavernous farmhouse, is down by the railway-line in Prémeaux-Prissey. The fruit is destalked, macerated for a long time with plenty of *pigeage*, kept up to twenty-four months in oak, up to 50 per cent of which is new, and bottled without fining. The results are well-coloured, full-bodied and rich, but rather brutal and four-square.

PONNELLE/CLAUDINE DESCHAMPS

These two domaines are run by Jean-Claude Boisset SA.

Ponnelle: 12.9 ha. Charmes-Chambertin (73 a); Bonnes-Mares (70 a); Le Musigny (21 a); Clos-de-Vougeot (36 a); Corton, Clos-du-Roi (49 a); Nuits-Saint-Georges *premier cru* in Les Damodes, Clos-des-Corvées-Pagets; Beaune *premier cru* in Les Grèves, Clos-du-Roi; village Chambolle-Musigny; village Vougeot *rouge et blanc*; Marsannay.

Claudine Deschamps: 6.73 ha. Gevrey-Chambertin *premier cru* in Bel-Air, Les Goulots; village Gevrey-Chambertin.

The winery is down in the back streets of Prémeaux. I had hoped, when I heard that responsibility for the wines had been given to Bernard Repolt of Jaffelin, that we might begin to see some exciting things here. Not so far.

In October 1996 Boisset further increased his vineyard holdings when he acquired the 20 ha Domaine Louis Violland as well as the associate *négociant* company. This estate owns land in Beaune *Premier Cru*, Corton-Charlemagne, Puligny-Montrachet and Savigny-lès-Beaune, Les Marconnets.

CHÂTEAU DE PRÉMEAUX

10 ha: owned and *en fermage*. Nuits-Saint-Georges *premier cru* Les Argillières; village Nuits-Saint-Georges; Côte-de-Nuits-Villages.

Alan Pelletier and his wife have a fine old building which dates back to medieval times and shows signs of the fortifications necessary in more lawless periods of history. Sadly the wine, stored partly in wood, partly in tank, is pleasantly fruity, but lacks real flair and concentration.

★DANIEL RION ET FILS

18.45 ha: owned and *en métayage*. Clos-de-Vougeot (73 a) (This is the only piece not owned. The *métayage* arrangement came to an end in 1995); Chambolle-Musigny *premier cru* Les Charmes; Vosne-Romanée *premier cru* in Les Chaumes, Les Beaux-Monts; Nuits-Saint-Georges *premier cru* in Clos-des-Argillières, Les Vignes-Rondes, Les Hauts-Pruliers; Les Terres-Blanches (both *rouge et blanc*); village Chambolle-Musigny; village Vosne-Romanée; village Nuits-Saint-Georges including the *lieux-dits* Les Lavières, Les Grandes-Vignes; Côte-de-Nuits-Villages.

This is an important domaine, whose public face is Patrice Rion, one of three brothers who work with their father out of a large, modern, Swiss-chalet-type building on the main road just above the Grandes-Vignes *climat*. Quality is high and dependable here, and if I find a 'house style' in the wines, a family resemblance, I don't quibble too much because the wines are clean and fruity and the tannins have become increasingly sophisticated over the years.

See Profile, page 591.

MICHELLE AND PATRICE RION

2.00 ha: owned. Village Chambolle-Musigny from the *lieu-dit* Les Cras.

The wines are made by the same person (this is the private domaine of Patrice and his wife Michelle), yet seem to have an individuality and a flair I sometimes search for in the parental establishment. I look forward to the time when this domaine expands into some *premier cru* land.

COMBLANCHIEN, CORGOLOIN AND SOUTHERN CÔTE-DE-NUITS-VILLAGES

The Clos-de-la-Maréchale marks the end of the appellation of Nuits-Saint-Georges. Between here and Ladoix, the first village of the Côte-de-Beaune, a distance of some 3 kilometres, the Côte is broken up by a series of marble quarries, and the stone, detritus and dust therefrom disfigure and dirty the landscape. This is a sort of no-man's land. But there are some vines. Together with the land of Brochon and Fixin these are the vineyards of Côte-de-Nuits-Villages (though Fixin has the right to village status as well, see page 54).

You get the feeling, however, that marble quarrying is more important than viticulture. Above the Nuits-Saint-Georges *premier cru* of Forêts they produce the pink limestone of Prémeaux. Here at Comblanchien it is milky coffee in colour. The stone is popular throughout France. According to Anthony Hanson it was used to decorate Orly airport. And it is much seen locally, on the counters of the *boulangeries* and *charcuteries* of Nuits-Saint-Georges, for example.

Part of Prémeaux-Prissey as well as the villages of Comblanchien and Corgoloin produce Côte-de-Nuits-Villages in these parts. The areas under vine are as follows: Prémeaux-Prissey (17.27 ha), Comblanchien (58.76 ha), and Corgoloin (84.41 ha). This is a total of 160.84 ha, rather more than half of the total permitted area in theory, and in fact, as Fixin is mostly bottled as such, the lion's share of the appellation.

A list of recommended Côte-de-Nuits-Villages sources is given on page 158.

PRÉMEAUX-PRISSEY

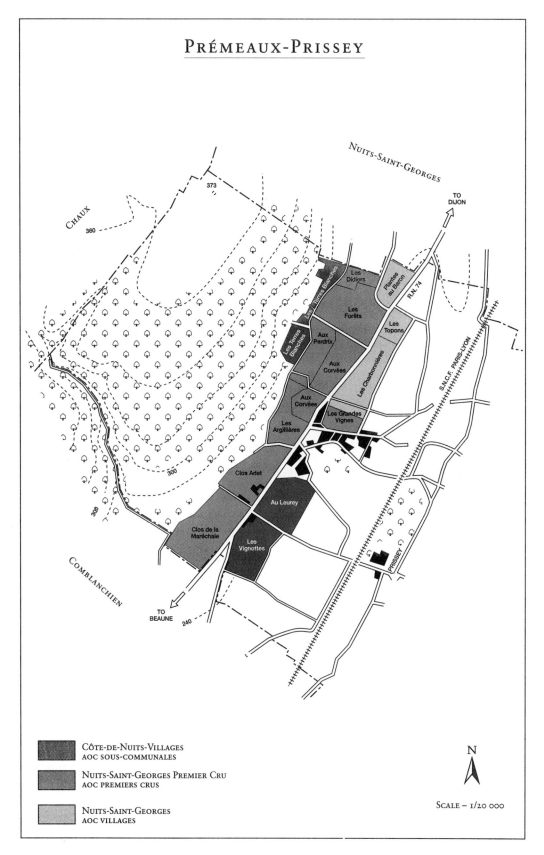

NUITS-SAINT-GEORGES

TO DIJON

CHAUX
360
373

Les Vignes Blanches
Les Didiers
Plantes au Baron
R.N. 74

Les Forêts

Les Terres Blanches
Aux Perdrix
Les Topons

Aux Corvées

Les Chaboeufières

S.N.C.F. PARIS-LYON

Aux Corvées

Les Argillières

Les Grandes Vignes

Clos Arlet

300

Au Leurey

300

Clos de la Maréchale

Les Vignottes

PRISSEY

COMBLANCHIEN

TO BEAUNE
240

Côte-de-Nuits-Villages
AOC SOUS-COMMUNALES

Nuits-Saint-Georges Premier Cru
AOC PREMIERS CRUS

Nuits-Saint-Georges
AOC VILLAGES

N

SCALE – 1/20 000

THE GROWERS

CHOPIN ET FILS, COMBLANCHIEN

13 a: owned and *en métayage*. Nuits-Saint-Georges *premier cru* Les Murgers; village Nuits-Saint-Georges; village Chambolle-Musigny; Côte-de-Nuits-Villages (*rouge et noir*).

André Chopin, now retired, is the brother of Daniel (see below), this domaine being run today by his son Yves and grandson Arnaud. Some 10 per cent of the stems are retained, the wine vinified at 25-30°C, and there is about 30 per cent new wood. In 1995 the domaine bought a pneumatic press. Quality here is good but not exceptional. A curiosity is the white Côte-de-Beaune-Villages. The Chopins' Côte-de-Nuits-Villages is neat, oaky and very stylish.

DANIEL CHOPIN-GROFFIER, COMBLANCHIEN

7 ha: owned and *en fermage*. Clos-de-Vougeot (35 a); Nuits-Saint-Georges *premier cru* Les Chaignots; village Vougeot; village Nuits-Saint-Georges; Côte-de-Nuits-Villages.

Escape from the main road by the mass of marble quarries, plunge into the village, and you will find a number of enterprising growers among the sad mixture of old houses and new bungalows that is today's Comblanchien. Daniel Chopin, small and balding, is the leading example. He is now approaching retirement, and what was once a 10 ha estate is being passed on to his children, principally his son-in-law Hubert Chauvenet of Nuits-Saint-Georges (see page 106). He no longer makes any Chambolle-Musigny, for instance, and the details above may well no longer be valid by the time this book appears on the shelves. What he does make is ripe, rich, vigorous and stylish. Chopin's wines last well.

RENÉ DURAND, COMBLANCHIEN

15 ha: owned and *en fermage/métayage*. Corton, Les Rognets (35 a); village Nuits-Saint-Georges; village Ladoix; village Aloxe-Corton; Côte-de-Nuits-Villages.

Durand is, or was the last time I met him, president of the *Syndicat Viticole* of Comblanchien. He acquired his Corton when the Charles Vienot estate was broken up and sold off in 1984. Apart from this wine, which can be good, I am underwhelmed with these wines, which spend part of their life in large oak *foudres*.

GÉRARD JULIEN, COMBLANCHIEN

12 ha: owned and *en fermage*. Echézeaux (23 a); Corton, Les Renardes (16 a); village Nuits-Saint-Georges; village Aloxe-Corton; Côte-de-Nuits-Villages.

M. Julien bottles a year after the vintage, to preserve the fruit, and retrieve the barrels for next year's crop. I have had some good wines from this cellar, but the results are uneven.

HAUTES-CÔTES-DE NUITS AND HAUTES-CÔTES-DE-BEAUNE

Above and behind the Côte d'Or in the Hautes-Côtes the countryside is peaceful and pastoral. There are valleys and plateaux, pastures and woodland, rocky outcrops and gently sloping fields. Up here it is cooler, often more exposed, and the soils are less fine, less complex. Only in carefully selected sites is the aspect suitable for the vine. This is the area known as the Hautes-Côtes.

There have always been vines in the Hautes-Côtes. Before phylloxera there were as many as 4,500 hectares in cultivation, although much was planted with non-'noble' grapes. But then, as elsewhere, the vineyards declined and as recently as 1968 there were barely 500 hectares of vines.

That was the nadir, but resurrection was already at hand. *Appellation Contrôlée*, with the prefix Bourgogne, had been bestowed on the Hautes-Côtes in 1961, and in 1968 a co-operative cellar called Les Caves des Hautes-Côtes - not up the back of beyond but sensibly on the main road outside Beaune where no passer-by could fail to notice it - was established. This now vinifies and sells 25 per cent of the combined appellation. Meanwhile, on the research station at Echevronne above Pernand-Vergelesses suitable clones of the Pinot Noir were being developed, and following a visit to Bordeaux, trials were being carried out with high-trained vines, thus avoiding the worst of the frost and, because they could be planted further apart for mechanical cultivation, thus economising on the expense of planting and maintaining new vineyards. Since then the fortunes of the Hautes-Côtes have blossomed. There are now well over 1,000 hectares under vine and production in 1994 reached a total of 57,724 hl (22,865 in the Hautes-Côtes-de-Nuits and 34,859 in the Hautes-Côtes-de-Beaune).

From a geographical point of view the two parts of the Hautes-Côtes do not quite correspond with the division between the Côte-de-Nuits and the Côte-de-Beaune. The northern section, the Hautes-Côtes-de-Nuits, begins at Ruelle-Vergy above Chambolle and continues to Echevronne and Magny-lès-Villers. Echevronne is in the Hautes-Côtes-de-Beaune while the land at Magny is divided between the two. There is then a separate section of the Hautes-Côtes-de-Beaune which begins at Mavilly-Mandelot above Beaune and extends south to Sampigny-lès-Maranges and Cheilly-lès-Maranges near Santenay.

There is a little - 15 per cent - white Hautes-Côtes wine. In my view this is less successful than the red wine, tending to be a bit lean. The customer is better off with a Mâcon villages. But it is the red wine, exclusively from the Pinot Noir, which is the corner of the appellation and the key to its deserved recent success. This is a wine to buy in a warm, ripe year like 1990 or 1989 - the wines are then delicious, and some of the best value in Burgundy. Avoid the wines of a cold rainy vintage.

THE GROWERS

This being a book about the Côte d'Or - the *vignoble* and not the *département* - I confine myself to those growers situated in the Hautes-Côtes who have their important holdings lower down.

DENIS CARRÉ, MELOISEY

11 ha: owned and *en fermage*. Pommard *premier cru* Les Charmots; village Pommard; Auxey-Duresses *premier cru* Les Duresses; village Saint-Romain (*rouge*); village Meursault in the *lieu-dit* Les Tillets.

The continually expanding Carré domaine dates from 1976, and its headquarters are in Meloisey, above Pommard. The reds are largely destemmed, depending on wine and vintage, and vinified in cement vats - for the better wines - or revolving *cuves auto-pigeantes*. Bottling takes place from twelve months onwards. This is one of the bigger and better of the Hautes-Côtes domaines.

YVES CHALEY, CURTIL-VERGY
DOMAINE DU VAL VERGY

Yves Chaley owns no vines in the Côte d'Or, but he is a *négociant* as well as an Hautes-Côtes grower, buying finished wine rather than grapes or must, and also *cuvées* from the Hospices de Nuits. A third occupation is that of *chambre d'hôtes* - he takes in bed and breakfast guests. Loquacious, rubicund and forthright in his opinions about wine in general and some of his colleagues in particular, a couple of hours' tasting with him can be an entertaining - if exhausting - experience.

FRANÇOIS CHARLES ET FILS, NANTOUX

11 ha: owned. Volnay *premier cru* in Clos-de-la-Cave-des-Ducs (*monopole*), Les Fremiets; Beaune *premier cru* Les Epenottes; village Volnay; village Pommard; village Meursault.

I find the Fremiets more interesting than the Volnay monopoly here (it is situated within the village, a stone's throw south of that of D'Angerville), and the Epenottes is a good example of what is rarely a riveting piece of Beaune. Another good Hautes-Côtes-de-Beaune source.

CLAUDE CORNU, MAGNY-LÈS-VILLERS

14.27 ha: owned and *en fermage/métayage*. Corton (61 a); village Ladoix; village Savigny-lès-Beaune; village Pernand-Vergelesses; Côte-de-Nuits-Villages.

Claude Cornu is a friendly, no-nonsense peasant who retains 20 per cent of the stems, vinifies at a relatively cool temperature, and uses about one-third new wood (more for the Corton). A few years ago he built a brand-new aircraft-hangar-type cellar. This coincided with the 1989 vintage. Things then began to look up. The 1989s and 1990s were definitely good. But sadly this improvement has not been sustained. Too often the wines are a bit rustic.

LUCIEN JACOB, ECHEVRONNE

14.60 ha: owned and *en fermage*. Beaune *premier cru* in Les Toussaints, Les Cent-Vignes, Les Avaux; Savigny-lès-Beaune *premier cru* in Les Vergelesses (*blanc et rouge*), Les Peuillets; Pernand-Vergelesses *premier cru*; village Savigny-lès-Beaune *blanc et rouge*.

The tall, bearded Jean-Michel Jacob, aided by his wife Christine and his sister Chantal Forey (married to Régis Forey of Vosne-Romanée), runs this expanding domaine. The fruit is completely destemmed, cold soaked for two or three days, vinified at 32°C for three days, and then at 25-27°C for six to eight days. There is no new wood, but one-fifth of the barrels are one year old. Well-made, stylish wines here.

ROBERT JAYER-GILLES, MAGNY-LÈS-VILLERS

11 ha: owned. Echézeaux (54 a); Nuits-Saint-Georges *premier cru* Les Damodes; village Nuits-Saint-Georges in the *lieu-dit* Les Hauts-Poirets; Côte-de-Nuits-Villages.

Robert Jayer, tall, moustached, straight-backed (he looks like a caricature of a regimental sergeant-major), is a cousin of the Jayers of Vosne-Romanée, and works with his own son Gilles (*sic!*). He is a very firm believer in new oak: 100 per cent for everything, including his Hautes-Côtes. His top wines can take it and are certainly very good, but for the lesser wines this is definitely an acquired taste: one I do not share.

MAZILLY PÈRE ET FILS, MELOISEY

13 ha: owned and *en fermage*. Beaune *premier cru* in Les Vignes-Franches, Les Cent-Vignes, Les Montrevenots; Pommard *premier cru* Les Potures; Savigny-lès-Beaune *premier cru* Les Narbantons; village Beaune in the *lieux-dits* Clos-du-Bois-Prévot (*monopole*) and Le Clou (*blanc*); village Pommard; village Volnay; village Monthélie; village Meursault.

Frédéric Mazilly is now in charge at this important domaine, father Pierre having retired. I would like to see a bit more attention to detail: smaller harvests, greater elegance.

THIERRY VIGOT-BATTAULT, MESSANGES

3.34 ha: owned and *en métayage*. Echézeaux (40 a); Vosne-Romanée *premier cru* Les Gaudichots; village Nuits-Saint-Georges in the *lieu-dit* Le Bas-de-Combe.

In the three *climats* quoted above, Thierry Vigot exploits the vines of Mme Gilberte Thomas, while he has his own vines in lesser areas, including that oddity, a *vin de pays de la Côte d'Or blanc*. Total destemming, a few days' cold soaking, vinification at 28-30°C, and a judicious but above all flexible attitude toward the use of new oak is the recipe here. I like the man. I like his wines. They are full, rich and concentrated. Sometimes they are a bit too sturdy. Sometimes they could do with a bit more finesse.

CÔTE-DE-BEAUNE-
VILLAGES

Unlike the Côte-de-Nuits-Villages, the Côte-de-Beaune-Villages is not a *terroir* specific appellation. Côte-de-Beaune-Villages can come from any one, or a combination, of fourteen communes and appellations from Ladoix to Maranges. These are: Auxey-Duresses, Blagny, Chassagne-Montrachet, Chorey-lès-Beaune, Ladoix, Maranges, Meursault, Monthélie, Pernand-Vergelesses, Puligny-Montrachet, Saint-Aubin, Saint-Romain, Santenay and Savigny-lès-Beaune.

While domaine-bottling growers use the appellation mainly for the produce of young vines and other lesser *cuvées* they deem not worthy of the village name, *négociants* may buy up wine sold under the village names and then make up their own blends.

The declarations are confusing. Statistics from the BIVB (*Bureau Interprofessionel des Vins de Bourgogne*) give a very small figure for the production of Côte-de-Beaune-Villages. Looking at the figures produced by the *Union Générale de Syndicats* one can see that this figure corresponds to already amalgamated wine, i.e. where a grower has vinified the produce of two villages together. In the UGS statistics one also notices that, say, Chorey has two declarations: one as Chorey-lès-Beaune, the other as Chorey, Côte-de-Beaune. If we take this latter figure as that which will be bottled as Côte-de-Beaune-Villages, we can add up a figure of about 2,600 ha of vines and production of 11,600 hl under this appellation, which is for red wines only. (But this figure does not include any contribution from Maranges, which is in the Saône-et-Loire *département* and not included, infuriatingly, in the UGS statistics). The main villages producing these wines, in order of size of provision, are Chorey-lès-Beaune, Auxey-Duresses, Chassagne-Montrachet, Saint-Romain, Ladoix, Saint-Aubin and Pernand-Vergelesses. The remainder only produce token amounts of Côte-de-Beaune-Villages.

The wine itself is soft, plump and fruity: an unpretentious Pinot Noir for early drinking: a useful gap between Bourgogne *rouge* and Hautes-Côtes and the cheapest of the village wines.

CORTON

AND THE WINES OF LADOIX, ALOXE-CORTON AND PERNAND-VERGELESSES

The Côte-de-Beaune begins, if not with a bang, then with a splendid isolated mound, the hill of Corton. This is an egg-shaped escarpment – the egg lying on its flatter side – and on top of it, perched like a toupée, is the Forêt de Corton, owned by Prince Florent de Mérode, *seigneur* of nearby Serrigny. Vines flow down on all suitable sides of this hill, from above Ladoix, facing almost as much north as east, via Aloxe, to above Pernand where they face as much west as south. All this is *grand cru*: the biggest in Burgundy, representing over one-third of the total *grand cru* surface area.

Not all of the land, arguably, is of true *grand cru* potential. Certainly not all the wine produced from it is of *grand cru* standard. But these vines are shared between these three communes. So it is logical to include them in a single chapter. And it is equally logical to deal with the *grand cru* first.

LADOIX-SERRIGNY

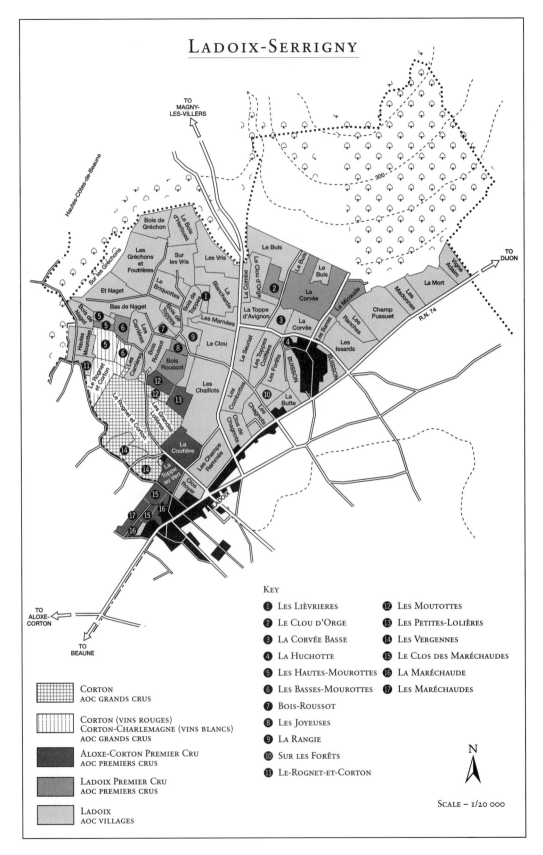

KEY

1. LES LIÈVRIERES
2. LE CLOU D'ORGE
3. LA CORVÉE BASSE
4. LA HUCHOTTE
5. LES HAUTES-MOUROTTES
6. LES BASSES-MOUROTTES
7. BOIS-ROUSSOT
8. LES JOYEUSES
9. LA RANGIE
10. SUR LES FORÊTS
11. LE-ROGNET-ET-CORTON
12. LES MOUTOTTES
13. LES PETITES-LOLIÈRES
14. LES VERGENNES
15. LE CLOS DES MARÉCHAUDES
16. LA MARÉCHAUDE
17. LES MARÉCHAUDES

CORTON
AOC GRANDS CRUS

CORTON (VINS ROUGES)
CORTON-CHARLEMAGNE (VINS BLANCS)
AOC GRANDS CRUS

ALOXE-CORTON PREMIER CRU
AOC PREMIERS CRUS

LADOIX PREMIER CRU
AOC PREMIERS CRUS

LADOIX
AOC VILLAGES

N

SCALE – 1/20 000

CORTON AND CORTON-CHARLEMAGNE

In total there are some 160.20 hectares of *grand cru* land on the slopes of Corton hill. Split up between the three villages this represents 22.43 ha in Ladoix, 120.51 in Aloxe-Corton and 17.26 in Pernand-Vergelesses. Out of the 160.20 ha, 71.88 *can* produce Corton-Charlemagne: this includes all the Pernand land, 48.57 ha in Aloxe-Corton, and 6.05 in Ladoix. I say *can*. The growers have the option in the Corton-Charlemagne appellation to plant either Pinot Noir or Chardonnay. And to complicate matters further, they also have the right – though few exercise it – to plant Chardonnay elsewhere on the hill, and to produce Corton *blanc* from it. There is, as Hugh Johnson puts it, a slight Alice in Wonderland air about the legislation on the Corton hill.

If you look at a map you will see that the area marked Corton-Charlemagne is that facing south-west towards the village of Pernand-Vergelesses and across the valley towards Savigny. The red wine area seems to be that overhanging Ladoix and Aloxe-Corton. In reality some red wine is produced in the lower slopes of the Charlemagne vineyard, while white wine – Corton-Charlemagne – is made all the way round the hill, albeit at the top of the slope.

As a further complexity, the hill is divided into a number of *climats*, and there will appear, prefixed by Corton on the labels: Corton, Clos-du-Roi, Corton, Les Bressandes, and so on. Le Corton is a *lieu-dit* in its own right. But Corton *tout court* will be a mixture of several different *lieux-dits*. And I must also mention the brand of Maison Latour here, a major proprietor in the area: Château Corton-Grancey.

HISTORY

Charlemagne, Charles the First and Great, as was befitting for a man who was Holy Roman Emperor and effectively the ruler of the western civilised world, was a giant of a man. He towered over his subjects, dominating them as much physically as by the force of his personality. One of his many domaines and the one producing one of his favourite wines was at Corton, itself named, one interpretation suggests, after an obscure first-century Roman emperor named Orthon: Curtis (domaine) d'Orthon become contracted to Corton. As with certain vineyards in Germany the story is related that, noticing the snows were always first to melt on this particular slope, Charlemagne ordered vines to be planted there, and lo, these produced excellent wine.

At the time the wine was red, but, as Charlemagne grew older, and his beard whiter, his wife Luitgarde, ever watchful over the dignity of her spouse, objected to the majesty of her emperor being degraded by red wine stains on his beard and suggested that he switched to consuming white wine. White grapes were commanded to be planted on a section of the hill, Corton-Charlemagne was born, and it continues still.

According to the Burgundian historian Camille Rodier, that part of the *vignoble* donated by Charlemagne to the *Collegiale* of Saulieu in AD 775 corresponds exactly to the current domaine of the Bonneau du Martray family, owners of the largest domaines and one of the best sections of the hill. Other later owners included Modoin, Bishop of Autun, who donated his Corton vines to the cathedral there in AD 858, the Abbots of Citeaux, the Knights Templar, the Dukes of Burgundy, Charlotte Dumay, who left her land to the Hospices de Beaune in 1534, and the Kings of France, whose tenure 400 years ago is still commemorated in the *climat* Corton, Clos-du-Roi.

The earliest extant document referring to Corton-Charlemagne dates back from 1375 and refers to a lease of the 'Clos le Charlemagne' by the Chapitre de Saint-Androche-de-Saulieu to a local farmer. A century later the abbot tried to wriggle out of this contract. In 1620 the lessee was a M. Esmonin. Again, ten years later, the clergy attempted to have the agreement revoked. In 1791, following the Revolution, the land was sold as a *bien national* and valued at 10,800 *livres*.

Legend apart, white wine production from the Chardonnay grape on the hill of Corton is a recent development. Jullien, in his *Topographie de Tous les Vignobles Connus*, 1824, makes no mention of white Corton. Le Corton is one of his *vins rouges de première classe*, and the reds from Pougets, Charlemagne and Les Bressantes (*sic*) among those of the *troisième classe*. There is no note of white Aloxe or Pernand at all.

By mid-century, however, the Chardonnay had arrived. Dr Lavalle in his *Histoire et Statistique de la Vigne et des Grands Vins de la Côte d'Or*, published in 1855, speaks of Pinot Noir on the mid-slope and lower lying ground and what he terms Pinot Blanc on the upper parts. In the 16 hectare section of Corton-Charlemagne lying in the commune of Aloxe, Messieurs Gouveau, de Grancey, Chantrier, Paulet and the Hospices de Beaune are listed as the main proprietors, while in the 19 hectares of land across the border in Pernand, only M. Bonneau-Véry (now the Bonneau du Martray family) is worthy of note. '*On ne recolte presque que des vins blancs dans ce climat*,' he states (the harvest in this vineyard is almost only white wine).

By the end of the century the owners included Louis Latour, who had acquired the Grancey domaine, and Jules Senard, two families who are still important proprietors in the area. Twenty years later, Camille Rodier brought out the first edition of his classic *Le Vin de Bourgogne*. In the 1948 edition he speaks of the Chardonnay grape being planted more and more widely, in what was by that time formally the appellation of Corton-Charlemagne, 'over the previous thirty years'. (This is a repeat of what he says in the first edition.) This grape, he writes, gives white wines of a fine golden colour and full flavour, the flavour combining cinnamon and gunflint.

As with the Charlemagne side of the hill, the Aloxe facing slopes also largely belonged in ecclesiastical hands in the Middle Ages. The monks of the Abbey of Sainte-Marguerite, up in the neighbouring valley of the river Rhoin near Bouilland, were one of the first to exploit the vinous possibilities of the *climat*, having received a donation of land in 1164. The Cistercians were soon to follow, as were the Templars, just as they were on the other side of the hill.

From the beginning of the seventeenth century onwards, as the power of the church waned, the land on Corton hill was progressively annexed by the local bourgeoisie, either by buying it outright, or by a simple matter of a cash lease rather than a more uncomfortable *métayage* arrangement. During the reign of Louis XV a number of important acquisitions were made. Two Dijon gentlemen, M. de Vergnette-Lamotte and M. le Bault, bought a sizeable amount of land from the Abbey at Citeaux; M. Larbalestier, another local, became proprietor of the vineyards of the Abbey of Sainte-Marguerite; and the brothers Thiroux of Beaune took over the famous *climat* of Clos-du-Roi. Another arrival was M. du Tillet, squire of the village of Serrigny (as well as Aloxe and Pernand). Le Bault was further to increase his domaine. His wife Jacqueline, as vivacious and intelligent as she was beautiful (there is a fine portrait dating from 1755 by Greuze) was in her own right heiress of 500 *ouvrées* (nearly 21 hectares) in Aloxe. It was the Bault family who constructed Corton-Grancey.

It was through Madame la Belle, as he addressed Jacqueline le Bault, that Voltaire acquired a taste for Corton (and it is to him that we owe our gratitude for having commissioned the Greuze portrait). Voltaire was an admirer, but Madame was not to be tempted. The one-sided passion was to continue for many years, during which many dozens of bottles of Bault Corton were despatched to Geneva or Ferney or wherever it was that Voltaire was nursing his frustration at the time. Incidentally the orders were for both red and white wine, in equal quantities. Sadly, however, Voltaire, great man of many parts, was not a real wine-lover. He was knowledgeable about wine, as you would expect a man of his catholicity of interests to be, but the nuances of connoisseurship passed him by. To him wine was merely a beverage.

The French Revolution caused its upsets in Corton as much as elsewhere. Much of the vineyard was declared *biens nationaux*. Other land changed hands as the fortunes of the *ancien régime* families withered and a newly rich bourgeoisie emerged. It is interesting to note that an *ouvrée* of Clos-du-Roi was worth half as much again as an *ouvrée* of Corton-Charlemagne. But as the Charlemagne was largely planted in Gamay at that time one wonders why the premium was not higher.

As we move further into the nineteenth century, into the picture come a number of familiar names. The ubiquitous Jules Ouvrard, proprietor of Clos-de-Vougeot, the Domaine de la Romanée-Conti and the Domaine de la Pousse d'Or, reconstituted the Clos-du-Roi, already divided. Jean Latour bought the château from the Granceys which had formerly belonged to the Baults. The Geisweiler family bought vineyards in Le Corton, Les Renardes and Les Languettes. Other important landowners included Auguste Dubois, mayor of Dijon, and the poet and gentleman of letters, Simon Gauthey.

Dr Lavalle, already mentioned, divided the red wines into four categories. The *têtes de cuvées* are Le Corton, Clos-du-Roi, Les Renardes and Les Chaumes (the upper part of Le Corton producing delicious white wine, he notes). The *premiers crus* include most of what is now the rest of the *grand cru rouge* vineyard: Les Bressandes, Les Perrières, Les Fiètres, Les Languettes, Les Pougets, Les Meix and La Vigne-au-Saint. Aloxe wines, he writes, are the firmest and most definitive of all the wines of the Côte-de-Beaune, and those of Corton itself possess these characteristics to the greatest degree.

When the commission that was to become the INAO delimited the territories of Aloxe, Ladoix and Pernand in 1936 they broadly followed the classification of Dr Lavalle, adding part of Les Maréchaudes, Les Paulands, Les Vergennes and Le Rognet, on the Ladoix side, and other parcels below the road that runs from Aloxe to Pernand to the *grand cru*. The result is that Aloxe possesses the least amount of *premier cru* vineyard of all the main Burgundy communes. Today there are, as I have said, across the three villages, a total of 160 hectares of land which can produce either Corton or Corton-Charlemagne.

THE SOIL AND WINE

The Chardonnay is planted on the upper slopes in a whitish-coloured marl with a high clay content on a hard limestone rock base – Oxfordian rather than the older Bathonian or Bajocian in the Côte-de-Nuits. Further down the slope there is more iron and pebbles but less clay in the soil, and the colour is redder. Here the Pinot produces the better wine, particularly on the more easterly facing slopes above Aloxe and Ladoix. Today, however, growers in Le Corton and elsewhere can get a better price for white wine than for red, and a switch of colour can be noticed. I remember Jean-Marc Voarick once telling me that the next time they come to replace their vines in the Languettes *climat* he would change to Chardonnay rather than Pinot.

On the Pernand side of the hill the soil is flinty, and the white wine will have more austerity, be steelier than that coming from above Aloxe. The whites from Aloxe *climats* are softer and *plus flatteur* in their youth, and develop faster.

This was particularly noticeable in the hot 1983 vintage. After a few years in bottle many of the Charlemagnes produced on the Aloxe-Corton side were already drying out, being high in alcohol and low in acidity. Those from the Pernand side, notably that of Bonneau du Matray, were still fresh and crisp.

The reverse, of course, is true with red wine. Pinots Noirs on the Pernand vines just do not get enough sun for long enough in the day – except in exceptional vintages – to get beyond ripeness to real concentration. Those above Aloxe-Corton with the classical aspect and

270-300 metres of altitude, in the middle of the slope, will provide the most perfect examples of red Corton. Clos-du-Roi is generally considered the best, followed in no particular order by Les Bressandes, Le Corton, Les Perrières, Les Pougets, Les Grèves and Les Renardes.

There are a large number of separate Corton *lieux-dits*. The most commonly declared separately are: Les Bressandes, Les Carrières, Les Chaumes, Clos-de-la-Vigne-au-Saint (*monopole* of the Domaine Latour), Clos-des-Meix (*monopole* of the Domaine du Comte Senard), Clos-des-Cortons-Faiveley (*monopole* of the Domaine Faiveley), Le Clos-du-Roi, Les Combes, Le Corton, Les Grandes-Lolières, Les Grèves, Les Languettes, Les Maréchaudes, Les Hautes-Mourottes, Les Basses-Mourottes, Les Perrières, Les Pougets, Le Rognet-et-Corton and Les Vergennes.

Surface Area: 160.19 ha • **Average Production:** 3,530 ha *rouge* (466,000 bottles)
2,075 hl *blanc* (274,000 bottles)

1994 declaration:
101 ha as Corton *rouge*
2 ha as Corton *blanc*
48.9 ha as Corton-Charlemagne

Principal Proprietors:

Corton-Charlemagne: *Bonneau du Martray (9.50 ha); *Louis Latour (9.00 ha); Bouchard Père et Fils (3.25 ha); Roland Rapet (2.50 ha); Château de Corton-André, La Reine Pédauque (2.12 ha); *Louis Jadot (1.88 ha); Marius Delarche (1.20 ha); Maurice Chapuis (1.12 ha); Dufouleur (1.09 ha); Albert Bichot/Domaine de Clos-Frantin (1.08 ha); Robert et Raymond Jacob (1.07 ha); Roux Père et Fils (1.00 ha); Michel Voarick (95 a); *Joseph Drouhin (91 a); Pierre Marey et Fils (89 a); *Michel Juillot (80 a); *Pierre Dubreuil-Fontaine (77 a); Baron Thenard (sold by *Remoissenet Père et Fils) (65 a); Rollin (63 a); *Joseph Faiveley (62 a); Pierre et Françoise Lassagne (59 a); Régis Pavelot (59 a); Chartron et Trébuchet (57 a); Hippolyte Thévenot/Antonin Guyon (55 a); *Pierre Bitouzet (53 a).

Growers with less than half a hectare whose wines can be recommended include: *Adrien et Jean-Claude Belland (35 a); *Bruno Clair (34 a); *Jean-François Coche-Dury (36 a); *Leroy (43 a); *Christophe Roumier (20 a); *Tollot-Beaut (24 a); *Thomas-Moillard (23 a).

The Hospices de Beaune possess 38 a (*Cuvée* Françoise de Salins) as well as 32 a of Chardonnay planted in Corton-Vergennes (Corton *blanc Cuvée* Paul Chanson).

Corton Rouge: Louis Latour (17.66 ha); Hospices de Beaune (6.45 ha); Château de Corton-André/La Reine Pédauque (5.90 ha); *Comte Senard (4.22 ha); *Prince Florent de Mérode (3.80 ha); Maurice Chapuis (3.15 ha); *Joseph Faiveley (2.97 ha); Domaine Baron Thénard (sold by *Remoissenet Père et Fils) (2.68 ha); *Chandon de Briailles (2.55 ha); Michel Voarick (2.37 ha); *Pierre Dubreuil-Fontaine (2.35 ha); Capitain-Gagnerot (2.21 ha); Hippolyte Thévenot/Antonin Guyon (1.94 ha); Didier Meuneveaux (1.94 ha); Adrien et Jean-Claude Belland (1.72 ha); *Maillard Père et Fils (1.70 ha); Marius Delarche (1.70 ha); *Louis Jadot (1.54 ha); Tollot-Beaut (1.51 ha); Chevalier Père et Fils (1.30 ha); Roland Rapet (1.25 ha); *Michel Juillot (1.20 ha); Gaston et Pierre Ravaut (1.00 ha); Michel Gaunoux (1.00 ha).

Growers with less than a hectare whose wines can be recommended include: *Thomas-Moillard (84 a); *Leroy (50 a); *Méo-Camuzet (45 a); *Joseph Drouhin (25 a).

The Hospices de Beaune offer the following Corton *rouge cuvées*: Charlotte Dumay (Les Renardes, Les Bressandes, Clos-du-Roi) and Docteur Peste (Les Bressandes, Les Chaumes, Les Voirosses, Clos-du-Roi, La Fièrte, Les Grèves).

Corton-Charlemagne is quite a different wine from the *grands crus* of Puligny and Chassagne. There should be a steely backbone, a raciness, which fleetingly suggests a *grand cru* Chablis. There will probably be a higher acidity. There should certainly be a certain austerity, and a need for long ageing, as much as a decade, before the wine comes round. This will not be because it has the pent-up, concentrated intensity of a Montrachet. It won't quite have that. But because it is a wine of sufficient size, depth and structure to require sufficient time to round off. But, like red Corton, sadly there are more indifferent producers than exciting ones.

Vintages, too, do not necessarily follow those of the south. The weather pattern may not always be similar and this will affect both the state of the fruit and the date it will arrive at maximum fruition. Corton-Charlemagne successes follow as much the successful vintages in red Corton and red wines generally as they do in the best years for Meursault, Puligny and Chassagne.

As for the red wines: what is the essential character of a Corton *rouge*? Firstly it is the biggest red wine of the Côte-de-Beaune. This is not so much a factor of its girth or its tannins – Pommards can make as large an impression – but in terms of its depth, its grip and its necessity to be aged before it is ready. Red Cortons need time to round off and naturally they last well in bottle. When they are young there is an austerity, almost a hard edge to a red Corton, the fruit has a herbaceous, leafy aspect to it. You have to wait to get the generosity.

And Corton, in the main, is only a second division *grand cru* for red wines. Often it is a bit lean. Only the vines from the heart of the appellation, from Clos-du-Roi and a few of the accompanying *climats*, can aspire to greatness. Only these seem to have the fat underneath the structure which will give rise when fully mature to that magic natural sweetness we look forward to on the finish of a great Burgundy.

LADOIX

Ladoix-Côte-de-Beaune, it says on the label, as if it might be confused with other Ladoix elsewhere – after all there are several Pouillys – but also because this is one of a number of lesser Côte-de-Beaune villages which have the option of also selling their wine under the label of Côte-de-Beaune-Villages.

Ladoix is the first Côte-de-Beaune commune one reaches as one drives south towards Beaune from Nuits-Saint-Georges. The vineyards begin north of the village up and behind the hamlet of Buisson. There is a road here just by the restaurant Les Coquines (which I recommend) where you can drive up the valley towards Magny-lès-Villers in the Hautes-Côtes. The appellation ends in the middle of the village of Ladoix. One step more and you are technically in the commune of Aloxe-Corton. There are even Aloxe-Corton *premiers crus* in the commune of Ladoix.

Much of the *vignoble*, then, is the continuation of the hill of Corton, as it turns round almost towards the north. The village wines lie up in less well-exposed slopes, lower down on the flatter land, and along the road towards the border with the Côte-de-Nuits. There are a sprinkling of *premier crus* on either side of the road to Magny.

It is this road, rather than the artificial line on the map a few hundred metres to the north, which really marks the difference between the Côtes of Nuits and Beaune, for it is here that the geology changes. North is Comblanchien limestone, south a younger Jurassic rock: Bathonian gives way to the softer, more marly Oxfordian, and the wine as a result changes too.

The village itself is jolly and bustling, and seems to consist almost entirely of houses which give on to the main road or the one which reaches it perpendicularly from the adjoining hamlet of Serrigny. There are a number of good growers, most of them remarkably welcoming. And prices for Ladoix *rouge* and *blanc* (the appellation covers both) are cheap. This is not a village the snobs and label hunters are likely to stop at. The wines are soft and plump, and if only they could be a bit more dependable and a bit less rustic, would present excellent value for money. But the locals are making progress all the time.

THE VINEYARD

Premiers Crus: There are seven *premiers crus*, in whole or in part. On the northern side we have Le Clou d'Orge (part), La Corvée (part) and La Micaude. On the Corton side lie Les Hautes-Mourottes (part) and Les Basses-Mourottes (both of which are also the extension of *grand cru* Corton), Bois-Roussot (part) and Les Joyeuses (part). In total these cover 14.38 ha and produce about 550 hl (72,600 bottles) of red wine and 58 hl (6,340 bottles) of white wine per year.

Village Wine: There are 117.92 ha of village land under vine. This will produce some 5,300 hl of wine a year. Much of this is sold as Côte-de-Beaune-Villages. In 1994 3,000 hl (400,000 bottles) of red wine was declared as Ladoix *rouge* and 556 hl (734,000 bottles) as Ladoix *blanc*.

THE *PREMIERS CRUS*

LE CLOU D'ORGE (1.58 HA) • LA CORVÉE (7.14 HA)
(*monopole* of the Domaine Capitain-Gagnerot)

LA MICAUDE (1.64 HA)

The wines from the northern *premiers crus* of Ladoix come from halfway up the slope (240–250 m), are oriented almost due south on a gentle incline, and have Comblanchien limestone as their base rock. There is a nice sturdy masculinity about these wines, and usually a better colour and grip than those from the hills opposite. But they can be less elegant.

Recommended Sources:
La Corvée: Chevalier Père et Fils, Edmond Cornu, André et Jean-Pierre Nudant (Ladoix).
La Micaude (monopole): Capitain-Gagnerot (Ladoix).

LES HAUTES-MOUROTTES (0.55 HA) • LES BASSES-MOUROTTES (0.93 HA)

BOIS-ROUSSOT (1.78 HA) • LES JOYEUSES (0.76 HA)

These are lighter, softer wines, with red fruit flavours such as cherry and redcurrant rather than black (*cassis*, blackberry). They mature quicker. They can be a bit thin and rustic.

THE GROWERS

CACHAT-OCQUIDANT ET FILS

11 ha: owned and *en fermage/métayage*. Corton, Clos-de-Vergennes (*monopole*) (1.5 ha); Aloxe-Corton *premier cru* Les Maréchaudes; village Ladoix; village Aloxe-Corton; village Pernand-Vergelesses.

Jean Marc-Cachet and his vigorous seventy-eight-year-old father Maurice make very good wine. There is plenty of new wood, and no old wood, which is just as important.

CAPITAIN-GAGNEROT ET FILS

16 ha: owned. Clos-de-Vougeot (17 a); Corton-Charlemagne (34 a); Corton, Les Renardes (33 a); Corton (1.82 ha); Aloxe-Corton *premier cru* Les Moutottes; Savigny-lès-Beaune *premier cru* Les Charnières (part of Les Lavières); Ladoix *premier cru* La Micaude (*monopole*); village Ladoix *rouge*; village Ladoix *blanc* in the *lieu-dit* Les Gréchons; village Aloxe-Corton; village Pernand-Vergelesses; village Chorey-lès-Beaune; Côte-de-Nuits-Villages.

The Capitain mansion is set back from the main road through Ladoix, an island in a sea of vines. Beyond is the winery. The Capitains, Patrice, Michel and father Roger, offer a wide range. And the standard is generally good. There is total destemming, a *cuvaison* for twelve to fourteen days at 25-28°C (maximum 30°) and 12.5 per cent new wood, but no barrels of over five years of age.

CHEVALIER PÈRE ET FILS

11 ha: owned and *en fermage*. Corton-Charlemagne (36 a); Corton, Le Rognet (1.15 ha); Ladoix *premier cru* La Corvée; village Ladoix *blanc* in the *lieu-dit* Les Gréchons; village Ladoix *rouge*; village Aloxe-Corton; Côte-de-Nuits-Villages.

Claude Chevalier, tall, handsome, in his forties, is now in charge here, as his father Georges, who first started bottling in 1959, is *en retraite*. Quality can vary here.

EDMOND CORNU ET FILS

12.50 ha: owned and *en fermage*. Corton, Les Bressandes (56 a); Aloxe-Corton *premier cru* Les Moutottes; Ladoix *premier cru* La Corvée; village Aloxe-Corton; village Savigny-lès-Beaune; village Ladoix including the *lieu-dit* Les Carrières; village Chorey-lès-Beaune *rouge et blanc*.

The genial, hospitable Edmond Cornu reached sixty in 1995, and has begun to hand more and more over to his son Pierre. Between none and 15 per cent of the stems are retained, fermentation takes place at 32-34°C, and there is 15 per cent new oak. Neat wines usually, sometimes a bit light, sometimes a bit rustic.

ROBERT ET RAYMOND JACOB

10 ha: owned. Corton, Les Carrières (50 a); Corton-Charlemagne (from the Hautes-Mourottes (1.00 ha); Aloxe-Corton *premier cru* Les Valozières; village Aloxe-Corton; village Ladoix *rouge et blanc*.

The brothers Jacob, no close relation to those in Echevronne, run this estate out of a splendidly large cellar, extended in 1990, in the hamlet of Buisson. The wines, of which the best receive one-third new wood, are supple, fruity and for the medium term.

JEAN-PIERRE MALDANT

7.34 ha: owned and *en fermage*. Corton (73 a); Corton-Charlemagne (33 a) (Les Maréchaudes, Les Grandes-Lolières); Aloxe-Corton *premier cru* Les Valozières; Savigny-lès-Beaune *premier cru* Les Peuillets, Les Fourneaux); village Aloxe-Corton including the *lieu-dit* Les Maréchaudes; village Savigny-lès-Beaune; village Ladoix including the *lieu-dit* Les Chaillots; village Chorey-lès-Beaune *rouge et blanc*.

I first encountered M. Maldant's wines when I scored his Corton-Charlemagne 1985 well at a blind tasting arranged by Claude Chapuis when he was writing his book. I then went to taste *sur place* and found a charming man in his fifties in a small cellar bang in the middle of Ladoix. He vinifies with 30 per cent of the stems for his Cortons, but none for the rest, lets the temperature rise as high as 35°C, and uses 10 per cent new wood. I like the man. I like his wines.

MICHEL MALLARD ET FILS

14 ha: owned and *en fermage*. Corton, Les Renardes (65 a); Corton, Les Maréchaudes (35 a); Corton (from Le Rognet and Les Lolières) (30 a); Ladoix *premier cru* Les Joyeuses; Savigny-lès-Beaune *premier cru* Les Serpentières; Aloxe-Corton *premier cru* (from Valozières, Toppe-au-Vert and Les Petits-Lolières); village Ladoix; village Aloxe-Corton; Côte-de-Nuits-Villages.

Tall, dark, handsome Patrick Mallard has taken over from his father here. Picking is by machine. The domaine likes to use 30 per cent new wood with a high toast. Sadly the wines inside do not inspire.

MAURICE MARATRAY

12.50 ha: owned and *en fermage*. Corton-Charlemagne (33 a); Corton, Les Bressandes (71 a); Corton, Les Grandes-Lolières (9 a); village Aloxe-Corton; village Ladoix *rouge et blanc*; village Chorey-lès-Beaune.

Next to Jean-Marc Cachat you will find Maurice Maratray. His wife was *née* Dubreuil-Fontaine of Pernand-Vergelesses. In a yard behind their house is a big modern *chai* with a cellar underneath. Some 8 per cent of the stems are retained, the red wine fermented at 28-30°C and 10 per cent new wood is used. Variable quality. But I liked the 1993 Corton-Charlemagne.

⋆PRINCE FLORENT DE MÉRODE

11.38 ha: owned and leased out *en métayage*. Corton, Clos-du-Roi (57 a); Corton, Les Bressandes (1.19 ha); Corton, Les Renardes (51 a); Corton, Les Maréchaudes (1.53 ha); Aloxe-Corton *premier cru*; village Pommard in the *lieu-dit* Clos-de-la-Platière; Ladoix *premier cru blanc* Les Hautes-Mourottes; village Ladoix *rouge* in the *lieu-dit* Les Chaillots.

Prince Florent de Mérode lives in the Château de Serrigny, a splendid moated castle, in part dating from the Middle Ages. His family has been here since 1700, and his wife is a member of the Luc-Saluces family of Château d'Yquem.

Quality has risen significantly in recent years. Today the grapes are totally destemmed, having been picked over to discard the unripe and rotten, and are bruised on a *table de tri*. There is a new wine-maker (it used to be Pierre Bitouzet of Savigny, into whose family hands some of the vines are leased out on a share-cropping basis), one-quarter new oak, and no filtration. The wines are now made in a spacious, insulated and temperature-controlled *chai* converted out of old stables and cowsheds, with an impressive cellar at the end, opposite the Château de Serrigny. More importantly, I feel, the vines are cropped to a lower *rendement*. The Prince de Mérode's wines are well coloured, rich, concentrated, individual and stylish. This is today one of the best sources for a range of quality Corton.

ANDRÉ ET JEAN-RENÉ NUDANT

12.55 ha: owned. Corton, Les Bressandes (61 a); Corton-Charlemagne (15 a); Aloxe-Corton *premier cru* La Coutière; Ladoix *premier cru* La Corvée; village Aloxe-Corton in the *lieu-dit* Les Valozières; village Savigny-lès-Beaune; village Ladoix including the *lieu-dit* Les Buis; village Ladoix *blanc* in the *lieu-dit* Les Gréchons; village Chorey-lès-Beaune.

The Nudant premises, now run by son Jean-René, are on the main road at the north end of the village. No stems, fermentation temperatures for the red wines at 30-32°C, and 10–20 per cent new oak is the rule here, and the wines are good. The domaine also produces a single vineyard Bourgogne *rouge*, La Chapelle-Notre-Dame, which comes from a twenty-five-year-old vineyard around the exquisite Romanesque chapel which lies under Valozières on the Aloxe side of the village.

PRIN

5.20 ha: owned. Corton, Bressandes (75 a); village Savigny-lès-Beaune; village Aloxe-Corton; village Ladoix.

The childless Louis Prin has now retired, leaving his nephew Jean-Luc Boudrot in charge here. The wines can be kept two years or more in cask if there are no orders for them, which is not to be recommended. They are also rustic.

GASTON ET PIERRE RAVAUT

14.50 ha: owned and *en fermage*. Corton, Les Bressandes (43 a); Corton, Les Hautes-Mourottes (58 a); Aloxe-Corton *premier cru* (Les Fournières and Les Valozières); Ladoix *premier cru* in La

Corvée, Les Basses-Mourottes, Bois-Roussot; village Ladoix including the *lieu-dit* Le Clos-Royer.

The quality has declined here since Pierre Ravaut took over from his father: a particular pity given the range this estate has to offer. From zero to 50 per cent of the stems are incorporated into the vinification, which is thermo-regulated at 38°–33°C, and the *cuvaison* lasts ten to fifteen days. Some 10 per cent new oak is utilised. But the results are weedy.

ALOXE-CORTON

The sleepy little village of Aloxe (the x is pronounced s) lies halfway up the hill away from the main road. It possesses neither bar nor village shop. Its inhabitants must make the 6 kilometre journey to Beaune for sustenance or conviviality. What it does have are some of the oldest cellars in Burgundy, dating from monastic times, and several fine buildings decorated with the typically Burgundian tiled roofs in different colours.

The remit of Aloxe's vineyards greedily stretches more than halfway round the hill towards Pernand-Vergelesses, and way back up and behind the village of Ladoix into territory which would much more logically be the fief of that commune, giving it the lion's share of the *grand cru* of Corton and the *premier cru* vineyards which lie beneath it. Aloxe-Corton can be red or white, but the proportion of white produced today is insignificant.

Aloxe-Corton, not just because it has adopted the suffix of the famous *grand cru*, is a better-known and rather more expensive wine that Pernand-Vergelesses and Ladoix. The vineyards are in general more favourably placed, oriented towards the south and south-east. The basic limestone is softer here than further north, decomposing into a flaky rock known as *lave*. On top of this in the *premier cru* vineyards the soil is quite deep, red in colour and rich in iron. There is a high pebble content, particularly on the Pernand-Savigny side (Les Vercots, Les Guérets, for example), these stones having been washed down the valley of the river Rhoin, which flows out from the village of Savigny-lès-Beaune.

This *terroir* gives a wine which is well-coloured, nicely sturdy: a meaty wine with a rich, robust colour and plenty of depth. The amount of *premier cru* vineyard, at 38 ha, is small, however. The *grand cru* has absorbed most of the land on the slopes.

THE VINEYARD

Premiers Crus: There are thirteen *premiers crus*, in whole or in part, some of which is technically in the commune of Ladoix. In Aloxe-Corton we have Les Chaillots (part); Clos-des-Maréchaudes; Les Fournières; Les Guérets; Les Maréchaudes; Les Meix (Clos-du-Chapitre); Les Paulands (part); Les Valozières (part); and Les Vercots. In Ladoix we have much more of the Clos-des-Maréchaudes and Les Maréchaudes; La Coutière; Les Petits-Lolières; Les Moutottes and La-Toppe-au-Vert.

Many of these *premiers crus* are the lesser, downward slopes of areas which are *grand cru* Corton and share their names. Confusingly, at least one – Paulands – is *grand cru* at the top, *premier cru* in the middle, but only village AC at the bottom.

In total these comprise 37.59 ha and produce some 1,400 hl (195,000 bottles) of wine a year.

Village Wine: Village Aloxe-Corton runs all the way down to the N74. There are 89.71 ha producing 4,000 hl (528,000 bottles) of red wine and 23 hl (3,036 bottles) of white wine a year. The white wine is as likely to incorporate some Pinot Beurot (akin to the Pinot Gris) in its *encepagement* as not, and, though rare, is worth pursuing, for it has an interesting, individual flavour.

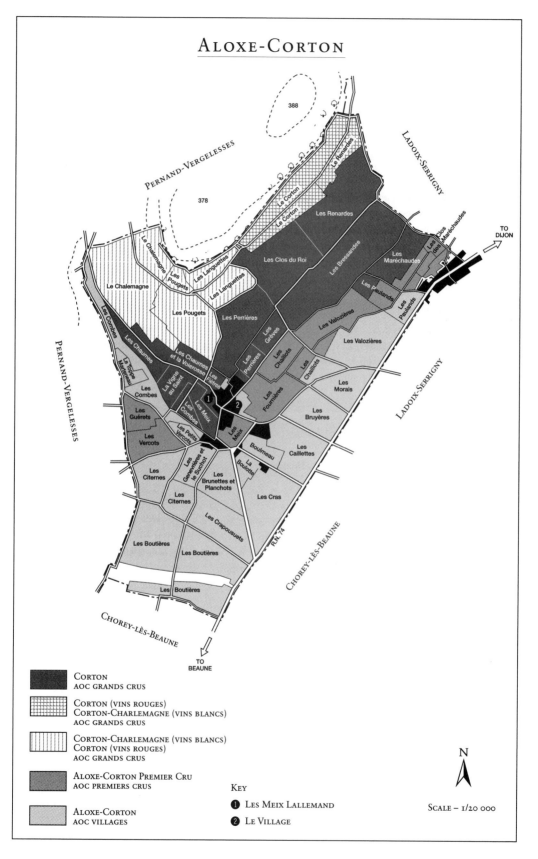

ALOXE-CORTON

388

PERNAND-VERGELESSES

378

Le Corton
Le Corton
Le Corton

Le Renardes

Les Renardes

LADOIX-SERRIGNY

Le Chalemagne

Les Languettes

Les Pougets

Les Languettes

Les Clos du Roi

Les Bressandes

Les Clos des Maréchaudes

TO DIJON

Le Chalemagne

Les Pougets

Les Perrières

Les Maréchaudes

Les Combes

Les Graves

Les Valozières

Les Paulands

Les Chaumes

Les Chaumes et la Voierosse

Les Perrières

Les Perrières

Les Chaillots

Les Valozières

Les Paulands

La Toppe Marteneau

La Vigne au Saint

Les Fietres

Les Chaillots

Les Morais

LADOIX-SERRIGNY

PERNAND-VERGELESSES

Les Combes

Les Meix

Les Fournières

Les Bruyères

Les Guérets

Les Combes

❶

❷

Les Petits Vercots

Les Meix

Les Vercots

Boulmeau

Les Caillettes

Les Citernes

Les Genevrières et le Suchot

La Boulotte

Les Brunettes et Planchots

Les Cras

Les Citernes

Les Crapousuets

R.N.-74

CHOREY-LÈS-BEAUNE

Les Boutières

Les Boutières

Les Boutières

CHOREY-LÈS-BEAUNE

TO BEAUNE

Corton
AOC GRANDS CRUS

Corton (VINS ROUGES)
Corton-Charlemagne (VINS BLANCS)
AOC GRANDS CRUS

Corton-Charlemagne (VINS BLANCS)
Corton (VINS ROUGES)
AOC GRANDS CRUS

Aloxe-Corton Premier Cru
AOC PREMIERS CRUS

Aloxe-Corton
AOC VILLAGES

KEY

❶ LES MEIX LALLEMAND

❷ LE VILLAGE

N

SCALE – 1/20 000

THE PREMIERS CRUS

LES MOUTOTTES (0.94 HA) • LES PETITS-LOLIÈRES (1.64 HA)
LA COUTIÈRE (2.52 HA) • LA TOPPE-AU-VERT (1.72 HA)
CLOS-DES-MARÉCHAUDES (1.41 HA) • LES MARÉCHAUDES (2.30 HA)
LES PAULANDS (1.59 HA)

These seven small *premiers crus* comprise those above the village of Ladoix, where the orientation varies between just north of east to the south-east. The wines are quite a bit fuller than those of the Ladoix *premiers crus* of this sector, but are often a bit hard, even a bit lean, even a bit rustic. They lack the depth, succulence and elegance of both the *grands crus* better situated further up the slope and the *premiers crus* to the south. Few of these names are ever seen on their own, except for Les Maréchaudes.

Recommended Sources:
La Coutière: André et Jean-René Nudant (Ladoix).
Les Maréchaudes: Jean-Pierre Maldant (Ladoix).

LES VALOZIÈRES (6.59 HA) • LES CHAILLOTS (4.63 HA)
LES FOURNIÈRES (5.57 HA) • LES MEIX (CLOS-DU-CHAPITRE) (1.90 HA)

Directly under Les Bressandes, Les Perrières and Les Grèves – all part of the best section of Corton – three *premiers crus climats* provide the best of Aloxe-Corton. The wines combine body and richness, together with a minerally spice which comes from the iron in the soil. They keep well.

Recommended Sources:
Les Valozières: Jean-Pierre Maldant; André et Jean-René Nudant (Ladoix); Comte Senard (Aloxe-Corton).
Les Fournières: Tollot-Beaut (Chorey-lès-Beaune).

LES VERCOTS (4.19 HA) • LES GUÉRETS (2.56 HA)

These two *premiers crus* lie on the other side of the village towards Savigny-lès-Beaune, and are separated from the *grands crus climats* of Clos-des-Meix and La Vigne-au-Saint by a little dip in the terrain, only authorised for village wine. One sees few examples of Vercots, and I have never been offered pure Guérets, but my impression is of a slightly less sturdy wine than a Valozières, but not necessarily less rich or less interesting.

Recommended Sources:
Les Vercots: Tollot-Beaut (Chorey-lès-Beaune).

Didier Meuneveaux of Aloxe-Corton makes a very good *premier cru* blend of Les Guérets and Les Fournières. Patrick Bize of Savigny's Domaine Simon Bize produces a very good Aloxe-Corton *village* from Les Suchots, which is nearby.

THE GROWERS
MAURICE CHAPUIS

10 ha: *en fermage*. Corton-Charlemagne (1.12 ha); Corton (1.30 ha); Corton, Les Perrières (1 ha); Corton, Les Languettes (85 a); Aloxe-Corton *premier cru*; village Aloxe-Corton.

Maurice, son of Louis, has been in charge here since 1985. Every year when I come to call I hope to see the breakthrough from merely good to the one-star quality which I feel instinctively this *cave* is capable of producing. So far not yet. In 1995 a new extension to the cellar was constructed. Is this the sign?

No stems, three days' cold maceration, fermentation temperatures up to a maximum of 33–35°C and 15 per cent new wood. The Chapuis family is conscientious about not over-producing, but sells 50 per cent off in bulk. Perhaps the *négoce* gets all the plums.

COLIN PÈRE ET FILS

5 ha: owned and *en métayage*. Corton, Les Renardes (1 ha); Beaune *premier cru* in Les Avaux, Les Sizies; Savigny-lès-Beaune *premier cru* Les Peuillets; village Aloxe-Corton.

One of the delights of visiting this cellar is that you pass from one old cellar into an even older, vaulted second one, which is said to date from the thirteenth century. Some 25 per cent new oak is used for the Corton here, which in my experience is very good. Half the crop is sold off in bulk.

CHÂTEAU DU CORTON-ANDRÉ; PIERRE ANDRÉ
DOMAINE DE LA JUVINIÈRE;
DOMAINE DES TERRES-VINEUSES

50 ha: owned. Corton, Les Pougets (1.34 ha); Corton, Les Combes (57 a); Corton, Clos-du-Roi (96 a); Corton, Les Renardes (2.07 ha); Corton, Les Hautes-Mourottes (63 a); Corton (33 a); Corton-Charlemagne (2.12 ha); Clos-de-Vougeot (1.10 ha); Vosne-Romanée *premier cru* Les Chaumes; Aloxe-Corton *premier cru* including Les Chaillots; Savigny-lès-Beaune *premier cru* Clos-des-Guettes; village Gevrey-Chambertin; village Ladoix *rouge* (Clos-des-Chaignots *monopole*) and *blanc* (Le Rognet); village Aloxe-Corton; village Pernand-Vergelesses; village Savigny-lès-Beaune; village Chorey-lès-Beaune; village Meursault; Côte-de-Nuits-Villages, Clos-des-Langres (*monopole*).

This large domaine is associated with La Reine Pédauque, owner of the tourist-trapping cellars-to-visit by the northern entrance to the centre of Beaune. The château itself is grand, fifteenth century, surrounded by a park at the foot of the *grand cru* Les Perrières. But elsewhere in the village is a large box of a factory which disfigures the landscape. This belongs in an industrial estate and should never have been allowed to be built there.

On the face of it, the wine-making is as it should be, but the results are uninspiring. The curious thing is that none of the 'home team' seem to realise it. Do they never taste anyone else's wines?

FRANCK FOLLIN-ARVELET

2.8 ha: owned and *en fermage*. Aloxe-Corton *premier cru* in Clos-du-Chapitre, Les Vercots; village Aloxe-Corton.

The tall, lean, somewhat unkemptly bearded Franck Follin took over the vines of his father-in-law André Masson in 1993. He lives along the road to Savigny on the edge of the village, but stores his wines in a fine vaulted cellar in the centre. My experience of what he does, naturally, is limited, but what I have tasted seems promising, the Vercots being better than the Clos-du-Chapitre. He destems completely, vinifies up to 35°C, uses a mere 10 per cent new oak and bottles without filtration.

LOUIS LATOUR

45 ha: owned and *en fermage*. Chambertin (80 a); Romanée-Saint-Vivant, Les Quatre-Journeaux (1.00 ha); Corton (15 ha) (mainly sold as Château Corton-Grancey); Corton, Clos-de-la-Vigne-au-Saint (*monopole*) (2.66 ha); Corton-Charlemagne (9 ha); Chevalier-Montrachet, Les Demoiselles (50 a); Aloxe-Corton *premier cru* in Les Chaillots, Les Fournières; Pernand-Vergelesses *premier cru* Ile-des-Vergelesses; Beaune *premier cru* in Vignes-Franches, Les Perrières, Clos-du-Roi, Les Grèves; Pommard *premier cru* Les Epenots; village Aloxe-Corton; village Volnay.

Maison Louis Latour is, of course, a major *négociant*. This sizeable domaine, based in Aloxe-Corton, provides about 10 per cent of the firm's turnover, perhaps a quarter of its Burgundian requirements.

Latour is notorious for having a policy of pasteurisation (to 70°C) for its reds. These are never very highly coloured, but often a bit heavy in alcohol. Sometimes I find them somewhat confected, lacking freshness; though the top wines (the Romanée-Saint-Vivant and the Chambertin, but not the Corton-Grancey) are usually very good indeed. Standards dipped in the mid-1980s. Have they risen again? Let's wait until we see the 1990s as mature wines.

Latour's whites have always been more reliable, though again I find them sometimes a bit over-alcoholic, occasionally a bit sulphury. These, if not the reds, certainly deserve a star.

DIDIER MEUNEVEAUX

6 ha: owned and *en fermage/métayage*. Corton, Les Bressandes (26 a); Corton, Les Perrières (66 a); Corton, Les Chaumes (31 a); Aloxe-Corton *premier cru* (from Les Fournières, Les Guérets); Beaune *premier cru* in Les Reversées; village Aloxe-Corton; village Pernand-Vergelesses; village Chorey-lès-Beaune.

The youthful Didier Meuneveaux has only recently assumed responsibility at this family domaine, whose headquarters is a substantial *maison bourgeoise* at the entrance to the village. But the first results are promising. Half the stems are retained, the temperature of the fermentation allowed to rise to 32°C, and 20 per cent new wood is used during the maturation. Some 40 per cent of the harvest is sold off in bulk. I have been impressed here by the cleanliness and originality of these wines.

★COMTE SENARD

8.70 ha: owned. Corton, Clos-du-Roi (64 a); Corton, Les Bressandes (63 a); Corton, En Charlemagne (*rouge*) (40 a); Corton, Clos-des-Meix (1.65 ha); Corton (from Les Paulands) (63 a); Corton Blanc (from the Clos-des-Meix) (45 a); Aloxe-Corton *premier cru* Les Valozières; Beaune *premier cru* Les Coucherias; village Aloxe-Corton *rouge et blanc*; village Chorey-lès-Beaune.

The *sympa*, balding Philippe Senard, a youthful forty-eight, turned towards the oenologist Guy Accad in 1988, and it took him a couple of years to adapt the general principles to his own estate. No excessive new oak here. The wines are bottled after as much as two years, without fining or filtration. Senard's wines now taste much more 'typical', right from the start, and they have colour, intensity and plenty of individuality and elegance: a major source of fine Cortons.

See Profile, page 634.

DOMAINE DES VERGELESSES

6.85 ha: owned. Corton-Charlemagne (35 a); Savigny-lès-Beaune *premier cru* Les Vergelesses, *rouge et blanc*; village Savigny-lès-Beaune; village Chorey-lès-Beaune *rouge et blanc*; village Beaune.

The wines of this domaine are made by Philippe Senard, and must be sold entirely to private clients, as well as the owners themselves. I don't think I have ever seen them offered on the open market.

MICHEL VOARICK

9 ha: owned and *en fermage*. Corton, Clos-du-Roi (50 a); Corton, Les Bressandes (54 a); Corton, Les Renardes (50 a); Corton, Les Languettes (83 a); Corton-Charlemagne (95 a); village Aloxe-Corton; village Pernand-Vergelesses *rouge et blanc*.

Jean-Marc Voarick believes in old-fashioned methods: no destemming, lots of *pigeage*, temperatures up to 35°C, and no new wood for the red wines. The cellars are very cold, which is perhaps one of the reasons he bottles late. These are big, brutal wines. They can soften up while the fruit is still there in very rich years. But in general the flavours are too rustic, I find.

PERNAND-VERGELESSES

In Pernand-Vergelesses I sometimes get the feeling that I have been translated to some *vieille village perchée* in the south of France. There is as much vertical to it as horizontal. It's a pretty village full of old houses, sharp corners and steep alleys clinging to the side of a hill which overlooks the western side of the Bois de Corton. Opposite, therefore, is the Charlemagne part of the Corton *vignoble*. Pernand also commands a fine view back over the flatter land toward Beaune.

Apart from Corton and Corton-Charlemagne, the main part of Pernand's vineyard is on the east-facing slopes of the Bois Noël which separates the village from Savigny-lès-Beaune. There are five *premiers crus*, of which the best is the Ile-des-Vergelesses. There is rather more communal land up behind the villages than is generally realised, and here the vines of Pernand flow imperceptibly into those of the Hautes-Côtes. Here also are the remaining vines of Aligoté for which Pernand used to have a fine reputation. Most of this Aligoté has now been replaced by Chardonnay, for which the growers can command a higher price. Régis Pavelot, though, retains his old vines and makes a very serious example.

Village Pernand-Vergelesses, whether white or red – the former used to represent about a fifth of the total production, but is now double that – can be somewhat lean in lesser years, but is usually good value. The red wine has a little more weight than the average Ladoix or Chorey-lès-Beaune, and is less rustic. Maison Louis Jadot of Beaune produces good examples of both colours from a *premier cru monopole* called La Croix-de-Pierre, and Bernard Dubreuil-Fontaine and his daughter Christine have the monopoly of the Clos-Berthet, a village wine (the Pinots Noirs were uprooted in 1995, but the Chardonnays remain). White Pernand, when it is good, is cool, crisp and appley with individual, slightly herbal, flowery tones to it. A third good example of this colour is that made by François Germain at the Château de Chorey-lès-Beaune.

The *terroir* under the Bois Noël is relatively similar to that of the Corton hill. Up-slope we find silico-calcareous marl on a limestone base, red in colour and rich in iron. Clay makes up about one-third of the soil. There are more stones on the lower slopes though. This is due to the effect of the river Rhoin which flows through Savigny.

THE VINEYARD

Premiers Crus: There are six *premiers crus* in whole or in part: La Creux-de-la-Net (part); En Caradeux (part); La Croix-de-Pierre; Les Fichots; Ile-des-Vergelesses; Les Vergelesses or Les Basses-Vergelesses. These cover 56.51 ha and produce 1,520 hl (200,000 bottles) of red wine and 225 hl (30,000 bottles) of white wine a year.

Village Wine: There are 137.63 ha of village wine and these come from three sectors: above and below the *premiers crus*, on the slopes opposite the Bois de Corton, and on either side of the road which continues up the valley towards Echevronne. Not counting any Aligoté which may be planted in village land, the average amount of village wine produced is 1,900 hl (250,000 bottles) of red and 1,350 hl (178,000 bottles) of white wine a year.

Pernand-Vergelesses *rouge* is also allowed to be sold as Côte-de-Beaune-Villages.

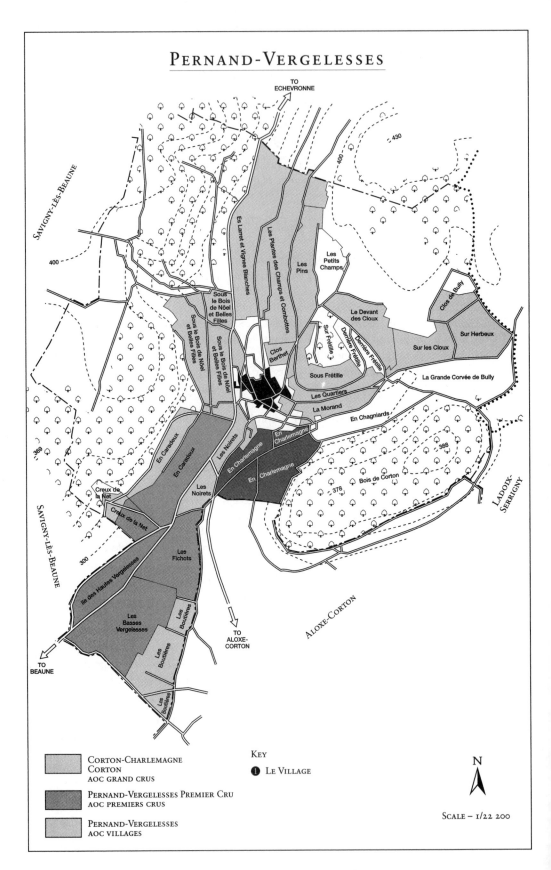

PERNAND-VERGELESSES

TO
ECHEVRONNE

SAVIGNY-LÈS-BEAUNE

430

400

400

Es Larret et Vignes Blanches

Les Plantes des Champs et Combottes

Les Pins

Les Petits Champs

Sous le Bois de Nöel et Belles Filles

Sous le Bois de Nöel et Belles Filles

Sous le Bois de Nöel et Belles Filles

Le Devant des Cloux

Clos de Bully

Sur Frétille

Derrière Frétille

Derrière Frétille

Sur Herbeux

Clos Berthet

Sur les Cloux

Sous Frétille

La Grande Corvée de Bully

Les Quartiers

La Morand

En Chagniards

En Charlemagne

369

En Caradeux

En Caradeux

Les Noirets

En Charlemagne

En Charlemagne

388

Creux de la Net

Les Noirets

En Charlemagne

378

Bois de Corton

LADOIX-SERRIGNY

Creux de la Net

300

Les Fichots

Île des Hautes Vergelesses

SAVIGNY-LÈS-BEAUNE

ALOXE-CORTON

Les Basses Vergelesses

Les Boutières

Les Boutières

TO
ALOXE-CORTON

TO
BEAUNE

Les Boutières

KEY

● LE VILLAGE

N

CORTON-CHARLEMAGNE
CORTON
AOC GRAND CRUS

PERNAND-VERGELESSES PREMIER CRU
AOC PREMIERS CRUS

PERNAND-VERGELESSES
AOC VILLAGES

SCALE – 1/22 200

THE *PREMIERS CRUS*

ILE-DES-VERGELESSES (9.41 HA)

Lying at an altitude of between 270 and 285 metres above sea level, on a relatively gentle slope facing exactly to the south-east, with Savigny-lès-Beaune's Les Vergelesses vineyard above and Pernand's Les Vergelesses (or Les Basses-Vergelesses) below, the oval-shaped vineyard of the Ile is ideally placed. It is surely a contender for elevation to *grand cru*.

The wine is individual: clearly better than the other *premiers crus*. It has medium-full body, an intense nose which recalls damson and black cherry, and a distinction and an intensity lacking in neighbouring wines. Yet, compared with the top *premiers crus* of Volnay and Pommard, the wine is cheap. It can be one of Burgundy's bargains.

Recommended Sources:

Chandon de Briailles (Savigny-lès-Beaune); Denis Père et Fils; Dubreuil-Fontaine; Régis Pavelot; Roland Rapet (all Pernand-Vergelesses).

LES VERGELESSES OR LES BASSES-VERGELESSES (18.06 HA)

EN CARADEUX (11.58 HA) • LA CROIX-DE-PIERRE (2.80 HA)

LA CREUX-DE-LA-NET (3.44 HA) • LES FICHOTS (11.23)

These *climats* can produce well-priced, good, honest bottles: medium-bodied, with both black and red fruit, and usually with good acidity. Wines for the medium term. You won't pay the earth. So don't expect the moon.

Recommended Sources:

Les Vergelesses or *Les Basses-Vergelesses:* Roger Rapet; Laleure-Piot (both Pernand-Vergelesses); Girard-Vollot; Jean-Marc Pavelot (both Savigny-lès-Beaune).
En Caradeux: Régis Pavelot (Pernand-Vergelesses).
La Croix-de-Pierre: Louis Jadot (Beaune).
La Creux-de-la-Net: Roger Jaffelin (Pernand-Vergelesses).
Les Fichots: Roger Jaffelin; Pierre Marey (both Pernand-Vergelesses).

THE GROWERS

*BONNEAU DU MARTRAY

11 ha: owned. Corton-Charlemagne (9.5 ha); Corton (*rouge*) (1.5 ha)

No other domaine in Burgundy, apart from the Domaine de la Romanée-Conti, sells only *grand cru* wine. The domaine's land on the Corton hill straddles the Pernand-Aloxe border and produces exemplary Corton-Charlemagne, vinified in oak, of course, of which one-third is new. In 1994 there was a dual change of generation here, Jean le Bault de la Morinière, who inherited the domaine from his aunt, giving way to his son Jean-Charles, while Henri Brochon in the cellar ceded responsibility to his sons Bernard and Jean-Pierre. Having reduced the area under Pinot Noir, at the bottom of the slope, retaining the oldest vines, and having made other improvements, the red wine, which tends to be a bit feeble, is getting better. But it is for its white wine that this domaine gains its star.

See Profile, page 346.

MARIUS DELARCHE PÈRE ET FILS

8.3 ha: owned and *en fermage*. Corton, Les Renardes (1.6 ha); Le Corton (8 ha); Corton-Charlemagne (1.2 ha); Pernand-Vergelesses *premier cru* in Ile-des-Vergelesses, Les Vergelesses; village Pernand-Vergelesses *rouge et blanc*.

Philippe Delarche is in charge here now, father Marius being *en retraite*. I don't get to see these wines often in bottle, as most is sold en *vrac* to the Beaune *négoce*. They seem clean, but a little anonymous.

DENIS PÈRE ET FILS

12.70 ha: owned and *en fermage*. Corton, Les Paulands (22 a); Corton-Charlemagne (40 a); Pernand-Vergelesses *premier cru* Ile-des-Vergelesses, Les Vergelesses; Savigny-lès-Beaune *premier cru*; village Pernand-Vergelesses *rouge et blanc*; village Savigny-lès-Beaune; village Aloxe-Corton.

It is the *fils*, Roland and Christophe, who are in charge here. Total destemming, fermenting temperatures at 32°C for red and 20°C for white, and between 10 and 25 per cent new oak is the recipe here. The Corton vines being young. It is the Ile which is the pick of the cellar. I have enjoyed recent vintages.

PIERRE DUBREUIL-FONTAINE

20 ha: owned and *en fermage*. Corton, Clos-du-Roi (98 a); Corton, Les Bressandes (97 a); Corton, Les Perrières (60 a); Corton-Charlemagne (77 a); Pernand-Vergelesses *premier cru* Ile-des-Vergelesses; Savigny-lès-Beaune *premier cru* Les Vergelesses; Pommard *premier cru* Les Epenots; village Pernand-Vergelesses in the *lieu-dit* Clos-Berthet (*monopole*) *rouge et blanc*; village Pommard; village Volnay.

Bernard Dubreuil has been in charge here for some years, and things have jollied along: pretty good, especially at the higher levels and in their village monopoly Berthet, but rarely dramatic. But now his daughter Christine is on the scene, I sense a change to something more exciting is on the way. I hope so. This is an important domaine, longer established than most. The Clos-Berthet *rouge* will be in abeyance for a few years. The vines here have just been replaced.

ROGER JAFFELIN ET FILS

10.5 ha: owned and *en fermage*. Corton-Charlemagne (23 a); Pernand-Vergelesses *premier cru* La Creux-de-la-Net *rouge et blanc*, Les Fichots; Beaune *premier cru* Belissand; village Pernand-Vergelesses in the *lieu-dit* Clos-de-Bully; village Savigny-lès-Beaune.

Pierre Jaffelin is responsible here, and operates from cellars which lie opposite one of Bonneau du Martray's at the top of the village. He retains 30 per cent of the stems for the red wine, vinifies for twelve to fifteen days at temperatures up to 30°C, and uses one-quarter new oak. Neat attractive wines here. They possess the lion's share of the Creux-de-la-Net.

LALEURE-PIOT PÈRE ET FILS

9.5 ha: owned and *en fermage*. Corton-Charlemagne (28 a); Corton (from Le Rognet and Les Bressandes) (53 a); Pernand-Vergelesses *premier cru* Ile-des-Vergelesses, Les Vergelesses; Pernand-Vergelesses *premier cru rouge et blanc*; Savigny-lès-Beaune *premier cru* Les Vergelesses; village Pernand-Vergelesses *rouge et blanc*; village Chorey-lès-Beaune; Côte-de-Nuits-Villages.

Jean-Marie and Frédéric Laleure make clean, competent wines, but they are rather dull. Even the *grands crus* lack real excitement.

PIERRE MAREY ET FILS

10 ha: owned and *en fermage*. Corton-Charlemagne (1.00 ha); Corton (50 a); Pernand-Vergelesses *premier cru* Les Fichots; village Pernands-Vergelesses *rouge et blanc*.

Father Pierre and son Eric Marey's *grands crus*, all on the Pernand side, are much morcellated. This is an up-and-coming domaine which does not export at present, but which makes wines with plenty of personality and a nice touch of oak.

RÉGIS PAVELOT ET FILS

7.41 ha: owned and *en fermage*. Corton (28 a); Corton-Charlemagne (58 a); Pernand-Vergelesses *premier cru* Ile-des-Vergelesses, Les Caradeux; village Pernand-Vergelesses *rouge et blanc*; village Aloxe-Corton.

Luc Pavelot has just finished his studies in Beaune and Dijon, and has joined his father at this estate. The cellar looks like a concrete bunker, and lies halfway down the slope below that of Roland Rapet. A feature of this domaine is its jealously guarded old vines, including one of the most serious Aligotés to be found in Burgundy. The other wines are very good too.

RAPET PÈRE ET FILS

19 ha: *en fermage*. Corton-Charlemagne (2.50 ha); Corton (from Les Pougets, Les Perrières) (1.25 ha); Pernand-Vergelesses *premier cru* Ile-des-Vergelesses, Les Vergelesses; Pernand-Vergelesses *premier cru blanc* (Les Caradeux); Beaune *premier cru* Clos-du-Roi; village Aloxe-Corton; village Savigny-lès-Beaune; village Pernand-Vergelesses *rouge et blanc*.

Vincent Rapet has now joined his father at this important domaine. Some 20 per cent of the stems are retained, the red wine fermented at a maximum of 33°C, and about 20-30 per cent of new wood is used, depending on the appellation. The wines are bottled after a year or so. The Rapets have been making wine here for more than two centuries, and they are usually good, but rarely exciting. The 1993s showed rather better in cask than I expected. So I am hoping this is a permanent sign for the better.

ROLLIN PÈRE ET FILS

11 ha: owned and *en fermage/métayage*. Corton-Charlemagne (60 a); Pernand-Vergelesses *premier cru* Ile-des-Vergelesses; village Pernand-Vergelesses *rouge et blanc*; village Aloxe-Corton; village Savigny-lès-Beaune.

Rémi, the *fils*, tall, dark, lean, bespectacled, in his thirties, is increasingly taking over from his father Maurice in this modern, efficient *cave* below the village on the road to Echevronne. Up to 20 per cent of the stems are used. There is four or five days' cold soaking before fermentation; and a quarter new oak in the top wines. The wines are competent but not exciting.

SAVIGNY-LÈS-BEAUNE

Up at the beginning of the valley of the river Rhoin, 6 kilometres north-west of Beaune, lies Savigny, one of the larger of the Côte-de-Beaune communes with 383 hectares of vines. Savigny is a modest little village. Some of the older houses may carry an enigmatic wall inscription such as *Les vins de Savigny sont nourrissants, théologiques et morbifuges* (the wines of Savigny are nourishing, theological [whatever that is supposed to mean – causing one to ponder on the meaning of life, I suppose] and will chase away every illness) or something equally inscrutable. These appeared between the seventeenth and eighteenth centuries, but no one knows who the authors were, or the reasons behind their execution.

The village can trace its ancestry back to Gallo-Roman times, when it was known as Saviniaco. But even earlier, the Romans themselves constructed a road through the valley, part of the connection between Autun and Langres, both important settlements at the time. Well-preserved traces of the road still exist. In the eleventh century Augustine monks built the exquisite Abbey of Sainte-Marguerite up in the valley near Bouilland. Back in Savigny the imposing château on the edge of the village, today a museum of old motor cars, dates from the beginning of the seventeenth century.

Another communal claim to fame is that it was here in the mid nineteenth century that the first viticultural tractor was invented, and as a consequence of this that vines were first planted in rows in the surrounding vineyards.

Savigny-lès-Beaune - the *lès*, with an accent, meaning 'by' or 'near to' - is the most divided *vignoble* in Burgundy. Part of the vineyard lies on the south-facing slopes of the Bois Noël, as it curves round from Pernand-Vergelesses. Opposite, on the north-east-facing flank of Mont Battois – down which the motorway thunders from the Morvan to the plain of Beaune – is the other half of Savigny's *premiers crus* adjoining those of Beaune. There is, incidentally, a rest site on the motorway above the village called the Aire de Savigny-lès-Galloises, from which there is a splendid panorama towards the hill of Corton. If you stop here you will find yourself exactly halfway between Lille and Marseilles. The flatter land between the *premiers crus* is village AC, as is an important but normally overlooked chunk of vineyard on south-facing higher ground beyond the village.

The soil on the Bois Noël side consists of gritty, sandy marl covered with ferruginous oolite on the top slopes, red-brown crumbly limestone below, not very stony and not very permeable, for the clay content is high. On the Mont Battois slopes the soil is more sandy, and even less stony, with deep limestone scree on the flatter land below.

The result, combined with the orientation, is wines which are quite separate in character. From the Pernand side the wines have medium weight, are elegant and persistent. The Mont Battois slopes opposite give more structured, more earthy, more *sauvage* wines, which get rounder and fatter as the slope turns round and approaches the boundary with Beaune.

There is also some white wine, not so much as in Pernand, but of an interesting character and similarly quite different from that of Meursault or the other villages to the south. To some extent this is the *terroir*, but it is also the consequence of the practice here of complanting Pinot Blanc or Pinot Beurot, the latter a sort of Pinot Gris, as used in Alsace. These Pinots ripen well, give good sugar readings but less acidity. More importantly they add a bit of spice. Growers like Patrick Bize can offer both Bourgogne *blanc* and Savigny *blanc* from various blends of Chardonnay and Pinot. And really good they are too.

There is plenty of Savigny, and the village can offer some very good sources of wine. Moreover prices are inexpensive compared with those of Pommard or Volnay. All this adds to the good value: a happy hunting ground for those who seek good inexpensive Burgundy.

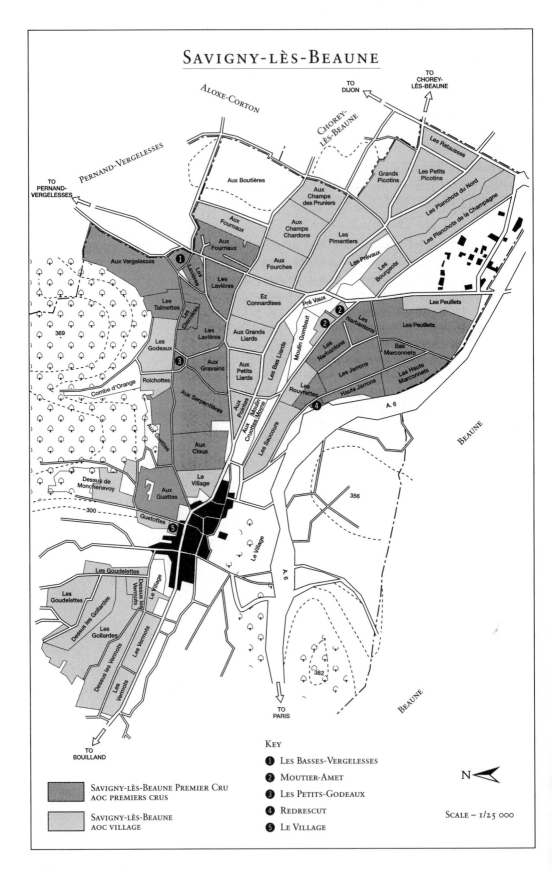

Savigny-lès-Beaune

TO DIJON

TO CHOREY-LÈS-BEAUNE

ALOXE-CORTON

CHOREY-LÈS-BEAUNE

PERNAND-VERGELESSES

TO PERNAND-VERGELESSES

Aux Boutières

Aux Champs des Pruniers

Grands Picotins

Les Petits Picotins

Les Ratausses

Les Planchots du Nord

Aux Fournaux

Aux Champs Chardons

Les Pimentiers

Les Planchots de la Champagne

Aux Fournaux

Aux Vergelesses

Les Lavières

❶

Les Lavières

Aux Fourches

Les Prévaux

Les Bourgeots

Les Talmettes

Les Chagnots

Ez Connardises

Pré Vaux

❷

❷

Les Narbantons

Les Peuillets

Les Peuillets

369

Les Godeaux

Les Lavières

Aux Grands Liards

Moulin Gombaut

Les Narbantons

Bas Marconnets

❸

Aux Gravains

Aux Petits Liards

Les Bas Liards

Les Jarrons

Les Hauts Marconnets

Roichottes

Combe d'Orange

Aux Serpentières

Aux Pointes

Les Rouvrettes

Hauts Jarrons

A.6

❹

BEAUNE

Aux Guettes

Aux Clous

Aux Pointes

Moulin Croûtté Moyne

Les Saucours

Dessus de Monchenevoy

Aux Guettes

Le Village

356

300

Guetottes

❺

Le Village

Le Village

A.6

Les Goudelettes

Les Goudelettes

Dessus les Vermots

Le Village

BEAUNE

Les Gollardes

Dessus les Gollardes

Les Gollardes

Les Vermots

382

Dessus les Vermots

Les Vermots

TO PARIS

TO BOUILLAND

Key

Savigny-lès-Beaune Premier Cru
AOC PREMIERS CRUS

Savigny-lès-Beaune
AOC VILLAGE

❶ Les Basses-Vergelesses

❷ Moutier-Amet

❸ Les Petits-Godeaux

❹ Redrescut

❺ Le Village

N

Scale – 1/25 000

THE VINEYARD

Premiers Crus: There are twenty-two *premiers crus* in Savigny-lès-Beaune, in whole or in part. On the Pernand side we have: La Bataillère (part of Les Vergelesses); Champ-Chevrey (part of Aux Fourneaux); Les Charnières; Aux Clous; Aux Fourneaux (part); Les Petits-Godeaux; Aux Gravains; Aux Guettes (part); Les Lavières; Aux Serpentières; Les Talmettes (part of Les Vergelesses); Aux Vergelesses; Les Basses-Vergelesses. On the Mont Battois slope will be found: La Dominode (part of Les Jarrons); Les Hauts-Jarrons; Les Jarrons; Les Bas-Marconnets; Les Hauts-Marconnets; Les Narbantons; Les Peuillets (part); Redrescut (or Redrescul); Les Rouvrettes (part). These cover 144.02 ha and produce around 5,350 hl (700,000 bottles) per year of red wine and 275 hl (36,000 bottles) of white.

Village Wine: There are 238.58 ha of village land in Savigny. Of this 150 ha lie in the plain on the east side of the village or on unfavoured slopes. The rest lies further up the valley of the Rhoin. Here you will find the *lieux-dits* of Les Gollardes and Les Vermots where I feel the best of Savigny's village wines come from. There is good Bourgogne, both red and white, from up here too.

The average production of village wine is 8,350 hl (1.1 million bottles) of red wine and 1,180 hl (156,000 bottles) of white wine a year.

THE PREMIERS CRUS

AUX VERGELESSES (15.38 HA) • LA BATAILLÈRE (1.81 HA)
LES BASSES-VERGELESSES (1.68 HA) • LES TALMETTES (3.10 HA)

The large Vergelesses *climat* and its three subsidiaries, all of which can call their wine Vergelesses, represent Savigny-lès-Beaune's best wine. Here Savigny is at its most refined, with the most intensity and depth. Here it is at its smoothest, its most velvety, its most complete. Savigny-lès-Beaune, Les Vergelesses lies in part above Pernand's Ile-des-Vergelesses and can often be its equal, rather superior to Pernand's (Basses) Vergelesses,

La Bataillère, once a *clos*, but having lost that designation – because the walls crumbled, apparently – has historically been considered the best part. It is really a continuation of the Ile. Today it is the *monopole* of the excellent Domaine Albert Morot of Beaune. The wine of Talmettes, a little further round the hill, under the forest at the top of the slope, makes slightly less distinctive wine.

Recommended Sources:
Aux Vergelesses: Simon Bize (Savigny-lès-Beaune); Lucien Jacob (Echevronne).
La Bataillère: Albert Morot (Beaune).

LES LAVIÈRES (17.66 HA) • AUX FOURNEAUX (6.42 HA)
CHAMP-CHEVREY (1.48 HA) • LES CHARNIÈRES (2.07 HA)

These four *climats* lie below Vergelesses and produce a soft, round, more loose-knit wine, but one with plenty of charm and succulent, plump, red fruit. This is perhaps the easiest Savigny to appreciate, both at the outset and a little later on, for it evolves earlier than most. Les Lavières is superior to Aux Fourneaux.

Recommended Sources:
Les Lavières: Pierre Bitouzet; Camus-Brochon; Chandon de Briailles (all Savigny-lès-Beaune); Tollot-Beaut (Chorey-lès-Beaune); Claude Maréchal (Bligny-lès-Beaune).
Aux Fourneaux: Simon Bize; Chandon de Briailles (both Savigny-lès-Beaune).
Champ-Chevrey: Tollot-Beaut (Chorey-lès-Beaune).

AUX GRAVAINS (6.15 HA) • LES PETITS-GODEAUX (0.71 HA)
AUX SERPENTIÈRES (12.34 HA) • AUX CLOUS (9.92 HA)
AUX GUETTES (14.08 HA)

Continuing round towards the village we come to the final group of *premiers crus* on the Pernand side. These wines are firmer that those of the Lavières, less refined than those of the Vergelesses, but nevertheless share much of the same characteristics: Savignys with style rather than raw substance.

Recommended Sources:
Aux Gravains: Jean-Marc Pavelot (Savigny-lès-Beaune).
Aux Serpentières: Simon Bize, Maurice Ecard (both Savigny-lès-Beaune).
Aux Guettes: Simon Bize (Savigny-lès-Beaune).

LES ROUVRETTES (2.83 HA) • LES NARBANTONS (9.49 HA)
LES JARRONS (1.46 HA) • LA DOMINODE (7.87 HA)
LES HAUTS-JARRONS (4.44 HA) • REDRESCUL (0.50 HA)
LES HAUTS-MARCONNETS (5.34 HA) • LES BAS-MARCONNETS (2.99 HA)
LES PEUILLETS (16.17 HA)

These are the Savigny-lès-Beaune *premiers crus* which lie under the motorway and Mont Battois. Les Rouvrettes lies nearest to the village. Peuillets marches with Beaune, Clos-du-Roi (with the motorway separating them); likewise Marconnets with its namesake in the next commune.

The wines don't *have* to be tough and *sauvage* here. What one is looking for is a combination of guts and balanced fruit, plus tannins which are properly sophisticated. The best, in my view, come from the Marconnets and that part of Jarrons normally sold as La Dominode. Bruno Clair of Marsannay has a plot of vines planted in 1902 here. This wine gives the lie to anyone who believes that Savigny cannot provide fine wine.

Recommended Sources:
Les Rouvrettes: Girard-Vollot (Savigny-lès-Beaune).
Les Narbantons: Camus-Brochon; Maurice Ecard; Girard-Vollot (Savigny-lès-Beaune); Leroy (Vosne-Romanée).
Les Jarrons: Maurice Ecard (Savigny-lès-Beaune).
La Dominode: Jean-Marc Pavelot (Savigny-lès-Beaune); Louis Jadot (Beaune); Bruno Clair (Marsannay).
Les Marconnets: Simon Bize (Savigny-lès-Beaune).
Les Peuillets: Capron-Charcousset; Girard-Vollot; Jean-Marc Pavelot (all Savigny-lès-Beaune).

THE GROWERS

PIERRE BITOUZET

22 ha: owned and *en fermage/métayage.* Corton, Les Maréchaudes (50 a); Corton-Charlemagne (50 a); Aloxe-Corton *premier cru* Les Valozières; Savigny-lès-Beaune *premier cru* Les Lavières; Savigny-lès-Beaune *premier cru blanc*; village Pommard in the *lieu-dit* Les Platières; Chablis; Chablis *premier cru.*

Pierre Bitouzet used to be the *régisseur* for the Prince de Mérode in Ladoix-Serrigny for whom both he and his daughter and son-in-law continue to be *métayers.* When I first began to visit him, he made all the Prince's wines in the fine vaulted cellar beneath his own elegant mansion in Savigny-lès-Beaune.

His own domaine contains a large amount (10 ha) of Chablis. He makes good reds, retaining 20–25 per cent of the stems, vinifying at 28-32°C and rotating the new wood on a one-third new per year basis. His best wine, though, is his Corton-Charlemagne.

★SIMON BIZE ET FILS

22 ha: owned and *en fermage/métayage*. Latricières-Chambertin (32 a); Savigny-lès-Beaune *premier cru* in Les Vergelesses, Aux Fourneaux, Les Serpentières, Les Guettes, Les Marconnets; village Savigny-lès-Beaune including the *lieu-dit* Les Grands-Liards; village Savigny-lès-Beaune *blanc*; village Aloxe-Corton in the *lieu-dit* Les Suchots.

The wines were very good here twenty and thirty years ago when Simon Bize was in charge – I have fond memories of the 1971 Vergelesses – but are even better now. His son Patrick is one of Burgundy's most sensitive and perfectionist wine-makers, ever seeking to add a touch here, modify a detail there. This is in my view clearly Savigny's best domaine.

Only the younger vines – which for Patrick means anything under twenty years – are destemmed here. There is a long *cuvaison*, controlled at 30–33°C, and 50 per cent new wood is used. Bize's wines are understated, slow to evolve, a little austere at the start. But they are beautifully poised and clear-cut in their flavours, with the individual characters of the five *premiers crus* visible for all to see. He additionally makes excellent generics, including whites from both Chardonnay and Pinot Beurot. An address not to be missed.

See Profile, page 341.

CAMUS-BROCHON

7.40 ha: owned and *en fermage*. Savigny-lès Beaune *premier cru* in Les Lavières, Les Narbantons, Les Gravains; Beaune *premier cru* Clos-du-Roi; Pommard *premier cru* Les Arvelets; village Savigny-lès-Beaune *blanc et rouge*, including a *vieilles vignes* red wine *cuvée*.

Half the stems are retained here, the fermentation temperatures allowed to rise to 35°C, and 20 per cent new oak is employed. Lucien Camus is a serious wine-maker who makes well-coloured, firm, intense wines, much on the lines of those of his friend, Patrick Bize.

CAPRON-CHARCOUSSET

6.89 ha: owned and *en fermage/métayage*. Savigny-lès-Beaune *premier cru* in Les Peuillets, Les Lavières; village Savigny-lès-Beaune *blanc et rouge* including the *lieu-dit* Les Pimentières (*rouge*); village Pernand-Vergelesses *blanc*; village Pommard.

Imagine a young, innocent Solzhenitsyn, without the cares of Mother Russia on his shoulders: that is Jean-Marie Capron, who runs this small estate with his wife Nicole. Traditional methods (100 per cent stems retained). There is a splendid cellar – three floors deep – it was once used for sparkling wine. The Pommard is currently from young vines. Nicely made, but quite old-fashioned wines. Some evolve to be very good bottles indeed.

★CHANDON DE BRIAILLES

13 ha: owned. Corton, Clos-du-Roi (44 a); Corton, Les Bressandes (1.74 ha); Corton, Les Maréchaudes (39 a); Corton *blanc* (25 a); Corton-Charlemagne (11 a); Aloxe-Corton *premier cru* Les Valozières; Pernand-Vergelesses *premier cru* in Ile-des-Vergelesses, Les Basses-Vergelesses; Savigny-lès-Beaune *premier cru* in Les Lavières, Aux Fourneaux; village Savigny-lès-Beaune including the *lieu-dit* Aux Fourneaux.

This important property is owned by Count Aymar-Claude and Nadine de Nicolay (pronounced Nicolaï) and their four children, and it is Nadine and her youngest daughter Claude who are in charge, together with cellar-master Jean-Claude Bouveret, known to one and all, even himself, for obvious reasons, as Kojak. Progress has been impressive here over the last decade, and this is now a prime source for Ile-des-Vergelesses (of which they are the largest land-holder) and a clutch of excellent Cortons.

See Profile, page 366.

DOUDET-NAUDIN

5.35 ha: owned (by Yves Doudet). Corton, Les Maréchaudes (50 a); Corton-Charlemagne (47 a); Savigny-lès-Beaune *premier cru* in Les Guettes, Redrescut; Aloxe-Corton *premier cru*; Pernand-Vergelesses *premier cru* Les Fichots; Beaune *premier cru* in Clos-du-Roi, Les Cent-Vignes; village Savigny-lès-Beaune in the *lieu-dit* Aux Petits-Liards; village Aloxe-Corton in the *lieu-dit* Les Boutières.

The merchants Doudet-Naudin possess this small domaine. Since 1990, following the death of old Marcel Doudet, there have been welcome changes here – at long last. There is still a long way to go yet. But one gets the feeling that the spirit is willing, at least.

MAURICE ECARD

13 ha: owned and *en fermage*. Savigny-lès-Beaune *premier cru* in Les Serpentières, Les Narbantons, Les Jarrons, Les Hauts-Jarrons (*blanc*), Les Peuillets, Les Clous, village Savigny-lès-Beaune *rouge at blanc*.

The rotund, bluff, genial Maurice Ecard works with his son Michel (under whose name some of the wines now appear). This is a modern, efficient set-up, and somehow you know you have stumbled on a good source of wine even before you have sampled a single cask. Some 30 per cent stalks retained, a twelve-day *cuvaison* at temperatures up to 33°C, and 15 per cent new oak is the programme here, and the results are plump, fruity wines for the medium term.

JEAN-MICHEL GIBOULOT

12 ha: *en fermage*. Savigny-lès-Beaune *premier cru* in Les Fourneaux, Les Serpentières, Les Gravains, Les Peuillets; village Savigny-lès-Beaune *rouge*, including the *lieu-dit* Les Grands Liards, *et blanc*.

Jean-Michel Giboulot, who has now taken over from his father Maurice, is turning more and more towards a completely biological approach in the vineyards. He has also planted ray-grass between his vines to prevent erosion. No stems, the fermentation temperature warmed up at the end to fix the colour and obtain a maximum of *matière*, and a mere 10 per cent new oak. I find the wines rather tough and artisanal.

GIRARD-VOLLOT

15 ha: owned and *en fermage*. Savigny-lès-Beaune *premier cru* in Les Peuillets, Les Narbantons, Les Rouvrettes; Pernand-Vergelesses *premier cru* Les Basses-Vergelesses; village Savigny-lès-Beaune *rouge et blanc*; village Aloxe-Corton.

Jean-Jacques Girard's family have been making wine since 1614. He retains a good proportion of the stems and makes Savigny which is a bit hard and sinewy. It needs time. The Rouvrettes, he finds, is never quite as good as it could be. The reason? The vines do not suffer enough.

PIERRE GUILLEMOT

7.7 ha: owned and *en fermage*. Savigny-lès-Beaune *premier cru* in Les Serpentières, Les Jarrons, Les Narbantons; village Savigny-lès-Beaune *rouge et blanc*.

Pierre Guillemot and his son Jean-Pierre are in charge here. This is fairly old-fashioned wine-making: most of the stems, and only a modicum of new wood. Quite a bit is still sold to the *négociants*. Their own wines are a little rustic, but have plenty of substance.

ANTONIN GUYON

48 ha: owned and *en fermage*. Charmes-Chambertin (10 a); Corton-Charlemagne (75 a);

Corton, Clos-du-Roi (75 a); Corton, Les Bressandes (1.00 ha); Corton, Les Renardes (25 a); Corton (25 a); Aloxe-Corton *premier cru* in Les Fournières, Les Vercots; Pernand-Vergelesses *premier cru* Les Vergelesses, Les Fichots; Volnay *premier cru*, Clos-des-Chênes; village Chambolle-Musigny including the *lieu-dit* Clos-du-Village; village Gevrey-Chambertin; village Savigny-lès-Beaune; village Beaune including the *lieu-dit* Clos-de-la-Charme-Gaufriot; village Pernand-Vergelesses *blanc et rouge*; village Chorey-lès-Beaune.

Some 23 hectares of Hautes-Côtes-de-Nuits in Meuilley make up almost half this estate, whose headquarters occupy imposing premises on the edge of Savigny. The bulk of the rest of the domaine came from Hippolyte Thevenot in 1965, and is still registered as such on the *déclaration*. Michel Guyon is in charge here, and there are some nice wines, the Volnay, Clos-des-Chênes always being one of the best. But there seems to be an absence of real flair here.

JEAN-MICHEL MAURICE, DOMAINE DU PRIEURÉ
11.5 ha: owned and *en fermage*. Savigny-lès-Beaune *premier cru* in Les Lavières, Les Hauts-Jarrons; village Savigny-lès-Beaune *blanc et rouge*.

The extended Maurice family produce light and quite pleasant wines, intended for drinking in the medium term. But they do not really excite me.

JEAN-MARC PAVELOT
12 ha: owned and *en fermage*. Savigny-lès-Beaune *premier cru* Les Dominodes, Aux Guettes, Les Narbantons, Les Peuillets, Aux Gravains; Pernand-Vergelesses *premier cru* Les Vergelesses; village Savigny-lès-Beaune *blanc et rouge*.

This is another top Savigny domaine which, like Maurice Ecard, produces Savigny without the hard *sauvage* aspect many of them present in their youth. Jean-Marc Pavelot's wines are elegant, plump and understated, letting all the fruit sing out, yet never simple. There is depth here; and the wines last.

CHOREY-LÈS-BEAUNE

It is only at Chorey-lès-Beaune and at Gevrey-Chambertin – and for precisely the same reason – that appellation village vineyards spill significantly over the main highway, the N 74, towards the east. Today neither the stream which runs down from the *combe* above Gevrey nor the river Rhoin which flows out of the Vallée d'Orée from Bouillard down to Savigny and beyond are major waterways. But in geological times they must have been. The mini-canyons they have left behind prove it. And over the aeons considerable limestone debris mixed with sand has been brought down the valley to spread out suitable vineyard land beyond the usual Burgundian confines. Chorey-lès-Beaune is unique. Most of the commune – as well as the village itself – lies on the 'wrong' side of the road. It is also the produce of that valuable item – so often overlooked by those in pursuit of the latest perfect score among the *grands crus* – red Burgundy at a price you can afford.

There are no first growths in Chorey, nor do you see many wines aggrandising themselves with the mention of a *lieu-dit*. Nearly all the wine is red, and more than half of this is sold as Côte-de-Beaune-Villages, the village being the major contributor to the appellation. Chorey-lès-Beaune is a soft, plump, fruity forward wine usually ready for drinking a couple of years at most after bottling. Those which come from the Aloxe-Corton side are richer, fuller and fatter than those from vineyards neighbouring Beaune and Savigny. There are some 130 ha under vines producing red wine, plus another handful planted in Chardonnay, some of the vineyards actually having been demoted from AC to generic in recent years, an almost unheard-of thing for Burgundy! Total production, including Côte-de-Beaune-Villages, is around 6,000 hl (792,000 bottles) of red wine and 140 hl (18,500 bottles) of white wine a year.

Chorey-lès-Beaune

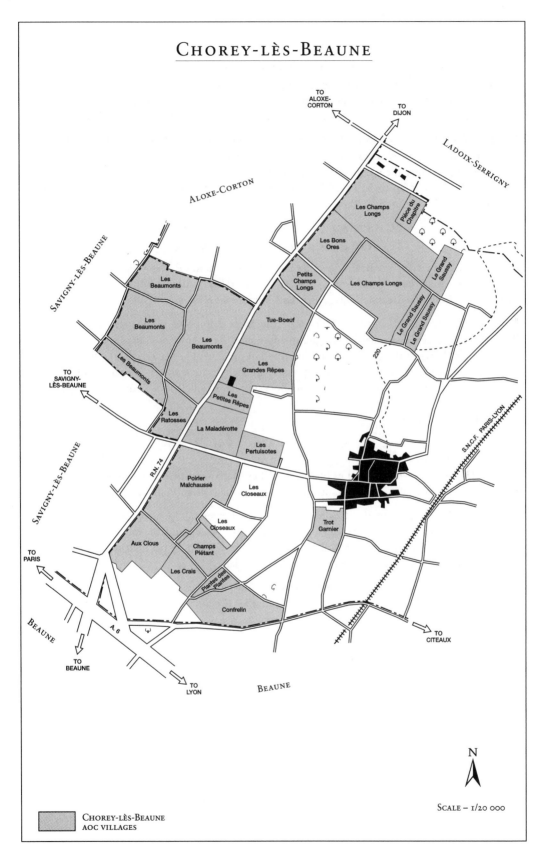

TO ALOXE-CORTON

TO DIJON

Ladoix-Serrigny

Aloxe-Corton

Savigny-lès-Beaune

Les Champs Longs

Pièce du Chapitre

Les Bons Ores

Petits Champs Longs

Les Champs Longs

Le Grand Saussy

Les Beaumonts

Tue-Boeuf

Le Grand Saussy

Le Grand Saussy

Les Beaumonts

Les Beaumonts

Les Beaumonts

Les Grandes Rêpes

TO SAVIGNY-LÈS-BEAUNE

Les Beaumonts

Les Petites Rêpes

Les Ratosses

La Maladérotte

S.N.C.F. PARIS-LYON

Les Pertuisotes

220

SAVIGNY-LÈS-BEAUNE

R.N. 74

Poirier Malchaussé

Les Closeaux

Les Closeaux

Trot Garnier

TO PARIS

Aux Clous

Champs Plétant

Les Crais

Plantes des Plantes

Confrelin

TO CITEAUX

BEAUNE

A. 6

TO BEAUNE

TO LYON

BEAUNE

N

SCALE – 1/20 000

Chorey-lès-Beaune
AOC VILLAGES

THE GROWERS

ARNOUX PÈRE ET FILS

23 ha: owned and *en fermage*. Corton, Les Rognets (33 a); Beaune *premier cru* Cent-Vignes; Savigny-lès-Beaune *premier cru* Les Guettes, Les Vergelesses; village Aloxe-Corton; village Pernand-Vergelesses *blanc*; village Savigny-lès-Beaune; village Beaune; Chorey-lès-Beaune.

Cousins of the Arnoux of Vosne-Romanée, the brothers Rémi and Michel, and Michel's son Pascal, run this efficient estate out of a hangar-like *chai* on the edge of the village. The domaine is three times the size it was twenty years ago. The Arnoux retain 10 per cent of the stems, vinify the reds up to 33°C, and employ one-quarter new oak overall. Good wines at all levels here. A very useful address.

★CHÂTEAU DE CHOREY-LÈS-BEAUNE
DOMAINE JACQUES GERMAIN

7 ha: owned and *en fermage*. Beaune *premier cru* in Les Boucherottes, Les Vignes-Franches, Les Cras, Les Teurons, Les Cent-Vignes, Sur-les-Grèves (*blanc*); Aloxe-Corton *premier cru* Les Valozières; Chorey-lès-Beaune; village Pernand-Vergelesses *blanc*.

Not surprisingly, the Château de Chorey is the most impressive edifice in the village: a properly moated castle, medieval in origin, in a fine park. The wines of François Germain (son of Jacques) and his son Benoît, now partially stored in the fine old cellars of the defunct Tollot-Voarick domaine, are finely balanced, expressive in their fruit, and very elegant. This is not only a fine source for *premier cru* Beaune, but also a supplier of a delicious Pommard-Vergelesses *blanc*.

See Profile, page 450.

DUBOIS D'ORGEVAL

13 ha: owned and *en fermage/métayage*. Beaune *premier cru* in Les Marconnets, Les Teurons; Savigny-lès-Beaune *premier cru* in Les Narbantons, Les Marconnets; Chorey-lès-Beaune; village Savigny-lès-Beaune; village Aloxe-Corton; village Beaune; village Pommard.

The Dubois are a large extended Chorey family. This domaine, which set up in 1985, united local land with the Orgeval's Beaunes and Pommards. One-third or so of the stems are retained, fermentation temperatures allowed to rise to 35°C, and 20 per cent new oak is used for the maturation. In my experience the wines lack flair.

FRANÇOIS GAY

6.38 ha: owned and *en fermage*. Corton, Les Renardes (21 a); Savigny-lès-Beaune *premier cru* Les Serpentières; Beaune *premier cru* Clos-des-Perrières; village Aloxe-Corton; village Savigny-lès-Beaune; Chorey-lès-Beaune.

François Gay, smallish, balding, in his mid-fifties, lives in an isolated house on the edge of the village. His barn-like *chai* hides his garden from much of the village. A small percentage of the stems is sometimes retained here. There is a three or four day period of cold soaking. The fermentation temperatures are allowed to rise to 34/35°C, and there is 30 per cent new wood. I much enjoyed tasting the 1994s and 1993s on a recent visit, but older vintages of the Clos-des-Perrières seemed not to have aged gracefully.

DANIEL LARGEOT

11 ha: owned and *en fermage*. Beaune *premier cru* Les Grèves; Chorey-lès-Beaune; village Savigny-lès-Beaune in the *lieu-dit*; village Aloxe-Corton.

Daniel Largeot, fifty-something, tall, balding and passionate, gives the initial impression of being somewhat haphazard. So does the appearance of the cellar. Deeper investigation shows this to be misleading. This man believes in low *rendements*, *saignées* if necessary, enzymes to help clarify the wine and one-quarter new oak for the better *cuvées*. Up to 1994 he did not destem; now he does, completely.

MAILLARD PÈRE ET FILS

17 ha: owned and *en fermage*. Corton, Les Renardes (1.5 ha); Corton (20 a); Aloxe-Corton *premier cru* Les Grandes-Lolières; Beaune *premier cru* Les Grèves; village Aloxe-Corton, village Ladoix; village Savigny-lès-Beaune; village Beaune; Chorey-lès-Beaune.

I first ran into the Maillard family and its wines at the *Salon des Jeunes Professionnels* exhibition which used to be held during the weekend of *Les Trois Glorieuses*. Subsequent tastings on the spot confirm this cellar as a good source for sound, consistently made wines which evolve in the medium term.

RENÉ PODECHARD

10.75 ha: owned. Beaune *premier cru* Les Cent-Vignes; Chorey-lès-Beaune *rouge et blanc*; village Savigny-lès-Beaune; village Aloxe-Corton.

There have been Podichards in Chorey since the sixteenth century, says René, a shortish man in his late fifties. This is a neat, tidy set-up in the centre of the village. The wines are good, and the domaine believes in holding them back until they are ready for drinking. A more-than-useful source.

TOLLOT-BEAUT ET FILS

22.28 ha: owned and *en fermage*. Corton-Charlemagne (24 a); Corton, Les Bressandes (91 a); Corton (60 a); Aloxe-Corton *premier cru* in Les Vercots, Les Fournières; Beaune *premier cru* in Les Grèves, Clos-du-Roi; Savigny-lès-Beaune *premier cru* in Les Lavières, Champ-Chevrey (*monopole*); village Aloxe-Corton; village Beaune in the *lieu-dit* Blanche-Fleur; village Savigny-lès-Beaune; Chorey-lès-Beaune.

This is a well-known and very reliable estate. The extended Tollot family work hard, do not spend their money on fripperies and keep an immaculate cellar. The wines – 10–20 per cent destemming, eight to twelve day *cuvaison* at, for reds, up to 32°C, and between 10 and 50 per cent new oak – have a particular signature: round, gently oaky, just slightly sweet in character and texture, and will never disappoint. But like a Bordeaux classed growth – La Lagune, for example – which never quite gives you super-second excitement, so the Tollot wines never make the hair on the back of your neck tingle. A good source nevertheless, and the Chorey is a good example of basic red Burgundy.

BEAUNE

If Dijon is the departmental capital of the Côte d'Or, Beaune is the wine nerve-centre of Burgundy. Inside the old walled city the atmosphere is still largely medieval. The streets are cobbled, the roads are narrow, the buildings ancient. Outside market days and away from the Place Carnot and the few shopping streets which lie nearby, Beaune is a sleepy, shuttered town, full of hidden alleys, quiet Renaissance courtyards and ecclesiastical remnants of its glorious religious and aristocratic past. There is a fine church, the Collégiale Notre-Dame, which dates from the twelfth century. There is a Musée du Vin, housed in a mansion formerly owned by successive Dukes of Burgundy in the fifteenth and sixteenth centuries. The Hôtel de Ville was once an ancient convent; another, the Couvent des Cordeliers, houses one of Beaune's wine firms, and is a trap for the unwary tourist. And of course there is the Hôtel Dieu, heart of the Hospices de Beaune, one of the most magnificent wine monuments in the world.

Beaune explodes to life during the weekend of *Les Trois Glorieuses*, three extravagant feasts which surround the Hospices de Beaune charity auction on the third Sunday in November. The city teems with people: local growers who have come up to show their wines in the massed throng of the Hôtel de Ville or the rather more sedate surroundings of the *Palais des Congrès*; and tourists, agents, buyers and friends of the local *négociants*, most of whom have their headquarters in the centre of the town, though today their cellars are housed in modern warehouses on the outskirts.

Everybody is there. For one hectic week countless litres of wine are drunk or sampled and spat, and it is impossible to find a parking space for your car, let alone a bed for the night. And then life returns to normal. The traffic whizzes round the *périphérique* without the metre-thick *bastions* which form the city walls, or avoids Beaune altogether by taking the nearby motorway, and the old medieval centre regains its traditional somnolence.

BEAUNE

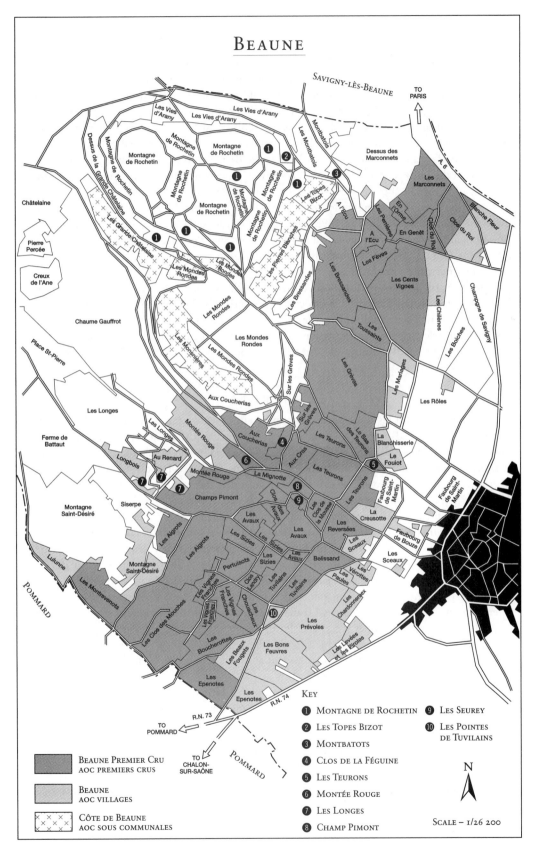

SAVIGNY-LÈS-BEAUNE

TO PARIS

Châtelaine

Pierre Percée

Creux de l'Ane

Chaume Gauffrot

Place St-Pierre

Ferme de Battaut

Les Longes

Montagne Saint-Désiré

Lulunne

POMMARD

Les Vies d'Arany
Les Vies d'Arany
Les Vies d'Arany

Montagne de Rochetin
Dessus de la Grande Châtelaine
Les Grande Châtelaine
Montagne de Rochetin
Montagne de Rochetin
Montagne de Rochetin
Montagne de Rochetin
Montagne de Rochetin
Montagne de Rochetin
Montagne de Rochetin
Montagne de Rochetin

Les Montbatois
Les Montbatois

Dessus des Marconnets

Les Marconnets

A 6

Blanche Fleur

Les Topes Bizot

Les Pierres Blanches

Les Mondes Rondes
Les Mondes Rondes
Les Mondes Rondes
Les Mondes Rondes
Les Mondes Rondes

Les Montrenières

Sur les Grèves

Aux Coucherias

Montée Rouge

Les Longes
Les Longes

Longbois

Au Renard

Montée Rouge

Siserpe

Champs Pimont

La Mignotte

Aux Cras

Montagne Saint-Désiré

Les Aigrots
Les Aigrots

Les Sizies
Les Sizies
Les Sizies
Les Sizies

Pertuisots

Les Vignes Franches
Les Vignes Franches
Les Vignes Franches

Les Clos des Mouches

Les Montrevenots

Clos des Avaux

Les Avaux

Les Avaux

Les Avaux

Clos de la Mousse

Clos Landry

Les Tuvilains

Les Tuvilains

Les Chouacheux

Les Boucherottes

Les Beaux Fougets

Les Bons Feuvres

Les Epenotes

Les Epenotes

R.N. 74

R.N. 73

TO POMMARD

TO CHALON-SUR-SAÔNE

POMMARD

À l'Ecu
À l'Ecu
Les Fèves

En Orme
En Genêt

Clos du Roi
Clos du Roi

Les Perrières

Les Cents Vignes

Les Chilènes

Les Boiches

Champagne de Savigny

Les Bressandes

Les Toussaints

Les Grèves

Les Mariages

Les Rôles

Le Bas des Teurons

La Blanchisserie

Le Fouiot

Les Teurons

Les Teurons

Les Teurons

Les Teurons

Faubourg Saint-Martin

Faubourg de Saint-Martin

La Creusotte

Les Reversées

La Cramotte

Faubourg de Bouze

Les Sceaux

Les Sceaux

Belissand

Les Vérottes

Les Paules

Les Chardonnergx

Les Prévoles

Les Lavées et les Erçles

KEY

① MONTAGNE DE ROCHETIN   ⑨ LES SEUREY

② LES TOPES BIZOT   ⑩ LES POINTES DE TUVILAINS

③ MONTBATOTS

④ CLOS DE LA FÉGUINE

⑤ LES TEURONS

⑥ MONTÉE ROUGE

⑦ LES LONGES

⑧ CHAMP PIMONT

N

SCALE – 1/26 200

BEAUNE PREMIER CRU
AOC PREMIERS CRUS

BEAUNE
AOC VILLAGES

CÔTE DE BEAUNE
AOC SOUS COMMUNALES

HISTORY

Beaune lies on a natural crossroads. The 'navel of Europe' was the extravagant boast of the local mayor, quoted by Christopher Fielden and John Arlott (*Burgundy*, 1976). It was where the old east-west road from Besançon to Autun met the old north-south *route* from Champagne and Dijon to Lyon and Marseilles; there was the added benefit of two natural springs which had their sources in the hills nearby. Colonised by the Romans as Belna or Belno Castrium in AD 40, the influence of Beaune grew as the importance of Autun, the capital of Burgundy in earlier Gallo-Roman days, fell, particularly after the destruction of the latter city by the sons of Clovis in the sixth century. The vine was already important. Gregory of Tours, who wrote a history of France in about AD 570, described the hills as 'covered in vines'.

Until the Duke of Burgundy moved to Dijon in the fourteenth century, Beaune was in all senses the capital of Burgundy. In 1395, Philippe Le Hardi published an ordinance prohibiting the plantation of the ignoble Gamay in favour of the noble Pinot, and from then on the best sites of the Côte d'Or were exclusively planted with members of the Chardonnay or Pinot family and the wines grew in fame.

The town of Beaune itself owes its character to the splendid pentangular fortified castle which was constructed during the reign of Charles XIII (1483–1498) and to the massive city fortifications which were built during the time of his predecessor Louis XI. This enclosed the town and has effectively preserved its centre. Unlike Dijon, Lyon, Mâcon or any other of the main cities of greater Burgundy, one can still imagine life as it might have been four or five hundred years ago.

LOCATION

Beaune is the Côte d'Or's third largest commune after Gevrey and Meursault. The slope of the *premiers crus* extends from the boundary with Pommard at the southern end towards the border with Savigny-lès-Beaune to the north and is divided in half by the road which goes up to Bouze in the Hautes-Côtes and along to Bligny-sur-Ouche. The soil structure, based on limestone, is complex. In general it is thin to the north (Marconnets, Clos-du-Roi, Fèves, Bressandes) especially on the steeper, upper part of the slope, and the vines have to stretch deep to find their nutrients. These wines are full, firm, even solid at the outset, and need time to mature. In the middle (Toussaints, Grèves, Teurons) there is some gravel (as the name Grèves would indicate) and the wine is of medium weight, plump and succulent. Bouchard Père's Vigne-de-l'Enfant-Jesus comes from an enclave in the Grèves. South of the road to Bligny there is some sand in the inclined *climat* of Montées-Rouge, and at Aigrots, Pertuisots and the upper part of Vignes-Franches; on mid-slope (Clos-des-Mouches, Vignes-Franches – from whence comes Louis Jadot's Clos-des-Ursules – Sizies, Avaux) the soil is very stony and hard to work; while at the southern end and lower down the slope (Boucherottes, Epenottes, Chouacheux) there is more clay and less gravel. Here the soil is deep, and production can be excessive if not restricted. This sector is known as *le puit* (the well) *de Beaune*, and produces soft, tender wines which evolve soon.

Though the colour of the soil is mainly a reddish brown, there are parts where it is a whitish marl, more suitable for the Chardonnay than the Pinot. On the upper part of the Clos-des-Mouches, Drouhin have vines which produce their celebrated white Beaune. Up-slope in the Grèves Jadot have Chardonnay. The results of these vines have a flavour which is somewhat more spicy than that of a Meursault. They also tend to evolve sooner. The production of white Beaune, however, is tiny, a mere 1,080 hectolitres or so per annum.

Which are the best *climats*? Beaune can boast forty-four which, in whole or part, are classed as *premier cru* (there are no *grands crus*) and no one seems to agree which are the best. Dr Morelot in 1831 cited Clos-de-la-Mousse (a small vineyard now the monopoly of Bouchard

Père et Fils), Teurons, Cras, Grèves, Fèves, Perrières, Cent-Vignes, Clos-du-Roi and Marconnets, all of which 'have the capacity to produce exquisite wines'. But he does not give any order of preference. Dr Lavalle (1855) lists Fèves, Grèves, Crais (now Cras) and Champs-Pimont as *têtes de cuvées*. Camille Rodier, writing in 1920, says the best is Fèves, with its finesse and delicate aroma; Grèves produces a very complete wine, with more body but not without finesse and velvet (*velouté*); Marconnets, on the Savigny border, is closed and solid, full but *bouqueté*. Clos-des-Mouches at the other end adjoining Pommard, is full-bodied, fruity, very elegant. Others (Cras, Champs-Pimont, Clos-du-Roi, Avaux, Aigrots) are supple and perfumed, and 'easy to drink' – a familiar phrase for damning with faint praise, I have always thought. He adds Marconnets, Bressandes and Clos-des-Mouches to Dr Lavalle's top *crus*. Poupon and Forgeot (*The Wines of Burgundy, 1964* and various editions subsequently) list Marconnets, Fèves, Bressandes, Grèves and Teurons as the best sites.

I would certainly agree with the last four of this final five, (Marconnets can be too muscular to have real finesse) and would add Cras, Vignes-Franches and Clos-des-Mouches, with the rider that, as always in Burgundy, the grower or *négociant* is of equal importance as the actual source. François Germain at the Château du Chorey always has a good range of Beaune *premiers crus*, as does Albert Morot, whose Beaunes come from the 7 ha family domaine and include Cent-Vignes, Grèves, Toussaints, Bressandes, Marconnets and Teurons. Bouchard Père et Fils are the largest land-holders in the commune of Beaune, with 48 ha of *premiers crus*. Chanson come next with 26, including the majority of Fèves which they sell as Clos-des-Fèves. The Hospices de Beaune have eight *cuvées* of Beaune and possess 19 ha. Drouhin have 15.5, Patriarche 12, Jadot 9, Louis Latour just over 4 and Remoissenet a couple. As one can see, most of the best land is owned by *négociants*. There are few important grower-only domaines in Beaune which market their wine in bottle.

How do the wines of Beaune compare with the other wines of the Côte? I find the wines of Beaune come midway between those of Pommard and those of Volnay. Pommards, particularly those of Rugiens, but equally from the best part of Epenots and elsewhere, are rich and sturdy. They can be somewhat four-square, but there should always be muscle. Volnays on the other hand are elegance personified: fragrance, delicacy, subtlety and finesse are the keynotes. The wines of Beaune are varied, as I have indicated above, but they lie somewhere in between. Only rarely, I would suggest, do they reach the quality of the best of these other two communes.

THE VINEYARD

Premiers Crus: As I have said, there are forty-four *climats* which, in whole or in part, are entitled to *premier cru*. In alphabetical order these are: Les Aigrots; Les Avaux; Les Beaux-Fougets (part); Bellisand; Blanche-Fleur (part); Les Boucherottes; Les Bressandes (part); Les Cent-Vignes; Champs-Pimont; Les Chouacheux; Clos-de-l'Ecu; Clos-de-la-Féguine (Aux Coucherias); Clos-de-la-Mousse; Clos-des-Avaux; Le Clos-des-Mouches; Clos-des-Ursules (Vignes-Franches); Clos-du-Roi (part); Clos-Landry or Clos-Saint-Landry; Clos-Sainte-Anne (Sur-les-Grèves); Aux Coucherias; Aux Cras; A l'Ecu (part); Les Epenottes (part); Les Fèves; En Genêt; Les Grèves; Sur-les-Grèves (part); Les Longes (part); Les Marconnets; La Mignotte; Montées-Rouge (part); Les Montrevenots or Montremenots; En l'Orme; Les Perrières; Pertuisots; Les Reversées; Les Seurey; Les Sizies; Le Bas-des-Teurons; Les Teurons; Les Toussaints; Les Tuvilains; La Vigne-de-l'Enfant-Jésus (Grèves); Les Vignes-Franches.

Some of these are very small, and by no means all are regularly seen. In thirty years I have never come across Les Beaux-Fougets, Les Longes, Les Montées-Rouge, En l'Orme or Les Seurey, and Blanche-Fleur only as a village wine. Altogether these cover 321.66 ha, of which about 20 are planted with Chardonnay and produce 11,500 hl (15.2 million bottles) of red and 730 ha (96,000 bottles) of white wine a year.

Village Wine: There are officially 128.13 ha of village land decreed as Beaune *tout court*. No doubt much more land would be suitable: as in the communes to the north and south, all that down to the main road. But as the town has expanded, the village land has shrunk. Today only some 98 ha (8 of which are white) is declared. Annual production is roughly 3,900 hl (515,000 bottles) of red wine and 350 hl (46,200 bottles) of white.

The village red wine, which is possibly supplemented by the lesser, young-vine *cuvées* of first growths, is a supple, early-maturing Pinot Noir of no great consequence. But the better *premiers crus* are quite a different kettle of fish. I describe these below. The white wine follows the same pattern. The village white wines are crisp, today wholly clean and 'modern', quite subtle and for early drinking. The *premiers crus*, of which the Clos-des-Mouches of Drouhin is the leading example, have an interesting spice, as if there were a little Pinot Beurot in the vineyard. These remind me of those of Savigny and Aloxe, where there is more likely to be some Pinot Beurot in the mix, but at a more concentrated level. Jadot's Beaune Grèves is another recommended example.

Côte-de-Beaune: Not to be confused with Côte-de-Beaune-Villages, this is a 52 ha appellation covering land up in the hill of the Mont Battois, between the Beaune-Savigny boundary and the route to Bouze. Behind the villas on the hillside, from which you get a splendid view of Beaune and the plain beyond, there are isolated blocks of vines. Why these are not AC Beaune I can't imagine. The wines are similar – light, soft and forward – though produced at a higher altitude. Or if not Beaune, why not Hautes-Côtes-de-Beaune? Annual production averages 850 hl (112,500 bottles) of red and 500 hl (66,000 bottles) of white. Only some 30 ha of the 52 ha delineated are currently under vine.

The Premiers Crus

I deal with these in a north-south order.

Les Marconnets (9.39 ha) • En l'Orme (2.02 ha)
Les Perrières (3.20 ha) • En Genêt (4.34 ha)
Clos-du-Roi (8.41 ha) • Blanche-Fleur (0.36 ha)

Though at the north end of the Côte, the aspect here is properly south-east (a little way further south, Grèves inclines more directly to the east), and the wines, especially from Marconnets, furthest up the slope, are fullish, plump and rich. There is a robust element as well, but this can sometimes detract from the finesse. Clos-du-Roi, underneath Marconnets, produces somewhat more earthy wine.

Recommended Sources:
Les Marconnets: Albert Morot; Remoissenet Père et Fils (both Beaune).
Les Perrières: François Gay (Clos-des-Perrières) (Chorey-lès-Beaune).
Clos-du-Roi: Camus-Brochon (Savigny-lès-Beaune); Tollot-Beaut (Chorey-lès-Beaune); Gabriel Bouchard (Beaune); Robert Ampeau (Meursault).

Clos-de-l'Ecu (2.37 ha) • A l'Ecu (2.65 ha)
Les Fèves (4.42 ha) • Les Bressandes (16.97 ha)
Les Toussaints (6.42 ha) • Les Cent-Vignes (23.50 ha)

The slope turns round to incline more directly to the east here, and not all the Cent-Vignes, which is practically flat, is probably really of first-growth quality. Bressandes and Fèves at the top of the slope can produce very good wine, almost on a par with Grèves and Teurons. Compared with the wines in the section above, there is an extra roundness, richness and style here, with the same sort of weight as Marconnets, but not the robust *sauvage* touch. The Clos-de-l'Ecu is the monopoly of the Beaune merchants Jaboulet-Vercherre.

Recommended Sources:

Clos-des-Fèves: Chanson (*monopole*) (Beaune).

Les Bressandes: Louis Jadot; Albert Morot; Jean-Claude Rateau; Remoissenet Père et Fils (all Beaune); Henri Germain (Meursault).

Les Toussaints: Louis Jadot; Albert Morot; Roland Remoissenet (all Beaune).

Les Cent-Vignes: François Germain, Château de Chorey; Arnoux Père et Fils; René Podichard (Chorey-lès-Beaune); Michel Duchet; Louis Jadot; Albert Morot (all Beaune); Vincent Bitouzet (Volnay); René Monnier (Meursault).

LES GRÈVES (31.33 HA) • LES TEURONS (21.04 HA)
AUX CRAS (5.00 HA) • LES BAS-DES-TEURONS (6.31 HA)
SUR-LES-GRÈVES (2.90 HA) • CLOS-SAINTE-ANNE (0.73 HA)
CLOS-DE-LA-FÉGUNE (1.86 HA) • AUX COUCHERIAS (7.70 HA)

The best *premiers crus* of Beaune, in my view, are Grèves and Teurons. Sur-les-Grèves in fact lies above Teurons, not Grèves, while part of the bottom of this *climat* is technically Le Bas-des-Teurons and is supposed to be inferior (but as in practice wine made here is labelled simply as Teurons there is no way the customer can differentiate). Another part of the upper slope above Teurons is Les Cras, next to the road up to Bouze, while Clos-Sainte-Anne, Clos-de-la-Fégune (a monopoly of Domaine Jacques Prieur of Meursault) and Aux Coucherias are the upper extensions beyond Les Cras as the hillsides turn round to face towards the south.

Cras, Teurons and Grèves, the former a little lighter than the other two, produce Beaune at its most elegant: fullish but properly round, rich and balanced, with plenty of depth. In cellars where they have both, Teurons is often the best, although this also depends on the age of the vines, and the precise location of the vines on the slope.

Coucherias is again just a little lighter than Cras, but flowery, elegant and with pleasant plump fruit. Sur-les-Grèves seems to be a favoured location in these parts for Chardonnay.

Recommended Sources:

Les Grèves (blanc): François Germain, Château de Chorey; Louis Jadot (Beaune).

Les Grèves (rouge): Daniel Largeot; Tollot-Beaut (Chorey-lès-Beaune); Michel Duchet; Joseph Drouhin; Louis Jadot; Albert Morot (all Beaune); Bouchard Père et Fils under Vigne-de-l'Enfant-Jésus (Beaune); Michel Lafarge (Volnay); Bernard Morey (Chassagne-Montrachet); Ropiteau-Mignon/Cottin Frères (Meursault/Nuits-Saint-Georges).

Les Teurons: François Germain, Château de Chorey; Bouchard Père et Fils; Louis Jadot; Albert Morot (all Beaune); Régis Rossignol-Changarnier (Volnay).

Aux Cras: François Germain, Château de Chorey.

Aux Coucherias: As Clos-des-Couchereaux, Louis Jadot (Beaune).

MONTÉES-ROUGE (3.75 HA) • CHAMPS-PIMONT (16.25 HA)
LA MIGNOTTE (2.40 HA) • LES AVAUX (11.52 HA)
CLOS-DES-AVAUX (3.70 HA) • LES SEUREY (1.23 HA)
CLOS-DE-LA-MOUSSE (3.37 HA) • LES SIZIES (8.58 HA)
LES TUVILAINS (8.94 HA) • BÉLISSAND (4.88 HA)
LES REVERSÉES (4.78 HA)

These are the *climats*, most of them small, which lie on the south side of the road up to Bouze. The slope is very gentle here, and there is quite a distance between the vines at the top (Montées-Rouge) and those in Reversées at the bottom.

I have had my best wines here from Les Avaux (though in her *négociant* days at Leroy, Madame Lalou Bize offered a splendid range of Beaune, including Sizies). But the wines here do not seem to have the definition, the flair and the character of Teurons or Grèves. Pleasant, medium weight, round and fruity is the style. For the medium term.

Recommended Sources:
Les Avaux: Champy; Louis Jadot (both Beaune).
Clos-de-la-Mousse: Bouchard Père et Fils (*monopole*) (Beaune).
Les Reversées: Jean-Marc Boulay (Volnay); Jean-Claude Rateau (Beaune).

LES AIGROTS (18.64 HA)

LES MONTREVENOTS OR MONTREMENOTS (8.42 HA)

LE CLOS-DES-MOUCHES (25.18 HA) • LES VIGNES-FRANCHES (9.77 HA)

PERTUISOTS (5.27 HA) • CLOS-LANDRY (1.98 HA)

LES BOUCHEROTTES (8.54 HA) • LES CHOUACHEUX (5.04 HA)

LES EPENOTTES (7.69 HA) • LES BEAUX-FOUGETS (0.27 HA)

These vineyards stretch from the hillsides of Montagne-Sainte-Désirée down towards the main road, from a point where the vines face almost due east, as in Les Aigrots, all the way round to due south, as in Les Montrevenots. The slope is very gentle, only rising slowly, even at the top.

Here we are on the border with Pommard. Is there a similarity, as there is in Marconnets, with Savigny? I have to say I don't see one, or only at the foot of the slope between Epenottes and some of the weediest Epenots. Vignes-Franches and Clos-des-Mouches (Jadot's Clos-des-Ursules in the former and Drouhin's example of the latter) are the best wines and *climats*. Here we can expect the same level of quality as Teurons and Grèves, but in a more expansive, opulent, slightly spicy sort of way. But most of the rest, as in the section above, lack excitement.

Recommended Sources:
Les Montrevenots: Jean-Marc Boillot (Pommard).
Le Clos-des-Mouches (*blanc*): Joseph Drouhin (Beaune).
Le Clos-des-Mouches (*rouge*): Joseph Drouhin (Beaune).
Les Vignes-Franches: Jacques Germain, Château de Chorey; Louis Jadot as Clos-des-Ursules (both Beaune).
Les Boucherottes: Jacques Germain, Château de Chorey; Louis Jadot (both Beaune).
Les Chouacheux: Louis Jadot (Beaune).

THE GROWERS

BERNARD BESCANCENOT

10.5 ha: owned and *en fermage/métayage*. Corton-Charlemagne (20 a); Beaune *premier cru* in Les Cent-Vignes, Les Teurons, Les Bressandes, Les Toussaints, Clos-du-Roi, Les Grèves, A l'Ecu; village Aloxe-Corton; village Beaune; village Pernand-Vergelesses *rouge et blanc*; village Chorey-lès-Beaune *blanc*.

With 3 ha, the tall fifty-plus Bernard Bescancenot is the largest owner in Cent-Vignes, one of the seven Beaune *premiers crus* in his portfolio. He retains 30 per cent of the stems, likes to keep the wine on its fine lees without racking, is not a great fan of new wood, and leaves his wines two years in cask before bottling. The wines are competent but not exciting.

ALBERT BICHOT ET CIE

This large *négociant* owns estates in Chablis, where I have tasted well, and the Domaine du Clos-Frantin in Vosne-Romanée (see page 129) where I have been less impressed. I am underwhelmed by the merchant wines too, and was disappointed to see the capable Joseph de Bucy, hired by Bichot from Jean Germain, depart almost as soon as he had arrived. Yet there is now a new generation, in the form of Albéric Bichot, at the helm, and Anthony Hanson writes that he is not above tasting blind alongside other Côte d'Or young growers. Is this a sign of better things?

GABRIEL BOUCHARD

4 ha: owned and *en fermage*. Beaune *premier cru* in Les Cent-Vignes, Clos-du-Roi; Pommard *premier cru* Les Charmots; village Savigny-lès-Beaune in the *lieu-dit* Les Liards; village Saint-Romain in the *lieu-dit* Les Perrières; village Beaune.

A rabbit warren of cramped cellars in the back streets of Beaune houses this Bouchard domaine, which claims only a scant relationship to better known Bouchards. Space prevents a total *élevage* in cask. After twelve months the wines have to go back into tank. Mixed results.

BOUCHARD AINÉ

This well-known *négociant* is now a part of the mighty Boisset empire. It is probably causing them some embarrassment. Up until recently, among a mere handful of Côte d'Or wines offered, this Bouchard was at least responsible for the Fixin and the Chambertin of the Domaine Marion. Now the Fixin is with Fougeray-Beauclair of Marsannay and the Chambertin has been entrusted to Henri Roch of Nuits-Saint-Georges. Bernard Repolt of Jaffelin (another firm that Boisset owns) is supposed to be in charge. But what is there to be in charge of?

BOUCHARD PÈRE ET FILS, SA

93 ha: owned. Chambertin (15 a); Bonnes-Mares (24 a); Clos-de-Vougeot (23 a); Le Corton (3.94 ha); Corton-Charlemagne (3.09 ha); Chevalier-Montrachet (2.32 ha); Savigny-lès-Beaune *premier cru* Les Lavières; Beaune *premier cru* in Les Teurons, Les Grèves, Les Grèves La Vigne-de-l'Enfant-Jésus (*monopole*); Marconnets, Clos-de-la-Mousse (*monopole*); Clos-Landry *blanc* (*monopole*); and more, see below. Pommard *premier cru* in Les Rugiens, Les Combes; Volnay *premier cru* in Les Caillerets (*ancienne cuvée* Carnot), En Chevret, Les Taille-Pieds; Le Chanlin, Les Fremiets Clos-de-la-Rougeotte (*monopole*); Meursault *premier cru* Les Genevrières; village Chambolle-Musigny; village Aloxe-Corton in the *lieu-dit* Les Paulands; village Ladoix in the *lieu-dit* Clos-Royer; village Beaune.

Beaune du Château *blanc et rouge* is a blend alternatively from 4 ha of *premier cru* planted in Chardonnay (Les Aigrots, Les Sizies) or 30 ha of *premier cru* planted in Pinot Noir (Les Aigrots, Les Sizies, Les Pertuisots, Les Avaux, Les Seurey, Clos-du-Roi, Les Cent-Vignes, En Genêt, Bressandes, Toussaints, Sur-les-Grèves, Champs-Pimont, Belissand, Le Bas-des-Teurons, A l'Ecu, Les Teurons, Les Reversées, Les Beaux-Fougets.

Bouchard Père et Fils are also *éleveurs* and bottlers of the wines of the Château de Vosne-Romanée (see page 136) (La Romanée *monopole*, Vosne-Romanée Aux Reignots) and the Domaine du Clos-Saint-Marc in Nuits-Saint-Georges (Clos-Saint-Marc *monopole* and Les Argillières).

Finally they distribute the wine of the Château de Mandelot in the Hautes-Côtes and were pioneers with Aligoté de Bouzeron.

In all Bouchard Père et Fils owns 93 ha, 71 ha of which are *grand* and *premier cru*: an impressive land-holding.

I have had plenty of splendid Bouchard wines of the 1940s, 1950s and early 1960s, and would still be happy to chance my arm today if any of these happened to come my way. But more recently, all the way through since the time I started writing *The Vine*, I have found the end results at Bouchard Père et Fils no better than competent, though occasionally there have been glimmers on the horizon. This is despite a splendid modern vinification centre and its change of policy from buying wine to vinifying bought-in grapes or must alongside the produce of its own vineyards. Something was missing. In 1995 the firm was taken over by Henriot of Champagne. I await the consequences of this change with interest. The indications so far are very promising.

In August 1996 Bouchard Père et Fils entered into an agreement with Domaine Ropiteau-Mignon to take over management of this 30 hectare estate. These wines will in future be made and sold by Bouchard Père et Fils.

See Profile, page 351.

HENRI CAUVARD ET FILS

16.5 ha: owned and *en fermage.* Corton-Charlemagne (20 a); Beaune *premier cru* in Cent-Vignes, Teurons, Bressandes; village Beaune including the *lieu-dit* Clos-de-la-Maladière *rouge et blanc* (*monopole*), Clos-des-Mariages *blanc;* village Chorey-lès-Beaune; village Aloxe-Corton; village Pommard in the *lieu-dit* Les Noizons; village Volnay; Côte-de-Beaune, *rouge et blanc.*

Henri Cauvard is large, dark, mustached and forty-something. His HQ lies a few houses down the road to Savigny from his father, now *en retraite.* No stems, one-sixth new wood (but no old wood) and bottling after a year and a half – though some 1993s were still unbottled in December 1995. The wines are quite sturdy, but the quality is unexceptional.

CHAMPY PÈRE ET FILS

Champy is the oldest *négociant* in Burgundy, and has archives dating back to 1720. Somewhat moribund, it was acquired by Jadot in the late 1980s, who were interested in the vineyards. They kept these, and some interesting reserves of old bottles dating back to mid nineteenth century, but sold the remainder – name and cellars – in 1990 to Henri Meurgey, a well-recognised *oenologue* and broker, and his son Pierre.

What Henri and Pierre offer today is a wide range of well-priced, well-chosen wines ranging from generics upwards, but not too far upwards. The emphasis is on affordable village wines rather than on a glitzy range of *grands crus.* They buy wine rather than must or grapes, and more than once, when I have correctly guessed the source, I have noticed that the wine in the Champy cellar showed better than it did in its original home, which I might have visited a day or two previously.

DIVA, handling estate-bottled Burgundy, is another Meurgey concern.

CHANSON PÈRE ET FILS

42 ha: owned. Corton, Vergennes (*blanc*) (12 a); Corton, Rognet (11 a); Beaune *premier cru* in Clos-des-Fèves (*monopole*), Les Bressandes, Les Grèves, Clos-des-Mouches, Clos-des-Marconnets, Clos-du-Roi, Champs-Pimont, Les Teurons, A l'Ecu, Vignes-Franches; Savigny-lès-Beaune *premier cru* in La Dominode, Les Marconnets; Pernand-Vergelesses *premier cru* Les Vergelesses, Les Caradeux (*blanc*).

Chanson was established in 1750, and has a large vineyard holding of its own. The wines are quite light in colour from the start, though this does not change much thereafter. There have been some very good wines of late, but in general I miss the concentration and fat, the richness and velvetiness I search for in top Burgundy.

See Profile, page 371.

LA COMPAGNIE DES VINS D'AUTREFOIS

Established in the late 1970s by Les Fils de Marcel Quancard of Bordeaux, but subsequently mainly Swiss-owned, this enterprising company, run by the ebullient Jean-Pierre Nié, himself from a wine-growing family in Santenay, specialises in domaine wines, which it buys early, whose *élevage* and eventual bottling it supervises. It also markets the wines of some larger, self-supporting estates. Late in 1996 the firm was taken over by Boisset.

A subsidiary label is Bertrand de Monceny.

★★Joseph Drouhin, SA

63.2 ha: owned and *en fermage*. Chambertin, Clos-de-Bèze (13 a); Griottes-Chambertin (53 a); Bonnes-Mares (24 a); Le Musigny (68 a); Grands-Echézeaux (48 a); Echézeaux (46 a); Clos-de-Vougeot (91 a); Corton, Bressandes (26 a); Corton-Charlemagne (34 a); Bâtard-Montrachet (10 a); Chambolle-Musigny *premier cru* including Les Amoureuses; Vosne-Romanée *premier cru* Les Petits-Monts; Volnay *premier cru* Clos-des-Chênes; Beaune *premier cru* including Clos-des-Mouches (*rouge et blanc*), Les Grèves; village Chambolle-Musigny; village Vougeot; village Chorey-lès-Beaune; village Beaune. Plus a domaine of 35.83 in Chablis.

Drouhin is also the exclusive distributor of Domaine Marquis de Laguiche in Chassagne-Montrachet (see page 291).

The firm dates from 1880, when Joseph Drouhin took over an already well-established Burgundian house, and then acquired the old cellars of the Dukes of Burgundy, near the Collégiale Notre-Dame.

This is one of the most perfectionist and least paternalistic of the Beaune merchants, dealing in nothing but Burgundy and Beaujolais, not even generics. The wines are now made in modern premises on the outskirts of Beaune, under the supervision of Robert Jousset-Drouhin, head of the firm, his son Philippe, who is responsible for the vineyards, and Laurence Jobard, chief *oenologue*, and are as good as any in the Côte, equally fine in both colours. Drouhin's daughter Véronique is responsible for the company's Oregon diversification: Domaine Drouhin.

See Profile, page 412.

Michel Duchet

5.50 ha: owned. Beaune *premier cru* in Les Bressandes, Les Grèves, Les Cent-Vignes, Les Pertuisots; village Beaune.

Behind the Eglise Saint-Nicholas in what used to be the old *vignerons' quartier* of Beaune you will find the cellar of the Duchet domaine, owned by a Parisian, the son of a local politician, and looked after on his behalf by Jean-Marc Durand (see below). The vines in the Bressandes and the Pertuisots are quite young at the time of writing, but I like the fresh, gently oaky, plump style of them.

Jean-Marc Durand

2.5 ha: owned and *en fermage*. Village Pommard including the *lieu-dit* En Boeuf; village Beaune.

As well as looking after the Duchet vines (see above), Jean-Marc Durand tends the Cuvée Maurice Drouhin vines for the Hospices de Beaune.

Camille Giroud, SA

Old-fashioned, in the best sense of the word, is how I would describe the wines of this merchant. Up to the present – though this will be changed when a new extension to the *cuverie* is completed in 1996 – Bernard and François Giroud have bought made wine, and it tends to be well-coloured, rich, full and long-lasting, sometimes a bit too robust. There is little new oak here, and the wines are bottled later than most. I have had some fine old bottles here, though others have been a bit tough.

There is now an embryonic domaine here: 32 a of Beaune *premier cru* Les Cras.

Hospices de Beaune

The Hospices de Beaune comprises two charitable institutions, the Hôtel Dieu, founded in 1443 by Nicolas Rolin, Chancellor of Philippe Le Hardi, Duke of Burgundy, and his wife

Guigone de Salins, and the Hospice de la Charité, endowed by Antoine Rousseau and his wife Barbe Deslandes in the seventeenth century. The Hôtel Dieu is a remarkable building in the centre of Beaune and is one of the world's great vinous tourist attractions. It is no longer used as a charitable institution for the sick and the poor, but is preserved as a museum. The central feature of the building is a huge dormitory, the Grande Salle or Chambre des Pauvres, its walls lined with curiously wide yet short beds – the inmates slept two to a bed – each with a sight of the altar at the far end so that, though bedridden, they could participate in the services.

The visitor will then pass into a central courtyard, view the medieval kitchens and pantries, and then move into a small art gallery whose central feature is a magnificent 'Last Judgement', commissioned by Rolin, executed by Roger van der Weyden. This is one of the masterpieces of the Northern Renaissance. Rolin and his wife also commissioned a picture of the Virgin from Jan van Eyck. This is in the Louvre.

Over the years both these charitable institutions were the fortunate recipients of vineyards, and these holdings now total some 62 hectares, nearly all of it *premier cru* or *grand cru*, and all but seven in the Côte-de-Beaune, making the Hospices one of the largest names in Burgundy. These 62 ha are split up into thirty-eight different *cuvées* which are often blends of a number of different *climats* within the same commune. They are sold each year under the name of the benefactor, by auction on the Sunday afternoon (and well into the evening: this is a lengthy, tedious auction *à la chandelle*) on the third weekend in November. In 1995 566 casks of wine (plus some of the previous year's *eau de vie*) were auctioned. This is not the entirety of the production as the produce of the younger vines is disposed of in bulk to the local *négociants*. The auction is the central event in the weekend of *Les Trois Glorieuses* and traditionally sets the trend of prices for the vintage, though the actual levels paid are grossly inflated.

The wines are sold when they are barely a month old, and as crucial as their initial quantity, is the competence of the firm (only local merchants may bid) who will look after it subsequently. It is wise to choose a merchant whose name you can trust.

Red Wine *Cuvées*

Charlotte Dumay: Corton, Les Renardes (2 ha); Corton, Les Bressandes (1 ha); Corton, Clos-du-Roi (0.4 ha).

Docteur Peste: Corton, Les Bressandes (1 ha); Corton, Les Chaumes and Les Voirosses (1 ha); Corton, Clos-du-Roi (0.5 ha); Corton, Le Fiètre (0.4 ha); Corton, Les Grèves (0.1 ha).

Rameau-Lamarosse: Pernand-Vergelesses, Les Basses-Vergelesses (0.65 ha).

Forneret: Savigny-lès-Beaune, Les Vergelesses (1 ha); Savigny-lès-Beaune, Les Gravains (0.65 ha).

Fouquerand: Savigny-lès-Beaune, Les Basses-Vergelesses (1 ha); Savigny-lès-Beaune, Les Talmettes (0.65 ha); Savigny-lès-Beaune, Aux Gravains (0.33 ha); Savigny-lès-Beaune, Aux Serpentières (0.14 ha).

Arthur Girard: Savigny-lès-Beaune, Les Peuillets (1 ha); Savigny-lès-Beaune, Les Marconnets (0.8 ha).

Nicolas Rolin: Beaune, Les Cent-Vignes (1.4 ha); Beaune, Les Grèves (0.33 ha); Beaune, En Genêt (0.2 ha); Beaune, Les Teurons (0.5 ha); Beaune, Les Bressandes (0.14 ha).

Guigone de Salins: Beaune, Les Bressandes (1.2 ha); Beaune, Les Seurey (0.8 ha); Beaune, Les Champs-Pimont (0.6 ha).

Clos des Avaux: Beaune, Les Avaux (2 ha).

Brunet: Beaune, Les Teurons (0.5 ha); Beaune, Les Bressandes (0.5 ha); Beaune, Les Cent-Vignes (0.5 ha).

Maurice Drouhin: Beaune, Les Avaux (1 ha); Beaune, Les Boucherottes (0.65 ha); Beaune, Les Champs-Pimont (0.6 ha); Beaune, Les Grèves (0.25 ha).

Hugues et Louis Bétault: Beaune, Les Grèves (1.1 ha); Beaune, La Mignotte (0.54 ha); Beaune, Les Aigrots (0.4 ha); Beaune, Clos-des-Mouches (0.33 ha).

Rousseau-Deslandes: Beaune, Les Cent-Vignes (1 ha); Beaune, Les Montrevenots (0.65 ha); Beaune, La Mignotte (0.4 ha).

Dames-Hospitalières: Beaune, Les Bressandes (1 ha); Beaune, La Mignotte (1.13 ha); Beaune, Les Teurons (0.5 ha).

Dames de la Charité: Pommard, Les Petits-Epenots (0.4 ha); Pommard, Les Rugiens (0.33 ha); Pommard, Les Noizons (0.25 ha); Pommard, La Refène (0.35 ha); Pommard, Les Combes-Dessus (0.2 ha).

Billardet: Pommard, Les Petits-Epenots (0.65 ha); Pommard, Les Noizons (0.5 ha); Pommard, Les Arvelets (0.4 ha); Pommard, Les Rugiens (0.35 ha).

Blondeau: Volnay, Les Champans (0.6 ha); Volnay, Les Taille-Pieds (0.6 ha); Volnat, Le Ronceret (0.35 ha); Volnat, En l'Ormeau (0.25 ha).

Général Muteau: Volnay, Le Village (0.8 ha); Volnay, Le Carelle-sous-la-Chapelle (0.35 ha); Volnay, Les Caillerets-Dessus (0.2 ha); Volnay, Le Fremiet (0.2 ha); Volnay, Les Taille-Pieds (0.2 ha).

Jehan de Massol: Volnay, Les Santenots (1.25 ha); Volnay (Santenots), Les Plures (0.25 ha).

Gauvain: Volnay, Les Santenots (0.65 ha); Volnay (Santenots), Les Plures (0.75 ha).

Lebelin: Monthélie, Les Duresses (0.88 ha).

Boillot: Auxey-Duresses, Les Duresses (0.5 ha).

Madelaine Collignon: Mazis-Chambertin (1.75 ha).

Cyrot-Chaudron: Beaune, Les Montrevenots (1 ha).

Raymond Cyrot: Pommard *premier cru* (0.65 ha); Pommard (1.10 ha).

Suzanne Chaudron: Pommard (1.37 ha).

Cyrot Chaudron et Georges Kritter: Clos-de-la-Roche (0.4 ha).

White Wine *Cuvées*

Françoise de Salins: Corton-Charlemagne (0.4 ha).

Baudot: Meursault, Les Genevrières-Dessus (0.65 ha); Meursault, Les Genevrières-Dessous (0.75 ha).

Philippe le Bon: Meursault, Les Genevrières-Dessus (0.13 ha); Meursault, Les Genevrières-Dessous (0.4 ha).

De Bahèzre de Lanlay: Meursault, Les Charmes-Dessus (0.13 ha); Meursault, Les Charmes-Dessous (0.4 ha).

Albert Grivault: Meursault, Les Charmes-Dessus (0.5 ha).

Jehan Humblot: Meursault, Les Poruzots (0.5 ha); Meursault, Les Grands-Charrons (0.1 ha).

Loppin: Meursault, Les Criots (0.5 ha); Meursault, Les Cras (0.2 ha).

Goureau: Meursault, Les Poruzots (0.35 ha); Meursault, Les Peutes-Vignes (0.2 ha).

Paul Chanson: Corton Blanc, Les Vergennes (0.35 ha).

Dames de Flandres: Bâtard-Montrachet (0.35 ha).

François Poisard: Pouilly-Fuissé (4.00 ha).

In recent years, the quality of the Hospices' wines has been much criticised, and rightly so. But in 1993/1994 a new wine-making centre, away from the centre of Beaune, was constructed. At the same time André Porcheret, who had been the Hospices' wine-maker until seduced away by Lalou Bize to be her right-hand man at the Domaine Leroy, was hired back. It became apparent that he was to be given greater control of the *vignerons* who tended the Hospices' vines (the job is leased out to locals who have neighbouring vines on an *à la tache* basis), and that a more rigorous attitude towards yield was to be inaugurated. A *table de trie* was installed at the winery and Porcheret was quoted as having extended the *cuvaison* following the fermentation. It seems a corner has been turned. Some are now beginning to suggest that the Hospices should act like a proper domaine, and look after the vines up to the time of bottling. To the Beaune *négoce*, of course, this is anathema, as it usurps their traditional role, indeed *raison d'être*. One further point of controversy is the Hospices' policy of putting everything into 100 per cent new oak. This, critics argue, is fine for the Mazis-Chambertin in a year like 1990, but inappropriate for an Auxey-Duresses in a much lighter year. Personally I find many of the Hospices' wines hopelessly over-oaked, even when racked into old wood immediately on receipt into the purchaser's cellar (this has to be by the 15th January following the sale). But perhaps Porcheret will be able to change this policy too.

★★LOUIS JADOT

59.44 ha: owned and *en fermage*.

This is split up between five domaines:

Domaine Louis Jadot: 23.62 ha. Chambertin Clos-de-Bèze (42 a); Chapelle-Chambertin (39 a); Bonnes-Mares (27 a); Le Musigny (17 a); Echézeaux (35 a); Clos-de-Vougeot (2.15 ha); Gevrey-Chambertin *premier cru* in Clos-Saint-Jacques, Les Cazetiers, La Combe-aux-Moines, Lavaux-Saint-Jacques, Les Estournelles-Saint-Jacques, Les Poissenots; Chambolle-Musigny *premier cru* Les Amoureuses; Savigny-lès-Beaune, La Dominode; Beaune *premier cru* in Les Avaux, Les Teurons; Marsannay (*rouge, rosé et blanc*); village Chambolle; village Santenay in the *lieu-dit* Clos-de-Malte (*rouge et blanc*).

Domaine des Héritiers Louis Jadot: 16.58 ha. Corton-Charlemagne (1.88 ha); Corton, Les Pougets (1.54 ha); Chevalier-Montrachet, Les Demoiselles (51 a); Pernand-Vergelesses *premier cru* (En Caradeux) Clos-de-la-Croix-de-Pierre; Beaune *premier cru* in Les Bressandes, Les Teurons, Clos-des-Couchéreaux (in Les Coucherias), Les Boucherottes, Les Chouacheux, Clos-des-Ursules (in Les Vignes-Franches); Puligny-Montrachet *premier cru* Les Folatières.

Domaine André Gagey: 3.67 ha. Clos-Saint-Denis (17 a); Chambolle-Musigny *premier cru* Les Baudes; Nuits-Saint-Georges *premier cru* Les Boudots; Beaune *premier cru* in Clos-des-Couchereaux (in Les Coucherias), Les Cent-Vignes, Les Grèves (*blanc*); Puligny-Montrachet *premier cru* Le Champ-Gain; village Chambolle-Musigny.

Domaine Robert Tourlière: 2.87 ha. Clos-de-Vougeot (64 a); Beaune *premier cru* in Les Grèves (*rouge et blanc*), Les Toussaints, Les Tuvilains.

Domaine Duc de Magenta: 12.70 ha. Chassagne-Montrachet *premier cru* Morgeot 'Clos-de-la-Chapelle' *rouge et blanc*; Puligny-Montrachet *premier cru* Clos-de-la-Garenne; village Puligny-Montrachet; village Meursault; village Auxey-Duresses.

The wine-maker here is the candid and enthusiastic Jacques Lardière: a fountain of knowledge and a man of genius. You will learn more about Burgundy in a morning tasting with him than in five years' trekking around on your own. And you will never be anything less than highly satisfied with his wines. This is a perfectionist. As you sample what is an exhaustive range and make your comments, you will often be told that yes, probably, this *premier cru* (not quite up to snuff) will be downgraded to the village *cuvée*; with this wine he did such-and-such, with another something quite different. And because.

See Profile, page 484.

JAFFELIN

Established in 1816, recently owned by Drouhin, but in 1991 sold to Jean-Claude Boisset, this *négociant* is managed by the able Bernard Repolt, who is responsible for Bouchard Aîné and the wines of the Domaine Ponnelle (see pages 156 and 205). Jaffelin offers a limited but well-chosen and well-priced range of wines, mainly village and lesser *premiers crus*. The wine-making, even when the firm was ancillary to Drouhin, is quite different, retaining more of the stems for instance.

★ALBERT MOROT

7 ha: owned. Beaune *premier cru* in Les Teurons, Les Grèves, Les Toussaints, Les Bressandes, Les Cent-Vignes, Les Marconnets; Savigny-lès-Beaune *premier cru* in Les Vergelesses, 'La Bataillère'.

Once a *négociant*, this family firm, today run by Mlle Françoise Choppin, now subsists on its domaine, which contains only *premiers crus* vines, and operates out of the gauntly gothic Château de la Creusotte, on the road to Bouze-lès-Beaune. Delicious wines, each separate and individual, can be found here. At the time of writing the Grèves is *jeunes vignes*.
    See Profile, page 554.

PATRIARCHE PÈRE ET FILS

This is a major *négociant*, owned by the ageing André Boisseaux and his family, with the sparkling wine house of Kriter as an associated company. The Château de Marsannay (see page 46) and the Château de Meursault (see page 250) are also part of the empire, and under various names the firm and family additionally possess 6.10 ha of Beaune *premier cru*.
    Patriarche, with their Couvent des Cordeliers in Beaune and their châteaux in Marsannay and Meursault, are focused toward the – perhaps less wine-knowledgeable – tourist. If that means 'commercial' wines, so be it. But commercial wines can be better than this.

JEAN-CLAUDE RATEAU

8 ha: owned and *en fermage/métayage*. Beaune *premier cru* Les Reversées, Les Bressandes, Les Coucherias; village Beaune; village Puligny-Montrachet; village Gevrey-Chambertin; Côte-de-Beaune.

Jean-Claude Rateau was one of the first of a now increasing number of Burgundian *vignerons* who are *biodynamique*, and as such has been something of a mentor to others. If this makes him sound like the wise old man of the hills it is not meant to. He is a vigorous, tall forty-something with a big black mustache, who started with one hectare in 1979. No stems, no new oak and a few days' cold soaking are other parts of the recipe. The results, especially the Reversées, a fine example of a not particularly well-sited *premier cru*, are very good. Currently the Coucherias is *jeunes vignes*.

★REMOISSENET PÈRE ET FILS

2.50 ha: owned. Beaune *premier cru* in Les Marconnets, Les Grèves, Les Toussaints, En Genêt.

Courtier as well as *négociant* (for a long while this firm was the supplier/broker for Nicolas and it was on the back of that the merchant business was established), Remoissenet buys wine, not must or grapes. Roland Remoissenet, today in his sixties, is shrewd, a man of frequent collecting enthusiasms, and a cat who walks by himself, decidedly not part of the sometimes self-important Beaune *négociant* 'mafia'. The firm distributes the wines of the Domaine Baron Thénard (see page 312) and these – Le Montrachet, Corton Clos-du-Roi, Grands-Echézeaux – are often the best wines. Today the problems of supply, with all of the best growers bottling all their best wines themselves, must be getting increasingly acute, but you can still get some very fine wines, which keep remarkably well, under the Remoissenet label, particularly in white.

BLIGNY-LÈS-BEAUNE

This village to the south of Beaune in the plain does not possess any *Appellation Contrôlée* vineyards. But there are a few sources worth noting.

CHÂTEAU DE BLIGNY-LÈS-BEAUNE

20.5 ha: owned. Echézeaux (34 a); Corton (Vergennes and Rognets) (76 a); Corton-Charlemagne (17 a); Corton *blanc* (Vergennes) (27 a); Vosne-Romanée *premier cru* Au-Dessus-des-Malconsorts; Nuits-Saint-Georges *premier cru* in Les Pruliers, Aux Thoreys, Aux Argillas; Beaune *premier cru* in Clos-des-Aigrots, Les Pertuisots, Les Grèves; Pommard *premier cru* in Clos-de-la-Charrière, Les Arvelets, Clos-Blanc, Les Charmots; village Vosne-Romanée; village Beaune including the *lieu-dit* Clos-Saint-Desiré *rouge et blanc*; village Pommard including the *lieu-dit* Les Vignots; village Volnay in the *lieu-dit* Clos-Martin; village Puligny-Montrachet; village Meursault.

The Château de Bligny belongs to the insurance company GMF (*Garantie Mutuelle des Fonctionnaires*), owners among other vinous interests of Châteaux Beychevelle and Beaumont in Bordeaux. I have not been very impressed by these wines, despite the impressive-looking list of vineyards and a perfectly normal wine-making recipe – no stems, five days' cold soaking, thermo-regulated fermentation at 30°C, one-quarter new wood. Up to 1994 they were coarse and neutral. Then they changed their *pigeage*-ing method. Now the wines seem to be thin and neutral.

JEAN GUITON

12.5 ha: owned and *en fermage/métayage*. Beaune *premier cru* Les Sizies; Pernand-Vergelesses *premier cru* Les Vergelesses; Savigny-lès-Beaune *premier cru* Les Peuillets, Les Hauts-Jarrons; Ladoix *premier cru* La Corvée; village Ladoix; village Aloxe-Corton; village Savigny-lès-Beaune; village Beaune; village Pommard; village Volnay.

Jean Guiton used to have an open mind about destemming, sometimes doing so completely, sometimes retaining most, but now he never utilises any. He vinifies at up to 33°C with two *pigeages* a day. He also tends vines in Savigny for the Hospices de Beaune. His own Savignys *can* be good (the 1993 Hauts-Jarrons) but like the rest of his wines are normally not much better than 'not bad'.

CLAUDE MARÉCHAL

9 ha: owned and *en fermage/métayage*. Savigny-lès-Beaune *premier cru* Aux Lavières; village Savigny-lès-Beaune; village Ladoix; village Pommard in the *lieux-dits* La Chanière, Les Vignots; village Auxey-Duresses *rouge et blanc*.

Not a very spectacular list of wines, but they are carefully made in the modern style, for drinking in the medium term. Maréchal, whose father was a mixed farmer, used to be an electrician. Most of his domaine is share cropped. He complains that his landlords wants quantity rather than quality. As a result he tends their half one way, his another. Some 5 per cent of the stems (for physical reasons), a week's cold maceration, controlled vinification at 32°C and one-fifth new oak is the formula here. A good address.

POMMARD

South of Beaune we come to the best red wines of the Côte-de-Beaune after the *grands crus* of Corton: Pommard and Volnay. The road forks after you pass the huge factory of the Cave des Hautes-Côtes. Keep to the left and you run along the plain towards Chagny. Turn right and you rise up into the hills towards Autun. This junction marks the transition from Beaune into Pommard; the Autun road – more or less – separates the higher-rising *premiers crus* of Pommard from the low-lying village wine.

The commune, roughly square, is divided into two by a stream – the river Dheune – which flows down from Nantoux in the Hautes-Côtes. On the Beaune side, therefore, the slope turns round to face the south, while opposite the aspect is in the reverse direction. Above the village, in contrast to the other communes, there is a large expanse of communal vineyard; rather more, indeed, than there is below on the flatter land. Here on the slopes on the Beaune side, the soil is a stony white marl, getting redder and less stony – except in the Epenots – as one descends into the *premiers crus*. On the south side of the village the incline is steeper, more rocky, and redder in colour – hence the name Rugiens – while lower down in Les Rugiens-Bas the subsoil is of Argovian limestone covered with a thick band of marly calcareous debris. Yet further down the slope, in the Fremiers and Poutures, the marl is mixed with an iron-rich oolite, while between the two main roads, where once again we are in village land, the soil is very clayey. Only below the Epenots on the Beaune side does the limestone debris contain much in the way of stone and pebbles and therefore drains well.

The percentage of active limestone in Pommard is high, and it is the reaction between this and the clays, of which Pommard also has more than Volnay and Beaune, which produces the typical fullness and sturdiness which is the Pommard character. Recent research has shown a similarity between the clays, or at least the electro-magnetic properties of their internal surface areas, with those of the villages of the Côte-de-Nuits.

POMMARD

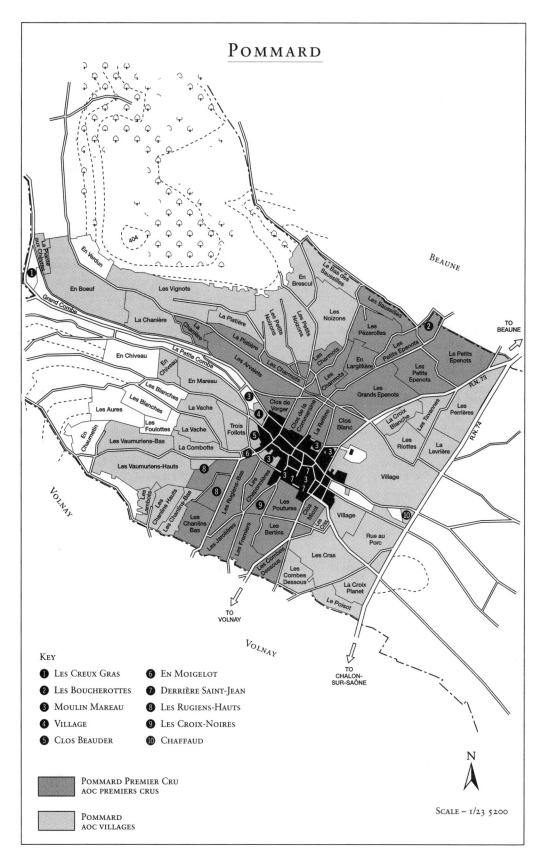

KEY

❶ Les Creux Gras
❷ Les Boucherottes
❸ Moulin Mareau
❹ Village
❺ Clos Beauder

❻ En Moigelot
❼ Derrière Saint-Jean
❽ Les Rugiens-Hauts
❾ Les Croix-Noires
❿ Chaffaud

▪ **Pommard Premier Cru**
AOC Premiers Crus

▫ **Pommard**
AOC Villages

N

Scale – 1/23 5200

HISTORY

The name Pommard is of malic origin (Pommarium, Pommone or Polmano are the ways it was written a millennium or so ago) and like much of Burgundy belonged either to the church or the Dukes of Burgundy and their vassals in the Middle Ages. The Abbey de Maizières, the Carmelites of Beaune and the Chevaliers of Malta (the Knights of St John of Jerusalem), were all landowners, as were the Counts of Vienne, *seigneurs* of Commarain commemorated to this day in the name of one of the *premiers crus* and one of the three local châteaux.

The main château, the one actually called the Château de Pommard, was constructed in 1802 in a neo-classical style. It stands in the middle of a huge *clos*, the largest single ownership in Burgundy, between the two main roads.

Once the property of the ubiquitous Marey-Monge family, it has belonged since 1936 to that of Laplanche.

Pommard has for long had a high reputation for its wines, though never having had any *grands crus* or *têtes de cuvée*. Perhaps this is because, as pointed out by Dr Lavalle in 1855, it had, along with Volnay and Beaune, been the most resistant to the 'invasion' of Gamay. If we were to contemplate a change in the hierarchy today I would nominate for elevation part – but part only – of two of the *premiers crus*: Les Rugiens-Bas and the central part of Les Epenots (the Clos-des-Epeneaux but neither all Les Grands-Epenots nor all Les Petits-Epenots). Clearly these produce the most distinctive wines of the village.

THE VINEYARD

Premiers Crus: In the commune of Pommard there are twenty-eight *premiers crus*, in whole or in part. These are as follows: Les Arvelets; Les Bertins; Les Boucherottes; La Chanière (part); Les Chanlins-Bas (part); Les Chaponnières; Les Charmots; Clos-Blanc; Clos-de-la-Commaraine; Clos-de-Verger; Clos-des-Epeneaux; Clos-Micot or Micault; Les Combes-Dessus; Les Croix-Noires; Les Grands-Epenots; Les Petits-Epenots; Les Fremiers; Les Jarolières; En Largillière (Les Argillières); Les Pézerolles; La Platière (part); Les Poutures; La Refène; Les Rugiens-Bas; Les Rugiens-Hauts (part); Derrière-Saint-Jean; Les Saussilles; Le Village.

Altogether these cover 125.19 ha and produce around 4,500 hl (594,000 bottles) a year.

Village Wine: There are 211.63 ha of village Pommard, producing some 9,400 hl (1.25 million bottles) a year.

Pommard, like Volnay but unlike Beaune, is an appellation for red wine only.

THE PREMIERS CRUS

LES PETITS-EPENOTS (15.14 HA) • CLOS-DES-EPENEAUX (5.23 HA)
LES GRANDS-EPENOTS (10.15 HA)

These three *climats* occupy the best land on the Beaune side of the commune, with the Petits-Epenots closest to the border to the north and the Grands-Epenots closest to the village. The slope here is very gentle but the presence of pebbles in the soil ensures good drainage and contributes to the considerable elegance which you find in a good Epenots once it has softened up. Opinions are divided as to which end, Grands or Petits, is the best. Most of the older books on Burgundy favour the former, present-day opinion the latter. Certainly as you get closer to the village the wine becomes a little fuller, but also sturdier and more four-square. This is because the soil becomes more alluvial. What no one would deny is the superiority of the Clos-des-Epeneaux in the middle. The monopoly of the Comte Armand, this is today one of the best wines in Burgundy. Most of the remaining wines simply say Epenots on the label, not differentiating their origin.

Recommended Sources:
Les Epenots: De Courcel; Parent; Daniel Rebourgeon-Mure (all Pommard); De Montille (Volnay); Pierre Morey (Meursault).
Clos-des-Epeneaux: Comte Armand (*monopole*).

LES BOUCHEROTTES (1.5 HA) • **LES SAUSSILLES** (3.84 HA)

LES PÉZEROLLES (5.91 HA)

EN LARGILLIÈRE (LES ARGILLIÈRES) (3.99 HA)

LES CHARMOTS (9.65 HA) • **LES ARVELETS** (8.46 HA)

LA PLATIÈRE (2.53 HA) • **LA CHANIÈRE** (2.78 HA)

These are the *climats* which start above Les Petits-Epenots on the Beaune border and continue round as the slope turns towards the south and the vineyards disappear up the valley towards Nantoux. The incline is steeper here, and the soil is a stony white marl.

Les Pézerolles and Les Charmots (I have rarely seen a wine from Les Argillières in between the two: the Domaine Lejeune in Pommard and Jean Monnier in Meursault are the only sources I am aware of) offer the wines of the greatest finesse in this sector, but they do not have the flair of the top Epenots. They are nicely substantial, occasionally a little robust; usually, as with all Pommards, well coloured. As you move into Les Arvelets and the *climats* beyond, the sun does not impinge properly on the vines until later in the morning, and the wines are less rich. The wine-making has to be precise here, to avoid a wine which is all substance and no generosity.

Recommended Sources:
Les Clos-des-Boucherottes (*monopole*): Coste-Caumartin (Pommard).
Les Saussilles: Jean-Marc Boillot (Pommard).
Les Pézerolles: Parent (Pommard); Lafarge; De Montille (both Volnay).
Les Charmots: Billard-Gonnet; Aleth Le Royer-Girardin (both Pommard).

CLOS-BLANC (4.18 HA) • **LA REFÈNE** (2.31 HA)

CLOS-DE-LA-COMMARAINE (3.75 HA) • **CLOS-DE-VERGER** (2.11 HA)

These four vineyards lie immediately to the north of the village, the first three under Les Arvelets and Les Charmots, and produce medium-full-bodied wines (though the Clos-de-Verger is never more than medium in weight) which I find rather ordinary: more *village* than *premier cru*. The Beaune merchants Jaboulet-Vercherre have the monopoly of the Clos-de-la-Commaraine.

LES CHANLINS-BAS (4.43 HA) • **LES RUGIENS-HAUTS** (6.83 HA)

LES RUGIENS-BAS (5.83 HA) • **LES JAROLIÈRES** (3.24 HA)

LES CHAPONNIÈRES (2.87 HA)

Here we are up-slope on the southern side of the village, and in the three last *climats* listed above, in very classy territory. Even if Les Rugiens-Hauts and Les Chanlins-Bas cannot boast such good wines, the difference is very small, and, in any case, as with Epenots, most growers do not differentiate which part of Rugiens their wines come from.

The vineyards lie on a steep, rocky slope, prone to erosion, with channels and pipe-lines organised to evacuate the rain efficiently whenever there is a violent storm. The terrain, and the wine, is quite different from that in the Epenots.

The basic difference between a top Rugiens and a top Epenots is one of energy and intensity. A Rugiens will show a rude power, to go with the size and richness, which is missing in the more laid-back, perhaps more elegant, Epenots. Chanlins and Jarolières betray their Volnay proximity and are somewhat hermaphroditic. Chaponnières is the closest to Rugiens.

Recommended Sources:

Les Chanlins: Bernard Vaudoisey (Volnay); Monthélie-Douhairet (Monthélie).
Les Rugiens: Billard-Gonnet; Jean-Marc Boillot; De Courcel; Aleth Le Royer-Girardin; Parent (all Pommard); Jean-Marc Boulay; Yvon Clerget; De Montille (all Volnay).
Les Jarolières: Jean-Marc Boillot (Pommard); Pousse-d'Or (Volnay).
Les Chaponnières: Billard-Gonnet; Parent (both Pommard).

LES FREMIERS (5.13 HA) • LES CROIX-NOIRES (1.28 HA)
LES BERTINS (3.54 HA) • LES POUTURES (4.13 HA)
LES COMBES-DESSUS (2.79 HA) • CLOS-MICOT (OR MICAULT) (2.83 HA)

Finally we come to the *climats* which lie down-slope from Rugiens *et al.* The last two of these are actually below the Autun road.

The wines are definitely lighter here, with Fremiers (bordering on Fremiets – notice the difference in spelling) having a real Volnay touch to it. Poutures and Clos-Micot can nevertheless be quite sturdy, as can Croix-Noires. In general this should be a sector for good, typical Pommards, which if not as powerfully rich as Rugiens or as intense as Epenots, are usually more satisfying, more complete, than those from the Pézerolles-Charmots area. Of course, as always, it depends on the grower . . .

Recommended Sources:

Les Fremiers: Coste-Caumartin; De Courcel (Pommard); Jean-Marc Boulay (Volnay); Monthélie-Douhairet (Monthélie); Lucien Boillot et Fils (Gevrey-Chambertin).
Les Croix-Noires: Lucien Boillot et Fils (Gevrey-Chambertin).
Clos-des-Poutures: Louis Jadot (exclusivity) (Beaune).

THE GROWERS

★★COMTE ARMAND
DOMAINE DU CLOS-DES-EPENEAUX

10 ha: owned. Pommard *premier cru* Clos-des-Epeneaux (*monopole*); village Pommard; Volnay *premier cru* Les Fremiets; village Volnay; village Meursault in the *lieu-dit* Les Meix-Chavaux; Auxey-Duresses *premier cru* (*rouge*); village Auxey-Duresses (*blanc*).

Until 1994 this was an estate which existed on its own single monopoly, but it has now begun to expand. The Count, a Parisian lawyer in his forties, had the perspicacity in 1985, when the standards were not what they should have been, to employ the young French-Canadian Pascal Marchand as his manager and wine-maker. Since then the improvement has been exponential. This Epenots – or perhaps I should say Epeneaux – is of a size and intensity that few others manage to achieve, yet retaining all the inherent finesse of the *climat*.

See Profile, page 331.

BILLARD-GONNET

10 ha: owned. Pommard *premier cru* in Les Rugiens, Les Chaponnières, Les Charmots, Clos-de-Verger, plus a *premier cru tout court* from Les Jarolières, Les Poutures, Les Bertins, Les Pézerolles; Beaune *premier cru* Clos-des-Mouches (*blanc*); village Pommard.

Philippe Billard is a good source for reliable if rarely mind-blowing Pommards. The fruit is completely destemmed, fermented at 30-34°C, and there is not so much a lot of new oak in the cellar as an absence of barrels which are too old.

★JEAN-MARC BOILLOT

10.50 ha: owned and *en fermage*. Bâtard-Montrachet (18 a); Beaune *premier cru* Les Montrevenots; Pommard *premier cru* in Les Rugiens, Les Saussilles, Les Jarolières; Volnay *premier cru* in Les Pitures, Carelle-sous-la-Chapelle, Le Ronceret; Puligny-Montrachet *premier cru* in La Truffière, Les Referts, Les Champs-Canet, Les Combettes; Beaune *premier cru* (*blanc*); village Pommard; village Volnay; village Meursault; village Puligny-Montrachet; village Chassagne-Montrachet.

This is one of the very few top-quality domaines in Burgundy which is equally as important in Pinot Noir as in Chardonnay in the variety and standard of its wine-making. Jean-Marc is part of the extended Boillot family, with cousins who make wine in Gevrey, a brother who makes wine in Volnay and a brother-in-law (Gérard Boudot of Domaine Etienne Sauzet) who makes wine in Puligny-Montrachet. Some of his estate comes from his rightful share of this latter source.

The Pinots are destemmed totally, given a week-long maceration at ambient temperatures and then vinified at 33–35°C. There is some 20–25 per cent new wood for both red and white wine. Jean-Marc has not been in business on his own account long (from 1984 to 1988 being wine-maker for Olivier Leflaive Frères), but I have a high respect for what he does. He told me once that he considers his Pommard, Saussilles produces better wine in softer vintages, such as 1989 or 1992, than in a firmer one, which is a point to ponder on. Boillot also has a *négociant* licence, but seems to exercise it most on the white wine front, with wines from the Côte Chalonnaise and extra Pulignys.

At the time of writing the Beaune *premier cru blanc* is young vines.

COSTE-CAUMARTIN

12 ha: *en fermage*. Pommard *premier cru* in Clos-des-Boucherottes (*monopole*), Les Fremiers; village Pommard; village Saint-Romain *blanc* including the *lieux-dits* Sous-Roche and Sous-le-Château.

Should you feel you are being watched, as you stand in the creepered, medieval Coste-Caumartin courtyard, complete with an old well, then look up. There is a gargoyled ancestor implacably staring down at you from within a mansard window. Despite the grapes being destemmed entirely, there is a character about these wines which is unmistakably rustic, but Jérome Sordet, whose ancestors have owned this estate since 1780, can offer you some very good wines at the top levels.

★DE COURCEL

8 ha: owned. Pommard *premier cru* in Les Epenots, Les Rugiens, Les Fremiers (also Les Croix-Noires but this is not bottled by the domaine); village Pommard.

Like the Comte Armand, the Courcels are absentee landlords. Gilles de Courcel, the member of the family who takes charge of the domaine, spends most of his life as export manager for Calvet in Bordeaux. The man on the spot in Pommard is Yves Tavant, fifty-ish, who took over from his father in 1971.

The domaine owns a large slice of Epenots, just on the Beaune side of the Clos-des-Epeneaux, in what they label as the Grand-Clos-des-Epenots. But their best wine is their Rugiens, perhaps the best example of this top Pommard. This wine is proof that Rugiens would be a worthy contender for *grand cru* status.

See Profile, page 407.

JACQUES FROTEY-POIFOL

5.34 ha: owned and *en fermage/métayage*. Pommard *premier cru* Les Charmots; Beaune *premier cru* Les Aigrots *rouge et blanc*; village Pommard.

The lean, straggly-bearded Jacques Frotey took over responsibility of this domaine from his grandparents in 1987. Much needed replanting and the clones that were available then were rather too productive. Despite that he doesn't green harvest. He employs up to 100 per cent of the stems, ferments right up to 38°C after three days' cold soaking, and employs only a modicum of new oak. He filters, but doesn't fine. The vines obviously are youthful here, especially in the Charmots. So far the quality is unexceptional.

JEAN GARAUDET

5.5 ha: owned and *en fermage*. Pommard *premier cru* Les Charmots; Beaune *premier cru* in Clos-des-Mouches, Belissand; village Pommard including the *lieu-dit* Les Noizons; village Monthélie *rouge et blanc*.

Jean Garaudet is a small middle-aged man who presides over a spotless *cave* under and behind his house off the main church square in Pommard. This branch of Garaudets is only distantly related to those in Monthélie. Some 15 per cent of the stems are used here. There are five days of cold maceration, temperatures up to 35°C for the reds and 30 per cent new oak. Careful wine-making is obvious here, and the wines prove it. A good source.

MICHEL GAUNOUX

10 ha: owned. Corton, Les Renardes (1.23 ha); Pommard *premier cru* in Les Grands-Epenots (one of the few domaines to specify this on the label), Les Rugiens; Pommard *premier cru tout court* from Les Arvelets, Les Charmots, Les Combes-Dessus; village Beaune.

This is one of two top domaines in Burgundy – Ampeau in Meursault is the other – where you are not allowed to taste out of barrel. They are not interested in letting you see the wine until the *élevage* is complete and the wine is in bottle. Even then, unless they have decided to put the wine on the market, they see no reason to pull any corks. Today it is Michel Gaunoux's widow who will receive you, and what you will be offered is a wine of size, power and alcohol. Sometimes there is a lack of grace, but I have had plenty of fine old bottles from this cellar. These wines are built to last.

A.F. GROS

8.22 ha: *en fermage*. Richebourg (60 a); Echézeaux (26 a); Savigny-lès-Beaune *premier cru*; Clos des Guettes; village Vosne-Romanée including the *lieux-dits* Aux Réas, Les Maizières, Les Chalandins; Clos de la Fontaine; village Chambolle-Musigny.

Anne-François Gros, daughter of Jean Gros of Vosne-Romanée, is married to François Parent, and it is he who is responsible for all their wines. In 1996 responsibility for all the Gros Richebourg passed into the hands of this domaine, and other changes were made as a result of the Jean Gros succession.

See Parent, page 222. See also Profile of the Gros family, page 473.

LAHAYE PÈRE ET FILS

23 ha: owned and *en fermage/métayage*. Corton, Les Renardes (30 a); Pommard *premier cru* including Les Arvelets; Volnay *premier cru* Les Santenots; Beaune *premier cru* Les Montrevenots; Meursault *premier cru* Les Perrières; village Pommard including the *lieux-dits* Les Vignots, Les Trois Follots; village Beaune in the *lieu-dit* Les Bons-Feuvres; village Meursault including the *lieux-dits* Les Meix-Chavaux, Les Grands-Charrons.

This is a large estate, and the wine-making recipe is similar to most, but I have to say I have never found their wines very inspiring. The property is owned by Serge Lahaye and his sons Michel, Dominique and Vincent. Each son now works independently, yet their wines are bottled with the same label.

RAYMOND LAUNAY

11 ha: owned. Chambertin (7 a); Latricières-Chambertin (7 a); Pommard *premier cru* in

Chaponnets, Clos-Blanc, Rugiens; village Pommard including the *lieu-dit* Les Perrières; village Santenay; village Ladoix.

Raymond Launay is now retired and his domaine is run today by his daughter Ghislaine Francis, the *caviste* being another lady, Eveline Bury. No stems, temperatures up to 32°C and 25 per cent new oak is the recipe here, and the wines are held two years in cask before bottling. I have never sampled the *grands crus*. As far as the Pommards are concerned I have found the quality improving in recent years, but not yet to be first-division stuff.

LEJEUNE

7 ha: owned and *en métayage*. Pommard *premier cru* in Les Rugiens, En Largillière, Les Poutures; village Pommard.

François Jullien de Pommerol has his own individual method of wine production, which involves placing the whole bunches, stems and all, into the vats, giving them a week or so to cold soak, and then crushing them by *pigeage* without ever letting the fermentation temperature rise above 30°C. The effect is of a semi-carbonic maceration. The wine then receives up to 75 per cent new oak. One cannot deny the richness and suppleness of the fruit extraction, but the flavours I find un-classic, and the oak a bit extreme. Good wines, but not to my taste.

ALETH LE ROYER-GIRARDIN
FORMERLY LES HÉRITIERS ARMAND GIRARDIN

6.5 ha: *en fermage*. Pommard *premier cru* Les Rugiens, Les Epenots, Les Charmots, La Refène; Beaune *premier cru* Les Montrevenots, Clos-des-Mouches; Meursault *premier cru* Les Poruzots; village Pommard.

Over the last decade this domaine has increasingly passed out of the hands of the charming Armand Girardin into those of the equally charming daughter Aleth, married to the actor Michel Le Royer. The wine-making has evolved too. At first there was far too much old wood – save for a new cask entered by their American importer or a *négociant* in Burgundy who had bought some of their wine – and the grapes were never destemmed. Now, slowly but surely, the old wood is being thrown out, and the grapes have been 70 per cent destemmed since 1991/1992. Yields are low, the vines for the most part are very old indeed, and the potential is high here. Sometimes, as in 1990, I have been exasperated by the hard, unyielding character of the wines, in other years very pleased with the quality – though I think 100 per cent new oak, which is the American *cuvée*, is excessive. But things are improving here. I feel they turned a corner in 1993. At the time of writing the vines in Pommard Refène are only fifteen years old, and Meursault Poruzots only five.

ANDRÉ MUSSY

6 ha: owned. Pommard *premier cru* Les Epenots; Pommard *premier cru tout court* from Les Pézerolles and Les Saussilles; Beaune *premier cru* in Les Epenottes, Les Montrevenots (Mussy spells it Les Montremenots); village Pommard; village Volnay.

In 1995 André Mussy, aged eighty-one, completed his sixty-ninth vintage. He is a vigorous and charming old boy, though with right-wing views M. Le Pen would relish but never dare utter in public. Here is another cellar the majority of whose barrels should be taken out and burnt. There is some new wood now, but that is not quite the point. Most of the barrels are far too old. Mussy also employs the practice of pumping back some of last year's wine into tank in order to free casks for the new vintage. This prevents their full evolution. Too often the wines are rustic here, I regret to say.

PARENT

11.38 ha: *en fermage/métayage*. Corton, Les Renardes (30 a); Corton-Charlemagne (28 a); Pommard *premier cru* in Les Epenots, Les Argillières, Les Chaponnières, Les Chanlins, Les Arvelets, Les Pézerolles; Pommard *premier cru tout court*; Beaune *premier cru* in Les Boucherottes, Les Epenottes; Ladoix *premier cru* Au Corvée; village Pommard in the *lieu-dit* La Croix-Blanche; village Ladoix; Savigny-lès-Beaune *premier cru* Clos-des-Guettes.

In addition to the above Jacques Parent, father of François, who is today responsible for the domaine, formed a *négociant* business some two decades ago in order to buy the produce of his relation Jean Parent. These vines, now owned by Jean Parent's widow and her daughter Annick, include Pommard *premier cru* Les Rugiens and a clutch of *premier cru* Monthélies, and used to be made exclusively by François. Since 1993, however, this agreement has come to an end.

The fruit is entirely destemmed, fermented at a low temperature – around 25°C – and the wine is given 25–33 per cent new oak. In the past I have suspected them of being over-chaptalised, but François, I feel, is a more sensitive wine-maker than his father, and this is not an allegation I would throw at the domaine today. These are rich, structured, quite meaty wines nevertheless. At the time of writing the Corton-Charlemagne vines are very young.

CHÂTEAU DE POMMARD

25 ha: owned. Village Pommard.

Jean-Louis Laplanche, psychoanalyst, Sorbonne professor and translator of Sigmund Freud, is the proprietor here, the largest *clos* in single ownership in Burgundy, the wine from which is put up in a dumpy bottle with an attractive label. Anthony Hanson is at pains to point out the perfectionist way in which the wine is made. I can only speak for the end product, which I have tasted on a number of occasions alongside those of Jadot in the USA (for Kobrand, Jadot's agents, also represent the Château de Pommard). I find it fullish, but pedestrian. It does not sing to me.

VIRGILE POTHIER-RIEUSSET

7 ha: owned. Pommard *premier cru* in Les Rugiens, Les Epenots, Clos-de-Verger; Beaune *premier cru* Les Boucherottes; Meursault *premier cru* Les Caillerets (*rouge*); village Pommard.

Virgile Pothier used to look after the vines of his sister, but this lady's daughter has now married Fernand Pillot of Chassagne-Montrachet, and taken her vines with her. The Rugiens is worthwhile here, as can be the Epenots, but the lesser wines lack substance.

DANIEL REBOURGEON-MURE

7.5 ha: owned and *en fermage*. Pommard *premier cru* in Les Epenots, Clos-des-Arvelets, Le Clos-Micault, Les Charmots; Volnay *premier cru* in Les Caillerets, Les Santenots; Beaune *premier cru* Les Vignes-Franches; village Pommard; village Volnay.

This estate has been growing as more and more land has been passed down the line from Daniel's father (Rebourgeon-Mignotte) and also from his wife's side. The style here is not for solid blockbusters, but for attractive plump wines which evolve in the medium term. Daniel Rebourgeon is one of Pommard's better wine-makers. His tidy, labyrinthine *cave* now holds a clutch of good Pommards. Currently the Epenots is *jeunes vignes*.

VIRELY-ROUGEOT

7.7 ha: owned and *en fermage/métayage*. Pommard *premier cru* in Les Chanlins, Clos-des-Arvelets; Meursault *premier cru* Les Charmes; village Pommard; village Beaune in the *lieu-dit* Clos-de-l'Ermitage; village Meursault.

With two cellars, one in Meursault to vinify the white wines – this is the Rougeot inheritance – and one in Pommard for the reds, plus a shop in the middle of the latter village to sell to passing tourists and a special emblazoned bottle, Patrick Virely, who has now taken over from his father Bernard, is well geared up to make the most of his domaine. The lesser *cuvées* of Meursault are sold off in bulk, leaving the Virely wine a blend of Narvaux and Limouzin. Nevertheless it is only 'quite good': there is a lack of flair and concentration. The same can be said of the Pommards.

VOLNAY

Volnay is one of the most delightful wines and one the most rewarding communes in the Côte d'Or. There is a large number of very fine and dedicated growers in the village, and the wine they produce is the epitome of elegance and delicacy, the most fragrant and seductively feminine expression of the Pinot Noir in the Côte-de-Beaune, directly analogous with the wines of Chambolle-Musigny in the Côte-de-Nuits. Volnay is as removed as it possibly can be from the souped-up, 'old-fashioned' brews which were fraudulently bottled as non-appellation Burgundy in our parents' day.

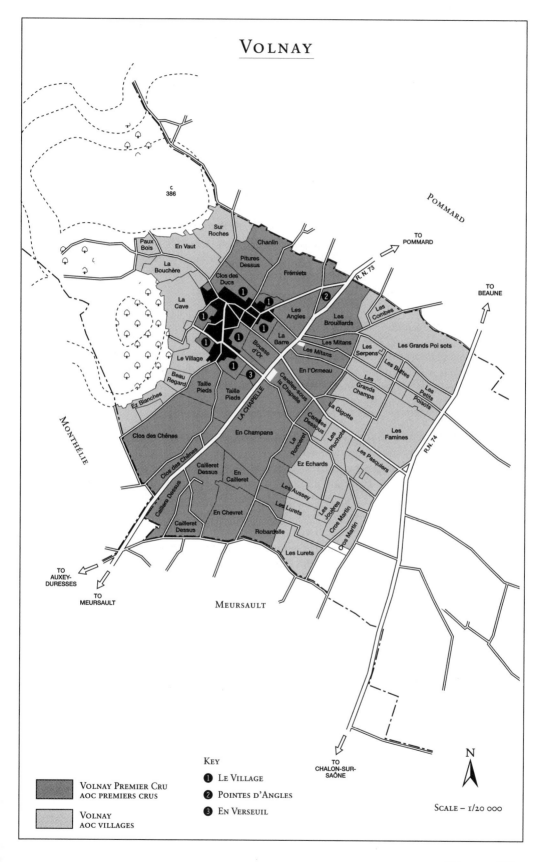

VOLNAY

c 386

POMMARD

TO POMMARD

TO BEAUNE

Paux Bois

En Vaut

Sur Roches

Chanlin

La Bouchère

Pitures Dessus

Clos des Ducs

Frémiets

R. N. 73

La Cave

Les Angles

Les Combes

Les Brouillards

Les Mitans

Les Serpens

Les Grands Poi sots

La Barre

Les Mitans

Les Buttes

Le Village

Bousse d'Or

En l'Ormeau

Les Grands Champs

Les Petits Poisots

Beau Regard

Taille Pieds

Taille Pieds

Carelles-sous la Chapelle

Carelles Dessus

Les Famines

Ez Blanches

LA CHAPELLE

La Gigotte

Clos des Chênes

En Champans

Le Ronceret

Les Pluchots

Les Pasquiers

R.N. 74

Clos des Chênes

Ez Echards

Cailleret Dessus

Cailleret Dessus

Cailleret Dessus

En Cailleret

Les Aussey

Les Lurets

Les Joutbes

Cros Martin

En Chevret

Robardelle

Cros Martin

Les Lurets

MONTHÉLIE

MEURSAULT

TO AUXEY-DURESSES

TO MEURSAULT

TO CHALON-SUR-SAÔNE

N

KEY

❶ LE VILLAGE
❷ POINTES D'ANGLES
❸ EN VERSEUIL

■ VOLNAY PREMIER CRU
AOC PREMIERS CRUS

▨ VOLNAY
AOC VILLAGES

SCALE – 1/20 000

HISTORY

Volnay is a small village tucked into the top of its slope above the vineyard and away from the main road. The name comes from a Celtic or early Gallic water god, De Volen. The village appears in medieval times as Vollenay and was spelt Voulenay by Thomas Jefferson when he toured around France just prior to the French Revolution.

Back in the Middle Ages, as with the rest of Burgundy, ownership of most of the land lay in the hands of the Church. The Order of Malta had vines in Les Caillerets, Le Champ-de-Caille (quail) as it was known in those days, the Priory of Saint-Etienne in Beaune was represented in Les Fremiets, Le Verseuil, Les Angles and La Carelle. The Abbaye de Maizières had a number of parcels in the best *climats*. The Dukes of Burgundy were also land-holders, and they and particularly their spouses spent much time here, after Hugues IV constructed a château in 1250: the view was excellent, the water pure, there was abundant hunting in the forests above . . . and of course there was the local wine, though it was more of a pale rusty red in colour in those days, what is called *oeil de perdrix* (partridge eye), for white and red grapes were commonly planted and harvested together.

An inventory taken on behalf of Louis XII, King of France, and, after the collapse of the Valois Dukes of Burgundy in 1477, inheritor of their land, mentions holdings in a wide number of what are now top *premiers crus*: En Cailleret, Chevret, Champans, Fremiets, L'Ormeau, Bousse d'Or, Clos-Blanc, Taille-Pieds. From then on its place at the royal table was secure.

Anthony Hanson has a delightful story concerning the Prince de Condé (*Burgundy*, Faber, 1995) which is well worth repeating. This worthy, enchanted with the quality of the wine, had the idea of transplanting some Pinot Noir vines from Volnay to Chantilly, his château in the Oise near Senlis, north of Paris. Obviously the wine did not come up to expectation. When he complained he was told: 'Monseigneur, you should also have taken the soil and the sun.'

Domaine-bottling in Burgundy can be said to have begun in Volnay. The present Marquis d'Angerville's father was a constant critic of the cynical fraud being perpetrated by local merchants in the 1930s. As a result they refused to accept his wine, and so he was forced to bottle it himself and to look outside the local *négoce* for his markets. He was soon joined by other growers, including his friends Armand Rousseau of Gevrey-Chambertin and Henri Gouges of Nuits-Saint-Georges, who were being similarly shunned. Encouraged by Raymond Baudoin, the French wine-writer and consultant to many top restaurants, by the American Frank Schoonmaker and later by Alexis Lichine, these fine growers were eventually joined by more and more top estates, leading to the situation today where almost everyone who makes good wine bottles and sells at least some of it him- or herself, and one expects that some of Beaune *négociants* are increasingly hard-pressed to find good wine to mature and sell. The tables have well and truly been turned.

LOCATION

Volnay is one of the smaller communes of the Côte-de-Beaune. On the one side lies Pommard, on the other the vineyards of Monthélie and Meursault. *Premier cru* vineyards lie on both sides of the Beaune-Autun road, with village wine extending all the way down to the Beaune-Chagny highway. There is more village land above the village itself on the steeper slopes.

While the geology is complex the soils of Volnay are in general lighter than they are in Pommard, and it must be this which largely explains the delicacy of the wines. Travelling up-slope from the Autun road from left to right, i.e. from south to north, we come first to the Clos-des-Chênes. This is Bathonian limestone, poor in nutrient, stony, light in colour, and on a steep slope which is oriented more toward the south than the remainder of the *premiers crus*. Next we come to Les Taille-Pieds and a number of individual clos or vineyards collectively decreed to be the *premier cru* Le Village (which I feel is a contradiction in terms) but which sell under their own, often monopoly, labels: De l'Audignac, Verseuil, Bousse d'Or, Clos-du-Château-des-Ducs, and so on. Here the limestone is of Argovian or Oxfordian origin, again light in colour, and hard to work, particularly up-slope in the Clos-des-Ducs. Further along still, alongside the Pommard border, there is Bathonian limestone once again in mid-slope in Les Fremiets (here spelled with a 't' rather than 'r' at the end, as in Pommard). The limestone is crumbly and the surface soil shallow. Up above in Les Pitures and Les Chanlins the limestone is Argovian again, and very stony.

Below Clos-des-Chênes we find various Caillerets. On the Meursault side the slope continues to be steep, the limestone is an Argovian and Oxfordian crumbly *lave*, but much redder in colour, stony again and very well exposed. At the top (Clos-des-Soixante-Ouvrées) there is little surface soil. Lower down it is deeper before we reach the base rock. This band of rock, over which is a reasonable depth of Bathonian scree and debris, but with a little more clay, continues north through the *climats* of En Chevret, Les Champans and Les Roncerets. Further along, though, in Les Mitans and Les Brouillards, the land becomes heavier, there is more clay; and the wines are sturdier.

Finally, an anomaly. Bordering on Les Caillerets and En Chevret, but over the border in the commune of Meursault, we have the large *climat* of Santenots. The land here is once again on Bathonian limestone, much harder than the *lave* of the Champans, red in colour, and quite stony — and larger stones at that — in parts. There is more clay than in the Caillerets and it is more suitable for red wine than white. Such Pinot Noir as is made here — and it is almost entirely printed in Pinot — is entitled to the Volnay appellation: Volnay, Les Santenots.

THE VINEYARD

Premiers Crus: There are thirty-five *premiers crus*, in whole or in part, in Volnay. They are as follows: Les Angles; Les Aussy (part); La Barre (Clos-de-la-Barre); Les Brouillards (part); Caillerets-Dessus (including the Clos-des-Soixante-Ouvrées); En Cailleret; Les Caillerets; Carelle-sous-la-Chapelle; Les Carelles-Dessous (part); En Champans; Les Chanlins (part); En Chevret; Clos-de-l'Audignac; Clos-de-la-Bousse-d'Or; Clos-de-la-Cave-des-Ducs; Clos-de-la-Chapelle; Clos-des-Chênes (part); Clos-des-Ducs; Clos-du-Château-des-Ducs; Les Fremiets; Les Fremiets (Clos-de-la-Rougeotte); La Gigotte (part); Les Grands-Champs (part); Lassolle (part); Les Lurets (part); Les Mitans; En l'Ormeau; Les Pitures-Dessus; Les Pointes-d'Angles; Robardelle (part); Les Roncerets; Les Taille-Pieds; En Verseuil (Clos-du-Verseuil); Le Village (part).

In the commune of Meursault, all the following have the right to the appellation Volnay, Santenots: Clos-des-Santenots; Les Plures or Pitures; Les Santenots-Blancs; Les Santenots-Dessous; Les Santenots-du-Milieu; Les Vignes-Blanches.

The *premiers crus*, including Santenots, cover 136.28 ha and produce about 5,200 hl (686,000 bottles) of wine a year.

Village Wine: There are 98.37 ha of village Volnay. This produces around 4,300 hl (568,000 bottles) of wine a year.

Volnay and Volnay *premier cru* are appellations for red wine only.

Which are the best of the grands crus?

Lavalle (1855) lists several as *têtes de cuvées*, though curiously neither Clos-des-Chênes nor Les Taille-Pieds, and in his preamble singles out Les Caillerets and Les Champans, while Les Santenots-du-Milieu is his sole *tête de cuvée* among the red wines of Meursault. Rodier promotes Les Taille-Pieds, but not Clos-des-Chênes, to *première cuvée* and earmarks Les Fremiets, Les Champans and Les Angles, with Les Caillerets the best of all.

For me there are five *climats* which seem to be a head or so above the rest: Les Caillerets, of course, Clos-des-Chênes, Les Taille-Pieds, Les Champans and Les Santenots-du-Milieu. Which of these is the best I find a pointless question. It depends on the grower, on the age of vines, and on the vintage; not forgetting personal choice. But it is at the southern end of the commune that I find the wines which give me the greatest satisfaction.

THE *PREMIERS CRUS*

CLOS-DES-CHÊNES (15.41 HA)

It is at this, the southern end of Volnay – Clos-des-Chênes, Les Taille-Pieds, Les Caillerets, and, indeed, over the border into Les Santenots-du-Milieu – that one will find Volnay's best wines. They are all subtly, intriguingly, seductively different. Clos-des-Chênes is a fuller wine than, say, Les Caillerets, but not as full as the Santenots-du-Milieu, maturing to velvet rather than silk. It is very pure in its expression of fruit, with a good grip of acidity and the ability to keep well. The structure is there, but it is hidden, and there is plenty of finesse. There is a combination of both austerity and lushness, but never a suggestion of anything four-square. The wines from higher up the slope in the large vineyard, and those on the Monthélie side, show less distinction.

Recommended Sources:
Vincent Bitouzet; Jean-Marc Bouley; Bernard Glantenay; Michel Lafarge (all Volnay); Maurice Deschamps (Monthélie); Joseph Drouhin (Beaune).

LES TAILLE-PIEDS (7.13 HA)

CLOS-DE-L'AUDIGNAC (1.11 HA)
(*monopole* of the Domaine de la Pousse d'Or)

EN VERSEUIL (CLOS-DU-VERSEUIL) (0.68 HA)
(*monopole* of the Domaine Yvon Clerget)

CLOS-DE-LA-BOUSSE-D'OR (2.14 HA)
(*monopole* of the Domaine de la Pousse d'Or)

CLOS-DU-CHÂTEAU-DES-DUCS (0.57 HA)
(*monopole* of the Domaine Michel Lafarge)

CLOS-DE-LA-CAVE-DES-DUCS (0.64 HA)
(*monopole* of the Domaine François Charles, Nantoux)

LA BARRE (CLOS-DE-LA-BARRE) (1.32 HA)

CLOS-DES-DUCS (2.41 HA)
(*monopole* of the Domaine Marquis d'Angerville)

Continuing around the slope above the main road the geology changes slightly, as described previously, and we come to a number of vineyards in private monopoly. Bousse d'Or, by the way, has nothing to do with gold. It comes from *bousse de terre*, local patois for 'good earth'. Wines from Les Taille-Pieds can be the complete Volnay: fullish in body, beautifully textured, supremely elegant. Those from other *climats* show a little more tannin in their youth, which can sometimes mask the elegance if you fail to take your time while sampling. But they are neither as stout or as heavy as the wines on the opposite side of the road, in Champans, for instance, and mature very gracefully indeed. There is a backbone to these wines which ensures a long life, and if they are a little austere in their youth, so what? They're not made for drinking when three years old.

Recommended Sources:
Les Taille-Pieds: Marquis d'Angerville; De Montille (Volnay); Comtes Lafon; René Monnier

(Meursault). Jean-François Coche-Dury produces a fine *premier cru tout court* from vines in Clos-des-Chênes and Taille-Pieds.

Clos-de-l'Audignac: Pousse d'Or (*monopole*) (Volnay).
Clos-du-Verseuil: Yvon Clerget (*monopole*) (Volnay).
Clos-de-la-Bousse-d'Or: Pousse d'Or (*monopole*) (Volnay).
Clos-du-Château-des-Ducs: Michel Lafarge (*monopole*) (Volnay).
Clos-de-la-Barre: Louis Jadot (exclusivity) (Beaune).
Clos-des-Ducs: Marquis d'Angerville (*monopole*) (Volnay).

LES PITURES-DESSUS (4.08 HA) • LES CHANLINS (2.86 HA)
LES FREMIETS (7.40 HA) • LES ANGLES (3.34 HA)
LES POINTES-D'ANGLES (1.23 HA) • LES BROUILLARDS (5.63 HA)

Wines from Les Chanlins and Les Fremiets show their Pommard vicinity in a certain muscular sturdiness here, and those from Les Angles and Les Brouillards can be a bit four-square. In general these Volnays lack the flair of the rest of the commune. They can nevertheless be thoroughly nice bottles, and should not be passed up. But it is correct to expect a small discount.

Recommended Sources:

Les Pitures-Dessus: Jean-Marc Boillot (Pommard); Vincent Bitouzet (Volnay).
Les Fremiets: Marquis d'Angerville (Volnay).
Les Angles: Lucien Boillot et Fils (Gevrey-Chambertin).
Les Brouillards: Lucien Boillot et Fils (Gevrey-Chambertin).
Régis Rossignol-Changarthier (Volnay) makes a good *premier cru tout court* from vines in Les Angles, Les Brouillards and Les Mitans. Bouchard Père et Fils produce Clos-de-la-Rougeotte (*monopole*) from vines in Les Fremiets.

LES MITANS (3.98 HA) • LES GRANDS-CHAMPS (0.24 HA)
EN L'ORMEAU (4.33 HA) • LA GIGOTTE (0.54 HA)
CARELLE-SOUS-LA-CHAPELLE (3.73 HA) • LES CARELLES-DESSOUS (1.46 HA)

Continuing back towards the south the wines here show more definition compared with those from the *climats* above, yet in Les Mitans can still be quite sturdy. Those from the Carelles are a little lighter in weight, if Yvon Clerget's is anything to go by. Curiously, for the *climat* is not insignificant, few growers offer L'Ormeau. I have no taste memory of it.

Recommended Sources:

Les Mitans: De Montille (Volnay).
La Gigotte: Darviot-Perrin (Monthélie).
Carelle-sous-la-Chapelle: Jean-Marc Boillot (Pommard); Jean-Marc Bouley; Yvon Clerget (Volnay); Paul Pernot (Puligny-Montrachet).

EN CHAMPANS (11.19 HA) • LES RONCERETS (1.90 HA)
LES AUSSY (1.70 HA) • LES LURETS (2.07 HA)
ROBARDELLE (2.94 HA)

En Champans and the *climats* underneath it, in many cases of which only a part is graded *premier cru*, produce a rich, fat, quite sturdy wine of more depth and distinction than those in the section above. It doesn't quite have the *élan* of a Taille-Pieds or a Caillerets, but it can nevertheless be a thoroughly rewarding fine Volnay. Champans itself is an excellent *climat*.

Recommended sources:

En Champans: Marquis d'Angerville; De Montille (both Volnay); Monthélie-Douhairet

(Monthélie); Comtes Lafon; Jacques Prieur (both Meursault); Jacques Gagnard-Delagrange (Chassagne-Montrachet).

Roncerets: Jean-Marc Boillot (Pommard); Paul Garaudet (Monthélie).

LES CAILLERETS (14.36 HA) • EN CHEVRET (6.35 HA)

These *climats* can produce Volnay at its very best; not quite as structured as Taille-Pieds or Clos-des-Chênes above the main road, nor as sturdy as both Santenots and Champans can be, but Volnay of real silk, lace and the complexity of all the *petits fruits rouges* you can imagine. The upper sections of this *climat*, where there is the least surface soil, produce wine with more finesse and distinction than the vines further down. It is here in Caillerets-Dessus that you will find the Domaine de la Pousse d'Or's Soixante-Ouvrées.

Recommended Sources:

Clos-des-Soixante-Ouvrées: Pousse d'Or (*monopole*) (Volnay).

Les Caillerets: Bouchard Père et Fils, Ancien Cuvée Carnot (Beaune); Vincent Bitouzet; Jean-Marc Bouley; Yvon Clerget; De Montille; Pousse d'Or (all Volnay).

En Chevret: Joseph Drouhin (Beaune); Jean-Marc Boillot (Volnay).

SANTENOTS (22.73 HA)

The best sector in this large vineyard is the Santenots-du-Milieu, of which the Domaine Jacques Prieur's Clos-des-Santenots is part. The land lower down (Les Santenots-Dessous), and further south (Les Plures) produce more common wine. A top Santenots-du-Milieu is full, rich, sturdy and will keep well. It is quite a bit less delicate than a Caillerets and it is not as elegant, but what it lacks in grace (certainly when it is young) it makes up in richness and depth when the wine matures. There is a lush sensuality about a good Santenots which is most attractive.

Recommended Sources:

Leroy (Vosne-Romanée); Robert Ampeau; Pierre Boillot; Comtes Lafon; Matrot; François Mikulski; Jacques Prieur (Clos-des-Santenots) (all Meursault).

The Marquis d'Angerville produces a Meursault, Santenots as does the Domaine Monthélie-Douhairet: a white wine. These are wines more of interest than pleasure. Pierre Boillot of Meursault makes a red Meursault, Caillerets. I'd say the same for this.

THE GROWERS

★★MARQUIS D'ANGERVILLE

15 ha: owned. Volnay *premier cru* in Clos-des-Ducs (*monopole*), Les Champans, Les Fremiets, Les Taille-Pieds, Les Caillerets, En l'Ormeau, Les Angles, Les Pitures; Pommard *premier cru* Les Combes; Meursault *premier cru* Les Santenots.

The Marquis d'Angerville produces a Volnay *tout court* which I imagine comes from the young vines and perhaps his holdings in the three or four *premiers crus* at the end of the list above. In fifteen years of visiting I have never been offered L'Ormeau, Les Angles, etc. to taste, nor the Pommard. But then it was ten visits before I sampled the Meursault, and that was only because I read elsewhere that it was in his portfolio, and I asked politely . . .

This is one of Burgundy's great domaines: marvellously pure expressions of Pinot, which last and last.

See Profile, page 321.

VINCENT BITOUZET-PRIEUR

11 ha: owned and *en fermage/métayage*. Volnay *premier cru* in Clos-des-Chênes, Les Caillerets, Les Taille-Pieds, Les Pitures, Les Aussy; Meursault *premier cru* in Les Perrières, Les Charmes,

Les Santenots; village Volnay; village Meursault including the *lieu-dit* Clos-de-Cromin.

This is another of those rare estates, one which is of equal note for Chardonnay as well as Pinot Noir. Bitouzet operates two cellars, making his Meursault on the spot in the *cuverie* of his in-laws, while the red wines are vinified back in Volnay. The Pinots are totally destemmed, cold-macerated for two to three days and then vinified at temperatures up to 35°C. Use of oak is minimal, a fifth for *premiers crus*. Bitouzet's wines have been steadily improving and the quality is now consistently good. Half of the produce is still sold off in bulk.

JEAN BOILLOT

13.5 ha: owned. Volnay *premier cru* in Les Chevrets, Les Fremiets, Les Caillerets; Beaune *premier cru* in Clos-du-Roi, Les Epenottes; Savigny-lès-Beaune *premier cru* in Les Lavières, Les Vergelesses; Nuits-Saint-Georges *premier cru* Les Cailles; Meursault *premier cru* Les Genevrières; Puligny-Montrachet *premier cru* in Clos-de-la-Mouchère (*monopole*), Les Pucelles; village Puligny-Montrachet.

This is an impressive-looking estate, almost entirely made up of *premiers crus*, with a 4 ha first growth Puligny monopoly. It is run by Henri Boillot, son of Jean and brother of Jean-Marc of Pommard. The cellars are clean and tidy, the wine-making details seem correct, and their approach to new oak is commendable (20 per cent new, the remainder one year old). But, though the wines are clean, they lack concentration and sometimes finesse. The Savigny-lès-Beaune, Les Vergelesses is currently young vines.

JEAN-MARC BOULEY

12 ha: owned and *en fermage/métayage*. Volnay *premier cru* in Les Carelles, Les Caillerets, Clos-des-Chênes; Pommard *premier cru* in Les Pézerolles, Les Fremiers, Les Rugiens; Beaune *premier cru* Les Reversées; village Volnay; village Pommard.

Jean-Marc Bouley practises a 60 per cent destemming for his first growths, 100 per cent for the lesser wines. There is a three-day cold-soaking before fermentation at temperatures up to 32°C, and 50 per cent new oak for the top wines. When I first began to visit him in the mid-1980s I found his wines too oaky, but this is less of a problem today. A good source: consistent too. The vines in Pommard, Les Pézerolles are currently rather young.

YVON CLERGET

6.0 ha: *en fermage*. Clos-de-Vougeot (34 a); Volnay *premier cru* in Les Caillerets, Clos-du-Verseuil (*monopole*), Les Santenots, La Carelle-sous-la-Chapelle; Volnay *premier cru tout court* from Les Chanlins, Les Mitans; Pommard *premier cru* Les Rugiens; village Volnay; village Pommard; village Meursault.

Yvon Clerget comes from one of the oldest families in Burgundy. They can trace their ancestry back to 1268. Total destemming here, thermo-regulated vinification at 33°C for reds and 16°C for whites, and one-quarter to one-fifth new oak. I have had some very good wines here, but I find the results inconsistent. There always seems to be one wine in the line-up which is not as good as it should be. The domaine has expanded recently as Clerget slowly takes over land belonging to his deceased uncle Felix Clerget of Pommard. But he will not take full charge of the Clos-de-Vougeot, for instance, until 1998. This is currently exploited by someone else on a *métayage* basis.

BERNARD ET LOUIS GLANTENAY

8.5 ha: owned. Volnay *premier cru* in Clos-des-Chênes, Les Santenots, Les Caillerets, Les Brouillards; Pommard *premier cru* in Les Rugiens, Les Saussilles; village Volnay; village Pommard.

Up above the village, near the '*panorama*', you will find Bernard Glantenay (his father Louis died in 1980). I have enjoyed vintages of his Clos-des-Chênes in the past, always the best wine here. But on recent visits I have found the wines a little weak. He didn't perform a *saignée*, for example, in 1992, when he certainly should have done so.

★★MICHEL LAFARGE

10 ha: owned and *en fermage*. Volnay *premier cru* in Clos-des-Chênes, Clos-du-Château-des-Ducs (*monopole*); Volnay *premier cru tout court*; Beaune *premier cru* Les Grèves; Pommard *premier cru* Les Pézerolles; village Volnay including a '*vendange selectionné*'; village Meursault.

Year after year, Michel Lafarge and his son Frédéric produce some of the most delicious wines in the village, all the way from a splendid Bourgogne *rouge* to the yardstick Clos-des-Chênes. See Profile, page 504.

★★HUBERT DE MONTILLE

7.5 ha: owned. Volnay *premier cru* in Les Taille-Pieds, Les Champans, Les Mitans; Volnay *premier cru tout court*; Pommard *premier cru* in Les Rugiens, Les Pézerolles, Les Grands-Epenots; Puligny-Montrachet *premier cru* Les Caillerets.

Another great Volnay estate, well known for its policy of minimal chaptalisation. This makes for very pure wines, perhaps a little lean and austere in their youth, but which mature magnificently. Responsibility is now shared between the *Maître* himself (Hubert de Montille is a top Dijon lawyer), his son Etienne and his daughter Alix, married to Jean-Marc Roulot of Meursault. The Puligny was acquired from the Domaine Chartron in 1993. See Profile, page 545.

★POUSSE D'OR

13.0 ha: owned. Volnay *premier cru* in Clos-de-la-Bousse-d'Or (*monopole*), Caillerets, Clos-des-Soixante-Ouvrées (*monopole*), Les Caillerets, Clos-de-l'Audignac (*monopole*); Pommard *premier cru* Les Jarolières; Santenay *premier cru* in Les Gravières, Clos-des-Tavannes.

Run on behalf of a consortium of owners, some of them Australian, by Gerard Potel, now assisted by his son Nicolas, this estate has been one of those pioneering with a Durafroid machine which evaporates excess water, thus reducing, indeed perhaps eliminating, the need to chaptalise. First results indicate this is a much more satisfactory way of creating a better solid to liquid ratio in the must than the traditional *saignée* (bleeding). I myself have strongly preferred the evaporated Caillerets to the 'ordinary'. A very good source. See Profile, page 578.

MICHEL ROSSIGNOL

5.0 ha: owned and *en fermage*. Volnay *premier cru* Les Pitures; Beaune *premier cru* Les Teurons; village Volnay; Côte-de-Beaune.

The fifty-year-old Michel Rossignol is one member of a hugely extended Volnay family, all of whom seem to make wine, but he has been at it, and bottling his own produce, longer than most. *Inter alia* he tends 2.5 ha for the Hospices de Beaune. I view with a certain amount of suspicion this domaine's policy of using revolving, *autopigeage* vinification *cuvées*, even for its best wines. The results seem empty and herbaceous to me.

RÉGIS ROSSIGNOL-CHANGARNIER

7.15 ha: owned. Volnay *premier cru* (a mixture of Les Angles, Les Brouillards and Les Mitans); Beaune *premier cru* Les Teurons; village Volnay; village Pommard; village Savigny-lès-Beaune; village Meursault.

The charming Régis Rossignol, approaching retirement age now, makes full, rich, sturdy, long-lasting wines from old vines and a low harvest. There is never any destemming here. The estate has been selling in bottle since the 1950s. Today – and very successfully according to M. Rossignol – he is doing experiments with the must-concentrating-by-evaporation Durafroid machine. A good source.

FRÉDÉRIC ROSSIGNOL-FÉVRIER

7.7 ha: owned. Volnay *premier cru*; village Volnay; village Pommard.

Frédéric Rossignol concentrates on his private clientele rather than exportation, 80 per cent of his production being sold in this way. My experience of this cellar, therefore, is mainly of wines tasted from cask. Some good things here.

BERNARD VAUDOISEY-MARTIN
CHRISTOPHE VAUDOISEY

10 ha: owned and *en fermage*. Volnay *premier cru* in Clos-des-Chênes, Les Caillerets; Pommard *premier cru* Les Chanlins-Bas; village Volnay; village Pommard; village Meursault.

One vinification, two labels. There are some stylish wines here. Destemming is total, fermentation temperatures are allowed to rise to 33°C, and there is some 20 per cent new oak. When I tasted their 1992s I preferred the Pommard Chanlins to the rather looser-knit Volnays, which is not surprising in a lighter year, particularly as they had not *saignée*-d. In 1993, when they did bleed their *cuvées*, the results were firmer but a little hard.

JOSEPH VOILLOT

10 ha: owned and *en fermage*. Volnay *premier cru* in Les Champans, Les Caillerets, Les Fremiets; Pommard *premier cru* in Les Rugiens, Les Pézerolles, Les Epenots, Clos-Micault; Meursault *premier cru* Les Cras; village Volnay; village Pommard; village Meursault.

Joseph Voillot has cellars both in Pommard and in Volnay, so could be listed under either village, but he lives in the latter, so I place him here. He is another who is experimenting with an evaporation machine (which I learn from Anthony Hanson he jointly owns with Michel Lafarge and Régis Rossignol). There are some very good wines at the top levels here, but sometimes I find his village *cuvées* a little rustic.

MONTHÉLIE

After Volnay there is an important break in the Côte. The first vineyards you come to are the continuation of Volnay's Clos-des-Chênes – and *premier cru* as well – but then the slope turns and doubles back on itself into the hills of the Hautes-Côtes. Across the valley there is another south-east-facing ridge and here the *premiers crus* begin again. But these are mainly within the jurisdiction of the next village: Auxey-Duresses.

Between the two, set back from the main Beaune-Autun road, lies the village of Monthélie, intimate, quiet and attractive without even a local bar to interrupt the sequence of houses, courtyards and farmyard outbuildings. It seems that everyone is involved in the wine business in Monthélie. If you don't make wine or work in the vineyards it's because you are not yet old enough. Or you've done your stint and are now *en retraite*.

MONTHÉLIE

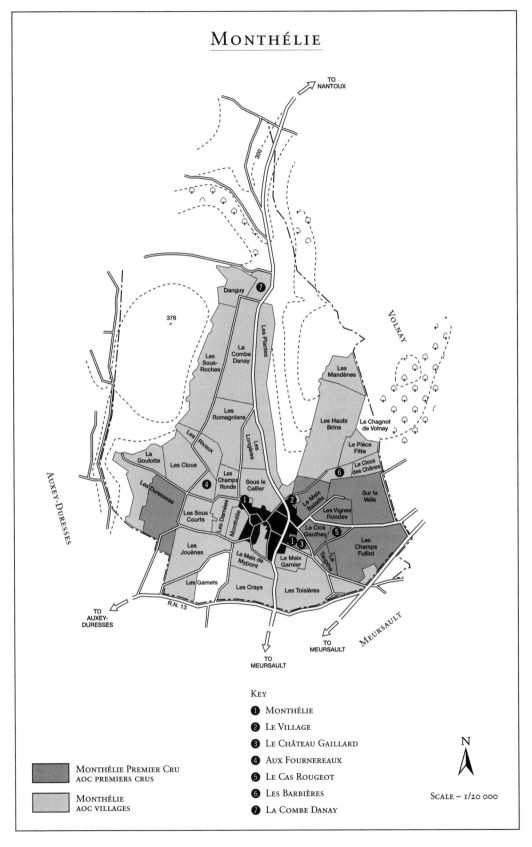

TO
NANTOUX

300

Danguy **7**

376

VOLNAY

La
Combe
Danay

Les
Plantes

Les
Sous-
Roches

Les
Romagniens

Les
Mandènes

Les Hauts
Brins

Le Chagnot
de Volnay

Les
Rivaux

Les
Longères

Le Pièce
Fitte

La
Goulotte

Les Clous

Les
Champs
Ronde

Le Clous
des Chênes

AUXEY-DURESSES

Les Duressess

4

Sous le
Cellier

6

Sur la
Velle

Les Sous
Courts

Les Darnées

Monthélie

1

2

Le Meix
Bataille

Les Vignes
Rondes

Le Clous
Gauthey

5

Les Jouènes

Le Meix de
Mypont

1

3

Le Meix
Garnier

La
Taupine

Les
Champs
Fulliot

Les Gamets

Les Crays

Les Toisières

R.N. 13

TO
AUXEY-
DURESSES

TO
MEURSAULT

MEURSAULT

TO
MEURSAULT

TO
MEURSAULT

KEY

1 MONTHÉLIE

2 LE VILLAGE

3 LE CHÂTEAU GAILLARD

4 AUX FOURNEREAUX

5 LE CAS ROUGEOT

6 LES BARBIÈRES

7 LA COMBE DANAY

N

MONTHÉLIE PREMIER CRU
AOC PREMIERS CRUS

MONTHÉLIE
AOC VILLAGES

SCALE – 1/20 000

HISTORY

According to the Abbé Courtépée the origin of the name Monthélie comes from Mont Oloye, suggesting a high place above an important road – the road in this case being the east-west route across Burgundy. In 855, in archives in Autun cathedral, it appears as Monthelio. Above the village there are remains of a look-out camp which dates back beyond the Romans to palaeolithic times.

In the early Middle Ages the land here belonged to the monks of Saint-Symphorien, followed by the Abbaye de Sainte-Marguerite. The Dukes of Burgundy then took over, only for Hugues I to make a donation to the Abbaye of Cluny in 1078. In the thirteenth century Pierre de Monthélie gave land to the ecclesiastics of Notre-Dame-de-Beaune. In 1523 vineyards in the village appear in the registry of the Kings of France.

It has never been either a village or vineyard of great importance though. Apart from the chapel belonging to the château, an attractive coloured-tiled-roofed building in the middle of the village, now belonging to the Suremain family (see page 238), Monthélie has never had a church. In the nineteenth century Dr Lavalle noted one *climat* (Les Champs-Fuillot) of *première ligne*, where the wine fetched 75 per cent of that of Volnay. Most of the rest of the commune was planted with Gamay. All this led to a certain sense of inferiority. When a village notice was put up on the main road in 1927 it rather plaintively had to insist 'Monthélie et ses Grands Vins'.

LOCATION

The continuation of the Volnay Côte, on which lie all but one of Monthélie's eleven *premiers crus*, is limestone of Bathonian origin. The land is quite steep, covered with red earth lower down, a lighter marl higher up. In the valley and climbing up towards Auxey on the opposite side the soil is an Argovian marl, light in colour, and low in calcareous matter. This gives an altogether different wine. While the *premiers crus* on the Volnay side can very justly be said to produce minor Volnay-style wines in character – not as concentrated, not as *fin*, but very pleasant (and often very well priced), the village land underneath is of much less distinction. It is often rustic. It frequently lacks that *sine qua non*: ripe plump fruit. While *premier cru* Monthélie is rather better than *premier cru* Auxey-Duresses, when it comes to village wine the reverse is often the case. This is not a question of altitude, but of exposition and a soil which is too alluvial.

THE VINEYARD

Premiers Crus: There are eleven *premiers crus*, in whole or in part. These are as follows: Le Cas-Rougeot; Les Champs-Fuillot; Le Château Gaillard; Le Clos-Gauthey; Les Duresses (part); Le Meix-Bataille; Les Riottes; La Taupine; Sur-la-Velle; Les Vignes-Rondes; Le Village (part). Several of these are small and obscure.

All except Les Duresses lie above the village on the extension of the Volnay *côte*.

These growths occupy 31.18 ha and produce about 1,250 hl (165,000 bottles) of red wine and 40 hl (5,280 bottles) of white wine a year.

Village Wine: There are 108.72 ha of village Monthélie producing about 3,700 hl (488,000 bottles) of red wine and 190 hl (38,000 bottles) of white wine a year.

The *Premiers* *Crus*

Les Champs-Fuillot (8.11 ha) • Sur-la-Velle (6.03 ha)
Les Vignes-Rondes (2.72 ha) • Le Meix-Bataille (2.28 ha)
Le Cas-Rougeot (0.57 ha) • La Taupine (1.50 ha)
Le Clos-Gauthey (1.80 ha) • Les Riottes (0.75 ha)
Le Château Gaillard (0.49 ha)

These are, roughly in order of descent down the slope, and also in order of quality, the *premiers crus* on the Volnay side of the village. Les Champs-Fuillot and Sur-la-Velle touch Volnay Clos-des-Chênes. The exposure here is to the south-east, and then, as one turns round, towards the south. The incline is gentle, but important enough to offer good drainage, and it is a propitious spot to make good wine.

And, yes, you can find it: of medium weight, with good cherry-redcurrant-strawberry fruit, if not the real complex fragrance of a Volnay, with perfectly satisfactory grip and style. Not great, but good honest Pinot Noir at a reasonable price.

Recommended Sources:
Les Champs-Fuillot: Eric Boigelot; Denis Boussey; Maurice Deschamps (all Monthélie). Denis Boussey also produces a very good Les Champs-Fuillot *blanc*.
Sur-la-Velle: Eric de Suremain, Château de Monthélie.
Les Vignes-Rondes: Dupont-Fahn (Monthélie).
Le Meix-Bataille: Monthélie-Douhairet (Monthélie).

Les Duresses (6.72 ha)

This *premier cru* touches Auxey's Les Duresses on the opposite side of the valley. The wine is a bit more four-square, a bit earthy, and less distinctive, the fruit less poised. But in good hands it can be well worth noting.

Recommended Sources:
Les Duresses: Paul Garaudet (Monthélie); Comtes Lafon (Meursault).

The Growers

Jacques et Eric Boigelot

8 ha: owned and *en fermage*. Volnay *premier cru* in Les Santenots, Les Taille-Pieds; Monthélie *premier cru* in Les Champs-Fuillot, Sur-la-Velle; village Volnay; village Pommard; village Monthélie; village Meursault.

Jacques Boigelot works jointly with his son Eric, and now out of a new winery behind Eric's house on the edge of the village. The father's share is sold off in bulk, Eric bottling his. I have had good wines here.

Denis Boussey

10.9 ha: owned and *en fermage*. Monthélie *premier cru* in Les Champs-Fuillot (*rouge et blanc*), Sur-la-Velle; village Monthélie *rouge et blanc*; village Volnay; village Pommard; village Aloxe-Corton; village Savigny-lès-Beaune; Meursault *premier cru* Les Charmes; village Meursault.

Denis Boussey shares tractors and other equipment with his brother Eric, who lives opposite. They have worked their vines independently since 1981. Everyone seems to say his whites were better than his reds, he complained to me once. I could only agree. But a good source, nevertheless.

★Didier Darviot-Perrin

8 ha: owned and *en fermage*. Volnay *premier cru* in La Gigotte (*monopole*), Les Santenots; Beaune *premier cru* Les Belissands; Chassagne-Montrachet *premier cru* in Les Bondues (*rouge*) and Blanchot-Dessus (*blanc*); Meursault *premier cru* in Les Charmes; village Volnay; village Beaune; village Monthélie (*rouge et blanc*); village Meursault; village Chassagne-Montrachet (*blanc*).

Didier Darviot produces very pure, stylish wines, true to their origins from his estate, much of which is inherited through his wife's family (the Perrin-Ponsots of Meursault). Apart from the Monthélies, of which there is not much, the average age of the vines is a respectable forty-five years. A very good source: the Chassagne-Montrachet, Blanchots-Dessus is delicious.

Maurice Deschamps

8.5 ha: owned and *en fermage*. Volnay *premier cru* Clos-des-Chênes; Monthélie *premier cru* Les Champs-Fuillot; village Monthélie *rouge et blanc*.

The handsome Maurice Deschamps completely changed his vinification methods in 1988: total destemming, longer maceration, more new wood. Another good source.

Dupont-Fahn

5 ha: owned and *en fermage*. Monthélie *premier cru* Les Vignes-Rondes; village Meursault in the *lieux-dits* Les Vireuils, Murger-de-Monthélie, Pré-de-Manche; village Puligny-Montrachet in the *lieu-dit* Les Grands-Champs; village Auxey-Duresses (*rouge*).

Michel Dupont and his American wife Lesley occupy a modern house and cellar close to the main road. He destems his grapes, ferments at 30°C, and uses 20 per cent new wood. The set-up is tidy, *sympa* and efficient. I like his wines.

Paul Garaudet

9 ha: owned and *en fermage/métayage*. Monthélie *premier cru* in Les Duresses, Le Meix-Bataille, Le Clos-Gauthey (all *rouge*), Les Champs-Fuillot (*blanc*); Volnay *premier cru* Les Roncerets; village Monthélie (*rouge et blanc*); village Volnay; village Pommard; village Meursault; village Puligny-Montrachet.

Paul Garaudet is the successor to his late father Georges, under whose label you will still see some of the wines on the domestic market. Total destemming, fermentation temperatures up to 34°C for the red wines, 30 per cent new oak. I've been visiting for a number of years now. Things are getting better and better.

Monthélie-Douhairet

6 ha: owned. Volnay *premier cru* Les Champans; Pommard *premier cru* in Les Chanlins, Les Fremiets; Monthélie *premier cru* in Les Duresses (*rouge et blanc*), Le Meix-Bataille; Meursault *premier cru* Les Santenots (*blanc*); village Monthélie (*rouge et blanc*) including the *lieu-dit* Clos-du-Meix-Garnier.

Mlle Armande Douhairet, eighty-five plus, was once described by another writer as a *monument historique*. No, she replied indignantly, but perhaps 'part of the natural heritage, somewhat in need of restoration'. Since François Lechauve, with André Porcheret of the Hospices de Beaune casting an avuncular eye over things, took over in 1989, there has been a dramatic improvement here. Some 30 per cent of the stems are retained, the wine given a long *cuvaison* (fifteen to twenty days) at temperatures up to 32°C, and between 30 and 40 per cent new oak is employed every year. The wines used to be tough when young, rustic when they evolved. This is no more.

Eric de Suremain, Château de Monthélie

8.85 ha: owned. Monthélie *premier cru* Sur-la-Velle; village Monthélie. Plus Rully (*rouge et blanc*).

A splendid environment, with a fine *manoir*, parts of which date back to the fourteenth century, overlooking the vineyards and situated in a little park. But the wines all too often are disappointing. When I called to sample the 1992s, not a very great vintage, I was impressed with the wines and I noticed that they had got rid of a lot of their old barrels. But the 1993s, a rather better vintage, were weak when I visited a year later.

AUXEY-
DURESSES

Auxey – pronounced Aussey – is the next village along the Autun road. But before you reach it, stop the car just outside Monthélie, before the road descends, and look at the view. It is one of the very best in Burgundy. In front of you lies the village of Auxey, sheltering under the Montagne de Bourdon. Further along the valley widens again and you can see the vines of Saint-Romain. To your right are the vineyards of Monthélie; to your left the village of Meursault, and beyond it the valley of the Saône; behind you there is Volnay and the *climat* of Santenots. You really are in the heart of the Côte-de-Beaune.

The village of Auxey lies in the valley between the afore-mentioned Montagne de Bourdon and the Mont Mellian, and two of the three sections which comprise the Auxey *vignoble* lie on the slopes of these hills. Those under the Montagne de Bourdon face south-east and then due south, and it is on the first part, before you come to the village, that you will find the *premiers crus*. This is a good site for the Pinot Noir. Opposite, on what is in effect the extension of the Meursault slope, the orientation is north-west, though the slope is gentle. Here the Pinot will not ripen successfully. This is land for Chardonnay, but not for *premier cru*. A kilometre or so further on, under the vineyard of Saint-Romain, is a third slope, facing south-east once again. You will find both varieties, but again no *premiers crus*.

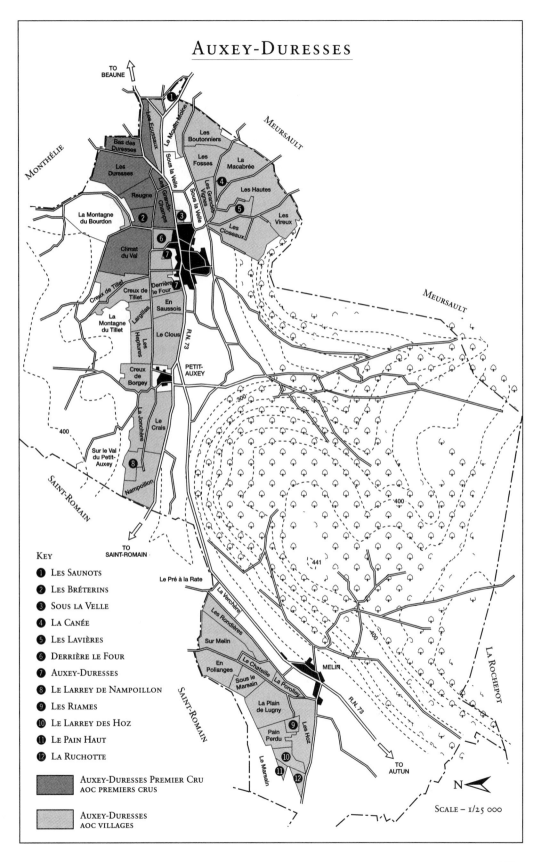

AUXEY-DURESSES

TO BEAUNE

MONTHÉLIE

MEURSAULT

MEURSAULT

SAINT-ROMAIN

SAINT-ROMAIN

TO SAINT-ROMAIN

TO AUTUN

LA ROCHEPOT

Les Écusseaux
Le Moulin Moine
Bas des Duresses
Les Boutonniers
Les Duresses
Les Fosses
La Macabrée
Sous la Velle
Reugne
Les Grandes Champs
Les Grandes Vignes
Sous la Velle
Les Hautes
La Montagne du Bourdon
Les Cloiseaux
Les Vireux
Climat du Val
Creux de Tillet
Creux de Tillet
Derrière le Four
En Saussois
La Montagne du Tillet
Largillas
Les Haptures
Le Clous
R.N. 73
Creux de Borgey
PETIT-AUXEY
La Jonchère
Le Crais
Sur le Val du Petit-Auxey
Nampoillon
Le Pré à la Rate
La Verchère
Les Rondières
Sur Melin
En Polianges
Le Chatelle
La Porollet
MELIN
Sous le Marsain
La Plain de Lugny
R.N. 73
Les Hoz
Le Marsain
Pain Perdu

KEY

1. LES SAUNOTS
2. LES BRÉTERINS
3. SOUS LA VELLE
4. LA CANÉE
5. LES LAVIÈRES
6. DERRIÈRE LE FOUR
7. AUXEY-DURESSES
8. LE LARREY DE NAMPOILLON
9. LES RIAMES
10. LE LARREY DES HOZ
11. LE PAIN HAUT
12. LA RUCHOTTE

AUXEY-DURESSES PREMIER CRU
AOC PREMIERS CRUS

AUXEY-DURESSES
AOC VILLAGES

N

SCALE – 1/25 000

HISTORY

Auxey was known in Gallo-Roman times as Aulaciacum, which slowly but surely contracted to Alcium or Aussey. In the eleventh century Cistercian monks created a vineyard and installed a water-mill in what was then the hamlet of Auxey. The village was subsequently ruled by a succession of *seigneurs* who have left their mark in the shape of the vestiges of at least two châteaux. You can still see what were the cellars of one of them, behind the church. The church itself is fifteenth century, and possesses a *tryptique* attributed to Roger van der Weyden.

Like many villages – in Auxey's case in 1928 – the village took on as a suffix the name of one of its top *climats*. Like Morey, it did not pick the very best. Les Duresses is not Auxey's top *premier cru*. That honour goes to Clos-du-Val. But I suppose Auxey-du-Val is a bit cumbersome.

THE VINEYARD

The *climat* of Les Duresses, the first and most easterly-facing of the *premiers crus* is, like its namesake in Monthélie, to which it is contiguous, of an Argovian limestone base: a stony marl, light in colour, the soil about 25–30 centimetres thick at the top. As you travel on, and the orientation charges towards the south, the soil becomes less calcareous, more marly, harder to work. Into Le Val and this tendency is even more exaggerated. This is the end of the *premiers crus*. This geology is continued in the vineyards which follow, but the soil colour gradually changes to red, and is mixed with more scree and limestone debris. The micro-climate is colder here, as a result of the forest on the opposite flank, despite the southerly exposure.

On the Mont Mellian slope the soil is a red-coloured, very stony limestone debris, and the rock underneath is more crumbly, the surface soil only 15–20 cm thick.

Premiers Crus: There are nine *premiers crus*, in whole or in part, and these are as follows: Les Bréterins (part); La Chapelle; Climat-du-Val; Clos-du-Val; Les-Bas-des-Duresses; Les Duresses (part); Les Ecusseaux (part); Les Grands-Champs; Reugne (part). These cover 31.78 ha and produce around 1,000 hl (132,000 bottles) of red wine and 16 hl (2,100 bottles) of white wine a year.

Village Wine: There are 137.87 ha of village wine producing 2,500 hl of red wine, including Côte-de-Beaune-Villages (330,000 bottles) and 1,700 hl (224,000 bottles) of white wine a year.

Premier cru Auxey *rouge* can vary from soft, forward, plump wines in the modern style to rather more substantial bottles which sometimes have a tendency to be a bit four-square, even rustic. The former aspiration, in my view, is fine at the village level, but one looks for more substance and depth of wine if one is paying *premier cru* prices. This sort of Auxey is usually a bigger wine than a Monthélie *premier cru*, and, with the weight but without the artisanal aspects, used to be rare, but one can now find it more and more. But – for here we are beginning to range into the Hautes-Côtes – there is nevertheless more of a difference in quality between the good years and the not-so-good than there is, say, in Volnay and Pommard.

Auxey-Duresses is also an important village for white wine. These are rather less expensive than village Meursaults, but can often be as good, so much better value. They need drinking reasonably soon.

THE *PREMIERS CRUS*

CLOS-DU-VAL (0.93 HA) • **CLIMAT-DU-VAL** (8.37 HA)
LES DURESSES (7.92 HA) • **LES BRÉTERINS** (1.69 HA)
LA CHAPELLE (1.28 HA) • **REUGNE** (1.98 HA)
LES BAS-DES-DURESSES (2.39 HA) • **LES GRANDS-CHAMPS** (4.03 HA)
LES ECUSSEAUX (3.18 HA)

I list these in order of my preference, the last three vineyards being those lower down the slope from the first six.

The Clos-du-Val, a monopoly of one branch of the extended Prunier family, and now divided between Michel Prunier and his first cousin Philippe (Domaine Prunier-Damy) is Auxey's best site, and seems to produce a wine which is quite a lot richer, fatter and more stylish than the other *premiers crus*. The rest of the Val *climat* and its immediate neighbours produce a more substantial wine than the vineyard of Les Duresses.

Recommended Sources:
Clos-du-Val: Michel Prunier, Philippe Prunier-Damy (both Auxey-Duresses).
Les Duresses: Jean-Pierre Diconne, Pascal Prunier (both Auxey-Duresses).
Les Ecusseaux: Robert Ampeau (Meursault).

The village Auxey-Duresses of the Duc de Magenta, both *rouge et blanc*, used to be produced by Maison Louis Jadot of Beaune and is now made by Pascal Marchand of Pommard's Domaine du Comte Armand. It's a fine example of the village wine.

THE GROWERS

ALAIN CREUSEFOND

10 ha: owned and *en fermage*. Auxey-Duresses *premier cru* in Le Val, Les Duresses; Meursault *premier cru* Les Poruzots; village Auxey-Duresses *rouge et blanc*; village Monthélie; village Meursault.

The forty-two-year-old Alain Creusefond makes his wine in capacious cellars under his house on the main road, eliminating all but 5 per cent of the stems, vinifying at 28°C and using 10 per cent new oak. Some wines are still bottled under the label of his father Gérard. I have had good wine in both colours here, especially the Duresses.

JEAN-PIERRE DICONNE

6.9 ha: owned and *en fermage/métayage*. Auxey-Duresses *premier cru* Les Duresses, Les Grands-Champs; village Auxey-Duresses *rouge et blanc*; Meursault including the *lieux-dits* Les Narvaux, Les Luchets.

The irrepressible, enthusiastic Jean-Pierre Diconne is one of Burgundy's eccentrics, and the wine-making here is a bit hit and miss. But I have had some good bottles in both colours.

ANDRÉ ET BERNARD LABRY

13 ha: *en fermage*. Village Auxey-Duresses *rouge et blanc*; village Pommard; village Monthélie.

When André Labry started off in the 1950s life was hard, and he didn't have the money to invest in Auxey-Duresses, so at first the exploitation consisted of new vineyards he had cleared and planted in the Hautes-Côtes. Today his son Bernard is in charge and the domaine offers neatly made village wine as well; but no first growths, to their regret. You will find them in Melin, the next hamlet along the road towards La Rochepot.

JEAN ET VINCENT LAFOUGE

7 ha: owned and *en fermage*. Village Auxey-Duresses *rouge et blanc* including the *lieu-dit* Les Vireux (*blanc*); village Meursault including the *lieu-dit* Les Meix-Chavaux.

This long-established domaine, located on the back streets of the village, has been bottling more and more of its own wine since Vincent Lafouge joined his father after wine school and national service. I've had some good wines here.

HENRI LATOUR ET FILS

16.06 ha: owned and *en fermage*. Auxey-Duresses *premier cru* from Les Grands-Champs and La Chapelle; village Auxey-Duresses *rouge et blanc*; Saint-Romain *rouge et blanc*.

Cousins of the Lafarges, but not of any Latours in the neighbourhood, Henri and his sons François and Sylvain are adherents of the Lyre system of training, tolerated but not encouraged by the authorities. With a Cordon-controlled pruning system, the engaging Henri Latour will explain, there is a much better sanitary condition of the fruit, and he obtains a better sugar level and a better colour. They also plant ray-grass to prevent erosion, are very *biologique* as regards treatments and have cropped 40 hl/ha for village wine and 30 for *premier cru* over the last decade. This immaculately tidy cellar produces very good wines.

★★MAISON LEROY

With Madame Lalon Bize-Leroy's acquisition in 1988 of the Charles Noëllat domaine in Vosne-Romanée (see page 132), one suspects buying activity here in Auxey must have come to a halt. But substantial stocks of high-quality old Burgundies remain in the cellar. The Leroy style has always been for wines which last well, bought in as wine when the vintage was a good one, and only when the quality was appropriate. Here is a treasure trove, but an expensive one.

JEAN-PIERRE PRUNIER
PASCAL PRUNIER

Jean-Pierre Prunier: 8 ha: owned and *en fermage*. Auxey-Duresses *premier cru* in Les Duresses, Le Val; Monthélie *premier cru* Sur-la-Velle; village Auxey-Duresses *rouge et blanc*; village Pommard; village Beaune; village Meursault; Saint-Romain *rouge et blanc*.

Pascal Prunier: 4.5 ha: owned and *en fermage*. Auxey-Duresses *premier cru* Les Duresses; Monthélie *premier cru* Les Vignes-Rondes; Beaune *premier cru* Les Reversées, Les Sizies; village Beaune; village Pommard; village Auxey-Duresses *rouge et blanc*; Saint-Romain *rouge et blanc*.

Pascal Prunier and his father Jean-Pierre, cousins of Michel (see below) now operate two maturation cellars, though some wines originate in the same vat. Following the Hospices de Beaune's acquisition of some Bâtard-Montrachet in 1990, some of their Beaune holdings were disposed of, via the agency SAFER, among the younger local *vignerons*, and the fresh-faced, curly-headed Pascal was able to acquire a parcel of Sizies. Some good wines here.

MICHEL PRUNIER

10 ha: owned and *en fermage*. Auxey-Duresses *premier cru* including Clos-du-Val; Volnay *premier cru* Les Caillerets; Beaune *premier cru* Les Sizies; village Auxey-Duresses *rouge et blanc*; village Meursault.

It is hard to think of the diminutive and somewhat self-effacing Michel Prunier as the doyen of his family. But he is certainly the best grower in the village, and the village seems to be largely populated by his relations. The village Auxey is destemmed 50 per cent, the lesser wines not at all, and there is one-third new wood for the *premiers crus*. His Clos-du-Val is my favourite Auxey.

Philippe Prunier-Damy

14 ha: owned and *en fermage*. Auxey-Duresses *premier cru* Clos-du-Val; Monthélie *premier cru* Les Duresses; village Pommard; village Beaune; village Volnay; village Monthélie; village Meursault; village Auxey-Duresses *rouge et blanc*.

This domaine used to be called Roger Prunier, the late Roger being Michel's older brother. Together the two domaines share the monopoly of the Clos-du-Val. Very good wines from a very clean and tidy cellar. Some 30 per cent new wood is used here.

Dominique et Vincent Roy

11 ha: owned. Auxey-Duresses *premier cru* in Les Duresses, Le Val; Volnay *premier cru* Les Santenots; village Auxey-Duresses *rouge et blanc*; Côte-de-Beaune-Villages.

Two brothers, Dominique and the lean, dark, bearded intelligent Vincent, run this emerging domaine, situated on the main road at the entrance to the village. Some 5 per cent of the stems, vinification controlled at 30°C, using natural yeasts, 20 per cent new oak and no fining after a light *Kieselguhr* filtration is the recipe here. The *cuverie* consists of squat round stainless-steel tanks equipped with automatic *pigeage* plungers over concrete vats, enabling *écoulage* by gravity. Behind this room is a fifteenth-century cellar dug out of the side of the slope. A good address: recent vintages of the Val are especially noteworthy.

SAINT-ROMAIN

Saint-Romain is really part of the Hautes-Côtes, but has enjoyed full village *Appellation Contrôlée* status since 1947. After Auxey-Duresses the road divides and the right-hand fork leads you through the Saint-Romain vineyards towards the village, surrounded by cliffs and perched below the remains of an impressive fortified château. The village is on two levels, Saint-Romain-le-Haut being within what were originally the bailey walls of the castle, the main village being below. Between the two the traveller will pass the impressive tiers of weathering oak staves of the cooper François Frères.

The soil is varied, but more suitable for producing white wine than red, as is the elevation of the vineyards (between 300 and 400 metres) and the ambient temperature. The vines are largely planted on a quite stony calcareous clay: the higher slopes are more marly, the lower terrains more iron-rich, and consequently red in colour.

There are no first growths in the commune, the only one in the Côte-de-Beaune apart from Chorey not to possess any. The 135 ha of village land produce about 1,950 hl (257,000 bottles) of red wine (including Côte-de-Beaune-Villages) and 1,800 hl (237,000 bottles) of white wine a year.

This is a village which is rather more successful in Chardonnay than in Pinot Noir. The red wines are hardly different from an Hautes-Côtes, at their best light, soft, fruity and for early drinking. In a poor year they are lean and herbaceous. The white wine comes into its own when the vintage is very warm, and Meursault and Pulignys are alcoholic, heavy and deficient in acidity. Then the advantages of Saint-Romain's cooler climate and consequent racier wines is an advantage. But even in lesser years this can be a good hunting ground for those seeking inexpensive white wine. Most *négociants* – Louis Jadot for example – will have one.

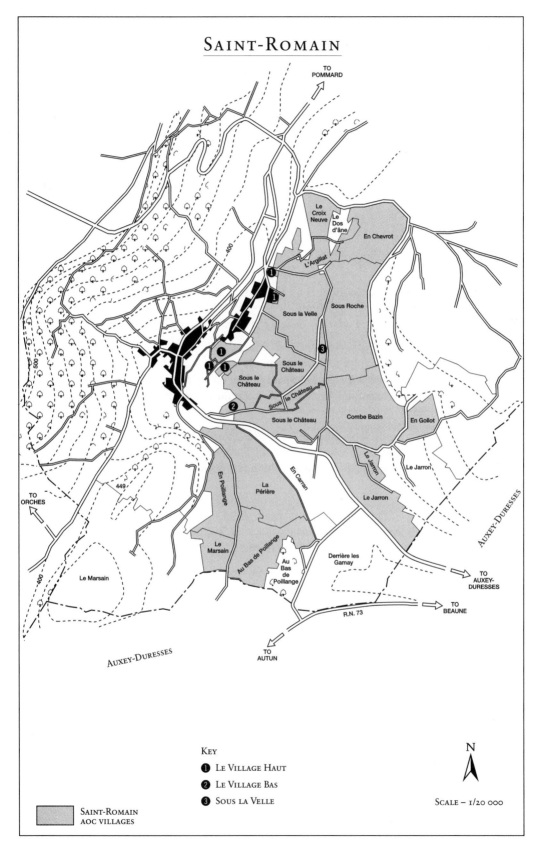

SAINT-ROMAIN

TO
POMMARD

Le
Croix
Neuve

Le
Dos
d'âne

En Chevrot

L'Argillat

Sous la Velle

Sous Roche

Sous le
Château

Sous le
Château

Sous le Château

Sous le Château

Combe Bazin

En Gollot

Le Jarron

Le Jarron

En Poillange

La
Périère

En Cléran

Le Jarron

TO
ORCHES

449

Le
Marsain

Au Bas de Poillange

Au
Bas
de
Poillange

Derrière les
Gamay

TO
AUXEY-
DURESSES

Le Marsain

R.N. 73

TO
BEAUNE

AUXEY-DURESSES

AUXEY-DURESSES

TO
AUTUN

KEY

1 LE VILLAGE HAUT

2 LE VILLAGE BAS

3 SOUS LA VELLE

N

SCALE – 1/20 000

SAINT-ROMAIN
AOC VILLAGES

Recommended Sources: See below.

THE GROWERS

★★D'AUVENAY

3.67 ha: owned. Mazis-Chambertin (26 a); Bonnes-Mares (26 a); Chevalier-Montrachet (16 a); Criots-Bâtard-Montrachet (6 a); Puligny-Montrachet *premier cru* Les Folatières; village Meursault including the *lieu-dit* Les Narvaux; village Auxey-Duresses *blanc*.

This is Madame Lalou Bize-Leroy's own private domaine, the produce of which is made and sold quite independently of the Domaine Leroy or Leroy the *négociants*. See pages 240 and 527.

HENRI ET GILLES BUISSON

14.43 ha: owned. Corton (33 a); Saint-Romain *rouge et blanc* in the *lieux-dits* Sous-la-Velle (*blanc*) and Sous-Roche (*rouge*); village Pommard; village Volnay; village Auxey-Duresses *rouge et blanc*; village Meursault.

Henri Buisson is now *en retraite* and it is his bearded, balding forty-something son Gilles who is in charge here. No stems, fermentation *en masse* (30°C for red, 21°C for white) and then *élevage* in wood, 10 per cent of which is new, is the formula. Lightish wines for early drinking is the result.

BERNARD FÈVRE

10 ha: owned and *en fermage/métayage*. Pommard *premier cru* Les Epenots; Beaune *premier cru* Les Montrevenots; village Savigny-lès-Beaune; village Pommard; village Auxey-Duresses; Saint-Romain *rouge et blanc*.

Bernard Fèvre additionally looks after 3 ha for the Hospices de Beaune. One of his share-cropping deals is with his uncle, André Mussy of Pommard, but the wine is made and *élevé* quite separately. He has been experimenting with *cuvées* matured almost entirely in new wood. I'm not impressed, however.

DOMAINE GERMAIN PÈRE ET FILS

13 ha: owned and *en fermage*. Saint-Romain *rouge* (Sous-le-Château) *et blanc*; village Pommard; Beaune *premier cru* Les Montremenots; village Beaune.

Patrick Germain has taken over responsibility from his father Bernard at this up-and-coming domaine and the wines have improved as they have progressively used less and less of the stems and increased the proportion of new oak. The whites are now entirely vinified in wood. There is a fine view from the terrace outside the Germains' home on the road up to Ouches.

ALAIN GRAS
RENÉ GRAS-BUISSON

14 ha: owned and *en fermage*. Village Auxey-Duresses *rouge et blanc*; Saint-Romain *rouge et blanc*; village Meursault in the *lieu-dit* Les Tillets.

Alain Gras' bastion lies high up in Saint-Romain-le-Haut among the ruins of the medieval château and church. The view from close by is impressive. He looks after 7 ha of his own and 7 ha belonging to his parents (still labelled as René Gras-Buisson, but it's all the same wine), and has been in the vanguard of putting Saint-Romain on the map. These are modern wines. 'I want to make *vins de plaisir*,' he says.

GUYOT PÈRE ET FILS

6.70 ha: *en fermage/métayage.* Saint-Romain *rouge et blanc*; village Beaune; village Puligny-Montrachet.

Thierry Guyot, plumpish, forty-ish, dark-haired, works alongside his Viking-looking brother-in-law Alain Lehais, father Marcel, whose name you will still see on some labels, having now retired. The domaine has been *biodynamique* since 1986. There is partial, but increasing destemming here, vinifications up to maximum of 34°C for the red (and in wood for the white) and 20–30 per cent new wood. These are fine, slow-to-mature wines of an intensity rarely seen in wines of these appellations. Recommended.

PIERRE TAUPENOT

9 ha: owned and *en fermage.* Saint-Romain *rouge et blanc*; village Auxey-Duresses *rouge et blanc.*

Pierre Taupenot is the twin brother of Jean of Morey-Saint-Denis. Anthony Hanson mentions an impressive inventory of old wines here. This I have not seen, perhaps because I have never been sufficiently impressed by the latest wines to want to stop and chat. I find Pierre Taupenot's wines both a bit lean and a bit unstylish.

MEURSAULT

Choose selectively, and you will perceive a natural progression in the Côte-de-Beaune. First the sturdy reds of Pommard; then the more elegant, softer wines of Volnay; and finally a white wine commune — Meursault. Meursault produces almost as much white wine as all the other communes put together. It is a large parish — only Gevrey and Beaune have more land under vines — and indeed a sizeable village with a seemingly limitless number of individual growers. For the last fifteen years I have visited twenty-five or so Meursault proprietors a year, usually eliminating three or four from the previous season in order to add new names. I have yet to arrive at the bottom of the list.

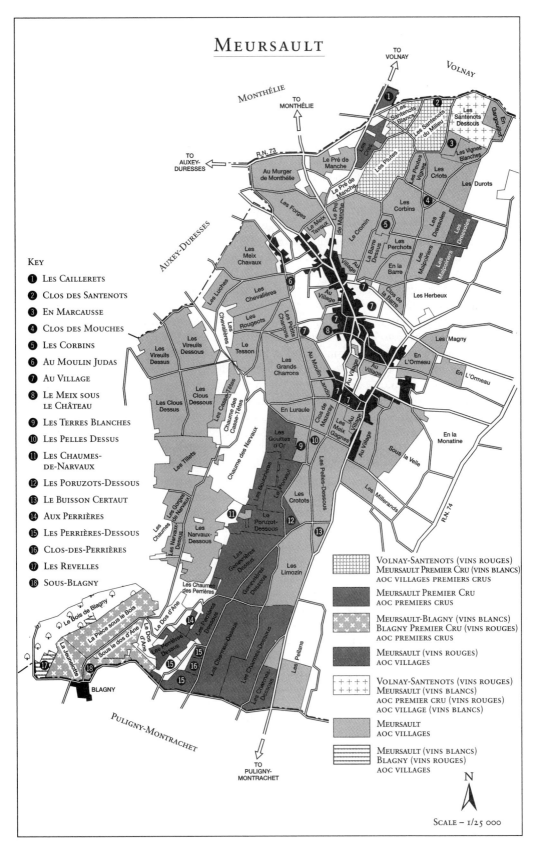

MEURSAULT

TO VOLNAY

VOLNAY

MONTHÉLIE

TO MONTHÉLIE

Les Santenots Blancs

Les Santenots du Milieu

Les Santenots Dessous

En Gargouillot

Les Vignes Blanches

Les Petites Vignes

Les Criots

Les Durots

TO AUXEY-DURESSES

R.N. 73

Au Murger de Monthélie

Le Pré de Manche

Le Pré de Manche

Le Pré de Manche

Les Cras

Les Plutes

Les Forges

Le Meix Tavaux

Les Corbins

Les Dressoles

Les Dressoles

Le Cromin

Les Perchots

Les Malpoiriers

Les Malpoiriers

AUXEY-DURESSES

Les Meix Chavaux

La Barre Dessus

En la Barre

Clos de la Barre

Les Herbeux

Au Village

Les Luchets

Les Chevalières

Les Chevalières

Les Rougeots

Le Tesson

Les Petits Charrons

Au Village

Au Village

Les Magny

Les Vireuils Dessus

Les Vireuils Dessous

Les Grands Charrons

En L'Ormeau

En L'Ormeau

Au Moulin Landin

Les Clous Dessous

Les Clous Dessus

Chaume des Casse-Têtes

Les Casse-Têtes

En Luraule

Clos de Mazeray

Les Meix Gagnes

Au Village

Les Gouttes d'Or

Les Tillets

Chaume des Narvaux

En la Monatine

Sous la Velle

Les Pelles-Dessous

Les Millerands

R.N. 74

Les Chaumes de Narvaux

Les Gorges de Narvaux

Les Narvaux-Dessous

Le Poruzot

Les Crotots

Le Poruzot-Dessous

Les Genevrières Dessus

Genevrières Dessous

Les Chaumes des Perrières

Les Limozin

Le Bois de Blagny

La Pièce sous le Bois

Sous le dos d'Ane

Le Dos d'Ane

Le Dos d'Ane

Les Perrières Dessus

Les Perrières Dessous

La Jeunellotte

Les Charmes-Dessus

Les Charmes-Dessous

Les Charmes-Dessous

Les Pellans

BLAGNY

PULIGNY-MONTRACHET

TO PULIGNY-MONTRACHET

KEY

1. LES CAILLERETS
2. CLOS DES SANTENOTS
3. EN MARCAUSSE
4. CLOS DES MOUCHES
5. LES CORBINS
6. AU MOULIN JUDAS
7. AU VILLAGE
8. LE MEIX SOUS LE CHÂTEAU
9. LES TERRES BLANCHES
10. LES PELLES DESSUS
11. LES CHAUMES-DE-NARVAUX
12. LES PORUZOTS-DESSOUS
13. LE BUISSON CERTAUT
14. AUX PERRIÈRES
15. LES PERRIÈRES-DESSOUS
16. CLOS-DES-PERRIÈRES
17. LES REVELLES
18. SOUS-BLAGNY

VOLNAY-SANTENOTS (VINS ROUGES)
MEURSAULT PREMIER CRU (VINS BLANCS)
AOC VILLAGES PREMIERS CRUS

MEURSAULT PREMIER CRU
AOC PREMIERS CRUS

MEURSAULT-BLAGNY (VINS BLANCS)
BLAGNY PREMIER CRU (VINS ROUGES)
AOC PREMIERS CRUS

MEURSAULT (VINS ROUGES)
AOC VILLAGES

VOLNAY-SANTENOTS (VINS ROUGES)
MEURSAULT (VINS BLANCS)
AOC PREMIER CRU (VINS ROUGES)
AOC VILLAGE (VINS BLANCS)

MEURSAULT
AOC VILLAGES

MEURSAULT (VINS BLANCS)
BLAGNY (VINS ROUGES)
AOC VILLAGES

N

SCALE – 1/25 000

HISTORY

The name Meursault – Murisault or Murassalt in old documents – is derived according to some authorities from the Latin for 'rat jump'. But Pierre Forgeot says the name comes from the fortified camp, dating from Bronze Age and Gallo-Roman times, which lies up in the hills above the village. Does the word *mur*, wall, have anything to do with it? The locals prefer the more colourful athletic rodents, which seems a bit far-fetched to me. But etymology, I fear, is far from being an exact science, and one can idle away a lot of time up its dark and twisted alleys.

Like the majority of communes of the Côte d'Or, the history of the parish is closely associated with the church. Even before there was a vine at Clos-de-Vougeot, the new Cistercian abbey at Citeaux, founded by the ascetic Robert de Molesmes in 1098 as a breakaway from the more comfortable order of the Benedictines at Cluny, had received a gift of land in Meursault from Duke Odo II of Burgundy. That was in 1102. This was followed by further donations in the next couple of centuries with the result that, after Vougeot, Meursault was Citeaux's most important viticultural territory, a situation which persisted until the French Revolution. Moreover, it is Meursault rather than Puligny which is the heart of the Hospices de Beaune's white wine holdings. In 1669 half the land belonging to the local *seigneur*, M. de Massot, was left to this institution.

Though most of Burgundy is equally as entitled to produce red wine as white, the commune seems always to have concentrated its production on white wines. Thomas Jefferson was told when he visited the area in 1787 that there was 'too much stone' in the soil for red wine production. No doubt the locals would have produced red wine if they could, for the former was much the most popular. Good Volnay sold for 300 francs the cask, but even the best Meursault (Jefferson refers specifically to Goutte d'Or) could fetch only 150. 'At Pommard and Voulenay [*sic*] I observed [the local farmers] eating good white bread; at Meursault rye. I asked the reason of the difference. They told me that white wines fail in quality oftener than the red, and remain on hand. At Meursault only white wines are made.'

André Jullien (*Topographie de Tous les Vignobles Connus*, written in 1815), refers to the Meursault reds of the Santenots *climat* on the Volnay border producing a wine similar to Volnay in style, and goes on to say that the majority of the commune's production was white wine. These, having left Burgundy, were often sold under the name of Montrachet, he adds. Perrières, Combettes (now – perhaps then – across the border in Puligny), Les Gouttes d'Or, Genevrièvres and Charmes, and in that order, he emphasised, were the best vineyards.

Forty years later, as far as the white wines are concerned, Dr Lavalle accords the *climat* of Les Perrières the accolade of *tête de cuvée*. Les Genevrières-Dessus, Les Charmes-Dessus, Les Bouchères and Les Gouttes d'Or are *premières cuvées*. By this time however, prices of the white wines seem to have caught up with the reds. A Perrières would fetch the same price (F 1,200 the *queue* in good years, direct from the press) as a Santenots-du-Milieu.

Today Les Perrières would head most people's list of the top *climats* in the commune, and I would put the best of the various parts of Charmes and Genevrières in second place, some way above the remainder. And I would also add the best of the white wines of Blagny, only considered part of Meursault since the days of *Appellation Contrôlée*.

The reason for the very large number of domaine bottlers in the village – well over 100, which is over four times that of Puligny-Montrachet and indeed double that of Gevrey, for instance – is twofold. Unlike in Puligny, where the water table is high, cellars can easily be constructed out of the bedrock beneath the village. The other concerns the fluctuations of fashion. Several times in the last thirty years, while Puligny-Montrachet has been in demand, Meursault has been out of favour. The Beaune *négoce* have not wanted to buy. There have been times when Meursault fetched less per bottle than a generic Chablis. So the growers have decided to go it alone.

THE VILLAGE

The large, sprawling village of Meursault lies in the middle of its *vignoble* and boasts a fine church dating from 1480, whose 57-metre spire can be seen from some distance away. This can be found near to the remains of a medieval fortress in the town's main square. Surrounding this *place* there are a number of narrow, winding streets and alleys, laid out to no coherent plan, reaching in one direction towards Auxey and Monthélie, and in another down towards the main road and across to Puligny-Montrachet. Within as well as without the village, hidden in their own parks behind secluding gates, there are a number of fine buildings, some dating back to the sixteenth and seventeenth centuries, or beyond. Chief of these is the seventeenth-century Château de Meursault, now the property of Patriarche. Across the main Beaune-Chagny road is the village of L'Hôpital de Meursault where you can see the ecclesiastical remains of the old leprosarium and eat cheaply but increasingly industrially at the Relais de la Diligence. It is in Meursault that the third and least stuffy of the *Trois Glorieuses* banquets, the *Paulée*, is held at lunchtime on the Monday after the Hospices de Beaune auction in November. Everyone brings and shares his/her own wine, and you are seated on long tables to facilitate this generosity. The last time I attended, I later counted no fewer than fifty-seven tasting notes in my *carnet*, my descriptions becoming progressively more indecipherable and unintelligible as the afternoon progressed!

LOCATION

The commune is divided by the village and has two distinct sections. The smaller northern part is an extension of the Monthélie-Volnay *côte* as it falls gently towards the south-east. The soil is based in Bathonian limestone and is a brown stony debris containing both pebbles and clay, more suitable for red wine than white. Here you will find the *climats* of Santenots and Les Plures. The red wine that is produced here is sold as Volnay, Les Santenots and is discussed in the Volnay chapter.

South of the village the soil is lighter in colour, rocky rather than pebbly, and the aspect is more to the east, even the north-east directly above the village. The vines lie sheltered under the forest of the Montagne du Chatelet de Montmellian, on the one side of which is the hamlet of Blagny and on the other side the village of Auxey-Duresses. It is close to Blagny that the best *climats* are located. The *terroir* here is of Bathonian origin: Callovian limestone, in parts Argovian white marl, covered in broken limestone debris, especially up-slope, where there is hardly any surface soil to speak of. In Les Perrières the soil is the lightest and stoniest of all. Beneath this is Les Charmes, similar in the upper part of the 'Dessus' (the *Dessus* goes quite a long way down the slope here!). Further down the earth is much deeper and the incline more gentle.

Next to this there is Les Genevrières, also divided into *Dessus* and *Dessous*. Again at the top the surface layer is thin but the soil a little redder in colour and deeper further down the slope. Next to this is Les Poruzots above part of which is Les Bouchères, and on the same level as Les Bouchères is the last of the *premiers crus* in this sector, Les Gouttes d'Or. Again the vineyards are very stony in the upper sections, but it is yet redder in colour and more clayey in consistency. It quite abruptly becomes less fine as we descend the slope.

Of equal importance is the nature of the underlying rock. In the top parts of Les Genevrières and in Les Perrières the base rock is hard. Further down in Les Genevrières and across the whole of Les Charmes there is *lave*, a shaley limestone which crumbles easily.

THE VINEYARD

Premiers Crus: Meursault and Blagny (for it is convenient to include Blagny here – though the terrain and wines will be discussed in the next chapter) possess twenty-nine *premiers crus* including the various Santenots and Les Plures which, if red (but they can be planted in Chardonnay), make Volnay, Les Santenots. These were discussed in the Volnay chapter.

In Meursault, these are: Les Bouchères; Les Caillerets; Les Charmes-Dessous; Les Charmes-Dessus; Les Chaumes-de-Narvaux (Genevrières); Les Chaumes-des-Perrières; Clos-des-Perrières; Clos-Richemont; Les Cras; Les Genevrières-Dessous; Les Genevrières-Dessus; Les Gouttes d'Or; Aux Perrières; Les Perrières-Dessous; Les Perrières-Dessus; Les Plures; Les Poruzots; Les Poruzots-Dessous; Les Poruzots-Dessus; Les Santenots-Blanc; Les Santenots-du-Milieu.

All the above can be both red or white. In practice only the *climats* near Volnay (Santenots, Plures, Les Cras, Clos-Richemont) are planted with Pinot Noir. However, while Meursault, Les Cras, Meursault, Les Caillerets, etc. can be red or white, Meursault, Les Santenots can only be white. If red, the wine is Volnay.

In Blagny, all have the right to the appellation Meursault-Blagny, *premier cru* if planted with Chardonnay: Sous-Blagny; Sous-le-Dos-d'Ane; La Jeunelotte; La Pièce-sous-le-Bois.

For Blagny *rouge,* see the next chapter.

These *premiers crus* cover 131.88 ha (this figure includes Volnay-Santenots) and produce around 4,100 hl (540,000 bottles) of white wine a year. Some 75 hl (9,900 bottles) of Meursault *premier cru rouge* is also declared.

Village Wine: There are 304.95 ha of village Meursault producing some 12,000 hl (1.584 million bottles) of white wine and 720 hl (95,000 bottles) of red wine a year.

White Meursault, said Camille Rodier in 1920, is at the same time dry and rich, with a flavour of hazelnuts. For Hubrecht Duijker (*The Great Wines of Burgundy*) it is ripe peaches which have just been picked on a hot day. Meursault, I would suggest, is an ample, sometimes gentle, wholly approachable wine, less sturdy but more opulent than Puligny, with less backbone too. It can occasionally be a little too fat and heavy, the broadness of the style not matched by sufficient acidity. The village wines can often be merely empty and anonymous. But all in all you have something which is round and ripe and fruity with a rich buttery flavour which should be supported but not overwhelmed by new oak. And then you will have something with considerable charm.

Moreover there are the '*deuxièmes crus*'. Nowhere in the Côte d'Or is the concept of a *lieu-dit* which is not a *premier cru* more important. Above the *premiers crus*, and taking over from them at the same altitude where they leave off, are what used to be termed (by Dr Lavalle and others) the *deuxièmes*. I see no reason not to avail ourselves of this description.

Up in the hills, going from south (above Les Genevrières) to north we have Les Narvaux, Les Tillets, Les Clous, Les Casse-Têtes and Les Vireuils. These tend to be steely and racy. The best have no lack of finesse.

In the line of the *premiers crus* after Les Gouttes d'Or, we have Les Grands-Charrons, Le Tesson, Les Rougeots, Les Chevalières, Les Luchets and Les Meix-Chavaux. These are fuller and rounder, but again have rather more distinction than ordinary village wines from lower down the slope or on the opposite side of the village.

THE PREMIERS CRUS

LES PERRIÈRES (13.72 HA)

This is the surface area of all the various Perrières combined (as are the equivalents below) and includes the 95 ares monopoly of the Clos-des-Perrières, belonging to Domaine Albert Grivault, which the owners, the Bardet family, are attempting to have elevated to *grand cru*.

Essentially there are two parts to the *climat*: that which lies immediately above Les Charmes (Les Perrières-Dessous) and that which lies further up the slope. In contrast to elsewhere it is the *Dessous* rather than the *Dessus* which is considered the best. Of course, as always, it depends on the grower (Jean-François Coche-Dury has his vines in the upper part, for example).

We are on the Puligny boundary here (next along are Les Champs-Canet and Les Combettes) and not surprisingly there are Puligny aspects to a wine from the Perrières. It is the most mineral, the most steely and the most racy of the Meursault *premiers crus*. It is floral, but then so are Genevrières and Charmes, but here the flowers are apple blossom and acacia, honeysuckle rather than honey itself, all quite high-toned. Above all, Perrières is perhaps the most elegant and persistent of the *premiers crus*. At its best it is positively brilliant, certainly comparable to Bâtard or Bienvenues, though perhaps not as fine – certainly not as powerful – as Chevalier or Montrachet itself.

Recommended Sources:
Robert Ampeau; Vincent Bitouzet-Prieur; Michel Bouzereau; Yves Boyer-Martenot; Jean-François Coche-Dury; Jean-Michel Gaunoux; Albert Grivault; Comtes Lafon; Matrot; Michelot; Pierre Morey; Jacques Prieur; Guy Roulot (all Meursault); Château de Puligny-Montrachet.

While none of the major *négociants* actually owns land in Les Perrières the *cuvées* of Joseph Drouhin, Louis Jadot and Olivier Leflaive Frères are usually worth recommending.

LES GENEVRIÈRES (16.48 HA)
Les Genevrières-Dessus is on the same level as Les Perrières-Dessous and produces better wine than Les Perrières-Dessus further up the slope. The vineyard does not, however, go all the way down to the Meursault-Puligny road, as does Les Charmes: the *climat* of Le Limouzin lies in between.

Genevrières is an opulent, even exotic wine: rounder than Perrières, if not fuller then certainly lusher; less steely and mineral; more fleshy, more spicy. Here the flavours are more musky, and there can be an element of citrus. Yet the result should be neither coarse nor heavy. A Genevrières should still have grip, should still be a wine of class. Virginal, however, it is not.

Is it better than Charmes? This is a question I find impossible to answer. There is certainly more of a variation in the quality of Charmes, whose lower sections should be excluded from *premier cru* status. But apart from that it is a question, as always, of which cellar you are in, the age of the vines, the vintage and personal taste. The two wines are very different.

Recommended Sources:
Guy Bocard; Bernard Boisson; Michel Bouzereau; Yves Boyer-Martenot; Charles et Rémi Jobard; François Jobard; Comtes Lafon; Michelot; François Mikulski (all Meursault). Plus the *négociants* listed above.

LES CHARMES (31.12 HA)
Larger than both Perrières and Genevrières put together, Les Charmes runs all the way down the slope until it reaches the Meursault-Puligny road, across which, in part, the land is not village AC but plain Bourgogne. It is perfectly valid to argue that the bottom third of Les Charmes should be down-graded to village status.

But that is not to denigrate the wine of the upper part. Here you will find a Meursault of equal interest and elegance to Genevrières, and in my view one of greater poise and style than Poruzots or Gouttes d'Or. There is an attractive, yet soft flowery character to a Charmes: peach blossom, delicately nutty, gently honeyed. The wine is less racy than Perrières, less exotically spicy than Genevrières. But it should be just as intense, just as stylish, just as harmonious.

Recommended Sources:
Robert Ampeau; Vincent Bitouzet-Prieur; Guy Bocard; Pierre Boillot; Hubert Bouzereau-Gruère (Charmes-du-Haut); Michel Bouzereau; Patrick Javillier; Charles et Rémi Jobard;

François Jobard; Comtes Lafon; Matrot; Michelot; François Mikulski; René Monnier; Guy Roulot; Marc Rougeot; Jacques Thevenot-Machal (all Meursault); Denis Boussey; Didier Darviot-Perrin (both Monthélie). Plus the *négociants* listed above.

LES PORUZOTS (11.43 HA) • LES BOUCHÈRES (4.41 HA)
LES GOUTTES D'OR (5.33 HA)

While Bouchères is rare – the only example I come across regularly being the Clos-des-Bouches-Chères *monopole* of Domaine René Manuel, bottled and distributed by Labouré-Roi of Nuits-Saint-Georges – the two other *climats* are easier to encapsulate. Poruzots and Gouttes d'Or are fullish wines, can be quite firm, but are always a little four-square, even a little *sauvage*. They can have plenty of fruit, depth and indeed interest: like Genevrières with a certain opulent spicy touch. But they cannot match either the flair or the complexity.

Recommended Sources:
Les Poruzots: Jean-Paul Gauffroy; François Jobard; François Mikulski; Michel Pouhain-Seurre (all Meursault); Olivier Leflaive Frères (Puligny-Montrachet).
Les Bouchères: René Manuel/Labouré-Roi, Clos-des-Bouches-Chères (*monopole*) (Meursault/Nuits-Saint-Georges).
Les Gouttes d'Or: Pierre Boillot; Alain Coche; Darnat; Jean-Michel Gaunoux (all Meursault).

LES CRAS (3.55 HA)

Les Cras is the only first growth on the Volnay side to be planted in any serious way with Chardonnay. Yet I feel this is nevertheless red-wine soil. The white wine, like the occasional Meursault-Santenots curiosity one comes across, never really convinces me. The Domaine Darnat has the monopoly of the 63 ares Clos-Richemont within Les Cras, and is the leading example, but even here I prefer their Gouttes d'Or.

BLAGNY (23.44 HA)

This is made up of La Jeunelotte (5.05 ha), La Pièce-sous-le-Bois (11.15 ha), Sous-le-Dos-d'Ane (5.03 ha) and Sous-Blagny (2.21 ha) but these separate *lieux-dits* are more commonly used to differentiate between Blagny *premiers crus rouges*.

Meursault-Blagny is a full wine, nicely steely and austere, very much a cross between a Puligny and a Meursault, but with more richness and backbone and less of the mineral aspect compared with a Perrières. It is a wine which should need time to mature, and should keep well. Strangely, you are more likely to come across it under a *négociant* label than directly from a domaine.

Recommended Sources:
Robert Ampeau; François Jobard; Matrot (all Meursault); Philippe Chavy; Henri Clerc (both Puligny-Montrachet); Maison Louis Jadot, Maison Louis Latour (both Beaune); Gilles Bouton (Saint-Aubin).

THE DEUXIÈMES CRUS

Here follows a selection of the best cellars for *deuxièmes crus*:
Michel Bouzereau: Les Tessons, Les Grands-Charrons.
Hubert Chavy-Chouet: Les Narvaux; Les Casse-Têtes; Les Grands-Charrons.
Jean-François Coche-Dury: Les Vireuils; Les Narvaux; Les Chevalières; Les Rougeots.
Jean-Philippe Fichet: Les Chevalières; Les Tessons.
Henri Germain: Les Chevalières.
Patrick Javillier: Les Tillets; Les Clous; Les Casse-Têtes; Les Narvaux.
Comtes Lafon: Clos-de-la-Barre.

Matrot: Les Chevalières.
Pierre Morey: Les Tessons.
Guy Roulot: Les Tessons; Les Luchets; Les Tillets.
All the above are in Meursault. See also the selections at Oliver Leflaive Frères and the Meursault, Les Narvaux of the Domaine d'Auvenay in Saint-Romain.

THE GROWERS

*ROBERT AMPEAU ET FILS

10 ha: owned. Puligny-Montrachet *premier cru* Les Combettes; Meursault *premier cru* in Les Perrières, Les Charmes, La Pièce-sous-le-Bois; Volnay *premier cru* Les Santenots; Beaune *premier cru* Clos-du-Roi; Savigny-lès-Beaune *premier cru* Les Lavières; Auxey-Duresses *premier cru* Les Ecusseaux; Blagny *premier cru* La Pièce-sous-le-Bois; village Meursault; village Pommard.

The Ampeaus, Robert and his son Michel, do not sell *en primeur*, holding back the vintage until they deem it ready for drinking. Moreover you cannot cherry-pick. You must take red as well as white, off-vintages as well as the good years. This is less of an imposition than it might be. Quality is high, even in the off-vintages, and the wines are built to last. I'd much rather be offered, say, a 1984 from here than a 1985 from many another Meursault establishment.

See Profile, page 316.

RAYMOND BALLOT-MINOT ET FILS
PHILIPPE BALLOT-DANCER
VEUVE CHARLES DANCER-LOCHARDET

14 ha: owned and *en fermage*. Meursault *premier cru* in Les Perrières, Les Genevrières, Les Charmes; Volnay *premier cru* in Les Santenots, Les Taille-Pieds; Pommard *premier cru* in Les Rugiens, Les Pézerolles, Les Charmots; Beaune *premier cru* Les Epenottes; Chassagne-Montrachet *premier cru blanc* in La Romanée and *rouge et blanc* in Les Morgeots; village Meursault *rouge et blanc* including the *lieu-dit* Les Criots; village Pommard, village Beaune, village Chassagne-Montrachet *rouge et blanc*.

Philippe Ballot is in charge of an impressive line-up, much of the result of which is sold off in bulk. The vines in some of the *climats* (Les Perrières, La Romanée) are young, but in Les Charmes and Les Genevrières the average age is thirty years and forty-seven years respectively. Ballot seems a conscientious wine-maker, but I confess I find his whites lack concentration.

VINCENT BITOUZET-PRIEUR
See Volnay, page 230.

GUY BOCARD

8.5 ha: owned and *en fermage*. Meursault *premier cru* in Les Genevrières, Les Charmes; village Meursault including the *lieux-dits* Le Limouzin, Les Grands-Charrons, Les Narvaux; Sous-la-Velle; village Auxey-Duresses; village Monthélie.

Guy Bocard took over from his father in 1988 or so and has gradually increased the amount he has bottled himself ever since. In 1992 he acquired a new pneumatic press. It produces much finer lees, he says, on which he can keep the wines longer. Bocard is hesitant, and rightly, about using too much new wood, and confines himself to a maximum of one-fifth, bottling after twelve months. Neat, well-made wines for the medium term.

PIERRE BOILLOT

2.5 ha: owned. Meursault *premier cru* in Les Charmes, Les Gouttes d'Or; Volnay *premier cru* Les Santenots; village Pommard.

'I well remember the 1947 vintage,' says Pierre Boillot, who is now in his mid-sixties. 'The grapes were picked in such a heatwave – and of course we had no temperature control in those days – so we left them outside the vineyard overnight, having hosed them down to cool them off. Others put ice in sacks in the red wine vats.'

   Slowly but surely this domaine is being passed on to his nephew, heir and immediate neighbour, François Mikulski. Pierre is a perfectionist, contemptuous of what he sees as sloppy corner-cutting by some of his peers. A good source.

BERNARD BOISSON-VADOT
DOMAINE BOISSON-MOREY

7 ha: owned and *en fermage*. Puligny-Montrachet *premier cru* Les Folatières; Meursault *premier cru* Les Genevrières; village Meursault including the *lieux-dits* Les Grands-Charrons, Les Chevalières; village Monthélie.

The tubby, balding, bespectacled Bernard Boisson makes round, ample, cheerfully fruity wines which evolve in the medium term. A good source.

HUBERT BOUZEREAU-GRUÈRE

12 ha: owned and *en fermage*. Corton, Les Bressandes (15 a); Meursault *premier cru* in Les Charmes (often two bottlings – Le Haut and Le Bas), Les Genevrières; Chassagne-Montrachet *premier cru blanc* Les Chaumées; Saint-Aubin *premier cru blanc* in Les Cortons, La Charmois; village Meursault including the *lieux-dits* Les Tillets, Le Limouzin, Les Grands-Charrons; village Chassagne-Montrachet *rouge et blanc*; village Puligny-Montrachet; village Santenay.

I had some good wines from the *sympa* Hubert Bouzereau, particularly the Charmes-du-Haut, where the vines were planted in 1957. Wines for the medium term here.

★MICHEL BOUZEREAU ET FILS

11 ha: owned and *en fermage*. Meursault *premier cru* in Les Perrières, Les Genevrières, Les Charmes, Blagny; Puligny-Montrachet *premier cru* in Le Champ-Gain, Les Champs-Canet; Beaune *premier cru* Les Vignes-Franches, Les Epenottes; village Meursault including the *lieux-dits* Le Limouzin, Les Tessons, Les Grands-Charrons; village Pommard; village Volnay.

This is the best of the Bouzereau cellars (there are yet others apart from Hubert, above). Michel and his son Jean-Baptiste recently acquired a pneumatic press and this has further accentuated the quality here. Fine, racy, stylish wines which can be held longer than most. A domaine to watch.

★YVES BOYER-MARTENOT

8.5 ha: owned and *en fermage/métayage*. Meursault *premier cru* in Les Perrières, Les Charmes, Les Genevrières; Auxey-Duresses *premier cru* Les Ecusseaux; village Meursault including the *lieux-dits* Les Narvaux, Le Pré-de-Manche; L'Ormeau; village Pommard; village Puligny-Montrachet; village Auxey-Duresses.

When I first started visiting Meursault regularly I found the wines of the diminutive Yves Boyer merely average. I called to taste the 1992s after an absence of a few years and found exciting things, and this progress has been confirmed by his 1993s and 1994s. This is now one of the best sources in the village. And the wines will keep well.

ANDRÉ BRUNET

7 ha: owned. Meursault *premier cru* in Les Genevrières, Les Charmes, Les Cras (*rouge*); Volnay *premier cru* Les Santenots; village Meursault including the *lieu-dit* Le Limouzin.

André Brunet is a charming old boy who lives with his wife in an impressive château in the middle of the village, with a huge immaculate vaulted cellar underneath. The wines, sadly, are not exceptional.

ROGER CAILLOT-MOREY

8 ha: owned and *en fermage/métayage*. Bâtard-Montrachet (49 a); Puligny-Montrachet *premier cru* in Les Pucelles, Les Folatières; village Meursault in the *lieux-dits* La Barre, Les Tessons, Le Clos-du-Cromin; village Santenay *rouge et blanc*; village Monthélie *rouge et blanc*.

The pearls of Roger Caillot's exploitation are in Puligny, not Meursault, where, *inter alia*, he is joint *métayer* for part of the Poirier family's Bâtard. This and the *premiers crus* are usually good, the Santenays and Monthélies are young vines. His reds are not as good as his whites.

HUBERT CHAVY-CHOUET

5 ha: owned and *en fermage*. Village Meursault including the *lieux-dits* Les Casse-Têtes, Les Narvaux, Les Grands-Charrons; village Puligny-Montrachet.

Hubert, brother of Philippe and son of Albert Chavy-Ropiteau, both of Puligny-Montrachet, has recently removed to Meursault, having married a young lady of the village. As more land gets passed down the inheritance ladder from both sides, this domaine will surely increase in importance as well as size. He's making neat, attractive wines with the village *climats*.

ALAIN COCHE-BIZOUARD
DOMAINE COCHE-DEBORD

8.5 ha: owned and *en métayage*. Meursault *premier cru* in Les Charmes, Les Gouttes d'Or; village Meursault including the *lieux-dits* Les Chevalières, Le Limouzin, L'Ormeau and 'Lupré' (Les Luchets and Le Pré-de-Manche); Monthélie *premier cru* Les Duresses; village Auxey-Duresses *rouge et blanc*; village Monthélie; Pommard *premier cru* La Platière.

Old vines and low *rendements* are the order of the day here, and 25 per cent new wood. This is one of only a few cellars in the village where the bottling of the white wines does not take place until eighteen months after the harvest. Very good white wines. The reds are less exciting.

★★JEAN-FRANÇOIS COCHE-DURY

9 ha: owned and *en fermage*. Corton-Charlemagne (30 a); Meursault *premier cru* Les Perrières; Volnay *premier cru* (from Clos-des-Chênes and Taille-Pieds); village Meursault including the *lieux-dits* Les Rougeots, Les Chevalières, Les Vireuils, Les Luchets, Les Narvaux; village Auxey-Duresses *rouge et blanc*; village Monthélie.

'Creamy, subtle and delicious,' is how Anthony Hanson describes Jean-François Coche's white wines. Here is a master wine-maker, a thinker and a perfectionist. The man is shy and self-effacing. There is no bombast, no chi-chi. And the results are excellent. Don't miss his reds either.

See Profile, page 395.

DARNAT

4 ha: owned and *en fermage/métayage*. Meursault *premier cru* Les Cras (*monopole* Clos-Richemont), Les Gouttes d'Or; Saint-Aubin *premier cru* En Remilly; village Meursault.

Henri Darnat is a capable young man, and seeking to expand the family exploitation. I remain unconvinced about Chardonnay in a *climat* like Les Cras, for this I believe is red-wine soil. But this is a good wine, and the Gouttes d'Or is even better.

BERTRAND DARVIOT

5.92 ha: owned. Beaune *premier cru* in Les Grèves, Les Belissands, Les Cent-Vignes, Les Marconnets; village Beaune including the *lieux-dits* Montagne-Saint-Desirée and Clos-des-Monsnières *blanc*; Meursault *premier cru* Les Caillerets; village Meursault including the *lieu-dit* Clos-de-la-Velle; village Savigny-lès-Beaune.

Brother of Didier Darviot of Monthélie, Bertrand and his wife Bernadette renovated the family château which had remained unoccupied for eighty years and installed themselves in the Château de la Velle in 1973. His red wine-making is original. The juice ferments at 18-22°C, a very low temperature, while the *chapeau* is at 30-32°C. This is obtained by a horizontally placed heat exchanger in the middle of the vat. The results are curious too.

SYLVAIN DUSSORT

5 ha: owned and *en fermage*. Village Meursault including the *lieu-dit* Le Limouzin; village Beaune in the *lieu-dit* Blanche-Fleur; Chorey-lès-Beaune.

Sylvain Dussort's father used to sell corks, viticultural treatments, etc and his brother teaches English and runs a neighbouring antique shop. I find the white wines good, but the reds, vinified with all the stems, rather less exciting.

JEAN-PHILIPPE FICHET

6.70 ha: owned and *en fermage/métayage*. Village Meursault including the *lieux-dits* of Les Clous, Les Tessons, Les Chevalières, Les Meix-sous-le-Château; village Monthélie; village Auxey-Duresses *rouge et blanc*; village Chassagne-Montrachet *rouge*.

The immaculately tidy cellar fills you with confidence, as does the demeanour of Jean-Philippe Fichet. And this is reinforced when you taste his wines. He used to farm some Perrières, but alas this is no more. But in the years to come he will inherit more land from his parents, as his father is about to retire. From 1997 he will have some Puligny-Montrachet, Les Referts and village Meursault in the *lieux-dits* Le Limouzin and Les Criots.

JEAN-PAUL GAUFFROY

13 ha: owned and *en fermage*. Meursault *premier cru* in Les Poruzots, Les Charmes; village Meursault including the *lieu-dit* Les Chevalières.

The leonine Jean-Paul Gauffroy's Poruzots is one of the best examples of this *premier cru*. As the vines in this domaine get older and older – he had to do a lot of replanting when he took over at the beginning of the 1980s – they get better and better. He bottles after eighteen months. A good source.

JEAN-MICHEL GAUNOUX

6 ha: owned and *en fermage*. Corton, Les Renardes (33 a); Meursault *premier cru* in Les Perrières, Les Gouttes d'Or; Volnay *premier cru* Clos-des-Chênes; village Pommard; village Meursault.

Jean-Michel Gaunoux is a diminutive man in his thirties who exploits the domaine of his mother and her parents. He shared premises with his father François until 1990 (his father has married again) when he installed himself in an impressively large (and immaculately tidy) cellar in another part of the village. The vines in the Perrières are still quite young, those in the Gouttes d'Or approaching fifty years old. One-sixth new oak. Good wines here.

CHÂTEAU GÉNOT-BOULANGER

19.08 ha: owned. Chassagne-Montrachet *premier cru blanc* (from Les Chenevottes, Les Vergers, Clos-Saint-Jean); Beaune *premier cru* Les Grèves; Volnay *premier cru* Les Aussy; Pommard *premier cru* Clos-Blanc; village Meursault including the *lieu-dit* Clos-du-Cromin; village Volnay; village Pommard. Plus Mercurey (11.5 ha).

The bulk of this estate, based in a fine château in the middle of the village, is the Côte Chalonnaise. It is managed by *régisseur* Claude Engelbert. He makes reasonable wines, but they have never struck me as anything special.

HENRI GERMAIN ET FILS

5.16 ha: owned and *en fermage*. Meursault *premier cru* Les Charmes; Chassagne-Montrachet *premier cru* Les Morgeots *blanc*; Beaune *premier cru* Les Bressandes; village Meursault, including the *lieux-dits* Les Chevalières, Le Limouzin; Clos-du-Cromin; village Chassagne-Montrachet *rouge*.

Henri Germain is the brother of François of the Château de Chorey (see page 196) and set up independently in 1973. His wife is a Pillot of Chassagne, which explains the vineyards further south. While the cellar, which he rents – he lives elsewhere – is not particularly cold, nor deep, the malos are always late to finish here. Germain is happy to let nature take its course. He doesn't bottle for eighteen months. A good source.

MAISON JEAN GERMAIN

1.61 ha: owned. Village Meursault including the *lieux-dits* Les Meix-Chavaux, La Barre; village Puligny-Montrachet; village Saint-Romain in the *lieu-dit* Clos-sous-le-Château.

This is a *négociant*'s business, buying must or grapes rather than wine, as well as vinifying and selling the produce of Jean Germain's own small domaine. Germain has been unwell. His right-hand man, Joseph de Bucy, departed for Albert Bichot (though soon left that establishment), and the last time I called I was told that I was not allowed to taste Jean Germain's own wines. No one knew why. What exactly is going on here I do not know. But I have had good, sensibly priced wines here in the past.

ALBERT GRIVAULT

5 ha: owned. Meursault *premier cru* Clos-des-Perrières (*monopole*), Les Perrières; village Meursault; Pommard *premier cru* Clos-Blanc.

The Clos-des-Perrières vines were planted in 1985, so are still young. But the other wines in this *premier cru* are old. The Bardet family, successors to Albert Grivault, are trying to get the Clos promoted to *grand cru*. Arguably the whole of Perrières-Dessous merits this. But then so do Puligny-Montrachet, Les Combettes, Les Caillerets, Les Pucelles . . . where does one stop? And the Bardet Clos-des-Perrières is not (or not yet, perhaps) a great wine.

★PATRICK JAVILLIER

8.6 ha: owned and *en fermage/métayage*. Meursault *premier cru* Les Charmes; village Meursault including the *lieux-dits* Les Narvaux, Les Casse-Têtes, Les Clous, Les Tillets, Les Murgers, Clos-du-Cromin; village Puligny-Montrachet; village Pommard; Savigny-lès-Beaune *premier cru* Les Serpentières; village Savigny-lès-Beaune *rouge et blanc*.

The engaging and capable Patrick Javillier not only vinifies *climat* by *climat* but even cask by cask, treating each one differently from each other in order to build up something of even greater complexity when the final blend is assembled. He makes splendid wines, and wines which last well.

CHARLES AND RÉMI JOBARD

7 ha: owned and *en fermage*. Meursault *premier cru* in Les Charmes, Les Genevrières, Les Poruzots; village Meursault including the *lieu-dit* Les Chevalières.

Charles Jobard is the brother of François (see below) and works his domaine with his son Rémi. One-sixth new oak here, and the wines are bottled after twelve months. A good source.

★FRANÇOIS JOBARD

4.71 ha: owned and *en métayage*. Meursault *premier cru* in Les Charmes, Les Genevrières, Les Poruzots, La Pièce-sous-le-Bois (bottled as Blagny); village Meursault.

The rather diffident, shy François Jobard makes fine and marvellously long-lasting wines, and keeps them at least eighteen months in cask before he bottles them. Not for those who like the fleshy, oaky Burgundy.

See Profile, page 500.

★★★COMTES LAFON

13 ha: owned. Le Montrachet (32 a); Meursault *premier cru* in Les Perrières, Les Charmes, Les Genevrières, Les Gouttes d'Or (the latter currently young vines); village Meursault including the *lieux-dits* Clos-de-la-Barre, Desirée; Volnay *premier cru* in Santenots-du-Milieu, Les Champans, Clos-des-Chênes; Monthélie *premier cru* Les Duresses.

This is one of the very few indisputably three-star white wine estates in Burgundy. But it is of equal importance in red wine. The white wines are held eighteen months in cask (the deep cold cellar helps) and are minimally handled. A great domaine.

See Profile, page 517.

LATOUR-GIRAUD

10 ha: owned. Meursault *premier cru* in Les Genevrières, Les Perrières, Les Bouchères, Les Poruzots, Les Charmes; village Meursault including the *lieux-dits* Les Narvaux, Le Clos-du-Cromin and 'Cuvée Charles Maxime'; Puligny-Montrachet *premier cru* Les Champs-Canet; Maranges *premier cru* in La Bussière; Meursault (*rouge*) *premier cru* Les Caillerets; Volnay *premier cru* Clos-des-Chênes; Pommard *premier cru* La Refène.

I gave up on this domaine for a few years, finding their wines excessively sulphury, but then went to call on them again. Jean-Pierre Latour is now in charge, father Pierre having retired, and a big improvement has taken place. There is less sulphur used, for a start, and no recourse to chaptalisation unless absolutely necessary. All the wine, apart from the generics, is now vinified in wood, one-quarter of which is renewed each year. Recent results have been very promising, which is to be particularly welcomed as the estate possesses no less than 2.39 ha (approx. one seventh of the total area) in Genevrières.

★MATROT

18.2 ha: owned. Meursault *premier cru* in Les Perrières, Les Charmes, Blagny; Puligny-Montrachet *premier cru* in Les Chalumeaux, Les Combettes; Volnay *premier cru* Les Santenots; Blagny *premier cru* La Pièce-sous-le-Bois; village Meursault; village Auxey-Duresses.

The wine is made by Thierry; but the labels can state Joseph (grandfather), Pierre (father) or Thierry himself, depending on the importer. It's all the same wine. This is old-fashioned wine-making in the best sense of the word: wines made for the long term, with minimal use of new wood and no concessions to being *flatteur* when they are young. Both reds and whites are very good here: but they need patience.

See Profile, page 535.

CHÂTEAU DE MEURSAULT

60 ha: owned. Meursault *premier cru* in Les Charmes, Les Perrières; Volnay *premier cru* Clos-des-Chênes; Pommard *premier cru* in Les Epenots, Les Fremiers, Les Charmots; village Meursault.

Here is a tragedy. This is a magnificent domaine with substantial holdings in the four first-listed *premiers crus* above, extensive territory in village Meursault and much else besides. All the Meursault is blended together, given far too much new oak, and bottled as Château de Meursault. It's like choosing the best *poulet de Bresse* and cooking it Tandoori style. The fifteenth-century vaulted cellars are magnificent; the wine-making set-up is ultra modern. The property belongs to André Boisseaux of Patriarche.

MICHELOT

23 ha: owned and *en fermage/métayage*. Meursault *premier cru* in Les Perrières, Les Genevrières, Les Charmes; Les Poruzots; village Meursault including the *lieux-dits* of Les Narvaux, Les Tillets, Les Grands-Charrons, Clos-Saint-Felix, Clos-du-Cromin, Le Limouzin, Sur-la-Velle; Puligny-Montrachet *premier cru* in Les Folatières, La Garenne; village Puligny-Montrachet; Santenay *premier cru* in Les Gravières, La Comme; village Pommard.

This long-established and well-known domaine used to have a high reputation. But then it went off the boil. I think the musts were over chaptalised. The *cave* was warmed to speed up the malo-lactic and the wines became rather heavy, blowsy and sulphury. Since the arrival of young Jean-François Mestre from Santenay (Mestre being married to Odile Michelot), things have begun to improve again, though they are not quite back to where they were in the 1960s and early 1970s. Now they have simplified the labelling. Up to 1992 they could appear under a number of Michelot Christian names, as Michelot-Buisson or as Mestre-Michelot. Now it's just plain Michelot, with the individual family name in the small print. At the time of writing the Perrières is young vines.

FRANÇOIS MIKULSKI

6 ha: owned and *en fermage*. Meursault *premier cru* in Les Genevrières, Les Charmes, Les Poruzots; Meursault *premier cru* (*rouge*) Les Caillerets; village Meursault (*rouge et blanc*); Volnay *premier cru* Les Santenots.

François Mikulski is Pierre Boillot's (see page 260) nephew and heir, and is married to one of the daughters of François Germain of the Château de Chorey. He's been in business on his own account since 1992. Good wines here.

PIERRE MILLOT-BATTAULT

8 ha: owned and *en fermage*. Meursault *premier cru* Les Charmes, Les Gouttes d'Or; Volnay *premier cru* Les Santenots; Pommard *premier cru* Les Rugiens; Beaune *premier cru* Les Epenottes; village Meursault.

The Millot-Battault estate operates out of a spacious cellar under a modern house between those of Roulot and Coche-Dury. One-fifth new oak is used for the white wines, 50 per cent or more for the top reds. A good address.

MONCEAU-BOCH

4 ha: owned. Meursault *premier cru* Les Gouttes d'Or; village Meursault including the *lieux-dits* Les Chevalières, Les Lurales; Volnay *premier cru* in Les Champans, Les Santenots; Auxey-Duresses *premier cru* Les Grands-Champs; village Auxey-Duresses in the *lieu-dit* Derrière-la-Tour.

The Monceau-Boch domaine is owned by Mme Louis Guidot, *née* Boch, and her son Hubert, but is leased out on a *métayage* basis, Guidot receiving his share as wine. Some 50 per cent new wood is used. I find the *élevage* here a bit insensitive.

JEAN MONNIER ET FILS

17 ha: owned. Meursault *premier cru* in Les Genevrières, Les Charmes; Pommard *premier cru* in Les Grands-Epenots, Clos-du-Citeaux (*monopole*), Les Argillières, Les Fremiers; Beaune *premier cru* Les Montrevenots; village Meursault including the *lieux-dits* Les Chevalières, La Barre, Clos-du-Cromin; village Puligny-Montrachet; village Volnay.

Jean-Claude Monnier and his son Nicolas make a little bit more red than they do white, and use about one-quarter new oak for the better wines. The domaine seems efficiently run, but the wines are rarely exciting in my experience.

RENÉ MONNIER

17 ha: owned. Meursault *premier cru* Les Charmes; Puligny-Montrachet *premier cru* Les Folatières; village Meursault including the *lieux-dits* Les Chevalières, Le Limouzin; village Puligny-Montrachet; Beaune *premier cru* Les Cent-Vignes, Les Toussaints; village Pommard in the *lieu-dit* Les Vignots; Volnay *premier cru* Clos-des-Chênes; village Monthélie; village Santenay in the *lieux-dits* Les Commes-Dessus, Les Charmes; Maranges *premier cru* Clos-de-la-Bussière.

The René Monnier domaine is guarded by a noisy Alsatian and run by Jean-Louis Bouillot and his wife, daughter of the late René Monnier. There is 100 per cent destemming for the red wines, two *pigeages* and two *remontages* a day – with temperatures being held at 28°C, and 25–30 per cent new oak. Bouillot recognises the importance of low yields, aiming for 35–40 hl/ha. A good source.

★PIERRE MOREY
MOREY-BLANC, SA

8.24 ha: owned and *en fermage/métayage*. Bâtard-Montrachet (48 a); Meursault *premier cru* Les Perrières; village Meursault including the *lieu-dit* Les Tessons; Pommard *premier cru* Les Epenots; village Monthélie.

The Morey family were long-time *métayers* for the Domaine des Comtes Lafon. Now this has come to an end Pierre Morey has set up a small *négociant* business to compensate for what he can no longer supply. And he is also *régisseur* for the Domaine Leflaive in Puligny-Montrachet. Morey combines these separate activities with great skill. He is a fine wine-maker.

See Profile, page 550.

MICHEL POUHIN-SEURRE

6 ha: owned and *en fermage*. Meursault *premier cru* Les Poruzots; village Meursault; village Puligny-Montrachet.

The stocky, genial, mid-forties Michel Pouhin runs this domaine from a base at the top of the village near the camping site. One-quarter new wood is used, and the wines bottled after a year. Another good source.

JACQUES PRIEUR

15.5 ha: owned. Le Montrachet (59 a); Chevalier-Montrachet (14 a); Corton Les Bressandes (73 a); Corton-Charlemagne (22 a); Clos-de-Vougeot (1.28 ha); Le Musigny (77 a); Chambertin, Clos-de-Bèze (15 a); Puligny-Montrachet *premier cru* Les Combettes; Meursault *premier cru* Les Perrières; Volnay *premier cru* in Les Champans, Clos-des-Santenots (*monopole*), Les Santenots; Beaune *premier cru* in Clos-de-la-Féguine (*rouge et blanc*) (*monopole*); Les Grèves; Chambolle-Musigny *premier cru* in La Combe-d'Orveau; village Meursault in the *lieu-dit* Clos-de-Mazeray (*rouge et blanc*) (*monopole*).

A truly mouth-watering line-up here, and now with the backing of Maison Antonin Rodet of Mercurey which owns half of the domaine. For far too long this estate only produced underwhelming, somewhat *suave* and oaky red wines and heavy whites. Now things are improving. An associate company at the same address is the Maison Duvergey-Taboureau. I do not know their wines.

ROUGEOT

14 ha: owned and *en fermage*. Meursault *premier cru* Les Charmes; Volnay *premier cru* Les Santenots; village Meursault; village Saint-Aubin; village Monthélie (*blanc*); village Pommard; village Ladoix; village Saint-Romain.

This somewhat disparate domaine is run by Marc Rougeot, and almost entirely consists of village wine, with several parcels where the vines are still young (Saint-Romain, Monthélie). Rougeot also has a merchant's licence. I have yet to be struck by the quality here.

★GUY ROULOT

11.4 ha: owned. Meursault *premier cru* in Les Perrières, Les Charmes; village Meursault including the *lieux-dits* Les Tessons, Clos-de-Mont-Plaisir (*monopole*), Les Luchets, Les Tillets, Les Vireuils, Les Meix-Chavaux; village Monthélie (*rouge*); village Auxey-Duresses (*rouge*).

An excellent domaine with a splendid range of '*deuxieme cru*' Meursaults, now run by Jean-Marc Roulot, who is married to Hubert de Montille's daughter Alix. Impeccable and conscientious wine-making, and wines which last well.

See Profile, page 609.

JACQUES THEVENOT-MACHAL

6 ha: owned and *en fermage*. Meursault *premier cru* in Les Poruzots, Les Charmes; Puligny-Montrachet *premier cru* Les Folatières; Volnay *premier cru* Les Santenots; village Meursault; village Puligny-Montrachet including the *lieu-dit* Les Charmes; village Pommard.

The red wines are made without destemming, the whites fermented entirely in barrel. I have found the quality irregular here.

VIRELY-ROUGEOT

See Pommard, page 222.

BLAGNY

Up in the hills between Meursault and Puligny lies the hamlet of Blagny. It is peaceful up here. Birds sing. The vineyards are divided by hedgerows and copses, a miracle of wild flowers in the spring, and the village itself is hardly more than a handful of houses centred round the old *manoir*, the property of the Comtesse de Montlivault. You are leagues away from the hustle and bustle of Beaune.

Blagny is a curious appellation, existing solely for red wines. If white, they become Meursault-Blagny, *premier cru*, or less commonly Meursault followed by one of the names of the Blagny *premiers crus*. And there is little village Meursault land. Alternatively, for the commune's dividing line runs through the middle, the white wine can be Puligny-Montrachet.

There is rather more communal Puligny up here (the *lieu-dit* of Le Trésin) than there is communal Meursault, and technically the Puligny-Montrachet *premiers crus* of Sous-le-Puits, La Garenne and Hameau-de-Blagny are Blagny *premier cru* if they produce red wine.

The vineyard land climbs up to 360 metres. The soil is an Argovian marl, covered in limestone debris. Up-slope the colour is red and there are plenty of pebbles. Lower down it is less pebbly. On the Meursault side the underlying rock is decayed and crumbly, white in colour, even with a blue tinge. You are facing south-east. On the Puligny side the orientation is more easterly, the soil is deeper, the underlying rock firmer, and redder in colour. Here there is the highest predominance of pebbles.

THE VINEYARD

There are seven *premiers crus*, as follows:

LA JEUNELOTTE (5.05 HA)
(Meursault)

LA PIÈCE-SOUS-LE-BOIS (11.15 HA)
(Meursault)

SOUS-LE-DOS-D'ANE (5.03 HA)
(Meursault)

SOUS-BLAGNY (2.21 HA)
(Meursault)

SOUS-LE-PUITS (6.80 HA)
(Puligny-Montrachet)

LA GARENNE OR SOUS-LA-GARENNE (9.87 HA)
(Puligny-Montrachet)

HAMEAU-DE-BLAGNY (4.28 HA)
(Puligny-Montrachet)

These make a total of 44.38 ha, 23.44 ha of which are in Meursault and 20.74 ha in Puligny-Montrachet. In addition there are 9.73 ha of village land, 1.77 ha of which are in Meursault, 7.96 ha in Puligny-Montrachet.

These produce around 220 hl (29,000 bottles) of Blagny premier cru rouge and 45 hl (6,000 bottles) of village Blagny rouge a year. Plus around 400 hl (52,800 bottles) of Meursault premier cru Blagny and 60 hl (8,000 bottles) of village Meursault.

Blagny *rouge* is a fairly sturdy, if not robust wine, a sort of cross between a Chassagne-Montrachet and Pommard, but a cross of good examples. In its youth it can be dumb and four-square. But given time it will mellow out to something with no lack of character or depth. It is unfashionable, and therefore cheap. It is certainly considerably more interesting than red Meursault. Like on the hill of Corton, Chardonnay is planted up-slope, Pinot Noir lower down, the best climats for red wine being La Pièce-sous-le-Bois and Sous-le-Dos-d'Ane.

Recommended Sources:

La Pièce-sous-le-Bois: Robert Ampeau, François Jobard, Matrot (all Meursault); Paul Pernot (Puligny-Montrachet); René Lamy (Chassagne-Montrachet).
Sous-le-Dos-d'Ane: Henri Clerc (Puligny-Montrachet).
Sous-le-Puits: Gilles Bouton (Saint-Aubin).
As Blagny *premier cru tout court*: Leflaive (Puligny-Montrachet).

PULIGNY-MONTRACHET

Puligny-Montrachet is the greatest white-wine commune on earth. Though with a mere 230 hectares of vineyards it is considerably smaller than either of its two neighbours, Meursault and Chassagne-Montrachet, the village can boast two of Burgundy's six white wine *grands crus* in their entirety, Chevalier-Montrachet and Bienvenues-Bâtard-Montrachet, plus roughly half, and, so the authorities would have us believe, the best sections of two others, Bâtard-Montrachet and Le Montrachet itself. Only Corton-Charlemagne and the diminutive Criots-Bâtard-Montrachet, of the six, do not lie, at least partly, in Puligny-Montrachet.

Puligny's *grands crus* lie at the southern end of the appellation, overlapping into neighbouring Chassagne-Montrachet, and this is where the Chardonnay grape reaches its most regal and supreme expression. Other parts of the world can and do produce plenty of competition with village Burgundy, particularly California and to a lesser extent Australia. But at *grand cru* level the best white Burgundies remain unequalled. Elsewhere the *terroirs* have not yet been found, or not yet correctly exploited. The top Montrachets, Chevaliers and Bâtards are wines to drink on bended knees, with heartfelt and humble thanks.

PULIGNY-MONTRACHET

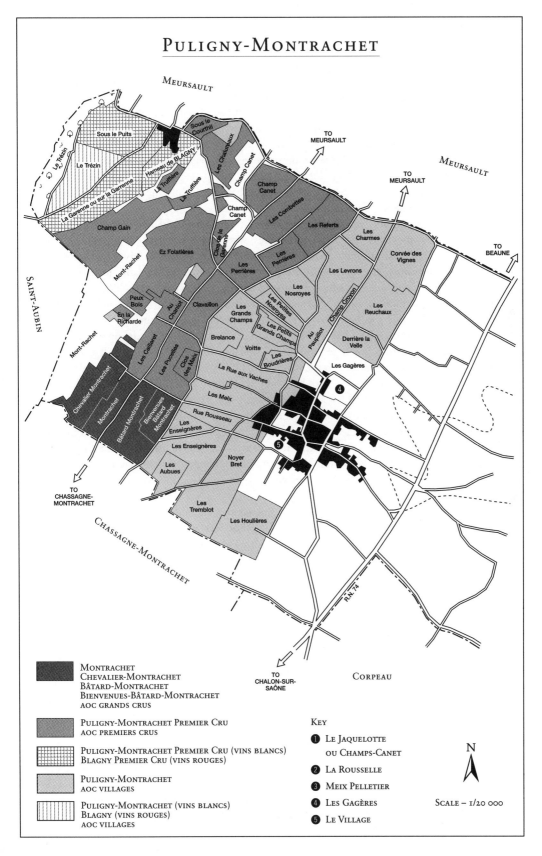

MEURSAULT

Sous le Puits

Le Trézin

La Garenne ou sur la Garenne

Hameau de BLAGNY

La Truffière

La Truffière

Sous le Courthil

Les Chaumes

Champ Canet

Champ Canet

Champ Gain

Ez Folatières

Clos de la Garenne

Champ Canet

Les Combettes

Mont-Rachet

Peux Bois

En la Richarde

Au Chaniot

Clavaillon

Les Perrières

Les Perrières

Les Referts

Les Charmes

Corvée des Vignes

Les Levrons

Les Nosroyes

Les Petites Nosroyes

Les Grands Champs

Les Petits Grands Champs

Les Reuchaux

Mont-Rachet

Les Caillerets

Les Pucelles

Brelance

Voitte

Les Boudrières

Au Paupillot

Champ Croyot

Derrière la Velle

Chevalier Montrachet

Montrachet

Bâtard Montrachet

Clos des Meix

La Rue aux Vaches

Les Gagères

Bienvenues Bâtard Montrachet

Les Meix

Rue Rousseau

Les Enseignères

Les Enseignères

Les Aubues

Noyer Bret

Les Tremblot

Les Houlières

SAINT-AUBIN

TO MEURSAULT

TO MEURSAULT

MEURSAULT

TO BEAUNE

TO CHASSAGNE-MONTRACHET

CHASSAGNE-MONTRACHET

TO CHALON-SUR-SAÔNE

CORPEAU

R.N. 74

MONTRACHET
CHEVALIER-MONTRACHET
BÂTARD-MONTRACHET
BIENVENUES-BÂTARD-MONTRACHET
AOC GRANDS CRUS

PULIGNY-MONTRACHET PREMIER CRU
AOC PREMIERS CRUS

PULIGNY-MONTRACHET PREMIER CRU (VINS BLANCS)
BLAGNY PREMIER CRU (VINS ROUGES)

PULIGNY-MONTRACHET
AOC VILLAGES

PULIGNY-MONTRACHET (VINS BLANCS)
BLAGNY (VINS ROUGES)
AOC VILLAGES

KEY

1 LE JAQUELOTTE
OU CHAMPS-CANET

2 LA ROUSSELLE

3 MEIX PELLETIER

4 LES GAGÈRES

5 LE VILLAGE

N

SCALE – 1/20 000

HISTORY

The origin of the village of Puligny-Montrachet is Gallo-Roman. In the first few centuries after the birth of Christ vines were first commercially planted in the area and the village was known as Puliniacus. Subsequently, particularly during the Dark Ages, it was the local Benedictine monastery at the Abbey of Maizières, between Dijon and Verdun-sur-le-Doubs, which carried on the traditions of viticulture and viniculture. From time to time the abbey would receive donations of land. In 1200 Guy de Saint-Sernin ceded half his *dîmes* (tithes) in Puligny and Blagny. In May 1252, the brothers Pierre and Arnolet of Puligny made a number of donations to Maizières including vines and land on 'Mont Rachez'. In 1286 Gui Berrier of Chagny also donated a plot of vines 'En Mont Raschet'. Gradually the Benedictine holdings became of considerable importance.

The fourteenth century was an unhappy time for the inhabitants of Puligny. Famine and pestilence roamed the land and these difficulties were further compounded locally when Philippe Hardi, Duke of Burgundy, confiscated the land of the *Seigneur* de Mypont, the lay ruler of Puligny and its immediate locality. In the interregnum, much of the land, formerly under vines, returned to scrub, and the Mypont baronial keep was allowed to crumble into ruins.

In the fifteenth century, a lawyer from Beaune, one Jean Perron, a new member of the *noblesse de la robe*, became *seigneur* of Puligny and Mypont. He had the vineyard slopes replanted and the Château de Puligny – what is today called Le Vieux Château, in the upper part of the village – constructed. In a much renovated and updated form this château still exists today. However, a newer building, nearer to the main road, built around the middle of the nineteenth century, but in a Renaissance style, is today's official Château de Puligny-Montrachet.

There is some disagreement about when exactly the fame of Le Montrachet began to surface. Jean-François Bazin (*Montrachet*) echoes the eighteenth-century Abbé Courtépée: compared with the top red-wine vineyards of the Côte-de-Nuits, Le Montrachet is something of a *parvenu* amongst *grands crus*. It was not even *en reputation* in the beginning of the seventeenth century, when 24 *ouvrées* (about a hectare) changed hands for a mere 750 *livres*. According to Dr Lavalle in 1855 the wines were first mentioned in 1482, by which time the land was already much divided.

Somewhat later, by which time its renown was assured, the majority of the *climat* belonged to the Clermont-Montoizon family. In 1728 the Abbé Arnoux, who published the smallest and slimmest of volumes (if my facsimile copy is an accurate reproduction) on Burgundy in London (but in French) says of Montrachet: 'the most curious and most delicate of all in France. A wine of which neither the Latin nor the French vocabulary is capable of describing its *douceur*'.

Naturally, Le Montrachet was noted by Thomas Jefferson in his tour of the French vineyards in 1787. The best wines of the Côte, he noted, were Chambertin, Romanée, Clos-de-Vougeot and Montrachet: the first and last at opposite ends. Montrachet sold for 1,200 *livres* the *queue* (a *queue* being two barrels) or 48 francs a bottle. This was the same price as the top three reds he cited. But at the time the rest of the whites only fetched half that of the equivalent red wines.

The majority of Le Montrachet was sequestered and sold as a *bien national* during the Revolution. That of the Clermont-Montoison family measured 100 *ouvrées* (about half the 8 ha) and was sold in two lots for 35,000 and 37,100 *livres* plus commission, to Henri Pourtalés. The one holding which seems to have survived the Revolution was that of the Laguiche family, who had married into the Clermont-Montoisons, and this despite the fact that Charles-Amable de la Guiche (as the name was spelled in those days) died on the guillotine in 1794. Perhaps, and it would not be a unique ruse for the time, the Pourtalés' sale was a bit of a blind.

By the mid nineteenth century, according to Dr Lavalle at the time, Le Montrachet was so far in a category of its own that its rating is *tête de cuvée, extra*. Next in line, as *premières cuvées*, comes, ahead of the rest, Chevalier-Montrachet, followed by 'Blagny-Blanc', Bâtard-Montrachet and Les Combettes, and then Les Platières, Les Referts and Les Charmes.

La Platière has changed its name since, but I assume, as all the other *climats*, not all of them today *premiers crus*, lie on the Meursault border, that this is where Platières was located. Interestingly Les Caillerets, Le Clavoillon and Les Pucelles were planted entirely with Pinot Noir at the time, while much of the rocky land further up-slope, Les Champs-Canet and Les Folatières for example, though noted by Lavalle, were very patchily planted. Such vineyards as existed would in the phylloxera times to follow be neglected and turn into *friche*. It would take the arrival of the *concasseur* in the 1950s, a machine which could pulverise the rock into something ploughable and plantable, before these *climats*, and those even further up-slope such as Champs-Gain, would be regained for the Chardonnay wine.

Curnonsky in the 1920s spoke of the five greatest wines of France: the Coulée de Serrant in Savennières, Condrieu and Château Grillet in the Rhône valley, the Vin Jaune of Château Chalon, and Le Montrachet. The first three, in the nineteenth century, were sweet wines. So I believe, in the best years at any rate, was Le Montrachet. I have had nineteenth-century Montrachets which, if no longer with any residual sugar to speak of, certainly had a botrytis-affected nose and an originally sweet mouth feel. I think nature was allowed to take its course, as today in Vouvray. And if the weather smiled, so much the better. Remember that almost all champagne, until Madame Pommery changed the fashion with her Brut 1874, was sweet. That was the mode of the times.

Puligny, as did Chassagne, appropriated the suffix Montrachet to its name in 1879.

The village of Puligny is tight and modest, centred round two squares, the Place du Monument and the Place des Maronniers. There are few shops and no bar, but a pleasant and Michelin-starred restaurant-hotel, suitably called Le Montrachet, with a *sommelier*, Jean-Claude Wallerand, who is passionate and knowledgeable about wine (not always the case, even in the top restaurants), and who has more than once pointed me in the direction of an up-and-coming young *vigneron*.

A noted feature of the village is its very high water-table, making the construction of underground cellars a costly, if not impossible business. Henri Clerc's — which is marginally lower than the road outside — has been flooded on more than one occasion. The solution, as with the Domaine Leflaive and the merchant Olivier Leflaive, is to make sure your above ground *chai* is temperature-controlled, for otherwise the ambient temperature might dry out the wine in a hot summer.

Puligny-Montrachet, which is almost entirely white, is a quite different wine from either Meursault or Chassagne-Montrachet. There is a structure, a raciness, a masculinity even, which is missing in the other communes. There seems to be more grip, and this gives the wines, however ripe and rich, a reserve which requires longer ageing. It also gives them a personality and breed which you rarely find in Chassagne, and only in Meursault in the three great *premiers crus*, Les Perrières, Les Charmes and Les Genevrières, which lie at the Puligny end of that commune. Puligny is where Burgundian Chardonnay is at its most complete.

LOCATION

The commune of Puligny-Montrachet lies on either side and up-slope from its village, the village itself being set back a few hundred metres from the main Beaune-Dijon highway. The *premiers crus* and *grands crus* begin where the incline begins to rise appreciably and when the altitude has reached 240 metres. Vineyard land continues up-slope, becoming progressively steeper as the altitude rises. Here and there the vineyards are pockmarked with patches of scrub and piles of larger stones, or the gradient interrupted by a series of step-like terraces. The further uphill you get, and above Blagny the vineyard continues to 400 metres (a marvellous view from up here), the more meagre the soil. It is just broken-up rock.

Le Montrachet itself lies at 260 metres and overlaps into the commune of Chassagne. The *climat* is perfectly exposed, very well drained, protected from the prevailing westerly wind and anything nastier that might whistle down the valley from Saint-Aubin by the hill of Mont Rachet itself. The soil is based on a hard Bathonian limestone topped with a light brown limestone debris. There is Bajocian marl at the top of the *climat*, pebbles in the lower part. Overall it is very stony.

What is so special about Le Montrachet? Scientists have been analysing the soil for ages. Yes, there is some iron here. The limestone is active (less so than in Chevalier above, more so than in Bâtard below). There is some clay (more so than in Chevalier this time, less so than in Bâtard). There is a marked amount of magnesium and of lead. Ditto gallium and beryllium. And there are copper, zinc, strontium, titanium, cobalt, tin, molybdenum, vanadium, nickel, chromium and even silver. We know what the presence of some of these trace elements will effect. Chromium is good for fruit-setting, zinc for reducing the acidity and increasing the sugar richness, cobalt speeds up the maturity, etc. But no-one has come any closer to explaining the miracle of Le Montrachet than the locals themselves: aspect and drainage are the real clue, according to them.

Up above, in Chevalier, the terrain is steeper. The rock is Bajocian marl and rendzina. There is less soil. Below, in Bâtard-Montrachet and its enclaves Bienvenues-Bâtard-Montrachet and Criots-Bâtard-Montrachet (which though it lies in the neighbouring commune of Chassagne is convenient to include here), there is more clay, the soil is deeper and richer, there is less fragmented rock and more gravel. Bâtard-Montrachet also overlaps into Chassagne.

The *premiers crus* of Puligny-Montrachet lie in the same line as the *grands crus* and continue up-slope on the northern side. Immediately next door we have Les Caillerets on the same level as Le Montrachet and Les Pucelles continuing on the other side of the road from Bâtard. It is not so much that the geology changes, though the Caillerets is even more pebbly than its famous neighbour, as the orientation, marginally less to the south, marginally more to the east. Beyond Les Pucelles, within which lies Clos-des-Meix, we have Clavoillon. Beyond Les Caillerets, and continuing up-slope, is Les Folatières. Le Clavoillon has quite deep soil, including some clay. Les Folatières is a large, steep *climat*, prone to erosion. Up-slope, and in Le Champs-Gain and La Truffière, vineyards quite recently rescued from the scrub and planted with vines, the soil is light red brown in colour. In mid-slope there is a white marly Bajocian limestone debris.

Les Perrières, which includes the Clos-de-la-Mouchère, extends from Le Clavoillon. The soil is marly, with plenty of pebbles and other stone fragments, as the name Perrières would suggest. We then come to the Meursault border. Les Chalumeaux and Les Champs-Canet up-slope: red earth, broken-up limestone rock on a crumbly limestone base (elsewhere the rock is much harder); Les Combettes and Les Referts marching with Meursault, Les Charmes: very little surface soil in the former; richer, deeper and more marly terrain in the latter.

THE VINEYARD

Grands Crus: There are five *grands crus* on the Puligny-Chassagne border: Le Montrachet, Chevalier-Montrachet, Bâtard-Montrachet, Bienvenues-Bâtard-Montrachet and Criots-Bâtard-Montrachet. These comprise some 32.5 ha and produce an average of 1,400 hl (186,000 bottles) per annum.

Premiers Crus: Puligny-Montrachet possesses twenty-three *premiers crus* in whole or in part. These are: Les Caillerets; Les Chalumeaux (part); Les Champs-Canet; Le Champ-Gain; Au Chaniot (in Les Folatières); Le Clavoillon; Clos-de-la-Garenne; Clos-de-la-Mouchère (in Les

Perrières); Clos-des-Meix (in Les Pucelles); Les Combettes; Les Demoiselles (in Les Caillerets); Hameau-de-Blagny; Les Folatières (part); La Garenne; La Jaquelotte (in Les Champs-Canet); Les Perrières; Le Peux-Bois (in Les Folatières); Les Pucelles; Sous-le-Puits; Les Referts; En-la-Richarde (part) (in Les Folatières); Sous-le-Courthil (in Les Chalumeaux); La Truffière.

As mentioned in the previous chapter the *climats* of Hameau-de-Blagny, La Garenne and Sous-le-Puits, if planted with Pinot Noir, produce Blagny *premier cru*, and not Puligny *rouge*. Apart from a little *premier cru rouge* from Les Caillerets, all *premier cru* Puligny-Montrachet is white. These *premiers crus* occupy 100.12 ha and produce about 4,350 hl (574,000 bottles) per year.

Village Wine: There are 114.22 ha of village land, and this produces about 5,300 hl of white wine (700,000 bottles) and 40 hl (5,280 bottles) of red wine a year.

The Grands Crus

Le Montrachet
Surface Area: 8.00 ha • **Average Production:** 393 hl (52,272 bottles)
(4.01 lying in Puligny-Montrachet
3.99 lying in Chassagne-Montrachet)

Principal Proprietors: ★Marquis de Laguiche (vinified and marketed by Maison Joseph Drouhin) (2.06 ha); ★Baron Thenard (mainly *élevé* and sold by Maison Roland Remoissenet et Fils) (1.83 ha); ★Bouchard Père et Fils (1.10 ha); ★Domaine de la Romanée-Conti (68 a); Jacques Prieur (59 a); Regnault de Beaucaron (50 a); ★Comtes Lafon (31 a); ★Ramonet (26 a); ★Marc Colin (11 a); ★Guy Amiot-Bonfils (9 a); ★Edmond Delagrange-Bachelet (8 a); ★Jacques Gagnard-Delagrange (8 a); ★Leflaive (8 a); Brenot-Petitjean (5 a); Château de Puligny-Montrachet (4 a).

Le Montrachet is, or should be, Chardonnay at its most perfect, the slowest to mature, the longest lived. Whenever you taste a range of *grands crus* there is yet another enormous step up after you have sampled the Chevalier – even if the Chevalier itself is twice as good as the Bâtard and the Bienvenues. In Le Montrachet itself there is an extra element of power, concentration, intensity and grip, such that makes it sometimes quite impossible to quantify and qualify seriously, even as late as the summer after the vintage, when many a village wine is being polished up for bottling.

Styles vary, as do *négociant* techniques, and you will see from the above that the merchants are in charge of the bulk of this *climat*, for the Beaucaron domaine is the supplier to Jadot, Latour and others, selling their grapes at the time of the vintage for these houses to vinify themselves; but Le Montrachet is always a fuller, richer wine than the other *grands crus*, with a better acidity as well as a great deal more depth and finesse. It can sometimes be a bit top heavy, but it is usually, in my experience, despite the obviously more inflated price, rather more reliable than the other *grands crus*, red or white. There are plenty more disappointing Chambertins than there are Montrachets! It needs at least ten years to ascend to its best.

Of the important names, Bouchard Père et Fils, Laguiche and Ramonet have their holdings in the Puligny half, while Lafon, Jacques Prieur, the Domaine de la Romanée-Conti, Baron Thenard and the remainder of the Chassagne growers own their vines in the Chassagne section.

Chevalier-Montrachet
Surface Area: 7.36 ha • **Average Production:** 255 hl (33,660 bottles)

Principal Proprietors: ★Bouchard Père et Fils (2.02 ha); ★Leflaive (1.92 ha); Jean Chartron (1.0 ha); ★Louis Jadot (51 a); ★Louis Latour (50 a); Château de Puligny-Montrachet (25 a);

*Michel Niellon (23 a); Dancer/Courlet de Vergille (19 a) (sold to *Maison Louis Jadot); *Georges Deléger (16 a) (made by Michel Colin-Deléger); *D'Auvenay (16 a); *Henri Clerc (15 a); Jacques Prieur (14 a); Romanée-Conti (13 a) (sold off in bulk).

Up-slope from Montrachet, and on much meaner soil, Chevalier-Montrachet never produces to excess, one explanation for the quality of its wines, which are clearly superior to Bâtard, Bienvenues and Criots. Chevalier-Montrachet is a full, firm wine, but not four-square, with a very good acidity and a masculine reserve. If it doesn't have quite the intensity of Le Montrachet itself it certainly has a great deal of depth and elegance, and I think it is this element of breeding, as well as harmony, which sets it above Bâtard and its neighbours. Once again, it is a wine which can be approached with confidence. The majority of the suppliers are consistent and reliable.

BÂTARD-MONTRACHET
Surface Area: 11.87 ha • Average Production: 514 hl (67,848 bottles)

Principal Proprietors: *Leflaive (2 ha); Charles et Paul Bavard (67 a) (sold to *Maison Antonin Rodet); *Ramonet (56 a); Bachelet-Ramonet (56 a); Paul Pernot (50 a); Jean-Pierre Monnot (50 a) (sold as must to Maison Louis Latour); *Pierre Morey (49 a); Roger Caillot-Morey (47 a) (both *en métayage* from Claude-Maxence Poirier); *Philippe Brenot (37 a); *Jean-Marc Blain-Gagnard (34 a); Madame Henri Jacquin (32a); *Jean-Noël Gagnard (30 a); *Richard Fontaine-Gagnard (30 a); *Hospices de Beaune (29 a); Jean Gallot (29 a) (sold to *Olivier Leflaive Frères); *Jacques Gagnard-Delagrange (27 a); Fernand Coffinet (26 a); Barolet-Pernot (23 a); Henri Clerc (18 a); *Etienne Sauzet (18 a); *Albert Morey (15 a); Marc Morey (14 a); *Jean-Marc Boillot (14 a); *Michel Niellon (12 a); Louis Lequin (12 a); René Lequin-Colin (12 a).
See also the *négociant* selections of e.g. *Louis Jadot, *Joseph Drouhin, *Roland Remoissenet.

Bâtard-Montrachet is a much fragmented *climat*, producing wines of a range of quality from excellent to beyond the pale. It is a fatter, more open, more exotic wine than Chevalier; usually with less grip and a more flowery, fleshy, honeyed, spicy richness. It can be four-square. It can also be blowsy. But I find it more consistent across the board than Bienvenues and Criots.

BIENVENUES-BÂTARD-MONTRACHET
Surface Area: 3.69 ha • Average Production: 178 ha (23,476 bottles)

Principal Proprietors: *Leflaive (1.15 ha); Jean-Pierre Monnot (51 a) (sold as must to *Maison Louis Latour); *Henri Clerc (46 a); *Ramonet (45 a); *Paul Pernot (19 a); Guillemard-Clerc (18 a) (exploited *en fermage*); Bachelet-Ramonet (13 a); *Etienne Sauzet (12 a); *Carillon (11 a); Jean-Claude Bachelet (9 a); Barolet-Pernot (9 a) (bought by Maison Louis Latour).

Bienvenues is, roughly speaking, the north-east quarter of Bâtard; down-slope, that is, marching with the bottom part of Les Pucelles. The wine has a fatness, a honeyed or honeysuckle fragrance, and a certain delicacy: feminine where Chevalier is masculine. It can sometimes be rather weak and feeble, and it is a wine whose grapes have a tendency to over-ripen more readily than most. But when you chance on a fine example you will find the complexity, accessibility and elegant harmony very seductive. It is usually a little cheaper, but not necessarily any worse, than Bâtard-Montrachet.

CRIOTS-BÂTARD-MONTRACHET
Wholly in Chassagne-Montrachet, but included here for readers' convenience.

Surface Area: 1.57 ha • Average Production: 69 hl (9,108 bottles)

Principal Proprietors: ⋆Joseph Belland (64 a); ⋆Richard Fontaine-Gagnard (33 a); ⋆ Jean-Marc Blain-Gagnard (21 a); Charles Bonnefoy (20 a) (sold in bulk); ⋆D'Auvenay (6 a); Hubert Lamy (5 a) (*en fermage* from Mme Marcelle Perrot); Blondeau-Danne (5 a).

This tiny *grand cru*, one of the smallest appellations in France, lies immediately to the south of Bâtard-Montrachet. Its wine is the most delicate of the five senior *climats* in the vicinity. Compared with Bienvenues, while the structure may be similar, the flavours are less honeyed, and the citrus element is expressed as lemon sherbet or limes. Again there is a flowery touch, but the flowers are less exotically perfumed, cooler, the effect more minerally. Criots can be elegant and exquisite. It can also be a bit empty.

THE *PREMIERS CRUS*

LES DEMOISELLES (0.60 HA) • LES CAILLERETS (3.33 HA)

Being the extension of Le Montrachet to the north, this is, or should be, the best of the *premiers crus*. The lion's share, the Clos-des-Caillerets, despite some recent sales to the Saier family (owners of Morey-Saint-Denis' Clos-des-Lambrays), to Madame Bize-Leroy and to Hubert de Montille of Volnay, belongs to Jean Chartron. And this wine is generally a cut above the standard of the *négociant* Chartron et Trébuchet wines. The enclave known as Les Demoiselles consists of the first thirty rows on the Montrachet side, underneath the end of Chevalier. At its best these are exquisite wines, not as powerful as Le Montrachet itself, but of pure breed, excellent grip and beautiful balance.

Recommended Sources:
Les Demoiselles: Guy Amiot-Bonfils; Michel Colin-Deléger (both Chassagne-Montrachet).
Les Caillerets: Jean Chartron (Puligny-Montrachet); Hubert de Montille (Volnay), both Clos-des-Caillerets.

LES PUCELLES (5.13 HA) • CLOS-DES-MEIX (1.63 HA)

Down-slope from the above we come to Les Pucelles, another *climat* which can often give you the same lift and delight as you get from a *grand cru*. The Clos-des-Meix is that part in the middle of the bottom of the *climat*, rather like a bite out of a sandwich. No-one seems to declare it as such these days. The largest owner here is the Domaine Leflaive, with over 3 ha, and this is frequently a very delicious wine, all silk, flowers and fragrance. I look for something feminine here, delicate, soft and honeyed, but with a good intense acidity underneath.

Recommended Sources: Leflaive; Jean Chartron (Clos-des-Pucelles); Henri Clerc; Paul Pernot (all Puligny-Montrachet); Jean Boillot (Volnay); Marc Morey (Chassagne-Montrachet). Plus the *négociant* selections of, e.g. Joseph Drouhin (Beaune), Olivier Leflaive Frères (Puligny-Montrachet).

LE CLAVOILLON (5.59 HA)

Le Clavoillon continues on from Les Pucelles, and is very nearly the monopoly of the Domaine Leflaive, who have 4.79 ha. The soil is obviously less fine here, with more clay in it, for we have a more four-square wine, in my view the least good of Leflaive's *premiers crus*. This is good stuff, but it does not aspire to *grand cru* status.

Recommended Sources: Leflaive, Gérard Chavy (both Puligny-Montrachet).

LES (OR EZ) FOLATIÈRES (17.65 HA)

This is the largest Puligny-Montrachet *premier cru*, and includes the enclaves of En-la-Richarde, Le Peux-Bois and Au Chaniot, none of which seem to be declared separately. Folatières is a fullish, meaty, mineral wine with plenty of weight of fruit and good grip – a typical Puligny *premier cru* in fact. The *climat* lies just above Clavoillon, next to Les Caillerets, but climbing further up the slope towards the hamlet of Blagny.

Recommended Sources: Gérard Chavy; Henri Clerc; Leflaive; Roland Maraslovac; Jean-Luc Pascal; Paul Pernot (all Puligny-Montrachet); Bernard Boisson; René Monnier (both Meursault); D'Auvenay (Saint-Romain); Louis Jadot (Beaune). Plus the *négociant* selections of, e.g. Joseph Drouhin (Beaune), Olivier Leflaive Frères (Puligny-Montrachet).

CLOS-DE-LA-GARENNE (1.53 HA)

This *climat*, which is quite separate from La Garenne, lies next to Les Folatières, on the north side of the road which climbs up to Blagny, and is the monopoly of the Duc de Magenta. The wine is made and sold, but under a special label, by Maison Louis Jadot of Beaune. Similar to a good Folatières, it is often one of Jadot's best Pulignys.

SOUS-LE-PUITS (6.80 HA) • LA GARENNE (9.87 HA)
LE CHAMP-GAIN (10.70 HA) • LA TRUFFIÈRE (2.48 HA)
HAMEAU-DE-BLAGNY (4.28 HA)

There is, I feel, a pioneering spirit here, much of the land having been converted from scrub by means of major engineering feats of pulverising the rock, clearing the bushes and smoothing out the terrain to make it economic to plant the vine. Fifty years ago, as old photographs will show you, this was nature's territory, not man's.

The wines are less fine and less fat than they are further down-slope – we are above 300 metres here, rising to 380 and more – and in lighter years they can be a bit thin. But there is usually good acidity, an absence of over-ripeness, and an attractive minerally quality. Jean-Marc Boillot's La Truffière is a lovely racy example.

Recommended Sources:
La Garenne: Château de Puligny-Montrachet (Puligny-Montrachet); Marc Colin; Gilles Bouton; Larue (all Saint-Aubin/Gamay).
Le Champ-Gain: Henri Clerc; Roland Maroslovac; Jean-Luc Pascal (Puligny-Montrachet); Roger Belland (Santenay); Louis Jadot (Beaune).
La Truffière: Jean-Marc Boillot (Volnay); Michel Colin-Deléger; Bernard Morey (both Chassagne-Montrachet).
See also the *négociant* selections, e.g. Olivier Leflaive Frères.

LES CHALUMEAUX (5.79 HA)

Incorporating Sous-le-Courthil, this is a *climat* whose wine I know best in the cellars of Thierry Matrot of Meursault. His example is not as fine as his Combettes, and has a herbal-flowery personality all of its own. On the basis of this example, I would rate Chalumeaux with the second division of Puligny *premiers crus*.

Recommended Source: Matrot (Meursault).

LES CHAMPS-CANET (4.06 HA) • LES COMBETTES (6.76 HA)
LES REFERTS (5.52 HA) • LES PERRIÈRES (8.41 HA)

The first three *climats* run down the Meursault boundary, marching with Meursault Les Perrières and Meursault Les Charmes. Puligny's Perrières occupies the land between Les Combettes and Les Referts and Le Clavoillon, and includes the 3.92 ha *monopole* of Clos-de-la-Mouchère, belonging to the Domaine Jean Boillot of Volnay. La Jaquelotte, which you will not see declared separately, is part of Les Champs-Canet.

The jewel here is not Les Champs-Canet, though that is directly on the line with Meursault, Les Perrières, but Les Combettes. Les Combettes is the most complete wine of the four *climats*, a mouth-watering and deliciously elegant combination of Meursault and Puligny, with the steeliness of the latter and the honeysuckle and hazelnut of the former. Les Champs-Canet is similar but not quite as fine, as three-dimensional; Les Referts is fatter, spicier, a little coarser; and Les Perrières, in my experience of Carillon's fine example (the Sauzet domaine's vines are currently young), the closest to Les Combettes. The Clos-de-la-Mouchère seems a little heavier.

Recommended Sources:
Les Champs-Canet: Carillon; Etienne Sauzet (both Puligny-Montrachet); Jean-Marc Boillot (Pommard).
Les Combettes: Henri Clerc; Leflaive; Roland Maraslovac; Etienne Sauzet (all Puligny-Montrachet); Ampeau Matrot (Meursault); Jean-Marc Boillot (Pommard).
Les Referts: Carillon; Etienne Sauzet (both Puligny-Montrachet); Jean-Marc Boillot (Pommard).
Les Perrières: Carillon; Etienne Sauzet (but young vines at present) (both Puligny-Montrachet); Jean Boillot (Volnay) as Clos-de-la-Mouchère (*monopole*).

Plus the *négociant* selections of, e.g. Maison Louis Jadot, Maison Roland Remoissenet et Fils (both Beaune); Olivier Leflaive Frères (Puligny-Montrachet).

THE GROWERS

★LOUIS CARILLON ET FILS

12 ha: owned. Bienvenues-Bâtard-Montrachet (11 a); Puligny-Montrachet *premier cru* in Les Combettes, Les Perrières, Les Champs-Canet, Le Champ-Gain, Les Referts; Chassagne-Montrachet *premier cru* Les Macherelles (*blanc*); Saint-Aubin *premier cru* Les Pitangerets (*rouge*); Mercurey *premier cru* Les Champs-Martin; village Puligny-Montrachet; village Chassagne-Montrachet *rouge et blanc*.

The Carillon family – it is now Jacques, grandson of Louis, who is in charge of the wine-making – have been resident in the village since 1632. Their wines are fine but understated. I quickly learned a lesson that it was a mistake to dismiss them for not flamboyantly waving a lush personality about when they were in cask; for when I sampled them blind in bottle later they always came out near the top. Now I know better, and admire them from the outset.
See Profile, page 361.

JEAN-RENÉ CHARTRON

9.00 ha: owned. Chevalier-Montrachet (1.00 ha); Puligny-Montrachet *premier cru* in Clos-des-Caillerets (*rouge et blanc*), Clos-des-Pucelles (*monopole*), Les Folatières; Saint-Aubin *premier cru* Les Dents-de-Chien.

In order to resolve inheritance problems with his sister, Jean-René Chartron has been forced to sell off parcels of both his Chevalier-Montrachet and his Caillerets. Moreover the domaine has also sold off fruit at the time of the harvest to other *négociants*, despite the fact that one assumes there is a contract with Chartron et Trébuchet (see below). In the Chartron et Trébuchet line-up, these domaine wines stand out. But they should be better still.

CHARTRON ET TRÉBUCHET, SA

Louis Trébuchet, who had worked in Beaune for other merchants, joined forces with René Chartron in 1984. The firm has always concentrated on white wines, and, of course, the plums are those of the Chartron domaine (see above).

The policy here is to bottle early. Frequently when I am in Burgundy in June, wines all the way up to the *premiers crus* are already in bottle. They are clean, but something in the wine-making has emasculated them, and they do not last in bottle. One can't help comparing

Chartron et Trébuchet with Olivier Leflaive Frères, set up at the same time and also concentrating on white wines (and about 200 metres away as the crow flies). Olivier Leflaive's Burgundies are real wines, Chartron et Trébuchet's are empty and soulless.

GÉRARD CHAVY ET FILS

11.5 ha: owned and *en fermage*. Puligny-Montrachet *premier cru* in Les Folatières, Le Clavoillon, Les Perrières, Les Pucelles; Beaune *premier cru* Les Cent-Vignes; village Puligny-Montrachet including the *lieu-dit* Les Charmes.

Run by the *fils* Jean-Louis and Alain, out of a tidy, modern cellar near the Vieux Château, this is a dependable estate, producing good fullish wines with plenty of personality. These Chavys are the only other proprietors in Le Clavoillon apart from Leflaive. At the time of writing the Pucelles are very young vines.

PHILIPPE CHAVY

3.5 ha: *en fermage*. Puligny-Montrachet *premier cru* Les Folatières; Meursault *premier cru* Blagny; village Puligny-Montrachet including the *lieux-dits* Les Nosroyes, Les Corvées-des-Vignes.

Philippe is a cousin of the Gérard Chavy brothers and brother of Hubert Chavy-Chouet, now removed to Meursault. Behind these two brothers lies the domaine of their father Albert Chavy-Ropiteau. Albert makes his wine in a large aircraft-hangar-type building in Puligny (which Philippe uses) but sells his wine off in bulk to Bouchard Père et Fils and others. Eventually Philippe and Hubert, both talented wine-makers, will come into their inheritance. Meanwhile Philippe farms some land which belongs to an uncle and is a share-cropper for the Château de Blagny. Good wines here.

HENRI CLERC

25.73 ha: owned and *en fermage*. Clos-de-Vougeot (31 a); Echézeaux (33 a); Bâtard-Montrachet (18 a); Chevalier-Montrachet (15 a); Bienvenues-Bâtard-Montrachet (46 a); Puligny-Montrachet *premier cru* in Les Pucelles, Les Combettes, Les Folatières, Le Champ-Gain; Meursault *premier cru* Sous-le-Dos-d'Ane; Blagny *premier cru* Sous-le-Dos-d'Ane; village Puligny-Montrachet (*rouge et blanc*); village Beaune (*rouge et blanc*); village Santenay.

The Clerc style is quite different from its neighbours. The wines are oaky, exotically fruity, rich and opulent. Sometimes they can be a little heavy. But I have had plenty of good wines here, and the evidence of the 1993s and 1994s indicates that things are becoming more elegant.
See Profile, page 390.

GUILLEMARD-CLERC

1.6 ha: owned and *en fermage/métayage*. Bienvenues-Bâtard-Montrachet (18 a); Beaune *premier cru* Clos-de-Coucherias; village Puligny-Montrachet in the *lieu-dit* Les Roucheaux.

Bernard Clerc's daughter Corinne is married to Franck Guillemard, whose family comes from the Hautes-Côtes. This is their own small estate.

★LEFLAIVE

21 ha: owned. Le Montrachet (8 a); Chevalier-Montrachet (1.91 ha); Bâtard-Montrachet (2.00 ha); Bienvenues-Bâtard-Montrachet (1.15 ha); Puligny-Montrachet *premier cru* in Les Pucelles, Les Combettes, Les Folatières, Le Clavoillon; Les Chalumeaux; Blagny *premier cru tout court*; village Puligny-Montrachet.

This is a famous domaine, and one where there has been much change in recent years, during which standards have not been what they were in the 1960s and 1970s. Vincent Leflaive, doyen of the village, and a man of great charm and wit, lost a long battle with cancer in 1993 aged eighty-two. The mantle first passed to his daughter Anne-Claude and nephew Olivier, it being the custom to have *co-gérants*, but Olivier has now left to concentrate on his own business (see below). There is a new *régisseur*, Pierre Morey of Meursault having replaced Jean Virot, and since 1990 part of the estate has been farmed along bio-dynamic lines.

There is certainly a perfectionism when it comes to cellar practice here. The *cave* is air-conditioned and scrupulously tidy (no spitting on the floor but into a bucket; no pouring back what you have not tasted into the barrel). But in the vineyard yields are definitely on the high side, declarations from the Clavoillon, where Leflaive owns 80 per cent of the *climat*, regularly being one of the highest of all the *premiers crus*.

Leflaive wines always taste well in cask, but of late have not aged well. The last really satisfactory vintage – by which I mean wines with aspirations to greatness, was 1985. But I have high hopes of the 1995s.

See Profile, page 510.

*OLIVIER LEFLAIVE FRÈRES, SA

8.75 ha: owned and *en fermage*. Meursault *premier cru* Les Poruzots; Chassagne-Montrachet *premier cru* Les Chaumées; village Puligny-Montrachet; village Chassagne-Montrachet (*rouge et blanc*).

Created in 1984, and with Jean-Marc Boillot, now of Pommard, as wine-maker, this merchant, which has since built up its own domaine, showed right from the start that they could produce high quality. Franck Grux took over as wine-maker in 1988, and, if anything, things are even better today. A wide range, mainly white. Recommended.

ROLAND MARASLOVAC-LÉGER

7.90 ha: owned and *en fermage*. Puligny-Montrachet *premier cru* in Les Folatières, Les Combettes, Le Champ-Gain; Saint-Aubin *premier cru* Les Murgers-des-Dents-de-Chien; Auxey-Duresses *premier cru* Les Breterins (*rouge*); village Puligny-Montrachet; village Meursault; village Chassagne-Montrachet (*rouge et blanc*); village Auxey-Duresses (*rouge*).

This is a reliable if never very startling cellar, and it is hosted by the cheerfully hospitable Roland Maraslovac. Some of his holdings are very small (6 a of Combettes for example), which must pose vinification problems on occasions. But there are good wines here.

STÉPHEN MARASLOVAC-TRÉMEAU

15.5 ha: owned and *en fermage*. Puligny-Montrachet *premier cru* in Le Champ-Gain, Les Referts, Les Folatières, Les Pucelles; village Puligny-Montrachet including the *lieu-dit* Clos-du-Vieux-Château; Meursault *premier cru* Blagny; village Santenay.

Father of Roland (see above), Stéphen Maraslovac sells most of his wine to the *négoce*, and I have had good examples *élevé* by La Compagnie des Vins d'Autrefois of Beaune. What he doesn't sell, perforce, he has to hang on to. But after a year they are transferred back to tank waiting for a buyer to come along. In June 1993 there were not only some 1991s still looking for a home, but even some 1990s. I fear M. Maraslovac is not really geared up for *élevage*.

VEUVE HENRI MORONI

6 ha: owned and *en fermage*. Bâtard-Montrachet (32 a); Puligny-Montrachet *premier cru* in Les Pucelles, Les Perrières; village Puligny-Montrachet.

Marc Jomain is the tenant of this estate, which includes land belonging to Mme Henri Jacquin. They have a shop and also a merchant's licence. Always seeking to increase my experience I called in here first in June 1989. I found the cellar dirty and the quality unimpressive. When I enquired over a rather weak Pucelles whether it was young vines, the response was that on the contrary, they were old: fifteen to twenty years old! This was obviously a venerable age in the view of the domaine. Subsequent visits have not persuaded me to change my mind that this is wine-making at its most cynical. *Caveat emptor!*

JEAN AND JEAN-LUC PASCAL

15 ha: owned and *en fermage*. Puligny-Montrachet *premier cru* in Les Folatières, Les Chalumeaux, Hameau-de-Blagny, Le Champ-Gain; Volnay *premier cru* Les Caillerets; village Puligny-Montrachet (*rouge et blanc*); village Blagny; village Meursault; village Volnay; village Pommard; village Auxey-Duresses.

This is another good reliable source which has yet to show me anything which sends me into raptures. Jean-Luc, son of Jean Pascal, is in charge. There is 25–50 per cent new oak for the whites, 20–35 per cent for the reds, which are entirely destemmed before vinification.

*PAUL PERNOT ET FILS

19 ha: owned and *en fermage*. Bâtard-Montrachet (60 a); Bienvenues-Bâtard-Montrachet (38 a); Puligny-Montrachet *premier cru* in Les Pucelles, Les Folatières, Les Champs-Canet, La Garenne, Les Chalumeaux; Meursault *premier cru* Blagny; Blagny *premier cru* La Pièce-sous-le-Bois; Volnay *premier cru* Les Carelles; Beaune *premier cru* in Les Teurons, Clos-du-Dessous-des-Marconnets, Les Reversées; village Puligny-Montrachet; village Pommard in the *lieu-dit* Les Noizons; village Beaune; village Santenay.

This large and expanding domaine must be a boon to the Beaune *négoce*, for quality is very high and Paul Pernot and his three sons only dispose themselves of some 20 per cent of the crop in bottle. I have consistent enthusiastic notes of Pernot wines. The Bâtard, though the results are very good, is relatively young vines. Currently the Bienvenues is the best wine here.

CHÂTEAU DE PULIGNY-MONTRACHET

23.5 ha: owned. Le Montrachet (4 a); Chevalier-Montrachet (25 a); Bâtard-Montrachet (4 a); Puligny-Montrachet *premier cru* in Les Folatières, Les Chalumeaux, La Garenne; Meursault *premier cru* in Les Perrières, Les Poruzots; Saint-Aubin *premier cru* En Remilly (*rouge et blanc*); Monthélie *premier cru* Les Duresses; Pommard *premier cru* Les Pézerolles; village Puligny-Montrachet; village Chassagne-Montrachet; village Meursault; village Saint-Aubin; village Monthélie (*rouge et blanc*); village Pommard; Saint-Romain; Côte-de-Nuits-Villages (*rouge et blanc*).

The bank Crédit Foncier de France, owner among other things of Châteaux Bastor-Lamontagne in Sauternes and Beauregard in Pomerol, acquired the Château de Puligny-Montrachet in 1989 from the Laroche company of Chablis. They have since built up the domaine from 15 ha to its present size, acquiring land from Jean Chartron and the Fleurot family, among others. There is a splendid modern vinification centre and a temperature- and humidification-controlled cellar. And one old-fashioned baby vertical press for the Montrachet. Quality is certainly good. It has the potential to be better still.

JACKY RIGER-BRISET

5 ha: owned and *en fermage*. Meursault *premier cru* Les Charmes; Saint-Aubin *premier cru* in Les Murgers-des-Dents-de-Chien (*rouge*) and En Remilly (*blanc*); village Puligny-Montrachet; village Meursault; village Pommard.

The Riger family arrived from the Saône valley to the east in 1979, and have built up this small domaine since. I have had some good wines out of cask here, but my experience of them in bottle is limited.

★ÉTIENNE SAUZET

8 ha: owned. Bâtard-Montrachet (18 a); Bienvenues-Bâtard-Montrachet (15 a); Puligny-Montrachet *premier cru* in Les Combettes, Les Champs-Canet, Les Referts, Les Perrières; village Puligny-Montrachet; village Chassagne-Montrachet.

Gérard Boudot, married to a grand-daughter of the late Étienne Sauzet, is one of Puligny's most gifted wine-makers, and produced his twenty-first vintage in 1994. The estate has lost a third of its holdings to Jean-Marc Boillot, Boudot's brother-in-law, but he has compensated by acquiring a merchant's licence, so it can buy in to fill up the gaps. Splendid wines here. At the time of writing the Perrières is young vines.

See Profile, page 628.

CHASSAGNE-MONTRACHET

Chassagne-Montrachet is the last-but-one important commune of the Côte d'Or before the hills fizzle out at Dezize, Cheilly and Sampigny-lès-Maranges, and the third of the three great adjacent white wine villages after Meursault and Puligny. Divided by the main highway between Chagny and Chalon to the south and Autun and Auxerre to the west and north-west, now to a large extent superseded by the Paris-Lyon motorway, Chassagne produces both red and white wine. Historically its vineyards have been planted with Pinot Noir. Today more and more Chardonnay can be found, and it is the white wines which have the greater renown and achieve the higher prices. This is not just because of the proximity of the *grands crus* of Le Montrachet and Bâtard-Montrachet, both of which *climats* straddle the Puligny-Chassagne commune boundary (indeed the smallest and most southerly of the white wine *grands crus*, Criots-Bâtard-Montrachet, falls entirely within Chassagne), nor solely as a result of the current demand for fine white Burgundy. The white wines, simply, are better.

The reds are good: full-bodied, stalwart, work-horse examples of the Pinot Noir, somewhat burly, occasionally rustic; similar in a way to those of Pommard or even the less distinctive examples of the Côte-de-Nuits. The whites too are full and firm; less definitive perhaps than those of Puligny, but with a better grip than the majority of Meursaults. When comparing generic examples of the same shipper I normally find the Chassagne more exciting than the latter, if not the former.

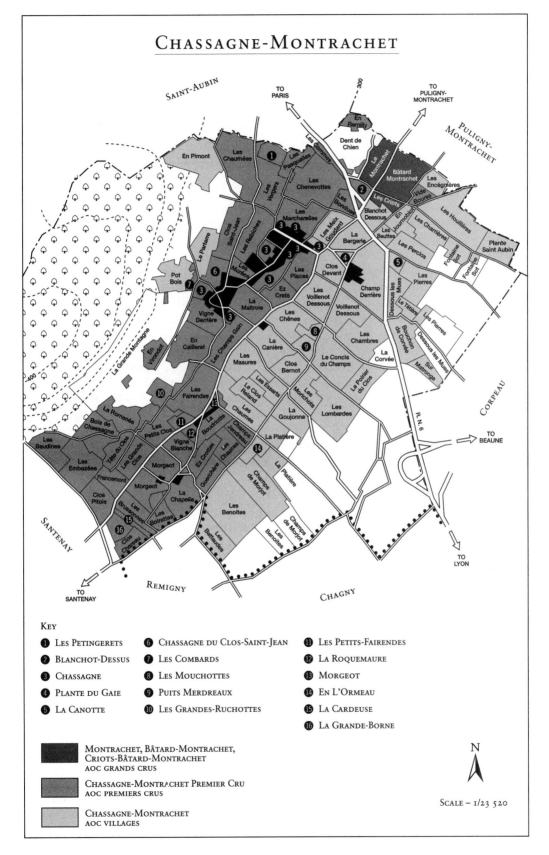

CHASSAGNE-MONTRACHET

SAINT-AUBIN

TO PARIS

TO PULIGNY-MONTRACHET

PULIGNY-MONTRACHET

En Remilly

Dent de Chien

En Pimont

Les Chaumées

Les Pasquelles

Les Gemmes

Le Montrachet

Bâtard Montrachet

Les Encégnières

Les Chenevottes

Les Criots

Vide Bourse

Les Houillères

Les Vergers

Les Bondues

Blanchot Dessous

En Journoblot

Les Charrières

Plante Saint Aubin

Clos Saint-Jean

Les Rebichets

Les Meix Goudard

Les Beuttes

Les Percils

Le Parterre

La Bergerie

Les Murées

Clos Devant

Les Pierres

Fontaine Bot

Fontaine Sot

Pot Bois

Les Placas

Champ Derrière

Dessous les Mues

Le Tellier

Les Pierres

Vigne Derrière

Ez Crets

Les Voillenot Dessous

Voillenot Dessous

La Maltroie

Les Chênes

En Cailleret

La Canière

Les Chambres

Bouchon de Corvée

Dessous les Mues

Sur Matronge

En Virondot

La Grande Montagne

Les Masures

Clos Bernot

Le Concis du Champs

La Corvée

Les Fairendes

Les Essarts

Le Clos Reland

Le Poirier du Clos

Bois de Chassagne

La Romanée

Les Chaumes

La Goujonne

Les Monchots

Les Lombardes

Les Petits Clos

La Boudriotte

Champs Jendreau

La Platière

Tête du Clos

Les Grands Clos

Vigne Blanche

Les Chaumes

La Platière

Les Baudines

Morgeot

Ez Crottes

Quercheau

Les Chaumes

En L'Ormeau

Les Embazées

Francemont

Morgeot

La Chapelle

Champs de Morjot

Clos Pitois

Les Brussonnes

Les Benoîtes

Champs de Morjot

Les Benoîtes

Clos Chareau

Les Golrettes

Les Battaudes

SANTENAY

TO SANTENAY

REMIGNY

CHAGNY

CORPEAU

TO BEAUNE

TO LYON

R.N. 6

KEY

1. LES PETINGERETS
2. BLANCHOT-DESSUS
3. CHASSAGNE
4. PLANTE DU GAIE
5. LA CANOTTE
6. CHASSAGNE DU CLOS-SAINT-JEAN
7. LES COMBARDS
8. LES MOUCHOTTES
9. PUITS MERDREAUX
10. LES GRANDES-RUCHOTTES
11. LES PETITS-FAIRENDES
12. LA ROQUEMAURE
13. MORGEOT
14. EN L'ORMEAU
15. LA CARDEUSE
16. LA GRANDE-BORNE

MONTRACHET, BÂTARD-MONTRACHET, CRIOTS-BÂTARD-MONTRACHET
AOC GRANDS CRUS

CHASSAGNE-MONTRACHET PREMIER CRU
AOC PREMIERS CRUS

CHASSAGNE-MONTRACHET
AOC VILLAGES

N

SCALE – 1/23 520

HISTORY

As in many places in this part of France the village has had a turbulent history. It was known as Cassaneas in AD 886, leading Christopher Fielden and John Arlott (*Burgundy, Vines and Wines*) to suggest a connection with a diminutive of the Latin *casa*, a house. And surely the *premier cru* La Romanée has a Roman connection. The local *seigneur* towards the end of the Middle Ages was Jean de Chalons, Prince of Orange. His castle, at the top of the côte, surrounded by what was then the village of 'Chaissagne', was besieged by the army of Louis XI at the end of the fifteenth century, for the Prince had sided with Louis' rival, Margaret of Burgundy. After much attrition the locals had to capitulate, and for their mischance in being on the losing side had their village burned to the ground.

Eventually a new village sprang up halfway down the slope. This was largely monastic in its origins. The Abbot of Maizières, recognising the vinous value of the local terrain, cleared much of the hillside and planted vines and built a local priory, the Abbaye de Morgeot, to house the brothers who worked on the vineyards. A sister establishment was established by the Abbess of Saint-Jean-Le-Grand. Morgeot and Clos-Saint-Jean remain two of the largest and most important *premiers crus*.

Historically, as I have said, Chassagne was a red-wine village like most in the Côte d'Or. Montrachet seems always to have been renowned for its white wines, but elsewhere, except in Meursault, what was made was red. Camille Rodier (*Le Vin de Bourgogne*, 1920) quotes a Dr Ramain who himself had dug up an inventory belonging to the then Marquis de Laguiche, lords of the village in the eighteenth century and still important landowners today. This document stipulated that a bottle of the Marquis' (red) Morgeot was worth two bottles of his Montrachet. As Rodier comments, for a moment God is eclipsed by one of his saints.

Jullien (*Topographie de Tous les Vignobles Connus*, 1816) cites the red wines of Chassagne among those of his third class, while noting that the wines of 'Morjot', La Maltroie and Clos-Saint-Jean are among his first class alongside lesser *grands crus* such as Clos-de-Tart and Clos-de-la-Roche in Morey and the *climats* of Musigny and Les Amoureuses in Chambolle. No mention is made of white wines in the village apart from Le Montrachet and its satellites. This dearth of Chardonnay is confirmed by Dr Lavalle, who wrote one of the most interesting source-books on Burgundy in 1855: 'If one excepts the vineyard producing the white wines called Montrachet, one finds only a few *ouvrées* here and there in Pinot Blanc, as in Ruchotte, for example . . . everywhere the Pinot Noir is planted in the good sites and Gamay in the poorer soils.' However he also mentions that Chassagne is the commune in Burgundy where one finds the Pinot Beurot or Pinot Gris (the so-called Tokay d'Alsace) also a white grape, in the greatest abundance.

The observation quoted above is repeated verbatim (without acknowledgement!) by Camille Rodier. The red wines, in Rodier's view, while less elegant than those of Volnay, have more colour and body. They last well. They have an 'indisputable similarity to some of the great wines of the Côte-de-Nuits'.

Yet by the 1930s there must have been more than just a token amount of Chardonnay outside the *grands crus*. I can remember bottles of the 1940s, though I have never sampled wines of the pre-war period. But Morton Shand writing in 1929, and even Warner Allen, as late as 1952, make no mention of the Chassagne white, concentrating their purple prose on Le Montrachet itself. It must be said, however, that their knowledge of France's vineyards was largely acquired at second hand, absorbed through the bottle itself. They probably never actually went and talked to a grower on the spot.

Old men with long memories of the village and its wines can remember when it was first decided to move from red wine to white. It was when the vineyards were being replanted after the phylloxera epidemic. Was this perhaps, I suggested, because the Chardonnay took to its graft better than the Pinot Noir? For this was one of the explanations why Sancerre, originally a red wine, became white. No, merely a response to a changing fashion. By the time of the introduction of the laws of *Appellation Contrôlée* in 1936 some 20–25 per cent of Chassagne's vineyards produced white wine. And, unlike most of the villages in the Côte d'Or, the top vineyards of Chassagne are allowed to produce *premier cru* wine of either colour. Since the war the move to white has accelerated. The grower Albert Morey remembers that when he bought his plot of Caillerets in 1949 the entire *climat* was planted in Pinot Noir. Today it produces one of the best Chardonnays in the commune. In 1982, 48 per cent of the village and *premier cru* wine was white but by 1992 the percentages had been reversed. Today over 55 per cent – but 73 per cent of the *premier cru* wine – of Chassagne's production comes from the Chardonnay. The cause is self-evident. A village Chassagne can today command F 67 a bottle if it be white but only F 36 if it is red. For a *premier cru* the gap is wider still: *rouge* from Morgeot at F 48, *blanc* from Caillerets at F 96, double the price.

LOCATION

Chassagne is one of the larger communes of the Côte d'Or with nearly 370 hectares under vines. This is similar to its neighbour Santenay, smaller than Meursault, but sizeably larger than Puligny. In addition one must count the entirety of the diminutive *grand cru* Criots-Bâtard-Montrachet (1.6 ha) and just under half of both Le Montrachet (8 ha) and Bâtard-Montrachet (12 ha).

The soil structure is complex. The rocky subsoil, like most of Burgundy, is basically an oolitic limestone. Here it is Bathonian, the same strata which is found in the Côte-de-Nuits. At Chassagne you can see a quarry halfway up the slope above the village, as well as the production therefrom of polished slabs of pink, beige or grey marble-like stone in the graveyards and fireplaces of the local growers. At various points in the village the surface soil, essentially limestone debris, has more or less clay, more or less gravel, and more or less chalk ('criot' is a corruption of *craie*: chalk), as well as changing colour; the heavier *terres rouges* being found lower down the slope at Morgeot, while higher up along the line from Embazées through Ruchottes to Caillerets you will find the lighter *terres blanches*. In general it is here in the leaner more chalky soils of the upper slopes of the village that the best white wines have their origins. North of the village the slope from the top of Clos-Saint-Jean down through Les Vergers and Les Chenevottes to the N6 is gentler, the soil contains both clay and gravel, and the Pinot Noir comes into its own, as it does at Morgeots, though much of this *climat* is now under Chardonnay. Finally round towards the border with the commune of Saint-Aubin, across which is this village's best *climat*, Les Charmois, the higher slopes above Les Chaumées have recently been reclaimed from the scrub. Again this cooler, north-east facing slope has been found to produce good racy white wines.

As I have said, it is the white wines which are the most distinctive. In general they are full and firm, more akin to Puligny than to the softer, rounder wines of Meursault. From the top of the slope on the Saint-Aubin side, vineyards like Les Chaumées produce lightish, racy wines with a touch of peach or crab apple, while lower down, say in Chenevottes, the produce is plumper and sometimes a touch four-square. For the best of the more masculine versions of white Chassagne you need to go to Morgeots. Caillerets and Grandes-Ruchottes up-slope are flowery, racy and feminine. Embazées and La Romanée 'all in finesse' and lighter still; while in Champ-Gain, halfway up the slope, you will get an elegant compromise: fullish, plump, succulent wines. My vote, though, would go to the Caillerets.

THE VINEYARD

Grands Crus: See under Puligny-Montrachet.

Premiers Crus: There are a great many: indeed a record fifty-two, but you will rarely see most of them, for many have the right to be sold under a more familiar name such as Morgeots.

In alphabetical order they are as follows: Abbaye-de-Morgeot; Les Baudines; Blanchot-Dessus; Les Boirettes; Bois-de-Chassagne; Les Bondues; La Grande-Borne; La Boudriotte; Les Brussonnes; En Cailleret; La Cardeuse; Le Champ-Gain; La Chapelle; Les Chaumées; Les Chaumes; Les Chenevottes; Clos-Chareau; Clos-Pitois; Clos-Saint-Jean; Les Grands-Clos; Les Petits-Clos; Les Combards; Les Commes; Les Crets; Les Criottes; Les Dents-de-Chien; Les Embazées (or Embrazées); Les Fairendes; Les Petits-Fairendes; Francemont; La Guerchère; Champ-Jendreau; Les Macherelles; La Maltroie; La Grande-Montagne; Les Morgeots; Les Murées; Les Pasquelles; Les Petangerets; Les Places; Les Rebichets; En Remilly; La Romanée; La Roquemaure; Les Grandes-Ruchottes; Tête-du-Clos; Tonton-Marcel; Les Vergers; Vide-Bourse; Vigne-Blanche; Vigne-Derrière; En Virondot.

These cover 158.79 ha and produce around 1,820 hl (240,000 bottles) of red wine and 5,000 hl (660,000 bottles) of white wine a year.

Village Wine: There are 179.51 ha of village Chassagne-Montrachet. Production averages 4,900 hl (647,000 bottles) of red and 3,000 hl (400,000 bottles) of white wine a year.

Readers will note that over 70 per cent of Chassagne-Montrachet *premier cru* is white wine, while under 40 per cent of village wine is this colour. This is logical. Most of the slope, excellent for Chardonnay, is *premier cru*. The lower lying land, more suitable for red wine, is village AC.

The Premiers Crus

En Remilly (1.56 ha) • Les Dents-de-Chien (0.64 ha)
Blanchot-Dessus (1.32 ha) • Vide-Bourse (1.17 ha)

These are the *premiers crus* on the north side of the N6 and they seem to produce nothing but white wine. Blanchot-Dessus lies directly next to Le Montrachet, on slightly lower land. Les Dents-de-Chien and En Remilly have been carved out of the rock above, while Vide-Bourse lies down-slope from Bâtard-Montrachet. I know of only one reputable producer of Blanchot *premier cru* but I am told that the Marquis de Laguiche has vines here, the produce of which is blended with others to produce the Chassagne-Montrachet sold under his name by Maison Joseph Drouhin.

Vide-Bourse can produce a rather four-square wine; En Remilly is really quite the opposite, all raciness and flowers. Darviot's Blanchot is a serious example, worth catching if you can.

Recommended Sources:
En Remilly: Michel Colin-Deléger (Chassagne-Montrachet); Philippe Brenot (Santenay).
Blanchot-Dessus: Didier Darviot-Perrin (Monthélie).
Les Dents-de-Chien: Château de Maltroye (Chassagne-Montrachet).
Vide-Bourse: Bernard Morey, Fernand et Laurent Pillot (both Chassagne-Montrachet).

Les Chaumées (7.43 ha)

Les Vergers (9.41 ha)
(including Petangerets, Les Pasquelles)

Les Chenevottes (9.26 ha)
(including Les Commes)

Les Bondues (1.73 ha)
(can be sold as Les Chenevottes)

Les Macherelles (5.19 ha)

On the opposite side of the N6, facing almost due east, lie these *premiers crus*. I list them from the top of the slope downwards. Here again most of the wines are white, the most racy from Chaumées, the richest, but perhaps a little lumpy, from Chenevottes and Macherelles. But a good composite site this.

Recommended Sources:
Les Chaumées (*blanc*): Michel Colin-Deléger (Chassagne-Montrachet).
Les Vergers (*blanc*): Guy Amiot-Bonfils; Michel Colin-Deléger; Richard Fontaine-Gagnard; Michel Niellon; Fernand et Laurent Pillot; Jean et Jean-Marc Pillot; Ramonet (all Chassagne-Montrachet).
Les Chenevottes: Bernard Colin-Chapelle; Michel Colin-Deléger; Richard Fontaine-Gagnard; Jean-Noël Gagnard; Château de Maltroye: Bernard Moreau; Jean et Jean-Marc Pillot (all Chassagne-Montrachet).
Les Macherelles (*blanc*): Guy Amiot-Bonfils; Jean et Jean-Marc Pillot (both Chassagne-Montrachet); Hubert Lamy (Saint-Aubin).
Les Macherelles (*rouge*): Bernard Colin-Chapelle; Jean et Jean-Marc Pillot (both Chassagne-Montrachet).

CLOS-SAINT-JEAN (14.16 HA)
(including Les Rebichets, Les Murées)

LA MALTROIE (11.61 HA)
(including Chassagne, Les Places, Les Crets)

Clos-Saint-Jean lies above the village, under the largest of the quarries, while La Maltroie lies on the other side of the road and houses which connect Chassagne-le-Haut with Chassagne-le-Bas. You would expect Clos-Saint-Jean to be preferred for white wine, La Maltroie for red.

Curiously the opposite is the case. There is a little Pinot Noir, which belongs to the village, and is vinified in turn by the local growers, in La Maltroie, but otherwise most of the wines are white, a major exception being those of the Château de Maltroye (spelled with a y) which has the majority of the Clos-du-Château immediately beneath the mansion.

Moreover, while many growers have replanted their Clos-Saint-Jean in Chardonnay I find it one of the least convincing *premiers crus en blanc*. The wine seems to me to lack both substance and fruit. No doubt the age of the vines comes into it. But I'm convinced this is not the whole explanation. There must be something in the soil which detracts from the character of the Chardonnay. Red Clos-Saint-Jean, on the other hand, can be rich, full, juicy and most enjoyable, slightly less heavy and less spicy than Morgeots.

Recommended Sources:
Clos-Saint-Jean (*rouge*): Guy Amiot-Bonfils; Richard Fontaine-Gagnard; Jean-Noël Gagnard; René Lamy-Pillot; Château de Maltroye; Ramonet.
La Maltroie (*blanc*): Michel Colin-Deléger; Richard Fontaine-Gagnard; Jean-Noël Gagnard; Château de Maltroye; Bernard Moreau; Michel Niellon.
La Maltroie (*rouge*): Château de Maltroye.

LES CAILLERETS (19.67 HA)
(including Les Combards, Vigne-Derrière)

LE CHAMP-GAIN (4.62 HA)

LA GRANDE-MONTAGNE (2.78 HA)
(including Tonton-Marcel, En Virondot)

Les Grandes-Ruchottes (2.13 ha)
(can be sold as La Grande-Montagne)

La Romanée (3.35 ha)
(can be sold as La Grande-Montagne)

Bois-de-Chassagne (4.38 ha)

Les Embazées (or Embrazées) (5.19 ha)
(can be sold as Bois-de-Chassagne)

Les Baudines (3.60 ha)
(can be sold as Bois-de-Chassagne)

These are the *climats* on the *côteaux* above the road that leads down from Chassagne to Santenay. This is the best section for white Chassagne. The vineyards lie at 250–330 metres, are well exposed, but sheltered, and face directly south-east. The wines here lose the somewhat clumsy, four-square aspect of other white Chassagnes, and gain in both raciness and depth. At the Chassagne end (Les Caillerets, Le Champ-Gain) the wines are fuller and less mineral in character than at the Santenay end (Les Baudines, Les Embazées). This *côteau* is almost entirely planted in Chardonnay.

Recommended Sources:

Les Caillerets: Guy Amiot-Bonfils; Bachelet-Ramonet; Jean-Marc Blain-Gagnard; Richard Fontaine-Gagnard; Jean-Noël Gagnard; Bernard Morey; Marc Morey; Michel Morey-Coffinet; Jean et Jean-Marc Pillot; Paul Pillot; Ramonet (all Chassagne-Montrachet); Marc Colin (Saint-Aubin); René Lequin-Colin (Santenay).

Le Champ-Gain: Guy Amiot-Bonfils; Jean-Noël Gagnard; Michel Niellon; Jean et Jean-Marc Pillot (all Chassagne-Montrachet); Marc Colin (Saint-Aubin).

La Grande-Montagne: Richard Fontaine-Gagnard; René Lamy-Pillot (both Chassagne-Montrachet).

Les Grandes-Ruchottes: Château de Maltroye; Bernard Moreau; Fernand et Laurent Pillot; Paul Pillot; Ramonet.

La Romanée: Bachelet-Ramonet; Château de Maltroye; Michel Morey-Coffinet; Paul Pillot.

Les Embazées: Bernard Morey (who spells it Embrazées).

Les Baudines: Bernard Morey.

Les Morgeots (54.23 ha)

The following *climats* can sell their wine as Morgeots: La Grande-Borne; Les Brussonnes; Les Boirettes; Clos-Chareau; Clos-Pitois; Francemont; La Chapelle; Vigne-Blanche; En Crottes; La Guerchère; Tête-du-Clos; Les Petits-Clos; Les Grands-Clos; La Roquemaure; Champ-Jendreau; Les Chaumes; La Boudriotte; Les Fairendes; Les Petits-Fairendes.

This incorporates not only all the *premier cru* land below the Chassagne-Santenay road, round the Abbaye de Morgeot itself, but the flatter land above the road, those vineyards which lie underneath those described in the section above. The only *climats* declared separately seem to be Boudriotte and Vigne-Blanche, and usually by growers who also offer a Morgeots.

Judging by production figures the land is equally divided between Chardonnay and Pinot Noir here, Morgeots being the major source for *premier cru rouge*. The whites, in my experience, can be a bit too fat and heavy-footed for comfort, for this, I believe, is really red wine soil. The reds are sturdy, quite muscular and dense when they are young, and fuller and spicier than Clos-Saint-Jean, but they mellow with age and can give some nice bottles when seven years old or so.

Recommended Sources:

Les Morgeots (blanc): Bachelet-Ramonet; Jean-Marc Blain-Gagnard; Michel Colin-Deléger; Jean-Noël Gagnard; Jacques Gagnard-Delagrange; René Lamy-Pillot; Bernard Moreau; Fernand et Laurent Pillot; Jean et Jean-Marc Pillot; Paul Pillot; Ramonet (all Chassagne-Montrachet); Duc de Magenta/Jadot (Chassagne-Montrachet/Beaune); Henri Germain (Meursault); Vincent Girardin (Santenay).

Les Morgeots (rouge): Richard Fontaine-Gagnard; Jean-Noël Gagnard; René Lamy-Pillot; Jean et Jean-Marc Pillot; Ramonet (all Chassagne-Montrachet); Duc de Magenta/Jadot (Chassagne-Montrachet/Beaune); Vincent Girardin; René Lequin-Colin (both Santenay).

La Boudriotte (blanc): Jean-Marc Blain-Gagnard; Jacques Gagnard-Delagrange; Château de Maltroye; Ramonet (all Chassagne-Montrachet).

Las Boudriotte (rouge): René Lamy-Pillot; Ramonet (who offer both Boudriotte and a Clos-de-la-Boudriotte) (both Chassagne-Montrachet); Larue (Saint-Aubin).

THE GROWERS

GUY AMIOT-BONFILS

8 ha: owned and *en fermage*. Le Montrachet (10 a); Chassagne-Montrachet *premier cru blanc* in Les Caillerets, Les Vergers, Les Macherelles, Le Champ-Gain, Clos-Saint-Jean; Puligny-Montrachet *premier cru* Les Demoiselles; Saint-Aubin *premier cru rouge* in Clos-Saint-Jean, Les Vergers; village Chassagne-Montrachet (*rouge et blanc*).

Unlike the others in the village, who have constructed new cellars and warehouses down on the plain, Guy Amiot and his son Thierry have just enlarged their own underground cellar. Amiot's father was an absentee landlord, and leased much of the land out to others on a *métayage* basis. These are now coming to their end. So until recently Amiot was not responsible for every aspect of his wine. The Montrachet and all the reds are bottled unfiltered. A very good source.

BACHELET-RAMONET

13.26: owned. Bâtard-Montrachet (56 a); Bienvenues-Bâtard-Montrachet (13 a); Chassagne-Montrachet *premier cru blanc* in La Romanée; Les Grandes-Ruchottes; Les Caillerets; Les Morgeots; La Grande-Montagne; Chassagne-Montrachet *premier cru rouge* in Clos-de-la-Boudriotte, Clos-Saint-Jean, Les Morgeots; village Chassagne-Montrachet *rouge et blanc*; village Puligny-Montrachet.

This estate used to produce marvellous wines, but went rapidly downhill in the 1980s, Jean Bachelet becoming old, tired and unwell, seemingly not up to the task. It is now his son-in-law Alain Bonnefoy who is in charge, and the whites, whose signature had always been an elegant delicacy, have improved. They have always been more interesting than the reds.

JEAN-MARC BLAIN-GAGNARD

7.70 ha: owned and *en fermage*. Bâtard-Montrachet (34 a); Criots-Bâtard-Montrachet (21 a); Chassagne-Montrachet *premier cru blanc* in Les Caillerets, Les Morgeots, La Boudriotte, Clos-Saint-Jean; Chassagne-Montrachet *premier cru rouge* in Les Morgeots, Clos-Saint-Jean; village Chassagne-Montrachet (*blanc et rouge*); village Volnay; village Pommard.

Jean-Marc Blain is the senior of Jacques Gagnard's sons-in-law, though married to the younger daughter. He produced his first vintage in 1980. Part of the Bâtard plus the yield of Le Montrachet are labelled as Edmond Delagrange-Bachelet, his wife's maternal grandfather. Blain's white wines, like those of the rest of the family, concentrate on the finesse and the fruit, and are delicate for Chassagnes. But they are all the more attractive as a result.

See Profile, page 440.

BERNARD COLIN-CHAPELLE

7.5 ha: owned and *en fermage*: Puligny-Montrachet *premier cru* Les Demoiselles; Chassagne-Montrachet *premier cru blanc* in Les Macherelles, Les Chenevottes, Clos-Saint-Jean (also Les Caillerets and Les Chaumées, but here the vines are very young); Chassagne-Montrachet *premier cru rouge* in Les Macherelles, Clos-Saint-Jean; Saint-Aubin *premier cru blanc* En Remilly; village Chassagne-Montrachet (*rouge et blanc*).

Bernard Colin, cousin of Michel and Marc, describes his approach as old-fashioned. I'd call it healthily ecological. Since joined by his son-in-law David Gourisse, the domaine has sold all its wine in bottle, but mainly to passing tourists via his *caveau* in the village. This Colin farms half the Demoiselles but his version is not as good as those of Michel Colin and Guy Amiot.

★MICHEL COLIN-DELÉGER

19.4 ha: owned and *en fermage*. Chevalier-Montrachet (16 a); Chassagne-Montrachet *premier cru blanc* in En Remilly, Les Morgeots, Les Chenevottes, Les Vergers, La Maltroie, Les Chaumées; Chassagne-Montrachet *premier cru rouge* in Les Morgeots, La Maltroie; Puligny-Montrachet *premier cru* in Les Demoiselles, La Truffière; Saint-Aubin *premier cru* in Les Charmois, Les Combes; Santenay *premier cru* Les Gravières; Maranges *premier cru*; village Chassagne-Montrachet (*blanc et rouge*); village Santenay.

Michel Colin is *fermier* for CCI Saint-Abdon, whose owners live in the north of France. The Demoiselles appears under his mother's name and some of the Chevalier under the name of Georges Deléger, though it is all now made by Michel Colin.

This is one of the best cellars in the village, with a splendid range of (mainly white) wines to offer. Balance and intensity of flavours are the keys here. Colin is one of the few who make a white Morgeots which is not heavy.

See Profile, page 399.

EDMOND DELAGRANGE-BACHELET

1 ha: owned. Le Montrachet (8 a); Bâtard-Montrachet (13 a); Chassagne-Montrachet *premier cru blanc* Les Caillerets; village Chassagne-Montrachet.

These wines are made by Jean-Marc Blain (see above).

RICHARD FONTAINE-GAGNARD

7.49 ha: owned and *en fermage*. Bâtard-Montrachet (30 a); Criots-Bâtard-Montrachet (33 a); Chassagne-Montrachet *premier cru blanc* in Les Caillerets, La Maltroie, Les Vergers, La Grande-Montagne, Les Chenevottes, Clos-Saint-Jean; Volnay *premier cru* Clos-des-Chênes; Pommard *premier cru* Les Rugiens; village Chassagne-Montrachet (*rouge et blanc*).

Richard Fontaine is the other Gagnard son-in-law, and made his first vintage in 1985. Again elegance and delicacy are to the forefront here. And he has some very good reds.

See Profile, page 440.

★JACQUES GAGNARD-DELAGRANGE

4 ha: owned. Le Montrachet (8 a); Bâtard-Montrachet (26 a); Chassagne-Montrachet *premier cru blanc* in La Boudriotte, Les Morgeots; Chassagne-Montrachet *premier cru tout court*; Volnay *premier cru* Les Champans; village Chassagne-Montrachet *rouge et blanc*.

Good as the wines of Blain and Fontaine are, Jacques Gagnard's are often better still. A master's hand here.

See Profile, page 440.

★JEAN-NOËL GAGNARD

8.5 ha: owned. Bâtard-Montrachet (37 a); Chassagne-Montrachet *premier cru blanc* in Les Caillerets, Les Morgeots, Les Chenevottes, La Maltroie, Le Champ-Gain; Chassagne-Montrachet *premier cru rouge* in Clos-Saint-Jean, Les Morgeots, La Maltroie; village Chassagne-Montrachet (*rouge et blanc*); Santenay *premier cru* Clos-des-Tavannes.

Jean-Noël is Jacques Gagnard's brother, a little taller, a little less solid, and a little less blunt in his disposition. The wines are different too: somewhat fuller and richer, less delicate, less easy to enjoy when they are young. But this is another very good source. Recent vintages have been most impressive.

MARQUIS DE LAGUICHE

4.75 ha: owned. Le Montrachet (2 ha); Chassagne-Montrachet *premier cru* Morgeot (*blanc et rouge*); village Chassagne-Montrachet *blanc*.

This famous estate sells its produce under contract to Maison Joseph Drouhin of Beaune. Is this perhaps the best Montrachet of them all?

While the vines are looked after by the domaine's own personnel, the viticultural programme is a joint effort between Philippe Drouhin and the Marquis, and it is Drouhin's team which harvests the fruit and makes the wine.

RENÉ LAMY-PILLOT

17 ha: owned and *en fermage/métayage*. Le Montrachet (5 a); Chassagne-Montrachet *premier cru blanc* in Les Morgeots, La Grande-Montagne, Clos-Saint-Jean, plus a *premier cru tout court*; Chassagne-Montrachet *premier cru rouge* in Les Morgeots, La Boudriotte, Clos-Saint-Jean; Blagny *premier cru* La Pièce-sous-le-Bois; Saint-Aubin *premier cru blanc* Les Pucelles; Saint-Aubin *premier cru rouge* Les Castets; village Chassagne-Montrachet *rouge et blanc*; village Saint-Aubin *rouge et blanc*; village Beaune.

Solid, burly, red-faced, with a handshake like a vice, René Lamy, brother of Hubert of Saint-Aubin, is continuing to build up his exploitation. The Montrachet arrived in 1990, the Beaune in 1994. He also has one of the largest collections of corkscrews I have ever seen: 730 examples, at the last count. Good wines here, especially in red, but I find the whites sometimes lack elegance.

DUC DE MAGENTA

In 1986 the Duc de Magenta entered into a long-term contract with Jadot (see page 000), who now take some 80 per cent of the yield, either in the form of grapes (for the red wines) or must (for the white). Until the harvest the vines are the responsibility of Magenta and his team, Jadot merely ensuring that the harvest is not too excessive.

CHÂTEAU DE MALTROYE

14.50 ha: owned. Bâtard-Montrachet (9a); Chassagne-Montrachet *premier cru blanc* in Les Dents-de-Chien, La Romanée, Les Grandes-Ruchottes, Les Morgeots, Clos-du-Château-de-Maltroye, Les Chenevottes, Les Macherelles, Les Baudines; Chassagne-Montrachet *premier cru rouge* in Clos-du-Château-de-Maltroye; Clos-Saint-Jean; Santenay *premier cru rouge* in La Comme, Les Gravières; Chassagne-Montrachet (*rouge et blanc*).

In the days of André Cornut this cellar was a shambles, and the quality of the wines reflected the mess. André's son Jean-Pierre has now taken over, put things in order, and the wine has improved. The lesser wines are kept partly in *foudre*, partly in small barrels. The red grapes are entirely destemmed. The three top wines (Bâtard, Les Dents-de-Chien, La Romanée) are given 100 per cent new wood.

BERNARD MOREAU

9.5 ha: owned. Chassagne-Montrachet *premier cru blanc* in Les Morgeots, Les Grandes-Ruchottes, Les Chenevottes, La Maltroie; Chassagne-Montrachet *premier cru rouge* in Les Morgeots; La Cardeuse (*monopole*); Saint-Aubin *premier cru blanc* En Remilly; village Chassagne-Montrachet (*rouge et blanc*).

We offer more choice in white, more volume in red is how the friendly Bernard Moreau and his son Alexandre explain their domaine. This is a good reliable source, but the wines are typical Chassagnes: sometimes they lack a zip of excitement. In 1994 though, Moreau bought a new pneumatic press, and proclaimed himself very pleased with the results.

BERNARD MOREY

11.80 ha: owned and *en fermage*. Chassagne-Montrachet *premier cru blanc* in Les Caillerets, Les Morgeots, Vide-Bourse, Les Embazées (spelled Embrazées), Les Baudines; Puligny-Montrachet *premier cru* La Truffière; Santenay *premier cru blanc* Les Passe-Temps; Santenay *premier cru rouge* Grand-Clos-Rousseau; Beaune *premier cru* Les Grèves; Saint-Aubin *premier cru blanc* Les Charmois; village Chassagne-Montrachet (*rouge et blanc*); village Santenay; village Maranges.

Brother of Jean-Marc (see below), Bernard Morey moved into a house on the road by the Abbaye de Morgeot, below which is an extensive cellar, a few years ago, but he still stores his white wine in cask in the cellars of his father Albert back in the heart of the village. In 1994 he extended his exploitation into Puligny and Maranges. I find this Morey more reliable than his brother.

JEAN-MARC MOREY

8 ha: owned and *en fermage*. Bâtard-Montrachet (15 a) (appears under the label of his father Alfred); Chassagne-Montrachet *premier cru blanc* in Les Caillerets, Le Champ-Gain, Les Chaumées, Les Chenevottes; Chassagne-Montrachet *premier cru* in Clos-Saint-Jean, Le Champ-Gain; Saint-Aubin *premier cru* Les Charmois; Santenay *premier cru rouge* Grand-Clos-Rousseau; Beaune *premier cru* Les Grèves; village Chassagne-Montrachet *rouge et blanc*; village Santenay (*blanc*).

Quality has been a bit uneven here in recent years.

MARC MOREY

8.5 ha: owned and *en fermage*. Bâtard-Montrachet (13 a); Chassagne-Montrachet *premier cru blanc* Les Caillerets, En Virondot, Les Chenevottes, Les Morgeots; Chassagne-Montrachet *premier cru rouge* in Les Morgeots, Les Caillerets; Puligny-Montrachet *premier cru* Les Pucelles; Saint-Aubin *premier cru blanc* Les Charmois; village Chassagne-Montrachet *rouge et blanc*; village Beaune.

This domaine lies within audible range of the local quarry and is run by Marc Morey's son-in-law Bernard Mollard. Quality used to be merely good, but is now getting better and better. 'Perfume and finesse is what I am looking for,' I was told. Quite so.

MICHEL MOREY-COFFINET

7.8 ha: owned and *en fermage*. Chassagne-Montrachet *premier cru blanc* in La Romanée, Les Caillerets, En Remilly; Chassagne-Montrachet *premier cru rouge* Les Morgeots; village Chassagne-Montrachet *rouge et blanc*.

Much of this domaine comes from Fernand Coffinet, Michel Morey's father-in-law; the rest from the domaine above, Michel being the son of Marc. Another good Chassagne source.

*MICHEL NIELLON

5 ha: owned. Chevalier Montrachet (22 a); Bâtard-Montrachet (12 a); Chassagne-Montrachet *premier cru blanc* in Clos-Saint-Jean, Le Champ-Gain, La Maltroie, Les Vergers; Chassagne-Montrachet *premier cru rouge* in La Maltroie, Clos-Saint-Jean; village Chassagne Montrachet (*rouge et blanc*).

Michel Niellon's cellars are almost as small as his domaine. He has two, one underneath his house, the other next to it, and both are exceedingly cramped. He believes in old vines and low *rendements*. Small is beautiful in this case. At the time of writing the Champ-Gain is young vines.

FERNAND ET LAURENT PILLOT

13.5 ha: owned and *en fermage*. Chassagne-Montrachet *premier cru blanc* in Les Vergers, Les Morgeots, Les Grandes-Ruchottes, Vide-Bourse; Chassagne-Montrachet *premier cru rouge tout court* (Les Morgeots and Le Champ-Gain) and Clos-Saint-Jean; Pommard *premier cru* in Les Rugiens, Clos-des-Vergers, Les Charmots, La Refène; Beaune *premier cru* Les Boucherottes; Volnay *premier cru tout court*; Saint-Aubin *premier cru rouge tout court*; village Santenay; village Puligny-Montrachet; village Pommard; village Volnay.

Since 1993 this domaine has boasted a total of twenty-two appellations (including generics). Laurent Pillot, son of Fernand, is married to a niece of Pommard's Virgile Pothier-Rieusset, and she has brought her family's vineyards with her, Virgile Pothier's exploitation suffering as a result. Good wines here. As with the domaine below the arrival of a new generation has had a positive effect.

*JEAN ET JEAN-MARC PILLOT

10 ha: owned and *en fermage/métayage*. Chassagne-Montrachet *premier cru blanc* in Les Caillerets, Les Morgeots, Le Champ-Gain, Les Vergers, Les Chenevottes, Les Macherelles; Chassagne-Montrachet *premier cru rouge* in Les Macherelles, Les Morgeots; village Chassagne-Montrachet *rouge et blanc*; village Santenay (*rouge*); village Puligny-Montrachet.

Jean-Marc Pillot, a trained oenologist, has taken over responsibilities here from his father Jean, and at the same time the domaine has relocated to a new, spacious cellar down on the flat land nearer to Chagny. Real progress has been made here. Very good wines now.

PAUL PILLOT

12 ha: owned and *en fermage*. Chassagne-Montrachet *premier cru blanc* in La Romanée, Les Morgeots, Les Caillerets, Les Grandes-Ruchottes, Le Champ-Gain, Clos-Saint-Jean; Chassagne-Montrachet *premier cru rouge* Clos-Saint-Jean; Saint-Aubin *premier cru blanc* Les Charmois; village Chassagne-Montrachet *rouge et blanc*.

Despite enlarging his cellar in 1993, Paul Pillot is still cramped for space, and the white wines are kept in his father's cellar a couple of hundred metres away. The best of these are very good. From 1994 the Morgeots, which belongs to his sister who is married to a Coffinet, became the responsibility of Michel Morey.

**RAMONET

17 ha: owned. Le Montrachet (25 a); Bâtard-Montrachet (70 a); Bienvenues-Bâtard-Montrachet (33 a); Chassagne-Montrachet *premier cru blanc* in Les Grandes-Ruchottes, Les Caillerets, Les Vergers, Les Chaumées, La Boudriotte, Les Morgeots; Chassagne-Montrachet *premier cru rouge* in Clos-de-la-Boudriotte, Les Morgeots, La Boudriotte, Clos-Saint-Jean; Puligny-Montrachet *premier cru* Les Champs-Canet; Saint-Aubin *premier cru blanc* Les Charmois; village Chassagne-Montrachet *rouge et blanc*; village Puligny-Montrachet (from 1998).

Noël and Jean-Claude Ramonet took over from their much revered grandfather, Pierre

('*Père*'), the creator of this marvellous estate, in 1984. Nothing much has changed, except that today everything is bottled on the spot (previously some buyers employed a local contract bottler).

The beauty of the Ramonet wines is that they are totally individual: more Ramonet than Chassagne. The work is done by instinct, not by the book. And neither Ramonet has had any technical training. Risks are taken, and they do not always come off. But when they (usually) do, they are brilliant. These are not wines for the faint-hearted.

See Profile, page 585.

SAINT-AUBIN
AND GAMAY

The N6 main road cuts a grand swathe through what is technically the commune of Chassagne – there are Chassagne vineyards on either side – but what feels like the border between Chassagne and Puligny. Just beyond where the Mont Rachet hill runs round to face the south-west you cross over from the terrain of both these villages into that of Saint-Aubin.

The first village you come to, however, will be that of Gamay. At this point the prevailing aspect of the hills veers round towards the south-east once again. As the N6 thunders off into the Hautes-Côtes you will reach the village of Saint-Aubin.

Up until recently the commune was one of those neglected, out-of-the-way villages of the Côte, producing more red than white, much of which went into the Côte-de-Beaune-Villages' melting pot. It was then discovered as a convenient source of inexpensive white, a sort of halfway house between Puligny and the whites of the Côte Chalonnaise, of a quality nearer to the former but a price nearer to the latter. Growers then turned to Chardonnay, which they planted in addition to what they already had. In the early 1980s there were 120 ha under production, two-thirds of which was red wine. Today there is twice as much, and over half of what is produced is white wine. Prices, sadly, are no longer the bargains that they were. But a good Saint-Aubin *premier cru*, at two-thirds that of village Puligny, can still be a good buy, and it will probably develop sooner.

The soil structure is varied, for we are dealing with two different hills, one on either side of the village of Gamay. The first, the Roche du May, is the continuation of the Mont Rachet slope, an Argovian marl covered by limestone debris and brown clayey limestone mixtures. Above the village of Saint-Aubin rises the Montagne du Ban. Here the limestone is Callovian, or Callovian mixed with the more marly Argovian in the sector of the *premiers crus*.

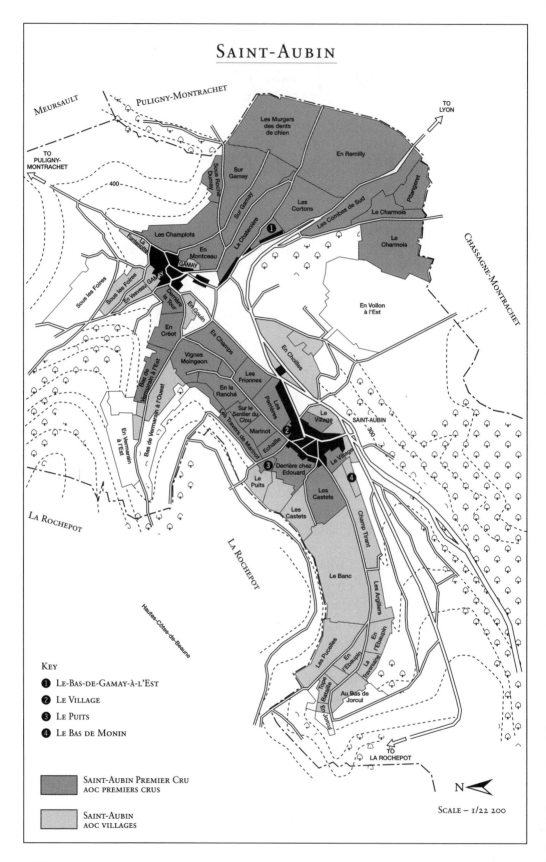

SAINT-AUBIN

MEURSAULT

PULIGNY-MONTRACHET

TO
LYON

TO
PULIGNY-
MONTRACHET

CHASSAGNE-MONTRACHET

400

Les Murgers
des dents
de chien

En Remilly

Sous Roche
Dumay

Sur
Gamay

Sur Gamay

Les
Cortons

Les Combes de Sud

Le Charmois

La Chatenière

Pitangeret

La
Fontenotte

Les Champlots

En
Montceau

Le
Charmois

GAMAY

Sous les Foires

Sous les Foires

En Vesveau GAMAY

Derrière
la Tour

En Goulin

En Vollon
à l'Est

En
Créot

Es Champs

Bas de Vermarain à l'Est

Vignes
Moingeon

En Cholles

Les
Frionnes

En la
Ranché

En Vermarain
à l'Est

Bas de Vermarain à l'Ouest

Sur le
Sentier du
Clou

Les Prefères

Le
Village

SAINT-AUBIN

300

Au Travers de Marinot

Marinot

Echaille

Le Village

Derrière chez
Edouard

Le
Puits

Le Village

Les
Castets

LA ROCHEPOT

Les
Castets

Champ Tirant

LA ROCHEPOT

Hautes-Côtes-de-Beaune

Le Banc

Les Argillers

Les Pucelles

En
l'Ebaupin

En
l'Ebaupin

La
Traversale

Tope Bataille

En Jorcul

Au Bas de
Jorcul

TO
LA ROCHEPOT

Key

❶ Le-Bas-de-Gamay-à-l'Est

❷ Le Village

❸ Le Puits

❹ Le Bas de Monin

Saint-Aubin Premier Cru
AOC PREMIERS CRUS

Saint-Aubin
AOC VILLAGES

N

Scale – 1/22 200

THE VINEYARD

Saint-Aubin is rich – one could argue too rich – in *premiers crus*. The whole of the vineyard between the Puligny border and the village of Gamay is *premier cru*, as is the little bit on the opposite side of the N6 which continues the Chassagne slope. Most of the section between Gamay and Saint-Aubin is also *premier cru*: only when you get beyond the village and the quaintly named vineyard of Derrière-Chez-Edouard (which reminds me irresistibly of the British expression 'It's brighter over Bill's Mum's') is there much village vineyard.

Premiers Crus: There are twenty-nine *premiers crus* in Saint-Aubin, in whole or in part. These are: Les Castets (part); Les Champlots; Le Charmois; La Chatenière; Ez Champs; Les Combes-au-Sud; Les Cortons; En Créot; Echaille; Derrière-Chez-Edouard; Les Frionnes; Le Bas-de-Gamay-à-l'Est; Sur-Gamay; Marinot; En Montceau; Les Murgers-des-Dents-de-Chien; Les Perrières; Les Petangerets; Les Puits (part); En-la-Ranché; En Remilly; Sous-Roche-Dumay; Sur-le-Sentier-du-Clou; Derrière-la-Tour; Les Travers-de-Marinot; Bas-de-Vermarain-à-l'Est (part); Vignes-Moingeon; Le Village (part); En-Vollon-à-l'Est.

The *premiers crus* make up 156.46 ha and produce 1,700 hl (224,400 bottles) of red wine and 2,800 hl (367,000 bottles) of white wine a year.

Village Wine: Village Saint-Aubin covers a mere 80.16 ha (barely half that of *premier cru*) and produces 1,450 hl (191,000 bottles) of red wine, including Côte-de-Beaune-Villages, and 750 hl (99,000) of white wine a year.

Both colours are light, soft, crisp wines which evolve in the medium term. Both can be a bit thin and ungenerous in poorer vintages. With the *vignoble* lying at 260–340 metres we are in more senses than one halfway into the Hautes-Côtes. The ambient temperature is cooler, the fruit needs longer to ripen fully, and therefore more liable to be caught by rain during the harvest.

In general the white wine is of far greater interest than the reds. The reds are no more than light Chassagnes, not usually too rustic, but with a tendency to attenuate. The white wines, especially those from the *climats* nearest to Chassagne and Puligny (La Charmois on the Chassagne side, En Remilly, Les Murgers-des-Dents-de-Chien and La Chatenière on the Puligny side) can have plenty of character and deftness, a sort of crisp raciness which can be most attractive. The *climats* above the village of Saint-Aubin itself – Les Frionnes, Les Perrières – have less definition.

Recommended Sources: See below.

THE GROWERS

JEAN-CLAUDE BACHELET

8 ha: owned and *en fermage*. Bienvenues-Bâtard-Montrachet (9 a); Puligny-Montrachet *premier cru* Sous-le-Puits; Chassagne-Montrachet *premier cru* La Macherelle (*blanc*) and La Boudriotte (*rouge*); Saint-Aubin *premier cru* Les Champlots (*blanc*) and Derrière-la-Tour (*rouge*); village Puligny-Montrachet; village Chassagne-Montrachet *rouge et blanc*.

The fifty-ish Jean-Claude Bachelet lives up in Gamay-le-Haut and claims only distant relationship with other Bachelets in the neighbourhood. He possesses a number of cramped cellars dotted around the village. All the whites are vinified in wood; the reds fermented without the stems. He holds the reds two years before bottling. There is reasonable quality here in both colours but a tendency to a heavy hand with the sulphur.

GILLES BOUTON

12 ha: owned and *en fermage/métayage*. Puligny-Montrachet *premier cru* in La Garenne, Hameau-de-Blagny, Sous-le-Puits; Meursault *premier cru* Blagny (in La Jeunelotte); Saint-

Aubin *premier cru blanc* in Les Murgers-des-Dents-de-Chien, En Remilly, La Chatenière, Les Champlots; Saint-Aubin *premier cru rouge* En Créot, Les Champlots; Blagny *premier cru* Sous-le-Puits; village Chassagne-Montrachet (*rouge et blanc*); village Puligny-Montrachet; village Blagny.

The energetic and *sympa* Giles Bouton took over the estate of his grandfather Aimé Langoureau in 1977 and has since enlarged it to its present size. He makes good wine in both colours, the Murgers-des-Dents-de-Chien and En Remilly being his best Saint-Aubin *blancs*, the Champlots the best *rouge*. But the pick of his cellar is the Meursault, Blagny and the Blagny *premier cru* (*rouge*) Sous-le-Puits.

MARC COLIN

16 ha: owned and *en fermage*. Le Montrachet (11 a); Bâtard-Montrachet (9 a); Chassagne-Montrachet *premier cru blanc* in Les Caillerets, Le Champ-Gain; Puligny-Montrachet *premier cru* La Garenne; Saint-Aubin *premier cru blanc* in En Remilly, La Chatenière, Les Combes, Les Charmois, Les Cortons, En Montceau; Saint-Aubin *premier cru rouge tout court*; village Puligny-Montrachet; village Saint-Aubin *rouge*; village Santenay.

Marc Colin has recently enlarged his cellar, installing a new pneumatic press, and has been joined by his sons Pierre-Yves and Joseph. The Bâtard-Montrachet belongs to his cousin Pierre. Michel Colin of Chassagne is another cousin. Most of the exploitation here, and certainly the more illustrious parcels, is in Chardonnay. A good address.

MICHEL LAMANTHE

7 ha: owned and *en fermage/métayage*. Puligny-Montrachet *premier cru* La Garenne; Chassagne-Montrachet *premier cru blanc* Les Vergers; Blagny *premier cru*; Saint-Aubin *premier cru rouge et blanc tout court*; village Chassagne-Montrachet (*rouge*); village Meursault in the *lieu-dit* Les Ravelles; village Saint-Aubin *rouge*.

Most of this domaine is rented on a share-cropping basis from the Comtesse de Montlivaut, proprietor of the Château de Blagny. Soft, forward wines for early drinking.

HUBERT LAMY-MONNOT

13 ha: owned and *en fermage*. Criots-Bâtard-Montrachet (5 a); Chassagne-Montrachet *premier cru blanc* Les Macherelles; Saint-Aubin *premier cru blanc* in Les Murgers-des-Dents-de-Chien, En Remilly, Clos-de-la-Chatenière; Les Cortons, Les Frionnes; Saint-Aubin *premier cru rouge* Les Castets; village Puligny-Montrachet; village Chassagne-Montrachet (*rouge*); village Saint-Aubin *rouge et blanc*; village Santenay.

Jean, the father of Hubert and René (see Chassagne-Montrachet) Lamy, was one of the first in the village to start domaine-bottling. For a long time this was a reasonably dependable if rarely exciting domaine. But the recent arrival of Olivier, Hubert's son, as wine-maker is edging quality forward. With a modern custom-built cellar on three floors, and plenty of space, there is no reason why this estate shouldn't go places.

LARUE

13 ha: owned and *en fermage*. Puligny-Montrachet *premier cru* in Sous-le-Puits, La Garenne; Chassagne-Montrachet *premier cru rouge* La Boudriotte; Saint-Aubin *premier cru rouge*; Saint-Aubin *premier cru blanc* in Les Murgers-des-Dents-de-Chien; Les Perrières; Blagny *premier cru*; village Puligny-Montrachet; village Chassagne-Montrachet *rouge et blanc*.

Didier and Denis Larue formed a GAEC (a family farming company) to exploit the vineyards they had inherited, in 1985. When I first came across them I felt that lack of space was inhibiting their ability to get the best out of their wines. This has now been resolved, and there has been a significant improvement here in the last couple of vintages.

DANIEL NICVERT ET FILS

13 ha: owned and *en fermage*. Auxey-Duresses *premier cru rouge*; Saint-Aubin *premier cru blanc* in Derrière-Chez-Edouard, Vignes-Moingeon, Travers-de-Marinot; Saint-Aubin *premier cru rouge* Le Village; village Puligny-Montrachet; village Meursault.

My experience of Jean-Marc Nicvert's wines is not very extensive. What I have seen leads me to expect soft, forward whites, somewhat rustic reds.

HENRI PRUDHON ET FILS

12 ha: owned and *en fermage*. Meursault *premier cru* Blagny; Puligny-Montrachet *premier cru* La Garenne; Saint-Aubin *premier cru blanc* in Les Chatenières, Les Murgers-des-Dents-de-Chien; Les Combes; Saint-Aubin *premier cru rouge* Les Frionnes; village Puligny-Montrachet; village Saint-Aubin (*blanc*).

Gérard Prudhon produces soft, attractive, early maturing wines. As elsewhere in the village the whites are more interesting than the reds. They are matured half in tank, half in wood, but the wood is new (20 per cent) or newish.

ROUX PÈRE ET FILS

25 ha: owned and *en fermage*. Saint-Aubin *premier cru blanc* in La Chatenière, Les Pucelles; Meursault *premier cru* Clos-des-Poruzots; Chassagne-Montrachet *premier cru* Les Macherelles; village Puligny-Montrachet in the *lieu-dit* Les Enseignières; Saint-Aubin *premier cru rouge* Les Frionnes; Chassagne-Montrachet *premier cru rouge* Clos-Saint-Jean; village Saint-Aubin (*rouge*); village Chassagne-Montrachet (*rouge*).

Marcel Roux has built up a considerable business since he started with 5 ha in 1960, and he also has a *négociant* licence which triples his turnover. Today he has been joined by his sons Christian and Régis. The set-up is clean and modern, there is plenty of new oak, but the wines fail to inspire me. At the time of writing the Macherelles are young vines.

GÉRARD THOMAS

9.5 ha: owned and *en fermage*. Meursault *premier cru* Blagny; Puligny-Montrachet *premier cru* La Garenne; Saint-Aubin *premier cru blanc* in Les Chatenières, Les Murgers-des-Dents-de-Chien; Les Combes; Saint-Aubin *premier cru rouge* Les Frionnes; village Puligny-Montrachet; village Saint-Aubin *blanc*.

Reliable, inexpensive and quite forward, is how I would describe Gérard Thomas' wines. Once again better in white than in red, but a good source for the former.

SANTENAY

With Santenay we come to the last of the important villages of the Côte d'Or. In fact we come to two, for there is Santenay-le-Haut and Santenay-le-Bas with a kilometre between them. Huddling under the Mont de Sène, Santenay-le-Haut is a largely medieval, straggly hamlet of narrow winding streets and ancient patched-up houses. Santenay-le-Bas, on the shores of the river Dheune and the Canal du Centre which links the Loire with the Saône, is rather grander and more modern. There are several noble mansions plus the renovated fortress originally constructed in the fourteenth century for Philippe le Hardi. In the grounds of this castle are two plane trees, said to be the oldest in France, planted by Henri V in 1599. Above the village is the hamlet and thirteenth-century chapel of Saint-Jean-de-Narosse.

The village dates from Gallo-Roman times when it was known as Santennacum or Santillacum. Archaeologists have excavated traces of a temple dedicated to Mercury at the top of the Mont de Sène. Already by this time it was a spa. The spring water is said to be extremely salty, but beneficial to those suffering from gout and rheumatism.

And because it is a spa, the village has a licence to operate a casino. There is a French law which connects the two. The casino is situated with the thermal complex and was re-opened – having been shut for some years – in 1957. Henri Cannard (*Ballades en Bourgogne*) reports that, at least in 1978, it was number two in France, immediately after Vittel and ahead of Vichy.

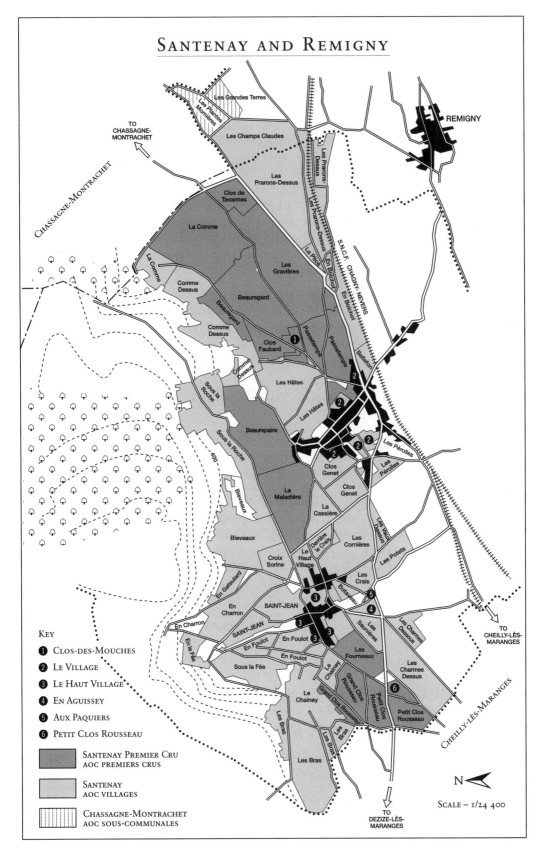

SANTENAY AND REMIGNY

REMIGNY

Les Grandes Terres

Les Plantes Momières

TO
CHASSAGNE-
MONTRACHET

Les Champs Claudes

Les Prarons-Dessus

CHASSAGNE-MONTRACHET

Les Prarons-Dessus

Les Prarons-Dessus

Clos de
Tavannes

La Comme

La Comme

La Pilce

En Boichot

S.N.C.F. CHAGNY- NEVERS

Comme
Dessus

La Comme

Beauregard

Les
Gravières

En Boichot

Beauregard

Comme
Dessus

Beauregard

Clos
Faubard

①

Passetemps

Passetemps

Baileton

Comme
Dessus

Les Hâtes

②

Sous la
Roche

Les Hâtes

②

Beaurepaire

Les Hâtes

Les Pérolles

② ②

400

Clos
Genet

② ②

Les
Pérolles

Bievaux

Clos
Genet

La
Maladière

Clos
Genet

Bievaux

La
Cassière

Les Vaux
Dessus

Derrière
la Crais

Les
Cornières

Croix
Sorine

Le
Haut
Village

Les Potets

En Gatsulard

Boleyeau

Les
Crais

⑤

En Charron

SAINT-JEAN

③

④

En
Charron

Les Champs
Dessus

TO
CHEILLY-LÈS-
MARANGES

SAINT-JEAN

③

Saumières

En Charron

En Foulot

③

③

En la Fée

En Foulot

En Foulot

Les
Fourneaux

Les
Charmes
Dessus

Sous la Fée

Le
Chalney

⑥

CHEILLY-LÈS-MARANGES

Le
Chalney

Grand Clos
Rousseau

Petit Clos
Rousseau

Petit Clos
Rousseau

Les Bras

Grand Clos Rousseau

Les
Bras

Les Bras

Les Bras

KEY
① CLOS-DES-MOUCHES
② LE VILLAGE
③ LE HAUT VILLAGE
④ EN AGUISSEY
⑤ AUX PAQUIERS
⑥ PETIT CLOS ROUSSEAU

SANTENAY PREMIER CRU
AOC PREMIERS CRUS

SANTENAY
AOC VILLAGES

CHASSAGNE-MONTRACHET
AOC SOUS-COMMUNALES

N

SCALE – 1/24 400

TO
DEZIZE-LÈS-
MARANGES

THE VINEYARD

Santenay is an important vineyard. Only Gevrey, Beaune and Meursault produce more wine. The vineyards continue the Côte below Chassagne, the slope gradually shifting its orientation in a gentle S shape until the exposure is more south than east, at which point one comes to the border with Maranges, and, indeed, the end of the Côte d'Or *département*.

In the northern part of the commune the vineyard soil contains gravel over a marly Argovian limestone – hence the name of Les Gravières for one of the best sites. This lies lower down the slope. Above, in La Comme, the soil is shallower but heavier, and there is more clay. Beauregard, which lies next door, is a mixture of the two.

Closer to the village is the *climat* of Passe-Temps, whose soil is gravelly in character but a touch more alluvial. There is then a gap in the *premiers crus*, with the isolated La Maladière and Beaurepaire above Santenay-le-Bas where the soil changes to a Bajocian marl, more commonly found in the Côte-de-Nuits. On the other side of Santenay-le-Haut the soil is richer, heavier and browner in colour, once again based on the hard Bajocian limestone. Here are the *climats* of Grand-Clos-Rousseau and Les Fourneaux.

Premiers Crus: There are fourteen *premiers crus*, in whole or in part. These are as follows: Beauregard; Beaurepaire; Le Chainey (Grand-Clos-Rousseau) (part); Clos-des-Mouches; Clos-des-Tavannes; Clos-Faubard; Grand-Clos-Rousseau; Petit-Clos-Rousseau; La Comme; Comme-Dessus (part); Les Fourneaux; Les Gravières; La Maladière; Les Passe-Temps.

These cover 124.29 ha and produce about 5,400 hl (712,000 bottles) of red wine and 340 hl (45,000 bottles) of white wine a year.

Village Wine: Village Santenay comprises 253.89 ha and yields about 9,400 hl (1.24 million bottles) of red wine and 800 hl (10,500 bottles) of white wine a year.

In general Santenay *rouge* comes in two styles: something akin to Chassagne-Montrachet, but earthier, solider and coarser, from the village *climats* and the southern end of the commune, and something lighter and rather more refined from the *premiers crus* at the north end. But even these 'lighter' wines have plenty of body. They are Beaune-ish rather than Saint-Romain-ish. They are not expensive, and they are becoming increasingly round, fruity and attractive as vinification techniques control the temperature, abandon the stems and forswear excessive *pigeage*.

The whites, too, have improved. They should be crisp, medium-bodied and fruity, less racy but fuller than a Saint-Aubin, perhaps with a touch of spice. They can of course be thin and anonymous, and in some cases heavy and rustic, but these examples, thank God, are getting rarer. There has been a lot of progress in Santenay in recent years, and wine-lovers could do well to pin-point the village as a source of good value in both colours.

THE *PREMIERS CRUS*

CLOS-DES-TAVANNES (5.32 HA)
(can also be sold as Les Gravières)

LA COMME (21.61 HA) • LES GRAVIÈRES (23.85 HA)
BEAUREGARD (17.91 HA) • CLOS-FAUBARD (5.14 HA)
CLOS-DES-MOUCHES (1.57 HA) • LES PASSE-TEMPS (11.47 HA)

This is the better part of the commune. There is a local saying that the best wines of Santenay come from east of the belfry. I would add that the closer you are to the Chassagne border, i.e. the most in danger of being out of earshot, the better the wine. According to Claude Muzard, the Clos-des-Tavannes, the north end of Les Gravières, is the '*grand cru*' of Santenay. This land is propitious for Chardonnay too, if you choose a good spot at the top of the slope. The red wines range from those which are Volnay-ish, in Les Gravières and Clos-des-Tavannes, to those which are more solid, Pommard-ish, in Les Commes. Both styles have rather more definition and finesse than most Chassagne-Montrachet *premier cru rouge*. Beauregard produces wines of medium weight, a sort of cross between the two but with marginally less flair. The wines of Passe-Temps are a little less weighty, and with less definition still.

Recommended Sources:

Clos-des-Tavannes: Pousse-d'Or (Volnay); Jean-Noël Gagnard (Chassagne-Montrachet); Gino Capuano; Lucien Muzard (Santenay).

La Comme: Adrien Belland; Roger Belland; Gino Capuano; René Lequin-Colin; Mestre; Prieur-Brunet (all Santenay).

Les Gravières: Pousse-d'Or (Volnay); Roger Belland; Gino Capuano; Vincent Girardin; Mestre; Lucien Muzard (all Santenay).

Beauregard: Roger Belland (Santenay).

Clos-Faubard: Mestre (Santenay).

Passe-Temps: Roger Belland; Philippe Brenot; Mestre (all Santenay).

BEAUREPAIRE (15.48 HA) • LA MALADIÈRE (13.56 HA)

These two *climats* produce wines which are medium-full, meaty and sturdy in character. There can be a hot pepperiness about them in their youth. There is good richness and depth though, and reasonable style: more so than the wines below, less so than the wines above.

Recommended Sources:

La Maladière: Vincent Girardin; Lucien Muzard; Prieur-Brunet (all Santenay).

GRAND-CLOS-ROUSSEAU (7.67 HA)

PETIT-CLOS-ROUSSEAU OR CLOS-ROUSSEAU (9.84 HA)

LES FOURNEAUX (6.06 HA)
(can also be sold as Clos-Rousseau)

LE CHAINEY (0.06 HA)

These are quite different wines to those produced in Les Gravières and are much closer to Maranges, with which they are contiguous. There is usually a good weight here, and a healthy, open, ever-so-slightly-rustic aspect to the fruit.

Recommended Sources:

Grand-Clos-Rousseau: Bernard Morey (Chassagne-Montrachet); Claude Nouveau (Marchezeuil).

Clos-Rousseau: Roger Belland (Santenay); Fernand Chevrot (Maranges).

THE GROWERS

ADRIEN BELLAND

11 ha: owned and en *fermage*. Chambertin (41 a); Corton, Clos-de-la-Vigne-au-Saint (49 a); Corton, Les Grèves (55 a); Corton, Les Perrières (69 a); Corton-Charlemagne (35 a); Aloxe-Corton *premier cru* Clos-du-Chapitre; Chassagne-Montrachet *premier cru* Les Morgeots; Santenay *premier cru* in Clos-des-Gravières, La Comme; village Aloxe-Corton; village Puligny-Montrachet; village Santenay.

The cramped, damp, mouldy cellars of Adrien Belland and his son Jean-Claude lie on the town's main square, the Place Jet d'Eau. Given the domaine's holdings in Corton and Chambertin it is a pity that the results are unremarkable. Indeed often the only wines worth noting are the Santenays.

ROGER BELLAND

23 ha: owned. Criots-Bâtard-Montrachet (62 a); Puligny-Montrachet *premier cru* Le Champ-Gain; Chassagne-Montrachet *premier cru blanc* Les Chenevottes; Chassagne-Montrachet *premier cru blanc et rouge* Clos-Pitois (*monopole*); Santenay *premier cru* in Les Gravières, La Comme, Clos-Rousseau, Passe-Temps, Clos-du-Beauregard, Beauregard; Maranges *premier cru* in La Fuissière, Clos-Roussots; village Santenay (*blanc et rouge*); Volnay *premier cru* Les Santenots; Meursault *premier cru* Les Santenots; village Pommard.

Roger Belland, son of Joseph, under whose label some of the wines have been bottled until recently, is the nephew of Adrien. The cellar is modern (though there is a more picturesque *caveau de dégustation* under the house); the barrels all reasonably new (30 per cent actually new each year) and the wines individual and stylish. One of the best sources in the village.

PHILIPPE BRENOT

5 ha: owned and *en métayage*. Bâtard-Montrachet (37 a); Chassagne-Montrachet *premier cru blanc* En Remilly; village Puligny-Montrachet in the *lieu-dit* Les Enseignières; village Chassagne-Montrachet *blanc* in the *lieu-dit* L'Ormeau; Chassagne-Montrachet *premier cru rouge*; Santenay *premier cru* Les Passe-Temps; village Santenay in the *lieu-dit* Les Pérolles.

Philippe Brenot is additionally a professor at the Beaune Wine School. He makes particularly good white wines.

JEAN-FRANÇOIS CHAPELLE
DOMAINE DES HAUTES-CORNIÈRES

20 ha: owned. Santenay *premier cru* in Les Gravières, La Comme, Beaurepaire; Chassagne-Montrachet *premier cru* Les Morgeots; village Santenay *rouge et blanc*; village Chassagne-Montrachet *rouge et blanc*; village Aloxe-Corton; village Ladoix; village Meursault.

Jean-François, forty-ish, dark, balding, took over this family domaine on the sudden death of his father in 1991. Geared very largely to its 7,000 odd mailing-list of domestic private clients, the domaine has a good stock of older vintages. My experience is mainly with the reds. They can be good. But they are variable.

LOUIS CLAIR, DOMAINE DE L'ABBAYE-DE-SANTENAY
GINO CAPUANO
(LUCIEN MUZARD ET FILS, see page 306)

14 ha: owned (leased out on a *métayage* basis to Capuano and Muzard). Santenay *premier cru* in Clos-des-Tavannes, Les Gravières, Clos-Faubard, Beauregard, La Maladière; village Pommard; village Chassagne; village Santenay (*rouge et blanc*).

Gino Capuano and the Muzard family (see page 306) are share-croppers for the late Louis Clair (he died in September 1995 aged eighty-nine) and the former uses the splendid cavernous cellars behind the house. The grapes are not destemmed, the *cuvaisons* are long, and the vines old. Quality is high. The Clair share is sold off in bulk (Louis Latour has always been a major customer, I'm told), but Capuano is increasingly selling his wine in bottle and very good the wines are too. An address to watch.

RENÉ FLEUROT-LAROSE
DOMAINE DE PASSE-TEMPS

11 ha: owned. Chassagne-Montrachet *premier cru* in Les Morgeots (*rouge et blanc*), Clos-de-la-Roquemaure (*monopole*) (*blanc*); Santenay *premier cru* Clos-des-Passe-Temps (*monopole*) (*rouge et blanc*).

This was once a great domaine. But slowly but surely the Fleurot family has sold off all its Le Montrachet and Bâtard-Montrachet and now – since April 1994 when the last was acquired by the Château de Puligny-Montrachet – there is nothing left. Impressive if decaying premises, but disappointing wine.

★VINCENT GIRARDIN

14 ha: owned and *en fermage*. Santenay *premier cru* in Les Gravières, La Maladière and Clos-du-Beauregard (*blanc*); Maranges *premier cru* in Le Clos-des-Loyères, Clos-Roussots; Pommard *premier cru* Les Chanlins; Beaune *premier cru* Clos-des-Vignes-Franches; Chassagne-Montrachet *premier cru rouge et blanc* Les Morgeots; village Santenay (*rouge et blanc*) including the *lieu-dit* Clos-de-la-Confrérie; village Pommard in the *lieu-dit* Clos-des-Lambots; village Meursault in the *lieu-dit* Les Narvaux; village Beaune.

Vincent Girardin is a rising star. In 1994 he acquired a new house, new wine-making premises, a very attractive wife, Véronique, more land (the Beaunes and Pommards) and a merchant's licence. This is probably the best domaine in the village today: the wines are very well-balanced and very stylish. The merchant wines are fine too.

CHÂTEAU PHILIPPE LE HARDI

88 ha: owned. Beaune *premier cru* Clos-du-Roi; village Aloxe-Corton; village Saint-Aubin; Mercurey *premier cru*; village Mercurey.

The vast bulk of this multi-national-owned domaine lies in Mercurey and not very good Mercurey at that. They have no land-holdings in Santenay. The red wine ferments in rotating, cylindrical auto-vinificators in, as you would expect, a very modern, almost industrial scale cellar, and the results are competent if unexciting. But the setting, in a path across the moat from the tastefully restored medieval château, is most attractive.

JESSIAUME PÈRE ET FILS

14 ha: owned. Santenay *premier cru* Les Gravières (*rouge et blanc*); Beaune *premier cru* Les Cent-Vignes; Volnay *premier cru* Les Brouillards; Auxey-Duresses *premier cru* Les Ecusseaux (*rouge et blanc*); village Santenay.

Underneath a spacious vinification and barrel cellar is an extensive rabbit-warren of a bottle cellar leading under the courtyard all the way back to the main road. The Jessiaume family have been here since the 1850s and own 5.5 ha in Les Gravières. Sadly the resultant wine could be rather better than it is at present.

LOUIS LEQUIN

7 ha: owned and *en fermage*. Bâtard-Montrachet (12 a); Corton, Les Languettes (9 a); Corton-Charlemagne (9 a); Chassagne-Montrachet *premier cru* Les Morgeots (*rouge et blanc*); Santenay *premier cru blanc* Clos-Rousseau; Santenay *premier cru rouge* Les Passe-Temps; village Santenay; village Pommard; village Nuits-Saint-Georges; village Maranges.

Louis Lequin and his older brother René (see below) jointly ran the domaine of their late father Jean (Lequin-Roussot) until they went their separate ways after the 1992 harvest. Louis remains at the old Lequin-Roussot premises near the level crossing. Lequin-Roussot wines were reliable if never very startling in the past. The Corton-Charlemagne is currently very young vines.

RENÉ LEQUIN-COLIN

8.16 ha: owned and *en fermage*. Bâtard-Montrachet (12 a); Corton, Les Languettes (9 a); Corton-Charlemagne (9 a); Chassagne-Montrachet *premier cru* Les Morgeots (*rouge*); Chassagne-Montrachet *premier cru* (from Les Vergers, Les Morgeots, Les Caillerets) (*blanc*);

Santenay *premier cru* in La Comme, Les Passe-Temps; village Nuits-Saint-Georges; village Pommard; village Chassagne-Montrachet (*rouge et blanc*); village Santenay (*rouge et blanc*).

René Lequin is now in new premises off the road up to Santenay-le-Haut. With no micro-fauna and flora in the cellar he found his malos late to take place in 1993. I have a hunch that he is going to be the better of the two sources in the years to come.

MESTRE PÈRE ET FILS

19.5 ha: owned. Corton (from Les Languettes) (37 a); Santenay *premier cru* in La Comme, Les Gravières, Clos-Faubard, Les Passe-Temps (all *rouge*) and Les Passe-Temps, Beaurepaire (*blanc*); Chassagne-Montrachet *premier cru rouge* Les Morgeots; Chassagne-Montrachet *premier cru blanc* in Tonton-Marcel (*monopole*); village Santenay (*rouge et blanc*); village Chassagne-Montrachet; village Ladoix (*rouge et blanc*); village Aloxe-Corton; village Maranges.

The extended Mestre family run this domaine, one of George Mestre's sons having left to take over at Michelot's in Meursault, and are a reliable source of wines which evolve in the medium term. You'll find them on the main square, the Place Jet d'Eau.

LUCIEN MUZARD ET FILS

21 ha: owned and *en fermage/métayage*. Santenay *premier cru* in Clos-des-Tavannes, La Maladière (under the label of Claude Muzard), Les Gravières, Clos-Faubard, Beauregard; village Santenay in the *lieux-dits* Clos-des-Hâtes and Champs-Claude (*rouge et blanc*); village Chassagne-Montrachet; village Pommard in the *lieu-dit* Les Cras; village Maranges; Côte-de-Beaune-Villages.

This domaine, now run by the brothers Claude and Hervé Muzard, is, in part, a share-cropper for the late Louis Clair's Domaine de l'Abbaye-de-Santenay (see page 000). The red grapes are not destemmed, allowed to macerate *à froid* for as much as a week, and vinified at a maximum of 32°C. Then there is up to 30 per cent new wood. All the white wines, even the Aligoté, is fermented in barrel. Since 1994 the domaine does not filter. Quality has improved considerably here in recent years. One of the stars of the village now.

LOUIS NIÉ, DOMAINE DE CLOS-BELLEFOND

8.5 ha: owned. Pommard *premier cru* La Platière; Volnay *premier cru* Les Santenots; Chassagne-Montrachet *premier cru* in Les Morgeots; Santenay *premier cru* Les Passe-Temps; village Santenay in the *lieux-dits* Clos-Genet, Clos-Bellefond (*monopole*).

The headquarters of this estate lie above its monopoly on the edge of the village: a fine château in a park with some impressive mature trees. Sadly the wine does not live up to its setting.

GUY PRIEUR, DOMAINE PRIEUR-BRUNET

20 ha: owned. Bâtard-Montrachet (8 a); Meursault *premier cru* Les Charmes; Chassagne-Montrachet *premier cru blanc* Les Embazées; Chassagne-Montrachet *premier cru rouge* Les Morgeots; Santenay *premier cru rouge* in La Maladière, La Comme; Santenay *premier cru blanc* Clos-Rousseau; Beaune *premier cru* Clos-du-Roi; Pommard *premier cru* La Platière; Volnay *premier cru* Les Santenots; village Meursault including the *lieux-dits* Les Chevalières, Les Forges; village Santenay including the *lieux-dits* En Boichot (*blanc*), Foulot (*rouge*).

This well-established domaine can trace its history back to 1804 when a pair of brothers from Change cashed in on the post-Revolutionary spoils of the Château Perruchot in Santenay. A more recent event was the marriage between Guy Prieur and Elizabeth Brunet of Meursault. Today the business is run by Dominique Prieur and his wife Claude Uny-Prieur. This is a good source.

PROSPER MAUFOUX

This *négociant* business dates from 1860 and occupies large premises which dominate the west side of the Place Jet d'Eau. I find their wines clean but unexciting: harmless but lifeless. A *sous-marque* is Michel Amance.

MARANGES

Maranges is where the 'Golden Slope' comes to its end. Beyond Santenay the hills curve round to face due south, and, shared between three villages, Cheilly, Dezize and Sampigny, combined in 1989 to form a single appellation, we have the *vignoble* of Maranges. Administratively we have crossed the border into the Saône-et-Loire *département* – which makes life complicated for the writer as wine-production details are not included in the Côte d'Or statistics – but this is nevertheless still part of the heart of Burgundy. The Côte Chalonnaise hills are a separate series of outcrops to the south-east.

Prior to the Maranges decree, this was not so much forgotten country as a part of Burgundy which was completely unknown. Most of the wine was red and went into Côte-de-Beaune-Villages blends. Since then people have started to visit the Maranges, and for good reason. There is good wine-making here, interesting wines and good value. It is also attractive country.

Dezize/Cheilly/Sampigny-lès-Maranges

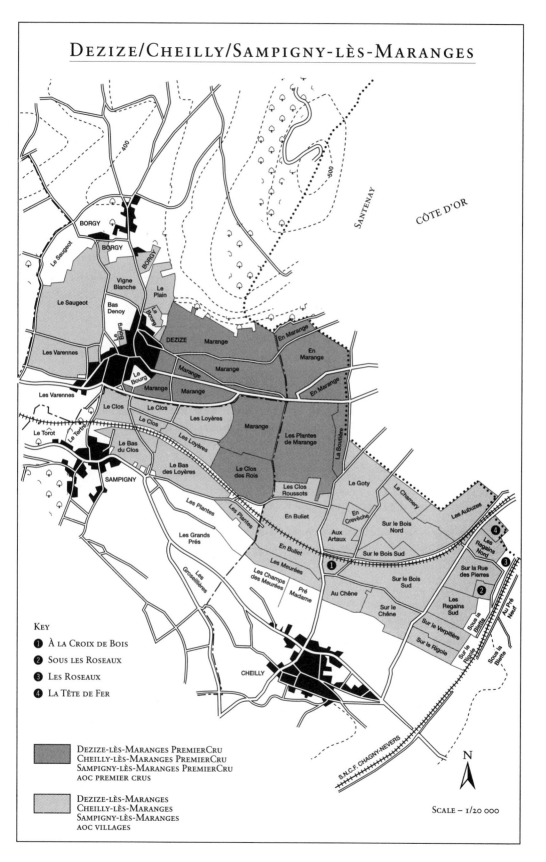

CÔTE D'OR

SANTENAY

BORGY

BORGY

Le Saugeot

Vigne
Blanche

Le
Plain

Le Saugeot

Bas
Denoy

Les Varennes

Le Bourg

DEZIZE

Marange

En Marange

En
Marange

Marange

Marange

Le Bourg

Marange

Marange

Marange

Les Varennes

Le Clos

Le Clos

Le Clos

Les Loyères

En Marange

Le Torot

Le Tertre

Le Clos

Les Loyères

Marange

Les Plantes
de Marange

La Boutière

Le Bas
du Clos

Le Bas
des Loyères

Le Clos
des Rois

Les Clos
Roussots

Le Goty

Le Chamery

SAMPIGNY

Les Plantes

Les Plantes

En Bullet

En
Crevèche

Sur le Bois
Nord

Les Aubuzes

Les Grands
Prés

Aux
Artaux

Sur le Bois Sud

Les
Regains
Nord

Sur la Rue
des Pierres

Les
Groseillières

En Bullet

Les Meurées

Les Champs
des Meurées

Pré
Madame

Sur le Bois
Sud

Les
Regains
Sud

Au Chêne

Sur le
Chêne

Sur le Verpillère

Sous la
Blette

Au Pré
Neuf

Sur le Rigole

Sur le
Rigole

Sous la
Blette

CHEILLY

S.N.C.F. CHAGNY-NEVERS

Key

❶ À la Croix de Bois

❷ Sous les Roseaux

❸ Les Roseaux

❹ La Tête de Fer

Dezize-lès-Maranges Premier Cru
Cheilly-lès-Maranges Premier Cru
Sampigny-lès-Maranges Premier Cru
AOC PREMIER CRUS

Dezize-lès-Maranges
Cheilly-lès-Maranges
Sampigny-lès-Maranges
AOC VILLAGES

N

SCALE – 1/20 000

THE VINEYARD

A gentle slope, rising up from 240 to about 360 metres, before you come to the trees, dominates the country to the south, and indeed the village of Cheilly, which lies on the lower land. In one block, shared between the three communes, is the *premier cru* land, towards the top of the slope. The soil is varied, a stony, brown limestone, getting heavier, more clayey and less stony as one journeys down-slope. The wine is almost entirely red; honest, sturdy and rustic in the best sense, useful for blending with the thinner reds of the lesser villages of the Côte-de-Beaune, but well worth examining in its own right. It has good acidity and it keeps well.

Premiers Crus: There are six *premiers crus*:
In Cheilly: En Marange; La Boutière; Les Plantes-en-Marange
In Dezize: Les Maranges (part); La Fuissière
In Sampigny: Le Clos-des-Rois; Les Maranges (part)

Together these comprise 75.34 ha and produce 2,700 hl (356,000 bottles) of red wine a year. Village Maranges occupies 151.13 ha and produces some 5,400 hl (713,000 bottles) of red wine and 150 hl (19,800 bottles) of white wine a year.

Recommended Sources: See below.

THE GROWERS

BERNARD BACHELET ET SES FILS

37.5 ha: owned and *en fermage*. Chassagne-Montrachet *premier cru* Les Morgeots (*rouge et blanc*); Meursault *premier cru* Les Charmes; Pommard *premier cru* Les Chanlins; Maranges *premier cru* La Fuissière; Santenay *premier cru* Clos-des-Mouches; Saint-Aubin *premier cru rouge*; village Puligny-Montrachet; village Meursault in the *lieu-dit* Les Narvaux; village Chassagne-Montrachet (*rouge et blanc*); village Santenay; village Gevrey-Chambertin; village Maranges including the *lieu-dit* Clos-Roussots.

Vincent, François and Jean-Louis, thirty-something sons of Bernard Bachelet, run this large domaine from the family headquarters in Dezize, but vinification takes place in Chassagne-Montrachet. I have found the standard good and reliable here in both colours.

MAURICE CHARLEUX

10 ha: owned and *en fermage*. Maranges *premier cru* in Le-Clos-des-Rois, La Fuissière; Santenay *premier cru* Clos-Rousseau; village Maranges *rouge et blanc*; village Santenay *rouge et blanc*.

Maurice Charleux's cellar is also in Dezize. He took over from his parents in 1970, having worked in the vineyards since he was fourteen. His style is for a typically sturdy Maranges, vinified with regular *pigeages* for twelve days, but they are neither too dense nor unduly rustic. The Clos-des-Rois is better than the Fuissière.

FERNAND CHEVROT

11 ha: owned and *en fermage*. Santenay *premier cru* Clos-Rousseau; village Maranges (*rouge et blanc*).

Fernand Chevrot took on responsibility for the family domaine on his father's early death in 1967. Now in his late forties, he is one of the few to make a speciality of the Maranges *blanc*. Good wine here. The winery is situated under a splendid mansion down in the flat lands of Cheilly.

YVON ET CHANTAL CONTAT-GRANGE

6 ha: *en fermage*. Maranges *premier cru* La Fuissière; village Maranges (*rouge et blanc*); village Santenay *rouge et blanc* including the *lieu-dit* Saint-Jean-de-Narosse.

Neither Yvon Contat nor Chantal Grange are Burgundians. They arrived from the Haute-Savoie in 1981 and have gradually built up this estate, entirely *en fermage*. A good source.

EDMUND MONNOT

10 ha: owned and *en fermage*. Village Maranges in the *lieux-dits* Clos-de-la-Boutenière (*monopole*) and Clos-des-Loyères; village Santenay *rouge* in the *lieu-dit* Les Charmes-Dessus; village Santenay *blanc* in the *lieu-dit* La Chainey.

From Edmond Monnot's terrace in Dézize there is a splendid panorama down the slopes of the Maranges vineyards to the south (from the Chevrots there is an equally impressive view in the opposite direction). Monnot's wines are perhaps the most elegant of the domaines in the area.

CLAUDE NOUVEAU

14.25 ha: owned and *en fermage*. Santenay *premier cru* Grand-Clos-Rousseau; Maranges *premier cru* La Fuissière; village Santenay including the *lieu-dit* Les Charmes-Dessus; village Santenay *blanc*; village Maranges.

Claude Nouveau's modern winery is in Marchezeuil, towards Nolay, but I include him here for convenience, rather than in the Hautes-Côtes section, as his vineyard holding is essentially similar to those listed above. The reds have good fruit and substance without being rustic; the whites are crisp and elegant. Good things here.

OUTSIDE THE CÔTE D'OR

Not everyone who is important in the Côte d'Or actually lives along the Côte. The following must be noted:

★DOMAINE MICHEL JUILLOT, MERCUREY

As well as the 30 ha this domaine owns in Mercurey – from which it makes excellent wine – the estate owns 1.20 ha of Corton, Les Perrières and 80 a of Corton-Charlemagne. Both are glitteringly clean, succulent examples; a reproach on much that is made in Pernand, Aloxe and Ladoix.

★MAISON ANTONIN RODET, MERCUREY

Under the aegis of Bertrand Devillard, this *négociant*, now partly owned by Champagne Laurent-Perrier, has made great strides. As well as owning two substantial estates in the Côte Chalonnaise, the Château de Chamirey and the Château de Rully, Rodet has had a half-share since 1988 in the Domaine Jacques Prieur in Meursault (see page 250). Devillard and his chief *oenologue* Mme Nadine Gublin make a fine team, and their merchant Côte d'Or wines are very good.

DOMAINE BARON THÉNARD, GIVRY

As well as 17.17 ha of Givry, this domaine has holdings in Le Montrachet (1.83 ha); Grands-Echézeaux (54 a); Corton Clos-du-Roi (90 a); Pernand-Vergelesses *premier cru* Ile-des-Vergelesses; and Chasssagne-Montrachet *premier cru* Clos-Saint-Jean.

The domaine works very closely with Maison Roland Remoissenet Père et Fils allowing them first choice of what they produce for delivery up to Beaune and eventual bottling under the Remoissenet label (see page 211). I have had Givrys bottled by Thénard, but never any Côte d'Or wines.

★MAISON VERGET, SARL, SOLOGNY

Jean-Marie Guffens, owner with his wife of the 3 ha Guffens-Heynen domaine in the Pouilly-Fuissé area, formed a *négociant* company in 1991. He is an impassioned, opinionated, excitable individual, and a good self-publicist. The business – it only deals in white wine – rapidly made a name for itself. Guffens has made the mistake of being somewhat indiscreet about his sources – or perhaps some journalists have been too foolish not to realise that this sort of information is off the record – and as a result some doors have been shut to him. But he has found alternatives. The wines are very good.

PART TWO

THE DOMAINE
PROFILES

THE DOMAINE
PROFILES

WITH SOME TREPIDATION I BEGAN TO APPROACH SOME OF THE TOP DOMAINES IN BURGUNDY A FEW YEARS AGO. I WOULD LIKE TO WRITE A PROFILE ON YOUR PROPERTY, I WROTE. COULD I MAKE A VERTICAL TASTING OF ONE OF YOUR TOP WINES? STOCKS, I KNEW, WERE LIMITED, UNOBTAINABLE ON THE OPEN MARKET IN THE RANGE I WANTED. SO THE ONLY PLACE TO MAKE THE TASTINGS, IN ORDER TO HAVE THE OPPORTUNITY OF COMPARING A SERIES OF MATURE WINES ONE WITH ANOTHER, WAS AT THE DOMAINES THEMSELVES.

It is in the tasting of mature wines that one may have a glimmer as to how today's immature vintages are going to progress, notwithstanding changes in viticultural and vinification techniques in the interim. The *terroir* does not change, nor does the personality of the wine-maker. Moreover, in the analysis of a complete range of the estate's wines, in the visit to the vines beforehand, and the discussion of the property's history and its wine-making afterwards, one is permitted access to a better appreciation of the domaine as a whole.

The response was better than I could have dreamt possible. Doors were opened. Cellars were raided. Wines dating back to the war and even earlier were produced. The generosity was overwhelming. My knowledge of Burgundy was immeasurably enriched. I welcome this opportunity publicly to thank the proprietors involved and their families.

The sixty-one properties which follow do not, however, represent exclusively my choice of the best. There are other domaines which should be included, but which for lack of stock of old wines, lack of a history of great wine-making that goes back sufficiently far into the past, or simply a lack of time and opportunity, are not here. But this, if not all the *crème*, is a very fine *crème de la crème* of nearly all that is finest in the Côte d'Or.

ROBERT AMPEAU ET FILS, *MEURSAULT*

I shall not forget the first time I visited the Ampeau domaine. It was in the spring of 1986, just about when old man Robert was handing over the reins to his son Michel. I had heard of Ampeau, of course, and I had some notion of his wines. But I had not visited him before because he didn't offer his wines *en primeur*, preferring to hold them back until he considered them ready for drinking.

So there I was, accompanied by my Falstaffian friend Bill Baker, towards the end of a day's sampling of young 1985s, ready for something a bit older.

The reception was typical. Here was a French *vigneron* determined to live up to the archetype: surly, suspicious, chauvinistic, doing his best to make us feel uncomfortable, to make us realise we were wasting his valuable time.

Hardly muttering a word, he led us down to a cellar stuffed to the rims with metal cages holding anonymous bottles. Seemingly at random Ampeau reached out for one, uncorked it, and sloshed a mouthful or two into our proffered glasses.

We looked at each other. There was a moment's silence. Battle had begun. At times like these, I find, it is best to rely on instinct. But instinct tempered with a little knowledge, a little imagination. Imagination suggested to me that *la politique* of Domaine Ampeau, only selling wines after five, seven, nine or whatever years, would result, in 1986, in a backlog of wines of the not-very-good vintages of the 1970s. Imagination also forcibly hinted that this first wine would be one of these off-vintages, but one that Ampeau was proud of. After all we were being challenged. He would expect us to find the wine very good, and then be amazed to hear that it wasn't 1978 or 1979, but 1977 or 1974. Knowledge reminded me what vineyards Ampeau possessed. After a pause for reflection I said 'Perrières 1977'. And I made it a statement, not a question. Lady Luck was with me. A hole in one.

Of course it would be satisfying to be able to report that at this juncture the entire atmosphere changed, collapse of stout party, *tapis rouge* for that great expert Monsieur Coates, etc., etc. Sadly, equally of course, this was not the case at all. Ampeau's attitude hardly budged a centimetre. But after a few other wines, which Bill and I also got pretty well right, he did begin to warm up. In the end we stayed tasting for about two hours - there being a big gap in the middle while he went off to collect some more bottles stored in a second cellar somewhere else in Meursault, during which we began to feel we had been abandoned. We continued to guess fairly accurately, as Ampeau stood by, poker-faced, determined to demonstrate that he at least could produce very good wine even in the worst of vintages. And he even allowed us to sample two Meursault 1979s, one machine harvested, one hand picked - quite different, the manually collected example much the better.

In the end I felt we had acquitted ourselves well; had shown, if that was the object of the exercise, that the British wine trade was *not* a bunch of total incompetents. And he had made it very clear that the Domaine Ampeau, both in red (60 per cent of his production) and in white, was a thoroughly reliable source. My friend Baker, who needs mature wine to sell to all the best restaurants in Britain - and sadly there are few others who can supply it - had found a more-than-useful source of good Burgundy. And I had made a new and classy contact among the many dozen small domaines in Meursault. I have been going back regularly ever since. And I haven't changed my initial impression. This is a very fine estate.

HISTORY

This is not a venerable domaine, steeped in history, handed down from father to son over the generations. It began with Robert Ampeau's father, Michel, who acquired some Perrières, some Charmes and some Volnay, Santenots in the early years of this century. His son took over in the 1940s, having married a Mademoiselle Robey who brought with her some vineyards in Beaune and in Savigny. In the 1950s he enlarged the land-holding by buying some Puligny-Montrachet, Les Combettes, more Volnay, Santenots and vines in Pommard and Auxey-Duresses. The final addition came in 1973 with 1.60 ha of Blagny and Meursault, La Pièce-sous-le-Bois. In total this adds up to just less than 10 hectares.

WINE-MAKING

The Ampeaus - and it is now Michel, Robert's son, an entirely different character, much less the traditional peasant, rather more relaxed, with a splendid sense of humour - are making *vins de garde*. In order to do this two elements are vital: concentration and high acidities.

Michel is a great believer in clonal selection. But it has to be the right clone, suitable not only for the particular location - soil, micro-climate - but one which marries well with the rootstock. And there has to be a variety of different clones within the same vineyard to maximise the complexity of the wine you will get out of it.

The next thing is to control the vigour of the vines, in order to keep the yields down. Michel Ampeau is much respected in the village, by others such as Dominique Lafon, for example, for the immaculate condition of his vines. They are pruned hard, excess buds are removed during the spring, excess foliage later, and a special ray-grass planted in July between the rows (it is ploughed in December) to combat erosion, to protect the soil compacting too much, and to act as an inhibitor to the lateral growth of the roots, forcing them to reach deep and bring up all the individuality and complexity of each *climat*.

In the cellar things start off, at least, traditionally. There is a pneumatic press, and the white wines are vinified in cask - 10-25 per cent new oak - with plenty of *bâtonnage*. The red grapes are mostly destemmed. Natural yeasts are used. Fermentation temperatures are held to a maximum of 30°C. Chaptalisation is carried out right at the end, to prolong the wine-making process. The whole thing is meticulously controlled.

Where the Ampeau domaine differs from most is in the length of its *élevage*. Both the reds and the whites remain in cask a mere nine months, being bottled after fining and a light filtration in August or September of the following year. The object is to preserve all the freshness, to ensure a long life in bottle. Wine develops considerably faster in cask, Michel will explain. They bottle early so that this ageing process will be slower.

THE WINES

In their youth, I would imagine - but you never see them in their youth - the Ampeau wines are rather lean and austere. The opulence comes with the maturity. As they round off they get fatter. Above all they invariably have excellent acidities, and this preserves the fruit and the elegance, revealing even in lesser vintages (1980 for white for instance) a surprising succulence and depth of interest. The wines *do* last exceptionally well.

Ampeau can offer red wines from Pommard, Auxey-Duresses, Savigny and Beaune, Clos-du-Roi. But the two best are the Blagny, La Pièce-sous-le-Bois and the Volnay, Santenots. The Volnay is the most classy, as you would expect, but the Blagny - sturdy, ripe and flavourful - is one of the best examples (alongside Matrot's) of this appellation.

There is a little white wine, under the Meursault prefix, from La Pièce-sous-le-Bois, and of course there is village Meursault. But the Ampeaus can offer three better *premiers crus*: Meursault, Les Charmes, Meursault, Les Perrières and Puligny-Montrachet, Les Combettes.

These are individual wines, well structured, concentrated and with very good grip. The Perrières is the one I know best. And this is my favourite.

What is currently on offer? At the time of my last visit to Ampeau in February 1995 he was offering various vintages of the early 1980s in white, but had not yet put the 1985 or anything later on the market. He had just begun to sell the 1987 reds, but not yet the 1986s nor the 1983s.

THE TASTING

I sampled most of the Meursault, Perrières and the Blagnys *chez* Ampeau in February 1995. Notes on the rest come from an Ampeau tasting I presided over for the North New Jersey Chapter of Wine Lovers International in October 1994.

WHITE WINES

Optimum drinking

Meursault, Perrières, 1984   Now–2004
This is surprisingly good. Fresh and rich and oaky and intense. Just a little lean on the nose. But real class and depth here. Very clean. Long. Vigorous. Will age well. Very good plus.

Meursault, Perrières, 1983   Now–2000
This is spicy and almost sweet on the finish. A definite touch of botrytis. Round and full. Good grip though. But I prefer the 1982. This is muscular, and slightly four-square.

Meursault, Charmes, 1982   Now–2000 plus
Very youthful colour. Full opulent nose. Quite a heavy wine indeed. Some alcohol is showing. Full, ripe and voluptuous. Plenty of fruit. Rich and fat. Surprisingly youthful. Very good.

Meursault, Perrières, 1982   Now–2004
Round, *à point*, concentrated, spicy and rich. This is a clean but opulent example. Good acidity. Quite full, ripe, balanced and still with very good grip. Lovely and generous. Very good indeed.

Meursault, Perrières, 1981   Drink soon
This is very good for a 1981, but has less to it than the 1980. Ripe, slightly suave. Slightly less vigour. But a little one-dimensional.

Meursault, Perrières, 1980   Now–2000 plus
Ripe, full, very fresh indeed. Remarkable for its age and vintage. This is soft but vigorous, and very, very good. It has got all the mineral quality of the *climat*, is fully mature, but round and ripe and not a bit old. *À point*. Very good.

Meursault, La Pièce-sous-le-Bois, 1979   Drink soon
Very youthful colour. Interesting quite youthful nose. This is fully mature. Medium body. Fruity and elegant but quite delicate. Lime and sherbet

flavours. Good acidity. An intriguing individual wine. Very good. Drink quite soon.

Meursault, Perrières, 1979   Now–2000 plus
Very youthful colour. Vigorous, harmonious, classy nose. No sign of age. Fullish, rich, *crème brûlée* elements. Yet very fresh and balanced. Very together. Very intense and complex ripe fruit at the end. Fine.

Puligny-Montrachet, Combettes, 1979   Now–1999
This comes as a bit of a shock after a series of Perrières. Round and supple, without the mineral edge. But some of this is the vintage, no doubt. Lovely elegant soft fruit. Still fresh. Very laid-back and poised. Very good length. Not a trace of blowsiness. Fine long finish. Fine quality.

Meursault, Perrières, 1978   Now–2000 plus
Just a touch lean and vegetal on the nose. But profound and stylish. And indeed quite powerful on the palate. Rich, still youthful. But well matured nevertheless. Good acidity. Was always a touch austere, I would judge. And I wonder if it isn't going to get a bit hard on the finish. But lots of quality here.

Meursault, Perrières, 1977   Drink soon
Interesting, well-matured but decidedly vegetal nose. It is getting a little tired now on the palate, especially at the end. But there is no lack of fruit or interest. Not too lean, nor hard. But beginning to lose its finesse.

RED WINES

Blagny, La Pièce-sous-le-Bois, 1987   Now–2000 plus
This has a very strong herbal taste of thyme and bay leaf. It is almost a vinous *bouquet garni*. Medium weight. Not a lot of fat. Indeed it is a little too lean and austere. Good acidity but not much charm.

Blagny, La Pièce-sous-le-Bois, 1985   Now-2008

Good colour. Rich and sturdy. Ripe and
flavourful. Plenty of wine here. Fullish, but not
too dense. Spicy and complex and freshly
balanced. This is just about *à point*. Very good.
Bags of life.

Beaune, Clos-du-Roi, 1985   Now-2000 plus

Medium colour. Still quite youthful. Quite
sturdy and earthy nose. Spice and caramel here.
This, in contrast to the whites, is fully mature.
Not particularly youthful for a 1985. Medium
body. A little one-dimensional. Clean, quite
classy. But only 'good'.

Volnay, Santenots, 1985   Now-2005

Medium to medium-full colour. Still quite
youthful. Ripe, sweet. Slightly boiled-sweet
raspberry-cherry fruit. Very Volnay. This is less
evolved than the Beaune, Clos-du-Roi. Good
grip. Stylish. Vigorous. Medium to medium-
full. Very clean. Complex. Lovely. Very good
indeed.

Blagny, La Pièce-sous-le-Bois, 1984   Now-1999

This is surprisingly round and fruity on the
nose. A touch astringent and stemmy but good
succulence, especially for a 1984, and good
vigour and elegance too. Positive at the end.
Will still keep well.

Blagny, La Pièce-sous-le-Bois, 1982
                                            Now-2000 plus

Good colour. A little rustic in a reductive sense
on the nose. Rich, ripe and meaty on the palate.
Good concentration. Good vigour. Fullish.
Attractive if not altogether very stylish.

Blagny, La Pièce-sous-le-Bois, 1979   Now-2000

Good colour. Just a little astringent on the nose.
But better on the palate. Soft. Not exactly very
stylish, but ripe, sweet even, and balanced.
Good positive finish. Good.

Blagny, La Pièce-sous-le-Bois, 1978   Now-2004

This is much more interesting than the 1979.
Fullish, rich, ample, succulent. Quite a sturdy
nose. But warm and generous, and meaty and
rustic (in the best sense) on the palate. Good grip.
Plenty of vigour. Plenty of depth. Very good.

Volnay, Santenots, 1978   Now-2010

Very good vigorous colour. Complex, lovely
nose. Splendid complexity of ripe fruit. Cassis
but also a cooked fruit element. This is lovely.
Deliciously balanced ripe fruit. Quite austere.
Fullish in substance. Better than the 1976. Very
classy and complex at the end. Good intensity.
Only just ready. Fine.

Blagny, La Pièce-sous-le-Bois, 1976   Now-2000

Fine colour. Lovely rich tannic nose: the best of
1976. Bitter chocolate and black cherry. Full,
earthy. Again artisanal in a good sense. Sturdy
and spicy but nothing lumpy here. Good grip.
Very rich. Very good.

Pommard, 1976   Now-2000

Full colour. Now mature. Some evolution on
the nose. Ripe but cooked and a bit dry. Structured on the palate. A little dense and astringent.
Good acidity. But a little burly and unbalanced.
Lacks a bit of class and definition. Quite good.

Volnay, Santenots, 1976   Now-2005

Full vigorous colour. Rich, full, spicy, aromatic
nose. Burlier than the 1978. Not as much
finesse. Full, fat, round. Burnt cooked fruit. The
structure shows a bit. More power than the
1978. Less finesse. Very good.

MARQUIS D'ANGERVILLE, *VOLNAY*

Jacques, Marquis d'Angerville, is the doyen of Volnay. The family has been making wines in the village for 190 years, was one of the very first in Burgundy to start domaine-bottling the entire produce of the estate, and has been producing high quality since at least the 1920s. D'Angerville is one of the greatest names in Burgundy, and the wines, despite being true Volnays, are built to last.

HISTORY

It was in 1805, the year of the Battle of Trafalgar, that the Baron du Mesnil, on taking up an appointment as *sous-préfet* of Autun, bought an estate in what was then called 'Vollenay'. At the time the two administrative centres in the area – and the two bishoprics prior to the Revolution – were Autun and Langres, not Beaune and Dijon. The diocese of Autun together with the nobility of the *ancien régime* had owned large amounts of land in the Côte-de-Beaune which was then sold off to the *bourgeoisie* in the 1790s and 1800s. Much of this would already have been leased out to local *vignerons* and *petits bourgeois* farmers who would have also owned a few vines and the odd cow on their own account. But some of the land would have been under their direct control.

The Baron had a country house, raised up on three floors over the cellars, constructed at the northern end of the village in a little park. The jewel in the crown of the estate, the 2.4 hectare monopoly of the Clos-des-Ducs *climat*, lies at the end of the garden beyond the more recently constructed swimming pool. The terrace, facing east across the vineyards commands a splendid view as far as the mountains of the Jura and beyond. It is a fitting site for one of the top estates in the region.

The Angervilles come from near Falaise in Normandy, and it was Jacques d'Angerville's grandfather who married a Mademoiselle du Mesnil towards the end of the last century.

It was their son, Jacques' father, also called Jacques, who bought up the estate after the death of his uncle, a Baron du Mesnil, in 1906. It was he who started the fashion for estate-bottled Burgundy. During the 1920s he was one of the few who spoke out vociferously against the corrupt practices of the local merchants in Beaune. In those pre-appellation days (sadly it was to continue long after the *Loi Capus* introduced AC in 1936), it was the custom of many merchants to ship up cheap wine from the south of France, even from Algeria, in order to blend it in with the local produce. D'Angerville *père*'s courage in denouncing this fraud led to no prosecutions, however, merely to his wine being blackballed by the trade.

So together with Henri Gouges, Armand Rousseau and a couple of others he was forced to bottle his own wine and seek out his clients direct. One was the Thienpont wine business in Belgium (and of Vieux Château Certan and other interests in Bordeaux) – 1899 Volnay, Champans at F 2.85 a bottle; another was a triumvirate of Americans – Frank Schoonmaker, Pierce, a merchant in Boston, and Senator Hollis. Schoonmaker's first visit was in 1935. D'Angerville shipped a lot of 1929 (Volnay, Fremiets at F 14), 1933 and 1934 to the USA before the war. There was even an order, placed but not shipped, in 1939, which was reserved quietly in Volnay until hostilities ended in 1945.

The market, of course, was different then, not so much by comparison with today, but in relation to what it had been in the period before the First World War. During the nineteenth century and beyond, Germany, Austro-Hungary and Russia were important markets for Burgundy; even, given its size, the USA. Afterwards, with Prohibition on the one side and economic ruin on the other, the Burgundians had to look elsewhere, to Belgium and Switzerland. Great Britain has never been as eager a Burgundian customer as it should be, or as it is for the wines of Bordeaux.

Jacques d'Angerville's first vintage was 1945. He was eighteen. He has been fully responsible for the wine since 1949, and proprietor of the estate since his father's death in 1952.

This Angerville is tall, dignified and white-haired. He seems a touch reserved when you first encounter him. But you soon begin to realise the warmth and passion for his wines that lie underneath, not to mention his awareness of his estate's position in the history of domaine-bottled Burgundy. While neither he nor his father had a formal wine education, he is certainly every bit as knowledgeable about the wine-making process as anyone in the Côte. And of the Burgundian wine economy. For six years he was president of the growers' side of the *Comité*

Interprofessionel des Vins de Côte d'Or et de l'Yonne. He is currently *Président de l'Institut Universitaire de la Vigne et du Vin*.

THE VINEYARDS

The Angerville domaine comprises just under 15 hectares, almost all of it (except for a 0.4 ha piece of village Pommard) of *premier cru* status, almost all of it in Volnay, except for some Meursault, Santenots, and all except this latter *climat* planted to Pinot Noir.

Pride of place is the Clos-des-Ducs, a *monopole*, as I have said, and lying between the Angerville mansion and the Pitures-Dessus. The soil here is *terres blanches*, very light in colour and very stony; the incline steep and very well drained, the rock underneath hard. The result is a wine which is firmer than a Champans or a Caillerets - which are really, as Jacques d'Angerville describes it, 'the heart of Volnay' - and which takes longer to develop. It has a Pommard touch.

The largest Angerville holding is in Les Champans, two sizeable chunks totalling a mite under 4 hectares. There is a little more clay in the soil here, but it is also stony and well-drained. The Volnay that the Champans produces is also a firm wine, even a touch solid at the outset. It is not quite as distinctive as the Clos-des-Ducs, but it is rich, structured and long-lasting for all that.

On the Pommard side of the commune the Angerville estate owns 1.5 ha of Fremiets. Here, and across the border in the Pommard *climat* of Jarolières, there is an Oxfordian, marly element in the limestone, and a thin surface of debris over decomposing rock. The result is normally a lighter wine, without either the intensity or the distinction of the Clos-des-Ducs or the depth of the Champans, but nevertheless, in the Angerville of sophistication of tannins.

The Angerville domaine has two further important holdings: in the Taille-Pieds *climat*, adjacent to Clos-des-Chênes, and in the Caillerets, below it: 1.07 ha of the former, 0.45 ha of the latter. Here Volnay produces its most glorious wines. The soil structure is not *that* different from the Champans, but the wines are less dense seeming. They are marginally less structured but more intense and concentrated. When these Angerville wines are young they are vigorous, rich and old viney, when they are mature they provide a splendid contrast to the Clos-des-Ducs, wines of great classic elegance, while the Clos-des-Ducs seems to have evolved something lush, exotic, and individually perfumed, with an underlying spice.

This is not the end of the Angerville Volnay line-up. The domaine owns vines in L'Ormeau, Les Angles and Pitures, but these are less regularly offered to the writer on his yearly visits, often blended together to make a *premier cru tout court*, and rarely seen on the export market. I confess to never having even tasted the Angerville Pommard.

WINE-MAKING

The two Jacques d'Angervilles, *père et fils*, are famous for having developed their own particular strain of Pinot *fin*, and suitably it bears their name. There are no clones in the Angerville vineyards and the average age of the vines is venerable, plants only being individually replaced when they give up the ghost.

Yields are low: 36 hl/ha in the prolific vintage of 1990, 30 hl/ha in 1991. The estate has never asked for the PLC. It is here that it all begins, says d'Angerville: old vines, low *rendements*, little interference and an absence of manipulation thereafter.

The grapes are completely destalked, vinified at quite a high temperature, macerated with the skins for eight to ten days, with *remontage* (pumping-over) rather than regular *pigeage* (treading down of the cap) and then matured using about one-third new oak for the top wines, and that only for the initial period of the wine's sojourn in cask. Angerville is against what he describes as the abuse of new oak. Thereafter the wine is fined and finally given a very light filtration before bottling, fifteen to eighteen months after the harvest.

THE WINES

The result is a style of wine which while intense and complex, is subtle and understated rather than flamboyantly expressive. These are wines which when young require concentration on the part of the taster fully to appreciate their own concentration. Length on the palate, individuality of *terroir*, and above all distinction is what Jacques d'Angerville and his son-in-law Renaud de Villette are after. They are also seeking to produce wines for the long term. They consider the prevailing view that a Volnay should be or will be mature after five years, rather than ten, a misnomer.

The Angerville wines are stayers, as the following tasting notes will amply demonstrate. They are also consistent. And they are first-class.

THE TASTING

I sampled the following vintages of Clos-des-Ducs in Volnay in June 1993.

VOLNAY, CLOS-DES-DUCS

Optimum drinking

1991   **1998–2012**

Bottled February 1993. Good colour. Fresh, plummy, ripe nose. Very elegant. A touch of gingerbread. Lovely fruit. Medium to medium-full body. Good tannins. Rich and ripe and stylish and long on the palate. This is very good. Will last well.

1990   **2000–2020**

Splendid colour. Firm, rich, concentrated nose. Not too masculine or untypically Volnay, but certainly a big full wine with plenty of depth. There is lots of wine here. Good structure. Cool. Composed. Real quality. Fine.

1989   **Now–2008**

Good colour. Abundantly ripe, seductive nose. More red fruity than the 1991 - wild strawberries and raspberries. Medium to medium-full body. Good acidity. Still plenty of reserves in this wine. Good grip. A very attractive wine. Very good.

1988   **1998–2015**

Not quite as full a colour as I would have expected. Less than the 1989. But the nose is ripe and stylish. This is more forward, more plump, less austere than others. Really very Volnay in expression. Slightly hard on the palate but very lovely on the finish. Complex, long, lots of finesse. Fine fruit. Very good indeed.

1987   **Now–1999**

Medium colour, just beginning to show signs of development. Fresh, round, plump straightforward nose. Now accessible. Just about ready.

Medium body. A little one-dimensional after the wines above but stylish and fruity and balanced. Most enjoyable. Positive at the end.

1986   **Drink soon**

Magnum. Lightish mature colour. No undue brown. Lightish fruity nose. Not much depth but not aged. On the palate this is also fruity. It is somewhat slight. But it is not dilute. A good effort, and plenty of enjoyment to offer.

1985   **Now–1999**

Medium colour. Now mature. The nose is ripe but spicy. It lacks a little finesse and there is a certain dryness. Medium to medium-full. Fruity enough, even fat, but the acidity and the definition are not quite what they ought to be. Slightly clumsy. I prefer the 1989 and 1991, let alone the 1990 and 1988. For the vintage the 1987 is better. But I have had better bottles than this: for example the following.

1985 (second note)   **Now–2016**

Tasted April 1993. Slightly better colour than the Champans alongside which it was served. This is a richer, fuller, more multi-dimensional wine. A lot of depth and class here. Very good grip. Very good complex fruit. This is still a little firm but has real quality and finesse. Fine.

1985 (Volnay, Champans)   **Now–2009**

Tasted April 1993. Medium-full colour. This is a little lean for the vintage. But perhaps it is still a little closed. The nose is classy and aromatic-nutty. The finish long and satisfying. The generosity I'm sure will appear. Very good but not the depth and class for great.

1984   **Drink up**

Surprisingly good colour. Fresh. This is a little short and a little slight, but neither tired nor astringent. Nor lacking fruit. Not great, but perfectly pleasant.

1983   **Now-2003**

Fullish colour. Not much maturity. No undue brown like some. Quite a full, four-square nose. Rich and fat and alcoholic but a little burly. Fullish, tannic. Uncompromising but rich and very concentrated. Marvellous essence of fruit. *Rôti* in character. Much better than the 1985 today. Needs food.

1982   **Now-2000**

Good fresh colour. Full for a 1982. Fine nose. Mature, mellow, elegant. Not a bit dilute. Still very fresh. This is excellent. Good grip. This has structure. Very long. Very lovely concentrated fruit. This too is better than 1985. Bags of life.

1981   **Drink soon**

Good colour. Quite substantial and not old. Mellow and fruity on the nose, without the depth of the 1982 but with more to it than the 1984. There is a hint of astringency at the end now but this is by no means a bad vintage. Ripe, clean and quite full. Even a dimension or two. Positive finish.

1978   **Now-2005**

Good full rich colour. No undue brown. Vigorous and meaty on the nose. Slight lack of nuance perhaps. This is fresh, structured, slightly rigid - compared with the 1982. Needed time to come out of the glass. It is a bit more old-fashioned. Lovely fruit as it developed. And a fine long complex finish. In the end very stylish. Very lovely.

1977   **Drink up**

This is getting towards the end, but once again wasn't *that* bad in the first place. Lightish. Not astringent. Not coarse. Still quite fresh and fruity.

1976   **Now-2000 plus**

Splendid colour. No undue brown. Fat blackberry-jam nose. Quite alcoholic, like the 1983. Not as dry or as burly as the 1983 though. Full, more typical, but quite a muscular wine nevertheless. Lovely ripe fruit. Fat, vigorous. This is complex and satisfying, and has bags of life. No lack of finesse either.

1973   **Drink soon**

Lightening colour: looking a little old. Still fresh on the nose if a bit rarefied. Very soft. Sweet. Delicate. Surprisingly lovely. Feminine. Very Volnay. Elegant.

1972   **Drink soon**

Medium and medium-full colour. Still quite vigorous. A touch lean on the nose, but not hard. I have had more generous 1972s. This is beginning to get a little too vegetal. Interesting, but not special. I prefer the 1973.

1971   **Drink soon**

Good colour. Still quite vigorous. Sweet on the nose. An aspect of *sur-maturité* that you find in 1976 Bordeaux, and the certain astringency that often goes with it. Ripe, mellow, medium body. Good fruity attack. Very plump and seductive. Positive enough finish, but not really quite enough zip to balance it and give it the class of great.

1964   **Now-2000 plus**

Very good full mature colour. Very very rich, complex nose. Heaps of wine here. This is a magnificent wine. Very rich and concentrated and vigorous. Marvellous fruit. Fat and ripe and without a suggestion of age. This is because it has such good grip. Classy, opulent, long. Very fine indeed. Still bags of life.

1959   **Past its best**

The colour is lightening now. And on the nose though ripe and full of roses it is fading. On the palate still sweet and elegant but really a bit past it. What a pity!

1945   **Now-1999**

Splendid colour. Still vigorous. This is a big burly tough uncompromising monster. On the palate it is more civilised. Full, rich, totally unchaptalised concentrated essence of Pinot. Very concentrated. Very lovely fruit. Not a hint of astringency. Took time to come out. Marvellous finish. Very fine indeed. Still has plenty of life.

1934   **Will still keep**

Very good colour. Slightly inky and dense on the nose but much better on the palate. Rich, full, very good grip. Quite a structured wine, made in the old-fashioned way, for keeping for twenty years before drinking with rich food. Very rich, even sweet on the finish.

L'ARLOT
NUITS-SAINT-GEORGES

There are a number of ways in which the Domaine de l'Arlot is different from most of the other four- and five-star estates of the Côte d'Or.

Firstly, the owners are outsiders, the insurance company AXA, whose main interests are not in wine. Today this is commonplace in Bordeaux; but it is - should I say, so far - unusual in Burgundy. Those that are - the Pousse d'Or, the Château de Puligny-Montrachet, and the Château de Bligny spring to mind - are very much the exceptions.

Secondly, the heart of the domaine consists of the monopolies of two Nuits-Saint-Georges first growths. The Domaine de la Romanée-Conti, of course, possesses the monopoly of two *grands crus*. But apart from them, possession of the whole of a *premier* or *grand cru* comes singly, and rarely. The Clos-des-Forêts-Saint-Georges measures 7.1 hectares, the Clos-de-l'Arlot four: 11 ha of exclusive prime land in Prémeaux, at the southern end of the Nuits-Saint-Georges appellation.

Thirdly, in its present format, this is a new domaine, one which has only made wine to be reckoned with since its take-over by AXA in 1987. The wines before were rustic. At a stroke, thanks to resident manager Jean-Pierre de Smet, born in 1946, a Niçois by origin, a talented skier and a passionate yachtsman, the quality was turned round and buyers began beating a path to his door. And finally Clos-de-l'Arlot is one of the major sources for that *rara avis*, a white Côte-de-Nuits, and delicious it is too.

ORIGINS

The name Arlot comes from that of a stream which flows out of the rock at the foot of the vineyard before disappearing into a culvert under the road. There is the opportunity here, I have suggested to Jean-Pierre, for the construction of a *vivier*, a natural protected pool - for trout or *écrevisses* perhaps. Above, towards the end of the eighteenth century, the vineyards were enclosed by Jean-Charles Vienot, a *vigneron* and merchant of Nuits-Saint-Georges. The nucleus of the estate has not been altered since.

The buildings, however, date from earlier, indeed the château itself from the time of Louis XIV. This was certainly an aristocratic mansion, but who the aristocrats were is lost in history. François Vienot, son of Jean-Charles, renovated the château, enlarged and reconstructed the dependent buildings, and laid out a park in the rear, complete with a box-hedge maze.

This folly of arboreal sculpture, at the foot of what was obviously an old quarry, is bizarre in the extreme. Cool, verdant, sombre, resplendent in birdsong, decorated with water-weathered, life-size pieces of limestone rock, some of which have been sculpted into the faces of animals, there is something spooky and theatrical about the place: a Greek tragedy waiting to be enacted.

François Vienot's children sold the estate to another *négociant* company, that of Jules Belin, after his death in the 1880s. And from 1891 to 1987 it remained in the Belin hands. This was at first a successful business, famous for its Marc à la Cloche, but most of the family were killed in a car accident at a level crossing in 1933. After that it limped on, but declining as others expanded. And it was no surprise when the estate was sold.

AXA AND JEAN-PIERRE DE SMET

Jean-Pierre de Smet, an accountant by training, is a lean, fit, handsome man of 50 or so. He ran his own business in New Caledonia for seven years, sailed his way around the world, and then got bitten by the wine bug. In 1977 he went to work the vintage at Domaine Dujac, for Jacques Seysses was an old friend, and he returned regularly in subsequent years, a fruitful contact which continues as a collaboration today. He went to the University of Dijon to study viticulture and wine-making and was then on the lookout for an estate of his own.

Another contact was Claude Bebéar, *président-directeur-générale* of AXA. De Smet heard that AXA, having acquired Château Franc-Mayne in Saint-Emilion in 1984, was interested in expanding into Burgundy. In 1987, just before they bought Château Pichon-Longueville-Baron, De Smet helped negotiate the sale of the Belin domaine. The set-up is unique in AXA *millésimes*, for while AXA own the *foncier*, that is the land and the buildings, De Smet and AXA jointly own the *Société d'Exploitation*, the company which runs the estate. De Smet is his own boss.

At the outset the new Domaine de l'Arlot found itself responsible for three *climats*: the Clos-des-Forêts-Saint-Georges, 7.1 ha which lie directly south of Les Saint-Georges on the Nuits-Prémeaux boundary, the 4 ha Clos-de-l'Arlot itself, and 1.8 ha of Côte-de-Nuits-Villages, Clos-du-Chapeau.

Late in 1990, having been pipped at the post by Lalou Bize over both the Charles Noëllat and Remy estates, the Domaine de l'Arlot acquired just under 25 ares of Romanée-Saint-Vivant. The vendor was Henri Poisot of Aloxe-Corton, the vines farmed by Michel Voarick in the same village. The price was 800,000 francs the *ouvrée*; high, and considered excessive by Louis Latour to whom the plot had been offered first. The Latour vines lie adjacent.

Subsequently more land was bought in Vosne-Romanée: 20 *ouvrées* (0.85 ha) of Les Suchots. The first vintage here was 1993. This makes a total of 14 hectares.

De Smet and AXA are still seeking to expand, particularly into a predominantly white wine domaine in the Côte-de-Beaune. This would logically complement the Côte-de-Nuits holdings, and it would also offer economies of scale. They have not stopped yet.

WINE-MAKING

The Domaine de l'Arlot vineyards are run under the supervision of Christophe Morin, who also works for Jacques Seysses, and the emphasis is on a *biologique* approach, and into keeping the harvest under control from the outset rather than undue recourse to green harvesting. In this part of Nuits-Saint-Georges the hillsides are steep, running abruptly down from the forests at the top of the slope to the main road. It is the thinnest part of the Côte. Most - indeed more and more - of the vines are ploughed, but a part of the vineyard is too steep to work and the weeds are controlled by herbicides. De Smet has had long and amicable discussions with the Gouges on the point of planting a special grass to counter erosion and eliminate other weeds, but is not yet convinced.

He does, however, believe in whole grape fermentation, and a minimum of destemming. You get greater complexity this way, he says. The must is cooled, not expressly to produce a period of cold maceration, but so that the fermentation temperatures do not exceed 33°C: 28 and upwards is the desired spectrum; the proposed differential between the start and the maximum being 15°. There is an average of 40 per cent new oak, De Smet buying in wood from the Allier together with Jacques Seysses which is weathered outdoors at the Domaine de l'Arlot. He prefers a light toast. The wine is fined, but not filtered, and bottled after fifteen to eighteen months.

Some 2 hectares, half the surface, of the Clos-de-l'Arlot is planted with Chardonnay (there is a small percentage of Pinot Beurot). But one of these hectares is young vines. Here the grapes are also not destemmed. After pressing the must is cooled, there is a 'severe' *débourbage* - more than usual - and the wine is decanted into another tank under inert gas to protect it from oxidation until the fermentation begins. It then takes place in wood, one-quarter of which is new, in a temperature-controlled cellar to keep the temperatures low. After a year it is lightly fined with bentonite, filtered and bottled.

THE WINES

This white wine, an instant success since the 1987, which is still a most attractive bottle, is an exemplar of modern wine-making. De Smet's whites are never blowsy, never over-alcoholic, never excessively oaky; always fragrant, pure and distinctive. Lesser vintages can come and go: this is always fruity, harmonious and full of character.

The Clos-des-Forêts-Saint-Georges is a typical Nuits. The wine has been very consistent, with a good colour (like other un-destemmed wines, it puts on colour for the first five years or so rather than losing it), a meaty, succulent character and very good acidity. The challenge, as elsewhere in Nuits, is to conserve or create the elegance to match the structure.

The Clos-de-l'Arlot is very much an oddball; not a Nuits in character, and more irregular in its results. 'I am still learning with this wine,' says Jean-Pierre. The colour is lighter than the Clos-des-Forêts, the wine has less body, and it evolves rather sooner. It has more elegance, indeed even a sort of Chambolle element, for the tannins are finer. But it has less fat, and can sometimes be too lean, even slightly astringent.

Quite naturally, for the methods are similar, and Jacques Seysses remains an avuncular mentor, though the men are of more or less the same age, the Arlot wines show similarities with those of the Domaine Dujac. They are finely made, with great attention to detail. Elegance and purity - sometimes at the expense of generosity and sex-appeal - are to the fore. If you like the one you will like the other. But whether you prefer these, or those of others, is a question of taste.

THE TASTING

I sampled the following wines at the Domaine de l'Arlot in June 1995.

CLOS-DE-L'ARLOT BLANC

1993 — 1998-2004

Light straw greeny gold colour. Soft, gently oaky, elegant nose. On the light side. This is well made and well balanced with good acidity and plenty of style. What it lacks is a bit of extra concentration and real ripeness. But it is crisp and most enjoyable. Very good.

1992 — Now-2005

Lightish colour. Ripe nose. Not so obviously oaky as the 1993. Expanded as it evolved in the glass. This has more depth and is more ample. Good oak on the palate. Rich, stylish. Fullish. Compared with the 1989 it is a little more herbal. Very good indeed.

1991 — Now-2000

Medium colour. Open nose. Broad. Little oak. Some vegetal aspects. More oak on the palate. Nicely rich, with good grip. This is surprisingly ample. Nutty. This is different. It is a more austere, masculine wine with good substance. Very good plus.

1990 — Now-2005

Slightly more colour than the 1989. Fat, rich, some oak, some honey on the nose. Ripe, fruit-salady, buttery. Richer and more aromatic. More depth. This is fine.

1989 — Now-2000 plus

Fresh colour. Aromatic, full of fruit. Gentle, ripe nose. Less body than the 1990, less grip too. But a very seductive wine. Good complex, ripe finish. Long. Compared with the 1992 this has a touch of apricots. Very good indeed.

1988 — Now-2000

Medium colour. Interesting mature nose. Still nice and fresh but complex, ripe and very slight touch of reduction. This went on aeration. On the palate a little lean but good acidity. Ripe but slightly four-square. Good plus.

1987 — Now-2000 plus

More colour than the 1988. Attractive nose. Open, ripe, accessible stylish. This is fresh, generous, gently oaky. Rather better than the 1988 and indeed one of the best of all. A touch of spice. Nicely round. Most attractive. Very good indeed.

1986 — Drink soon

De Smet didn't make this. Plump nose. Still fresh. No *sur-maturité*. It is a little diffuse. The colour a little light gold. The acidity less. But if with less style and no new oak it is recognisably the same thing. Not losing its grip. Quite good.

CLOS-DE-L'ARLOT ROUGE

1993 — Now-2005

Good colour. Soft and round (softer and rounder than the Forêts). Full of soft red fruit on the nose. More developed than the Forêts. The wine is lighter, but it is classier. The fruit is purer. This is very intense even if it only seems to have the structure of a 1992. Very long. Very elegant. Very complex. Very good indeed.

1992 — Now-2000

Medium colour. On the nose this is ripe and attractive. But perhaps a little too soft. On the palate light to medium body. Here I prefer the Forêts. This is a little slight. And it doesn't have the dimension or intensity to compensate. Quite good plus.

1991 — Now-2005

Good colour. Lovely soft, quite intense fruit on the nose. This has plenty of depth. A fat, ripe wine. Very good grip. Seems just about ready at first, but there is a backbone here, a reserve which needs to soften. Very finely balanced. Long. Here I prefer the 1993. It is more elegant. The tannins are finer. Very good plus.

1990 — Now-2009

Very good colour. Rich, fat, opulent nose. The fruit just a little cooked. The whole thing very exotic, even erotic. A cornucopia of fruit here. Medium-full. Very, very ripe. Lovely ripe tannins as well. Very good grip. This is immensely plump and seductive. Yet cool at the end. Very classy.

1989 — Now-2000

Medium colour. No undue development. Soft, fragrant, soft fruity nose. Not a lot of intensity though. Yet medium body. A touch astringent still. Good ripe fruit. But a slight lack of zip. Just about ready. Good at best.

1988 — Now-2003

Medium colour. No undue development. Very stylish balanced fruit. Rather more class and dimension than the 1989. Medium to medium-full. Composed. Ready. Fresh, stylish, balanced. Long. This is an accessible, most attractive example. Much more together than the Forêts. Very good.

1987 — Now-2000

Medium colour. Now mature. Round, ripe, spicy nose. This is not as fine as the Forêts. It has a good attack and quite a complex follow-through. But it lacks the weight and depth. Good.

CLOS-DES-FORÊTS-SAINT-GEORGES

1993   **1999-2007**

Good colour. Very good ripe blackberry nose. Just a little adolescent at present. High-toned. Medium to medium-full. Good grip. Nicely ripe tannins. Good intensity on the palate. Stylish. Very good. Very good plus.

1992   **Now-2002**

Medium colour. No development yet. High-toned, soft, blackberry and raspberry nose. Medium body. Soft and ripe. Lovely style. Good balance. Succulent and forward but not a bit wishy-washy. Very seductive. Good plus.

1991   **1998-2012**

Good colour. Fine nose. Poised, very clean positive Pinot fruit. Youthful, vigorous and with a lot of depth. But the family resemblance between these three (1993, 1992 and 1991) is very obvious. This seems richer and more concentrated than the 1993, though it is hard to tell. It is certainly fuller and more intense. Very lovely fruit. Very elegant. Good tannins. The Nuits-Saint-Georges masculinity in the background. Naturally ripe and sweet. Very good indeed.

1990   **1999-2012**

Very good colour. Rich nose. Concentrated, backward, slightly solid and dense, inky even. Full, spicy, much more of a cooked fruit taste. This is very, very rich and intense. Splendid grip. Currently rather more adolescent than the 1991. But more to it. Yet perhaps the 1991 will always be more stylish. Needs time. Fine.

1989   **Now-2003**

Medium colour. Still fresh. Open, accessible nose. Heaps of soft red fruits. This seems fully ready. This is very like the 1992. Medium body. Lots of lovely fruit. Very ripe. Evolving in the short term. Nicely fresh. Very seductive. Very good.

1988   **Now-2005**

Light to medium colour. A little development. A little mixed up on the nose. Ripe but a little chunky and solid at the end. Medium body. The tannins are quite evident. The fruit is finely balanced. Very stylish and very intense; surprisingly so, giving the wine class, length and potential for development. Give it another year. The least integrated on the attack, but all resolved on the finish.

1987   **Now-2010 plus**

More colour than the 1988. Still youthful. Cleaner, rounder, much more stylish than the 1988. Lovely fruit. A frank, classy expression. An excellent 1987. Fullish, very fresh, lovely fruit. Complex and concentrated. Very good grip especially for the vintage. Still needs time. This is fine.

1986   **Now-2003**

Not made by De Smet. Fullish, mature colour. But no undue age. Robust, slightly inky, old-fashioned nose. A little sweet-sour. Better on the palate. Indeed good for the vintage. Slightly ungainly but ripe, balanced and fruity. Slightly solid.

COMTE ARMAND, CLOS-DES-EPENEAUX, *POMMARD*

Hard by the church in the centre of Pomerol, an arch leads you into a small gravel courtyard and a gaggle of late medieval buildings. Over the entrance are carved the words 'Clos-des-Epeneaux'. This is the headquarters of the domaine which produces Pommard's finest wine.

The spelling - Epeneaux, not Epenots - is idiosyncratic but long established. Up until 1994 the estate produced only one wine from a single piece of land. And the vineyard's ownership can be traced back in an unbroken line to its inception before the French Revolution. All this is rare in Burgundy.

Like its great rival across the church square, the Domaine de Courcel, the Clos-des-Epeneaux has an absentee proprietor. The present Comte Armand, Vicomte Gabriel, is a lawyer in his forties who lives mainly in Paris. The man on the spot in Pommard is a thirty-five-year-old French-Canadian, Pascal Marchand. Marchand has been in charge since 1985. The enviable reputation of today's Clos-des-Epeneaux is largely due to him.

HISTORY

Approximately two centuries ago, in the last fifteen years of the eighteenth century, what is now the Clos-des-Epeneaux was slowly pieced together, bit by bit. Its creator was a man from a wealthy family in Nuits-Saint-Georges, Nicolas Marey. Marey's father-in-law was the influential Gaspard Monge, local politician and minister in the post-Revolutionary administration. A *place* in the centre of Beaune is named after him. As the old ecclesiastical and aristocratic estates were dismembered and sold off, the pair built up a considerable vineyard holding, not the least part of which was the lion's share of the *climat* of Romanée-Saint-Vivant.

Nicolas and his wife Charlotte had a number of children. One of these was Clothilde, and it was through her line that ownership of the Clos-des-Epeneaux would pass. Clothilde married a man with the same profession as her grandfather's. Jean-François Armand was a *champenois*, and *député* for the Aube *département*.

Their son, Ernest, was destined for a diplomatic career. At the end of the 1850s he found himself Ambassador to the Vatican, just at the time when Garibaldi, in his progress towards the unification of Italy, was menacing the Papal States. Garibaldi's power base was the north, but Rome, the Eternal City, had already been targeted as the natural capital, as of course it had been when last the country was a political whole a millennium and a half previously. On the progressive side was Garibaldi and the new monarchy of Victor Emmanuel II, on the other was an unholy alliance between the Curia and the King of Naples. For additional support the Pope looked to his other natural ally, Napoléon III of France, and as the emperor's ambassador, Ernest Armand was influential in persuading Napoléon to lend assistance. In gratitude the pontiff appointed Ernest a count. Gabriel Armand is the fourth generation on. And the family still possesses the Clos-des-Epeneaux.

PASCAL MARCHAND

Pascal Marchand was born in Montreal in 1962. He studied history and literature, and was briefly in the merchant marine. But in 1983 he decided to go and work the vintage in Burgundy. He spent a month or so with François Germain at the Château de Chorey-lès-Beaune. He returned a year later, enrolling himself at the *Lycée Viticole* at Beaune, and working for Bruno Clair in Marsannay. It was through Bruno that Pascal met the Comte Armand.

The Count, not being entirely happy with the way his domaine was being run, was looking for a new *régisseur*. The incumbent at the time was Philibert Rossignol, aged seventy-one, who had worked at the domaine for thirty-five years, but in practice most of the work was being done by his son Michel. When Rossignol *père* came to announce his impending retirement, Comte Armand seized his chance. The twenty-two-year-old Pascal was offered the position. He took over in January 1985.

There was much to be done. The domaine was over-manned. One of the first things Pascal had to do was to declare two of his staff redundant. While the Clos was full of old vines, the cellar was equally full of old casks, seriously overdue for replacement. The wine, though full and rich, was often rustic. Both vinification and *élevage* - though a proportion of the crop was sold off in bulk - would have to be made more sophisticated.

Was there local resentment at the new, young and foreign upstart? Yes, Pascal admits, things were a bit sticky at first. But luckily the Rossignols were Volnaysien not Pommardien. And they were no longer around. The Count had suggested that one of them remain for a few months in an advisory position, but they had refused. Marchand continued with his studies, installed himself in a small apartment above the cellars, and swiftly turned round the quality of the wines, declassifying the entire 1984 crop to village Pommard on the way. The quality had been fine before; it was soon to become so again.

THE CLOS

The Clos-des-Epeneaux is a walled vineyard, roughly square, and lies between the Petits-Epenots on the Beaune border and the Grands-Epenots towards the northern end of the village. Technically it has a foot in each. The slope here is quite gentle, but thankfully very well drained. A thin layer of relatively heavy soil, mixed with stones, lies on a crumbly limestone base, rich in iron.

The vineyard is divided into quarters, and subdivided again into vines of different ages, making it easy to isolate into different *cuvées* of different ages. Moreover, says Pascal, the *sélection massale* of the old vines was very well done. He is proud of his vines, some of which are sixty years old, and of their high density - 12,500 *pieds à l'hectare*. From 1995 he will gradually begin to replace the most fragile, at the rate of 2 per cent a year, to maintain an average age of fifty years.

The vineyard has been bio-dynamically run since 1988, treatments being applied not only according to the calendar and the lunar cycle, but to the movements of the planets. No herbicides or systematic fertilisers are used; only the barest modicum of farmyard manure is applied. Marchand is an advocate of pruning late, when the sap has already begun to rise. It lessens the risk of disease, he maintains.

The vines are pruned hard, and the yield is deliberately limited. Even in vintages prolific elsewhere the Clos-des-Epeneaux yield is kept well below 40 hl/ha. In 1991, a year of frost and *coulure*, it was as low as 20. Pascal Marchand aims for a mean of 35/37 hl/ha.

WINE-MAKING

Under the old regime the domaine had usually vinified with at least some of the stalks, and, as I have indicated, there was little new wood. Both of these Pascal changed immediately. He removed all the stems, and introduced 35 per cent new wood for the wine until the first racking in March or April. Today the must is given a three- or four-day cold maceration, after which the temperature is allowed to rise as far as 33°C. The maceration lasts between twelve and seventeen days, longer than hitherto. And the wine is deliberately allowed to take its time over its malo. 'That way it can enrich itself on its lees,' says Pascal. There are usually four *cuvées*, that of the youngest vines being sold off *en vrac* to the Beaune *négoce*. The other three are kept separate until the fining which takes place in the winter of the following year. Bottling is by gravity, without filtration, in the spring or summer which follows. Only recently has all the old-vine wine been estate-bottled.

THE WINE

I have watched the evolution of 'modern' Clos-des-Epeneaux since I first visited the domaine to taste the 1985s, and I have frequently sampled three or four or so of the more recent vintages together when I have tasted with Pascal. Not only, obviously, do you see the contrast between the vintages, but you are also aware of a progression.

The wines, indeed, *have* become more sophisticated. The tannins have been tamed. Pommard is, or should be, a full-bodied tannic wine, but it doesn't have to be sturdy. If you compare the 1985 with the 1990 the former retains a certain rusticity. It tastes as if it might have been vinified with some of the stalks. As a result it hasn't as much finesse as the wines of today.

The other progression has been in terms of intensity. There is today simply more flavour in the Clos-des-Epeneaux than there used to be: a volume of fruit and a multi-dimensionality of character which are more usually found in the Côte-de-Nuits. Moreover the fruit flavour is more black fruit than the cherries and redcurrants of most Côte-de-Beaunes, even most Pommards. The Clos-des-Epeneaux is a splendid wine today which normally needs a decade to mature. I can't say I am deeply enamoured of the 1986, but that is largely the vintage. Apart from that Pascal Marchand has not put a foot wrong.

Scoop

I have a scoop for you, said Pascal as I was finishing the tasting below. For the first time since the late 1850s, when Jean-François Armand sold off his other Pommards to concentrate on the Clos, the domaine will no longer be confined to one wine. Some 9 *ouvrées* (about 0.4 of a hectare) of Volnay, Fremiets have just been acquired. From whom, I demanded. He wouldn't say. It will be fascinating to see what the Clos-des-Epeneaux team makes of this!

The Tasting

I sampled the following wines in Pommard in February 1994.

Pommard, Clos-des-Epeneaux

Optimum drinking

1991   2001–2020

Good colour. Very fine concentrated nose. Plenty of depth and flesh here. As well as structure and grip. Closed in. Full, rich, tannic. Very well balanced. Very stylish. The finish is extremely ripe and classy. Very very long. This is a splendid example of the vintage. Needs time.

1990   2003–2025

Very good colour. Backward nose. A hint of reduction at first. Rich, solid and classically Pommard. Uncompromising. Even brutal on the palate. Very full. Very tannic. But behind an enormous concentration, intensity and richness. Marvellous fruit. Real breed, very powerful. Very long. Brilliant.

1989   1998–2012

Medium-full colour. This, again, is rather firmer and more backward than most 1989s. On the palate the attack is a little austere - not that there is anything wrong with that - but in no way round and plump and generous like most 1989s. This is a serious *vin de garde*. Rich, fullish, backward. A lot of depth. Needs time. Very good indeed.

1988   1999–2015

Full colour. The nose is beginning to lose its initial roughness. Marvellous fruit. Very well balanced. Subtle and classy. On the palate the tannins aren't quite as well-mannered as they are in the three wines above. And the wine is still backward and austere. But the finish is long and generous. Fine.

1987   Now–2005

Good medium-full colour. No sign of age. Slightly hard on the nose. On the palate the wine is full and rich for a 1987. Good meaty structure. Plenty of concentration. The hardness evident at the start is not there at the end. And the finish is rich and classy. A fine example of the vintage. Hardly ready. Will last well.

1986   Drink soon

Medium to medium-full mature colour. Soft, slightly spicy nose. Not a lot of class, but not weedy. On the palate a bit of astringency, and underneath that a wine which is a little rustic and flat. No great shakes. Will dry out.

1985   Now–2008

Medium-full colour. Still youthful. There is a certain rusticity to the tannins here on the nose. As if some stems had been left. But 100 per cent *éraflé*. Better as it evolved. Fullish, balanced, ripe and still youthful, the tannins still not quite resolved. Not quite as classy and harmonious as the wines later but certainly very good indeed.

1982   Now–1999

Medium to medium-full, mature colour. Gamey, vigorous, rich nose. Not a lot of class perhaps but plenty of fruit, attraction and guts. Fullish and vigorous for a 1982. Good acidity. Ripe and seductive. Long. A very good example indeed. No hurry to drink up.

1980   Drink soon

Very good colour. Barely mature. Full, rich and glowing. Full nose. Maturer than the colour would suggest. A touch vegetal. Fullish body, not as fat as the 1982. Higher acidity. A touch lean, a touch artisanal and one-dimensional. A little astringent at the end. But a very good Côte-de-Beaune 1980, nevertheless.

1979   Drink soon

Medium to medium-full colour. Fully developed. Not a patch on the 1980. Yet on the nose more succulent, more lively. There is an interesting element of old Burgundy here, gamey and complex. Slightly lumpy and austere. But very good indeed. Evolved very well in the glass. Best with food. Finishes very well.

1978   Now–2000 plus

Full, rich, mature colour. Lumpy and slightly shitty on the nose at first. Fat, succulent and rich after a bit of aeration. Fullish, meaty and fleshy. Good grip. This has all it needs except the class. Still vigorous nevertheless. Held up well and seemed to get cleaner on aeration. Fine. Better than last time out.

1973   **Drink up**

Surprisingly good colour. Not a bit too aged. The nose a little dried-out. On the palate equally a little pinched and astringent. But underneath one can see some succulence. Was very good in its time. Still enjoyable, just. But it held up well in the glass.

1972   **Drink soon**

Lightening up on the colour. A mixture of nuts, madeira-like high acidity and wood on the nose. Still alive, though losing its fruit and class now, and lightening up. But not astringent. This has interest, even length and complexity. Held up very well on evolution. Even acquired more life. Very good indeed.

1970   **Drink soon**

Light colour. Now old looking. On the nose it lacks vigour and seems to have lightened up. Still enjoyable. The palate is a little more alive. Good succulent fruit. Fine acidity keeping it fresh. Medium-full body. Has lost a bit of class but still very enjoyable. Again it held up well.

1962   **Drink up**

Colour has lightened up now. But not too old. Soft, evolved - well-matured - but classy nose. This is old but not past it. Delicate but balanced, fresh, not astringent. Even complex. Class here. Lovely.

1961   **Drink up**

Not a bad colour. Brown but some life. Less succulence on the nose than the 1962. Slight touch of gingerbread. On the palate still sweet. A little all on the surface but again has attraction. Decidedly more concentrated and more fruity on the follow-through than the above. Lovely too. Positive at the end.

GHISLAINE BARTHOD-NOËLLAT,
CHAMBOLLE-MUSIGNY

A generation ago the idea of a woman wine-maker in such a hands-on region as Burgundy would have been viewed with suspicion. Wine-making was man's work, the old guard would have grumbled. There was even a myth that the very presence of a woman in the cellar at *that time of the month* would somehow taint the wine. Women were tolerated in the vineyard - they have been largely responsible for the *taille* for centuries - but not in the cellar; and not in the decision-making.

Happily the wind of change which has blown through the Burgundian *vignoble* since the late 1970s has dispelled this aspect of male chauvinism as it has opened doors and eyes and ears in a host of other respects. There are probably as many women studying at the *Lycée Viticole* in Beaune or undergoing oenological training at Dijon today as there are men. And there are at least a dozen ladies in charge in the top division of Burgundy's *négociants* and domaines. One of them, producing some of the best wines in Chambolle, that most elegant of all Burgundy's villages, is the attractive, blonde thirty-six-year-old Ghislaine Barthod. Ghislaine can boast no *grands crus* in her portfolio, but her over 6 hectare domaine extends over no fewer than nine first growths in the village, and a tasting in her cellar provides a fascinating opportunity to compare the nuances between them.

HISTORY

Just as there are two distinct branches of Grivots in the Côte-de-Nuits, so are there two separate families of Noëllats, one based in Chambolle, the other in Vosne-Romanée. And as, once upon a time, a Vosne-Romanée Grivot married a homonym who was not a cousin, so the two Noëllat branches have been united in marriage. Marcel Noëllat, the Chambolle resident, was one of the first – in 1929 – to start domaine-bottling in the village. He had an uncle who lived in Paris and could promote his wines to restaurants and private customers in the capital. Marcel had two daughters: one married Gaston Barthod, an ex-soldier from the Haut-Doubs; the other married Michel Noëllat – no relation – of Vosne-Romanée.

Until 1977, when Marcel Noëllat retired, Gaston Barthod worked alongside his father-in-law. For many years he was secretary, subsequently becoming president, of the local growers' syndicate, and is still, though now himself retired, on the administration board of the association of wine-growers of the entire Côte d'Or.

On Marcel Noëllat's retirement the domaine was split between the two sisters, but Gaston Barthod's sister-in-law continued to let him exploit her vines in a *fermage* basis, and this arrangement persists today.

Ghislaine has been in charge for a decade now and from henceforth the label will bear her name. She has enlarged the domaine by buying land in the *premier cru climat* Les Combottes (the wines were replanted in 1986, and the wine currently goes into the village *cuvée*), by extending her ownership in Les Châtelots, also a *premier cru*, and by clearing scrubland up-slope from the Bonnes-Mares, alongside where Bruno Clair has done the same. The holding in village AC has also been increased, by old vines in a *lieu-dit* called La Croix, under the Combottes. In 1987 Ghislaine bought the house and cellar of the Veuve Modot and removed the Barthod-Noëllat HQ to these potentially rather fine premises (they need redecoration, but currently all available funds are being spent in the vineyard and in the cellar), where she lives with Louis Boillot, one of the *fils* of Domaine Lucien Boillot *et fils* of Gevrey-Chambertin.

THE VINEYARD

Ghislaine, a past student of the Beaune viticultural college, is an imaginative wine-maker. But it is in the vineyard, she insists, that it all starts. The domaine consists of vines which are for the most part impressively old, and it is the maintenance of this average age, and restrictive pruning to minimise the yield, which are of prime concern. If you prune short, wipe out the *contre-bourgeon* and take out one of the flowers if the bud has produced two, there will be no need for green harvesting later in the season.

The *premiers crus* lie on both sides of the village. On the north side, in the line of Bonnes-Mares, is the largest holding, 0.86 ha of Les Cras. Next to this lies 0.25 ha of Les Fuées, above which, recently partly elevated to *premier cru*, is 0.37 ha of Les Véroilles. The slope is steep here, the soil a light-coloured limestone debris, and in the first two mentioned *climats*, the vines forty to fifty years old.

On the other side of the *route des vins* Ghislaine is one of four proprietors in the *premier cru* section of the Beaux-Bruns (0.72 ha), and has 0.19 ha of Baudes and a few rows of Sentiers, not enough to produce a separate *cuvée*. Below the village lie the Chatelots (0.23 ha) and the young-vine Combottes, and in the direction of Vougeot 0.25 ha of Charmes. There is a number of parcels of village wine, and a hectare or so of Bourgogne *rouge* across the main Nuits-Dijon road in a *lieu-dit* called Les Bons-Bâtons.

WINE-MAKING

The Barthod wine is vinified in open-top wooden *cuves*, using a maximum of one-third unstemmed bunches, placed deliberately in the centre of the vat in order to assist an even and slow extraction of colour and aromas. After a two- to three-day maceration *à froid* the fermentation will start to get going, gently at first, but up to a temperature of 32°C, interrupted by a *pigeage* morning and evening. This continues until the juice is racked off the pulp after a fortnight. There is one-quarter new oak and the wine is bottled after about twenty months.

There is greater control and greater attention to detail than there was in Gaston Barthod's time, as exemplified by the recent introduction of a *table de trie* at the winery, which supplements the elimination of suspect fruit in the vineyard during the picking. There is now more *pigeage* and less *remontage* than there was a decade ago, racking is later, allowing the wine to thrive on its gross lees, and the wines are either fined or filtered, but rarely submitted to both treatments. Having for the past six years had the wines bottled by a contract bottler, Ghislaine has now bought her own bottling machine.

THE WINES

The range is impressive; the wines intense and persistent, but soft and elegant, as all Chambolle's should be, and since 1987, at the very least, quality has been top-notch. What is particularly noteworthy are the differences which can be demonstrated between the various *premiers crus*, each indicative of its *terroir*, none obliterated by too much new oak.

A good measure of the competence of any domaine is what they make out of their village vines, especially in the lesser years, those where there was rain at the time of the harvest. This criteria would be particularly pertinent in Chambolle, with its tendency to wines of delicacy rather than substance.

On this count Ghislaine Barthod scores highly. Her village Chambolle, even in a vintage such as 1992, shows no lack of depth or grip, and no lack of style either. It is an exemplary wine which usually comes into its own after four to five years.

The Beaux-Bruns is a typical Chambolle from the Morey side: plump, lush and ripe, with good backbone and definition, and often a hint of maple syrup. The Véroilles certainly does have a Morey touch, one can see its proximity to Bonnes-Mares. This is a firmer but leaner wine, with less charm at the outset, but no lack of depth.

The Fuées is new, from the 1992 vintage onwards, and when I was there in the autumn of 1993 had recently been racked. More easy to describe is the Cras, one of my favourite wines in the Barthod cellar: fruit flavours of cassis, raspberry and plums expressed in a beautiful fresh, elegant, intense style, overlaid with a hint of violets and under-pinned by just the right measure of new oak.

Again new, from the 1991 vintage, are Châtelots and Baudes. The former seems the lightest of the *premiers crus*, a supple, fragrant wine which is very typically Chambolle. The Baudes is altogether more ample and has more backbone - the *climat* lies directly underneath Bonnes-Mares after all - and is a wine of real richness: meatier than the Cras, but less pure perhaps.

To end this line-up we arrive at the Charmes, traditionally offered last for sampling. It is even better than the Cras. It has a breed and an intensity which have more than once made me write down '*grand cru* quality' in my notes. It is not that it has the most size, but it is the most concentrated. Here, as in the Cras and most of the other *premiers crus* we need to wait seven or eight years after the vintage before the wine reaches full maturity. But as the notes below will show, this is only the beginning. These Barthod Chambolles can easily keep twenty years with no sign of deterioration. It is a fine domaine.

THE TASTING

The following range of wines was sampled in Chambolle in February 1994.

CHAMBOLLE-MUSIGNY, LES CRAS

1992   **1998-2010**

This will be bottled in March or April. Medium colour. A raw wine on the nose. This is *sur colle* in preparation for the bottling, and shows a little astringency and hardness. But underneath good fruit and very good acidity. The finish is the best bit. Long, ample, seductive. Medium to medium-full body only. But plenty of intensity. Very good.

1991   **1999-2015**

Good colour. Splendid nose. Lovely fruit. There is no lack of backbone here but the structure is not too apparent. Real Chambolle finesse. Just a hint of new oak. Medium-full, intense, rich, multi-dimensional. Good ripe tannins. Very good grip. The follow-through is very harmonious and very classy. Lovely.

1990   **2000-2020**

Very good colour. Full, fat, concentrated, firm and rich on the nose. This has closed in now, so it is not as voluptuous as the 1991. There is more to it, and the flavours are more exotic, nevertheless. Fullish, not so much structured as a wine with real dimension and depth. Slightly adolescent now but marvellously rich and opulent on the finish. Splendid fruit. Very fine.

1989   **Now-2015**

Good colour. Very fragrant. Soft, refined, ripe fruit. Very Chambolle. Medium body. This is a gentle example, which is coming forward quite quickly. Just a little tannin to be resolved. Lots of intense and subtle fruit backed with very good acidity. Classy, harmonious and very long indeed. Will last well.

1988   **1999-2018**

Very good colour. The nose is still hidden. But the fruit is classy. Quite a structured wine. Fullish. Good tannins. Very fine slightly plummy fruit - the 1989 is more strawberry and cherry flavoured. Cool, composed, balanced. Still some tannin. This is for the long term. Fine quality. Impressively stylish at the end.

1987   **Now-2005 plus**

Good colour. Just a hint of maturity. Fresh nose. Good fruit. Really quite stylish. Approaching maturity now. Medium to medium-full body. Open, fruity, fat and quite rich, with good refreshing acidity. This is a very good 1987 indeed. The finish is very long and lovely. Classy for the vintage. *Bravo!*

1986   **Drink soon**

The colour is a little light and certainly brown at the rim. But the nose, though soft, is not weedy and the fruit is still fresh. Somewhat dilute and one-dimensional on the palate. But not - or not yet - astringent. Still positive on the finish. But the wine lacks backbone.

1985   **Now-2005**

Very good colour. Still very youthful. The nose is ripe, but it is a little caramelly and rustic. I had hoped for better after above. Medium-full. Still youthful. Reasonable grip. Plenty of fruit. But it is clumsy. It lacks class. There is no nuance here. Good acidity. But no dimension at the end.

1985   **Now-2015**

Second bottle. Still a bit closed. Fullish. Very good acidity. Lovely stylish raspberry fruit. Very concentrated. Very subtle at the end. But unlike most 1985s this needs time still. Very long. Fine.

1984   **Drink soon**

Very good colour for the vintage. Fullish, no undue brown. Surprisingly good nose for a 1984. Fresh, ripe. Positive. Medium body. This has vigour and even concentration. Even a bit of fat as well. Amazingly good. A splendid example. Really long and positive.

1983   **Now-1999**

Medium-full colour. Mature. Not too brown. Ripe and spicy. Not a touch of a hail taint. Nor is it too dry and evolved. Medium-full body. Very 1983 in character on the attack. Yet is sweet and has good freshness on the follow-through. Lacks a little class but ripe and attractive and finishes well.

1982   **Now-2000**

Medium colour. Fully mature. Fresh, open, accessible nose, if without a lot of depth. Yet more to it on the palate. Medium to medium-full. Good acidity here. Stylish. Plenty of fruit. No lack of dimension, especially for a 1982. Long, positive, even complex, finish. Fine for the vintage. Still has plenty of life.

1980   **Drink soon**

Medium colour. Fresher than the above. Mature nose, good fruit, complex. But still fresh. Soft, round, plump and elegant. Very Chambolle. Discreetly classy. By no means a blockbuster but good intensity and a long positive finish. Less vigour than the 1982 though. Very good indeed. But in this line-up the least good of the 1982-1978 flight.

1979   Now-1999

Medium to medium-full colour. More vibrant than the 1980, as well as a little fuller. More aromatic than the 1980 on the nose. Slightly more evolved. Slightly less classy. Fuller, fatter, richer and more vigorous on the palate. More to it. Very good intensity. There is fine lovely fruit. Very concentrated. And plenty of future.

1978   Now-2000 plus

Fullish colour. Only a hint of brown. Ripe nose. Quite exotic. Slightly gamey. Plenty of complexity and depth. Fullish, delicate. Very classy fruit. Lovely harmony. More discreet than the 1979. More intense. More breeding. Complex and concentrated and very long and very lovely. Very fine. Indeed much better and much more vigorous than the 1979.

1977   Drink up

Good colour for the vintage. A little weedy on the nose which I suppose is natural for a 1977 at this stage. But on the palate there is still fruit - if in a lean sort of way - and there is personality and elegance. Very good for the vintage.

Chambolle-Musigny, 1961   Now-2000

Mature colour. Medium-full. Fragrant, complex, very fresh. Now soft mellow and subtle. Medium-full, real depth. Very lovely ripe concentrated fruit. Long, multi-dimensional. Very classy. Amazing vigour. Splendid finish. Very fine, especially for a village wine.

SIMON BIZE,
SAVIGNY-LÈS-BEAUNE

'You have to be philosophical,' says the forty-five-year-old Patrick Bize. 'One year nature is against you. The next year you may produce marvellous wine, but the economy has gone sour and no-one wants it. When there is a short vintage you find you could have sold everything three times over. Then you have a plentiful vintage but the market has gone to sleep.'

And, he could have added, the problem is exacerbated for anyone whose estate is based in Savigny. Savigny is not as fashionable as Vosne-Romanée or Gevrey-Chambertin. Good as its wines may be, they sell for half the price. It costs as much to produce the wine: there is the same amount of new oak and the same necessity for a meagre *rendement*. But the rewards are less.

HISTORY

The Bizes come originally from the Savoie. In the early 1800s one branch settled in Savigny and another went to Paris. The first family records denoting wine-making refer to a Simon Bize who bought some village Savigny and Bourgogne, Les Perrières in 1868. His son, Patrick's grandfather, also called Simon, built up the domaine in the 1920s, and it has gradually been added to since, the last additions being in 1993, to make up a present-day holding of 22 hectares. There was a time, during the 1940s, when Patrick's father, again a Simon, was unwell, and the domaine was run by his brother René; but this Simon took back control in the 1950s. He formally retired in 1988.

Patrick, born in 1952, joined his father in 1978. 'No, I didn't go to wine school. My training was more practical. I can count as my tutors Ramonet *père*, Aubert de Villaine, Henri Jayer, Jacques Seysses, the Marquis d'Angerville and Hubert de Montille. They taught me not only the viti- and vinicultural side but the commercial aspects as well. And look at the bad advice that has come out of the wine schools in the last twenty-five years!'

The Bize domaine was one of the first in the village to go it alone. Grandfather Simon was already estate-bottling before the war. Father Simon increased the percentage in the 1950s and since 1972 the entire production has been marketed in bottle. The familiar name of Frank Schoonmaker crops up as the first American client back in the early 1960s.

Land was a great deal cheaper in those days. When Patrick's father bought another hectare of Savigny-lès-Beaune, Les Vergelesses in 1952 the price was 100 (new) francs an *ouvrée* - negligible! His mother had inherited some vines in her home village of Chassagne-Montrachet. At this time the land had so little value it was given away to those members of the family who remained on the spot.

THE VINEYARDS

Savigny is divided into two by the river Rhoin which rushes down the Vallée Dorée from Bouilland and beyond. On the one side the vines cling to the south and south-east facing slopes of the Bois Noël and join those of Pernand at the Ile-des-Vergelesses. On the opposite flank the vineyard is exposed to the east, even to the north, and meets that of Beaune at the motorway. The soils, and of course the wines, are quite different.

So too are the village wines. One plot occupies the lower land in the valley between the hillsides. Another and better site is the prolongation of the slope under the Bois Noël above the village and further into the Vallée Dorée. This is where the Bize domaine has most of its village wine, and adjoining it, its generics too.

It is fresh and peaceful up here, well away from the hectic traffic on the main Beaune-Nuits-Saint-Georges road. The soil is arid, shallow and poor; very stony, the limestone rock breaking through at intervals. But the wine, in contrast to that from the higher vineyards in the plain, is full of character and individuality, the white as well as the red. Patrick Bize produces Bourgogne *blanc* from both Chardonnay and Pinot Beurot from his Champlains vineyard, and a splendid generic white from older vines in the adjoining Perrières. There is red from this *climat* too and village wine of both colours from Les Bourgeots. Even in the least of these vineyards the *rendement* was no higher than 40 hl/ha in 1992, elsewhere a prolific vintage.

Three years ago Patrick Bize rented some Aloxe-Corton, Les Suchots, the first venture outside Savigny for the domaine. This is village AC (Aloxe has little *premier cru*), but so far I find the results less interesting than those from the more established Grands-Liards, a village Savigny which lies under the *premier cru* Lavières (1.6 ha).

On the Beaune side the Bize estate owns land in one *premier cru*: 0.6 ha in Savigny-lès-Beaune, Marconnets. The soil here is deeper than on the opposite slope: there is clay and gravel too. And the wine is rich and sturdy and tannic, with an earthy *goût de terroir* and a vinosity typical of this side of the village. Perhaps the wine is less elegant than that from the Vergelesses. But it makes up for this in substance.

Guettes, Fourneaux, Talmettes and Vergelesses are where the Bize domaine has its *premier cru* vineyards on the south-facing side of Savigny. As the name Lavières will suggest, the soil here is mainly decomposed limestone rock (*lave*). There is little earth as such. In the Guettes (0.48 ha), nearest to the village, the colour is redder and the slope steep. The wine can be a bit tight and four-square to begin with, but opens out to a typical Savigny: meaty and rich, nicely substantial, good with game. Fourneaux, which lies underneath Les Vergelesses, is half *premier cru*, half village AC, but the Bize hectare is in the upper, better part. I usually prefer this to the Guettes: the fruit is more ample, the wine has more finesse and depth. But it is in the Vergelesses (of which Talmettes is a part) that Patrick Bize produces his largest *cuvée* and best wine. The combined holding is 3 hectares. The wine is the most complete, the most elegant. Above all it has intensity and complexity. A Bize Vergelesses can rival the best of the Ile which lies just below - and is in the commune of Pernand. It needs a decade to come round in the best vintages.

A few years ago Patrick was approached by a company who intended to invest in Burgundian vineyards and wanted to entrust Bize with their management. The first results of this new venture lie in Latricières-Chambertin - 32 ares of it - enough to make five or six barrels. It was only subsequently that Patrick found out that this was the parcel formerly farmed by Laurent Ponsot of Morey-Saint-Denis, for he had not been involved in the negotiations over the purchase. The first vintage is the 1995.

VITICULTURE AND WINE-MAKING

'Old vines and low yields are what is important,' says Patrick Bize, 'otherwise there are no rules. We do what the vine demands.' He has experimented with Cordon training, but gave it up: there were problems of oidium. So he continues with Guyot, pruning very short, and debudding (rather than green harvesting) to keep the harvest down. In 1992 his overall yield, generics included, was 37 hl/ha. In 1993 it was 33.

The wine is fermented in open wood or enamelled steel *cuves*. There is no conscious pre-fermentation maceration. 'If the fermentation starts immediately, we are not worried. If it doesn't, we don't push it.' The *cuvaison* lasts fifteen to twenty-one days, depending on the volume of the *cuve*, and when the wine is racked off, a little sugar is added to prolong the fermentation. This rounds off the wine and adds to its finesse.

The amount of stems which are left in the fermenting must depends more on the state of the vines than on the vintage. Vines which are younger than twenty years are always destemmed. Older vines usually not. Some 50 per cent of new Nevers wood, very lightly charred, is employed for the *premiers crus*, 10 per cent for the rest, but only until the first racking which usually takes place in August, eleven months after the vintage. Thereafter the wine is assembled and fined if necessary with white of egg (it depends on the state of clarification) and bottled in the following March or April. Sometimes it is filtered, sometimes not. Again it depends on the wine.

What has been changed since Patrick took over? The most visible difference is the size of the cellar, a large extension having been completed in 1991. All the red wine is now vinified and matured here. Elsewhere in the village the old *cuverie* is now used only for the barrel fermentation and *élevage* of the white wine; while a third *cave*, shared with the Chandon de Briailles domaine, is used for sundry storage.

'My father,' says Patrick, 'didn't destem at all, and the wines had a shorter maceration because of a lack of space. But we still used the same amount of new wood. We only use the first pressing now. The rest we throw away. In the past we used both pressings.'

Is Vergelesses Always the Best Wine of Savigny?

I posed Patrick the question. The man is modest. He can only speak of his own wines, he says. (For he knows what I am really driving at is whether the Bize Vergelesses is the best of all.) The Marconnets often has the best colour, and is the biggest and most ample. It is easy to appreciate. It is certainly the best *climat* on the southern flank of Savigny. Equally the Guettes may last the longest, despite being a bit hard at the outset. But, he says, Vergelesses is the synthesis, the summation of all the good qualities you find in the other *climats* in the commune. And, he points out, in the olden days – before AC – it sold for the same price as a second-division Corton.

Personally, as I find second-division Cortons even more disappointing than first-division Cortons (and these are inconsistent enough), I would rather have the Bize Vergelesses. Bize is the best domaine in Savigny, and this is its best wine.

The Tasting

I sampled the following wines *chez* Bize in February 1994.

Optimum drinking

Savigny-lès-Beaune, Blanc, Les Bourgeots, 1992
Now–2000 plus

Bottled in September. Ripe, spicy; plenty of style and complexity on the nose. Gently oaky. Quite good grip. Medium-full. The attack hasn't quite come together yet, but the finish is fresh and shows plenty of depth. Good.

Savigny-lès-Beaune, Aux Grands-Liards, 1991
Now–2004

Medium to medium-full colour. Ripe, substantial nose. Plenty of depth here. Medium to medium-full body. Balanced. Succulent fruit. Gently oaky. Good ripe tannins. This is very good indeed for a village wine.

Savigny-lès-Beaune, Aux Guettes, 1991
1999–2012

Medium to medium-full colour. More closed on the nose. Still a little bit tight. On the palate fuller, more intense, more concentrated and more structured. Best on the finish where the wine is rich and meaty with very good grip. Long, classy. Very good. Proof that Savignys were a great success in 1991.

Savigny-lès-Beaune, Les Fourneaux, 1991
2000–2015

Less harvest because of hail in August. 10 *pièces* for 1 hectare was the result. As a consequence a very good colour. Much more so than the Guettes. It was also bottled later, not until August 1993, because the malo took a long time to complete. Much more youthful on the nose. But much more concentrated on the palate. Full, tannic. Rich and profound. Fine. Splendidly complex finish.

Savigny-lès-Beaune, Aux Guettes, 1990
2000–2020

Fine colour. Splendidly rich concentrated nose. Opulently ripe and crammed with fruit. Full, fat and delicious. This is a very rich wine, but with splendid grip to balance it. On the finish long and classy. Very good indeed. Needs time.

Savigny-lès-Beaune, Aux Guettes, 1985
Now–2010

Fine colour. No sign of age. Beautifully balanced, complex and stylish on the nose. Medium-full. Approaching maturity. Very good grip. This is refined and long and subtle. A very good example.

Savigny-lès-Beaune, Les Vergelesses, 1985
Now–2012

Good colour. Rich, round ripe nose. This is medium-full bodied and has very good intensity. Very elegant, concentrated fruit. Very good acidity. A nice lean touch to the character of this wine which will give it plenty of life for the future. Fine.

Savigny-lès-Beaune, Les Vergelesses, 1984
Drink up

Magnum. Lightish colour. Quite brown. Lightish nose. A little dilute and vegetal, though not attenuated. On the palate this hasn't got much vigour or concentration but it is not beyond the pale. Quite fruity. Quite fresh. Not bad. But drink up.

Savigny-lès-Beaune, Les Vergelesses, 1983
Now–2005

Very good colour. Full and rich and vigorous. Not too dry on the nose. But the fruit is cooked. On the palate the tannins are evident on the attack but the wine has grip and the finish is rich and clean. Better with food. Still needs a year. A bigger wine than the 1985. Richer but not as stylish. Very good.

Savigny-lès-Beaune, Les Vergelesses, 1982
Drink soon

Surprisingly good colour. Ripe, plump nose. Reasonable style. On the palate a quite full wine, still fresh, quite rich and meaty. This has good vigour and depth for a 1992, if not a lot of elegance. Positive finish. Good.

Savigny-lès-Beaune, Aux Guettes, 1979
Now-2000 plus

Good fresh colour. Rich, fat, slightly gamey nose. Still plenty of life ahead of it. Ample, even sweet, elegant. Very good grip. Fullish. Surprisingly plump and generous. Long. Very alive. Fine. Very lovely stylish finish.

Savigny-lès-Beaune, Les Vergelesses, 1979
Now-2000 plus

Even better colour. Full and rich and concentrated. This is even better. Splendid nose. Fat and vigorous. Rich, full, very good grip. A very ripe concentrated wine with lovely classy fruit. Complete. Very long. Very fine.

Savigny-lès-Beaune, Les Vergelesses, 1971
Drink soon

Quite an old brown colour now. Laid-back, subtle, soft and fruity on the nose. Refined. Complex, soft, generous. Beautifully balanced. Still vigorous at the end, despite the colour. Rich and lovely. Long and classy. Very fine.

Savigny-lès-Beaune, Les Vergelesses, 1964
Now-2000 plus

Fullish, vigorous colour. No undue brown. Fat, rich and sweet. The ripeness and *rôti* quality of a hot year. Yet not over-tannic. Full body. Meaty rather than gamey. Plenty of structure but no trace of astringency. Rich, slightly spicy and caramelly. Less class than the 1971 but very enjoyable. Fine.

Savigny-lès-Beaune, Les Vergelesses, 1952
Now-1999

Amazingly good colour. Hardly a hint of maturity after forty-two years! Small harvest, small berries, hot and dry summer. One can still smell the tannin and structure, though there is no astringency. Full, aromatic, fat and voluptuous. Even sweet. Plenty of vigour and concentration. Almost creamy in its richness. Lovely. Still has plenty of life.

Savigny-lès-Beaune, Les Vergelesses, 1929
Will still keep

Even more of an amazing colour. Rich, full, very very vigorous. Marvellously youthful nose. Splendid acidity. Not as muscular as the 1952 or 1964. Fullish, smooth as silk. Quite oaky. Very rich and concentrated. Very intense. Very elegant. Marvellously complex and vigorous at the end. Splendid quality.

Savigny-lès-Beaune, Blanc, 1952   Drink soon

Golden colour. At first rather four-square. After a while opened out. Rich. Ripe. Some *surmaturité* Beurot here. Caramelly. Fat. Opulent. Not exactly very refined. But good grip. Not too evolved. Yet in the end a bit rustic.

BONNEAU DU MARTRAY,
PERNAND-VERGELESSES

The domaine which is now called Bonneau du Martray was probably created out of the ashes of the old ecclesiastical land-holdings when these were taken over by the state and sold as *biens nationaux* at the time of the Revolution. It was not the local *vignerons* who benefited; they could not raise the capital. It was the wealthy bourgeoisie. One of the latter was the Bonneau-Véry family. Dr Lavalle, whose book on the history and the wines of the Côte d'Or, published in 1855, is an important source work for those like myself who delve into the origins of the top wine estates, lists the Bonneau-Vérys as owning 19.7 hectares of Corton-Charlemagne at the time, which produced an average of 20 hectolitres per hectare. The family owned the totality of the part of the *climat* which lay within the commune of Pernand (or Pernant, as Dr Lavalle spells it), and together with other land, enjoyed an estate of 24 hectares.

The vines, however, were not yet Chardonnay. They were Pinot Blanc, even Gamay. And they were not very fashionable either. At the time of the Revolution the red wine parts of Corton sold for 250-300 francs an *ouvrée*, the white for barely 150.

Some time after 1855 the domaine was split, and one of the heirs sold his share. Later, following the phylloxera crisis, some of the land at the top of the slope was planted with pines rather than vines. During the miserable 1930s, yet another hectare was amputated. Today, therefore, the size of the domaine is 11 hectares, 9 of which produce white wine, 1 of which is planted in Pinot Noir, and 1 of which is in the process of being converted from red to white.

In 1969 the late Comtesse Jean le Bault de la Morinière inherited the domaine from her uncle René Bonneau du Martray. Her husband, despite his Parisian residence, is descended from Burgundian stock – the Le Bault family, who live in Dijon, were owners on the other side of the Corton hill before the Revolution – and is related on his mother's side to Madame de Sevigné. It was Madame de Sevigné (1626–1696) in one of her many affectionate and revealing letters to her daughter, the Comtesse de Grignan, who uttered the immortal prediction embracing the fashion for coffee, the plays of Racine and the wines of Bordeaux: 'It won't last!'

In the time of Uncle René the totality of the Bonneau du Martray harvest was sold to the local *négoce*, and Jean le Bault could well have continued the part of absentee, disinterested landlord. But no. He had different ideas. He set himself to study viticulture and oenology, and, helped by the rising profitability of top-class wine-making in the 1970s, decided to switch over to bottling and marketing his wines on a direct basis. Today the entirety leaves the domaine in bottle, and 90 per cent is exported.

At the beginning of 1994 there was a dual change of generations at the domaine. Jean-Charles le Bault de la Morinière took over from his father, and in the cellars Henri Bruchon, formerly in charge, took his *retraite* and was succeeded by his sons Bernard and Jean-Pierre.

THE WHITE WINE

The white wine, of course, is now entirely from Chardonnay. Steps have been taken in recent years to limit the harvest even further than hitherto, but nevertheless, with 43 hl/ha in 1993 – more or less the same as the other major land-holder, Louis Latour – I feel it could be reduced even more. This was a vintage, of course, where there was rain during the harvest. Taking their tip from Christian Moueix and Château Pétrus, Jean le Bault and his son Jean-Charles, the latter now living permanently in Pernand with his wife Anne, ordered a helicopter, at 3,000 francs an hour, to hover over the fruit in the vineyard in order to help dry it out.

Just above the church in one of Pernand's steep, winding alleys, an old manoir has been converted into one of the most up-to-date wineries in Burgundy. In the safe hands of the brothers Bruchon, now responsible for the *cave* and the vines, the juice, having been extracted by means of two pneumatic Bucher presses, installed in 1991, begins its fermentation in small 15 hectolitre stainless-steel vats, and once this is under way, it is transferred to oak barrels, one-third of which are renewed each year. There may be as many as eight *cuvées*, which, assuming they are all up to standard, are gradually incorporated together before bottling takes place in March, eighteen months after the vintage. The wine does not spend all its time in cask. Before the second winter it is returned to the tanks in order that it should not become too *boisé* (woody) or dried out.

As far as the white wine is concerned this is clean, meticulous, intelligent wine-making, and the result is a classy product which, if a touch leaner than some Corton-Charlemagnes (because the vines face south and south-west rather than east, overlapping the *sub-climats* of En Charlemagne in Pernand-Vergelesses and Le Charlemagne in Aloxe-Corton, and do not enjoy quite as much direct sunlight during the day), has depth, elegance and harmony. Bonneau du Martray produces the true steely sort of Corton-Charlemagne which is built to last.

THE RED WINE

The red wine, however, has been a disappointment for far too long. For more than two decades – as far as one can see the vintages prior to 1970 were structured enough, if not very elegant -- the Bonneau du Martray Corton *rouge* was slight; sometimes quite fragrant but generally rather light in colour and feeble on the palate. Several explanations were proffered: that the vines were young; that the fruit was prone to rot, being at the bottom of the slope with air circulation prevented by the brick wall below, constructed to combat erosion. Perhaps the plants employed were unsuitable clones; perhaps they were on the wrong rootstock; perhaps they were just simply over-cropped.

Yet it seemed curious that next door to this excellent white was this perennially weedy red. In the early 1990s it was decided to uproot half of the plot and move this land over to Chardonnay. Perhaps what was ripped up was the worst half; perhaps they started to take the red wine seriously. But in 1993 I suddenly saw the red wine becoming serious. Let's hope it lasts. It is made in the traditional manner, being cold macerated for a few days before the fermentation is allowed to begin. The proportion of the stems utilised varies with the vintage: 50 per cent sometimes. None at all in 1995. The wine is bottled after a year and a half, during part of which time, like the white, it may be stored in *cuve* rather than barrel.

THE TASTING

The following wines were sampled in Pernand-Vergelesses in June 1995. From a comprehensive tasting I made in November 1989 I can comment on older vintages as follows:

White Wines

1983 Powerful, alcoholic, better-mannered than most.

1982 Round, generous, fullish. Holding up well.

1979 Very delicious. Complete, harmonious, fragrant. Will last well.

1978 A little austere and not as lovely. Good though.

Red Wines

Generally speaking don't bother. The only one I really liked was the 1959. The 1978 isn't too bad though.

WHITE WINES

Optimum drinking

1993   **2000–2015**

Bottled end April: no undue sulphur. This is very poised. Gently ripe and plump. No undue austerity or leanness. It has plenty of fruit. On the palate very good concentration and intensity for a 1993. Excellent grip. Gently oaky. Lovely vigorous finish. Very classy. Very fine.

1992   **2000–2010**

Fat, ample nose. Nicely reserved and austere for a 1992. Rich on the palate. Gently oaky again. This is a bigger, more muscular wine than the 1993. Excellent depth. Really a lot of class again here. But for a 1992 could have been even *more* concentrated. Fine for the vintage nevertheless. Long and opulent.

1991   **Now–2007**

Ripe and vigorous on the nose for a 1991. Nothing weak or vegetal here. On the nose there is good Chardonnay, and the end on the palate is vigorous. But on the attack it is a touch simple and one-dimensional. Very good style and very good oak nevertheless.

1990   **1998–2015**

Adolescent at first, taking time to come out in the glass. At first it seemed a bit neutral, and I was more than a little disappointed. It is still a firm wine, reserved, but underneath is a splendid opulence, marvellous concentration of fruit and great class. Better than the 1989. Fine quality.

1989   **Now–2008**

A little more colour. Similarly backward. This is a little heavier and more four-square, and the oak shows a little more, for the wine has a little less acidity. Full, very ripe, just a little spicy. Best with food. Very good indeed. But the 1990 is classier.

1988   **Now–2010**

Good firm nose. Fragrant, classy and oaky. Developed in the glass. Slightly linear, ripe, clean, nicely austere. Less to it, but I think it has more class than the 1989 and 1990. Slightly lean, but a fine complex wine. Very long on the palate. This has depth. Fine.

1987   **Drink soon**

This is losing its fruit and class a little now on the nose. But underneath, on the palate, it is still most enjoyable. There is noticeable sulphur on the palate too. With these vintages it is obvious that they had a heavier hand with the sulphur than today.

1986   **Now–2000 plus**

Slightly more colour. A little heavy on the nose. A little SO_2. Fat and rich. A suggestion of over-ripeness. Full, abundant, spicy. A wine for food. It is not exactly exceptionally stylish. But it is warm, generous, masculine and voluptuous. Fresher than a large number of Pulignys and Meursaults. Very good.

1985   **Now–2010**

Again a little more colour. At first a little SO_2 curtails the expression. But this has kept the wine very fresh. On the palate excellent grip. Fine fruit. Very pure and racy. Masculine, firm, complex and really quite concentrated. Just went on getting better and better. Quite structured. Very fine.

RED WINES

1993   **2000–2010**

Very good colour. A feminine example, rich and ripe. But Chambolle-ish rather than Corton-ish. Fragrant, succulent. Medium to medium-full. Classy, complex. Very good indeed. At last something serious!

1992   **Now–2001**

Very good colour for the vintage. Light, ripe nose. Similar on the palate. A little too much of the cherry-flavoured fruit-drops. But pleasant. Yet it lacks a bit of elegance.

1991 **Drink soon**

Medium colour. The nose is a bit hard, more structure and stems than fruit. Medium body. A little sweet. Lacks depth and strength.

1990 **Drink soon**

Light to medium colour for 1990. Again more structure and stems than fruit. The nose is a little weak. And the palate is even more so. This is poor.

1989 **Now–2000**

Medium colour. Much fresher on the nose than the 1990. This is very pleasant. Medium body. Ripe, crisp and fragrant. Generous, charming. Good positive finish. No undue stemmy taste. Very good. Nevertheless a little slight and one-dimensional.

1988 **Now–2000**

Medium colour. Quite brown. Stems on the nose. Better on the palate. A bit lean, a little thin. But quite classy, quite ripe. Rather better than the 1990, though not as charming as the 1989.

1987 **Drink soon**

Light colour. Weak. Thin. Nothing here.

1986 **Past its best**

Light colour. Even worse. Slight decay on the nose.

BOUCHARD PÈRE ET FILS, *BEAUNE*

In April 1995, after several years of rumours that they were in financial difficulties - that, for instance, they had attempted to buy Bouchard Aîné, in order to absorb the name, when this latter firm was sold to Jean-Claude Boisset, but had been prevented from doing so by their bankers - it was announced that Bouchard Père et Fils had been taken over by Champagne Joseph Henriot.

At this stage - I have not yet had a chance to taste the 1995 vintage - it is too early to say what changes will be made by the new owners. The basic change that I for one am hoping for is the injection of a bit of flair into the wine-making. The logistics are already there. Bouchard Père et Fils are by far the biggest landowners on the Côte: 93 hectares of vines of which 71 are *premiers* and *grands crus*. Their winery, built in 1984 and reconstructed after a fire in 1990/1991, is capable of giving them all the control over their vinification and maturation processes that they would wish for. And history, in the form of a record of fine old bottles in the 1940s, 1950s and 1960s, is on their side. Even the will is there, for the Bouchards have been experimenting, and often the results were offered to invited guests at a special tasting during the weekend of the Hospices de Beaune. I remember one year sampling top white wines that had been *bâtonnés* or not, or made with natural versus selected yeasts. Another year there we were asked to pronounce on the effects of different origins and chars of oak. A third discussed filtration. They certainly seemed to be trying to improve.

Yet as other established *négociants* forged ahead in the 1980s, and were joined by an ever-growing number of excellent wine-bottling domaines, poor old Bouchard was left standing. The fizz had evaporated. The stamp of authority had disappeared. An opportunity had been missed.

HISTORY AND THE BUILDING OF A DOMAINE

You have to go back nine generations and over 250 years to find the first Bouchard in the wine business. This was Michel, who was born in 1681, and died in 1755. The family came originally from the Dauphiné, and were cloth merchants. A book of Michel's textile samples still exists.

From cloth – there is a parallel here, at almost exactly the same time, with the champagne house of Ruinart – Michel Bouchard turned to selling wine. The first transaction dates from 1731.

At first the Bouchards only dealt in finished wines. It was not until after the Revolution, during the time of Michel's grandson, Antoine-Philibert, the *centenaire* (he lived from 1759 to 1860), that the first vines were acquired, some 7 hectares in Volnay. Part of this was subsequently to pass out of the hands of the Bouchards, being inherited by Antoine-Philibert's daughter Philiberte Judith, whose daughter married a notary from Nolay called Jean-François Carnot. But a couple of generations later it was to return to the family when Joseph Bouchard, sixth in the line (1862-1941), married his cousin, a descendant of Judith and Jean-François. The Volnay, Caillerets is still commemorated with the suffix '*ancienne cuvée Carnot*'. Perhaps it had always been made and sold by the Bouchards.

Slowly but surely, little by little, the family enlarged their vineyard holdings. Naturally these would be concentrated in the immediate locality. The distance a vineyard-worker could walk, or could be transported by horse and cart from the Beaune headquarters, precluded ambitious forays into the Côte-de-Nuits. In 1909, for instance, Bouchard Père et Fils bought a 6.85 parcel of Corton, divided roughly equally into Corton-Charlemagne and Le Corton. Back in 1838 they had made their first *entrée* into Montrachet, with the purchase of a hectare and a bit from the Comte de Bataille de Mandelot. This has been supplemented with a 2.54 ha parcel of Chevalier-Montrachet (in which *climat* they are the largest land-holder, with 1.39 ha of Meursault, Genevrières, with Chassagne-Montrachet, *premier cru*, En Remilly, with Savigny-lès-Beaune (3.91 ha of Les Lavières), with Pommard and with much else.

But the heart of the domaine lies in Beaune itself. Bouchard Père et Fils possess no less than 46.59 ha of *premier cru* Beaune. Much of this is blended together and sold as Beaune du Château, *premier cru*. Vinified and marketed separately, however, is the 3.36 ha *monopole* of Clos-de-la-Mousse, the 1.98 ha of Clos-Saint-Landry, another monopoly, and, best of all, the 3.91 ha parcel of Beaune, Grèves subtitled Vigne-de-l'Enfant-Jésus.

More recently the Bouchards have expanded both to the north and to the south and into exclusivities. In 1972 they acquired 15 ares of Chambertin. They also own 71 a of village Chambolle-Musigny. They were one of the first to exploit the possibilities, particularly in Aligoté, of Bouzeron, where they now own 1.38 ha of Bourgogne *générique* and 5.57 ha of Aligoté de Bouzeron. Finally in 1995, following the sale to Henriot, further acquisitions were made in the Côte-de-Nuits: 7 *ouvrées* (24 a) in both Clos-de-Vougeot and Bonnes-Mares.

In 1976 they took over (from Bichot; before that it had been Leroy) the marketing exclusivity of the Comte Liger-Belair's Domaine du Château de Vosne-Romanée. This gives them 68 a of Les Reignots, *premier cru*, and the sales exclusivity of the smallest *Appellation Contrôlée* in France, the 85 a of La Romanée itself. The vines are tended and the wine made by Régis Forey in Vosne-Romanée. Bouchard take delivery in cask after the malos have completed.

Another exclusivity is the Nuits-Saint-Georges *premier cru* – and *monopole* – Clos-Saint-Marc, which lies partly in Les Argillières, partly in Les Corvées-Pagets. This is in fact a *métayage* arrangement (but with Bouchard getting both half-shares of the fruit). The owner is Guy Hamonic, director of the National Jurisprudence library at Saint-Cloud in Paris. The parcel measures 93 ares.

THE CHÂTEAU DE BEAUNE

The Château de Beaune, part of the great bastion which used to form the outer walls of the city, lies on the eastern side. After the French Revolution it passed into the hands of the celebrated Dr Morelot, author of one of the first books on Burgundy's wine. His son-in-law was Bernard Bouchard, son of Antoine-Philibert, the *centenaire*, and it was to Bernard that the château, its outbuildings and the cavernous cellars beneath the city walls were to pass, just at the time the Bouchard business was beginning to expand and become a serious affair, a domaine as well as a major *négociant*.

WINE-MAKING

The Bouchard vines in Beaune are tended by their own salaried teams, but elsewhere they are worked *à la tâche*, a local paid so much a year to look after a plot rather than being employed on an hourly basis. Nevertheless the Bouchards exercise plenty of control over what is done. In 1991, for instance, it was decided to plant a special ray-grass between every other row of vines, particularly the young ones, in order to restrain their vigour. As well as this, and as well as combating erosion, they have found that the incidence of rot has been reduced.

In vineyards likely to suffer from drought, i.e. in the stony arid Chevalier-Montrachet, in the upper slopes in Corton, and in the light, shallow soils of the Beaune, Grèves, the Bouchards mulch the soil with bark. In these sort of soils, they will tell you, it would be an error to prune to the Cordon du Royat system. In the deeper soils, however, Cordon-training seems to work, the grapes are naturally riper, there is less risk of rot, and the harvest can be kept low.

Whatever else the explanation for the wines of Bouchard Père et Fils not being as splendid as they could and should be, excessive harvesting is not one of them. Overall, in their *premiers crus* in 1993, they harvested 42.13 hl/ha, in their *grands crus* 34.09 (Jadot's figures are 43.39 and 36.76).

The Pinots Noirs are mostly destemmed – it varies from year to year – and vinified in temperature-controlled tanks using the natural yeasts after several days' cold maceration, *pigeage* and *remontage* being carried out mechanically and the cap kept submerged. Thereafter there are the usual treatments, neither too much nor too little new oak, and bottling is by gravity, the top wines hand bottled.

Are the wines manipulated too much? Is the whole thing *too* technical? Too mechanised? Too safe? There has certainly been some improvement in the 1990s (over the quality during the 1980s) as the new vinification centre has given Christophe Bouchard, born 1949, a qualified *oenologue* and responsible for the wines, more control. But nevertheless if you compare the Vigne-de-l'Enfant-Jésus 1990 with the 1971 and the 1964 . . .

The whites are better, it has to be said, but still, except at the very top levels, leave something to be desired. A Meursault, Genevrières, 1986, sampled in February 1995, was everything that could be desired, and this vintage today can often be a disappointment. But other vintages, other wines, have not inspired me. Yet the presses are the most up-to-date and the cellars are temperature-controlled. It is easy to say what is wrong: an absence of flair. But why? The future of Bouchard Père et Fils, however, is undoubtedly going to be interesting.

THE TASTING

I sampled the following wines at the Château de Beaune in June 1995.

Beaune, Grèves, Vigne-de-l'Enfant-Jésus

Optimum drinking

1993   **1998–2004**

Medium to medium-full colour. Plump nose. Plenty of fruit. Perhaps it lacks a little austerity and grip. It seems quite evolved already. There is a slight lack of freshness. Medium body. Decent acidity but it is a little weak-kneed and the fruit is not very classy. The finish is a bit thin. Quite good for the vintage at best. This is not as good as it seemed in cask.

1992   **Now–2002**

Medium colour. Fresh, attractively fruity nose. Not much substance. But the wine is stylish and balanced. An engaging charming wine. Good harmony, attractive fruit. Has a bit of backbone so still needs a year or two. The good acidity will keep it fresh. A better result within the context of the vintages than the 1993.

1991   **Now–2004**

Good colour. Better than the 1990. Ripe nose. But a little sweet and sweaty. It lacks flair. Better - plumper - as it evolved in the glass. The attack is good. The tannins not unsophisticated. But the follow-through lacks a bit of succulence and real richness. Will this get astringent? It is bigger but a bit more earthy than the 1993. Quite good for the vintage.

1990   **1998–2008**

Medium-full colour. Some evolution now. Firmer and fuller - rather richer and more substantial - on the nose than the 1991. The fruit is slightly cooked, and again a little sweaty. On the palate the wine is rich, but the tannins seem a little rude. The follow-through shows the fruit to the fore, and there is good acidity. But there is no real harmony and finesse. Again quite good for the vintage.

1989   **Now–2002**

Good colour for the vintage. Still very fresh. Plump, fruity nose. No lack of substance. But a slight lack of definition. This is a bit diffuse. On the palate the wine is medium-bodied, is rich and round and a touch sweet. It lacks a bit of what I can only call pure Pinot. There is some substance here so the wine still needs a year. Reasonable acidity but a lack of flair again.

1988   **Now–2000**

Slightly less colour than in the 1989. And more evolved. This is weak and unstylish for 1988. It has a slight element of reduction on the nose. On the palate the fruit is ugly and the tannins are coarse. The whole thing is decidedly pedestrian. Surprisingly for a 1988 there is a lack of acidity. I fear it will get astringent. More like a not-very-good 1987 than a 1988. Disappointing.

1987   **Now–1999**

Medium colour. Now mature. There are dry, slightly over-ripe elements here on the nose which remind me of 1983. The tannins are to the fore. Like many 1983s the wine is better on the palate. There is good acidity, and quite ripe fruit. But the whole thing is a bit tight and ungainly, and a bit astringent at the end. Earthy finish. Not very exciting at all.

1985   **Now–2000 plus**

Medium-full colour. Reasonable freshness and vigour still. Fully mature on the nose. Quite sweet and ripe. Now round and mellow. But it lacks a bit of definition and certainly class. Medium body. Ripe. Mature. There is some balance and style here. And the finish is reasonably attractive and positive. But it lacks real concentration and thrust. More style than some of this series of Vigne-de-l'Enfant-Jésus though. But over-chaptalised and didn't hold up well in the glass. Quite good.

1982   **Drink soon**

Good colour for the vintage. Fully mature. Pleasant nose. Now soft. Is it beginning to lose its fruit? On the palate this is beginning to lose its style. Not that it had a lot to begin with. And the finish shows some signs of astringency. An agreeable wine without hard edges. Quite good.

1971   **Now–2000**

Magnum. Very good colour. Fresh, mature, stylish Pinot nose. This is very good. The wine is mellow but shows no sign of weakness. Medium to medium-full, silky-smooth. Very good fruit. Clean, classy. Still complex. Still long. Still fresh. Most attractive. Very good.

1964   **Now–2005**

Magnum. Fine mature colour. The nose is splendidly rich and meaty. Still vigorous. Round and spicy, sweet. Rich and full on the palate. Concentrated. Classy. An ample, balanced wine. Fine.

1947   **Now–2000 plus**

Deep colour. A little volatile acidity on the nose. Not so much in a second bottle. Marvellously ripe without being over-ripe. Surprisingly good vigour and backbone. Full, really quite masculine and structured. Very rich without being blowsy or inelegant. Firm. Long. Fine. Still a lot of life ahead of it.

La Romanée

1993   **2003-2020**

Very good colour. This has a very fine nose. Rich, almost chocolatey, profound fruit here. Plums, raspberries and cassis. Marvellously complex and integrated. This seems to be in an altogether different league from the rest of this series. Firm, full, good rich ripe tannins. Splendidly concentrated fruit and very good grip. A masculine wine. Slightly leaner than Romanée-Conti or the DRC's Richebourg but certainly of top *grand cru* quality.

1992   **Drink soon**

Very good colour for the vintage. Lots of sulphur on the nose, hiding a very over-blown wine, harvested far too late, with very low acidity. This is already beginning to fall apart. Plump and fruity, but unbalanced and very sulphury on the palate. A good wine ruined by bad *élevage*. I had a sample from the top of the bottle. A top-up was less sulphury.

1991

Not declared.

1990   **1998-2006**

Good colour. But not brilliant in the context of the vintage. And now showing some brown at the edge. This is ripe on the nose, but it isn't exactly rich or concentrated: not in 1990 *grand cru* terms. But it is lush and attractive if a little lacking finesse. Fullish and rich, but the tannins are a bit coarse and the wine lacks flair. Good grip. You can see the potential. But the wine-making was not up to it. Pedestrian.

1989   **Now-2002**

Similar colour to the 1990, but if anything, less brown at the rim. A bit over-ripe on the nose. Not quite as clean as it could be. I wondered if it was a bit corky at first. We tried another bottle. It was similarly over-ripe and seemed to be already thinning out. Medium-full. Some sulphur on the palate. Reasonable fruit and acidity but the whole thing once again coarsely constructed. Rather weak. Thin finish. Poor.

1988   **1998-2010**

Very good colour. Much more to it than the 1990. Slightly old-fashioned meaty nose. Sweet-sour. There isn't much Pinot purity about this, I regret. Better on the palate. This is better than both 1990 and 1989 in my book. The whole thing seems cleaner. There is better fruit. Good acidity and the tannins are reasonably under control. Some elegance at last. Full, masculine, backward again. Very good plus.

1987   **Now-2007**

Good fullish, mature colour. Rather lumpy and four-square on the nose. The tannins are unsophisticated. They lie underneath the wine, dense and slightly unripe. On the palate however, like the 1988, the wine is better. It is not brilliant, but it is a pretty good effort for the vintage. Rich, reasonably balanced and fresh. Long and positive at the end, even generous. Will still improve. Very good indeed for the vintage.

1985   **Now-2000**

Medium-full, well-matured colour. On the nose this shows rather rude, dry tannins for a 1985 - why so tough? Well-matured for a 1985. Medium-full, rather coarse and unbalanced. This is tasting far older than it should. The fruit is nice and ripe, and there is no lack of acidity. But where is the class?

1982   **Now-2000**

Very good colour for the vintage. Soft, mellow, quite classy nose. On the palate the wine is fresh, classy, mellow and smooth. Good vigour for a 1982. No hurry to finish this up. Ripe, nicely concentrated. Very well put together. Really classy. Fine for the vintage.

1976   **Now-2000**

Full, still fresh looking. Like all 1976s this is a bit tough on the nose. On the palate though there is no undue tannin or astringency. The wine is rich, quite exotically fruity, still very fresh. There is just a little rigidity. But this would not be apparent with food. The follow-through is ripe and mellow. Perhaps there is a little lack of concentration here. The power and intensity one can see in the 1982 is not here. Also the acidity is less. Is this lack of thrust the age or was it always like this? Very good but not great.

Chevalier-Montrachet

1993   **1999-2009**

Youthful nose. Good richness, good acidity, good oak. All slightly separate at present. On the palate this is highly promising. Firm, backward, very clean, very classy. Long and nicely poised and harmonious. Nothing untoward sticks out. I think this will be very fine.

1992   **1998-2012**

This has a curious whiff on the nose. High toned, daffodils and celery. Underneath pure, scintillating, ripe, not a bit too muscular or too woody. This is very well put together. Nicely racy. Very concentrated. Really poised and harmonious. Lovely fruit. Excellent definition.

Very floral. A hint of honey. Gentle but intense and persistent. Less acidity than 1993. Not larger than life. Fine plus.

1991   **Now-2001**

A very good result for the vintage. Nicely firm. Good fruit and oak. Plenty of character. There is less here than in the 1993. What it lacks is a bit of natural intensity. But it has the grip and the fruit, and, if not *that* abundant, is quite classy. It will always be a little one-dimensional, but that is the vintage, and for a 1991 it is very good indeed.

LE MONTRACHET

1991   **Now-2007**

Fat, rich, aristocratic nose. On the palate fullish, nicely ripe. Still closed. Not a *lot* of grip though. But I like the fruit. Classy. Still a little hardness on the follow-through. Good length.

1990   **Now-2012**

Lovely fruit here on the nose. An opulent wine but with a good reserve of acidity. This is very elegant and very delicious. Full, intense, youthful - but not aggressively so. Very splendid fruit above all. Real flair and style. Very lovely. Very elegant.

1989   **1999-2015**

On the nose this is richer and more powerful than the 1990, but with slightly less acidity - or freshness of acidity. Fuller, just a hint of reduction and *sur-maturité*. The oak is also more evident. This is more adolescent. Fatter. Spicier. More alcoholic. At present it is the 1990 which sings. But this may last longer and end up better. Virile. Powerful. Bags of life.

1971   **Drink soon**

Golden colour. A little reduction on the nose at first. This is quite evolved - more so than it should be. Good acidity. But the fruit has disappeared a bit. This is by no means great. Classy, but a lack of real dimension and concentration and vivacity. Yet lush, fruity. And it got better and better - fatter - in the glass. Ripe, ample. Fine.

ALAIN BURGUET,
GEVREY-CHAMBERTIN

Sometimes I wish I were a French wine dictator, able to confiscate prime land from perennial under-achievers and present it, *carte blanche*, to some small grower who had shown that he or she had merited it. Sadly, Gevrey-Chambertin possesses a number of the former. The waste of opportunity is tragic. The village, though, also boasts a number of the latter, domaines built up from scratch from nothing, without much in the way of illustrious *climats*, whose owners deserve all the encouragement that they can get.

For the last decade I have organised, every June, a party in Burgundy. I invite all the growers I know best and everyone arrives with samples of the vintage which is ten years old. It is not a competition but a celebration. The best that Alain Burguet can offer is a Gevrey-Chambertin *vieilles-vignes* – not a *grand cru*, not even a *premier cru*. But it has never once failed to hold its own against much more illustrious wines.

Alain's Gevrey is a *vin de garde*, as sturdy and as uncompromising as the man itself. It is not made to be enjoyable when young. Alain is totally unconcerned whether it is *flatteur* at the outset or not. This is a wine for the ten-year term. It is a yardstick example and proof that even 'lesser' Burgundy can be very fine, and last and last.

HISTORY

There have been Burguets in the Gevrey locality for some time now. But more as *vignerons* than as *propriétaires*. Alain's grandfather Arsène Burguet, originally from the Savoie, arrived in Gevrey when he married a local girl soon after the First World War. This marriage produced Yvon, who was one of the vineyard workers for the Domaine Tortochot, but managed to scrape together a couple of hectares of his own on the side. And Yvon had two sons, Gilles in 1947, and then Alain, born in 1950.

Alain and his father did not get on. Indeed it would seem that relations between Yvon and Gilles were not that hot either, for Gilles upped sticks and became a long-distance lorry-driver for a number of years, only returning to take over his share of the family vines after Yvon's death in 1991.

Alain left school at fourteen, apprenticed himself alongside his father and *chez* Tortochot, but after a monumental family row determined to go off on his own. In 1974 an elderly farmer decided to retire, and Alain took over his 2.10 ha estate on a *métayage* basis. His first vintage was the 1975, a difficult, rot-infested year, which he freely admits he screwed up. But the 1976 he got right, and he has hardly put a foot wrong since.

Slowly but surely Burguet has expanded his exploitation. It has not been easy, and it has not been cheap. But when he can he has bought or leased new land, and he now looks after 5.60 ha, 3.5 ha of which he owns in his own right. 'All the profit I make has to be immediately paid out – back to the bank,' he complains. But he admits the financial discipline is good for him. In 1985 he acquired land in the *premier cru* Les Champeaux, which he re-planted the following year. From the 1993 vintage this has been isolated as a separate *cuvée*, all three *pièces* of it. At first he produced solely a village *vieilles-vignes cuvée* under his own label, selling the rest off in bulk, for reasons of cash flow. Today he bottles all he makes, including some Bourgogne *rouge*. It is still not a great deal, but is an improvement on the amount of Burguet wine that was available a decade ago.

At the beginning it was hard to find customers, and the well-known family difficulties, as well as his own character – for this is a no-nonsense man: he doesn't dissemble – made the locals somewhat suspicious of him. But Becky Wasserman sampled his 1978, and started to sell his wines on the US market, and one day Jean Troisgros dropped by, just on the off-chance, liked what he tasted – it was the same 1978 – and once you are in one three-star restaurant it is much easier to sell into others.

WINE-MAKING

'I have not changed my methods,' says Alain. In most respects this is absolutely true. But there is an exception. Alain used to be wary of new oak, fearing that his wines would dry out, and believing that they were already tannic enough. But one year Becky Wasserman sent him a new barrel, complete with a pink ribbon, for his birthday, in order that he could experiment. Gradually the Burguet attitude mellowed. In 1988 he only used 5 per cent new wood, and that only in his *vieilles-vignes cuvée*. Today the percentage is 30, Alain buying ten to fifteen new barrels a year. And the wine, in my view, is better.

Alain is a great believer in the natural acidity of the wine. This is essential if you are producing a *vin de garde*, he says. This is one of the reasons he ploughs his land, doesn't use herbicides, and tends to pick early. In 1988 he started two days before the official *Ban des Vendanges*. This is in theory illegal. But his friends came to his support and he escaped prosecution.

He is also, naturally, for a low harvest. Old vines and vigorous pruning keep the yields low and concentration high – and means that the crop is riper earlier. After that it is a hands-off approach. Minimal sulphuring, minimal chaptalisation – if the grapes are at 12° he'll only add half a degree, to compensate for what is lost during the fermentation process, and at the end of the fermentation, in order to prolong it as efficiently as possible - and otherwise letting nature take its course. He usually destems entirely, allows the temperature to rise to 35°C before cooling, and after a quick malo-lactic keeps the wine on its fine lees, bottling early, thirteen to fourteen months or so after the harvest. He doesn't fine the wine, preferring to keep the CO_2 in it, but lightly filters instead.

The wine is vinified in a temperature-controlled winery at the back of his house in the Rue de l'Eglise and the barrels stored in the cellar underneath. Burguet now has a new, temperature-controlled cellar at the top of the village, part of a building which is probably 400 years old. This will replace the three bottle-storage cellars he used to have, dotted round the village.

LE ROI CHAMBERTIN

Petty jealousies abound in wine-making villages, and Gevrey is no exception. You might have imagined the rugged, independent Burguet continuing to do his own thing, aloof from the back-biting that went on. But no. He was one of the originators of the *Roi Chambertin* September festival, aimed at grouping all the local growers together to present a common promotion of Gevrey to the world. Together with Gabriel Tortochot (who lives two houses down the road), Jean Trapet, M. Jacquin, a local businessman, and the writer and historian Jean-François Bazin, Alain helped launch the idea in the early 1980s. It was difficult to get off the ground at first, and to this day one or two growers still stand apart. But ten years on it is now one of the landmarks in the Burgundian calendar. Next to the imposing, bearded Gérard Vachet and the svelte Sylvie Esmonin, all in their robes and finery, the short stocky Alain Burguet, not quite as wide as he is tall, comes as a contrast. But the reception he gets shows that this one-time outsider is now acknowledged as one of the super-stars of the village.

THE TASTING

I sampled the following wines *chez* Alain and Dominique Burguet in February 1995.

GEVREY-CHAMBERTIN, VIEILLES-VIGNES
(all in magnums)

Optimum drinking

1993   1999–2009

Good colour. Rich fat nose with a lot of depth. Good tannins. Sturdy but well covered. Some 30 per cent of new wood in this *cuvée* now. Fullish, balanced, meaty. Very good grip. Lovely plump stylish fruit. Long. Complex. Very good indeed.

1992   Now–2004

Very good colour for the vintage. Ripe, plump, raspberry and cherry-flavoured nose. Plenty of substance but no hard edges. Some tannin but the tannins nicely ripe. Good grip. Fresh and fruity. Plenty of depth for the vintage. A most attractive example. Ready soon.

1991   1998–2010

Excellent colour. Very good nose. The tannins are firm but not hard, fully ripe. Medium-full, more structure than in the 1993, and on the palate a certain hardness still. But this will disappear. Good grip. Cassis fruit, and plenty of it. Rich, ripe, long positive finish. Quite sturdy, but certainly very elegant. This will keep very well. Very good indeed.

1990   2000–2020

Marvellously full rich colour. Not a hint of development. Nicely firm, like the above, but hugely abundant: rich, exotic, very concentrated. This is beginning to go into its shell, having lost its puppy fat. Full, powerful, intense and concentrated. Very good grip. Marvellous rich finish. Excellent.

1989   Now–2004

Good vigorous colour. Less development than most. On the nose not the size of the above. A wine which though not quite ready seems delicately poised, even fragile. Sweet fruit here. On the palate the wine is less evolved and less delicate than it seems on the nose. Indeed better structured. Medium to medium-full. Less sturdy than most of Burguet's wines. Full of fruit. Good acidity. Just a little tannic astringency still. Fine finish. Great charm. Very good.

1988　　　　　　　　　　　　　**1998-2018**

Splendid colour again. Not a trace of development. This is back to the usual Burguet style: sturdy and tannic, rich and meaty. This is particularly youthful. Very good grip. Fullish. Still quite a lot of unevolved tannin. But marvellous raspberry-cassis fruit. A classic. Very very long. Really classy. Fine: as good in its own way as the 1990.

1987　　　　　　　　　　　　　**Now-2005 plus**

Good vigorous colour. Fullish, not a lot of development. Very good nose. Nothing unstylish or ungainly here. Good round tannins. But fresh and plump. This is medium to medium-full, nice and fresh. Good backbone. Ample, balanced stylish fruit. Clean and classy. Very fine indeed for the vintage. Harmonious and elegant. This is a great 1987. Plenty of life ahead of it.

1986　　　　　　　　　　　　　**Drink soon**

Medium fully mature colour. This is not in the same league as the 1987. A slight dryness and astringency on the nose, and a bit diffuse. It is a bit better on the palate. Fruity, even a bit sweet and artificially so. Medium body. Not short. But the follow-through lacks elegance and the finish is a bit meagre. Drink soon.

1985　　　　　　　　　　　　　**Now-2015**

Fine colour, hardly any sign of development. As a result of spring frost Alain made 18 hl/ha. Splendid nose. Ample mulberry fruit. Good structure, the usual Burguet firmness. Good grip too. A lovely generous wine, still fresh. Very good ripe tannins which still need time to soften up. Plump, complex, harmonious, nicely abundant. Very long. Very lovely. Still needs a year or two.

1984　　　　　　　　　　　　　**Drink soon**

Fully mature colour. Evolved nose. But this is certainly very respectable, and by no means at its end. Good fruit. A little lean but not astringent. Not tired. Not a bit unclassy - as at the end of the 1986. Fresh and balanced. Plenty of enjoyment to be had. I prefer this to the 1986.

1983　　　　　　　　　　　　　**Now-1999**

This again is more than respectable. Fully evolved colour. On the nose none of the undue astringency or aspect of chicken shit that you get in some 1983s. Ripe and sweet on the palate. Medium-full. Spicy and not exactly elegant but clean, rich, and with no lack of grip. It is less concentrated and not as weighty as I had expected, but much better mannered, better harmony and freshness. *À point.*

1982　　　　　　　　　　　　　**Now-2000**

Really quite an evolved colour, despite it being in magnum. But quite full. Lovely mature nose. Full of fruit. No weakness at all. Very good freshness and grip. Medium to medium-full, round, vigorous, complex, ripe. This is quite substantial. Good positive long finish. A very serious example of the vintage. Will still keep well. Better than both 1983 and 1984.

1981　　　　　　　　　　　　　**Drink soon**

Much better colour. Fuller, more vigorous. A tiny harvest for Alain; he made 17½ *pièces*. On the nose no lack of balance or freshness, but slightly lean and austere. Yet really quite ripe and substantial. Plenty of interest, even in its slightly cool way. And, despite a little astringency now, no lack of charm and attraction.

1980　　　　　　　　　　　　　**Drink up**

Good colour. Also full, also vigorous. But more so than the 1981. Firm and even masculine on the nose. Slight hardness on the tannic front. On the palate there is a touch of astringency now. Medium to medium-full body. And the wine has become a little lean. But good grip. A certain lack of generosity here. For a Côte-de-Nuits so it is now marginally disappointing, especially after the 1981 and 1982 which are surprisingly good within the context of their vintages. The acidity shows at the end.

1978　　　　　　　　　　　　　**Now-2005 plus**

Very good colour. Vigorous, full and rich looking. On the nose a wine of richness, substance and depth. A bit more rustic (the stems seem to show more) than the wines today. Fullish, meaty, good acidity. Now the secondary flavours of a mature wine without having lost the vigour and structure of its youth. Lovely complex finish. More stylish on the palate. Long and complex. Fine. Bags of life ahead of it.

1977　　　　　　　　　　　　　**Past its best**

Old colour. Light, old, a bit sour. Rather astringent but not dead or unbalanced. Was perfectly respectable once.

LOUIS CARILLON ET FILS, *PULIGNY-MONTRACHET*

'There are seventy people who make wine in Puligny today,' estimates Louis Carillon, 'but only twenty who live off it, and only seven or so who bottle a serious amount of their produce themselves.' There have been Carillons in the village for centuries – they can trace their history back even further than the Leflaives – but it is only in the last few years that they have been part of the serious seven or so. As recently as 1985 they sold half of their harvest to the *négoce*. Today it is 10 per cent.

This is a dynasty which is steeped in wine, pursuing a tradition which has been passed down from father to son since 1632, the date they boast on their label, when a Carillon *viticulteur* is recorded; or since 1611, the date engraved on the lintel above the entrance to one of their cellars; or even since 1520, when a Jehan Carillon is mentioned in archives. The family still occupy the same premises as they did then, between the church and the old château which belonged to the original *seigneurs* of the village. Today – for with the high water-table, underground cellars in the village are precluded, and so one has to expand sideways – the Carillon network of buildings for vinification, barrel and bottle storage, plus the living quarters the various members of the family occupy, make up a positive rabbit-warren of ancient courtyards, secluded alleys, and sudden private gardens, the old and the new in happy but haphazard confusion.

HISTORY

Recent history begins with Louis, born about two-thirds of the way through the last century. He was followed by his son Prosper, who was in charge at the time of the Second World War, and then Robert, the current head of the family, born in 1914. Grandfather Robert, though he has now turned eighty, and suffers somewhat from the after-effects of a stroke, is still active, still ready with a comparison between the latest vintage and one of thirty or forty years ago.

Louis, the Louis after which the domaine is currently named - fifteen years ago it was Carillon Père et Fils - was born in 1937. Burly and dark-haired, with a no-nonsense manner about him, he recalls Puligny and the Carillon domaine when he was young. 'We had a horse then. It was much later that tractors began to appear. And much less land was under vine. The land below the village, towards the Nationale, was polycultural, a garden of vegetables and soft fruits. Up on the hillsides most of the steeper land, the Folatières, for example, was *en friche*.' The Carillon family worked 6 hectares, but quite a lot of this produced only generic wine.

Slowly but surely, from the late 1940s onwards, the Carillons expanded their domaine. Some 3 *ouvrées* of Bienvenues-Bâtard-Montrachet, their single *grand cru*, were acquired in 1955, needing replanting. A further 6 *ouvrées* of Perrières, little by little, augmented grandfather's 16. Up to the end of the 1950s, apart from a few hundred bottles sold to private customers, the Carillons sold their entire harvest in bulk. But from then on they began to hold more and more back, and they even began to export a bit. The domaine was further extended when Louis married. His wife comes from Chassagne-Montrachet. Through her - for Chassagne is a much inter-married village - the couple's sons, Jacques, born in 1962, who makes the wine, and François, born in 1968, who looks after the vines, have cousins throughout Chassagne as well as in Puligny.

THE VINEYARD

The Carillon domaine now occupies 12 hectares, and of this the vast majority lies in Puligny. There is Saint-Aubin, Chassagne (both red and white) and even Mercurey, and of course the usual generics, but no less than 5 hectares of village Puligny, scattered over eleven different *lieux-dits*. Some of this village wine is sold in bulk, as is the produce of 23 ares of Champ-Gain.

On the Meursault border, the domaine has vines in all three of the *premiers crus*. Referts lies furthest down the slope, and the soil is pebbly, lying on hard rock. Here there are 21 ares, planted in 1961. At the top, with crumblier rock, the friable limestone known as *lave* but with much less earth, is Champs-Canet (55 a planted in 1952 and 1972). In between, at present very young vines (planted 1989) are 47 a of Combettes.

Further south, towards Clavoillon and Pucelles, is the *climat* of Perrières, not to be confused with the Meursault vineyard of the same name. The official surface area of this Perrières is 8.40 ha, but 3.92 of this sells as Clos-de-la-Mouchère, and is a *monopole* of the Domaine Jean Boillot of Volnay. If one excludes this, the Carillon family, with 94 a of vines of various ages, is the largest grower in the *climat*. The soil, as the name suggests, is pebbly, as in the Referts, but the colour is less rich, a pale ochre rather than a reddish brown. The wine is different. The Referts, I remember Jacques Carillon telling me once, produces a wine with more acidity: an advantage in the ripe years, the reverse in the leaner vintages.

Finally there is the Bienvenues, that strange little bottom right-hand chunk (as you face the mountain) within the Bâtard-Montrachet. The Carillons own 12 ares, the vines dating from 1959.

WINE-MAKING

On either side of the Rue de l'Église, one building entirely covered in creeper, lie the Carillon vinification cellars. In here you will see a Vaslin press, a new pneumatic machine, first employed in 1992, and a rotating horizontal stainless-steel *cuve* for vinifying the red wines.

The entire domaine is still picked by hand, and all the grander wines, plus about 70 per cent of the village Puligny, of which there will originally be up to five different *cuvées*, are fermented in barrel.

Jacques Carillon has decided views on the wines he likes and dislikes. He does not like wines with too exotic a flavour: so he doesn't ferment at too low a temperature, doesn't exaggerate the *bâtonnage*, and doesn't subject the wine to too much new oak. All these three can produce wines which are *flatteurs* in cask: but they don't last. They will dry out.

He also dislikes the taste of over-ripeness. What you will be left with eventually will be alcohol, not enough acidity, and a lack of elegance. What he is looking for is wines for the long term. Since 1991 they have been pruning harder, reducing the crop from the outset. The result, he says, is more concentrated wine which takes longer to open out.

So there is only a modicum of new oak: one new cask in four or five for the grand wines, one in seven or eight for the village wine. And some of the casks are the larger *demi-muids*, though of recent construction.

Adjoining one of the *cuveries* – you step down marginally, and now have to dip your head – is the first of the barrel cellars. There is another one out beyond a house which is no longer occupied, which is even more claustrophobic. This cellar is cooler. The wines mature more slowly. In these two cellars the wines will remain on their lees for nine to twelve months, before the wood and the space are released for the next vintage. Bottling of the village wine begins in September, after a *Kieselguhr* operation to eliminate the finings and later a membrane filtering. The better wines are held in tank for a further three to six months.

These tanks occupy yet another cellar. This is one of the dependencies of the old château, and is reached either by driving round three sides of a square, past buildings seemingly untouched since the Revolution, or by following a meandering series of alleys, carefully constructed, I'm sure, so that the uninitiated would get completely lost. This cellar is modern, air-conditioned and functional. A travelling machine will arrive to do the bottling, but the Carillons do their own labelling and cartoning. Here the bottles and cases are stored until despatch.

THE WINES

The Carillon village Puligny is exemplary: a yardstick example of what it is, and a splendid representation of the Carillon style. It is clean, poised, elegant and plumply fruity, with just the merest suggestion of new oak; a most attractive bottle.

The Referts is an ample wine, the most Meursault-ish of the range. It can have a flavour of honeysuckle. But underneath there is a good steely acidity and plenty of fat. The Champs-Canet is similar, usually richer and fatter, perhaps a little more honeyed, but equally lovely. There is no general rule, in my experience, as to which is the better.

The Perrières, however, is a wine of different character, though again whether it is the best of the three or not varies from vintage to vintage. It is a more austere, mineral wine, though not necessarily more structured. There is an aloof but feminine, flowery character on the nose, good depth, and plenty of complexity at the end. All three are excellent.

From their 3 *ouvrées* of Bienvenues the Carillons produce one of the best examples of this *grand cru* in Burgundy. There is racy peachy fruit here as well as honeysuckle, no exaggerated new oak, subtlety, complexity and intensity. Some Bâtards can be a little heavy and four-square. I have never found even a suggestion of this in the Carillon Bienvenues. It is a delicious example. This is a seriously good family domaine.

THE TASTING

I sampled the following wines in Puligny in June 1994.

Puligny-Montrachet, 1992   **Now–2004**

Fullish, plump, ripe, but a touch adolescent at the moment. This is rich and generous. Very gently oaky. Good grip. Slightly rigid just at present. But very good.

PULIGNY-MONTRACHET, PERRIÈRES

1992   **1998–2010**

Ripe, fat, silky-smooth nose, with just a touch of wood. This is very elegant and very impressive. Very classy and complex. Fullish. Very good grip. An ample wine. Very well balanced. Shows very well indeed. Marvellous finish.

1991   **Now–2001**

Leaner on the nose, but nevertheless plenty of depth and style. Less acidity than the 1993 (sampled from cask) though. A slighter wine. Quite advanced. Medium body. Plenty of interest. Balanced and ripe. Soft and quite forward. But good grip. Elegant and positive. A very good result for this vintage. Long and satisfying.

1990   **Now–2009**

This is a bit between two stools on the nose, having lost the fresh exuberance of the 1992 and not having yet gained the maturity of the 1985. On the palate the wine is full, fresh, peachy and harmonious. Very good grip again. Fatter and less flowery than the 1992. Fine finish. A more structured wine. Perhaps just a little less elegant. But fine.

1989   **Now–2002**

More positive on the nose than the 1990. Rich, concentrated, ample. Not as fat or as concentrated on the palate as the 1990. Seems to have less backbone and excitement. The alcohol is more obvious. And it doesn't seem to have quite as much acidity. Less substance. Less vivacity. Good grip. But not nearly as interesting. Very good merely.

1988   **Now–1999**

Youthful colour. A little unforthcoming on the nose. Not a lot of richness, dimension and intensity, but clean and fruity. Surprisingly good on the palate. Fresh, balanced and plump. Not a lot of depth but has harmony, definition and length - even depth. Medium body. *À point.* Very good. I'd rather drink this than the above.

1987   **Drink soon**

Slightly deeper colour. More evolved slightly vegetal nose. A little neutral, a little lean and mean on the attack. The finish is more attractive. Fresh because of the acidity. Yes, and positive too. Not bad at all. Plenty of enjoyment here.

1986   **Now–2005**

Good fresh colour. Soft nose. Quite evolved; a slight touch of *sur-maturité*. Not the grip of the 1985. Plump, round and generous. Ripe and ample and buttery. Very attractive, but in the final analysis lacks the grip for a wine of the depth and real seriousness of 1985. Fresher than the 1989 though. Fine nevertheless. Very very long.

1985   **Now–2015**

Fuller colour than the above. This is excellent. Full, distinguished. Youthful, very concentrated, quite structured nose. Full, rich, and very impressive on the palate. It is still a touch adolescent. Still very fresh. Marvellous complex fruit, only now beginning to come out. Very long, very concentrated, very subtle. Excellent. Will still improve.

1984   **Now–2000**

This is extraordinarily good. Fresh colour. Good fresh nose. Not a bit lean and vegetal. On the palate neither lean or mean but ample, indeed generous. Upright, round, one can see just a touch of oak. A little austerity, naturally, but amazingly enjoyable. Will still last well. Stylish, long, complex finish. Fine.

1983   **Drink soon**

Deepish colour. Really quite golden. Nose of a dry Sauternes. Not too blowsy though. A slight sweet-sour element but nevertheless fresh. Fat, rich, honeyed, quite alcoholic. But not too old. A little heavy perhaps and not exactly elegant. A wine for food.

1982   **Drink up**

Quite a deep colour. Maderised touches on the nose, with a touch of reduction. Better on the palate. Medium body. Well matured. Loosening up a bit and losing its elegance. Never really very very concentrated. Not bad, but a bit past its best.

OTHER WINES SAMPLED

Bienvenues-Bâtard-Montrachet, 1985 Now–2005

Good colour. Ripe and concentrated and gently oaky, but more evolved than the Perrières. Now absolutely *à point*. Rich, ample, generous. Delicious. Very good grip. Very long. Very fine indeed.

Bienvenues-Bâtard-Montrachet, 1966 Now-2000

Well-matured but still fresh, even crisp, without having lost any of its fruit. Youthful but beeswaxy. Lovely fruit. Long, discreet. Lemony-appley but in the best, ripest sense. Fine. Still bags of life.

Saint-Aubin, *Premier Cru*, 1985 (*rouge*) Now-2000

Fresh, fragrant, soft and brisk. Very good stylish fruit. This is youthful for a Saint-Aubin. Still has bags of life, even if lightish. Elegant finish. Very good for what it is.

Chassagne-Montrachet, 1978   Now-2000

Mature colour. A mix of village and *premier cru* Macharelles. A meaty example, with a touch of cooked fruit and liqueur cherries. Good vigour. Fresh. Fullish. Good if no real elegance. A bit four-square.

Mercurey, 1969   Now-2000

A mixture of village and *premier cru* Champs-Martin. This is round, mature, fragrant and surprisingly fresh. Indeed elegant. Good grip. Raspberries and redcurrants. Long. Not a bit rustic. A fine example of a Côte Chalonnaise. Plenty of life still.

CHANDON DE BRIAILLES,
SAVIGNY-LÈS-BEAUNE

The Savigny-based Domaine Chandon de Briailles has been bottling and exporting longer than most, since the 1950s if not earlier. The wine it made enjoyed a high reputation in those days - well deserved, judging by the 1959s today - and sold in top Parisian restaurants such as Lasserre, Prunier and La Tour d'Argent. But sadly after that standards declined, a result of a lack of interest on the part of the proprietors, absentee landlords who lived in Paris, and sloppy cellar techniques on the spot. Happily the last decade has seen a renaissance. Since 1989 this has once again been a source for that *rara avis*: top-notch red Corton.

HISTORY

The estate last changed hands in 1834 when it was bought by Pierre Guillemot, a councillor at the royal court at Dijon. Count Aymar-Claude de Nicolay inherited it from his grandmother the Countess Chandon de Briailles and is now sole owner, having bought out his brother's share in 1971. He is a cousin of the Chandons of Moët.

The base for the domaine is a fine Louis XIV *manoir* built in 1704 by Isaac Theureau, a local squire, the dependencies being constructed over Cistercian cellars. There is a large garden, laid out in the style of Le Nôtre, full of mature trees, standard roses and box hedges, and containing at the far end what looks like a family tomb, but is merely some other sort of architectural *jeu d'esprit*, a grotto with statues of Greek deities. Over all the stonework are encrusted rustic carvings, bosses, gargoyles and the like, now somewhat worn by the wind and the rain. These add to the charm and the individuality of the place. But I would suggest that they are an acquired taste.

As the name Guillemot does not appear in Burgundian books of the last century I assume the vineyards that the domaine owned, and there were even more then, were leased out to local *vignerons* during this period. In the time of the Chandon de Briailles they were taken back, and the estate started to bottle and market at least some of its produce itself. But then, after the old Countess died, things went into decline. Count Aymar-Claude was busy in Paris with his property company, and Nadine, whom he had married in 1956, was occupied with their four young children. Meanwhile the average age of the Chandon vines had declined, as a result of quite a lot of replantation in the early 1960s.

But no-one was interested. Indeed some parcels of Serpentières and Guettes, both *premiers crus* next to the village graveyard on the Pernand side of Savigny, were sold off. When I first started to visit on a regular basis I formed a distinct could-do-better opinion of what the estate was producing, but the resident cellar manager, François Pacquelin, didn't seem very bothered.

Enter the whirlwind. As her daughter Claude puts it, Nadine de Nicolay, having finished rearing her family, needed something to occupy herself. Tall, blonde and handsome, with bounteous energy and an indefatigable determination to pour her heart and soul into the domaine and its wine, Nadine was just what this sleepy under-achieving estate required. She first started to get involved in 1982; but it was really from 1984 onwards that she took over responsibility. Pacquelin was persuaded to retire, and in his place the young shaven-headed Jean-Claude Bouveret, known to one and all, even himself, as Kojak, for obvious reasons, was appointed cellar-master. The third of Nadine's daughters, Claude, born in 1967, decided that she too was interested, and enrolled herself to take diplomas in viticulture and oenology at the University of Dijon. Sometimes, I get the feeling, there is a clash between Nadine's enthusiasm and her daughter's quieter professionalism. But it is a good team, and the results are there for all to see.

THE VINEYARDS

In total the Chandon de Briailles domaine comprises some 13 hectares. On the Pernand side of Savigny-lès-Beaune under the Bois Noël there are 2.61 ha of *premier cru* Lavières. Below it, on similar crumbling limestone rock, but on flatter land, lie 2.1 ha in Fourneaux, in both *premier cru* and village appellation land.

Turning round the corner into the commune of Pernand-Vergelesses we have 1.27 ha of Les Basses-Vergelesses, and, up-slope, no less than 3.78 ha – a quarter of the *climat* – in the Ile-des-Vergelesses itself. Some of the parcels here date back to 1938. Replanted in 1988/1989, and only just now coming back into production, are 29 ares of Aloxe-Corton, *premier cru*, Les Valozières. Curiously, in the days before the old vines were grubbed up, this used to sell for more than the Ile.

Double the price of the Ile are the domaine's three Cortons: 40 ares of Maréchaudes at the bottom of the hill, above Ladoix; the largest parcel, 1.76 ha, in Bressandes, in mid-slope; and 46 a in Clos-du-Roi, perhaps the best *sub-climat* for red wine in the *grand cru*. The average age of all three parcels is not that high, being only now some thirty years, but is improving all the time.

White wines are somewhat recent in the Chandon de Briailles portfolio. Between 1986 and 1992 they planted 90 ares of Chardonnay in the Ile-des-Vergelesses. Six years earlier 14 a in Corton, Bressandes and 12 in Les Chaumes, another part of the Corton *grand cru*, next to Pougets, had also been devoted to white wine, but under that rare appellation, Corton *blanc*: not Charlemagne. In the last years a further 10 *ouvrées* (40 a) of Bressandes have been turned over to Chardonnay. Finally, in 1990, the domaine managed to acquire a small parcel of Corton-Charlemagne, right up under the lip of the forest, on the edge of the appellation above Ladoix. These 2½ *ouvrées*, however, will only produce fifty cases of wine. So this may be blended in with the rest.

VITICULTURE AND WINE-MAKING

Over the last decade the entire viticultural and wine-making processes at the Chandon de Briailles domaine have become more tightly controlled and more sophisticated.

In the vineyard the emphasis, naturally enough, has been for less but better fruit, and a more characterful representation of the *terroir*. Herbicides have been dispensed with in favour of ploughing and hoeing, the composting reduced to a minimum and the pruning is more rigorous, with the young vines held in check by Cordon training. Replanting is generally by *sélection massale* rather than by clones.

Once the shoots have appeared the potential crop is reduced by removing excess buds, particularly those of the second generation of fruit which produces the *verjus*. Later on in the season, if necessary, there is a *vendange verte*, and some of the leaves are removed to expose the maturing bunches. This improves the colour.

In the cellar, having hitherto not destalked, the approach has become more flexible. The young vines are now destemmed, and in the 1992 vintage half of the older vine fruit was passed through the *égrappoir*. In other years this has been merely crushed, to liberate some of the juice. There is now a *table de trie*, which rolls from side to side to eliminate excess water.

In the old days the wine was fermented at 30°C, without any cold maceration at the outset. This again has changed. The must is now cooled at the beginning, so some pre-fermentation maceration can occur, and the fermentation temperatures are a little cooler. The intention is to avoid the harsh, herbaceous tannic flavour which would arise if the temperature was allowed to go too high. Thereafter, the *élevage* techniques have been tightened up too, the wines are manipulated as little as possible (the 1992s, for instance, neither being fined nor filtered), and the date of bottling decided by the state of the wine, not according to rote. Older vintages were bottled after fifteen to eighteen months, the 1991s after eighteen to twenty-one, and by gravity. There is 50 per cent new oak for the *grands crus*, one-quarter or less for the rest, but, not wishing to extract too much of a woody taste, the wines are racked back into older wood after the malo-lactic.

THE WINES

Over the last few years the quality at Chandon de Briailles has improved considerably: the colours are more intense; the wines have become plumper; there is now more definition and greater elegance. They are no longer, at the lower levels, occasionally a little slight. For these are, for Savignys and Cortons, wines of only medium weight. Fruit rather than muscle or the Savigny *goût de terroir* is the keynote.

Firstly the whites. The Ile-des-Vergelesses *blanc* is neat and elegant, with, from 1992, very good oak integration. But it is delicate. It is very clear that the vines are still young.

After a dozen years of visits I was finally able to announce, when I sampled the 1992 Corton *blanc* for the first time, that I could find in it the same sort of class as I search for in a Corton-Charlemagne. Prior to this there had always been something rather four-square about it. I have now seen it again in bottle. It is in the style of Bonneau du Martray rather than Louis Latour, despite its origins. And this 1992 is fine.

The red wine range begins with the village Savigny. This is round, soft and fruity: a wine of charm which will evolve in the medium term. The Fourneaux is similar, with just a little bit more intensity and backbone, but the Lavières is a considerable step up: both more substance and more style.

Between these last two, in quality, and usually in serving order in the Chandon de Briailles cellars, will come the Pernand-Vergelesses, Les Basses-Vergelesses. This can be a slightly leaner wine, but it has more dimension than the Fourneaux, and will need another year in bottle.

Vastly superior, and one of the gems of the *cave*, is the Ile. The wine from this *climat*, which in the Chandon de Briailles case merits being elevated to *grand cru*, is described in books as a 'Corton for the ladies'. I have always found myself nonplussed by this remark, as, for me, the wine has nothing in common with any Corton, even those in the same cellar. An Ile is, as you would expect from its location, a synthesis of all that is best in Savigny and Pernand, and then some. The Chandon de Briailles' Ile today is a wine of real intensity and originality, with a velvety black-cherry fruit, good structure, and a lot of class. And it is excellent value.

Of the Cortons the least sophisticated and the most overtly muscular is the Maréchaudes. There is an animal touch in wines of this *climat*. The vines are younger here too. I prefer the Ile.

The Bressandes is much better: more depth and persistence; proper *grand cru* dimension and class. It is more austere at the outset, but that is no criticism. And it will last much longer. The Clos-du-Roi is even more closed in its youth, but there is more concentration and even better fruit. Both these are fine, but the Clos-du-Roi is the finer.

There have been great strides at the Chandon de Briailles domaine in recent years, with 1990 better than 1989, 1991 better still, within the context of the vintage, and even the 1992s are a great success. Things can only get better. This is an estate to watch.

THE TASTING

I sampled the following range of wines in Savigny-lès-Beaune in June 1994.

WHITES

Pernand-Vergelesses, Ile-des-Vergelesses, 1992

Optimum drinking
Drink up

In tank from September. Bottled in January. Eight-year-old vines. This is elegant, gently oaky, delicate, but nicely crisp and soft. Yet not without length and depth.

1993   2000–2010

Good medium-full colour, lighter than the 1993. Soft plummy nose. Good acidity. Medium to medium-full. Elegant. Still obviously very youthful. But it seems to have good intensity, plenty of fruit and very good length.

Corton, 1992   Now–2007

Fine nose. Very good stylish, cool (Bonneau du Martray-ish) oak and fruit. Fullish, long, delicious. This is very complex and very elegant. Lovely.

CORTON-BRESSANDES

1992   1998–2006

Bottled in April. Medium colour. Gentle, stylish, soft now with a touch of oak. A pretty wine on the nose, but a lack of real intensity. Cherry flavours. Medium body. Quite marked by the oak on the palate. Ripe. Attractive. Balanced. Good length and class. Very good for the vintage.

1991   **2000–2015**

Very good colour. Good, firm, abundant, balanced, classy nose. Gently oaky underneath. Medium-full body. A slight touch of bitterness from the stems, but this will go. Fine follow-through. Good grip. Rich. Plump and ample. Very good length. Fine.

1990   **1999–2010**

Both the colour and the nose are less intense than the 1991. Less elegant too. There is a slight touch of the rustic here. The oak is a little more apparent than in the above. Better on the palate. Round. Medium-full. Good fruit. But after the 1991 it lacks the extra concentration and style you would expect in this vintage. Very good plus.

1989   **1999–2012**

Good colour for the vintage. Not far short of the 1990. Nicely firm and fat and plump. Medium-full body for the vintage. Just as sizeable as the 1990. Good fatness and depth. Nicely concentrated and consistent from start to finish. This is better than the 1990. Very good indeed within the context of the vintage.

1988   **Now–2009**

Good colour. The nose is austere, as one might expect, but also a little pinched. After a while very cassis in aroma, abundant and gently oaky. Medium to medium-full body. Ripe and attractive attack, but a certain hardness and astringency behind it. How will it soften up? Good acidity. Seems very good. But the 1989, 1990 and 1991 are better.

1987   **Now–2000**

Magnum. Good colour. No undue brown. Fullish. On the nose a touch of spice, a touch of hardness. Medium body. Pleasant, but a slight lack of really ripe fruit. Not too lean. But it could have been more generous, more charming. And not a lot of dimension either. Quite good.

1986   **Drink soon**

Magnum. Good substance on the colour, not too developed. Developed nose. A lack of real class. But fruity. Medium body. A little astringent. Plump if a little contrived. But quite

positive. Not at all a bad effort. Yet one-dimensional and a bit pedestrian.

1985   **Now–2000**

Amazing colour. Very full. Little development. Is it as dense as it looks? Yes it does seem a bit tough on the nose. Solid and tannic and a little rustic, but at the same time rich and ample: more so than the 1990, for example. Good vigour and length. Little class. But good for food: a couscous, for example.

1982   **Drink soon**

Magnum. Good vigorous colour for the vintage. Plump nose, a touch spicy. Medium body. A little coarse but ripe and balanced. The acidity beginning to show as the fruit was never very concentrated. Quite good.

1978   **Now–2000**

Magnum. Big colour. Like the 1985, surprisingly so. Nicely animal on the nose. A bit of reduction. Somewhat gamey. Full-bodied, meaty, balanced, rich and indeed very attractive. A touch artisanal but a fine success nevertheless. Bags of life.

1976   **Drink up**

Magnum. Very good colour. Still very vigorous. This is artisanal on the nose. Dense, solid, astringent and, despite the colour, over-developed. Now rather dry. The fat has gone - so has the fruit. Only the structure is left. On the follow-through a little better.

1959   **Now–2000**

Fine colour. Still very vigorous. Very very lovely nose. Rich, complex old Pinot Noir. Ripe, a touch of spice. Balanced and soft and multi-dimensional. Very very complex, fat, yet vigorous still. This is a very fine example of a very fine vintage. Lovely.

CHANSON PÈRE ET FILS,
BEAUNE

Together with Bouchard Père et Fils, Drouhin, Jadot and Latour, Chanson Père et Fils are one of the 'Big Five' wine-merchants in Beaune. They are also one of the oldest: one of six eighteenth-century companies still active, according to the firm's brochure. Like the other big four, Chanson are major vineyard-holders, in their case very largely on the *premier cru* slopes of Beaune itself - a total of 42 hectares. And like Bouchard, on the other side of town, Chanson occupy one of the five 'bastions', look-out fortresses, which are part of the medieval fortifications of the city.

HISTORY

The history of Chanson begins with one Simon Verry or Very. Not much is known about this gentleman's origins, but it is assumed he was a kinsman of the Verys who were the owners of what is now the Domaine Bonneau du Martray. Very was originally a broker, but became registered as a merchant in 1750. Voltaire and the British lords Montague and Naisborough were among his early customers. A sideline was a stud-farm for the breeding of race-horses.

In 1774 Very became associated with a M. Gaboreau who had rented a cellar on the edge of town, in the Bastion de l'Oratoire. This round, four-storey, massive brick structure, with walls of immense thickness - 7.5 metres at the base - capable of storing the entire production of even a plentiful vintage for the Beaune vineyards, was constructed by the king of France, Louis XI, when his forces took over Burgundy following the death of Duke Charles the Bold in 1477.

Gaboreau died at the time of the French Revolution, but the Verys continued, and indeed it is assumed profited by it to the extent of acquiring at that time one of their prize possessions, today, the monopoly holding of the Beaune *premier cru*, Clos-des-Fèves. In 1804 Charles Very, son of Simon, and now getting on in years, brought Alexis Chanson (1787-1855) in to manage the business. By this time the firm had taken over the entire Bastion. It took its present-day form - young wines in barrels at the top, older wines in bottle below - in 1826. Chanson bought out the Very heirs in 1846, changed the name of the company and was to be succeeded by his son Paul and grandson Edouard (1863-1953).

Edouard Chanson and his wife produced a daughter, Thérèse (1896-1977), and as his brother Alexis had no children, it was through the female line that succession was to pass. Thérèse wed Maurice Marion (1890-1970), and he became the *patron* in the 1920s. It is his children, François (born 1929) and Philippe (born 1932) who are in charge today.

THE DOMAINE

The Chanson's long line-up of Beaune *premiers crus* embraces 3.80 ha (95 per cent) of the Fèves (and the monopoly of the Clos-des-Fèves), 3.77 ha (44 per cent) of the Marconnets (and the monopoly of the Clos-des-Marconnets) and 5.80 ha (30 per cent) in Les Teurons. Moreover there are sizeable holdings in Clos-des-Mouches (3.46 ha of which 1.42 ha are under Chardonnay), Bressandes, Clos-du-Roi, Champs-Pimont and A l'Ecu.

In Savigny the firm possesses vines in Dominode and Marconnets (the later Chardonnay as well as Pinot Noir); in Pernand-Vergelesses they own over 5 ha in Les Vergelesses and 2.60 ha of Chardonnay in Les Caradeux; and in Corton a dozen ares each (two barrels' worth) in Vergelesses (*blanc*) and Rognet (*rouge*). Apart from a little village Savigny, presently fallow, the domaine lies entirely in *premier* and *grand cru*. Their policy of uprooting the vines after forty years though, keeps the average age at a mere twenty years old.

WINE-MAKING

Wine-making, under the direction of Marc Cagnier, *chef de cave*, now takes place in modern premises outside Beaune on the road to Savigny.

The Pinot Noir fruit is now destemmed, a departure from the procedures prior to 1985, allowed to warm up gently as the fermentation starts, and vinified in revolving *auto-pigeante* tanks or horizontal ones with automatic *pigeurs*, at 30-32°C. To avoid having to fine, which Philippe Marion considers dries out and removes some of the stuffing from the wine, enzymes have been added to the wine at the time of de-vatting. There is from 10-40 per cent new wood, depending on the vintage and the wine's status, and it is bottled after a light plate filtration after fifteen to eighteen months, a little earlier, i.e. before the second Christmas, in the case of weaker vintages.

THE WINES

Chanson wines have been criticised in the past for being a bit light and weak, and for appearing prematurely dried out. It has been suggested that the vines were over-cropped, that the *cuvaisons* were too short, and that the wines were held in cask too long.

As if to counteract some of this, Philippe Marion pointed out to me that the 1993s had been macerated for longer than was usual. (This hasn't given them any extra colour, but in the case of the Clos-des-Fèves it has led to the best example for years.) And I myself had looked up the declarations for this vintage. Chanson's yields varied considerably in 1993: 26.5 hl/ha in the Grèves, but 36 in the Teurons, 39 in the Marconnets, 42.75 in the Fèves and 47 in Clos-du-Roi and Les Vergelesses.

The wines certainly could be more concentrated, and should have more flair and definition. With the exception of the 1993, already mentioned, and the 1988, even the Clos-des-Fèves, their flagship wine, is normally no better than merely 'good'. It should be better.

THE TASTING

I sampled the following wines in Beaune in January 1996.

BEAUNE, CLOS-DES-FÈVES

Optimum drinking

1994   **1999-2006**

Bottled ten days ago. Good colour nevertheless. Nicely ripe on the nose, with a touch of astringency from the bottling. This is ripe and balanced with a good grip holding it together and no lack of fruit and depth. Good plus.

1993   **2000-2012**

Medium colour. Still fresh and purple. This isn't 100 per cent clean. Slightly corked? Second bottle much better. Rich and succulent. Ripe and very elegant, with a flair missing in the 1994 and 1992. A very good example, with more elegant fruit and slightly more concentrated than the 1991. Lovely finish.

1992   **Now-2002**

Good colour for the vintage. Similar to the 1991. Plump ripe nose. Good substance for a 1992, though not a lot of succulence. Medium body. Just a little tannin to resolve itself. Good freshness. No weakness. But a little straightforward. Yet pleasant and positive. Good plus for the vintage.

1991   **1998-2008**

Medium to medium-full colour. Very good nose. Rich, fat and substantial. Classy and complex too. Fullish. Very good tannins. This has depth and even concentration. Very good grip. This still needs time. Long. Very good.

1990   **1998-2010**

Quite evolved and not very full in colour for the vintage. Slightly adolescent. Firm, but a little lumpy. Fullish. Very ripe, almost over-ripe. Good acidity. A plump, rich example. But without the class of the 1993. Merely good.

1989   **Now-2000**

Good colour. A little more evolution than the 1990. Ripe, cedary, aromatic nose. A touch of mocha. This is fully ready. Plump and spicy, and medium to medium-full, but with a certain lack of freshness and elegance. Slightly sweet. It won't improve. Good but not special.

1988   **Now-2009 plus**

Very good colour. Still very youthful. Refined, ripe, very elegant, very well-balanced fruit on the nose. This has a lot of class. Quite full. Fresh. This has real length, depth and dimension, and plenty of complexity. Very very long and lovely. Better in a year. Fine.

1987   **Drink soon**

Good but fully evolved colour. Slightly sweet, slightly rustic nose. But fresher than many 1987s today. Medium body. A bit astringent on the palate and coarse on the finish. A good example though. The fruit is still positive.

1986   **Drink up**

Evolved colour. Light, evolved, slightly diffuse nose. A little fluid. Lightish, yet reasonably fruity and balanced. This, for the vintage, is better than the 1987, though the above has more to it.

1985 Now–2003

Good fullish mature colour. Ripe and quite substantial on the nose. But it lacks a little flair, a little concentration, a little grip of acidity. In this way it reminds me of the 1990 - one feels it ought to be better. Reasonably balanced but coarse at the end. Quite good.

1983 Now–2003

Half bottle. Good full colour. No undue brown. Rich, full, spicy, quite tannic on nose and palate. But if a touch brutal still, not unbalanced. Good concentration and acidity. Very good with food. Still has good vigour. Better than the 1985.

1982 Drink up

Light to medium evolved colour. Soft plump nose. Not too old. Medium body. A touch coarse at the end but a perfectly pleasant wine. A bit one-dimensional. Only quite good, even for the vintage.

1980 Drink up

Reasonably full, but brown colour at the rim. Fully evolved. This is an old wine now. But it is not too faded. There is a sweet, old roses fruit still and no coarseness. I prefer this to the 1982. A little more weight; much more elegance.

1978 Now–2000 plus

Good full colour. Still plenty of vigour. Rich on the nose. There is a little more new wood behind it. And also a smell of a loft full of stored apples. Medium-full. Slightly rigid. Slightly hard. The acidity rather dominant. The finish isn't as good as the nose. Slightly four-square. Good but not special.

1976 Now–2000

Fullish, mature colour. Opulent, mocha nose. A little evolved, a little diffuse. But not astringent. This is a wine for food but it is not too tannic or too lumpy. I prefer it to the 1978. It is more generous. But it isn't very elegant.

1971 Drink up

Fullish, mature, but not too aged colour. Evolved, slightly fading, but very complex, elegant, fragrant nose. On the palate a little astringent and it will lose its elegance from now on. But a very good, harmonious example. Long, complex, multi-dimensional.

1970 Drink soon

Surprisingly full colour. Rather less evolved than the 1971. Plump, open, succulent nose. Plenty of freshness, plenty of fruit. This has much more vigour than the 1971; more weight too. But less class. Surprisingly good though.

1969 Now–2000

Half bottle. Full mature colour. Still vigorous. Firm, hard, youthful even, on the nose. Evolved well. Fullish, rich, spicy, concentrated and ripe. There is a little suggestion of dryness at the end, but this would not be evident with food. Long, multi-dimensional, complex and classy. Very good.

Beaune, Bressandes, 1966 Now–2000

Good fullish mature colour. No undue brown. Ripe, aromatic, very accessible. This is medium to medium-full, ripe and charming and harmonious. It lacks just a little grip and concentration. But still today very fresh and certainly very stylish. Very good.

1959 Now–2000

Good colour. No undue age. Lovely ripe, cedary mocha nose. Fullish, aromatic, rich and sweet. Good vigour and substance. Good grip. Not a trace of astringency or undue structure. Lovely. Very very long and complex. Fine.

1947 Will still keep well

Amazingly youthful colour. Lovely nose. Very rich, very opulent and aromatic. Very complex and fresh. This is very fresh and very concentrated. Velvety if the 1959 is silky, though the structure showing just a bit more and the acidity just a touch more rigid. But fine. Still bags of life.

Beaune, Clos-des-Mouches, 1937

Can still be kept

Full, mature but no undue age. Slightly hard and old on the nose. But not faded or fruitless. Fullish, still a bit tannic. But good fruit and a firm acidity. Slightly rigid, like a muscular 1978. But still in good condition. And will still keep.

PHILIPPE CHARLOPIN,
GEVREY-CHAMBERTIN

Once upon a time, in the mid–1980s, a young Burgundian *vigneron* approached a much respected older wine-maker with a sample of his wine. 'Very nice,' said the elder statesman, 'but you have retained too much of the stems.' Next year the young man returned with his new vintage. 'That's better,' opined the guru, 'but still too many stems.' Another twelve months passed. The wine was again both commended and criticised. Finally there came a great vintage – 1990 – and unqualified approval from the older man. 'Now you have learned how to make wine,' he said. 'The stems are unnecessary.'

The older man, as you might have guessed, was Henri Jayer. The young man was, of course, Philippe Charlopin. And the story is typical of the progress that has been achieved in Burgundy over the last decade. Today's Bourguignon or Bourguignonne has an enquiring mind. He or she is in and out of friends' cellars tasting and comparing. There is an ambition towards perfectionism in the air.

THE CREATION OF THE DOMAINE

Philippe Charlopin was born in 1956. His father, André, an orphan, was brought up in the Arrières Côtes, moved down to Gevrey-Chambertin as a worker on other people's domaines, and slowly began to parcel together an estate for himself. When he died in 1977, from a stomach ulcer, he left Philippe an estate of 3.5 ha, half owned, half rented, including 18 ares of Charmes-Chambertin.

Philippe was then twenty-two, and about to get married. He had worked for a couple of neighbouring domaines before joining his father. He was ready to take over, and keen to expand.

His first venture was in Marsannay, where he and his wife Sonia had installed themselves on the *Route des Grands Crus*. In 1983 he acquired some Morey village and 18 ares of Clos-Saint-Denis from the Amiot-Bertrand family. In 1986 he stopped vinifying in the cellars beneath his mother's house in Gevrey and installed a new *cuverie* beneath his own house in Marsannay. More village wine followed in subsequent years: Vosne in 1989, Chambolle in 1991, yet more Gevrey in 1993 and 1994. And in 1988 he was entrusted with the upkeep of 21 ares in Le Chambertin itself. The land belongs to Madame Barron, a member of the extended Latour family. The wine is bottled with both of the Charlopin and Barron names on the label.

Today Charlopin manages an estate just short of 12 hectares, and has moved back to Gevrey to take over part of the erstwhile Charles Quillardet premises on the main road towards Dijon.

WINE-MAKING

'Extracting the flavour out of Pinot Noir is more of an infusion process than vinification,' says Charlopin. 'Every origin must be treated in a different way. It is a learning process to find out which is best. The first time I fermented Chambolle-Musigny I got it all wrong. I made it the same way I did my Morey-Saint-Denis, and the result was a wine which was too solid. It didn't taste like Chambolle at all. Pinot doesn't need the long *élevage* of Syrah and Cabernet, and while with these grapes oxygenation is beneficial, with Pinot Noir it is not.'

His methods have changed considerably over the years. He is a supporter of the idea of a long cold-soaking process before the fermentation is allowed to begin, and also seeks not to lose all the CO_2 generated by both the alcoholic and malo-lactic fermentations. The presence of this gas helps protect the wine and prevents reduction.

From 1990 he has had a *table de tri*, and with the better *matière première* he gets as a result has found that it is not necessary to *piger* as much as hitherto. 'At first I thought that it was in the *cuve* that I made the wine. So I did a lot of *pigeage* to squeeze out the flavour. Now I realise that it is all in the fruit in the first place. This of course has to be in prime condition if one is to cold macerate. But I can now let the wine make itself.'

Charlopin believes in a long *cuvaison*, the wine protected from the air by a bucket of SO_2 solution added at the top and a maximum temperature of 30°C. In a sense the lower the acidity and concentration the more the maceration should be prolonged. The 1993 had fifteen days; the 1992 twenty-five. Sometimes he does a *saignée*. The downside, he will admit, is the risk of a certain hardness and inbalance in the wine. So he avoids it if possible. The opportunity to control the size of the crop lies earlier in the season.

In the last two years, Charlopin has *bâtonné*-ed his casks, to accelerate the enriching process. Because his *cave* is above ground, and not particularly cool, the evolution of his wines is quite quick (another reason for retaining so much CO_2 in the wine). This is also an explanation of why he keeps some of his lesser wines in bulk rather than casks, why he does not rack his wines at all, and why he generally bottles in August after the harvest, without fining, but after a light *Kieselguhr* filtration for some of the wines.

THE WINES

Charlopin's two main wines are his village Gevrey and his Marsannay. Marsannay, he avers, should not be too full-bodied a wine. If it is it tends to be coarse: size without depth. You have to pick and choose where to plant your Marsannay vines, he says, for there are several areas up above the village where both the soil is too heavy and a cool wind comes whistling down the *combe* from the hills above. The wine from here should be de-classed to Bourgogne *rouge*. Round the corner are the sheltered *lieux-dits* of Longeroies and Montchevenoy, and even further north there is the gritty Clos-du-Roi on the Chenôve border. These are the best sites. Sometimes, Charlopin points out, you have to wait a whole week later after picking your Gevrey-Chambertin for the Marsannay vines to come to full fruition.

In Gevrey he sells off the produce of the younger vines in bulk, retaining only a *vieilles-vignes cuvée* from 2 hectares of vines on the Brochon side. This is the best of his village wines. The Morey-Saint-Denis comes from three parcels averaging sixty years old, and is also an exemplary *cuvée*, a little less structured and meaty, but with excellent fruit. I find these two have more definition than the Vosne and the Chambolle.

The three *grands crus* come in small quantities – two to three casks of each – and are reared in 50 per cent new wood. The Clos-Saint-Denis lies plumb in the heart of the *climat*, between the vines of Jadot and Jean-Paul Magnien, but the Charmes is right down by the main road. Both parcels of vines are forty years old. Nevertheless I usually prefer the latter. It seems to have a refreshing plump individuality and, yes, plenty of charm.

With the Barron/Charlopin Chambertin we are aiming for the super league. The vines lie between those of Rousseau and the rest of the Héritiers Latour, are thirty years old, and have now been in Charlopin's hands for seven vintages. I have yet to find the wine great. But it is now very fine, and a significant step up from the Charmes, as it should be.

Charlopin, a tubby rubicund enthusiast with a mass of curly black hair, now well installed back in Gevrey, is busy enlarging the cellar, and has constructed an attractive apartment from what must have been an old granary above the cellar. He hasn't stopped learning yet, though the quality of the wines he produces is now very good indeed. And he hasn't stopped expanding either. The latest acquisition is 71 ares in the Gevrey vineyard of Les Justices, behind the house. 'What sort of wine will you get from here?' I ask. 'Look at the soil,' says Philippe, 'very stony. Look at the average age. Not bad, eh? I think I will produce a very nice, but more feminine wine here. Not as *charpenté* as the *vieilles vignes*, but elegant.' Yes, indeed, this is a very good source. And in 1996 there will be some Mazis-Chambertin as well.

THE TASTING

I sampled the following wines in February 1995.

CHARMES-CHAMBERTIN

Optimum drinking

1993 — **2000–2010**

Good colour. Has recovered well from bottling two months previously. Rich, plump, fat, oaky nose. Lovely ripe cassis-raspberry fruit with a touch of chocolate. Fullish, very good grip. Nicely cool but not austere. Classy tannins. Lovely fruit. Very long. Fine.

1992 — **Now–2004**

Medium to medium-full colour. Soft, harmonious, fruity, persistent nose. Real charm, no lack of depth. The oak shows a little more here than in the above. Medium to medium-full body. Plenty of wine here. Plump, more red-fruity than the 1993. Less structure but this has plenty of intensity and class. Long on the palate. Fine for the vintage.

1991 — **1998–2008**

Good colour. On the nose quite substantial and tannic. More animal and meaty than the two above. A more sturdy and masculine wine. Good grip. Medium-full. Some tannin. Underneath not as fat or as composed as the 1993. But balanced and stylish and with no lack of fruit. Long on the palate. Very good.

1990 — **1998–2012**

Fine colour. Velvety rich, opulent, ample,

smooth, gently oaky nose. Fullish, hugely rich, very flamboyant. Very plump. A most seductive example. Balanced, classy, generous. Finishes long. Fine.

1989   **Now–2007**

Very good colour. Very rich, almost over-ripe nose. The stems have added to the backbone and grip of this wine, much to its advantage. Good substance, some tannin. Backward for the vintage. Lovely fruit, and well balanced. Very good indeed.

1988   **1998–2015**

Excellent colour. Quite amazing. Very fine nose, really rich and concentrated. A substantial wine with excellent acidity. A lot of stems in here, so naturally it is more herbaceous at present than the 1990. This is currently a bit adolescent. Fullish, more austere than the 1990. But a lot of depth and class here. This will perhaps last the best of all. This is one of Charlopin's favourites. Fine.

1987   **Now–2003**

Good colour. Fullish, still youthful. Stylish nose. Good harmonious fruit here. No hard edges. Medium to medium-full body. Just a touch of tannin still. Ripe underneath. Not *that* fat but by no means lean. Balanced and elegant. Just about *à point*. Good acidity. Finishes well. A very good example.

1986   **Now–1999**

Magnum. Medium to medium-full colour. Good fresh aspect. Fresh on the nose. Nicely plump fruit. Not a blockbuster. A gentle wine. But fruity, stylish and reasonably balanced. Enjoyable if no great depth and dimension. Very good for the vintage.

1985   **Now–2010**

Magnum. Medium-full colour. Not a lot of maturity. This is still very young, even firm on the nose. Took a bit of time to come out. Very lovely succulent fruit. Medium-full. A sturdier, more rustic sort of wine than Charlopin makes today. The structure shows more. Yet very good acidity and very good fruit. It is still youthful. Good grip and plenty of thrust at the end. Fine.

1984   **Drink soon**

Good fresh colour. Fresh nose, a little light, and one can see the wood. As 1984s go this is not at all bad. Reasonable ripeness, structure and depth. Even some class, though this is on the wane now. A very good effort.

1983   **Now–1999**

Evolved colour. But reasonable depth. On the nose gamey and pruney on the one side, dry and tannic on the other. Better on the palate. A little

astringent, but ripe and concentrated, and fresh too. A bit tough, especially on the attack, but the finish is rich and positive. Good.

1982   **Drink soon**

Magnum. Charlopin's last magnum. Medium colour. Fully mature but no real age. Good vigorous nose. Plenty of ripe fruit if a touch diffuse. The new oak also shows a little. This is soft and sweet and elegant, though beginning to loosen up at the end. Good grip. A very good effort. But drink soon.

1981   **Drink soon**

Good colour. Mature but quite substantial. Less evolved than the 1980. A little lean on the nose, but no lack of interest. On the palate this is a bit one-dimensional, and now getting a bit astringent. But perfectly agreeable.

1980   **Now–1999**

Good colour. A little *tuilée* now. A bit diffuse on the nose. Better on the palate. Not exactly rich or fat, but concentration and with dimension. Classy, balanced, even intense. Full of interest. Very good.

1979   **Now–2000 plus**

Magnum. Very good colour. Vigorous too. Gevrey was hailed in parts, but not south of Mazis and Ruchottes. A masculine, full, somewhat old-fashioned wine. A little dilute on the nose. And hollow in the middle. Yet fatter and more ample than the 1980. This has the brawn, the 1980 has the manners. Yet this is more ample. Better with food. And a lot more vigour. Very good indeed.

1978   **Now–2000**

Very good colour. Splendid vigour. Fullish, sturdy, slightly old-fashioned meaty wine on the nose. More rustic than the above. Rather four-square. On the palate a touch 'hot' - one can see the chaptalisation. Full, a bit lumpy, a touch astringent. Yet rich and with plenty of interest. Better with food. Seems a bit more four-square than the 1979. And not as elegant. Very good.

1977   **Drink soon**

Magnum. Very good colour. Vigorous. Stylish nose. There is still fruit here. Not vegetal, though a bit lean, naturally. This is a surprisingly good example. Fullish, a bit 'assisted', but the result is very successful. A bit 'hot' at the end. But good acidity without being too lean. Very good indeed for the vintage.

1976   **Drink soon**

Splendid colour. Solid nose. Dry, over-macerated. A rather astringent wine on the palate. Full, quite rich. But not exactly very sweet and generous. A bit lumpy. Tough going. Will never really round off.

ROBERT CHEVILLON,
NUITS-SAINT-GEORGES

Among the select few Nuits-Saint-Georges domaines who can safely be accorded stars – Faiveley and Gouges spring readiest to mind – is the 13 hectare domaine of Robert Chevillon. Robert, tall, handsome, greying, slightly fleshy, was born in 1938. He lives with his wife and one of his grown-up sons in a modern but unpretentious house in the back streets of Nuits, not far from his cousin Michel, also proprietor of a wine estate of note.

Like many, the origins of this Chevillon domaine can be traced through generation after generation of *petits vignerons* who worked for the local *négociants* while operating a few rows of their own vines or land they share-cropped in their spare time. There was a Symphorien Chevillon who was born in about 1860 and died in 1926. His son Eugène-François was a military bandsman in the 1914-1918 war, and formed his own dance orchestra in Nuits when he returned to supplement the meagre income he made from his vines. Maurice and Georges (father of Michel) divided their inheritance, such as it was in 1946, and went their separate ways. But when Robert, son of Maurice, joined his father after his own *service militaire* in 1968, the exploitation was a mere 3 hectares, the produce of which was sold in bulk to the local merchants.

The Chevillon domaine as it stands today is therefore a recent creation. The 13 hectares are a mixture of vineyards directly owned, land leased and vines worked under a share-cropping arrangement. The Perrières, for instance, all 53 ares of it, was acquired from seven different owners between the years 1982, when Maurice Chevillon retired, and 1985. The domaine has only been seriously bottling its own wines since 1977. It has only been exporting since 1979.

And yet, even preceding these dates, this Chevillon domaine had established a reputation for excellence. Older vintages, the late 1960s and early 1970s, were already deemed very good. And the early 1980s consolidated confidence in the consistency of Robert Chevillon's wine-making. Year in, year out, even in minor vintages such as 1981 and 1984, the wines were worth buying. They have a finesse and a concentration and a distinct individuality, *climat* from *climat*, which is rare in the commune. They are poised and rich and harmonious. They last well. How does he do it?

THE DOMAINE

The domaine consists entirely of vines in Nuits itself and the lower land nearby which produces generics. In addition to the Cailles, the Vaucrains, the Saint-Georges and the Perrières, already mentioned, there are four others: Bousselots, usually sold off in bulk, Chaignots, Pruliers and Roncières: a total of eight. And a tasting session in the Chevillon's *cave* is an exemplary introduction to the variety of wines produced in the commune.

A tasting will start with the village Nuits. Parcels from throughout the commune, from the Vosne marches to Prémeaux, plus the young vines of the *premier cru climats*, make up this blend. It is well-coloured, as are all Chevillon's wines, fullish and rich, firm with a certain rusticity - that is typical Nuits - but plump and ripe as well. It needs four years to mature, even in softer vintages such as 1992.

Bousselots is a *premier cru* south of the Chaignots on the Vosne side of the commune. Chevillon usually sells this off to the *négoce* (he currently disposes of about 25 per cent of his crop in bulk in order to maintain cash flow), and the only vintage I have ever sampled was the 1991. I found it supple, feminine and full of fruit, without the usual Nuits sturdiness, but balanced and elegant. Even in this vintage, which is less structured than the 1990 or the 1988, the wine had dimension, depth and length. Chevillon has two-thirds of a hectare here, and the vines are thirty years old.

Chaignots will be the next wine you are offered. The parcel measures just over 1.5 hectares and the vines are twenty-five plus years old. This is similar, but a bit richer, a bit more structured. You can see the Vosne-Romanée proximity.

Chevillon has almost two-thirds of a hectare of twenty-five-year-old vines in Les Pruliers, one of the best-known of the *premiers crus* immediately south of the town of Nuits-Saint-Georges. Here the wines are more masculine, more virile, than those on the Vosne-Romanée side. This wine is fuller and more tannic than the Chaignots, and usually with more richness and depth. But which you prefer is a question of taste.

Even better, in my view, is Chevillon's Roncières, a 1 hectare parcel in the *climat* immediately to the south. Chevillon used to share-crop this parcel, but he now leases it so he gets the full harvest from the vines rather than only half of it. It tastes as if the vines are old, which they aren't - indeed they are only marginally more venerable than those in the Pruliers. The wine has an extra element of concentration and opulence. It is very seductive.

Up-slope you will find Chevillon's 0.5 hectare of Perrières. The soil is lighter, as the name indicates containing an element of gravel, and the wine is softer and more feminine. Is it better? I preferred the Perrières 1990 in cask, but the Roncières 1990 when it came to tasting them in bottle.

Cailles, Vaucrains and Les Saint-Georges itself, just above the Nuits-Prémeaux boundary line, are the heart of the commune; in principle the three best *climats*. Chevillon boasts 1.2 ha of the first, 1.5 ha of the second and 0.6 ha of the last, all of them planted with vines which date from the 1920s or earlier. All three wines are yardstick examples of all that is glorious about fine Pinot Noir. The Cailles is the one that comes forward earliest, combining the finesse of the Perrières and the depth and fruit of the Roncières. Vaucrains is sturdier, firmer, richer, even more intense, but it needs a year or so longer. Les Saint-Georges is even more profound and concentrated and backward. All three, in Chevillon's dedicated hands, are wines of finesse and complexity as well as structure.

And finally, as you take a deep breath to gird your loins after this splendid gamut of *premier cru* reds, you will be offered that *rara avis*, a white Nuits-Saint-Georges. Scattered throughout his empire are Pinot Noir vines which have degenerated and produce white wine. He also has a little Chardonnay planted in the *climats* of Damode and Argillières. The balance is roughly 70 per cent of the former, 30 per cent of the latter. Prior to the 1985 Chevillon incorporated this fruit with the red wine *cuvées*. Now he produces a separate white wine. It is vinified in wood, one-third of which is new, and bottled without filtration after twelve to fifteen months. I love it. It doesn't taste like Chardonnay. Indeed the aroma fleetingly recalls red fruits such as raspberry and redcurrant, with its own, almost Pinot-Gris-like spice. It also keeps well. Robert gave me a bottle of 1985 once which I opened in 1993. It was delicious. I still could have kept it five more years.

VITICULTURE AND WINE-MAKING

Trying to get explanations out of some *vignerons* is like trying to get acknowledgements of past mistakes out of ruling politicians: a fruitless exercise. This is not to say Robert Chevillon is not friendly and receptive, though he is, like many of his peers, a little suspicious at first, and it takes time to break this down. It is just that he can't see what you are driving at. The secret is that there are no secrets. It is not what those who succeed do, it is more what those who produce worse wine don't do. The bad wine-makers over-fertilise and over-crop, have dirty cellars and sloppy *élevage*, over- or under-oak, filter the guts out of the wine and bottle too late. Robert Chevillon, of course, does none of these. What he does do seems so logical to him that he can't understand why everybody else doesn't do it as well.

Robert is happy to have some vines of considerable age in his land-holdings. The Cailles was planted in 1920, as was the majority of his Vaucrains (there is a parcel here which is over a century old). The vines in the Saint-Georges *climat* also date from the early 1920s.

Chevillon likes old vines. The production therefrom does not need to be restrained and the wines have more concentration. He is content to let his vines die of a natural old age, and will only replace them one by one as a hole falls vacant. These new vines are picked separately and the fruit vinified with the village wine.

He also, you feel, understands his vines. You don't have to be a magician to realise after a time that one vineyard - Roncières or Pruliers, in the Chevillon instance, because of the aspect of the vineyard and the nature of the soil - ripens earlier than the others, and that the fruit on the village vines on the Vosne side, because they are lower down the slope and the soil is often quite humid, has a tendency to rot, and must be watched like a hawk. Nor do you have to be a genius to comprehend that some particular vines, or plot of vines, will always be over-productive than others; because of their age, or the clone, or the rootstock, or because of the *terroir* itself. But it is then being meticulous, sagacious enough to do what is necessary to counteract these phenomena that counts. That is what distinguishes the good *viticulteur* from the mediocre.

Chevillon has a healthy contempt for many of what he would consider the fads of modern wine-making. *Saignée*? You don't need to *saigner* if you don't over-crop. Cold maceration before fermentation? He gets enough colour anyway and a better extraction of flavour is obtained in alcoholic solution during the fermentation than in aqueous solution before. Low-temperature fermentation? Chevillon considers his results are better - more fat and more fruit - at anything up to 33°C. New oak? Why submerge the fruit? One-quarter to one-third is quite enough, depending on the vintage. And much less for the village wine.

Robert is an adherent of the long, slow *cuvaison* faction. The fruit, destemmed some 75 per cent, macerates for three or four weeks, longer in 1990, and the wine is then allowed to proceed with its malo at its own pace. The wine lives on its fine lees throughout the summer, the second racking, at the time of the next vintage, is done *à l'abri de l'air* (without oxygenating the wine), and the wine is then fined, and subsequently bottled about sixteen to eighteen months after the harvest, with only the very lightest of filtrations. Chevillon does his own bottling. 'These contract bottlers! Imbeciles!' There is a visible shudder.

CONSISTENCY

Robert Chevillon is a proud man, a little aloof at first, and protective of the domaine he has built up. There was a suggestion, a couple of years ago, that his elder son, Denis, would set up on his own with a part of the vineyard. This idea, however, seems to have evaporated. Father and sons work alongside each other. This may occasionally create its own tensions, but I'm sure it is for the best – from the point of view of us, the consumers – if it can be managed. I have sadly seen too many domaines degenerate into impossible-to-manage minute morsels.

Chevillon produces consistent wine; impressively so, even in mediocre vintages. This is what impressed Kermit Lynch, his US importer. 'What I found in Chevillon, when I first went to see him in 1979 or so,' says Kermit, 'was a Hubert de Montille of Nuits-Saint-Georges.' What *I* like about the Chevillon domaine is that year after year it produces one of the best ranges of wines in the commune.

THE TASTING

The following wines were offered at a tasting organised by The Wine Treasury in November 1992.

Optimum drinking

Nuits-Saint-Georges, Blanc, 1990   Now–2006
As usual it doesn't exactly smell like Chardonnay. Some 70 per cent Pinot Noir mutated into white; 30 per cent Chardonnay. Nice touch of sweetness and oak. Flowery. Very stylish. Ripe, balanced, very grapey. Good. Long.

Nuits-Saint-Georges, 1990   Now–2005
Good colour. Meaty, rich nose. Good richness and substance here. Fullish, balanced. Very good grip. Fat and ripe. Still a little tannin. A good basic example. Finishes long.

Nuits-Saint-Georges, Les Roncières, 1990   1998–2010
Good colour. Fragrant, ripe, stylish nose. This is very complex. Medium body. Just a little tannin. Intense. Lovely ripe Pinot fruit. Long, subtle. Very good indeed.

Nuits-Saint-Georges, Les Perrières, 1990   1998–2009
Good colour. This is slightly leaner, more minerally on the nose. The extra gravel shows. I prefer the above. Medium body. Good fruit, but not quite the intensity and concentration. Good but not great.

Nuits-Saint-Georges, Les Chaignots, 1990   1998–2012
Good colour. Fat, ample and a touch spicy on the nose. Medium to medium-full body. Coffee and chocolate. A little more tannin. Ripe and opulent. Most attractive. Very good.

Nuits-Saint-Georges, Les Vaucrains, 1990   1999–2015
Very good colour. Firmer, richer and more concentrated than the Chaignots. More backward. Medium-full. Good tannin. Ripe, rich and typically earthy. A fleshy gamey wine. Very good plus.

NUITS-SAINT-GEORGES, LES SAINT-GEORGES

1991   Now–2005
Good colour. Good nose. This has plenty of fruit and style, good balance, and if not the structure of the 1990, certainly plenty of interest. Medium body.

1990   1999–2015 plus
Good colour. This has the most depth and concentration, as well as class, of all the 1990s. It is the sweetest and most intensely fruity. Full, very good ripe tannins. Very good grip. This is a fine example. Excellent balance. Ample, supple, intense. Very long. Best of the series.

1989   Now–2004
Medium-full colour. Still very young. Fragrant, violet scented, cranberries and raspberries. Medium body. This is quite soft, but has good intensity on the follow-through. Good acidity. Attractive if a little adolescent at present. Finishes well. Very good for the vintage.

1988   Now–2012
Good colour. The colour is just beginning to show signs of development. Plenty of depth here on the nose. Slightly hard edges at present. Medium-full. Good tannins. Very good acidity. Lots of depth. Very good indeed. Plenty of potential for a very long life.

1987   **Drink soon**

Good fresh colour for the vintage. On the nose just a little dryness of tannin. The attack is quite full, ripe and ample. In the background there is a little hardness but the finish is more attractive. Reasonable acidity. More to it than the 1986. Good.

1986   **Drink soon**

Good colour for the vintage. Quite intense and full. Soft on the nose, but not a bit weak. Now a hint of the vegetal, but in the best sense. Medium body. Good plump fruit. Good depth. Good grip. This is a surprising success. Only one and a half dimensions but ripe and pleasant.

1985   **Now–2004**

Medium colour. Fully mature looking. Soft, fragrant, spicy nose. Velvety and a touch exotic. Medium-full, concentrated, intense. The tannins now soft. Lots of wine here, and very good grip. This is not as good as 1988 or 1990 but is long and complex. Fine.

1984   **Drink soon**

Surprisingly good colour for the vintage. No sign of age. Full. The nose shows plenty of fruit still. No hard vegetal touches. Medium to medium-full. Ripe. Most attractive. Plenty of depth. Even fat and sweet at the end. A fine result.

1983   **Now–2000**

Medium-full, brown colour. Fully mature. On the nose, fat, opulent, fleshy, exotic. On the palate very spicy, slightly burnt aspects, but no hardness, dryness or undue tannins. This is exotic and concentrated. Intense and fleshy/gamey. A typical successful 1983. Plenty of grip and plenty of life.

BRUNO CLAIR,
MARSANNAY

Burgundy's biggest news in 1985 was the division of the famous and extensive (38 hectares) Clair-Daü domaine, and the acquisition of 29 per cent of it through both a purchase and the creation of a farming arrangement by Maison Louis Jadot of Beaune. It was a stroke of luck for Jadot, giving them on a plate a comprehensive helping of the best wines of Gevrey-Chambertin. It marked the beginning of the end of a family feud which was increasingly resembling the histrionics of a soap-opera like *Dallas*, but it was the start of the independence of a young man, now forty years old, who has over the past decade established himself as one of the best wine-makers in Burgundy: Bruno Clair.

HISTORY

The history of the Clair-Daü domaine begins in the First World War. Joseph Clair from Santenay met Marguerite Daü from Marsannay. He had been wounded and came back to Burgundy to convalesce. They were married in 1919 and were to produce three children: Bernard, born in 1921; Noëlle, who eventually married a M. Vernet, in 1923; and Monique, who was to wed a M. Bart. Marguerite and her sister Hélène Trinquier had inherited 8 hectares of vines in Marsannay. But these had been allowed to degenerate as a result of the phylloxera epidemic. Joseph Clair took them over, replanted the vineyards, and the Clair-Daü domaine was born.

Gradually the domaine was extended. Land was not as expensive then as it is today. An *ouvrée* (there are roughly 24 *ouvrées* to the hectare) from which you would normally expect to produce three-quarters of a *pièce* of wine, cost the same price as the value of that cask.

The first acquisitions were in Gevrey, in 1924 and 1925 in the *premier cru climats* of Combe-aux-Moines and Estournelles-Saint-Jacques, up-slope from the church and the old château. In the 1930s the holding in Marsannay was itself extended, some village Gevrey was acquired, and the domaine reached further south to embrace the *climats* of Chambolle-Musigny, Amoureuses and Bonnes-Mares. More of the latter was acquired in the early 1950s, as was some Clos-de-Vougeot.

Two more Gevrey-Chambertin *premiers crus* followed later in the 1950s: Cazetiers in 1951 (by Bernard) and Clos-Saint-Jacques from the Comte de Moucheron in 1952. In 1960 Joseph Clair successfully competed against Aymar de Nicolay of the Domaine Chandon de Briailles to purchase some venerable vines - already about sixty years old - in Savigny-lès-Beaune, La Dominode. The year afterwards a rich widow in Gevrey sold Joseph and Bernard almost an hectare of Clos-de-Bèze, and finally in 1970 Bernard took over a two-thirds-of-an-hectare parcel of Gevrey-Chambertin, *premier cru* Clos-du-Fonteny, and the following year a hectare of Vosne-Romanée in the *lieu-dit* of Aux Champs-Perdrix (300 metres up-slope from Romanée-Conti, they proudly claim).

Bernard Clair started working alongside his father in 1939, and married Geneviève Bardet in 1946 (the couple were divorced in 1972), producing five children. Also in 1954 the ownership of the domaine was entrusted to a family-owned *Société Civile*.

It was after the death of Joseph Clair in 1971 that the troubles began. The children, it seemed, had never got on that well among themselves, but the lid on family dissension had been firmly held in place by Joseph, from all accounts somewhat of a patriarch.

Things were not too bad at first but in 1981 the Clair-Daü affair went from bad to worse. Bernard, naturally, wanted to re-invest his profits in the vineyard and in the cellars, to buy new wood and the equipment necessary to control the vinification and maintain the reputation of the domaine. The sisters (one of whose husband's business was failing to thrive) wanted their money out. Meanwhile, though Bernard, responsible for the vinification, was producing a fine *matière première*, the *élevage* in the cellars was increasingly being mishandled by cellar-master M. Ploy. He was nearly always drunk, remembers Bruno Clair. But he was a dab hand at *boules*.

Matters reached a head in 1981. In frustration Bernard Clair walked out. In retaliation the sisters boarded up the front door of his house, for it gave on to the courtyard of the domaine. Clair had to come and go by the rear entrance. Noëlle Vernet took over, assisted - if that is the word - by the now totally incapable M. Ploy. But this was merely a stop-gap. The Clair-Daü domaine was up for sale. It was a sad time. The vines were neglected. All the competent people had left. The quality of the wine declined.

Following the death of Joseph Daü, ownership of the Clair-Daü domaine was divided into four parts. Bernard possessed almost two-thirds of the vines of the *Société* Clair-Daü. Then there was Roger Trinquier, son of Hélène, *née* Daü. And there were the two other Clair-Daü children. It was Noëlle Vernet's share, plus the *fermage* of Roger Trinquier's part, i.e. 29 per cent of the domaine, which passed into the hands of Louis Jadot in 1985 together with the existing stocks. Monique Bart runs her quarter from a large modern cellar elsewhere in the village, the wines now being made by her son Martin, and Bernard Clair, not wishing to put all his eggs in one basket, kept his 1.6 ha of Bonnes-Mares and some Marsannay vines for himself. This is now rented to the Domaine Fougeray-de-Beauclair. Since the 1986 vintage the remainder of the domaine has devolved to Bruno Clair, son of Bernard and Geneviève Bardet: he therefore runs more than half of the original Clair-Daü domaine.

BRUNO CLAIR

Bruno is the youngest of the family. There is an elder brother, Michel, a lawyer, and three sisters. He started working at the Clair-Daü domaine in 1978 but left after the family rows to build up his own domaine, mainly by taking on parcels in Marsannay *en fermage*. During the next five years he built up a domaine of 9 hectares, a third of it, like the parcels he has recently resurrected up-slope from Bonnes-Mares and the Clos-de-Tart, in plots which had been *en friche* since the aftermath of the phylloxera epidemic. He teamed up with Philippe Brun, a young man who had worked for Drouhin, and began by leasing the Savigny-lès-Beaune, La Dominode from his father.

Now he tends 21 hectares. The lion's share is still in Marsannay, *Appellation Contrôlée* in its own right since the 1986 vintage; white (from Pinot Gris as well as Chardonnay), red and the famous *rosé*, now sadly declining in popularity but nevertheless quite delicious, indeed my favourite *rosé* of all. In addition there is the venerable Savigny, Dominode, the bulk still vines planted in 1902 - the young vines are vinified separately and labelled as Savigny *tout court*. There is village Gevrey, Morey, Chambolle and Vosne including a rare Morey-Saint-Denis *Blanc*; *premier cru* Gevrey in Bel-Air, Cazetiers, Clos-du-Fonteny, and Clos-Saint-Jacques (this is labelled under his mother's name) and the *grand cru* Clos-de-Bèze. Since the 1993 harvest there has been some village Aloxe-Corton and some Corton-Charlemagne.

WINE-MAKING

Bruno Clair, like all good wine-makers, is nothing if not flexible. Vinification techniques are adjusted to the vintage, to the fruit which arrives in the first place. To ensure that this fruit is as fine as possible the vines are pruned short and fertilisation is kept to a minimum. 'One must understand the vines and the *terroir*.' This is what everyone will tell you, but if you travel round his vineyards with Bruno, you really do feel that he knows every plant individually, and is aware of every subtle nuance and variation in the soils they are planted in.

On arrival at the winery in Marsannay, a large barn with an underground cellar beneath it, the bunches are partially destemmed, the percentage depending on the state of maturity of the wood as much as the fruit, a *saignée* is performed in some vintages (in 1986, for example), and after a few days' cold maceration, the fermentation is allowed to progress up to a maximum of 32°C. There is a regular *pigeage* in the early stages, and a *cuvaison* of up to three weeks, again depending on the vintage.

Thereafter the lesser wines are kept partly in bulk, in oak *foudres*, partly in barrel; the better wines entirely in small oak of which a third is new, and bottled from about fifteen to twenty-one months after the vintage, depending on the wine. Sometimes the wines are fined but not filtered as in 1988; sometimes filtered but not fined, as in 1987. It all depends on the year.

THE WINES

Bruno's wines are structured, elegant, and age well. The colours are not dense black, but the wines have no lack of intensity. I find them nicely austere when they are young, with good grip and plenty of sophisticated tannins. This is a fine domaine which is a worthy successor to the reputation of Clair-Daü at its best.

THE TASTING

I sampled the following wines in Marsannay in June 1993. As you will see, Bruno had assembled a range of Gevrey-Chambertin, Cazetiers to sample alongside a sequence of Gevrey-Chambertin, Clos-Saint-Jacques. It was a fascinating comparison. Both *climats* were planted in 1957/1958. But while the average *rendement* in recent years in the latter has been 35 hectolitres per hectare, itself a commendably low figure, that of the Cazetiers, where the soil is more meagre, and the vines suffer more, is as low as 27 hl/ha.

GEVREY-CHAMBERTIN, LES CAZETIERS

Optimum drinking

1991   1998-2011

Bottled a month previously. This is in the middle of its *maladie de la mise*. The colour is good, but the nose rather upset. Good grip. Medium to medium-full. Good fruit. Judgement deferred though.

1990   1999-2015

Good fullish colour. Fine rich Pinot nose. Now beginning to close in. Ripe, quite opulent. Fullish on the palate. Not a blockbuster, but a wine of lovely depth and style. Good acidity. Potentially very silky. This has lovely complexity and balance. Very good indeed.

1989   Now-2009

Good colour. On the nose this is just a touch less fat than the Clos-Saint-Jacques. Ripe, balanced, generous, accessible. Medium body. Round and soft, good balance. This has great charm. Finishes very well. Very good.

1988   1999-2015

As always, a little more colour than the Clos-Saint-Jacques. Fullish. Reserved on the nose, a little austere. Ripe but the acidity is apparent. Medium-full body. Good fruit. Clean classic Pinot. Not a wine of great density, but one of harmony and class and complexity. Marvellously rich, even fat finish. As good as the Clos-Saint-Jacques, perhaps better.

1987   Now-2000

Medium colour. Less brown than the Clos-Saint-Jacques. Fresh, stylish but not *that* substantial nose. Medium body. Balanced, ripe, gentle, even quite rich and intense. But a soft wine without real backbone. Positive finish. Attractive. Will keep well.

1986   Drink soon

Splendid colour. Fullish, still immature. Fuller,

richer, more intense nose than the 1987. But there are mature slightly vegetal elements which are not quite as stylish. Fat, rich, opulent, medium-full body. But just a little coarse. This will get progressively less elegant as it develops. So drink soon. I prefer the above.

1985   Now-1998

Vinified by Clair-Daü (M. Ploy), *élevé* Jadot. Medium to medium-full body. Mature. Soft, ripe nose. Fruity, but not exactly very elegant. Better on the palate. Rich, slightly caramelly. Good grip. Highish alcohol. This is a bit rustic and fiery. Lacks style.

1984   Drink up

Once again a bigger colour than the Clos-Saint-Jacques. Medium. Mature. Ripe nose. Still has fruit and style. A little astringent. Medium body. Not bad. But towards the end of its life now

GEVREY-CHAMBERTIN, CLOS-SAINT-JACQUES

1991   1998-2014

Bottled a month previously. Showing a little better than the Cazetiers. Slightly richer. Seems to have more to it. But not the right moment to judge it.

1990   1998-2018

Medium-full colour. Rich, concentrated nose. There is a lot of depth here. Fullish, rounder and more rich and concentrated, more intense than the Cazetiers. A fine example. Quite austere. The tannins very ripe. Harmonious, elegant. Very long on the palate. Fine.

1989   Now-2011

Good colour. Voluptuous, rich and creamy nose. Rather more closed than the Cazetiers, more adolescent, the tannins a bit more apparent but much richer. The finish is ripe and potentially opulent. Very good grip. Lovely fruit. Very good indeed.

1988 1999-2018

Medium-full colour. Rich nose, good depth, plenty of backbone and grip. But more ripeness than the Cazetiers. Fullish, with more backbone and tannin. More concentration and potential opulence of fruit as well. Has real grip and intensity. Lovely. Fine quality. But more adolescent.

1987 Now-2005

Medium colour. Some maturity. Lightish nose. Very stylish and harmonious though. There is an attractive ripeness of fruit here. Just a little more substance than the Cazetiers. Certainly quite a lot more grip and depth. Medium to medium-full. Still some unresolved tannin. This is a fine example for the vintage. Very good future.

1986 Now-2005

Much better colour than the 1987. Not as full or as fresh as the Cazetiers though. Rich, plump, fat nose. Lovely fruit. Round and ripe and seductive. Good structure. Good grip. A lot more style than the Cazetiers, a lot more depth. Lovely ripe fruit. Here I prefer the 1986. Elegant, long, fat, seductive. Fine.

1985 Now-1999

Vinified by Clair-Daü, *élevé* by Jadot. Medium-full colour, better than the Cazetiers, less advanced. Slightly more old-fashioned on the nose. Chunkier, more stems, than today. Some tannin, a little rustic. Quite powerful. Some alcohol evident. Lacks real style.

1984 Past its best

Lightish, slightly over-mature colour. This is dried-out on the finish. Rustic. Poor.

1983 Drink soon

Medium colour. Well matured. Spicy, raisiny, a little astringent, a little vegetal. Oddly sweet-sour on the nose, even a little oxidised. Like a 1969 claret. There is ripeness here, but no style. Reasonable grip too. Unexciting.

1982 Drink up

Light to medium colour. Well matured. Quite obviously a very stretched harvest. This is light, somewhat fiery in alcohol. But the fruit is lightening up. Unexciting.

1980 Drink soon

Medium colour. Well matured, a little dull. Better, fresher on the nose than the 1982 and 1983. Some structure. Some fruit. Not a lot of finesse though, and now at the end of its life. But the best of the three. Not bad.

1978 Drink soon

Medium to medium-full colour, but really very old looking. Touch of maderisation. Touch of lactic. Has lightened up, and lost its fruit. Now lean and a bit vegetal and not very exciting. Wasn't ever that special.

OTHER WINES TASTED

Marsannay, Vaudenelles, 1988 Drink soon

Medium colour. Fresh, stylish, ripe Pinot on nose and palate. Soft, plump, *tendre*, balanced, delicious. Lightish. Plenty of character, plenty of finesse. *À point.*

Bonnes-Mares, 1983 Now-2000

Medium-full mature colour. Spicy nose. A touch of cloves and prunes. But clean, and not a bit overbalanced. Good acidity. Medium to medium-full body. Elegant, smooth. Good grip. Quite rich and sweet. Long and complex. Very good indeed. This is rather better than the Clos-Saint-Jacques.

Gevrey-Chambertin, Clos-du-Fonteny, 1989 Now-1999

Round, *tendre*, ripe and elegant. Supple. Fruity. Very good depth though. But a medium-bodied wine which will be ready soon. Great charm. Very good. Lovely fruit.

Gevrey-Chambertin, Clos-Saint-Jacques, 1967 Drink soon

Half bottle. Mature fullish colour. This is serious. Rich and chocolatey on the nose. Well matured. Ripe, quite rich. Concentrated and stylish. This has held up well. Fresh. Cool. Positive. Complex. Long. Surprisingly fine.

Savigny-lès-Beaune, La Dominode, 1962 Drink soon

Half bottle. Quite a vigorous colour. Much less brown than I would have expected, though it has lightened up at the edge. Just a little sweaty on the nose. Quite substantial. Old but fresh. Just a little rigid or chunky. Yet the fruit is fresh, sweet, long, lovely. Unexpectedly good, indeed fine for the vintage.

Gevrey-Chambertin, Clos-Saint-Jacques, 1963 Drink up

Half bottle. Really quite old on the colour. This is getting towards the end, if not already there. The nose is fragrant, sweet, elegant, old-rose-y. Soft, has lightened up, but still has style and fruit. Not astringent, just gently fading away. A great surprise. Perhaps 1963 wasn't really *that* bad after all.

HENRI CLERC,
PULIGNY-MONTRACHET

The Clerc domaine and its wines are in many respects the odd ones out among the top estates of Puligny. The style of the wine is controversial, and its quality can be patchy, disaster being equally as common as excellence. Some of the techniques – centrifuging of the must, picking by machine, and anointing the outside of the barrels with linseed oil – are frowned on by perfectionists. Yet this is a large domaine of prime land, with its tentacles spread wide, as far as Clos-de-Vougeot and Echézeaux in the north, down to Santenay in the south. The potential here could be as high as you could go. But will it ever be realised?

HISTORY

Bernard Clerc, son of the eponymous Henri, who died in 1971, can trace his ancestors back – residents in Beaune to the thirteenth century on his father's side and in Puligny since the sixteenth century on his mother's. But their involvement in wine is more recent. The Clerc family were *tonneliers* and *foudriers* in the last century, manufacturing wooden vinification vats as well as small barrels, not land-holders. The nucleus of the wine estate comes from Bernard's mother, the daughter of Joseph Patriarche. It was Patriarche who started to build up the domaine in the first half of this century, acquiring land in Bâtard-Montrachet in 1903 and more in 1908, Chevalier and Bienvenues in 1923. Various other bits followed, but when Bernard Clerc took over in 1965 the exploitation covered a mere 6 ha. Under the new regime the domaine was considerably enlarged, particularly in generic and village AC, Bernard replanting land formerly under cereals, and buying and exchanging other parcels. Today it is 22 ha. As much as 15 ha of this is generic wine.

With 60 per cent of the estate's production being sold to private clients, Bernard Clerc has for long been concerned with the discrepancy between the amount of quality white wine he has to offer as opposed to red. Firstly he bought some village Beaune. Jointly with the Gerbet sisters, he managed to acquire the Piat (IDV France) parcel of Clos-de-Vougeot, via SAFER, early in 1984 (together with the wine of the 1984 vintage). The land lies in the middle of the bottom half of the *climat*, and the Clerc's share measures 30 ares. Finally in 1991 he signed a three-year lease with Jean Mongeard of Vosne-Romanée and Roger Belland of Santenay: Echézeaux from the former and Santenay from the latter in exchange for village Puligny.

The recent years have been troublesome times for Bernard Clerc. He and his wife separated, and the business was hit by the recession. As a result he was forced to sell some land in order to make ends meet. He chose to dispose of 4 *ouvrées* (16 ares) of Bienvenues-Bâtard-Montrachet, being fortunate enough to have 65 a in the first place. This he sold to a Swiss company, a consortium of wine-lovers, but was able to arrange it that his daughter Corinne and her husband Frank Guillemard are the *métayers* for this parcel. So half the wine remains in the family.

Bernard Clerc has a son as well as a daughter. Laurent was the heir apparent. He married Véronique Michelot, grand-daughter of Bernard Michelot of Meursault. This marriage broke down, and whether because of this or not Laurent decided to pursue another career outside the Côte-de-Beaune *vignoble*. Like the prodigal son, he has now returned and has his own small domaine. Meanwhile the delightful Corinne, whose husband Frank hails from a domaine in the Hautes-Côtes, occupies herself both with her father's estate and the embryonic Domaine Guillemard-Clerc.

THE VINEYARD

Looking at the average age of the Clerc domaine, it becomes apparent that Bernard's succession coincided with a major replantation of much of *premier cru* land. The biggest slice is in Folatières (1.49 ha). There is 0.67 of Combettes, 0.32 of Champ-Gain and 8 ares of Pucelles, all dating from the late 1960s. The *grands crus* present a different picture: the vines in Bâtard (18 a) are old, approaching their fiftieth birthday, but those in Chevalier (15 a) and Bienvenues (49 a) are relatively young, a mere fifteen years or so. Village Puligny from a *climat* called Charmes (26 a) is usually produced separately: now by Laurent Clerc. And there is a further 2.89 ha of other village wine, 27 a of which makes red wine.

Outside the commune, both Pinot Noir and Chardonnay are planted in Blagny, Sous-le-Dos-d'Ane, and there is the village Beaune (44 a) and the Clos-de-Vougeot, already mentioned.

VITICULTURE AND WINE-MAKING

Much of the Clerc land is worked *à la tâche*, the *tâcherons* or vineyard-workers being paid by the surface area for which they are responsible, rather than by the hour. Some of the generic land is leased out to young *vignerons*.

Bernard Clerc bought his first harvesting machine in 1982, replacing it by a more sophisticated version four years later. He is quoted (by Simon Loftus, *Puligny-Montrachet*) as claiming that the quality of machine-harvested juice was as good as with the hand-picked crop. Loftus alleges further that Clerc uses, or used the machine wherever he could. Today, I am told, the machine is only used to pick in generic and village *climats*, not in the *premiers* and *grands crus*.

On arrival at the winery the juice is centrifuged, pressed using a new Bucher *pneumatique*, the generic wine fermented in tank, and the village, *premiers* and *grands crus* in wood. There is 35 per cent new oak for the *grands crus*, and progressively less for the lesser wines.

The Clerc HQ is a large courtyard, fronted by an imposing house on the first floor, below which is the *cuverie* and cellar. Beyond, across a back road, is a much larger, more modern warehouse, and up in the hills below Blagny, where Corinne and her husband and children used to live in an absurd Swiss-chalet-type folly, is a splendid *cave* dug into an old quarry. The cellar in the village, however, is partly underground, and, with Puligny's water table being so high, subject to periodic flooding. It is for this reason, perhaps, that the barrels are coated with linseed oil. Bernard Clerc likes a high toast, and vinifies at a high temperature. These two elements in the wine-making equation ensure an opulence and an exotic aspect to the flavour, one which is an integral part of the Clerc style. As a result of this insistence on the centrifuge – for it must eliminate malo-lactic bacteria – malos are late to finish at the Clerc domaine. In June 1994 one of the 1993 wines had not even finished its sugar-alcohol fermentation.

Again perhaps because of the way it is handled, the wine is difficult to clear. The wines are fined, later *Kieselguhr* filtered, and filtered again before bottling. Bottling takes place from September onwards.

THE WINES

Until about 1988, Bernard Clerc sold a good third of his produce in bulk to the local *négoce*. I remember in the 1970s Roland Remoissenet being an important customer, though the wine under his labelling had none of the Clerc style.

This style, as I have said, is different to those of the other major domaines of the village: lush, toasty, fat and voluptuous, with a distinctly exotic flavour of honey and citrus and roasted nuts. Sometimes, as with the 1988s, when they confess to having made a mistake with the choice of wood and its charring, the wines have a curious smell of smoky bacon. Often, on ageing, the wines dried out, indicating a lack of freshness and zip at the outset. Often too, the wines are very obviously chaptalised, alcoholic, even sweet. Delicate and subtle they ain't.

But they can be good. They are larger-framed than most, firm as well as oaky, and in some vintages they seem to be holding up rather better than you expect.

Overall, however, there is – or there used to be, for I have found the 1993s and 1994s, in bottle, rather better – a lack of finesse, an absence of the laid-back, steely intensity which is Puligny at its most magnificent. The wines make a statement, but it is heavy metal rather than Mozart.

THE TASTING

I sampled the following wines in Puligny in June 1994.

CHEVALIER-MONTRACHET

1992   **Now–2007**

Good colour. Rich, opulent nose. Fat, quite toasty, quite exotic in flavour. On the palate it is more evolved than most at this stage. Good acidity. Juicy fruit. Slightly four-square at the end. Just a little heavy. But long on the palate. Very good indeed but lacks a little bit of real elegance for fine.

1991   **Drink soon**

Good nose. Not too slight. Good fruit and substance. Elegant. Medium-full, plump, quite forward. The finish is getting a little blowsy. But this has more to it than most.

1990   **Now–2009**

Quite marked by the oak on the nose. A toasty wine: rich and fat. On aeration the oak diminished and the fruit began to come out. There is a lot of concentration here. Firm and full and meaty, but really quite oaky. Fresher and more elegant than the 1992. More depth too. Very good indeed. But not the backbone of the 1986.

1989   **Now–2005**

Higher toned nose with an aspect of banana and asparagus. Curious. Plenty of oak support. A lighter wine than the above. Less grip. The fruit a little dominated by the oak. But attractive nonetheless. Could have done with a bit more zip and concentration. Finishes long though. Very good.

1988   **Now–1999**

Quite a yellow colour. At first the nose smelled oddly of bacon. Ample and plump. Quite fresh. But a little loose-knit. Yet for the vintage, despite the smoky-bacon flavour, a wine of depth and interest.

1987   **Drink soon**

Surprisingly good nose for a 1987; has depth, and a good dollop of oak hasn't done it any harm. Fullish for a 1987, rich, meaty. No lack of substance and interest. Not exactly very classy. But a good effort.

1986   **Now–2010**

Fresh, honeyed and concentrated. The nose here is very promising. No less youthful, it seems, than the 1985. Firm and oaky on the palate. A full, meaty wine which still needs time. Good grip. Exotic oaky finish but a fine example. Holding up much better than most.

1985   **Now–2015**

Rich and full and firm on the nose. This is even better. Very full, very very rich and concentrated. Firmer. Even more grip. This is still very young. Oaky and toasted. And underneath rich, complex and creamy. This is excellent. Very very long. Very classy.

1984   **Now–1998**

Not a bit too lean and vegetal on the nose. Still fresh. Medium body. Gently oaky. No lack of fruit. This is classier than the 1987. More composed. Really most enjoyable. Flowery and long. No hurry to drink up. A very good result for the vintage.

1983   **Drink soon**

This is corked, but behind it the wine is rich and concentrated, neither too dry or evolved. Has grip, even. An opulent attack. A little short and blowsy at the end. But a very good result for the vintage.

1982   **Drink soon**

Round, open nose. Soft and plump. Plenty of fruit. Gentle and quite long enough on the palate. A medium-full wine. Not without elegance. Still holding up well. Good.

1981   **Drink up**

Magnum. Deep colour. Ripe and honeyed, perhaps just a suggestion of maderisation on the nose. Spicy and oaky on the palate. Just a little hard and now getting a bit old. But by no means undrinkable.

1980   **Drink soon**

Not as deep a colour as the 1981. Good fresh nose. This is really not bad at all. A bit one-dimensional, but reasonably balanced, reasonably long. Still has interest. Very good for the vintage.

1977   **Past its best**

Quite a deep colour. A little reduction on the nose (a touch of gas; malo not completely finished before bottling?). But not acid or fruitless. But it is getting there. On the palate it is obvious this has seen better days.

1974   **Drink soon**

Deep colour. Quite ample on the nose and a touch vegetal. But not at all beyond it on the palate. The alcohol shows a bit hot at the end. But there is fruit here. And it has not dried out. This is even quite enjoyable still.

1973   **Now–2003**

Deep colour. Rich, honeyed, almost *crème brûlée* nose. Stylish, complex, multi-dimensional. A concentrated, very spicy wine, the finish is toffee-ish. But vigorous and rich and lovely. Full and firm. Quite alcoholic I would judge. Fine.

1962   **Past its best**

Golden colour. This is showing a bit of age on the nose. It smells like an old dry Sauternes. On the palate it is really a bit past it. Thin at the end. The acidity showing. A pity.

1952   **Will still keep well**

Lighter colour than the 1962 or 1947. Firm, fresh, concentrated, stylish nose. Very lovely. Still vigorous. Long, fragrant, very complex. After the 1962 this is a surprise. Quite the contrary. Well matured but not old. Rich, powerful, intense. Fine.

1947   **Will still keep well**

Golden colour. Rich nose. Sauternes aspect, but not heavy or oxidised, nor too petrolly. Full, firm, plump and very concentrated, with a surprisingly fresh peachy acidity at the end. This leaves the follow-through fragrant and complex and very very stylish. Very fine. Will still keep well.

JEAN-FRANÇOIS COCHE-DURY,
MEURSAULT

Coche-Dury is one of Burgundy's super-stars: a name to conjure with and rank alongside those of Lafon and Ramonet. But the fame is recent. It was only subsequent to Jean-François' succession to the helm in 1973, following his father's early retirement as a result of back problems, that this estate began to export. (It is Becky Wasserman who can be said to have 'discovered' him for the American market.) Only in the last dozen years has the meagre production – for the exploitation is less than 9 hectares – been so sought-after as to be virtually unobtainable.

HISTORY

It was Jean-François' grandfather, Léon, who began to establish the domaine in the 1920s. He bought a few parcels - Bourgogne *blanc*, village Meursault, including Les Vireuils, Auxey-Duresses and Monthélie - rented a few more, and began to bottle himself as well as selling to the *négoce*.

Some of this land passed to his son Julien, and is now the responsibility of Alain Coche (Domaine Coche-Debord). Some devolved to his daughter Marthe, mother of Madame Guy Roulot. The rest was inherited by his son Georges, father of Jean-François.

Georges took over his share of the domaine in 1964, and continued to enlarge it. A further 16 parcels, including Volnay *premier cru* in Clos-des-Chênes and Taille-Pieds, and Meursault, Perrières were added. Some of these plots were leased on a *métayage* (share-cropping) basis, but since Jean-François has been in charge, most of these have been transformed into a simple leasehold arrangement, allowing him to keep all the fruit, and making the estate more of a commercial proposition.

By this time more and more of the production was being estate-bottled, and the reputation of the Coche wine was rising. Coche *père* entered his wines into *concours*, winning numerous gold medals. He placed them on to the lists of the top restaurants. Both increased the domaine's private clientele. By the time Jean-François took over the domaine was already on the local map. It was time to go international.

THE VINEYARDS

The Coche-Dury domaine measures 8.93 hectares, a third of it producing generics: Aligoté, Bourgogne Chardonnay and Bourgogne Pinot Noir. Most of the rest is in Meursault. There are no fewer than twelve different parcels of village AC, one of which is red, and only one *premier cru*: two parcels of Perrières, both about a quarter of a hectare. Coche sells about one-third of his production in bulk, the same *cuvées* every year, to Latour and Jadot.

Some of the village parcels are bottled separately. These are from land on the slope, either above the *premiers crus*, as in the case of the Narvaux, or in the same line, further to the north, nearer to the village itself. In 1989 and in 1993, as a result of the short crop, he blended the Narvaux and Luchets together (38 and 32 ares respectively). The other individual bottlings are Vireuils, where he has 61 a of old vines, Chevalières (12 a), and Rougeots (65 a - average age also old).

Sadly Coche does not get all the fruit of his sole *premier cru*, the magnificent Perrières. One parcel is owned by him (the vines date from 1947), but the other (vines planted in 1960 and 1974) is leased *en métayage* from a businessman in Saint-Etienne. Half of this is sold in bulk to the *négoce*.

Above Aloxe-Corton, in a *lieu-dit* called Sous-la-Croix, Coche produces about six casks a year from an acquisition dating from 1986: Corton-Charlemagne. The vines here were planted in 1960. The proprietor lives in Chambery. In 1985 Coche moved into Puligny, acquiring some village Les Enseignères.

In all the adulation over his white wine, Coche-Dury's reds tend to be overlooked. There is, as well as the generic wine, a small amount of red Meursault, some Auxey-Duresses (there is a little white Auxey too) and some Monthélie. But the *crème de la crème* comes from 16 ares of Volnay, Clos-des-Chênes, planted in 1960. There are also 21 a in the Caillerets, planted in 1989, and very often, especially if the harvest is small, Coche blends the two together.

VITICULTURE AND WINE-MAKING

Quality begins in the vineyard, says Jean-François Coche, and the first thing you must do is to restrict the harvest. Even young vines can produce good wine, though it tends to evolve rapidly, if you can ensure that the production is controlled. But of course old vines with deep root systems are better. He prefers to plant using his own material: clones are too uniform, he says.

Coche is also sceptical about green harvesting - by that time it is too late. You have to start earlier. While there are now many who like to Cordon du Royat prune their Pinot Noir, Coche is one of the few who trains some (about 30 per cent) of his Chardonnay this way. It produces smaller bunches of smaller grapes, he says, and so more concentrated wine. The harvest needs to be limited from the outset.

Jean-François Coche has only recently acquired a pneumatic press, and it was first used in the 1994 vintage. When I raised an eyebrow at this, for most top growers have 'gone pneumatic' for some years, he defended his old Vaslin (horizontal hydraulic) machine. 'All that is necessary is not to press too strongly.'

After pressing and *débourbage*, and cooling to 16°C if necessary, the entire white wine harvest, even the Aligoté, is vinified in wood in the cellar behind his house. (The house was built in 1974. He constructed an additional functional bunker of a cellar in 1982 and has since enlarged it twice. Yet he still has an additional cellar elsewhere in the village.)

Coche likes new wood, and as a result his wines are oakier than most, making them very engaging in their youth (and ensuring good marks in the reviews). While there is a maximum of 50 per cent, the wines are kept in the original Allier wood longer than most. He is also a great believer in *bâtonnage*. The wines are racked twice, fined but not filtered, and bottled by hand some twenty months after the vintage.

The reds are entirely destemmed, finish their alcoholic fermentation (as well as undergo their malo-lactic) in cask, of which one-fifth is new, are racked but once, fined during the second winter, and again hand-bottled without filtration, normally a couple of months earlier than the whites.

THE WINES

The Coche style is for wines which are plump, radiantly succulent and generous, immensely attractive from the start, and, of course, rather more oaky than most. This immediate appeal, the result of the new oak and the *bâtonnage*, can be misleading. With all the flavours up-front and out in the open, one is inclined to be suspicious. Will the wines last? After all, there are plenty of others who produce sexy wines which fail to stay the course. Would a bit more restraint be in order? Should they be more austere?

The secret, of course, lies in the small *rendement*. Underneath the opulence there is concentration. In the best vintages such as 1989 and 1985 - the later vintage the best of the decade, according to Jean-François - there is also a splendid balancing acidity. The result is something rich and creamy, with no lack of style or depth even in 1987, no lack of freshness and complexity even in the 1982 at twelve years old. The wines *do* last.

This is careful, dedicated wine-making from one of the most thoughtful, punctilious wine-makers in Burgundy. Coche is a shy man, tall, and youngish-looking for his age. You feel he is somewhat bemused by his success and the attention it has brought. But then you realise he is proud too, determined also; even, dare one suggest it, a touch arrogant. But he is entitled to be. This is one of the finest white wine domaines in the world.

THE TASTING

I sampled the following wines in Meursault in June 1994.

MEURSAULT, PERRIÈRES

1992   **1999-2015**

Fat, oaky, plump and generous on the nose. This shows splendidly despite being bottled a month previously. Very good grip and concentration. A touch of spice. Very ripe fruit without a suggestion of over-ripe. Full, fat, intense, substantial. Very long on the palate. An exotic touch here. Fine.

1991   **Now-2001**

The nose here is still a little closed. But ripe enough, elegant enough, and with plenty of grip and depth. Soft and flowery. Less closed, less dimension obviously compared with the 1992. Good class, but I fear it will get less classy as it develops. Reasonable acidity. Good.

1990   **Now-2008**

Fat, quite opulent and exotic nose. The oak quite evident. It is a little over the top? Oaky, slightly over-ripe palate. Good grip. But a very ample wine. Loads of fruit. Very seductive indeed. It is a bit adolescent, but it doesn't have the freshness and style of the 1989. Very good indeed.

1989   **Now-2017**

Firmer and richer, more stylish nose than the 1990. This is more classic. Very good grip. Full, firm, gently oaky. Plenty of fat but the wine is fresher and more stylish in my view than the above. Very fine long finish. Very complex at the end. Still quite closed. Excellent.

1987   **Now-2000**

Very impressive indeed. This is cool, flowery, very elegant, and with no lack of style and depth. It is a lot better than the 1991, and indeed I am not sure I don't prefer it to the 1990. Medium-full. Very lovely gently oaky fruit. Very good acidity. Elegant, has dimension, will still last. Very good indeed.

1986   **Now-2004**

Fresh nose. Ripe, concentrated and oaky. Quite spicy underneath. But no hints of over-ripeness or botrytis. Medium-full. Quite opulent again. Good attack, but some evolution on the finish. This is much better than most but it is not a patch on the 1985. Yet it held up very well. Remained fresh and classy. Very good indeed.

1985   **Now-2020**

Splendid nose. Youthful, radiantly clean and composed. Marvellous fruit. Fresh and very fine acidity. Full and concentrated. This is still a bit closed in. The attack is not really open yet. But the follow-through is rich, balanced, aristocratic and intense. Not quite as concentrated as the 1989 but very fine indeed.

1983   **Now-1999**

Quite a deep colour. Over-ripe, slightly botrytised nose. Now rather inelegant. Ample and rich and fat on the palate. Full, flamboyant. Not really lacking freshness but it lacks a bit of style. Yet the finish is cleaner. Better with food. Certainly enjoyable.

1982   **Now-1999**

Lovely nose. Flowery, gentle, *tendre*, still very fresh. Medium-full, plump, very engaging. On the follow-through surprisingly long, stylish and complex. Most attractive. Absolutely *à point*. A fine example, and a wine of great charm.

MICHEL COLIN-DELÉGER,
CHASSAGNE-MONTRACHET

One of the finest but most obscure white wines of Burgundy comes from a 60 a parcel in the *climat* of Puligny-Montrachet, Les Caillerets. These vines lie at the southern end of the vineyard next to Le Montrachet itself, directly underneath Chevalier-Montrachet, and are bottled as Puligny-Montrachet, Les Demoiselles. You can find them under four different labels. The best, a top *grand cru* in all but classification, is from Michel Colin-Deléger.

HISTORY

Today's Colins are descended from Emile who was born in Chagny, was apprenticed to a baker, but gave it all up to move 5 kilometres up the road and become a *vigneron* in Chassagne in 1878. His son Joseph had three children - François who died in 1975, André and Louis - and it is from them that the current three Colin domaines are descended: Michel in Chassagne, his cousin Marc in Gamay, and their cousin Bernard, also in Chassagne.

Michel, born in 1949, is married to Bernadette, one of the daughters of Georges Deléger, and they have two sons who have just recently joined the exploitation, Philippe and Bruno. He is now in control of 19.4 ha of vineyard. Some of this is his own, some is from the Deléger side, more comes as a result of a *métayage* arrangement with the SCI Saint-Abdon, whose owners, erstwhile *négociants* and childless, are pharmacists in Valenciennes on the Belgian border, while the most recent addition results from a farming agreement with what was once the Domaine Laurence in Dézize-lès-Maranges. Michel Colin has divided the 8.5 ha with his friend Bernard Morey.

THE DOMAINE

The estate is extensive. At the top of the tree is a 16 a nibble in Chevalier-Montrachet. This in fact is not the Georges Deléger parcel, as might be imagined (Georges still being personally responsible for this wine) but that of Georges' brother Robert. Robert tends the vines and Michel buys the grapes from him. The vines are adjacent to one another and were purchased by Deléger *père*, Edmond, in 1936.

In Chassagne-Montrachet *premier cru blanc* there are as follows: 1.50 ha in Les Chaumées, 1 ha in Les Vergers, 75 a in Les Chenevottes, 70 a in En Remilly, 40 a in La Maltroie and 65 a in Morgeots; in Chassagne-Montrachet *premier cru rouge* a further 15 a in La Maltroie and 24 a in Morgeots. And in village wine there are 1.50 ha of white and 5.05 ha of red.

There are two Saint-Aubin *premiers crus blanc*, 20 a Les Combes and 34 a Les Charmois; Santenay *premier cru rouge* Les Gravières and Maranges *premier cru rouge* - both 90 a; plus village Santenay *rouge* (1.40 ha), Côte-de-Beaune-Villages (40 a), and Puligny-Montrachet, La Truffière (50 a).

LES DEMOISELLES

But it is the Demoiselles which is the most interesting. Until the 1940s Caillerets was a red wine vineyard, and the Demoiselles end - no-one seems to know the origin of this separate designation - was rather larger than it is today. After the AC laws of 1936 both Louis Jadot and Louis Latour managed to have their parcels upgraded to Chevalier-Montrachet (in 1938), as did the Domaine Chartron after the war. And it was presumably on these occasions that these parcels were first planted in Chardonnay. Joseph Colin had acquired his 30 a at the turn of the century and perhaps at the same time the domaine which would later be called Saint Abdon - after a *clos* in the Chaumées - bought the remaining 30 a. These I suggest were converted to white wine in the post-war years, at a time when much of the Chassagne vineyard on the slopes to the south was similarly being replanted.

Joseph Colin's section has now been divided: 15 a to Michel and 15 a to his cousin Bernard. But to complicate matters the SCI Saint-Abdon vines are leased out *en métayage* to Guy Amiot but their share made into wine by Michel Colin. Amiot gets two-thirds of the crop. Michel Colin takes the remaining third but vinifies it separately from his own fruit. This is bottled under the Saint-Abdon label and is mostly consumed by the owner's friends. While Guy Amiot's Demoiselles is very good (the Bernard Colin wine you can buy in this Colin's boutique in the village, but it is in my experience less exciting), Michel Colin's is superior, a real beauty, but as there are usually only 7 hectolitres of it, 77 cases for the whole world, it is difficult to get hold of. It is currently one of a small number of his wines which bear his mother's name (Madame François Colin) on the label.

WINE-MAKING

After a *triage*, both in the vineyard and back in the winery - preferably, says Michel '*dans les vignes*', the white wine grapes are gently broken before being pressed in a *pneumatique* (acquired in 1987). There is only a *débourbage* in years where there is rot. The must begins its fermentation, using natural yeasts, in thermo-regulated stainless-steel vats. Once this is under way the emerging wine is decanted into barrels, one-fifth of which are new, the wood coming from the Vosges and the Allier. The casks are *bâtonnés*, usually until the end of the malo-lactic fermentation, depending on the vintage; the wine kept on its fine lees until the end of July; and bottling takes place in September. 'I don't want my wines to be too heavy,' says Michel Colin. 'What I am looking for above all is the aroma and the fruit.'

THE WINES

The Demoiselles, as I have said, is *grand cru* in all but name. The Truffière, from a little further up the slope and to the north, is flowery, crisp, racy and elegant: a splendid example of this *climat*.

Among the Chassagne *premiers crus* the one I normally prefer is En Remilly. This is a directly south-facing vineyard at the same level as the Truffière, on exposed bare rock above Le Montrachet. Very dry years can be a problem here, as there is hardly any surface soil and the vines can suffer from drought. But in most years this is a wine of real distinction, poised like a ballerina, crisp but intense.

Opposite, above the main road that divides the northern part of Chassagne from the much larger southern section, Colin has vines in three adjoining *climats*: Chaumées, at the top of the slope; Vergers in the middle and Chenevottes at the bottom. I normally prefer the Vergers, as would be logical. It is fuller than the En Remilly, ripe and honeyed, but also racy and steely. The Chenevottes is a little more four-square, the Chaumées flowery but with less depth.

The vines in La Maltroie are still young, but one can find a very pleasant honeysuckle aroma in the wine if rather less definition and grip on the palate. Better, surprisingly - for they are often rather clumsy - is Colin Morgeot *blanc*. This is often the most elegant of all Chassagne's white Morgeots, and as nearly everyone has vines in this large (50 plus hectares) conglomerate *climat*, there is a lot of competition.

Michel Colin and his boys produce lovely white wines - and the reds are good too - which are now housed in a new *cave de stockage*, lower down in a mini *zone industrielle* towards Chagny. Their signature is in their definition and their purity of fruit. It is not just the faint possibility of acquiring some Demoiselles which should tempt you in the direction of this cellar.

THE TASTING

I sampled the following wines in Chassagne in June 1996.

CHASSAGNE-MONTRACHET,
LES VERGERS

Optimum drinking

1994   **1998-2004**

Very good fresh nose. Ripe, fully, very good grip for the vintage. Nutty and rich. Fullish for the vintage. Stylish, long and harmonious. Very good - especially for a 1994.

1993   **Now-2003**

Gentle but quite broad nose to take in some suggestions of the herbal-vegetal as well as flowery. Good acidity. No lack of ripeness. Good oaky base underneath. This is evolving quite fast and doesn't have the grip for the long term. Good though.

1992 Now-2005

Firm on the nose. Rich and ripe and concentrated and nutty. This has a lot of depth. Fullish, rich, almost-but-not-quite over-ripe. Good grip. This is an abundant, even slightly voluptuous example. Slightly blowsy at the end but not short or inelegant. Beginning to round off now. Good ripe finish. Long too.

1991 Now-2000 plus

Good fresh nose. Stylish and even concentrated as well. No age, nothing unripe or vegetal either. Only at the end, on the palate, is this a little unplentiful. But the attack is rich and ripe and surprisingly good. And the finish is positive and gently oaky.

1990 Now-2005 plus

Good fresh colour. Firm, concentrated nose. Still vigorous. Fresh, youthful and concentrated on the palate. This is just about ready now. A ripe, very well-balanced, well-mannered, elegant example. Good grip. Nutty. Long. Complex. Lots of depth and dimension. Very classy. Will still improve. Fine.

1989 Now-2005

Rather more golden colour here. Softer, fatter and more honeyed on the nose than the 1990. Ample and more exotic than the 1990 on the palate. Less grip and structure and acidity. But enough to keep the wine fresh and generous and very seductive. Long. Most attractive. *À point*. Very good indeed.

1988 Now-2000 plus

Good fresh colour. Fresh, even slightly closed, on the nose too. On the palate this is now *à point*, and has plenty of dimension and character for the vintage. Fresh. Balanced. Very good. Lots of finesse and lots of charm. Nothing weak or ungenerous at all.

1987 Drink soon

Colour quite evolved now. On the nose fully mature too, but still balanced, under control. There are hints at the end that this is beginning to fall apart, but the grip and style are still there. Ripe, balanced. Has held up well. Very good for the vintage.

1986 Drink soon

Quite an evolved colour too. On the nose a touch of over-ripeness but only a touch. Still fresh. But certainly honeyed, with an addition of barley sugar. Fat, rich, a little blowsy. But this has better acidity than most. Good length. Very good for the vintage.

1980 Now-2000

Not too old on the colour. And the nose is ripe and vigorous and has surprising depth and attraction. On the palate the wine is full, vigorous and complex. Still fresh. Nothing old. Good grip. Very good fruit. I would have said it was a 1979. Much fresher than the 1986. Delicious. Will still keep. Fine.

1975 Drink soon

Michel's first vintage. Quite an old colour but not a bad wine. Still quite fresh. But a wine without depth or interest. Still drinkable.

JEAN-JACQUES CONFURON,

NUITS-SAINT-GEORGES, PRÉMEAUX

One of the newest of today's stars in the Nuits-Saint-Georges area is the Domaine Jean-Jacques Confuron. As recently as 1988 it sold the vast majority of its wine in bulk. Since then, with the arrival of Alain Meunier, husband of Sophie, *née* Confuron, progress has been remarkable. Quality has been consistent and improving, and this is now one of the cellars I most enjoy visiting. There is no *chichi*; merely a quietly industrious and welcoming couple who produce very good wine, including perhaps the best Nuits-Saint-Georges, Les Boudots in all Burgundy.

HISTORY

The domaine was born when Jean Confuron (1904-1965) of Vosne-Romanée married Anne-Marie Bouchard of Prémeaux in 1926 and installed himself in the latter village. The Chambolle vines, and some of the Clos-de-Vougeot came from his side of the family. Some of the Nuits-Saint-Georges and the Côte-de-Nuits-Villages came from the Bouchard side.

The marriage produced two children: Christian and Jean-Jacques (1929-1983). (Jacky Confuron-Cotetidot of Vosne-Romanée is a direct cousin.) Jean-Jacques qualified as an oenologist and married Andrée Noëllat of Vosne-Romanée. From her share of the important Noëllat domaine came more Clos-de-Vougeot, the Nuits-Saint-Georges Boudots and half a hectare of Romanée-Saint-Vivant. All this totalled 12 hectares, which the brothers worked jointly until the death of their mother in 1980, when the domaine was split and Christian went back to live in Vougeot.

Soon after, Jean-Jacques fell ill, and from 1982 until 1988 the domaine was run by Andrée Confuron and her daughter Sophie, then in her early twenties. They continued in the way Jean-Jacques had done, picking later than most, sometimes, as in 1982, producing rather too much wine, and selling most of the wine off after the harvest to the local *négoce*. There was little new wood, the *cave* and the vines needed attention, but the wine cannot have been too bad. Anthony Hanson in the first edition of his *Burgundy* (1982) mentions that the wine was selected by the Belgian court.

ALAIN MEUNIER

Alain Meunier, lean and hungry - as opposed to the more ample proportions of his wife - is the son of an Auxois agriculturalist. His first speciality was that of an agricultural mechanic, and as such he was employed by the *Lycée Viticole* at Beaune, which has its own viticultural domaine. He looked after their tractors and wine-making equipment and, *inter alia*, helped take the students round the vineyards. It was there that he and Sophie met. She was taking the viticultural and oenological course, something which Alain was soon to embark on after their marriage in 1988. They are today both thirty-five, and now have three children. In 1989 the couple took over the domaine and Alain produced his first Jean-Jacques Confuron vintage.

THE DOMAINE

The estate today measures 7 ha. At the top of the hierarchy is the half-hectare of Romanée-Saint-Vivant, old vines at the north of the *climat*, sandwiched between those of Leroy and Alain Hudelot. In the Clos-de-Vougeot there are two quarter-hectare parcels, both at the top of the slope. One of these was bought by a Confuron ancestor when the Léonce Bocquet domaine was split up and sold in 1920, the other comes from the Noëllat side.

In Chambolle the property holds 35 a of *premier cru* Châtelots and Feusselottes in the ratio of two-thirds of the former, one-third of the latter, vinified together, and 1.15 ha of village land; in Vosne there are 30 a in Les Beaux-Monts; and in Nuits-Saint Georges 30 a of Boudots, 44 a in Les Chaboeufs and 1.23 ha of village Les Fleurières, lying between Les Pruliers and the main road.

As well as all this there are 1.40 ha of Côte-de-Nuits-Villages, 35a of Bourgogne *rouge* and 50 a of Aligoté. It is a nice little empire.

WINE-MAKING

There was much to do, a lot to fine-tune, when Alain took charge in 1989. One of the first and most important tasks was to construct a new vinification cellar. The second was to look after the vineyards better and to reduce the potential crop. Over the next two years Alain gradually transformed his entire viticultural approach into *biologique*, dispensed with chemical fertilisation, cut down on composting and systematically began to remove duplicate buds and flowers.

As an agricultural engineer, Alain knows only too well how easily bad-quality machinery can ruin good-quality fruit. An ancient crusher-destemmer is worse than useless. An insensitive pressing machine will only result in undue astringency in the wine. Even something as basic as transporting the grapes from vineyard to *cuverie* in too large a container will crush the fruit at the bottom prematurely and lose vital aromas.

With a lower crop Alain obtains healthier and riper grapes, and unlike his late father-in-law can therefore pick earlier, preserving the acidity and freshness of the fruit, and avoiding any risk of rot. There is a *table de tri*, and more or less 100 per cent destemming - though Alain may add back a few of the stems to improve the physical efficiency of the fermentation. There is now no crushing. Cold soaking takes place for four or five days, the vat closed with a plastic top to retain the aromas, and during this period there is a very gentle *remontage*. The vat is then warmed to get the fermentation going, retaining the plastic top in order to guard the CO_2 from escaping. ('For me this is a vital element. This protects the wine. It keeps the fruit fresh.') Chaptalisation takes place in stages (up to a maximum of 13°C); there are three *pigeages* a day; and the wine is racked off as soon as the fermentation is finished, i.e. when there is less than 2 g of sugar.

Alain adds a modicum of gently pressed *vin de presse* (there is a new press machine now), allows the wine to fall bright, and decants into barrel to await the malo, which he allows to proceed at its own pace in the spring and following summer. The wine is not racked there-after until bottling, unless it begins to show a reduction in taste. Alain prefers to let it lie on its lees, protected by the CO_2, as long as possible There is no fining, since 1990 no filtering, and bottling takes place after fourteen to eighteen months in wood.

Alain Meunier is a fan of new wood. Overall 50 per cent of the barrels are new, ranging from 70-80 per cent for the top wines to 10 per cent for the generics. There was a time I feared he was exaggerating in this respect - the Boudots 1991, 1992 and 1993 all had 100 per cent new wood; and at the behest of Bobby Kacher, his American importer, there were village *cuvées* in 100 per cent new wood too - but I now feel this is under control. The wine having become more concentrated, it can absorb more new wood. For a time, across the board, there were two *cuvées* of each wine: one European and one (rather more oaky) destined for Kacher's US customers. Today, apart from one or two generic new barrels, there is but one wine in each appellation. The oak is noticeable, but it is not too extreme. Some 75 per cent of the Confuron wine is now exported, but, not wishing to put all his eggs in one basket, no more than 10 per cent of the crop is sold to any one client.

The Future

Since 1992 or so prospective buyers have been banging on Alain Meunier's door, and he now has insufficient stock to meet the demand. The solution, as has occurred to other growers elsewhere, was to develop a *négociant* business.

In association with a Lyon lawyer, Jean-Louis Féry, whose small domaine, based in Echevronne, Alain also supervises, Alain buys in grapes - they are currently vinified in a cellar in Savigny, but will probably, eventually centralise in Echevronne - and the produce is sold under the label of Maison Féry-Meunier. Currently there are four wines: Gevrey, Morey, Pommard and Corton-Charlemagne, a total of some 80-100 *pièces*. Alain doesn't want this development to get too big. The tail mustn't start to wag the dog, or get out of control. But at least he has enough wine to meet the demand.

THE WINES

Rich, concentrated and very pure, with a firm new oaky support and very good *terroir* definition, is how I would describe the J. J. Confuron style. They remind me of the wines of Faiveley. They have progressed in style from the slightly 'hot' 1990s - when with hindsight Alain feels he chaptalised a bit too much - to the almost perfectly poised 1993s, a vintage of very fine Confuron wines right across the board from Côte-de-Nuits-Villages to Romanée-Saint-Vivant. There is real class now. Jean-Jacques Confuron wines deserve to be in everyone's cellar.

THE TASTING

I sampled the following wines in Prémeaux in June 1996.

NUITS-SAINT-GEORGES, AUX BOUDOTS

Optimum drinking

1994   1998-2005

Bottled December 1995. Medium to medium-full colour. Soft, elegant nose. Round, the tannins ripe and velvety. Good acidity and depth. Very fresh. Gently oaky. This is still young, even a little raw. But there is no lack of substance or *terroir* definition here. This is rather better than the 1992. Long. Classy. Very good indeed.

1993   2002-2012

Good fullish colour. The oak here is rather more pronounced, and the toast seems higher. Lots of depth here. Rich, fat and ample. Fullish on the palate, where there is no undue oak. Good intensity and concentration. Very Vosne-ish in character. Long, very stylish. Fine.

1992   Now-2002

Surprisingly good colour. Soft and round on the nose. But no undue oak. Not as sophisticated as the 1994. Medium-full. Ripe and pleasant. Well balanced but compared with the 1994, a slight lack of personality and finesse and complexity. Very good.

1991   Now-2004

Good colour. Fresh upright nose at first, though it held up to air less well than I expected. Medium-full. Good fresh clean fruit on the attack. Well supported by oak. Underneath as it evolved I get a whisper of attenuation, which is odd, as there is no lack of acidity here. But the wine is rather flat at the end. Curious.

1990   2000-2015

Very good colour. Rich substantial nose, but rather more of a typical Nuits-Saint-Georges than the refinement of Vosne. Full, tannic, rich, much more of a blockbuster. Very good grip. A certain element of cooked fruit. Adolescent. But fat, ample and exciting. Bigger but not as classy as the 1993. Slightly 'hotter'. Fine.

1989   Now-2002

Good colour. No real browning at the rim yet. Mellow, ripe, very attractive nose. On the palate, however, not quite as fresh or as clean as it might have been. Not as sophisticated as the wines today. Good balance but a slight absence of fat and vigour. Merely good. Yet the finish is sweet and ample.

1988   Drink soon

A little lighter in colour than the 1989. More developed too. The tannins on the nose not as sophisticated as today. But there is good depth here. This is more rustic than the 1989, and there is even a certain dryness and astringency. This won't get any better. Only fair.

COURCEL,
POMMARD

Though their main holding is in Pommard, Epenots, the gem of the Courcels' cellar is their Pommard, Rugiens. Pommardiens have long argued that Rugiens should be accorded the status of *grand cru*, and most dispassionate observers would agree with them (perhaps adding one or two other nearby *climats* as well). To those who remain unconvinced I say: go and taste this Courcel wine. Put it up alongside a Corton or an Echézeaux. You will change your mind.

Like the Comte Armand, proprietor of Pommard's other top estate, the Courcels are absentee landlords. Gilles de Courcel, the member of the family who is today responsible for taking the major decisions, lives mainly in Bordeaux. Having worked for Champagne Piper-Heidsieck and the Burgundian *négociant* Albert Bichot, he is currently export director for Calvet, and makes the arduous trip across country back to Pommard about once a month to confer with resident *régisseur* Yves Tavant.

HISTORY

This was once a much larger domaine. Its lineage can be traced back to a M. Gautey in the seventeenth century. By the mid nineteenth century the holdings had passed to the Lejeune family, and they built up a 20 plus hectare domaine only to see it split for the usual inheritance reasons some time at the beginning of this century. This provided both the current De Courcel estate and that which still retains the Lejeune name and is today run by François Julien de Pommerol. The present title of the former comes from Gilles de Courcel's grandmother, Madame Bernard de Courcel, whose mother was a Lejeune.

Since the division the Courcel family holdings have been further diminished. Until 1975 they owned the entirety of the Grand-Clos-des-Epenots. In that year 3 of the 8 hectares of the Grand-Clos were disposed of in favour of Patriarche's Château de Meursault. Their section divides the current Courcel vineyard in two. One parcel lies immediately next door to the Clos-des-Epeneaux of the Comte Armand; the other closer to the Beaune boundary.

On the face of it this might seem a sadness, to have lost such a large slice of prime land. But, as Gilles de Courcel will point out, the size of their *cuverie* was inadequate. In abundant vintages prior to 1975 they didn't really have the space to vinify their Epenots properly. Most *cuves* would have to be used twice, reducing the opportunity for proper long-term maceration.

After Madame Bernard de Courcel's death in 1951 - the year, incidentally, of Gilles de Courcel's birth - responsibility devolved to one of her five children, Gilles' maiden-aunt, Marie. She lived in Pommard in the imposing house next to the winery opposite the church and was in charge until she herself passed away in 1983. This building is now occupied by Gilles' sister and her family when they are in the region. Gilles de Courcel himself has a house in the plain, on the other side of the motorway near the River Saône.

THE VINEYARD

The Courcel estate currently comprises some 8 hectares, 5 of which lie in the afore-mentioned Grand-Clos-des-Epenots. Some of the vines here are sixty years old; the average is forty-five years. This is also the average age of the Courcel's 1 hectare of Pommard, Rugiens. Rugiens lies on the opposite, Volnay side of the village of Pommard. The incline is steeper, erosion is much more of a problem, and the bed of surface soil, red further down-slope, more of a buff-coloured orange higher up where the Courcels have their vines, is barely a few centimetres deep. The limestone bedrock shows through in a number of places.

Elsewhere in the village there are two-thirds of a hectare of Fremiers (average age twenty-five years old, and only marketed under the domaine label in recent years), 60 ares of Croix-Noires and 35 ares of village Pommard. These lesser *cuvées*, together with the young vine element of the better *climats*, are sold off in bulk. It is also the Courcel's policy to dispose of around 30 per cent of even their serious wines to the *négoce* in this way.

YVES TAVANT

Day-to-day responsibility at the Courcel domaine lies in the hands of Yves Tavant. Yves, born in 1945, a slight wiry man aptly described by Remington Norman (*The Great Domaines of Burgundy*) as having the mien of a jockey, is the third generation of his family to fill this post. He has been in charge since 1971.

WINE-MAKING

On entry into the winery the fruit is decanted into a sophisticated *tapis de triage*, installed in 1990. This is set at an incline, so that water can roll away should the grapes have been collected in the rain. Press a button and the belt will begin to riddle gently from side to side, shaking off more excess water. Press another button and a draught of warm air will dry the fruit off even more effectively. Not surprisingly de Courcel and Tavant are very proud of this new machine.

After three or four days' cold maceration the fermentation takes place in open wooden *cuves*, the temperatures being allowed to rise to 33°C. At the outset there are three *pigeages* per day. Once their fermentation has died down the vat is closed and the maceration continues under a blanket of CO_2, with only one *pigeage* every twenty-four hours. Eventually the press wine - or some of it - and the *vin de goutte* are assembled, the gross lees allowed to settle out, and the wine racked off into barrels, as much as 80 per cent of which can be new (but in less structured vintages such as 1992 only 25-30 per cent), in the cellar below. Fining takes place in bulk, and the wines are bottled after fifteen to eighteen months in cask after a light plate filtration.

In the old days there was no cold maceration before fermentation, the must being warmed up immediately, but the new method, employed since 1990, has been found to give the Courcel wine an extra richness and element of fat, and indeed more sophisticated tannins. This has also been achieved by limiting the amount of stems left in the macerating juice. The domaine used to destem very little. Now they have a destemmer which does not crush the fruit and two-thirds of the harvest goes through this machine. When wet, de Courcel will point out, the stems will add a lot of unwanted water.

THE WINES

The baby of the cellar is the Pommard, Fremiers, a *climat* which lies on the Volnay border lower down-slope from the Rugiens. I have watched the evolution of this wine since it was retained by the Courcels for bottling under their own label in 1988. At the time the vines were seventeen years old and it was felt that at last they were worthy of the Courcel name. While it is neither as powerful as the Rugiens or as elegant as the Epenots it is certainly now a true Pommard: rich, substantial and meaty. The 1992, for a 1992, is better than the 1989 and 1990 were within the context of their vintages.

Paradoxical as it may seem, the Grand-Clos-des-Epenots lies in that section, nearer to the Beaune boundary, otherwise known as the Petits-Epenots. And the Petits-Epenots provides better wine than the Grands-Epenots which lies on the other side of the Comte Armand's Clos-des-Epeneaux.

The reason for the superiority of the Petits-Epenots over the Grands is a question of geology. The former lies on limestone rock, the second on a mixture of rock and ancient alluvial soil. The difference is subtle, but nevertheless important.

The Courcel wine comes from both sides of the Grand-Clos. It is stylish, concentrated and intensely flavoured. Compared with the Fremiers there is an extra dimension of definition, of depth, and of character. Compared with the Clos-des-Epeneaux it is softer, more Beaune-ish; less brutal in its youth, with the finesse more apparent. In the best vintages - 1990 for example - it needs eight or nine years to come round, a year or two less than Comte Armand's wine.

The Rugiens, though, is yet finer, perhaps the best example of this *climat* in all Burgundy. We have more size and more power here. The wine is more tannic and more masculine. The fruit flavours are black as well as red. A 1990 vintage of this wine needs a decade to reach maturity. But then, what a delight is in store! *Grand cru* quality, which should be rewarded with a *grand cru* appellation.

THE TASTING

I sampled the following wines in Pommard in February 1994.

POMMARD, RUGIENS

1992   **1999-2009**

Bottled mid-December 1993. Good colour. Ripe nose. Good substance and character. Has recovered well from the bottling. Fullish for a 1992. Good tannins. Rich, gently oaky. Good grip. This has style and generosity. A very good example indeed. Plenty of depth and character here. Long elegant finish.

1991   **2000-2015**

Very good colour. Rich nose. Substantial. Closed. Full, ample, well structured. Vigorous and tannic without being hard. Rich and fat and plump at the end. Plenty of depth. Plenty of succulent fruit. A fine example. Very long. Very lovely fruit.

1990   **2001-2020**

Very good colour indeed. Splendidly rich and concentrated on the nose. Fat and generous but underneath structured and intensely flavoured. This is beginning to go into its shell now. Full, tannic, very good grip. Enormous black fruit concentration. Fine finish. Excellent.

1989   **1999-2015**

Good colour. The nose of this wine is less opulent than it was a year ago. Medium-full, very ripe but very good grip. The tannins are very ripe too. Blackcurrant and redcurrant fruit. Nicely fresh. Gently oaky. Complex and very classy at the end. Lovely.

1988   **1998-2010**

Good colour. Similar to the 1989. Here again the nose is rather hidden. But there is more substance and fat than in the 1989. On the palate a plump wine, but less lean, less grip than I had expected. This is quite open, more like a 1985. It lacks a little concentration and intensity at the end. Very good but not great.

1987   **Now-2006**

Very good colour for 1987. As full as the 1988, no real sign of brown. Getting towards maturity. Slight touch of spice. But good class and substance. Medium to medium-full. Some tannin on the attack. Fresh and stylish and fruity though, and a long, clean ample finish. Very good indeed for the vintage. Just about ready.

1985   **Now-2001**

Medium to medium-full colour. Some maturity. The nose is a little stringy, a touch disappointing. Medium body. Ripe on the palate. Fully mature. Cherry-flavoured fruit. Somewhat lacking backbone and grip. So only good. And

I feel that before too long it will begin to get astringent. So far the finish is certainly positive though.

1981   **Drink soon**

Surprisingly good colour. Slightly lean on the nose. But not without fruit and interest. Full for the vintage. Ripe too. Plenty of depth. Even ripe and concentrated. Still vigorous. Surprisingly good.

1979   **Drink soon**

Good colour. Not too old. Lovely fruit on the nose. Ripe and fat and complex. This is *à point*. Fullish, fresh and has a lot of dimension for a 1979. Round and subtle and long at the end. Still plenty of life. A fine example.

1978   **Now-2000 plus**

Fine colour. Fullish and virile. Rich meaty, quite oaky nose. Fullish, very ripe and concentrated, very lovely classy fruit on the palate. This is still fresh. But fat and complex and very long indeed. Very lovely. Excellent.

1976   **Now-2000 plus**

Very good colour. Full and intense to the rim and no sign of brown. Full on the nose. Not too solid or dense. Certainly full and structured on the palate. There is still tannin here. Rich and concentrated, very very ripe. A wine for food. A little hard. But still ample and fresh. Not overbalanced. Very good.

1972   **Drink soon**

Medium colour now, quite brown at the rim. Aromatic nose. Not too firm and acidity, but a certain leanness nevertheless. Lightening up on the palate. A little vegetal. Not mean but it lacks class. The wines of the Côte-de-Nuits are better.

1970   **Drink soon**

Medium-full colour. Quite brown at the rim. Ample, plump, ripe, straightforward nose. Open, easy to drink. Comfortably fruity. Still fresh. Not a wine of great intensity but surprisingly vigorous. And plenty of interest. Medium to medium-full. Positive finish. Most enjoyable. Very good indeed.

1964   **Now-2000 plus**

Fine full vigorous colour. Splendidly vigorous and rich slightly gamey nose. Full, rich, almost sweet. Copious fruit; very, very ripe; very good balance. Good structure. Plenty of life. Very seductive. Very lovely.

1962   **Drink soon**

Fine colour. No undue maturity. Ripe, ample, fresh but stylish nose. Open but still vigorous.

Lovely fruit. A little more evolved than the 1964. A little earthier, slightly less structured. But nevertheless plenty of vigour, plenty of depth. Plenty of fruit. Plenty of class. Very good indeed.

1961   **Now–2000 plus**

Similar colour. A little more intensity. Concentrated nose, still youthful. Very, very ripe. This is very concentrated. Ripe, slightly caramelly-spicy. Intense and very very rich. Very good grip. This has very classy fruit. Subtle. Very long. Fine. Even more to it than the 1964. Aristocratic. The fruit is brilliantly intense and long lasting on the palate.

1959   **Drink soon**

Splendid colour. Rich, full and very vigorous looking. Splendid nose. Rich and concentrated. Very intense, even over-ripe and caramelly. This has less grip than the 1961 and 1964, but its own velvety plummy fruit and a touch of gingerbread. Lovely nevertheless. But slightly less vigour.

1945   **Drink soon**

Fine colour. Still plenty of vigour here. (17 *pièces sur* 13 ha – so probably a mixture – Pommard *premier cru*.) Caramelly and slightly maderised on the nose. This is curious but not undrinkable. Very concentrated indeed. More aromatic than fruity. Spice, wood (? sandalwood). Rich. Good grip. Yet a little astringency here. But there is still a good acidity. This wine is holding up well.

JOSEPH DROUHIN,
BEAUNE

Forty years ago Burgundy was a completely different *vignoble*. The *négociants* ruled the roost. Domaine-bottling was negligible. Life was traditional; it had hardly changed for centuries. If a *vigneron* from 1857 had happened to re-emerge in a cellar a century later he would have noticed little new apart from the introduction of electric light. These were the last flickering embers of the pre-scientific age. There were no oenologists, no fertilisers, no artificial yeasts, no tractors, no clonal selection. Growers grew grapes, the wine made itself and shortly afterwards the merchants' drayman would arrive and take the barrels away to Beaune or Nuits-Saint-Georges. Quality was a bit hit-and-miss, but the ancestral methods had been tried and tested, and they worked more often than not, though nobody really understood why.

Now all has changed. We've all been to wine school, and roles have reversed: the domaines have become *éleveurs* and bottlers and sellers; the merchants have become vineyard-owners and vinifiers of their own and other people's grapes. Modern technology has arrived. We now know why: we can control what goes on. Standards have also considerably improved, but not every innovation has been for the best, however. The Burgundian vineyard was grossly over-fertilised in the 1960s. The infamous Pinot Droit was planted too widely, and usually on to the equally disastrous SO4 rootstock. Yields are too high. Quality is often cynical. And prices even more so; though since 1985 they have become more realistic. But by and large it has been a change for the better.

One man who has seen this all happen, and who in fact started his Burgundian career in 1957, is Robert Drouhin, today's owner and director of Joseph Drouhin. Maison Joseph Drouhin is rightly one of Burgundy's most respected wine firms; Domaine Joseph Drouhin one of its most important estates; and Robert and his children one of Burgundy's most intelligent wine dynasties. And for all his patrician, somewhat shy and aloof bearing, Robert Drouhin is one of Burgundy's most refreshingly honest ambassadors as well as one of its most important innovators. Listen to this man. You will learn much.

HISTORY

The firm dates from 1880, the domaine from forty years later. In the former year Joseph Drouhin took over a merchant business originally founded in 1756. Maurice Drouhin, son of Joseph, came back from the war in 1919 and took over the direction of the business. He decided to specialise at the finer end of the market and to invest in land. Vineyards were cheap, a lot of them *en friche*, having been allowed to go fallow following the disaster of the phylloxera epidemic. He first acquired the 13.7 ha Clos-des-Mouches, a *premier cru* Beaune at the southern end of the commune, and other local parcels. But none of them very far away. One used horses in the vineyards in those days, and there were limits to how far one could travel as a result.

In 1938 (or 1926 according to Jean-François Bazin), Maurice Drouhin bought almost two-thirds of a hectare of Clos-de-Vougeot. It was his first venture outside the purlieus of Beaune. It was not, at that stage, a profitable move.

Robert Drouhin, nephew and heir-apparent, was born in 1933. It was intended that he should serve a long apprenticeship before succeeding, and to this end after military service he enrolled himself at wine school to take an oenological degree. It was not to be. In 1957 Maurice Drouhin suffered a stroke. Robert was thrown into the deep end at the tender age of twenty-four.

Poor Robert! It was easy to be seduced by the counsels of all the newly qualified *ingénieurs agronomes* and *oenologues*. Vines? They were old; they were feeble; they looked decrepit. They had to go. A large part of the domaine was replanted in 1961 and 1962. Fertilisers and compost? Far more efficient! Pile 'em in! Herbicides? Much better than using tractors that might harm the vine roots! Rootstocks? Well, we've got this amazing new productive SO4! Fermenting must? Can't have warm and cloudy! You must only vinify cold clean juice.

I don't want to suggest that all was disaster. But mistakes were made. I quote from Remington Norman's *Great Domaines of Burgundy*: 'I don't know whether I am a man of experience,' confesses Robert Drouhin, 'but I have certainly made enough mistakes.' The trouble is it sometimes takes twenty years to realise that it *is* a mistake.

But Robert Drouhin learned fast. And he continued his uncle's policy of vineyard acquisition. In 1961, the year he got married, he bought vines in Chambolle, including some Amoureuses, Bonnes-Mares and Musigny. Parcels of Volnay and Corton followed, as did Clos-de-Bèze, Griottes-Chambertin, Echézeaux, Grands-Echézeaux and Bâtard-Montrachet. Moreover, since 1947 Drouhin has farmed and marketed the estate of the Marquis de Laguiche, owner of the largest portion of Montrachet. In 1968, when the fortunes of Chablis were at their lowest ebb, he started building up what is now an extensive holding in the best part of the commune. There is now a total domaine of 63.2 hectares: 25.5 ha in the Côte d'Or, nearly all of it in *grand* or *premier cru climats*, and 37.7 ha in Chablis.

THE DROUHIN PHILOSOPHY

With the exception of its domaine in Oregon, a separate company, Drouhin deals entirely with Burgundy. There are no *vins de table*, no branded *ordinaires*, no wines from the Rhône or the Ardèche, no wines from Provence or Languedoc-Roussillon. 'We work exclusively with the grapes of Burgundy: Chardonnay, Pinot Noir, Gamay and Aligoté.' And Pinot Gris. Traditionally, Burgundian red wine producing vineyards have contained a small percentage of white grapes. This is still authorised. But only Drouhin adheres to this time-honoured practice.

Moreover, Robert Drouhin is convinced that *sélection massale* produces better wine than clones. 'The *Comité Interprofessionnel des Vins de Bourgogne* has experimented with many clones, but they only feel they can recommend five each of Pinot Noir and Chardonnay. This limited selection is bound to reduce the complexity and individuality of the wines. I can't prove it.

But I'm sure I'm right.' Some 75 per cent of Drouhin's new plantations are with his own rootstocks, generated from sixty-year-old vines in the Clos-des-Mouches.

'During the last twenty years, we have experimented and innovated. And we have tested the new against the old. Mostly we find the traditional has much to commend it. This is nowhere more true than in our own vineyards, where our wines receive their genetic input.'

To this end grafting is on to Riparia Gloire rootstock, infrequently used elsewhere in Burgundy because of its low yields. Vineyard density is the highest in the Côte d'Or: 12,500 vines per hectare as against 8,000 or 10,000 elsewhere. Vines are pruned down to eight buds – and Drouhin were one of the first to practise *éclaircissage* (crop thinning) and to remove leaves so that the bunches could receive the full rays of the sun – and the vineyards are rarely if ever fertilised or composted. In the Côte d'Or the vineyards are ploughed rather than the weeds removed by herbicides. In Chablis, because of the frost protection equipment it is necessary to use topical herbicides, but in Drouhin's case only lightly.

But biological? 'We've experimented,' says Drouhin, 'but more in the direction of using less chemicals; nothing really dramatic. I'm not convinced that organic viticulture is necessarily the best approach. Perhaps the good results are merely the result of reduced yields and because this method attracts the perfectionists and the radicals.' But you only have to look at the Drouhin vines to realise that their approach is equally perfectionist.

It is typical of Robert Drouhin's open-minded approach that his relationship with his children, particularly Philippe and Véronique who take an active part in the business (Véronique is a trained oenologist, and responsible *inter alia* for the new development in Oregon), and with his senior employees, is one of equal cooperation with colleagues rather than one of master and servant. The contrast with some of the other local *négociant* businesses is refreshing. His chief wine-maker, one is therefore not surprised to discover, is the elegant Laurence Jobard, not a gnarled, forelock-tugging old boy whose status is little more than that of *maître de chai*.

The Drouhin grapes are only partially destemmed, the unstemmed bunches are poured into the vats whole, and the *cuves* cooled to allow forty-eight hours pre-fermentation maceration. Artificial yeasts are abhorred. 'Technically perfect wines which do not reflect the typicity of their *terroir* have no appeal for me. We may have less consistency but in the long term we have greater elegance, complexity and fidelity to the earth with the wines we produce at Drouhin,' says Robert.

The percentage of new oak is low. 'We are not carpenters. We make our wines with grapes, not wood! Oak, properly used, helps determine the personality of the wines and their balance. Nothing should dominate, not alcohol, not tannin, not over-oaked vanillin. Young, these wines might not make as big a statement, but over time they are better.'

Drouhin uses a variety of French oak: Vosges, a dense grain with a lot of tannin, oak from northern Burgundy, Nevers and the Allier – the last with delicate, soft tannins, particularly suitable for white wines. The origin should not be discernible after six months, Drouhin believes. The treatment – he buys and ages the oak himself – is more important than the origin.

Finally, in the cellar and in the bottle nothing is hidden. Each barrel has the name of wine printed on it, and even a bar code, which makes for easy stocktaking. Each bottle has a branded cork with the name of the wine and the vintage, not some fatuous '*mise en bouteille dans nos caves*'.

THE WINE

Tasting is everything. The laboratory is only the back-up. And if necessary a wine might be declassified one or even two rungs down the ladder, from *grand cru* to village. 'It is here,' says Drouhin, 'that a producer secures his reputation. The degree to which he insists on excellence and authenticity is the degree to which his wines will be respected internationally.'

Drouhin's wines are lighter in colour than some, and may seem, to the uninitiated, at first somewhat lighter on the palate. Delicate is the word used, and feminine. But this is deceptive. Underneath there is a lot of intensity. Above all there is a great integrity of *terroir*. Above all there is breeding and finesse. Moreover there is no discernible difference between the wines from their own domaines and what is bought in. (Much of this is in grapes; otherwise in wine or must from long-term contracts.) Yet it is not for nothing that Drouhin's main holdings outside Beaune are in Chambolle-Musigny. The elegance and fragrance of Chambolle obviously resound an echo in the Drouhin psyche. These are fine wines, pure Pinot Noir, never blockbusters. They may not seem very structured, but they are complex and they will certainly keep. A very fine domaine. A very fine *négociant*.

THE TASTING

The February 1992 Studley Priory Fine Wine Weekend featured the wines of Joseph Drouhin, notably their excellent Beaune, Clos-des-Mouches. Here are my notes.

BEAUNE, CLOS-DES-MOUCHES, BLANC

Optimum drinking

1986   **Drink soon**

Deeper colour than the 1985. Ample oaky nose. Ripe and just slightly overblown. Fullish, fully ready. Interesting spices. Doesn't taste as if it is pure Chardonnay. An ample, fleshy, exuberant wine. Reasonable grip. But it doesn't have the class of the 1985.

1985   **Now-2000**

Fullish but light colour for its age. Rich, fuller, crisper and firmer than the 1986. This has more class and more depth. Full, still with plenty of vigour. Will last well. This is ripe and ample but has very good grip. Very good indeed. But it also has an un-Chardonnay spice.

BEAUNE, CLOS-DES-MOUCHES, ROUGE

1989   **Now-2000 plus**

Good fresh colour. Medium-full, still has purple tinges. Ripe, lush, abundantly fruity nose. Medium body. Good grip. I like the fat. I like the high-toned fruit. It lacks a bit of weight and backbone but it is by no means short. Not much tannin. Good style and complexity. Long. Will evolve soon. Just needs to lose its rawness.

1988   **Now-2006**

Good fresh colour. Medium-full. Still youthful. Closed nose. Good grip. A little unforthcoming at present. Very good raspberry Pinot fruit, plenty of depth. More austere than the 1989. Less rich it seems, but a lot of depth here. This has gone into its shell a bit. Medium-full. Good tannins. Very good grip. Best of all on the finish which is long and complex. Classy.

1987   **Now-2000**

Youthful, medium colour. No sign of brown yet. Medium intensity on the nose. A little superficial after the 1988. Round and fruity with a touch of dry spice about the residual tannin. Medium body. A touch astringent. This has good depth and plenty of interest. Just beginning to adopt the spice and gameyness of mature Burgundy. More profound than I thought on the nose. Very good for the vintage.

1985   **Now-1998**

Fullish colour. Little sign of development. Good freshness on the nose. This is fat and generous. Very succulent. Strawberries and blackberries as well as raspberries. The most appealing of the first four, but, paradoxically even, the least grip. Ample, round, rich. Not short, but it lacks extra complexity on the finish. Good but not great.

1984   **Drink up**

Good fresh colour. No undue age. Just a little decay on the nose. But soft and not too ungenerous. It is beginning to lose its grip and intensity now. Medium body. This isn't bad for a 1984 but now needs drinking.

1983   **Now-2000**

Medium-full colour. Now some brown. Firm, spicy, slightly dry, leathery nose. There is weight and backbone here if perhaps a lack of grace. On the palate quite a rugged wine, with a certain tough astringency. Underneath there is fruit and grip, but it is a little out of kilter. A wine for food, definitely. Not short, nor dry, but destined to be dominated by its structure. The finish is long and clean. Will still evolve. Will it improve? Good but not great.

1982   Drink soon

Medium colour. Fully mature. Soft, fragrant nose. Slight touch of mint or camomile, but not too vegetal or herbal. There is plenty of fruit here, and no undue age. *À point* now, and not for long-term keeping. This is medium bodied, has reasonable grip if not real depth and dimension. Will decline from now on. But has charm still. Even elegance.

1980   Drink soon

Full colour. Mature but not unduly so. Attractive gamey nose. Good fruit. No real concentration, depth or class though. Fully ready. This has more to it than the 1982, but is similarly getting towards the end of its life. Medium to medium-full. Good acidity if not a lot of depth or concentration. A good bottle for drinking now.

1978   Now-2000

Good colour. Still vigorous. Fragrant, complex, stylish, if slightly cool nose. Medium body. If it lacks a little fat and concentration, the fruit is multi-dimensional, the wine subtle, balanced and long. Best of all on the finish. By no means a blockbuster but very lovely, lingering and subtle. Held up very well in the glass.

1976   Now-2000 plus

Good colour. Full and still quite purple. Fresh nose. Full. Still youthful. Rich. Still primary aromas to the fruit. Full, rich, meaty, tannic. But has very good succulence. Quite cool fruit. Not a bit too jammy. Good grip. Still very young. Almost unnaturally so. It is just a touch rigid. But I like it very much indeed. Ready but will keep well.

Grands-Echézeaux, 1976   Drink soon

Full rich colour, barely mature. On the nose at first a hint of hot bitter chocolate, then Marmite, finally leather. An animal wine. Rich and caramelly. Full, some tannin, but not excessively so. Meaty and rich. Good acidity. But earthy. There is a certain driven quality, but the wine has depth, fat and length. Will still keep well. Very good.

Musigny, 1976   Now-2000 plus

Magnum. Full, rich colour. Just about mature. Compared with Drouhin's 1976 Grands-Echézeaux this is more evolved, but more fragrant and much, much more elegant. Silky-smooth. Very lovely ripe fruit. This has much more intensity and *the* most splendid raspberry flavour, without being the slightest bit sweet. Balanced, long, very complex and subtle. Still vigorous. More so than I thought on the nose. Quite lovely. Very fine indeed. Very very long and full of interest.

DUJAC,
MOREY-SAINT-DENIS

There are Burgundy domaines which are long established and long renowned, having estate-bottled for fifty years or more. There are others which have only recently become stars, because it is only in the last decade that they have themselves bottled a significant portion of their produce, though they might have been producing wine for generations. And there is a third category: domaines which have been created from scratch. Of these, none has had such a meteoric rise to super-stardom as the Domaine Dujac in Morey-Saint-Denis. It is only thirty years since Jacques Seysses first arrived to work in Burgundy, and 1997 will represent only the twenty-eighth vintage of his wines. But the quality of the Seysses wine was recognised from the outset. And the reputation of Domaine Dujac has not looked back since.

BEGINNINGS

Jacques Seysses was born in 1941. His father, Louis, was head of Biscuits Belin, since sold to Nabisco, and, importantly, president of the Club des Cent, a club of wealthy continental oenophiles and gastronomes dedicated to the art of good living. Three-star restaurants and five-star domaines were the happy hunting grounds of these ladies and gentlemen, and from an early age Jacques was party to the entertainment. He remembers being taken to La Tour d'Argent at the age of seven; and visiting *Père* Ramonet and the Domaine de la Romanée-Conti when his father went down to re-stock his cellar. 'Thanks to my father I drank the great 1934s and 1929s in their prime. He gave me a marvellous introduction to all the best domaines and châteaux in Burgundy and Bordeaux. My yardsticks were implanted from an early age.'

Jacques was a lazy student. His father sent him to work for the Morgan Guarantee Bank in Paris and in New York for two years, and after he returned appointed him Marketing Director at Biscuits Belin. But, as Jacques says, 'I was always more interested in creating a product, not just selling it.'

One of Louis Seysses' colleagues in the Club des Cent was Jean Ferté, uncle of the Potels and chief shareholder in the Domaine de la Pousse d'Or (in which Seysses *père*, too, had a slice of the action). Thanks to this connection the young Jacques, aged twenty-five, arrived in Burgundy in 1966. He spent two vintages in Volnay, learned a lot, and decided that this was the path he wished to follow. So the search was then on for land to buy.

The nucleus was found in the Domaine Marcel Graillet in Morey-Saint-Denis. Graillet *père*, a distant cousin of the Mongeards of Vosne-Romanée, was an absentee landlord, a diplomat who was resident consul for the French government in China and in Turkey. Back in Morey he owned 4.5 hectares, including land in Clos-de-la-Roche, Clos-Saint-Denis and Gevrey-Chambertin, Les Combottes (which he had unsuccessfully attempted to get elevated to *grand cru*). The HQ was at Le Petit Labussière, once upon a time a monastic establishment, and the Graillets had once owned the monopoly of the *premier cru* Clos-de-la-Bussière next door (now owned by the Domaine Georges Roumier of Chambolle-Musigny). The domaine was for sale because Marcel Graillet had married a Niçoise. She missed the sun and wished to return to the south of France. Late in 1967 a deal was struck. Louis Seysses bought out the Graillets, and Jacques had his foothold in Burgundy.

The Graillet domaine, however, did not bottle. Their produce was collected in bulk by the Burgundy *négoce* in the spring after the malos had finished. The house was in reasonable order, if not very *soignée*, and so were the cellars below, though they were a bit primitive, and inadequate for a domaine which intended to bottle itself.

But of course, with only 4.5 ha, the domaine was not large enough to be self-supporting. Jacques continued to work in the family business, and as other suitable land came up for sale, slowly but carefully enlarged his estate.

GETTING OFF THE GROUND

Jacques Seysses' first vintage was the unfortunate 1968. He sold it all off in bulk. By the next year, 1969, he had constructed a new *cuverie* after tearing down an old garage opposite his entrance courtyard and replaced the old concrete *cuves* with enamelled-steel vats. The construction was not completely finished and insulated however, and as the winter was cold, the wines were slow to evolve. But the quality was good. Jacques acknowledges the generous help he received from Charles Rousseau, as well as what he had learned from Gérard Potel. And there was now another wine in the portfolio: 0.69 ares of Echézeaux acquired from members of the Dufouleur family.

Through his father's contacts Jacques Seysses had an open door into the top restaurants in France. Vivarois, in Paris - which had three stars at the time - was an early customer. Allard was another. Jacques packed and delivered the wine himself, and sold other bottles to his family and friends.

A year or so later, thanks to an introduction from Aubert de Villaine, Colonel Frederick Wildman came to call and taste the 1969s and 1970s. Jacques remembers the occasion well. 'He was a gaunt, rather frightening old man. He didn't say much. And I thought the wines weren't showing very well that day. He tasted around the cellar in complete silence, and not hearing any grunts of approval I was beginning to think: well, that's it, he doesn't like my wine. And then suddenly he said: "I will take the lot." I was stunned. But I didn't want to put all my eggs in one basket. I said I would sell him half.' It was the beginnings of a fruitful arrangement. Wildmans would represent the Domaine Dujac in the USA for the next twenty years.

On the domestic front recognition was also not slow to arrive. The magazine *Gault et Millau* discovered Domaine Dujac through the restaurant Vivarois. Christian Millau came down to taste in 1972 and subsequently published a favourable article. Jacques Seysses was soon besieged by private customers. Eventually, also through the exposure in the top restaurants, he even gained a foothold in Britain, at the time the last bastion of *négociant* wine.

By 1973, now with a wife, Rosalind *née* Boswell, daughter of an American general, whom he had met when she came to pick the 1971 harvest, Jacques Seysses felt confident enough to give up Biscuits Belin and settle in Burgundy. He extended the cellar and the Domaine Dujac was up and running.

THE GROWTH OF THE DOMAINE

Today the Domaine Dujac covers 11.5 hectares and produces eleven appellations. The Clos-de-la-Roche, arguably the best wine in the cellar, has been increased from half a hectare to 1.95 ha by acquisitions from Bertagna and the Domaine Alfred Jacquot, the latter in 1977. The vines date from between 1945 and 1985. Nearby, in the Clos-Saint-Denis, the original hectare has been enlarged by half, again from Jacquot in 1977. Two-thirds of this was planted before 1950. The parcel of Gevrey-Chambertin, Les Combottes, just to the north, now comprises 1.15 ha, and, again from Jacquot in 1977, five parcels of Charmes-Chambertin make up a holding of 0.70 ha. There is the Echézeaux, already mentioned, and 0.43 ha of Bonnes-Mares, bought from Paul and Joseph Hudelot in 1969. In this latter *climat*, the vines until recently have been young, having been replanted in stages between 1971 and 1984. But as these vines age it is becoming apparent that this is perhaps destined to be the most serious wine in the Dujac stable. We shall see. The parcel lies in Chambolle but nonetheless on the *terres rouges* rather than on *terres blanches*.

There are three other small elements in the portfolio: a parcel of old vine Chambolle-Musigny, Les Gruenchers, which makes five casks of a wine I always find most impressive; half a hectare of village Chambolle and a quarter hectare of young vine Vosne-Romanée, Les Beaumonts, rented rather than owned. The rest of the exploitation is 3.5 ha of Morey-Saint-Denis village, lying mainly below the house, towards the main road. Some 60 ares of this is planted with Chardonnay rather than Pinot Noir.

Is this the limit? 'Certainly not,' says Seysses. 'I had my eye on the Remy domaine. I had it all set up until I was gazumped by Lalou Bize. When I realised that she was determined to get the land irrespective of the price she had to pay, I had to back off.'

VITICULTURE

Jacques Seysses is a great believer in clones, and was one of the first to appreciate their importance. 'We use a wide variety, and a mixture of rootstocks as well. Each new development, each new generation, is producing clones which are better, *plus fin* than before. I am convinced that if one controls the *rendement* properly clones are better than a *sélection massale*. There is less danger of viral degeneration and other infection, and the harvest is more even. What we are now working towards is a *sélection massale des clones* . . . Before 1983 we had no clones in production at the domaine and the average age of the Dujac vines was very old. I did a lot of replanting between 1978 and 1983, all with clones, and I am very satisfied with the results.'

Since 1987 he has had Christophe Morin, a native of the Loire, working for him as *chef de culture*. 'This was my best investment of all,' says Jacques. Morin also works the vines of the Domaine de l'Arlot of Nuits-Saint-Georges, Arlot's manager, Jean-Pierre de Smet, being an erstwhile Dujac apprentice.

'The most important object of pruning and training the vines is to have a maximum, at least in potential, of productive buds in the right place on the plant. So we must adapt to the vine. We use all the four permitted pruning and training systems: *éventail* and *crochet* for young plants, to control their vigour, Guyot and Cordon thereafter. We prune short, of course, to six buds per vine, and then we do subsequent debudding and green harvesting if necessary.'

The vineyard is alternately hoed and ploughed. Herbicides are abhorred. Hoeing is good for aerating the soil without decreasing the micro-flora, but it makes the vineyard more susceptible to erosion. The vines are trained high, to increase the foliage and the air-circulation. The former maximises ripeness ('The leaves are the factory of the fruit. They produce the sugar'); the latter reduces the risk of rot.

'All in all I am looking for a *rendement* of less than 40 hl/ha,' says Jacques Seysses. But it varies. 'I produced 10 per cent less in 1989 than in 1988 or 1990. Absurdly little in 1991, when I had to go around after the hail, taking out all the bruised grapes individually with tweezers – not really economic, I have to say: but I was determined to avoid a recurrence of 1983' (not a favourite vintage in the Dujac camp). 'And in 1993 I produced 28 hl/ha in the Clos-de-la-Roche. Even in 1992 we only made 40 hl/ha there.'

One of the best investments he has made, Seysses believes, is to take on more pickers at vintage time. They can take more time, and so the *triage* is more efficient, and yet the domaine can still be cleared in a week. 'We used to be great believers in picking late,' he says, 'but experiments have shown that this can be carried to excess.'

WINE-MAKING

Tasting a range of Dujac vintages demonstrates clearly that there have been four phases to date in the development of the Dujac style and quality since the domaine's inception: before 1978, 1978-1984, 1984-1988, and after 1989. Partly this is the learning process, partly it is the equipment used. A pneumatic press replaced the old Vaslin in 1984. Since the arrival of Christophe Morin the *matière première* is better. Before 1984 the tannins were less sophisticated, the taste of the stems more apparent, the taste of oak less well integrated. None of these criticisms would be justified today.

From the start, emulating his friend Aubert de Villaine at the Domaine de la Romanée-Conti, and indeed Gérard Potel, who used to destem only the young vine Pousse d'Or fruit, Jacques Seysses has vinified his bunches whole. Why? 'The stems act as an anti-oxidant. Uncrushed berries exude less juice so the fermentation is slower and more flavour is extracted.' At first Jacques Seysses would be quoted as saying that if he could destem without crushing the fruit, this is the policy he would adopt. But he has changed his mind now he has his gentler pneumatic press. 'I think the stems absorb the hard tannins and add complexity.'

So there is no *égrappage*. 'We must not separate the calf from the cow too early.' After a short pre-fermentation maceration – Seysses got the idea from André Tchelitchieff in California, and first did this consciously in 1978, though because of the cold cellar it had occurred unwittingly in 1969 – the fruit is given a long, slow (sixteen to twenty-one days) *cuvaison* at relatively low temperatures, below rather than above 30°C - usually at 26-28°. There is now an automatic *pigeage* apparatus. The press wine is vinified separately.

There is, and always has been, a lot of new wood in the Dujac cellar. Jacques Seysses was party to a research project into the effect of new oak in 1976. He found he marked the new wood wines higher, and since then has put all his *grands* and *premiers crus* entirely in new oak, saving these casks for next year's village wine. They are then sold. The wood comes from the Allier, and Seysses insists on a light toast. The wine is racked once after the malo, sometimes lightly fined but never filtered, and bottled by gravity any time from the early months of the following year (January 1994 for the 1992s). Having experimented with bottling at twelve months, eighteen and twenty-four, Seysses is convinced that earlier is better than later. It preserves the fruit.

WHITE WINES

There are, of course, white wines as well as red. The first is the Morey-Saint-Denis *blanc*, produced since 1986. This is vinified in wood, without any prior skin contact, and kept on its fine lees, with *bâtonnage* at the beginning, until bottling the following September. Seysses' objective is not so much to produce a real *vin de garde* but a wine for the medium term. 'My taste is for the fruit above all. Why wait ten years if the wine is already delicious at five years old.'

There is also a *négociant* Meursault (and sometimes a Puligny-Montrachet) produced under the name of Druid. This again dates from 1985. The enterprise was initiated by (and still belongs to) Rosalind Seysses' side of the family. The name was chosen because Rosalind's mother discovered by chance that there had been an ancient family of Druids called Seysses in Toulouse, the town where Jacques was born. Twenty-five barrels' worth of grapes are bought in every year from the producers in the village. The wine is only sold outside the European community, and the concept is being maintained at this level - now that Jacques has subsequently developed the 46 ha Domaine de Triennes in the Var with Aubert de Villaine - for the Seysses' three children, all boys, to develop in the future if they so wish.

RED WINES

The red wine range begins with the village Chambolle-Musigny (the Vosne-Romanée, Beaumonts is rarely shown because the quantity is negligible). This is a good example, full of vibrant fruit; very Chambolle. The Morey-Saint-Denis comes next. Seysses adds the young vine fruit from the better *climats* in this *cuvée*. It is more black fruity than the Chambolle; lush, opulent and with more depth. The Gevrey-Chambertin, Combottes and the Charmes-Chambertin follow. Both are wines of intensity rather than power, but very good indeed, with blackberry, cassis and plum fruit. The *grand cru* is not necessarily better than the *premier cru* though, and I often prefer the Chambolle-Musigny, Les Gruenchers to both. This is a wine of splendid balance and real elegance.

The Clos-Saint-Denis and the Clos-de-la-Roche are an intriguing contrast. The former is velvety and feminine, the latter firmer, richer and finer. Each is an excellent example of the *climat*, among the top two or three in the whole of Burgundy.

Both the Bonnes-Mares and the Echézeaux are from younger vines, and getting better and better by the year. Perhaps, as I have suggested, the Bonnes-Mares is potentially the finest of the lot. It is already the biggest wine in the portfolio. The Echézeaux comes from the same selection of clones, planted at about the same time, and it is fascinating to see quite how different it is: a little leaner and more austere on the attack, less muscular in the middle, yet with no lack of richness at the end.

'I see myself as a doctor,' says Jacques Seysses. 'I'm there in case of trouble. But I am not there to change nature. Scientific knowledge is not strong enough to give us advance rules. It is better to let nature take its course.'

What I like about the Dujac wines is their purity. Chaptalisation is low - though the 1977s were probably under-chaptalised; under 12° the wine lacks glycerol, which only appears at the end of fermentation when the degree of alcohol has already reached 11.5°; and without glycerol the wine lacks richness and *velouté*, and will not keep.

These are wines of lightish colour but intense fruit, and great elegance and definition. They are very individual, with a particular style which is only echoed elsewhere, and for obvious reasons, by Jean-Pierre de Smet at the Domaine de l'Arlot. But nevertheless they are 'un-manufactured'. Other domaines' and *négociants'* wines naturally have their own particular character. But sometimes this thumbprint imposes too much, obliterating the *terroir*. Not so at the Domaine Dujac. The explanation, I believe, is this modest, hands-off approach. 'We have a tendency to think that the miracle is in the sophistication of the equipment,' says Jacques Seysses. 'In reality the miracle comes from the *matière première*, from the grape. I rely more and more on tasting to decide what to do. These days the scientists and *oenologues* have given us the courage to rely on our palates and not merely on analysis.' Jacques Seysses produces wines which reflect his own taste and personality. Thirty years' experience has proved that this is a style which is enthusiastically appreciated throughout the world. A deserved success. A very fine domaine.

THE TASTING

I sampled the following wines *chez* Seysses in January 1994.

CLOS-DE-LA-ROCHE

Optimum drinking

1992   **Now-2009**
Good colour. This has recovered well from its bottling a month ago. Ample, plump, attractively balanced fruit on the nose. No lack of grip. Medium-full. Stylish. Balanced. Lush and succulent. Plenty of depth. This will be more 1985ish than 1982ish. Very good indeed.

1991   **1999-2015**
Half *égrappé*, because he lost many berries through hail. So equalising fruit and stalks. Seysses borrowed the destemming machine from Etienne Grivot. Good colour. More marked by the wood than the 1992. Very good. Slightly blacker fruit than 1992 on the nose. Fullish, intense, very rich. Surprisingly opulent on the follow-through. Good grip and backbone. Very long. Very complex. Classy at the end. Fine.

1990   **2000-2020 plus**
Excellent colour. On the nose it seems to have gone into its shell. Closed, firm, but full. This is now adolescent. Full body. Tannic. Very good acidity. Lots of wine here. At present a little disjointed. Not together. But the finish is very rich, very complex and very concentrated. Very fine. But needs time. Much more powerful and intense than the 1991.

1989   **Now-2012**
Good colour. Ripe, luscious, red fruit nose. Rich, almost a suggestion of sweetness. Fat too. Medium-full, beautifully balanced. Very seductive. Heaps of fruit but plenty of acidity to harmonise it. Long and complex. Not as structured as the 1991 but perhaps more intense. An engaging, charming wine. Fine.

1988   **Now-2006**
Medium colour. Not as deep as the 1989. Discreet, complex, very subtle nose. Classy, balanced and distinguished. On the palate, though, it is not as exciting. It is like a greengrocer who puts all his best fruit at the front. Medium-full body. A slight lack of zip and intensity. Fruity, correct, but it lacks excitement after the wines above. It lacks a little acidity. They produced more in 1988 than in 1989 contrary to the norm and consider they suffered from the drought. The progress toward maturity was *bloqué*.

1987   **Now-2000 plus**
Very good mature colour. Fullish and vibrant. Fine rich nose. Fleshy and succulent. Fruity and charming. This is now *à point*. If it doesn't have the depth or concentration, or the class of fruit of the 1989-1991 trio, it is nevertheless balanced, fruity, fresh and most enjoyable. The finish is round and vigorous. Even quite stylish. A fine example for a 1987.

1985   **Now–2010**

Very good colour. No sign of maturity. An attractive grilled hazelnut touch to the nose. On the palate this is approaching maturity but it is nevertheless at a slightly in-between stage still, though it has softened up and the tannins are now well integrated. Medium to medium-full. Good fruit. It lacks a little strength and grip but it is amply fruity and well-balanced and has very good length. But very good indeed rather than great.

1983   **Now–2000**

Full but mature colour. Not too brown. This is the one wine where the stems are evident on the nose. On the palate ripe and sweet but a touch astringent, a touch tainted. The follow-through shows good acidity, cleaning the dryness and even some of the taint. Overall not an unattractive wine because the aftertaste is clean. But a problem for the consumer nonetheless.

1982   **Drink soon**

Very good colour. Well matured. But not a bit aged. Open, plump, ripe nose. Just lacks a little intensity. Similar on the palate. Medium body, a touch of astringency from the stems (is this because the fruit is lightening up?). Yet the finish is plump and clean and not a bit short. Gently classy. Long. Held up very well in the glass. More vigorous than it at first appeared. Very good indeed for the vintage. Better than 1980.

1980   **Drink soon**

Very good colour. Only a little brown. A late harvest: the latest Jacques Seysses has ever vintaged. More structured than the 1982. Slightly cool fruit. Now lightening up. Some unripeness to the tannins which are now sticking out in an astringent form. The wine now needs drinking quite soon, while it is still fresh. Good acidity. But I fear it will get a bit attenuated.

1978   **Now–2000 plus**

Excellent colour. Still youthful. Round, rich, mellow but quite masculine nose. Fullish, the stems show just a little. A slightly old-fashioned wine. Muscular. Rustic in the best sense. Good grip. Fat and mellow if not exactly sweet and generous. Long. But not the finesse of the wines ten years later. Not the weight or the grip of the 1976.

1976   **Now–2005 plus**

Fine colour again, just a bit more evolved. Fat, rich, quite structured nose. But expressed here in a fleshy sense, not a tannic sense. Not over-ripe. Full, rich, tannic, sturdy and with the structure showing. Yet with food no problem. Merely ample and very satisfactory. Not a bit cooked. Fine acidity. Not that classy but a very fine example. Rich. Very long. Fatter than the 1978.

1972   **Now–2005 plus**

Full mature colour. Not entirely brilliant. As always, though, a wine of great individuality. Fullish. Marvellous natural acidity. Mellow and complex fruit, with a touch of coffee and bitter chocolate, even caramel balanced or completed by an almost Madeira-like grip. Still very fresh. In its way classy, as well as intriguing. Will last for ages.

1969   **Now–1999**

Fine colour. Barely mature. Lovely nose. Mellow, honey cake and gingerbread. Similar palate. Good grip. Spicy and fruit. Generous, slightly over-ripe elements yet certainly very very fresh. *À point.* A lovely wine. Long and complex on the finish. Still plenty of life.

RENÉ ENGEL,
VOSNE-ROMANÉE

Praise the Lord and pass the orchids, a new super-star has arrived in the Burgundian firmament! The Engel domaine has always had a good reputation, though up to 1981 two-thirds of the produce was sold off in bulk so there wasn't a great deal to judge it by. But today the quality is exceptional. When I made my first appraisal of the 1992 vintage in November 1993 I remarked that my Engel visit ranked with that of the neighbouring Domaine Leroy as the highspot of a three-week sojourn in Burgundy. Anyone competent can make good wine in a good vintage. But it takes a bit of genius to make excellent wine in a lesser vintage. This Philippe Engel showed he could do in 1992, and the vintages he has made subsequently have continued this high level. The world as a result is now a happier place.

René Engel, professor of oenology at Dijon for thirty-five years, one of the founders of the *Confrérie des Chevaliers du Tastevin*, historian and *belle-lettriste*, was born in 1892. Twelve years later his mother Eugénie was widowed, and as a second husband she chose Paul-François Faiveley. This branch of the Faiveleys, distantly related to the Faiveleys of Nuits-Saint-Georges, had been in Vosne-Romanée for four generations. The two pooled their vineyards, the holdings later to be added to by René Engel, and the Domaine Engel was born. Today it consists of 7 hectares: 3 of village Vosne-Romanée, 1 of Vosne-Romanée, Les Brûlées, half a hectare each of Echézeaux and Grands-Echézeaux, and 1.36 ha at the top of Clos-de-Vougeot, acquired when the Léonce Bocquet estate was broken up in 1920. The residue is a Passetoutgrains *vin de table* (into which goes all the young vine wine) whose origins come from the plain on the other side of the railway-line next to the village of Flagey.

Originally the estate was much larger. René Engel inherited 10 hectares and increased it to 15, though he had the habit of occasionally rewarding faithful vineyard-workers by ceding an *ouvrée* or two to them on their retirement.

René Engel was a patriarch, with all the qualities, good and bad, that this entails. On the plus side, as a scientist and humanist, he was humble as well as wise, as his grandson puts it. He continued to learn right until the end of his long life. There are three criteria for good wine-making, he would say, and they are all about cleanliness: the fruit should be totally healthy; the cellar and its equipment should be scrupulously clean; and one should have a clear idea of what one intends to do with the harvest, how to make the best possible wine out of it.

During the 1930s, somewhat by accident, René Engel became a *négociant*. He went up to Paris to try to sell his wine to a particular chain of grocery shops. He was rebuffed. An hour or so later he remembered he had left his umbrella. When he returned he found his erstwhile interlocutors in the middle of a tasting of wines from all over France. René Engel was invited to join them, found the wines nondescript, and persuaded them that he could do better. He was hired as the firm's wine supplier on the spot.

His son, Pierre, was a man of culture, with a thorough knowledge of literature and mythology. He would have liked to be a poet, but he found it difficult to escape from the shadow of his father. Even after René Engel officially retired in 1949 he made his presence felt. The elder Engel continued to interfere, and Pierre found himself tied. In 1970 he fell ill, lost his enthusiasm and let the domaine fall into neglect. When Philippe, born in 1955, began to play his part after his studies at the *Lycée Viticole* in Beaune, the quality of the wine was at its lowest ebb. Most of the wine was sold off in bulk. Even in the good years only about one-third was domaine bottled. The majority of the wood in the cellar was old. The vineyards had been over-fertilised, and results were somewhat haphazard. 'I think my father made very good wine in the good years,' says Philippe. 'They seem better than my neighbours'. But they were proportionately less good in the minor vintages.'

Pierre Engel died in 1981, a year when everything was sold off under contract to Moillard. Philippe and his mother were now in charge. They were determined to change things for the better. Though in 1982 they continued to sell two-thirds to the *négoce*, from 1983 onwards he began to bottle more and more under his own label. And from 1988 all the Engel wine has been bottled *sur place*.

Improvement in the quality of the Engel wines was remarkably swift. Once he had established his authority by forcibly removing his grandfather from the cellar during the 1982 vintage (René Engel lived to be ninety-four, dying in 1986), Philippe Engel was able to do things his way. He and his grandfather had always understood each other. But they were now on equal terms. Their respect for each other was shared, and Philippe remembers him with great affection. The counsel of the older man was often valuable. When Philippe was worried that his 1985 temperatures were too high, his grandfather told him not to worry. 'The fruit is very ripe and very clean. It is a *grande année*. It won't do the wine any harm.' As it turned out the results were splendid. The Engel Clos-de-Vougeot is brilliant: one of the wines of the vintage.

Perhaps in 1986 René Engel, had he still been alive, would have prevented one of the few mistakes Philippe has perpetrated. The vintage was large, and in the week prior to the harvest there was rain. Philippe decided to *saigner* his *cuves*. However when he saw the intense colour he had achieved in his Clos-de-Vougeot he decided to re-introduce the *saignéed* juice. The Echézeaux and the Grands-Echézeaux, where he didn't, are better.

The results in recent years have been startling, showing that the 1985s were no fluke: the 1989s are poised and classy; the 1990s as fine as you would hope in this magnificent vintage; and the 1991s show the high quality of this as yet under-rated vintage.

WINE-MAKING

'What have I changed - modified - adapted?' says Philippe in response to my question. 'Just about everything!

'Though my grandfather added some of the stems - he said you should chew them first to ensure they were ripe rather than bitter - my father eliminated all the stalks, and this I continue. I have also reduced the harvest, though again my father also kept the crop small . . . But we now have a *table de tri*, a proper one I bought in 1990. Before that we used a "home-made" version I had built. There is much more *pigeage*, and no pumping during the vinification, a *cuvaison* of twenty-one days, and much more new wood, 50 per cent for the *grands crus*.'

Philippe likes a high temperature, up to 35°C, during his maceration, has reduced the amount of sulphur he employs, now racks less frequently, and only filters when he has to. The 1992s, for instance, have not been filtered. The approach, and the resulting wines - and it is no coincidence - parallels that of Henri Jayer, a wine-maker Philippe Engel much admires. These are rich, oaky, sturdy, fleshy wines built to last. They are flamboyant but not obvious. Underneath there is all the richness and purity of Pinot Noir you hope to find in great Burgundy.

Experiments continue. In 1988 he exchanged some grapes with Alain Burguet of Gevrey-Chambertin. Each produced a separate *cuvée*. Curiously the Vosne grapes transported to Gevrey seemed to acquire a Gevrey character, and vice-versa. I suspect it has something to do with the yeasts. But neither result was a great success, perhaps because the quantities employed were too small. The wines seemed good at the outset but have not improved with ageing. In 1994 I tasted the Vosne-Romanée '*cuvée* Gevrey-Chambertin'. I found it was beginning to get a little stringy and artisanal at the end.

PHILIPPE ENGEL

You will find the Engel headquarters in the main square of Vosne-Romanée. It is a square, barn-like building constructed in 1900. The winery is on the ground floor, guarded by a hairy Alsatian, the cellar beneath and the living quarters, separate apartments for Philippe and his mother, above. In his spare time, as well as the duties he has inherited from his grandfather on the *conseil* of the *Chevaliers du Tastevin*, Engel has a passion for motor-cycling and keeps a boat in the south of France - a good area to find Engel wine in the local restaurants. I had assumed for years that Philippe, a sturdy, balding, ruddy-cheeked man with vivid blue eyes and full lips, was an only child. But he has two sisters and a brother, an antique-dealer who lives in Paris. This, no doubt, is another area where you can enjoy the increasingly good Engel wine.

The Tasting

I sampled the following wines in Vosne-Romanée in February 1994.

CLOS-DE-VOUGEOT

Optimum drinking

1992   1999-2012

Bottled without filtration. Round, soft, rich, oaky nose. Fullish good grip. Soft tannins but plenty of backbone. Lovely succulent fruit. Long, seductive. Very fine for the vintage.

1991   2001-2020

Full, rich colour. Firm nose. Quite structured. Good tannins. Nicely austere. Fullish, very good grip. Very good backbone. Rich plummy fruit. Nicely balanced with its oak. Long and succulent at the end. Will last well. Fine.

1990   2002-2025

Very fine colour. This has closed in but nevertheless shows a splendid richness and concentration. Powerful. Full, profound, very intense and concentrated. Marvellously structured. Splendid fruit. This has heaps of dimension. Really splendid. Very very long and complex. Needs time. Brilliant.

1989   1998-2010

Full colour for the vintage. Delicious oaky-raspberry nose. Very perfumed. Refined. Subtle. Medium-full. Beautifully poised, very ripe complex fruit. Very lovely. Finely balanced. Very long lingering finish. Real class this year.

1988   1998-2015

Not as full or as youthful as the 1989. Closed, firm, rich, fat oaky nose. Fullish, still youthful. Very good acidity. Lovely nicely austere fruit. Not a powerhouse, especially after the 1990, but very long and complex. Very elegant. Very good indeed. But in its context perhaps the least good of these first five vintages. It lacks a little intensity and concentration.

1987   Now-2010

Good colour. As full as the 1988, but more maturity. Very good nose. Rich, substantial, ripe, oaky and stylish. This is a really fine 1987 because it has breed. Full and ample. Some tannin still. Very good grip. Rich, fat and plummy at the end. Very long. Still very youthful.

1986   Now-2004

Good fullish mature colour. Ripe, soft, fruity nose. Quite classy. Good acidity. This is less virile than the 1987, less substantial. But round, plump, ripe. Just beginning to come round. Classy fruity and fresh for a 1986. Very good but the 1987 is better.

Grands-Echézeaux, 1986   Now-2009

Very good colour. This is much richer and more concentrated than the Vougeot. Firm, and very vigorous still for a 1986. An ample, rich, meaty wine. Very good structure. Lovely classy fruit. Long and fresh and complex. This is a very fine example. Better than the 1987 Vougeot as well as the 1986.

Echézeaux, 1985   Now-2015

Very good colour. Just a touch of maturity. Splendid nose. Fat and rich and concentrated and old viney. Quite full. A very round and intense wine. Splendidly ripe fruit. Similar to the 1990 but less structured. This is very lovely.

1984   Drink soon

Neither fined nor filtered. Mature colour. Doesn't look weedy at all. Smells a little of fennel and cinnamon. On the palate this has plenty of fruit and is not at all feeble or *passé*. Nor is it too lean. Has class and respectability. A fine example.

1983   Now-1999

Brown colour. Reasonably full. No hail, rot or dryness on the nose. But really quite developed, even a little aged. Medium-full, round, plump, good fruit, reasonable acidity. A touch of astringency. And a lack of vigour for a ten-plus-year-old wine. But cleaner than most, and has length and even attraction at the end.

Vosne-Romanée, Les Brûlées, 1982 Drink soon

Really rather light and evolved in colour. Pleasant but a bit diffuse on the nose and palate. Yet balanced and fruity, with a slightly caramelly spice. Not too short. Nor astringent. Indeed the finish is positive. Quite good for the vintage.

Vosne-Romanée, 1978   Now-2000 plus

Good fully mature colour. The nose of a mature Burgundy, with all the complexities and spices of a Pinot with plenty of bottle age. Medium-full, round, balanced, rich and plump. Plenty of depth. Lovely. Still fresh at the same time as gamey and well matured. Very good indeed for a village example. Improved - took on vigour - with aeration.

1961   **Now–2000 plus**

Fine full colour. Still very vigorous. Splendidly rich nose. Black cherries, coffee, caramel and chocolate. Quite sturdy and tannic still. But very concentrated. Fullish. Luscious and succulent. Old viney. Very very rich. But nevertheless a structured wine. Still very very vigorous. Lovely long succulent sweet finish. Very fine quality.

1923   **Drink soon**

Mature colour. Quite brown at the rim. But not aged. 'This,' said René Engel, 'was the best wine I ever made.' Soft, delicate, exquisitely classy and complex nose. Very very subtle and multi-dimensional. Sweet, softly spicy. This is *grand vin*. Still, though silky, very intense. Very very long. Still hardly a hint of real age.

MICHEL ESMONIN
ET FILLE,
GEVREY-CHAMBERTIN

This is a story much more about the *fille* than about Michel
Esmonin, for it is only since she arrived that this Gevrey estate
began to make one-star wine and to sell it off direct. Hitherto
it was good, but nothing to write home about. Since 1990, but
particularly since 1993, we have wines of great class, including
most importantly a large slice of that pretender to *grand cru*
status, Clos-Saint-Jacques. The *fille* is Sylvie, born in 1961,
ingénieur agronome at Nancy and *diplômée d'oenologie* at
Montpellier, and as able – as well as attractive – a successor as any
father could wish.

HISTORY

There have been Esmonins in Burgundy, they say, since before the Revolution. Our story begins in 1905 with the birth of Henri, one of eight children, and still going strong at the age of ninety-one. Henri and his brother Gaston worked the 4–5 ha family vineyard, but this was in village wine and in generics, and it was not sufficient to support both of them and their families. So in addition they found work elsewhere, in the vast estates of the Comte de Moucheron. Gaston went off to Meursault, where the Count owned the Château itself, Henri remained in Gevrey, tending what was then Moucheron's monopoly, the Clos-Saint-Jacques, plus other vines of his in Chambertin itself and in Lavaux and Estournelles-Saint-Jacques. First of all this was on an employer-employee basis, but over the years the arrangement turned into one of *métayage*: Henri Esmonin producing his own percentage of Clos-Saint-Jacques and the rest to sell in his own right.

Henri Esmonin had three children. The first, Jean, had a weak chest, and was unable to work in the vines. He became a local politician. Michel was born in 1938, and André - from which comes the André et Frédéric Esmonin domaine - in 1940.

In 1954 the Comte de Moucheron sold his estates. The Clos-Saint-Jacques was divided into four parcels. Armand Rousseau bought that to the south-west (2.20 ha); roughly 1 ha went to the Fourrier family and 2 ha to the Clair-Daü domaine (since divided between Louis Jadot and Bruno Clair, who looks after his mother's portion); and finally, on the north-east side, 1.6 ha were acquired by Henri Esmonin. Michel took over this and Henri's other vines on his father's retirement. And Sylvie took over in 1989.

SYLVIE ESMONIN AND HER WINES

'At first I was hesitant,' says Sylvie. 'I wanted to work at the domaine but I wasn't prepared to commit myself to when I would start. I didn't want to be superfluous. I wanted to be in charge.'

It seems, though, that this is precisely what Michel Esmonin had been prepared to let her be. He had begun, in a small way, to bottle some of the wine under the domaine label in 1987. He'd installed temperature control of the fermentation in 1986 after one of the *cuvées* of 1985 Clos-Saint-Jacques had climbed to 39°C. And he'd luckily never been tempted to over-fertilise the vineyard. The rootstock is the unpopular - because disease prone - but nevertheless fine from the quality point of view 161-49. So the ingredients were there. In 1989 he stepped aside and let Sylvie make the running.

The vineyard work was changed so that it became entirely *biologique*. The harvest was reduced, and rather more new oak, 50 per cent for the top *cuvée*, was introduced into the cellar. Year by year the domaine held back more for estate-bottling, and now, apart from a little to Switzerland, nothing is sold off in bulk.

From having been 100 per cent Pinot Noir, Sylvie has started replacing the odd dead vine with some Pinot Beurot, as in the old days. It is perfectly legal to have as much as 10 per cent other Pinot in your Gevrey vineyards, the advantage being that Pinots such as the Beurot produce very high levels of sugar.

There is a *triage* in the vineyard; there is 100 per cent destemming, and the fruit is passed through a *fouloir* to gently break the grapes before maceration. After four or five days' cold soaking the fermentation begins. Sylvie is not '*obsédée*' (obsessed) with the maximum temperature, but what she seeks is a gentle fermentation - as long as possible - and a reasonably long total *cuvaison*. So the temperature is kept lowish, at a maximum of 32°C.

After *écoulage*, the pulp is pressed in a *pneumatique* installed in 1991. Some of the juice is added to the free-run wine, the tank allowed to settle out and the wine then decanted into barrel. Sylvie is anxious to avoid racking as long as possible, leaving the wine to feed on its lees protected by the carbon dioxide rather than by sulphur. The first racking will therefore be delayed until June or July, and there will be only one other, before the bottling eighteen months or so after the vintage. A very light filtration takes place on the rare occasions, such as 1994, when the wine was not naturally bright.

THE DOMAINE

The line-up is simple, a direct progression upwards from Bourgogne *rouge* (42 a) and Côte-de-Nuits-Villages (69 a) to village Gevrey-Chambertin (3.9 ha) - of which there are two *cuvées*, a regular and a *vieilles vignes* - and the Clos-Saint-Jacques (1.6 ha) whose average age is thirty years old. In 1995 however, Sylvie took on the lease of 19 a of Volnay Santenots and 24 a of Bourgogne *blanc*. Will she expand further? 'I am not interested in any more local village wine. What's the point? But if a bit of *grand cru* came my way …'

THE WINE

There is a clear family resemblance between the wine Sylvie Esmonin makes and the Clos-Saint-Jacques Bruno Clair produces in the parcel next door. The wines are lighter, and less fat and lush than Charles Rousseau's example. The Fourrier domaine is currently under-achieving, and the Jadot wine, vinified at much higher temperatures, has quite a different style. But certainly four out of five Clos-Saint-Jacques, at the very least, each in their individual ways, show the *grand cru* quality of this *climat*. And Sylvie's is as delicious as any of them.

THE TASTING

I tasted the following range of wines in Gevrey-Chambertin in June 1996.

GEVREY-CHAMBERTIN, CLOS-SAINT-JACQUES

	Optimum drinking

1994 — 2002-2015
Good colour. Profound cassis-blackberry Pinot Noir. Gently oaky. Firm, closed even. Good ripe tannins. Quite full. A generous mouthful. Intense. Long. Lots of dimension here. Fine.

1993 — 2002-2015
Fine colour. Profound on the nose. Very straight. Very pure. Good oak support. Firm and full on the palate. A composed wine. Ripe, generous, very well balanced. Nicely cool. Long and complex. Fine.

1992 — Now-2002
Good colour. Ripe Pinot on the nose. Soft and succulent on the palate but shorter than the 1994, and not as much personality. Medium body, round, balanced enough. Easy to drink. Very pleasant.

1991 — 2000-2010
Very good colour. Similar to the 1993. No undue age. Rich nose. Not quite as full of fruit or as stylish as the 1993 but very good nonetheless. Medium-full. Good tannins. A little drier - not as succulent as the 1993 - but

good grip and plenty of style. The same cool, understated character. Very good.

1990 — 2002-2015
Fine colour. Fat and rich on the nose. But not as sophisticated as the 1993. Slightly drier. The tannins more evident. Somewhat tougher. This is full and ample and has more of a cooked fruit flavour. *Confit de fruit*, says Sylvie. Very good grip. Very long. A plentiful, fat rich wine but not as stylish as the 1993. Fine though.

1989 — Now-2006
Very good colour. Better than the 1988. Lovely nose. Very soft ripe cherry-raspberry fruit. Quite intense. Most attractive. This is a delicious 1989. Very good grip. Quite full enough. Long, complex and very stylish. Really multi-dimensional and generous. Lovely. Just about ready.

1988 — Now-2002
Good colour but both the 1987 and the 1989 are deeper. A little meagre on the nose. Not just cool, but a little under-extracted. Medium body. This is quite pretty but it is a bit too simple. Reasonably balanced but no real grip. And it lacks real structure. Pleasant but a bit one-dimensional for a 1988. Fully ready.

1987   Now–2004

Very good colour. Full and still fresh. Rather more animal on the nose than the wines today but rich and fat and meaty. Quite sweet. Good structure and tannin. Nothing dry or *sous-bois* about this. Fat, old-fashioned in a sense, slightly hot at the end. But long and positive. A very good example for the vintage. Still plenty of vigour.

1986   Drink soon

Reasonable colour. No undue age. Gently fading on the nose. Loose-knit. Some dead leaves. Not astringent though. On the palate a bit light. Still fresh and fruity though. Reasonably stylish. Reasonably long and positive. Good for the vintage.

1985   Drink soon

Good colour. Mature. There is something definitely rustic on the nose. And rather more age than there should be. On the palate the wine is light - has lightened and loosened up - and quite fruity. But lacks grip and depth and real style. This is not very special.

1984   Drink up

Reasonable colour. Slightly weedy on the nose. But not too faded. Nor too terrible in the mouth either. The *terroir*'s quality can be discerned. Soft, reasonably round. Still fresh. Perfectly pleasant.

1983   Now–2000

Quite brown on the colour. A bit dry and astringent on nose and attack. But no rot. And indeed under the toughness quite rich and vigorous on the palate. Good grip. Rich even. OK it is a tough wine. But good, if not very good, with food. Will still last.

1980   Drink up

Quite an old colour and quite an old nose now. Soft and quite pleasant on the palate. Some sweetness. But a bit loose and diffuse now. Yet the finish is fresh. Not bad at all.

1977   Drink soon

Not at all a bad colour. Fresher nose than the 1980. Here is another vintage where the quality of the *terroir* comes out. There is class here. Good length. Medium body. A lack of fat and richness of course but the wine is pleasant and positive.

JOSEPH
FAIVELEY,
NUITS-SAINT-GEORGES

In one of the back streets of Nuits-Saint-Georges a rather ugly but functional concrete office block lies over the cavernous traditional cellars of a former sparkling Burgundy house (it still says Veuve Labouré on the decaying portals through which the grapes make their entry). This is the headquarters of one of the biggest and best domaines in Burgundy, a domaine which is also a *négociant*: Maison Joseph Faiveley, '*le plus important domaine viticole de Bourgogne*'.

Faiveley is run today by the forty-five-year-old François, sixth in a direct line from the original Pierre Faiveley who founded the business in 1825. François, tall, dark, attractive and bespectacled, with just the merest suggestion of a lisp, lives next door with his Anglo-French wife Anne and their family, two boys and the first female Faiveley to be born since 1772, suitably christened Eve. He began to take over from his father Guy in the mid-1970s, and has been solely in charge since 1978. The wines were fine before - a Faiveley bottling from the 1940s and 1950s, if you can find one, is one of the best guarantees of a fine old Burgundy - but they have improved even more since. This is classic, expert wine-making. Burgundy at its best.

THE DOMAINE

The Faiveley domaine, 115 hectares divided between Mercurey (70 ha) and the Côte d'Or (45 ha, almost entirely in the Côte-de-Nuits) is not just one of the largest in Burgundy, but is probably the richest in terms of its concentration in *premier* and *grand cru climats*. From the start, unlike other merchants at the time, François Faiveley's predecessors re-invested their profit in real estate, in order, as he puts it, to control the quality chain right through from the plantation of the young rootstock down to the day the bottle arrives in the cellar of the client.

In *grands crus* the estate comprises vines in Clos-de-Bèze, Mazis, Latricières, Le Musigny, Echézeaux and Clos-de-Vougeot. In *premiers crus* the main vineyards are located in Combe-aux-Moines and Cazetiers (Gevrey-Chambertin), in Chambolle-Musigny (Les Fuées, La Combe-d'Orveau), and in the Nuits-Saint-Georges *climats* of Les Saint-Georges, Porrets-Saint-Georges, Chaignots, Vignerondes, and Damodes. In addition the domaine has a lease until 2002 of the entirety of the 9.55 ha Clos-de-la-Maréchale, the most southerly of the great vineyards of the Côte-de-Nuits.

There are also a few hectares of *grand cru* Corton, right up at the top of the slope above Aloxe and Ladoix. Here you will find 62 ares of Corton-Charlemagne and just under 3 hectares of Rognet-ez-Corton (the word *rognet* indicates a piece of land which was once upon a time transferred as dowry from a young heiress to her husband). In 1930, before *Appellation Contrôlée* was introduced, incidentally, the Court of Dijon granted the Faiveleys the right to call their wine from this parcel Clos-des-Cortons-Faiveley. 'The best customers for my Cortons,' says François, 'are the rabbits of the Prince de Mérode [who owns the forest which sits like a *toupée* at the top of the Corton hill]. They eat the vine's young shoots. But they keep the harvest within bounds.'

VITICULTURE

'I am convinced,' says François Faiveley, 'that the quality of any wine is three-quarters (or more) determined by the quality of the fruit in the first place.' Like many of the more progressive proprietors in the area, he has employed Guy Accad as viticultural consultant (though not in the cellar). Together they have carried out an exhaustive analysis of the state of the soil in the Faiveley vineyards. This produced the decision either to stop fertilising completely or to reduce it to a minimum, to continue with a policy of largely reproducing vines from their own stocks (*sélection massale*) rather than a widespread use of clones, and to prune to a maximum of five or six buds per vines. If, despite this, the harvest looks like being excessive, as in 1990, the vines are green harvested, just prior to the *véraison*, the bunches furthest from the trunk being knocked off.

Successful wine-making? 'The secret is that there is no secret,' says François. In the Alps, you come across cairns, little pyramids made up of small stones. Wine-making is like this: a mass of interlocking, coherent detail. The time of vintaging is crucial. Everything, from Clos-de-Bèze to Bourgogne *rouge*, is sorted through a *tapis de triage* (there is an interesting wind-tunnel to blow away excess juice if the fruit arrives wet). 'We employ fifteen to twenty people just for this, because the sanitary state of the fruit is so important. We destem entirely now; have *saignée*-d when the juice has been diluted by rain (trials in 1982, a lot in 1986); cold macerate for a few days; and we vinify, using the indigenous yeasts, not artificial ones, at about 26°C, macerating the wine with the skins for as long as possible. Why do we vinify at a "low" temperature? Because the aromas are essentially volatile. A "hot" fermentation in my view produces wines which lack grace. As Professor Peynaud says: the higher the temperature the quicker the nose disappears. Pinot Noir is more fragile than Syrah or Cabernet.' Faiveley is adamantly against controlling the temperature by means of pumping the wine through a heat-exchanger ('A serious oenological error. It oxidises the wine'). Cooling is achieved by running cold water down the side of the fermentation tanks.

Thereafter? Pressing using a pneumatic press (much more gentle than the old system, and the wines then fall bright quicker and more naturally), plenty of new oak (up to 50 per cent for the top wines) and bottling by hand without filtration, for the top wines, usually fourteen to sixteen months after the harvest.

THE FAIVELEY PHILOSOPHY

François Faiveley is a man of taste and culture (you will hear the slow movement of Mozart's piano concerto K 467, Elvira Madigan, if you are kept waiting on the business telephone), and he has a healthy disrespect for - if not fame - certainly fortune. The majority of Faiveley's needs can be supplied by its own domaine, and François would rather keep the activities of his enterprise within a boundary he can personally control himself. Quality should be paramount. He has no ambition to be master of a mammoth empire. *Some* addition to the in-house supply is usually called for. The estate comprises a mere 3 hectares of village wine and it boasts nothing in Morey or Vosne (not that I can ever remember sampling a Vosne in the Faiveley cellars). Nor do they own any Côte-de-Beaune apart from their Corton. What he buys he buys as grapes; only occasionally, as in 1990 when the *rapport qualité-prix* was so good - and when he bought as much as he could, even to the risk of over-stocking himself and over-burdening his bank balance - does he venture hungrily into the *négoce* market.

Expansion is continuing in the Côte Chalonnaise, however. Having been farmers there since before the First World War, Guy Faiveley, father of François, purchased the nucleus of the existing Mercurey domaine in 1964. François has recently extended this by acquiring 10 hectares of land in Montagny (it produced its first harvest in 1992). He has also bought 5 prime hectares of Hautes-Côtes-de-Nuits, in the valley directly above Nuits-Saint-Georges itself. But what about expansion in the Côte d'Or? 'The prices are excessive.'

And the future? There is going to be more and more competition, François is convinced. And Burgundy is not going to be able to compete price for price with 'new' countries like Australia - or indeed with the south of France. The only way it is going to be able to survive is to produce higher and higher quality. The sole solution, not so much for Chambertin, Clos-de-Bèze, which will sell on its name and past reputation, but for middle-of-the-road *premiers crus*, is that the quality must be stunning.

'If I had been able to pursue a second career,' says François, 'it would have been as a *parfumier*. I am obsessed by the bouquet of fine Burgundy.' (One of his favourite books is Susskind's *Perfume*.) Burgundy has been wrongly thought by outsiders to be a heavier wine than Bordeaux. 'I still get people coming up to me saying they can't take Burgundy because it is too heavy, too powerful, too alcoholic. But Burgundy isn't like that. Above all it is a wine of finesse. The great thing about Pinot Noir is its marvellous perfume. A Burgundy may be technically correct, but if it doesn't exude this elegance it is nothing.'

François is a civilised man, a man with an enquiring mind and a wide range of interests. Music is one of his great loves, particularly the music of Bach. Painting, especially Turner, is another great passion. And to relax he has his boat. The boat is named Glenn II (there was originally a Glenn I). John Glenn the astronaut? No. Glenn Gould the pianist, supreme executor of the Partitas and other suites of Johann Sebastian Bach.

THE WINES

Faiveley's wines are, above all, supremely clean and elegant: definitive examples of Pinot Noir (I must not forget the Corton-Charlemagne, which, though rare, is equally classic). They are full, rich and concentrated, oaky but not too aggressively so, and sumptuous in the potential opulence of their fruit. But above all they have richness and breed, the thumbprint of a master wine-maker.

THE TASTING

The amalgamation of two wine weekends here. The Cortons were offered to the Hollywood Wine Society (Hollywood, Miami) in March 1992. The Mazis-Chambertins were sampled at Studley Priory Hotel, near Oxford, in November 1994.

Optimum drinking

Corton-Charlemagne, 1988   1998–2010

This is still very young. Slightly austere but very concentrated and stylish. Gently oaky. Very good grip. This is extremely classy. Very, very long and complex. Lovely.

CORTON, CLOS-DES-CORTONS-FAIVELEY

1990   1999–2016

Good colour. Rich, fat, Pinot nose: a lot of depth here. Still youthful and firm. Fullish. Good tannins. Very good grip. A wine of structure, concentration, class and potential. There is a lot of wine here. Very long. Fine plus.

1989   Now–2009

Medium-full colour. Ripe, lush nose. Abundant fruit and no lack of acidity. Most attractive. Medium-full. Open, rich, fragrant, almost sweet Pinot. Soft and fleshy, plum and abundant. Good grip. This is much less firm and backward. But very good. A lot of sex appeal.

1988   1999–2019

Good colour. Closed, austere but subtle nose. This is very lovely and complex. Youthful, fullish, some tannin. Very good acidity. Not as concentrated as the 1990 or as abundantly fruity as the 1989, but perhaps more class and balance and complexity in the long run. Fine.

1987   Now–2000

Medium colour. Softer nose. Reasonable intensity. Good ripe Pinot fruit. This is approaching maturity. Stylish, ripe and harmonious. Very clean Pinot if without the depth and concentration of the three vintages above.

1986   Drink soon

Good colour. A little dry and barnyardy on the nose. It lacks a bit of bite but again the acidity is good on the palate and the wine has style. I prefer the 1987 though.

1985   Now–2004

Medium-full colour. Some evolution on the nose. Ripe, but does it lack a bit of grip? This is

a little bit of a disappointment. It doesn't sing. Better as it evolved in the glass but it is not *that* much better than the 1987. Fuller, some depth, better length and complexity, but not up to 1988, 1989 and 1990. Very good rather than fine. My note on this wine, when sampled in Nuits-Saint-Georges in November 1991, was more enthusiastic. (See also page 000.)

1984   Drink soon

This is a light wine but not old. Still fresh. Simple but agreeable. By no means beneath consideration.

1983   Now–2000 plus

Medium colour. No undue brown though. Gamey, fleshy, animal nose. Fat and rich. There is a little dryness from the tannins underneath. But on the palate nothing rude about it. Fullish, rich, slightly cooked black cherry fruit. Good grip and concentration. This is still vigorous. Very good indeed.

1982   Drink soon

Medium colour. Soft aromatic nose. Medium to medium-full body. Good acidity if no real concentration or depth. Round, slightly spicy. Perhaps just a touch coarse, but finishes positively. But lacks real style and complexity.

1981   Drink soon

Good colour. Slightly dry on the nose and austere on the palate. Good acidity but a lack of real lushness and class. Lacks a bit of fruit. Not at all bad though. Better, and more elegant, than the 1982.

1980   Drink soon

Magnum. Good colour. A touch vegetal on the nose. Medium to medium-full. More personality and fruit than the 1981 and 1982. Ripe, plump and quite interesting nose. There is a slight boiled-sweet aspect, but this is the best of the three. Good grip.

1979   Now–2000

Magnum. Good colour. Not a bit dry but now mature. But this is fragrant, ripe and complex on the palate. Soft, round, medium-full, supple and subtle. Good long finish. Will keep well. Very good.

1971   **Drink soon**

Good mature colour. No undue age. Soft
fragrant nose. On the palate a wine of great
refinement, with just a suspicion of beginning
to coarsen up. Medium body. Round. Spicy.
Good grip still. Very good. Quite complex but
not the breed of fine.

Latricières-Chambertin, 1966   Now-2000 plus

Fine colour. Rich, concentrated, meaty nose.
Still vigorous. Full, rich, oaky, plump,
blackberry-flavoured wine. Fat and profound.
Plenty of wine here and plenty of life ahead of
it. Concentrated. Lovely. Fine.

Latricières-Chambertin, 1964   Drink soon

Very fine colour. Still youthful. Fullish but less
exuberant nose than the 1966. More evolved.
Now a complex wine, with the flavours of quite
an old bottle. This is long, harmonious,
originally a little hotter and more structured,
but without quite the grip of the above. Yet still
long and fragrant. Very good.

1962   **Drink soon**

Good colour. Fine, complex nose. A touch of
caramel and cinnamon. Lovely. Medium-full,
balanced, fragrant Pinot fruit. *À point*. Delicate
but still very positive. Very long and subtle. Fine.

1929   **Can still be kept**

Fine mature colour. No undue age. Very
complex nose. Still fresh. Slightly more volatile
acidity than usual today. Soft fruit. Touch of *pot-
pourri*, cinnamon, orange peel, cloves, burnt
sugar and strawberries. Soft, mellow, sweet,
delicious, still very fresh. Not so much full as
very, very intensely flavoured. Exquisitely
balanced. *Grand vin!* Will still keep well.

MAZIS-CHAMBERTIN

1992   **Now-2004**

Medium colour. Attractive, cherry-raspberry
nose. Not a bit sweet. Very elegant. Certainly
positive. Medium body. A little tannin. The
follow-through is very ample, not a bit weak.
And the wine has plenty of style. Even better as
it developed. Very good for the vintage.

1991   **1999-2015**

Good colour. Splendid rich, gently oaky
concentrated nose. Lots of depth and
complexity here. This has more to it than the
1989. This is most impressive. Fullish, very good
grip. Not a bit sweet. Lovely fruit. Very lovely
finesse and harmony. But real dimension as well.
Long. Classy. Very fine.

1990   **2000-2025**

Very good colour. Closed, adolescent, powerful
nose. Very full and rich, a meaty wine of great
intensity, fat, vigour and depth. Splendidly
concentrated fruit. Lots of wine here. And one
which is going to need time. Excellent.

1989   **Now-2009**

Medium to medium-full colour. Just a touch of
development. Fragrant, gently oaky, very stylish
ripe nose. Generous, engaging, classy. The
attack shows lovely fruit. Medium-full body and
good grip. A most attractive example. But it
doesn't have the volume, depth or vigour of the
1991. Fine for the vintage though.

1988   **Now-2015**

Good colour. Some development now. Fullish.
Clean, totally un-souped-up nose. Not too
austere though. On the palate medium-full
body. A little tannin. Underneath this a soft
wine, quietly concentrated and laid back. As
1988s go it is not too lean and unforgiving. It is
already generous. Very classy. And very subtle
too, especially on the finish.

1987   **Now-1999**

Good fresh medium-full colour. Touch of spice,
touch of tannin and astringency on the nose. A
touch of sweetness as well. Medium body. A
cheerful ripe, easy-to-drink wine, now ready. It
is fresh but it lacks a little fruit and quite a lot of
real finesse. A little barnyardy. But it finishes
better than it starts. Long. Very good.

1986   **Drink soon**

Medium colour. Just about mature. Soft nose.
Not unstylish. No undue age. Lightish, but not
coarse. Good acidity. Much lighter but more
elegant than the 1987. Soft but long, even a
little complexity. Very good again.

1985   **Now-2004**

Full colour. Now mature. Plump open nose.
Beginning to adopt the spices of maturity, the
gameyness of mature Burgundy. Seems to be of
a slightly different style than the wines made
later. Medium-full. Good balance. Ample but
slightly sweeter and spicier than the rest. It lacks
just a little grip, bite and concentration. It is just
a little diffuse. Harvested a little late. Not
enough acidity. So not fine. Merely very good.

1982   **Drink soon**

Medium-full colour, now mature but not
unduly so. Ample nose. Rich, fat and a little
sweet, but good style and vigour. Lovely and
fragrant. Cherry-like. Medium body. Ripe and
spicy. Plump, long, stylish. Soft. Very 1982. Very
good.

1981   **Drink soon**

Splendid colour. Very good nose. This has an aspect of 1972. But less austere and acidic. Very classy if lean. More oaky than the 1982. Medium to medium-full. Not too animal, certainly not vegetal. And no lack of ripeness and depth. Not that concentrated of course. No lack of vigour. Not fat but long. Very good indeed for the vintage. More finesse than the 1982.

1980   **Drink soon**

Very good vigorous colour. Lovely nose. Fragrant classy nose. Quite concentrated but not *that* rich. Violets. Fullish, mellow. Rather more structured than the 1981 and 1982. This is rich and full and stylish. Balanced, plenty of vigour, still a touch firm. Plenty of dimension. Fine.

Jacques Gagnard-Delagrange, Jean-Marc Blain-Gagnard and Richard Fontaine-Gagnard,
Chassagne-Montrachet

Nowhere is vinous Burgundy more confusingly arcane than in Chassagne-Montrachet. The village is small, betraying its medieval origins in small clusters of houses giving on to tiny secluded courtyards. The people live huddled together. And everyone seems related to everyone else.

As is the custom, most of the domaines have double-barrelled titles. The wife's maiden name, provided she has brought vineyards with her as dowry, is tagged on to that of her husband. So we have the estate of Jacques Gagnard, known as Gagnard-Delagrange. Jacques' father's domaine was called Gagnard-Coffinet, Coffinet being his maternal grandfather. That of his wife, Marie-Josèphe, was known as Delagrange-Bachelet. When Jacques, born in 1928, divided his inheritance with his brother Jean-Noël, born in 1926, and the two went their separate ways in 1960, the Gagnard-Delagrange domaine was born. Now, to save inheritance taxes, much of this domaine has been passed down the line to the Gagnards' two daughters: some as a straight gift, some on a *métayage* basis. The eldest, Laurence, born in 1955, married Richard Fontaine in 1982. The second daughter, Claudine, born in 1957, had already married Jean-Marc Blain in 1980. So today we have two further estates: Fontaine-Gagnard and Blain-Gagnard.

But to complicate matters further, while the land has been passed on, the older generation have in some cases retained the right to the resulting crop on an *usifruitier* basis. So while the Fontaine and Blain domaines may nominally own the land, and may indeed make the wine, some of the harvest may be bottled under the name of Jacques Gagnard, or even his father-in-law Edmond Delagrange.

Moreover, while each of the three domaines is independently responsible for its vines in the first place, and will equally have separate control over the *élevage* of the wine in the second place, the harvest in the middle tends to be more of a communal family affair. Some of the parcels are tiny. It makes sense to collect them and vinify them together. Only after the juice has been pressed is it then shared out.

WHO OWNS WHAT?

Officially, then, Jacques Gagnard is owner of 4.15 hectares. This includes 8 a of Montrachet, 27 a of Bâtard-Montrachet, *premier cru* white in Boudriottes and Morgeots, *premier cru* red in Morgeots and Clos-Saint-Jean and some Volnay, Champans. Some 2 hectares, however, have been given to the next generation *en métayage*.

Jean-Marc Blain is responsible for 7.70 ha. There are 21 a of Criots-Bâtard-Montrachet and 37 a of Bâtard-Montrachet, *premier cru* white in Caillerets, Boudriottes, Morgeots and Clos-Saint-Jean, and in this latter parcel red wine too. This son-in-law is the *métayer* for Jacques Gagnard's Volnay, Champans. He also owns the 8 ares of Montrachet from which Jacques gets his fruit, 35 a of Volnay, Chanlins and 42 a of Pommard.

Richard Fontaine's exploitation is of similar size - 7.49 hectares - and he too owns 8 ares of Le Montrachet. But this time the *usifruitier* is his wife's grandfather, Edmond Delagrange, still vigorous at the age of eighty-five. Fontaine looks after 33 a of Criots, 30 of Bâtard, *premier cru* Chassagne *blanc* in Caillerets, Morgeots, Vergers, La Maltroie, Chenevottes (*en métayage* from an outside family), Grande-Montagne (these are young vines) and Boudriottes, *premier cru rouge* in Morgeots and Clos-Saint-Jean, and further vines in Volnay, Clos-des-Chênes and Pommard Rugiens. Furthermore he looks after another 14 a parcel in Bâtard, the fruit of which is bottled in Blain under the Edmond Delagrange label.

While the three parcels of Bâtard - all on the Chassagne side - are quite separate, and have different origins, the Criots is a divided plot, inherited from the Delagrange-Bachelet side of the family. The Montrachet, also now divided, was bought by Jacques and his father-in-law from the Fleurot family in 1978. This, the Caillerets and the Boudriottes are pressed together, the juice separated thereafter.

WINE-MAKING

With a close-knit family such as the Gagnards - the daughters live side by side - you would expect a certain similarity in the way the wine is made and in its resulting style. This is only partly true.

The bluff, stocky, handsome Jacques Gagnard is in many ways the traditionalist. He employs the least new oak (15 per cent), but leaves the wine longest in cask, until January or February of the second year. He prefers to employ the indigenous yeasts, believes in plenty of *bâtonnage*, but thereafter likes to disturb the wine as little as possible. Without having measured it, I would guess that his cellar is probably cooler - as well as older - than those under Blain and Gagnard's adjoining houses lower down in the village.

Jean-Marc Blain is the shorter and shyer of the two brothers-in-law. His father was a Sancerrois vet, and he had decided to go into wine long before he fell into the Gagnard family. He met Claudine when both were studying oenology at the University of Dijon. Like his father-in-law his aim is for *vins de garde*, so he too likes a long lees contact, to get as much richness into the wines as possible. He uses 25 per cent new oak and bottles after a year.

Richard Fontaine is tall, blue-eyed, and has the nose of someone who used to be an amateur boxer (though in fact it was broken in an accident while doing his military service). He arrived later in Chassagne, his wife Laurence having already begun to sell some of her wine under her own name. His methods are much like those of Blain, except that he retains at least some of the stems in his red wine-making, and uses a touch more new oak during the *élevage* of the whites.

THE WINES

The tasting below gave me a splendid opportunity to sample the wares of the three domaines side by side, as well as serving as an illustration of the differences between the various

442   JACQUES GAGNARD-DELAGRANGE, JEAN-MARC BLAIN-GAGNARD AND RICHARD FONTAINE-GAGNARD

Chassagne white wine *climats*.

To the north of the village the family has vines in Les Vergers and Clos-Saint-Jean. The latter are still young, and the wine here is correct but not as yet particularly exciting. Fontaine's Vergers comes from twenty-year-old vines, but is again good rather than great.

On the southern side Richard Fontaine exploits the vines in La Maltroie. These are not young but the wine therefrom is not the best in the combined portfolio. Go further south, and down-slope, and you will come to the Boudriottes and the Morgeots. Here the wines are fat and sturdy, the vines more than a generation old, and the results rather better: stylish, rich, persistent, built to last. The Boudriottes under Jacques Gagnard's label is perhaps the best.

The final *premier cru*, lying up-slope from Les Boudriottes, is Les Caillerets. Blain and Fontaine share the must, but vinify separately. This is one of Chassagne's best vineyards, and the wine is suitably more steely, more flowery than the two above. Except for the 1991 vintage, where Richard Fontaine's results are a bit feeble, I would find it hard to suggest which is the better of the two. The same applies to the Criots-Bâtard-Montrachets. The family is one of the very best sources for this tiny (1.57 ha in total) *grand cru*.

It is when you come to compare the respective Bâtard-Montrachets that a hierarchy begins to emerge. There is not a lot of difference in the age of the vines; if anything those of Jacques Gagnard are marginally the least old. But regularly throughout the tasting his wine was the best of the three, and better than either of the Criots. There have been a number of *grand vin* vintages of Jacques Gagnard's Bâtard in recent years. And in his masterly hands the Montrachet itself is even greater. As he also regularly produces one of the best of the *premiers crus,* I can't help suggesting that the sons-in-law still have something to learn from his lifetime's experience. And to hope that, despite now being over the official retirement age, he continues to remain in charge of his part of the family vineyard. This is starry wine-making without a doubt.

THE TASTING

I sampled the following wines in Chassagne-Montrachet in February 1995.

Optimum drinking

1993 CHASSAGNE-MONTRACHET

Morgeots   1999-2009
Jacques Gagnard-Delagrange
Bottled a fortnight ago. Ripe, full of fruit. A certain solidity from the Morgeot *terroir* but ample, good grip. Plenty of future. Slightly closed at present but a stylish example.

Boudriottes   1999-2009
Jacques Gagnard-Delagrange
More floral, but more persistent. Lovely fruit. Rich and complete. This is a step-up. Very stylish. Very well balanced. Has put on weight and personality since I saw it last. Fine.

Clos-Saint-Jean   Now-2004
Blain-Gagnard
Young vines, planted in 1987. Bottled in September. Round and ripe, but not a lot of character. A little one-dimensional. Correct and clean and balanced. Nevertheless a bit dull. Forward.

Boudriottes   1999-2009
Blain-Gagnard
Bottled in September as well. A little dry and austere on the nose, compared with Jacques', but this is the bottling. The finish is round and complex. Long and succulent for a 1983. Good richness. Very good indeed if not fine. Lovely finish.

Morgeots   1999-2009
Blain-Gagnard
Round and fat. Good apply aspect. Round and ripe. More recovered from the bottling than the above. Good length. I prefer this to Jacques' example. Very good.

Vergers   Now-2004
Fontaine-Gagnard
Bottled in September. This is ample, flowery, even a touch spicy. An ample wine, but it doesn't have the style of the Boudriottes above. A little fleshy. A little simple.

La Maltroie   1998-2007
Fontaine-Gagnard
Rich, slightly smoky - in a bacon sense - fat and

ample on the nose. Better than the above. But again a little facile. Ripe and sweet even. Good grip. Good plus.

Caillerets   1999-2009
Fontaine-Gagnard
Also a slightly smoky nose. But richer, more style, better balanced. This is closed and backward. More new oak. Fine follow-through. But it lacks just a bit of grip. Very good though.

Bâtard-Montrachet   2000-2012
Jacques Gagnard-Delagrange
Bottled fifteen days ago. Fat and slightly heavy on the nose. Ample on the attack. Good fruit and style. Reasonable length. Tails off slightly but this is the effect of the bottling. Lovely elegance, nevertheless. I am sure this is very fine.

Bâtard-Montrachet   2000-2012
Blain-Gagnard
Bottled in September. Rich nose. Round and masculine. Spicy and quite full, even a slight bit heavy. But the follow-through is fine. Plenty of depth and grip here. Lovely fruit. Very fine.

Bâtard-Montrachet   2000-2012
Fontaine-Gagnard
Bottled in September. Very rich, composed nose. Plenty of depth here. The most backward. Just a little more oak. Very concentrated. Very backward after the above. Persistent. Masculine. Intense. Very concentrated. Splendid fruit. Very fine indeed.

Criots-Bâtard-Montrachet   2000-2012
Fontaine-Gagnard
This has a lovely nose. Fragrant, just a touch of new oak. Very concentrated. Beautiful Chardonnay fruit. Elegant. Long. Fully *grand cru* quality. Excellent.

Criots-Bâtard-Montrachet   2000-2012
Blain-Gagnard
Slightly dumber and less advanced. Perhaps richer. A full ample wine with very good depth. Just a little floral. Hidden but profound. Excellent too.

Le Montrachet   2000-2015
Jacques Gagnard-Delagrange
Serious nose. Profound, rich, high quality. This is rather closed at first. And doesn't sing like the above. But it is shy, subtle and deceptive. The finish is very long. Very fine. But not as much of a jump-up today as one usually finds between the other *grands crus* and Le Montrachet. However it has only just been bottled, so I will give it the benefit of the doubt.

1992 CHASSAGNE-MONTRACHET

Clos-Saint-Jean   Now-2004
Blain-Gagnard
Slightly herbal on the nose, a touch sweet. Pleasant but a little built-in sulphur. Not exciting. A bit simple.

Morgeots   1999-2009
Blain-Gagnard
Slightly more colour than the wine below. A nice big sturdy, slightly four-square wine. Still closed. Full, meaty. Good grip. Plenty of depth. But needs time. Good plus.

Morgeots   1999-2009
Jacques Gagnard-Delagrange
A little more evolved, but perhaps a little less depth. Fresh and fruity. Round, uncomplicated, balanced, very good extract. An elegant wine with a long classy finish. I prefer this to the above. Very good.

Vergers   1999-2009
Fontaine-Gagnard
Quite a full colour. Fat and rich but a little four-square on the nose. Quite stylish. Ripe and balanced certainly. But it doesn't quite sing. Yet perfumed, attractive. Good depth. Very good.

La Maltroie   1998-2006
Fontaine-Gagnard
Quite a full colour. Aromatic nose. This has got a better attack but seems a little similar on the finish. Good but doesn't have the depth of the above.

Boudriottes   1999-2009
Jacques Gagnard-Delagrange
Light colour. Fine nose. Ripe, composed, stylish. Laid-back. Medium body. Very good balance. Lovely fruit. Very good finesse here. Not as heavy as the Caillerets. Lovely.

Caillerets   1999-2009
Blain-Gagnard
Ample and rich, opulent, honeyed. A closed-in wine. But a lot fatter than the above. Very ripe on the palate. Quite alcoholic. Good grip but slightly hot at the end. Very good plus.

Caillerets   1999-2009
Fontaine-Gagnard
This seems more evolved than the above, even a suggestion of *pourriture noble*, of *sur-maturité*. Seems more loose-knit, less closed, but perhaps a better grip. I prefer the finish here. Slightly less heavy. Very good indeed.

Bâtard-Montrachet   2002–2015
Jacques Gagnard-Delagrange

As usual the least colour. On the nose gently honeyed, stylish, ripe. On the palate oaky, with a smoky-bacon aspect. Rich, balanced, masculine. Very fine grip. Concentrated fruit. Slightly adolescent. But excellent. Really fine finish.

Bâtard-Montrachet   2000–2015
Blain-Gagnard

A little leaner than the above on the nose. But plenty of depth. Closed, adolescent. Perhaps, as on the nose, a touch heavy, even a bit alcoholic. This may be as good eventually as the above. But I doubt it. Very good indeed.

Bâtard-Montrachet   1999–2010
Fontaine-Gagnard

Much more evolved on the nose. Round, open, but a little blowsy. An ample wine but it is a bit too forward. Round, plump, voluptuous. But it doesn't have the grip or the finesse.

Criots-Bâtard-Montrachet   2000–2015
Fontaine-Gagnard

Fine nose, though just a touch heavy for comfort. On the palate quite different from the wine below. Round, rich, but a touch rigid. This is still closed. Good grip. But the structure seems to be too present. Yet a fine finish. Long. Full of finesse.

Criots-Bâtard-Montrachet   2002–2015
Blain-Gagnard

This is very fine. Rich, succulent, composed. Fat, and balance, and delicious. This is very fine indeed. Youthful. Concentrated. Harmonious. Very lovely fruit. Delicate touch of oak. Really intense. Better than the Bâtard.

Le Montrachet   2002–2020
Jacques Gagnard-Delagrange

This is really serious. Firm, aristocratic, virile nose. More concentrated than the Bâtard. No aspect of smoky bacon and other strange flavours. Full, concentrated, splendid grip. This is a brilliant example. Perfectly poised. Very subtle. Splendidly elegant and complex. Very very long.

1991 CHASSAGNE-MONTRACHET

Clos-Saint-Jean   Drink soon
Blain-Gagnard

This is a simple wine, and has also a bit of SO$_2$. Even more SO$_2$ on the palate. Not for me.

Vergers   Now–2006
Fontaine-Gagnard

Quite an evolved colour. But no meanness or leanness on the palate. Good fruit. A touch of oak. Ripe, fresh, plenty of complexity. This has style and length. Very good, especially for a 1991.

Morgeots   Now–2006
Jacques Gagnard-Delagrange

This is poised and elegant for a Morgeots, both on the nose and on the attack. Indeed the nose is very fragrant and stylish. The follow-through is a touch heavier. A little neutral. But a very good effort.

Maltroie   Drink soon
Fontaine-Gagnard

Fat, rich, honeyed, a little too blowsy and rich. Rather too evolved. On the palate there is a bit of honey but it lacks style. Heavy and a bit sweet and blowsy at the end. It won't last.

Boudriottes   1998–2008
Jacques Gagnard-Delagrange

Crisp, ripe, balanced, classy. A little austere but ripe and harmonious. Medium weight. Balanced. Unexpected depth. Very good indeed.

Boudriottes   1998–2008
Blain-Gagnard

Similar but a little more evolved. A little less classy. The nose after a bit showed a little oxidation. A slight taste of reduction on the palate. And a little less grip. But certainly good. The finish is correct.

Caillerets   1998–2008
Blain-Gagnard

This is fresh and ripe and has very good elegance and harmony. Medium-full. Fat, good concentration. Good grip. For a 1991 this has very good depth and character. Fine for the vintage.

Caillerets   Drink up
Fontaine-Gagnard

This I find a bit too evolved, rather like his Maltroie. Short. Tired.

Criots-Bâtard-Montrachet   1999–2010
Blain-Gagnard

Rich, concentrated, vigorous. Fat and full. Good depth. Fresh and succulent. Ripe and elegant. Long and fine.

Criots-Bâtard-Montrachet   Now–2004
Fontaine-Gagnard

This again, sadly, is a bit too evolved on the nose. Ripe on the palate. But a little sweet, a little short. Unexciting.

Bâtard-Montrachet   1999–2010
Jacques Gagnard-Delagrange

Fresh nose. Fine concentrated fruit. Nothing a bit off-vintage about this. Deliciously fruity. Really quite exciting quality here. Very lovely on the palate. Good concentration. Very good grip. Fine.

Bâtard-Montrachet   1999–2010
Blain-Gagnard

Fat, austere, concentrated, crisp, fine nose. Good depth. Not quite as stylish or as good a grip as the above. But fine, long, complex. Fine finish. Very good indeed.

Bâtard-Montrachet   1997–2004
Fontaine-Gagnard

Blowsy and flat, again. Why so? Ripe but flat. Richard admits his 1991s are disappointing. But I don't know why.

1990 CHASSAGNE-MONTRACHET

Clos-Saint-Jean   Now–1999
Blain-Gagnard

Ripe and quite rich, but, as always, a bit one-dimensional. This was the first vintage, so very young vines. A bit simple but well-made.

Vergers   1998–2006
Fontaine-Gagnard

This is very, very good. Rich, concentrated, very good grip. Lovely ripe fruit. A fine example with heaps of depth. Good acidity. Slightly toasted aspect to the fruit. Youthful, slightly austere. Very good indeed.

Boudriottes   Now–2004
Jacques Gagnard-Delagrange

Slightly lean, but very stylish on the nose. Lovely flowery fruit. Yet on the palate quite evolved. Good balance. Quite crisp. A slight lack of grip and fat underneath but delicious now. Very good.

Boudriottes   Now–2005 plus
Blain-Gagnard

A bit heavier and four-square on the nose. Slight aspect of SO_2. Less evolved than Jacques' wine on the palate. Round, ripe, stylish. Just about ready. Very good grip. Long. Very good indeed.

Morgeots   Now–2005
Blain-Gagnard

Full, firm, slightly four-square, just a touch of SO_2, but ripe and rich on the nose. Good depth and grip. A little heavy. But rich, if not very elegant.

Caillerets   Now–2006
Fontaine-Gagnard

Slightly more developed but a lot more elegant. Less size, more finesse. This is fullish, *à point*, ripe and succulent. Good grip. Very elegant and stylish. Fine.

Criots-Bâtard-Montrachet   Now–2006
Blain-Gagnard

Backward, very elegant and very concentrated. Full, a slight touch of sulphur. Rich and a bit four-square and solid. Backward but I don't think there is any more depth to come out. Fine but not great.

Criots-Bâtard-Montrachet   Now–2004
Fontaine-Gagnard

Quite a different wine. A little crisper, slightly less heavy; a touch of orange peel. A lot more evolved. This has more noticeable new oak behind it. It is fresher. It has more style. And it is more ready for drinking. But also it is fine without being great.

Bâtard-Montrachet   Now–2020
Jacques Gagnard-Delagrange

This is very serious. Lovely concentrated nose. Very fine fruit. Beautifully balanced. Very aristocratic. Very excellent on the palate. Marvellous fruit. A real explosion of flavour. Delicious fruit. Very fine grip. Splendid harmony. Great wine.

Bâtard-Montrachet   Now–2005
Blain-Gagnard

Classy fruit but a little restrained on the nose. On the palate this is quite developed, and after the above seems a bit one-dimensional. Generously ripe. Reasonable grip. Very good indeed.

Bâtard-Montrachet   Now–2003
Fontaine-Gagnard

This is the most evolved on the nose. A touch of wood. A touch of spice. Expansive yet has good grip underneath. Slightly looser-knit but very good indeed as well. More toasty. Less SO_2. Very good indeed.

Montrachet   2002–2025
Jacques Gagnard-Montrachet

This is even more closed in than his Bâtard. Very concentrated indeed. Still an infant. It doesn't sing like the above. But there is heaps of depth. Slightly less grip, it seems. Yet very, very long, complex, succulent. Very excellent. This is superb. And indisputably great wine.

1989 CHASSAGNE-MONTRACHET

Criots-Bâtard-Montrachet   Now–2005
Blain-Gagnard

Very slight hint of reduction on the nose. But rich, ample, greengagey, fullish. This is a fine example, good grip. A little delicate but lively. Now mature. But plenty of vigour if no real weight or backbone. Fine.

Bâtard-Montrachet   Now–2003
Fontaine-Gagnard

Expansive nose. A slight hint of *sur-maturité*. Crisper, good acidity and backbone on the palate. Slightly all over the place. And indeed just a touch corky. But very good indeed nevertheless.

Bâtard-Montrachet   Now–2020
Jacques Gagnard-Delagrange

Closed, but very lovely rich nose. Full of fruit and not a trace of age or over-ripeness. This is excellent, as was his 1990. Round, fat, ripe, beautiful fruit and balanced. The complete wine. Excellent finesse and very, very long at the end. Real class here. Brilliantly long and subtle on the finish. Great wine.

Le Montrachet   2000–2020
Jacques Gagnard-Delagrange

Brilliant nose. Even after the delights of the above, this is a step above. And it is less in its shell than the 1990. The nose is super-concentrated. And the palate is extra-opulent, closed. Perhaps the 1990 is more complex, has greater depth. This is a bit more open, easier to appreciate. Very fine indeed. Even greater than the above.

1988 CHASSAGNE-MONTRACHET

Bâtard-Montrachet   Now–2000 plus
Blain-Gagnard

Somewhat meagre on the nose, a touch hard. But stylish nevertheless. Good acidity. Somewhat one-dimensional, and a little lean. But it is better than the 1987 below. Very good. There is definition and class here.

1987 CHASSAGNE-MONTRACHET

Criots-Bâtard-Montrachet   Drink soon
Fontaine-Gagnard

This has a lot of built-in sulphur on the nose. Rather diffuse and blowsy as well. And the colour is orangey. Rather blowsy. No depth. Disappointing. And needs drinking soon.

Bâtard-Montrachet   Now–2000
Blain-Gagnard

Good straight nose. Clean, positive, vigorous and fruity. A lot going for it, especially in this vintage. Ample and ripe if without any real depth. Fresh and very pleasant if without real class. But long enough, enjoyable enough. Very good. No trace of fatigue.

1986 CHASSAGNE-MONTRACHET

Boudriottes   Drink soon
Blain-Gagnard

Fresh nose for a 1986, just a touch of orange peel and blowsiness. On the palate a little more evolved. Round and aromatic. But a little short, a little lacking style. Good.

Bâtard-Montrachet   Drink soon
Fontaine-Gagnard

A bit reductive and overblown on the nose. Rather short on the palate. Nothing much here. Reasonably fresh fruit for a short while in the middle. But that's all.

1985 CHASSAGNE-MONTRACHET

Boudriottes   Drink soon
Blain-Gagnard

Firm but round nose. Plenty of fruit here, but still immature. Yet on the palate there is a little coarseness. Good freshness. But doesn't quite sing. A little diffuse.

Maltroie   Now–2000 plus
Fontaine-Gagnard

Full nose. Expansive and succulent. No hard edges here. Now *à point*. This has plenty of future. Good balance. Nicely fat and fresh. Long, succulent. Elegant. Fine.

Criots-Bâtard-Montrachet   Drink soon
Blain-Gagnard

Mature, very stylish nose. Lovely ripe succulent fruit and very good acidity. *À point* but no sign of age. Now *à point* on the palate. Ripe, rich, opulent. Mature. This is fully mature and is beginning to lose its vigour at the end. Fine but drink soon.

Criots-Bâtard-Montrachet   Now–2000
Fontaine-Gagnard

Just a touch of reduction on the nose. But good grip. And, like the above, still fresh. On the palate round, rich, succulent and most attractive. More vigorous than the above. Very good grip. Fullish. Fine.

Bâtard-Montrachet   Now–2010 plus
Jacques Gagnard-Delagrange

Lovely nose. Rich, concentrated, classy, backward. Really profound. Fat, opulent, rich, full. Very good acidity. This is very classy, very concentrated, and very fine indeed. Marvellous finish. Subtle. These Chassagne-Bâtards are not a bit heavy. This has real class and is very complex, very, very long. *Extra!*

1984 CHASSAGNE-MONTRACHET

Boudriottes   Now–1999
Jacques Gagnard-Delagrange

Fruity, very fresh. Very stylish. No sign of age here. No lack of depth either. And the wine is surprisingly ripe and elegant. Good concentration. No lack of fruit. Fresh. Delicious. Very good indeed. Bags of life.

1983 CHASSAGNE-MONTRACHET

Morgeots   Drink soon
Jacques Gagnard-Delagrange

This is quite evolved in colour, and on the nose. But is rather more distinguished on the nose. And less astringent at the end than I had expected. But nevertheless orangey, evolved, slightly coarse. Still fresh. But not really elegant.

1982 CHASSAGNE-MONTRACHET

Morgeots   Now–2000 plus
Jacques Gagnard-Delagrange

Ripe, fresh and succulent. Good acidity. This is not super-stylish but is very generous and delicious, without the usual heaviness of Morgeots. Good acidity. Unexpectedly good.

Bâtard-Montrachet   Now–1999
Blain-Gagnard

Intriguing nose. Candied peel and nuts. Roasted almonds here. On the palate it is a little blowsy. Richer and fatter and with good apparent grip. But the elements are a little disappointing for a *grand cru*.

Criots-Bâtard-Montrachet   Now–2000 plus
Fontaine-Gagnard

This is rather good. Ripe and fresh, very good fruit. Long and rich. Not as full as the above, or as fat. But the acidity is full. Round, balanced, very stylish. Very good indeed. Plenty of life.

1979 CHASSAGNE-MONTRACHET

Boudriottes   Now–2000
Jacques Gagnard-Delagrange

Fragrant, succulent, very fresh, lovely fruit.

Peachy. Delicious. Fully mature but no sign of age. Round, fullish, long, stylish, complex. Fine.

Criots-Bâtard-Montrachet   Drink soon
Edmond Delagrange

Quite an evolved colour. But not too tired on the nose: not a bit. A little bit less fresh than the above. But plumper and richer and riper. Still enjoyable. But not really what it was in its prime.

1976 CHASSAGNE-MONTRACHET

Boudriottes   Drink soon
Jacques Gagnard-Delagrange

Nicely rich and stylish on the nose. Not a bit too over-ripe or heavy. Good freshness and personality. A fine example. Rich, good acidity. Somewhat exotic in its fruit. So not *that* elegant. But a very good example.

Bâtard-Montrachet   Drink soon
Edmond Delagrange

Round, rich, expansive. This is full and fine, with very good acidity. Opulent. Slightly spicy. Exotic. Still fresh. Still enjoyable. Still stylish. This is much better than the Criots 1979.

1973 CHASSAGNE-MONTRACHET

Boudriottes   Drink soon
Jacques Gagnard-Delagrange

Fragrant nose. Not too evolved. Fresh and stylish. Some age on the palate. Yet rich and even quite profound. Good fruit. Elegant. Aromatic. Very good indeed.

Bâtard-Montrachet   Drink up
Edmond Delagrange

The colour is a little evolved now. And the nose is a little tired. Yet there is fruit here. Rich. But it is now at the end of its life. The above is better.

1971 CHASSAGNE-MONTRACHET

Boudriottes   Drink up
Jacques Gagnard-Delagrange

Oldish colour. Slightly white porty on the nose and on the palate. There is a suspicious touch of residual sugar here. Quite alcoholic. Walnutty. Ripe, fresh if well-matured. Interesting rather than agreeable. I prefer the 1973.

Bâtard-Montrachet   Drink up
Edmond Delagrange

Oldish colour. This is really quite evolved. But is still soft and ripe, even slightly apply. Round, smooth, stylish and complex. A lovely finish - if you like old wine.

Premier Cru (? **Boudriottes) 1966**   **Drink up**
Jacques Gagnard-Delagrange

Light golden colour. Less rich than the above but fresher. Good acidity. Good fruit. A little hard at the end. But interesting. And no lack of style.

Premier Cru (? **Boudriottes) 1959**   **Drink up**
Jacques Gagnard-Delagrange

This is rich and honeyed. Vigorous and quite alcoholic still. Peachy and apply. A bit hard and fiery. But rich, fat, masculine. Still sweet. Still not without vigour. Better and more vigour than the 1966. Very good indeed.

JACQUES GERMAIN AND THE CHÂTEAU DE CHOREY-LÈS-BEAUNE,

CHOREY-LÈS-BEAUNE

Reconstructed in the 1660s on the ruins of a fortification built in the thirteenth century, the Château de Chorey-lès-Beaune gives the impression of being as much a proper castle (*château fort*) as an imposing country residence (a *château* in the Loire sense), though on a small scale. It is encircled by a moat, deep in places, which is said to contain fish. Within this lies the château and its dependencies. Without there is a park, surrounded by a stone wall. It is owned by François Germain and his four children and is the headquarters of a 17 hectare domaine which can boast no fewer than six *premier cru* Beaunes, one of them a rarity, a Beaune *blanc*. François Germain also makes an excellent white Pernand-Vergelesses. Today the château takes in paying guests on a *chambres d'hôte* (bed and breakfast) basis. This would be a splendid place to stay for anyone who wants to build a holiday round the wines of Burgundy. You will be in the peace of the country, able to enjoy the charm of a romantic old building and its surroundings, yet only five minutes by car from the centre of Beaune.

HISTORY

It was François' great-grandfather Pierre, born in 1845, who acquired the Château de Chorey around the start of the twentieth century. Pierre Germain was the proprietor of a 20 hectare estate, which included some Clos-de-Vougeot, and had bought his way into Maison Poulet Père et Fils, one of Beaune's oldest *négociants*.

Pierre died in 1936, to be succeeded by his son Paul, born in 1875. The economic climate had changed, sadly. Times were hard. Poulet was unprofitable, and part of the domaine had to be sold off. Paul would have sold the château too, but ownership also belonged to his sister Berthe, Mother Superior of the Dames Hospitalières of the Hospices de Beaune, and she wouldn't allow it.

After the war the succession passed to Paul's son Jacques, born in 1907. He was the first member of his family actually to live in the Château de Chorey. He resurrected Poulet Père et Fils, which interested him more than the domaine, now dwindled to 7 hectares, but he renovated the château. It was here that François, born in 1936, and his siblings remember their childhood.

Jacques died suddenly of a heart attack in 1968. The children decided to dispose of their interest in Maison Poulet, and François then used his share to buy out his brothers and sisters in order to become sole owner of the Château de Chorey (Henri Germain, *vigneron* in Meursault, is one of his brothers). He has since built up the domaine by acquiring some vines in Chorey-lès-Beaune itself, which the family had never owned before. He also bought the Pernand-Vergelesses and more Chorey in 1980.

THE DOMAINE

Today the domaine - Germain Père et Fils since François' eldest son Benoît took over responsibility in the cellar in 1993 - includes 5 hectares of Chorey-lès-Beaune, 2.8 ha of Pernand-Vergelesses, all of it producing white wine, and 2.5 ha of generic red and white Bourgogne.

Pride of place, however, are the Beaunes. In ascending order of interest there are 60 ares of Les Cent-Vignes, youngish vines, and with a little sand in the soil, so spicy, *tendre*, feminine; 1 ha of Les Boucherottes, plump, cherry-flavoured, supple, easy to drink; another of Les Vignes-Franches, ripe, succulent, fat and persistent; 1.30 ha of Les Cras, sturdy, rich and concentrated, very classy, with very good grip; and finally Les Teurons, no less than 2 ha of it, the most complete, the most intense, the most elegant and the longest-lasting.

The white Beaune comes from Sur-les-Grèves, up-slope from the Grèves itself. The Germains possess 15 ares, enough to make a couple of casks. The flavour reminds me of quinces. The wine has both body and good acidity, and a touch of spice. It is individual and intriguing. And it keeps well.

WINE-MAKING

François Germain is adamantly against excessive harvesting. A maximum of 35 hl/ha for *premier cru*, 40 for village is what he is after. Even in 1989 he didn't exceed this figure, though he did, for the first time since 1973, in 1990, one year when the yield *could* have been a little high but not have resulted in dilution.

For this reason he prunes his vines hard, debuds in the spring, and trains his Chorey vineyards to the Cordon du Royat system. This is preferable to green harvesting. When necessary he will do a *saignée de cuve*.

Today he destems completely, allows three days' cold soaking, and extends the maceration more, closing the vat after the fermentation has finished and leaving the wine on its skins for a further week. The temperatures are allowed to rise to 34°C. Thereafter the *premiers crus* are given one-half new wood, filtered with *Kieselguhr* but not fined. This procedure, the Germains consider is much gentler than fining and plate filtration.

THE WINE

The result, says Benoît, is richer wines, which, while supple and easy to drink after four or five years, nevertheless can be kept ten to fifteen years, or even more.

I find the style of François and Benoît Germain's wines admirable. The gently oaky, plump and racy Pernand *blanc* is excellent value - the name makes it hard to sell, and this keeps the price down - and the reds are balanced, pure and intense. They hold their colour well, are surprisingly complex and stylish, and last well in bottle.

This is an open, friendly, hospitable family. Despite living in a grand château they do not stand on their dignity. And they make very good wine.

THE TASTING

I sampled the following wines at the Château de Chorey in June 1995.

BEAUNE, TEURONS

Optimum drinking

1993   **2000-2010 plus**

Good colour. Rather more than 1991, it seems. Very fresh *coulis* of red fruits on the nose. Fine acidity, even a little austere at present. Ample, fullish, ripe cherry-flavoured wine. Nicely complex. Very well balanced. Good depth and weight and thrust. Lots of class. Very good.

1992   **Now-2002**

Lightish colour. Attractive, stylish, ripe nose. No lack of intensity here. Plump, certainly not a bit weak. A generous example with heaps of attractive fresh fruit. Medium body. Balanced. Ripe. Very good indeed for the vintage.

1991   **1998-2005**

Medium-full colour. This is very good on the nose. The tannins are more sophisticated than some, the wine nicely round and rich. Lush for a 1991. A bit more earthy than the 1993. The tannins a little firmer and drier. Good grip. Not quite the flair of the 1993 but very good.

1990   **1998--2015**

Full colour, still very youthful. Full, vigorous, rich nose. Still very young. Only the fresh *primeur* fruit aromas so far. Splendidly concentrated fruit on the palate. Really concentrated. Very classy. Lovely pure Pinot. Extremely ripe, but, here, not cooked. Very good grip. This is super. Will make a really seductive bottle. Very vigorous. Very long.

1989   **Now-2005**

Medium to medium-full colour, still very fresh. Ample, abundant, soft and generous on the nose. Perhaps the first which is ready for drinking. Round, very ripe indeed. But with very good acidity. Medium-full. Nicely intense. Essentially soft. Long, generous, most attractive. Still needs a year.

1988   **Now-2005**

Good, youthful colour. Again the nose is still very fresh. Nicely ripe and generous, but the usual austerity of the vintage at this stage. This has the tannins sticking out a bit. Good acidity. Attractive fruit. But it lacks just a touch of fat. This may come as it rounds off. But today doesn't sing as much as the rest.

1987   **Now-2002**

For the first time, a colour with a bit of brown in it. Still vigorous though. This is ripe, full of interest and surprisingly classy on the nose. This is now ready. A fresh, plump, ripe wine with good depth. Nothing coarse about it. Very good tannins. Long. Complex. Very good indeed for the vintage.

1986   **Drink soon**

Quite a lot browner than the 1987. Evolved nose, but not past it. There is a reasonable substance here to back it up. On the palate the weakest so far despite some richness. But there is an element of astringency. I would say, overall, not bad. But drink soon.

1985   **Now-2005 plus**

Very good full, fresh colour. Lovely nose. A cornucopia of fresh fruit. Surprisingly virile and youthful for the vintage. Good acidity too. Fat, rich, full, meaty. Plenty of grip. Today the wine would be even more elegant. But this is very good anyway. Will still keep. No undue signs of age.

1984   **Now–2000**

Very good colour for the vintage. Fullish and still very fresh-looking. Some fruit on the nose. Not disagreeable. Still fresh too. This is a very good 1984. Slightly lean. But not coarse. Still fruity if a little austere. Medium body. Drink with food. Very good.

1983   **Now–2000**

Full, very fresh colour. Rich and full, slightly sturdy but this is not too astringent, nor over-ripe. On the palate it is a bit lumpy. And there is some astringency. But good vigour. Nice and fruity. Finishes cleaner than it starts. Good plus for the vintage.

1982   **Drink soon**

Good mature colour. Very stylish and positive. But the fruit surrounding it has dried up a little. On the palate the wine is more vigorous. It has very good substance and it is rich and positive at the end. Will still last well. Very good for a 1982.

1981   **Drink soon**

Surprisingly good colour. Amazingly fresh looking. Quite full too. Slightly faded. And the fruit is becoming neutral. But still enjoyable on the palate. It is fresh. It is not too astringent. And the fruit flavours are balanced and positive. Very good for the vintage.

1980   **Now–2000 plus**

Good fullish mature colour. But no sign of age. This is very good. Rich and concentrated. Blackberries and whortleberries. Fully mature. Slightly four-square at the end. I like this. Complex. Good structure. Balanced. Needs food for there is a little structure apparent, but fresh, stylish and surprisingly complex.

1979   **Now–2000 plus**

Ample, ripe nose. Quite exotic. More evolved, more spice and toffee than the 1980. This is surprisingly concentrated. It is rich, it is fresh and it is lovely. Splendid fruit. Lots of depth. Still very vigorous. A fine example of the vintage.

1978   **Now–2005 plus**

Fine colour. Just about mature. Fine nose. Real class and depth here. A lovely concentrated wine. Very good grip. And this of course, is even better than the 1979. You don't often get a Beaune with this richness and concentration. Great class. Splendid vigour. Essence of fruit. Brilliant!

1977   **Drink up**

Surprisingly good fresh colour for the vintage. Splendid nose too. Still very fruity, only a touch of old tea. On the palate a bit one-dimensional. A little dirty. Yet the fruit that remains is very praiseworthy.

1976   **Now–1999**

Splendid full fresh colour. Still very vigorous. Roasted nose. But good richness. Good depth. Fresh fruit. A big, meaty wine for food. Full, rich, very well balanced. A little four-square, even dense. But it has good grip. Nicely ripe.

1975   **Drink up**

Lightish mature colour. But no undue age. This is a bit thin, unsurprisingly. But there is no rot, no real lack of fruit considering that it is twenty years old. Indeed this is cleaner and more agreeable than the 1977.

1974   **Past its best**

I am sure this colour is surprisingly vigorous for a 1974. Not much on the nose except for a bit of SO$_2$. This is the least good of all. Now weak and blowsy. Nothing left.

1973   **Drink soon**

Very good colour for the vintage. No undue maturity. Fresh on the nose, but a little light. This is not at all bad. Now just a bit astringent. But not dirty. Medium body. Fruity. A bit one-dimensional. But a most pleasant bottle in its prime.

1972   **Now–2000**

Surprisingly deep colour. Still very vigorous. Full, meaty nose. Ripe and stylish. Not austere. Full, firm. Good acidity. A bit, vigorous, classy wine. Plenty of depth. Rather more opulent and fat and less lean and austere than most. Will still keep well. Very good indeed.

1971   **Now–2000 plus**

Full, vigorous colour. No undue maturity. Lovely nose. Class, depth, concentration and very complex fruit here. Plenty of vigour. Full, round, ripe and very elegant. This is concentrated, smooth and velvety and has real class and depth. Fine. Long. Vigorous. Lovely.

HENRI GOUGES,
NUITS-SAINT-GEORGES

Senior in Nuits-Saint-Georges in terms of both age and quality is the Domaine Henri Gouges. Henri Gouges was one of the very first in the whole of Burgundy to market his wines in bottle, back in the 1920s; and, with the exception of a dip in the early 1980s, when the average age of the vines in the exploitation was less than desirable, the quality of the Gouges wines has always been of the very highest. The older wines are splendid. The vintages since 1987, and particularly so since 1990, are equally exciting.

The Domaine Henri Gouges has been a pioneer in a number of ways. Not only in domaine-bottling but in the production of a white wine, rare in the Côte-de-Nuits, and in the Gouges' case uniquely from degenerated Pinot Noir which produces white grapes. Moreover the domaine run by Pierre and his cousin Christian, in charge of the vineyards and the wine respectively, has been one of the first to plant a special grass in order to prevent erosion, which as a beneficial side-effect persuades the roots to delve deeper, resulting in a wine with better acidity and extract than hitherto. Visiting the Gouges domaine today is a refreshing experience. Elsewhere there are prima donnas, some of whom cannot tolerate even a suggestion of criticism of their wines. The Gouges cousins are naturally proud of their heritage and perfectionists about what they do, but there is an engaging readiness to accept past mistakes and to learn by them which is rare even today, and a coherent philosophy of respect for *terroir*, *cépage* and *millésime* for which the unprejudiced viewer can have nothing but the highest regard.

HISTORY

There have been Gouges in Burgundy since the seventeenth century. Not unnaturally, they have been involved in the wine trade. Before the First World War a Henri-Joseph Gouges was *chef de culture* for the *négociants* Misserey-Rollet in Nuits-Saint-Georges. Additionally, not only did he own a few parcels of vines on his own account, but he was a *pépiniériste*: he produced grafted cuttings for the first generation of post-phylloxera plantings. This Gouges had married a Grivot. So the family are distant cousins of today's Grivots of Vosne-Romanée.

Henri-Joseph's eldest son, also called Henri, was born in 1899. On his return from the war in 1919 he presented his father with an ultimatum. Either you sell me your vines or I shall remain in the army - he was the deputy head of music in his regiment. Father acceded, and today's Domaine Henri Gouges was born. During the 1920s and 1930s the estate was enlarged: the Pruliers and the Saint-Georges were acquired in 1920 and 1921; the *monopole* of Clos-des-Porrets in 1934. The domaine has not been altered since.

Henri had two sons, Michel and Marcel, but remained in charge until the day of his death in 1967. His portrait - a photo in one of the downstairs reception rooms - shows a rather severe, moustached, heavy-jowled man with a large forehead: not exactly a beauty, but quite evidently someone of great force of character, a bit of an autocrat.

Christian Gouges, the youngest of his grandchildren, remembers him and the formal, interminable (for a small boy), regular Sunday lunches. Henri Gouges was a gourmet, indeed himself something of a chef, and he was acquainted, naturally enough, with all the great *hôteliers* and *cuisiniers* of the region. These would be invited to swell the family ranks on the weekend. There would be much serious talk about wine, and course after course of fine food accompanied by great bottles, leaving the children bored and restless at the other end of the table until relief came and they were paroled, able to go away and play in the garden.

The weekend was usually the occasion when all the children had their weekly bath. But not always. On occasion the bath (there was only one in the house) would be occupied by large pike, still alive, awaiting their Sunday doom. The fish thrashed about, slopping water all over the place, exhibiting their fierce, razor-sharp teeth in a menacing fashion. It was not permitted to toy with them.

THE DOMAINE

The Gouges domaine extends over a little more than 14.50 hectares, all of it (except generics) in Nuits-Saint-Georges, and all except the 0.43 ha of Chaignots, a *premier cru* on the Vosne-Romanée side (the vines here are relatively young: seventeen years old), located between the town of Nuits and the commune boundary with Prémeaux.

Pride of place must be given to a 1-hectare-plus parcel in Nuits' greatest *climat*, Les Saint-Georges. Here, as in most of the rest of the domaine, the average age is now around forty years old. The holding in nearby Vaucrains is 0.98 ha, and that in the Pruliers, a couple of hundred metres to the north, is 1.80 ha. There is 1.3 ha of plain village Nuits-Saint-Georges.

But if pride of place goes to the Saint-Georges, the *climat* closest to the Gouges' hearts is their 3.5 ha monopoly of the Clos-des-Porrets-Saint-Georges. This is the triangular northern end of Les Porrets or Les Poirets. In the time of grandfather Henri this was the Gouges' best wine: the vines were the most venerable of the domaine. He, sadly, refused to replant, so when his son took over quite a lot of renovation was required. The average age of the vines throughout the domaine declined, and particularly that in the Clos-des-Porrets. Now the vines in the domaine have regained a respectable average age, that in Clos approaching thirty, and there is a planned programme of replantation to keep the average age high.

In addition to the above, Michel and Marcel Gouges, sons of Henri and fathers of Pierre and Christian, own a further 2.5 ha on their own account, not technically part of Domaine

Gouges, and the produce of this, up to now, has been sold off in bulk. This land was *en friche*, which the brothers replanted in the late 1950s. One parcel consists of a hectare - about half this steep *climat* - of the obscure *premier cru* Les Chaînes-Carteaux, adjacent to Vaucrains and up-slope from Les Saint-Georges.

Despite the proximity of the parcels, the soils - and so, of course, the wines - are different. A couple of years ago the Gouges cousins helped instigate a major review, *climat* by *climat*, of all the Nuits vineyards and the wines they made. Geologists and soil engineers were sent in to analyse the *terroir*. Major tastings, some of which I was able to attend, took place. The result is a very useful booklet, *Crus et Climats de l'Appellation de Nuits-Saint-Georges*, produced by the local *Syndicat Viticole*.

From this one can see that the essential difference between Les Saint-Georges and Les Vaucrains, its immediate neighbour up the slope, is that the first is limestone, the second more often calcite. The former contains more clay, the latter a little sand. Both are very stony, but the Vaucrains contains pieces that it would be no exaggeration to call rocks. And the Vaucrains lies on the steeper slope.

If you compare these with the Clos-des-Porrets and the Pruliers you will notice that in the former there is a lot of gravel, in parts deep, and there is gravel too, though to a lesser extent, in the latter. But while the limestone base of the Saint-Georges is varied, containing Comblanchien stone, the two more northern vineyards lie purely in the pink limestone of Prémeaux. Such are the nuances of Burgundy, and the root cause of the diverse fascination of its wines.

RAY-GRASS

The land is the responsibility and passion of Pierre Gouges, born in 1948, slight, somewhat shy, and *diplômé* in viticulture. He joined his father and uncle in 1967, and was himself joined by his younger, taller, curly-haired cousin Christian, born in 1956, in 1974. Christian holds a *brevet professionnel* in oenology and is responsible for the cellar and the commercial side. The two have been jointly in charge since 1986.

Erosion is a perennial problem in Burgundy. Sudden thunderstorms can wash down the precious soil from the prime vineyards on to the village land on the flat, and has to be laboriously recuperated. Occasional curious indications stand out where the *wrong* soil has been replaced, and this will naturally affect the flavour and character of the wine.

In order to try to combat this threat Pierre had the idea of planting some ray-grass in the Chaînes-Carteaux in 1975. The grass would hold the soil together. But would it increase the risk of frost? Would the taste of the wine be changed? Would its quality?

As far as the Gouges are concerned the experiment was a triumphant success, and ray-grass has now been planted throughout the domaine. Yes, there is a slightly added risk of frost, but all the other side-effects are beneficial. The grass prevents the rooting of weeds. By competing in the surface soil it controls the vigour of the younger vines and forces the roots to go deeper. It removes excess humidity. Moreover, as the vines' nurturing roots are existing in deeper soil which is better balanced than that on the surface, the result is riper fruit, much better natural acidity, and more complex wine.

WINE-MAKING

The Gouges domaine has never over-cropped. Even in prolific vintages such as 1990 and 1992 the overall yield is as low as 35 hectolitres per hectare.

On arrival at the winery the bunches are completely destemmed, the unripe and rotten fruit removed, and the must and pulp vinified in closed vats complete with automatic *pigeage* plungers at temperatures which are allowed to rise to 30–32°C. Vinification lasts ten to twelve days and the temperature is kept high by chaptalising, when this takes place, in stages, rather than all at once at the beginning.

Thereafter the wine is racked, retaining its fine lees, and transferred into barrels in the first-year cellar where it undergoes its malo-lactic fermentation. The Gouges are not keen on a large proportion of new wood, preferring to let the wine speak for itself. 'The fruit must provide the essential character of the wine, not the wood. And the wood must certainly not be over-toasted.' Only 10 per cent of the barrels are renewed annually. After the previous year's crop has been bottled in the early spring the new wine is moved into the second-year cellar, under the house. Today it is neither automatically fined, nor filtered as a matter of rote. It depends on the vintage and the wine. The 1992s, for instance, were bottled without filtration.

RECENT CHANGES

Christian and Pierre Gouges, as I have said, took over in 1986, at a time when the domaine was under criticism. What has been modified since then, I asked?

Firstly the vines have attained a proper average age. Secondly there is a greater control over such things as the temperature of fermentation. This has been raised from around 27-28° to over 30°C, and the length of maceration has also been extended, both enabling greater extraction of flavour and intensity. Thirdly the approach is more flexible. The cousins *saignée*-d in 1986, as should have been done in 1982. The automatic *pigeage* machines were installed in 1987, again aiding extraction. But above all there is the beneficial effect of the ray-grass. This, say the Gouges, has enabled them to maximise the expression of each of their *terroirs* at their disposal, as well as producing better wine.

THE RED WINES

The Gouges portfolio opens with their village wine. This is a true Nuits-Saint-Georges: somewhat severe at the outset, but rich and meaty underneath. It develops well. The next wine you will be offered is the Chaignots. This is beginning to get more *sérieux* as the average age approaches twenty years, and to demonstrate more and more of its Vosne-Romanée proximity. The Clos-des-Porrets is full, rich and complex, with a classic 'central Nuits' structure, a little solid in its youth, but now with plenty of depth. Les Pruliers is barely 200 metres away, but what a contrast: less solid but more massively concentrated and structured with a fine black-fruit nose, and hints of leather and chocolate. Les Vaucrains is often the most brutal of all, always very closed and unforthcoming in cask, and despite its richness and intensity often the least easy to appreciate. At the top of the tree comes Les Saint-Georges, more classy, especially in its youth, full, with excellent fruit and marvellous depth of character. *Chez* Gouges you can clearly see the strong arguments for according *grand cru* status to this *climat*.

THE WHITE WINES

It was back in 1936 that Henri Gouges first noticed that some of his old-vine Pinot Noir in the Clos-des-Porrets was producing white grapes. Intrigued he took cuttings, which he carefully propagated in a gravelly *premier cru* nearby called Les Perrières. Eventually, in 1947, he had enough to produce a barrel or two of white wine. The land-holding here now comprises 0.39 ha, and about 150 cases of Les Perrières *blanc* are produced each year. Fermentation starts in tank, is finished in cask, of which one out of five is new, the temperature being controlled at 18-20°C. The wine is kept on its lees, with *bâtonnage* once a week until Christmas and bottled the following September. There is now, in addition, one barrel's worth of a Clos-des-Porrets *blanc*. This has been produced since 1990.

THE GOUGES STYLE

Gouges Nuits-Saint-Georges are made for keeping. There are no compromises, no nod in the direction of making something easy to enjoy (and therefore to mark highly) after a few months in cask or a year in bottle. The wines in fact often do not show as generously or as stylishly as some others if broached in their youth. But this is no fault. Indeed, as elsewhere, it is a mark in their favour. Wine, after all, is made for drinking during a meal when in its prime. That is the time it can properly be judged. When the 1990s and 1991s are opened in fifteen years or so, no-one will be anything less than deeply impressed with the products of Christian and Pierre Gouges.

THE TASTING

I sampled the following wines in Nuits-Saint-Georges in February 1992.

Nuits-Saint-Georges, 1991 *Optimum drinking* **1999-2012**

Very good colour. Ripe nose, closed-in, but plenty of depth. Fullish, very sophisticated tannins. Very good grip. Rich and meaty and masculine. Firm. Good concentration. Fine for a village wine. Needs time.

Nuits-Saint-Georges, Les Vaucrains, 1991 **2000-2018**

Fine colour. Splendidly rich nose. Real intensity, concentration and depth. Full, very light touch of new oak. Beautifully poised. Lovely black-fruit flavours. Very good grip. Fine tannins. Very classy. This has a lot of dimension. Very long complex finish. Very fine.

Nuits-Saint-Georges, Les Vaucrains, 1990 **2002-2025**

Very fine colour. Very rich, opulent chocolatey nose. Concentrated and ripe. Fatter and more voluminous than the 1991. But beginning to go into its shell. On the palate the style is more exotic than the 1991. Very full. Fine tannins. Marvellous fruit. Very good grip. A big wine. A magnificent one. Splendid finish. Excellent.

Nuits-Saint-Georges, Les Vaucrains, 1989 **1998-2010**

Good colour. Nicely austere on the nose. Quite substantial. Even a touch hard. Typically Nuits-Saint-Georges. Ripe and succulent and seductive on the palate. Medium-full body. Balanced, cherry-raspberry fruit. Fresh and complex and classy. Fine. The 1991 is more *sérieux*, though, and is built for the longer term.

Nuits-Saint-Georges, Les Saint-Georges, 1988 **1998-2018**

Very good colour. Hardly a hint of evolution. A very classy nose here. Complete. Balanced. Poised and intense, if without the same weight or muscle as the 1990. Medium-full. Round

tannins. Very good grip. This is cool and long, classy and complex. Very lovely long lingering finish. Very fine.

Nuits-Saint-Georges, Les Saint-Georges, 1987 **Now-2008**

Good fullish colour. Some maturity. This is a very classy 1987. Ripe, plummy nose. Nicely cool. Just a touch of spice - butterscotch-caramel. Medium-full, ripe, sophisticated flavours, balanced and long. Quite supple. Good structure. Well-integrated tannins. Plenty of class and depth here. Very good plus.

Nuits-Saint-Georges, Les Saint-Georges, 1986 **Now-2003**

Good colour. Again fullish. A little more brown. The nose is not as balanced or as stylish as the 1987. There is a touch of dryness here. A slight lack of freshness. On the palate medium to medium-full. A little looser-knit. Yet there is no lack of structure and no astringency. Good grip. Ripe and long and positive. Good finish. Very good.

Nuits-Saint-Georges, Clos-des-Porrets, 1985 **Now-2005**

Medium-full colour. Fully mature. Soft nose. Fruity but lacks a little intensity. 1986 and 1987 seem better within their context. On the palate ripe, just a suspicion of oak, balanced and elegant. But fully ready. Just a touch diffuse. One and a half dimensions rather than three. Pretty rather than compelling. For the vintage good plus. But at the time the vines here were quite young.

Nuits-Saint-Georges, Les Saint-Georges, 1984 **Drink soon**

Light to medium colour. Fully mature. Surprisingly good nose. Fresh, elegant, fruity. Not too lean. Not a bit tired. Lightish, gentle, even complex, even plump. Long positive finish. This is really enjoyable. Classy. Hats off!

Nuits-Saint-Georges, Les Vaucrains, 1983
Drink soon

Medium colour for a 1983. Some brown. Somewhat hard and dry on the nose like many 1983s. And like many of them it lacks charm and fat. Better on the palate. Plumper, reasonable grip. But a little astringent. Not spoiled. Would be better with food. But rather dry and hard and stemmy. Quite good at best for the vintage.

Nuits-Saint-Georges, Les Saint-Georges, 1982
Drink soon

Rather a light colour. Fully mature. Soft, fragrant nose. But like many 1982s, a little loose-knit. Yet the style of Les Saint-Georges is clearly here. Lightish to medium body. Fully evolved. Reasonable grip. Good fruit, but a little empty at the end. A little fluid. Quite good for the vintage at best.

Nuits-Saint-Georges, Les Vaucrains, 1980
Drink soon

Medium to medium-full colour. Fully mature. Slightly loose but stylish nose. Just a touch lean and vegetal to the fruit. Lightish on the palate. Balanced but getting a little short at the end. But if the structure is a bit feeble it is nevertheless fresh and pleasant. But I have had more exciting 1980s - and ones with plenty more guts. Quite good for the vintage.

Nuits-Saint-Georges, Les Vaucrains, 1979
Drink soon

Better than the 1980. More colour, no undue maturity. More substantial on the nose and palate. A little gamey and rustic on the nose. But no lack of weight in this quarter. There is something charmingly unsophisticated about this wine. The *sauvage* character of Vaucrains is noticeable. Ripe, balanced. Medium-full. Still positive. But no real elegance. Just a hint of astringency at the end.

Nuits-Saint-Georges, Les Saint-Georges, 1978
Now-2005

Medium to medium-full colour. Fresher than the 1979 but still fully mature. Good nose. Rich, round, classy, complex. This is a very good mature Burgundy: *à point* but with bags of life. Medium-full, rich, gamey. Good freshness. Good tannins. Good grip and structure. Plenty of vigour. Ripe and complex. A fine example.

Nuits-Saint-Georges, Les Vaucrains, 1977
Drink up

Lightish, well-matured colour. The nose is still fresh and by no means unattractive. Light, of course: but gentle. And still alive and kicking if a little lean and vegetal. No astringency. Has not coarsened up. Surprisingly good.

Nuits-Saint-Georges, Clos-des-Porrets, 1976
Now-2000 plus

Very good, fullish, rich, vigorous colour. Burnt caramel and some tannin on the nose. But not unduly dense. Full and rich, fat and slightly over-ripe in its fruit. A structured wine which shows a touch of astringency as well as the tannin. Plenty of depth and follow-through, if a little ungainly, and lacking velvetiness. Yet still fresh. And will keep. Long, positive, even complex finish. A wine for food. This is a very good example indeed.

Nuits-Saint-Georges, Clos-des-Porrets, 1975
Drink up

Reasonable colour. But well-matured. Not undrinkable. Some fruit. The dryness of the rot of 1983, but in a much more all-pervasive way. Underneath lean and fruity, with an almost Madeira acidity. This has kept it quite fresh.

Nuits-Saint-Georges, Les Vaucrains, 1974
Drink up

Good colour. Quite full, not too brown. Not a lot on the nose. Soft on the palate. But the character is like a slightly larger 1977. A little riper perhaps. But nonetheless lean. And now a touch of astringency at the end. Not bad.

Nuits-Saint-Georges, Les Pruliers, 1973
Drink soon

Really quite a fullish vigorous colour for 1973. Rich nose, no undue age. Fat and meaty. Not too gamey. Fullish, nicely ripe, charming, plump. Open and accessible. Perhaps it is now beginning to shorten and coarsen. But a lot of pleasure to be had here. Very good for the vintage.

Nuits-Saint-Georges, Les Vaucrains, 1972
Drink soon

Good colour. Like the 1973, but even fresher. There is a certain *sauvage* aggression on the nose which comes from the Vaucrains. High acidity. On the palate a little astringency. A bit lumpy. And a lack of class as well as charm. I prefer the above. I have had better 1972s.

Nuits-Saint-Georges, Clos-des-Porrets, 1971
Drink soon

Oldish colour now. Not too light, but almost a green touch to the brown at the rim. Slightly ungenerous and hard on the nose. Is this a hail taste? Less hard on the palate. Fully mature. Very ripe but really quite evolved. Good acidity and you feel this is beginning to take over, that the wine was fatter and more succulent a decade ago. Yet the finish is still long, classy and complex. Lovely.

Nuits-Saint-Georges, Les Pruliers, 1970

Past its best

This again is really quite old. The nose is light but not disagreeable. And it is pretty dilute and feeble on the palate. Yet it's not dried out. Very obviously a large harvest.

Nuits-Saint-Georges, Clos-des-Porrets, 1962

Now-1999

Good colour. Fresh, vigorous. An intriguing nose. Complex woods and spices and a gently wild raspberry smell. Very classy. On the palate a wine of vigour and concentration and very lovely ripe, complex fruit. Still very sweet. Full, subtle. Long. Splendid. Plenty of life. A fine lingering finish.

Nuits-Saint-Georges, Les Saint-Georges, 1945

Now-2000 plus

Splendid colour. Rich and full and barely mature. On the nose still powerful and structured. Big, tannic. Rather hard at first. Yet very very ripe and concentrated. But nevertheless a little tannic and astringent. But this is only apparent on the attack. The finish is ripe and succulent. Satisfying. Vigorous. Splendid. Best with food.

Nuits-Saint-Georges, Clos-des-Porrets, 1934

Drink soon

Very good colour. Deep rich, only marginally brown. A full structured wine. Fresh. Has been kept longer in cask than is usual these days. Full, quite high acidity. Lots of fruit here and just a faint hint of maderisation. A sturdy vintage, evidently. Long. Best with food. Delicious.

Jean Grivot,
Vosne-Romanée

Opposite the walls which contain the cellars and dependent buildings of the old Marey-Monge estate, recently resuscitated by the Domaine de la Romanée-Conti, along an anonymous road which runs briefly north towards the village cemetery of Vosne-Romanée, you will find the headquarters of the Grivot family, proprietors of one of the village's most important and most parcellated estates. This domaine has long been established as one of Vosne-Romanée's best, and has been bottling and selling direct since before the war. But in recent years it has been surrounded by controversy. Why the fuss? The reason can be expressed in one word: Accad.

Much has been written, most of it ill-informed nonsense, about Guy Accad and his methods. A lot of this has been the fault of the man himself, a hopeless communicator. He may like to cover himself in mystery; but the results have been unfortunate, not least for the criticism levelled at those who have adopted his approach to viticulture and viniculture. The impression has been given that there are simply two camps in Burgundy: Accad on the one side and 'proper' Burgundy on the other. This is to forget that not only are there 101 non-Accad ways of making wine – just permutate different amounts of new oak, percentages of stems, length of maceration and varying temperatures of fermentation for a start – but that each of the so-called Accadiens have responded with their own personal interpretation of the maestro's ideas; and these have evolved with the times. Critics have rushed to judgement, the techniques have been glossed over, and the basic philosophy behind the ideas has been obscured. Evaluation has not been easy, not least because the youthful Accad wines have not sung out, and have even tasted alien. But Etienne Grivot now has nine Accad vintages under his belt, and the oldest are approaching maturity. We can now taste the results. The proof is today apparent. Put simply: it works.

HISTORY

The origins of the Grivot family lie in the upper reaches of the river Doubs, 100 kilometres to the east in the Jura, but Grivots have been established in Burgundy since the French Revolution. At first they lived in Nuits-Saint-Georges, farming vines at Arcenats in the Hautes-Côtes and at Corgoloin, but raising other crops as well. A branch then moved to Vosne-Romanée, and slowly but surely the activities of this side of the family concentrated on wine production. Gaston Grivot, son of Joseph and father of Jean, sold his vines in these lesser areas in 1919 in order to buy an important piece of Clos-de-Vougeot from a M. Polack. He was one of the first to pursue a proper oenological degree at Dijon University in the 1920s. And he had the foresight to marry Madelaine, daughter of Emile Grivot of Nuits-Saint-Georges in 1927 - no close relation, but surely a distant cousin - who brought vines in Pruliers and Roncières with her as a dowry. Jean Grivot, the present head of the family, was born in 1928. He too studied at Dijon, married a Jayer, inheriting vines in Chambolle, Vosne-Romanée, Les Rouges and Echézeaux from her and her sister Jacqueline, and, in 1984, acquired a parcel of land in Richebourg, formerly owned by the Vienot estate, dividing it with Jean Mongeard. Little by little, therefore, a sizeable (by Burgundian standards) domaine has been created. There are currently forty parcels of vines spread over 14.35 hectares, and twenty different wines. From 1959 all has been sold in bottle.

Currently the Grivot domaine can boast three Nuits-Saint-Georges *premiers crus*: Boudots (seventy-five-year-old vines), Pruliers (half sixty-year-old vines, half replanted in 1993), and Roncières (average age forty years old); five Vosne-Romanée *premiers crus*: Beaux-Monts, Brûlées, Chaumes, Suchots and Rouges - all thirty to fifty years' average age; 0.31 ha of sixty-year-old Richebourg; 0.61 ha of forty-five-year-old Echézeaux; and the largest and most important piece of all, 1.86 ha of Clos-de-Vougeot, a substantial section several rows of vines wide which ranges uphill from the main road in the centre of the *climat*. 'I'm no chicken,' says the sixty-five-year-old Jean Grivot, 'but there are plenty of vines on our domaine which are older than I am.' The Grivot aim is to preserve this venerable age in the vineyard. Each year, as vines die or become semi-recumbent, some 800 individual vines, one-sixtieth of the total, are replaced. Only occasionally, as with half the Pruliers recently, is it reluctantly necessary to replace whole parcels of vines.

ÉTIENNE GRIVOT

Étienne Grivot, son of Jean, born in 1959, and now married to Marielle, daughter of Simon Bize of Savigny-lès-Beaune, joined his father after his own viti- and vinicultural studies and work experience elsewhere in France and in California in 1982.

Like his father, Étienne is a thinker, an intelligent, serious man, the last to rush after the latest fad, someone who works things through carefully before he acts. Why then should it be he, of all people, who would succumb - as some might put it - to the seductions of Guy Accad? Let him speak for himself.

'I felt,' says Étienne, 'that our wines of the early 1980s, the 1970s and even the 1960s were elegant and harmonious, but except in the very great vintages they lacked staying power. Modern-day wines seemed to lack the concentration and structure of those of earlier times. Yet the vines were old; we didn't over-produce [the Grivot domaine, both pre- and post-Accad, makes no more than 38 hl/ha even in its village appellations, around 30 hl/ha in the top *climats*], and we didn't under-macerate. What had gone wrong? I wanted to know how I could add more *puissance* to something which was already generous, complex and balanced. The potential was there. How could I make it actual?

'In my school I had a very imaginative teacher, and when I met Guy Accad I realised I had been thinking on the same lines for years. We knew already that Burgundy had been excessively over-fertilised for years, that the addition of too much nitrogen, phosphorus and potassium had undermined the equilibrium of the soil; that moreover it had blocked the magnesium necessary for effective photosynthesis to take place. The result was a deficiency in the production of chlorophyll. The fruit was simply not ripening, and therefore concentrating, as well as in the past. Without proper grape maturity one cannot produce wines of power and longevity. . . . My approach therefore is biological. We treat the vineyard as a complex, integrated mechanism. We need to establish an equilibrium. Upset one element and you destroy the whole thing.'

So far, so uncontroversial. Just about everybody producing serious Burgundy would agree. Indeed there are many domaines who follow these tenets in the vineyard whether they employ Guy Accad as a viticultural consultant or not. Fertilisation has been dispensed with; treatments have been reduced, and are less necessary as the vines themselves are more healthy and therefore more resistant to infestation; the amount of vines per hectare has been increased, from 8,000 to 10,000 to 12,000 to 15,000; and pruning is drastically short. Étienne is sceptical about green harvesting, for reducing the quantity of grapes and producing more or less the same quantity, which is what usually happens, will only produce less concentrated wine, for the ratio of juice to grape-skins, which is where the flavour lies, is only increased. In his view a *saignée* is preferable. Even better, he suspects, may well be the possibility of enriching the must by evaporating out some of the water - the technique known as *évaporation à pression atmosphérique*, and now undergoing experimental trials in certain domaines.

THE ACCAD METHOD

Where the controversy arises is in the cellar, after the harvest has taken place. The principle, having produced fully mature, concentrated fruit in the first place - and this may mean significantly delaying the harvest; but with healthy vines this should present less of a problem than with grapes grown on neutral, over-fertilised soil - is to maximise the potential of this fruit by giving it a structure which will sustain it, i.e. to maximise the body, the tannin and the acidity. In order to produce a wine which is capable of long ageing the must needs to be protected against oxidation both while it is being transformed into wine and thereafter.

The Accadiens believe that a better extraction of both tannins and flavour compounds occurs in aqueous solution, i.e before the fermentation has taken place. The must is therefore deliberately cooled, if necessary, sufficiently sulphured to kill the oxidase enzymes, and allowed to macerate for several days, even as long as a week, before the fermentation is allowed to take place. There is then a long *cuvaison*, again at a relatively cool temperature, in order to obtain a further extraction of tannin, extract and aroma.

In the Grivot cellar, having originally macerated *à froid* for six or seven days, Étienne now finds that four or five days are sufficient. He used to use artificial yeasts, but has now reverted to natural yeasts. Believing both that a lot of new wood accelerates ageing, producing wines which are both ready to drink sooner and do not last as long in bottle, and that an excess of new oak masks *terroir* individuality, Grivot only employs about 5 per cent new barrels a year overall. Moreover the wine spends the whole of its first winter in tank, before being racked into small casks.

It is current practice in Burgundy to rack as little as possible, perhaps only twice during the wine's *élevage*. Grivot disagrees: 'I don't think a great Burgundy is as fragile a wine as this would suggest. It certainly shouldn't be if it is vinified properly. I rack in January, in May after the malo, when I transfer the wine into cask, in September and then again before bottling. Equally, a great Burgundy can easily sustain a full two years in wood. I bottled my 1990s in August and September 1992, though I considered three months earlier suitable for the 1991s.' The wines are not fined, filtered very lightly, if at all, and bottled by gravity.

DEVELOPMENTS

Étienne Grivot has always maintained that he did what *he* wanted to do, not just because Guy Accad said so, and he describes his approach now as much less Accadien than in 1987 and 1988, when he first adopted the guru's vinification ideas. Over the years he has learned by experience, and modified the techniques. Flexibility, he points out, is the keynote to the Accad approach. The methods are in fact *less* rigid than elsewhere. And he has now severed his contract with Guy Accad. 'But I have no quarrel with him,' Grivot explains. 'I have no regrets and I have learned an enormous amount. But Accad has created a lot of ill-feeling. He has been clumsy. There was not enough communication.'

CRITICISMS

There are a number of interlocking criticisms levied at wines made by the Accad technique: that they are over-sulphured, that they do not taste like Burgundy, that they will not last.

Accad wines certainly *do* taste strange when they are in cask, though in the case of Étienne Grivot's wines less so today than they did at the outset. The 1987s took more than a year to finish their malo-lactic fermentations, and I found them almost impossible to judge in November 1988. (Grivot will point out, however, that this had nothing to do with the Accad method, nor the sulphur dioxide, but was because he harvested too early.) But nevertheless they are odd, and in a blind tasting of wines only recently in bottle - for instance the 1988s in January 1991 - I have marked them down purely because they did not seem true to type. This is to their disadvantage. But that a wine seems atypical at the beginning need not necessarily mean that it will always be so.

The techniques of prolonging the *macération à froid*, and the necessity of protecting the must from oxidation, means adding more sulphur at this stage than is usual, but equally there is no reason to add any more later. The wines when bottled contain no more than those of any non-Accadien wine-maker.

At the outset it was said that the method would not produce *vins de garde*. As the whole point of the exercise was to do precisely this I never quite understood this allegation. After all, whatever one might have thought about the technique itself, one could not escape the fact that neither Étienne Grivot nor Guy Accad - nor indeed Jean Grivot himself - are total fools. Indeed quite the opposite.

Sampling the 1987 wines today proves this allegation to be totally false. This is a mixed year, and some wines have not evolved well. Some are prematurely brown at the rim, some are attenuated, some have rather unsubtle tannins. Not so the Grivot wines. They have a fine colour, plenty of dimension and vigour, plenty of fruit, and plenty of style. Sampling the other recent vintages shows that these wines, if anything, will have a longer life than those produced by more traditional methods.

TYPICITY

This is the thorny problem. Are Accad wines typical of Burgundy? Of course the first obvious retort is typical of what? Typical of the sort of weak wine which even in an excellent vintage like 1971 was unable to last the course? Or typical of 'real' Burgundy as it was in the 1940s and 1950s, and before the war? The difficulty is that only the old-age pensioners among us tasted these wines when they were very young.

One thing must be obvious. The viticultural approach of Grivot and his friends must produce wines which are potentially at least more true to their *terroir* than those from vineyards which are over-protected and over-fertilised. Denser planting, later harvesting and a reduced crop must similarly be a plus in the direction of site specificity.

But does the vinification method obliterate this, as say the critics, or re-establish this, as say the Accad adherents?

While we will really have to wait for another ten years, in order to be able to sample the 1988s, 1989s and 1990s in their prime as fully mature bottles, one can already, I believe extrapolate from the way these vintages and the 1987s show today to answer the question in the positive sense. The *terroir* has not been displaced. The wines are not atypical. The Accad method works.

And while we are about it we should acknowledge that this idea of cold pre-fermentation maceration is not so revolutionary after all. Before the days of temperature control, Burgundy being Burgundy, October harvests being more usual than not, and northern Europe normally being quite cool by this time, especially at night, grapes were frequently gathered at sub-10°C temperatures, and the fermentation process would equally often take four or five days to get going. Wine in the old days therefore followed the same process. Except that the thing was more hit and miss.

CONCLUSION

Let's leave the last word to Jean Grivot. What had his reaction been when Etienne first proposed changing his vinification methods? 'I agreed that we must do everything possible to maximise the intensity and *puissance* of our wines. And as soon as we compared our 1987s with those of our neighbours I was convinced we had done the right thing. Ours were so much better.'

And *do* the current Grivot wines resemble those which were made in the old days? 'I remember the 1937s and the 1945s and the 1949s. When they were young they were almost undrinkable: harsh, rough and even coarse. But look how they turned out! Today wines are made to be accessible for tasting after six months. You could criticise them for being too *flatteurs*. Our own wines today remind me of how the old wines tasted when they were young. And I am sure they will last just as well.'

THE TASTING

I sampled the following wines *chez* Grivot in June 1993.

1991

All had been recently bottled.

Optimum drinking

Vosne-Romanée Now-2006

Medium colour. The nose is suffering a bit from the recent bottling. Ripe enough. Medium body. Good grip. But it is difficult to see the nuances and the elegance. On aeration: plump, soft, good depth.

Nuits-Saint-Georges, Les Boudots 1998-2008

Medium-full colour. Ripe, rich, definitive nose. More accessible. Fuller, rounder, rich, old-viney. This has plenty of grip and depth and intensity. Long. Very good indeed.

Clos-de-Vougeot 1999-2012

Fullish colour. A bit shocked by the bottling. Ripe, gently oaky. Fullish, certainly complex. But difficult to really judge. On aeration: very good fruit, concentration, very good style, very complex.

1990

Bottled end August/beginning September 1992.

Vosne-Romanée 1999-2009

Fullish colour. Plump and rich, cool and stylish on the nose. On the palate this is medium-full, ripe and has good intensity. Ample and accessible. A wine of real charm. Very good for a village example.

Nuits-Saint-Georges, Les Boudots 1999-2012

Fullish colour. Complex nose. Poised Pinot Noir fruit. Medium-full body. Fragrant, harmonious, classy, complex. Underneath it has the Nuits backbone, but this is a well-mannered example. Rich, intense. Long. Very good indeed.

Clos-de-Vougeot 2000-2018

Full colour. Fat, ample and concentrated, and of course rich on the nose. Fuller than the Nuits. More tannin, more backbone. But has more depth. This is a bit adolescent at present. Is closing in. But a fine example. Very long. Very promising.

1989

Bottled August/September 1991.

Vosne-Romanée   **Now–2006**
Medium to medium-full colour. Soft, ripe, generous nose. Plenty of fruit here. Medium full, ample, even rich on the palate. Good acidity. Once again this shows well. Plenty of future.

Nuits-Saint-Georges, Les Boudots   **1998–2010**
Medium to medium-full colour. This has a very lovely nose. More noticeably oaky. (New oak in this *cuvée* but not nearly as much in 1990.) Refined fruit. Round, seductive. Medium-full body. Generous. Long. Lovely.

Clos-de-Vougeot   **1998–2012**
Medium to medium-full colour. Rich, fat, full, concentrated nose. This has plenty of depth and vigour. Still very young. This has a faint touch of reduction about it. On the palate I find a slight lack of intensity at first, but after a bit of aeration, the wine was concentrated, gently oaky, intense and elegant. Harmonious and long and complex too. Fine.

1988

Bottled August/September 1990.

Vosne-Romanée   **Now–2009**
Very good colour. Fine, firm nose. Lovely Pinot fruit. Nice combination of richness and austerity. Touch of oak. Fullish. Masculine. On the palate still unresolved. But the finish is ripe and long. Very good indeed. Lovely.

Nuits-Saint-Georges, Les Boudots   **1999–2012**
Very good colour. Fine nose. Excellent depth and style. Complex and concentrated and - despite Accad methods - classic. This is a very fine example. Full, rich, concentrated, nicely austere. Follows through very well indeed. Very good intensity. Very long and complex.

Clos-de-Vougeot   **2000–2015**
Very good colour. The most closed on the nose. The most adolescent on the palate. Expanded in the glass. Rich, marvellously balanced. Fullish. Very good structure. This has lovely fruit. Excellent grip.

Richebourg   **2004–2020**
This had been decanted at 8 o'clock that morning. Marvellous colour. Excellent nose. Marvellous blackberry-raspberry Pinot nose. Still very very youthful. Very profound, very concentrated. Fullish, balanced, very intense.

Real breed. A wine of huge concentration and potential. Substantial and concentrated. *Grand vin.*

1987

Vosne-Romanée   **Now–2000 plus**
Good colour. No undue brown. Ripe and fresh on the nose. This is vigorous and plump. Good fruit. Ample, round, generous, stylish. Good backbone. Above all, good finesse. Plenty of life. Long, balanced. Very good indeed.

Nuits-Saint-Georges, Les Boudots   **Now–2005**
Good colour. A little brown. Concentrated nose. Very good straight Pinot. Complex too. Ripe, quite substantial. Very good stylish fruit. Very good acidity. Long. Subtle. Vigorous. Very good finish. Finesse here. Fine for the vintage.

Clos-de-Vougeot   **Now–2009**
Good colour. A little brown. A fatter wine, more aromatic, than the Nuits, Boudots. Fullish, very good grip. Very good class, concentration and intensity. Very fine finish. Lots of vigour.

VOSNE-ROMANÉE, LES BEAUX-MONTS

1978   **Now–2000 plus**
Magnum. Very good colour. Still very vigorous. Fine nose. Good grip of acidity. Ripe, elegant. Youthful. Medium-full, round, plump, elegant. Subtle. This is composed. Long, lovely complex finish. Still young. High class.

1976   **Now–2000**
Good colour. Still very youthful. Ripe and rich and aromatic. A little dryness of tannin on the nose. Richer and sweeter than the 1978. Fatter, slightly more alcohol. Not quite as elegant or complex, but fuller, more ample and more substantial. Very good indeed. And still with plenty of life. Long on the palate.

1972   **Drink soon**
Medium colour. Mature. No undue age. This is medium bodied. Fresh and ripe. Fragrant on nose and palate. No undue acidity. Subtle, stylish. Long. Really fine finish. Very good.

1969   **Drink soon**
Fullish, mature colour. This is rich and meaty and mellow on the nose. On the palate ripe, aromatic, a little evidence of alcohol. Sweetly perfumed, a touch of caramel and cooked fruit.

1964   **Now–2000 plus**
This is a lovely wine. Fine vigorous mature nose. Fuller, richer and sweeter and more vigorous than the 1969. Dynamic, velvety. Very good grip. Marvellous fruit. Complete. *Grand vin.*

Clos-de-Vougeot

1959 **Now–2000 plus**

Fine colour. Ample full nose. Still very vigorous. Quite structured. Meaty. Rich and ripe and concentrated and sweet also. A bigger wine than the Beaux-Monts 1964. Real depth and quality. *Grand vin* again.

1937 **Drink soon**

Amazing colour. Slightly austere on the nose and lightish acidity on the palate. Yet ripe, vigorous, fresh. Slightly chunky. Fullish. Surprisingly vigorous. Not a trace of astringency. Long. Fine.

ROBERT GROFFIER,
MOREY-SAINT-DENIS

Here is a question for a wine quiz: name a leading grower in Morey-Saint-Denis who doesn't have a single vine in the commune. A clue? He's the biggest land-holder in Chambolle-Musigny, Les Amoureuses - which of all the *premiers crus* is the leading contender for *grand cru* status. The answer is Robert Groffier.

Robert Groffier is like his wine. As pets are said to resemble their owners, so do wines. Groffier is self-effacing, gentle, pacific. His wines are soft but intense, elegant but understated, delicate and subtle. They are, naturally, mainly Chambolle-Musignys. He resides in a nineteenth-century mansion set in a courtyard surrounded by wine-making buildings which lies on the *Route des Grands Crus* directly below the Clos-de-Tart. But his 7 hectare domaine contains no Morey vines. In the past you could criticise the Groffier results for sometimes being too insubstantial and for sometimes being not quite as stylish as they could be. But today, with a reduced *rendement* and greater control, they are more consistently some of the finest in all Burgundy. If you are looking for real Pinot Noir - complexity, purity and finesse, rather than power, muscle and gaminess - this is the place to come.

HISTORY

Groffier is not an uncommon name in the Côte d'Or today; and if you look back into the archives you will see the name listed in 1855 among the owners of Musigny, Bonnes-Mares and Chambolle-Musigny, Les Fuées. These Groffiers, however, do not have anything to do with today's Groffier in Morey-Saint-Denis. The origin of this domaine was a Frédéric Groffier towards the end of the nineteenth century. One of his children, Jules (1898-1974), was a champion both in boxing and cycling, and became president of the Sporting Club of Dijon. It was he, from the 1930s onwards, who built up the present estate. He acquired his Amoureuses, Bonnes-Mares and Hauts-Doix from a firm of *négociants* called Peloux in 1933. After the war some Sentiers followed and in 1953 he bought 42 ares of Chambertin, Clos-de-Bèze from another merchant, Gauvin, based in Chalon.

In 1960 he passed his inheritance down the line. One-third went to a daughter, Madame Gérard Peirazeau (whose share has always been sold off in bulk) and the rest to his sons Robert (born 1931) and Jean-Claude. Jean-Claude was a haemophiliac - infected with contaminated blood, he died recently of AIDS - and was less interested in the vine. Helped by money from his wife's side - she comes from Nuits-Saint-Georges - Robert was able to buy Jean-Claude out, and it was from this time that the domaine began to bottle itself and seek out export customers. Since 1973 the majority of the crop has been sold in bottle, and though they continued to reserve a little for Drouhin up to relatively recently, nothing is today sold off in bulk. Before the war, however, Jules had already experimented with estate-bottling, and had even opened a shop in the village to sell his wine to passers by. But this was more of a reaction to the pittances paid by the local merchants during the slump. The endeavour didn't last.

Today Robert is assisted by his son Serge, who is in his early forties, and the two make a good team. Serge does most of the work in the vineyard, and lives with his wife and small family next door; Robert is in charge in the cellar. And Madame Groffier, women having a better head for figures than men, is in charge of the accounts.

THE DOMAINE

We drive first to Chambertin, Clos-de-Bèze. Groffier's 10 *ouvrées*, enough to make seven or eight barrels in a good year, lie to the north of the *climat*, above Chapelle-Chambertin and below the *premier cru* of Bel-Air. Since 1991 he has changed the training method to Cordon du Royat, enabling him to space the bunches (six to eight per vine) out more. Not only does this give him a greater control over the size of his crop, but he avoids the threat of rot. Moreover, he gains half a degree of potential alcohol. The grapes are riper. The vines here are forty years old.

Opposite the Mazoyères part of Charmes-Chambertin, on the 'wrong' side of the road, lie Groffier's village vines. There are various parcels of various ages, totalling 82 ares. Further along, below the delimitation of Morey, he produces Bourgogne *rouge* and lesser generics - there is more generic land below Clos-de-Vougeot - and he has his *potager*. All his vines, except one or two of the most venerable plots, are today ploughed and hoed.

Drive up from Vougeot to the village of Chambolle-Musigny and you will see, uncharacteristically flamboyant, the name Robert Groffier et Fils, Les Amoureuses picked out in white capitals on the face of the rock. There are faults in the limestone here, and above Vougeot several small cliffs step up from the village wines to Amoureuses and Le Musigny itself like a giant staircase. Robert owns 1.12 hectares of Amoureuses made up from three adjoining sections on slightly different levels. The vines average twenty-six years old. Next door lies his Hauts-Doix: 1 hectare of thirty-year-old vines. To prevent erosion the prunings are minced up and left to mulch on the ground.

We turn back towards Morey. Above the road is Bonnes-Mares, where Groffier owns 1 hectare of thirty-year-old vines next to the plots of his sister and Georges Lignier towards the Morey end of the *climat*. Below is a further hectare of his third Chambolle *premier cru*, Les Sentiers.

WINE-MAKING

Much has changed in the last decade or so. How much of this is Serge's influence, how much the general Burgundian increased concern for perfectionism I do not know, but it goes a long way towards explaining the greater consistency and higher quality of the Groffier wines.

For a start the *rendement* has been reduced. While Robert considers that you don't gain anything by going as low as 25 hl/ha, he now crops all his *grands crus* and *premiers crus* at 30–35 hl/ha. That's the optimum, in his view. Because he has stopped fertilising and uses less organic compost he obtains a better colour. There is more solid matter, less juice in the fruit. He now picks later but quicker, giving him more time to supervise the wine-making. He and Serge now pass through the vines before the harvest, cutting out what is sub-standard, to aid the job of the harvesters. And, since 1994, there is a *table de tri*.

The wine is vinified in enamelled- and stainless-steel tanks, with the help of a *pigeoir automatique*. While up to 1984 he vinified with all the stems there is now almost total destemming, except for the Clos-de-Bèze. Groffier likes to see his fermentation temperatures go up to 35°C, to extract the '*matière*', and this he can do without anything rustic being created because he employs selected yeasts. The top wines get 80 per cent new oak, the *premiers crus* 60 per cent. Having filtered using *Kieselguhr* in the 1980s, he now doesn't filter at all, bottling directly off the fining (which is done with white of egg) in the March of the second year. Some of the 1993 was not fined either.

THE WINES

At the start of the Groffier portfolio lies the Gevrey-Chambertin. The soil below the *grand cru* of Charmes where the vines are planted is gravelly, well-drained, and the wines here are less sturdy than they are above the village on the Brochon side. In Robert Groffier's hands this becomes very much a Chambolle-lover's Gevrey: soft, plump, intense but atypical.

The Hauts-Doix and the Sentiers repeat, at a lower level, the difference between Musigny and Bonnes-Mares; the former all grace and texture, the latter more black fruity, firmer, richer and more succulent, but with no less finesse. Groffier's Amoureuses is one of the best in the Côte d'Or, more intense than the Hauts-Doix, more classy too, long, complex and more oaky: a lovely example.

Then we come to the Bonnes-Mares. Groffier's example is more like that of Freddy Mugnier than that of the Domaine Roumier, that is on the lighter side, but this is nevertheless a firmer, more vigorous, more masculine wine than the rest of his Chambolles. The Clos-de-Bèze is similarly softer than most. Sometimes I seek a bit more structure here. But I can't fault the fruit or the harmony. This is a top domaine, and the wines have all the elegance and purity of Pinot Noir that you would wish.

THE TASTING

I sampled the following wines *chez* Groffier in February 1995. Unless stated otherwise, all vintages are Chambolle-Musigny, Les Amoureuses.

CHAMBOLLE-MUSIGNY, LES AMOUREUSES

1992   **Now-2005**

Medium to medium-full colour. Lovely round, elegant, fragrant nose. At present just a little lean on the palate. It appears a little lightweight at first, but it is certainly fruity and persistent. Long and stylish on the palate. A typical 1992. It will evolve soon into a most satisfactory and charming bottle. Very complex at the end.

1991   **1999-2015**

Medium-full colour. Rich, concentrated, gently oaky nose. Very stylish. Excellent depth. Very classy. The malos were very late to finish here. But the result in bottle is splendid. Fine acidity. Very good ripe tannins. Medium-full. Long. Delicious. Very lovely Chambolle fruit. Fine for the vintage.

1990   **2000-2018**

Very good colour. On the nose this is a little disturbed and adolescent at first, but after a quarter of an hour it was much improved. Fine on the palate though. Deliciously rich and concentrated. Fullish, fat and ripe. But with heaps of Chambolle fruit. Some tannin. Very good grip. Lush, succulent and very good indeed.

1989   **1998-2015**

Very good for 1989. Rich, fullish nose for this vintage. Plenty of lovely elegant complex fruit. Plenty of depth and substance. Rich and succulent. Intense and fragrant. Still very youthful. Very good grip for a 1989. Very long, lovely finish. Fine.

1988   **1998-2015**

Very good colour. Still quite closed on the nose. Good touch of wood here. Concentrated, subtle, vigorous. Good grip. On the palate this starts off well, but then the follow-through lacks just a little thrust and consistency. The finish is a touch hard and a little vacant. But this is still adolescent. After a quarter of an hour it seems to gain strength and length at the end. On evolution I rate it very good plus for the vintage. Still needs time.

Bonnes-Mares, 1987   **Now-2004**

Good colour for the vintage. A little dry on the nose at first. Much better on the palate. Round and soft. Quite fat and rich for a 1987. Good touch of spice. Fresh, fullish, plenty of depth here. This is a fine 1987. Classy, vigorous, very good acidity. No hard edges. Good length. Not the class of the wines above nevertheless.

1986   **Now-1999**

Reasonable colour. Still really quite fresh. A little gamey on the nose. Finish and plump on the palate. It doesn't have the concentration of the Bonnes-Mares 1987, but it is well matured and plump. Still fresh, still elegant. A touch diffuse of course but a very good example of the vintage.

1985   **Now-2004**

They had a very small harvest here in 1985, because of frost, which even hit in the Amoureuses. Good colour, now mature. Sturdy nose, ripe and plummy, but slightly four-square. Fullish on the palate, rich and ripe. Good acidity. But a slightly hard, spicy edge. It lacks a bit of harmony. It could have been so elegant and velvety! Will still round off though. So perhaps in three to four years it will show better. Very good for the vintage at best.

1984   **Drink soon**

Fresh colour still. And fresh on the nose. There is still fruit and sweetness here though it is beginning to get lean and vegetal. But as 1984s go it goes very well. This is more elegant than the 1985. Plump and agreeable still. Plenty of enjoyment to be had. Long, complex finish. A fine example of a 1984.

1983   **Now-2000 plus**

Fully evolved colour. On the nose soft, quite succulent, alcoholic. But the alcohol not excessively marked. On the palate a suggestion of a hail taste. Yet the wine is not too dry, tannic or astringent. This is not undrinkable. Rich, fresh, really quite plump. A pity about the hail taste. Yet this is less apparent on the finish, and would be with food. For a 1983 this still has plenty of vigour. But a funky wine.

1982   **Drink up**

A well-matured, light to medium colour. Slightly weedy on the nose. Light on the palate, pleasantly fruity, but rather insubstantial. This was very obviously a huge vintage. Yet it is not too old, nor is it too short, nor is it coarse.

1981

All sold to the *négoce*.

1980   **Now-2000 plus**

Good youthful colour. This is round and fresh and succulent. Good freshness. A delicious bottle. Vigorous, ripe, balanced, stylish. Medium to medium-full. Still plenty of fruit. Elegant, complex and harmonious. Not a blockbuster, but a most attractive bottle. And it doesn't lack grip and backbone either.

Bonnes-Mares, 1979   Now-2000

Lots of hail at the flowering. Good, substantial, vigorous colour. A little dumb on the nose at first. There is some CO_2 here, but this has kept the wine fresh. Slightly fuller than the 1980, a little more four-square, a little rigid and spicy. But not as long on the palate. Nor as much finesse. Peppery finish. Very good indeed but the 1980 is more fragrant and more stylish. Yet the finish is long and sweet and poised.

1978   Now-2015

A special *cuvée* with 100 per cent new wood. Fine colour. Full and vigorous. I don't get any excessive oaky flavours here. Lovely rich nose. Still very youthful. You could keep this another twenty years. A full wine. Rich and meaty. A slight touch of solidity. Very good grip. Lovely ripe fruit. Concentrated. Long. Succulent.

1977   **Drink up**

Evolved colour. But not undrinkable on the nose. On the palate a little sour, especially on the follow-through, but not totally fruitless. Nor too evolved and dry and astringent. This had elegance once, and attraction too.

1976   Now-2005

Good vigorous full colour. Animal, gamey nose, old-fashioned. On the palate full, rich, exotic, larger than life. Very good grip. This has rather better poise, elegance and generosity than most. It is really quite concentrated. Best with food. Full, tannic, spicy. Alcoholic. Long. Delicious but un-Burgundian.

1972   Now-2000

This was the first year they started bottling seriously. Good colour. Still very vigorous. Ripe, interesting nose. Good roundness coupled with a certain austerity. Medium to medium-full body. Rather more generous than most 1972s are today. Finishes well. Very good.

THE GROS
FAMILY AND
THEIR WINES,
VOSNE-ROMANÉE

Vosne-Romanée is a commune rich in *grand cru climats*, and a village replete with growers of the highest quality. One of the longest-established of this first division, owners *inter alia* of the monopoly of an excellent *premier cru*, Clos-de-Réas, and of no less than 2 hectares, one-quarter, in the best part of Richebourg, one of the grandest *grands crus* of them all, is the Gros family. Though there are now four separate Gros exploitations – and to further complicate matters, what is exploited does not necessarily correspond with what is owned, especially in Richebourg, which you might imagine to be a cause of friction – the members of the Gros family seem to get on surprisingly well. This enabled me in June 1992 not only to sample a fine range of older Gros *grands crus*, but to compare alongside each other several recent vintages of each of the four village examples of the different Gros estates: Domaine Jean et Michel Gros, Domaine Gros Frère et Soeur, Domaine Anne et François Gros and Domaine A.F. Gros.

HISTORY

The dynasty begins with Alphonse Gros, born in 1804 at Chaux, a hamlet in the hills behind Nuits-Saint-Georges. He married a Latour and arrived in the village of Vosne in the 1830s, where he bought a substantial house, later divided, which had formerly belonged to the Abbey of Citaux prior to the Revolution. In 1860 he acquired the 2-plus hectare walled vineyard of the Clos-de-Réas, a triangular *climat* at the southern end of the village, down-slope from Malconsorts and Chaumes, and like them a *premier cru*.

Following his retirement a few years later, responsibility passed to Louis-Gustave, one of his two sons, who had married a Mlle Guenaud, and it is under the name Gros-Guenaud that the wine was first sold. Louis-Gustave must have been one of the first small growers to sell his wine direct. In a price list of 1 November 1868 he points out that as there are no middle men between him and his clientele he is able to offer his wines 20-30 per cent cheaper than the *maisons de commerce*: the Clos-de-Réas at 5 francs the bottle for the 1858, 3.50 for the 1861 and 1862, and 2.50 for the 1864, in minimum quantities of twenty-five bottles per order, delivered to the railway station at Vougeot or Nuits. He adds that the 1868 vintage is a good one, which the consumer would do well to stock up on.

The domaine continued to expand. In 1882 Louis-Gustave acquired 2 hectares of land in Richebourg, up in the Veroilles section of the *climat*, between Cros-Parentoux and Brûlées. In 1920 Louis-Gustave's grandson Louis Gros - the domaine was now trading under the name of his father (Jules) Gros-Renaudot - bought two substantial parcels of Clos-de-Vougeot, one directly under the vineyard of Musigny in the north-west corner of the *grand cru* adjacent to the château, called Clos-de-Vougeot, Le Musigni (sic), the other a little further south but also at the top of the slope, called Grand-Maupertuis. Some Grands-Echézeaux followed, and, in 1970, a further few rows of Clos-de-Vougeot, next to the Grand-Maupertuis, was bought by Jean Gros, son of Louis, from Madame Machard de Grammont, *née* Dufouleur.

Louis Gros died in 1951, and for a while the domaine continued to be run in common by his four children: Gustave, Jean, François and Colette. François did the paperwork and managed the finances, Jean looked after the vines and Gustave ran the cellar. Sadly none of the three men seems to have enjoyed the best of health. Nevertheless, with the exception of Gustave, who died in 1984, this generation still survives, though it has been the next who has been making the wine for some time.

In 1963, when François got married, the Gros-Renaudot domaine was split up. Jean received the Clos-de-Réas, François the Clos-de-Vougeot Maupertuis, and Gustave and Colette, neither of whom had married, pooled their interests together under the name Gros Frère et Soeur, and took over the Grands-Echézeaux and the larger Musigni section of the Clos-de-Vougeot. The Richebourg was divided.

Thirty and more years on the land is in the process of being passed on to the next generation. Under French inheritance law, whatever is relinquished before the age of sixty-five (which Jean attained in 1993) attracts a lower rate of death duty. In the meanwhile Michel and Bernard, sons of Jean, have bought land for themselves in the Hautes-Côtes, Anne-Françoise, their sister, has married François Parent of Pommard, and taken some of her inheritance along with her as dowry, and Anne, daughter of François, has herself expanded her father's domaine.

THE GROS EXPLOITATIONS

Who owns what, and who looks after what - and as I have said these do not exactly correspond - is currently somewhat complicated. See also page 479. This was the position up to and including the 1995 vintage.

Under the Jean Gros label - the wines made by his tall, moustached eldest son Michel, born in 1956 - you will find the yield from 22 ares of Richebourg, 21 a of Clos-de-Vougeot (vines replanted in 1987), the 2.13 ha of Clos-de-Réas, nearly 2 ha of village Vosne, small parcels of village Nuits and Chambolle, 2 ha of Hautes-Côtes and a hectare and a quarter of Bourgogne. Under Michel's label there are the wines from another 18 a of Richebourg (obviously the two parcels are vinified together, so it is the same wine), two-thirds of a hectare of village Vosne, and 9 ha of Hautes-Côtes-de-Nuits, white as well as red.

It is Michel's younger, stockier, dark-haired brother, Bernard (born 1958), who runs Gros Frère et Soeur. This consists of 69 ares of Richebourg, 1.6 ha of Clos-de-Vougeot (the Musigni part), 40 a of Grands-Echézeaux, 3.25 ha of village Vosne, 6 ha of Hautes-Côtes-de-Nuits and 1.5 ha of Bourgogne.

Anne-Françoise Gros, their sister, owns 20 ares of Richebourg. This is vinified by Michel with the yield of the other two parcels he exploits, but labeled as A.F. Gros. She and husband François Parent make the wine from 1.3 ha of village Vosne, 26 a of Echézeaux and 2 ha of Hautes-Côtes-de-Nuits, planted with Pinot Noir.

Anne, daughter of François, took over from her father in 1988. She looks after 60 ares of Richebourg, almost a hectare of Clos-de-Vougeot, 1.1 ha of village Chambolle and 1.5 ha of Bourgogne. In addition she has 0.4 ha of village Vosne *en métayage* which she took over completely from the 1991 vintage.

WINE-MAKING DIFFERENCES AND SIMILARITIES

Michel Gros made his first vintage in 1975. Though his mother Jeannine, originally from the Jura, runs the business side of Domaine Jean Gros - she has also been mayor of Vosne since 1971, one of her first duties being to marry Aubert de Villaine, co-owner of the Domaine de la Romanée-Conti, to his American wife Pamela - father Jean seems to live a life of leisure. He prefers hunting and fishing to wine-making, as does his brother François. In fifteen or more years of regular visits to Domaine Jean Gros I have never succeeded in meeting him. (Originally I surmised Madame Jeannine was a widow. I mentioned this in *The Vine*, and though I corrected the mistake as soon as it was pointed out to me I was rather dismayed to see the error repeatedly copied by other writers who should have bothered to do their own research.)

Michel prefers to maintain the harvest within limits by pruning short and rubbing off excess buds early in the season, rather than by green harvesting in late July, a process whose efficacy he regards with a certain healthy scepticism. He generally leaves about 20 per cent of the stems in the must, more for its physical effect, easing the fermentation, than for the tannin contribution. Vinification takes place in a variety of vats, mainly cement, following a gentle crushing of about half of the fruit. There is no prior *macération à froid*, but *pigeage* twice a day, and temperatures up to a maximum of 34°C. After a *cuvaison* of ten to twelve days the fermented wine is lodged in oak casks (100 per cent new for the *grands crus* and the Clos-de-Réas, half or one-third for the rest). It is racked but once, and filtered through *Kieselguhr* prior to bottling.

All this is what you might expect when you get to know Michel, a kind but somewhat shy man at first, but one whose character is evidently both perfectionist and cautiously conservative. (When I asked him what changes he had made since he took over from his father he was able to offer little except the installation of cooling systems.) Where there is a break with the norm is that he is a firm believer in selected yeasts. There is a more efficient transference of sugar to alcohol, in his view, and the resulting wine has more finesse.

I find the Jean Gros wines very pure in their expression of Pinot. There is an essence of fruit, an intensity of flavour, and a breed in these wines which is wholly admirable.

Bernard's wines, those bottled as Gros Frère et Soeur, are also made with selected yeast cultures, and by broadly the same procedures, except that the grapes are always wholly destalked and filtering is by *cartouche*. He started making the wines with his uncle in 1980. In those days Gustave did not employ new wood, and he used the natural indigenous yeasts. Bernard changed this after 1987. He uses less new wood (50 per cent for the Richebourg in 1989) than Michel, but his wood has a higher toast and comes from Chatillon in northern Burgundy, so the effect is more aggressive when the wine is young, and he bottles a couple of months earlier. I find his wines chunkier. Like the man himself they are more exuberant. But perhaps they have marginally less finesse. Here, however, because nearly all the land he exploits has been replanted since 1984, the average age of the vines is currently young.

The wine of Domaine A.F. Gros - or perhaps it is more accurate to say that of François Parent - is similarly produced: 100 per cent destemming, ten days' *cuvaison* at temperatures up to 32°C, but perhaps three *pigeages* a day rather than two, and filtering both by *Kieselguhr* and through plates. The results are sturdy, like Bernard's, but seem to have an extra element of spice.

Anne Gros (Domaine Anne et François Gros up to 1994, Domaine Anne Gros *tout court* thereafter) is newer to the game, having only graduated from wine school in 1985. Prior to this, three-quarters of this domaine's wine was sold off in bulk to the local *négoce*, and only since the 1990 vintage was the entire harvest domaine-bottled. The quality of this domaine's wine used to be the lowest of the four, but here we have seen the greatest improvement. Anne has learned fast, and I much admired her 1990s. Here we have a little destemming or none at all, it depends on the year, the use of natural yeasts, and fermentation in open wooden vats, or stainless steel for the small *cuvées*, with a maximum temperature of 32°C. There was 80 per cent new wood for the Richebourg 1989, but it was bottled in April and May 1991, rather than June-August for Bernard's and August-September in the case of Michel's. The wine is delicious! And, yes, her wines *do* have a certain femininity about them.

THE HAUTES-CÔTES

Before I settled down to sample and discuss the wines of the Gros family I asked them to take me round their vineyards.

We began in the Hautes-Côtes at Concoeur, directly above Vosne. Here Bernard has a 6 hectare plot he has been progressively planting since 1988. The soil is excessively rocky, and you walk through a field entirely covered in limestone rubble, taking care not to twist your ankle. The vines are high-trained - better for photosynthesis - and planted 5,000 vines to the hectare, half the density of down below.

Further south, at Chevrey, almost on the borders of the Hautes-Côtes-de-Nuits and Hautes-Côtes-de-Beaune, the three children of Jean and Jeannine Gros share another 9 hectares. This is less rocky soil, and, being on a slope, grass is planted in the spaces between the alternate rows to prevent erosion. Here the density is 3,000 vines per hectare. The vines are trained to a double cordon and the oldest part of the plot dates from 1970. Michel Gros has a further 4.5 ha vineyard of Hautes-Côtes, planted with Chardonnay as well as Pinot, at a *lieu-dit* called Le Lieu-Dieu. Though the wines from all these locations are quite different, the law prevents the Gros from labelling them with separate site names. Michel blends his together. But if you arrive to sample early enough, he will be pleased to show you them side by side. You'll be able to taste the difference.

The Richebourg vines date mostly from the 1930s, and are now gradually being replaced. Bernard has replanted most of his in the last few years. This is prime land, up behind the vines of the Domaine de la Romanée-Conti and in the north-west corner of the vineyard on a decided slope. The soil is friable, and looks good enough to eat; the vines are mostly gnarled and stumpy, pruned close to the ground and grudgingly short. Richebourg is a substantially ample and concentrated wine, opulent as well as firm and concentrated. And some of my greatest vinous experiences have been with Richebourgs. I had to pause and incline my head in admiration.

A short drive away, through a hole in the top wall, opposite the DRC's Grands-Echézeaux, you will gain access to Anne and Michel's adjoining parcels of Clos-de-Vougeot. Anne's is the larger parcel, 93 ares, and the vines date from the first plantations after the phylloxera epidemic: shortly before the First World War. Michel has ten rows. A few years ago his vines were even older, but sadly after the 1985 vintage they had to be grubbed up. So today this is an infant plantation.

These vines run east-west, up and down the slope. Bernard's 1.5 hectare parcel in the lee of the château is also young vines, and is planted north-south, unusual in the Côte. A better exposure to the sun, he says. But worse if it hails. Let's keep our fingers crossed.

THE TASTING

I sampled the following splendid range of wines in Vosne-Romanée in June 1992. My thanks to all the members of the Gros family for their hospitality and generosity. It was an unforgettable experience. The wines noted as Anne (or François) are bottled as Domaine Anne et François Gros; those marked Bernard (or Gustave) are Gros Frère et Soeur; those marked Anne-Françoise are Domaine A.F. Gros; those as Michel or Jean are Domaine Jean Gros. The oldest three wines are merely individual family labellings of what was originally all the same bottling.

Optimum drinking

Vosne-Romanée, 1990, Anne　　Now-2003
Not yet in bottle. Made two barrels. Les Barraux above Richebourg. *En métayage.* Good succulence. Good colour. Plenty of grip and depth here. Very good for a village example. A lot of concentration here. Perhaps the best of the four.

Vosne-Romanée, 1990, Bernard　　Now-2003
Not yet in bottle. Racked yesterday. Partly declassified young vine Grands-Echézeaux. One-third new oak evident. Medium-full colour. Firmer, slightly more dry and astringent. But this may be the racking.

Vosne-Romanée, 1990, Michel　　Now-2003
Not yet in bottle. From Aux Réas. 100 per cent new oak (this sample) – the eventual wine will be 50 per cent. Medium-full colour. The oak is certainly evident. But underneath plenty of style and depth.

Vosne-Romanée, 1990, Anne-Françoise
　　Now-2003
In bottle eight days ago. From Les Maizières just under Echézeaux by the cemetery. 20 per cent new oak. Good colour. Fragrant, ripe, very well-balanced wine. Not suffering too much from the *mise*. Long. Delicate but forceful.

Vosne-Romanée, 1989, Anne　　Now-1998
The lightest of the four colours. Medium colour. Plump, generous nose. Ripe. Perhaps the least full of the four. Medium body. Good

balance and tannins but quite forward. Not a lot of depth. Stylish finish.

Vosne-Romanée, 1989, Bernard　　Now-2001
The most purple of the four colours. Medium-full colour. Firmer, plummy, sturdier. This is more closed but has plenty of grip and depth. Long. Very good.

Vosne-Romanée, 1989, Michel　　Now-2002
Medium-full colour. The most marked by the wood. Fine and stylish, especially on the follow-through. Ripe and intense. Very good indeed. Very long. Very good grip.

Vosne-Romanée, 1989, Anne-Françoise
　　Now-2000
This one from Aux Réas - says so on the label. This is like Bernard's on the nose. Fat and plump. Good fruit, but not as intense. Not quite as much grip. Quite long. Good plus.

Vosne-Romanée, 1988, Anne
Not produced.

Vosne-Romanée, 1988, Bernard　　Now-2003
Medium-full colour. Not very expressive on the nose. Very good fruit on the palate though. Good grip. Quite concentrated but lacks a little complexity and style for better than good plus. The most supple and approachable of the three.

Vosne-Romanée, 1988, Michel　　Now-2003 plus
The most developed in colour. Marginally the lightest. But the most fragrant on the nose. Fullish, harmonious, very promising. Lovely stylish fruit and fine acidity. Very good indeed.

Vosne-Romanée, 1988, Anne-Françoise
                                    Now-2003 plus
From Aux Réas. The fullest colour. The most closed and concentrated. This is a bit adolescent. On the follow-through ample and fleshy with a touch of spice absent in the above. Very good.

Richebourg, 1989, Anne   1998-2015
Medium-full colour. Marvellous nose. Rich, oaky, succulent. Very concentrated. Fullish, harmonious, stylish. Lovely fruit. Disarmingly delicious.

Richebourg, 1989, Bernard   1999-2015
Full colour. The nose is a bit closed. Almost as if it were still bottle sick. Full, ample palate. More structure but not on so much form. Very good grip though. The finish is fine.

Richebourg, 1989, Michel (et A.F. Gros)
                                    Now-2015
Fullish colour. Firm, concentrated nose. Quite dominated by the oak. This is full, tannic, concentrated. Less flexible than Anne's. But real flair and marvellous fruit and depth. Fine.

Richebourg, 1988, Anne   1998-2008
Medium-full colour. Lovely fragrant nose. Medium-full. Ripe and quite concentrated but not the depth and style of a *grand cru*. The 1989 is *much* better.

Richebourg, 1988, Bernard   2000-2020 plus
Full colour. Rich but a little rigid on the nose. Closed, fullish, very good concentration. Lovely fruit here and very good grip. Very fine on the finish. This is more adolescent than Michel's.

Richebourg, 1988, Michel (et A.F. Gros)
                                    2000-2025 plus
Much the deepest colour. Brilliant nose. Full, very rich, very concentrated. Marvellous complexity and harmony. This is a splendidly powerful, complete wine. *Grand vin*. Essence of fruit here.

Richebourg, 1987, Bernard   Now-2002
Fullish colour. A little development. Fine stylish oaky nose. Fresh, plump and not short of concentration. Medium to medium-full. Still a little tannin. This has good grip and freshness and plenty of depth. Shows very well.

Richebourg, 1987, Michel   Now-2006
Full colour. Little development. Youthfully firm oaky nose. Good depth of fruit. More structure, more oak. Very good concentration and grip. Just a little more complex and more positive. A fine example of the vintage.

Richebourg, 1986, François   Now-1999
Medium colour. Quite evolved nose. Lightish but soft and fragrant nose. Not dry. But it doesn't really have a lot of concentration. Pretty and quite stylish, nevertheless. Ready now.

Richebourg, 1986, Bernard   Now-2000
Just a little more colour and less development than his 1987. On the nose a little dry and blowsy, like a 1976 Bordeaux. Fullish, spicy, a little hard, but much better on the finish, which is fat and has no lack of grip. Very good. But the 1987 is better.

Richebourg, 1985, Bernard   Now-2012
Fine colour. Still very young. Rich and concentrated on the nose. Just beginning to acquire the nuances of a mature wine. This is very fine. Full, tannic, old viney and concentrated on the palate. Intense and powerful. Very fine rich finish. Still needs time.

Clos-de-Vougeot, 1985, Michel   Now-2015 plus
Medium-full colour. Just a little development. Marvellous nose. Very very concentrated and complex. Quite brilliant. Persistent and intense. Powerfully flavoured. Very good grip. Essence of wine. *Grand vin*.

Richebourg, 1984, Michel   Drink soon
Fullish mature colour. Fullish, plump nose. No lack of ripeness and finesse, if not *that* concentrated. Medium body. Now ready. Needs drinking soon while it still has its style but now a most enjoyable bottle. Not a bit off-vintage. Best on the nose and attack though lacks real grip and complexity.

Richebourg, 1983, Michel   Now-2005 plus
Medium-full mature colour. Browner than the above. Smoky nose, not as fresh or as enjoyable as the 1984 today. Less stylish. More developed. More *viandé*. Quite different on the palate. Very rich and concentrated but with the dry tannins, especially on the attack of the vintage. Yet the finish is quite clean and very ripe. Very good grip. Still needs a few years. Fine quality.

Richebourg, 1978, Michel   Now-2000 plus
Medium-full mature colour. Marvellous mature Burgundy nose. Very lovely gamey character but multi-dimensional. This is very lovely. Mature, complex, round and persistent. Very brilliant. Very fine indeed. Mature Burgundy at its best.

Clos-de-Vougeot, 1976, Michel   Drink soon
Medium-full mature colour. A little fuller than the Richebourg 1978. Good sturdy nose with just a hint of dryness and burnt toast. Similar palate. Ripe and rich. Good grip. Better with food. Very good.

Richebourg, 1976, Michel   Now-2000 plus

Very fine, rich full colour. No undue maturity. Ample rich nose. Much more dimension and fat. This dominates the structure in a most admirable way. Very full and concentrated. Very ripe also. A lot more concentrated than the 1978. Even better. More youthful too. Excellent. *Grand vin.*

Richebourg, 1969, Gustave   Now-1999

Very good fresh colour. Rich, aromatic, spicy, sandalwoody. A lot of depth and style here. Beautiful ripe complex fruit. Very good acidity. Medium-full. Balanced. Discreet. Very aristocratic. Surprisingly so for this vintage. Bags of life. *Grand vin.*

Clos-de-Vougeot, 1966, François   Drink soon

Good mature colour. Full, muscular; gamey. Slightly less stylish. Fullish. Quite sturdy. Just a little astringent now. Very good but not the depth or the succulence of the Richebourgs above.

Clos-de-Vougeot, 1964, Jean   Drink soon

Very good colour. Better than the Richebourg 1964. Over-ripe nose. Lush, lovely, very seductive, very sexy and animal. On the palate a touch more rustic than the Richebourg and a little more astringent. Very good indeed though.

Richebourg, 1964, Gustave   Drink soon

Fully mature colour. Fragrant, well-matured, lovely violet aspects. On the palate lovely ripe fruit. Good grip. Fullish and fine. But at the end showing signs of loosening up.

Richebourg, 1959, Gustave et Jean Will still keep

Splendid colour. Still vigorous. Marvellous nose. Really very very complex and lovely. Still ripe and fresh. Great style here. This is *grand vin*. Fat, vigorous and very concentrated still. Marvellous. Can still be kept. Not hot, but a touch burnt and concentrated. *Rôti* is the word.

Clos-de-Vougeot, 1959, Gustave et Jean
                            Drink soon

Mature colour. Spicy, gamey nose. Rather harder and more *sauvage* than the above. A little astringent but hot and rich and with a touch of *crème brûlée*. Fullish, rich, ripe.

Clos-de-Vougeot, 1955, Gustave et Jean
                            Drink up

Lightening mature colour. Fragile but *tendre* and delicious. Old roses. No decay. No undue astringency on the nose. Still alive on the palate. For those who like old wine without being necrophiliacs. Soft, ripe, fragrant. Long. Still lovely.

Richebourg, 1949, Gustave et Jean   Drink soon

Magnum. Recorked three years ago. Lightening colour. Fragrant very classy nose. This is getting towards the end of its life but a wine of real elegance and balance. Everything in place. Lovely complex fruit. Medium body. Soft. Ripe. Delicious. *Grand vin* but drink soon. Half an hour later, with a meal, this seemed to have gained vigour. Indeed it was fresh and even deeper in colour. Remarkably lovely. Marvellous ripe complex fresh fruit which lasted for ages.

Richebourg, 1945, Gustave et Jean   Now-2000

Magnum. Very good colour. Concentrated but a little astringent on the nose. Tough. Got better and better in the glass. Structured but very very concentrated. Still very very youthful, because the acidity is high. I think this will still improve, even. It certainly expanded with aeration. Austere. Fresh. Concentrated. Long. But not generous.

Clos-de-Vougeot, 1944, Jean   Drink up

Old colour but not clouding over. A touch of maderisation on the nose. But not too bad on the palate. Still has fruit and fragrance. Made without the assistance of chaptalisation or anything. (And not at all a bad effort.)

In 1996 further changes were made in order to complete the inheritance share-out, as the label of Jean Gros ceased to exist. Michel took the monopoly of the Clos de Réas. All the Richebourg passed to Anne-Françoise as well as the Chambolle-Musigny and village Vosne-Romanée, Clos de la Fontaine. See pages 130 and 220.

ALAIN HUDELOT-NOËLLAT, *VOUGEOT*

Life is not always a smooth ride. And in Burgundy, where jealously guarded vineyards can be seized and broken up, *force majeure*, as a result of the laws of succession, resentment can linger, feuds can simmer on for decades and one side of the family be at daggers drawn with the other. All because of a few begrudged vines.

Often, too, someone is left like the piggy in the middle to shoulder the brunt of the burden for no real logical reason, having committed no obvious fault themselves. One such was Alain Hudelot. He has survived nevertheless. And he is one of the unsung heroes of Burgundy for he makes excellent wine, although his efforts are largely unrecognised.

HISTORY

There have been Hudelots in Chambolle since before the Revolution. Alain's grandfather was the *régisseur* of L'Héritier Guyot in Vougeot and in his own right a vineyard proprietor in Chambolle. His son Noël further extended the domaine, having married a Mongeard. Auguste Mongeard was one of those who bought up part of the Léonce Bocquet holdings in Clos-de-Vougeot in 1920; some of this passed to his son-in-law.

Alain Hudelot was born in January 1940. He left school early and started work in the vineyards in 1954. He worked for his father, for other proprietors in the area and for some of the local merchants. When he was twenty he rented some vineyards in Chambolle from his family and set himself up in his own right. It was the early days of tractors. Alain saved up for one, offered his services to his neighbours, and invested the proceeds in further vineyards. By the time his father ceded him some of the vines in Clos-de-Vougeot ten years later he had built up a domaine of some 5 ha; some owned, some rented.

In 1963 he got married. Madame Hudelot, as she became, was the granddaughter of Charles Noëllat. The Noëllat family, however, were against the marriage. Not only did they refuse to welcome Alain into their midst, they tried to deny Madame Hudelot her rightful dowry.

The battle was long, it was bitter, and it was costly. Charles Noëllat being long deceased and his daughter a widow, the domaine was being run by her brother, a M. Morou. Morou refused to let Alain have access to his wife's vineyard land. Having tried peaceably but vainly, over a period of six years, to wrest the inheritance out of the Morou clutches, Alain Hudelot was forced to instigate a *procès*. This was in 1969. Things were not resolved until after Morou's death in 1976. Hudelot found himself not only having to pay all his own legal costs, but death duties on the value of the vineyards he took over. It doesn't really seem fair to me. It certainly didn't to him. But I can't say he seems bitter about it, merely resigned. For to this day, even after thirty years of marriage, he's still never been invited to his mother-in-law's house.

THE VINEYARDS

The domaine's holdings began with those which come through the Hudelot and Mongeard side: Chambolle-Musigny village, Chambolle-Musigny, Les Charmes and Vougeot, Les Petits-Vougeots: a total of 4 hectares. This latter wine is a rarity, for there is little communal or *premier cru* land outside the Clos-de-Vougeot itself.

In Vosne-Romanée there are vines on the Nuits-Saint-Georges side in Malconsorts (0.2 ha), not far from which is Alain's sole Nuits-Saint-Georges, Les Murgers (0.67 ha). Here the vines are partly quite young. Those on the northern side of the commune are venerable: some seventy-year-old vines in Les Suchots (0.45 ha); equally old, but now partly ripped out, waiting to be replaced, in Beaumonts (0.32 ha), plus 0.68 ha of village wine. There are three separate parcels in the Clos-de-Vougeot, originating from both sides, comprising a total of 1.05 ha. Here too Alain makes the wine of his father, Noël Hudelot-Mongeard. The produce of this 0.43 ha parcel is usually sold off in bulk. Once again the vines here are of considerable age: that of Hudelot *père* being planted in 1920 and 1921.

The jewels in the crown, though, are the vines in Richebourg (0.28 ha) and Romanée-Saint-Vivant (0.48). In the former *climat* Hudelot has his rows of vines between those of Grivot and the Domaine de la Romanée-Conti and those of Liger-Belair (farmed by Denis Mugneret) and Jean Mongeard. In Romanée-Saint-Vivant his lie next to those of Domaine Jean-Jacques Confuron. Like Alain's the Confuron vines have also been inherited from the old Charles Noëllat domaine. Again, as in the Clos-de-Vougeot, the vines here are very old.

All this makes a domaine of some 12 hectares. Together with his Bourgogne *rouge* Alain makes twelve different wines. This is typical Burgundy!

Alain Hudelot is very proud of his old vines which he jealously preserves, but he is not necessarily convinced about the efficacy of paring the harvest to the bone. Look at Lalou Bize, he scoffs - Madame Bize having bought up the bulk of the Charles Noëllat domaine after the death of Madame Morou in 1988. He's sure the wines are splendid - he's never tasted them - but at 13-15 hectolitres per hectare he feels they are hardly economic. Hudelot is quite content to make twice as much, or more, and to perform a *saignée* if necessary. Back in 1964, when he used to be one of Alexis Lichine's suppliers, the great man organised a blind tasting of the local *grands crus*. Alain's Clos-de-Vougeot beat the lot of them: but he had produced a *pièce* an *ouvrée* (55 hl/ha). Most of his perfectionist peers would regard two-thirds or three-quarters of this amount to be the maximum that should be allowed in a *grand cru*.

WINE-MAKING

Behind the Hudelot home in Vougeot - a few houses on a lay-by by-passed by the main road - you will find a large barn-like construction. On the ground floor, apart from the orange trees and other fragile plants which winter here, there are a series of enamelled-steel fermentation vats, the bottling line and various piles of pelleted cases awaiting dispatch. It is orderly, neat and spacious. Underneath is the barrel cellar. As usual the best wines, the impressive names and those matured using the most new oak, are closest to the bottom of the stairs, so you see them first.

The wine is usually vinified with a small proportion (10 per cent or so) of the skins, and given a long maceration at temperatures up to 32°C. There is 100 per cent new oak for the *grands crus*, a quarter or a third for the rest. For fifteen years this Hudelot has sold all his own wine in bottle. Up to 1986 he used a contract bottler, the same Maurice Ninot of Beaune Lichine had himself used. Increasingly though, he began to feel that Ninot did too much of a belt and braces job, over-filtering the wine - taking too much out of it - in order to protect himself. In this year he confronted Ninot with two bottles: the Clos-de-Vougeot he had always bottled himself under his father's name, and that under Alain's label bottled by Ninot - the identical *cuvée* in the first place. Which do you prefer? he demanded of Ninot. Oh, this one, most definitely, said Ninot pointing to the Hudelot bottling. Yes, I agree, replied Alain grimly. And from then on he resolved to bottle everything himself. Since the 1990 vintage he has neither fined nor filtered his wines.

THE WINES

Alain Hudelot's wines have always shown very promisingly in cask, but sometimes were let down by the over-zealous protection against future contamination of the contract bottling of M. Ninot. Older Ninot bottlings under the Alexis Lichine label seem to be fine in my experience, but after Lichine ceased his interest in Burgundy the quality of Hudelot-Noëllat wines went through a patchy phase: sometimes excellent (the Romanée-Saint-Vivant 1980, the same wine in 1982, almost all the top wines in 1983), usually fine (the Clos-de-Vougeots of 1976, 1978 and 1982, and even of 1981), but occasionally disappointing. Some of the lesser wines lacked stuffing and rapidly lost their vigour. The Vougeots, Les Petits-Vougeots has always been a little weak. The Hudelot-Noëllat 1986s are unexciting, and he missed the boat in 1979. Moreover, even after he sacked Ninot, the 1988s are not really up to scratch.

But this period now seems far away. I have long considered Alain's Romanée-Saint-Vivant and Richebourg, the former discreetly oaky and intensely perfumed, the latter rich, opulent and aristocratic, two of the best wines in all Burgundy, and blind tastings of the 1989 and 1990 vintages proved this emphatically. His Clos-de-Vougeot is ample and seductive, but at the same time firm and concentrated, one of the best from the variable *climat*; and the *premier cru* Vosnes are classy and dependable. All these need a good seven to eight years - or more - before they come round. I'm still not convinced by his Vougeot, Les Petits-Vougeots, but then I remain unconvinced about Vougeots in general. But apart from that you can rely on the Domaine Hudelot-Noëllat to provide you with some of the best wines in the middle section of the Côte-de-Nuits. It is a very good estate, and it deserves greater recognition.

THE TASTING

I sampled the following wines at the domaine in February 1994.

Optimum drinking

Clos-de-Vougeot, 1991   **2000-2015**

Fine colour. Splendid rich nose. Fat and opulent with a touch of wood. Fullish, very good ripe tannins. Plenty of structure and power here but excellent acidity. Not a bit dense. This is a very fine 1991. Lots of depth. Lovely classy fruit. Very long.

Clos-de-Vougeot, 1990   **2000-2020**

Splendid colour. This is exotically rich, chocolatey, a little new oaky, with a lot of intensity and structure behind it. It is beginning to go into its shell now. But this is an excellent example. Succulent, concentrated and balanced. Very very long and complex and lovely.

Clos-de-Vougeot, 1989   **1998-2012**

Good colour. Ripe and plump on the nose. But without the intensity and the depth of the above. Lovely ripe stylish fruit though certainly quite full, and with an excellent complex follow-through. A meaty 1989 which finishes with real dimension and class. Fine.

Clos-de-Vougeot, 1988   **Now-2002**

Not as much colour as the 1989. Lacks volume and intensity. This is a little light and inconsequential for the vintage. Medium to medium-full. Correctly balanced. Fruity. But no real backbone. Just about ready. Only quite good.

Vosne-Romanée, Malconsorts, 1987   **Now-2004**

Medium to medium-full colour. Some sign of maturity. A little adolescent and rustic on the nose. On the palate just about ready. Medium to medium-full. Plump. Reasonably balanced. Quite fat and fruity. Attractive if without being very classy. Good.

Romanée-Saint-Vivant, 1987   **Now-2010**

Good colour. Lovely nose. Rich, plump, gently oaky. Much more stylish than the above. Full, very concentrated. Really lovely fruit. This is delicious. Rich, raspberry flavoured. Very good grip. Long and satisfying. Fine quality. Plenty of vigour.

Clos-de-Vougeot, 1985   **Now-2005**

Medium-full colour. Quite mature now. Soft nose. Spicy, warm but quite evolved. On the palate medium to medium-full. Open, plump. Accessible. Good grip. This is good but lacks a bit of class and intensity. A little disappointing. But better than the 1988.

Nuits-Saint-Georges, Murgers, 1981 Past its best

Lightish colour. Still reasonably fresh. Soft, spicy, but a little weak as well as hard. On the palate lean, now light and a bit watery. Nothing much here.

Vosne-Romanée, Suchots, 1979   **Past its best**

Lightish colour. Really quite old looking. Old nose. Light on the palate. The fruit is beginning to dry out, but the wine still has acidity, now getting dominant. Rather disappointing.

Chambolle-Musigny, 1978   **Drink soon**

Medium to medium-full colour. Fully mature. No undue age. A little hard and rustic on the nose. Better on the palate. Firm, quite full. A little austere. Good acidity. Better with food, because it is a little four-square. Good.

Clos-de-Vougeot, 1978   **Now-2000 plus**

Good full rich colour. Barely mature. A faint touch of reduction on the nose. On the palate fullish, with a touch of the animal about it. Quite structured. Ripe. Mulberry flavoured. Rich. Satisfyingly vigorous. Slightly *louche*. Very good.

Clos-de-Vougeot, 1972   **Now-2000 plus**

Good vigorous colour. Fine nose. Mellow, rich and complex, not too lean. Still very fresh. Fullish, round, even sweet. This is a fine example of a 1972. Plenty of richness and depth. Good class. Lovely. Still very vigorous.

LOUIS JADOT,

BEAUNE

The firm of Louis Jadot was founded in 1859. It is now one of the largest and most important of Beaune's *négociants*, among the top three in terms of the quality and consistency of their wines. Today Jadot have a domaine of some 60 hectares, including the important addition of the majority of what used to be the Domaine Clair-Daü in Marsannay, which they acquired in 1985. They also make and market the wines of part of the estate of the Duc de Magenta in Chassagne and (up to 1994) the Clos-des-Corvées in Nuits-Saint-Georges, as well as having a number of other local agreements.

On the death of the third Louis Jadot in 1962 André Gagey, at the time assistant to M. Jadot, was asked to run the company as regent for Louis-Alain Jadot. Unhappily Louis-Alain was killed in a car crash at the age of twenty-three in 1968. Gagey was appointed general manager and later managing director. In 1985 the Jadot family sold the firm to the Kopf family, owners of Kobrand, Jadot's US agents. Nevertheless André Gagey, who officially retired in 1992, and his son Pierre-Henri, today in his late thirties, have had a completely free hand, and the firm continues quite unencumbered by outside influences, now vinifying the vast majority of its wines itself under the direction of the able and engaging Jacques Lardière.

JACQUES LARDIÈRE

Jacques Lardière, a youthful, energetic, curly-haired fifty-year-old, is the genius behind Maison Jadot. He started in 1970, at the age of twenty-three, working alongside an old boy called Forey who was in charge of the cellars. Before too long he had to deal with the problems of the 1971 vintage, a year when hail damaged much of the Côte. 'I am going to have to vinify with the skins for only a very short time, and so at an unnaturally high temperature if I am going to extract any colour,' he told André Gagey. 'Let me sleep on it,' was the response. Gagey gave him the go-ahead the next day, though at first he was doubtful of the results. But when the wines turned out fine, with no lack of colour and substance, and when they later found out that they were the only *négociant* in Beaune without a single tainted wine, he apologised to Lardière for his initial suspicion. Lardière has had *carte blanche* ever since.

THE DOMAINE

The origins of the Jadot family lie in Belgium. There is, I am told, a Jadotville somewhere in that country. Towards the end of the eighteenth century a Louis Jadot arrived in Burgundy, and no doubt took advantage of the dismemberment of the ecclesiastical domaines to acquire a few vineyards. His son married the daughter of a small *négociant* in the 1850s, thus creating the Maison Jadot we know today. Its cellars used to be in the Couvent des Jacobins, a fifteenth-century convent located near the Hôtel de Ville. The chapel, a construction with a splendid vaulted roof whose side pillars are surmounted with fantastic gargoyles, has been converted into two storeys and its architectural significance destroyed. Underneath, in side chapels and what used to be the crypt, the location was ideal for storing wine. Today Jadot have an efficient modern warehouse on the road out to Savigny-lès-Beaune but they still use the Couvent des Jacobins for special tastings and receptions.

The 60 hectare domaine is made up of five elements. Firstly there is the Domaine Louis Jadot. This includes what used to be Clair-Daü, a new purchase in Santenay, the Clos-de-Malte, and a couple of *premier cru* Beaunes the company acquired when it took over Maison Champy a few years ago: a total of 23.62 ha.

Secondly there is the Domaine des Héritiers Louis Jadot. These are the early purchases by the Jadot family: lots of other Beaunes, a good hunk of Corton, Chevalier-Montrachet, Les Demoiselles and some Puligny-Montrachet, Les Folatières. But it also includes the Clos-de-la-Croix-de-Pierre in Pernand-Vergelesses, which is another recent purchase. The total here is 16.58 ha.

Thirdly and fourthly are two in-house family domaines with whom the firm has an exclusivity. These are the 3.67 ha estate of André Gagey himself and the 2.87 ha property which comes from his wife's side of the family, the Domaine Robert Tourlière.

Finally there is the 12.70 ha domaine of the Duc de Magenta. This is based around holdings in Chassagne and Auxey-Duresses and has been under the Jadot wing since 1985. But the wines maintain a special label.

WINE-MAKING

Over the last fifteen years I have spent many a happy morning - at least two per year; one in June for the whites, one in November for the reds - in the Jadot cellars tasting the latest vintage and talking to Jacques Lardière. At some of the other *négociants* I am ushered into the tasting room, confronted with a line of bottles, and left to get on with it. Not so *chez* Jadot. Jacques wheels up an upright barrel on to which to line up the glasses. I move over to a wide step-ladder on top of which I can park my notebook and off we go, from generic up to *grand cru*, wine by wine, discussing each as we go. What is remarkable, even before you absorb the passion and total competence of this remarkable man, and indeed even before you start thinking about the high quality of the wines, is that he remains totally unphased by the size of the job he is doing. Jadot may well be responsible for 10 per cent of quality village and *premier cru* white Burgundy. Lardière will casually mention that this year's *cuvée* of Meursault is 400 barrels' worth. He normally makes as many as ninety different wines a season. In November 1994 I sampled fifty-seven different 1993 red wines; in June 1995 thirty-three 1994 white wines. And that is counting by appellation, not by *cuvée*. Doesn't he tremble at the knees that something might go wrong? Not that I have noticed.

For Lardière there are only a few simple rules and only one single object. The object is the expression of the *terroir*, whether that of a humble Santenay or a grand Clos-de-Bèze. The way to achieve this is an illogical (on the face of it) mixture of interfering as little as possible and being prepared to take risks. Some of the things he does would be shot to bits by the teachers of any wine school. He would be equally criticised for not doing a lot of what he doesn't do.

For the red wines the point at where the eyebrows rise up is when you hear that he prefers to vinify at 35-40°C, a point where most *vignerons* would expect the fermentation to stick and the wine to become infected by vinegar bacteria. It doesn't worry Lardière. He destems the fruit, ferments in open wooden vats with two *pigeages* a day, using the natural yeasts, having neither cooled nor raised the temperature during a pre-fermentation soaking. He also likes to macerate for as long as a month. Most others are content with half this.

Having talked to many another talented wine-maker who does things differently, you sail into the attack, playing devil's advocate. Come on Jacques, you say, at 35-40°C all your aromas are going to volatilise and disappear. If you macerate for a month especially with natural yeasts you will only be left with coarse tannins. The delicacy will be lost . . . Then you stop and feel foolish. For you have tasted the wines, and they are anything *but* lacking in aroma, elegance, delicacy and anything else you search for in fine Burgundy.

Lardière's attitude to oak is also a little bizarre. The accepted theory is that fine concentrated vintages are balanced by lots of new oak, light vintages dominated by it. *Chez* Jadot the '*grands millésimes*' are given 15-20 per cent new oak, the '*petits millésimes*' 50 per cent. It doesn't seem to upset the wine. There is a single racking only, and bottling without either fining or filtration. Here at least we are on secure ground. And Lardière takes care that you realise that every single barrel, every *cuvée*, is tasted and analysed continually. It is not all left to chance.

With the white wines there are also one or two points in the evolution from grape juice to wine in bottle where the method is different to accepted theories and procedures. Most wine-makers believe in *débourbage*, the settling out of the gross - and possibly dirty - lees. Like the Domaine Ramonet, Lardière does not allow the juice to settle. The grapes are pressed and the must poured straight into the barrel for fermenting. Little new oak is used, especially in the richer, fatter vintages - in the opposite, leaner years the wine might be given extra time in cask to round off - and the wine given one racking, a light casein fining and a light plate filtration. The latter is as much for show - customers like star-bright wines - as for anything else.

Where the Lardière white wine-making method differs most from that of his peers is that he habitually blocks the malo somewhere along the process. This is to conserve the acidity. To add tartaric acid would be anathema. It never integrates properly with the wine, in his view. (He is not really concerned that it is illegal in Burgundy if you have chaptalised as well.) Others will suggest that a blocked malo Chardonnay never weathers well. Jacques will quietly, or noisily, depending on circumstances, disagree.

This is a man of passion and sensuality. Wine for him is part of the magic of life. Wine is made by God, but all too often screwed up by the ignorant human, he once said to me. 'Look at all the boring wines,' he says. 'Many of them are technically impeccable, but they have no soul, no personality in them. They could have been manufactured by robots. I sometimes wonder if the people who make them ever taste them. You must use your tastebuds, your imagination, your intelligence. Not a rule book!' And look at all the Jadot wines, you could reply. They are not all perfect. But on the scale that they are made the overall quality is remarkable, mind-boggling even. Jadot are lucky to have him. And, as customers, so too are we.

THE TASTING

In June 1995 I sampled a range of Jadot's Chevalier-Montrachet, Les Demoiselles and Corton, Pougets in Beaune.

CHEVALIER-MONTRACHET, LES DEMOISELLES

1985   **1998-2018**

Good colour. Still very fresh. Youthful oaky nose. Still very young. Concentrated and oaky. Firm and vigorous. Very full, very intense. Marvellously concentrated. Very good grip. This is masculine. Rich. Still very young. Very fine indeed. Potentially a great bottle. Very complex. Marvellously long at the end.

1983   **Now-2005 plus**

Good colour, not too evolved. Higher-toned, toasted nose. Quite alcoholic but not too heavy. One of the most composed 1983s I have had for a long time. Very fresh on the palate. Full. Opulent, very rich and fruity. But excellent acidity. Fat, plump and very fine. Very long too. Less austere. More exotic.

1979   **Now-2005 plus**

Good colour. Delicious, harmonious nose. Lovely rich fruit. Fresh, honeyed, nutty. A lot of depth and quality here. This is very, very lovely. Splendidly fresh complex fruit. Real class. Real poise. Fullish nose. Very subtle. Very lovely harmony. Long and very complex at the end. Excellent.

1975   **Now-2000**

This colour is quite deep and almost golden. Very interesting nose. A touch of candied peel, a touch of raisins. Honeyed. Vigorous. Fresh. This is now well matured. Fullish, quite a lot of alcohol. A touch four-square, and the flavours untypical. But a splendid result for the vintage. And a most enjoyable wine.

1973   **Drink soon**

Good colour. Still fresh. Just a little light and unexpressive on the nose compared with the 1971. Better on the palate. This is beginning to show its age now. But the fruit is ripe, gentle and even a little *tendre*. Good acidity but never had quite the strength of the 1971 (or the 1985). Yet very classy. Gentle, round and honeyed. Fine.

1971   **Now-2000**

Rather more of a golden colour than the 1973.

Seems fatter, richer and fresher on the nose though. This is splendid. Full, plenty of backbone. Very good grip. Holding up better than the 1973. Allowing the class and concentration to come searing out. Very fine intensity of fruit. Marvellous finish. This is very fine indeed. Real class and depth here. *Grand vin*.

1967   **Now-1999**

Rich golden colour. Well-matured nose. Opulent, honeyed. But a touch vegetal on the nose. This is only medium-full, but surprisingly harmonious and well integrated still. Ripe, nutty, very good grip and intensity. It is not as great, as intense and concentrated as the 1971, but it is most attractive. Very well balanced and still long and complex at the end. Holding up very well. Fine.

1964   **Now-2000**

Fresh colour for a wine of this age. Fat, ripe, almost a touch of caramel (or at least caramelised peaches) here. This has almost the volume and natural residual sweetness of a red wine. Full, ripe, opulent but not a bit heavy. Very well balanced. Still has plenty of life. Not quite as special perhaps at the end (as complex) as on the attack. But certainly very, very long. Fine.

CORTON, POUGETS

1988   **2000-2020**

Fine immature colour. Marvellous pure Pinot on the nose. Still very youthful. Not a bit hard though, as some Cortons can be in their youth. Fullish, excellent grip. Some tannin. This is very fine, very, very harmonious, poised, intense and stylish. Long. Very fine.

1985   **1998-2012**

Good colour. Just beginning to show some brown now. The nose is a bit closed. Rich and fat but not really composed. Fullish, a little burly. Just a little four-square. Sweet and spicy. An element of slightly cooked fruit - different from the 1988. Not quite as much elegance or as definitive at the end. Good intensity though. Very good plus.

1983   **Now-2012**

The colour is fuller and browner than the 1985. No undue age though. Some astringency and stemminess of the tannins on both nose and palate (especially on the attack), but the follow-through is very rich and satisfying. Rather more to it than the 1985. Very, very rich and concentrated. Fine with food. Excellent finish.

1973   **Now-1999**

Medium-full, mature colour. No undue age. Soft, mature wine. This is elegant and still fresh, if never a wine of really great intensity. Medium to medium-full, balanced, fresh, harmonious. Very nicely ripe generous Pinot. Elegant, long, complex. Holding up very well indeed. Surprisingly good.

1971   **Now-2000 plus**

Mature full colour. No undue age. Really quite firm and youthful on the nose. The masculine aspect I associate with Corton. Fullish, plenty of concentration. An ample wine, good concentration. Lots of intensity. This is rather more elegant than the 1973 - or indeed the 1983 and 1985. Splendid acidity. Very, very aristocratic. Fine plus.

1964   **Now-2000 plus**

Fine full mature colour. Splendidly ripe, complex, fragrant nose. This is now round, sweetly rich, intense and totally seductive and generous. Mature but still very, very fresh. Long. The 1971 is slightly more austere and perhaps a little more classy. But this is lovely. Very, very long. Fine quality.

1953   **Drink soon**

Really deep mature colour. Very complex aromatic nose. Undergrowth and all sorts of mature spices. Yet absolutely no sign of age on the attack. The wine is full, opulent, sensual. Not as classy as the 1971 or as generous as the 1964. But nevertheless a lovely complex mature wine. Perhaps just beginning to get a little diffuse now. No sign of astringency though.

1947   **Now-2000 plus**

Fine colour. Full, mature but not a bit unduly so. Splendidly concentrated, full, chocolatey caramel nose. Full, rich. Very, very concentrated. A marvellously fresh vibrant example. Splendid grip and vigour. Hugely fruity. Complex and aromatic. This is excellent. Very, very lovely long naturally sweet ripe finish.

BEAUNE, CLOS-DES-URSULES

The exclusivity Clos-des-Ursules is part of the *premier cru* known as Vignes-Franches, a *climat* plumb in mid-slope in the lower part of the Beaune *côte*. The vineyard (2.20 hectares) used to belong to the sisters of the Compagnie de Sainte-Ursule, a teaching order which was set up in Beaune in 1626. Like most religious foundations, this convent was the recipient of donations from grateful local residents, and by the time of the Revolution they had a domaine of 574 *ouvrées* (about 24 hectares) of vines as well as other land in the area. The first Louis Jadot bought the Clos in 1826.

Clos-des-Ursules is an excellent example of a Beaune *premier cru*: medium-full, round and fruity, generous and approachable, velvety and perfumed. It is very typical of the plump, attractive, open *premier cru* wines, maturing in the medium term, that one gets from this part of the Beaune *commune*. Delightful as it may be at five years old, it nevertheless can keep well, as the following notes will amply demonstrate.

In September 1988 I was invited to a tasting of thirty-two vintages of Clos-des-Ursules, spanning a century of wine-making. Needless to say it was a fascinating experience. It was also impeccably organised by André Gagey and his team; with plenty of space, plenty of time, and a delicious lunch afterwards prepared by Jean Crotet, of the sumptuous Hostellerie de Levernois on the outskirts of Beaune across the motorway. With the lunch we drank Corton-Charlemagnes from the Jadot domaine: a 1928, which must have been quite a robust alcoholic wine in its prime; a 1962, honeyed, complex and delicate yet vigorous and powerful, a lovely bottle, still very youthful; then, even better, an exquisite 1971, aristocratic, rich, luscious and concentrated, with amazing depth and surprising freshness and vigour, indisputably *grand vin*; and finally (yes, we had them in an atypical order) the 1983, full, quite chunky, rich and sweet and quite alcoholic, but with a better grip than most 1983s.

1986 **Now-1999**

Medium colour; a little maturity. Quite good Pinot, fresh and fruity without any great depth. Similar on the palate. Fresh, raspberry fruit. A bit one-dimensional. Honey and vanilla from oak underneath. Not mean though. If anything it lacks a bit of bite. *À point*. Reasonable quality. For early drinking.

1985 **Now-2002**

Medium-full colour. Very youthful. Fresh, ripe and youthful on the nose. Slightly oaky, reasonable concentration. Medium body, a little tannin, a cheerful, pleasant, seemingly uncomplicated wine for reasonably early drinking. Ripe, oaky and seductive, nevertheless. Good balance.

1983 **Now-2003**

Full colour. Little maturity if any. Full, slightly lumpy, slightly cooked nose. A sturdy wine, rather solid and youthful. Full, rich and tannic. This has good concentration and grip in a masculine slightly solid sort of way. Better on the palate than on the nose. Will develop. Rich finish and not too spicy or hot. Very good.

1980 **Drink soon**

Medium-full colour. Some maturity, the most of this first series. Somewhat diffuse on the nose and a certain dryness. Medium body, ready and possibly already getting a bit loose. Good fruit though a bit uncomplicated. Has good grip, though, which gives it more style than I had expected.

1978 **Now-2003**

Fullish colour, just a bit of maturity. Slightly ungracious and spicy on the nose. Rich in a slightly lumpy way. Fullish, rich and quite high acidity on the palate, not lacking either interest or even a certain finesse. Always a slightly ungenerous wine but not too mean. A bit rigid really to have real class.

1976 **Now-2003 plus**

Fullish colour. No maturity. Youthful, quite full, concentrated wine; potentially a lot here but in its shell at present. Fullish, youthful and tannic on the palate. Good depth, good grip; classy Pinot. Very good indeed. This is the proof that 1976s can be really quite exciting in the Côte-de-Beaune.

1973 **Drink soon**

Medium colour. Not a lot of maturity. Good, quite youthful nose; a shade austere. Ripe but has acidity. Lacks a bit of generosity. Full and black fruits. Reasonable acidity. Ripe but

slightly one-dimensional. Lacks real complexity perhaps. Did not evolve very well in the glass and finished a bit short. Still enjoyable though.

1971 **Drink soon**

Good fullish, mature colour. Something a bit green and hard and mean on the nose. This doesn't smell like a good vintage. Tastes like a good example of an off-vintage. Medium body, a lack of real concentration of ripe fruit. A bit disappointing. One-dimensional. Very strange. I understand that there was a short maceration because of there being hail damage to the fruit.

1969 **Drink soon**

Good full, mature colour. Concentrated, new oaky nose. Ripe and crammed with red fruit. Good acidity as well. A full wine, fully mature, quite developed. Open and freshly fruity. Quite complex but lacks the spice and complexity and grip of the 1961 and 1962. It evolved in the glass quite fast to the point where it got a bit lumpy. Good but not great.

1966 **Drink soon**

Good, medium-full, mature colour. Mature Pinot with a touch of vegetable/farmyard. Quite fragrant, on the lighter side with a touch of spice. A medium-full generous mature wine. No great weight but good balance and dimension. This is fine and delicate and has slightly better acidity than the 1964 which has kept it fresher and more vigorous and complex. Long. Very good indeed. My third favourite of the 1960s.

1964 **Drink soon**

Good, medium-full, mature colour. Full, round and honeyed. Vanilla and oaky on the nose. Fragrant, on the feminine side for a 1964 but full and powerful. Complex. Balanced. Well matured, if not showing a touch of astringency and perhaps also shortening. Better on the attack than on the finish, but generous, medium bodied. Certainly good.

1962 **Drink soon**

Very good, full, mature colour. Ample, plump, generous, accessible and fat. A concentrated nose. Youthfully oaky indeed. Good rip, fresh Pinot though and plenty of richness. Very attractive and seductive. Lovely nose, lovely palate. Full, ripe, very well balanced. High-class fruit and concentration. Still very vigorous. Very long and complex. Will even improve. High class. The second best of this decade.

1961 **Will still keep**

Very good, full colour. Not a lot of maturity. Full, still youthful. Concentrated and sturdy. Depth and dimension here. Slightly closed. Full and concentrated, if not quite structured, even solid. Still very youthful. Still needs time. Rich, concentrated, fresh, lovely fruit and very good palate. Potentially excellent. Fine, very ripe finish. The best of this series (1961-1971).

1959   Drink soon

Medium-full, mature colour. Mature, fragrant, feminine wine, flowery rather than spicy. Delicate and complex (reminds me of a 1953 claret). This is older than the 1954 but is in the same style. Lovely blackcurrant and raspberry. Less spice though more as it developed. Long and balanced but less life and vigour. Very good nevertheless. Oaky background. Third best of the 1950s.

1957   Drink up

Very full colour, just a little brown. Full, rich and concentrated on the nose. Lovely fruit. Plenty of depth here. A fine vintage. Fully mature if not lightening up a bit. Fullish, just a shade vegetal and lumpy. As it evolved it was not as good as I thought at first. Quite old. Lost vigour and interest in the glass.

1954   Drink soon

Good fullish, vigorous, mature colour. Less muscle. Fine, fragrant, ripe, mature Pinot. A touch of spice and coffee. Quite complex but on the lighter side. Medium-full, mature and complex. Very harmonious. Very long on the palate. A lovely example of carefully made Pinot Noir now in its prime. Very well balanced. Will keep very well indeed. Fragrant and multi-dimensional. Very classy. Second best of this series.

1952   Drink soon

Full colour. Little sign of age at the rim. Fullish, youthful, rich, fat and chocolatey on the nose. Quite a sturdy wine with a slight four-square element. Fullish, a little tannic. Ripe and fruity, a little spice and pepper on the follow-through. Fine but not great. Finishes reasonably.

1949   Drink soon

Similar colour to the 1947. A little fuller, a little more age perhaps (slightly muddier). Older on the nose. Fine but now perhaps dying/loosening a little. Some age here. Fullish, slightly spicy, sweet. Quite a fat, sturdy wine, an element of tannin which threatens to become slightly astringent. Good but not the harmony and elegance of some. This is very ample. It is just it doesn't have the life. Third best of the 1940 series. À point.

1947   Will still keep

Fine, full, vigorous colour. Like the 1945 but more youthful. Slightly less sturdy on the nose.

This is elegant, fragrant, complex and ripe. Slightly less full than the 1945. Just a touch of spice, lovely fruit. Medium-full. Ripe, complex, ample. Very fine. Long. The best of this series.

1945   Will still keep

Amazingly full colour. Still almost black. No brown, no lightening at the rim. Solid, masculine, very concentrated, almost tough. Port element and a certain austerity/rigidity. Full and tough, oak and vanilla, some astringency. A fat wine as well as solid. Coffee-chocolate as well as black fruits. Reasonable length but not the finesse of the 1947 in my view.

1937   Will still keep

Good vigorous colour. Quite sturdy and originally tough Pinot Noir. Now old Pinot, slightly gamey aspects. A shade dry but good fruit and grip underneath. Spicy elements, tobacco and coffee, as it evolved. Fullish, rich, originally a firm, even hard wine and still has this structure and muscle. Slightly austere but not tough. Still vigorous. Long finish.

1933   Drink soon

Good colour. Not originally as sturdy as the 1937, I would have thought. Slightly dry and vegetal now on the nose. Medium-full. A fragrant, ripe wine, rather more exciting on the palate than the nose would indicate. Good vigorous fruit. Less dense and muscular than the 1937. Fresh, almost peachy as well as raspberry. Less spice. Very good. Finishes long. Essentially a wine of greater finesse and charm.

1928   Will still keep

Similar colour to 1933. Fine, ripe, concentrated fruit with a touch of honey, caramel and spice on the nose. Fine quality and plenty of vigour. Fullish, a fine, rich, concentrated wine with both depth and complexity. Plenty of dimension here. Good, quite firm structure coupled with concentrated fruit. Ample, full character. Very distinguished.

1926   Drink soon

Slightly more colour. Slightly lighter nose with an element of oxidation as it developed. Medium-full body; rich, aromatic, plump and generous. Now just a hint of age. Ample fruit coupled with a hint of spice: cinnamon. Nevertheless more vigorous on attack than the nose would indicate. The finish is long still but just lacks the punch now of a wine like the 1928, indicating it will start lightening and shortening before too long.

1923   Will still keep

Very fine, full, vigorous colour. Fullish, fat, ample, vigorous. A generous, plump wine, still alive and complex. Very fine. This is excellent if not quite as classy as the 1928. Fullish, rich and ample, still round and warm and plump - even voluptuous. Fresher and more vigorous than the 1926. Lovely ripe fruit. Strawberry, raspberry and cherries. A touch of spice. Just a hint of astringency on the finish. Yet vigorous and fragrant still. Will still keep well. Very lovely and seductive.

1919   Drink soon

Good fullish colour. A little more aged than the wines of the 1920s and 1930s but by no means too old. Quite a bit older than the 1923 on the nose. But not faded. Just fine, ethereal, complex, slightly old roses. Delightful. This has now lost a bit of its original weight but a finely balanced wine with good acidity; fragrant and fruity rather than spicy. Real finesse. Still lovely and no hint of astringency. Might get a bit lean as it develops.

1915   Drink soon

Good colour, more vigorous than the 1919. Generous and highly spicy on the nose. Still sweet and aromatic. Feminine and complex, barley sugar and ginger biscuits. Similar on the palate. Quite full, vanilla and oak evident. Sweet and rich and very generous and seductive. Still very vigorous but has grip rather than acidity as it is very, very ripe. Lovely. One of the best of the pre-1945 wines. Very long on the palate.

1911   Drink soon

Quite a good colour but a little age. Also a little age on the nose. Fragrant but lightening. A distinguished old gentleman. Certainly plenty of finesse here. Dried up as it evolved. Better on the palate, quite spicy, even peppery. Was probably quite a tough wine originally; though sweet, there is a certain austerity. A hot vintage? Now there is a bit of astringency at the end but though muscular this is rich and ample and still finishes well. Third best of this final series.

1906   Drink up

Also a bit of age now on the colour and definite age on the nose. Astringency is very evident, a bit hard and tough and ungenerous now. This is also evident on the palate. The fruit in its sturdy way was always slightly leaner than the above and this is now fading leaving the acidity. A full wine, not without quality and interest but now lacks generosity.

1904   Drink soon

Very good colour. The most full and vigorous since the 1923. Obviously quite highly sulphured when bottled or re-corked because there is an element of hydrogen sulphide, but this has kept the wine alive. Old but fullish, plump and complex. Similar on the palate. Not quite the length and complexity on the follow-through; though fullish and fat and fresh still and plump and fruity there is a certain lack of concentration and bite especially at the end. Still very vigorous though. A lot of interest. Definitely oaky and not without length. Very fine.

1895   Drink soon

Remarkable colour, even better than the 1904. This could be a wine of the 1950s or even 1960s! Yet a bit of maderisation on the nose. Still enjoyable though. Got more and more maderised as it evolved. Fullish, spicy, a shade astringent on the finish. Not at all without interest. Still has length and freshness (in terms of intensity and lack of dryness).

1887   Drink soon

Very good colour for its age. Medium-full, still quite vigorous. Old but not too faded at first on the nose. Distinguished, old, concentrated Pinot, plenty of depth and character. Subtle. This is a lovely wine. Slight hints of astringency but medium bodied, mellow, complex, rich and concentrated. Very lovely. Perfect balance. Quite remarkable. No undue age. *Grand vin*! Still sweet. Magnificent!

A Postscript: A Tasting of Nineteenth-Century Burgundy

Beaune, April 6 1992. I was in Bourgueil yesterday. I shall be in Bordeaux tomorrow. Why this crazy Burgundian detour? Because I have been invited, as one of forty-five prestigious guests (I quote from the press release, of course), to celebrate the forthcoming retirement, after forty-five years in the business, of André Gagey, doyen of the Burgundy *négoce* and *président-directeur-générale* of Louis Jadot.

We assemble in the vaulted cellars beneath the old Couvent des Jacobins. The place is heaving with stars. If a bomb was to explode French gastronomy would be ruined for a generation. Haeberlin of the Auberge de l'Ill is there, Pic from Valence, Troisgros from Roanne and Sanderens, Vrignat and Pacaud from Paris. All of Burgundy's top restaurateurs are also present of course: Lameloise, Blanc, Loiseau, Lorain and Meneau. And there are Robert Parker and Clive Coates and a few other hacks.

Places have been allotted. I find myself next to Roger Vergé and opposite Paul Bocuse. Bocuse tells me funny story after funny story about the formidable Fernand Point, whose last and arguably greatest sous-chef was Paul himself, before he left to work up the family business on the other side of Lyon. One incident concerns an inadvertent mix-up between some old Bollinger and some even older Château Grillet, which resulted in a party of Americans driving off convinced Condrieu was a sparkling wine. Vergé counters with an anecdote concerning *fromage de tête* (brawn) and the confusion this caused when the adjutant of an important English diplomat arrived to set up a dinner for his boss. My eyes though are more for the list of wines that has been set before us. Four vintages of Montrachet, the youngest being 1904; eight red wines, starting with Clos-de-Vougeot 1898 and ending with La Romanée 1865. The eyes boggle. My taste-buds begin to salivate.

Most of the wines, I later find out, have been lying in the Jadot cellars since time immemorial. Some date back to Jadot's nineteenth-century predecessor, Lemairre-Fanleux of Nuits-Saint-Georges. Others were unearthed when Jadot took over Champy a few years ago. All have been pre-tasted by Jacques Lardière, Jadot's wine-maker, by André Gagey and his son Pierre-Henri.

Not all the wines, surprisingly, are from great vintages. The 1898 vintage is described as *fruité, un peu maigre et mince* (fruity but a bit lean and thin). 1875 produced dilute wines because the year was too abundant. But the bottles we taste are remarkable: uniformly high quality and amazingly vigorous.

The biggest surprise, though, is that two of the Montrachets were clearly made from botrytised fruit. I knew that Coulée de Serrant and Château Grillet used to be sweet wines, but Montrachet? This is a discovery.

This is a privileged and special occasion, and as it should be it is followed by an august banquet in the Chambre du Roy of the Hospices de Beaune. The lunch is prepared by the two best chefs in the immediate locality, Jean Crotet of the Hostellerie de Livernois and Jean-Pierre Silva of Le Vieux Moulin in Bouilland. Both these gentlemen have earned two stars in the Michelin guide. Do they feel somewhat nervous serving up a meal to so many three-star chefs? It would not appear so. The meal is excellent. This time I am seated next to Michel Roux, one of France's most successful exports to the United Kingdom. Why don't you come and eat more often at the Waterside? he complains. I try to explain that it is not so much the price of the meal and the wines, but the taxi there and back. It is 31 miles from Château Coates to Bray, door to door, and the cab drivers would charge you for the round trip, both ways. It would cost as much as the meal itself!

There are more old wines with the Hospices de Beaune luncheon: Corton-Charlemagne 1982, and Corton-Pougets 1959 and 1915, the latter the best of the decade in Burgundy.

There are speeches, of course; and commentaries on the wines. Everybody congratulates everybody. And in the middle of it all, calm and benign, sits the happy André Gagey, a lifetime of making good Burgundy behind him. And, we trust, with a long and healthy retirement to look forward to. *Merci*!

Here are my notes.

WHITE WINES

Le Montrachet, 1904

The colour of an old fino - or a Sercial. Rich and fat on the nose and still very much alive. There is honey here, as well as nuts. Even a touch of botrytis. Good acidity too. Full and concentrated, quite powerful, and, I would judge, also quite alcoholic. On the palate the fruit has dried just a little, but there is no decay. The wine is still rich and persistent. But it has lost just a little of its sweetness. A full vintage in the style of 1976 or 1983. Fine. Held up well in the glass though it became a little bitter.

Le Montrachet, 1899

Very light amontillado colour. Sparkling clean. A touch of Madeira and mushrooms on the nose. This has lost a little of its fruit - what comes out on top is the acidity. But a very elegant, stylish, more delicate wine than the 1904. A little petrolly on the nose, in the sense of old Riesling. Yet (originally) deliciously elegant: splendid fruit. Once lovely.

Le Montrachet, 1889

Light amontillado colour. Full, fat, rich, waxy, sweet nose. An element of botrytis. A touch of maderisation. Also definite residual sugar. Fullish, but a certain astringency. Curiously, yet still enjoyably, sweet-sour. Elements of fusel oil as it developed in the glass. Perhaps always just a little heavy and four-square.

Le Montrachet, 1881

Light amontillado colour. The nose has lost intensity now. A little dilute. Yet style and depth here originally. Like the 1889 a wine of pronounced sweetness. But no botrytis. Soft, Vouvray-ish, oaky and waxy. A little astringent. A little bitter on the finish.

RED WINES

Clos-de-Vougeot, 1898

The colour is still remarkably full and vigorous. On the nose this is lush, sweet and ripe; very lovely, coffee and chocolate flavours still. Full but not hard, nor any sign of decay or drying out. Fullish on the palate. Complex and gently sweet. Good intensity. Remarkable vigour for a wine nearly 100 years old. Long. If the acidity shows just a little it doesn't detract a bit. Fine.

Beaune, Clos-des-Ursules, 1895

Medium colour. Quite an old wine. There is a certain astringency and hardness. Gamey, even shitty, at first. A dense wine at the start. But quite powerful and masculine and yet rich on the palate. Good grip. Long, still a bit tough. Vigorous. Very good indeed, if not that stylish. But oaky and full of quite cooked fruit - a cherry tart.

Corton, 1894

Good colour but fully mature. Rich firm nose. This is ripe, very Pinot and very vigorous. Remarkable for a ninety-eight-year-old wine. It still has the structure, the hard edge of Corton. Even better on the palate. Fat and very concentrated. Lovely black fruit elements. This is very vigorous. Really rich and fat. Seems as if it will keep for ages. Gently sweet on the finish. Brilliant. *Grand vin*.

Clos-de-Tart, 1887

Deep colour. A touch cloudy, quite mature at the edges. This shows a little age. The nose has dried up and closed up a bit. Aspects of dry violet cachous - almost talc. Better on the palate. A little rigid but full, ripe blackcurrant/violet fruit. Plenty of sweetness. Good acidity. But lacks a little suppleness now. It is rich but not sumptuous. Yet the fruit must have been really lovely once. Fine.

Richebourg, 1877

Good colour. Well matured of course. Slight hardness on the nose. I can still smell the stems. Yet rich and full at the same time. On the palate this is quite evidently a wine of size and intensity - even solidity, even austerity. Like a 1972. But concentrated and rich and full on the palate. Interesting almost vegetal elements. Yet ultimately a slight lack of charm. Very good indeed.

Pommard, 1875

Very good vigorous colour. The nose has dried up a little. But underneath a typically sturdy nose with a hint of molasses. Spice here. Gameyness. Rich and full and sweet on the palate. Slight elements of caramel. Another hot year, I would judge. Fatter than the nose would indicate. A structured wine. Very good indeed if not with enormous style: typically Pommard in fact.

Bonnes-Mares, 1870

Very good vigorous nose. This nose is a rare glimpse of heaven. Delicate, complex, gloriously sweet and fruity. All in lace and subtlety. And without a hint of real age or decay. On the palate the wine is round but intense, fat and very very concentrated. Simply marvellous fruit and breed and dimension. A really *great wine*. Positively fabulous. And astonishing vigour.

La Romanée, 1865

Very good colour. This is a wine of great delicacy – though originally full and meaty – complexity and finesse but it is not quite as vigorous as the Bonnes-Mares 1870. There is a certain age here; not so much decay as elements of *sous-bois* and mushrooms; but at the same time quite delicious and original in its flowers and fruit. Justifiable proof of its great *provenance*. Really subtle and complex. Still sweet and still holding up well in the glass. Great finesse. *Grand vin*.

WINES SERVED WITH THE BANQUET

Corton-Charlemagne, 1982

Full, round and sweetly ripe, if not very elegant. A little alcohol shows on the nose. Fat with reasonable acidity but a little heavy. No better than 'good'.

Corton-Pougets, 1959

Fine colour. At first a little closed, even dry. Balsamic flavours. Took some time to come out – the malo having taken place in bottle, probably. Full. Somewhat rigid. Alcoholic. Roasted, cooked fruit. Sweet. A little clumsy, yet rich and enjoyable. A little astringent and four-square. Perhaps residual gas. A second bottle was softer, oakier, rounder, more aromatic, caramel and molasses. Fatter and more seductive. Less colour in this second bottle. Different wood? Chocolatey with a touch of mint. Third bottle: a bit more age. CO_2 and a bit of volatile acidity.

Corton-Pougets, 1915

Good nose. Nose at first of ivy, then *champignons* and *sous-bois*. On the palate round and rich and succulent, but with a certain reserve. Highish acidity. There is a certain rigidity about this. The second bottle retained this highish acidity, and was a bit austere. A third was softer. Long, round, rich and complex. Good grip. A fourth was even better. This had vigour and substance. Depth and life. Indeed all the bottles were very young for a vintage as old as 1915.

HENRI JAYER,
VOSNE-ROMANÉE

'80 per cent of red Burgundy is good at the outset, but only 20 per cent after bottling,' Henri Jayer was quoted as saying in 1985. I am sure this was true then. That this is no longer valid twelve years on is in no small measure due to his own influence as father-figure and guru to the younger generation. This fit, young-looking seventy-four-year-old - you'd take him for sixty - is, like Philippe de Rothschild and *Père* Ramonet, a vinous legend in his own lifetime. The history of present-day Burgundy could not be written without him.

HISTORY

Henri was born in 1922, the third son of Eugène Jayer. Eugène was a local - being born in Boncourt-les-Bois, in the plain outside Nuits-Saint-Georges - but he was not originally a *vigneron*. He had installed himself in Vosne-Romanée before the 1914–18 war, working for others, manufacturing the straw protections for bottles in wooden cases, and preparing the grafts between Pinot Noir and rootstock. Gradually he pieced together a 3 hectare domaine, largely from land which had been allowed to go dormant after the phylloxera epidemic, in Echézeaux, Vosne-Romanée, Les Beaumonts and elsewhere.

The name Jayer is familiar in vinous circles in this part of the Côte, and they are all related. Jacqueline Jayer, whose wines are today made by the Grivot family, is a cousin, so too are Madelaine, wife of Alfred Haegelen, and her brother Robert, of the domaine Jayer-Gilles, based in Magny-lès-Villers in the Hautes-Côtes. But Henri's direct relations are his elder brothers Lucien and Georges.

Georges became a *forestier*, and the wine that has been sold under his label has always, to all other extents and purposes, been identical with that bottled as Henri Jayer. The wine of the other brother, Lucien, though made by Henri, was separately *élevé*. It was always Lucien who has tended the family vines, Henri who was responsible in the cellar.

In 1942 Henri married Marcelle Rouget, whose uncle worked at the Domaine de la Romanée-Conti. Shortly afterwards he was entrusted with a large part of the Méo-Camuzet domaine on a *métayage* basis. Together with further leasing arrangements that Lucien entered into when he came back from the war, this gave the Jayers enough to live on.

Over the years Henri was able to increase his own land-holdings, in village Vosne-Romanée, in generics - Bourgogne *rouge* in Couchey, to the north - and particularly, in Vosne-Romanée, *premier cru*, Cros-Parentoux. This 1 hectare *climat*, next to Richebourg, which Henri himself cleared and planted in the immediate post-war years, is divided 70:30 between himself and the Méo-Camuzet domaine.

For many years Henri Jayer continued to make the wine of the vines he was entrusted with in the traditional manner: fermenting with most of the stalks at a high temperature, and using some but not a great deal of new oak. The Méo-Camuzet share was sold off in bulk. So, largely, was everything else.

But Henri has an enquiring mind. Fascinated by cellar work, and quite happy to leave the vines to Lucien, he began to experiment, to increase his knowledge of other wines, and to fine-tune his own wine-making. Gradually over the years the Jayer method changed, and at the same time he began to bottle and sell more on his own account. By the mid-1970s, the Jayer style, as we know it today, had been fully developed.

LE STYLE JAYER

It starts in the vineyard. When Anthony Hanson asked François Faiveley what was the Jayer secret (*Burgundy*, 1995), the reply was: 'Yield, yield and again yield.' That is, a reduced one. There are two other aspects: the *terroir* and the individual signature of the *vigneron*. The latter is important, but it must not obliterate the former. 'OK,' Henri Jayer said to me once, 'if you are offered Cros-Parentoux you know it is either mine or Méo's. But Echézeaux? It could be anybody's. The wine must be unmistakably Echézeaux. But mine must be equally unmistakably Henri Jayer's.'

And further: 'The wine must be clean and pure, above all. It must be full and fleshy, fat and concentrated, but discreet, supple and soft at the same time. It must be vigorous and succulent, underpinned by the tannin and the new oak. But not dominated by either of these. And it must have definition' - which goes back to the previous paragraph. This is exactly what he produces.

Purity and concentration are the epitome of the Jayer signature. This is achieved by the restricted crop in the first place, and then by total destalking, a five- to seven-day pre-fermentation cold maceration – not achieved by excess sulphur dioxide but by temperature control – and fermentation in cement vats (better than wood, because of the risk of bacteriological infection; better than stainless steel because the heat is retained), at temperatures of up to 34°C, with a long maceration. 'I wait,' says Jayer, 'until the cap begins to sink into the wine. This is when the CO_2 produced by the fermentation has begun to die down.' There are two pumpings over a day for the first few days. Then *pigeage*. And, of course ('I insist!'), natural yeasts. 'Thank God,' says Henri Jayer, 'for two things which have made the life of the *vigneron* so much easier. The first is anti-rot treatment, the second is the thermo-regulation of the vinification.'

The wine then goes into 100 per cent new oak. Is this not more than it can take? you ask. Not if the wine is concentrated enough, replies Henri Jayer mildly. 'I rack it after the malo and again before the fining a year or more later. I fine with two whites of egg per cask, and when this has settled down I bottle by hand, off the finings, with no filtration.'

This is a bluff, bullet-headed man speaking, relaxed and genial when you know him well. But a man, you are aware, who doesn't suffer fools too gladly. 'There is too much sloppy *élevage* around,' he said to me in the early days. 'You only have to look at the colours. A prematurely brown wine is a faulty wine. It has been allowed to oxidise. Either the fruit was not completely ripe or there has been bad hygiene in the cellar. People don't look after their wine properly.'

But then again, seemingly contradicting himself: 'You must let the wine make itself. You can protect it *too* much. You have got to take risks. People manipulate their wine excessively.' The explanation is the care taken in the first place: the low harvest, the totally healthy fruit, and the concentration. The wine then has the vigour and the substance to look after itself. In Henri Jayer's hands the results are staggering. The man never had any formal education, yet he produced some of the finest wines in the Côte.

EMMANUEL ROUGET

Produced, not produces. Today Henri Jayer is *en retraite*, and all the Jayer family vines – Lucien's in 1985, Georges' in 1986 and Henri's in 1991 – have been passed on.

The lucky recipient is Henri Jayer's nephew, Emmanuel Rouget. Rouget, born in 1958, a tall and sturdy dark-haired man, not yet as relaxed and urbane as Jayer, trained as an automobile mechanic, found it hard to find work, and was rescued by his uncle in 1976. He set up on his own account in 1985, buying the old Louis Gouroux premises in Flagey. He too has not had any formal vinous education. But who could have a better teacher?

Today it is Rouget who tends the vines and makes the wine. No doubt Henri Jayer is still involved, as he is in a sort of advisory capacity at the domaine Méo-Camuzet, whose vines he had to turn back in 1988.

The arrangement with Rouget is the usual share-cropping one. Rouget gets half the fruit. In fact all the wine is made together, so what happens in effect is that half is labelled as Emmanuel Rouget – half of each of the three family plots of Echézeaux (totalling 1.43 ha), for instance – the rest is bottled under one of the Jayer brothers' names. But it is all the same wine. Rouget also has vines on his own account, and looks after a small estate in Savigny-lès-Beaune on behalf of Jean Crotet, proprietor of the two-star hotel and restaurant at Levernois, outside Beaune. In total he looks after 6 hectares.

Has Rouget changed anything since he took over? He looks at me incredulously. How dare I suggest such a thing? Then he reflects. Well, we collect the fruit in plastic containers rather than wooden baskets now. And, I remember to myself, he did not impose 100 per cent new wood on the 1992s. This was wise.

This aspect of new wood is my sole reproach over the Henri Jayer 'method' and the resulting wines, though it is not a factor which regularly worries me when I sample the wines in cask. At that time the oak, though present, doesn't seem to impinge too much. But it is when you are drinking the wine many years later, over a meal which may take an hour and a half or more - which, of course, is how most consumers are going to meet their Henri Jayer wines - that the oakiness sometimes obtrudes. I was on my way to Sancerre once, in the early summer of 1994, and I stopped at the two-star, Relais-et-Château, Hostellerie Les Bézards, north of Pouilly-sur-Loire. I felt like pushing the boat out, and when I saw Henri Jayer's Vosne-Romanée, Cros-Parentoux, 1985 on the list, even at an inflated price, I decided to go for it.

At first my notes were ecstatic: marvellously pure and concentrated Pinot Noir; tannins totally under control; oaky, obviously; but very well balanced. Delicious. It was when we came to cheese, some time later, that a doubt began to intrude. The fruit in the wine seemed to have got submerged under the wood. As it evolved further the wood became more and more dominant. In the end, and this is unlike me, I didn't even finish the bottle.

I had the same problem with the same wine and the 1985 Vosne-Romanée, Les Brûlées in February 1985, when I held a 1985 tasting in London. The remains of these two wines, and others which had showed well, were drunk at the lunch afterwards. Yet other wines, Jayer's 1980 Cros-Parentoux, such 1982s, 1986s and 1987s that I have seen, seem to have absorbed the oak better. Perhaps it is just this vintage. Most of the other mature wines are as uniformly splendid as the Jayer reputation would suggest, and the quality shows no signs of having changed since the Rouget takeover.

THE TASTING

I sampled the following wines at a tasting of The Wine Club of Philadelphia, organised by John McNulty in October 1994.

Optimum drinking

Vosne-Romanée, Cros-Parentoux, 1988
Now-2016

Medium to medium-full youthful colour. Lovely ample oaky nose. Very clean. Rich, chocolate-coffee nose. Medium-full body, beautiful fruit. Ample and full of fruit. Lovely balance. Very classy. Not a lot of tannin. But real intensity and class. Very fine.

Vosne-Romanée, Les Brûlées, 1983
Now-2000 plus

Light to medium colour. Brown at the rim. Slightly cloudy. Very 1983 on the nose. Pruney sweet. Slightly alcoholic. On the palate medium to medium-full. A little astringent. Quite fresh but a slight lack of real grip and intensity and fat. Elegant certainly, and no lack of acidity. Perhaps not macerated long enough. I have had better Jayer 1983s. No hail. No rot. Very good.

Echézeaux, 1991
2000-2015

Medium-full fresh colour. Firm nose. Backward, ripe, very cassis-raspberry, not a bit sweet. Still very young. Lovely fruit. Nicely austere. This is cool but classy. Fullish, still quite

tannic. On the attack a little austere. On the follow-through real thrust and intensity. Lovely finish. Very fine. But not quite as good as the 1989 or 1985.

Echézeaux, 1989
1999-2019

Fullish, vigorous colour. Big, full, chocolatey, oaky nose. Very ample. Still youthful. A wine of richness and backbone. Fullish, rich and fat. Good black-fruit flavour. Very good acidity. This is youthful but very fine indeed. Real intensity at the end. Cool. Lovely.

Echézeaux, 1985
Now-2020

Full, rich, voluptuous colour. Closed coffee-flavoured, rich nose. Gamey exotic elements. Full, fat, rich and tannic. This is meaty. Very good acidity. Youthful. Potentially great. Real concentration. Real depth. Very, very lovely.

Echézeaux, 1983
Now-2000

Fullish, well matured colour. The colour is a bit cloudy. Fat, rich, slightly hot nose. Fullish, some astringency. But fat and intense and powerful. Good grip. Quite a gamey wine, yet fresh. Lost its fruit quite fast. But quite classy. Quite some alcohol here. A wine for food.

Echézeaux, 1982   Now–2009

Medium colour. Now mature. Round, sweet,
slightly boiled sweet nose. Good vigour if not
very full and substantial. Medium-full, still a
little youthful. Ripe, a little simple. Good thrust
but not the fat and concentration of the best.
Good length. Just about ready.

Echézeaux, 1981   Now–2009

Fullish colour; just about mature. Fragrant,
fruity, elegant nose. Not a lot of oak. Lovely
sweet redcurrant-raspberry fruit. On the palate
a little less interesting. Medium-full. Still
youthful. A touch of tannin. Good intensity.
Quite good acidity. Not exactly fat. Nor really
very, very complex. Less fat and spicy, less easy
to drink, but better class than the 1982. Still a
bit hard. But very good nevertheless. Especially
for the vintage.

Echézeaux, 1979   Now–2004

Quite a mature colour. Medium-full, brown at
the rim. Here there is a slight gamey/tobacco
pruney-ness on the nose. A touch of astringency.
Fullish, ripe. Quite intense. It has more power
and more fat. Again totally clean. Good freshness.
Long. Bags of life. Slightly faded, but not exactly
classy. Fine for the vintage.

Richebourg, 1986   Now–2004

Quite full, mature colour. Rich, ripe, gamey,
but not exactly classy nose. A little over-ripe.
On the palate a plummy wine. Medium-full.
Reasonable structure and grip. A clean, well-
made wine. But not a wine of complexity and
depth. Fine for an 1986.

Richebourg, 1985   1998–2025

Very good colour. Still very, very young. Very
concentrated on the nose. Delicious at first.
Quite firm and oaky later. Much more black
fruity and plummy than I had expected.
Backward. Very, very concentrated, and fresh
too. Very intense. Cool, elegant, very lovely
indeed. This is excellent.

FRANÇOIS JOBARD,
MEURSAULT

Discreet, understated, slow to show their quality and personality - the very opposite of the glossy, the flamboyant and the upfront - are the wines of François Jobard, one of the very best growers in Meursault. You could use some of these same adjectives to describe the man himself. He is very shy. Trying to get information out of him is like getting blood out of the proverbial stone. Even after fifteen years of regular visits he still calls me *Monsieur*. Have patience though. Dig deep. Involve Marie-Claire, his wife, and Antoine, his son, now at the local *Viti*. And your perseverance will eventually be rewarded. As at every fine cellar the visitor can learn much.

HISTORY

There have been Jobards in Meursault since the French Revolution, and today, as well as at two domaines there, the name can be found at Maison Joseph Drouhin, in the person of their wine-maker, Laurence Jobard, and at Maison Louis Latour, where the cellar-master is another Jobard. These, however, are distant cousins, it seems, and indeed only tenuously related to each other.

The Meursault domaine was built up by François' father and grandfather, both called Pierre, and by the first Pierre's father – whose name François cannot recall but who was the *régisseur* of another domaine – in the aftermath of the phylloxera crisis. As with most domaines it has been expanded, only to be divided among the next generation, who have then been forced to repeat the process.

This last happened in 1971. Pierre number two was *en retraite* (he died in 1982), François (born 1940) and his elder brother Charles had already been going their separate ways for half a dozen years or so, and in this year it was decided to divide things formally. Combined, the estate was not large, divided it was barely economic, but in the previous year François had bought some Genevrières for himself, and in the subsequent decade he was able to expand further. He now exploits just under 5 hectares, most of it owned, but some of the village wine leased *en métayage*. In Pierre's time very little had been bottled, but François, abandoned by the *négoce* in the mid-1970s (in 1978 the price of village Meursault was a mere 18 francs per bottle, less even than Chablis and Pouilly-Fuissé which were 20) had perforce to go it alone. In those days, he muses, we were uprooting generic Chardonnay and replacing it with Pinot Noir. Now we do the reverse.

THE DOMAINE

Pride of place, not because it is necessarily the best but because it is the largest parcel, is the Meursault, Poruzots: 71 ares in the upper part of the *climat*. The soil is redder and less stony here than further along in the Genevrières and Perrières, and François' vines come from several different parcels, one dating back to 1944. Nearby lie 54 a of Genevrières, 16 a of Charmes, again in the upper part of the *climat*, and, up in the hamlet of Blagny, 21 a of Chardonnay and 29 a of Pinot Noir in La Pièce-sous-le-Bois. A more recent purchase is a small parcel in Puligny-Montrachet in the vineyard of Le Trézin, the only village parcel above the *premiers* and *grands crus* on the hill.

François Jobard's village Meursault comes from two sources, En-la-Barre, behind his house, and Les Tillets, above Poruzots. It is this parcel which is leased. Together these total some 2 hectares.

Rather more than most growers, Jobard is keen on Cordon training for his Chardonnay (others may prune to Cordon for Pinot Noir, but keep to Guyot for the white grapes). Roughly half his vines, particularly the young ones, are trained this way. The Guyot weakens the vines, he says, necessitating more manuring. The Guyot method, he points out, is relatively new in Burgundy, only being widely adopted in the 1930s. But, showing me some very old, neighbouring, Cordon-trained plants, where the buds are far too far away from the main root, you can go too far. You can't Cordon-train for ever. He prunes to six bunches only, being contemptuous of green harvesting (it means you haven't done it properly before), but nevertheless doesn't believe that you have to be *that* exigent about Chardonnay quantity. 'In the *premiers crus* that I possess the vine can well support 45 hl/ha and still produce concentrated wine.'

Initially in the spring he will use herbicides against weeds, ploughing and hoeing later on, and his approach is basically organic. He stops treating his vines earlier than most, the last being at the end of July or the beginning of August, and he doesn't believe in anti-rot sprays, which he feels retard the progress towards maturity.

WINE-MAKING

After a *triage* in the vineyard the fruit goes straight into the *pressoir*, a newish pneumatic apparatus, and the juice is then racked directly into barrel without a preliminary *débourbage*. Why doesn't he settle out the gross lees first? His father didn't, and he has always been pleased with the results. And he has never had any off flavours.

Natural yeasts are used, a minimum of new oak, and the wines kept in wood as much as two years with a minimum of manipulation. For three years he hasn't fined, and a light filtration is all the wine gets before bottling by gravity.

He is also no great fan of excessive *bâtonnage*. 'You have to be very careful or you will chase out the CO_2 and let the aromas escape,' is how he puts it.

THE WINE

The result is a wine which is pure, backward, inexpressive at the outset, but which has a real depth of character and great elegance. It lasts a long time.

Above all the Jobard wines have an excellent acidity. How does he think this comes about? (Because he certainly doesn't tartrate the must, a procedure he abhors – 'It dries up and hardens the wine. It never marries.') Why the high acidity? Jobard ponders. 'Perhaps because we did not over-fertilise the soil with potassium in the 1960s and 1970s. Perhaps it is the Cordon training. Perhaps because we have very little SO4 rootstock.' It seems to be something he takes for granted.

Why the Jobard wines need time is perhaps easier to answer. The *cave* below the house, extended in 1992, is cool, though not as damp as, say, Lafon's. Moreover the wine is concentrated, and its *élevage* not hurried along. It is deliberately not a wine made for creating orgasms in its early life. But for those who have the sense and patience to leave them to mature quietly for a decade or so, this is certainly not a bad thing. The result is all the better, all the richer and more profound in the end.

THE TASTING

I sampled the following wines *chez* Jobard in July 1995.

MEURSAULT, PORUZOTS

1992 *Optimum drinking* **1998–2006**

Honeyed on the nose, with a touch of seed cake. There is a little *sur-maturité* here. An adolescent wine. There is no lack of grip. But it is a little disjointed. Finishes rich, long and austerely. Needs time. Not at its best. Plenty of complexity on the finish. Surely very good. But not in the league of the 1990 and 1989.

1991 **Now–2001**

Flowery on the nose. Delicate and complex. This is a very elegant if slightly vegetal, herbal sort of wine. Medium body. Good fruit and dimension if no great richness. Good grip. This is just about ready now. Finishes with a lot more character than most 1991s.

1990 **1998–2009**

This is fat, and evolved for a 1990 and for

Jobard. Rich, mellow, opulent, oaky. Full. On the palate more grip and raciness than the nose indicates. Very rich and fat and concentrated. Lots of depth. But austere. This is long and splendid and will still develop.

1989 **Now–2012**

Lovely nose. Classic hazelnuts, nicely austere buttery Chardonnay flavours. A ripe, youthful but nevertheless gently poised wine. Beautifully harmonious. This is very fine. On the palate there is real intensity and persistence. Excellent fruit. Very good grip.

1988 **Now–2005**

Fresh nose. Nicely fruity. Balanced, ready, open and accessible without any great depth or complexity. This is a fine example from what was only an averagely good vintage. *À point*. Fresh, fruity, round, plump and ripe. Long. Positive finish. Improved in the glass.

1987   **Now–2001**

Gentle slightly herbal nose. Good freshness from the acidity. Another very good result. Attractively fruity. No lack of balance. Ripe. Good finish. Neither too acidic nor too vegetal. A splendid result. This is almost as pleasant as the 1988.

1986   **Now–2003**

Fresh, slightly scented. Quite a lot of *sur-maturité* nose. This is very 1986, lots of botrytis on the palate. Yet good grip. The wine is honeyed, rich, and has a reasonable acidity. It is not tired or too evolved. The finish is very fresh. This would go very well with *foie gras*. Better perhaps than a really sweet wine.

1985   **Now–2025**

Very youthful on the nose. An open, profound wine. Totally pure and clean. Full, very very ripe and concentrated. Splendidly fresh. Gently honeyed. Marvellous harmony. Excellent fruit. This is a great wine. Much more masculine than the 1989 and better balanced than the 1990. Only just ready.

1984   **Drink soon**

This has had the benefit of being a small harvest. Because it is surprisingly concentrated. And the acidity has now mellowed. Mineral, apply, but not tired, herbal or weedy. Interesting nose. I get a lot of pleasure here. It is a little austere, but it is not under-ripe. Nor is it over-evolved.

1983   **Drink soon**

Plump rather than fat on the nose. Not too forceful, nor is it astringent, nor alcoholic. It is a big fat wine, muscular and spicy. But I prefer it to the 1986. It is fresher, it doesn't have that faded botrytis character. Though there is no lack of botrytis here. It is because it has the grip and the concentration. Slightly heavy, nevertheless. Needs food. Larger than life.

1982   **Now–1999**

Flowery, ample and fresh - surprisingly so - on the nose. This is full and concentrated. Has a touch of smoky bacon. Lovely plump ripe vigorous fruit. This has plenty of body and plenty of depth. Another example of how good this vintage can be for white wine. Fine grip. Long finish. Will keep well. No sign of age.

1980   **Drink soon**

Lean, apply but not a bit tired. Very elegant. It lacks a little generosity and the acidity shows a bit at the end. But it is very stylish and surprisingly youthful.

1976   **Now–1999**

One can sense the alcohol, but, like the 1983, there is a splendid acidity. This has kept the fruit very ripe and fresh. Delicious fruit-salady flavours with a touch of nuts and spice. Full, fat, plump, harmonious, long. A larger than life wine. But very fine. Will still last well.

1971   **Now–2005 plus**

Lovely almost perfumed nose. Very concentrated, very ripe (almost sweet - but no botrytis). High acidity. Very very fresh. This in its own way shows how the 1990 Moselles (very very concentrated, very high acidity) will go. It is like a 1947 white Burgundy. Soft, mellow, intense finish. *Grand vin*!

OTHER WINES

Meursault, Blagny, 1989   **Now–2015**

This is richer, firmer and more masculine and more racy. More Puligny-ish - than the Poruzots. Clean, very concentrated, very well balanced, very stylish. A fuller wine. Long, still needs time. Lovely.

Blagny, La Pièce-sous-le-Bois, 1988   **Now–2006**

This is now beginning to round off. Good colour. Some maturity. Ripe, gently spicy, aromatic plump nose with good acidity. The tannins are now soft. Nicely fragrant. Not a bit lumpy. Indeed more Volnay-ish (like Santenots) than the usual run-of-the-mill Blagnys. Good plus.

Blagny, La Pièce-sous-le-Bois, 1978
                                             Now–2000 plus

Half-bottle. Mature colour. On the nose just a touch vegetal, but rich and round and aromatic nevertheless. Ripe on the palate. No rusticity or aggressivity here. Shows well. Nicely mellow. Very good.

Blagny, La Pièce-sous-le-Bois, 1976   **Now–1999**

Good full colour. This has good size - without being too tannic and structured. The fruit is cooked. But there is good acidity. A muscular wine. Full, rich, but slightly dense. The 1978 is rounder and more stylish. But very good.

Blagny, La Pièce-sous-le-Bois, 1973   Drink soon

The first vintage after he acquired the parcel. Fully mature colour. This is still fresh, not astringent. And quite full. But it has lost a bit of its elegance. Quite good.

MICHEL

LAFARGE, *VOLNAY*

Away from the main roads, tucked up at the top of its vineyards under a hill where once the Dukes of Burgundy had a hunting lodge, lies the medieval village of Volnay, a maze of narrow steep roads and silent little alleyways. Below and on either side are the best of the commune's *premiers crus*: the large Clos-des-Chênes overlooking Monthélie to the south; underneath it Caillerets, and Santenots across the Meursault border; in the middle Champans, Taille-Pieds and Bousse d'Or; to the north Fremiets, Chanlins and Pitures, beyond which lie the vineyards of Pommard. We are in the heart of the red wine sector of the Côte-de-Beaune. We are at the home of one of the most elegant and delicate expressions of the Pinot Noir.

For an example of the finest red Burgundy that is fragrant and feminine, yet intense and long-lasting, you need look no further than the wines of Domaine Michel Lafarge. Lafarge and his ancestors have been making wine in the village since at least the French Revolution, almost certainly earlier. Lafarge and his father and grandfather have been mayors of the village and Henri Lafarge, Michel's father, was additionally *régisseur* of the Hospices de Beaune. So there is a sense of family tradition and communal responsibility here. Along with those such as the Angervilles and Boulays, the Boillots and the Rossignols, Lafarge is part of the continuing history of Volnay, a history which has had the production of fine Burgundy as its *raison d'être* since the Middle Ages.

HISTORY

The Lafarge family are *vignerons*. Originally, no doubt, they worked for the great patrician land-holders, ecclesiastical or aristocratic, who held sway in the area for so long. Piece by piece since the early 1800s the family turned from being *laboureurs* for others to vineyard-owners in their own right. An ancestor, Jean-Baptiste Gillotte, is recorded as owning land in Volnay, Mitans in 1855. His son acquired a piece of Clos-des-Chênes towards the turn of the century and the Clos-du-Château-des-Ducs was added by Michel's grandfather a few years later. Henri Lafarge bought the Beaune, Grèves in 1954, and Michel, in his turn, has tagged on the Pommard, Pézerolles, a parcel of Volnay, Brouillard and some more village and communal wine.

In all this adds up to 7.8 hectares, a reasonable domaine by Burgundy standards, one that is self-sufficient and will support a family.

Where the Lafarges have been prudent, by luck and by design, is to preserve the unity of their *vignoble*. When Henri Lafarge died in 1967, the domaine could have been split among his three children. Luckily neither of Michel's two brothers wanted to be a *vigneron*. One is the manager of a firm which produces plastics, the other a director of a wine-distribution company in Lyon. Over the years, Michel Lafarge has slowly bought back his brothers' inheritance.

The same will eventually happen, one assumes, in the next generation. Michel and his wife Noëlle have four children, two sons and two daughters. But only the eldest, Frédéric, is following in his father's footsteps. Frédéric, born in 1958, has, unlike his father, taken viticultural and oenological courses at the local wine schools. He worked in Champagne and did a *stage* at Château Palmer in 1976. He and his wife Chantal, together with the next generation of Lafarges, live next door.

WINE-MAKING PHILOSOPHY

Michel Lafarge is a tall, lean, fit and handsome man, now in his mid-sixties. With his straight white hair and piercing blue eyes he exudes an atmosphere of calm authority, decisive in his opinions but cautious in his approach. There is dedication and an open, questioning mind here, but also a healthy scepticism; there is generosity and much charm, but you sense also an unspoken contempt for the sloppy methods of some of his neighbours and the way others are easily led astray by the blandishments of 'experts' and the vagaries of fashion.

It all starts, of course, in the vineyard. Michel, with his natural suspicion of unproven new panaceas, was one of the few to resist over-fertilising his vineyards in the 1960s. He is hesitant about clones, preferring, in the main, to generate his own plant material from the best of his own vines. 'Most clones are too productive,' he says, 'and there is not enough variety among them. I've noticed that the same clone on the same rootstock produces quite differently, in volume and in quality of fruit, even in adjoining *climats* in Volnay. There is much more research still to be done.'

On the other hand, he is a firm believer that for the Pinot Noir, in most of his vineyards at least, as he will add, Cordon pruning - a spur from which the canes are pruned very short - is better than the Guyot system. The harvest can be controlled more efficiently, and the risk of rot, as the fruit will be wider spaced, is reduced. 'To produce quality fruit - and you can only produce quality wine with top-class fruit in the first place - you must have old vines, and a small crop. We rarely produce more than the *rendement de base*. Then you must have a severe *triage* - it is of paramount importance to eliminate the second generation of fruit and the *verjus* - and long *cuvaisons*.'

'Pick early when the weather is bad. Pick as late as possible if it is fine,' is another Lafarge maxim. The *premiers crus* are picked first, the generics later. The grapes are 80-100 per cent destalked, totally in the poorer vintages, for the wood will be unripe too, and might impart a herbaceous taint to the wine, but on the other hand a small percentage of stalks helps prolong the fermentation. In most vintages there is a short pre-fermentation maceration. Indigenous yeasts are invariably used. Lafarge considers that artificial yeasts do not produce as well. Paradoxically this is because they are too efficient. And because there are fewer different strains, the wine is less complex.

Lafarge, to quote Remington Norman (*The Great Domaines of Burgundy*) 'places a high value on the traditions of transmitted experience.' He worked alongside his father from 1946, when he left school, until 1966, when his father was ill. From 1966 to 1978 'I was all on my own, and then Frédéric joined me. It is a good thing to have one's son with one. One is not only teaching him, but one can profit by a second opinion, an alternative view, someone to bounce an idea off.' This is no patriarchal domaine.

While no two vintages are alike, similarities and parallels can obviously be drawn between one vintage and another, and this can enable the Lafarges to decide precisely how long to macerate, and at what temperature, how much *vin de presse* to add (rarely any at all in this cellar: 'one must be very prudent'), whether to *saigner* (Lafarge is generally against, believing that it unbalances the wine, but accepts that it is a useful process in some vintages), and how long and often to perform a *pigeage*. To quote Remington Norman again, Michel Lafarge says 'The only way of improving quality is to review what has been done and achieved before.'

In general the *cuvaison* lasts fourteen days, and is held at a maximum of 30°C. Only in the poorer years is it shorter and hotter. 'Long fermentations fix the colour and tannins better and make more complex wine.'

Lafarge is not an excitable man, but he is vehement about one thing: 'The greatest error one can make is to leave the *pressoir* on automatic. One must be there! Today not enough people pay enough attention. They seem to think all these modern machines will make the wine themselves!'

He is also vigorously against pumping the wine around all over the place. 'Wine is fragile. One must pump as little as possible. A heat exchanger is a disaster!' If you cool the cellar, says Lafarge, this will do the trick.

Thereafter, in the cellars under the houses of Michel and Frédéric, part of which date back to the thirteenth century, the wine is left to mature – in about 25 per cent new oak – for fifteen to twenty months. There are two rackings and a fining with white of egg, but the wines are rarely filtered.

THE WINES

'Burgundy keeps much longer than people imagine,' says Michel Lafarge. 'I remember the great years of my father's and grandfather's days – 1911 and 1929, for instance – and in my time 1945, 1959, 1961 and 1964. Most of these will still keep for ages. More recently we have had vintages such as 1976, 1978 and 1983. One must wait. One must have patience.' With many of the older Lafarge wines I've tasted in Burgundy, particularly those which have never been moved from Michel's cellar, I get the impression that they've remained stable, hardly evolving once they reached maturity, and will continue to remain this way for years to come.

The Lafarge style is of wines which are true to their *terroir*. The Beaune, Grèves tastes like a Beaune, Grèves – plump, succulent, quite meaty; the Volnays are the epitome of all that is grace; and the Pommard, Pézerolles, as it should be, is more structured and brutal when it is young, more rugged and muscular when it is mature. From vines on the Volnay-Meursault border Lafarge produces a little Meursault and Côte-de-Beaune-Villages.

Judge a *vigneron* though, as you judge a wine merchant, by the quality of his lesser wines, his generics. Michel Lafarge produces a spirited, stylish Aligoté, a fragrant, *primeur rosé* in the years he practises a *saignée*, and one of the very best Bourgogne *rouges* in the whole of Burgundy. He has a hectare of Pinot Noir on the west side of the N74 which directly touches the Volnay appellation. I'd much rather drink this, at half the price, than most of his neighbours' communal wine! Drink the 1989 now, retain the 1988 for a year or so, and then move on to the brilliant 1990. You're in for a treat!

There is Volnay, Volnay *Vendange Selectionnée* (from the oldest vines), Volnay *premier cru* (from a number of *climats* including Mitans and Chanlíns), and Volnay, Clos-du-Château-des-Ducs. This comes from an enclave, directly below the house, within the *premier cru* misleadingly called Le Village. Up until the end of the Second World War it was labelled as Clos-du-Château-des-Ducs, but then the title was disallowed by the authorities as it had never been registered and the wine had to be bottled as Le Village. A few years ago Michel Lafarge won back the right to the original name.

The village wine is a neat, elegant example: pure Volnay, evolving in the medium term, with lovely raspberry fruit. The *Vendange Selectionnée* is fatter and richer. The *premier cru* is fuller and more intense, as one might expect. It is worth the extra. With the Clos-du-Château-des-Ducs (which should not be confused with, nor does it bear any geographical resemblance to, the Marquis d'Angerville's Clos-des-Ducs) one is in the realm of high-class Burgundy. The vines are from parcels of eighteen and fifty-seven years of age, and they produce a wine with more obvious tannins than the Clos-des-Chênes but with a fine persistence of concentrated fruit.

The best wine in the Lafarge cellar, invariably, is the Clos-des-Chênes. The parcel is just under 1 hectare in extent, planted during the war, in 1950, and at various times in the early 1980s (the produce of the young vines is vinified separately and not added to the Clos-des-Chênes *cuvée*) and is situated just above the road to Monthélie.

This is one of the great Volnays. 'I think it is the epitome,' says Michel Lafarge. 'The structure is there, but it is hidden.' The wine seems supple, not marked by the tannin, but in fact it has plenty of depth and reserve behind it. The fruit is rich and concentrated; lush, opulent, complex and harmonious. And always with enormous finesse. A complete wine from one of the best domaines in the Côte d'Or.

THE TASTING

I sampled the following wines in Volnay in June 1992.

VOLNAY, CLOS-DES-CHÊNES

Optimum drinking

1990
1998–2015

Bottled at the beginning of May, six weeks ago. Fine colour. Has recovered well, but then only fined, not filtered. Lovely rich velvety-concentrated nose. Marvellous fruit with subtle underlying oak. Intensely flavoured. Fullish. Very well balanced. Lots of depth. Lots of class, and above all the wonderfully velvety persistent style of fine Volnay. Splendid finish. Excellent.

1989
Now–2008

Good colour. Delicate, fragrant but subtle Pinot Noir. Still just a little bottle sick. This is not evident on the palate though. Medium-full. Very ripe. Almost chocolatey-black cherry. On the palate there is very good acidity, but it is a touch adolescent at the moment. Long, complex, subtle finish. Very good indeed. A wine of great generosity and charm, potentially.

1988
Now–2015

Very good colour. No sign of development. Closed nose. Just a touch animal. Medium-full. Quite reserved. Good structure and very good grip. A little closed-in, even hard on the attack, but opening up on the finish. Persistent, classic, very classy indeed. This is multi-dimensional and if less fat than the 1990 very close to it in complexity and depth.

1987
Now–2007

Medium colour. Now some sign of brown. A little adolescent still on the nose. A touch of caramel and spice here. Medium to medium-full. Good structure. Plenty of fruit. Good acidity. This still needs a few years. But remarkably concentrated and profound, as well as stylish, for a 1987. Evolved, in the best sense, in the glass. Very graceful. Very long finish. Very good quality.

1986   **Now-2000**

Surprisingly good for the vintage. Deeper but a little browner than the 1989. Open, accessible plump nose. Not a bit dry or weedy. It doesn't have the structure and grip of the 1987. But very Volnay, very good fruit and harmony. Fullish for a 1986. Not a bit dry. The harvest was halved by hail before the flowering. Excellent for the vintage. Just about à *point* now. But plenty of vigour.

1985   **Now-2010**

Good colour. Only a touch of maturity. Ripe, mature Pinot. But still a touch adolescent. Not on form. More presentable on the palate. Medium-full. Good grip. Very well structured. A concentrated wine but one which is still a bit awkward. Best on the finish which is long, complex and subtle. Excellent grip for a 1985. Fine.

1984   **Drink soon**

Full colour for the vintage. Vigorous, only just about mature. Good style on the nose. Fresh. Sufficiently ample and complex if not *that* fat or persistent. Medium body. Just a little astringent but quite plump and with good acidity. A fine result for the vintage.

1983   **Now-2015**

Fine vigorous colour. Very full, only a little brown. Fascinating nose. At first distinctly hot chocolatey - in a profiteroles sense. Then a little dry and funky and animal, with a separate sweet *rôti* aspect. Finally less astringent, more fragrant, with a hint of caramel and coffee as well as the chocolate. On the palate a wine of vigour, richness and structure. Quite muscular on the attack. With better manners on the finish. Long, complex, fat, rich. A much bigger, more concentrated wine than the 1985, with much more vigour and life. Potentially very much better. Very long at the end. Very fine quality.

1981   **Now-1997**

Full, vigorous colour. Ripe, complex nose. Nothing off-vintage about this. Medium to medium-full. Good grip. Plenty of fruit. Really quite concentrated. There is lots of depth here, and no undue astringency or lack of class. Surprisingly vigorous, surprisingly good. Will still last well.

1979   **Now-1999**

Medium-full colour. Mature but no undue brown. Aromatic, round, cedary, a little caramelly on the nose. Medium to medium-full body. Just a hint that it may be loosening up and drying out. But it lost this as it evolved in the glass. It is two- rather than three-dimensional, but balanced, ripe, fresh and stylish and still persistent on the finish. Very good.

1978   **Now-2002 plus**

Fine, full mature colour. Still youthful. Splendidly concentrated nose. Fat, full, vigorous nose, with a touch of coffee and chocolate. Still young. On the palate this is lush but fresh and balanced. Fullish, ample, profound and with a very lovely complex continuation. Lots of life still. Very fine. Will still improve.

1977   **Drink soon**

Good colour. Fullish, a little browner than the 1978. This is remarkably good on the nose. And on the palate, too. Less structure, obviously, than the 1978, but no lack of fruit and flesh. No sign of age. Not mean. Still fresh and stylish. A surprisingly charming and enjoyable bottle.

1976   **Now-2005 plus**

Very good colour. Full, still hardly mature. Fat, ripe, spicy, gamey. But not a bit dry or brutal. Really quite civilised. Full and rich and structured on the palate. Roasted fruit. Almost burnt and caramelly. Good tannins though and plenty of grip. This will still improve. Fine.

1972   **Drink soon**

Good mature colour. Intriguing complex nose. A touch sweet-sour. A touch vegetal-herbal. Medium body. Not lean, but cool and austere in the best complex sense. Soft and round now. Mellow and complex. Long and with a lot of character. Very good.

1970   **Drink soon**

Good mature colour. A little more age than the 1972. A lot of hail at the beginning of August, three storms in one afternoon, reduced what threatened to be too large a harvest. Beginning to show the nose of an old wine. Fresh and fruity still but losing its grip and concentration. Round and ripe. Caramel and nuts. More vigorous on the palate. By no means gone. Medium to medium-full. Ample. Good grip. Lacks the intensity and finesse for fine but very good indeed nevertheless.

1968   **Drink up**

Light to medium colour. Still alive. A little faded on the nose but more vigorous on the palate. Still pleasant. Ripe if a little one-dimensional but balanced and stylish. A fine effort for the vintage, and by no means finished. Positive finish.

1966   **Now-2000 plus**

Good mature colour. Fuller, more spicy and more vigorous on the nose than the 1970.

Definitely caramelly. Interesting fruit. Somehow more peaches and apples than *petits fruits rouges*. Medium to medium-full. Good complexity and balance and more style and vigour than the 1970. Plump, fresh, complex. Long. Fine.

1957   Drink soon

Good colour. Nicely spicy - nutty, caramelly - nose. Soft and cedary underneath. This has ripe, fresh fruit. Good acidity in a slightly austere 1972-y sense. But fatter, richer, bigger. But peachy-apply rather than strawberries and cherries again. Complex finish. Still plenty of enjoyment. Very good.

1952   Now-2000 plus

Very good colour. Full and still quite vigorous. Full and tough on the nose at first. Still powerful. Needed to be allowed to come out of the glass. A big wine. Concentrated, rich, vigorous. On the palate really fine and multi-dimensional. Fat and velvety. Long and complex and very lovely and distinguished. Very fine indeed. Plenty of life still.

1937   Drink soon

Good fullish colour. No undue age. Slightly vegetal aspects at first. These dissipated in the glass. Ripe, complex. Not aged. On the palate a wine which is ripe, fragrant, gentle but vigorous. Still fresh. Lovely. Old roses. Kept very well. Two hours later, at the end of lunch, this was still virile and full of fruit. No hint that it was nearing its end. Can still be kept.

COMTES LAFON,

MEURSAULT

It is a strange fact of Burgundian life that there are many more great red wine domaines than there are white. My own list of two- and three-star estates (see Appendix Three, page 986) comprises four domaines which have been awarded three stars, and twenty which have gained two. But only three of these – Coche-Dury, Ramonet, and, of course, Lafon – are chiefly known for white wines.

It is not that there are more red wine-makers than white. There are at least 100 domaine-bottling estates in Meursault alone. So what is the explanation? Is it harder to make fine white wine than red? Have the growers had it easier for longer? Does the average age of the people responsible come into it? Or is it just plain incompetence? Why are there not more Coche-Durys and Ramonets? Where are the white-wine equivalents of Denis Bachelet and Alain Burguet?

The Domaine des Comtes Lafon, however, is indubitably three-star. At the helm, in the person of the thirty-eight-year-old Dominique Lafon, it has one of the most talented wine-makers in all Burgundy, and one of its most enquiring minds. It is only recently, though, that the Lafon domaine has been fully in charge of its vines and its wines. For most of the post-war period the land was leased out on a *métayage* (share-cropping) basis to other local vignerons, notably the Moreys of Meursault and the Bouleys of Volnay. It is only since 1987 that these leases have one by one come to an end, and it was not until 1994 that they totally ceased.

HISTORY

In 1865 Jules Lafon, a lawyer by profession, arrived in Burgundy from his native Gers – he was born in Auch, in the middle of Armagnac country – to take up the position as *Inspecteur des Finances* in Dijon. He wooed and married a Marie Boch from Meursault, and in 1867 the couple set about constructing a substantial Victorian home in a little park in the northern outskirts of Meursault. They were not the only ones. There are a number of patrician mansions dating from this period in this *quartier* of the sprawling village. The original Lafon property included the buildings and gardens which are now those of the Domaine Prieur. This was where Lafon installed his in-laws.

Jules Lafon was rich and successful. He was also an intransigent Roman Catholic. When church and state were separated in 1905 he was unwilling to allow his tax inspectorial post to be used to force the ecclesiastics to declare their wealth. Instead he resigned his position and retired into private legal practice. In gratitude the Vatican appointed him a Pontifical Count.

He was also active in the affairs of the vine. Marie Boch had inherited a substantial estate. There were holdings in Champans, Santenots-du-Milieu ('*une grande pièce*'), Genevrières-Dessus, Goutte d'Or and Poruzots, as well as lesser vineyards in Meursault, according to Lavalle in 1855, and Lafon bought more. In November 1918 he attended the auction of nearly 1 hectare of Le Montrachet belonging to Charles Drapier, a grower and *négociant* in Puligny. This auction seems to have been a very strange affair. The asking price was apparently 30,000 francs but eventually after some haggling the parcel was knocked down to Auguste Fleurot and Jules Lafon for 32,500. There then arrived a third potential buyer, Léon Roizot, who was prepared to offer more. You might have thought that Fleurot and Lafon would simply have told him he was too late, but French auctions seem to be different from those in Great Britain. Rather than defer the outcome to a second auction the trio decided to share the parcel between the three of them, so each acquired approximately a third of a hectare. The Roizot parcel now forms part of the Montrachet holding of the Domaine de la Romanée-Conti. The Fleurot land was later divided and sold off piece by piece, one of the last remaining fragments being acquired by the Domaine Leflaive in the summer of 1991.

Perhaps the greatest of Jules Lafon's achievements was the creation of the Paulée, the last and infinitely the most enjoyable of the three gastronomic festivities which surround the Hospices de Beaune auction. In 1923, being mayor of Meursault, he had the idea of reviving the traditional end-of-harvest meal when the owner celebrates the vintage with his workers. Lafon invited thirty-five of his friends to a small feast. Today some 600 manage to squeeze their way in, each bearing an interesting old wine or three. It is the greatest bottle party in the world.

Count Jules finally passed away in January 1940, well into his nineties. Responsibility then devolved to his two sons, Pierre and Henri. Pierre died in 1944 and with the war soon to be over Henri wanted to sell up. This was resisted by René, Pierre's son, an engineer by profession who lived in Paris. Then followed one of those bitter family quarrels. Neither side could afford to buy the other out but both could thwart the other's wishes, in Henri's case by preventing René from making any capital expenditure on the estate or borrowing against its assets. It was 1956 before the issue was resolved. In the meanwhile the land was leased out on a share-cropping basis, but somehow, with the help of a man on the spot, René managed to vinify his half of the grapes, the wine from which was sold off in bulk.

In 1957 René Lafon married Marie-Thérèse – she hails from the Bresse – and in 1961 he decided to start bottling all his own wine. He still thinks this is the best vintage he ever made. In 1967 he decided to move back from Paris and live in Meursault. The reputation of the Lafon wines was steadily rising, and wine-making was beginning to become profitable.

DOMINIQUE LAFON

The next step was the arrival of Dominique Lafon, his eldest son. In 1978 Dominique enrolled at the *Lycée Viticole* at Beaune and began to be involved in the wine-making at the domaine. Between 1982 and 1986, following the completion of his oenological and viticultural courses, he worked for the broker Becky Wasserman in Bouilland. 'These were some of the best years of my life,' says Dominique. 'It was a marvellous experience to visit and taste other people's wines, indeed to buy and sell them, and to visit the United States and other countries and wine regions.' He arranged his holidays so that he would be available during the harvest, and gradually took over responsibility for the wines. René's last vintage was the 1982.

From 1987 onwards the *métayage* arrangements began to come to their end, and Dominique began to become involved in the vineyards as well as in the cellar. Has he changed much? 'Most of our *métayers* have been first class. Pierre Morey – who had most of the white wine vineyards, including the Montrachet – is particularly good. But some of the others were not as meticulous as I would have liked. As far as the wine-making is concerned I have not altered things to any great extent. In my father's day his red wines were macerated using a grill to keep the *chapeau* below the surface of the wine, and by pumping over. Today we do this by *pigeage*. But the white wines have always been bottled late. They were kept two years on their lees in the time of my great-grandfather.'

THE VINEYARDS

The impressive roll-call of Lafon wines and *climats* begins in Volnay: Champans, Santenots and Clos-des-Chênes, three of the top five *premiers crus* – Caillerets and Taille-Pieds are the others – in the village.

Uphill of the Volnay-Monthélie road, indeed on the border of the two communes, rises Clos-des-Chênes, gently curving round under the Bois de Chaignot where once the Dukes of Burgundy owned a hunting lodge, so that it faces south as well as east. Lafon owns a third of a hectare here, next to the vines of Michel Lafarge. The Clos-des-Chênes soil is arid and thin, decomposed rock only a couple of dozen centimetres thick over the limestone subsoil. The wine is pure Volnay, supremely fragrant and complex, intensity rather than muscle.

Below the road lies Champans. The soil here is dry, with little clay, and lots of small stones. Underneath there is a flaky limestone the locals call '*lave*'. Here Lafon has half a hectare of vines, and will make eight barrels of wine (200 cases) in a normal vintage.

The largest of the Lafon Volnay holdings is in Santenots, technically across the commune border into Meursault, but, if planted with Pinot Noir, entitled to be labelled as Volnay. Lafon has more than half – 3.8 ha – of the best part of the *climat*, Santenots-du-Milieu. The soil here is different; the underlying rock harder, and nearer to the surface, the pebbles larger, the incidence of clay greater.

What is the difference between the Champans and the Santenots-du-Milieu? Both are fuller than the Clos-des-Chênes. The Champans is lush and rich, fuller and sturdier, and usually more tannic than the Santenots, but the Santenots usually has more depth and intensity. The Clos-des-Chênes vines are relatively young, twenty years or so. Those in the Champans are mostly very old – a large parcel was planted in the mid 1920s – while those in Santenots are middle-aged, averaging just over thirty years.

The last of the red-wine vineyards is in the Duresses *climat* of Monthélie, on the Monthélie/Auxey border. This is not a wine which has been long under the Lafon label. The vines were planted in 1985, and Lafon until recently has sold his wine in bulk to the *négoce*, one year to Jaffelin, as I remember. But he is pleased with the way the vines have developed, and has now added it to his portfolio.

The Chardonnay vineyards begin with three village Meursault parcels: 2.1 hectares of Clos-de-la-Barre, 60 ares of En-la-Barre and 50 a of Désirée. The Désirée lies in the Plures *climat* under the local camping site and is planted on the SO4 rootstock (most of the rest is 3309, plus 161/49 for Pinot Noir and 161 - which latter Lafon prefers - for Chardonnay). SO4 is very vigorous, early maturing and produces wines with a tendency to low acidity. Careful treatments, adding a bit of magnesium to balance the excess of potassium, composting as little as possible, and severely restricting the yield, have reduced the harvest and improved the balance. This is a better wine since Dominique Lafon took the vines back in 1988.

Technically this is a *premier cru* wine. Lafon was told by the authorities that if he changed the name from Désirée to Plures he could call the wine *premier cru*. But both because he doesn't consider the wine good enough, and because he has established the name Désirée he has decided not to proceed in this direction.

The Clos-de-la-Barre lies literally behind the garden but within the walls of 'Château Lafon', a fine nineteenth-century mansion on the northern edges of the village. The soil is shallow and marly and based on rock. The vines flower early but ripen slowly, resulting in good acidities despite normally being the last plot to be harvested. Clos-de-la-Barre is fuller and more masculine than the Désirée; a village wine of considerable depth and personality. 'It is my favourite vineyard,' says Dominique. 'I feel at home here.'

South of the village the first Lafon *premier cru* one reaches is Gouttes d'Or; shallow, reddish soil holding a little clay, and usually making quite firm, sometimes four-square wine. There is a third of a hectare here. The vines were badly degenerated as a result of the virus known as *Court-Noué*. When Lafon took them back he ripped them all out, replanting in 1990. Presently, therefore, there is no wine under this label.

Genevrières, a few hundred metres further on, also has a red soil, but there is less clay and more stones here. Lafon's vines are on the distinctly steep, upper part, next to those of the Hospices de Beaune and Henri Boillot. Just over half a hectare produces around eight barrels of wine. The vines now being forty years old, Lafon will soon begin a very gradual replanting programme to maintain the average age at this level.

In the Perrières *climat*, adjacent to the south, there are two parcels, one at either end, and the soil is less red in colour, very shallow, and very much more stony. At the northern end Lafon has about two-thirds of a hectare of forty-year-old vines. On the Puligny border the parcel is small, 2 *ouvrées* (about one-eighth of a hectare) and the vines are nine years old. The wine from this parcel is usually added to the village wine. Being on SO4 rootstock, and from clones, a lot of green harvesting is necessary to keep the yield within limits. What are these limits? In the young vines five Pinot Noir or eight Chardonnay bunches will produce 40 hectolitres per hectare. 'This is the limit,' Dominique says. One can't help noticing the difference between a Lafon vine, neat, uniform in ripeness, with a few healthy bunches, and some of the neighbours, haphazard tendrils drooping all over the place, and a plethora of fruit, not all of it ripe, some indeed rotten.

Finally in Meursault, underneath the Perrières at the southern end, lies Lafon's largest slice of *premier cru*, 1.75 ha of Charmes. Again it's all dessus, the upper part. The soil is equally stony, but more water retentive. The subsoil is the shaly limestone called '*lave*'.

Which of the three is the best? And what are their individual characters? It is easier to answer the second question than the first, for though the Perrières is normally the superior, this is not always the case: 1986 is an example.

The Charmes is usually the most accessible, the roundest and the most typically Meursault. This is a wine of honey and hazelnuts and hot buttered toast; all silk and soft pillows. The Genevrières is fuller, often the least appealing in its youth, less sensual, more intellectual. The Perrières is a synthesis of the two with an element of Puligny floweriness and steeliness: the most complete, the most refined, the most complex.

In 1991 Dominique Lafon finally took back his family's third of a hectare of Le Montrachet. Puligny and Meursault, just as much as Puligny and Chassagne, enjoy a rivalry which is not always friendly. When he first emerged in his tractor in the vineyard lanes of Puligny, on his way to tend his Montrachet vines, there was a distinct hush in the air. He could feel the native *vignerons* wondering: Who the hell is this interloper? This man has no business here!

Lafon's vines are the most southernly in this famous climat, in the Chassagne section below those of the Domaine de la Romanée-Conti, under those of Baron Thenard. The vines are twenty and fifty years old; the soil a light yellow brown, almost beige, and very stony indeed. In a good year he will make five *pièces*: 125 cases of the best white wine in the world. All in all, the 12.5 hectare Lafon domaine will make 50,000 bottles a year.

FURTHER DEVELOPMENTS

One of the things which takes up a great deal of Dominique Lafon's time today is having to say 'No, sorry. We haven't any wine to sell.' Naturally, therefore, he is seeking to expand. In recent years he has further increased his village land, having bought 6 *ouvrées* of Puligny-Montrachet, Le Champ-Gain (first vintage 1995).

THE CHÂTEAU AND THE *CHAI*

The Lafon château still gives a distinctly mid-Victorian impression. One feels little has been changed since the time of Jules and Marie. Prominent is an imposing picture of Marie's brother, a naval lieutenant who was born in 1825 and killed at Sebastopol at the age of thirty. He suffered a wound in his shoulder which necessitated amputation of his arm. He refused chloroform, then just beginning to be available as an anaesthetic, but regarded by some as unmanly. Sadly the shock of the surgery led to his demise.

Across the courtyard is a large shed which serves as the winery, below which is one of the deepest, coldest cellars in Burgundy. This now has a new extension, joining it up to further cellars which lie under the main house.

René and Marie-Thérèse Lafon live in the château. Dominique and his wife Anne, and their young family, live a few minutes' drive away in the village of Tailly, on the other side of the main Beaune-Chagny road.

VINES AND WINE-MAKING:
THE LAFON PHILOSOPHY

Dominique Lafon belongs to a group of young or youngish Burgundian wine-makers (I call them the Burgundy Tigers) which includes his brother-in-law Christophe Roumier, Étienne Grivot, Jacques Seysses, Jean-Pierre de Smet, Patrick Bize, Philippe Senard, François Faiveley, Véronique Drouhin and others. Long gone are the days when Burgundy was a region of jealous, uneducated peasants who never communicated with one another. If Lafon has a problem, or an idea, he will phone around to get advice or bounce an opinion off someone, and he is equally ready to reciprocate or help out with someone else's difficulty. The group exchanges information, tastes wine from all over the world together, and meets regularly over a meal, and a large number of bottles, in the top local restaurants. What is very evident, talking to Dominique and his peers, is that there are few hard and fast rules. Wine-making has become flexible. Low yields and the pursuit of excellence are the paramount aims, but how you get there depends on individual circumstances.

He'd had a good grounding from his father René. 'At the *École Viti* at Beaune I was a bit confused at first,' he says. 'I didn't know enough to challenge what I was being told, like machine-harvesting being better than manual collection of the fruit, and other practices we did not follow at the domaine. But I instinctively knew some of them to be wrong.' René

Lafon's philosophy, as he will put it, was 'to have the courage to do nothing'. It was father René who demonstrated how correct was the domaine's attitude towards bottling. The received view was that the Lafons bottled too late. So in 1980 René Lafon bottled one cask of 1979 at the same time as he bottled the 1978s. This lot oxidised fast, which the 'late-bottled' wine did not, proving that the lees served as an anti-oxidant. 'I'm not saying what I learned at the *Viti* was useless,' says Dominique, 'but it needed to be taken with a pinch of salt. It gave me the background to understand what could be applicable to my wines and what was best discarded.'

In the vineyard the overriding concerns are keeping the harvest in check and the fruit healthy. In the Désirée *climat* Lafon always has his worst problems with grape-worm. He's tried introducing a predator. He has also been careful to add all his chemicals in a natural, organic form. The effect is more even and more efficient, and it will last longer, he will explain. Since he has taken over the vines he has cut out fertilisation entirely. There is merely a little compost for the older vines.

As far as the clones versus *sélection massale* argument is concerned Lafon is agnostic. He is happy with the clones now available for Chardonnay - the new Gouttes d'Or vineyard is entirely clonal - but adopts a 'bit-of-each' approach to Pinot Noir, taking some cuttings from his oldest vines in Champans on the one hand, but expressing satisfaction with the development of the clones planted in the Monthélie, Les Duresses *climat* in 1985 on the other.

I asked him about training vines by the Cordon du Royat method, as opposed to Guyot. 'I've been thinking about it,' he replied, 'but I haven't tried it yet. I feel the vine ages too quickly. There is also a problem with the Chardonnay in that it makes too dense a leaf canopy. So there is a risk of rot unless you are very careful to take out these leaves, which of course is time-consuming.'

Time is also a factor when it comes to ploughing. He'd like to do more, but, especially if it rains, time is the one thing he hasn't got. So he ploughs all the young vines, but treats the older vines with a weedkiller once a year. A further element in the argument is that some of these older parcels of vineyard which have not been cultivated for some time may be vulnerable to the plough. The roots may be too shallow.

The date of harvesting is crucial. Vines which have SO4 rootstocks, Lafon will explain, accelerate towards maturity particularly fast. You have to watch them like a hawk in order to collect the fruit at the right moment. A couple of days too late and they will be over-mature. Grapes with too low an acidity - which will happen if you over-crop - rot more easily, he adds.

Nevertheless the Lafon vineyards tend to be harvested later than most. 'If you keep the yield low,' he says, 'you don't have to worry too much about the acidity. And I'd rather wait for the extra concentration.'

Lafon wines are made to last. The vinification and *élevage* processes are not rushed, and the wine for the most part left to develop in its own way. The white wines are fermented in barrel (new oak for the Montrachet and the *premiers crus*), kept on their fine lees in the very cold deep cellar, and racked only once after the post malo-lactic *assemblage*. They are fined but not filtered, and bottled twenty to twenty-two months after the vintage. The 1990s were bottled in July 1992.

The black grapes are usually entirely destemmed, and the pulp then cooled so that there is three- or four-day maceration before fermentation starts. Lafon considers this delay helps extract better fruit and leads to more noble tannins. But the higher temperatures produced by the fermentation itself, up to 32°C, fix the colour and tannin. The red wines are matured in one-third new oak and usually bottled after two years, though the 1989s were bottled after eighteen months.

So the wheel has come full circle, and the domaine of Jules Lafon is safely back in the capable hands of his great-grandson. But what of the poor *métayers* who have lost the land they and their parents have looked after for so long? One can't help feeling sorry for Pierre Morey. He had the most to give up.

From what one can see the change-over seems to have been handled with tact and sensitivity. The longest possible notice was given, and most of the *métayers* seem to have accepted the inevitable with good grace. Pierre Morey, in fact, has had the luck to have been appointed wine-maker at the Domaine Leflaive, has set up his own *négociant* business to make up for what he has lost, and he still has responsibility for Bâtard-Montrachet that he has *en métayage* from the Poirier family, as well as other vines in Meursault of his own.

THE TASTING

The following wines were sampled in Meursault in September 1992. Once again my thanks to Dominique Lafon and his family.

1990

Optimum drinking

Meursault   Now-2004

Bottled two months ago, in July 1992 like all their 1990s. Ripe, fresh, plump. Stylish and with good depth. Best on the finish. Very good. Very long for a village wine.

Meursault, Clos-de-la-Barre   Now-2006

Slight 'do not touch me' about this. Fullish. Slightly four-square. Rich underneath. Plenty of depth and individuality. Best on the finish. Long, subtle. Potentially very good. Lovely balance.

Meursault, Désirée   Now-2004

This is much more accessible. Finer it seems. Ample and generous. Ripe and sexy. But the above has more future.

Meursault, Charmes   Now-2009

Round and ripe and gently oaky. Very good harmony. This is a definite step up. Intense, long. Very attractive. Shows very very well. More sensual than intellectual, opposite to the Genevrières.

Meursault, Genevrières   1998-2010

Suffering more from the bottling on the nose. A little more wood. A little rawer. Yet the follow-through is very rich and intense. Better acidity. More depth. Fatter and fuller and more power-ful. Very good. I prefer this to the Charmes.

Meursault, Perrières   1998-2010

Very subtle nose. Soft and delicate but intense. Rather more recovered from the bottling on the nose. Rich and fat without being a blockbuster on the palate. Round, ripe, subtle, complex and very long. Lovely. Complete. Fine. Less structure but more finesse and depth and harmony.

1989

Meursault   Now-2000

Oh, if all village Meursaults could be like this! Honeyed, citronelle. Fat and concentrated. Ripe. But plenty of depth. Fine for a village example.

Meursault, Clos-de-la-Barre   Now-2003

Very good ripe acidity here. Stylish, complex, fresh. Flowery fruit but with the Clos-de-la-Barre structure underneath. Long. Fullish. Very good.

Meursault, Désirée   Now-2000

As always this is lighter and softer. More feminine perhaps. Also good balance and length. But I prefer the virility of the Clos-de-la-Barre. This has less grip.

Meursault, Charmes   Now-2008

This is really very serious. Subtle, honeyed and lovely. Complete. Rich and concentrated. Very stylish fruit. Very good grip. Medium-full. Long, complex, intense. Very fine. Extra special.

Meursault, Genevrières   1998-2008

Firmer, richer, more backward. More structure. Today it is a bit the ugly duckling after the swan of the above, but the after-taste is very long and intense. This needs time. Could be just as good. We'll just have to wait and see.

Meursault, Perrières   1999-2010 plus

Quite lovely nose. Flowery, honeyed, aristo-cratic, rich. Brilliant fruit. This has the structure of the above and the finesse and aromatic amplitude of the Charmes. The complete Meursault. Great depth. Brilliant. Knocks the others into the sidelines.

OLDER WINES

Meursault, Gouttes d'Or, 1988   **Now-2000 plus**

Original nose. A quite four-square wine with a crab-apple flavour. Good acidity. But in comparison with the rest of the 1989 *premiers crus* a touch rustic. Slightly hard. Medium-full. What it lacks is a bit of fat. But no lack of thrust and substance. Good, but one and a half dimensions only. Very good for the vintage.

Meursault, Charmes, 1987   **Now-2000**

Soft, elegant but mature nose. Quite round and certainly charming and fruity. Eighteen hl/ha here this year, and the first year Dominique looked after these vines, having got them back from the *métayer*. For a 1987 this is very good indeed. There is a little astringency here - from the wood - but good grip, good acidity and good length. One and a half dimensions only again.

Meursault, Charmes, 1986   **Now-2003**

Seems to have quite a lot of alcohol on the nose. But only 13.0°. Quite full and even heavy. This is rich but a touch blowsy, and I'm not sure whether it will hold up its elegance. But this, says Jasper Morris MW (one of Lafon's major UK customers) is more elegant than at the outset. Perhaps this slightly heavy, spicy style is just not my taste. Others liked it better than me. Fat, rich, good acidity. But essentially a burly wine.

Meursault, Charmes, 1985   **Now-2005 plus**

Now this is much more my style, and I cannot agree the 1986 is better. More structure, and much much more elegance. Splendid concentrated nose. Lots of fine fresh complex fruit. Very good grip. Fullish, very vigorous. Very intense. This is very fine. Very long complex finish. Best wine so far.

Meursault, Perrières, 1982   **Now-2002**

Last vintage of René Lafon. Bottled January 1985 (by Dominique). This has a fine, ample, aromatic nose. Violets and raspberries; Pinot Noir-ish. Beeswax and hazelnuts also. Soft, vigorous, quite rich, round nevertheless. Intense and very harmonious. Very good acidity. Very fine. Complex. Bags of life.

Meursault, Gouttes d'Or, 1979   **Now-1999**

Intriguing smoky nose. There is a slight herbal, vegetal aspect - the mark of Gouttes d'Or. Good acidity. Slightly four-square. Lacks a little *rondeur*. Best with food. Good vigour. Quite full. Mineral. Good but not great.

Le Montrachet, 1979   **Now-2005 plus**

Quite a deep colour. But a fresh, very very ripe, concentrated nose. Lovely. This is balanced, subtle and fragrant. Very *petits fruits rouges* as well as Chardonnay. Fine acidity. Great breed. The complete wine. *Grand vin*. Bags of life.

Meursault, Désirée, 1976   **Drink soon**

Three and a half years in cask, because the malo occurred so late. Honeyed, with a herbal, camomile, *tilleul* aspect. No undue acidity. Most attractive. No sign of age. Fullish, vigorous. Round and ample. Very good acidity. Plump, slightly crab-apply. Complex. Quite structured still. A substantial, very slightly four-square wine. A red wine in white-wine clothes. Held up very well in the glass. Nose got more and more interesting. A great surprise.

Le Montrachet, 1974   **Now-2000 plus**

Full but absolutely no age on the colour. This is remarkably good. Rich, complex and concentrated. Very good style. Very vigorous. It has, despite the vintage, the distinction and class and intensity of Montrachet. Lovely. Extraordinarily good. An experience. Still very youthful.

Meursault, Charmes, 1971   **Now-2000 plus**

Quite a mature colour. Pinot Noir nose. Raspberry as well as peach and hazelnuts and butter. Some maturity. Full, fat, meaty. This is fine, complex, concentrated. Very good acidity. A very rich classy wine. Lovely. Improved in the glass and held up very well. Very very long.

Meursault, Gouttes d'Or, 1966   **Now-2000**

Fresh colour. Lovely healthy round, ripe nose. Very clean and fresh. Delicate and complex with none of the usual Gouttes d'Or four-square character. Gentle, velvety. Very good acidity. Really peachy in flavour. Very subtle. Long. Medium to medium-full body. Very good indeed.

Meursault, Perrières, 1962   **Now-2000**

Quite a well-matured colour. Absolutely lovely nose. Fresh, fragrant, complex. Honey and delicate multi-dimensional fruit, flowers and herbs. Medium-full. Concentrated but gentle. Very good grip. Amazing vigour and real harmony. Everything from start to finish in place.

Le Montrachet, 1961   **Drink soon**

Quite a powerful nose. After a while - improving in the glass all the time - rich, fat, concentrated, even alcoholic. Yet not very high. A little evolved now. Spicy aspects. The fruit loosening its persistence and elegance. Very good but not great. Slightly four-square.

Le Montrachet, 1935   **Drink soon**

Golden colour. Lovely nose. Considerable class

and complexity. A fragrance and youthfulness which is quite amazing. This is very fine indeed (much better than the 1961). Very complex fruit. Very much a concentrated, *vendange tardive* character. Excellent. Great wine in fact. Very very long and vigorous.

Volnay, Santenots-du-Milieu, 1979   Drink soon
Bottled two and a half years later. Good, fresh, fullish colour. This is very fresh. All the *petits fruits rouges* without any *gibier* or *renard*. Elegant. Delicious. Quite delicate. Long. Medium-body. A gentle wine. But complex. Drink quite soon. Very raspberry. Didn't hold up very long in the glass.

Subsequent to the above tasting, which concentrated on white wines, Dominique Lafon and his father decided to organise a tasting of their Volnay, Santenots-du-Milieu. This took place in June 1996.

Le Montrachet, 1986   Now-2005 plus
This is much, much better and more vigorous and balanced than most. Rich, fragrant, fat and concentrated with good grip. Lovely ripe wine with splendid intensity. Long and complex. More vigorous than the 1982. Very lovely indeed and bags of life.

Le Montrachet, 1982   Now-2005
Marvellous nose. Opulent and yet fresh. Marvellous fruit. Soft yet persistent. Full, fat. Still very youthful. Deliciously balanced. Long. Very complex. Very classy. Very fine indeed.

Meursault, Genevrières, 1869   Drink up
Slightly old colour but on the nose not completely dead. Rather dilute more than faded. But the fruit is nearly finished. This was the first year Lafons were here. Fresh.

VOLNAY, SANTENOTS-DU-MILIEU

1993   2003-2015 plus
Very fine colour. Splendid ripe plummy nose. Quite a substantial wine. Full, tannic but the tannins well covered. This has a lot of grip and vigour. Quite sturdy. Excellent fruit. Lots of class. Youthful, vigorous. Long. Fine.

1992   1998-2008
Good colour. Now developing gently. Supple, plump, blackberry-flavoured nose. Good vigour on the palate. Medium to medium-full. Good tannins. Ripe and succulent. Good acidity. A little tannin now rounding off. Very good length. Very good (fine for the vintage).

1991   2000-2012
Very good colour. Still youthful. Round nose. Nutty. Fresh and vigorous. Good oaky base. Medium to medium-full. Ripe, complex and very good. Showing well. Youthful and elegant and complex and promising. Mocha and chocolate as it developed. Fine for the vintage.

1990   2002-2026
Fine colour. Very rich, full and opulent, marvellous fruit. This is not adolescent. Very lovely. Full, well-rounded tannins. Lots of concentration and grip here. This is extremely good. Very long. Very complex. Very intense. Very very balanced and concentrated. Very fine indeed.

1989   1999-2005
Very fine colour for a 1989. Very lovely ripe, rich, round nose. Doesn't have the vigour of the 1990 but fragrant and more substantial than most. This was harder than most in its youth. Now rounding off. Very satisfactory. Long. Still fresh. The structure just a little evident. Slightly more extraction than concentration. As it evolved a little hard on the nose. Drink when ready. Very good but not fine.

1988   1999-2010
Good youthful colour. This is still fresh, firm, classic. You can see the 50 per cent *rafles* used at the time (since 1989 the grapes are totally de-stemmed). It is a little dry. On the palate a little sturdy. Very good grip. Firmer than the 1990. Though the fruit is as ripe the wine is less generous. This is a wine for food. Slightly rude at the end.

1987   Now-2002 plus
The first year Dominique was in control of the vines. Medium to medium-full mature colour. This is fresh, meaty, fruity, of no great depth and elegance, but with interesting flavours, enough harmony and it is *à point*. Medium body. Good finish. Nothing *sous-bois* dead leaves about it. Might lose its elegance and get a bit astringent soon. (This was a very very small year here: 15-17 hl/ha.) Very good plus for the vintage.

1985   Now-2000 plus
Only one racking before bottling in those days. Bottled by assembling four *pièces* at a time. Good colour. Medium to medium-full. No great age. Some development on the nose. A little rustic. A touch of CO_2. Ripe, round, balanced. *À point*. Still very vigorous due to the carbon dioxide. Very good for the vintage.

1979   Now-2000
Mature colour. Delicate nose. Fine fruit. *Papa Lafon never sulphated at the time of the harvest.*

'When the grapes arrived I would taste them, and then form an idea of what I wanted to do. Then I would have the wine analysed - acidity, pH, potential alcohol etc. - and the next day perhaps I would modify my intentions in the light of the results.') Slightly gamey. Softer and more evolved on the nose than most 1979s. Balanced, elegant. Rather more elegant than the 1985. Fresh raspberry flavours. Long. Fine. Silky. Holding up better than the nose would indicate.

Volnay, Champans, 1978 2000-2005

95 per cent *égrappé*. Vigorous but mature colour. Plump, complex and very elegant on the nose. Velvety ripe and round. Medium full. This has very lovely fruit. Not a bit too austere. Ripe, generous, succulent and because of the acidity very very long and very very fine and elegant. Will still last well.

Volnay, Champans, 1976 Now-2000 plus

Splendid colour. Still very very youthful. Opulent, fat rich nose with a touch of *confit* fruit character as in the 1990. Full, tannic, meaty, structured. This is not tough at all. Nor too tannic either. No dryness. Fine grip. This is an excellent example. Just a little rigid. Still bags of life.

Volnay, Clos-des-Chênes, 1971 Drink soon

Because of hail two barrels in nine *ouvrées*. Last year of old vines before they were ripped up. Medium to medium-full, fully mature colour. Lovely nose here. Delicate like the 1979 is now. But elegant like the 1978. Hail taste on the palate but not on the nose - dry tannins. Good acidity. Holding up well. Concentrated. Very good but I find the taint on the palate a little too much.

An anonymous bin in the cellar. Tasted recently and marked Rouge Bon! ?1969 Now-2005

Thought to be Champans. Certainly a wine of some age, and typical of 1969. Rich. Some alcohol. Not as fine or as fragrant as it could have been but a ripe wine with good grip. Very good indeed.

1959 Drink soon

Very good mature colour. Lovely fragrant aromatic nose. Really fine. On the palate perhaps it lacks a little strength and virility. Other 1959s I have had recently have been richer and fatter but this is long, complex, balanced and lovely.

1929 Now-2005

The colour is still very much alive. Very very delicate nose but complex and fresh. Fragrant, mocha, touches of hazelnuts and even candied peel. Even more fine on the palate. This has the fragrance of the 1959 but with rather more puissance. Rather more intensity than the nose indicated. Very long and fine. Really intense. Magnificent. Still very vigorous and graceful. Marvellously fresh.

1871 Still holding up

This is just about on its last legs. The colour is still alive. The nose is a bit maderised and mushroomy, but the palate is fresh, clean and long. Very fine fragrant fruit. Not too astringent. A little aeration did it no harm. Still sweet. Still a little intensity and vigour.

LEFLAIVE,
PULIGNY-MONTRACHET

In 1991 a curious anomaly was rectified. It seemed hardly credible, given that the 8-plus hectares are divided between fifteen different proprietors, that not a single Le Montrachet vine should belong to a domaine based in Puligny. The Domaine Leflaive, like others I imagine, had at times been in the market when a sale was in the offing, but had hitherto been put off by high prices. Then in 1991 they acquired 2 *ouvrées*, enough to fill one rather over-sized new cask they had specially made. It was a fitting complement to one of the greatest white wine domaines in Burgundy, one which could boast substantial parcels in three of the four other local *grands crus* and four of the best *premiers crus*, and a total of 22 hectares in all.

Two years later this purchase achieved a greater significance: as an epitaph to one of Burgundy's greatest men. Vincent Leflaive, doyen of Puligny and a man of great charm, wit, hospitality and wine-making genius, passed away after a long battle with cancer on 11 September 1993. The fitting complement has become an even more fitting memorial. Vincent Leflaive was a personal friend: a man I loved. Every time I come into the cellar to taste the wine and see the 500 litre Montrachet barrel lurking behind the door I think of him.

HISTORY

The Leflaives can trace back their family tree to one Marc Le Flayve who married a Jeanne Corney and lived in Cissey near Beaune, dying there in 1580. From Cissey the family moved to Poil and at the beginning of the eighteenth century moved again to Puligny when Claude Leflaive married Nicole Vallée, a local girl, the wedding taking place on 3 February 1717. The marriage document, witnessed by various members of the Leflaive and Vallée family, and countersigned by Mutin the *curé*, is still preserved. Eight generations later – and nearly all, from father to son, christened Claude or Joseph – the Leflaives are still there.

Over their many years in Puligny the Leflaive family have gradually built up their vineyard holdings. Claude Leflaive the second inherited some vines from his mother Nicole in 1735. Perhaps more were acquired when the Marquis d'Agnan, Seigneur de Puligny et Mypont, emigrated to Austria at the time of the Revolution and his lands were sequestered and sold off. Nevertheless as subsequent generations came and went, and at each death land had to be divided in equal portions among the heirs, it became impossible to retain a sizeable vineyard. In 1835, in a *donation-partage* Claude Leflaive transferred 5 hectares of vines, including land in Bâtard-Montrachet, to his children. By 1905, when his grandchild Joseph received his inheritance on the death of his father, the domaine – if you can call it by such a grand word – was down to 2 hectares of vines.

JOSEPH LEFLAIVE

Joseph Leflaive was born in 1870, a year which pin-pricks all French consciousness, and was not originally reared to be a *vigneron*. One can imagine, with a family property at an uneconomic 2 hectares, that most if not all the Leflaives must have had to earn their living away from the vine. Joseph was a brilliant student, by career a marine engineer, and took part in the construction of the first French submarine. In 1898 he married Camille Biétrix du Villars, a lady of Dauphinoise extraction, and settled in her home town of Saint-Étienne to manage an engineering factory.

Nevertheless, he did not neglect his patrimony. In the aftermath of the phylloxera epidemic, more and more land was falling into disuse as smallholders, unable to replant in a time of depression and falling prices, simply gave up their vineyards. For those with means, the patience and the foresight, it was a golden opportunity. Between 1905 and 1925 Joseph Leflaive built up his own holdings by acquiring parcels in the most illustrious *climats*: Le Chevalier, Le Bâtard, Les Bienvenues, Les Pucelles, Le Clavoillon . . . some 20 hectares of prime vineyard.

In 1918, still the absentee landlord – in theory at least – Joseph appointed François Virot as *régisseur* of his expanding domaine. Virot was a local man, son of a *vigneron* in Chorey-lès-Beaune, and a cousin of the *régisseur* for Baron Thénard, proprietor then and now of a sizeable part of Le Montrachet and a friend of Joseph Leflaive. Finally in 1926 Leflaive gave up the engineering business, and returned to Puligny personally to take charge of the estate. He died in 1953.

The mantle then passed to a new generation: to Joseph (or Jo) (1908-1982) and his younger brother Vincent (1912-1993). The property was turned into a *Société Civile* and Jean Virot took over from his father as *régisseur*.

Vincent Leflaive officially retired in 1990, leaving his daughter Anne-Claude and nephew Olivier as *co-gérants*. Since Vincent's death, enabling Olivier to be freer to concentrate on his expanding *négociant* business, which he set up in 1984, Anne-Claude has run the domaine on her own.

In recent years there have been parallel changes both in the cellar and in the vineyard. Pierre Morey of Meursault was slowly but surely losing all the vines he was exploiting *en métayage* as they returned to Lafon. He was appointed *régisseur* on Jean Virot's retirement early in 1989. There was a similar change when Jean Jafflin replaced Michel Mourlon as *chef de culture*. But more radically in 1990 it was decided to initiate experiments with bio-dynamic culture in a few carefully selected parts of the domaine's vineyards. Anne-Claude was the instigator here, and is not one to be rushed. Converting the domaine so that it is truly *biodynamique* is a long-term process, and it will be seven to ten years before the results are clear for all to see.

THE DOMAINE

The Leflaive domaine is an impressive holding. In terms of surface area the family own 1.91 ha out of 7 in Chevalier-Montrachet, 2.00 out of 12 in Bâtard, 1.15 (almost half) of Bienvenues, nearly 3 ha of *premier cru* in Pucelles, 4.67 (84 per cent) of Clavoillon, 0.73 of Combettes, 1.3 ha of Folatières and over 4 ha (some planted in Pinot Noir) of village wine. In addition there is the Montrachet and a further 1.63 ha of red Blagny, Sous-le-Dos-d'Ane. Only a few *négociants* - Latour in Aloxe-Corton, for example, and Bouchard Père et Fils in Beaune - can boast as much as 21 ha of *premier cru* and *grand cru* land in a single commune.

WINE-MAKING

You will find the headquarters of Domaine Leflaive behind a heavy wrought-iron gate off one of the several *places* in Puligny. Puligny is a peaceful, indeed sleepy village, and running down some of the smaller more obscure growers is a difficult business. But everyone knows where Leflaive is. Surrounding a courtyard are several above ground *chais* where the wine is stored, bottled and despatched. The office of Anne-Claude Leflaive is up a double staircase to the right. A short walk across the square towards the church and up an alley will take you to the *cuverie* and first-year 'cellar'. All these again are above ground. As in many places in the Médoc the water-table is too high to enable underground cellar construction.

One thing will strike you forcibly. While many wine cellars, in Burgundy and elsewhere, are untidy if not downright scruffy, the Leflaive installation is spotless. You will even be asked to spit, when you expectorate your tasting sample, into a bucket, and not discreetly behind the barrels. This passion for cleanliness is no mere idiosyncratic fetish, it is emblematic of the Leflaive approach to wine-making. Clean hands and clean equipment make clean wine. Clean wine needs to be 'mucked about with' less than unclean wine. And the more you treat a wine - rack it, fine it, filter it, move it, sulphur it - the more you destroy the delicate flavours within it and the less opportunity the flavours which remain have to shine through.

After a severe *triage* in the vineyard, the grapes are pressed in two new Bucher pneumatic presses, speedily after harvesting, and the must is then allowed to settle overnight. Part of the harvest, the *crus*, is fermented in oak, the lesser wines in wooden *foudres*, the temperature of the fermentation being maintained at 18°C. They then remain in these receptacles until the malo-lactic fermentation is finished. Unlike occasionally elsewhere, the *cave* is not exaggeratedly warmed to speed this process up. Sometime towards the end of the summer the wines are transferred back - they used to be filtered at this point, but since 1991 no longer - across the village where they are stored in stainless-steel tanks preparatory to a light fining with casein and eventual *mise en bouteilles*. The cold of the second winter helps settle out and clarify the wine and so only a light filtration is necessary. The bottling takes place about eighteen months after the vintage.

The wood used is both *foudres*, large oak tuns of varying capacity, and *pièces*, the traditional Burgundy 228 litre barrel. About a third to a quarter of these *pièces* - Allier or Vosges in provenance, not Limousin, which would impart too strong a taste - are annually renewed.

RECENT CHANGES

What have the new team - Anne-Claude Leflaive and Pierre Morey - altered or added since they took over, I asked Anne-Claude at a recent Studley Priory wine weekend?

'I think the most important thing is our attitude towards the vineyards,' she said. 'Not only are we increasingly *biodynamique*, now about 6 ha being cultivated in this way, but the rest is *biologique*. We have used no fertilisers since 1989, nor herbicides either . . . We now regard each plot as a separate unit. In the time of my father we tended to pick, say, all the Pucelles in one go. Now we treat and harvest all of them - and we have thirty-eight - separately. We prune later,' she added, 'when the sap has already begun to rise. You get less chance of disease that way . . . Another thing we have changed is our attitude towards *bâtonnage*. We now do this two or three times a week until Christmas. This is rather more than we used to. And because we are stirring the lees up, we find we no longer need to use added yeast to finish the fermentation properly.'

QUANTITY

The Leflaive domaine has been accused in recent years of both a slightly cavalier attitude towards *rendement*, and a falling-off in standards. After a splendid success in 1985 the domaine's 1986s are disappointing, with too much of a *sur-maturité* flavour. They have not aged gracefully. In both 1989 and 1990, potentially very fine vintages, the standard, for Leflaive, was below par. The wines were pure and very stylish, but should have been more concentrated.

The average age of the domaine vines, at a mere twenty-five years in 1995, must play a part. But surely there is more to it than this. Is the yield to blame? It has never been one of those estates that boasted of the paltry quantities it produced. Nor would Vincent Leflaive in his time and Pierre Morey today offer any protestations about the importance of low yield. Indeed the opposite. Like others - and I emphasise that even among five-star domaines they are not alone - they believe that you can produce up to 48 or 50 hl/ha, even in *premier* and *grand cru* (the legal maximum, with PLC, is 48 and 54 respectively) without a falling-off in quality.

And the statistics show correspondingly. In 1993 the domaine produced 48 hl/ha, the very most it was allowed to, in its Chevalier, its Bâtard and its Bienvenues - and in its Montrachet. But then so did Sauzet. So did Carillon in its Bienvenues. And so did Henri Clerc in its Chevalier and Bâtard, though not in its Bienvenues. This, mind you, is the harvest in finished wine, *after* the severe *triage* to eliminate sub-standard fruit.

So the figures seem to bear out that the Leflaive view is not unique. One just wonders how different the wine would be if the *rendement* were reduced to 38.5 hl/ha, which, in fact, was the *average* production in Chevalier-Montrachet in 1993. (In Montrachet itself it was 42, in Bâtard 44.6.)

THE WINES

'I like to make a wine of elegance and harmony, avoiding excessive alcohol,' Vincent Leflaive said to me once. Finesse is the keynote; a subtle, complex, almost deceptive delicacy hides a wine of enormous depth, quality and great concentration. Above all the pure and delicious fragrance of the Chardonnay grape comes singing through the wine. Leflaive wines are infinitely seductive and enticingly drinkable when young. But do not be hasty. Given time they get even better, and they last for ages. 'Too many people drink my wines too young, alas,' I quote Vincent again.

The range begins with the Puligny *tout court*: classic, impeccable, ripe and balanced. Then Clavoillon, of which Leflaive produce the lion's share: a firm wine, masculinely Puligny, rich and nutty, plenty of depth, but sometimes a bit four-square. Next comes the Folatières. The vines are rather younger here. But I think in principle that the *climat* offers more depth and nuance. Combettes from near the Meursault border is feminine and peachy, soft and honeyed, plump with beautiful fruit. Pucelles in the Leflaive hands is in my view a *grand cru*: a prima-ballerina of a wine, with enormous elegance, great depth, and magnificent fruit. Bienvenues is a firm wine of staying power, both steely and fat at the same time, certainly masculine if Combettes is feminine. Bâtard can be simply great. Chevalier simply magnificent. And now they have Le Montrachet as well. You could run out of superlatives.

THE TASTING

The Pucelles were sampled at a dinner held in London in October 1992; the Chevaliers *chez* Leflaive in June 1993; and the Combettes and others at the Studley Priory Wine Weekend in November 1995.

PULIGNY-MONTRACHET, LES PUCELLES

Optimum drinking

1989   **1998–2008**
Light colour. Lovely rich, gently oaky, very stylish nose. Still youthful. Reserved. Peachy. Very good concentrated fruit. Full. Very good grip. Oaky on the palate. This is fine. Very long and complex. A subtle wine but needs time to mature. But it doesn't quite have the length on the palate for perfection.

1987   **Now–1999**
Light gold colour. Soft nose. Plump but without vigour. Medium body. This is rather better than a Bâtard I had two days ago. Good fruit. Good balance. Plenty of interest. A little short but full of charm. *À point* but will last well.

1986   **Drink soon**
Light gold colour. Fat, aromatic, nutty, voluptuous. Creamy and oaky. Medium body. Slightly over-ripe and lacking real freshness. This means it is losing its finesse. I prefer the 1987. A touch disappointing.

1985   **Now–2012**
Light colour. Firm, closed, real depth here though. Still a little adolescent. Full, lovely fruit. Expanded considerably in the glass. This has real depth and concentration. The best of the series. Still needs time.

1983   **Drink quite soon**
Full old colour. Rich but slightly blowsy. Slightly sweet/sour. Medium body. Plump, fresh compared with most 1983s, but I find the 1982 more stylish. This is just a touch ungainly.

1982   **Now–2000 plus**
Good fresh medium gold colour. *A point.* Round, full of stylish fruit. Good freshness, quite oaky, really quite concentrated. Medium body. This is very elegant. A lovely wine. *A point.* Much more style than the 1986. Third

best of the series. Long, complex. Very good indeed.

1981   **Drink soon**
Fullish colour. Lean but interesting nose. Medium body. A little lean. A bit one-dimensional. A bit short. But has style. Linear but attractive. But got light in the glass.

CHEVALIER-MONTRACHET

1990   **1999–2019**
Ripe nose, a touch of mint. But not, it seems a lot of reserve behind it. It is ripe and full, but not austere. On the palate it shows a little SO_2, and seems a little lacking zip. Rich, fat, good but adolescent. Slightly disappointing at first. Much much better later. Fine. But the 1985 is better.

1989   **1998–2015**
Rich, ripe, nutty, fine nose. Aromatic and spicy. There is also a little SO_2 on the palate. Slightly less backbone but rounder and riper and more opulent in fruit. Good grip, but not as much as the above. This showed better than the 1990 at first, but after aeration the 1990 was finer. Fine.

1988   **Now–2010**
On the nose this is austere and a little lean. On the palate only a little SO_2 is evident. Good oaky base. Slight element of grilled nuts to add to the fruit and give it a bit of extra personality. Once again it expanded considerably in the glass. Rich, fat and complex for a 1988. Fine for the vintage. Long. Good acidity. Very good, but by no means great, but better than 1986 and 1987.

1987   **Drink soon**
A little vegetal on the nose. Green. Lacking richness. With a slightly overblown vegetal aspect. Better on the palate. Once again the oak has given it a bit of sweetness and helped it to round off. Not *that* exciting, and an absence of real class. But that is the vintage. *À point.*

1986   **Drink soon**

Evolved nose. Somewhat disappointing. Not much elegance here like a lot of other 1986s this has matured badly. Fat but unstylish. On the palate ripe, over-ripe, blowsy, alcoholic. Not much future here. Hardly better than the 1987. I think the Pucelles is better.

1985   **Now-2020**

This is fine. Firm, aristocratic, full and complete. Still needs keeping. Very lovely. Marvellous harmony. Full, ripe, balanced and with marvellous depth. Very, very long, complex, splendid finish. Excellent. This is *grand vin*.

1984   **Drink soon**

Magnum. A little lean, obviously, but stylish enough and indeed ripe enough, especially on the palate. Yet not obviously over chaptalised. For this vintage is really very fine and most enjoyable. Not unripe. Not faded. Still has life. Elegant even. Not too vegetal and herbaceous. Not uncomplex. Surely one of the best of the vintage.

1983   **Drink soon**

Quite high alcohol evident on the nose. Slightly heavy and astringent. But better on the palate. It lacks a little freshness but it is not unclean, nor astringent, nor unstylish. Very plump and certainly slightly over-ripe. Would go well with *foie gras*. Not short of acidity. Nor lacking depth. Fine for the vintage. Will still keep. But lacks real finesse. Didn't develop well.

1982   **Now-2000 plus**

The colour is now getting golden. Soft, poised, ripe and very engaging. This is gentle but long. Deceptively stylish and complex. Well balanced too. Plump and very elegant and silky. I find this lovely. Still has vigour. Very fine indeed.

1981   **Drink soon**

Deeper colour still. Slight hints of pine needles at first. Lean and showing a little fade in vigour. As it developed it got a little rounder and sweeter on the nose. Still a little herbal. This lacks style though it is not too old. But it needs drinking now. It is beginning to lose what fruit it ever had and get astringent. I prefer the 1984.

1980   **Drink soon**

This has a round, slightly oaky, slightly acetaldehyde nose. A bit sweet-sour. Rather better on the palate. Decent structure, reasonable finesse. Has fruit and grip if not much concentration or style. Now needs drinking soon. But not at all bad. Still enjoyable. Has length. Good.

1979   **Now-2000 plus**

Magnum. Lovely nose. Complex, laid-back, very concentrated, but round and *tendre* like the 1982. More concentration and depth, vigour and backbone than the 1982 though. Good acidity. Fullish, still fresh. Mature without anything coarse about it. Peachy, hazelnutty, a touch of fresh mushrooms. This is excellent. Silky. Very long and fragrant. Lovely lingering finish. Will still keep.

1978   **Drink soon**

Magnum. More golden in colour. Lichees and white truffles and angelica on the nose. The acidity is more dominant than in the above. There is more structure but it is less round. After 5 minutes in the glass it began to soften a bit. Quite firm, ripe, peachy, good acidity. This is complex but not as integrated or as harmonious or as stylish. Fine. Better with food. Still has life.

1977   **Drink soon**

Surprisingly good. Soft, not a bit too lean and vegetal. Nor too obviously chaptalised. Fruity, round, positive and consistent from start to finish. Has no obvious sign of age. Fresh still. Fine for the vintage. Elegant. Surprisingly good. Drink soon, but no rush to drink up.

1976   **Now-1999**

On the nose this reminds me of the 1983. But it is better. Fat, rich, opulent, spicy. No undue alcohol. Nor is it too aged. In fact it is a lot fresher, rounder, more complete and more elegant. This is still very young in fact. Good grip. Plump and rich and not without finesse. Long. Fine. Plenty of life ahead of it.

1949   **Drink soon**

Not disagreeable. Not totally finished. Olivier bought at auction. Re-corked, topping up with 1978. Honeyed, even a touch of caramel on the nose. Faded, but there is still fruit. Voluptuous. Certainly full of interest. Only a hint of maderisation.

PULIGNY-MONTRACHET, LES COMBETTES

1993   **1998-2006**

Good colour. Lovely, fragrant nose. Not *that* powerful, but a good soft steeliness here. Mineral. Medium body. Slight touch of the vegetal to the palate at present. Riper and more stylish on the follow-through. A very good example, but it doesn't have the concentration of the best Perrières.

1992   **Now–2003**

Good full colour. Fat and ample on the nose. A little closed. But a little lacking grip at the same time. I would have hoped for more thrust, more depth. This is quite a delicate example. Lovely fruit at first but a bit blowsy at the end of the palate. It will develop soon. But I don't think it will gain anything by keeping. Only good.

1991   **Now–2000**

Youthful, light colour. Neat, ripe, stylish. Good concentration for the vintage. Certainly elegant. Quite fragile. This is a fine example of the vintage. Medium body. Balanced. Very stylish. Not that much concentration but pure and harmonious. Long and highly satisfactory. Very good fruit. Complex too. Give it another year.

1990   **Now–2000**

Slightly more colour than the 1989. Fat and rich on the nose. An opulent wine with plenty of depth and balance but not an enormous amount of grip and concentration. Ample, fat and rich on the palate. Good acidity. The attack is ripe and plump, and the finish is quite long. But a slight lack of elegance as it leaves the mouth. Slightly heavy. More Clavoillon than Pucelles. Very good at best.

1989   **Drink soon**

Rather over-evolved on the nose. *Sur-maturité* here, and it seems already a bit tired and faded. Slightly better on the palate. Honeyed, peachy, good oaky base. But already a touch of astringency. This needs drinking soon. Today it is good plus. It will soon be worse.

1988   **Now–1999**

Youthful, light colour. This is a little neutral and herbal on the nose. Better on the palate. Nice honeyed touch to go with the slightly herbaceous elements. A bit austere. And not very elegant. But a pleasant wine with a positive finish. Very good for the vintage.

1987   **Drink soon**

Light nose but fresh and stylish. Neatly made. Attractive if lightweight and delicate. Soft, gentle, complex. More honeyed, more Meursault-ish and rather more attractive than the 1988. A bit more developed. But very good indeed.

1985   **Now–2010 plus**

Good fullish colour. Firm nose. This is by far and away the best of the series. Full, still very young. Rich, concentrated, impeccably balanced. Marvellously ripe harmonious fruit. Oaky and concentrated underneath. Very, very long. Still will get better. Bags of life. Very fine.

OTHER WINES

Puligny-Montrachet, Le Clavoillon, 1989
                                            Now–1999

Fresh nose. Rather better than the Combettes. Not a lot of grip but good and fat, quite mature already. Fullish, a little blowsy on the palate. But fresher than the Combettes. Rich, round, slightly sweet at the end. Quite high alcohol and not enough grip. Lacks class and dimension. But very good.

Puligny-Montrachet, 1979   **Now–2000 plus**

Slightly less colour than the 1978. Fresher, more fragrant on the nose. Lovely finesse and very good concentration and poise for a village wine. Long. Peachy. Will still last very well. Very good indeed.

Puligny-Montrachet, 1978   **Drink soon**

Golden colour. Firm, rich but slightly vegetal aspects on the nose. This is not as stylish and as complete as the 1979, and the sweetness at the end is less elegant. Full and meaty. But very good, and better still with food.

LEROY,
VOSNE-ROMANÉE

How do you determine great? Is it size? Is it quality? Is it price? Is it 'reputation' (whatever that is)? Is it the amount of media coverage? However you do compute it, the greatest domaines of Burgundy today must be those under the control of Lalou Bize: the Domaine Leroy and her own Domaine d'Auvenay. The estates of Jadot, Faiveley and Bouchard Père et Fils are far larger, that of Romanée-Conti the most splendid in terms of the percentage of *grand cru terroir*, but for the nobility of its wines, pride of place must go to Leroy and to Domaine d'Auvenay. The sheer concentration, depth and intensity Lalou Bize manages to squeeze into her bottles is breathtaking.

Much of the domaine, of course, is new, additional parcels having been joined to the initial 12 ha Charles Noëllat estate acquired in 1988. But this has only replaced an equally impressive *négociant* business based in Auxey-Duresses. Maison Leroy is as much of a cachet on the label as Domaine Leroy, and it is because of the quality and vigour of these merchant wines that we can extrapolate into the future with the confidence that we do when we today taste out of cask at the Domaine Leroy headquarters in Vosne-Romanée.

HISTORY

Henri Leroy, a third-generation wine and spirits merchant, was born in 1894. The business dealt in fine wine, but made its profits from selling brandy to Germany, particularly to Asbach, and by selling lesser bulk wine into that country to be made into *sekt*. During the 1930s Henri became firstly a client of the Domaine de la Romanée-Conti, and then a good friend of Edmond Gaudin de Villaine, the *gérant* and co-owner with his brother-in-law Jacques Chambon.

These were hard times. Financially, the DRC was a bottomless pit, necessitating yearly expensive investment on the one hand, but yielding no profit on the other. It seemed inevitable that it would have to be sold. And if it were to pass out of the Chambon/De Villaine hands, Henri Leroy and his friend knew only too well, it would be the start of the slippery slope. Before too long the vineyards of Romanée-Conti and La Tâche would be as morcellated as that of Clos-de-Vougeot.

Some years later, in 1942, with the financial structure of the domaine having been changed into a *Société Civile*, Jacques Chambon decided to sell out. Henri Leroy bought the Chambon share and became co-owner of the Domaine de la Romanée-Conti. For the meantime, however, he was content to take a back seat, at least officially. It was not until 1950, after Edmond Gaudin de Villaine's death, that he became a *co-gérant* alongside Edmond's son, also Henri. The two were to run the DRC jointly until 1974. Henri Leroy passed away on 21 February 1980. As he had commanded, the domaine's Richebourg 1952 was opened after the funeral in his memory.

LALOU

Henri Leroy and his wife Simone (*née* Brun) had two daughters, Pauline, born in 1929, and Marcelle (universally known as Lalou) in 1932. It was the latter, adored and adoring younger daughter, who was to inherit her father's passion for wine.

Lalou, born in Paris, was brought up in Meursault, in the mansion today occupied by her daughter Perrine. 'From the word go I was fascinated,' she says. 'I was a cellar rat, watching and helping the *cavistes* rack the wines, taste them, bottle them. My mother kept calling me to come out of the cellar and play with my friends like a normal schoolgirl, but as soon as I could I crept back.' Henri Leroy, his attention diverted by the DRC, had somewhat neglected his *négociant* business. Lalou remembers 1937s still in cask long after the war. In 1955 she persuaded her father to let her take over. She was twenty-three. 'He gave me *carte blanche*,' she says. 'I started as I meant to go on. I bought finished wine, and only that which pleased me. I insisted on having no contracts, no moral obligations. If the wine wasn't *extra*, I didn't buy it.'

The turnover of Leroy wines has always been modest, the stock to back it up enormous: totally uneconomic. But it has always been subsidised. Firstly by the bulk German business, later by the Leroy sales exclusivity of the DRC wines. Except for the UK and the USA, this all passed through Leroy. Three-quarters of the Leroy turnover came from selling DRC wines.

In 1974 the co-managership at the DRC passed down a generation, to Lalou, representing her sister (they both owned 25 per cent) and Aubert, son of Henri de Villaine, representing his brothers, sisters and cousins (there are ten of them). From the start this was a fiery relationship. Lalou is not an easy character: emotional, insecure, arrogant, temperamental and combative, she must have been a trial to the pacific, intellectual Aubert. It was a fire awaiting a match. Early in 1992, following a boardroom dispute, Lalou was relieved of her position as *co-gérante*.

CHARLES NOËLLAT

Meanwhile, at the other end of Vosne-Romanée, lay the headquarters of the Charles Noëllat domaine. The land-holdings were impressive: nearly a hectare of Romanée-Saint-Vivant, over a hectare and a half of very well-placed Clos-de-Vougeot, 78 ares of Richebourg, parcels of substantial *premier cru* vineyard in Nuits-Saint-Georges, Les Boudots and Vosne-Romanée, Les Beaux-Monts and Les Brûlées. Charles Noëllat had died in 1939, and despite some of the land passing to other members of the family, notably what are today the Alain Hudelot-Noëllat and J. J. Confuron estates, the residue still amounted to 12 hectares. But it was moribund. Quality was unremarkable and inconsistent. Yet the potential was high. 'Yes, the wines they produced were terrible,' says Lalou, 'but the quality of the vines was great. All honour to Charles Noëllat. The vines were old, reproduced by *sélection massale*. And in the Romanée-Saint-Vivant they are particularly superb, giving very small fine berries. Yardstick Pinot Noir fruit. I have never seen anything so fine in all of Burgundy.'

In 1988 the estate came on the market. It is said that AXA were interested. But Leroy made a better offer. Subsequently, in July, Lalou and Pauline sold one-third of their interest in Leroy to their Japanese agents Takashimaya in order to finance the 65 million franc acquisition of Charles Noëllat, including buildings and stock. (After a number of years offering the plums of this stock around the trade the residue was sold at jumble-sale prices in an auction in Dijon in 1992.)

FURTHER PURCHASES

At a stroke, the addition of the Charles Noëllat domaine to that of Leroy, mainly based in Auxey and Meursault, but with tiny holdings in Chambertin, Clos-de-Vougeot (at the bottom) and Musigny, transformed it into one of Burgundy's major players. But things did not stop here. In 1989, for 19 million francs, Lalou acquired the Gevrey-based 2.5 ha Domaine Philippe Remy. This added 50 a of Chambertin, 57 a of Latricières, 67 a of Clos-de-la-Roche, as well as *premiers crus* in Gevrey-Chambertin, Les Combottes and village land in Gevrey and Chambolle. It neatly complemented the Noëllat estate. A year later Lalou increased her holding in Le Musigny by buying a parcel from the Moine-Hudelot family. Some Corton, both red and white, has followed, as has some Volnay, Santenots. Today the domaine measures just under 22.5 ha.

The cellars at Charles Noëllat were renovated, the vat house gutted and replaced, and André Porcheret seduced away from the Hospices de Beaune to help her run it (he has since been seduced back).

At the same time, in her own right, Lalou has been making further acquisitions. High up on the plateau above Saint-Romain is an ancient farm - records go back to a donation from Raynaud, *seigneur* of Saint-Romain, to Messieurs de la Ferté in 1180 - known as the Domaine d'Auvenay. It used to belong to Henri Leroy's bachelor brother. It is here that Lalou lives with her husband Marcel Bize. They married in 1960. While she occupies herself with wine, he runs the farm.

Under the name of Auvenay Lalou has added on to the land in Auxey and Meursault that she inherited from her father: 51 a of Puligny-Montrachet, Les Folatières in 1989, 6.4 a of Criots in 1990, 16.3 a of Chevalier-Montrachet (from Jean Chartron) in 1992, 26 a of Bonnes-Mares in 1993, and lastly, 26 a of Mazis-Chambertin (Lalou had always bought the wine) from the Collignon family in 1994. The total is now 3.67 ha. Vinification of this has to be separate from that of Domaine Leroy. In 1994 a brand new *cuverie* was installed up at Auvenay.

BIO-DYNAMISM

In many ways the seemingly hard-nosed Lalou Bize is the last person you would expect to be seduced by any new fad. That bio-dynamism is not a fad is proven by the fact that the Domaines Leroy and Auvenay have joined the increasing number who have gone not just *biologique* but the full way.

Nicolas Joly's Coulée de Serrant at Savennières was Lalou's Road to Damascus. 'I shall never forget,' says Nicolas. 'There was Lalou, dressed up as if she had just stepped out of some *maison de haute couture* in Paris, on her knees, running the soil of the Coulée de Serrant through her fingers, and exclaiming, *"Ça, c'est la vérité".*' Actually, Lalou maintains she was probably wearing jeans.

'The soil was alive,' says Lalou. 'Everything was alive, and in place, in harmony with one another: the earth, the plants, the fruit and the wine. I really do believe that cosmic rhythms should determine when we do things. And that we should encourage the vine to build up its own resistance and allow it to express its own *terroir*. So we have proscribed all chemical treatments except very minimal doses of sulphur against oidium and copper sulphate against mildew.' In 1993, to avoid further compacting the soil with yet another tractor treatment, Lalou sprayed against mildew by helicopter. Sadly this proved ineffective, and as a result her crop was reduced almost to nothing.

WINE-MAKING

In many ways the Leroy wine-making methods are deeply traditional. Pruning is excessively strict. There is no destemming, a severe *triage*, two *pigeages* a day – there are automatic plungers but they have now reverted to *pigeage à pied* – and a long *cuvaison* at temperatures up to 33°C. Each vat at Vosne-Romanée is equipped with an internal temperature-controlling stainless-steel coil. 100 per cent new wood is used, there is no filtration, and not always a fining either.

THE WINE

Superficially, the above sounds very much like what they do at the DRC. Yet curiously the results are quite different. In the DRC wines you can occasionally taste the presence of all the stems during the fermentation. *Chez* Lalou never. The DRC wines are well coloured but not as full, almost densely thick, as at Leroy. Lalou's are even more concentrated, even more tannic, even more long-tasting. Yet never too solid and impenetrable. They are hugely intense, and from the outset manifest quite extraordinary depth of fruit. They are great wines.

The problems of her abrupt sacking from her position as *co-gérante* of the Domaine de la Romanée-Conti now largely behind her – and she will admit the Noëllat acquisition brought with it an inevitable conflict of interest which she was slow to acknowledge – Lalou is now happy at the Domaine Leroy and on her own. 'Look at my vines,' she will say. 'Look how healthy and comfortable they are.' And, being Lalou, she will not fail to point out a neighbour's plot of excessively abundant, uncontrolled growth. 'And come and taste the wine.' And this you do, accompanied by a yapping, manic mongrel she once found abandoned up in the hills. (This dog finally passed away in 1995, but has been replaced by another.) Lalou's wines, according to her, are always '*extra*'. But today, once you have inveigled your way in, and won the confidence of this essentially shy, and for all her faults, lovable as well as admirable woman, you are allowed to beg to differ, and she will occasionally yield that this particular *cuvée* is perhaps not quite as good as it could be. The one-time cellar rat is now a master in her own right, which she never really felt herself to be at the DRC, and the wines she produces, admittedly at very high prices (but if you produce 20 hl/ha rather than 40 or 50 then they have to be, and there is no subsidy now) are triumphantly brilliant.

THE TASTINGS

I sampled the following range of Volnay, Santenots and Mazis-Chambertin in Auxey-Duresses in February 1995. On my return Farr Vintners offered a range of her 1989s and other wines over a dinner in London, to which I have added wines sampled at a dinner in Kansas City in

October 1994. Finally, in March 1994, I was invited to a Burgundy Club dinner at the Montrachet restaurant in New York. The feature was a range of Leroy Richebourgs of the 1950s.

VOLNAY, SANTENOTS

Optimum drinking

1992   **1999-2012**

Splendid colour. Rich, profound nose. Pure Pinot. Unexpectedly concentrated for a 1992. Fullish, very good tannins. A touch adolescent. But ripe, intense. Even long. Certainly very, very stylish. Very good indeed.

1991   **2000-2020**

Excellent colour. Fine rich cassis fruit on the nose. Very stylish. Fullish, good tannins, good grip. This is just a touch rigid at present, but the follow-through is splendidly rich and complex. Fine.

1989   **1998-2012**

Fine colour. Very delicious fruit on the nose. A charming bottle, on the forward side for a Leroy wine. Very sumptuous, well-balanced seductive fruit. Fine acidity. Silky smooth at the end. Very good length. Fine.

1986   **Now-2002**

Good colour. This is unexpectedly good for the vintage, though not as good as the 1992. Fresh plump nose. A touch astringent on the palate. But the finish is ample, ripe and charming. Very good.

1985, *cuvée* No. 1   **Now-2005 plus**

Fine colour. Lovely ripe nose with a touch of caramel and spice. This is lovely, and fully ready. Round, balanced. Good structure. Very good grip. Ample, lovely complex velvety finish. Fine.

1985, *cuvée* No. 2   **Now-2010**

The same origin as the above. Richer, firmer, more masculine, more vigour. Lovely rich finish. This is only just ready. Very ample. Even better.

1978   **Now-2010**

Splendid colour. Marvellous nose. Profound, aristocratic, pure. Magnificent fruit here and very fine balance. Fullish, vigorous. Very complex, very intense. Excellent finish. A profound example. Very very long. This is very fine indeed.

1976   **Now-2000 plus**

Fine colour. Slightly tough tannins on the nose. Animal. Better on the palate because there is plenty of richness and concentration. Fine fresh finish. Not a bit too heavyweight. Good grip. This has plenty of life ahead of it. A fine example of the vintage.

1973   **Now-1999**

Good colour. Evolved nose. But there is still sweetness here. And class. Still fresh. Nicely sweet on the palate. Plenty of charm. Remarkably good for the vintage. Still very positive. Long.

1972   **Now-2004**

Good colour. Soft nose. A little austere but complex, very stylish, lots of depth. I like this very much. It is profound, intellectual. A little aloof. But it is clean and pure, subtle and very long and positive on the palate. Lovely.

1970   **Drink soon**

Now the colour is getting a little pale. The nose shows quite a lot of evolution. Soft, ample palate. Somewhat similar to the 1973. A little more classy but more evolved. This is at its best now. Very stylish.

1969   **Now-2005**

Fine colour. Lovely nose. Rich, fat, caramelly, vigorous. This is very fine indeed. Full, very concentrated, really quite structured. Excellent grip. Lovely fruit. Ample, sumptuous. Very very long. Bags of life. Flamboyantly exciting.

1964   **Now-2000**

While the colour has now lightened a bit, the wine is still superb and vigorous. Cooked fruit. Rich, fullish, round and sweet. Not as exciting as the 1969 today. But a really lovely example.

1962   **Now-1999**

Reasonable colour, especially for the age. This has a little CO_2 in it but is sweet and ripe, velvety and subtle. Medium weight. A touch of astringency at the end. But fine as well. Still plenty of life. Round, gently sweet finish.

1959   **Now-2005**

Fine colour. This is much better, much more vigorous, than the 1964. The nose is very rich; spicy and has the same cooked fruit aspect. Fullish. Lovely fine fruit. A big, muscular but excellently structured example. Very 1959. Lovely rich finish. Excellent.

1955   **Drink soon**

Fullish colour. Coffee flavours on the nose. Now quite evolved. On the palate this has plenty of vigour still. Ripe, fresh, complex. Plenty of depth. Original. Delicate. Still very positive at the end. Delicious. Very fine.

1949   **Now–1999**

Good positive colour. Deliciously fragrant on the nose. Old but not a bit decayed. Plenty of vigour. Really very classy indeed. Marvellous lingering complex fruit. Delicate at the end but still very very long. Multi-dimensional. Great wine.

MAZIS-CHAMBERTIN

1987   **Now–2012**

Fine colour. This is excellent for the vintage. Rich nose. Fine fruit. Fullish. Good round tannins. Old viney concentration. Classy. Very good grip. Fine positive finish. Long, ripe, fat. Very fine indeed.

1985   **1999–2025**

Excellent colour. This is very special. Brilliant old-vine concentration. Very ripe. Impeccably balanced. Marvellous colour. Hugely rich fruit. Very ample. Excellent grip. A very splendid wine. Very very fine indeed. *Grand vin*!

1983   **1999–2025**

Full colour. Fine, very rich nose. On the palate a bit hard and tannic. Aggressive but not a bit tainted. Full, meaty. Long and very very rich and concentrated. This is as grand in its own way as the 1985. But quite different. Splendidly long on the finish. Excellent.

1982   **Now–2005**

Fine colour. Brilliant nose. Not a touch of evolution and very very concentrated. Could be a 1978. Lovely harmony and freshness, class and complexity. Medium-full. Beautifully balanced. Excellent – really excellent for a 1982. A very lovely wine. *À point* now. Very very long and subtle at the end.

1978   **1998–2025**

Fine colour. Superb nose. Rich, profound, aristocratic, slightly austere but hugely ripe and complex and classy. Full, still a little tannic. It will still improve. Splendid grip. Marvellous, marvellous fruit. Very very harmonious, complex, multi-dimensional. Very very long on the finish. *Grand vin*. Quite brilliant.

1972   **Now–2002**

Good colour. Soft and subtle on the nose. Very 1972. Slightly austere and vegetal but at the same time round, even ripe. Medium-full. Round and fruity. Plenty of depth. Nicely fresh and charming now. Very good indeed.

1971   **Now–2000**

Good colour. This is soft, evolved, totally clean. But quite old for a twenty-three-year-old Leroy

wine. Rich and round and soft and supple. Fresher on the palate than on the nose. Complex. Lots of finesse. Soft, long amply fruity finish. Still sweet. Delicate but lovely.

1967   **Drink soon**

Fresh colour. Fragrant nose. Still rich. Round, fruity, still vigorous. Gentle, soft, but lots of finesse here. Still has plenty of life. Very elegant. Very fine for the vintage.

1966   **Now–2004**

Very good colour. Still full, still vigorous. Round, sweet, good substance. Rich and caramelly at the end. Very good grip. Plenty of depth. This is a very lovely example. Profound. Classy. Balanced. Vigorous. Very very long. Very fine.

1962   **Now–2000**

Good colour. Lovely nose. There is an aspect of grilled almonds and warm biscuits on the nose. On the palate just a touch of CO_2. But ripe and rich if a bit rigid at first. Good grip. Round, long, subtle, very stylish fruit on the finish. Still very long. Fine.

1959   **Now–2009**

Excellent colour. Marvellous rich nose. Fabulous concentrated ripe old viney fruit here. Full and very very rich. Still incredibly youthful. Now mellow, now very complex, very profound. This is sweet and complex, velvety rich, marvellously multi-dimensional. *Grand vin*.

1955   **Now–2000**

Marvellous colour, for a wine of this age. Really lovely subtle nose. Ripe, delicate in a feminine sense. Very ripe. Very beautifully balanced. Mellow. Long. Fine.

DOMAINE LEROY 1989

Pommard, Les Vignots   **1999–2012**

Good colour. Lovely rich plummy nose. Very good concentration and style for a village wine. Like a number of Leroy 1989s, this is beginning to lighten up. Fullish, quite meaty. Very good grip. Fine redcurrant and raspberry fruit. Fine for what it is.

Nuits-Saint-Georges, Les Lavières   **1999–2014**

Good colour. Pleasant nose. Quite lean though. Medium-full. Very good grip. Good tannins. Very stylish fruit underneath and very good depth. Highly satisfying. Despite the austerity, very good for a village wine.

Nuits-Saint-Georges, Les Boudots
                                   2000–2020 plus

Very good colour. Brilliant nose. Very very lovely Pinot fruit. Excellently covered tannic structure. Shows a bit more new oak than the Beaux-Monts. Fullish, sumptuous. Very very rich and concentrated. This is very very lovely. Great length. Great harmony. Complete.

Vosne-Romanée, Les Genevrières   1999-2014
Very good colour. Soft, compact, quite rich on the nose. But not that ample. On the palate it is just a touch rustic. A bit more obvious tannin than the Lavières.

Vosne-Romanée, Les Beaux-Monts   2000-2020
Very good colour. Quite closed on the nose. More so, and a bit more muscular than the Boudots. Full, lush, meaty, fat, gently oaky. Very good tannins. This is currently a little adolescent. Came out in the glass. Fine (plus).

Richebourg   2002-2030
Fine colour. Very rich and concentrated. Enormous depth. But now closed. Real finesse. Brilliant fruit as it opened up. Marvellous texture and intensity. Splendid richness. Full. Very very ripe indeed. Soft tannins but plenty of structure. Excellent grip. This has splendid fruit. Great length and harmony.

Romanée-Saint-Vivant   2001-2025
Fine colour. Very rich, but more silky-smooth than the Richebourg. Marvellous elegance. On the palate just a touch of astringency. Real intensity on the follow-through. Soft, fullish, creamy rich and lacy. Marvellous acidity. Excellent fruit. Marvellous length. Goes on and on.

Clos-de-Vougeot   2000-2018
Fine colour. Fat, robust, animal nose. Less class than other Leroy *grands crus*. Full, tannic, rich, almost sweet. Lovely mulberry fruit. Good balance. This is fine, but lacks the finesse and real length for great. Voluptuous and seductive though.

Chambolle-Musigny, Les Fremières   2000-2020
Good colour. Quite closed on the nose. Good grip. Very good fruit. Lovely ripeness. Very Chambolle, plump, generous, sexy. Finely balanced. Very long. Very very harmonious. Fine by any standards. Particularly lovely for a village wine.

Clos-de-la-Roche   2000-2020
Fine colour. Very fine black-cherry fruit on the nose. Hugely rich and voluptuous. Fat. Sexy. Very harmonious and stylish. Very ripe indeed. A little closed on the palate. Very good grip. Long. Potentially luscious. Good length. Very fine plus.

Latricières-Chambertin   2000-2018
Fine colour. Tighter than the Clos-de-la-Roche. Good richness. But more adolescent than most at this stage. Leaner than the Clos-de-la-Roche. Less fat, less ripeness. This is the least exciting of the Leroy *grands crus*. Very good indeed at best. Yet fullish, balanced. But not as hugely rich and elegant enough.

Chambertin   2005-2030
Fine colour. Hugely concentrated fruit. Very excellent class and concentration. Very backward. A complete wine. Full, very round ripe tannins. Gently underpinned with oak. Fine grip. This has intensity, great distinction. Marvellous slightly austere fruit. Very very long and complex. Excellent.

OLDER WINES

Gevrey-Chambertin, *Premier Cru*, 1985
                                    Now-2007
This has a fine colour. On the nose still a bit closed and adolescent and on the palate also a bit awkward. Quite pronounced acidity. This is a bit lean and lacking generosity. Not much attraction here. But a bit awkward at present. Quite good at best. Will still improve.

Pommard, 1983   Now-2005
Full colour. Rich and chocolatey. Typically 1983 tannins. Fat, sweet, rich. Meaty but opulent. Very good acidity. Not exactly classy. Indeed tarty and *gavroche*. But very good indeed for a village wine. Very vigorous.

Côte-de-Beaune-Villages, 1978   Now-2004
Good colour. Slightly four-square. Ripe but a little solid, high acidity. Quite full. But a bit lean. Lacks generosity. Quite good. Still has vigour but will it ever get round and generous?

Beaune, Sizies, 1978   Drink soon
This has some development now. Fullish colour. Aromatic nose. A touch vegetal. But the soft heart of Beaune is underneath. Indeed the wine, if a bit over-evolved, is elegant. But the finish is now a little lean and difficult to enjoy. Will not improve.

Chambolle-Musigny, 1980   Now-2002
Reasonable colour. Mature nose. This is round and developed and elegant. Not great depth or intensity, but it is only a village wine. And it is enjoyable, soft, composed and quite long. Good.

Chambolle-Musigny, 1978   Now-2000
Good colour. This lacks a bit of elegance on the nose. There is something rustic and H$_2$S about

it. No better on the palate. Tough, lean, lightish acidity. A bit rigid. Slightly coarse. Not special.

Nuits-Saint-Georges, Les Chaboeufs, 1972
Now-2002

Good colour. Nicely fat and plump for a 1972 on the nose. On the palate also a balanced wine. Ripe, classy, medium weight. Velvety at the end. No undue acidity. This has composure and charm. Very good plus.

Bonnes-Mares, 1971   Drink soon

Medium to medium-full colour. Fully mature. Fully evolved nose. Light and discreet but sweet. This is fully evolved on the palate. On the attack it is soft, fragrant but lacks a little backbone and vigour. But on the follow-through it is more intense than you would think at first. Raspberry fruit. Sweet. Balance, classy. Long, fragrant. Very good indeed. But not great. Held up very well in the glass, which surprised me after the initial impression.

Meursault, 1969   Drink soon

Quite a gold colour. Really quite deep. This is round and very ripe and opulent and fresh. A fat wine. Still vigorous. Very good.

Musigny, 1969   Now-1999

Medium-full fully mature colour. Very lovely sweet fragrant nose. Complex, balanced. Lovely fruit. Medium-full. At first quite a lot more developed than the Chambertin (as it looks), but the follow-through is intense and vigorous and very very lovely. Very classy. Splendidly aristocratic finish. Very fine indeed.

Chambertin, 1969   Now-2000 plus

Fine full vigorous colour. Splendid nose. Rich and full and fat. Fat and creamy and rich on the palate. Full body. Very good acidity. Marvellous classy fruit. Very high quality indeed. Vigorous. Very very long. Excellent. Real finesse.

Pommard, Epenots, 1964   Now-2000 plus

Very good colour. Still vigorous. Typically 1964, typically Pommard. Structured, fat, slightly caramelly, full of fruit. Plenty of vigour. Full, still quite tannic. Very good acidity. Just a little 'old-fashioned'. But vigorous, balanced, intense. Very good. Just a little dense perhaps.

RICHEBOURG

Richebourg, 1959   Now-1999

Full, youthful colour. Rich and vigorous, very ripe indeed, but classy rather than too *rôti*. Fullish, marvellous concentrated fruit. But mellow now. Very good grip. This is long, intense; beautifully clean. Splendidly balanced. Round and complex, very fine indeed. Still plenty of life. But slightly softer than I expected. Very classy yet not exactly very rich. Just a touch lean but as it developed sweeter and more intense than the rest.

Richebourg, 1957   Drink soon

Medium to medium-full colour. No undue age. Soft, oaky, mellow and cedary, even a touch sweet on the nose. Medium-full. More substantial than the colour and the nose would indicate. Good acidity. Not a bit hard and lean. Not as rich or as complex as the 1959 but fine. Quite nutty. Lovely finish.

Richebourg, 1955   Drink soon

Full colour. Mellow oaky nose. Fragrant, old roses aspects, with a touch of roast chestnuts. Ripe and classy. Distinguished. Mellow, soft, ripe and delicate. A little more age than the 1957 and 1959. Medium-full. Long. Silky. Fine plus.

Richebourg, 1953   Past its best

Full colour. This seems to be a little drier on the nose, having lost some of its fruit. Medium body. A touch of astringency. A touch vegetal. This is a little past its best. A lack of fat, the acidity is beginning to show.

Richebourg, 1952   Now-2000 plus

Very full colour indeed. Very youthful still. Rich, robust, structured, very good grip. Much richer, sweeter and more oaky than the 1959 to 1953 series. Quite a different style. Fat, mellow. Full, vigorous. Very fine. But quite different.

MATROT,
MEURSAULT

'Wine-making? I don't know what I am going to do until the vintage arrives. I wouldn't do the same things or make the same wine if I was *chez* Lafon, and Dominique likewise if he were to exchange places with me. Not only are the *terroirs* and the vines different. So also are our *caves*.'

Flexibility above all is the keynote at the Matrot domaine, and Thierry Matrot, tall, gentle and balding, born in 1955, having thought long and hard about it, has rejected many of the nostrums advocated by his peers in favour of an empirical and reactive approach. 'For me the fascination of wine is that with each location and each variety one has an identity and individuality. My job is to enable every one of these to express itself fully. And every vintage is going to be different. So every year the wine-making techniques are going to be a little bit different as a result.'

Here is a philosopher speaking, a lean blond with an earring who lives in a small, somewhat haphazardly extended cottage with his wife Pascale, three girls, a large sleepy Saint Bernard and several modern paintings up in the quiet hamlet of Blagny. There is a calm and a privacy here which matches the Matrot temperament, one you feel which was more at home with the ethos of the late 1960s than with the materialistic 1990s. But do not mistake the peaceful Matrot *laissez-faire* for something diffident and lackadaisical. He knows what he is about. And his is one of the few Meursault domaines which really does produce wines which last.

HISTORY

Joseph Matrot was born in 1881, lived in the Château d'Evelle in the Hautes-Côtes, and was a *négociant*. In 1904, he married Mademoiselle Amoignon who had some vines in Meursault. He gave up his business, took up residence in the imposing premises his wife had inherited, and set about developing the estate.

At first it was more of a farm than a wine domaine. Horses were still used for vineyard work and other transportation. There were cows and chickens. Cereals, fruits and vegetables were produced. But he had dealt in bottled wine before and had a network of customers. So he continued to do so, and did not sell in bulk to the wine trade in Beaune.

Pierre, his son, was born in 1923. He joined his father in the vineyard and his sister Thérèse looked after the office work.

Thierry himself is one of five – he has four sisters. He started work at the domaine in 1976 after taking an oenological diploma at Beaune and further studies in Mâcon, and has been in sole charge since 1983.

THE DOMAINE

The domaine, it would appear, has been sizeable since the 1920s and it now extends over 18 hectares; into Puligny, Volnay and Auxey, as well as Meursault. It makes red as well as white wine. In the 1950s though, Joseph and Pierre increased it by buying about 4 hectares – Meursault, Perrières for the first time, more Meursault, Charmes and the Puligny-Montrachet, Combettes – and in 1976 Thierry and his father further increased their Perrières holding by sharing a new piece of land with Guy Roulot. More recently Thierry has acquired on his own account 0.5 ha of village Meursault (Les Gargouillots) which lies under Volnay, Santenots. This he rents to the family domaine.

The red wines come mainly from Volnay, Santenots and Blagny. There are three parcels in the former *climat* comprising 1.4 ha whose wines complement each other. That in the Plures gives delicacy and finesse, that in Le Milieu gives balance, and that from higher up the slope brings body and weight and staying power. The blend is a sturdy wine, rich and concentrated and repaying cellaring.

Up in Blagny, in a natural sheltered amphitheatre, the vines are planted as they are on the hill of Corton, the Chardonnay up-slope, the Pinot Noir lower down. The red is labelled La Pièce-sous-le-Bois, and there is 2.2 ha of it. The white is Meursault, Blagny, and makes up the rest of a total holding of 4 hectares. Blagny *rouge* is another sturdy wine, with an earthier, slightly spicier flavour than Volnay, Santenots. Matrot's, like that of his neighbour Ampeau, is one of the best. The white, too, has the backbone typical of its origins, and again needs time to come out of its shell.

Above the village of Meursault, in the area of what I call the *deuxièmes crus*, you will find Les Chevalières. Half of Matrot's holding is rather young vines, but the older half is bottled as a separate village *cuvée* reserved for Robert Haas of the USA. This is a firm, racy, mineral wine. A little further along is Les Vireuils, a fine, delicate, elegant wine. Further along still, under the Poruzots and the Genevrières, are the *lieux-dits* of La Pelle, where the wines are also young, and Limousin. Here the wines are fat and rich, but can be heavy and bland. They are not to Thierry's taste. All in all there are 4.7 ha of village white Meursault, and, at least originally, a number of *cuvées*, later blended together.

In Meursault *premier cru*, as well as the Blagny, the Matrot domaine owns 1.12 ha of Charmes, mainly in the best part, and mainly fifty-year-old vines – the ideal age, according to Thierry – and 0.53 ha of Perrières, again mainly from very old vines. Across the border into Puligny there are 6 *ouvrées* (0.31 ha) in the Combettes, the vines here being thirty years old, but beginning to degenerate, and, above Champs-Canet, on the road to Blagny, a large parcel

(1.32 ha) of Chalumeaux. If Combettes is honeyed and nutty, betraying its Meursault proximity, Matrot's Chalumeaux is understated, delicate and *nerveux*. Finesse, not strength, is the character here.

VITICULTURE

If you really do suppress the vigour of young vines, pruning down to four bunches per vine, you can produce some surprisingly interesting wine, maintains Thierry Matrot. You can not only express the *terroir*, but bring out the complexity and character of the *cépage*. 'I am a bit sceptical about the notion of *vieilles vignes*,' he says. 'Obviously old vines are essential. But the yield is even more important. If you persist with your *vieilles vignes*, what happens when you have to rip them all up? It is much more important to maintain a high overall average age, and to prune closely. Green harvesting is something I am also cynical about. I have tried it and I would estimate the gain is only about 20 per cent. It is much more efficient to control the harvest from the outset.'

While Thierry has been experimenting with Cordon training in a parcel of young vines in his Volnay, Santenots - he has an open mind about it, and wants to compare the results - the rest of the Pinots and all the Chardonnays are always Guyot pruned. He likes a long cane, the lowest buds rubbed out, and plenty of space and allowance for aeration between the rest. 'The problem number one with the Pinot is rot.' Six to eight bunches for Pinot Noir will give 35-40 hl/ha. The Chardonnay is allowed one bud more, eight to ten bunches. Overall he aims for 35-40 hl/ha for *premier cru*, 40-45 for village wine. In fact his ten-year average is towards the lower limit of these parameters in white, and around 30 hl/ha for red wine.

Since he persuaded his father to stop chemically fertilising in 1973 there has been a bare minimum of organic manure added to the Matrot vineyard: 'I am seeking an equilibrium and a living soil,' is how Thierry puts it. Yet even after twenty years there is still a bit too much potassium in some of the vineyards. Yet it is here, and not in the cellar, says Thierry, that the wine is made: '*Vignerons* can make great wine with only a bare knowledge of oenology, but an oenologist could never make great wine without a very thorough understanding of his vines and the land they lie in.'

THE CELLAR

On the south side of the village of Meursault the Rue de Martray runs down from the church to the Place de l'Europe. Halfway down a perennially open double metal gateway gives access to a large courtyard. On the left is the office, in front of you a hangar shelters the agricultural machinery, on the right is the building where the wine is made. More importantly, underneath you is a deep, cold, damp barrel and bottle cellar. Since 1985 Thierry has made a conscious effort to hold back more and more stock until it is ready for drinking, believing that he should supply at least his restaurant customers with wines that have come out of their adolescence. One should aim, he says, for five vintages in one's *cave*: three complete vintages worth of stock.

If rot is the chief problem for Pinot Noir, what causes Thierry the greatest concern as far as Chardonnay is concerned is *sur-maturité*. The evolution of white wine made from over-ripe grapes, he says, is always a catastrophe. This happened in many estates in 1986, and in 1983 much of the Chardonnay was even affected by noble rot. In order to eliminate these berries Thierry was forced to destem his Chardonnay. He then had to press by hand because his old hydraulic press couldn't cope. Next year he bought a modern pneumatic press.

Fermentation for the white wines begins in tank, after the must has been allowed to settle and cooled down to 16°C. Once it gets going the juice is transferred to cask. Matrot dislikes new oak for his white wines, preferring to have his casks broken in by a friend. 'Newish is more important than new,' he says. But he is prepared to tolerate a small proportion for the maturation of his red wines. Nor does he approve of *bâtonnage*. He considers the carbon dioxide in the wine keeps the lees gently moving, providing sufficient extraction without having to resort to 'artificial' means.

The white wines are kept on their fine lees until bottling just before the next harvest, the reds being bottled at the same time. Neither are wines which are very showy in their youth. They need patience. You have to give them the benefit of the doubt. But if you give them time you will reap a rich reward as the following notes will indicate. Matrot's wines are built to last.

THE TASTING

The following wines were sampled *chez* Matrot in February 1994.

Optimum drinking

Meursault, Charmes, 1990   1998-2008

Good full colour. Rich, fat, full but slightly adolescent nose. Nicely austere and firm on the palate. Good grip. Ripe fruit. Good depth. Plenty here. Very good indeed. Fine classy finish.

Meursault, Charmes, 1989   Now-2004

Good colour again. Softer on the nose. More fragrant. Slight element of *sur-maturité*. Good acidity though. Peachy. Stylish. Ripe and fruity in a more feminine juicy sense than the above. Very complex at the end. But the 1990 is superior and will last better. Fresh. Long. Very good indeed again.

Meursault, Charmes, 1988   Now-2002

Slightly lighter colour. Slightly leaner nose. Good acidity but less depth and weight. Less richness. But racy and nutty and stylish on the palate. This will continue to develop. Very good. Especially for the vintage.

Meursault, Charmes, 1987   Drink soon

Deeper colour. The nose is a little attenuated and dry-herbal but it is better on the palate. Here it is reasonably fresh and fruity though not very classy or generous. Or indeed very long and complex. But gentle and appealing. Quite good plus.

Meursault, Charmes, 1986   Now-2002

Good fresh colour. This is a great deal fresher, less over-ripe, less botrytis, than most. But there is nevertheless an element here. Soft, honeyed, fat and ripe on the palate. Now *à point*. This is very good but there is a slight lack of real dimension and class at the end.

Meursault, Charmes, 1985   1998-2015

Good fresh colour. Surprisingly austere on the nose. Almost apply on the attack. Fullish, rich, closed-in. Still slightly hard and severe. But the follow-through is complex, very well balanced.

Discreet but has a lot of dimension. Potentially fine plus. But needs time.

Meursault, Charmes, 1984   Drink soon

Fresh colour. Shows a little evolution. Plenty of fruit and attraction on the nose. Beeswaxy. Good acidity. This is not a bit off-vintage-y. It lacks a bit of generosity though. But the finish is long and attractive. Very good indeed for the vintage.

Puligny-Montrachet, Les Chalumeaux, 1982
Now-2000

Good fresh colour. This is *à point*. Ample, plump, mature. Complex. Fullish on the palate, round, ripe, succulent, balanced. No sign of dilution or weediness. Long and subtle at the end. Very good indeed. Will last well.

Meursault, Charmes, 1981   Drink up

Good colour. Plenty of interest on the nose. A touch of mint. This is a good result for the vintage. But it is beginning to show a bit of age now. Ripe enough, but a little lacking finesse and freshness at the end.

Meursault, Charmes, 1979   Now-1999

Good fresh colour. Lovely nose. Complex, honeyed, classy and ripe. Very subtle. Still very fresh. This is of fine quality. Medium-full, concentrated but round soft and succulent. Lots of dimension. Still very young. Bags of life. A lovely mellow mature wine.

Meursault, Charmes, 1973   Drink up

The colour is still fresh. On the nose one is given hints of a plateau of *fruits de mer*. It is a little faded now (Thierry says he's had better bottles). But underneath ripe and complex. Still long, but some of the fruit and class has disappeared.

Meursault, Charmes, 1971   Drink soon

An old colour now. Curious nose: fat, honeyed, slightly rancid and sweet-sour. On the palate full, rich, quite high in alcohol. Individual, indeed very bizarre. Beeswaxy. Would be fabulous with *foie gras*. Raisiny and peachy. Slightly sweet but less so than on the nose. I love it. But a distinct oddball.

Meursault, Charmes, 1970   **Now-1999**

Splendidly vigorous colour. Fine nose. I find this rather more vigorous than the 1973. Rich, fat, complex, nutty. Medium-full, very good acidity. Complex and ripe on the follow-through. Less delicate than the 1979. Slightly more four-square. But plenty of depth. Fine. Still very very young. Even better as it evolved. Very lovely.

Meursault, Perrières, 1961   **Now-1999**

A very light touch of gold to the colour. Marvellous nose. Concentrated and profound. Aromatic. Slight touch of old champagne yeastiness-mushroomness. Rich. Fat. Even a suggestion of sweetness on the palate. Full, concentrated, an explosion of intensity and flavour and concentration. Very fine fresh acidity. Very vigorous indeed. Very very ripe. This is *grand vin*. Very very long. Brilliant.

(Believed) Meursault, Charmes, 1947   **Drink soon**

Not Perrières – because there wasn't any. Nor Combettes. Very light fine colour. Ripe nose. Complex and nutty. Just a faint touch of age. This wine finished its malo in bottle. Very ripe, a definite suggestion of sweetness. Good more and more interesting and fresh and classy as it developed, even on the nose. Mellow. Spicy. Complex. Fresh. Very fine indeed.

Blagny, La Pièce-sous-le-Bois, 1947   **Now-1999**

Vigorous colour. Fullish, still fresh. Fragrant, very fresh, marvellous ripe nose. Round, mellow, sweet but ripe on the palate and not at all volatile. Fresh, gentle but with vigour and very very lovely fruit. Long and complex. Lingering finish. This is really splendid. Silky, very classy, marvellous fruit. Beautifully harmonious. Plenty of life.

MÉO-CAMUZET,
VOSNE-ROMANÉE

The Méo-Camuzet domaine produces indisputably two-star wine, and even in Vosne-Romanée, where there is no lack of competition, it is among the top handful of leading estates. But its fame is recent, as until 1983 everything was sold off in bulk. Only recently has the domaine been responsible for the produce of the majority of its vines, for these were leased off on a share-cropping basis. For forty years the *métayers* not only tended the fields but made the wine. But since 1988 these leases have slowly but surely begun to come to their end, and it was in this vintage that the Domaine Méo-Camuzet began to market the entirety of its share of the crop in bottle.

HISTORY

The vines come from the Camuzet side, but the ownership, and today the management of the estate, belongs with the Méos. The Méo family hails from Selongey, a town north of Dijon, some halfway towards Langres. A Jean Méo arrived in Nuits-Saint-Georges at the end of the nineteenth century, and set himself up as a schoolteacher. He had a son called Gaston, a civil engineer, who married a Marcelle Lamarche, of the well-known Vosne-Romanée family, and they had a son, Jean, born in 1927.

Jean was destined for great things. A petroleum engineer by profession, he graduated into politics, becoming a member of General de Gaulle's cabinet at the end of the 1950s, and subsequently a *député* in the European parliament and a Parisian councillor. For a number of years he was president of the *Institut Français du Pétrole* in Paris.

Etienne Camuzet, his great-uncle, was born in 1866, and was *député* for the Côte d'Or from 1902 to 1932. When the widow of Léonce Bocquet and her children decided to sell the Château du Clos-de-Vougeot and its vines in 1920, it was Camuzet who purchased the building itself. After the war he sold it for a nominal sum to the *Société Civile des Amis du Château du Clos-de-Vougeot*, in order that, in effect, it should belong to the *Confrérie du Tastevin* who held their regular banquets there and were in charge of the celebration and promotion of the wines of Burgundy.

Camuzet died in 1946, and his estate passed to his daughter Marie, who had married the Dijon *négociant* Georges Noirot-Carrière. This marriage was childless, and when Marie died in 1959 the inheritance passed to Jean Méo.

HENRI JAYER AND THE OTHER *MÉTAYERS*

It was towards the end of the war when Étienne Camuzet, mayor of Vosne as well as former *député* for the region, approached Henri Jayer, then in his early twenties, and recently married. 'Would you like to take on some of my vines on a *métayage* basis? The Brûlées, and the Nuits-Saint-Georges, Les Murgers?' Jayer said yes. There also happened to be some land *en friche* in the Cros-Parentoux, which he was later to develop.

Other Camuzet vines were contracted out elsewhere: Clos-de-Vougeot, Vosne-Romanée, Les Chaumes and village Vosne to Louis Faurois; the same plus Nuits-Saint-Georges, Les Boudots, to the father of Jean Tardy. At first these *métayers* were entirely free. They looked after the vineyards, they were responsible for making the wine. One-half of what was produced belonged to the domaine. The rest was their own. But just about all of it was sold off in bulk. Affairs did not change when the succession devolved to Jean Méo. He was far too busy with his own career in Paris.

THE 1980s

Things began to change at the beginning of the 1980s. Henri Jayer, having changed his vinification methods, began increasingly to sell off his share - and his own family vineyard produce - in bottle, and rapidly began to make a name for himself. Louis Faurois had ceded his share-cropping arrangements to his sons Jacques and Jean, and the son of Jean, Christian, had taken up the position of cellar master at the domaine, and was responsible for the *élevage* of the Méo-Camuzet share of the wines.

It was time for decisions to be made. 'We had,' says Jean-Nicolas, son of Jean Méo, born in 1964, 'to go one way or another. Either we sold the domaine, or we took charge ourselves. That's when I became involved. My two elder sisters had their own careers, and I was the only one left. I decided I wanted to become involved, so we decided to continue.'

JEAN-NICOLAS MÉO

Jean-Nicolas Méo, tall, dark and handsome, now married to a Polish young lady of the Walewska family, studied business and economics in Paris, took an oenological and viticultural degree at Dijon, and worked in California with Domaine Chandon and others. He took up responsibility for the domaine towards the end of 1988.

Coincidentally - or perhaps not - this was the last vintage share-cropped by Henri Jayer. Most *métayage* agreements run on an on-going nine-year basis until the *métayer* reaches sixty, retirement age (when, of course, if the landlord so wishes, the arrangement can pass to the *métayer's* son or daughter). Jayer reached sixty in 1988, Jean Faurois and his brother Jacques a few years later. Only the lease with Jean Tardy will still last for some time, for Tardy is younger. This will continue in operation until 2007.

Even before the Faurois brothers' leases ceased, however, the control over what went on was much more exigent. Their autonomy no longer existed. There was much more vineyard management by Jean-Nicolas Méo and his number two, Christian Faurois, and the domaine harvested and vinified its own share of the grapes. 'Since I took over things have been more homogeneous,' says Jean-Nicolas. 'The different wine styles which resulted from the different share-cropping arrangements are no longer apparent.'

Naturally Jean-Nicolas acknowledges a huge debt to Henri Jayer. 'He is a marvellous wine-maker,' he says, 'and we largely continue to make our wine according to his recipe.' But there is now more emphasis in pre-production, in improving the quality of the fruit in the first place. 'The most important progress in Burgundy being made today is in viticulture.' The domaine is as organic as possible. It replaces dead vines with its own stock, rather than clones as hitherto. There is green harvesting now, nearly every year, and a *triage* on arrival in the winery.

WINE-MAKING

On arrival the fruit is completely destemmed, without crushing, cooled to 15°C, and given three to five days' cold maceration, or even longer. Natural yeasts are used. The fermentation temperature is allowed to rise to 34°-35°C, and maceration lasts fifteen to eighteen days. Thereafter the wine is matured, except for the generics, entirely in 100 per cent new oak. 'Our handling is gentler than hitherto,' says Jean-Nicolas. 'There is less pumping.'

Jean-Nicolas Méo doesn't like over-chaptalised wine. *'Il faut la main légère sur le sucre.'* Why chaptalise in the first place, you ask? It extracts more flavours, Méo explains. 'Because you add the sugar at the end of the fermentation, you prolong it, and the high temperatures, by one or two days. We aim for a maximum of 13-13.5°C. Remember that you lose half a degree during the *élevage*. In less ripe vintages, paradoxically, one must chaptalise less in order to preserve a perfect equilibrium.'

Another point Méo has reflected on is the vexed question of yield. You can't establish a precise point at which the diminishing returns begin, he says. It depends on the year. In a vintage like 1990 you can produce far more - 30 hl/ha rather than 25 (for *premiers* and *grands crus*) before the wine becomes dilute than - in 1991 and 1992. Moreover, and this is the tricky part, you can't tell until after the event, after the harvest is over.

THE VINEYARD AND THE WINES

The Méo vineyard is some 15 hectares (it depends how you calculate it: with or without what is lost through the *métayage* arrangements). What they are responsible for directly has of course grown considerably, necessitating an extension to the cellar on the road that leads up from the centre of the village towards the foot of La Tâche.

The range is extensive. Firstly there is now some Bourgogne, Hautes-Côtes-de-Nuits *blanc*. It comes from land above Beaux-Monts. The wines are still very young but the wine is crisp, stylish and crab-apply. Next follows the village Vosne and the village Nuits. The latter is from older vines, and I usually prefer it. Of the various *premiers crus* there are two Nuits: Boudots and Murgers; and three Vosnes: Chaumes, Brûlées and Cros-Parentoux. Of these the Chaumes is the first to be offered. It is less interesting than the others (no fault of the wine-making, merely the position lower down the slope) and the least expensive. Then come the Nuits-Saint-Georges. The Murgers is meaty, oaky, expansive and muscular; the Boudots more refined, usually more intense.

Instead of being offered the Vosne-Romanée *premiers crus* next, as you might expect, the Clos-de-Vougeot and the Corton follow. Méo-Camuzet are the second biggest proprietors in the Clos, and the domaine's large block of vines lies directly beneath the château, averaging over thirty years old. Yet, curiously, I am never enthused by this wine. And the Tardy example, from the same parcel, never really sings to me either. These are certainly both very good, even fine, but not as great as the greatest of Clos-de-Vougeots. Is it me? Is it something to do with the clones and the rootstocks? It is the only one of the Méo-Camuzet wines I cannot come to terms with.

The Corton, on the other hand, is certainly very exciting. Like another Côte-de-Nuits Corton, that of the Thomas-Moillard domaine, it has the depth, concentration and intensity of fruit you hope for, as well as the austerity of this *climat*. The vines are old. The parcel, at 45 ares, nicely extensive.

We now come to two very exciting wines indeed. Vosne-Romanée, *premier cru* Brûlées and its neighbour Cros-Parentoux. The vines in the Brûlées occupy 70 ares, and are over sixty years old. In the Cros-Parentoux they are thirty-five to forty years old, and take up 30 a (Jayer and his nephew Emmanuel Rouget exploit the remaining 72 a of this tiny *climat* up above Richebourg.) The Brûlées is very rich, almost to the point of being sweet, quite crammed with fruit; potentially extremely lush, yet firm for a Vosne-Romanée. The Cros-Parentoux, though the vines are less old, has even more to it: a better grip still, another dimension of flavour, and a startling slightly austere individuality. Vosne-Romanée doesn't come better than this!

And finally we come to the Richebourg. The vines are a generation old, just getting into their prime, and there are 35 a of them. This is a classic: opulent, extremely rich and concentrated, creamy-ripe; almost exotic. Lucky Burgundy, lucky consumer for most Richebourgs are fine these days. But this is indisputably one of the best.

Jean-Nicolas Méo is a proud man, a little serious perhaps, and you wonder sometimes whether he regrets having taken up his vinous inheritance. But a quote from Bazin (*La Romanée-Conti, La Côte de Nuits de Vosne-Romanée à Corgoloin*) is revealing. 'I was trained for an intellectual *métier*,' said Méo, 'and I now find myself in what is essentially a physical occupation. But I am enthralled by the product. And don't think the brain doesn't have to be used. Intelligence, attention to detail and prudence are required all the time.' And, I would add, flair and imagination too. The domaine is in good hands. It can only rise to even more exciting heights in the years to come.

THE TASTING

I sampled the following wines at a tasting put on by one of Méo-Camuzet's leading British importers, Bibendum, in April 1994.

Nuits-Saint-Georges, Aux Murgers

1991 1999–2015

Good colour. Rich, fat, oaky but very stylish nose. Not *sauvage*. One can see the Vosne proximity. Fullish, good tannins. Good grip. This is certainly a keeper. Good rich fat oaky follow-through. Very good plus.

1990 2001–2020

Good colour, but no more than 1991. This is much tighter on the nose than the 1991. Concentrated but closed. Black fruits. More *sauvage*. More structured. Full-bodied. Chocolatey and leather aspects. Very very rich and concentrated. Very good grip. Fine. Needs time.

1989 Now–2007

Very good colour. Soft cherry fruit on the nose. Less concentrated than the 1991. Indeed in comparison with 1991 and 1988, let alone 1990, a bit feeble. Better on the palate. Medium-full, inherently soft sweetly ripe. Good acidity. Has a lot of charm. Very good.

1988 1998–2018

Good colour. Medium weight, balanced, intense, raspberry-cherry nose. Not a blockbuster but very elegant. Fullish, ripe but harmonious and nicely austere. Subtle, long. Lovely. A wine of great seductive appeal. Really complex at the end. Very good indeed.

Clos-de-Vougeot

1990 Now–2007

Good colour. Much more open than the Nuits, Murgers on the nose. Spicy and oaky - bits of cinnamon and allspice. But not a blockbuster. Medium-full. Ripe and seductive, but lacks a bit of backbone and real class. Good plus. Will come forward soon.

1989 Now–2007

Very good colour. A little flat on the nose. Lacks zip, and the fruit, while plump, is a bit flabby. Better on the palate, but, like the 1990, a slight lack of concentration. Medium body. The finish also lacks a bit of style. But the wine has satisfactory length. Good plus.

1988 Now–2006

Very good colour. Firm, balanced and very stylish on the nose. Lovely blackberry-raspberry flavours. Less good on the palate. Medium body. A little astringency as much as tannin (from the oak?) making the fruit a bit stringy. Again not the class of a *grand cru*. Good.

Vosne-Romanée, Aux Brûlées

1991 1999–2015

Good colour. Fine nose. Balanced and intense. Lovely blackberry-raspberry fruit. Very classy. Good oaky base. Medium-full. Abundantly ripe, sweet and oaky. Good grip. Long, stylish. Very good indeed.

1990 1999–2025

Very good colour. Immensely concentrated on the nose. Impeccably put together. Real potential here: real depth. Marvellous on the palate. Full, hugely concentrated, crammed with fruit. Splendidly ripe. Goes on and on on the palate. Very very long finish. Very fine.

1989 1998–2012

Very good colour. Ripe, spicy nose. Rather more open than the 1991, and a little less zip. A little astringency hint on the palate but quite full. Good grip and intensity on the follow-through. Ripe. Long. Very good indeed.

1988 1998–2018

Good colour. A touch of mint on the nose. Even herbaceous. This has less charm as yet than the Murgers. Opened up as it evolved. Fullish, firm, concentrated, very well balanced. This is complex and subtle. Very long. Lovely.

Vosne-Romanée, Cros-Parentoux

1990 2001–2030

Fine colour. Very concentrated, hugely rich, oaky nose. This is much less evolved than the Brûlées. But has much much more to it. A brilliant wine. Full and firm, marvellously structured. Splendid grip and hugely fruity. Very very long. Excellent.

1989 1999–2015

Very fine colour for a 1989. Much fatter, richer and spicier than the Brûlées. Sweeter too. Does it have less zip? Fullish, opulent, certainly plenty of grip on the palate. This is very seductive. Very very long and voluptuous. Excellent for a 1989.

HUBERT DE MONTILLE, *VOLNAY*

At a crossroads in Volnay's Rue de Combe, hidden by a large wooden door, a huddled cluster of medieval buildings and a creeper-covered *chai* surround a gravel and cobbled courtyard. Move behind, into a rather fine park, where there are some venerable old trees and a swimming pool in the distance, and you can take a proper look at an imposing mansion, only the servants' entrance side of which has been on view before. This is the headquarters and summer home of the de Montille family and their 6.5 hectare estate. The wines are some of Volnay's purest and finest; six *premiers crus*, three in the commune and three across the border in the neighbouring Pommard, which regularly call for attention as being among the best examples in the Côte-de-Beaune.

Maître Hubert de Montille is a lawyer as well as the proprietor of this domaine. His domed shaven head, robust figure and impressive intelligence give you some idea of his thrusting performances in court. An aggressive but a worthy advocate, you think to yourself. I'll make sure he is acting for me if I ever have to plead in a French court. This is a man of determined views, but one who seems to thrive in his dual life. And he obviously enjoys food as well as wine. 'I remember as a young man,' he told me, 'doing a service for the Gros family after the death of Louis Gros in the 1950s. As well as my fee they sent me a brace of woodcock and a bottle of Richebourg 1947.' His eyes glaze over with the memory. 'And there was another occasion,' he remembers, 'I went up to Saulieu to have lunch with Loiseau, the proprietor. We were both very young. It was the restaurant's day off, and we ate in the kitchen. He made a soup of oysters and sea urchins . . . and we had a bottle of Romanée-Saint-Vivant 1953 from Leroy with the cheese.'

HISTORY

The de Montille origins lie with a family of *parlementaires, noblesses de la robe et de l'épée* in the eighteenth century. Before the French Revolution they owned land in Volnay and Pommard. Part of the family moved up to Chambolle and Morey. Indeed one of them lived in what is now the house of Bernard Maume in Gevrey-Chambertin.

The domaine in the Côte-de-Beaune was built up, little by little, during the nineteenth century. Perhaps the vineyards at this time were leased off to other wine-makers, for the name De Montille does not figure in the pages of Dr Lavalle's *Histoire et Statistique de la Vigne et des Grands Vins de la Côte d'Or*, published in 1855. Yet according to Hubert de Montille the estate totalled 10 hectares at the time, and in addition it bought in grapes from local *petits vignerons* who did not have their own wine-making equipment.

After phylloxera, certainly, the size of the domaine dwindled for a while. The family concentrated its energies on the rearing of cattle further north in the Auxois, while the men normally followed a military profession and married late.

Hubert de Montille's grandfather had five children. When the estate was divided after his death, the eldest took the château at Créancy near Pouilly-sur-Auxois. Hubert's father inherited some of the vines and the house in Volnay. Other bits were sold off.

Hubert himself was born in 1930, an only son. His father François, already an old man, died five years later, so during Hubert's infancy the De Montille estate was run by his mother and an uncle. His first vintage was in 1947 - Hubert remembers that the only way to keep the temperature under control was to hose down the grapes with cold water before allowing them to ferment - and he took over in 1951.

He inherited a mere 2.5 hectares, and this was obviously insufficient to live on, particularly in those less profitable days. Hence the law, and the build-up of a thriving advocate's practice in Dijon. But during the 1960s De Montille began to enlarge the domaine. He acquired some more land in Pommard, Rugiens to supplement what he already had. He added Pommard, Les Pézerolles, the Volnay, Mitans, a small section of Pommard, Grands-Epenots. Before too long the estate reached its present size.

And he had already noticed that the difference in price paid by the *négoce* for the good, the bad and the indifferent was negligible. He decided, now that his legal business was doing well, that he could afford the delay in payment that would be entailed if he bottled and sold his wines direct. 'I was young and ambitious,' he says. 'I thought I made good wine, and I thought I could get a better price for it if I established my own name.' Back in 1950 he had even bottled 10 per cent of his harvest. From 1959 onwards domaine-bottling was undertaken seriously. 'The last good vintage that I sold to the Beaune wine merchants was the 1961.'

Today Hubert de Montille has been joined at the domaine, at least part time, by his son Étienne. While a student at Dijon, Étienne assisted his father from the 1983 harvest onwards. He was responsible for the 1988 vintage. He is now working for Coopers and Lybrand and is currently based in Budapest, but nevertheless manages to spend most of his free time, especially during the vintage, at Volnay. He will soon be back in France and will be able to be more involved in the domaine.

THE VINEYARDS

There are three separate Volnay *premiers crus* in De Montille's portfolio: Taille-Pieds (0.8 ha), Mitans (0.73) and Champans (0.66). In addition 70 a of vines from Carelles-sous-la-Chapelle, Brouillards, Les Angles and Le Village (despite its name a first growth) produce a Volnay *premier cru*, and there are 15 ares of Volnay *tout court*.

In Pommard the holdings in both Rugiens and Pézerolles are just over a hectare each, and there is a quarter of a hectare of young vine Grands-Epenots. Until 1993 when De Montille acquired 51 a of Puligny-Montrachet, Les Caillerets from the Domaine Chartron there were no white wines.

The age of the vines, overall, is not particularly venerable. 'You can't keep the vines in the Taille-Pieds and elsewhere until they are sixty years old,' says De Montille, nothing if not forthright. 'The soil is too meagre; not rich enough. They degenerate long before this.' The average age in the De Montille domaine is around twenty-five years old. The Volnay, Taille-Pieds, perhaps his best wine, was planted in 1978 and 1979. There is a mixture of clones - he was one of the first to go down this path - plus a little *sélection massale* to give extra variety. One thing De Montille has rejected, common elsewhere, is Cordon training. He has reverted to a simple Guyot system.

WINE-MAKING

De Montille's wines are made with the object of extracting the pure, unadulterated flavour of the Pinot Noir grape, and establishing it in a structure which will enable the wine to last until the flavours are mature and complex, but without the size overwhelming it at any stage. Subtlety is everything. Solidity is anathema. As is chaptalisation, except to a very small degree in the poor vintages.

Triage is important. In 1971 there was hail all over the Côte. One of the worst-hit vineyards was the Volnay, Taille-Pieds. '*J'ai trié à mort*' (I can't translate this literally. Let's just say he sorted the good from the bad until he felt nearly dead from exhaustion.) 'And I fined the wine with milk, but I still couldn't eradicate the taint completely.'

De Montille expresses horror at over-chaptalisation: alcoholic wines which taste fiery and leave a flavour of beet-sugar in the mouth; 12-12.5° is quite enough. The grapes are partially destalked - it depends on the vintage and the ripeness of the wood; but normally 50 per cent of the stems are left - fermented at a relatively high temperature with a lot of *pigeages* in the first few days, and macerated for a fortnight or so. Not surprisingly, given his objectives, now wood is sparingly employed, a quarter or a third for the *premiers crus* (only one-fifth in 1991: 'This is not Chambertin!'). The wines are fined, not normally filtered, and bottled twenty to twenty-four months after the vintage.

THE WINES

Of the Volnays, it is the Champans, where the soil contains a little clay, which is the fullest and the richest: fat and concentrated, with plenty of depth, and a fine capacity to age. The Taille-Pieds up-slope from the Pommard-Monthélie road is more refined, less structured, perhaps the more intense and classy, equally long-lasting. The Mitans falls somewhere in between in structure, but does not have quite the complexity of either.

The vines in the Grands-Epenots date from 1984, so are currently not producing truly representative Pommard. At present the wine tastes more like a Beaune. The Pommard, Pézerolles, from further up the slope, is a wine of good backbone and fruit, if marginally less breed. Better still is the Rugiens. This is a fine Pommard, the meagre, stony, quite steep *terres rouges* giving a wine of depth as well as structure; ample, harmonious and nicely austere - without it being a bit dense - when it is young; rich and voluptuous, yet restrained and classy when it is mature. Generally I prefer de Montille's Volnays to his Pommards. But what I like about all this domaine's wines is their elegance and harmony, the pure expression of their Pinot Noir fruit.

THE TASTING

I sampled the following wines in Volnay in July 1993. The 1991s were still in cask.

1991

Volnay, Premier Cru   1998–2009

Good colour. Rich. Some tannins sticking out. Quite a sturdy wine but it has grip and good blackberry fruit. Shows well.

Volnay, Taille-Pieds   1999–2012

Good colour. Good nose. This is positive, fresh and elegant. The same size but better tannins, more complexity and finesse. Good balance. Long finish. Very typical Volnay.

Volnay, Mitans   1998–2010

Good colour. Rounder but a little less complexity. A bit more straightforward. Balanced. Correct. Good.

Volnay, Champans   2000–2015

Full and rich and meaty. Fat and concentrated. Plenty of depth here, and more structure than the Taille-Pieds. Even better.

Pommard, Pézerolles   2000–2012

Good colour. A little more jammy in style. The tannins slightly more aggressive. A good wine but lacks the nuance of the above.

Pommard, Grands-Epenots   1998–2010

The vines are quite young. Good colour. Ripe and appealing. Medium to medium-full body. But it lacks just a bit of real intensity. Long and fragrant. Beaune rather than Pommard. Stylish.

Pommard, Rugiens   1998–2010

Good colour. Less developed nose. This also lacks a little thrust. The wine is more closed, the tannins more evident. The finish is ample and there is harmony. But an absence of real grip and concentration. The Volnays are superior this year.

1990

Volnay, Mitans   2000–2015

Fine colour. Full, structured nose. Rich and concentrated but quite sturdy. Tannic but real grip and depth. Backward, meaty. Long. Very good.

Volnay, Taille-Pieds   2000–2025

Fine colour. A rounder, richer, more composed wine than the Mitans. Better mannered, the tannins less aggressive. Very intense. Very lovely fruit. Very long and complex. Lovely. Fine.

Volnay, Champans   2002–2025

Excellent colour. Very rich on the nose, but a bigger more closed-in wine than the Taille-Pieds. Full, structured, indeed quite Pommard-ish in style. Today it is the Taille-Pieds which

sings: it shows all its nuances. This will need longer to mature and last longer. Will it be as good? It will certainly come close.

OLDER VINTAGES

Volnay, Taille-Pieds, 1989   Now–2009

Medium-full colour. Soft nose. Ripe, opulent. Fullish, quite structured, backward for a 1989. Rich and meaty. Good grip and reserved. There is plenty of wine here and plenty of vigour. But it needs time. Very good.

Volnay, Taille-Pieds, 1988   1999–2020

Fullish colour. There is a lot of depth and a lot of finesse here. But on the nose it is very closed in. Marvellous fruit. Full, intense, concentrated and vigorous. Very good acidity of course. Potentially very silky and opulent, and very profound and classy. But it is very youthful. Lovely finish nevertheless. Very high class.

Volnay, Taille-Pieds, 1987   Now–2000

Medium to medium-full colour. Fresh. Just a hint of maturity. Not a lot of nose. But after a while a certain dry, slightly rigid fruitiness was apparent. Palate similar, but suppler, riper. Slightly hard still, but approaching maturity. Very good for the vintage but lacks a bit of real nuance and real charm. Finishes well.

Volnay, Taille-Pieds, 1985   Now–2005

Good colour. Fullish, mature, vigorous. Lovely nose. Rich, ample, lovely ripe fruit. Good structure and grip as well. This is a highly successful 1985. It has all the fruit and charm. But good backbone and vigour as well. Just about ready. Very long. Very complex. Lovely.

Volnay, Champans, 1983   Now–2005

Full, vigorous just about mature colour. Quite a sturdy nose, but not over-tannic, or too dense. One can see plenty of fruit. The attack is rich and full, the follow-through a little tannic and dry but the finish once again ample. Obviously a wine whose structure is more than apparent. But a rich, concentrated one. Splendid mulberry-raspberry fruit. Just about ready. Fine but the 1985 Taille-Pieds is better mannered and more elegant.

Pommard, Pézerolles, 1982   Drink soon

Medium to medium-full mature colour. Soft, well-matured nose. A ripe wine, not perhaps a very elegant one, but one with reasonable grip and depth. Enjoyable but lacks nuance especially at the end which is getting a little meagre. Good but not great.

Volnay, Taille-Pieds, 1978   Now–2005

Very good colour. Full, just about mature, very

vigorous. Fullish, ripe, a certain austerity but it is not too lean. Just dignified. Quite prominent acidity. Very old-viney concentrated fruit. Complex. Stylish. Long. Lovely. Bags of life.

Volnay, Taille-Pieds, 1976   Now-1999

Even better colour than the 1978. Barely mature. The nose is quite closed at first, but not too chunky. On the palate a ripe wine with a touch of spice, but a little four-square, a little astringent. Yet not short. The finish is clean and positive and long. Would be much better with food. Very good nevertheless.

Volnay, Taille-Pieds, 1972   Now-1999

A little ullage but the colour is fullish, still vigorous-looking. This is an example of how good the 1972s can be. Ripe, vigorous, medium to medium-full. Now beginning to show slightly earthy and clumsy at the end, but still elegant, not coarse: positive and plump at the end - and by no means lean. Very good plus.

Volnay, Taille-Pieds, 1971   Drink soon

Some ullage here. Medium-full colour, mature. Not too aged. The nose is soft and harmonious. Very ripe but with good grip. On the palate there is a touch of decay and hail-taint at the end, but only a trace. The attack is fullish, very ripe and fruity. Didn't hold up very well in the glass. The hail taste became more dominant. Drink soon and don't decant.

Volnay, Taille-Pieds, 1969   Now-1999

Good fullish mature colour. Mellow nose. Ample, rich, all the spice of maturity here. Nutty and complex. One can see it was once rather a muscular wine. Slightly rigid. Good acidity. Fullish on the palate. This doesn't quite live up to the nose. A bit four-square. Yet very good mature Burgundy. To be drunk with food. Plenty of life.

Volnay, Taille-Pieds, 1966   Drink soon

A little ullaged. Well-matured colour. Soft nose. Beginning to get ethereal, but still sweet and elegant. Light, supple, losing its structure. Yet not astringent. Nor coarse in any way, and still having its fruit. The acidity is beginning to show on the finish. But still very good. And I find it more elegant than the 1969.

Volnay, Taille-Pieds, 1964   Now-2000 plus

Full, vigorous colour. Full vigorous nose. This is lovely: fat and rich and nutty. Lots of depth and complexity. Hearty and warm. On the palate bigger and sturdier even than the 1969, but much more depth grip and concentration. This is fine. Multi-dimensional. Spicy and *rôti*. Exuberant. Plenty of life.

Volnay, Taille-Pieds, 1949   Now-1999

A little ullage here, but I suppose that is to be expected in a wine of this age. Splendid colour. As good as the 1964. Marvellous nose too. Lots of vigour. Heaps of fruit. A very lovely wine. Fullish, very complete, very rich, very velvety. Concentrated but not muscular. Very good grip. Very vigorous. Very very long. The flavour is getting just a little vegetal so not the greatest of finesse. But fine wine nevertheless. And it will still keep.

PIERRE MOREY,
MEURSAULT

Pierre Morey leads a triple life. In the first place he is the proprietor of an 8 hectare domaine. As the major *métayer* for the Domaine des Comtes Lafon he used to exploit more, but this arrangement evaporated piece by piece from 1987 onwards as Dominique Lafon took his patrimony back, and has now ceased. To replace what he has lost - Meursault from the three greatest *premiers crus* of Perrières, Genevrières and Charmes, not to mention Le Montrachet - Pierre formed a small *négociant* company (Morey-Blanc - Blanc being his wife's maiden name) in 1990 and now buys in grapes and must. And for this, the law not permitting domaine and *négociant* wine to occupy the same *cave*, he has had to find separate premises. Thirdly Pierre Morey is *régisseur* at the Domaine Leflaive. He worked alongside about-to-retire Jean Virot from September 1988 and took over at the beginning of 1990.

All this gives the quiet, shrewd, cautious Pierre Morey a unique perspective over the wines, mainly white, of the best part of the Côte-de-Beaune. Morey's blood runs with wine. The experience of this forty-eight-year-old, ruddy-cheeked man is unrivalled. And his own wines, made for the long term, are excellent. But how he now manages to find time for all his responsibilities I do not know.

HISTORY

Pierre Morey likes to recount the history of how Alexis Morey, a Chassagne-based *vigneron* – where the name Morey is two-a-penny – travelled as guard to a priest, secreted in a coach at dead of night, as they came down to Meursault in 1793 at the height of the Terror to celebrate an illicit mass. One of the communicants was a young lady, Benigne Millot, the daughter of the man whose cellar had been lent for the service. Alexis fell instantly in love with her. He remained in Meursault, and a new line of Moreys was founded, now only distantly related to their cousins a few kilometres south.

August Morey-Genelot, Pierre's father, was born in 1912. This Morey saw no future in the wine business – it was a time of savage slump and unprofitability, especially for the wines of Meursault, ignored by the *négoce* in favour of Puligny – and became a travelling salesman. He sold pharmaceutical products until his own father, a sick man as a result of wounds in the First World War, and now ageing, persuaded him to return and take charge of the family domaine. It was 1937. Auguste did not consider it worth buying land, but he did agree to become *métayer* for Lafon, and later on in 1963, in Bâtard-Montrachet and Pommard, Epenots, for the Poirier family, based in Reims.

Pierre Morey, born in 1948, is one of eight, with a brother who is an engineer with the aeronautical firm Dassault and six sisters, as well as half-siblings, for Auguste's first wife died during the Second World War and he married again. He started working alongside his father in 1966 and took over responsibility in 1972. He himself has two children, a daughter aged twenty, and a son Guillaume, disabled, aged sixteen. His wife Christine is a qualified teacher of physical education.

THE VINEYARD

Sadly, says Pierre ruefully, most of my estate is now in generics. The Lafon vines are all gone. Even the Bâtard-Montrachet is now split with his brother-in-law, Roger Caillot. Pierre's plot of vines measures 0.48 ha, right up under Montrachet itself, but he only gets half of this. The rest is delivered in bulk to Louis Latour. He has 0.52 ha of Perrières which he has exploited since 1973 and owned since 1987; 1 ha of Tessons and Forges; 26 a of red Meursault; 0.81 ha of Monthélie, *en fermage*; and 0.50 ha of Pommard, Epenots, also *en métayage*, thirty-year-old vines on the village side of the Clos-des-Epeneaux. The rest of the 8 ha make Bourgogne *blanc*, Aligoté and *rouge*. He is looking for more land, but only in prestigious *climats*.

VITICULTURE AND VINIFICATION

Pierre Morey, as he puts it, has returned to the viticultural methods of fifty years ago: ploughing rather than the use of herbicides, composting – and a light hand at that – rather than fertilisation, and no systematic chemicals. In short, the *méthode biologique*.

He also has carefully thought-out views on the effect of *rendements* on the wine's quality. There are some very precise circumstances, he says, where the volume can be quite high without the quality of the wine suffering as a result. It doesn't appy with Pinot Noir, but only with Chardonnay. It doesn't apply where the soil is thin, such as in the Tessons and the Perrières. It doesn't apply where the vines are young. And it doesn't apply to every vintage. But if you have old vines in a deep soil such as Bâtard, in some vintages you can produce up to the maximum allowed and still achieve wines of concentration. If you vintage late you will get good alcoholic degrees and no lack of acidity.

In principle Morey *does* harvest late, picking up both the Bâtard and the Perrières on the same day. 'These are my most prestigious *cuvées*, and I want the wines to be as concentrated as possible. I wait until the optimum moment.'

After pressing in a new *pneumatique*, installed in 1991, the wine is descended into the *cave* by gravity, fermented in cask with regular *bâtonnage* until Christmas. There is about one-quarter new wood on average, from both the Allier and the Vosges, to give an extra dimension of complexity. The wine is then kept on its lees until the following December before the first racking and left for a total of eighteen months before bottling after a fish fining and a light filtration.

THE WINE

The result is a wine of good rich colour - fish fining not bleaching the wine as casein tends to do - which is built to last. These are not sexy wines in their youth. They can be hard and unforthcoming at first. But patience will be rewarded if you care to wait. And this means a minimum of eight or nine years for the Meursault, Perrières, yet more for the Bâtard. The wines will last for a quarter of a century. Why does his Perrières last so well? you ask. 'It is a more mineral wine than Genevrières or Charmes. The acidities are usually higher.' Pierre Morey's example is a classic.

THE TASTING

I sampled the following wines in Meursault in June 1994.

MEURSAULT, PERRIÈRES

Optimum drinking

1992　　　　　　　　　　**1999-2015**

Lovely rich, fat, opulent nose. Gently oaky. Abundant fruit. But laid-back. A subtle expression. Very good. Still closed. A wine made for the long term. Full. Fine.

1991　　　　　　　　　　**Now-2007**

Fine nose. Flowery, not a bit too evolved. Fresh and surprisingly concentrated. Not a touch 'off-vintage' here. Fullish, cool, classy. Still needs time. The finish is very impressive for a 1991. Very long. This has plenty of future.

1990　　　　　　　　　　**1998-2010**

Firm nose. Still closed. Rich and ripe, nutty and *sous bois*, even bonfires. Underneath more opulent, and with a very good grip. Fresh. Long. Adolescent but potentially very fine. Needs time. This has a lot of depth and dimension.

1989　　　　　　　　　　**Now-2015**

Quite a different nose. Less plump. Rich and opulent, more flowery, more fruity. Less adolescent. A fat ample full wine with an abundance of flavour. Very good grip. On the palate there is a touch of sulphur but the finish is very meaty, very classy. Very concentrated and complex. This is even better than the 1990 though it has less size and perhaps less grip. But it has more flair and complexity. Very fine indeed.

1988　　　　　　　　　　**Now-2005**

Firm nose, a little unforthcoming. Not as opulent as the two vintages above. But very good depth nevertheless, and no lack of attractive plump fruit. On the palate fullish, the attack is just a touch rigid, but the finish is long, full of fruit, complex and fine. Again a splendid example for the vintage. Will keep well.

1987　　　　　　　　　　**Now-2000**

Good fresh nose. Plump too. No undue evolution. Nor weakness either, once again surprisingly good for the vintage. On the palate a good oaky base. Not a lot of dimension to the fruit but ample enough, balanced enough, stylish enough and classy enough. Good positive finish.

1986　　　　　　　　　　**Now-2005**

Honeyed in the best sense on the palate. Soft opulent fruit. No *sur-maturité* on the palate. Round, fat, plump, voluptuous. This is an abundant wine, almost viscous. But it has a very good acidity. No trace of blowsiness. Very fresh at the end. Fine.

1985　　　　　　　　　　**Now-2020**

A firm, very very rich and concentrated wine on the nose. Marvellous fruit. Aristocratic in its bearing. Still a little closed on the palate. But real depth and dimension here. Abundantly ripe. A brilliant example. Splendidly long ample finish. Excellent. For the long term.

1984   **Drink soon**

Evolved nose, but neither thin nor vegetal. Nor without style. This is fresher and more concentrated and fruity than most of the other examples I have seen recently. Soft finish. Lots of interest. Very good.

1983   **Now-2000**

The colour is quite deep here. And the wine has the usual 1983 nose. But it is not tired or flabby: there is a slight flowery-herbal element. On the palate it is like a plate of mixed exotic-fruit sorbets: ripe and opulent but nevertheless fresh. Not exactly very stylish. But very good. For drinking with food.

1982   **Now-2000**

Lovely nose. Soft, silky, ripe and fresh and honeyed. Some evolution now on the palate. This doesn't have quite the class and grip of Coche-Dury's wine, for instance. It is fuller and a little heavier. But it is rich and ample and balanced on the finish. Very good again.

1981   **Past its best**

Quite a deep colour. A bit thin on the nose. With a bit too much built-in sulphur. As far as off-vintages are concerned, this is not in the league of 1984/1987/1991 by any means. It is better on the palate, at least on the attack, but the finish is now tired. A good effort for the vintage but now past its best.

1980   **Drink up**

An even older colour. Soft nose. Curiously a little sweet as well as dry. A bit of sulphur. A bit coarse and oily on the palate. Somewhat rustic. Again now a bit over the hill.

1979   **Drink soon**

Rich, fat, old-fashioned nose, with a touch of reduction. A sturdy example. This is disappointing by comparison with other 1979s. A little aged. A little too much sulphur. Full but lacks grace. Will not improve. Pedestrian.

1978   **Now-2000 plus**

This is very classy on the nose, with a light herbal element. Much better than the 1979. Velvety. Ripe. Individual. Fullish. Very good grip. Long. Nicely austere at the start perhaps. But certainly very ripe too. Fine. Plenty of life.

1976   **Drink soon**

Exotic fruit nose like the 1983, but a little less fat now. Fat and rich, slightly oily, opulent palate. But not lacking interest, even class. This has held up surprisingly well. Not too lumpy, not too blowsy, not too coarse. Very good.

1974   **Drink soon**

Deep colour. A soft wine but not too tired, even if it lacks elegance and dimension. Reasonable fruit. No great depth. But not bad at all. Drink soon now.

1973   **Drink soon**

Fragrant nose. Complex. Full, even a touch solid - like the 1979 - but much more harmonious. Just a little four-square on the palate. Rich and meaty. Balsamic flavours. Still vigorous. Still has style. But a wine for food.

1971   **Now-2000**

A well-matured nose but not coarse. What it has is a slight vegetal, slight petrol hint of an old Riesling. On the palate very lovely complex, stylish ripe fruit. Silky smooth. Beautifully balanced and very very long. Excellent. Still has vigour.

1970   **Drink soon**

This is another very fine wine. Less fragrant and complex but fullish, smooth, alive and concentrated with a lovely velvety character and very good grip. Not quite as exciting as the 1971, but much better, for instance, than the 1973. Much more composed. Real old-vine concentration.

1966   **Drink soon**

Well-matured, spicy, beeswaxy nose. Has begun to lose a bit of fruit on the palate but nevertheless classy, not short, not lumpy. Good structure. Still fresh. Still enjoyable. Just a faint hint of oxidisation and maderisation.

1964 (possibly Perrières)   **Past its best**

Now this really is quite old on the nose - and we are not sure whether it's Perrières or straight Meursault or what. But it is of little consequence. On the palate the wine is really past it.

ALBERT MOROT,
BEAUNE

Next to the *Lycée Viticole* on the outskirts of Beaune, just below the *premier cru* slopes of the Teurons, lies the Château de la Creusotte. This is the headquarters of a business which was once a fully-fledged *négociant* but now simply exists to sell its own domaine wine. The domaine, however, comprises 7 hectares of choice land, all of it *premier cru*, including no fewer than six different *climats* in the best part of the commune of Beaune. Just as you would go, say, to Ghislaine Barthod for an overview of the differences between Chambolle-Musigny's first growths, so the Domaine Albert Morot is a very good place to start investigating Beaune.

HISTORY

The Domaine Albert Morot is owned by Guy and Françoise Choppin. The pair are brother and sister, neither of them is married, and the former, sadly, is today an invalid. Since 1984 the business has effectively been run by Françoise on her own. And it was from this date that *négociant* activity ceased, the last vintage Mlle Choppin bought in from the outside being 1983.

The original Morot, Albert, set up the *négociant* business in Beaune in 1820. Following the phylloxera epidemic one of his succesors set about acquiring vineyards from the Duvault-Blochet family (owners at the time of a vast estate which included the Domaines of Romanée-Conti and Pousse d'Or), the Marey-Monge family and others, and towards the end of the century established himself on the present site. The château is not, as one might hope, a fine, late medieval construction complete with the coloured slate roof so common in the area, but a more pedestrian, rather solid gentleman's residence of less architectural interest. It was built in 1898.

Following the First World War this Morot extended his activities as merchant. He acquired further cellars in the centre of town, later sold to Patriarche and Bouchard Aîné, and began exporting to Britain and the USA. The business was one of the first to open its doors to the passing tourist, enabling the firm to build up a substantial mailing list for *vente directe*. Guy Choppin - the inheritance following the female line - took over in 1952 and was in able charge for the next thirty plus years.

THE VINEYARD

Today, as I have said, the Morot business has contracted back to that of a domaine, and there are three employees rather than the eight of a generation ago. The largest parcel in the portfolio is the one outside the commune of Beaune, 1.8 hectares in an enclave of Savigny-lès-Beaune, Les Vergelesses called La Bataillère: a *monopole*. This has always been considered the best element of the *climat*, lying as it does on the same level as the Ile-des-Vergelesses. A century and a half ago it belonged to the widow Vauchey and was dignified with the connotation of *clos*. The authorities have since objected. Part of the wall has fallen down, and it is not totally enclosed. The name has no connection with any battle however. Legend has it that the owner was once a M. Bataille. Albert Morot bought it from cousins of the Senard family of Aloxe-Corton.

In the commune of Beaune, all in the northern sector of the *vignoble*, there is 1 hectare of Teurons, planted in 1963, 13 ares (two casks' worth) of Grèves (young vines dating from 1992), 0.77 ha in the small *climat* of Toussaints (1969), 1.27 ha of Bressandes, up-slope from Toussaints, mainly dating from 1946, 1.28 ha of Cent-Vignes (1958/1959) and 68 ares of Marconnets at the extreme north of the commune. The distance between Marconnets and Teurons is hardly 2,000 metres. But there are in all six distinctly different *premiers crus*, and all but one in reasonable quantity: 1 hectare will produce sixteen to eighteen barrels of wine.

VITICULTURE AND VINIFICATION

Françoise Choppin is proud of the average age of her vines. This by itself, provided the pruning is severe, will keep the harvest within bounds, though she admits to having green-pruned in recent years, and having *saignée*-d in others. The depth in the resultant wine is unmistakable, she feels. And she is somewhat contemptuous of those who are prepared to rip up a vine before its sixtieth birthday. The previous generation in the Grèves dated from the first decades of this century.

On arrival at the winery - 'we always start harvesting on a Wednesday,' she told me once - the fruit is completely destalked ('they only impart bitterness, and what I am after is the fruit') and given a long *cuvaison*, with temperatures which are allowed to rise as high as 33°C at the beginning. There is plenty of *pigeage*. They used to heat up the cellar to encourage the malo-lactic, but this has now been discontinued. 'I prefer to let the wine achieve its malo itself. I am in no hurry.' The wines are racked after the malo and bottled by gravity about a year later, today without filtration, and without even being fined in the 1991 vintage.

'I don't like the taste of new wood, especially if the toast is high,' says Mlle Choppin firmly. And here she finds herself somewhat at odds with her American agent, the Washington-based Bobby Kacher. Kacher knows that lots of new wood produces high marks in American wine magazines, and is adept at imposing new barrels on some of his suppliers. Françoise Choppin has resisted, but only in part. When I began to call on her a decade or more ago the new wood percentage was 20 per cent. Then it became about a third, though it used to be one out of two for the Grèves before the vines were ripped out. Now it is an overall 50 per cent. I trust she will not succumb to pressure to increase the amount further. The wines won't be able to take it. They aren't Chambertins, after all.

Thankfully Françoise Choppin is a shrewd and independent character, and Kacher has already blotted his copybook once. A few years ago he persuaded her to buy a *Kieselguhr* filter, only to come back a year or two later, having discovered that *Kieselguhr* filtration was disapproved of by Robert Parker, and forbade the Morot domaine from using it after all. Today the machine stands forlorn in a corner of the cellar: unwanted, unused.

THE WINES

The Morot range begins with the Savigny: rich, substantial, and not a bit rustic, profound for a wine of this commune. You then move into the Beaunes. The most different from the rest is the Marconnets, betraying its origins on the Savigny margins with a *goût de terroir* and an almost Pommard-like density and tannic structure. It takes time to come round, and perhaps never aspires to the same amount of finesse as the remainder. But it is a good example nevertheless.

The four remaining wines - or five if you include the Grèves - are more similar to one another: extensions of the pure, raspberry blackberry plumpness of middle Beaune, each with a particular nuance. The least interesting is the Cent-Vignes. It is medium to medium-full-bodied, supple and soft. There is good intensity but not quite the depth and definition of the rest. But it is '*très fin*', to quote Françoise Choppin. Bressandes comes from higher up the slope, has more body, and a slight aspect of exotic spice, sometimes coffee and chocolate. It is one of my favourites. Lower down lies the Toussaints: the same weight, always good acidity, but not quite as fat. Finally the Teurons, which Mlle Choppin insists should be spelled without an H ('Theurons is quite wrong'). This is the most complete, usually the most structured of the whole range. The tannins are the ripest and most sophisticated, the balance is excellent, the fruit showing great breed. It is a fine example.

THE FUTURE?

There is a quaintness about the Morot set-up. The house is out of bounds and in some state of disrepair. With an invalid to look after, Françoise Choppin does not socialise much. She doesn't even drive a car. The office is determinedly old-fashioned, the most up-to-date element being the small flat upstairs used by the regular *stagiaires*. The cellars, on three levels, the lower one regularly flooding, are cavernous, the meagre harvest almost lost. Until you taste the wines you feel the whole thing is dilapidated, decaying, rather sad. Though Françoise Choppin is a robust lady, she must, like her brother, be approaching retirement age. What is the future? Will the vineyards get snapped up by Jadot, as they gobbled those of Champy, and the name cease to exist? There have already been approaches from outsiders.

I am told that there are *petits cousins*, who live in Le Havre. Thankfully one of these has followed a course in viticulture and oenology and is earmarked to take over. For this we should be thankful: it would be a sad loss if the Domaine Albert Morot was to lose its independence.

THE TASTING

I sampled the following wines in Beaune in February 1994.

Optimum drinking

Beaune, Teurons, 1991　　　**1999-2014**
Very good colour; as deep as the 1990. On the nose still a little bottle sick, but good richness and substance here. Fullish, better on the palate than on the nose. Good grip. Positive, concentrated and intense in flavour. There is structure here, but the tannins do not impose. Very fine follow-through and finish. Impressive quality.

Beaune, Teurons, 1990　　　**2000-2018**
Very good colour. Firm, rich, closed nose. This has gone into its shell. Black fruit flavours compared with the 1989. Here the tannins do show a bit. I don't find the fat I had expected. There is very good acidity and the wine is long and concentrated and stylish at the end. But the middle is a little dry. But after 15 minutes it began to fill out. It became much more complex. Very fine indeed.

Beaune, Teurons, 1989　　　**1998-2012**
Medium-full colour. Splendidly ripe and succulent on the nose. Raspberries, strawberries, cherries, even a touch (but naturally) sweet. Yet on the palate still quite a long way from maturity. Rich and fullish. Round but with a certain backbone and tannic structure to round off. Needs time. Lovely rich finish. Very good indeed.

Beaune, Teurons, 1988　　　**1999-2020**
Fine colour. More so than the 1990. Also quite closed on the nose but a little more accessible. Less weight and tannin. A little more red fruits than the 1990. Fullish body. Very good grip. This is very stylish and complex. Slightly more austere but subtle, multi-dimensional. Very, very well balanced. Very, very long. Fine.

Beaune, Teurons, 1987　　　**Now-2003**
Very good colour. No sign of maturity. Ripe, quite concentrated, good style and depth. A low yield is very apparent. On the palate medium-full body. Good fruit, but not the intensity and class of the 1988. Approaching maturity. Has balance and length. But there is a certain lack of depth and succulence and real style. Good though.

Beaune, Teurons, 1986　　　**Now-1999**
Medium, mature colour. Not weedy on the nose by any means. Plump and fruity. Even rich. Just a little one-dimensional after the wines above. Fresh on the palate. Round. Fruity, medium-bodied. Positive. A great success for a 1986. Will still keep well.

Beaune, Teurons, 1985　　　**Now-2005**
Just a little more colour than the 1986. Lovely nose. Ripe and ample. Accessible but subtle. Well balanced. Good attack but even better on the finish. Warm, rich, generous. Very good grip. Medium-full. Just about ready. Most attractive. Fine.

Beaune, Teurons, 1983　　　**Now-2008**
Very good colour. Barely brown. Full and intense. Not a bit dry or lumpy on the nose. Rich, slightly cooked fruit of course. Full, balanced, spicy, not a bit dry or astringent. Very good grip. This is meaty - gamey even - but still structured. Very good indeed.

Beaune, Bressandes, 1982　　　**Drink soon**
Quite brown at the edge but still vigorous within. Good and fullish. Soft and gentle on the nose. Round and juicy on the palate. Balanced, stylish, even quite complex. This has class and lingers nicely on the palate. A very good example.

Beaune, Teurons, 1982　　　**-**
Very brown colour. Not weedy though, but looks like an Oloroso sherry. Half bottle - because that was all that was left. Oxidised.

Beaune, Teurons, 1976　　　**Now-2000 plus**
Splendid colour. Hardly a hint of brown. Very very full. Meaty, slightly tough, old-fashioned nose compared with the wine today. But that is also the tendency of the vintage. Full, structured, intense and concentrated. Very good grip. This is a slightly four-square example, and will always be a bit solid. But it isn't dry or astringent. This is good. Would even be very good with food. Still young.

Beaune, Teurons, 1972   Now-1999

Good fullish mature colour. Lovely soft intense nose. Not a bit austere. Medium-full, round, velvety. The acidity *is* a bit apparent, but the fruit is classy and the wine finishes very long on the palate. A very good example indeed.

Beaune, Marconnets, 1964   Now-1999

Despite a marked ullage the colour is full and fresh, and the nose is rich, full, ripe and generous. Full and concentrated on the palate. Balanced. Vigorous. Rich and complex. Lovely old Burgundy at its best. Fat, meaty, mellow but quite sturdy, as befits a 1964.

Denis Mortet,
Gevrey-Chambertin

No other *vignoble* in France has seen as much change as Burgundy over the last fifteen or twenty years. Sometimes the evolution can be gradual, as a wine-maker refines his techniques or gradually hands over to his children. Sometimes the adjustment is abrupt. A domaine can be split. A parcel of old vines can be ripped out. But inevitably the progression is fundamental. Burgundy today has been transformed. A time-traveller from as recently as the early 1970s would hardly recognise it.

HISTORY

As an example I could site no better case than that of Denis Mortet, aged forty-one, and his Gevrey-based domaine. Denis' father, Charles - a cousin of Charles Rousseau, incidentally - started off with 1 hectare. Seeing little future in the neighbourhood, and having married a lady from Daix, on the other side of Dijon, he decamped and concentrated on mixed farming. He kept his vines, however, and added to them when the occasion arose. But he didn't bottle himself, let alone think of exporting.

Denis, the elder by six years of Charles Mortet's two sons, was born in 1956. He started working alongside his father in 1977. When brother Thierry joined them in 1982 the family business was turned into a GAEC (*Groupement Agricole d'Exploitation en Commun*). Meanwhile Denis was continuing to enlarge the exploitation by taking on his own vines *en fermage* or *en métayage*. He started bottling the Mortet wine, and in 1984 he began to export it. I remember first encountering the wine at a London tasting a year later. And he had moved back to Gevrey-Chambertin when he got married in 1978. It was more logical, despite the fact that his wife Laurence was a local Daix girl.

So, by the end of the 1980s Charles' original hectare had been enlarged to nearly 8, in thirty different plots from Daix to Clos-de-Vougeot. Gradually the wine-making was being fine-tuned. Certainly the quality was improving. A new star had emerged, which bottled practically everything it produced. The name of Mortet was on the map.

In 1991 Charles Mortet officially retired, though he still today works in the vineyard, and the GAEC was broken up. Thierry Mortet - after all, it is difficult being the much younger brother - wanted to go his own way. The domaine was split up. From being a reasonably-sized estate for the two of them it looked as if each brother would be left alone with a rump.

But then, like a fairy godmother, along comes a local *vigneron*, one Bernard Guyot. He, like Charles, was about to retire. He had seen the care with which Denis Mortet tended his vines. He'd tasted the result. Obviously he had been impressed. 'Would you like to take over my land?' he suggested to Denis. With one bound Mortet was free, as they say in adventure stories. Guyot exploited 4.5 hectares. Together with a further 50 ares from another leasing arrangement this would push up the Denis Mortet domaine to nearly 10 hectares, the new parcels coming onstream with the 1993 vintage. Denis has lost his Gevrey-Chambertin, Clos-Prieur to Thierry. It wasn't worth splitting up. And the parcel of Chambolle-Musigny, Beaux-Bruns, bought in 1987, as with a lot of the rest, has been divided. But Mortet now has a good chunk of Lavaux-Saint-Jacques, has doubled his slice of Champeaux, taken on several interesting old vine plots of village Gevrey, has retained all the Clos-de-Vougeot and the Chambertin, which were his own private *en fermage* arrangements, and can now offer a Marsannay, 0.48 ha in Les Longeroies, where a neighbour is Bruno Clair. He's got even more to sell than he had in 1991.

THE VINEYARD

In total the domaine now covers 9.8 ha and offers fourteen different *appellations*. At the bottom of the range there are the usual generics: Aligoté and Chardonnay, Pinot Noir *rouge* and Passetoutgrains. Much of this comes from Daix, in the Côte Dijonnaise, north of the city.

There is 2.8 ha of village Gevrey, very little of it on the 'wrong', east side of the N74, plus a village *monopole* 'En Motrot' (0.50 ha) and two other separately-bottled village wines: 1.20 ha of 'Au Velle' and 1 ha of 'En Champs' *vieilles-vignes*. Then there are the *premiers crus*. Two of these are in Gevrey-Chambertin; 50 a of Champeaux and 1.17 ha of Lavaux-Saint-Jacques. The latter lies next to the Clos-Saint-Jacques, and the former further to the north adjacent to the commune boundary with Brochon. In Chambolle-Musigny there is the third: Beaux-Bruns, down-slope from the Bonnes-Mares.

Finally there are two *grands crus*, both leased. In Chambertin, next to the vines of Trapet, Denis exploits 4 *ouvrées* (0.15 ha). This belongs to Noëlle, wife of Charles Quillardet. The vines were planted in 1955/1957. Right down in the bottom right-hand corner of Clos-de-Vougeot, as you look up from the main road, just where those who don't have vines in the sector consider the land not worthy of being rated *grand cru* (but they haven't tasted the Mortet wine), is Mortet's 32 ares parcel. The land belongs to Pierre Charvet of Daix and Maurice Henry of Marigny. Half the vines date from 1960; the other half from 1985.

VITICULTURE AND VINIFICATION

The average age of the Mortet vines is old, and of this Denis is very proud. He is exigent about their care too. It wasn't that he doesn't trust those who work them for him, but just to be sure he had been down at 9 p.m. in the evening of the day before I called on him in June 1994 to check what had been done that day.

The land is ploughed and hoed, herbicides being abhorred, and because Denis wants the vine roots to dig deep. He is meticulous about pruning hard, debudding, and eliminating excess shoots. 'The *rendement* is everything,' he says. 'There is no escape from a low harvest.' He has green harvested, in 1988 and 1989, for instance. 'But it is a last resort. It is better to reduce the harvest earlier. I'd prefer not to have to do it in future.'

At harvest-time there is a very severe *triage* in the vineyard, and, since 1993, a second one on a *table de tri* in the winery, a building on the outskirts of the village which looks like a bus garage.

The fruit is entirely destemmed, and vinified in concrete open *cuves* of various sizes. After a short *macération à froid* there is a long *cuvaison* at 29-32°C. When the fermentation is at its most violent, for a couple of days, there are three or four *pigeages* a day. Thereafter two, and the *cuves* covered over.

Once the *cuvaison* is over the wine is descended into casks in the cellar. There is a mixture of oak. Vosges for the better wines: the evolution is slower but better, says Mortet. And between one-third and 75 per cent new oak, depending on the status of the wine. After the malo the wine is racked, for the one and only time. Since 1988 it has been bottled unfiltered, usually eighteen months after the vintage, and it is sometimes not fined either.

THE WINES

Denis Mortet is an independent character and, rightly, proud of what he does. You feel he could be a hard task-master, not putting up readily with fools. He sacked his first American agent, Bobby Kacher, because he didn't like the way the man wanted to impose himself and his wine-making ideas. He now deals with Martine Saulnier in California, a native Frenchwoman who, as he puts it, understands wine better.

But it is clear Mortet is a man of passion as well as perfectionism. Touring round his vineyard parcels shows quite plainly his commitment. You feel he knows every single vine personally. And the wines, full, generous, multi-dimensional, rich and expansive, have a lot more to them than most. This is a splendid domaine. And the wines are getting better and better.

THE TASTING

I sampled the following wines in Gevrey-Chambertin in June 1994.

Gevrey-Chambertin, Champeaux, 1992
1999–2007

Bottled a bit earlier than usual (December rather than end March). Very good colour for a 1992. Very good nose. Plump and oaky and with plenty of depth. Very generous. Medium-full. Good structure. Good balance. This has more to it than most. Lovely ripe fruit. Long. Very good indeed. Great charm.

Gevrey-Chambertin, Champeaux, 1991
2000–2015

Good colour. Firm but balanced and stylish on the nose. Good plummy austerity. Lots of dimension. Medium-full. A little hidden on the attack. More expansive on the follow-through. Good grip. Very long. Very good indeed. Very classic.

Gevrey-Chambertin, Champeaux, 1990
2001–2020

Splendid colour. Rich, meaty, closed nose. Some tannin here. Has gone into its shell a little. Fullish. The slight robustness of the Champeaux *climat* accentuated by the adolescence of the wine. Rich underneath. Good grip. A slight lack of real elegance at the moment. But I am certain there is enough here.

Gevrey-Chambertin, Champeaux, 1989
Now–2010

Good colour. A little development. Soft nose. A touch of sweetness and spice. A touch of reduction. Fine on the palate. Velvety rich. Good backbone. Very good acidity. Quite full, especially for a 1989. Lovely fruit. Long. Very seductive. Plenty of future.

Gevrey-Chambertin, Champeaux, 1988
Now–2009

Good colour. Less oaky on the nose. Rich and quite full, balanced, cool and fragrant. On the palate this is good but it lacks a little concentration and grip by comparison with the vintages above. Medium-full. Not a lot of tannin. Still a little of the austerity of the vintage, but beginning to round off now. Ripe on the finish. Very good. But a little dimension is missing. I prefer the 1989.

Gevrey-Chambertin, Champeaux, 1987
Now–2000

Medium colour. Now some development. Fresh, plump nose with a touch of spice. No weakness. But perhaps no great elegance either. Medium body. Ripe, plump and attractive. No uncomfortable edges. Quite stylish. Quite balanced. Good for drinking now. Good for the vintage. Long and positive.

Gevrey-Chambertin, Champeaux, 1986
Drink soon

Medium colour. Mature. Soft, evolved nose. This now shows a little astringency on the palate. It has less grip and less definition than the 1987. Medium body. Only a little fruit, and this is drying up. Average.

Gevrey-Chambertin, Champeaux, 1985
Now–2010

Medium-full colour. Still youthful. Fine nose. Lovely rich fruit, very good acidity. Round and generous. Has both the elements: grip and warmth, that the 1986 lacks. Medium-full, very good balance. Ripe and ample. Still has a bit of unresolved tannin. Very long. Very good indeed.

Gevrey-Chambertin, 1982   Drink soon

Medium-full colour for the vintage. Fully mature. Ripe, pleasant nose. No great thrust behind it but attractive and balanced. Medium to medium-full. Now showing a few signs that it is getting a little old. But ripe and fresh and plump still. And still positive at the end. A very good example of a village wine.

Gevrey-Chambertin, Champeaux, 1980
Drink up

Good colour. Still vigorous. Still quite full. The nose is beginning to lighten up now. But there is good fruit and style nonetheless. On the palate now a little thin and astringent. I had expected better especially after the village 1982. Pleasant fruit but a little weak.

Gevrey-Chambertin, 1978   Drink up

Good full mature colour. Quite evolved, even a little too much so on the nose. On the palate there is a slight metallic, sour touch. But at the same time there is structure and fruit. Got a bit maderised as it evolved. Other bottles, apparently, have been better recently.

Gevrey-Chambertin, Champeaux, 1976
Now–2000

Fine colour. Still youthful. This is a good example. Very ripe but not a bit dense and lumpy. Structured, of course. A full-bodied meaty wine. Slightly exotic. Larger than life. Over-ripe in places. But glamorously fruity. The backbone shows but with food this is very good indeed. No lack of grip and length.

GEORGES MUGNERET AND MUGNERET-GIBOURG, *VOSNE-ROMANÉE*

One of the last times I met Dr Georges Mugneret, who sadly died in November 1988, was at vintage time in the previous year. I was in the region making a video on Burgundy, and one of those we had chosen to interview on film was Madame Jeannine Gros, mayor of Vosne-Romanée and proprietor with her husband of Domaine Jean Gros. The Gros and the Mugnerets share a large nineteenth-century house, built over cellars excavated in about 1750. Almost as soon as we began to set up in the communal courtyard out scurried Dr Georges; not, as I thought at first, because he wanted to be filmed as well, but because he was fascinated by cameras and the whole filming process. Here was a man, it was confirmed again, of polymathic interests: an ophthalmic surgeon who just happened in his spare time to be responsible for one of the best domaines in Burgundy.

HISTORY

There have been Mugnerets in Vosne-Romanée - and in the wine-producing business - for generations, and there are now a number of estates with this name somewhere in their title in the village (prompting the Georges Mugneret domaine to demand on its letterhead that one *En raison des homonymes, prière de préciser noms et prénoms*). The Gibourgs, however, were farmers, polyculturalists, out in the plain of the Saône: cereals and cattle were their concerns, not wine.

Towards the beginning of this century a branch of the Gibourgs installed themselves in the village. One of these married Georges Mugneret's father, and the Mugneret-Gibourg domaine was born. He produced Bourgogne *rouge*, village Vosne-Romanée, from the large field between the village and the main road, and Echézeaux. At one time the estate also possessed some Clos-de-Vougeot, but - to the later fury of Dr Georges - this was sold off in the 1930s.

Dr Georges Mugneret, his medical activities subsidising the wine business, then unprofitable, began to enlarge the domaine after the war. Some Clos-de-Vougeot, once part of the Léonce Bocquet estate, was acquired in 1953 and replanted the following year. In 1971 came some Nuits-Saint-Georges, Les Chaignots. A decade later followed some Nuits-Saint-Georges, Les Vignes-Rondes, lower down the slope, but also on the Vosne side of the commune. The soil from the former erodes into the latter when there is a violent storm. Meanwhile in 1977 the Thomas-Bassot majority in the Ruchottes-Chambertin was divided between Charles Rousseau, Michel Bonnefond, a businessman from Rouen (who appointed the Christophe Roumier as his *métayer*) and Dr Georges Mugneret. Finally, in 1985 Mugneret bought almost half a hectare of Chambolle-Musigny, Les Feusselottes.

Georges and his wife Jacqueline had two daughters. The first, Marie-Christine, qualified as a doctor of pharmacy, married Eric Teillaud and has two daughters. The second, Marie-Andrée, married Loic Nauleau and has recently produced their first child (a daughter again).

When Dr Georges Mugneret fell seriously ill in 1988, Marie-Christine started to lend a hand with the wine-making process; her mother meanwhile continuing with the commercial side. She took the oenological diploma at Dijon and gradually, as she became more and more involved, gave up the pharmaceutical side of her life. She and Eric made the vintages from 1988 to 1991. Now that Marie-Andrée, also a qualified *oenologue*, is working at the domaine the two husbands are only needed when something heavy, such as racking, is required to be done.

THE VINEYARDS

The estate now covers 8.88 hectares, the original sections - 0.85 ha of Bourgogne *rouge*, 3.80 ha of village Vosne-Romanée and 1.25 ha of Echézeaux being leased to others on a *métayage* basis and sold under the Mugneret-Gibourg label. The newer parcels acquired by Dr Georges - 0.34 ha of Clos-de-Vougeot, 0.64 ha of Ruchottes-Chambertin, 1.27 ha of Nuits-Saint-Georges, Les Chaignots, 0.26 ha of Nuits-Saint-Georges, Les Vignes-Rondes, and 0.46 ha of Chambolle-Musigny, Les Feusselottes, are sold under his name: Dr Georges Mugneret. Four of these (the Clos-de-Vougeot, the Ruchottes, the Feusselottes and the Vignes-Rondes) are looked after by others *à la tâche*: the *vignerons* (André Esmonin in the case of the Ruchottes) being paid an annual sum for the work, but allowed to decide for themselves when to do it. The remainder are rented out *en métayage*.

The plums of the domaine are the Clos-de-Vougeot and the Ruchottes. The latter, much split up within this tiny *grand cru*, is from vines which are thirty-five years old. The Clos-de-Vougeot, now forty years old, consists of eighteen rows which lie between those of Méo-Camuzet and Lamarche and run down from the château itself towards the Château de la Tour.

There are two plots producing wines which are complimentary to each other, in

Echézeaux. The first, 59 ares, lies up-slope in Les Rouges, next to those of Dujac, and consists of seventy-year-old vines. The second, 64 ares, is in the Quartier des Nuits, outside the south wall of the Clos-de-Vougeot. Here the vines are younger, and there is a tendency to over-produce, necessitating a regular green harvest. Twenty harvesters are employed for one day to collect the fruit from the four parcels farmed *à la tâche*: the *métayers* deliver the Mugneret's share to the winery in grapes.

WINE-MAKING

Have you changed things since you took over? I asked Marie-Christine. 'Well, we have a *table de triage* now, and we have found it very useful. And in 1993 we installed an automatic *pigeage* machine. But the wines my father made were fine, and I have seen no need to alter the wine-making process.'

The grapes are destemmed (here there has been a change, for Dr Georges used to leave 20 per cent in, provided they were ripe), allowed to macerate for two to three days before the fermentation gets going, and vinified in wooden and cement vats for fifteen to twenty-one days, at reasonably high (30°C plus) temperatures. With Marie-Christine's scientific back-ground it is not surprising that she prefers to use artificial yeasts. The result, she says, is longer fermentations, more glycerol extraction, and a more efficient translation of sugar into alcohol.

The wine is matured in 40 per cent new wood for the lesser wines, 80 per cent for the *grands crus*, racked twice, after the malo and again six to eight months later, fined *en masse* in the early months of the second year before the bottling which takes place from April to June.

THE WINES

At the bottom of the hierarchy, after a sturdy but not rustic Bourgogne *rouge*, is the village Vosne-Romanée. This benefits from the economies of scale; for the produce of the young vines - a part of the parcel had to be replanted after the 1985 frost - can be vinified separately and set aside. It is a splendid village example, full and sturdy, but succulent, rich and ample, with a good base of oak.

The Nuits-Saint-Georges, Les Vignes-Rondes, is a tiny parcel, and looking through my notes I see I have never been offered it for tasting. Is it sold off in bulk? The Chaignots, from up on the slope above the Vignes-Rondes, betrays its Vosne-Romanée proximity to give a wine which combines the structure of Nuits and the purer black-cherry, cassis elegance of Vosne. I like it very much. It needs seven years in a top vintage.

The Chambolle-Musigny, Les Feusselottes, is a lighter wine which comes forward a year earlier, but one with more style and no lack of intensity. There is fragrance here; raspberries and violets, and sometimes more obvious oakiness. Sometimes it is more subtle than the Chaignots. Sometimes the Chaignots stands out because it has more substance.

The Echézeaux is in the same mould as the Clos-de-Vougeot, but there is less dimension, and an element of the rustic. It may not have the weight or drive for 'fine' but it is usually plump and seductive. Another very good example of the *climat*.

The Clos-de-Vougeot is often the best wine in the cellar: indeed it is one of the best of all in this uneven *grand cru*. This is full and structured, concentrated and plummy, elegant and profound. In a fine year it needs a decade before it is ready.

Less flamboyant but sometimes with more power, more grip and more depth is the Ruchottes. This is a wine of real intensity and finesse; less mulberry, more cassis in flavour. It takes longer to open out. Again it needs keeping ten years.

Georges Mugneret was a genial, enthusiastic man who embraced life to the full, and the wine he made - which tradition his daughters are most ably carrying on - is a reflection of this approach. The wines are well-coloured, though not immensely deep in hue, generous, rich, oaky and long lasting: above all they are pure Pinot Noir.

THE TASTING

I sampled the following wines in Vosne-Romanée in June 1994. My thanks to the elegant Mesdames Mugneret for their generosity.

Optimum drinking

Clos-de-Vougeot, 1992   Now-2004

Medium colour. Bottled one month previously, this wine has recovered well. Fresh and plump on the nose. Good substance and grip. But soft and *tendre* nevertheless. Medium body. Round, generous, charming. Good touch of oak. Long. Not a blockbuster but balanced and attractive. Good.

Clos-de-Vougeot, 1991   1999-2015

Medium-full colour. Rich, firm nose. A bit closed at present. But heaped with fruit and very stylish. Fullish. Good tannins. At present the elements do not knit together but the fruit is ripe, the wine balanced and there is plenty of complexity. Long. Subtle. Very stylish. Very good indeed.

Clos-de-Vougeot, 1990   2000-2025

Medium-full colour. Marvellous nose. Very very rich and concentrated. A big wine with splendidly ripe tannins. This is very exciting. Full and very very rich and concentrated on the palate. Very ample velvety black-fruit flavours. A lot of grip. And a great deal of finesse too. Very fine indeed.

Clos-de-Vougeot, 1989   Now-2000

Medium-full colour. Higher toned nose than the 1991. A bit closed still. Less structure though. Medium to medium-full body. Round and generous, but it doesn't have quite the grip it should have. I fear this may get a little astringent. Very good but not for the long term.

Clos-de-Vougeot, 1988   1998-2018

Medium-full colour. Firm, but poised on the nose. Lots of class here. This is not as reserved as most. It is not a bit hard on the palate. The wine is a little austere, but this is no bad thing. The fruit is ripe, potentially ample. The wine fullish. Very well balanced and very very long and complex. Lots of finesse. Fine.

Clos-de-Vougeot, 1987   Now-2005

Medium-full colour. Little development. Attractive, plump nose. Now soft. Medium-full. Good acidity. Ample and clean. Not a wine of great depth but well made, with good length and class. Much better than the 1986, and with a better future than the 1989. Very good.

Clos-de-Vougeot, 1986   Now-1999

Medium-full colour. Good for the vintage but there is now some brown at the rim. Soft and plump. This is a bit like the 1992 on the nose. Clean but only medium body and of medium intensity, structure and grip. On the palate ripe but a little one-dimensional. But fresh and charming. Will still last a few years. Good.

Echézeaux, 1985   Now-2005

Not a lot of colour. Now beginning to mature. Fresh on the nose though. Good grip. Plump, elegant fruit. But inherently soft, like the 1989 but a bit fuller and fresher. Quite meaty, as befits an Echézeaux, on the palate. Even a little hard still. Some stems here, evidently. Very good plus, but not the style and dimension for better. Slightly dilute at the end.

Echézeaux, 1983   Now-2003

Fuller colour but more brown. Very 1983 on the nose at first. Slightly astringent/stemmy overtones. Seemed to get fresher as it evolved. Rich in a caramelly chocolatey sort of way. A tougher wine than the 1985, and for food. But I prefer it. It is a bit animal but rich and fat and generous and meaty. Fine.

Echézeaux, 1982   Now-2000

Medium to medium-full colour. Mature but not unduly so. Plenty of class, vigour and depth on the nose. This is excellent for a 1982. Rich, vigorous and classy. Quite full. Plenty of dimension. *À point* now. Generous sweet finish. All a good old Burgundy should be. Will keep well.

Clos-de-Vougeot, 1978   Drink soon

Good colour. Fully mature. On the nose this is good but not glorious. Fully mature, slightly gamey, lightening up. On the palate this shows a wine with reasonable grip, but a lack of real concentration. For a 1978 it is a bit disappointing. Elegant and reasonably long nevertheless. But a little weak.

Echézeaux, 1976   Now-2000 plus

Good colour. Still quite fresh. Rich, fat, vigorous and chocolatey on the nose. Like the 1983 without the astringency. Fullish, ripe, sweet and rich. Good acidity. This is plump and vigorous and I like it very much. Even better with food. Lovely finish. No undue structure. Plenty of life still.

Echézeaux, 1974   **Drink soon**

Medium colour. Fully mature. Still fresh. Light but fruity on the nose. Light but still sweet, still plump, still pleasant. Not yet past it. A surprisingly good result. Hats off!

Clos-de-Vougeot, 1973   **Now-1999**

Medium colour. A little fresher than the above but fully mature. Not at all bad on the nose. There is substance and ripeness here. Again no sign of real age. This, surprisingly, is bigger, richer and more vigorous than the 1978. Fat, fullish, ample. Good freshness and good length. Fine for the vintage. Most enjoyable.

Clos-de-Vougeot, 1969   **Now-2000 plus**

Magnum. Very fine colour. Full, ample, rich, sweet, meaty nose. Still fresh and vigorous. Full and plump and generous on the palate. Good acidity. Heaps of fruit. Bags of life. Very fine.

Echézeaux, 1966   **Drink soon**

Good colour. Fully mature. Soft nose. But fragrant and attractive. Good finesse. Good fruit. Medium full. Good acidity. Round, getting a touch delicate but gentle and sweet. The acidity will tend to dominate from now on. But this is very good. Still long and classy.

Clos-de-Vougeot, 1964   **Now-2000**

Very good mature colour. Rich nose. Plump, very concentrated. Rather more laid back than the 1969. Very lovely. Excellent. Fullish, marvellous, distinguished and balanced. More finesse than the 1969. Very very long. Very very complex and harmonious. Beautiful. Great wine!

Clos-de-Vougeot, 1961   **Drink soon**

Very good mature colour. A little less vigorous-looking than the 1964. Slight touch of astringency. A density missing in the above. Full and rich, but the vigour is beginning to diminish and a little astringency beginning to set in. Yet still fat, ample, long. Fine. Was even better ten years ago.

Clos-de-Vougeot, 1957   **Drink up**

Soft, fragrant nose. Fading a little. On the palate the wine is still sweet, and certainly very elegant. But lightening up. Gentle, long. Still a lot of pleasure to be had.

Clos-de-Vougeot, 1929   **Drink soon**

Full, mature but vigorous colour. Earthy, reductive gamey flavour on the nose. But it is full and ample. Full on the palate. Ripe, good acidity. Animal, slightly artisanal. But sweet, soft, fragrant and surprisingly lovely at the end. Not a touch of astringency.

JACQUES-FRÉDÉRIC MUGNIER AND THE CHÂTEAU DE CHAMBOLLE-MUSIGNY, *CHAMBOLLE-MUSIGNY*

'We used to keep chickens,' remembers Freddy Mugnier, lord of a substantial but somewhat decaying mansion at the top of the village of Chambolle-Musigny. 'But there was one snag. The cockerel decided to roost in a bush just underneath our bedroom window. Every time a car went past, whether it was the middle of the day or the darkest hour of the night, he would crow. . . . But he made a splendid *coq au vin*.'

The domaine of the Mugnier family, substantial at the turn of the century but much reduced since as a result both of the usual inheritance laws and through disinterest on the part of Freddy Mugnier's ancestors, has recently been resurrected. For Freddy Mugnier, the last decade has been a learning curve. But the curve is pointed very positively in the right direction. The domaine covers a mere 4 hectares, but it includes some choice parcels, and the wine that it produces today rivals the very best of the village.

HISTORY

François Mugnier, known as Frédéric, was born in 1826 at Champforgueil near Chalon-sur-Saône in southern Burgundy. At the age of thirty he established a liqueur business in Dijon, dealing in *cassis*, *mûre* and *pêche de vigne*, which rapidly became very successful. Naturally he decided to branch out into wine. He bought several parcels from the Marey-Monge family, and in 1899 the Château de Chambolle-Musigny itself from them. This rather gaunt edifice - it would make a splendid site for a horror movie - had been built in 1832.

François/Frédéric died in 1911, and his son Ernest in 1924. The succession passed to one of the latter's eight children, Charles, and then to a nephew, Jacques-Frédéric, born in 1923, who took over in 1944. This Jacques-Frédéric, father of today's Freddy, was a lawyer by training and a *financier* by profession. His business was based in Paris, and his career often took him abroad. None of his relations, it seems, was interested in taking up the reins at Chambolle. Fairly soon after the war the family sold their distillery business to Maison L'Héritier-Guyot. Bits of land slowly eked out into other hands, particularly that of Drouhin, to whom part of the family sold their inheritance in 1948/1949, and further parcels were leased off on a *fermage* basis, principally the 9.55 hectare monopoly of Nuits-Saint-Georges, Clos-de-la-Maréchale which together with 43 ares of Clos-de-Vougeot, was rented to Maison Faiveley in 1950. For some years the Chambolle vines were farmed by Maison Faiveley, and then from 1977 to 1984 by Bernard Clair of Marsannay. On his retirement in 1977 - he died in 1980 - Jacques-Frédéric would occasionally return to Chambolle, but merely as a visitor. The farming contracts were renewed. Vinously, the name of Mugnier had all but disappeared. Their portion was sold off in cask.

FREDDY MUGNIER

Frédéric Mugnier was born in 1955. His mother hailed from Alsace, where she was a champion at curling, and in his youth Freddy spent much time at Guebwiller, though he was born in Geneva, where his parents were briefly resident after having returned from Indo-China. He became an off-shore oil engineer, with little thought for the family vineyard until in 1984 he decided to take a sabbatical. Instantly he was hooked. He installed himself at the *Lycée Viticole* for a six-month crash course, and, the Bernard Clair lease having come to its end, decided to take over himself. His first vintage was the 1985.

But were 4 hectares, even in illustrious *climats*, going to be enough to support him and his young family (he and Jocelyne were married in 1989)? Freddy had always had a passion for flying. In 1988 he obtained a commercial pilot's licence, and has since then worked three days a week for the French airline TAP. It gives him a certain financial freedom. The vineyards remain, as they were, worked by outsiders *à la tâche*, but it is Freddy who is responsible for the wine, and, since 1988, all of it has been domaine-bottled.

THE DOMAINE

The domaine totals 4.05 ha, all of it in Chambolle-Musigny. At the base of the *tarif* lies 1.3 ha of communal Chambolle. This comes from three parcels: Les Plantes, which in fact is *premier cru*, Les Combottes-Bas, lower down from the part which is classified as first growth - both these lie down-slope from the village itself - and La Combe-d'Orveau. This last *climat*, where one of Freddy Mugnier's neighbours is Étienne Grivot, lies at the end of a valley the other side of Musigny to the south. Why is Les Plantes de-classified? you ask. 'The vines were planted in 1968,' says Freddy, 'and the clone was a Pinot Droit. Moreover the site is that of an old quarry. Some of the soil is alluvial, and has been brought up from the other side of the main road. I found the wine lacked finesse. But now I have managed to control the harvest I am more satisfied with the results. I might declare it separately one day.'

Adjacent to Bonnes-Mares, Mugnier owns 70 ares of Les Fuées. He feels these are potentially his best raw material, but some of the vines are virus-ridden. The parcel is square, missing a small piece in the middle, precisely in mid-slope.

On the other side of the commune, next to Le Musigny itself, are 55 ares of Les Amoureuses. This lies in two sections, above and below the small road. In the steeper, lower-down bit, Freddy says, there is a lack of potassium in the soil. The excess of fertilisation in the 1960s and 1970s means that most of the Côte d'Or still retains too much potassium in the soil, leading to wines which have a tendency to lack intensity, but here and in the other Mugnier parcels the wines suffer no shortage of this element.

Travelling back to the other side of the village, we come to Bonnes-Mares. Mugnier owns a band of vines which stretch from the road back into the trees, from *terres rouges* lower down to *terres blanches* up above. The parcel covers 35 a, most of which is forty-year-old vines. Currently part of the *climat*, planted in 1980, but on unsuitable *portes-greffes*, is being replanted.

Top of the tree is Le Musigny, where Mugnier points out he is the second largest owner after the Comte de Vogüé. He owns 1.15 ha, in two parcels, the one to the north having the older vines.

But what of the other parcels rented out to other people? The Clos-de-Vougeot has been sold. In 1978 the nine-year-old lease came to an end. The law insists that the existing tenant is in a commanding position. You can't cancel a *fermage* unless you are able and willing to take it on yourself. You are not allowed to transfer. At this time Mugnier *père* decided to sell it. The parcel was '*dans le bas*', at the bottom of the *grand cru*. The Clos-de-la-Maréchale, however, will eventually revert back to Freddy, but not until 2002. All he has to do is to be patient.

WINE-MAKING

While Freddy has no day-to-day responsibility over the vines, he certainly takes pains to make his views felt. There has been no use of herbicides for five years now, nor any fertilisation for a long time until a light natural compost was added to balance the soil in 1995. Pruning must be short in the first place. By the time you come to do a green harvest or a *saignée* it is too late.

There is a severe *triage* in the vineyard, at the time the fruit is collected, quite a lot of destemming - retaining some more for physical purposes rather than for the flavour they impart - and the must, after a four-day cold maceration, is vinified at a high temperature (maximum 32-33°C), Freddy having lengthened the maceration to as much as three weeks, with lots of *pigeage*. The press wine is vinified separately, and some of it may well be blended back with the free-run wine. Overall 25 per cent new oak is used. Mugnier has produced an average 33.85 hl/ha over the ten years he has been in charge.

Has he changed his vinification methods over this period? I have adapted it to the vintage, Mugnier will reply. 'In 1988 I fermented at a cooler temperature, with less *pigeage*. It seemed to suit the Musigny. In 1989 I went the other way: there was more *pigeage* and at the end of the maceration I heated part of the wine up to 40°. I was worried I wasn't extracting enough *matière*. This was the first vintage I did a bit of cold soaking. But overall the main permanent change has been a longer maceration, and now a maximum temperature of 33°. . . . I like the challenge of making red wine,' he adds. 'The risks are greater than with white wine.'

THE WINES

I have followed the wines of the Château de Chambolle-Musigny since the beginning: that is, since the 1985 vintage. Looking back over my notes I find myself continually noting 'Freddy Mugnier's wines get better and better!' There are only five wines to taste, in the splendid cellar beneath the house - though there have occasionally been six in the past when he has produced a separate *vieilles-vignes cuvée* of Musigny - and I often wish there were more. But, though the price of land has halved since the peak it reached at the height of speculation a few years ago, Freddy still considers the levels too high. They would need to halve again before it became economic, in his view. He would rather buy something in the Midi.

Mugnier's wines are true Chambolles: the epitome of delicacy, elegance and persistence. They are in the style of the Domaine Georges de Vogüé rather than that of Roumier next door: feminine in the best sense of the word. Sometimes they can be lighter still.

The first wine you are given to sample is the village Chambolle. As I have explained this has *premier cru* Les Plantes fruit in it, and it exhibits very good concentration for a village example and excellent Pinot Noir class.

The Fuées (like the Bonnes-Mares) has an element of black fruit as well as red, in this case a suspicion of blackberry. Obviously it is fuller and fatter and more generous. But is also much longer and more complex.

More closed-in, but yet at the same time more sumptuous and intense, is the Amoureuses. It is the same size, but there is more to it.

Currently the average age of the vines in the Bonnes-Mares is relatively low: fifteen rather than the thirty-four-year-old average overall. And this shows in two ways: the wine is very obviously Chambolle-Musigny, rather than the sort of masculine halfway house it normally is; and it can in some lighter years, like 1992, lack a little backbone. But the class and cornucopia-like fruit are usually there, even if the wine isn't a blockbuster.

Today Freddy Mugnier's Musigny (and I am relieved he has stopped producing two *cuvées*) rivals that of De Vogüé. And that means a wine at the summit of what Burgundy can produce. I look forward to seeing the 1993 again when it has settled down in bottle. In November 1994, out of cask I summarised my notes with two words, the first time I had had occasion to use them *chez Mugnier*: indisputably great.

THE TASTING

I sampled the following range of wines in Chambolle-Musigny in February 1995.

LE MUSIGNY
(unless otherwise stated)

Optimum drinking

1992   1998–2008

Medium to medium-full colour. Bottled May-June 1994, and not quite back on form yet on the nose. Soft, plump, freshly balanced. Improved on aeration. Medium to medium-full body. Delicious fruit. Very good acidity. This has vigour and class and no lack of depth. It is not as structured as the 1991, for instance, but it is not a bit lightweight. Fine, long complex finish.

1991   1999–2014

Medium-full colour. Very stylish nose. All silk and violets and raspberries and cream. Soft but intense. This really sings. Medium-full, very round sophisticated tannins, just a suggestion of new oak. Very good grip. Really splendidly classy fruit. Harmonious, persistent, complex and generous at the end. Very lovely. An excellent example of the vintage.

1990   2000–2020

Full colour. Abundantly rich nose. Coffee, chocolate and even leather as well as fruit, even a touch of *crème brûlée*. Very profound. This is slightly adolescent, indeed is not as much on form as the 1991. But there is splendid concentrated fruit. Plenty of structure with very good grip. Quite some tannin. But not a bit brutal. The fruit is fat and fine and ample. This again is a very fine example.

1989   1998–2014

Medium-full colour. Very fine nose. Not as adolescent as the 1990. Harmonious, intense, very perfumed, very complex. Medium-full-bodied. Nicely rounded tannins. Again a touch of oak. There is a certain austerity on the follow-through. Very long, very good grip. Lots of dimension. Once again a very lovely example.

Vieilles-Vignes, 1989   2000–2019

Just a little more colour. A little bit bigger. Certainly rather more youthful. This is currently a bit hidden and it doesn't shine out as much as the above. But obviously it has got more to it. Excellent acidity and concentration for a 1989.

1988   **1998–2020**

Good colour. Quite a fullish, animal, spicy nose. Generous and fat. Good acidity but not too austere. Indeed lovely and ripe and succulent. Fullish, very good acidity. Excellent complex fresh fruit. Marvellously ripe and marvellously vigorous. The fruit almost obscures the structure. Fullish, excellent tannins. A wine of real finesse and great intensity. Immense length. Will last for ever. Very very fine. Brilliant.

Vieilles-Vignes, 1988   **(? bad bottle)**

More of a deposit. The colour is more evolved, and so is the nose. This is less stylish and a lot less vigorous than the above. Something has happened here. Rather evolved. Not representative.

1987   **Now–2000 plus**

Medium to medium-full colour. Some evolution. Good nose. Ripe, fresh. A touch of spice. But no lack of finesse. Beginning to round off. On the palate the tannins lack a bit of sophistication, and the fruit, though ripe, is a little one-dimensional. Yet the wine is balanced, the finish very long and positive. It just lacks a little class. But the *terroir*'s beauty cannot be denied. The finish is most agreeable.

1986   **Now–1999**

Good fullish vigorous colour for a 1986. Slightly diffuse on the nose but fresh and plump. Stylish and no lack of definition. There is a little astringency here. It is looser-knit than the 1987, and again there is a lack of real class and definition. But it ends better than it starts. Like the above the *climat* shows. But I prefer the 1987. It is less loose-knit.

Vieilles-Vignes, 1986   **Now–2005**

Just a little less colour. Better nose. More vigour, more concentration. Fresher and more ample. Very good for a 1986. Open, generous and accessible. This is remarkably good. An extra element of concentration, vigour and class. This is better than both of the above. Very good grip. Still lots of life.

1985   **Now–2015**

Splendid colour. Full, vigorous, not a bit mature. Splendid nose. Marvellous fruit. Very concentrated and very good grip. All the red fruit in the world is here. Quite brilliant. On the palate it is just beginning to round off, but it is still a bit adolescent. Fullish, fine acidity. Ample, vigorous. Very long. A splendid wine. And it is going to get even better!

1984   **Drink soon**

Good colour. Not aged. A delightful example. Soft and sweet and fresh. A little one-dimensional of course. But not a bit weak. And the finish is still positive. A very good effort.

1980   **Drink soon**

Very good colour for the vintage. No undue age. Fresh nose. A touch lean but still supple. On the palate medium bodied. Not an enormous length but a little bigger than the 1984, a little rounder, a little fatter, a little better. But drink soon also.

1978   **Now–2004**

Huge vigorous colour. Could be a 1976. Rather a solid, four-square, slightly dense wine on the nose. It lacks a bit of grace. On the palate the wine is fullish, a little muscular. Good fruit and still lots of vigour. But it lacks finesse and harmony. And I don't think it will age gracefully.

Bonnes-Mares, 1949   **Now–2000 plus**

Fullish, vigorous colour. Quite spicy on the nose. Sweet, concentrated, plump and profound on the palate. Beautifully balanced. A very lovely wine which is gently harmonious, complex, very profound and very classy. Very long. Excellent. Plenty of life still.

1945   **Now–2005 plus**

Very full colour. Still very youthful. Rich, fat, vigorous and very concentrated. On the nose. Similar on the palate. Essence of fruit here. Marvellous grip. Full and majestic but not a hint of being too dense like some Bordeaux. This is still amazingly vigorous. A *grand seigneur*!

Bonnes-Mares, 1943   **Drink soon**

Excellent colour. Full and with no sign of age. Very lovely nose. Silky-smooth, ripe, succulent. Still very fresh. Splendid fruit. On the palate there is a hint that the wine is beginning to lose its beauty. It is still sweet, but it is a little lighter than it once was. Gentle. Almost fragile. Still lovely, because very fragrant and very classy and extremely complex. Very, very fine. But drink soon.

1926   **Now–2000**

Marvellously vigorous colour. Splendid vigour for a wine of nearly seventy years old. A touch of spice but splendidly concentrated old-vine fruit. A full wine, brutal once. Some astringency here. Certainly was vinified with the stems. Sweet but structured. Better with food. Fine but not great.

PONSOT,
MOREY-SAINT-DENIS

The view from the terrace in front of the Ponsot house, high up above the village of Morey-Saint-Denis, is breathtaking. Directly below you are the vines of Clos-de-la-Roche and Clos-Saint-Denis. Beneath the village *premier cru* land gives way to communal, with generic vines on the other side of the main road. Further on, usually showing little signs of movement, is the railway; beyond that, quite the opposite, the busy autoroute. Yet further, the great swathe of the Saône valley and its tributaries, rich agricultural land punctured with forests and pools, leads you to the foothills of the Jura mountains. On a clear day you can even see Mont Blanc. But if you can, say the locals, you can bet that next day it will rain.

The Ponsot domaine, potentially - and indeed very often in practice - one of the very best not only in Morey but among the whole of the Côte, has had its ups and downs recently. Laurent Ponsot, the heir apparent, suffered a terrible car accident in March 1988. Though he walks almost normally now, jogging and skiing are out, and his recovery was slow. Father Jean-Marie, long-time mayor of Morey and committee member of numerous wine associations, has had his problems too. There have been some inconsistencies in the standard of the wines, and indeed one or two whole vintages where the quality was not as good as it should be. Judging by the 1993s, however, the domaine is once again right on form. Let's hope it stays this way.

HISTORY

The Ponsot family hails originally from Saint-Romain. In 1872, one of their line, a lawyer in Dijon, bought the Liébault domaine in Morey-Saint-Denis on behalf of his son William. It measured some 3 hectares, which William proceeded to enlarge by renting other parcels from absentee landlords. William died childless in 1926, but not before his god-child and nephew had been roped in to learn the *métier* and prepare himself to follow the succession. This was Hippolyte, father of Jean-Marie, himself father of Laurent.

By this time, several of the leases having come to their end and been taken back by their rightful owners, the Ponsot estate was back to the original 3 ha. Hippolyte had been a captain in the army during the First World War, and had then become a solicitor's clerk. This he didn't enjoy, and he was delighted when his uncle William invited him to join them. The two decided to increase the domaine in their own right, and the first of many purchases was made in 1925 when they acquired 50 ares of Clos-de-la-Roche. Hippolyte died in 1972.

Jean-Marie Ponsot, his son, was born in 1927, and he started working for his father in 1947, by which time the domaine had increased to 6 ha. He took over responsibility in 1957. The year before he had further augmented the Ponsot exploitation by entering into a number of *métayage* (share-cropping) arrangements. One of these was with a member of the Rémy family in Latricières and in the Clos-de-la-Roche (where the Ponsots had bought a further hectare in 1952). Another later lease, in 1982, was with the Mercier family, whose estate is called the Domaine de Chézeaux. Here the vines lay in Griottes-Chambertin, Chambertin itself, Chambolle-Musigny, Les Charmes and Clos-Saint-Denis.

PIONEERING WORK WITH CLONES

The significant contribution of Jean-Marie Ponsot has been in the field of clones. Together with Bernard Clair, and under the supervision of Professor Raymond Bernard of the viticultural faculty at Dijon University, he made a selection of cuttings of the best of his vines in the early 1960s, seeking a happy medium between health of the vine, the quantity it produced and the quality of the resulting vine. Some of the most celebrated clones in Burgundy today have their origins in Ponsot's vineyards.

FURTHER SALES AND DEVELOPMENTS

Jean-Marie and his wife have a son, Laurent, born in 1954, who has been responsible for the wine-making since 1983, and three daughters who live in Paris. Laurent went to the Hotel School in Nice, decided the hotel business was not his *métier*, and changed to general commerce. He then worked in the travel business in Paris until 1981 before joining his father, and taking the oenology course at Dijon.

Since returning to Burgundy he has lived with his Eurasian wife and three children out in the plain near the Abbey of Citeaux. The change of environment at the end of the day he finds refreshing.

Recently there have been a number of changes in the *métayage* arrangements between the Ponsots and the Mercier family and others. These have only served to further complicate what is already quite a confusing picture.

The first thing to point out is that not all the Mercier/Chézeaux vines are exploited by the Ponsots. The Domaine de Chézeaux also owns vines in Fixin. These are leased to the Domaine Berthaut in the same village.

Secondly, there is the Griottes-Chambertin. The Merciers bought a second parcel in 1984, but under an arrangement whereby the erstwhile proprietor would continue to have the produce of the vines until his death. This parcel was under a *métayage* contract to André Esmonin of Gevrey. For the first two years there were therefore two Griottes-Chambertins coming out under the Domaine de Chézeaux label: one that André Esmonin made, the other produced by Ponsot. But you could tell the difference. Thereafter, between 1987 and 1991, the labels were identical. In 1992 it was agreed that the two *cuvées* should be blended together before bottling, simplifying things a great deal. But in 1994 the old proprietor died. The Merciers then passed over *métayage* control of those vines to René Leclerc. But it has been agreed to continue with the policy of blending the Domaine de Chézeaux share before bottling takes place. As far as I am concerned it would have been far simpler to have entrusted that bit too to the Ponsots.

One of the other share-cropped parcels has also changed hands. The owners of the Latricières and a bit of Clos-de-la-Roche sold out in 1994. The Ponsots were offered all of it, but could only afford to buy the 7 *ouvrées* (28 ares) of the Clos-de-la-Roche. The rest they have lost. From 1995 Patrick Bize of Savigny-lès-Beaune has been entrusted with the Latricières-Chambertin. But the Chézeaux contract continues until 2002.

THE DOMAINE

The Ponsot domaine, from the 1995 vintage, covers 8.73 ha, of which 1.99 ha is leased on a share-cropping basis, the domaine getting two-thirds of the crop. This latter exploitation covers 89 ares in Griottes-Chambertin, 38 ares in Clos-Saint-Denis, 14 ares in Chambertin itself, and 58 ares in Chambolle-Musigny, Les Charmes.

In their own hands, and the pride and joy of the Ponsot family, is 3.31 ha of Clos-de-la-Roche. The Ponsots are by some margin the largest land-holders in this *grand cru*. It can be brilliant. The younger vines are de-classified into Morey-Saint-Denis *premier cru* where they join the produce of 66 a of Morey-Saint-Denis, Les Monts-Luisants. This is a sizeable *climat* which lies next to the Ponsot home and cellars, above the Clos-de-la-Roche.

The family have a further 1.18 ha of Monts-Luisants land planted with white grape varieties - Morey-Saint-Denis *premier cru* Les Monts-Luisants *blanc*. There used to be some Pinot Noir mutated into giving white grapes - what I call Pinot Gouges - but this has been ripped up. There also used to be a substantial majority of very old Aligoté dating from 1911. Currently the *encépagement* is 50 per cent of this old Aligoté, 50 per cent Chardonnay. The wine seems never to undergo malo-lactic, occasionally goes completely strange and is not bottled (as in 1993). But when it is on form, if not a great wine, it is certainly worth investigating, full of individuality. In my view it is best drunk young. (But Laurent Ponsot points out I have never sampled the 1964 or 1970.)

The village Gevrey-Chambertin (51 a) and Morey-Saint-Denis (20 a) are dignified as *Cuvée des Grives* and *Cuvée de l'Abeille* respectively. While the average age of the vines is the same, given as thirty-five years, I usually find the Morey the more interesting wine. This leaves the Chapelle-Chambertin (47 a). This is a competent wine, but as the vines are young it does not offer the same interest in the Ponsot line-up as the Latricières or the Griottes, just as the Clos-de-la-Roche and the Clos-Saint-Denis (the latter equally as fine as the former) are superior, in the Ponsot stable, to the Chambertin.

WINE-MAKING

There are few rules in the Ponsot cellar, and a direct question - do you do this? - is often met with a quizzical response, as if the question had been of the 'Have you stopped beating your wife?' variety. Laurent, you feel, although having been officially responsible for wine-making since 1983, is still fighting his corner.

In the vineyard, where he is considerably helped by the fact that the family haven't used fertilisation for thirty years, Laurent Ponsot lays much emphasis on the choice of the plants and rootstock in the first place. They must be adapted to both the soil and the subsoil, as well as to each other. The search, as with clonal selection today, is for a small quantity, and small but concentrated berries.

Stems, both Ponsots believe, don't add anything. Their utility is physical. They, and the introduction of whole uncrushed bunches, prevent the temperature rising too high too quickly; they trap oxygen for use by the yeasts; and they prolong the fermentation. There is no deliberate pre-fermentation cooling. The grapes are today very largely destemmed, rather more so than in the mid-1980s, but whole bunches are still partially employed.

Vinification temperatures vary - the domaine only investing in a cooling unit in 1986 - as does the length of the *cuvaison*, and sometimes there is a pre-fermentation *saignée de cuvée*. And so too varies the length of time the wine remains in cask. It can be up to twenty-four months before the wines are bottled. Since 1985 there has been neither fining or filtration, and a very minimal use of sulphur. But there is a dislike of new oak, which has been passed down from father to son. Even when the domaine discards an old cask, and has to replace it, the barrel is then put through a leaching procedure to get all the 'new' effect out of it before any new wine is allowed to be poured into it.

THE WINES

There is an individuality about all the Ponsot red wines, as well as the Monts-Luisants *blanc*. A plummy toffee spice, an element of the exotic, and sometimes a more-than-usual flavour of gamey cooked fruit is the key. The result can be wines which are somewhat over the top, somewhat unclassic. It does not always work. But you have to credit the Ponsots for taking risks. When the wines hit it right they can be brilliant.

(Laurent Ponsot vintaged very late in 1994, but, despite this - for the weather improved - was dissatisfied with his results. All the *grands crus* were declassified, to Morey and Gevrey *premier cru* respectively. And the prices reduced accordingly: a piece of honesty and realism which deserves congratulations.)

THE TASTING

I sampled the following wines *chez* Ponsot in February 1995.

CLOS-DE-LA-ROCHE, VIEILLES-VIGNES

Optimum drinking

1992   **1998–2010**
Good colour. Animal, spicy nose. Good, intense, sweet, cherry-perfumed on the nose and palate. Medium to medium-full. Round tannins. Good grip. This is long, substantial for a 1992, and very intense and stylish. An individual wine, plenty of character. But no new oak. Fine for the vintage.

1991   **1999–2015**
Very good colour. Serious, complex, classy nose. A touch of coffee, a touch of cherry-brandy chocolates. Plenty of depth. Quite full. Some tannin. But this shows only a touch of hardness. Very good grip. Lovely fresh ripe fruit. Long, subtle, elegant. Very well put together. A delicious harmonious bottle. Very fine quality for the vintage.

1990   **2000–2020**
Splendid colour. Splendid nose. Rich, concentrated, toffee spice, plummy cassis fruit; bitter chocolate and cherry as well. Fullish, fat, voluptuous, ample. Very good grip. Ripe and powerful on the follow-through. Some tannin, still unresolved. The finish is very intense and larger than life. Still youthful. Very fine.

1989   **Now–1999**
Very good colour. Still very youthful looking. Broad nose. Spicy and sweet. Just a little diffuse. Quite ample on the palate, but a lack of real grip and backbone. Now evolving, with even a slight astringency at the end. It is a little blowsy, essentially. It is ripe, but it lacks real style. Merely good. I prefer the 1992.

1988   **Now–2000**
Medium-full colour, a little evolution. Spicy-toffee nose. Some sweetness. A lot less austere than most 1988s. I find this a bit loose-knit. Medium to medium-full, not much tannin, and,

very surprisingly for a 1988, rather low in acidity. The follow-through is even a little dilute. Atypical. And merely good again.

1987   **Now–2003**

Medium to medium-full colour. Now just about ready. Good positive fresh, complex mature fruit on the nose. Vigour and class here. No hard edges or astringent corners. Medium-full, balanced, just about ready. Good acidity. Lovely ripe fruit. Very long. Good dimension. Very fine for a 1987. Most enjoyable. Will this last better than the two wines above?

1986

Déclassé.

1985   **Now–2010**

Fine colour. Only just about mature. Ripe but a little burly on the nose. The tannins lack sophistication. Good grip and depth and richness otherwise. Fullish, fat, ample, ripe slightly spicy wine on the palate. Good acidity. Long and voluptuous and slightly exotic. Fully mature. Tastes older than it is. But fine quality. Very well balanced. On the palate the tannins do not stick out at all. Good vigour.

1982   **Now–2000**

Very good mature colour. Classy nose for 1982. Laid-back, fully mature but not a bit too diffuse or faded. Medium body. Delicate but balanced. Good complex fruit, especially on the follow-through. Very stylish. Good length. Still fresh, even vigorous. Very fine for the vintage.

1981   **Drink up**

Very good colour. Slightly less evolved than the above. A little austere on the nose. A little lean on the palate. This is a bit light, and getting a bit feeble. But there is still enjoyment to be had. The class of the *climat* is evident. A very good result.

1976   **Now–2000 plus**

Fine full vigorous colour. Substantial nose. Evident tannins but blackberry and leather flavours, fat and spicy. Just a little tough. But plenty of fruit on the palate. Fullish. No over-ripeness of the fruit. Very good acidity. A fine example. Very good vigour. Not a bit of astringency at the end.

POUSSE D'OR,
VOLNAY

Some of us are born with silver spoons in our mouths; others, so to speak, have the silver spoon thrust at them. One who has thoroughly earned the bounteous advantage of a fairy godmother - in this case his wife's uncle - is Gérard Potel of Volnay's Domaine de la Pousse d'Or. *Heureux qui!* But wrap up the envy, my friends. It couldn't have happened to a more deserving man.

The 13 hectare Domaine de la Pousse d'Or has only been in its present form since 1964. The land comprises several of the choicest parcels of two long-standing estates, whose histories can be traced back into the eighteenth century or beyond. It was created through the efforts of one of France's leading *amateur gastronomes* and *oenophiles* of the post-war era, and has at its helm today, in Gérard Potel, one of Burgundy's most respected wine-makers. Yet Potel is not a native Burgundian, and part of the shareholding in the domaine has since 1985 belonged to a consortium of Australians. Since its re-creation three decades ago this has always been an estate which has looked outwards rather than inwards, and it is therefore no coincidence that it should have been chosen as one for carrying out research into techniques of re-balancing the must by means of water evaporation - a process I am sure we will hear much of in future years.

HISTORY

One of the two estates in which lie the origins of today's Pousse d'Or is that of the Duvault-Blochet family. A century ago this was a giant domaine: the Romanée-Conti itself was part of it, as was the Clos-de-Tart, and so was what was then called En-Bouze-d'Or, a 2-hectare monopoly in Volnay, acquired by Jacques-Marie Duvault-Blochet from the Du Mesnil family sometime after 1855. In all it comprised 100 hectares of prime land.

Duvault-Blochet himself died in January 1874. For the next fourteen years, until November 1886, his land-holdings were exploited in common by his successors, the families Guyot, Massin and Chambon. The Clos-de-la-Bousse-d'Or and most of the rest of the Côte-de-Beaune holdings passed into the hands of Armand Massin after the split in 1886, and when he died in 1913, were left to his sons-in-law, Messieurs de Chavigné and Lavoureille.

The headquarters of this domaine - it comprised 25 ha in 1955 and may well have been even larger in the first place - were in Santenay, in the imposing construction in the Place Jet d'Eau now occupied by the *négociants* Prosper Maufoux, and briefly owned by Harveys of Bristol.

Meanwhile, back in Volnay, there was another imposing edifice. In the 1893 *Danguy and Aubertin*, a sort of Burgundian Cocks and Féret, a photograph of it is described as the Château de Volnay et Clos d'Audignac, the property of M. Delaplanche-Garnier. He too owned a large estate, with vines in Caillerets, Taille-Pieds and Clos-des-Chênes in Volnay, and parcels in Pommard, Meursault, Auxey and Puligny-Montrachet. This is the building which is the home of today's Domaine de la Pousse d'Or.

FERTÉ

We now come to Jean-Nicolas Ferté. Ferté was a gentleman farmer and businessman who hailed from the Aisne. He was a bachelor, a lover of huntin', shootin' and fishin', but above all, passionate about food and wine: a *bon viveur*, a gourmet, a master of the art of good living. He was a member of the *Académie des Vins de France*, the *Académie des Gastronomes* and the *Club des Cent*, a gathering of the richest cream of these wine- and food-lovers. Ferté knows everybody, all the great chefs and *maître d's*, all the top wine-makers and château-owners. In his youth he had even organised things so that he did his military service in Burgundy and could visit the likes of the Marquis d'Angerville, Rousseau, Gouges and '*père*' Ramonet - his almost exact contemporary - on his days off.

HOW THE ESTATE WAS FORMED

Ferté had a favourite niece, Florence, and Florence had a bright young man whom she intended to marry: Gérard Potel. Ferté decided to 'adopt' the young pair - Potel refers to him as 'my' uncle to this day - and help them set themselves up. He picked the right man.

Gérard Potel's father's family were well-to-do farmers from Château Thierry, on the edge of the Champagne area. His mother was Catalan in origin, and her family had spent time in Algeria. Gérard himself is one of eight children, and was brought up near Carcassonne where his parents produced table wine. He took a degree in agricultural engineering in Paris and then went to Beaune to study oenology under Philippe Trinquet. It was here he met Florence and came under the wing of Jean Ferté.

Ferté, of course, was not disposed to invest his largesse in table wine. This was greatly beneath the old man's dignity. The three of them therefore went on the hunt for something suitable, something which would make fine wine. And Ferté told all his friends to look out for something on his behalf.

It was through '*père*' Ramonet that the nucleus was found in the Chavigné-Lavoureille estate. Ramonet was someone who never wrote letters. But nevertheless he wrote to Ferté to let him know that this domaine was up for sale. Ferté, however, happened to be on holiday in Algeria, and no-one opened his correspondence. So in the end Ramonet telephoned. This was an even more extraordinary occurrence. The old boy *hated* the telephone.

Eventually the message got through. Eventually a consortium, which included Louis Seysses (father of Jacques Seysses of Domaine Dujac) who had just sold his Biscuits Belin to Nabisco, was set up. They bought about half of the Chavigné-Lavoureille estate, other parcels being snapped up by Matrot, De Montille, Ampeau and others, and on 8 May 1964, the Domaine de la Pousse d'Or - they had to change the B into a P because the authorities wouldn't allow a title based on the name of a *climat* - came into being.

Why was the Chavigné-Lavoureille domaine put on the market? Because the successors to the original Massin sons-in-law didn't get on. And the business was not making money. Various parcels of land had been sold off over the years, and the winery in Santenay had just been sold to Harvey's, who had at the time extravagant plans in Burgundy to complement their shareholding in Château Latour (this didn't last long, as neither did the appointment of a young Lavoureille as director of their Burgundian operation).

The Potels installed themselves in Savigny, hired part of what was then Harvey's premises, and started looking for somewhere more permanent to live in and run their estate from. Meanwhile Gérard continued to make the arduous journey to Carcassonne to supervise proceedings down there.

In Volnay, the daughter of M. de Laplanche-Gandier, a Madame Raoult, had died at the age of ninety-two in 1962. Her house, bequeathed to an association of retired priests, lay closed and empty - though the cellars were leased by Bouchard Père et Fils - for there were no retired priests who could make use of it. In October 1964 it was put up for auction. Ferté and the Potels, having almost bought what is now the Savigny HQ of the Domaine Antonin Guyon, bought it. With it, beyond the garden, came another monopoly, the 80 ares of the Clos-de-l'Audignac.

FURTHER DEVELOPMENTS

It was, of course, through Ferté and his friend and fellow member of the Club des Cent, Louis Seysses, that Seysses' son Jacques should come down to Burgundy and get bitten by the wine-making bug. Jacques worked two vintages with Gérard Potel in the mid-1960s. After Louis Seysses had acquired the Domaine Dujac for his son in 1967 he wanted to sell his shareholding in the Pousse d'Or. But only at a profit, which at that stage could not be paid. For a long time, even beyond the death of Jean Ferté in 1978, there was an impasse, the dearth of domestic interest in taking over the Seysses shareholding dropping to zero after the election of François Mitterrand in 1981. In 1985 a group of Americans expressed interest, but not on terms to which Gérard Potel could agree. But finally, thanks to the good offices of the Burgundian-based American wine-broker Becky Wasserman, and to Potel's friendship with Bill Pannell, founder of the Moss Wood estate in the Margaret River area, a consortium of Australians was found to buy up the Seysses interest. Thanks to that marvellous new invention, the fax machine, the whole thing was finalised in six hours, and on the last day of August 1985 Pannell and his associates became shareholders in the Domaine de la Pousse d'Or.

THE VINEYARDS

'It is a major convenience,' says Gérard Potel, 'that all my parcels are sizeable. Unlike others I don't have the inconvenience of vinifying in minute quantities.'

The most northerly parcel lies across the Pommard boundary in the *premier cru* of Jarolières, just below Rugiens. The parcel here now measures 1.5 ha, the domaine having recently bought 40 ares it rented *en métayage* from an American called Harris.

Between the village of Volnay and the main road up to Auxey-Duresses a number of small parcels are collectively (and misleadingly, for this too is *premier cru* land) grouped under the name Le Village. Most proprietors prefer to use any other name which is available, especially if they can then claim the monopoly of it. Lafarge has his Clos-du-Château-des-Ducs. Potel has two: the 2.14 ha Clos-de-la-Bousse-d'Or and the 80 a Clos-de-l'Audignac. The vines in the former *climat* average forty years old. The latter, enlarged and flattened by Gérard Potel when he arrived, was replanted in 1965.

In the *premier cru* of Caillerets, at opposite ends, the Domaine de la Pousse d'Or has two large parcels - Bouchard Père et Fils is the other major land-holder - and one of these is a monopoly too. At the bottom, eastern end, next to the Champans where there is more soil, and where the wines are the most precocious, lies 2.27 ha of plain Caillerets. Up-slope, just under the road, is the 2.39 ha Clos-des-Soixante-Ouvrées (*monopole*). The vines here have an average age of over forty years old. Here the soil is meagre, just really broken-up rock. The wines are quite different.

The remaining two parcels of the Pousse d'Or domaine lie in Santenay. Immediately adjacent to the Chassagne border, within the northern end of the Gravières *climat*, is the 2.10 ha parcel known as the Clos-des-Tavannes. Again there is little soil here. Further south, in the Gravières proper, but not quite so well situated, nor planted with Pinots which are as *fin*, though dating from 1952, are 2.16 ha more. Above here (indeed the intention is gradually to expand over all the upper part of the slope) for Gérard Potel is convinced that there is a similarity with the hill of Corton - there are now 15 ares of Chardonnay: 'To give Nicolas' (the Potels' son, aged twenty-five) 'something to do.' This is the only white wine element in the Pousse d'Or portfolio. This is, to all extents and purposes, a Pinot Noir domaine.

VITICULTURE AND WINE-MAKING

Along with many of his peers, Gérard Potel has ceased treating his vineyards with weedkillers and now ploughs his vineyards several times a year. It aerates the soil and eliminates superficial roots, forcing the vine to dig deeper. Fertilisation is kept to a bare minimum and the only regular sprayings are the traditional treatments against oidium and mildew, the latter a real problem in 1993.

The vineyard has been renewed partly by *sélection massale*, partly by clones, Potel having no strong views either way, with the young clones being pruned and trained into a Cordon du Royat, the older vines being Guyot.

One of the impressive things about a visit to the Pousse d'Or domaine at vintage time is its order. This is inevitably a somewhat haphazard time. Yet here things are definitely under control. The place is clean, the temperatures of each *cuve* firmly regulated - Potel likes to vinify at 28-30°C - and the *pigeages* regular.

He used to destem only the young vines. 'It is very important that the stems are ripe, if you are going to use them,' he says. But since 1989 he destems more. 'The stems are an anti-oxidant,' he explains, 'good if there is any risk of rot. But one can *trier* more efficiently if one destems.' He now pays great attention to pH. This is a better measure of the balance than calculating the acidity on a grams per litre basis.

Vinification lasts about a fortnight, and the wines are then matured using about 25 per cent new oak and bottled after sixteen to eighteen months (fourteen months for the 1992s) after fining and a light filtration if this is necessary. Flexibility above all is the keynote here. The *rendement* is kept to a minimum, but after that 'you must react to what nature brings in. Not impose your own rules.' Potel was one of the first to practise a *saignée*, a technique he learned from Bernard Clair-Daü and first used in 1973. Now, of course, he is experimenting with *évaporation à pression atmosphérique*, on which his son Nicolas wrote a thesis in 1993. His 1992

Caillerets *cuvée* was subjected to this process, and as a consequence was not chaptalised. It made one of the best wines in the cellar.

This is not the only thing you will learn if you are prepared to listen to Gérard Potel. In some weaker vintages, for instance, the colour will begin to leech out of the wines after eight or so days' *cuvaison* if you vinify with all of the stems. So what he does then is raise the temperature up to 35°C at the beginning of the fermentation, extract the colour, and then cool it down to 25°C to prolong it as long as possible. This technique enabled him to produce very much better 1986s, a rainy vintage in the Côte-de-Beaune, than the majority of his neighbours.

THE WINES

Gérard Potel has now been producing very fine wines for thirty years, his first vintage being the great 1964, still vigorous and very exciting. The range begins with the Santenays. Of the two I find the Clos-des-Tavannes clearly superior to the Gravières. The two are similar in style, not surprisingly, but the Tavannes is richer, a little fuller, and has more style and definition. Neither, being Santenays, are expensive.

The Pommard, Jarolières is Volnay-ish for a Pommard, not being as meaty as the best Rugiens. It is nevertheless quite a distinct wine from Potel's Volnays: a little four-square and chunky, full, ripe, rich and fat, if without being as elegant.

The first Volnay you will be offered to taste is the Clos-de-l'Audignac. The vines here are now getting middle-aged, and the wine is a true Volnay, round, plump, gently caressing the palate with its fruit and finesse. The Caillerets comes next: less delicate, but nevertheless medium-full rather than full bodied, more austere, yet plump, concentrated and generous. It is a better wine.

The Soixante-Ouvrées has yet more depth, is fuller in structure and has much more definition. It can show less agreeably in its youth, but is a wine for the longer haul. When mature it is a wine of unmistakably great finesse: a yardstick example.

Sometimes I prefer the Soixante-Ouvrées, sometimes the Bousse-d'Or. The vines in the Bousse-d'Or are older. The geology of the soil makes for a fuller wine. It is more tannic in its youth - this sometimes masking the elegance - and so there can be a suggestion of Pommard about it. Underneath, when the wines come to maturity, there is velvet, while the Soixante-Ouvrées is silk, and a splendid expression of the richness and intensity of old-vine fruit. As the tasting notes below will suggest, it is an impressive wine.

THE TASTING

I sampled the following wines *chez* Potel in June 1994.

VOLNAY, CLOSE-DE-LA-BOUSSE-D'OR

Optimum drinking

1992   **1998-2007**

Good colour. Bottled three months previously. Elegant, soft, gently oaky nose. Very stylish. Very good acidity. On the palate a little shaken up by the bottling. Good substance and plenty of balanced fruit and a little tannin on the attack. Long on the finish. Very good for the vintage, I am sure.

1991   **1999-2015**

Very good colour. Firm nose. A little closed. Plummily rich. Again good grip. This shows

very well indeed. Fullish. Good structure. Lovely rich fruit. Black fruits as well as red. Fat, ample and potentially generous. Lots of finesse and complexity here. Very long on the palate. Fine quality. Lots of future.

1990   **2002-2025**

Excellent colour. Nose has gone into its shell here. On the palate it is adolescent, full bodied, tannic, even dense. All a bit impenetrable. The follow-through is marvellously rich and concentrated and profound though. But the character is Pommard rather than Volnay. A fine example of a great vintage. Patience is required.

1989   **Now-2001**

Medium to medium-full colour. Not as concentrated as the 1991. Soft, plump, charming nose but a forward wine without much underneath it seems. Plenty of fruit, but it is not exactly fat and velvety and smooth. The follow-through is a little thin. Disappointing. Quite good at best. Potel had problems with cork weevil with this wine, and had to re-cork. The Caillerets 60 Ouvrées is better.

1989   **Now-2006**

Magnum. (Not re-corked.) Good full, youthful colour. Plump abundant plummy fruit on the nose. Good attack. Medium to medium-full, ripe tannins. Not the greatest of complexity and depth. But this is fresher and more interesting than the bottle size. Certainly very good.

1988   **Now-2015**

Good full colour. Still very young. Marvellously perfumed, very pure raspberry and cassis and redcurrant fruit on the nose. Not too austere - or as austere as others - here. Medium-full, balanced. Long. This is very classy and the tannins are ripe but it needs a couple of years to round off. Then it will be lovely.

1987   **Now-2000 plus**

Medium to medium-full colour. Not a lot of development. This is round, slightly spicy, and surprisingly ample on the nose. On the palate there is a little astringency, and the follow-through as a result lacks a bit of fat and class. Yet it is not short. The finish shows classy fruit. A bit of a curate's egg. Good plus.

1986   **Now-1999**

Surprisingly good colour. Deeper but slightly more developed than the 1987. A little dry, but not astringent on the nose. Good substance on the palate. An unexpected amount of fruit and depth. Not a bit suspiciously sweet. This has a good positive follow-through and a long and satisfying finish. Excellent for the vintage.

1985   **Now-2010**

Very good colour. Still youthful. Splendid nose. Marvellously ripe ample fruit. But very good acidity. Very classy indeed. Fullish, very complex, balanced rich wine on the palate. Very long. Very classy. Very fine. And it will keep well.

1983   **Now-2000 plus**

Very good colour. Now mature, but not a bit aged. The usual dry tannins of the vintage on the nose. On the palate a mix of the rich and the gamey and the slightly decayed. Some astringency on the attack. The finish is better; rounder richer and more stylish. Very good for the vintage.

1982   **Drink soon**

Medium, mature colour. Plump, attractive, slightly spicy nose. Medium body, beginning to lighten up and perhaps even coarsen up. But fruity and accessible, clean and not a bit astringent. The acidity is good, and threatens to obtrude as the wine ages further. A very good example. But drink soon. It is getting to the end of its useful life.

1981   **Drink soon**

Unexpectedly good colour though a little cloudy. Not over-evolved either. Not much nose. Medium full. Slightly austere on the attack but surprisingly classy fruit, though without real richness. A little astringency lurks underneath. But a brave and successful example for the vintage. No lack of pleasure here.

1980   **Drink soon**

Good colour. Fullish, mature. No lack of interest on the nose. Fresh and plump. Less fruit and spice than the 1982, but with more class because the grip is better. Even more impressive on the palate. There is depth here. A certain astringency is hovering but nevertheless the wine finishes long and positively. Very good for a Côte-de-Beaune of this rainy vintage. Improved well in the glass.

1979   **Drink soon**

Medium to medium-full but quite an evolved colour. Sweeter than the above, but a little superficial. Easier to enjoy. But it is a little more astringent, and has less depth and freshness. Medium body, a touch of spice, a slight lack of finesse. Good but not exciting. Once again much better on aeration. Seems to have gained vigour and class. Very good.

1978   **Now-2000 plus**

Good full mature colour. Rich, fat, concentrated nose with a touch of spice. This is lovely. Still fresh, even to the extent where one can see a element of new oak. Ripe, medium-full, balanced, complex and very long and classy. A very lovely example. Bags of life.

1977   **Drink up**

No undue age on the colour. There is a definite sour streak here but apart from that - and it is apart - there is style, even fruit. And life, or at least not its opposite. I have had worse.

1976   **Drink soon**

Marvellous colour. Very very full, hardly any brown. Looks like a Hermitage. Big, fat, roasted, astringent nose like the 1983 but less stemmy. On the palate a rich, fresh but *confit* fruit, muscular, tannic wine. A bit astringent at first, but so ripe that this structure gets submerged on the follow-through. Dense on the after-taste though. A wine for food. It will get increasingly astringent.

1971   **Drink soon**

Fullish colour but quite evolved. The nose has got very gamey, even a touch vegetal. But on the palate we have a soft, mature, complex, not over-aged wine. Balanced, classy, gentle, long. I like this. (And no trace of hail.)

1966   **Drink soon**

Well-matured colour, lighter than the 1971. Spicy, plump, almost caramelly on nose and palate. Medium to medium-full. Nicely rich and seductive. But very round and soft. Good length. Good style. Lots of attraction. Very good indeed.

1964   **Now–2000 plus**

Splendidly full, vigorous mature colour. This is very fine indeed. Sumptuously rich, concentrated and balanced. Lots of fruit. Full and ample, sweet and spicy, complex and vigorous. Splendid. Very very long. A great wine. Bags of life.

RAMONET,
CHASSAGNE-MONTRACHET

It is the spring of 1978. A small man, seventy-two years of age and very much a peasant, with an old stained pullover, baggy trousers and the inevitable *casquette* on his head, arrives at a lawyer's office in Beaune. He is about to buy 25 ares and 90 centiares - enough to make about four and half barrels - of Le Montrachet, the finest white wine vineyard in the world. The vendors are the Milan and Mathey-Blanchet families: gentle people. Pierre Ramonet is a man of the soil. Apart from the occasional meal at some of his clients - Lameloise, Alan Chapel, Troisgros, Bocuse - he never ventures outside Chassagne-Montrachet. He hates the telephone. He rarely writes a letter. Such paperwork that needs to be done is achieved by Mother Ramonet, *née* Lucie Prudhon, whom you will never see dressed otherwise than in black, as befits old ladies throughout France, in an old school exercise-book which she keeps in a drawer in her kitchen.

There is the question of payment. 'Ah, yes,' says Ramonet. He fishes in one pocket for a thick wad of notes, in another for a second, in the back of his trousers for a third, and so on. The stacks of money pile up on the attorney's desk. He has never seen such an amount of *espèces* in his life. 'I think you'll find it all there,' says Ramonet, uncomfortable in the formal surroundings of the lawyer's office. And he leaves, anxious to return to the familiarity of his cellar and his vines.

'*Père*' Ramonet was more than a character. He was, to use the old cliché - but it is true in this instance - a legend in his own lifetime. More or less from scratch, by dint of sheer hard work and a genius for wine, he built up one of the finest white-wine domaines in Burgundy. Today the name of Ramonet is synonymous with top Chardonnay. The allocations for bottles are fought over, for every collector considers it his or her right to own some. They sell at auction for astronomical sums whenever they appear. On the rare occasions, as in January 1995 at the Montrachet restaurant in New York, when someone puts on a special vertical tasting and dinner, the tickets - and they are not cheap - are over-subscribed ten times. Ramonet in white is the equivalent of Henri Jayer or the DRC in red.

Pierre Ramonet died in 1994 at the age of eighty-eight. He is much missed. But his echo lives on, and the wines, in the able hands of his grandsons Noël (born in 1962) and Jean-Claude (born in 1967) since the 1984 vintage (*mais sous ses ordres*, stoutly avers Noël), continue his reputation. They are very fine. More importantly, they are also very individual. A Ramonet wine is a Ramonet wine before it is a Chassagne, or a Bienvenues, or a Bâtard ... or a Montrachet.

HISTORY

The original Ramonets came from the Bresse on the other side of the river Saône from Chalon. A branch settled in Beaune in the nineteenth century, where they were millers. The mill failed, and one of them, Claude, moved to Chassagne, where he became a *tâcheron* - a vineyard worker who is paid by the amount of land he tends rather than by the day as a direct employee - for Colonel Vuillard, owner of the Château de Maltroye.

This Claude had three children; a daughter who married Georges Bachelet (from whence comes today's Bachelet-Ramonet domaine) and two sons, Pierre, born in 1906 and Claude, born in 1914. This Claude never married, and died in 1977. Pierre married Lucie Prudhon, daughter of the Duc de Magenta's *chef de culture* at the Domaine de l'Abbaye de Morgeot. (For a time the wine was sold as Domaine Ramonet-Prudhon.) They had a single child, their son André (born in 1934), father of Noël and Jean-Claude. André has never enjoyed good health and for some time has been more or less of an invalid. He has never had total responsibility for the Ramonet domaine.

Pierre Ramonet left school at the age of eight to help his father in the vineyard. His first vineyard purchase was in Chassagne-Montrachet, Les Ruchottes, early in the 1930s. Exhibiting at the Beaune wine fair in 1938, he found himself being addressed by Raymond Baudoin, one of the founders of the *Revue des Vins de France*, and adviser to many of the nation's top restaurants. Baudoin had obviously encountered something disagreeable at a neighbouring stand. 'Have you got anything to take the taste away,' he asked. And was given some Ruchottes 1934. 'Excellent!' pronounced Baudoin. 'Do you have any for sale? Can I take away a couple of bottles?' Six months later he arrived in Chassagne with Frank Schoonmaker, one of the first Americans to seize the opportunity provided by the abolition of Prohibition. Schoonmaker took 200 cases of both red and white - though the Ramonets did not get paid until after the war!

Baudoin was of similar assistance in getting the Ramonet wine on to the lists of the top restaurants in France: Taillevent in Paris, Point in Vienne, the Côte d'Or in Avallon - and this encouraged the opening up of a market for *vente directe*. And of course, after the war, and his settlement of the bill for the 1934s, Schoonmaker continued as the major export customer.

Slowly but surely the Ramonet domaine began to expand. They now possess vines in seven Chassagne *premiers crus* (Ruchottes, Morgeots, Caillerets, Clos-de-la-Boudriotte, Clos-Saint-Jean, Chaumées and Vergers) and most of these were acquired in the 1940s and 1950s. In 1955, two adjoining parcels, one in Bâtard (45 a), one in Bienvenues (56 a), were obtained from Henri Coquet.

More recently the domaine has expanded into Saint-Aubin (Les Charmois) and into Puligny-Montrachet (Champs-Canet and village wine) and some Boudriottes white has been bought. The total now exploited is 17 hectares.

WINE-MAKING

In theory Noël is responsible in the cellar and his brother Jean-Claude in the vineyard. But in fact it seems to be a joint effort. Neither has had technical training, and so if you ask why they do this, or not do that, you will be unlikely to receive a coherent answer. The approach is empirical and instinctive. But it seems to work.

The Chardonnays are pruned to the Guyot system, the Pinots Noirs Cordon trained. In the vineyard the yields are kept low, the average age of the vines maintained high, with no *repiquage* after a certain time. This means that, as has happened in Le Montrachet, whole parcels eventually have to be ripped up. The produce of the younger vines can then be vinified apart, and down-graded. This is the case today with half of the Montrachet.

The red wines, village Chassagne, Clos-Saint-Jean, Clos-de-la-Boudriotte and Morgeots, are partially destemmed, usually 50 per cent, cold soaked for a few days, vinified in cement vats – there is a resistance to stainless steel here – macerated for ten days, and matured using one-third new oak for a year, being both fined and lightly filtered.

There is a very noisy cooling unit for temperature control in the cellar. Above ground what looks like an ugly garage-type hangar stands over an extensive underground cellar hewn out of the rock. But the Ramonets express no interest in being able to cool down or warm up the wine in order to facilitate the malo-lactic. 'We like to let nature take its course.'

Unusually the Ramonets do not allow the gross lees to settle out before the fermentation of the white wine begins. 'There are elements in the gross lees which are good,' maintains Noël. Perhaps as a result of this, the wines are *bâtonné*-ed much less than elsewhere: only once a month for four months. Why? Because they fear that these gross lees would taint the wine. Fermentations are begun in tank, continued in wood – overall about one-third new – at 20-25°C, and the finished wine kept on the lees as long as possible before the first racking. A second racking takes place after a year or fifteen months. The white wines, like the reds, are both fined and lightly filtered.

The cellar, both upstairs and downstairs, is not the neatest, most orderly cellar you have ever been into. Odd bits of machinery, adaptors for pipes, and boxes of this or that lie all over the place. You feel they have never had a tidy-up or thrown anything out. As you squeeze between a beaten-up truck and a redundant pumping machine to get below to sample the wines you find that the staircase is used as a cupboard for yet more accumulation of bits and pieces. It is like an ironmongers' nightmare.

But all this seems fitting when you meet Noël Ramonet. The man is in his mid-thirties, stocky, usually unshaven, in a dirty old T-shirt and jeans, with piercing blue eyes, a loud voice, and peremptory way of expressing himself. Finesse, order and method, and reflection are alien. Energy, passion and forthrightness define his manner. But when you listen, you realise that this is truly a chip off the old block. He reveres his grandfather. But he has his own full understanding of his *métier*. (He has also got one of the most magnificent – and eclectic – private cellars I have ever seen. All bought; none exchanged.)

'*Moins fins mais plus profonds,*' he will agree with you, when you sample the Chassagne, Morgeots white after the Saint-Aubin, Charmois. And the Boudriottes is more mineral, less fat and heavy, because this is on the semi-*coteaux*, while the Morgeots is in the plain. The Chaumées, despite being very young vines, and the Vergers, show more finesse. They are properly on the slope. And the Caillerets and the Ruchottes are best of all. 'Where the soils are really well drained, as here,' explains Noël, 'you will always have much less problem with botrytis.' This is the heartland of Chassagne white.

Why is there such a sharp contrast between the Bienvenues – composed, accessible, discreet – and the Bâtard – closed, powerful, masculine? After all the vines are adjacent, and the same age. Noël shrugs. You feel he knows the answer. But he can't articulate it. And is his Bâtard his most consistently successful wine? Is it better even than the Montrachet, which can be totally brilliant, but over the seventeen years since the Ramonets have produced it, certainly not always? Is this a question you even dare ask?

I find the Ramonet reds refreshingly direct. They are full, ample and plump, nicely concentrated but nicely succulent at the same time. Chassagne reds will never be great, and can be over-extracted. But the Ramonets get theirs right.

The whites, on the other hand, are exceptional. They are distinctive, full-bodied and long-lasting. They are rich and masculine, firm and concentrated. They can be magnificent.

And they can also be flawed. This is a result of risks being taken. But often the flaws are by no means disagreeable; they lend individuality; they give character; they add an element of dimension. For me, a great wine often *does* have something just a little bit 'wrong' about it. And a squeaky-clean 'perfect' wine is very rarely as interesting.

THE TASTING

I sampled the following wines *chez* Ramonet in June 1995.

BÂTARD-MONTRACHET

*Optimum
drinking*

1989   1998–2010

Green-gold colour. Rich, firm, honeyed nose. An ample wine, full of *fondant* and citronelle flavours. Not yet fully resolved. On the palate one sees the honey mixing in with the oak to give a wine which is really *moelleux*. Very good grip. Just at the point of being over-ripe and *vendange tardive*-ish. Adolescent.

1988   Now–2008

Lighter colour. Interesting nose. A touch of reduction at first, which then blew off. Then afterwards, a touch of truffles. This is fatter, richer and more interesting than the vast majority of 1988s. Indeed it has a lot of depth. And it has a lot of finesse: dare I say it, more than the above. Good grip. Long. Delicious. Just about ready.

1987   Now–1999

Good colour. Herbal nose. A little unbalanced, for there is too much size and alcohol for the fruit. Hot at the end. Not too lean. But it lacks real class. Quite good only. But a very good example for the vintage.

1986   Now–2005

Not too deep a colour – the 1989 shows more – but the nose is quite typical of 1986: a little dry, a hint of over-ripeness. Not too blowsy though: but just a little. Ripe, abundant, oaky. Reasonable acidity. Good fruit. But I prefer the 1989, let alone the 1988 and 1985. By comparison this is a little simple. But it is very fine for a 1986. It has much better class and length than most.

1985   1999–2020

This is a huge wine. Still immature. No undue age to the colour. Voluminously rich nose. Very good grip. Still hidden. On the palate very powerful, very full. Excellent acidity. Yet a certain over-ripeness, even sweetness. This is a brilliant example. Completely adolescent today. Alcoholic, monstrous, even ugly in places. But potentially splendid. All the elements are here.

1983   Now–2010

Good colour. A big wine again. Very, very rich on the nose. Almost sweet. This is again powerful and over-ripe, but it is much better than the 1986. Indeed it suggests the beneficial aspects of *pourriture noble* rather than the reverse.

Very full. Alcoholic again. Exotic ripe fruit. Lovely honeyed elements. Almost sweet. The point is there is a good acidity here. A *confit* of fruit. Lots of future. Fine.

1982   Now–2005

Just a little more colour, but very fresh for a 1982. Lovely ample nose. Silky smooth, extremely seductive, very well balanced. Quite full but not heavy. Yet very good intensity. This is very lovely, still very vigorous. The finish is fine. An example of how fine some of these 1982s can be. Very lovely. Very complex.

1979   Drink soon

Properly mature colour. On the nose this is a bit of a shock after the 1982. Very evidently an old wine. Yet, Noël Ramonet says, this is not a rogue bottle. On the palate the wine is ripe, there are interesting vegetal elements, there is good acidity and the finish is complex. But it is a touch old. I prefer the 1982 by some way.

1978   Now–1999

Just a little less colour than the 1979. Very complex nose. Austere at first. Now a combination of biscuit, vegetal elements and nuts. Nicely complex. Certainly individual. Medium-full body. A touch lean – indeed it reminds me of a 1972 white. Good length. Not exactly sexy or generous. Best with food.

1976   Now–2003

Golden colour. This is lovely. It is over-ripe and abundant, without the *pourriture noble* of the 1983. And it has a splendid acidity keeping it elegant and fresh and plump. In fact as it evolves it gets more nutty and less over-ripe. Just merely succulent, abundant and lovely. Very fine.

1972   Drink up

Old colour. A bit tired and oxidised on the nose. Better on the palate. Indeed perfectly drinkable and acceptable. Not falling apart. Still classy, ripe and enjoyable. It is the acidity which has preserved it. But drink up.

1969   Now–2000

Golden colour. This is very special. Rich, concentrated, well-matured nose. Obviously was a very powerful wine in its youth. It still has a lot of structure and volume. Nutty on the nose. Very complex, ripe ample and well balanced on the palate. A great wine. Very long on the palate.

1964   **Now–2000 plus**

Golden colour. This is even better than the 1969. Slightly less powerful, but more integrated. Ripe, sweet, very, very complex. Multi-dimensional. Fresh. Complete. Beautifully harmonious. Velvety. Extra-fine. Real finesse. Great length. This is *grand vin*. One of the loveliest bottles of old white Burgundy I have ever had.

1961   **Drink soon**

Deep golden colour. This is now getting really quite old. There is a gentle element of maderisation here but a lovely residual ripe sweetness and very good concentration and intensity. Getting a little pinched on the finish, perhaps.

1959   **Now–2000 plus**

Golden colour. Aromatic, fresh, honeyed, classy, ripe nose. This is extremely lovely. Full, round, ripe and balanced. This is still very fresh and even powerful. Marvellous concentration. Great breed. Very long and complex. Really classy. A beautiful wine. This is even better than the 1964. It is longer, sweeter, even more vigorous. *Grand vin!*

DANIEL RION,
NUITS-SAINT-GEORGES

'Look at the road,' says Patrice Rion, from high up in his Clos-des-Argillières. 'See how, as it leaves Nuits–Saint-Georges, it starts at the bottom of the slope, but then seems to traverse it, so that most of the village of Prémeaux lies further down the slope on the opposite side. That is why there is one *premier cru*, Les Grandes Vignes, on the "wrong" side of the road. We have got almost a hectare of vines there. Our bit is not *premier cru*, but it makes much better wine than some of the *climats* on *this* side of the road, down below Les Saint-Georges and Les Porrets.'

Patrice, born in 1956, is one of three brothers who together with their father run the Domaine Daniel Rion et Fils. But he is the wine-maker and the public face. It was he, at the age of seventeen, having returned from a *stage* in Alsace where *vente directe* was commonplace, who decided to put up a notice outside the winery and start selling bottles to passing tourists. In 1973 this was rare in Burgundy. It is Patrice's wine-making skills which have put this Rion domaine on the map. And it is as a result of his imagination and shrewdness that Domaine Daniel Rion is one of the first to present its wines on the Internet. With 18.5 ha the domaine is able to offer a wide range of wines from generic to *premier cru* in Nuits-Saint-Georges, Vosne-Romanée and Chambolle-Musigny, and even some Clos-de-Vougeot, though this latter, the only part of the estate farmed rather than owned, has from 1995 left the Rion hands.

Pierre Rion, known as Rion *le cadet* (the younger brother), was born in Switzerland and was a farmer in the Haute-Savoie, a tenant of the Château de Boncourt. Following a fire which destroyed much of his livelihood, he upped sticks and settled in Vosne-Romanée. It was the last years of the nineteenth century.

Pierre had one son, Louis, and together they began to build up a wine domaine, subsisting at first as vineyard workers but gradually evolving into leaseholders, even proprietors. But the estate was never large. When the first of Louis' sons, Daniel (it is from the second, Marcel, who died in 1989, that the other Rion domaine, that of Armelle and Bernard, comes) came back from military service in 1955, Louis gave him 2 hectares: 'Here's your patrimony. Get on with it.'

Daniel was about to get married. His bride was Gisèle Truchetet, daughter of Raymond, a family of polyculturalists based in Prémeaux. She brought with her 1 hectare of vines, and the pair installed themselves close to Daniel's in-laws.

The rest of the domaine has been built up since; much of it from scrubland at the top of the slope which Daniel bought, cleared and planted. The Clos-des-Argillières, the Terres-Blanches and the Hauts-Pruliers in Nuits-Saint-Georges, as well as the Beaux-Monts in Vosne-Romanée, are all new or reclaimed vineyard land. 'This makes it easier,' explains Patrice, 'to look after our vineyards in as *biologique* a way as possible. Normally we only have neighbours on one side.' But on the other hand, I feel, the cooler micro-climate at the higher reaches contributes a certain leanness and austerity to the Rion style.

Daniel and Gisèle have four children, a daughter, Pascale, and three sons: Patrice, Christophe, born in 1958, and Olivier, born in 1961. Today Olivier is responsible for the vines, while Christophe partly looks after the Truchetet 50 ha farm. Since 1980 Patrice has been responsible for the wine.

The winery, a rather ugly Swiss chalet-type edifice facing on to a large car-park, lies in the middle of Prémeaux, almost opposite the buildings of the Domaine de l'Arlot. The *cuverie* is on the ground floor, the cellar underneath. It is efficient and functional. What it lacks, perhaps, is a little romance. But only the hard-nosed professionals get this far. The tourist is received elsewhere, by various members of the family in their own homes and cellars, where the location is *plus sympathique*.

THE DOMAINE

A tour of the main elements of the Rion domaine may begin by driving up into the vineyards above Prémeaux. Look at the colour of the stone, Patrice will say. In the Clos-de-l'Arlot the rock is a sandy-coloured Comblanchien limestone, in the Clos-des-Argillières, above Les Argillières itself, the stone is the pink Prémeaux limestone. The Domaine Rion possesses 72 ares here. It gives quite a different wine.

Continue along at the top of the vineyards (admire the view!) and you reach the Terres-Blanches. As the name suggests, the stone, decomposed rock, is white. It is almost entirely stony in parts, and there is sand, much less clay. The wine as a result is more mineral. Two-thirds of a hectare are under Pinot Noir. A new section, making up 37.5 ares, rescued from *friche* by Olivier, has been planted with Pinot Blanc (not Chardonnay, which would produce too lean and acid a wine). The vines here are still very young.

Not all the Hauts-Pruliers is entitled to *premier cru* status, says Rion. But ours is, he goes on happily. You can see the soil change, and the difference in height and exposition between the different parcels. Here the Rion holding is 42 ares.

Turn through the back streets of Nuits-Saint-Georges, wriggle about a bit, and you will come out near a rather scruffy Inter-Marché supermarket off the road up into the Hautes-

Côtes. Behind this a road – if you can call it that – runs through the northern vineyards of Nuits-Saint-Georges towards Vosne-Romanée, dividing the upper *premiers crus* from the lower village wines. The lateral extent of the *vignoble* is here five or six times wider than it is in Prémeaux, and it is here that the Rions have the last of their *premier cru* Nuits-Saint-Georges, Les Vignes-Rondes (46 ares). Here we are not at the top of the slope, for above Vignes-Rondes lies Chaignots, and above *that* is En-Perrière-Noblot. So this is not a vineyard that the Rions have created from scratch.

Further on, but down-slope and across the Nuits-Vosne boundary, lies Vosne-Romanée, Les Chaumes, *premier cru* (42 ares). The Rion parcel lies next to that of Grivot, and contains the oldest vines of the domaine: fifty-five years old, or more.

To achieve the impressive 2.25 ha land-holding in Vosne-Romanée, Beaux-Monts, roughly half of which is *premier cru*, the remainder in the Hauts-Beaux-Monts and village wine, Daniel Rion had to piece together forty-eight parcels acquired bit by bit over five years in the early 1960s, then clear the land, wrench out the largest stones, replace them with suitable soil, and build walls to protect what he had created from erosion. Quite a task!

In Chambolle-Musigny the domaine owns 41 ares of *premier cru*, Les Charmes, and 32.5 ares of village land. 'Notice how the vine leaves are yellower in colour,' says Patrice. 'This is a result of a higher amount of active limestone in the soil, and more efficient drainage. Chambolle vines are always the first to suffer if there is a drought. But the soil composition makes the wines more elegant.' Across the main road is perhaps one of the best spots for generic Burgundy in the whole Côte. The *lieu-dit* is called Les Bons-Bâtons. Ghislaine Barthod of Chambolle also has vines here.

Finally the Clos-de-Vougeot. Here the Daniel Rion domaine shared a parcel *en métayage* with their cousins. The landlords were the Cheron/Misset family, associated with Maison Pascal Frères and Naigeon-Chauveau of Gevrey-Chambertin, and the parcel is situated in the middle of the slope on the Vosne-Romanée side. The lease, which began in 1945, came to its end with the 1994 vintage and the vines thereafter reverted back to their owners. While the wine in the Daniel Rion hands is good, I have never found it startlingly so. There is better value for money elsewhere in the portfolio. This Rion domaine exploited 72 ares, of which they got half the fruit.

WINE-MAKING

'Thankfully my father never succumbed to the temptation to over-fertilise, as so many did in the 1960s and 1970s,' says Patrice, 'and so I have never had any problem with the acidities in my wine.'

They now eliminate all the stems, having previously retained 20 per cent. After a short period of cold soaking, the fermentation temperatures are very strictly controlled at 31.5-32.5°C, with selected yeasts added at the end of the process, after the indigenous varieties have done their work. The *cuvaison* can be prolonged up to eighteen days, unless the fruit is very concentrated, as in 1990, when the *écoulage* is earlier. There is one racking, in April or May after the malo has finished; from 20 up to 50 per cent new wood; and bottling takes place after a further ten to twelve months, after a fining, but without filtration.

'At the beginning,' says Patrice, 'we were criticised for our wines being a bit hard. So in 1985 we shortened the maceration and did a little less *pigeage*. But I wasn't entirely satisfied. So we then reverted back to longer macerations and more *pigeage*. But I think we are more flexible now, and the tannins we extract are nobler. This is where temperature control is so important. Too high and the wine is coarse, too low and it lacks body and structure.'

THE WINES

The Daniel Rion wines have their own character: sturdy, long-lasting, rich but at the same time a little austere and four-square. Often I found myself admiring them without being seduced by them, and wishing both that they had more generosity and more definition.

What was curious was the difference between the Daniel Rion wines and those under the label of Michelle et Patrice Rion, for the two (Michelle being Patrice's wife) have a small vineyard of their own: Chambolle-Musigny, Les Cras (but village Les Cras not *premier cru*) and Bourgogne *rouge*.

These are made by the same man on the same winery, I said to myself. Yet they are different. They have a certain flair that the Daniel Rions lack.

What does he do that is different? I asked him in June 1995. But I didn't receive a satisfactory answer. But then in November, when I came to sample the 1994s out of cask, I found a change had occured. Given the difference in the vintage between 1994 and 1993 the wines nevertheless had an extra refinement. There had obviously been a number of small adjustments to the wine-making process. The results were for the first time not merely 'very good', but fine.

THE TASTING

I sampled the following wines in Prémeaux in June 1995.

VOSNE-ROMANÉE, LES CHAUMES

Optimum drinking

1993 — 2000-2010

Good colour. Still very purple (bottled end February). Nicely plump on the nose. Pure Pinot, very stylish. Good backbone underneath. Quite firm, quite full, a youthful rawness at present. Ripe, stylish, good grip and plenty of thrust. Ample and long and expansive at the end. Very good.

1992 — Now-2002

Medium colour. No lack of substance or fruit here. But the fruit is more cherry-redcurrant than the raspberry of the 1993. Good weight and balance on the palate. Quite meaty for a 1992. Good crisp acidity. Ripe, plenty of dimension. Very good for the vintage.

1991 — 1998-2008

Good colour. Still youthful. The nose seems to have gone into its shell a bit. There is plenty of volume here, and a touch of oak. This is earthier than the 1993, a little spicier, a little less pure, for it has acquired some of the spice of maturity. Good fullish ample ripe wine. No aggressive tannins - these are nicely ripe. Balanced. Long. But not as long or as stylish as the 1993. Very good.

1990 — 1999-2012

Very good colour. The nose is rather hidden at first. This is quite burly, and will probably always be so. A little four-square. Certainly very, very ripe underneath. And no lack of grip. But will the muscle change into velvet? Currently rich, full, balanced. But could be more stylish. Good plus for the vintage.

1989 — Now-2000 plus

Good colour. Some evolution. But looks bigger and more backward than most. More developed, more accessible but much more elegant, it seems, on the nose. This is lovely. Quite full. Excellent acidity. Sumptuous fruit. Very long. Subtle. Just about ready. A big wine for the vintage. Fine for the vintage.

1988 — Now-2002

Very good colour. Still youthful. No less full-looking than the 1990. Slightly lean. Lovely fruit here: crisp and very clean and pure. There is a little unresolved tannin on the attack but the finish is round, vigorous and highly promising. Very good grip. Very well balanced. Very good indeed for the vintage.

1987 — Now-2000 plus

Very good colour. Mellow nose. Nicely fresh. No aggressive tannins. Just a touch of caramelly spice. Medium-full body. Just about ready. This has no hard edges and plenty of fruit and thrust. Still youthful. Certainly fresh. But it is now *à point*. Long and positive. Unexpectedly smooth and elegant. Very good indeed for the vintage.

1986   **Drink soon**

Good colour. Fullish, no undue brown. More evolved than the 1987 on the nose. But no astringency. No undue fade or age. Mellow, complex, spicy, still fresh. Medium body. A touch of astringency on the palate. But a very good result for the vintage. Positive at the end. Not short. Still enjoyment to be had.

1985   **Now-2005**

Fullish colour. Just about ready. Fresh, plump nose. Not as voluminous as perhaps I had expected. On the nose high toned, just a touch lean. Medium to medium-full body. Still quite young. It lacks an element of fat and also all-embracing definition. Quite high in acidity. Complex. Very good quality. But somehow I feel just a little something is missing. Improved on aeration. Perhaps it needs food.

1984   **Drink up**

Good fresh colour. Slightly animal and vegetal on the nose. But no lack of interest or vigour. Getting a little light, a little astringent now, but no lack of fruit or vigour and the finish here, if a touch 'hot', is still positive. A very good effort. Doesn't lack elegance.

1983   **Now-2005 plus**

Very good colour. No undue brown. It has the 1983 dry and tannic nose (though no stems). But on aeration more and more of the fruit began to come out. Rich, full, tannic and concentrated. A meaty wine, slightly aggressive. Certainly very ample. No sign of undue dryness on the palate. Larger than life. Needs food.

1982   **Drink up**

Fresh, medium mature colour. Interesting nose. It is drying out a bit, but there is fruit here and the spicy wood of an old wardrobe. Lightening up on the palate. But still enjoyable, still has a reasonable grip. Good fruit.

1981   **Past its best**

Good colour. Not a lot of volume but not really very brown at all. Not too faded. This is a light wine which is not too faded at first, but really quite astringent on the follow-through. Acidity is beginning to show. There was certainly no lack of fruit and style here, but now a bit past its best.

1980   **Now-2000 plus**

Very good fullish mature vigorous colour. Most attractive nose. Quite rich, still fresh and vigorous, but now mellow and complex. Full, meaty, lovely fruit, plenty of life ahead of it. Good grip. Good tannic structure but no undue structure. Probably was rather hard at the outset. Finely poised masculine wine. Lovely. Lots of life ahead of it. Vigorous. For food. I prefer this to the 1985.

1972   **Now-2000 plus**

Fine colour. No undue maturity. This is not at all too austere. Slightly lean, naturally, but plenty of classy fruit. Ripe enough. Long. Complex. This is very good indeed for the vintage.

ROMANÉE-CONTI,
VOSNE-ROMANÉE

The scarcest, most expensive – and frequently the best – wine in the world is the Romanée-Conti from the aptly-named Domaine de la Romanée-Conti. If you can lay your hands on a case – and it is a big 'if' – you would have to pay £5,000 or more for a young vintage, double or treble for a wine in its prime.

The vineyard is tiny. As a *grand cru* it is entitled to *Appellation Contrôlée* in its own right, and at 1.81 hectares it is one of the smallest appellations in France. Production is meagre: 22 hectolitres per hectare in 1990, elsewhere a prolific vintage. This means the equivalent of around 400 cases per annum at the end of the day: less than 5,000 bottles for the whole world. But if you *do* get the chance to drink the wine in its prime you will be transported to heaven. This is the purest, most aristocratic and most intense example of Pinot Noir you could possibly imagine. Not only nectar: a yardstick with which to judge all other Burgundies.

THE VINEYARDS

Vosne-Romanée is the first of the six great - in the sense that they possess *grands crus climats* - communes of the Côte d'Or as one travels north out of Nuits-Saint-Georges. The village of Vosne is small and tranquil, set a few hundred metres away from the main road, and centres round a square, at one end of which lies a modest church and at the other a more imposing *mairie*. Beyond this square, at the north-west corner of the village, along a little road which abruptly stops at the entrance to the vineyard of Romanée-Saint-Vivant, the traveller will find, not without difficulty if this is his first visit, the grey-painted metal gate which leads into the small courtyard of the Domaine de la Romanée-Conti. Beneath the offices to the left lie part of the cellars; across the road, under what looks like an anonymous garage, lie further cellars, where the wines will spend their first year or so in cask. A short walk in the opposite direction will bring you to the old *manoir* of the abbey of Saint-Vivant, which the domaine has recently taken over for use as a second barrel cellar.

The contrast with the grand country estate atmosphere of the leading growths of the Médoc, or the tourist-attracting, rather over-restored buildings of some of the *négociants* in Beaune is very apparent. There are no neon lights, no flamboyant *panneaux*. Visitors, though warmly received when they *do* arrive, come only by appointment. The casual tourist is discouraged.

Above and behind this small complex of houses, offices and *chais* lie the vineyards, literally the bed-rock on which the fortunes of the domaine are based. Nearest is Romanée-Saint-Vivant, the largest vineyard. Further up the slope is the tiny, gently inclined La Romanée-Conti itself. As the hill curves round to the right to face more north-east than south-east lies the steeper Richebourg. To the left, across the narrow files of vines which make up the *climat* of La Grande-Rue, runs the slope of La Tâche, again steep at the top. On either side of this memorable roll-call of names are two of Vosne's top *premiers crus*, Les Malconsorts, on the Nuits boundary, marching with Les Boudots, in my view Nuits' best site, and to the north Les Suchots, across which are the various stony Echézeaux vineyards.

The Domaine de la Romanée-Conti owns the entirety of two *climats*, La Romanée-Conti and La Tâche. They possess approximately half of Richebourg, over a third of Grands-Echézeaux and one-seventh of Echézeaux, this last holding being in the *lieu-dit* Les Poulaillères, the best part of this large *grand cru*. It also used to farm, but since 1988 has owned, the portion - over half of the appellation - of the Domaine Marey-Monge's Romanée-Saint-Vivant. The total Vosne-Romanée *grand cru* holding is as follows:

	Hectares	Average age of vines
La Romanée-Conti	1.81	47 years
La Tâche	6.06	45 years
Richebourg	3.51	28 years
Grands-Echézeaux	3.53	45 years
Echézeaux	4.67	30 years
Romanée-Saint-Vivant	5.29	25 years

In addition, the domaine owns 0.68 ha of Le Montrachet, 0.17 ha of Bâtard and about 1 ha of communal Vosne. The last two are not sold under the domaine label but in bulk to local merchants, as is the produce of vines on the more famous slopes which are less than ten years old.

The Abbé Courtepée in the late eighteenth century, echoed by Camille Rodier in the twentieth, said of Vosne-Romanée, '*Il n'y a pas de vin commun*' (there are no common wines in the village). The wines were famous then, and they are just as highly regarded now. The mixture of the right exposure, on a well-drained slope facing east or south-east, soil which is essentially an oolitic, iron-rich limestone on a base of marl, rock and pebbles, and vines which lie approximately between 250 and 300 metres above sea level, sheltered from the west and north by the trees at the top of the slope, is as good as you can get. The *grand cru climats*, plumb in the middle of the slope, are the best of all, and the Domaine de la Romanée-Conti has the lion's share of these.

HISTORY

The Domaine as it stands today was brought together by Jacques-Marie Duvault-Blochet about a century ago, but its individual constituents have of course an older history.

The prime section, La Romanée-Conti itself, can count but nine owners in eight and a half centuries. In the twelfth century it belonged to an influential local family called Vergy. In 1232 Alex de Vergy donated a piece of land known as Le Cloux-de-Vosne (Cloux is a common *lieu-dit* in Burgundy and denotes a particularly well-regarded piece of ground) to the nearby Abbey of Saint-Vivant, a subsidiary of the great endowment at Citeaux. Almost exactly 400 years later, in 1631, the site was sold to a Monsieur de Croonembourg (to raise money for a 'crusade' to Palestine, it is said; though it sounds a little late to me for crusades - perhaps it was to be more of a pilgrimage).

It was the Croonembourg family who decided to change the name to Romanée. Was there some tangible evidence of Roman occupation at the time? Or was this just in memory of the people who had first introduced the science or art of vine-cultivation to Burgundy?

The Croonembourgs also bought the neighbouring vineyard of La Tâche, and it was under their ownership that the wines first received renown.

In 1760, after the death of Philippe de Croonembourg, his son André decided to sell his domaine. There was great competition to become owner of La Romanée, already regarded as the best vineyard in Burgundy. After a while, only two contestants remained in the ring, the Marquise de Pompadour, the King's mistress, and one of the King's distant kinsmen, Louis-François de Bourbon, the Prince de Conti. Thanks to the efficacy of his agent, François Joly, it was the Prince who was the victor, much to the chagrin of La Pompadour - but no doubt the King himself was the final arbiter, and as has unkindly been pointed out, the Pompadour was then somewhat on the wrong side of fifty, and perhaps had less influence on the King than she had previously enjoyed. The price, though, was astronomical, 8,000 gold *livres*, particularly as taxes continued to be payable to the Abbot of Saint-Vivant.

The Prince added his name to La Romanée, and Romanée-Conti it has been ever since. The Pompadour forswore Burgundy and turned to the delights of Champagne.

Conti, however, reserved all the produce of his vineyard for his own pleasure. Not even his friends, who according to Beaumarchais, would go down on their knees in front of him and mockingly plead for an indulgence of one single bottle, could move him from his avarice. La Tâche, now under a separate ownership, was able to take La Romanée-Conti's place as the most sought-after Burgundy in France.

During the Revolution Conti emigrated, and the vineyard was sequestered by the State and sold as a *bien national* in 1793. As John Arlott and Christopher Fielden point out (*Burgundy*, Davis-Poynter, 1976), 'Even the prosaic valuers . . . dug deeply into their resources of evocative language when they described it on the Bill of Sale.' A celebrated piece of vineyard, they said; the most advantageous position in Vosne; the fruit reaches the most perfect maturity; the site bares its breast to the first rays of the sun which stimulates it with the softest heat of the day; and so on. The document even goes on to claim that the Romanée-Conti vineyard 'did not suffer from *coulure* or frost like many of the other *climats*'. This contrasts intriguingly with the Document of Sale under similar circumstances and at the same time, which is today preserved, framed at Lafite. Lafite's Bill of Sale says simply that it was 'Le Premier Cru du Médoc et produisant le premier vin'; moreover, the property was in good order - and it also did not suffer from frost.

The purchaser was a Parisien, a Nicolas Defer de la Nouerre, about whom little seems to be known. Subsequently, in September 1819, it changed hands again. The new owner was Julien Ouvrard, at one time Napoléon's banker, later to be imprisoned for fraud, and already proprietor of Clos-de-Vougeot and also, according to Fielden, of properties in Bordeaux (though no famous ones as far as I am aware). The price was once more fabulous. At 78,000 francs, it worked out at 45,000 francs per hectare, at a time when Chambertin, La Tâche and Richebourg could not attain more than a third of that amount.

Finally in 1869 Romanée-Conti changed hands for the last time. The new purchaser was the afore-mentioned M. Duvault-Blochet, probably the most important vineyard-owner Burgundy has seen since the Revolution. He it was who constituted most of the present domaine by acquiring the holdings in Richebourg and both of the Echézeaux *climats*, and his holdings extended throughout the Côte d'Or, including the Domaine de la Pousse d'Or in Volnay.

La Tâche and the Rest

According to my French dictionary, the word La Tâche signifies 'work which was remunerated' as well as merely a task. 'À la tâche' is a form of payment by the job completed rather than by the hour or day, and here perhaps refers to the difficulties of working this particular vineyard in order that it would produce of its best; perhaps as the cliché puts it, 'beyond the call of duty'.

In the eighteenth century, according to some records, it was also in the hands of the Croonembourg family. At some time before the Revolution it belonged to the Chapitre de Nuits, and while La Romanée-Conti was off the market sold for the high price of 1,200 francs the *queue* - a Burgundian measurement which like the Bordeaux *tonneaux* has no cooperage actuality but which is the equivalent of two 228 litre *pièces* or Burgundy barrels. In 1791 it was bought by a M. Marey, whose family also owned part of Romanée-Saint-Vivant. It was acquired by the Domaine de la Romanée-Conti in 1933.

Originally La Tâche only covered 1.5 hectares. However, during the 1930s most of the *climat* of Les Gaudichots was absorbed, for the Domaine de la Romanée-Conti and its predecessors in a series of lawsuits were able to prove that a 'local, loyal and constant' precedent of selling the wine from this additional section as La Tâche had been set, and this was confirmed by the AC regulations when they appeared in 1936. La Tâche now covers 6 hectares.

Romanée-Saint-Vivant takes its name from the Abbey of Saint-Vivant, owners also in the Middle Ages of what is now Romanée-Conti. The abbey acquired part by donation, part by purchase in the mid thirteenth century, and were large vineyard-holders in the Côte-de-Nuits and in the Hautes-Côtes, more extensively planted with vines in pre-phylloxera times than now.

At the time of the Revolution all ecclesiastical vineyard holdings were sold off, and part was bought by the Marey-Monge family of Nuits for 91,000 francs. The Domaine de la Romanée-Conti took over management of this parcel in 1966, and have re-constituted about half of this holding since then. In September 1988 they bought it.

The Present Proprietors

One of the present day co-administrators of the Domaine de la Romanée-Conti, representing the large number of members of his family, is Aubert de Villaine, a great, great, great-grandson of Jacques-Marie Duvault-Blochet. De Villaine, who originally had ambitions to be a poet, is a quietly purposeful, studious-looking, bespectacled man in his mid fifties. His mother was

Russian. He has an American wife, an art historian, and lives in an attractively converted *manoir* in the village of Bouzeron in the Côte Chalonnaise.

De Villaine started working at the domaine in 1964, alongside his father Henri and Henri Leroy, who had bought half the domaine from other descendants of Duvault-Blochet in July 1942. De Villaine had previously trained with Leroy SA in Auxey-Duresses. He acquired his own property in Bouzeron - of which he is deputy mayor - in 1973, and since then has been the driving force behind the creation of Bouzeron as a separate AC for Bourgogne Aligoté. His example is a classic, and his Bourgogne *rouge*, from Pinot Noir, and *blanc*, from Chardonnay, are equally delicious. Five years ago he embarked (on behalf of his nephews) on a new project in the Provence with Jacques Seysses of Domaine Dujac and another friend, not in the wine business. Together they acquired the Domaine de Triennes in the Var near Saint-Maximin-de-Saint-Baume. They have quickly transformed the 46 hectare vineyard to Syrah, Cabernet Sauvignon, Chardonnay and Viognier. The results so far are very promising.

For many years, following the death of her father, the counterpart to Aubert de Villaine was Lalou Bize-Leroy, and the two - the scholarly De Villaine on the one side and the flamboyant Lalou Bize on the other - provided an interesting contrast. Early in 1992, there was a boardroom putsch, and Madame Bize was relieved of her position as joint manager.

Following this departure it was decided to appoint Charles Roch, eldest son of Lalou's sister Pauline, as *co-gérant*. Tragically Charles was killed in an automobile accident a month later. His brother Henri, today aged thirty-two, proprietor from a base in Nuits-Saint-Georges of his own expanding estate, has taken his place.

THE VINES AND WINE-MAKING

It has been said recently that the Domaine de la Romanée-Conti is run on bio-dynamic lines, or that bio-dynamic trials were being carried out. This is not strictly true: *biologique* (no systematic products, artificial fertilisers or treatments) yes; but *biodynamique* no.

'We want to get the maximum of character and individuality from the soil and from the vine,' I was told on a visit in 1983. As evidence of this, in reaction to the widespread replanting in the early years of this century following the phylloxera epidemic, the owners refused, despite declining yields - in only one vintage during the 1920s did the harvest produce more than 20 hectolitres per hectare, and in 1933 only 6 hl/ha - to plough up the vineyard and plant grafted vines in the Romanée-Conti *climat*. They only finally replanted in 1946 with a *sélection massale* from the old Romanée-Conti rootstocks, still preserved today, and it was not until 1952 that the next harvest appeared under the Domaine de la Romanée-Conti label. Propagation is done using shoots from their own vineyards. Behind the offices, what at first sight seems to be a *potager* turns out on closer inspection to be a field of newly grafted young vine shoots.

The object of the biological approach is to produce a natural equilibrium in the soil, in a way which by itself controls the vigour of the vines. Thus together with an elimination of all but the barest essential in composting and a careful selection of only the best plant-stock and rigorous pruning is a low harvest ensured. Elsewhere, if the harvest looks like being too abundant, some of the young bunches are piteously knocked off. Past experience at the Domaine de la Romanée-Conti has shown that here it is not necessary. Pruning has traditionally been done by women, wives of the cellar-workers; the wife of the late André Noblet, erstwhile cellar-master, who died in 1986, reserving for herself the vineyard of Romanée-Conti itself.

There is a total of twenty-five permanent employees: one per hectare. At the time of the vintage these are naturally supplemented so that there is a team of sixty pickers, enabling the Domaine de la Romanée-Conti to complete its harvest in eight days.

The *rendement* is normally scant - in a region now notorious for over-production. In the twenty years to 1980 40 hectolitres per hectare was reached occasionally (in 1959, 1970, 1972 and 1973), but never surpassed, and the average yield was a mere 30.8 hl/ha. Elsewhere almost half as much would today be the norm. Even in 1989, a prolific vintage, the domaine harvested no more than 32 hl/ha; in 1990 only 30 hl/ha.

The domaine also prides itself on the late date of its picking. This is always at least a week after everyone else has commenced their harvest, often a fortnight. In 1978 the Domaine de la Romanée-Conti did not start until 16 October, after the rest of Burgundy had finished. Before the real harvest commences a *passage de nettoyage* is undertaken. Experienced staff work through the rows of vines cutting out anything substandard. I was in Burgundy with a wine tour at the time of the 1987 harvest, and took them up to worship at Romanée-Conti. The earth was covered in rejected bunches or half bunches of grapes not considered up to scratch.

On arrival at the press house the bunches undergo a *triage*. They are poured on to a conveyor belt, and each is systematically and assiduously picked over to eliminate anything rotten or unripe. This technique was first introduced in 1977, and, though much copied since, was for a long time the only one in Burgundy. 'Only with the finest fruit can you produce the finest wines,' says Aubert de Villaine. Next the bunches, stems and all, are moved into the vats, where the must undergoes a long *cuvaison* - often for as much as a month. Fermentation used to take place at a temperature of between 30 and 32°C; nowadays 29-30 is the norm. The juice from the first pressing is added, and the wine matured entirely in new oak from François Frères in Saint-Romain, increasingly today exclusively from the forests of the Vosges, for sixteen to twenty months before bottling - it used to be longer. The 1990s were bottled in April 1992. One advantage of such a painstaking *triage* is that the wine can be kept on its lees as long as possible. Often there is not a single racking, as in 1979, 1980 and 1981; otherwise one only. If there is a fining, and this also does not always take place, it is done with white of egg; four whites per barrel. Up to 1985 - with the exception of the 1982 - the bottling was straight from the cask, and cask by cask without any prior *égalisage* or filtering, into a special heavy, old-fashioned bottle. Today after a prior *assemblage* of the entire *cuvée* five or six casks at a time are blended before bottling in order to eliminate any minute bottle variations which might occur.

THE WINES

Of the red wines, the two Echézeaux - particularly the Grands-Echézeaux, which is the more expensive of the two - are burly wines. This is not to say they are not ripe and full of fruit, but they can occasionally lack breed, and sometimes the stems are evident. The Romanée-Saint-Vivant - a significant step up - is lighter, softer, much more elegant and more feminine - Musigny in character. There is a higher proportion of marl and clay in the soil. The Richebourg is big, but fat and ripe, and lasts a long time. La Tâche is a classic, but a classic in a Mouton-Rothschild sort of way, that is if Romanée-Conti can be said to be Lafite. The improvement over the Richebourg is immediately apparent. There is more breed, concentration, depth and more density of fruit. It is not merely because the vineyard is older - forty-five years overall as opposed to twenty-eight - simply, the Tâche *terroir* is superior. Finally at the top of the tree - usually, though there are vintages when I prefer La Tâche - is Romanée-Conti itself: a wine of great richness, harmony, concentration and finesse; silk rather than velvet as in La Tâche. Throughout the whole range, but especially in these last two, the glorious, true, clean flavour of the Pinot Noir comes shining through. At their best - and there has been a lot of best in the last decade - these are yardstick examples of all that is glorious about Burgundy.

THE TASTINGS

I sampled the 1994, 1993 and 1992 red wine vintages in Vosne-Romanée in November 1995; the remainder in stages towards the end of 1992.

This is a rather better vintage for the Domaine de la Romanée-Conti than 1992, indeed a conspicuous success. The domaine produced 25 hl/ha.

Optimum drinking

Echézeaux   2000–2008

Surprisingly good colour. Lovely generous oaky nose. Medium-full body. Good grip. Ripe and sophisticated. Good tannins. A substantial example. Fat and succulent at the end. Fine.

Grands-Echézeaux   2002–2012

Splendid colour. Most impressive. Very lovely nose. Marvellous fruit and real class and concentration here. Very, very rich, succulent and abundant. Very good tannins. This is a wine of much more depth, complexity and fruit. Very fine.

Romanée-Saint-Vivant   2002–2012

Excellent colour again. Lovely nose. Really silky complex fruit. Great texture. The attack is fine, the follow-through very good, but lacking just a little fat and grip. But the finish is very long, very opulent, with plenty of depth. Very fine.

Richebourg   2005–2017

Excellent colour again. Marvellous nose. This is very opulent and rich. Very, very lovely and concentrated, with a good new oaky support. A step up. This is absolutely delicious. Marvellous class, intensity and richness. Very, very good grip. Long. Well structured. Even quite powerful. Excellent.

La Tâche   2005–2020

Another very fine colour. This is sturdier, more rigid, less lush in texture on the nose. Very good acidity. A firmer wine. The oak quite present. On the palate this is full and backward, rather more masculine and muscular. Another barrel was more supple. But this is quite solid and quite powerful nonetheless. Rich, fat and intense. Very fine indeed.

Romanée-Conti   2003–2018

Much more delicate, very intense and perfumed fruit. Feminine. Very silky, marvellous class. Exceptional balance. This is very discreet. And this year it really sings. Splendid ripe complex fruit. Very, very long. Subtle and very, very lovely. Top class.

Le Montrachet   2000–2012

Malos very late here, some barrels not yet finished. Lovely rich concentrated nose. Quite a big powerful example. Rich and peachy, fat and oaky. Very good grip. Not a trace of *sur-maturité*. Very fine.

An excellent vintage: lovely pure Pinot fruit, excellent acidities and very sophisticated tannins: 26 hl/ha.

Echézeaux   2002–2015

Fine colour. Lovely rich oaky concentrated nose. On the palate this is structured, masculine, quite tannic but the tannins very ripe and mature. Excellent grip. Lovely and fresh. A mixture of red and black fruits. Fine long succulent finish. Fine quality. Better than usual.

Grands-Echézeaux   2002–2018

Fine colour. Lusher and riper on the nose. More succulent. Well structured but the hard edges are less than the above. Perhaps a little less backbone. Very good acidity. This is a little austere. Fullish, long. Fine as well.

Romanée-Saint-Vivant   2002–2018

Fine colour. Lovely nose. Very poised and elegant. Gently oaky, velvety-smooth, rich wine. Fullish, ripe, very good acidity. Intense and lush and very lovely and complex. Long, subtle, understated. Very, very long. Very fine.

Richebourg   2005–2025

Better colour. This has begun to close in on the nose. Very rich, much fuller and more substantial. But a hint of the stems and of mint today. On the palate this is most impressive. Full, very rich, very youthful. Good tannins and quite a lot of them. A touch of liquorice and coffee. Marvellous fruit. Very good grip. A little more adolescent than the wines above but very delicious. Very fine indeed.

La Tâche   2005–2025

Marvellous colour. Firm nose, but very, very rich. Real finesse here. Aristocratic and very, very concentrated. Full, slightly adolescent but really rich, really profound. A marvellously impressive, old-viney wine on the palate. Real length. Real dimension. This is going to be a *grand vin*.

Romanée-Conti   2005–2025

Marginally less colour. More adolescent on the nose. This is a lighter wine than the Tâche. Less impressive today. Very silky, more feminine, as usual. On the palate softer but equally intense. Very lovely fruit. But it is the Tâche which sings today. Yet this has fabulous fruit and marvellous complexity and class. Also a great wine. But much more subtle.

Le Montrachet   **2002–2015**

Good colour. Very lovely nose. Finely perfumed, very concentrated, very laid-back. Full on the palate. Not a bit heavy or too powerful. Very good intensity. Long. Subtle. Beautifully balanced. A refined complex example. Better than the 1994. Less power, more finesse. Very fine.

1992

Malos were very tumultuous, leading to, initially, colours which were less than expected. But the wines have put on weight and colour since bottling. There is yet more to come, says Aubert de Villaine, who compares them with the 1982s. I find them a bit light, but not short of either complexity or elegance.

Echézeaux   **Now–2003**

Good colour. Soft and fruity on the nose. Shows a touch of the stems. Medium body. Good acidity. This is gentle and composed, rich, naturally sweet. Good grip at the end. Elegant, positive, lacks a bit of strength but certainly very good, and certainly very long on the palate.

Grands-Echézeaux   **1998–2006**

Good colour. Quite a bit fatter on the nose. Medium-full, ripe, spicy. Rather more opulent. Good freshness. Good acidity. This is lush and succulent. Nicely sweet at the end. Very good indeed.

Romanée-Saint-Vivant   **Now–2004**

Good colour. A little closed on the nose. Ripe, medium-bodied wine. This has less weight to it than the Grands-Echézeaux or the Richebourg. But it has good intensity and fruit. A delicate wine. Persistent and complex and elegant nonetheless. Very good indeed.

Richebourg   **1999–2009**

Good colour. Rich, firm, opulent nose with a touch of spice. Fullish, fat, rich and plump. This is more voluminous and has better grip and depth than the Romanée-Saint-Vivant. Lovely fruit. Very well balanced. A concentrated wine. Very fine follow-through. Fine.

La Tâche   **1999–2009**

Good colour. Slightly closed on the nose. The stems show a bit. This is rather more adolescent than the Romanée-Saint-Vivant. Good richness, but more on the follow-through than the attack. Delicate for La Tâche. Best at the end today. Lovely classy fruit. Quite substantial. Sweet very elegant finish. Fine plus.

Romanée-Conti   **2000–2010**

Good colour. Fragrant nose. But a bit light. This again has gone back into its shell. But the fruit is very fine here, and it is balanced with very good acidity. Complex, fragrant, persistent at the end. Really classy finish. Less substance, more nuance and intensity. Complex in texture. Very, very long. Fine plus.

Le Montrachet

Not produced.

1991

It is now apparent that 1991 is a really very good vintage for red Burgundy indeed: better than the 1986 vintage, and more structured than the 1987s. They made 25 hl/ha.

Echézeaux   **1999–2012**

Quite a different kettle of fish to the 1992. Very good colour. Not aggressively stemmy on the nose. Full, rich, meaty. Very good grip. Long and very stylish. Very good indeed.

Grands-Echézeaux   **2000–2015**

Good colour. More closed and unforthcoming. Stems show a bit. More brutal. On the palate fuller, more tannic, more intense and on the finish richer. But more adolescent. Fine long finish. Fine quality.

Romanée-Saint-Vivant   **2000–2015**

Good colour. The nose is elegant and smells of violets and damsons. Medium-full, good tannins. Very lovely complex fruit. Slightly reserved, but a great deal of finesse. Lovely rich oaky finish. Very very long and complex wine.

Richebourg   **1999–2015**

Good colour. Fatter and richer, but slightly less grip. Slightly less concentration. It is most attractive but it lacks a bit of intensity. It doesn't have the fat in the middle. Very good indeed.

La Tâche   **2002–2020**

Fine colour. Here there really is intensity. This is a wine of real power. The nose is closed. The palate shows cassis and plums. Marvellous concentration. Full. Splendid balance. Super. Really excellent. Marvellous finish.

Romanée-Conti   **2000–2015**

After the Tâche this is a bit disappointing. Good colour. Plenty of depth. Rather more adolescent and brutal. Certainly fine. No lack of grip. But it doesn't seem to have the intensity today.

1990

A theatrical vintage: a cathedral full of arch-bishops in their finery. Better than 1988. Mind-blowingly magnificent.

Echézeaux   **2000-2020**
Very good colour. This is still a little bottle-sick on the nose. But after a bit of aeration one could see a lot of plump, ripe fruit. Fullish, good grip. Fat and tannic. But not really on form. The Grands-Echézeaux seems a great deal better.

A second bottle was quite different. Fresher, lovely ripe fruit. Very good.

Grands-Echézeaux   **2001-2025**
Very good colour. A lot of depth and concentration here. More tannic and more austere. Full bodied. Very good ripe tannin. Good grip again, but altogether richer and with more definition. This is very good indeed.

Romanée-Saint-Vivant   **2001-2025**
Medium-full colour. Fine nose. Racy, lacy, intense, individual. Excellent fruit on the palate. Really lovely *petits fruits rouges*. Medium-full. Complex, discreet. Not powerful but very, very intense, long and persistent. Fine.

Richebourg   **2003-2030**
Fine colour. Super-concentrated blackberry fruit on the nose. Very impressive. Full, tannic but very very ripe. Excellent acidity. Fat and really very, very rich. This is a brilliant success this year. Marvellous fat intense long finish. Powerful even. Excellent.

La Tâche   **2005-2035**
Excellent colour. Powerful, closed nose. The brooding giant. This is not necessarily a bigger wine than the Richebourg but one of excellent concentration and great intensity. More powerful, more persistent. A marvellous wine. Well integrated with the oak. *Grand vin*.

Romanée-Conti   **2005-2035**
Fine colour. This is more closed. Marvellous nose. Like the Romanée-Saint-Vivant there is an aspect of alpine flowers. Less powerful, but more intense than La Tâche. Marvellous discreet, very concentrated fruit. Fullish, very very concentrated. Great intensity. Silky smooth potentially. Disarmingly brilliant. *Grand vin* without a doubt. 22 hectolitres per hectare. It shows!

1989

Beginning to close up on the nose – though more expressive on the palate.

Echézeaux   **Now-2012**
Good medium-full colour. Plump, ripe, marvellously strawberry-fruity nose. Fat and accessible. Fullish, abundantly charming. Generous and open.

Grands-Echézeaux   **1998-2012**
Fullish colour. Rather more purple than the above. Firmer, richer and oakier. Rather more depth and complexity. Rather more structured and backward. Fine fruit, raspberries as well as strawberries. Good acidity. Good long finish. Very good.

Romanée-Saint-Vivant   **1998-2012**
Medium-full colour. Little development. Fragrant nose. Lovely fruit and style. A splendid, positive very elegant example. Medium-full. Long. Marvellously balanced. A super result this year.

Richebourg   **1999-2015**
Good colour. Lush, rich, voluptuous on the nose. Fat and plump on the palate. Fullish, tannic. Masculine. Exotic. Very good grip. But perhaps the Romanée-Saint-Vivant is better this year.

La Tâche   **2000-2020**
Good colour. Excellent nose. Very stylish, lovely fruit and balance. This has begun to close in a little and the attack is less definitive than the finish. Long. Fine. Complex. Classy.

Romanée-Conti   **2000-2020**
Good colour. This is considerably superior to La Tâche. Super concentrated fruit. Very lovely balance. Rather more complex and concentrated than the above. Real extract here. Excellent. Marvellous finish.

1988

These have gone into their shell. Excellent quality though: not as good as the 1990s, but better than the 1985s.

Echézeaux   **1998-2015**
Medium-full colour. Fine nose. Round, ripe, slightly aromatic. Gingerbread aspects. Balanced and accessible. Fullish, very concentrated. Excellent acidity. Very good fruit. This is very good indeed. Plenty of backbone and, because of the fruit, not a bit austere.

Grands-Echézeaux   **1999-2018**
Fullish colour. Less accessible. Richer and fuller. But more awkward and adolescent. On the palate fuller and more concentrated. Best on the finish which is long and complex and satisfying. Fine.

Romanée-Saint-Vivant   **1999-2018**

Medium-full colour. Delicately complex, oaky, multi-dimensional nose. This has a lot of intensity. Medium-full body. The oak dominates a little at present. But lots of fruit underneath. Persistent. Lovely.

Richebourg   **2000-2020**

Fullish colour. Very, very rich and plump on the nose. Creamy and velvety. Extremely impressive. Structured, very concentrated, very intense. I prefer this, by quite a lot, to the above. Persistent. Complex. Intense. Very fine indeed.

La Tâche   **2002-2030**

Full colour. Fine nose. Powerfully intense *cassis*, blackberry fruit. Delicious. Much more concentrated than the above. Full bodied. Virile and vigorous. Mineral and disarmingly brilliant. Marvellous richness and balance and complexity. *Grand vin.*

Romanée-Conti   **2002-2030**

Full colour. Lovely nose. Closed but concentrated and aristocratic. Quite full, marvellous balance and intensity of flavour. Good grip. Subtle and complex. Tannic and concentrated and multi-dimensional. Even better. *Grand vin.*

1987

Right from the outset I have found the Domaine de la Romanée-Conti 1987s to have less charm than the 1986s. In the long run they will no doubt turn out better. But today they seem a little austere.

Echézeaux   **Now-2004**

Medium colour. Quite brown at the edge. Fragrant nose. There is some substance and fruit here, but not quite enough to balance the structure. Good grip but a touch bitter. Lacks a little fat and therefore charm. Good but not great.

Grands-Echézeaux   **Now-1999**

Medium colour, with just a suspicion of brown. Soft, succulent, ripe fruit on the nose, with just a hint of the stems. Good cherry-like flavours. Good freshness. But not a lot of weight. Medium to medium-full body. Still a bit raw, even harsh. The tannins still evident. Less robust on the follow-through. Good fruit. Good grip at the end.

Romanée-Saint-Vivant   **Now-2006**

Very developed and already supple nose. This has good fruit; there is succulence here. Stylish, balanced, fragrant. Quite complex. Very good.

Richebourg   **Now-2005**

Medium colour. Quite brown at edges. A little dry on the nose. Not as good as Romanée-Saint-Vivant. The attack is a little hard and although there is more fruit and less astringency on the follow-through the effect is a little vegetal. Lacks a little class as well as fat. A bigger wine than the Echézeaux. Good plus.

La Tâche   **Now-2010**

This is decidedly superior. Much fresher colour. Lovely nose. Much more concentrated fruit and a lot of style. Ripe, oaky. Quite complex. This is medium-full, long, and positive. Not too backward though.

1986

A great success for the domaine: fully mature.

Grands-Echézeaux   **Now-2000 plus**

The colour of this is very similar to the 1987. No undue maturity by any means. A little more developed on the nose than the 1987, in the sense that it is more gamey. But it seems more substantial. Medium to medium-full body, nicely rounded with a hint of spice. I find this more interesting and more elegant than the 1987 today. Good grip. Plenty of dimension on the finish. Very good for a 1986.

Romanée-Saint-Vivant   **Now-2002**

Good mature colour. Slightly cool and austere. Yet a lot of class both on the nose and on the palate. Medium body. A certain dryness as it developed, and the stems showed. But this is only in the middle. The finish was long and complex, and fresh. Very good indeed.

Richebourg   **Now-2004**

Ripe, fat, spicy nose. Good substance here. Rather better than the Romanée-Saint-Vivant. Plenty of depth and attraction. Just about ready. Medium-full body. Just a vestige of unresolved tannin. Positive follow-through. Rich, bramble fruit. Good grip. Quite fat. Will still improve. Shows well.

La Tâche   **Now-2008**

Medium to medium-full colour. Good nose. Rich, ample, potentially velvety. Complex fruit: cherry, mulberry and *cassis*: a lot of nuance. Fine on the palate. Superior in class, depth, size and dimension by some way. Finely balanced. An exciting superior wine. There can't be many better 1986s.

Adolescent. The best wines should not be touched for at least five years. The Domaine de la Romanée-Conti wines have a lot more structure, depth, grip and potential for longevity than most 1985 burgundies.

Grands-Echézeaux   Now-2009

Good colour. Fat, very ripe mulberry fruit on the nose. Still a little reserve on the palate. Good acidity. Medium full. Long and satisfyingly plump and generous. Fine complex finish.

Richebourg   1998-2015

Medium-full colour. Slightly adolescent nose. Touch of green olives, honey and oak as it evolved. Big, fat, rich and ripe. Round and sweet and fragrant and rich. Full, some tannin. Really fine, full, almost voluptuous Pinot Noir fruit. Good grip. A lot of concentration.

La Tâche   1999-2020

Full colour. Similar nose but extra richness and depth and roundness and ripeness on nose. Very fine concentrated fruit. Great concentration of everything. More body, more tannin. Better grip. More closed. Very long and complex on the finish.

Romanée-Conti   1999-2020

Medium-full colour. Less sturdy but greater finesse. Touch of coffee/chocolate. Lafite rather than Mouton. Enormous intensity of flavour without being a blockbuster. Breed here, even delicacy. Marvellous fruit. Again very young. Quite lovely.

1984

A surprisingly good result, showing that location (and expertise) are more important in Burgundy than the vintage.

Echézeaux   Drink soon

Medium colour. Not too brown. Slightly gamey on the nose. But there is fruit here and the wine is still fresh, reasonably plump and interesting. Medium body. Good. Very good for the vintage.

Grands-Echézeaux   Drink soon

Medium-full colour. Fuller, riper nose than the Echézeaux. This is fresh and plump on the palate. Nothing off-vintage about it. Fragrant raspberry fruit. Balanced, stylish, long.

Romanée-Saint-Vivant   Drink soon

Medium-full colour. Not too brown. Softer and more vegetal on the nose. Animal and soft. Ripe and fragrant on the palate. Just a suspicion of age

on the follow-through. Good grip though. Plenty of merit here.

Richebourg   Now-2000

Better colour. Fine nose. Has class and depth. Again this is a positive wine. Slightly bigger and possibly less subtle on the finish. But plenty of ripeness and fruit. Good though.

La Tâche   Now-2000

Medium-full colour. Not too brown. Indeed still vigorous. Good classy plump fruit on the nose. This is ripe and has plenty of interest. This is really astonishingly good for this sad vintage. Very good depth and grip. Long complex ripe finish. Will still last well.

1983

The controversial vintage; unjustly condemned by the ignorant. In some of the wines a hail taint is evident and/or the tannins are rather dry, but only in the Echézeaux and the Romanée-Saint-Vivant does this show – and even in these two it is hard to judge the wines as spoiled. The three top wines are indisputably great. What one has to accept is a completely different flavour than is usual in Burgundy: cooked fruit, roasted nuts, hot chocolate, mushrooms and prunes, and above all, considerable quantities of spice and tannin.

Echézeaux   Now-1999

Medium colour. Mature. Some hail taint still. Not too dirty on the palate, and certainly good concentrated plummy fruit. But a taint of hail unmistakably there. Yet I can enjoy this. Just about ready.

Grands-Echézeaux   Now-2000

Quite a bit fuller and more vigorous colour. Fatter, fuller, a little drier on the attack. Again the taint is there on the attack. But much less so than the above on the finish. Not exactly very elegant though. A little bit bulky. But it will get more appealing as it continues to round off.

Romanée-Saint-Vivant   Drink soon

The colour looks a little old, if anything, now. This is a little more astringent than the two above. Yet riper on the finish. I find this the least agreeable. The most tainted on the follow-through.

Richebourg   Now-2015

Good colour. Youthful, tannic nose. Alcohol shows. Liquorice as it developed. Slightly green twiggy at first but neither hail nor rot. As it evolved became full and plump, but still with a refreshing hint of mint. Full, tannic, masculine. Sturdy. Great richness and very good acidity. Quite a noticeably bigger, more austere, more backward wine than the 1985. Equally as fine - or indeed better: it is a question of taste.

La Tâche   1998-2020
Medium-full colour. Big fat concentrated oaky nose. A lot of concentration. Full and tannic. Still backward if not burly. Big, closed, rich. Lacks a bit of charm but no hail taint. Not the finesse of the 1985 at present but plenty of potential. It is a much fuller, richer wine. Both more austere but eventually more exotic. Very fine indeed.

Romanée-Conti   1998-2020
Slightly more colour. Slightly more vegetal on nose. But marvellous rich plums and blackberry fruit at the same time. This is an exceptionally concentrated wine. No hail taint. Big and full but very very ripe and concentrated. Simply splendid. The masculine answer to the femininity of 1985. Equally good. Even fat on the finish.

1982

Plentiful, generous, *à point*. No great finesse but plenty of enjoyment to be had.

Echézeaux   Now-2000
Slightly better colour than the 1984. Interestingly spicy - cinnamon, allspice, coffee - nose. Rather more oak in evidence than 1984. This has depth and good grip for the vintage. Long and stylish. Ripe.

Grands-Echézeaux   Now-2004
One bottle better than another. A little more backward and seems a shade leaner. There is a certain resinny almost metally bitterness somewhere within. Yet the follow-through is fatter and more concentrated. Good plumpness underneath. Long, ripe, fat. Will develop.

Romanée-Saint-Vivant   See note
Slightly lighter and browner colour. Light fragrant nose and palate. Quite classy but not as much to it. Slight astringency beginning to lurk. This needs drinking soon. (Was this a bad bottle? The same wine at a 1982 Ten Years On tasting in 1992 was much better.)

Richebourg   Now-2005
Medium, mature colour. Ripe, plump quite spicy but slightly loose nose. Better on palate. Ripe and rich and spicy. Medium body. Good depth and balance if not a great deal of class. Ready. Will keep well.

La Tâche   Now-2008
This has the same sort of weight but is much more classy. A little more backward. Indeed could do with a year or two. Long. Quite easily the best. Ripe, concentrated wine with very good depth and grip for the vintage.

1981

Surprisingly fine. A bit lean but certainly classy.

Richebourg   Now-2002
Medium colour. Brown at edges. Broad, quite ripe nose. No meanness. Some maturity now. Medium to medium-full body. Good grip but not lean. Vigorous but the tannins now absorbed. Stylish, ripe, has interest. Excellent for the vintage.

La Tâche   Now-2000
Fuller colour. Medium-full. Similar slight aspect of barley sugar. Richer, fuller but slightly broader, slightly more tannic. But slightly blowsy and open on finish. Good though. Still has length. Better acidity and more to it but slightly less style. Slightly diffuse on the finish.

Romanée-Conti   Now-2008
Slightly less colour than the above. Fuller, richer and more concentrated, surprisingly meaty. Still needs time. Has fruit, concentration and good vigorous structure. Surprisingly good for vintage. Long warm finish.

1979

A much smaller harvest than the 1981 at the domaine. The concentration shows.

Richebourg   Now-2005
Medium colour. Fine mellow oaky nose. Similar palate. Medium-full, just about ready. Quite marked by the oak. Good grip. Ripe, complex. Just about ready. Most attractive. Will keep well. Long, warm finish. Delicious.

La Tâche   Now-2008
Good colour. Ripe, full, *crème brûlée* nose. Fullish, rich, still a little tannin. Only just ready. A touch of tannin. Good ripe acidity. No lack of concentration. Long finish. Rich. Excellent.

Romanée-Conti   Now-2000
Medium-full colour. Sturdier nose. Some tannin. More backward. Full, fat, meaty. Slightly less full but more finesse. Again very fine. Positive and fresh, especially for the vintage. Long, complex, very high class. Excellent.

LE MONTRACHET

I confess to having changed my mind about the Domaine de la Romanée-Conti's Montrachets. They are certainly better than they were: the tendency to being four-square and over-alcoholic, about which I had reservations, has been reduced. The wines now have a lot more breed. And they are equally certainly made to last. Production is very small.

1994   **2003–2012**

Malos very late here, some barrels not yet finished. Lovely rich concentrated nose. Quite a big powerful example. Rich and peachy, fat and oaky. Very good grip. Not a trace of *sur-maturité*. Very fine.

1993   **2002–2012**

Good colour. Very lovely nose. Finely perfumed, very concentrated, very laid-back. Full on the palate. Not a bit heavy or too powerful. Very good intensity. Long. Subtle. Beautifully balanced. A refined complex example. Better than the 1994. Less power, more finesse. Very fine.

1992

Not produced.

1991   **Now–2010**

Light ripe golden colour. On the nose still a little dumb. On the palate good concentration, good personality, good acidity. Certainly very stylish and plenty of interest. But one and half dimensions only. More honeyed as it developed.

1990   **1998–2010**

Deeper colour than the 1989. Rich, full, voluptuous nose. Just a touch heavy after the 1989. Less concentrated. But firm and balanced. Very ripe. Quite powerful. Very good indeed.

1989   **1999–2015**

Mid-gold colour. Lovely nose. Discreetly ripe and concentrated fruit, beautifully balanced on the nose. On the palate a reserved but concentrated wine of great depth and power of flavour. Very fine indeed. A lot of potential here. Best of all on the finish.

GUY ROULOT,
MEURSAULT

Terroir or wine-maker: which exerts - or which *should* exert - the greatest influence? This is a continuing debate. I myself have taken part - at the Oregon Pinot Noir Celebration and elsewhere - in seminars on the subject. If in California and Australia, where sometimes wine-makers change positions like football super-stars, some give exaggerated importance to the individual, in Burgundy you will find most *vignerons* consider the land the crucial factor. This is only natural. If there *isn't* an essential difference between Genevrières and Perrières, why vinify and bottle them apart?

For proof of the French viewpoint you only have to look at the Domaine Guy Roulot in Meursault. Not only does it produce seven different Meursaults, only two of which are *premiers crus* - and they are all indeed different, the same characters in each being discernible whatever the vintage - but it has had four different wine-makers in the last fifteen years; and the effect of this in the wine is much harder to uncover. The wines also, as it happens, are extremely good.

HISTORY

There have been, at the very least, five generations of Roulots in Meursault, the earliest traceable being Guillaume, registered as a *viticulteur* in 1830. But primarily, in those far-gone days, they were distillers and millers. The milling activities were given up towards the end of the century, but the distilling continued, Paul Roulot, grandfather of Jean-Marc, today's wine-maker, buying new premises for this process on the road to Auxey near the *tonnellerie* Damy shortly after the First World War. This Roulot also bought some vines in the *climat* of Meix-Chavaux at this time, and though originally he worked for a local merchant called Giraud, little by little, as he built up his domaine - some derelict land in the Charmes, for instance, at the end of the 1930s - he became self-supporting. Paul Roulot died in 1976.

It was his son Guy, though, who really created today's 11.4 hectare Domaine Roulot. He had the fortune to marry a Coche (Geneviève Roulot is a first cousin of Alain Coche) and from this side came the Meursault, Tillets, the Auxey-Duresses, Les Duresses, the Monthélie and the Bourgogne Aligoté. Guy Roulot bought some Luchets and the Tessons at the end of the 1950s, more Luchets in 1975, and shared a parcel of Meursault, Perrières with Pierre Matrot, a great friend, in the following year. Meanwhile the couple had produced two children - Michèle in 1951 and Jean-Marc in 1955 - and moved into their existing house in the Rue Charles Giraud in 1963. Guy Roulot was one of the first to consider separately vinifying and bottling not just his *premiers crus* but his other Meursaults, all of which come from the slopes in the same line as first growths, and which in pre-AC times were regarded as *deuxièmes crus*.

Tragically Guy Roulot died in 1982 at the early age of fifty-three. The natural successor was Jean-Marc, then aged twenty-seven, but he had another career, that of classical actor, and was naturally reluctant to give it up. Ted Lemon, a Californian at the time learning his *métier* in Burgundy (and today wine-maker at Château Woltner) took over for a couple of years, and made the 1983 and 1984. On his departure a cousin, Franck Grux, now wine-maker at Olivier Leflaive Frères, was appointed. Franck made the next four vintages. Finally, in October 1988, Jean-Marc Roulot decided to return to Meursault. He has since expanded the domaine further into Monthélie (there is now some *premier cru blanc* Les Champs-Fulliot). And in September 1994 he married Alix, daughter of Hubert de Montille of Volnay.

THE DOMAINE

The Roulot domaine owns vineyards in two of the greatest Meursault *climats*: 28 ares of fifty-two-year-old vines in Charmes, but right down on the lowest slopes of this vineyard; and 26 a of thirty-year-old vines in Perrières. There are five Meursault '*deuxièmes crus*': 49 ares of Tillets, which lies above Poruzots and Gouttes d'Or (the vines are relatively young here, dating from 1974); 67 a of Vireuils, further along towards the commune boundary with Auxey-Duresses; 85 a of Tessons, lower down, dating from 1959 and 1961; 1.03 ha of Luchets, again under the Vireuils; and finally, adjacent, 95 a of Meix-Chavaux. Here the oldest vines date from 1929, and will be replanted soon. There is village Auxey and *premier cru* Les Duresses and Grands-Champs (71 a, 32 a and 41 a respectively, all planted in Pinot Noir. This is leased *en métayage* to the Guidot family). In Monthélie there is village red and the *premier cru* white, already referred to (both young vines); and finally Aligoté, Bourgogne *blanc* and Bourgogne *rouge*.

VITICULTURE AND WINE-MAKING

Almost the entire estate is trained Guyot - there is a little Cordon - and it is all ploughed and hoed: no herbicides are used. The harvest is restrained by the removal of excess buds and double shoots, rather than by recourse to green harvesting, and there is a severe *triage* at the time of the harvest. All in all the estate and its vines are kept in meticulous order.

In 1987 the Roulot domaine acquired a pneumatic press, giving Jean-Marc even more control of the wine-making process. Since 1993, the *cave*, which is not normally excessively cool, has been *climatisée*. This may eventually lead to a change in the length of time the wine is kept in wood before it is bottled. Hitherto the Roulot domaine has always bottled after eleven months, just prior to the next harvest. Jean-Marc would like to keep the *premiers crus* longer, up to eighteen months, but as the cellar can rise to 16°C in the summer, fears that this would not work. I point out that the extra six months are winter, not summer months. He is thinking of doing some trials.

All the white wines except for the Aligoté are entirely fermented in wood, and there is now 20-30 per cent new, mainly from the Allier for the whites (though from the Vosges for the red wines). This is a little less new wood than in Franck Grux's time. The must is cooled if necessary at first so that the fermentation begins at 16°C.

Unlike some, Jean-Marc is not a great believer in *bâtonnage*. 'It does, I admit, create richness, but it also creates heaviness, and one loses purity.' Purity is something he feels very strongly about. 'I prefer to lose a little volume and power on the palate in order to obtain the *ligne droite* and the purity. What I like - and in red wines as well as in white - is that when one noses the wine one gets an idea of what is to follow on the palate. I consider it essential that there is a correspondence between the one and the other. So I give the wines a gentle *bâtonnage* only once a fortnight, and only at the beginning. To get the most elegant, most profound wines one should stir up less, and even be prepared to accept a wine which at the outset seems lighter, less fat and exotic.'

On the other hand Jean-Marc does consider the lees important. There is one racking of the wine, after the malo, but then the wine, having been unified, goes back into barrel on its lees.

The fining agent is another thing this quietly passionate man has put under his microscope. Having done trials he is convinced that for some of his wines fish fining is superior to casein, bentonite and the rest. The aromas are finer. But, curiously, it works for some but not for others. The Meix-Chavaux, the Luchets and the Charmes for instance, rounder and richer wines, turn out better if fined with casein.

THE WINES

There are not many top-quality *caves* where, as here, one gets the chance to compare such a wine range of the second division of the Meursault *climats*.

In the Vireuils, land they farm *en métayage* from Abel Garnier, I find a peachy fruit. It is a racy wine: a good example. The Meix-Chavaux has more structure, is plumper and fatter. You can see that it comes from lower down the slope. This is a nutty wine, sometimes with a honeysuckle flavour. It has more depth. Luchets, which lies in between has the advantages of both, and is yet better. Roulot's is a lovely example.

The Tillets is the most original of all the five '*deuxièmes crus*' in this cellar, for the *climat* lies away from the rest. But the vines' age is younger. In a vintage such as 1992 this did not matter too much, though I preferred the Luchets, but in 1993, for example, the wine seemed a little thin. There is a mineral, flowery raciness here. It can only get better as the vines get older.

Best of all, however, is the Tessons. Here, like the Luchets, we are in mid-slope. And in Roulot's hands we have wine of really serious *premier cru* quality, as the tasting notes which follow will show. Depth, balance, breed: it's all here. It's the slowest to evolve, needing seven years in the best vintages.

Roulot buys casks with a slightly higher toast for his Charmes, deliberately to match and differentiate what he considers a rich wine from a rich soil. What this means, when you sample the Charmes after the Tessons out of cask, is that you are in for a shock. The Tessons is closed in, restrained, aloof. The Charmes is open and exuberant, oaky and peachy, much more accessible. But it is, ultimately, also the better wine, as it should be.

But best of all is the Perrières, as is also logical: firmer, steelier, more closed-in, more mineral, but with greater finesse, more definition, more dimension. All in all, a splendid end to a fine sequence of wines: impressive quality, and wines which keep well.

THE TASTING

I sampled the following wines *chez* Roulot in June 1994.

MEURSAULT, TESSONS

Optimum drinking

1992   **Now–2007**

Quite rich and fat on the nose but a touch closed. More accessible on the palate. Ample, rich, good grip. Certainly very stylish. Medium-full. Good melon, apricot and honeysuckle fruit. Long. Elegant. Very good. Has begun to close in.

1991   **Now–2003**

Delicate, flowery, stylish nose. This is surprisingly racy for a 1991. Harmonious. Very good fruit. But a gentle example. Long on the palate. Very good indeed for the vintage. Very stylish and complex.

1990   **Now–2010**

This is a bit adolescent on the nose. Took a bit of time to come out. Yet even then not lacking a little heaviness. Better on the palate. Full, rich, plenty of fruit. A touch rigid. But good grip. The finish is better than the attack. Good depth. Complex. Masculine. Quite powerful. But difficult to see the elegance. On evolution and aeration after half an hour I preferred this to the 1987.

1989   **Now–2009**

Open, plump, flowery nose. Not a bit adolescent. Very classy. Full, intense and very complex. For some reason just a touch more wood. But a lovely ample rich wine. Very very subtle, fresh and harmonious. Long, lovely, delicious. Excellent.

1988   **Now–1999**

This is quite a bit more evolved than the wines above. A little flat on the nose. A bit fresher on the palate. Quite lush and fruity but at the end it lacks a bit of elegance, and dimension too. OK but not special. The least good of the last ten vintages.

1987   **Now–2000**

The nose is much fresher than the above, and I prefer the wine's style on the palate. More austere. Quite complex. A fine example for the vintage. This is balanced and stylish. Good long positive finish. Most enjoyable.

1986   **Now–2003**

No undue colour here. Honeyed and fresh, but not over-evolved. Nevertheless it lacks a little zip. On the palate beeswaxy. Some age, just a touch heavy. And the end is a touch flat. Evolved quite quickly in the glass. Full but not exactly very harmonious, nor very classy. Naturally very high in alcohol – more than 14° – and one can see this on the finish. Rather a hot end to it. Second worst wine of the decade. Not really my style. Did not last in the glass.

1985   **Now–2015**

Good fresh colour. Fine nose. Full, concentrated, just a slight vegetal touch – but in a good sense. Rich. Complex. This is full and firm on the palate. Just a little solid and rigid at first, but it evolved well. The follow-through is balanced and ample. A lot of wine here; and one for food. Will still improve. Rich and oaky and very complex as it evolved. Fine.

1984   **Drink soon**

A little more colour. Gentle nose. No lack of fruit. Even elegance. Not a bit faded or sour. Plenty of fruit and life on the palate. This is better than Roulot's Perrières. Still fresh. Medium body. An elegant wine. Plenty of attraction here. Surprisingly good. Finishes ripe and long.

1983   **Now–2000 plus**

This is a fat, rich, honeyed wine with high alcohol, but though 14.5° and with certainly an element of *sur-maturité*, it is not too heavy. Full bodied, yes; and certainly a wine for food, like the 1985. Rich on the finish, very ample; a touch rigid. But very good. Much better than the 1986. But, as always, atypical.

1979   **Now–2000**

Very fresh colour. Lovely fresh, slightly herbal, complex nose. Finesse here. Round, gently oaky, very stylish fruit. Ripe and even honeyed. But very lovely balance. Great purity here. Definitive. Very fine. Still bags of life. Still very vigorous. Delicious.

1978   **Now–2000**

Magnum. A touch more colour. A bit more age, a bit more structure, a bit more rigidity. But a lot of interest on the nose. A touch of *sous-bois* wood. Fullish, meaty. A little more vegetal and solid. Needs food. More wine here than the 1979, but less style.

1976   **Drink soon**

Magnum. Good colour. Fresh, youthful, rich but not a bit heavy. Very good fruit, not a bit over-ripe. Harmonious. But not quite as good on the palate. A little heavy. A little four-square. A little alcoholic. Yet fresh. Much better than most. Still positive. Still enjoyable.

1973   **Drink soon**

Some development on the colour. But not too old. Nice touch of fresh honeycomb on the nose. Very complex, fresh and delicious. On the palate soft, complex, feminine. Evolved but really elegant. A medium-bodied supple wine. Surprisingly fresh. Excellently balanced. Very fine. Lovely finish. Very long, even complex. Held up well in the glass.

1971   **See note**

Much older colour than the 1973. Old and gently honeyed on the nose. But a little maderised and oxidised. Not too bad on the palate. It has loosened and shortened but not coarsened. But really a little past its best. Are other bottles fresher?

1966   **Will still keep well**

Magnum. Fullish colour. Highish acidity. Slightly austere and just a little mineral, even herbal on the nose. Expanded considerably in the glass. Very elegant. Very complex. A full wine with a lot of concentration. On the palate this is very lovely. Rich and velvety and complex. Very good grip. Extremely fresh. Held up very very well. Indeed got better and better.

GEORGES ROUMIER,
CHAMBOLLE-MUSIGNY

For Chambolles with a difference – wines which are substantial, even sturdy, as well as velvety and elegant – the best source is the Roumier domaine: to be precise, because there is another in the village, the Domaine Georges Roumier. This is one of the longest-established estate-bottling domaines in the Côte d'Or, and one of the very best of all.

HISTORY

The nucleus of this domaine lies in the dowry of Geneviève Quanquin, who married Georges Roumier in 1924. Georges came from Dun-les-Places, in the Charolais cattle country near Saulieu. When he arrived in Chambolle he took over the Quanquin family vineyards, enlarged the exploitation by taking on a small part of Musigny *en métayage* and buying additional land in the commune, and set up on his own, independent of his parents-in-law, who also had a *négociant* business. (This ceased to exist after the Second World War.)

The domaine was further enlarged in the 1950s. More Bonnes-Mares, from the Domaine Belorgey, arrived in 1952. Two parcels of Clos-de-Vougeot were added in the same year. And in 1953 the 2.5 ha *monopole* of the *premier cru* Clos-de-la-Bussière in Morey-Saint-Denis was acquired from the Bettenfeld family. In the 1930s this parcel had belonged to the Graillet estate, the residue of which was subsequently to form the base of the Domaine Dujac.

Georges and Geneviève had seven children, five of them boys, and I get the feeling he must have been a bit of a martinet, not willing to let go of the reins. In 1955, Alain, the eldest son, left to take up the position of *régisseur* for the neighbouring De Vogüé domaine. Another son, Paul, became a *courtier*. Jean-Marie, the third, did not play a part in the domaine until his father retired in 1961 (Georges died in 1965). In this year, wishing to keep the domaine intact, the brothers formed a limited company for their inheritance, which together with the sisters' holdings, was rented to the domaine. Since his retirement from De Vogüé Alain has retrieved his share, these vineyards now being exploited separately by his son Hervé.

Today the wine-maker at the Domaine Georges Roumier is the thirty-six-year-old Christophe, son of Jean-Marie. Christophe was born in 1958, studied oenology at Dijon University, did a *stage* at the excellent Cairanne co-operative in the Côtes-du-Rhône in 1980, and joined his father the year after. The wines were fine in Georges and Jean-Marie's time. They have reached even greater heights under the aegis of Christophe.

More recently there have been three significant additions to the Roumier portfolio. In 1977, when the Thomas-Bassot domaine was being sold, a substantial slice of Ruchottes-Chambertin came on the market. Two parcels were quickly snapped up by Charles Rousseau and Dr Georges Mugneret. The third was acquired by a businessman and oenophile from Rouen, one Michel Bonnefond. At Rousseau's suggestion Bonnefond entered into a *métayage* arrangement with the Roumiers, and Christophe now gets two-thirds of the yield of this 0.54 ha parcel.

In the following year, Jean-Marie Roumier finally managed to buy the parcel of Musigny - just under one-tenth of a hectare; it only produces a cask and a half - which the family had been share-cropping since the 1920s.

Seven years later, in 1984, a French *négociant* in Lausanne, Jean-Pierre Mathieu, bought a small section (0.27 ha) of Mazoyères-Chambertin. This again is rented *en métayage* to Christophe Roumier. The financial arrangements are a little different here, and Roumier only gets half of the crop - which, like most Mazoyères, is labelled as Charmes, a name easier to pronounce and sell.

Somewhat earlier than this, back in 1968, Christophe's mother, Odile Ponnelle, bought a parcel of land, *en friche*, on the Pernand-Vergelesses side of Corton-Charlemagne, up under the Bois de Corton. The land was cleared and replanted, the first vintage being 1974. It is delicious, but there is little of it: three *pièces* from 0.2 ha.

THE VINEYARDS

The heart of the 12.6 hectare Roumier domaine, as always, lies in Chambolle-Musigny. A number of parcels in the village, comprising a total of 6.8 ha, and including some *premier cru* Les Cras and some Fuées which is not *premier cru* but is likely to be so some day, produce a splendid village wine. There are originally six *cuvées* of this, eventually blended together, and within this wine will be the yield of some old vines of Pinot Beurot, a sort of Pinot Gris, the residue of the old days when a few white vines were planted in with the red in nearly every Burgundian *climat* to add balance and complexity to the wine.

On the other side of the village, just under the northern end of Le Musigny, there is 0.4 ha of Amoureuses, Chambolle's finest *premier cru*. This plot was planted in three stages, in 1954, 1966 and 1971. The vines in the parcel of Musigny itself, lying nearby, date from 1934.

Roumier's most important wine, though, is not this Musigny - or not always - but the Bonnes-Mares. (A *pièce* and a half is difficult to vinify. And though Christophe considers Musigny in principle the grandest *grand cru* in the Côte d'Or he finds the results of his Musigny less regular.) There are four parcels of Bonnes-Mares, one currently naked awaiting replanting, all in the Chambolle part of this *grand cru*, totalling 1.45 ha.

There are two distinct soil types in Bonnes-Mares. At the Morey end the soil is *terres rouges*. But, coming down the slope in a diagonal line from above the Clos-de-Tart and continuing south towards Chambolle the soil changes to *terres blanches* (if you look carefully you will see a large quantity of small fossilised oysters) and this makes up most of the *climat*. Three of Christophe Roumier's parcels are *terres blanches*, one *terres rouges*. He normally vinifies them separately and blends them together afterwards. What is the difference? The *terres rouges* gives the power, the backbone, the concentration, says Christophe. Wine from the *terres blanches* is more spiritual. From here we get the finesse, the intensity, the definition. But a blend is yet greater than the sum of the parts.

Below the northern, Morey, end of the vineyard and the Clos-de-Tart the land sinks into a hollow as it comes down the slope (this is the *premier cru* of Ruchot) and then rises up a little. Here we find the enclosed vineyard of Bussière. In a house in the middle live Jean-Marie Roumier and his wife.

Finally there is the Clos-de-Vougeot. Originally there were two parcels, vinified together and both sold under the Georges Roumier label. After 1984, the upper part was taken back by Alain and Hervé Roumier, leaving 32 ares in the lower part of the *climat*. It is certainly a good wine. But in Christophe Roumier's view: 'It is not really of *grand cru* quality.'

VITICULTURE AND WINE-MAKING

'We don't make Pinot Noir,' Christophe Roumier is quoted as saying (*The Great Domaines of Burgundy*, Remington Norman), 'we make wines from *terroir* which expresses itself through Pinot Noir.' There is a lot more to fine wine than merely the variety it is made from. Roumier sees his role as an intermediary, as a facilitator. The *vigneron's* duty is to allow the vines to produce fruit which, when vinified, will be unmistakably typical of its origins. The wine-maker's job is to effect this translation from fruit into wine. But it is a question of control rather than creativity. The creation is being done by the vine, by its location, by mother nature: not by man.

Along with most of the progressives in the region Christophe Roumier has turned his back on weedkilling sprays, preferring to plough the vines. This is sometimes difficult where a vineyard has not been cultivated for some time, as important roots may be cut in the process. But an ancillary benefit where it is done is that the roots are encouraged to penetrate deeper.

The average age of the vines in the Roumier domaine is high, but they don't make a fetish of it. Once a parcel has reached, say, fifty years old, individual vines are not replaced as they die off. So eventually, as currently in one part of their Bonnes-Mares, the whole parcel can be cleared, the land disinfected against viral contamination, and eventually replanted. At first the young vines are Cordon trained, when their youthful vigour has died down this is replaced by the traditional Guyot method.

Pruning is severe, and the harvest is further contained by an elimination of excess buds and shoots during the spring. This is much more effective, says Christophe, than a green harvest later in the season. By then it is too late, he maintains, though he admits he had to do it in 1986. But he has no time for those who have to do it every year. It shows they didn't restrict the crop properly in the first place. This discipline is reflected in the Roumier harvest: 41 hl/ha in village wine, 34 in *premier cru*, 30 in *grand cru* in 1992, elsewhere a very large harvest. This is the key, says Christophe, to the production of great wine.

The next part of the jigsaw is the quality of the fruit. Trials have convinced Christophe that the ratio of leaves to fruit, and their exposure, is critical. So he prefers a large canopy, trained a little higher than some, at least during the early part of the season. It is also important, he believes, to eliminate the second generation of fruit, the *verjus*.

There is a careful *triage*, both in the vineyard and later when the fruit arrives in the *cuverie* up at the top of the village, but a flexible attitude to the quantity of the stems which are kept. In 1983 the harvest was entirely destemmed; in 1985 and 1986 not at all. Usually at least 20 per cent of the stems are retained. The wine is vinified in open-top wood, concrete or enamelled-steel vats. The first two materials are preferable, says Christophe, for the heat generated by the fermentation is slower to dissipate.

Fermentations at the Roumier domaine begin slowly, so there is always a brief period of pre-fermentation maceration. Thereafter, Christophe likes to prolong the extraction, maintaining the temperature just under 30°C, as long as possible. The temperature level is one of the wine-maker's most important points of intervention, Christophe believes. It should not go too high, for you begin to lose the subtleties of the aromas above 33°C.

As you would expect from the Roumier approach to *terroir*, this is a domaine which does not approve of a lot of new oak. 30 per cent is about maximum. 'I want to taste the wine, not the cask,' says Christophe, pointing out that new wood is the best mask for wine faults. The wine is kept on its lees until racking the following September, fined with one egg white only per *pièce*, and not filtered unless absolutely necessary. The 1989s and 1992s were bottled after fifteen to sixteen months, but normally bottling takes place later, between April and June of the following year.

THE WINES

Christophe Roumier is refreshingly open about the quality of his wines. I have referred already to his view on his Clos-de-Vougeot and to the irregularity of the Musigny as a direct consequence of the size of the *cuvée*. 'It should be the best, but it isn't always.' In principle, he will tell you, Mazis, in the line of Chambertin and Clos-de-Bèze, should be better than Ruchottes. It gets more sun later in the evening in September. The reason Ruchottes has the higher reputation, I suggest to him, is that the three most important producers, Rousseau, the Mesdames Mugneret and himself, are all highly competent wine-makers, while in Mazis there are a dozen or so, some good, some less so. The real Charmes, Christophe will also insist, is a better *terroir* than that of the Mazoyères.

The Roumier range begins with the Corton-Charlemagne. The vines are now of a respectable age, and since 1985, at the very least, have been producing wine of really top quality. This vintage, 1990, and especially 1992 are the plums, the 1989 marginally disappointing in the context, but even 1991, even 1988, even indeed the now tired 1987, are, or were, very good.

The reds, as I have said, are more muscular than most: full, virile, austere, made to last; not necessarily wines which sing in their youth. Time is required - a decade for the best wines in the best vintages. The series begins with a Bourgogne *rouge* (2 ha). This is a sturdy example, but none the worse for that, even in 1992 it had good structure and good acidity. The village

Chambolle follows next. It is a bigger wine than those of Ghislaine Barthod or De Vogüé, and it takes longer to open out. But there is no lack of finesse, no lack of Chambolle fragrance. The Morey, Clos-de-la-Bussière is firmer and chunkier, with a touch of the rustic about it. Again it lasts well.

You will usually be offered – wine-makers normally giving you the wines to taste in their order of preference – the Clos-de-Vougeot next, before the Amoureuses. And it is certainly true that the latter is the finer wine. The Clos-de-Vougeot is not the very best example of this *grand cru* available in Burgundy, but it is by no means the worst. It is plump but just a little four-square. That bit of sparkle which elevates a wine from the merely very good to the fine or great is not there. The *terroir* is simply not good enough. The Chambolle-Musigny, Les Amoureuses, though, is delicious. Here we really do find distinction and class, as well as the supreme fragrance of the commune. It is a fitting example of the village's greatest *premier cru*. In Roumier's hands clearly a wine of *grand cru* quality.

The next two wines in the range are from the *climats* in Gevrey that Christophe farms *en métayage*, the Charmes and the Ruchottes. The latter is clearly finer than the former – indeed I rate the Amoureuses better than the Charmes – and it can be the best wine in the Roumier cellar. Perhaps it is in 1992. Here we have intensity as well as weight and richness, the lush flamboyance of Gevrey-Chambertin, and all the finesse you would expect in top-quality Burgundy.

The Bonnes-Mares, by contrast, is always much more closed-in; somewhat solid at the outset, much less expressive. It seems to go through more of an adolescent phase, and it is only on the finish – but of course, when a wine is young, the finish is what you should concentrate on – that you can see the breed, the complexity and the depth. Is this Burgundy's best Bonnes-Mares? It needs at least a decade to come round.

When the Musigny is good – and it usually is – it is brilliant. It has less backbone than the Bonnes-Mares, less density. But it can be equally backward, needing just as much time to come round. Sometimes, as I suspect in 1991, the Bonnes-Mares has more concentration and a better balance. Sometimes, as perhaps in 1992, the reverse is the case. It is a pity there is so little of it.

In sum, this is one of Burgundy's greatest domaines and Christophe Roumier is one of its most intelligent and knowledgeable wine-makers. The combination of the two produces magic.

THE TASTING

I sampled the following range of wines in Chambolle-Musigny in February 1994.

Corton-Charlemagne, 1992   *Optimum drinking*   **2000–2020**
  Infanticide. But a great wine. Marvellously clean and crisp. Fine grip. Yet underneath very concentrated, very subtle and laid back. Marvellous concentrated fruit. Beautifully balanced. Enormous class. Brilliant!

Corton-Charlemagne, 1991   **Now–2006**
  Ripe, just slightly on the heavy side. Aromatic. On the palate rather more elegant. Rich, gently oaky. Classy. Medium-full. Fine positive finish. Very good indeed.

Corton-Charlemagne, 1990   **1998–2014**
  This is very closed-in on the nose. But round and ripe and sexy on the palate if without the concentration and intensity of the 1992. Fullish, balanced, classy. Lovely and round and succulent at the end. It is not a particularly steely Corton-Charlemagne. Yet very fine and complex and very long.

Corton-Charlemagne, 1988   **Now–2008**
  Nicely austere. Rich, closed and backward. This has real class. Good grip. Mineraly. Virile. More typically Charlemagne. This is not as complex as the 1990 but nevertheless very good indeed.

Bonnes–Mares, 1992   **1998–2008**
  Good colour. Gently oaky. Rich, balanced and certainly very concentrated. A lovely fat, medium-full wine. Velvety. Accessible and immediately attractive. Really classy. Lovely long lingering finish. A very fine 1992.

Chambolle-Musigny, Les Amoureuses, 1991
          Now-2005

8 hl/ha. This was where the hail hit most. Very good colour. Touch of chocolate and almost pine-resin on the nose. A little pinched. Medium-full body. Some tannin. This has reasonable acidity but it lacks a bit of generosity. It is a little tough and over-extracted. A touch dry and disagreeable at present. Will get better as it rounds off. Only 'good' though.

Ruchottes-Chambertin, 1991   **Now-2010**

Slightly less colour. 22 hl/ha. Full, rich, masculine nose. Nicely austere. Very good grip. This is fullish, has a lot of attraction and concentration and is very long and stylish on the finish. Blackberry and black plums all the way through. Fine.

Bonnes-Mares, 1991   **1999-2014**

Very good colour. 14/15 hl/ha. A more structured, more backward wine than the Ruchottes. Full, rich and masculine again. But more tannin evident. More concentration and a better grip though. Firmer and more closed but the follow-through shows real breed and depth. Very long on the finish. A little adolescent. Lovely complexity. Very fine indeed.

Musigny, 1991   **Now-2014**

Extremely good colour. Even better than the Bonnes-Mares. 20 hl/ha. Little hail. Very lovely fruit on the nose. A certain amount of tannin on the attack, but does it quite have the concentration of the Bonnes-Mares? Is the grip of the above better? Fullish. Classy. Very fine. Indeed lovely. But not quite as good.

Bonnes-Mares, 1990   **2000-2025**

Splendid colour. Enormous depth and concentration but has really gone into its shell now. This really is a wine of power. Yet nevertheless despite the size a richness and generosity are apparent. Very full. Splendidly ripe tannins. Almost sweet in its fruit. Fine grip. This is less adolescent than the 1991. Excellent finish. *Grand vin*!

Bonnes-Mares, 1989   **Now-2012**

Quite full colour. Much more red fruits on the nose. And much less backward and structured. Medium-full. Abundantly ripe. Good acidity. Quite round. Still just a little raw, rather than very tannic. Outclassed by both 1990 and 1988 but still very good indeed. Long if not very fat and concentrated.

Bonnes-Mares, 1988   **1998-2015**

Full colour. This is very lovely on the nose. Very ripe and concentrated. Very lovely ripe fruit and very good grip. So a lot of style and finesse. At present, especially after the 1990, the attack is a little austere. But fullish, balanced, very very long and classy. Very good acidity. Just needs time. Fine.

Bonnes-Mares, Vieilles-Vignes, 1988 1999-2020

This year Christophe didn't make *terres blanches* and *terres rouges cuvées* but old and young vines. Slightly less colour than the above. Slightly less evolved but much more intense and classy. The nose is brilliantly complex. On the palate just a little fuller. A little more concentrated and tannic. Above all more finesse and intensity. Marvellous finish. A classic! *Grand vin*!

Bonnes-Mares, 1987   **Now-1999**

Medium colour. Now just about mature. Interesting nose. Some structure and a little caramel shows. But not a lot of real finesse. Medium-full. Fresh. Quite balanced, but a certain hard edge from attack to end. Lacks a little charm. Not as good as the 1986. Quite good.

Bonnes-Mares, 1986   **Now-2000 plus**

Fresher colour. More depth. Less evolution. Rather better than the 1986. Round, plump, cherries and raspberries. A lot of attractive fruit here and no lack of freshness. Quite full. Plenty of weight. Even some grip. Generous open fruit, not too sweet. Very good positive finish. Complex. Long. Unexpectedly good. Most seductive. Very good plus.

Bonnes-Mares, 1985   **1999-2015**

Full, fresh colour. No real sign of maturity. Closed on the nose. Rather dominated by the stems (only 25 per cent *éraflé*). Yet on the palate full, rich, concentrated, ample. Very good grip. This is adolescent but will be fine in five years. Long and stylish. Needs time. On aeration improved considerably. I think this is rather better than the 1989. Good grip. Fine plus?

Bonnes-Mares, 1984   **Drink up**

Lightish colour. But not old or weedy. Evolved fast in the glass. At first fresh and enjoyable. Not too lean. But got a little weedy. It seems dilute as well as unripe. Not special. Drink up.

Bonnes-Mares, 1983   **Now-2000 plus**

Fullish colour. Mature but not unduly so. Full, rich, spicy, animal, slightly caramelly on the nose. As always the dry tannic attack, with its own slightly curious funky taste. Yet full and rich. Not too dry on the follow-through. Good grip. Positive, rich, concentrated finish. Fresh. Just about ready. Better with food. Fine.

Bonnes-Mares, 1982   **Now-1999**

Medium to medium-full colour. Still fresh though never very deep. Mature but not unduly so. Fresh and plump and attractive. Medium-full, very well balanced, fruity and not at all without complexity, class and dimension. A fine 1982. Can still be kept. Very good.

Bonnes-Mares, 1981   **Drink soon**

Similar weight of colour. A bit more age, a little lighter. This I find rather better than the 1984. One dimension, of course, but fresh and positive. No undue age. There is plenty of enjoyment here. Not too weak or attenuated by a long way. Medium body. Quite good.

Bonnes-Mares, 1980   **Now-2000 plus**

Again a very similar colour, especially to the 1982. Fresh on the nose. Still youthful. Fuller, richer, classier and with more dimension and depth than the 1982. Really quite concentrated. Once again a proof of how good these top Côte-de-Nuits are in this vintage. Balanced and complex. Long and still very vigorous. Very good finish. Very good indeed.

Bonnes-Mares, 1978   **Now-2000 plus**

Medium-full mature colour. This is at first a little hard on the nose. More destemming than the 1985, but nevertheless a little more vegetal/herbal than fruity at first. On the palate though, ripe and balanced and succulent. Good acidity. Just a slight lack of fat and generosity. And perhaps not an enormous amount of finesse. Long, nevertheless. Vigorous. Very good indeed. But the 1985 is better.

Bonnes-Mares, 1959   **Now-2000 plus**

This has an incredible vigour. Splendid colour. Full, rich, meaty nose. Still quite full and still very very young. Fat, ripe, very concentrated. Almost sweet. This is very lovely. Generous and rich and balanced and very very long and stylish. Very fine indeed. One of the best 1959s I have had for ages. And bags of life. *Grand vin*!

ARMAND ROUSSEAU, GEVREY-CHAMBERTIN

There are few finer domaines in the Côte d'Or than that of Armand Rousseau. With land in Le Chambertin itself, Chambertin, Clos-de-Bèze, Mazis, Chapelle, Clos-Saint-Jacques and Cazetiers, all in Gevrey, as well as in Clos-de-la-Roche in Morey-Saint-Denis, this 14 hectare estate can boast some of the finest sites in the northern part of the Côte. The vines are old, the *rendement* low, and the wine-making perfectionist – and the wines themselves are stunning.

Charles Rousseau himself – he took over on his father's death in a car accident in 1959 – is one of nature's gentlemen. Small, ebullient and shrewd, he is generous with his time and his willingness to impart information. He has the refreshing ability to be dispassionate about the quality of both his own and his neighbours' wines. He will admit that there were problems with rot in 1983, and that as a result of a strange bacteria or enzyme in his cellar, his 1978s and 1979s are not up to scratch. This openness, this honesty, though now on the increase, especially among the younger generation, is rarer than one might think. A grower's wines are as precious and as personal as his own children. Criticise them and you wound the proprietor himself. I remember a day I received a rather aggrieved letter from an important French *personnage*. I had written that I had found his 1988s disappointing. He thought that it was presumptuous of me to have said so. But someone, I could have replied, must tell the emperor that he has no clothes on.

ARMAND ROUSSEAU

Armand Rousseau, Charles' father, was a wine-broker before the First World War. He lived in Gevrey and was a middle-man between his neighbours, the local growers, and the wine-merchants in Nuits-Saint-Georges and Beaune. As such he must have known the area and its wines as well as anybody. He would have been aware in advance that a parcel of vines would be coming on the market. He would have seen land going to waste as the old original pre-phylloxera *vignes françaises* were not replaced. He saw the opportunity to build up a domaine of his own and he gradually began to buy.

At first, like his neighbours, he sold his wine in bulk, shortly after the vintage, to the local *négoce*. It was the great Raymond Baudoin, editor of the French magazine *Revue des Vins de France*, and consultant to a clutch of the finest French restaurants of the time – to Point in Vienne, Pic in Valence, Darroze in Mont-Saint-Marsan and Taillevent in Paris, among others – who persuaded Rousseau to set aside some of his best *cuvées* for domaine-bottling and direct sale. During the 1930s the local merchants were over-stocked, sales of wine to them were moribund, and prices were very depressed. Baudoin's pioneering work, to *sortir les vignerons dans le monde*, as he put it, was invaluable. Through the restaurants Rousseau was able to build up a private clientele. Through Baudoin he was introduced to Frank Schoonmaker and began to export. And all this gave him the means further to expand his holdings in Gevrey.

Yet progress was slow. When his son Charles took over in 1959 the size of the domaine was only 6.5 hectares. It has since more than doubled. In 1961 Charles acquired land in Clos-de-Bèze (this has recently been enlarged by the purchase of a half hectare of vines from the Nousbaum family). In 1965 and again in 1975 he bought his Clos-de-la-Roche; in 1968 more Chambertin to add to his father's holding; in 1978 the Clos-des-Ruchottes when the Thomas-Bassot estate was wound up. (The rest of the Ruchottes was shared between Dr Georges Mugneret of Vosne-Romanée, and a businessman from the north of France who entrusted his share to the Georges Roumier domaine of Chambolle-Musigny) and in 1983 yet more Chambertin from Jaboulet-Vercherre. More recently he has acquired yet more Chambertin and Chambertin, Clos-de-Bèze. The Clos-Saint-Jacques had been acquired in 1954 from the Comte de Moucheron, then owner of the Château de Meursault. You have to be patient, says Charles. Not everything that comes up is entirely suitable; and today prices are high.

Today, and for all I know this will be already out of date by the time this book is published, there is 2.20 ha of Chambertin, 1.5 ha of Clos-de-Bèze, 1.06 ha of Clos-des-Ruchottes, 0.53 ha of Mazis, 1.36 ha of Charmes and Mazoyères, 2.21 ha of Clos-Saint-Jacques, 1.48 ha of Clos-de-la-Roche, 75 ares of Cazetières, 50 a of Lavaux-Saint-Jacques and 2.26 ha of village Gevrey.

WINE-MAKING

Careful wine-making, short pruning, a rigorous selection, and, of course, old vines in the best sites. It all sounds so simple, but so few manage it!

It all starts in the vineyard. The average age of the vines is deliberately kept high: sixty years in Le Chambertin; forty-five in Clos-de-Bèze. Every year Charles Rousseau rips out about a sixth of a hectare across his domaine – a few vines here, a few vines there – to maintain this important average.

The object, of course, is to keep the harvest low and the concentration of the vines high. In his Clos-Saint-Jacques, for instance, his average *rendement* during the 1980s was under 30 hectolitres per hectare. Even in the prolific 1986 vintage it was only 35.

As a result of this Rousseau never has to practise a *saignée*. It is more important, he will tell you, to reduce the crop in the vineyard by having old vines in the first place and then by pruning hard. And finally by a severe *triage* of the fruit. 'You should have seen my vineyards in

1986,' he told me. 'The ground was carpeted with rotten berries which had been eliminated at the time of the harvest. It was necessary to examine every single bunch. As a result I had to employ fifty harvesters for twelve days to pick the 1986s. The 1985 was collected by half the number in half the time.'

Vinification takes place in open stainless-steel vats. Rousseau uses about 15 per cent of the stems, not so much for the extra tannins the stems will add to the must, but for physical reasons, to give aeration to the mixture of juice, skins and pulp. To vinify all the stems would be a grave mistake, in Rousseau's view. You would get too much tannin, and tannins of the wrong, hard and unripe sort, as well as an excess of bitter acidity.

Maceration takes place for about a fortnight, the temperature being controlled at a maximum of 31°C, with *pigeage* and *remontage* (treading down and breaking up of the pulp, and pumping over) twice a day. The wine is then decanted into a fresh vat or straight into cask to await the malo-lactic fermentation. There is 100 per cent new oak from the Allier for the Chambertin, the Clos-de-Bèze and the Clos-Saint-Jacques, and 60 per cent for the other top wines. Bottling normally takes place between eighteen months and two years of the harvest; the lesser wines in May, the top wines in September.

THE WINE

What exhilarates me about Rousseau's wines is their concentration and their class. The concentration, naturally, is readily apparent in rich vintages such as 1990, 1988, 1985 and the more structured years such as 1983 and 1976. (Incidentally, as the best 1983s are softening, and their rather rigid tannins are being absorbed, I am beginning to notice an element of cooked fruit; something similar in its way to the 1982 clarets, though of course the 1983 Burgundy is a great deal less consistent). The class is not only obvious in these vintages, and not only in lighter years such as 1986, but in for example the 1984s. Not being dominated by excessive quantities of unripe tannins, as perhaps you might find in a claret in a less ripe vintage, Rousseau's 1984s, now that they have softened up, are really surprisingly good. These are the proof of the thesis I have put forward elsewhere in discussions of Burgundy and the Pinot Noir. Go for old vines and expert wine-making in the poorer vintages. You will get much more interesting wine than by buying lesser, village examples in a so-called great vintage.

THE TASTING

I sampled the following wines *chez* Rousseau in June 1995.

Optimum drinking

Gevrey-Chambertin, 1993　　　**1998–2005**

This shows even better than it did last November. It is not yet in bottle. Very good colour. Lovely fruit. Very good acidity. Medium-full body. Stylish for a village wine. Good intensity. A lovely generous wine. Long on the palate.

GEVREY-CHAMBERTIN, CLOS-SAINT-JACQUES

1993　　　**2001–2015**

Fine colour. Lovely, lush, quite oaky nose. A bit adolescent at present but a ripe and unaggressive mouthful. Splendid fruit. Excellent grip. Very good intensity. Rich, complex, concentrated flavours. Very classic. Very lovely indeed. To be bottled very soon.

1992　　　**1999–2008**

Very good colour. This is really quite full. And gives every indication of remaining like this. This is quite closed at present on the nose. It has very good substance and depth for the vintage. Good oak. Really quite full body. Rich and fat. Good tannins. Not as lush or as generous as the 1993, nor as concentrated and as classy. But a splendid example. Long, elegant. Needs time.

1991　　　**1999–2013**

Very good colour. A fine nose. Rich, a touch spicy, the oak a gentle base. Seems a little bit more evolved than the 1992 and a little less sophisticated than the 1993. Fullish, round and rich, aromatic. Good tannins. Plenty of fat and *matière*. But like the nose a bit more spice. Fine for the vintage.

1990   2000-2020

Excellent colour. Still very youthful indeed. Marvellous nose. Expansive, opulent, very very rich, splendid depth and intensity of fat ripe fruit. Brilliant. Very well balanced. Splendid grip. Marvellous richness and length on the finish. *Grand vin*!

1989   Now-2007

The colour has lightened a little but still looks youthful. And it is still fullish. Ripe, plump, flowery nose. Obviously not as powerful or as chocolatey as the 1990 but generous, balanced, very seductive. Medium-full body. Quite supple. Good acidity. Like the 1992 not a wine of great power but one of great attraction. Long. Very good indeed.

1988   1999-2020 plus

There is now a suggestion of evolution on the colour. Lovely nose. Really sophisticated complex fruit. Fine acidity but rich enough so not hard or austere. Fullish. This is a beautifully composed wine and one for the long term. Good tannins but they don't stick out. Very very subtle and complex at the end. Very, very lovely indeed. May indeed last longer than the 1990. *Grand vin* again.

1983   Now (just)-2010

Fine full colour. Little brown. Very vigorous. Ample, rich, and above all concentrated nose. This is powerful, but it is now, finally, ready. Yes the tannins are a bit dry and stemmy, but this element has been almost submerged by the richness of the wine on the nose, and is completely absent on the palate. Fullish, very good grip. Fat. Spicy. Still very youthful. The finish is ample, concentrated, generous, vigorous. And very fine. A wine for food. Still bags of life.

The following wines were shown at the Atlanta Wine Festival in August 1992.

Le Chambertin, 1989   Now-2009

Medium-full colour. Luscious, but quite *tendre* new oaky nose. Medium-full, splendidly ripe. Complex, balanced but soft. No undue tannin or austerity. Long. Quite fat. Good grip. Fine.

Le Chambertin, 1988   2000-2025

Full colour. Firm, slightly closed nose. Splendidly concentrated fruit. Very good acidity. Fullish, good tannin. A lot of depth and class. This is still young. Excellent.

Le Chambertin, 1987   Now-2006

Good fullish colour, just a hint of brown. Aromatic, spicy nose. Slightly animal now. Good richness and depth and good reserves. Ripe. Medium-full. Just a touch of astringency but this will go as it mellows. Long. Complex and classy. And structured. Not far short of the 1989. Surprisingly good.

Le Chambertin, 1986   Now-1999

Medium to medium-full colour. Fully mature. Soft, slightly dry nose. But gentle and ripe and quite complex as well. Medium to medium-full. Stylish fruit. Good balance. More depth on the finish than the attack. Certainly very good. Long and classy finish.

Chambertin, Clos-de-Bèze, 1985   Now-2020

Medium-full colour. Little maturity. Splendid fruit. Silky smooth. Ripe, rich and complex. Good depth and structure, about halfway between 1988 and 1989. Good grip. Very, very long. Marvellous dimension. This is excellent. Very concentrated.

Chambertin, Clos-de-Bèze, 1983   Now-2020

Full colour. Little maturity. Dry, animal nose. Rich, full, fat, succulent palate. Very complex. Slightly cooked fruit. Good grip. This is better than the 1985. And very different. A structured, tannic wine, but not a bit too astringent on the finish. And not a trace of rot, it goes without saying. Splendid.

Chambertin, Clos-de-Bèze, 1982 Now-2000 plus

Good fullish colour. Only just mature. Soft, velvety-fruity nose. Surprising succulence and class. Good acidity. Medium-full on the palate. Ripe, fresh, complex. A lot of depth. This is surprisingly fine. Just about ready but will last very well.

Le Chambertin, 1980   Drink quite soon

Good colour. Still very fresh. The nose is fresh and fruity and so is the palate, but both are a little one-dimensional. Not as good as the 1982 by a long way. Pleasant but lacks real depth and length.

Le Chambertin, 1976   Drink quite soon

Medium-full colour. No undue maturity. Fine *rôti* nose. Animal, roasted nuts, caramel. Rich and fullish, but it lacks the acidity it needs to give it real complexity. Fine but not great. It lacks a bit of concentration. Is it beginning to loosen up now? Best drunk quite soon.

The opportunity to sample the following came through an invitation to lunch with Bill Baker of Reid Wines in September 1995.

Mazis-Chambertin, 1972 Now-2000

Good fresh-looking medium-weight colour. Light 1972y nose. Fresh but rather lean. Medium body. Aloof. Slightly vegetal. Good but no marked acidity. Slight lack of generosity but plenty of class. Complex. Very good indeed.

Gevrey-Chambertin, Les Cazetiers, 1969
Now-2000

Good mature nose. Earthy, rich, quite robust nose. Aged *sauvage* flavours with a slight lack of class but good sweet fruit and succulence. Medium-full body. Slightly spicy. Good balance. Enough dimension, depth and finesse for at least very good. Vigorous and generous.

Gevrey-Chambertin, Clos-Saint-Jacques, 1969
Now-2010

Fine mature colour but still plenty of vigour. Splendid concentration. Twice as much as the Cazetiers. This is seriously good. Full, vigorous, classy and with real depth. Fat, succulent, rich and still very fresh indeed. Very long and complex. Excellent.

Gevrey-Chambertin, Clos-Saint-Jacques, 1966
Now-2000

Very good colour. Lush aromatic, fat nose. Getting just a little four-square as it developed. This is fullish, has good acidity and is a lovely wine. But it doesn't have the richness and dimension of the 1969, or the nuance of the Clos-de-la-Roche. Drying out slightly on the palate. Very good plus.

Clos-de-la-Roche, 1966 Now-2000

Medium colour. Quite evolved. Rather older than the Clos-Saint-Jacques. Delicate. Soft, refined, very complex nose. This is older, but beautifully ethereal. Sweet and plump, medium to medium-full. Complex, very classy. Better by a long way. Still long, fresh and fine at the end. Subtle and intense. Lovely.

Gevrey-Chambertin, Clos-Saint-Jacques, 1964
Now-2000

Good fullish colour. Still quite purple for a thirty-year-old wine. Firm, full, rich, meaty. Plenty of vigour. Plenty of depth. This is very fine. Full, rich, very concentrated, still very young. Ripe and generous. Fat and multi-dimensional. Long. Excellent.

Mazis-Chambertin, 1964 Now-1999

Good fullish colour. Vigorous but mature. Sweet, succulent, better mannered than the Clos-Saint-Jacques, but less structured. And it did not last as well in the glass. Medium to medium-full, refined, but getting a little loose. But still long and fine. Still has life.

Charmes-Chambertin, 1964 Now-2000

Very good colour. Somehow more glowing that the Mazis. Just a little tight on the nose. A touch of the stems perhaps on the nose, more so than the Mazis. Vigorous, full and rich and structured. A meaty wine. Slightly less class than the Mazis. But more vigour and sweetness. Long. Plenty of life. Very good indeed.

Chambertin, Clos-de-Bèze, 1964 Now-2000

Fine full vigorous colour. Big, fat, muscular, vigorous and underneath marvellous fruit. Splendid richness, almost over-ripe. Still very youthful. This is sweet, full, decadent, hedonistic, voluptuous, a little exotic. Not great but very fine indeed. Not as good as the 1962 though. As it evolved, just a little four-square.

Chambertin, Clos-de-Bèze, 1962 Now-2000

Fine full colour. Still youthful. Lovely nose. Complex, beautifully balanced. This is a fullish, soft, velvety wine. Not as voluptuous as the 1964 or as structured but more composed, less over-ripe. More classy. Very fine indeed but not quite complex enough for great.

Clos-de-la-Roche, 1959 Now-2000 plus

Full, rich colour. But a little more evolved than the Charmes 1959. This shows a little age on the nose. Slightly vegetal, slight decay. Slightly stemmy. Full, meaty, very rich, a masculine example, brutal, lots of vigour. Getting better and better in the glass. Lots of depth. Brilliant but in an old-fashioned way.

Charmes-Chambertin, 1959 Now-2000

Very good colour. Full, rich, glowing, mature. Rich and fat and complex. Still fresh and sweet and succulent. Very lovely. Medium-full body. This is not great, but it is a lovely bottle, robust, warm and spicy, quite structured, not *that* refined. But certainly fine. Plenty of life.

The following Domaine Armand Rousseau wines were offered at the Studley Priory Wine Weekend in December 1989.

Gevrey-Chambertin, Clos-Saint-Jacques, 1987
Now-2004

Good fresh colour. Ripe, fat, oaky nose. Fresh, insistent. Not too disturbed by the recent bottling. This seems to have more depth than the 1986. Rousseau agrees, though he prefers his 1986 Ruchottes to the 1987. A little unsettled on the palate. Lovely fruit, gently oaky. Quite full. Good, ripe tannins. Plenty of depth and style. Very fine.

Chambertin, Clos-de-Bèze, 1987   Now–2006

Good colour. Fine, ripe, rich mulberry nose. Less austere and more opulent than the Chambertin. A delicious, fullish, voluptuous wine on the palate. Lovely, complex, rich fruit. Quite firm. But balanced, harmonious, long and elegant. Excellent.

Chambertin, 1987   Now–2006

Good colour. Lovely, concentrated plummy-blackberry fruit on the nose. This is more closed in - less seductive. At present it seems a trifle leaner. Fullish, again quite firm. Very good grip. Also excellent.

Gevrey-Chambertin, Clos-Saint-Jacques, 1986
                                                    Now–2003

Medium colour only. Rich, slightly spicy nose. Quite full. Good fruit and grip, but not the concentration or quite the style of the 1987. Ripe if not really concentrated. Stylish, positive finish. Very good.

Gevrey-Chambertin, Clos-Saint-Jacques, 1985
                                                    Now–2016

A little more colour than the 1986. But surprisingly not a great deal more. Full, concentrated nose. A lot of depth here. Closed in. Coffee, chocolate and caramel as it evolved. Fat, rich and multi-dimensional. Great depth. Very fine Burgundy here. Intensely concentrated. Good acidity. Excellent.

Gevrey-Chambertin, Clos-Saint-Jacques, 1984
                                                    Drink soon

Light to medium colour. Some development. Surprisingly good nose. A little lean but neither mean nor too vegetal. Not without class either. Light to medium body. A little slight, but not weak; one-dimensional is the better word. Elegant, a touch austere. But finishes riper than it starts. Surprisingly good.

Clos-de-la-Roche, 1984   Now–1998

Good colour. Still very youthful. Fine plummy fruit, high toned. Younger vines than the Ruchottes. This is a medium-bodied, fragrant wine. Not at all without class or depth.

Ruchottes-Chambertin, Clos-des-Ruchottes, 1984   Now–1999

Very good colour. Even better than the Clos-de-la-Roche. More closed. Richer, more black-berry nose. More tannin. Old viney. Quite hard, more tannic but rich nevertheless, and full for a 1984. Good depth. Quite firm. Very good indeed.

Chambertin, 1984   Now–2001

Fine colour. Rich and fat on the nose, nothing 'off-vintage' about this. Just as fine on the palate. As much tannin as the Ruchottes but the tannins are more covered by the richness and concentration. Long, classy, fullish, excellent. Will keep very well.

Gevrey-Chambertin, Clos-Saint-Jacques, 1983
                                                    Now–2016

Best colour of the series, must a little brown. Big, full, rich, meaty nose. No undue tannins though. And - it must be emphasised, absolutely without a taint of rot. Full-bodied, structured, tannic, very, very rich and concentrated and with a slight cooked fruit flavour. This is a bigger wine than the 1985. More depth, full, richer. Fine grip. Very long. Even better than the 1985.

Charmes-Chambertin, 1982   Drink soon

Medium colour. This is now charming and open. Ripe, fresh and full of fruit. A lovely plump wine with a lot of class. No pretension to *grand vin* though. Ready but will last well. Fine acidity and concentration for a 1982.

Gevrey-Chambertin, Clos-Saint-Jacques, 1982
                                                    Drink soon

Medium colour. No undue astringency. Pleasant, open, spicy nose. Medium body. Round, soft, plump wine. Lacks a bit of grip and vigour and complexity on the follow-through but plump and charming. And with more depth than the Charmes. Good ripe fruit and certainly not short.

Gevrey-Chambertin, Clos-Saint-Jacques, 1981
                                                    Drink soon

Better colour than the 1982. No undue age. Pleasant, fresh nose. I prefer this to the 1982 because the better acidity makes it more positive. A little fuller, more tannic and a little more concentrated. Much more personality. Good, positive fruit. No lack of elegance. Very good.

Gevrey-Chambertin, Clos-Saint-Jacques, 1980
                                                    Drink soon

Better colour still. Medium-full, still vigorous. This reminds me a bit of the 1972. Slightly lean and acid but has richness, complexity and depth. Medium-full, ripe, slightly spicy. Now ready. With some of the complexity of maturity. Very good indeed. (Not exceptional because it lacks just a little real breed, like the 1972s.)

Chambertin, 1976   Drink soon

Medium-full colour. Now mature but no undue sign of age. Full, ripe, baked cherry tart fruit. But no lumpy dry tannins: not a trace. Ripe, spicy in a liquorice way. Fat, voluptuous. Very good balance. Complex, ample finish. Still very fresh.

Chambertin, 1972   Now–1999

Fullish colour. No undue breed. Lovely nose. Very classy and fresh with the just-a-bit-lean fruit of the 1972 vintage. Vigorous, full, complex and mellow. Not as spicy as the 1976, and has more class. Fuller, more concentrated, more depth, better grip.

Chambertin, 1969   Now–2000

Very fine full, rich mature colour. Lovely complex, mellow nose. This has real class and absolutely lovely mulberry fruit. Delicate even. Beautifully balanced. Round, delicious. Beautiful harmony. *Grand vin*.

ÉTIENNE SAUZET, PULIGNY-MONTRACHET

A number of years ago, as if these things were not an everyday occurrence in Burgundy, a lot of fuss was created in certain wine media circles when the Puligny-based Sauzet domaine, one of the most celebrated sources of great white Burgundy, was split up. Following the 1990 vintage, Jean-Marc Boillot, one of the three children of Colette, *née* Sauzet, and Jean Boillot, took over his share - approximately one-third - leaving Gérard Boudot, husband of Jeannine, one of the other Boillot children, responsible for the remainder. The impression was given of a family at war, no-one speaking to one another, of bad blood in the air. Jean-Marc was depicted as the villain, Gérard represented as the poor injured innocent. And it was implied that Sauzet would never be the same again.

As you can imagine, a great deal of this was exaggerated nonsense. It was simple for Gérard Boudot to arrange matters so that he could buy in grapes to augment the production he had lost. These changes are inevitable anyway, as one generation gives way to its successor. The inevitable has been accepted, and no-one has lost out, not least the consumer, for he now has two addresses to go to in his search for top Chardonnay, that of Jean-Marc Boillot as well as Étienne Sauzet, for each produces excellent wine.

HISTORY

Étienne Sauzet was born in 1903 and died in 1975. He inherited 3 hectares, gained more when he married in 1924, and while he acquired some 14 ares of Bâtard-Montrachet on the Puligny side in 1936, essentially built up the domaine in the 1950s until it reached some 12 hectares, including another small plot of Bâtard, some Bienvenues, and *premiers crus* holdings in no fewer than five of the top Puligny vineyards.

Étienne and his wife had a single child, Colette, who married Jean Boillot of Volnay. Jean Boillot was a major vineyard-holder in his own right, indeed rather more important in this respect than his father-in-law. The two didn't get on, and this may explain why the Sauzet domaine was never integrated into that of Jean Boillot, but has always continued a separate existence.

Colette and Jean had three children: Jean-Marc (born in 1951), Jeannine (born in 1954) and Henri (born in 1955). It is Henri who today runs the Jean Boillot domaine, while Jean-Marc, who was Olivier Leflaive's *régisseur* from 1984 to 1988, now has his own separate domaine and *négociant* business based in Pommard. Jeannine married Gérard Boudot in 1974, and in this year he took over at Sauzet from his ailing grandfather-in-law.

GÉRARD BOUDOT

Gérard Boudot was born in 1950 in Le Creusot. His original intended *métier* was land-management, but he failed the exam to get onto an '*Eau et Forêts*' course. He chose viticulture and viniculture instead, another agronomous discipline, and it was while he was at the *Lycée* in Beaune that he met Jeannine. An ardent rugby player, he joined the local team. Jean Boillot was the vice president. And as neither Jean-Marc or Henri was at that time interested in taking on the reins at Sauzet, it was to Boudot that the succession fell, working for Madame Sauzet after Étienne's death in 1975. It was from this time onwards that the domaine began to sell the entirety of its production in bottle.

THE DOMAINE

Following the separation, Gérard Boudot is today responsible for some 8 ha of Sauzet vines, buying in, ideally in grapes, about half as much again to make up for what he lost at the end of 1990. The *Société Anonyme Sauzet*, created the following year, is a *négociant*, and is the customer of the *Société d'Exploitation Sauzet*, as well as these outside suppliers, enabling all to be vinified and matured together under the same roof, a cramped interlocking rabbit warren of stone-vaulted cellars under the family house on the outskirts of Puligny-Montrachet.

WINE-MAKING

Above everything one must be flexible, says Gérard Boudot: '*jamais systématique*'. And if there is anything which has changed over the years it is this, and the updating of the hardware so that greater control can be applied to the wine-making. There is now a *pneumatique* wine press, for example, and the cellars themselves are *climatisés*.

Like many, Boudot is contemptuous of green harvesting. 'You get fewer bunches, but they are larger in size to compensate, so you produce less concentrated wine.' Controlling the harvest starts earlier, at the pruning stage, and then later when you rub out excess buds.

Unlike some in Puligny, Gérard Boudot is in favour of anti-rot treatments, essential in a vintage such as 1994, and as a result has no problem with botrytis. The Sauzet 1986s are splendid, while many of his neighbours' wines have not lasted the course. In none of his other vintages have I found that over-ripe, suggestion-of-Condrieu flavour when I have sampled the wines out of cask. As a result the acidities are always very good, and the wines hold their elegance.

'Maximum finesse and an individual expression of the *climat*, is what I am after,' says Boudot. He vinifies with selected yeasts, lowering the temperature of the cellar so that this takes place at 18-20°C. There is always a long, thorough *débourbage*, so that the lees are as fine as possible and that the wine can be left on them as long as possible, in order to extract all the flavour and richness out of them. There is *bâtonnage*, but not to excess, or the flavours would be too ephemeral. The wines are matured in 25-50 per cent new oak of different origins and bottled after a year or a year and a half, 'when the wine is ready,' says Boudot.

THE WINES

From 40 ares of generic vines, the Sauzet domaine produces a fine, if quite highly-priced, Bourgogne *blanc*: Puligny in all but its label. Of the village wine itself there are normally originally three *cuvées*: old vines from the Meix, under Pucelles; from the Charmes and the Corvées on the Meursault side of the commune; and from Trézin, the only plot of village AC up in the hills, above Les Garennes: a total of 2.6 ha. These spend some of their life in wood, some in tank, before being blended and bottled. The result is a yardstick example, complementing the much smaller *cuvée* of Chassagne, a Puligny-ish wine from the Enseignières, under Bâtard.

The least - at present, for the vines are young - of the village wines is currently the Perrières, only now in the 1994s vintage coming into its own. This is a lean, racy, flinty wine with good acidity. It will acquire more depth and fat, which will complement its essentially minerally character, as the vines age. The domaine exploits half a hectare in this *climat*.

Having lost the whole of the Truffière to Jean-Marc Boillot's capable hands, the remaining three *premier cru* Sauzet wines come from one above the other on the Meursault border, marching with the Charmes and the Perrières. Lowest on the slope is Les Referts (70 a). Highest is Champs-Canet (1 hectare). Between the two, ideally placed, is Les Combettes (1 hectare also).

To taste the three alongside each other, as I did in the tasting below, is to be shown an emphatic proof of the importance of *terroir*. There are barely a few hundred metres from the top of the Champs-Canet to the bottom of Les Referts. Yet the wines are strikingly different. Intense and minerally - the soil being essentially broken up limestone rock - in Champs-Canet; lush, ripe, but slightly heavier, with the least class, in the Referts; the most backward, the most concentrated, the most finesse, a synthesis of the two (biased towards the Champs-Canet) but with an extra dimension, in the Combettes. This latter wine can be extraordinarily good!

There are just over 15 ares of Bienvenues-Bâtard-Montrachet in the Sauzet portfolio, the vines planted in 1936. It is the smallest *cuvée* and the oldest vines. Three and a half casks were produced in 1993 and 1994. This is a flowery wine, like a Pucelles, feminine (if one's allowed to use the word these days), gently honeyed, without the greatest structure but often with tremendous elegance.

Finally the Bâtard. The Sauzet domaine retains the original piece, acquired before the war. The wine is masculine where the Bienvenues is feminine, and rich, fat and opulent. In Boudot's hands it comes out rather more elegantly than most.

THE SAUZET STYLE

'Spicier, more pungent, with a directness and vigour,' says Simon Loftus in his elegant book on Puligny-Montrachet, comparing Sauzet to Leflaive, which is 'more subtle'. With this assessment I must demur. Indeed, forgetting the spice, I think Loftus has it the wrong way round.

I find the Leflaive wines direct and expressive, easy to assess. The Sauzet wines are more delicate, more subtle. There is a purity about both. But perhaps the Sauzet wines, in the best sense, are the most discreet.

POSTSCRIPT

What of the future? Having lost one-third, is the domaine to be truncated again when the bell tolls for Henri and Colette? The answer, suggests Gérard Boudot, is, in principle, no, for Jeannine will be entitled to a share of her father's estate. This can be exchanged for her brother Henri's portion of Sauzet. So both domaines, allowing for Jean-Marc's share, can continue as they are. It would certainly be the simplest and most efficient solution.

THE TASTING

I sampled the following wines in London in January 1995. My thanks to Bill Baker of Reid Wines, Stephen Browett of Farr Vintners, Barry Phillips of The White Horse at Chilgrove, Harold Porter and Bruce Templeton for their assistance in amassing the samples.

Optimum drinking

Referts, 1992 — 1998–2009

Slightly heavier colour than the other two 1992s. A little heavier and more obviously marked by SO_2 on the nose. But good style and depth underneath. Currently a bit adolescent. But rich and very well balanced. Good grip. An ample example. On ullage the SO_2 not at all apparent. Very good.

Champs-Canet, 1992 — 1998–2009

Rich, oaky nose. Lovely character and balance here. Slightly leaner than the above. Less full, quite a lot less fat. Minerally, very stylish, beautifully balanced. Very long. Very good plus. Quite a contrast.

Combettes, 1992 — 1999–2012

Refined nose. A little more backward than the above, but more concentration and depth. The sum of the two and then some. Delicate but intense. Poised, gently ripe and peachy. Very persistent at the end. A bit adolescent at present but potentially fine. A distinct step up.

Referts, 1991 — Now–2002

Flowery, slightly scented nose. Citronelle and apple blossom. Not the greatest structure but very attractive. On the palate medium to medium-full. Ripe and stylish. Not the greatest of weight and power but has plenty of character and no lack of balance. Give it a year. Good for the vintage.

Champs-Canet, 1991 — Now–2004

Leaner and more neutral than the Referts on the nose. More to it on the palate. Ripe in a slightly herbal sort of way. Better grip and more intensity than the above. A touch lean, but a wine with a lot of interest for a 1991. Finishes long and with plenty of dimension. Very good.

Combettes, 1991 — Now–2006

Good depth, unexpectedly so for a 1991, in a delicate sort of way on the nose. On the palate this is quite concentrated, and quite backward. It has a power and an intensity lacking in the above. Currently a bit adolescent. But very good indeed.

Referts, 1990 — Now–2006 (?)

Adolescent and a bit sulphury on the nose. Why is it the Referts should be more sulphury than the others? On the palate the sulphur rather overwhelms. Difficult to judge. Good ripe acidity certainly.

Champs-Canet, 1990 — Now–2010

Cleaner, leaner, most attractive nose. Excellent balance. Fullish, excellent acidity, lovely fruit. A very fresh wine with a lot of intensity. This is fine. And it will last and last.

Combettes, 1990 — Now–2015

Similar nose to the above: but rather more depth and concentrated. Again fullish. Splendidly harmonious and multi-dimensional. The follow-through here is very classy and very complex. Most exciting. Quite delicious fruit, beautifully put together. Very fine.

Referts, 1989

Corky.

Champs-Canet, 1989 — Now–2004

Rather more evolved than the 1990 on the nose. Lots of depth. This is not as good as the vintage above. There is less fat and less grip; less dimension, in fact. But it is nevertheless a balanced, nicely fruity very charming wine. Very good plus.

Combettes, 1989 — Now–2008

More closed than the above. Rich, nutty, and ripe, but seriously concentrated. Yet neverthe less not a patch on the 1990. But it has a lot more to it than the above. Very good nicely austere acidity. Splendid fruit. Very very long. Fine.

Referts, 1988   **Drink soon**

Light nose. Suggestions of orange peel. Soft, round, *à point*. This has less to it. Indeed it finishes a little hollow. And, once again there is a suggestion of SO_2. Quite good at best.

Champs-Canet, 1988   **Now–2000**

Rather more to it on the nose. There is good depth here, especially for a 1988. Medium to medium-full. Fresh, ripe and fruity. But a little one-dimensional. Certainly stylish though. An attractive wine. Rather significantly better than the above. Very good indeed.

Combettes, 1988   **Now–2004**

Similar nose. But just that bit more to it. This is richer and rounder, and has more depth and dimension. Really properly positive at the end. Good grip. Pure fruit. Very elegant. Very long. Remarkably good for an 1988. Will still improve. Fine plus for the vintage.

Perrières, 1987   **Now–2000**

The last vintage before they replanted? Fresh minerally nose. Good character here. No weakness. No vegetal-ness. This is better than the Referts 1988. Good acidity. No great complexity, depth or class but ripe, charming, attractive and with a positive finish.

Combettes, 1987   **Drink up**

A little tired on the nose. A bit of built-in sulphur. This is not a patch on the 1988. A little fatigued now, even a touch oxidised, losing its elegance especially at the end. Are there better bottles?

Referts, 1986   **Now–1999**

Flowery, plump, very slightly blowsy on the nose. Ripe and honeyed. This is the best Referts so far. Medium-full. Not the greatest of grip and concentration. But lovely ripe fruit-salady fruit. Good acidity. But inherently soft. Great charm. Very good indeed. *À point.*

Champs-Canet, 1986   **Now–2002**

Ample, rich nose. Not a touch of *sur-maturité*. Rich, nutty and fat. Plenty of vigour and grip. This has a lot of promise. A much more closed-in wine, and at first sight, less charming. The follow-through is very much more promising: rich, very good grip. Even quite firm. Excellent freshness and class especially for a 1986. Very fine, complex finish. Fine.

Combettes, 1986   **Now–2002**

Fat but firm, lush but very well balanced. Splendidly ample nose. This is richer and fleshier and more exotic. Less firm, less obvious grip. But no lack of acidity and harmony. A very ripe, abundant example. Delicious.

Perrières, 1985   **Now–2005**

Firm nose. Nicely minerally and stylish, very complex slightly crab-apple, quince and peach fruit. On the palate not the greatest of weight but real style, real balance and real length here. Lovely fruit. Very subtle at the end. Fine.

Champs-Canet, 1985   **Now–2008 plus**

Slight melon aspect on the nose. Very ample, very rich, lovely class, real depth. Fullish. Excellent fruit on the palate. This shows what a great vintage the 1985 is. Rich, marvellous grip. Really classy. Very very long. Still an infant. Very fine.

Combettes, 1985   **Now–2010 plus**

Very rich nose. Very fine quality. Still very young and even a little closed-in. This is fuller and firmer than the Champs-Canet. Even more concentration and dimension. Excellent. An absolute classic. Only just ready. Marvellous finish.

Champs-Canet, 1984   **Drink soon**

Slightly more colour than the Combettes. Not a lot on the nose. This is unexpectedly good. No great depth. But ripe enough, even rich enough, elegant enough, balanced enough. Fresh, complex, long. Really surprisingly delicious. Better than the Combettes for once.

Combettes, 1984   **Drink soon**

A bit more vegetal on the nose than the Champs-Canet. On the palate this is a little more astringent than the Champs-Canet. It has less charm. But underneath it is still ripe and enjoyable. Certainly good.

Champs-Canet, 1983   **Drink soon**

Fresh colour. Surprisingly fresh on the nose. No over-ripeness, no botrytis. This is fat, rich, honeyed, a little lumpy. But certainly very enjoyable. There is a slightly burnt, roasted aspect on the follow-through and it is probably quite alcoholic. But it is full and vigorous and not without class. Very good.

Combettes, 1983   **Drink soon**

Fresh colour. A touch of botrytis on the nose. This seems more tired on the palate than the above. The fruit has dried up a bit. There is the same slightly lumpy, burnt quality. Good acidity though as well. But I prefer the above. It has more vigour.

Referts, 1982   **Drink soon**

Surprisingly deep colour. The only one of the series. Ripe, slightly over-ripe nose, like a well-matured apple. On the palate this is ample and round and fullish. Just a little one-dimensional. But still fresh and expansive. Very good.

Champs-Canet, 1982   **Now-2000**

Fresh colour. Rather fresher and more stylish than the Referts. Slightly less ample. But much better class, grip, vigour and concentration. On the attack it seems a little vacant, but the follow-through is rich, balanced and elegant. Fine.

Champs-Canet, 1979   **Drink soon**

This is a fresher example than last time. Good colour. No undue age. Just a touch of tiredness and built-in sulphur. But ripe, succulent, charming and with plenty of fruit. But it is now beginning to get a little short.

Combettes, 1979   **Now-2000**

Good colour. No undue age. Lovely fresh nose. This is very fine, and much better and more vigorous than the Champs-Canet. Rich, balanced, harmonious and complex. Very good grip. Very very classy. Very very complex. Very fine quality. Quite lovely.

COMTE
SENARD,
ALOXE-CORTON

'There is no such thing as the *"méthode Accad"*,' says Philippe
Senard. 'It doesn't exist. It is a philosophy, not a method. A
concept, not a do-it-yourself wine-making manual. And the
vinification part of it is only the tip of the iceberg. It is the
viticulture underneath which is of far greater importance. Guy
Accad, don't forget, is an *ingénieur agronome* as well as an
oenologue. He is one of the few who has thought about the
importance of the soil.'

Like many, Senard is one of those, disappointed with what
they produced in 1982 and 1986, who 'went Accad': in his case
in 1988. As he describes it, in this first year neither he nor Accad
had any idea of what they were doing. After the wines had
settled down in cask he decided he would have liked to have
done some things rather differently. In 1989 he did alter a few
things. And in 1991 he made the wines entirely as he wished to.
He has now split up with Accad - this also seems to be common
- but he continues to make wine according to the general Accad
principles, having adapted these to his 8.7 hectare domaine.
With a string of Cortons under his belt, Senard is today one of
the leading producers of this appellation.

HISTORY

Philippe Senard was born in 1948. He almost died of carbon-dioxide asphyxiation at the outset. He was born in the old Hospices maternity home, situated over the old vinification cellar. It was during the vintage.

He has inherited the estate from his father Daniel, now eighty-two years of age. Daniel, past president of the Beaune Chamber of Commerce, long-time mayor of Aloxe-Corton, and *grand maître* of the *Chevaliers de Tastevin*, took over from his father Jules in the 1930s, but the origins of the domaine go back a generation further, to 1865.

The Senard domaine was larger fifty years ago than it is today. In 1929 it controlled over 30 hectares, and also operated as a *négociant*. But inheritance problems whittled down the estate, and during the slump the merchant business was sold to the Naigeons in Gevrey and has since disappeared.

Philippe went to the *Viti* in Beaune, and then spent some time in Kenya before coming back to do his National Service. He wanted to go back to Africa, but his father said he needed him in the family business. This was not the wine estate, but a factory producing plastic chips for casinos, apparently one of only two in the world. Senard spent five years as commercial director of this establishment before deciding he'd rather be in wine. Daniel Senard had never taken an active interest in his inheritance, employing Paul Meurgey as his *régisseur*. Philippe took over from him and produced his first vintage in 1971.

As well as running the Comte Senard domaine - the family are Papal Counts, the decree being issued in the 1870s - Philippe Senard is a director of another estate, the Domaine des Terregelesses. This was created by a businessman/wine-lover (who wishes to remain anonymous) in 1983. It owns 6.5 hectares, including some Corton-Charlemagne, Savigny-lès-Beaune, Les Vergelesses red and white, and village Beaune and Chorey. Philippe vinifies the wine in his premises in Aloxe-Corton, but the *élevage* takes place in a cellar off the Place Madelaine in Beaune.

Moreover Philippe Senard has also acted as a local broker. In 1986 he had an operation on his spine, and his doctor advised him to reduce his manual activity in the vineyard. This gave him some free time, and so he started to sell other growers' wines, to act as a middle-man between seller and buyer. He has now delegated much of this to a couple of young *protégés*, but still does the selection himself. 'It gives me the chance to taste plenty of other wines.'

THE DOMAINE

The Senard domaine encompasses 8.7 hectares. Surrounding the family houses - Daniel and his wife live opposite Philippe and his wife Béatrice - at the foot of the Corton hill is the largest element in the portfolio: 2.10 hectares of Corton, Clos-des-Meix, a *monopole*. Currently part of this is virgin land. Some 4-5 ares of old Pinot Noir vines have been uprooted. Senard will replace them with Chardonnay: it will be Corton *blanc*, not Charlemagne.

Up the hill, next to the water tower, lies the *lieu-dit* of Paulands. The vines are old here and Senard labels this wine as simply 'Corton'. To the west, round the slope towards Pernand-Vergelesses, he possesses 40 a of red 'En Charlemagne'. In the other direction lie his best Cortons: 64 a of Clos-du-Roi and 63 a of Bressandes. Before you descend the slope to inspect his Aloxe-Corton, *premier cru* Les Valozières (70 a), his 2.6 ha of village Aloxe and his 51 a of village Chorey, Senard will point away towards the horizon. Beyond Serrigny and the motorway the family possesses a farm in the plain. The main building, in the days before the land was cleared, was a thirteenth-century *maison de chasse*. More recently, Philippe can remember when the lower lying land between the village of Aloxe and the main road, today producing village AC, provided grazing space and cereals for the horses which were used in the vineyards.

Senard's attitude towards viticulture is profoundly *biologique*, obviously influenced by the teachings of Guy Accad. He ploughs and hoes, rather than using herbicides. He prunes hard and debuds in the spring rather than green harvests. And he keeps composting and the various treatments against insects, mildew and oidium down to the minimum. 'It is all in the fruit,' he will tell you. 'Get the fruit right and you have done 90 per cent of the work. What I want are healthy clusters of small grapes, but not too much of them.' He picks his village Chorey by machine but the rest, of course, by hand, and rather later than he did in pre-Accad days. 'You have to be courageous!' he says.

WINE-MAKING

Philippe Senard's fine, low, vaulted cellar is one of the oldest in Burgundy. It was excavated by Dominican monks, Antonins of the nearby Abbaye Sainte Marguerite - whose ruins can be inspected up in the valley of the river Rhoin at Bouilland - in the fourteenth century. Apparently the building constructed above the cellar burnt down soon afterwards. The Black Death all but wiped out the local population. And the ruins covered up the entrance to the cellar. It was rediscovered, quite by chance, by the Senard's gardener in 1880. In the last war the entrance was once again blocked up, in order to protect the cellar's contents from the invaders. Late in the 1980s the cellar had its own *concierge*, a toad named Nestor, after a Homeric hero famous for his age and wisdom.

Senard destems his fruit by about a half or three-quarters, depending on the vintage, and then cools the must to 10°C where it macerates for five days. He vinifies at a cool temperature (25°C), prolongs the *cuvaison* to twenty to twenty-five days, and gives his top wines 25-30 per cent new wood. Like many he abhors an excessive taste of new oak. The wine is then simply left for two years with neither fining nor filtration. Enzymes have clarified the wine instead.

THE WINE

Philippe Senard, balding but young-looking, enthusiastic, perspicacious and full of humour, has a more cosmopolitan outlook than many in Burgundy: the result of his upbringing and other non-vinous activities. It was perhaps this that made him more readily move over to the Accad camp than some of his peers. Does he regret it? Not for a minute. He regrets that Accad has been ham-fisted over both his public relations and his private relations with his clients, which has blown up a concept which is deeply logical into one of controversy. People harp on about the cold maceration as if that was all there was to it, he complains. But when you look at the wines - and from 1989 Senard has really got it right - you can have no doubts as to the efficacy of the concept. The Cortons taste like Cortons, and they all taste different: they are true representatives of their *terroir*.

At the 'feminine' end, we have the En Charlemagne: a red wine made in white-wine soil. This is juicy, floral and fragrant. The Clos-des-Meix is similar, but with a little more weight, a little more fat: less mineral, but perhaps less elegant.

The Corton, from the Paulands, is rather more closed, with good backbone and intensity. There is a meaty power here which bodes well for the future. But it is sometimes less expressive in its youth.

Bressandes and Clos-du-Roi are the two top *sub-climats* in this large (50 ha-plus) *grand cru*. They are a significant step-up. Bigger, richer, more concentrated, with both more class and more persistence, they are both fine. But the Clos-du-Roi usually has that extra bit of brilliance. Senard's is today one of the best Cortons on the market.

THE TASTING

I sampled the following range of Philippe Senard's Cortons in Aloxe in February 1995.

CORTON
(from Les Paulands)

1992   **1998–2006**

Good colour. Soft, aromatic, ripe nose. Gently stylish. Medium body. Round, ripe, plump and balanced. Good grip for a 1992, but it doesn't have the elegance of the 1991 (or the 1993 for that matter) nor the depth. But a good example. Positive and stylish at the end.

1991   **1999–2012???**

Good colour. But no more than the 1992, for instance. Fresh, composed, elegant nose. Not a blockbuster but plenty of depth. Excellent on the palate. Very well balanced. Lovely fruit. Fullish, long, intense. Classy. Complex. Very good indeed.

1990   **2000–2015**

Fullish, backward colour. Quite a lot more than the above. Rich, backward nose. Very good acidity. Cassis fruit and a lovely quietly harmonious expression of it. Fullish, gently oaky. Lovely fruit. Very, very ripe. An opulent and charming wine. Long, very seductive. Fine.

1989   **Now–2009**

Medium-full colour. Plenty of fruit on the nose but lacks a little backbone. Put on more weight as it evolved in the glass though. Fat, rich, fullish, good tannins. Good acidity. Not quite the balance and definition of the 1991. But very good. And much better than it appeared at first.

1988   **Now–2009**

Medium-full colour but less to it, it would appear, than the 1989. A touch austere on the nose. Not currently a wine with a smile. This has good grip, some weight and tannin. But not as much flair or elegance as it should have. Somewhat awkward, even with a slightly metallic taste.

1987   **Drink soon**

Medium colour. Plump nose. Quite evolved now. Rather a small wine. And a little blowsy. Now ready. Pleasantly fruity and quite fresh. But nothing special. No depth. Lacks freshness. An improvement on the 1986.

1986   **Drink up**

Medium colour. Evolved now. This is even weedier than the 1987. Now beginning to get astringent. This is poor: thin, unsophisticated, sweet and unbalanced.

1985   **Now–2017**

Good colour. Fullish, still youthful. Ripe, plump and plummy. Good reserves. Very good

grip. This is still youthful but is of very good quality indeed. Just a touch rigid on the attack. But ample and composed. Elegant, harmonious, long. Bags of life. Will still improve. Still needs time.

1984   **Now–1999**

Unexpectedly good colour here. Medium to medium-full, mature. But not undue brown. The nose is pleasantly fruity and still fresh. And the palate is equally agreeable. Classy, long, ripe. No sign of age. An excellent example of the vintage.

1983   **Now–2005**

Fullish, mature colour. Full rich nose. Chocolatey. A little four-square perhaps but not a bit dry and astringent. Plenty of ripeness and plumpness. This is a very good 1983 indeed. Fullish, rich, spicy. Quite structured. The fruit slightly cooked. A wine for food. Good fruit. Good grip. Still needs to soften. But the finish is very good.

1982   **Drink up**

Medium colour. Fully mature. A bit diffuse on the nose. A bit over-evolved on the palate. This is light and rather hollow. And is now beginning to lose what grip and elegance it ever had. Somewhat dilute. Not special.

1981   **Drink up**

Lightish colour. Fully mature. There is even less to this, but that is understandable. Some fruit but now a bit hard and vegetal and coarse as well. And very slight.

1980   **Now–2000 plus**

Good fullish fresh colour. As big as, but more vigorous than the 1978. This is very good. Alive and plump and elegant on the nose. Fresh and with very good fruit. On the palate this is similar. A most attractive example. Fresh, virile, plummy. No hard edges. No coarse corners. Long. Fullish. Bags of life. Very good indeed for the vintage.

1978   **Now–2005 plus**

Fullish, mature colour. Very good nose. Fresh, quite concentrated, full of finesse, lots of depth. Fullish on the palate. Rich and ripe with a touch of spice. Nicely classy. Nicely profound and very long on the palate. Fully ready but bags of life. Fine.

1976   **Now–2005 plus**

Full, mature but vigorous colour. Attractively ripe, meaty and animal on the nose. Fullish, but unlike the 1983 no undue tannins. Just a good backbone. Very good grip of acidity. Opulent, fresh, lots of dimension. Lots of vigour.

JEAN TARDY,
VOSNE-ROMANÉE

Jean Tardy is a neat, fit, handsome man in his fifties who runs a 5 hectare domaine with his son Olivier from a modern house on the *Route Nationale* in Vosne-Romanée. He makes very good wine indeed. Since he started bottling seriously in 1985 or so he has rapidly attracted an enthusiastic clientele, and now could easily sell twice as much as he produces. This fills him with both pride and exasperation, for he would love to increase his exploitation, but current prices prohibit it.

THE VINEYARDS

Like his father, from whom he inherited his vineyards in 1970, Jean Tardy is a *métayer*, a share-cropper. And this, potentially, is the worrying thing about the domaine's long-term future. For Tardy's landlord is the Méo-Camuzet estate, and while they were quite happy to let him take over twenty-five years ago when his father retired, it is unlikely that the lease will be extended to Olivier when Jean decides to go *en retraite*. Jean-Nicolas Méo is now firmly in charge of his patrimony. The Henri Jayer lease exists no more, and other arrangements the Méo-Camuzet family made in the past have come to an end. Eventually there will be no more Tardy Clos-de-Vougeot, nor Nuits-Saint-Georges, Les Boudots and Vosne-Romanée, Les Chaumes, the gems in the Tardy portfolio.

Tardy is the sole *métayer* of the Méo-Camuzet Nuits-Saint-Georges, Boudots. The *climat* clings to the rock immediately to the south of Vosne-Romanée, Aux Malconsorts and the forty-year-old parcel measures 1.04 ha, Tardy tending the vines and rendering half the crop to the Méo domaine at vintage time. In Vosne-Romanée, Les Chaumes the vines are much younger, having been planted in 1976. Tardy's share is half the produce of 1.55 ha. Potentially the best of the three, though not always, are the results of 0.23 ha of Clos-de-Vougeot, excellently placed high up the slope in the *lieu-dit* Les Grands-Maupertuis, and from forty-year-old-plus vines.

While Tardy *père* had no vines of his own, Jean has attempted to build up his own estate. In 1972 he bought some regional vineyards - Bourgogne *rouge* and Passetoutgrains, and a 45 ares parcel of village Nuits-Saint-Georges, Le Bas-de-Combe. This lies down-slope from Les Boudots, but in the same line as the Chaumes, and the vines are thirty-five-plus years old. The 1990 is delicious. More recently he bought a third of a hectare of village Chambolle-Musigny. It lies in a *climat* called Les Athets, touching the *Nationale*.

VITICULTURE AND VINIFICATION

Tardy is meticulous both in the vineyard and in the cellar. 'It all rests,' he says, 'on a small crop and on healthy fruit.' So there is strict pruning and careful debudding, a minimum of treatments, and a careful *triage* at the time of the harvest. He is much more exigent about keeping a control of the quantity today than he was in 1989, he says, comparing that vintage with the 1992.

Like his erstwhile fellow Méo *métayer*, Henri Jayer, Jean Tardy believes in 100 per cent destemming and 100 per cent new oak: the former because he wants his wine to be rich and sturdy, but not hard; the latter because, provided the yield is kept to a minimum, the new oak is a natural complement to the fruit. To ensure this, even in the most concentrated years, even with his old vines, he habitually *saignées* all his *cuvées*. *Cuvaisons* are extended as long as possible, usually to twenty days, the temperature is highish, about 30°C rather than below, and after one post-malo racking, the wine is left untouched: no fining, and a light filtration only when absolutely necessary.

THE WINE

All this, bar one aspect, I find wholly commendable. Where I have a doubt, a suspicion, is the invariable recourse to a *saignée*. The trouble with a *saignée* is that, as well as surplus water, some of the most delicate of the aromatic flavours are leached out. The result, and this is occasionally apparent in Tardy's wines, is something which is full and rich and oaky and concentrated, but which lacks nuance. Others have found this in his Nuits-Saint-Georges, Les Boudots. I have found it in some of Tardy's Clos-de-Vougeots. And when I tasted the Boudots 1988 after an hour on ullage (see below) I was unimpressed by its evolution. (Tardy, by the way, considers the 1988 vintage superior to the 1990. It is, he says, finer, more complete, *plus de longue garde*.)

Nevertheless, this is a quality domaine, and with his son Olivier, a capable young man, now on board, things can only get better. Let's hope, both that the Tardys can gain control of more quality vines, and that it is many years before Jean decides to retire. The leasing arrangement with the Méo-Camuzet domaine runs until the year 2007.

THE TASTING

I sampled the following wines in Vosne-Romanée in June 1994.

NUITS-SAINT-GEORGES, LES BOUDOTS

Optimum drinking

1992   **Now–2005**

Bottled in March. Very good colour. Plump, vigorous nose. On the palate very good fruit. No lack of depth or grip. This is a fine example of the vintage. Gently oaky, nicely plump and supple. But good substance. Very good indeed. Very elegant. Very complex.

1991   **1999–2012**

Very good colour. This has firmed up and closed in on the nose. The tannins show a bit. On the palate fullish, rich. Good grip. At the moment a bit adolescent. But ripe and expansive. Rich and balanced. Plenty of depth. Long on the palate. Very good indeed.

1990   **2001–2020**

Excellent colour. Here again the wine is closed and adolescent on the nose. Powerful, intense and full bodied. A masculine wine of full structure. Quite tannic but very very rich. Very good grip. Lots and lots of depth. Fine.

1989   **Now–2002**

Reasonable colour. This shows some evolution and even dilution on the nose. Plump and ripe and pleasant. But one can see the size of the vintage here. Charming. Not short nor dry. But a little one-dimensional. Lacks the elegance of the 1992. Yet a generous, very pleasant bottle. Still long and positive. Very good plus.

1988   **1998–2020 plus**

Fine colour. Still a bit closed on the nose but a marvellous fruit and consistency on the palate. Full, good structure. Very good acidity. But the fruit is exceedingly rich and ample, long, elegant and aristocratic. The best so far. Even better than the 1990. Very very long. (Yet later, with food, I found it had become thin and stringy, while the 1986 was still most attractive.)

1987   **Now–1999**

Good colour. A bit of evolution on the nose. On the palate a little bit of astringency and a slight lack of grip and zip. Quite plump. Medium to medium-full. Good. Not short. But it lacks a little excitement and finishes a little dry.

1986   **Now–2000**

Rather better colour than the 1987. On the nose fatter and plumper. Medium to medium-full also. A fatter wine, with good ample fruit. Not a lot of grip. But plump on the follow-through, round and soft, and with good length. Rather more attractive and satisfactory than the 1987. Charming. Gently oaky, ripe and persistent. Very good indeed for the vintage. The 1992 will turn out like this.

1985   **Now–2004**

Very good colour. Velvety rich on the nose but the necessary grip and zip. On the palate ample and plump, more substance and depth than the 1986, but not combining to make a wine of real top-class interest. Very good indeed, certainly, but not the grip and finesse and depth of the 1988; or to be classed as fine.

1983   **Drink soon**

Good colour. The nose, frankly, is rather rustic. But the palate, especially after 5 minutes' aeration, is better. A bit astringent, but nonetheless rich and ripe. Not exactly a lot of concentration, nor much finesse. Indeed it is dry and artisanal at the end, as well as sweet and plump. Nevertheless 'quite good' for the vintage.

1979   **Drink soon**

This has a very good colour and surprising plumpness and vigour. While at the same time there is a touch of the artisanal, it is rich and fat, round and complex. Good acidity. Shows very well. Full for a 1979 Nuits.

THOMAS-MOILLARD,
NUITS-SAINT-GEORGES

As a result of one of those laws which seems eminently sensible in theory but which is sometimes an infernal nuisance in practice, the wines and wine-making of the Domaine Thomas-Moillard have to be kept apart from those of its sister company, the *négociant* Moillard-Grivot. They can't even use the merchant bottling line for the domaine wines! Rather than invest in a second line, a travelling contract-bottling machine is employed. As a result, next to the larger merchants' premises on the Vosne side of Nuits is a smaller but equally modern installation which houses the produce of a 33 ha domaine, and a very good domaine at that. Thomas-Moillard wines, I feel, do not get the recognition that they deserve. I have been visiting and tasting for fifteen years or more, yet I seldom see them on merchants' and restaurants' lists, and they don't crop up at tastings of wines in bottle as often as do the wines of, say, Faiveley, Drouhin or Jadot. Nevertheless what I have seen leads me to expect quality and consistency. And, as elsewhere in Burgundy, an increased level of success in the vintages of the last dozen years or so.

HISTORY

The history begins with one Symphorien Moillard, scion of a family long established in Nuits-Saint-Georges, and possessor in the 1840s of a good-sized domaine which his ancestors had assembled at the time of the Revolution. This had been further augmented by his own marriage to a Mlle Grivot, daughter of another vineyard-owner.

In 1850, Moillard was visited by a Belgian from Namur who had descended into the region on what was then the brand new Paris-Lyon-Marseilles railway. This man was on the look-out for someone who could act on his behalf as a buyer and broker of top Burgundy. A friend put him in touch with Moillard. Moillard invited him to stay *chez lui*, and a week later the Belgian, a lawyer we are told, but perhaps a budding wine-merchant as well, had placed an order for 14 *feuillettes* of top wine, leaving Moillard to look after their *élevage*, bottling and eventual dispatch.

The wines pleased the Belgian lawyer's friends, and a year later he sent down for double the quantity to be delivered. This was beyond the possibility of Moillard's own domaine. He had to buy in wine to fulfil the order. He was now a *négociant*.

Symphorien Moillard's son, also called Symphorien, was killed in Algeria in 1870 during the French war of conquest, so the succession passed down through the female line. Jeanne Moillard, daughter of the first Symphorien, married Maurice Thomas, a vineyard-owner himself, in 1873. It was under Maurice's reign over what was a rapidly-expanding empire that the present-day Moillard cellar - capable of holding 1,000 barrels under a single roof - was constructed to the orders of the Dijon architect Charles Suisse.

Moillard, or Moillard-Grivot - today the simple surname is used for the *grande distribution*, the double-barrelled for private clients and top restaurants - was soon one of the most powerful in Burgundy. It was able to withstand the loss during the First World War of its entire stock held in Belgium - a coincidence that this happened to be in Namur? - and the compensation for this arrived just in time to keep the business secure during the economic crises of the 1930s. Indeed Moillard was able (and willing) to act as banker and stockholder for other merchants such as Liger-Belair and Chauvenet during this miserable time.

In the meanwhile, prompted by their American clients, the Moillards had diversified into fruit juices. Juvigor, which has disappeared, was one of their brands. Pampryl, which is certainly still vigorous, was another. (This is now owned by Pernod-Ricard.)

The business survived the Second World War, despite the second loss of the Belgian stock - after that the Moillards gave up stocking wine in Belgium! - and indeed thrived sufficiently to necessitate the construction of a second immense barrel cellar, parallel to that of the original, this time with a capacity of 1,500 casks.

Today it is the fifth generation of Thomas-Moillards who are in charge: Denis and Henri-Noël, together with their father Yves, who officially stepped down as *président-directeur-générale* in 1988, and their cousin Charles-Olivier. Their chief *oenologue* is Gérard Sauvaget, in charge of the wines since 1971.

THE DOMAINE

The Thomas-Moillard domaine occupies 32.74 ha, 13 ha of which is in the Hautes-Côtes. Most of the rest is in the Côte-de-Nuits - the exceptions being a 2.20 ha chunk of Beaune, Les Grèves, some Savigny and some Corton - and nearly all of this is red wine.

The vines are looked after by others, not by Thomas-Moillard themselves. These include André Esmonin in Gevrey for the two Chambertins (5 a of Chambertin itself and 24 a of Clos-de-Bèze) and the Bonnes-Mares (15 a); Sylvain Cathiard and André Perrin (-Rossin) in Vosne-Romanée (17 a Romanée-Saint-Vivant, 60 a Clos-de-Vougeot, 2.94 ha Vosne-Romanée, Les Malconsorts, 93 a Les Beaux-Monts); and Michel Chevillon in Nuits-Saint-Georges. Michel

Thomas, a younger son, also tends some vines. While these farming arrangements are on a *métayage* basis, the domaine buys the *métayers'* share in grapes, so in fact it gets the entire yield of wine from each parcel. One of the contracts Moillard-Grivot have is with a Georges Thomas, no immediate relation, and his 40 a of Echézeaux.

The heart of the Thomas-Moillard domaine lies in Nuits-Saint-Georges. Here it owns two monopolies: that of the 2.12 ha Clos-des-Grandes-Vignes in Prémeaux, the only *premier cru* on the 'wrong', i.e. east side of the main road; and the Clos-de-Thorey on the Vosne side of the town.

The story behind the latter *climat* centres round Charles Thomas, a grandson of the original Symphorien. Charles was a bit of a *bon viveur*, and seems to have specialised in selling to the Moillard's Belgian clientele. After one visit, no doubt well wined and dined, he succumbed to a serious heart attack. Convalescing back in Nuits-Saint-Georges, and having been told to take more exercise, he used to walk among the vineyards with his wife, especially up in the scrub above the vines, in places which had returned to nature following the phylloxera epidemic. Here was a piece of land called the Clos-de-Thorey which had once belonged to the Marquis de Montmaure, the proprietor of Romanée-Saint-Vivant. It is said that this proprietor often blended the two together in pre-appellation days. Now the locals were using the land for grazing cattle.

Charles bought the terrain and succeeded in resurrecting about three-quarters of it. The vines were planted in 1922. His son Yves, helped by present-day bulldozers and tractors, renovated the rest in the 1950s, and now the domaine can boast a vineyard of 4.23 ha. The vines are old, and as you can read in the notes which follow, produce a typical 'northern' Nuits: rich and full, opulent and ripe.

THE WINES

The red wines are totally destemmed, given a three- or four-day cold soaking, and vinified at 28 to 30°C, both in traditional vats, for the smaller lots, and larger stainless-steel *cuves* with revolving arms inside to break up the *chapeau*. There is usually one fining, a light filtration, and bottling, by the contract bottler as I have said, takes place after a year to eighteen months in wood, about 30 per cent of which is new.

The house-style is for very well-coloured, sturdy wines, quite tannic, and not necessarily very easy to appreciate in the year or two after they have been put into bottle (although they normally taste very well in cask, twelve or so months after the vintage). They can appear a little hard in this period of their adolescence, and are made for the long term. But the quality, certainly in the years since 1983, is very good indeed.

THE TASTING

I sampled the following range of wines in January 1996.

NUITS-SAINT-GEORGES, CLOS-DE-THOREY

Optimum drinking

1994 — **2000-2008**

Bottled three weeks previously (15 December). Good full colour. The nose is a little subdued by the sulphur, but there is plenty of depth here. Medium-full body. The tannins are ripe but a little hard at present. Good acidity. A typical sturdy Nuits. Lacks a little succulence but this will come. Good depth.

1993 — **2002-2015**

Good colour. Firm, rich nose. Plenty of depth here. But has retired into its shell a little. A little ungainly because of the sulphur. Better on the palate. Full, good ripe tannins but slightly hard at present as well. Good grip. Plenty of wine here. Nicely austere, and good concentration. Needs time. Very good.

1992 — **1999-2007**

Good colour. Again the nose is a bit ungainly. But there is good structure and depth for the vintage. Quite full for the vintage on the nose.

Very good rich blackberry fruit, and good grip as well. This has a lot of substance for a 1992, and it is long, harmonious and sophisticated. Very good for the vintage.

1991   **1999-2012**
Good colour. Very attractive, quite firm, damson fruit on the nose. Violets as well. Certainly has Vosne touches. But no lack of weight or backbone. Full, a lot of depth here. Nicely firm. Concentrated, very good acidity. Easier to see the quality than the 1993 today. Long. Very good indeed.

1990   **1998-2015**
Fine colour. Rich, full and tannic on the nose. Lots of depth. On the palate this is medium-full, but slightly more evolved than I expected after the wines above. Lovely rich fruit, opulent and ripe. Good acidity but the 1991 has more. The finish is long and succulent. Very good plus.

1989   **Now-2009**
Very good colour. Still youthful. Lovely ripe nose. Lots of *petits fruits rouges* as well as *noirs*. This is a medium-full-bodied wine of real flair, grip, succulence and charm. Long, complex. Lovely fruit. Fine.

1988   **1998-2015**
Good colour. But not as full as the 1989, and just as evolved. Slightly unforthcoming on the nose. Certainly good and rich and no lack of grip. Better on the palate. Fullish, rich, concentrated, well structured. Above all a grip and a drive which are very promising. Fine finish. Complex. Persistent. Fine.

1987   **Now-2003**
Medium-full mature colour. No undue age. Slightly spicy on the nose, and a certain lack of elegance as well. But vigorous and full of fruit by comparison with most. Fullish, opulent. Lots of ripe fruit. Now round and soft. Only a slight lack of freshness and elegance at the finish detracts from this wine. But a very good plus example for the vintage.

1986   **Now-2001**
Excellent fresh colour for the vintage. Full too. Slightly lighter and more loose knit than the 1987 on the nose. But good fruit and more elegance. Medium-bodied. Very charming fruit. Fresher and more elegant than the 1987, if not as structured. Long, balanced, complex. Not a trace of age.

1985   **Now-2005**
Fine colour. Barely mature. This is still very youthful on the nose. Quite structured. Very good ripe rich fruit. Fullish, ripe and ample on

the palate. Not quite the acidity to finish it off really elegantly but a round, plump wine which is just about à *point*. Very good for the vintage.

1983   **Now-2005**
Good fullish mature colour. Still fresh. No undue brown. This is fresh, but a bit hard on the nose. On the palate there is good ripeness and concentration. Good grip, and a touch of spice. Despite the over-the-top presence of the tannins a very good wine. Needs food. Still youthful. Very good indeed for the vintage.

1982   **Past its best**
Medium colour. Fully evolved but no undue age. Lightish nose. Rather too much compost heap and H$_2$S. Light to medium body. Rather sweet, rather attenuated. This is blowsy and poor.

1981   **Drink soon**
Surprisingly good, fresh colour. Slightly lean on the nose. But the fruit is fresh and elegant. Not too lean on the palate. Fresh and fruity if a bit one-dimensional and only medium body. But long and positive enough and very enjoyable. A surprisingly good result.

1980   **Now-2000**
Very good mature colour. Fine rich nose. Full, balanced and stylish. Yet another proof of how good this vintage can be in the Côte-de-Nuits. Medium-full. The tannins are not as sophisticated as those of today, so it is not as good on the palate as on the nose.

1977   **Drink up**
Medium colour. But no undue age. A little vegetal on the nose. Light, fruity, one-dimensional. Fading slightly. But balanced and elegant. A good result. But only a curiosity now.

1973   **Past its best**
Medium colour. Lightening up a bit now. Nose getting vegetal and diffuse. Slightly sweeter and slightly more substantial than the 1977 but now breaking up.

1971   **Drink soon**
Good fresh medium-full colour. On the nose fully evolved. Complex, refined but is it beginning to lose its fruit? On the palate this is nice mature Burgundy with a good combination of ripe, genuinely sweet fruit and slightly gamey spice. But good rather than great.

1964   **Now-2000 plus**
Good fresh vigorous fullish colour. Rich and fullish on the nose. More vigour than the 1971. Fatter and more succulent. This is full, rich and lovely. Much better than the 1971. Velvety

smooth with plenty of grip and depth. Lots of dimension and vigour and complexity and length on the finish. Fine quality. Still has plenty of life.

1963   **Drink soon**

Says 1963 on a typed slip in the punt. But I don't believe it. Colour not far removed from the 1964. Nose is ripe, with a touch of mocha, and plenty of substance underneath. On the palate a little lighter, a little more evolved. But good balance and plenty of fruit and dimension. Positive, round, slightly spicy finish. Good acidity. A mis-labelled 1962?

1959   **Now-2005 plus**

Splendid colour. Just a touch inky on the nose but fat, rich, structured and vigorous. On the palate a full, concentrated, powerful wine. This has splendid backbone, really rich, almost sweet, old viney fruit. A chewy wine. Caramelly rather than gamey. Vigorous. Very intense. Still bags of life. (This got better and better while the 1945 became a little rigid in the glass.) Very fine indeed.

1945   **Now-2000**

Very fine colour. Just as vigorous as the 1959. Splendid nose. Real concentration. Full but not a touch of out-of-place structure or rigidity: not too much tannin. Velvety rich, marvellous grip. Full and intense. And fresh as a daisy. Seems – at first, but see above – as if it will last for ever. Very fine indeed.

1922   **Past its best**

A Nuits-Saint-Georges but not the Clos-de-Thorey which was planted in 1922. Huge colour. But not inky and 1937-y on the nose. Slightly gamey-vegetaly. Some fruit. Yet not really very elegant. On the palate it starts better than it finishes. But after being quite pleasant and fruity on the attack the wine is a bit empty and acid at the end. And a bit coarse. A curiosity only.

CHÂTEAU DE LA TOUR, *VOUGEOT*

The Clos-de-Vougeot occupies just over 50.5 hectares and is divided into 107 plots, shared among eighty-two different owners. There is only one wine, however, which is actually vinified on the spot. This is the wine of the Château de la Tour, owner of the other château down-slope from the Château du Clos-de-Vougeot itself, and the largest single proprietor in the Clos, with 5.48 ha of vines. From 1975 this domaine has been in the hands of Madame Jacqueline Labet and her sister Madame Nicole Déchelette, and from 1986 Madame Labet's son François has been responsible for the wine. A disciple of the Lebanese oenologist and viticulturalist Guy Accad, François is one of a number of today's Bourguignons who combine a solidly biological approach in the vineyard with a cold-soaking, cool fermentation regime in the cellar. He is a young man, and he is still learning, but at the Château de la Tour he is one of the few who can enjoy the benefits of scale in a vineyard which is *grand cru*. Many of the wines he has produced since 1988 I have rated very good indeed, and one or two have been better still. This is a place to watch.

HISTORY

For the history of Château de la Tour we have to go back to the history of the Clos-de-Vougeot itself. In 1791, 693 years after it had first been delimited, the vineyard was torn from the grasp of the local Cistercian monks and put up for sale. After passing through several hands it was acquired in 1818 by Victor Ouvrard on behalf of his nephew Jules. The Ouvrards had amassed a fortune in Napoleonic times as both bankers to the Government and Empire and as suppliers to the army. Jules Ouvrard died in 1861, and the Clos once again passed through several hands before a consortium of six local *négociants* bought the vineyard in 1889. The six rapidly became fifteen and the fragmentation has continued to this day.

Up until this time Ouvrard and his successors had sold off the produce of the Clos in bulk to the local merchants. One of these, who had bought heavily in the 1885 and 1886 vintages, had organised that their purchase should be bottled and stocked at the old château so as to guarantee authenticity. This was the Maison Beaudet Frères, based in Beaune in the Clos-du-Chapitre in the Rue Paradis. They were not one of the original six, and so they were faced with the problem of removing their wine from the château, now owned by a rival *négociant*, Léonce Bocquet of Savigny.

Not wishing to lose their *cachet* of *mise en bouteilles au château*, Beaudet were quickly on the lookout to acquire part of the Clos, and this they managed to do a couple of years later. It was then that the Château de la Tour was constructed, and a makeshift railway line was set up within the Clos to move all their bottles of 1885 and 1886 - some 20,000 of them - down from the old château to the new, without them having to leave the Clos. It was the firm's proud boast, not only that the bottles were pure and authentic, but that none left the Clos until ready for drinking.

The successor to the Beaudets of 1889 and 1891 was a son, Charles. He was badly gassed during the First World War, and lost a lung. Advised to retire to a hot and wet climate he decided to sell up and move to Brazil, where he became a coffee planter. In 1920 the *négociant* business was sold to Jaffelin and the Château de la Tour to another merchant, Maison Morin Père et Fils of Nuits-Saint-Georges. He died in 1964. Whether by coincidence or not, his only daughter married Jean Morin in 1925. It is the two daughters of this marriage, Mesdames Labet and Déchelette, who are today's owners.

THE VINEYARD

The Château de la Tour is the largest owner in the Clos, with 10.9 per cent of the total surface. Its vines run almost from the very top to the very bottom. Behind - that is, to the south of - the old château there is one substantial plot. A second one, much the biggest of all, occupies the middle of the northern end, about halfway down, and runs right in the very middle of the Clos itself, and this is connected to two narrow strips which straddle the Grivot parcel and run down to the main road.

Naturally the vines are of different ages - from seventy years old down to infants. A significant replanting took place following the 1985 frosts, and a further parcel replaced one which suffered from *eutypoise* in 1990/1991. The produce of these very young vines is not incorporated into the *grand vin*, but sometimes recently, as in 1993, a small quantity of *vieilles vignes* is bottled separately.

WINE-MAKING

Up until 1975 wine-making responsibility had been in the hands of Morin Père et Fils. The wine was vinified on the spot, but distributed by them, and often sold off in bulk.

In that year - a terrible vintage, and no Château de la Tour was produced - Jacqueline Labet took over. The wine was made by the *maître de chai*, one Henri Legros, and a serious amount of château-bottling began to take place. The year of 1979 was another disaster. The Clos was badly hailed on 11 June, more or less wiping the crop out. At the Château de la Tour a small amount of 6° *rosé* was harvested on 11 November. It was later distilled.

Nevertheless, in the other post-1975 vintages, as you will see in the notes which follow, while the wine was somewhat artisanal, it wasn't bad at all. There is little wrong with the 1985, for instance.

It was the year afterwards, 1986, that Jacqueline's son François took over. This was a difficult year. There was rain just before the vintage, and there was a threat of rot. This was not a success at the Château de la Tour, and moreover François was not convinced that in general the property was doing as well as it should. The next year he got in touch with Guy Accad, and from 1987 to 1992 Accad was employed as a consultant.

The first changes were made in the vineyard. The soils were analysed. Clos-de-Vougeot encompasses a wide variety of soils, from limestones and marls of different epochs down to alluvial deposits, changing in colour and stoniness quite considerably from the upper slopes down to the bottom.

Labet began to prune a lot harder, in order to avoid both the necessity to green harvest later in the year, and to have to do a *saignée*, which he considers unbalances the wine. He also started to harvest much later than hitherto. If the fruit was concentrated enough, i.e. if the harvest was not excessive, there would be no danger of feeble acidities, it was considered. It was also decided, eventually, to reduce to half the amount of stems retained in most vintages and to use enzymes to aid clarification and thus eliminate the need to fine and to filter except in rare circumstances.

The must is today cooled to 5°C and macerated at this temperature for up to a week. The fermentation temperature is also kept low, within the 25-27°C range, and the *cuvaison* extended to fourteen to eighteen days. Thereafter the wine goes partly into new oak - from 15-50 per cent according to the *cuvée*, and is bottled after a year and a half. They have occasionally sold to Jadot in the past - Jacqueline Labet is a cousin of the Gagey family - but today the Château de la Tour is almost entirely sold off in bottle.

THE WINE

As well as the Château de la Tour, François Labet is responsible for the Beaune domaine of his father Pierre. This consists of 5 hectares: Beaune, *premier cru*, Les Coucherias, Beaune, Clos-des-Monsnières red and white, Savigny-lès-Beaune, *premier cru*, Les Vergelesses *blanc* and Bourgogne *rouge*. These are vinified and *élevé* at the Château de la Tour. I find the red wines sometimes a little slight, but the whites are commendable, with just the right amount of oak, nicely crisp fruit, and plenty of individuality.

The Château de la Tour has evolved over the last half a dozen years. In cask, after a year or so's evolution, it can sometimes lack succulence. Yet this seems to come after the wine has settled down in bottle. I find Accad-inspired wines often put on fat and richness later than more traditionally made wines, as do other red Burgundies where the fruit is not destemmed. This Clos-de-Vougeot is no exception. It is also becoming more distinctive, more original, year by year, as François Labet learns by experience, and this is a progression in the correct direction.

THE TASTING

I sampled the following wines at the Château de la Tour in June 1995.

CHÂTEAU DE LA TOUR, CLOS-DE-VOUGEOT

Optimum drinking

1993   1998-2004

Good colour. Full and intense and purple. Plump on the nose. Good fruit. Ripe and with no hard edges. But not a lot of intensity or depth. Expanded as it evolved. Medium to medium-full. Good acidity. Good tannins. Currently it is adolescent. It lacks a little weight and structure. But the fruit is ripe. 'Good' merely.

Vieilles-Vignes, 1993   1999-2009

Slightly less colour than the 'regular', less purple too. Fresh, raspberry and chocolate nose. Fatter and more intense than the above. This has got the fat and depth that the 'ordinary' lacks. Medium full, well balanced, very ripe. Rather better. Very good indeed.

1992   Now-2002

Good colour for the vintage. Medium to medium-full. Soft nose. A touch lean. On the palate there is plenty of volume and dimension. Lots of lovely ripe fruit. Long and positive. Very good - at the very least - for the vintage. Lots of charm.

1991   Now-2209

Good fullish colour. Good fruit, but slightly alien on the nose at first. Less so after a bit of aeration. And it seemed to get fatter in the glass. On the palate it seems to have more backbone and depth than the regular 1993. This is very promising. Fullish. Good tannins, rich and plump. Good grip. Very good indeed.

1990   1999-2020

Good fullish colour. A little more evolution than the 1991. Full, rich, concentrated, very well balanced. Lots of wine here. Lovely fruit. Very good style. Deliciously concentrated and rich. Abundant, expansive fruit. Very good acidity. This has character and depth. Fine.

1989   Now-2006

Good fullish colour. Vigorous too. No more evolution than the 1990. Interesting smoky, roasted aromas on the nose. Less evolved than I expected. More structure too. On the palate there is a suggestion of astringency. Otherwise it is ripe, balanced, slightly more austere than most 1989s. And it doesn't have the fat of the 1990. Good plus.

1988   1998-2008

Fullish colour. More brown than the 1989. Curious aromas here. Chocolate blancmange

and cough mixture at first. But got riper, sweeter and classier as it evolved. This again I find a bit astringent on the attack. Again slightly lean, a slight absence of fruit. It lacks a bit of concentration and a bit of generosity. But these may come. It is still a long way from maturity.

1987   Now-2000

Most impressive colour. Full, just a little brown. Very good nose. Rich, poised, classy. Totally composed. Lovely ripe fruit underneath. This is very good indeed. Rich, fat, gently oaky. Lots of concentration. No strange flavours. Lots of intensity here on the finish. Drink quite soon for it will not age gracefully, I fear. The stems are showing on the after-taste.

1986   Drink soon

Medium to medium-full mature colour. This is a little weedy and evolved on the nose. A bit thin. But more importantly, a bit coarse. Too much stems. Not enough fruit. A bit astringent. This is drying out.

1985   Now-2000 plus

Medium-full mature colour. Fullish, rich, nicely abundant nose. I like the style here. The Pinot is quite pure and the wine is long on the palate. Medium-full. Mature. Not the greatest of class but ripe and generous. Reasonable length. But lacks a bit of grip and dimension for great. Very good plus.

1983   Now-2000 plus

Good full colour. No undue brown. This has much less dry tannin on the nose than I would have expected. But the fruit began to dry out and coarsen on aeration. On the palate there is plenty of fruit. But there is a savage astringency which dominates almost immediately. No rot or hail smells though. And the finish is lush. Needs food. Very good for the vintage.

1981   Past its best/drink up

The colour is still quite fresh looking. Slightly lean on both nose and palate but by no means a disaster. Now it is getting a bit sour, rather than really astringent. But it wasn't too bad once.

1980   Drink up

Lightish colour, which *visibly* deepened. I have never seen it happen quite this quickly. Good fresh, stylish nose. On the palate though the wine is a little coarse at the end now, and though the attack is quite fresh and fruity, the after-taste is much less exciting.

1978   Drink soon

Medium-full colour. Fully mature. Rich, controlled, classy nose. On the palate a fullish meaty example. Not exactly very stylish. (All these older examples show more class on the nose than on the palate.) It starts well but it gets a bit animal and astringent at the end. Good plus.

1976 **Drink soon**

Magnum. Good full colour. Not too evolved looking. A bit tough and dense, but nicely sweet on the nose. Rather muddy and astringent on the palate, with the stems showing. Old-fashioned is the word. And now it lacks grace. Medium-full. Reasonable fruit and length. Getting a little short now at the end. Good plus though.

1966 **Now–2000 plus**

Splendid colour. Still showing and vigorous. Lovely nose here. This has the class the late 1970 vintages lack. Fullish, concentrated, aromatic. Very smooth. This has all the beauty of mature Pinot. Balanced, poised and complex. Long on the palate. Still a lot of vigour. This will outlive the 1976 and 1978 because the balance is so good. Fine.

COMTE GEORGES DE VOGÜÉ,
CHAMBOLLE-MUSIGNY

Delicate, feminine and fragrant, the epitome of finesse: lace, silk and taffeta; violets and dog-roses; raspberries and blackcurrants with a finish of liquorice; amplitude and generosity; intensity without a trace of hardness. All this has been said by those attempting to describe the taste of Le Musigny. It goes further: an ode by Keats; the oboe solo from the Sixth Symphony of Beethoven; a Fabergé egg. What is it about Musigny which excites the imagination to such realms of fantasy?

Musigny is indeed an individual and distinctive wine. It is totally dissimilar from the other *grand cru* of Chambolle, Bonnes-Mares. But then the two are separated by the village, the valley of the tumbling river Grosne and several hundred metres of vineyard. But it is also quite different from its contiguous neighbour, the Clos-de-Vougeot. Musigny lies higher up the slope, at a point where the rise becomes distinctly steep. The soil is stony and thin, there is barely 30 centimetres of surface earth before you strike the crumbling limestone rock underneath. There is red clay in the upper part of the climat, rare in itself, but in general there is less clay than further down or in Bonnes-Mares, less nitrogenous matter, and hence more breed, and more definition in the wine, but less structure. The soil of Musigny is friable, and this contributes to the fragrance of the wine.

And the wine, when it is good, *is* perfumed and silky-smooth, not rugged and masculine. The tannins are there, but they are supple; the vigour is present, but the feel is essentially soft. If Musigny has a similarity with any other *grand cru*, it is with Romanée-Saint-Vivant, just as the wines of Chambolle find their echo in those of Volnay in the Côte-de-Beaune.

OWNERS

Le Musigny consists of two sub-*climats*, Le Musigny itself and at the same altitude next door to the south, Les Petits-Musigny. In addition the owners of a couple of isolated parcels of the Combe-d'Orveau seem to have been able to prove to the authorities that they have always produced Musigny wine and have been added on. Altogether this comprises 10 ha, 85 a, 55 ca.

Four proprietors own 90 per cent of the surface area. The Château de Chambolle-Musigny (Frédéric Mugnier) owns 10.5 per cent, Jacques Prieur 7.05 per cent and Joseph Drouhin 6.2 per cent. Other landowners include Pierre-Julien Hudelot, Daniel Moine-Hudelot, the Domaine Ponnelle, Georges Roumier and Lalou Bize. But the lion's share, 7 ha, 24a, 21 ca, almost 70 per cent, and including the totality of Les Petits-Musigny, belongs to the Domaine Comte Georges de Vogüé. Not for nothing does this estate proclaim itself the Domaine des Musigny.

HISTORY

Not many estates in the Côte d'Or can trace their origins as far back as the Vogüé domaine of Chambolle-Musigny. Around 1450, when what was to become today's tightly-knit community of houses was but a straggling hamlet, a Jean Moisson endowed money for the construction of the Chambolle village church. When his granddaughter married a Dijon merchant called Michel Millière in 1528 she brought as dowry the nucleus of the future Vogüé domaine. The deed of marriage settlement is the first extant mention of Musigny vines. The Millières residence - it still exists - lay in the Rue de la Chouette in Dijon. For most of the fifty-two years the late Comte Georges de Vogüé ran the family domaine he lived next door. A bizarre coincidence.

In 1575, again through the female line, the vines passed into the hands of the illustrious Bouhier family, prominent members of the local parliament. And two centuries after that, in 1766, Catherine Bouhier de Versalieu, last of her line, espoused Cerice François Melchior de Vogüé, eldest son of a long-established noble family from the Vivarais. Once again the Musigny vines are mentioned in the marriage deed.

Six generations on, following the death of the late Comte Georges in 1987, the management of the Vogüé estate is in the hands of Elizabeth, Baronne Bertrand de Ladoucette, only daughter of Comte Georges, and the domaine belongs to her, and to her daughters, Comtesse Gérard de Caussans, and Marie de Vogüé.

GEORGES DE VOGÜÉ AND ALAIN ROUMIER

Georges de Vogüé took over the domaine on the death of his father in 1925. A man of military bearing, cooly precise, aristocratic but by no means self-important, he was complemented by his resident *régisseur*, Alain Roumier, whose father and grandfather had also occupied the same post. Roumier, who retired in July 1986, was the opposite of De Vogüé. Short of stature, excitable and voluble, every meagre inch the peasant, he was as passionate about his wines and his responsibilities as was his *patron*. Merely the expression was different.

Today there is a new *équipe*. The vines are tended by Gérard Gaudeau, the wine by François Millet, and the sales by Jean-Luc Pépin. Briefly, after the retirement of Roumier, it was Gérard de Caussans, son-in-law of Madame la Baronne, who was in charge of the marketing and financial management. Tragically he was overtaken by a rapid cancer and his tenure was brief.

THE DOMAINE

Located in one of the thin side roads in the heart of the village, you gain access to the large Vogüé courtyard through a fifteenth century porch. Opposite you lie the *chais*. Above the porch and round the sides, in a mixture of architectural styles, is the château itself: a grand stone staircase to the main rooms on the first floor: monumental fireplaces; hammer-beamed ceilings; escutcheons of the Moissons everywhere as are portraits of past De Vogüés. But otherwise it is sparsely furnished. Beneath the *chais* is the cellar, a vast vaulted room, replete with barrels of young wine, and cool and tranquil as all cellars should be.

The domaine itself comprises 12.4 hectares. As well as the 7.25 ha of Musigny, there are 2.75 ha of Bonnes-Mares, located entirely in the southern, Chambolle end of this *climat*, 60 ares of Amoureuses, 1.80 ha of *premiers crus* (Baudes and Fuées) and a small parcel of village wine. The Musigny vines average forty years - it is all sold as Musigny *vieilles-vignes*; the rest are twenty-five to thirty years old.

WINE-MAKING

How do they make the wine? François Millet, you feel, is wary of committing himself, as if he is still feeling his way, but, as he will hasten to assure you, flexibility is the key. The first thing is a low *rendement*: 30 hectolitres per hectare is the paramount objective. After that the fruit is largely if not totally destemmed. It depends on the vintage, the origin of the grapes and the ripeness of the stems themselves. Fermentation takes place at relatively high temperatures - above 30°C rather than below, and where possible the length of the maceration is prolonged. There is a judicious, but not excessive, use of new wood, only a light filtration, and the wines are bottled after a year to eighteen months.

MUSIGNY BLANC

As well as the red wines, the Vogüé domaine produces 100 cases - and the monopoly - of Musigny *blanc*. This is a *rara avis*. One is rarely permitted to sample it out of cask. It is an odd wine, exclusively Chardonnay, but grown on Pinot Noir soil, but in no way resembling even Nuits-Saint-Georges *blanc*, let alone a Corton-Charlemagne or a Montrachet.

One-third of a hectare is planted with Chardonnay, the residue of a period when it was commonplace to mix about one-tenth white grape bearing vines amongst your red. Old records will show you that in pre-phylloxera times even a Chambertin *blanc* was occasionally produced.

The wine is most individual. A little four-square, quite heavy in alcohol, yet rather austere, it is full and almondy - blossom as well as nuts. You would have difficulty placing it. It does not do well in blind tastings.

My experience is limited. I am tempted to say that it is more of a curiosity than an experience, but I am looking forward to the opportunity of being persuaded to change my mind.

THE RED WINES

It has become a commonplace in recent years to decry the De Vogüé domaine as an under-achiever. This accusation is only partly just. To be fair, Burgundy as a whole had a lean time during the years between 1971 and 1985. But to be equally dispassionate it is true to say that in the later years of the Georges de Vogüé/Alain Roumier epoch the standard did slip, and it has taken the new team a few vintages to learn how to cope. Yet, if the 1983 - badly hailed - was a disaster, the 1978 is fine; and though the 1976 (a hirsute wine, Alain Roumier is quoted as describing it) and the 1982 are unremarkable, as are the 1986 and 1987, the progression since 1988 is very encouraging. The 1989 has all the class and fragrance you would expect, and the 1990, 1993 and 1995 are very exciting indeed. Things are looking up. The domaine is in good hands. The future is bright.

THE TASTING

The following wines, amassed by Bob Feinn and Greg Cook and their friends, were sampled in Connecticut in March 1992. At a vote at the end, the 1949 was almost unanimously decreed the best wine followed by the 1953 and the 1942 *vieilles-vignes*. Readers are additionally referred to the Remoissenet Musigny *vieilles-vignes* of this period - even up to 1972. The domaine at this time sold off a sizeable portion in cask to this excellent *négociant*, and I can recommend many of their bottlings.

MUSIGNY BLANC

Optimum drinking

1983 Drink soon

A little hot and alcoholic on the nose at first. Quite flowery as it developed. But ripe and ample and fruity on the palate. Rich, balanced and generous. Good grip. Good character. This is individual and very good indeed. Will keep well.

1982 Drink soon

Slightly lean on the nose, with a little built-in sulphur. On the palate the fruit seems a little pinched, though the acidity is reasonable. But the wine is a little ungenerous and ungainly. A bit dull.

1970 Drink soon

A bit varnishy on the nose. Slighly attenuated. Quite high acidity on the palate. Lean but reasonably stylish. But rather austere.

1969 Now-2000

Quite a full colour. Ample, rich, plump, almost sweet nose. Still fresh and flowery. This is most attractive. Quite similar to the 1983 but less marked by alcohol. Better class and balance. Ripe and generous. Complex and harmonious. Long, and intense on the finish. Will still keep very well.

MUSIGNY, VIEILLES-VIGNES

1989 Now-2018

Good colour. Ripe, cherry-raspberry nose. Rich, ample and with plenty of depth. Good grip as well. This has concentration and balance, complexity and class. Medium-full. Above all it has very good acidity. Lovely fruit. Violets and other fragrances. Intense and long. A fine example.

1988 Now-2005

Medium-full colour. Soft and fragrant on the nose. Very Chambolle, a wine of style and delicacy and delicious complex fruit. But on the light and forward side for a 1988. This is not as good for the vintage as the 1989. Good. Stylish,

balanced fruit, but two dimensions rather than three. Medium to medium-full. A little raw and rigid. Merely good.

1987 Drink soon

Lightish colour. Fruity but light and one-dimensional on the nose. Fully ready. Lacks a bit of depth and grip. More elegance and depth than the 1986 though. Lightish, one-dimensional, pleasant but forward. Not bad at best.

1986 Drink soon

Rather slight on the nose. Has style though. Not too dry but rather short and much less interest and elegance than the 1987. Weak. Unexciting.

1985 Now-2003

Medium colour. Now mature-looking. On the nose it lacks depth and intensity for a 1985. Merely pretty. Medium body. Ripe raspberry fruit. Just a little tannin still. Like the 1988 it lacks real dimension and depth but it has good grip. Quite long and complex. Good plus but not great. Yet I find this more interesting than the 1988.

1983 Drink up

Medium to medium-full colour, quite mature. A little astringency on the nose but there is at least some fruit. A touch musty, but no hail damage at first. Better than expected. Got coarser as it evolved in the glass. Became vegetal and astringent quite quickly. On the palate dry and mean and certainly tainted. Disappointing. Died in the glass. Nothing to commend it.

1982 Drink soon

Just a little more colour than the 1983. Soft, ample nose. No great concentration but not too bad. On the palate this is a medium-bodied wine with some fruit and balance, but not enough class, concentration, depth and individuality for a *grand cru*, even in this vintage. Pleasant but not great by any means.

1978 Now-2000 plus

Medium-full colour. Mature. Ripe, ample nose. But lost its intensity quite quickly. On the palate, though, a wine of real class and character.

Delicate and soft, very Musigny. It doesn't have much size, but it certainly has delicious complex fruit and a lovely long finish. This is fine.

1976   **Drink soon**

Full mature colour. Cooked plum tart on the nose. Ample and fat, slightly roasted. On the palate it is a bit awkward. Rigid and ungainly. Somewhat tough and a little coarse. Reasonable acidity but not very harmonious. Quite good.

1973   **Drink soon**

Medium-full, mature colour. Light nose, elegant and distinctive, but losing a little of its grip now. But very elegant. On the palate this has no pretention to being a great wine but is balanced, fresh and fragrant - indeed complex. Much more harmony and class than the 1976. Long. Very *gouleyant*. Surprisingly good. Will still keep.

1972   **Drink soon**

Good colour. Very cedary nose. Intense, individual, fresh, full of interest. Smoky, bonfires and chocolate aspects. Still plenty of vigour here. Good structure. High acidity of course. Just a touch - the merest hint - of maderisation. Lots of depth and concentration here. But like many 1972s, a bit austere. Will still last well. Very good plus.

1970   **Drink soon**

Good mature colour. Delicate nose. Soft, just beginning to fade a little. Very soft now. Has less grip than the 1973. A little looser-knit and not as fresh. But similar in character. Medium body. Still balanced, fresh and classy. Good plus.

Bonnes-Mares, 1969   **Now-2000 plus**

Splendid colour. Fragrant, complex, spicy, gamey and lush. Sweet and succulent. Stylish and balanced. Long. Will still last very well.

1969   **Drink soon**

Good mature colour. Quite an old nose now. Has dried up and lightened up a little. Soft and fragrant though, and certainly elegant. Plenty of fruit and freshness on the palate. Round and intense. Old viney. Medium to medium-full. This is very good but I feel it has seen better days. I've had better bottles of this wine - very good indeed - and I prefer it to the 1971.

1967   **Drink soon**

Well-matured colour, now lightening. Quite a vigorous cedary-animal nose. Caramelly. Good fruit and vigour. As it evolved there was a hint of maderisation. Medium body. Plump, vigorous and fresh. No enormous complexity but holding up well. Still long and positive on the finish. Good plus.

1966   **Drink soon**

Mature but vigorous medium-full colour. Refined, very stylish nose. Balanced and complex. But didn't after 10 minutes shine as much on the palate. Medium-full, plump, ripe, complex and elegant. This is very classy. Soft and sweet on the finish. I like this a lot. Very good plus. Spicier than the 1967: more concentrated too.

1962   **Drink soon**

Very good colour for the age. Fullish, no undue maturity. Smoky, aromatic nose. This is sweeter than the three wines above. Almost over-ripe. Cinnamon aspects. Coffee and spice. This is even plumper than the above: fatter and creamier and more vigorous. Really old-viney. A gamey, intensely flavoured fragrant wine. Very good also but the 1966 is more elegant.

1959   **Drink soon**

Very good colour. A touch of maderisation on the nose. But certainly intense. Rich, meaty full and still vigorous. Quite high volatile acidity. Ripe, gamey, exotic, caramelly flavours. Long and satisfying. Not exactly elegant but plenty of pleasure to be had here. Raisiny. Very good plus.

1958   **Drink soon**

Lightish colour. Slightly simple nose. Fragrant and a bit attenuated. Very soft now but by no means too old. Still stylish. On the palate the wine is sweet and fragrant. Lightish. Somewhat one-dimensional but the grip is still here and there is nothing short or astringent about it. A very good example for the vintage.

1957   **Drink soon**

Good fullish mature colour. This is plump and fat and round and ample on the nose. Youthful. Cedary. A little raw and rigid on the palate. The fruit has begun to dry up a bit. What it lacks is fat and generosity. Evolved fast. Still very good though.

1955   **Drink soon**

The cork fell into the bottle as it was being opened. Good, fullish, mature colour. At first a little dry on the nose. Oxidised fast. A pity. There is sweetness and elegance, if not, it appears, a great deal of complexity here.

1953   **Now-2000 plus**

Good full colour. Fat, spicy, old-viney nose. Sweet and complex. Fullish, just a touch of astringency. There is quite a muscular wine here. Rich and meaty, but just a bit rigid now. Fine and fragrant on the finish. Long and very satisfying. Will still keep well. Very classy. Very fine. Better than the 1947.

1949   **Now–2000 plus**

Fine colour. The fullest and most vigorous since the 1980s. Fine nose, at first totally dreamy. I've had better 1949s. This nevertheless has the most aristocratic, harmonious, subtle nose of the entire tasting. Fullish, ripe, complex, fragrant. Vigorous and amply fruity. *Great wine.* Very very long. Real class. Will still keep well.

1947   **Drink soon**

Medium colour. Fully mature. A little 'hot' on the nose. A little dry and alcoholic. On the palate the wine is almost sweet. Crammed with fruit. Not too burnt, but very old-viney concentration, almost raisiny. Still long, still vigorous. A lot of appeal here. Still intense on the finish. Will still keep well. Fine plus.

1943   **Drink soon**

Fullish colour. Fully mature. This is the only wine which has been re-corked and it is a corky bottle. Yet, despite this the wine is rich and sweet and vigorous.

non Vieilles-Vignes, 1942   **Drink soon**

Good colour. Lovely, elegant, creamy nose. But is this 100 per cent Pinot Noir? Medium-full, ripe and rich, but a little rigid as it developed. I think this now needs drinking soon. Very good indeed though. The finish is still sweet, complex and fragrant.

Vieilles-Vignes, 1942   **Drink soon**

This is a significantly fuller and more vigorous colour than the regular bottling. Excellent nose. Really lovely concentrated perfumed fruit. My second favourite wine of the 1940s. This is plump and soft and complex. More complete, more intense and much more classy and harmonious than the above. Long. Lovely. Very fine indeed.

1937   **Drink soon**

Excellent colour. Tarry, dense, Rhônish, cedary. Full, rich and sweet, but un-Burgundian. A little solid and rigid.

1934   **This bottle too old**

Pronounced ullage, very low shoulder indeed. The colour is still reasonable though. Some age. Maderised, oxidised and raisiny-pruney, but not so much as to be disagreeable. Full, concentrated, old-viney. Fat and I'm sure excellent in its day. Still very good and enjoyable.

Part Three

Vintage Assessments

When I first started to plan this book it became obvious to me that in one respect at least it would have to be radically different from my book on Bordeaux, *Grands Vins*, and that is in this, the Vintage Assessments section. In Bordeaux you have approximately 150 châteaux of *cru classé* quality. Apart from the Graves, each produces a single *grand vin*. Moreover quantities are large. It is therefore not too difficult to assemble a representative selection, taste them in one or two or three sessions, and base a vintage assessment on the results. Elsewhere in *Grands Vins*, additionally, the very same wines had been vertically sampled.

Burgundy, obviously, is different. Most domaines will make a number of wines worthy of note. But quantities are minuscule and they disappear into the cellars of private consumers, never to be seen again, right from the word go. Assembling a range of even fifty or so, some years after the event, is hard work. To do justice to the 1,500 wines which are perhaps worthy of assessment is almost impossible. To repeat the process until one becomes familiar with the evolution of every single wine is quite without the bounds of possibility.

I therefore decided it would be ludicrous to base these Vintage Assessments on a single tasting. Even if I assembled all the Burgundies I had tasted over the last six or so years it would hardly do justice to the range that would be dispersed over the world's wine cellars. But this would be better than nothing, and will have to do.

I therefore set out to sample as many fine Burgundies as possible. In this I have been immeasurably assisted by many dozen groups of friends and wine-lovers' associations. Will you come and talk to us, they asked? Only if it is over a serious range of Burgundy, I generally replied. The response was generous in the extreme. As a result I have probably sampled more fine Burgundy in the last six years than most might do in a lifetime. It has been a splendid few years!

The tastings roughly fall into three parts. Firstly there are the newer vintages (*wines not yet safely in bottle have not been noted: I refer readers to my regular coverage of new vintages in* The Vine *for that*). Notes on these come from a multitude of opportunities in the United Kingdom and the USA: private tastings, trade opportunities and the like. Secondly there is my *Ten Years On* yearly celebration. This takes place in Burgundy in June. I invite all the top growers to join me with a sample or two. I descend with a few cases of champagne, a side or two of smoked salmon and some farmhouse English cheese (far better for red wine than the vast majority of French cheeses!), and *le tout Bourgogne* descends on Becky Wasserman's Le Serbet in Bouilland (from whom I rent a room when I am in the region), and we all have a splendid time. It is a celebration, not a competition. But it is a fascinating opportunity to see a range of wines a decade old alongside each other. Finally, for vintages even older than a decade, I have been deeply indebted to my friend Bob Feinn and his group of New Haven CT based Burgundy lovers. Thanks to their generosity I have been able to indulge myself with wines of vintages as far back as 1949.

As you will see, for all the notes are dated (usually the most recent representative comment for the wines I have had the opportunity of tasting more than once), I have in the main only listed those wines sampled since 1 January 1990. But there are one or two exceptions: a 1949/1959/1969 session in October 1989 was too important to be left out, plus there are a few notes on other older wines of such importance, sampled just prior to my self-imposed deadline – a 1979 tasting ten years on, for instance – which I felt should be included, despite the assessments being somewhat dated. Better that, I decided, however inadequate, than no mention at all. My justification for this is that once a wine is ten, fifteen or twenty years old its path has been established. You can see where it has come from and predict confidently where it is going to. A note, even if a decade old, can still therefore be valid.

I remind readers that other notes from a single vertical tasting occasion, which usually took place at the domaine itself, will be found in the second section of this book. These have *not* been included here.

A Further Important Point

Generalising is hazardous - particularly in Burgundy. If you are rating something like the quality of a vintage, or its state of maturity, do you go by the best, or the average? What, indeed, in Burgundy, *is* the average?

I have based my assessments of the vintage as a whole on the premise that those who have been kind enough to invest in a copy of this book are those who take Burgundy seriously and therefore have bought the best (and I don't mean only *grand cru* wine) from the best growers: the 300 or so I review regularly in *The Vine*. We all know that this is not representative of Burgundy in general, but it corresponds to what has been carefully selected by merchants in the UK and the USA and elsewhere, out of all the dross that is available, for offering to you, their customers.

On the basis of this selection, and my experience when I return to investigate even the meanest of vintages, I can safely say that in every year there are some surprisingly good wines. Good *terroir* and good wine-making will out. A 1984 may not have the richness of a 1985, nor a 1992 the depth and concentration of a 1993, but it can still be good. Mistakes obviously are made, even in the best of vintages, but if you stick to the best growers you will nearly always find something which will give you pleasure, even in vintages rated only 11 out of 20.

Please Note

1. All tasting notes are of wines safely in bottle, having recovered from the bottling, subsequent shipping, etc. Cask samples have been excluded.

2. In many cases I have tasted the wines on a number of occasions. For these wines I have usually inserted my most recent tasting note.

3. State of maturity comments ('drink soon' etc.) refer to the wine's state of play in 1997 when this book is published. For instance, a note taken in 1994, where I originally wrote 'drink now to 1998' has been amended to 'drink soon'.

4. The marks accorded are out of 20, and can be translated into value judgements as follows:

12.0	Poor	16.0	Very good
13.0	Not bad	17.0	Very good indeed
14.0	Quite good	18.0	Fine plus
15.0	Good	19.0	Very fine indeed

5. In all vintages, however bad, the best growers will produce surprisingly good wine (Burgundy, and the Pinot Noir especially, is particularly favoured in this respect): not so rich and concentrated perhaps, but showing the elegance of the *climat*, and not without complexity and balance. Sadly the reverse is also true. Even in the very best of vintages the incompetent will ruin what nature has given them.

For this reason, wines are marked within the context of the vintage. A successful result, despite the weather, needs applauding. A disappointing effort, when the sun smiled, needs equally to be criticised. My assessment of the vintage as a whole, as well as its future development from 1997 onwards, will be made clear in the preambles to the chapters which follow.

1996

RATING FOR THE VINTAGE

Too early to say but certainly well above average.

SIZE OF THE CROP

Abundant. First reports indicate up to 10 per cent more than 1995.

This book goes to press even before the wines have finished their malos and are ready for a preliminary sampling, let alone a final judgement. Nevertheless, a glance at the weather conditions and the vintage comments of some of the leading figures in the region gives us an idea of what to expect. The following is what I wrote in *The Vine* in December 1996:

After a winter which began cold, but turned milder, March and April were very dry months, leading to a delayed bud-break during the first fortnight in April. May was cool, overcast and wet, but this led to a smooth acceleration of a vegetative cycle, and when the sun and the warm weather began at the beginning of June, the vines were able to flower within the period of a week, very rapidly, and very successfully. Suddenly, instead of being a week behind, we were five days ahead of schedule. The fruit setting was also rapid and without incident, despite a return to cooler temperatures at the end of June.

July was statistically normal, i.e. fine and sunny, without thunderstorms, and the fine weather continued into the first half of August despite a drop in temperatures. Throughout the summer, the north wind was dominant. This had the benefit of reducing the risk of oidium and mildew, but it meant cool nights, however hot and sunny it might have been during the day.

By the end of August the state of the fruit was again behind the norm, but September, while not being particularly warm, was very dry and very sunny. The precipitation for the month was one-third of the norm: 23 mm as opposed to 67. The vines caught up, the berries increased in sugar without increasing too much in volume, and when the vintage started (officially on 18 September for white wines, on 20 September for reds) the cycle was again five or six days in advance. The harvest continued in good weather save for two hours of rain on one day and a morning's-worth on another. The size of the crop is large, both for Pinot Noir and for Chardonnay. This will inevitably lead to a variation in quality - perhaps wide - between the conscientious, who have not exceeded the *rendement de base*, and the rest.

While we need sunshine to effect the photosynthesis, we need warm weather to turn the malic acidity into tartaric and to concentrate the berries. And, paradoxically, we need at least some rain to break down the potassium and avoid pHs which are too high. September was a month of very even temperatures, degrees not varying by more than 1° or 2° from day to day, and this has helped the fruit to make the utmost of the weather conditions. Where the harvest was reduced to reasonable levels, therefore, we had grapes with thick skins, good sugar levels, in some cases higher than 1990, high acidities and plenty of tannin. And in a perfect sanitary condition. The resulting wine has a splendid colour, plenty of backbone and grip and plenty of concentration. It is early days, and much remains to be seen after the malo-lactic fermentations are finished. But it augurs well: a *vin de garde* which may be an amalgam of 1966, 1978 and 1990; certainly a vintage to save up for.

The white wines also seem to be very successful, with the same high degrees of sugar when harvested and high (malic) acidities. Those who cropped low, and those who were able to take their time and pick each parcel at its optimum, will have made the best wines, and at present these seem full, rich and concentrated. But, as with the reds, we will get a very much better picture after the malos have completed.

(A full report on barrel tastings of the white wines will be published in *The Vine* in October 1997; that on the reds in February and March 1998. Write to *The Vine*, 76 Woodstock Road, London W4 1EQ, Great Britain, or fax (44) 0181 995 8943 for further details.)

1995

RATING FOR THE VINTAGE

Red: 17.5   **White:** 16.0

(provisional)

SIZE OF THE CROP

(Hectolitres, excluding generic wine)

	Red	White
Grands Crus	11,720	3,286
Village and *Premiers Crus*	173,727	46,575
Total	185,447	49,861

A smaller harvest than 1994 (5.36 per cent less in red, 7.76 less in white), but compared with the five-year average 1.2 per cent more abundant in red and 2.0 per cent less plentiful in white: so really not far from the average.

This book goes to press after I made a preliminary barrel-sampling survey of the white wines (published in *The Vine* in November 1996) but before I have had a chance to sample the reds. (Report in *The Vine* February and March 1997. Write to *The Vine*, 76 Woodstock Road, London W4 1EQ, Great Britain, or fax (44) 181 995 8943 for further details.)

WEATHER CONDITIONS

There was no real winter in 1994/95. The early months of the vegetative cycle were dry and mild, indeed fine in March and April. This produced a good *sortie* of buds in both the Chardonnay and Pinot Noir.

The bad weather arrived in the middle of May. It snowed, the snow remaining on the upper slopes, on 13 May. Two days later there was frost on the flatter land below. The weather remained cool and unsettled right through until 21 June or so - indeed throughout my visit to sample the 1994 whites in cask I was wearing a jacket or pullover, rather than the normal short-sleeved shirt.

The result, naturally, was a long and drawn-out flowering with the inevitable losses due to both *coulure* and *millerandage*. The harvest in parts of Chassagne was reduced even further by hail. There were also sporadic outbursts of mildew all the way up and down the Côte.

While the bad flowering affected the red-wine crop more than the white, the Chardonnay harvest was nevertheless seriously affected too, as the figures above suggest.

After 21 June the summer arrived, and it became then, paradoxically, too dry and hot: to the extent of placing a stress on the vine and blocking the progress towards maturity.

The fine weather continued until September. The two weeks after 4 September were unsettled, the latter half of this fortnight distinctly rainy, but after the 18th the weather cleared. Bouchard Père et Fils began to collect their Pinots on 21 September, their Chardonnays on the 23rd. Drouhin followed two days later. The Domaine Leflaive harvest took place between the 25th and the 30th, the date the red grapes began to be picked in the Côte-de-Nuits. And in general, especially so after 24 September, the weather was fine, the fruit dry and the risk of rot minimal.

THE STYLE OF THE WINES

WHITE WINES

Compared with 1994 the fruit was much more healthy. There was little rot, no great degree of *sur-maturité*, and so cleaner musts, with less risk of reduction and less need to perform a very heavy *débourbage*.

Acidities were high, and at the outset the wines seemed a bit linear. This caused Drouhin to *bâtonner* more than usual. At Olivier Leflaive Frères, on the other hand, they employed a bit more *cuve* (as opposed to fermentation in barrel) than usual with their lesser wines: expressly to preserve the racy fresh aspects of the wines.

Malos have taken their time to complete. But this has not posed problems. The lees are healthy and there is no rush to rack. Meanwhile what might have seemed linear at the outset has been able to fatten and enrich itself as the spring has progressed into summer.

'Racier than 1992 but with the same fat and substance,' said Bernard Moreau, who makes Chassagnes. 'Better balanced than 1989,' said his neighbour Michel Colin, 'like 1990 but with more up-front fruit.' According to Jean-François Coche the vintage is certainly better than 1992 and 1990. He prefers 1989 to 1990, and is not sure whether to place the 1995s at this level. The latest vintages will keep well, he thinks, just like the 1985s. Dominique Lafon also prefers 1995 to 1992.

Perhaps the best summary can be left to Noël Ramonet: 'Where 1995 really scores over 1992 is in the elegance and structure of the fruit. The wines are not as ripe but they have better acidity and potential to age well. They have the power and intensity of the 1989s, but the grip of the 1990s.'

This is the growers' view. The *négociants* are less enthusiastic. Jacques Lardière pointed out that outside the first division, most domaines were picking grapes with an alcohol potential of only around 12°: not really ripe and concentrated enough. He prefers his 1992s. 'They are a lot better,' he told me.

RED WINES

As with the whites, but even more so, the malos were long to take place. Normally, in Meursault cellars in June, I sample at least some Volnays, etc., just out of curiosity. This year there was hardly a single wine that was ready.

It does seem, however, that this is a fine vintage for red wines. The best growers have harvested low quantities. Tannins and acidities are good, indicating *vins de garde*, and the wines have plenty of fruit, depth, elegance and extract. No-one is suggesting a vintage with the opulence of the 1990s. But most seem to agree that 1995 is on a par with - or better - as well as in many ways similar to 1993.

1994

RATING FOR THE VINTAGE

Red: 13.0-14.5   **White:** 13.5

(variable)

SIZE OF THE CROP

(Hectolitres, excluding generic wine)

	Red	White
Grands Crus	12,605	3,504
Village and *Premiers Crus*	183,337	50,549
Total	195,942	54,053

The 1994 harvest was marginally larger (2.7 per cent in white, 1.6 per cent in red) than the five-year average: that is, relatively abundant. The yields varied from 42 hl/ha and 44 hl/ha in village and *premier cru* Côte-de-Nuits and Côte-de-Beaune *rouge* respectively, to an average of 48 hl/ha for village and *premier cru* white wines in Meursault, Puligny and Chassagne.

Nevertheless, while in general the figures do not appear to differ greatly from 1992 and 1993, most of the best growers, as a result of both severe *triage* and then a *saignée*, are at pains to point out that in their cases they produced rather less. The Domaine de la Romanée-Conti made 25 hl/ha, Roumier averaged 32, the Clos-des-Epeneaux 35 and Philippe Charlopin, including his generics and Marsannay, 40 hl/ha overall. At the Domaine Leroy, Lalou Bize produced 107 *pièces* from 25 ha, as against 101 in 1993, an average of 12.84 hl/ha. This paltry amount can hardly be economic, even at her high prices!

WEATHER CONDITIONS

A wet winter built up a high water-table in the soil, which was to prove important in a summer which was largely dry. The *sortie* was not particularly abundant but a swift early flowering at the end of May, some fifteen days in advance of the norm, ensured both a large harvest and the probability of an early one.

Then, on 20 June, came a notorious hail-storm. According to the local newspaper, the *Bien Publique*, and a press release which rapidly followed from Chartron et Trébuchet, the *grands* and *premiers crus* in the heart of Puligny-Montrachet were 'devastated'. In fact the damage was inflicted, for the second time in a row, in a swathe down from Blagny towards the *premiers crus* on the Meursault-Puligny border, not in the centre, except in Chevalier-Montrachet and Le Montrachet itself. Pucelles, Folatières and Clavoillon all eventually produced over 50 hl/ha (the legal maximum is 54 hl/ha) and Bienvenues and Bâtard-Montrachet over 43 hl/ha (max. 48), while the Puligny *premiers crus* of Chalumeaux, Champs-Canet, Combettes and Referts and the Meursault *premiers crus* of Perrières, Genevrières and Charmes all produced much less, though rather more than in 1993. In retrospect you could say that the Meursault-Puligny border harvested a normal crop, the rest of Puligny, as so often, an excess quantity.

Following this scare the summer was excellent. August was dry, and in some areas the fruit began to lag behind in development, but a couple of days of rain at the end of the month speeded up the progress towards maturity again, and by the first week of September, with everything looking splendidly ripe and healthy, everything was pointing towards an exceptional vintage.

It was not to be. A thunderstorm during the weekend of the 10th ushered in a week or more of heavy rain. Thankfully the temperature also dropped, and at first these downpours gave no real cause for concern. But as they continued – most growers starting their harvest on Monday 19 September or the weekend before – it became apparent that acidities were threatening to be dangerously low, that there was a risk of mildew, and that the fruit in some areas had passed the point of no return and were already over-ripe.

It is this factor of *sur-maturité* which is the key to the vintage. According to the Carillon family and others, the thunderstorm at the beginning of the rains caused the Chardonnays, already more or less ripe in Puligny-Montrachet, to 'turn' almost overnight. Botrytis set in quickly and the grapes passed from being marginally ripe to over-ripe without ever attaining the optimum of being really concentrated in the middle.

Many domaines, aware of the danger, rushed out to collect the fruit as fast as possible. 'It was a vintage to harvest very quickly,' said Jean-François Coche-Dury. Leflaive completed their harvest within a week, instead of the usual ten days, Carillon in five and a half instead of nine. 'It was best,' said Franck Grux of Olivier Leflaive Frères, to harvest earlier, albeit with a lower than desirable degree, but at least with some fruit and balance, than later, and get more alcohol but wines without finesse and acidity. Roger Caillot of Meursault echoed this, and pointed out that he had harvested his best vineyards first. Not only were they, naturally, the ripest, but: 'I'd rather lose the Bourgogne *Blanc* than the Bâtard-Montrachet.'

All this was wise, up to a point. It depended where your vineyards were. Towards the end of the week of the 19th the weather cleared. Would there have been an advantage in waiting? Some did: Thierry Matrot in Meursault, Gérard Boudot at Domaine Étienne Sauzet, and Jean-Marc Morey in Chassagne-Montrachet. None had fruit that suffered from botrytis. Both Matrot and Morey make red wine as well as white and are used to using anti-rot treatments, which solely white-wine producing domaines – or some of them – consider unnecessary (but not Gérard Boudot). Matrot *began* with his generics, unlike Caillot, and his *premiers crus* are nicely full and reserved for the vintage. So are Boudot's; and neither *cave* shows the *sur-maturité* prevalent elsewhere in Puligny-Montrachet.

The lesser villages – Saint-Aubin, Saint-Romain, Auxey-Duresses, etc. – can often provide excellent value. But their vines and their owners suffer under several disadvantages. Their fruit ripens later, a process which can be further retarded if the grower feels it is economically necessary to crop up to the limit to make up for the lower prices. (Thankfully most don't, for which they deserve our applause: indeed Saint-Aubin etc. normally crop less than the greedy growers in Puligny.) Secondly, however ripe the fruit, the wines lack the inherent structure of the three main villages. If less voluminous in the first place, then, if rain affected, more dilute in the second place. This, rather than botrytis, is the failing of these 1994s. There was just too much rain in the middle decade of September for the Saint-Aubin fruit not to have been affected. You have to go back to 1990 to find a really good vintage in these villages.

Further north, however, there *was* an advantage in waiting. The effect of the rain was less. The fruit in most cases – except in parts of Corton-Charlemagne – was less ripe. And there was no threat of *sur-maturité*. Here growers could take advantage of the improvement in the weather after 22 September. Here the 1994 white wine harvest is at its best – or certainly at its most uniform.

The improvement in the weather conditions after 22 September is more visible in the quality of the red wines, and this is particularly noticeable in the Côte-de-Nuits, where many growers were able to wait until the beginning of October. Not all succeeded. It is a question of luck, size of the harvest and the efficacy of anti-rot treatments. 'I had a choice,' said Laurent Ponsot. 'To pick rotten grapes on the 23rd – when most of the Côte-de-Nuits started picking

- or rotten but ripe grapes a week later. The fruit didn't get any worse. But it did get riper.' Nevertheless he has declassified much of his harvest down to village level.

THE STYLE OF THE WINES

WHITE WINES

'A vintage not of *terroir* but of date of harvest. A vintage of *coteaux* rather than plain,' said Jean-Marie Guffens of Maison Verget. Robert Drouhin echoes the first bit: 'There are 1994s which are disappointing because they were picked too late. Thankfully most of the Chardonnay was ripe enough before the rain began to have too much effect. If you picked reasonably fast the rain didn't do too much damage.' 'Quite the opposite of 1993,' said Dominique Lafon, 'and much more difficult to vinify.' For Thierry Matrot the vintage is a blend of 1982 and 1989. This, I think, is putting it a bit strongly. Personally I fear that too many wines will go the disappointing way of many of the 1986s, and others are simply dilute versions of the 1992s.

But just as the 1994 vintage is not consistently good, neither is it consistently bad. It is at its most disappointing in the Puligny-Chassagne *grands crus*. Here you have to search very hard for a wine of real *grand cru* quality, concentration and, above all, grip. Many are ripe enough, but too many are dilute and *pommadés* and blowsy. There will be no Baron Thenard/Remoissenet Le Montrachet this year. There was too much rot, and it has all been sold off in bulk.

Lower down the scale many Puligny-Montrachet *premiers crus* and village wines are similarly disappointing, and it is noticeable, in a *cave* where the grower offers Puligny as well as Meursault, that even where the Puligny vineyard has been harvested first, it is the least good wine. Lovers of Puligny, this is not the vintage for you. The few exceptions include those who had sprayed against rot, those who had stopped the malo, and those with vineyards on the Meursault border: the estates of Carillon and Sauzet, and at the merchants Drouhin and Jadot, and in one or two examples elsewhere, such as the Pucelles of Olivier Leflaive, the domaine wines (but not the *négociant* wines) of Jean-Marc Boillot and the Caillerets of Maison Rodet.

There was a lot less rot and *sur-maturité* in Chassagne, and the wines are rather more consistent. The tendency with Chassagne whites is to be a bit four-square, and some of the 1994s can be faulted not so much for a lack of structure as a lack of flair and personality: as usual. But very good wines can be found at Jean-Marc Blain, Colin-Deléger, Jacques Gagnard, Jean-Noël Gagnard, Jean et Jean-Marc Pillot, Paul Pillot and Ramonet, as well as the *négociants* above. Maison Verget, whose 1994s are a bit up and down, has a very good La Romanée.

The best wines of the three villages will be found in Meursault. Indeed the twenty-five domaines I visited in June 1995 provided few disappointments. Meursault harvested less, especially on the southern side in the three famous *premiers crus* of Charmes, Genevrières and Perrières and along the slope towards the north in the so-called '*deuxièmes crus*' of Narvaux, Tillets and so on. There was also much less rot and over-ripeness. The plums will be found at the domaines of Michel Bouzereau, Yves Boyer, Coche-Dury, Jean-Philippe Fichet, Jean-Michel Gaunoux, Patrick Javillier, François Jobard, Lafon, Matrot, Michelot, Pierre Morey, Jacques Prieur and Roulot. You will also find plenty of good Meursault at the usual top *négociants*.

RED WINES

A vintage to separate the sheep from the goats. Those who produced up to the maximum allowable found themselves with a much more severe rot problem than those who had curtailed their crop to below 30/35 hl/ha (for the top wines) and 35/40 (for the rest). Given this rot they would not have been able to macerate as long as they should have to get the right amount of colour and extract from the skins and pulp. And therefore they will have produced weak, insipid wine, perhaps with a taint of rot, certainly with dirty lees, so another important wine-making element, the enrichment of the wine on its fine lees before and after malo-lactic, would have been denied them.

The competent and dedicated, on the other hand, had a smaller harvest in the first place, and with soils which were biologically managed, fruit which had less rot and was less rain-affected. They were able to delay their harvest and benefit from the better weather which ensued after the equinox. They were freer to make the wine as it should have been made.

In the Côte-de-Nuits the 1994 vintage is better than 1992. The crop in the top domaines was smaller. The wines put on weight over their first year, and show more definition and class, a satisfactory structure, and a character of fruit which is much more identifiable with their *terroirs*. There is a similar softness and accessibility, a roundness and generosity, but the wines are more structured and austere, and have more depth and finesse.

In the Côte-de-Beaune opinions are divided and the quality is more variable. But even there the successful 1994s have, as Pascal Marchand of the Domaine du Comte Armand put it 'more interesting fruit, more volume' (than the 1992); or, are 'better, more concentrated', to quote Nathalie Tollot of the Domaine Tollot-Beaut. And let us not denigrate the (in some places) unfairly assassinated 1992s. Now they are in bottle, approaching maturity, and available for all to sample, they are selling like hot cakes. Restaurateurs and their customers love them. The 1994s, if carefully chosen, will be a highly satisfactory follow-on vintage.

WHERE ARE THE BEST WINES?

A summary can be made of the generalisations.

★ 1994 is a vintage where you can clearly see the difference between the serious grower with his reduced harvest and those who are lazy, incompetent and harvest up to the legal limit.

★ The reds of the Côte-de-Nuits are better than the reds of the Côte-de-Beaune.

★ Within the Côte-de-Beaune, Maranges, Santenay and Chassagne are more even than Volnay, Pommard, Beaune, Savigny and Chorey. No one Côte-de-Nuits village is spectacularly better than another.

★ The best of the whites will be found in Meursault. This is in general a poor vintage for Puligny-Montrachet.

★ But in general the reds are better than the whites, especially in the Côte-de-Nuits.

★ This is not a vintage for the out-of-the-way villages and the Hautes-Côtes.

★ But otherwise it is a respectable vintage which will come on stream early, and will follow 1992 as being a more-than-useful vintage for the restaurant and hotel side of the wine business.

At the time this book went to press (August 1996) it was too early to come to a firm judgement of the wines in bottle.

STATE OF MATURITY TODAY

White: With the exception of the very top and very concentrated wines, the 1994s are loose-knit, not very high in acidity and will evolve soon. Drink the Pulignys fast, they will not make elegant old bones. The village wines can be drunk now, the *premiers crus* from 1998-99, and over the next three to five years.

Reds: This is an early-maturing vintage. The lesser Côte-de-Beaunes are for drinking soon (1997-2000), the better wines will keep for a year or so. But beware the dilution. Most of the Côte-de-Nuits will come on stream from 1999 or so, and these will last better. But this is not a year for locking away and then forgetting for a decade or more.

TASTING NOTES

BLANC

Auxey-Duresses   Henri Latour

Light, forward, pleasant. Reasonable balance. Seems cleaner than the 1992. Finishes well – better than it starts. Good. **(12/95)**

Drink soon   14.0

Beaune   Clos-des-Mouches   Joseph Drouhin

Full, rich, spicy nose. Slightly dry as a result of bottling. Fat and with plenty of depth. Gently oaky. A meaty example. Very good indeed. **(10/95)**

1999-2006   16.5

Chassagne-Montrachet   Caillerets   Guy Amiot

This has a good grip for a 1994. Peachy and ripe on the nose. Good structure on the palate. Elegant and gently oaky. Very good. **(06/96)**

1998-2004   16.0

Chassagne-Montrachet   Laguiche   Joseph Drouhin

Firm, full, concentrated nose. Slightly dumb on the attack but good backbone, depth and grip underneath. Very good indeed. Steely in a Puligny sense but a lot more to it than Pulignys of this vintage. Very good indeed. **(10/95)**

1999-2006   16.5

Chassagne-Montrachet   Vergers   Guy Amiot

A soft gently oaky wine with a pear-peach nose. It lacks a little grip but it is ripe, honeyed and stylish. Quite long enough. Good plus. **(06/96)**

1998-2003   15.5

Corton-Charlemagne   Louis Latour

Opulent, oaky. Rich and fat. Fullish, somewhat exotic and tropical in flavour. Lacks a little Corton-Charlemagne austerity. Ripe. Some alcohol. Not too much sulphur. Elegant but more 1994 than Corton-Charlemagne. **(03/96)**

1999-2005   16.0

Meursault   Charmes   René Monnier

Quite full and firm for a 1994. Some oak. Ripe. Not a lot of acidity. Quite tropical in fruit. Already very drinkable. Shows well but though positive, lacks a little intensity at the end. **(03/96)**

Drink soon   14.0

Montrachet   Guy Amiot

Splendidly firm and austere on the nose for the vintage. This is instantly in a much higher league. Rich, fat, concentrated, very good grip. A wine which really will keep, unlike the vast majority of the rest. Lots of dimension. Very fine. **(06/96)**

2000-2008   19.0

Morey-Saint-Denis   Monts-Luisants   Ponsot

Light, forward, pleasant. Reasonable balance. Seems cleaner than the 1992. Finishes well – better than it starts. Good. **(11/95)**

1999-2005   15.0

Puligny-Montrachet   Les Demoiselles   Guy Amiot

This has very good raciness and style for a 1994. Again not for the long term though. Medium-full, flowery-peachy. Concentrated. Individual. Fine. **(06/96)**

1999-2004   17.5

Puligny-Montrachet   Folatières   Joseph Drouhin

Less structured than the Beaune, Clos-des-Mouches. Good fruit. But a quite forward wine. The acidity is good though and the wine not over-ripe. Stylish. Long but soft and gentle and forward. Very good. **(10/95)**

1998-2004   16.0

Puligny-Montrachet   Truffière   Bernard Morey

Good concentration and richness. This has plenty of depth. The fruit is a bit confit and the acidities gentle. But there is depth and class here. Good. **(6/96)**

1999-2003   15.0

1993

RATING FOR THE VINTAGE

Red: 17.5   **White:** 15.0

SIZE OF THE CROP

(Hectolitres, excluding generic wine)

	Red	White
Grands Crus	11,895	3,577
Village and *Premiers Crus*	181,477	49,681
Total	193,372	53,258

Overall 1993 (there are sadly always a few disappointments) is an exciting red-wine vintage. The colours are excellent, the acidities fine, the fruit lush, the structures very good, the tannins sophisticated. The vintage combines, in the words of Freddy Mugnier, 'At best the velvet texture and richness of 1990, the fruit of 1989 and the acidity of 1988.'

The white-wine crop, however, was much higher: 45.3 hl/ha in Meursault (despite hail damage on the Puligny border), 49.8 in Puligny and 57.0 in Chassagne (village and *premier cru* wine only).

It seems as if some parts of Meursault and Puligny over-performed in order to make up for the hail losses in Perrières and elsewhere. Rumours circulated that *le fruit a monté la côte,* i.e. that some growers added village AC wine to their paltry *cuvées* of *premier cru*. Some wines, indeed, taste like it.

WEATHER CONDITIONS

Following the 1992 vintage, the autumn was grey and wet but the winter largely dry. A hot spell in the last fortnight of March encouraged an early bud-break, and the *sortie* of potential grape bunches turned out to be abundant. The flowering took place successfully and a few days earlier than normal during the first decade in June.

Spring and summer, right through until August, were warm but wet, frequently interrupted by thunderstorms. As a result it was the worst season for mildew since 1953. Growers were forced to treat the vines twice as frequently as usual, Jadot spraying their domaine ten times rather than five. Oidium was also a problem.

One of the storms took place during the night of 19-20 June. A swathe of hail caused damage in some of the vineyards of Saint Aubin and in Blagny, but most seriously in the *premiers crus* of Perrières, Genevrières and Charmes in Meursault and in those *climats* across the border in Puligny: Referts, Combettes and Champs-Canet. The harvest here was more than halved as a result, Dominique Lafon producing eight and a half *pièces* from his 1.2 hectares of Charmes (16 hl/ha), Thierry Matrot 18 hl/ha in his Perrières and Gérard Boudot of Domaine Étienne Sauzet 15 hl/ha in his Combettes.

The *véraison* took place at the beginning of August, and this was accompanied by a change in the weather. The month that followed was warm and dry - a precipitation of a mere 17 mm - and in this heat the grape-skins thickened, a factor that was to be crucial when it came to the harvest. Some of the progress of the fruit towards maturity was retarded, however. The grapes remained *bloquées*, particularly in the best-drained, most meagre soils further up the slope. This seems to have affected the Chardonnays more than the Pinots Noirs.

With the arrival of September there was a two-day period of rain. This jump-started the ripening process again and the must-weight rose rapidly in the ten days which followed, the *Ban des Vendanges* being announced on 15 September in the Côte-de-Beaune.

The vintage then began. The long-range forecast was unpromising, and most growers rushed out to pick their grapes. The reds were now ripe, and generally were cleared first, leaving a brief period before the weather changed in which to clear some of the ripest white-wine vineyards. Usually it is the best exposed sites, the *grands* and *premiers crus* which arrive at maturity first. But in 1993 it was exactly these which had been *bloquées* in August. The grower was therefore in a dilemma: pick now, just a little unripe - a full degree of alcohol less than in 1992 - or wait and perhaps suffer dilution when the announced rain commenced. A no-win situation indeed!

The weather did break, as feared, and on the day of the equinox. But after three days of rain it cleared a little, enabling the rest of the Côte-de-Beaune harvest to be collected before it deteriorated again at the beginning of October. Conditions were by no means perfect during this period; it was a question of dodging in and out of the showers. But at least the rains were not heavy, nor were they continuous. And it was cool. There was little incidence of rot.

In the red-wine areas the hail damage had occurred earlier, on 16 and 27 May, though the June thunderstorm was also deleterious, and the mildew onslaught was if anything even worse.

All in all, things were not looking too good as the *grandes vacances* approached. The August weather, though, thankfully, was excellent. A storm on 10 September was beneficial rather than the opposite, for it helped further ripen and soften the tannins, and the *Ban des Vendanges* was declared, amid some optimism, on 15 September.

Sadly there was rain during the harvest. It rained at the beginning; it rained during the middle; and it rained at the end. But it certainly did not rain everywhere all the time, and most growers were able to stop and start, and collect their fruit while it was dry. Few Burgundian domaines are very large and in this respect Burgundy benefited in 1993. Most can be picked in a week. With the help of the long-range weather forecast most growers were able to adapt their picking programmes to the best days of the fortnight between the 15 September and 1 October.

THE STYLE OF THE WINE

WHITE WINES

The fruit which arrived at the winery, if a little sodden on occasion, was at least healthy. But maturity levels were somewhat less than perfect, and in the majority of the region that had escaped the June hailstorm the quantity that was coming in was abundant. Most growers with unaffected vineyards report harvest quantities similar to those of 1992: 40 hl/ha rather than an ideal 35 in *grand cru*, 45 rather than 40 in *premier cru* and as much as 60 in village wine. In 1992 the extra quantity did not seem to affect the quality of the wine. In 1993, I regret, it has.

The lower than optimum degree of ripeness has, of course, meant chaptalisation, and in most cases to the full 2° of potential alcohol which is permissible. It was a mistake, though, said Jean-Marie Guffens of Maison Verget, to over-chaptalise. In his view a wine which would potentially have realised 11.5 or 12.0 should only have been chaptalised by a degree. More would result in imbalance. The wines did not have enough substance to sustain any higher a degree of alcohol. Equally, he averred, 1993 was also a vintage where one had to be very careful not to over-oak the wines.

The wines at the outset were marked by their acidities, and seemed to lack fruit. Faces were long. Fermentations took ages to complete, and malos were the tardiest to finish for many years. 'I've never known a year when they were so late,' said Gérard Boudot. But this seems to have done the wines no harm. Quite the contrary. At the end of the malos one could see a wine with a much higher level of fruit and personality than had been feared at the outset, and no undue acidity levels either.

A year later, when I was in the region sampling the 1994 whites, I took the opportunity to sample a wide range of top 1993s. I was impressed by their progress. What was crucial, of course, was a reasonable rather than excessive harvest. This together with the thick skins, under which most of the flavour elements reside, resulted in fruit with plenty of character, despite the inclement weather, and the result, helped by the naturally high acidity, was wine with plenty of depth, interest and even concentration at the top levels. In many cases the 1993s, though quite different, are better than the 1992s. They are certainly fresher, and will last longer. The run-of-the-mill, however, are like the 1988s, though not as severe, and a small step ahead of the 1991s. But the best are surprising. Really very good indeed.

RED WINES

Small berries - so a greater concentration of solid to liquid - and not much of them; plus fruit, provided the pickers had performed a *triage*, which was healthy, and, if not cropped during rain, of high acidity: all this added up to a promising start.

Yet at the beginning the wines seemed rather neutral with high acidities. It was only after the malos - which were long and drawn-out - that the true contours and quality of the 1993 reds began to emerge. In retrospect these long-lasting malos transformed the vintage. The lees were clean, the wines could slowly enrich themselves without danger of mercaptan contamination, and they just went on tasting better and better as summer turned into autumn.

A feature of the 1993s is their excellent healthy colour. Another is a refreshing acidity; not too high, just what is required to preserve the fruit and maintain the elegance. A third is an intensely perfumed, pure Pinot fruit. If they are a little less structured than the 1991s in some cases, at least the tannins are riper and more stylish. There are no hard edges. In sum the 1993s are more harmonious than the 1991s, and have a lot more stuffing than the 1992s, but the same charm of the best of this vintage. They have better acidities than the 1989s and do not possess the austerity of the 1988s. 'As good as the 1990s, but different,' says Denis Bachelet. '*Ils pinottent*,' says Christian Gouges, meaning that they show a more typical expression of Pinot Noir fruit than this earlier, magnificently rich, but atypical vintage. 'They have a flavour of *glacé* fruit,' says Jean-Luc Pépin of Domaine Comte Georges de Vogüé. 'Harmonious,' says Jacques Lardière of Maison Jadot. 'An engaging personality,' says Robert Drouhin.

Bottle tastings have confirmed the quality of the 1993 reds. The words 'classic', 'pure' and 'yardstick' occur frequently in my notes. The wines are not as rich or as voluminous as the 1990s, but they are perhaps more elegant. With 1991 and 1995 as well, not to mention 1989 and 1988, we Burgundy-lovers have a very pleasant *embarras du choix* before us.

WHERE ARE THE BEST WINES?

To summarise:

★ Some surprisingly good white wines, especially in Meursault, which will last well. They show plenty of breed.

★ Somewhat lean white wines elsewhere.

★ Not a particularly good vintage for the lesser known villages or Hautes-Côtes.

★ A lovely red-wine vintage. It should be in every cellar.

★ As far as the red wines are concerned there is no great difference in quality between the Côte-de-Beaune and the Côte-de-Nuits, though Chambolle-Musigny is particularly fine and uniform, and short in quantity.

STATE OF MATURITY TODAY

White: The best Meursaults are concentrated, will need time, and will last very well indeed. The remainder, certainly at village level, can be started now. *Premiers crus,* those with good acidity, are ready but will last well. The others will not make old bones and much beyond 2001 will be pushing it.

Red: This is a classic vintage which needs keeping not so much because the wines need an undue length of time to mature but because the complexity and the harmony of a good mature 1993 will give such joy it is a shame not to wait until all the flavours of true maturity have had time to form. Drink lesser wines, such as good generics and lighter villages, from 1998. The fuller village wines and *premiers crus* need keeping until 2001 while the *grands crus* need guarding until 2004. Drink the 1992s and 1994s first.

A comprehensive tasting of the red wines of the 1993 vintage will be published in *The Vine* towards the end of 1997. Write to 76 Woodstock Rd, London W4 1EQ, Great Britain, or fax (44) 181 995 8343 for further details.

TASTING NOTES

BLANC

Auxey-Duresses   Labry
Light, neat, fruity, forward. But well made. Not hollow. **(12/95)**
Drink soon   14.0

Auxey-Duresses   Henri Latour
I find this a little neutral. The wine has good acidity but it lacks ripeness and succulence. Yet reasonably long. Boring though. **(12/95)**
Drink soon   13.5

Bâtard-Montrachet   Leflaive
Firm, closed nose. Fine but very backward. Fullish, rich. Good grip. Slightly closed, slightly adolescent. Not great but fine. Elegant and intense at the end. **(10/95)**
1999-2007   17.0

Chassagne-Montrachet   Boudriotte
Jacques Gagnard-Delagrange
Just a touch of SO$_2$. But good acidity. This has elegance and perfume. Nicely austere. Good depth underneath. Nice touch of oak. This is very good. And it will get better. **(06/96)**
1998-2005   16.0

Chassagne-Montrachet   Caillerets
Louis Jadot
A pleasant, quite crisp, clean wine, but one with a lack of real richness and depth. Medium-full. Balanced. But a little dull. Merely good. Slightly better than the Meursault Charmes. **(06/96)**
Now-2002   15.0

Chassagne-Montrachet   Caillerets
Bernard Morey
This has good richness for a 1993. Slightly four-square. Not a lot of depth and dimension. But there is good fruit and good balance. This has good length and more to it, on aeration, than there seemed at first. Long. Rich. Good depth. Very good plus. **(06/96)**
1999-2004   16.5

Chassagne-Montrachet
Morgeots, Duc de Magenta   Louis Jadot
Good depth, ample and ripe, but a little clumsy and four-square. Some built-in SO$_2$. Clean on the follow-through. Fullish. Quite rich. But lacks a bit of real concentration, zip and flair. Merely good plus. **(06/96)**
Now-2003   15.0

Chassagne-Montrachet   Morgeots
René Lamy-Pillot
Soft, ripe but rather sulphury. The fruit is reasonable, as is the balance. But this is too dominated by the sulphur. If this goes, this will be good, even very good, for there is some concentration here. But will it? **(06/96)**
1998-2003   13.5

Chassagne-Montrachet   Morgeots
Olivier Leflaive Frères
Subdued nose but good oak. Good grip. A little austere on the attack. But there is good depth here. Finishes long and positively. Classy. Very good. **(10/95)**
1998-2004   16.0

Chassagne-Montrachet Morgeots
Bernard Moreau

Some dose of SO$_2$ as in the 1992 but much less of a built-in sulphur taste. Indeed clean, crisp, fullish and racy. Very good depth and style. Plenty of fruit. Good grip. Long and stylish. Very good. **(06/96)**

Now-2003   **15.5**

Chevalier-Montrachet Henri Clerc

Firm, backward. Still very closed. Fine. Clerc's wines seem to have become less heavy and exotic, and more refined and complex over recent years. **(03/95)**

2000-2009   **17.5**

Corton-Charlemagne Louis Jadot

Very youthful. Rather dumb on the attack. Rich and fullish, but I am not really that convinced. Finishes long but not really very lush. Very good at best? **(10/95)**

1998/99-2000   **16.0**

Fixin Louis Jadot

This is extremely good - better than many a Meursault. Just the right touch of wood. Ripe. Full flavoured. Excellently balanced. Round, ripe. Delicious for what it is. **(12/95)**

Now-2000 plus   **15.0**

Meursault Bouchard Père et Fils

The nose has interest but it is a little bland on the palate. Good acidity but not enough depth. **(10/95)**

Now-2001   **13.5**

Meursault Sylvain Dussort

Delicate, poised, good acidity. This is very good. Good definition here. **(12/95)**

1998-2004   **15.5**

Meursault Olivier Leflaive Frères

Slightly closed on the nose. Lovely fruit here. It is not as intense as the very best but there is good grip. Quite firm and backward. Rich, balanced and classy. Very good complex fruit. Medium-full. Very good indeed. **(10/95)**

1998-2005   **16.5**

Meursault Virely-Rougeot

This is a perfectly correct example with good fruit and a touch of wood. Balanced but not exactly very elegant. But quite a young wine still. Quite good plus. **(12/95)**

1998-2004   **14.5**

Meursault Charmes
Vincent Bitouzet-Prieur

Only the merest vestige of SO$_2$ here, curiously (after his 1992s). Crisp, gently oaky, round and stylish. Good fat and fruit for the vintage. Nice long persistent finish. Good plus. **(06/96)**

1999-2004   **15.5**

Meursault Charmes Louis Jadot

This is plump and fruity but a little one-dimensional. It lacks a bit of intensity and flair. Currently a touch of built-in SO$_2$. No great grip. Merely good. **(06/96)**

Now-2002   **15.0**

Meursault Clous Dujac/Druid

Some oak, but essentially a lightish, quite ephemeral wine. Stylish, fruity, ripe, but doesn't have the grip of Druid Puligny. Quite good plus. **(10/95)**

Now-2004   **14.5**

Meursault Goutte d'Or
Jean-Michel Gaunoux

A softer, more ample, more flowery nose than his 1993 Perrières at present. This is a little more advanced. Good ripe fruit. But not as concentrated or as stylish. Good plus. **(06/96)**

Now-2002   **15.5**

Meursault Limouzin Dujac/Druid

This is similar to the Clous, but has more style and a better grip. Also a 'feminine' example. Good. **(10/95)**

Now-2004   **15.0**

Meursault Narvaux Morey-Blanc

Racy, very good oak integration. Lovely fruit. Very good grip. This has enormous class. Crisp. But gamey. Very good. **(10/95)**

Now-2005   **16.0**

Meursault Perrières
Vincent Bitouzet-Prieur

A little bit more sulphury than his 1993 Charmes, but not as bad as the 1992s. But it kills the nose a bit. Fullish, ripe. Good substance and depth. But I don't get the nuance and style of the Charmes. Good merely. But will it improve? **(06/96)**

1999-2004   **15.0**

Meursault Perrières
Jean-Michel Gaunoux

Very good nose. Ripe with good structure and acidity. Slightly vegetal in its fruit but good oaky base, good concentration and good dimensions. Stylish. Long. Will keep well. Very good plus. **(06/96)**

1998-2005   **16.5**

Meursault Perrières Louis Jadot

This has good depth and plenty of class. Medium-full, complex, lots of personality. Clean long elegant finish. Just about ready. Real flair. Very good indeed/fine. **(06/96)**

Now-2005   **17.5**

Meursault Perrières Pierre Morey

There is a bit of sulphur here on the nose at present, though less so on the palate. But the wine is rich and concentrated and gently oaky, and there is plenty of depth as well as grip. Fine positive finish. Very good concentration. White peach fruit. Will last well. Fine plus. **(06/96)**

1998-2008   18.0

Meursault Poruzots
Jacques Thevenot-Machal

Plenty of depth but just a little lean. It has got class, indisputably. But while balanced and mineral I would not say it was a great 1993 Meursault. **(12/95)**

1998-2004   14.5

Meursault Tessons Pierre Morey

Slightly more depth, a little more backward than the Narvaux of Morey Blanc. Slightly more citronelle than peachy. Slightly less marked. Very good. **(10/95)**

1999-2005   16.0

Pernand-Vergelesses Rollin Père et Fils

Fresh colour. Reasonably clean and substantial, but rather anonymous. **(12/95)**

Drink soon   13.0

Puligny-Montrachet Bouchard Père et Fils

More interest than the Meursault, especially on the nose, but similarly rather dull on the palate. Good grip again. But a more positive finish. Good. **(10/95)**

Now-2003   14.0

Puligny-Montrachet Henri Clerc

Fresh, classy, fullish. Good fruit and good acidity. A very good example. Long, ripe finish, and just a touch of oak. **(12/95)**

Now-2002   15.5

Puligny-Montrachet Dujac/Druid

A lovely example. Quite oaky. But a good deal of fat and depth as well. Rich. Very good acidity too. Will develop. Fine. **(10/95)**

1998-2008   16.5

Puligny-Montrachet Thierry Guyot

Complex, concentrated nose. This has a good oak base. Lots of lovely fruit. Quite full. This has good structure and depth. Long, lots of potential. Needs time. **(12/95)**

1999-2005   16.5

Puligny-Montrachet Louis Jadot

The nose is a bit unformed but there is nice crisp fruit and balance - even depth - on the palate. Very good for a village wine of 1993. **(10/95)**

1998-2005   15.0

Puligny-Montrachet Caillerets
Hubert de Montille

Nicely elegant. Very good, slightly delicate, but intense Chardonnay sweetness. Very typical. A touch of oak. Good acidity. Quite forward. Could have had a bit more concentration but very elegant. Long, but a delicate expression of Puligny. Very good plus. **(03/96)**

1998-2004   16.5

Puligny-Montrachet Champ-Gain
Henri Clerc

Slightly closed on the nose. A touch of SO_2. On the palate quite clean. Firmer, richer, more to it compared to the village wine. Less evolved. There is good depth here but it is rather hidden at the moment. Rich, concentrated, full of fruit. This is gently oaky. Very elegant and composed. Fine. **(10/95)**

1999-2014   17.5

Puligny-Montrachet Clavoillon Leflaive

Accessible, classy oak integration. Elegant fruit. Nicely ripe. More evolved than the Olivier Leflaive wines. Concentrated, persistent and very elegant (more so than usual for Clavoillon). Very good indeed. **(10/95)**

1998-2004   17.0

Puligny-Montrachet Clos-de-la-Garenne,
Duc de Magenta Louis Jadot

This is lovely. Real flair here. Good grip. Slightly less rigid than the Folatières. Very fine concentrated fruit. This has the concentration and intensity I am looking for. A lovely example. Flowery and complex and very classy. And it will keep. Very fine. **(06/96)**

Now-2007   18.0

Puligny-Montrachet Combettes
Henri Clerc

A wine of depth. Lovely concentration. This is very good. Long and complex. Very good fruit. **(03/95)**

1999-2005   16.0

Puligny-Montrachet Folatières
Henri Clerc

More open on the nose than the Champ-Gain and the Combettes. Flowery. Good acidity. Not the greatest depth but stylish. **(03/95)**

1998-2003   15.5

Puligny-Montrachet Folatières
Louis Jadot

This has very good depth and flair and concentration. Lovely fruit. Not a bit heavy. Good class and grip. Fresh and fine. But not great. Yet the finish is warm and ample and elegant and long. **(06/96)**

Now-2005   17.0

**Puligny-Montrachet Perrières
Louis Carillon**

This is a very elegant example, with plenty of fruit underneath. Ripe. Medium to medium-full. Very well balanced. Delicate but intense. Peachy. Very long and complex. As usual very understated. Very good indeed, even fine. **(11/95)**

1998-2005   **17.5**

Puligny-Montrachet Pucelles Leflaive

A little over-blown, it seems, on the nose. Pity! Where is the grip? Or is it the recent bottling? Elegant fruit and oak attack but it seems to lack the grip it should have. Ample and rich. Forward. Slightly disappointing. Only good. **(10/95)**

Now-2003   **15.0**

**Saint-Aubin Les Champlots
Jean-Claude Bachelet**

There is a bit of SO$_2$ here, but the wine is ripe and stylish. Light and quite forward. Quite good plus. **(01/96)**

Now-2001   **14.5**

Saint-Romain Germain Père et Fils

Clean, ripe and racy. Good balanced fruit. This has depth and is nicely fat. A soft fruity wine. Very good. Now ready. **(12/95)**

Now-2000   **15.5**

Saint-Romain Thierry Guyot

Good grip, ripe and concentrated and complex. But very closed still. Good depth though. This is good plus, but needs two years. **(12/95)**

1998-2003   **15.0**

**Saint-Romain Sous-la-Velle
Henri et Gilles Buisson**

Touch of SO$_2$ on the nose here. Fat and rich, but not blowsy, on the palate. Good grip. Nice ripe fruit. This has depth and length. Just about ready. Good. **(12/95)**

Now-2000 plus   **14.5**

Santenay Clos-Genêt Brenot

Quite a deep colour. But not a bit over-evolved on nose and palate. Good oaky base. Very stylish balanced fruit. Vigorous but fragrant. Ripe. Long. Very good. **(12/96)**

1998-2004   **15.5**

Savigny-lès-Beaune Louis Jadot

Quite firm, a little lean. Needs a year or two to mellow. Quite good but not great. **(10/95)**

Now-2001   **13.0**

Savigny-lès-Beaune Jean-Marc Pavelot

Not a lot of oak. Crisp, lemon-limey fruit. Good acidity. Ripe. Good length. **(10/95)**

Now-2001   **14.0**

Vougeot Clos-Blanc L'Héritier-Guyot

This is a little spicy, with a touch of austerity behind it. But ripe and long and stylish. I prefer the 1994 though. It has more dimension. Quite good. **(12/95)**

1998-2003   **14.0**

ROUGE

Aloxe-Corton Franck Follin

Good colour. Nose still a bit blunted. Some SO$_2$ evident. On the palate this is good and sturdy. Ripe and balanced. Quite full. But it lacks a bit of elegance. Slightly hard. Lacks succulence. Quite good. **(12/95)**

1999-2006   **14.0**

**Aloxe-Corton Clos-du-Chapitre
Franck Follin**

Good colour. This is richer and more interesting than the village wine. Plummy. Quite full. Good grip. A sturdy wine, as usual, for an Aloxe, but underneath rich and long. Good. **(12/95)**

2000-2008   **15.0**

Aloxe-Corton Vercots Franck Follin

Good colour. This is riper and more succulent than the Clos-du-Chapitre. Good depth and concentration. Again good grip. Quite full. This is again sturdy but has plenty of concentration and richness underneath. Very good. **(12/95)**

2001-2010   **16.0**

Auxey-Duresses Labry

Soft, ripe, elegant. Good intensity. Forward but good. **(12/95)**

1998-2002   **14.0**

Auxey-Duresses Henri Latour

Good colour. Rich on the nose. Ample and succulent. Very good style and balance. Fullish. Very good tannins and grip. Above all complex and intense and long on the palate. This is very good indeed for what it is. Lovely finish. **(12/95)**

2000-2010   **16.0**

**Auxey-Duresses Clos-du-Val
Philippe Prunier-Damy**

Medium colour. Not a lot of weight but elegant, balanced and stylish. The tannins are round. This is Volnay-ish and finishes well. Medium body. Good. **(12/95)**

Now-2003   **15.0**

**Auxey-Duresses Les Duresses
Alain Creusefond**

Good colour. Very good plump, ripe nose. Rich Pinot here. Good fullish structure. Succulent. Firm. Balanced. This is very good indeed for what it is. **(12/95)**

2000-2008   **16.0**

Auxey-Duresses   Le Val
Dominique et Vincent Roy
Medium to medium-full colour. Fresh, plump nose. Good depth. This is ripe and with plenty of depth. Long, stylish. Intense. Very good. **(12/95)**
2000-2010   16.0

Beaune   Arnoux Père et Fils
Good colour. Rich plummy, gently oaky nose. Quite full. Good tannins. Rich and fat on the palate. Good grip. Quite firm at present. Very good depth. Very good grip. Very good. **(12/95)**
2000-2008   15.5

Beaune   Louis Jadot
A touch appley on the nose. Youthful. Slightly raw. Lacks a little real concentration and personality. But quite ripe and stylish. Quite good. **(10/95)**
1998-2007   14.0

Beaune   Jean-Claude Rateau
Very good colour. Nicely lean and austere. Very good fruit. A slight lack of fat. But intense, balanced. Very good depth. **(12/95)**
1999-2006   16.0

Beaune   Blanche-Fleur   Sylvain Dussort
The colour is light. There is rather more intensity on the nose. But essentially a supple wine without a tannic backbone. Good acidity. Nice ripe fruit. But rather lean. **(12/95)**
1998-2003   13.5

Beaune   Cent-Vignes   Bernard Bescancenot
Good colour. The nose is a little closed in. The palate shows a good balanced, ripe wine, even rich, with no lack of richness or grip. No sign of new wood here. Meaty, succulent. Long. This is good. But it could have been a bit more elegant. **(12/95)**
1999-2005   15.0

Beaune   Clos-des-Couchereaux   Louis Jadot
Rather better than the simple *premier cru*. Rich, ripe, stylish. Good intensity. Very good. **(10/95)**
1999-2012   16.0

Beaune   Clos-de-la-Maladière
Henri Cauvard et Fils
Monopole. In tank, not yet bottled. Good colour. It is a little rigid. A little forced. But it needs an aeration. Some substance and fruit. But little grace. **(12/95)**
1998-2003   13.0

Beaune   Clos-des-Mouches   Joseph Drouhin
Medium colour. A bit less than expected (? the recent bottling). The nose is closed and tight. I get a suggestion of smoked ham. On the palate this is rather less expressive than I had hoped. There is balance and intensity here and plenty of class. But today not the fat and opulence of their Volnay Chevret. Good grip. Medium-full. Very good at least. **(10/95)**
1999-2012   16.0

Beaune   Grèves   Daniel Largeot
Good colour. This is ripe and rich, with a good touch of wood. Ripe tannins. Full. Good grip. Very nice black-fruity style. Balanced. Stylish. Long. Very good. **(12/95)**
2000-2009   16.0

Beaune   Perrières   François Gay
Rich, fullish, clean, meaty. Very stylish. A persistent example with good grip and intensity. Lovely raspberry fruit. Quite full for a Beaune. **(12/95)**
1999-2009   16.0

Beaune   Reversées   Jean-Claude Rateau
Good colour. Fat, abundant nose. Fullish, splendidly balanced and intensely flavoured. Nicely austere. Very good grip. Good tannins. Quite full and substantial. Long. Needs time. Very good. **(12/95)**
2000-2009   16.0

Bonnes-Mares   Auvenay
Fine colour. Cool, oaky nose. Quite a high toast. Very concentrated. Very backward. At first very unforthcoming. Spicy, fullish, rich. A little bit too tannic on the palate for the wine, though long and classy. Lacks a little fat and concentration. Very young. Very good indeed. But perhaps not fine. **(10/95)**
1999-2012   17.0

Bonnes-Mares   Bart
Very fine colour. Slightly animal nose. Beginning to go into its shell. Full, oaky, rich. Very good tannins. There is plenty of wine here. Good grip. But a little lumpy. Lacks a little real elegance. Needs time. Good merely. **(12/95)**
2001-2011   15.0

Bonnes-Mares   Dujac
Still quite closed on the nose. This again is less on form than some of the others. Concentrated, fullish, intense. Masculine. Surely fine. **(10/95)**
2000-2015   18.0

Chambertin   Clos-de-Bèze   Bart
Very fine colour. Compared with their Bonnes-Mares this is cleaner and more stylish. A lot of wine here. Full, tannic, rich and oaky. Very good grip. Rather adolescent now. But a fine example. **(12/95)**
2002-2012   17.5

Chambertin Clos-de-Bèze Joseph Faiveley
Very good colour. Marvellous nose. Really rich and concentrated. Real depth and finesse. Full body. The tannins so ripe they hardly seem there. Marvellously rich. Fat and profound and very very distinguished. Excellent. (12/94)
2004-2018   19.0

Chambolle-Musigny Joseph Drouhin
Medium to medium-full colour. Lovely fragrant raspberry nose. Soft, very gently oaky, very fragrant. Delicate but intense. Very very classy and poised for a village wine. Lovely long finish. Fine for a village example. (10/95)
1999-2009   16.0

Chambolle-Musigny Dujac
Light and fragrant. A bit young viney. But the follow-through shows no lack of depth or fruit. But the Morey is better. (10/95)
1998-2005   14.5

Chambolle-Musigny Hubert Lignier
Medium colour. Fragrant nose. Soft and charming. This is a little slight. And it lacks a little concentration and richness. But the wine is elegant and the fruit is pure. Good acidity. Quite good. (05/95)
Now-2002   14.0

Chambolle-Musigny Baudes Hubert Lignier
Good colour. A touch of new oak on the nose. Fine velvety Chambolle fruit. Good thrust and grip. Medium-full on the palate. Stylish, ripe and balanced. A slight lack of real grip. Very Chambolle. Potentially opulent. But very good indeed. (05/96)
1998-2007   17.0

Chapelle-Chambertin Joseph Faiveley
Very good colour. Plump, fruity nose. Medium-full body. Good acidity. Very lovely fresh, fragrant complex fruit on the palate. A feminine wine. Very well balanced. Very good indeed. (12/94)
2000-2010   17.0

Charmes-Chambertin Dujac
Slightly raw on the nose still. Lovely soft fruit on the palate. Slightly less oak apparent than the Combottes and not any better I think. (10/95)
1999-2012   16.5

Charmes-Chambertin Hubert Lignier
Medium-full colour. Ample, ripe, not that concentrated. This doesn't have the intensity of his Combottes, it would seem. On the palate a bit better. Reasonable acidity. Medium to medium-full. A slight lack of fat and grip hinting at a little astringency for the future. But certainly 'good'. (05/95)
1998-2007   15.5

Chassagne-Montrachet Boudriottes Jean-Claude Bachelet
Good colour. Ripe and sturdy. A bit tannic on the attack. But round and rich and vigorous on the follow-through. Medium-full. Ripe fragrant Pinot. This is elegant and stylish. Good touch of new oak. (12/95)
1999-2009   15.0

Chassagne-Montrachet Morgeots Olivier Leflaive Frères
The colour is a bit on the light side. A soft fruity wine - Drouhin-ish - elegant but a little too soft perhaps. A touch 1992-ish. Very good fruit. Forward. (10/95)
Now-2005   14.5

Chorey-lès-Beaune René Podechard
Very good colour. A touch of new wood. Lovely rich ripe fruit. Very clean and positive. This is a delicious example. Fine for what it is. Fullish, very good grip. Ample and generous. (12/95)
1998-2004   15.0

Clos-de-la-Roche Dujac
Fine full colour. Very intense, aromatic, concentrated nose. A definite touch of the stems. Essence of wine here. Full, very, very ripe. Splendid grip. Very, very ripe tannins. Real quality, concentration and intensity here. (03/96)
2000-2018   18.0

Clos-de-la-Roche Robert Gibourg
One barrel. New oak. Good colour. Rich and meaty. The oak is a little marked. But there is good concentration here. Lots of succulent balanced fruit. Very good indeed. (12/95)
2001-2012   17.0

Clos-de-la-Roche Hubert Lignier
Very good colour. Ripe, concentrated and opulent on the nose. Plenty of class. Plenty of intensity. Good weight here. Quite structured. Good grip. Black cherry, plum and mocha fruit with a new oaky base. Not really startlingly brilliant. But fine plus. Lovely long finish. (05/96)
1999-2012   18.0

Clos-Saint-Denis Dujac
Excellent composed, complex fruit on both nose and palate. This is very lovely and very intense. Medium-full. Fine plus. (10/95)
2000-2015   18.0

Clos-de-Vougeot René Engel
Less colour than Rion. Very closed on the nose. Very very rich and concentrated. I prefer this to Rion. Slightly less oaky. More classy. Very sophisticated. Fullish. Fine. (10/95)
2000-2015   17.5

Clos-de-Vougeot   Joseph Faiveley

Very good colour. A little less exciting on the nose than the above. Lovely fruit here as well. Slightly more muscular. Very good acidity. Fullish, a little more hidden. Fine. But is it better? **(12/94)**

2002-2015   **17.5**

Clos-de-Vougeot   Jean Grivot

Very good colour. Slightly lean and twiggy on the nose. Backward. Lacks a bit of generosity though. Slightly lean and rustic on the palate. This is very good indeed. But backward. Lacks real richness. Very, very long. Very good plus. **(03/96)**

2001-2015   **16.5**

Clos-de-Vougeot   L'Héritier-Guyot

Medium-full colour. Oaky nose. Quite spicy and burnt-toasted. This again has good depth. Fullish. Good tannins. But it lacks a bit of individuality and sex appeal. Good grip. Plenty of depth. Perhaps it will become more generous as it rounds off. Good plus. **(12/95)**

2000-2008   **15.5**

Clos-de-Vougeot   Lamarche

Medium-full colour. Slightly solid nose. The tannins show a bit. Fat and meaty. The tannins are rather apparent on the palate and the wine is a little rough-hewn and rustic. Good fruit though. Good length. Very good but by no means fine. **(03/96)**

2000-2010   **16.0**

Clos-de-Vougeot   Méo-Camuzet

Very good colour. Rich, full, rich nose. High quality here. Lots of depth. Full and rich. Fat and balanced. Lovely fruit. Very good grip. Long. Backward. Very positive. Fine. **(03/96)**

2002-2015   **17.5**

Clos-de-Vougeot   Daniel Rion et Fils

Very good colour. Very good nose. Quite oaky on both nose and palate. Good substance. Classy for Rion. Not quite the succulence and dimension of the Engel. Fullish. Very good indeed. **(11/95)**

2000-2015   **17.0**

Corton   Bouchard Père et Fils

Full, rich colour. Really quite oaky. This is ripe and has finesse, redcurranty and cherry in flavour. Youthful, fresh, tannic. A promising depth here. Not a bit burly or alcoholic. Very good fruit. Medium-full body. Long, intense, complex classy finish. Very good plus. **(03/96)**

2000-2013   **16.5**

Corton   Michel Mallard et Fils

(Rogents and Follières.) Good colour. A little rigid on both nose and palate. Slightly lean. But good substance. Balanced but it could have been richer and more generous. **(12/95)**

1999-2007   **15.0**

Corton   Bressandes   Prin

Colour a bit light. Nose rather thin and without any class. This is still in cask (in January 1996) and has loosened up. But it was never very concentrated. Nor was it ever stylish. Some fruit. But one-dimensional. Medium body. Undistinguished. **(01/96)**

1998-2003   **12.0**

Corton   Carrières   Jacob

They declassed the 1994. Medium to medium-full colour. Not a blockbuster. Medium body. A bit lean and rustic. This is clean on the palate but doesn't really have enough stuffing. **(12/95)**

1999-2005   **13.0**

Corton   Clos-des-Cortons   Joseph Faiveley

Very backward but very serious. Concentrated. Good oaky base. Really rich, really classy. Nicely 'masculine' as Cortons should be. Fine plus. **(10/95)**

2000-2015   **18.0**

Corton   Clos-du-Roi   Comte Senard

Good colour. Opulent, blackberry nose. Almost over-ripe. Some new oak. Splendidly rich and ripe on the palate. Fullish. Very good intensity and depth. This is an impressive wine. Marvellous follow-through. At this stage still 'different' but not un-Pinot. Fine plus. **(10/95)**

2000-2015   **18.0**

Corton   Maréchaudes
Michel Mallard et Fils

Good colour. More generous, more elegant than the Renardes. The oak is more evident. Slightly less structure. But more fruit. Good balance. Good, but not the concentration and depth for great. **(12/95)**

1999-2006   **15.0**

Corton   Renardes   Robert Gibourg

Not quite so marked by the new oak, though all three *pièces* are 100 per cent new. Rich, chocolatey, caramelly nose. Firmer, less fat and less succulence in the middle. Not as intense as his Clos-de-la-Roche. But very good. **(12/95)**

2000-2010   **16.0**

Corton   Renardes   Michel Mallard et Fils

Meaty, satisfying, rich. Slightly more substance. But a bit slight for the vintage. **(12/95)**

1999-2004   **13.5**

Echézeaux   Dujac

Fullish, meaty nose. Lovely classy old-viney fruit. Rich, ample oaky. More exotic than their Clos-Saint-Denis. Very ripe and voluptuous. Lovely. **(10/95)**

2000-2012   **17.5**

Echézeaux   Joseph Faiveley

Very good colour. Lovely nose. Very rich and very stylish. Beautifully balanced. Fullish. Very good tannins. Splendid opulent fruit and very good grip. Classy though. Real intensity. An exciting example. (12/95)

2002-2015   18.0

Echézeaux   Forey Père et Fils

Full colour, rich, closed nose. Opulent and meaty on the palate. Fullish. Very good acidity. Good oaky base. Rich at the end. Abundant. Very good grip. Long. Lots of finesse and complexity. Fine plus. (12/95)

2004-2015   18.0

Echézeaux   Fabrice Vigot

Good colour. Slightly closed on the nose but fat, rich and substantial. On the palate fullish. Rich, balanced and stylish. This has lovely ripe fruit. Very good indeed. (12/95)

2000-2012   17.0

Fixin   Vincent et Denis Berthaut

Good colour. Ripe, quite sophisticated for a Fixin. Fullish but no hard edges. Good fruit and grip. Medium-full. Shows well. Long positive finish. (12/95)

1999-2007   15.0

Fixin   Régis Bouvier

Good colour. Very good fruit, but a little hard at first. Soon this was round and ample, a medium-bodied to medium-full-bodied wine with lovely fruit. Not *sauvage*. But plenty of grip for the meantime. (12/95)

1998-2004   14.5

Fixin   Champs-Perdrix
Gilbert Moniot-Defrance

Always a bit more *corsé* than his Maizière. Ripe. Quite substantial. Nothing *sauvage*. A fullish meaty, succulent wine. Good style and grip. Good stuff. (12/95)

2000-2008   14.0

Fixin   Clos-du-Chapitre
Dufouleur Père et Fils

Good colour. Ample, good depth. This (obviously from Gelin) is ripe, stylish, well made. Very good. (10/95)

1999-2008   15.5

Fixin   Crais   Vincent et Denis Berthaut

Good colour. More substance and depth. Good rich fruit. This is surprisingly elegant. And it has recovered well from the bottling. Long, complex. Sturdy but not *sauvage*. Very good. (12/95)

2000-2008   16.0

Fixin   Hervelets   Bart

Good colour though not a blockbuster. This is sturdier and also more *sauvage* than the 1994. Good acidity. A little austere at present but that is no bad thing. Individual and stylish. Ripe and positive at the end. Medium to medium-full body. Good. (12/95)

1999-2007   15.0

Fixin   Hervelets
Charles Bernard, Clos-Saint-Louis

This is a bit light, but it is elegant and balanced and has a cherry-raspberry fruit and is positive. A touch of new wood here. Quite good. (12/95)

1998-2002   13.5

Fixin   Hervelets   Vincent et Denis Berthaut

Better colour. This has richness and depth. And rather more definition and class. Plenty of wine here. Good grip. A very good meaty example with elegant fruit underneath. Will last well. (12/95)

2001-2009   15.0

Fixin   Hervelets   Derey Frères,
Domaine de la Croix-Saint-Germain

Good colour. This is rather better than the Marsannay. Old vines here (forty years old). Good fruit, succulent and not too solid. Good ripe tannins and balancing acidity. Not *sauvage*. Plenty of depth. Finishes long and complex. But not the style for better than good. (12/95)

2000-2006   14.5

Fixin   L'Olivier   Charles Bernard,
Clos-Saint-Louis

The wine is a bit light. A bit more astringent than the 1994. But no more substance. This is really a bit too weak. (12/95)

Drink soon   12.0

Fixin   Maizières   Gilbert Moniot-Defrance

Some of this still in cask - he bottles when he receives orders. Another bottling *tasteviné*. Sturdy, a bit dry on the nose. Good substance, richness and grip but lacks a little flair. Quite good. (12/95)

2000-2006   13.5

Gevrey-Chambertin   Alain Burguet

Very good colour. Firm nose. Quite closed. Very good acidity but still raw and youthful. Medium-full. Slightly raw and tannic. Slightly vegetal. Needs time to round off. (10/95)

1999-2009   14.5

Gevrey-Chambertin   Chezeaux

Medium colour. Ripe succulent nose - a little assisted perhaps. Medium body. Plump and ripe but not a lot of depth and distinction. Slightly coarse. Quite good. **(03/96)**

1998-2006 **14.0**

Gevrey-Chambertin   Robert Gibourg
Good colour. This is rich and meaty. Perhaps a little sturdier than the Morey. Good tannins. Good acidity. This is very good again. **(12/95)**

2000-2008 **15.0**

Gevrey-Chambertin   Louis Jadot
Medium colour. Plump, ripe, fruity, rich and ample. This is balanced and stylish. Lovely fruit. Real positive finish. Very good indeed for a village wine. **(10/95)**

1999-2009 **16.0**

Gevrey-Chambertin   Hubert Lignier
Good colour. Quite a meaty nose. Rich and fat. A lot more weight than his Chambolle. Good plummy fruit. This has just a little unresolved tannin still. Medium fruit, ripe, rich, gently oaky. Good depth. Very good for a village example. **(05/96)**

1998-2005 **15.0**

Gevrey-Chambertin   Denis Thibault
The style of this domaine is for quite delicate, very fragrant and elegant wines, and this is no exception. Lovely fruit. Very subtle and well balanced. Rich at the end. But quite forward. Very good. **(12/95)**

Now-2005 **15.0**

Gevrey-Chambertin   Vachet-Rousseau
Good colour. This is a bit adolescent but it is ample, balanced, juicy and seductive. Ripe fruit. Ripe tannins. Very good for a village wine. **(11/95)**

1998-2005 **15.0**

**Gevrey-Chambertin   *Vieilles-Vignes*
Denis Bachelet**
Medium colour. Quite firm on the nose. Very pure Pinot fruit underneath. Quite delicious. Fullish, intense, very cool, very complex. This is remarkably good. Very lovely. Very, very long and classy. Fine. **(03/95)**

1999-2009 **17.5**

**Gevrey-Chambertin   *Vieilles-Vignes*
Alain Burguet**
Fullish colour. Full and rich, forward and voluptuous. Very fine example for a village. Lovely fruit here. Full. Slightly burly at present on the palate. Some tannin. Rich, opulent and meaty. But very lovely. Marvellous finish. Fine quality. **(03/96)**

2000-2012 **17.5**

**Gevrey-Chambertin   *Vieilles-Vignes*
Michel Esmonin et Fille**
Good colour. A fragrant wine. Rich, very good grip. Long. Medium to medium-full. Not as full as most, but the fruit is fine and the wine very persistent at the end. Very good. **(12/95)**

2001-2010 **16.0**

**Gevrey-Chambertin   *Vieilles-Vignes*
Michel Guillard**
Very good colour. Rich, fullish and meaty. Lovely ripe fruit. Very very good tannins. This is a lovely old-viney example. Rich long finish. Fine. **(12/95)**

2002-2012 **17.0**

**Gevrey-Chambertin   Cazetiers
Joseph Faiveley**
Splendid colour. Quite closed on the nose. A neat example. Fullish, stylish, gently oaky. Not a powerhouse but a wine of real poise and depth. Very long. Fine plus. **(12/95)**

2001-2015 **18.0**

**Gevrey-Chambertin   Clos-Saint-Jacques
Michel Esmonin et Fille**
Good colour. This is more closed in than the *Vieilles-Vignes*. On the palate the oak is evident but the fruit is very concentrated and intense. Lovely complex Pinot flavours. Very well balanced. Classy, long. Fine. **(11/95)**

2002-2012 **17.5**

Gevrey-Chambertin   Combottes   Dujac
Fine fragrant nose. Good oak. Very intense. Lots of depth. This is very stylish indeed. Very lovely fruit. Very complex. **(10/95)**

2000-2015 **17.5**

**Gevrey-Chambertin   Combottes
Hubert Lignier**
Good colour. Good nose. Quite firm, with good concentration and nicely pure masculine fruit. Very Gevrey. On the palate this is now oaky, fat and stylish. Good intensity. Lovely long finish. Lovely ripe fruit. This is fine. **(05/96)**

1998-2010 **17.5**

**Gevrey-Chambertin   Corbeaux
Michel Guillard**
This is well coloured, meaty and with good ripe tannins and heaps of rich fruit. Nice touch of oak. Plenty of depth. Very good indeed. **(12/95)**

2002-2012 **16.5**

**Gevrey-Chambertin   Lavaux-Saint-Jacques
Vachet-Rousseau**
Very good colour. Lovely rich velvety, gently oaky nose. This is fullish, very intense, very classy. Excellent balance and very lovely

concentrated fruit. Ample and very ripe. Fine. (11/95)

2000-2015   17.5

Gevrey-Chambertin   Les Marchais
Joseph Faiveley

Very good colour. Plump nose. Ripe and rich. Good depth for a village wine. Fullish. A wine with no hard edges. Good grip. Balanced. Stylish. Long. Very good for a village example. (12/95)

1999-2008   15.0

Ladoix   Les Joyeuses   Michel Mallard et Fils

A little rustic but plump and firm. Yet a bit slight. Forward. (12/95)

1998-2004   13.5

Latricières-Chambertin   Joseph Faiveley

Very very good colour. More reserved on the nose. Good depth here. And on the palate a wine of real style. More than most Latricières. Here we can see the Chambertin proximity. Marvellous concentration and depth. Very fine indeed. (12/95)

2003-2015   18.5

Latricières-Chambertin
Newman, Gilbert Vadey

Good colour. Fresh plummy nose. This is plump and essentially soft in its tannic structure. Good grip. But not quite the structure, depth and class, indeed even the richness, for better than very good. (11/95)

2000-2015   16.0

Marsannay   Champs-Perdrix
Huguenot Père et Fils

Ample, fatter, richer than his Marsannay Echézeaux. This is a bit softer, more evolved. But no lack of depth. Nicely abundant fruit. Long and satisfying. Very good. (12/95)

1998-2005   14.5

Marsannay   Clos-du-Roy
Régis Bouvier

Good colour. Slight smell of filter-papers at first but this blew off. Quite substantial but not coarse or hard. Good tannins. Good grip. Rich and concentrated. Plenty of wine here. This will last well. Very good. (12/95)

2000-2006   14.5

Marsannay   Echézeaux   Marc Brocot

Good colour. Slightly coarse on the nose. But on the palate shows very good fruit and grip. Rich and ripe, balanced and fragrant. A good plus example. Good acidity. Ripe tannins. Long. Needs time. (12/95)

1999-2006   15.0

Marsannay   Echézeaux   Jean Fournier

Good colour. A little dry on the nose and palate. Ripe and fruity. A little thin at the end. Not bad. Quite clean. Not rustic. (12/95)

1998-2002   13.0

Marsannay   Echézeaux
Huguenot Père et Fils

Good colour. Fresh stylish plump wine. Good fruit. Slightly austere at the back but clean and unassisted. Finishes long. Good style and elegant. (12/95)

1998-2003   14.0

Marsannay   Vignes-Marie   Derey Frères,
Domaine de la Croix-Saint-Germain

Vines more than thirty years old. A lightish wine. Not very elegant. The fruit is a little hard but otherwise nondescript. Just about ready. (12/95)

Now-1999   12.0

Mazis-Chambertin   Joseph Faiveley

Very good colour. A little hidden on the nose. Fullish, very ample. Very well balanced. Very rich. Fine, I am sure, but judgement deferred. (12/95)

2002-2012   17.5

Mazis-Chambertin   Dominique Laurent

Splendid colour. Very very intense. Very lovely fruit. Quite oaky. Powerful in its intensity. But not its alcohol, only 12.5°. Cool, very elegant, very complex. Very harmonious. Lovely subtle finish. Very fine. (11/95)

2003-2013   18.0

Mazis-Chambertin   Philippe Naddef

Full, immature colour. Full nose. Austere, concentrated, quite powerful. Quite oaky. High acidity on the palate but a lot of *matière* here. This has an 1988 touch. A little tough. High extract. This needs time. Very good indeed. But perhaps it lacks a little class and nuance. But very youthful. (10/95)

2003-2013   17.0

Mazis-Chambertin   Vachet-Rousseau

Fine colour. Lovely nose. This is very fine. Very very concentrated and intense. Very classy ripe fruit, beautifully balanced. Good tannins. Good oaky base. Very very long and complex at the end. Very fine. (11/95)

2002-2020   18.5

Morey-Saint-Denis   Régis Bouvier

This is quite stylish but a little thin. Quite high acidity. Seems young-viney (but twenty-two-year-old vines). Unexciting. (12/95)

Drink soon   12.0

Morey-Saint-Denis   Dujac

Medium body. Fragrant, intense, stylish, balanced. Not too oaky. Nicely plump. Very good acidity. Very good for a village example. **(10/95)**

1999-2009   15.0

Morey-Saint-Denis   Robert Gibourg

Very good colour. Rich nose. Good acidity. This is meaty and fragrant, full without hard edges. Ripe and balanced. The tannins are nice and ripe too. Good plus. **(12/95)**

2000-2008   15.0

Morey-Saint-Denis   Chaffots
Hubert Lignier

Good colour. Quite oaky on the nose. A refined wine: complex, lots of *petits fruits rouges (et noirs)*. Medium to medium-full. Good attack. Laid back. Ripe and rich and gentle. Lacks just a little grip for fine, but balanced and elegant. Very good plus. **(05/96)**

1998-2005   16.5

Morey-Saint-Denis   Chaffots
Michel Magnien

Medium to medium-full colour. Fresh, very Pinot fruit on nose and attack. Medium body. It tails off a little at the end, and it doesn't have the dimension of some. But a good plus wine nevertheless. Positive and very pretty fruit and long enough. **(12/95)**

1999-2004   14.5

Morey-Saint-Denis   Façonnières,
Vieilles-Vignes **Hubert Lignier**

Very good colour. Just a touch barnyardy on the nose. Fullish, fat and rich and concentrated. Quite a spicy earthy flamboyant wine: in complete contrast to the Chaffots. Not quite the purity and style for fine but very good indeed. **(05/96)**

1999-2008   17.0

Morey-Saint-Denis   Riotte
Henri Perrot-Minot

Medium full colour. Firmer, more concentrated, richer and more intense than the Rue de Vergy. More depth. More backward. Fullish, quite oaky, rich and concentrated. Very good grip. Splendid classy balanced fruit. Long, intense. Lovely. Very good indeed/fine. **(03/96)**

2000-2015   17.0

Morey-Saint-Denis   En la Rue de Vergy
Henri Perrot-Minot

Full, rich colour. Quite firm, even a little adolescent on the nose. As it developed very lovely raspberry, blackberry fruit. Medium-full. Very clean intense classy fruit. Very good grip.

Gently oaky. Fat, nicely ripe and rich. Very good. **(03/96)**

1999-2012   16.0

Nuits-Saint-Georges   Fabrice Vigot

Good colour. Fruity nose and palate. The tannins could be a little more sophisticated. But the balance is here. Lacks a little elegance but quite good. Finishes well though. **(12/95)**

2000-2005   14.0

Nuits-Saint-Georges   Argillas
Joseph Faiveley

Good colour. Soft, quite spicy nose. Medium weight. Not a lot of tannin. This is suave and elegant, fruity and balanced. Not a bit *sauvage*. Vosne-ish. Very good. **(12/95)**

1998-2008   16.0

Nuits-Saint-Georges   Chaboeufs
Philippe Gavinet

Medium colour. This is quite developed already and shows a little attenuated and rustic. Fruity, oaky, soft. But badly handled. **(10/95)**

1998-2003   13.0

Nuits-Saint-Georges   Chaignots
Joseph Faiveley

Very good colour. Ripe, rich, fragrant nose. Very lovely fruit and style. Medium-full. Slightly leaner, but very good grip. Not as soft and seductive. A more masculine example. Backward. Long. Very good indeed. **(12/94)**

2000-2010   17.0

Nuits-Saint-Georges   Chaignots
Christian Gavignet-Bethanie et Filles

Good colour. Rather more elegant on the nose. Full and meaty. Rather over-chaptalised 'hot' feel. The tannins a bit over-extracted. Clumsy. **(12/95)**

2000-2004   12.5

Nuits-Saint-Georges   Clos-des-Argillières
Daniel Rion et Fils

Much more sophisticated than the Grandes-Vignes. More depth and concentration perhaps than the Vosne Beaux-Monts. Richer, spicier, creamier but not quite the class. **(10/95)**

1999-2012   16.0

Nuits-Saint-Georges   Clos-des-Forêts
Arlot

Medium to medium-full colour. Soft, composed, laid-back, plump nose. Medium to medium-full. Round and ripe and nutty. Good length and dimension. Complex and classy. This shows very well especially at the end. Very good indeed. **(03/96)**

2000-2012   16.5

Nuits-Saint-Georges   Clos-de-la-Maréchale
Joseph Faiveley
> Fine colour. As always, rather animal and
> *sauvage*. This year very, very rich at the same
> time. Full, good grip. Opulent and sensual. But
> not as stylish as most of the rest of his Nuits-
> Saint-Georges. (12/95)

2002–2012   15.5

Nuits-Saint-Georges   Damodes
Joseph Faiveley
> Very good colour. Slightly leaner but more
> backward. Somewhat different in character. Not
> as brutal as the Chaignots. Not as lush as the
> Vignerondes. Ripe. Balanced. Very stylish.
> More depth. Very very long. Fine. (12/95)

2000–2010   17.5

Nuits-Saint-Georges   Damodes
Christian Gavignet-Bethanie et Filles
> Bottled end July. Rather rustic. Quite sturdy
> and ripe but lacks nuance and elegance. Good
> colour. (12/95)

2000–2006   12.5

Nuits-Saint-Georges   Grandes-Vignes
Daniel Rion et Fils
> Compared with his Beaux-Monts this is more
> *sauvage*, more sinewy. Masculine. Good texture.
> Good. (10/95)

1998–2008   15.0

Nuits-Saint-Georges   Lavières
Joseph Faiveley
> Very good colour. Quite a different character.
> Rich, tannic, full, exotic and chocolatey. More
> concentrated. Fat. Fine finish. Very seductive.
> Very good grip. Very good plus. (12/95)

2000–2010   16.5

Nuits-Saint-Georges   Murgers
Chopin et Fils
> Very good colour. A little reduction on the
> nose. *Sauvage*, meaty, plenty of richness
> underneath. Full, tannic, very Nuits-Saint-
> Georges. This is a bit adolescent at present.
> Good acidity. Seems a bit brutal at first. Lacks a
> little richness. A bit coarse. Only quite good.
> Long though. Plenty of wine here. May
> improve as it ages. (12/95)

2000–2009   13.5

Nuits-saint-Georges   Perrières
Forey Père et Fils
> Fine colour. Lovely nose. Good oak. Very rich
> and concentrated. Very stylish. Opulent and
> succulent. Very good grip. This has a lot of
> depth. Very lovely. Black-fruity. Fine plus. (11/95)

2001–2012   17.5

Nuits-Saint-Georges   Porrets-Saint-Georges
Joseph Faiveley
> Elegant and rich on the nose. A civilised Nuits-
> Saint-Georges. Firm, full, very good tannins. A
> typical Nuits-Saint-Georges in its sturdiness.
> Needs time. Very good indeed. (12/95)

2000–2012   17.0

Nuits-Saint-Georges   Pruliers
Château de Bligny
> Good colour. Chunky, inky-tannic nose. No
> flexibility here. Reasonable acidity. Quite full.
> But no style. Over-extracted. (12/95)

1999–2004   12.0

Nuits-Saint-Georges   Saint-Georges
Joseph Faiveley
> Very good colour. This is very lovely.
> Marvellous complex elegant nose. Fullish.
> Crammed with fruit. Tannic but the tannins
> very very ripe and stylish. Long, complex. Real
> depth. Very, very lovely. Very fine. (12/95)

2000–2012   18.5

Nuits-Saint-Georges   Vaucrains
Jean Chauvenet
> Full colour. Firm, rich, oaky nose. Quite
> chunky and tannic. Acidity shows. A robust
> example. Good and full bodied. Plenty of grip
> and depth. But it lacks a little finesse. (03/96)

2000–2012   16.0

Nuits-Saint-Georges   Vaucrains
Alain Michelot
> Good vigorous, medium-full colour. Some oak
> on the nose. Some tannin. Quite good
> concentration but good acidity. It lacks a little
> succulence and fat but it is good plus. Still
> youthful, just a little dense. (03/96)

2000–2010   15.5

Nuits-Saint-Georges   Vignerondes
Joseph Faiveley
> Very good colour. Slightly closed on the nose. A
> touch of caramel and spice here. Very seductive.
> Fullish. Good oaky base. Rich. Very good grip.
> This is more accessible on the palate. Long.
> Delicious. (12/94)

1999–2009   16.5

Pernand-Vergelesses   Rollin Père et Fils
> Reasonable colour. A bit flat on the nose.
> Slightly vegetal. Medium body. Quite fresh. But
> lacks style and richness. Pedestrian. (12/95)

Drink soon   12.0

Pernand-Vergelesses   Ile-des-Vergelesses
Laleure-Piot
> Good colour. Slight toffee-butterscotch elements
> on the nose but good round ripe fruit as well if

not really that concentrated. Nor that classy either. This is fruity and plump and enjoyable but it lacks the definition and finesse of a top *premier cru* such as this. Not hard or lean though and finishes better (plumper, more concentrated) than it starts. Good. **(10/95)**

1998-2006   15.0

Pernand-Vergelesses   Ile-des-Vergelesses
Denis Roland Père et Fils

Good colour. This is round, intense and concentrated, without being a blockbuster. Very good style. Rich and meaty. Very velvety. Long. Very good plus. **(12/95)**

1999-2008   16.0

Pernand-Vergelesses   Ile-des-Vergelesses
Rollin Père et Fils

Good colour. Serious fruity nose. This has good depth. But on the palate only medium body and intensity. Quite concentrated but not very fat and rich. Needs more depth to be really good. **(12/95)**

1999-2004   14.5

Pommard   Joseph Drouhin

Medium to medium-full colour. Very ripe, plump nose. Good backbone. Nicely rich and nicely stylish. An impressive example of a village wine. Very lovely clean fruit. Very well balanced. Some substance but not a bit dense or out of place. Long. Very good. **(10/95)**

1999-2009   16.0

Pommard   Olivier Leflaive Frères

Good colour. Clean fragrant nose. Good substance. This is balanced and stylish. Very good indeed for a basic. Nice little touch of oak. Ripe, harmonious. Very good. **(10/95)**

1998-2010   15.5

Pommard   Chaponnières   Raymond Launay

Good colour. Bottled two years after the vintage. This is a sturdy beast of a wine. Firm, tannic, brutal nose. Ditto palate. Rich underneath but there is a dry touch on the attack, and though the finish is mellower the net effect remains a bit hard. Good but not great. Yet long. **(12/95)**

2000-2015   15.0

Pommard   Charmots   Jacques Frotey-Poifol

Good colour. Charming nose. This attacks with good fruit but then it tails off a bit. It lacks intensity and real grip. Quite good only. **(12/95)**

1999-2004   14.0

Pommard   Clos-des-Arvelets
Lahaye Père et Fils

Good colour. Soft and a little rustic on the nose. Fresher on the palate. Medium to medium-full.

Some structure. Some tannin. But essentially rather an artisanal wine. The tannins are not really sophisticated enough. The wine is a bit over-evolved. Will be ready soon. Quite good. **(12/95)**

1998-2004   14.0

Pommard   Clos-des-Arvelets
Daniel Rebourgeon-Mure

Good colour. Fat, rich but with a slightly *tendre* aspect for a Pommard. But this is no fault. Elegant and intense. Very harmonious. This has a lot of depth and complexity. Very good plus. **(12/95)**

2000-2010   16.5

Pommard   Clos-des-Arvelets
Virely-Rougeot

Good colour. This is ripe and quite stylish. But a little thin and hard. It lacks concentration and fat. Good acidity but a little lean. Not bad at best. **(12/95)**

1998-2002   13.0

Pommard   Epenots   Pierre Morey

Good colour. This is rich, oaky and profound on the nose. Quite austere. On the palate there is an element of darkness at first. But this may be the bottling. Slightly sweet/sour. Doesn't really sing. But certainly good. Not very Pinot at present. **(11/95)**

2000-2007   15.5

Pommard   Noizons   Jean Garaudet

Good colour. Nicely substantial and sturdy on the nose and palate. Quite austere - it could have done with a bit more richness. But no lack of depth or fruit, or even elegance. And it will get more generous as it rounds off. Very good for a village wine. **(12/95)**

2000-2010   15.0

Pommard   Noizons   Jean-Luc Joillot

Good colour. Ripe, ample, expansive nose. This is a good meaty village example. Substantial, balanced. Very good fruit. Even quite elegant. Very good. **(10/95)**

1999-2012   15.5

Saint-Romain   Sous-le-Château
Germain Père et Fils

Good colour. A bit closed on the nose. On the palate good fragrant elegant Pinot fruit. Slightly austere at the moment, but will get more generous as it rounds off. Good. **(12/95)**

1998-2002   14.5

Saint-Romain   Sous-les-Roches
Henri et Gilles Buisson

Medium colour. This is soft fruit. Has a little backbone of tannin which needs to soften up.

But the wine is ripe and quite intense. Ready in a year. Lacks a little succulence. Quite good plus. (12/95)

Now-2001   **14.0**

Santenay Champs-Claude
Lucien Muzard et Fils

Good colour. Old vines here. Mocha, dark chocolate, black cherries on the nose. Fullish, ripe tannins but really quite structured. Yet not solid or dense. Rich, long, intense. Very good. (12/95)

2000-2010   **16.0**

Santenay Clos-Faubard
Lucien Muzard et Fils

Good colour. A wine of medium weight and reasonable fruit. But it lacks a bit of elegance and zip, as if it had been allowed to get very slightly oxidised during its *élevage*. Another bottle seemed a little - but not a lot - fresher. Average quality. (12/95)

1998-2002   **13.0**

Santenay Gravières Hautes-Cornières
Jean-François Chapelle

Good colour. Sturdy nose, even a bit inky. Fullish, tannic. Plenty of good rich fruit. No lack of grip. A wine for food. Just a touch foursquare. But not rustic. Quite good plus. (12/95)

2000-2010   **14.5**

Santenay Maladière
Lucien Muzard et Fils

Good colour. Fresh, stylish, generous nose and palate. Medium body. Good intensity. Not a blockbuster but nicely persistent, long and elegant. (12/95)

1999-2009   **15.0**

Savigny-lès-Beaune Jean-Marc Pavelot

Very good colour. Plump nose. Good ripe fruit. Very good grip. This is really quite rich. Very elegant. Fine for a village. (11/95)

Now-2007   **15.5**

Savigny-lès-Beaune Hauts-Jarrons
Jean Guiton

Medium colour. A ripe wine with nice round tannins and plenty of charm. Good intensity at the end. Finishes long. Good. (12/95)

1999-2005   **14.5**

Savigny-lès-Beaune Hauts-Jarrons
Jean-Michel Maurice, Domaine du Prieuré

This is a bit unripe. And it is rather lean and thin for a 1993. Unexciting. (12/95)

Drink soon   **12.0**

Savigny-lès-Beaune Lavières
Claude Maréchal

Good colour. This has real depth and intensity. Ripe, concentrated and very poised. Fullish. Harmonious. Classy Pinot. Very good indeed. (12/95)

2000-2007   **16.0**

Savigny-lès-Beaune Narbantons
Dubois d'Orgeval

Good colour. Nice and meaty. A bit hard. A proper Savigny. Ripe, but it lacks a bit of richness and finesse. Good acidity. Fullish. Quite good. (12/95)

1999-2005   **14.0**

Savigny-lès-Beaune Narbantons
Mongeard-Mugneret

Ripe, slightly spicy nose. A little *sauvage*. Balanced. Medium body. Meaty. Lacks a bit of nuance but quite good plus. (10/95)

1998-2005   **14.5**

Savigny-lès-Beaune Peuillets
Denis Roland Père et Fils

Bottled in July. Good colour. Slightly old-fashioned (all the stems). Juicy, meaty, a bit lacking richness and slightly hard on the follow-through. Not rustic. But artisanal. Balanced and fresh though. (12/95)

1999-2004   **14.0**

Savigny-lès-Beaune Serpentières
Maurice et Jean-Michel Giboulot

Bottled September. Good colour. Quite a tough wine. A bit raw and over-macerated. High acidity. Rather too extracted. Heavy. Yet you can see the fruit. Not bad. Tannic. May soften up. (12/95)

2000-2005   **13.0**

Volnay Caillerets Pousse d'Or

Lovely fragrant nose. Very Volnay. Beautiful fruit. Just a touch of oak. Delicious fruit. Lovely complexity. This is fine. (10/95)

1998-2012   **17.0**

Volnay Caillerets, Clos-des-Soixante-Ouvrées Pousse d'Or

Not as expressive on the nose as the plain Caillerets. But concentrated and stylish. Backward. On the palate plenty of depth. Slightly less fat at present. But even better. (10/95)

2000-2015   **17.5**

Volnay Caillerets, Cuvée Carnot
Bouchard Père et Fils

A touch thin and lean on the nose after Pousse d'Or. Better on the palate. Slight lack of richness though but has class and balance. Certainly good plus. (10/95)

1999-2009   **15.5**

Volnay Champans Marquis d'Angerville

Medium-full colour. Ripe, concentrated, fullish nose. A little closed. Medium body. Good richness but lacks a little concentration and new oak. Slightly one-dimensional for what it is. Very good but not great. **(03/96)**

1999-2008   16.0

Volnay Champans
Jacques Gagnard-Delagrange

Lively nose. Very stylish fruit. Lovely soft ripe cherries here. On the palate very Volnay. Good intensity. Round and stylish. Ripe tannins. Long. Subtle. Very good indeed. **(06/94)**

Now-2008   17.0

Volnay Chevret Joseph Drouhin

Good colour. Very lovely nose. Very classy and concentrated and complex. Very ripe. Most impressive. Fullish, very complex, very harmonious, very Volnay, very elegant. Lovely long lingering finish. Fine. **(10/95)**

1999-2012   17.5

Volnay Clos-de-la-Bousse-d'Or
Pousse d'Or

Very good colour. A little richer and more powerful than the Caillerets, Soixante Ouvrées. Fullish, long, intense. Ripe tannins. Splendid fruit. Fine quality. **(10/95)**

2000-2015   17.5

Volnay Clos-des-Chênes Michel Lafarge

Very good colour. Firm, rich, concentrated nose. A lot of class here. This is full and fat and nicely austere. Lovely individual fruit. High class. Very Volnay. Fragrant, cool, balanced, long, lovely finish. Fine. **(03/96)**

2000-2015   17.5

Vosne-Romanée René Engel

Fine colour. Lovely nose. Really fat, concentrated and stylish. Lovely fruit. Chocolatey-rich. Really ripe. This is excellent. Very good acidity. **(10/95)**

1998-2012   17.5

Vosne-Romanée Denis Thibault

A bit more substance than the Gevrey. This is a delicious example. Rich, almost meaty, fat. Very good grip. Lovely intense fruit. Long, fine. **(12/95)**

1999-2009   16.5

Vosne-Romanée Fabrice Vigot

This is a bit more stylish than the Nuits-Saint-Georges. Similar weight. Again very nice fruit. More elegant. The whole is more sophisticated. Medium-full. Round, balanced. Good finish. **(12/95)**

2000-2008   15.0

Vosne-Romanée Beaux-Monts
Daniel Rion et Fils

Fine colour. Lots of depth, lots of class. Very good grip again. Medium-full. Very very long and complex. Very elegant. Slightly leaner than the Nuits, Clos-des-Argillières but more depth, more elegance. Fine. **(10/95)**

1999-2012   17.5

Vosne-Romanée Gaudichots
Forey Père et Fils

Fine colour. Austere, cassis nose. Almost lean at first. Ripe, rich and perfumed on the palate. Fullish, individual. Slightly leafy still. Not as opulent as the Nuits, Perrières. But long, fine and complex. Fine. **(11/95)**

2002-2012   17.5

Vosne-Romanée Reignots Château de Vosne-Romanée, Bouchard Père et Fils

Medium to medium-full colour. Not that much of a blockbuster. Nicely, but gently, fat, rich and oaky on the nose. Elegant but not very powerful. This is more like what I expected from the 1992. For 1993 it is elegant and persistent but it lacks weight and backbone. Balanced, long and stylish though. Good at best. **(10/95)**

1998-2003   15.0

Vosne-Romanée Suchots Robert Arnoux

Medium-full colour. Still very youthful. Splendid nose. Real intensity. Very concentrated. Marvellous fruit. Fullish. This is balanced, poised, has heaps of fruit and just the right touch of oak. Very Vosne-Romanée. Very classy and cool. Quietly confident. Fine plus. **(10/95)**

2002-2025   18.0

Vosne-Romanée Suchots Jean Grivot

Fine colour. Very rich on the nose. Has gone into its shell a bit. Opulent, fullish, very classy, nicely cool. Clean and nicely austere. Very, very rich. The finish long, intense, velvety, complex and very high class. Fine plus. **(11/95)**

2003-2013   18.0

Vougeot Cras L'Héritier-Guyot

Medium to medium-full colour. Fragrant nose. Good depth. Medium-full body. Good acidity. It is a little austere. It has the substance but not the charm. Good balance though. Long enough. Quite good plus. **(12/95)**

1999-2005   14.5

1992

RATING FOR THE VINTAGE

Red: 14.0   **White:** 15.5

SIZE OF THE CROP

(Hectolitres, excluding generic wine)

	Red	White
Grands Crus	13,278	3,600
Village and *Premiers Crus*	182,261	48,606
Total	195,539	52,206

Though not as prolific as 1990, the 1992 vintage nevertheless produced a huge crop, especially in red wine, and this, together with rain at the time of the harvest, has led not only to soft wines which have evolved in the medium term, but also to even greater inconsistency up and down the Côte than usual.

The best growers, of course, did not exaggerate their harvest. Lafon produced 40-45 hl/ha in his village and *premier cru* whites, 34 in red. Thierry Matrot's figures are similar. Pascal Marchand at the Domaine du Comte Armand made 37 hl/ha in the Clos-des-Epeneaux. In Nuits-Saint-Georges Gouges made 35 hl/ha, Robert Chevillon 42 and Alain Michelot 50. In Vosne-Romanée the Domaine de la Romanée-Conti produced 30 hl/ha, Engel 32, Grivot and Méo-Camuzet 35-38 (both equal to their 1991 *rendements*), but the respective Gros domaines rather more and Jacques Cacheux 45-48 hl/ha. Christophe Roumier produced 41 hl/ha in his village wines, 34 in his *premiers crus* vineyards and 30 in his *grands crus*. Charles Rousseau made 35-40 hl/ha.

On the other hand Vincent Bitouzet produced 47 hl/ha overall in white, Jean-Philippe Fichet 52 in his Meursault Perrières and the Domaine Michelot 50-55 hl/ha ('a normal harvest'). In Morey Georges Lignier and others made up to 48 hl/ha and even had to send wine away for distillation. Given these statistics you hardly even have to taste the wines!

Overall the yield in Puligny was 49.0 hl/ha, in Pommard 44.6 and in Gevrey-Chambertin 46.1. This is really too much. It had the effect in 1992 of reducing *terroir* differentiation.

WEATHER CONDITIONS

May was warm and dry; June overcast, wet and somewhat muggy; July and August largely fine, and dry enough to retard the development of the fruit until some welcome rain at the end of the second month de-blocked the ripening process. Then followed, and it was this which made the vintage, a ten-day period of great heat immediately prior to the harvest which began around 14 September in the Côte-de-Beaune, a week ahead of normal. Must weights rapidly climbed, acidities quickly changed from malic to tartaric, without falling too fast as the grapes concentrated, and the first week of the vintage took place in excellent weather. Nevertheless, not all the parcels ripened at the same time. It was necessary to monitor each vineyard very carefully in order to collect the fruit at the optimum moment.

Most of the Côte-de-Beaune, red grapes as well as white, had been collected before two days of rain set in on 22 September. The weather then cleared until the following weekend (27 September) after which conditions were mediocre. In the case of red wines that final push from maturity to concentration never came. But, unlike Bordeaux, which harvested a week or more later, most of Burgundy was vintaged in fine weather: both reds and whites are better than average.

THE STYLE OF THE WINE

WHITE WINES

'A *flatteur* vintage,' said Jacques Lardière of Maison Jadot, 'without the backbone or depth of a great vintage but certainly very good. It will come forward early.' Roland Remoissenet was more positive: 'Where the yields were not too high the wines are very ripe and concentrated. *Extra!*' 'Not quite as good as 1989,' said Dominique Lafon, who prefers his 1989s to his 1990s, 'but as good as 1985.' He pointed out that he makes better wines now. Jean-Marc Roulot, who prefers his 1990s to his 1989s, said that the wines were less structured (than his 1990s) but more elegant. François Carillon described them as less mineral but more ample. Thierry Matrot said that they resemble the 1986s, but are not as over-ripe.

One thing everyone agreed on was that the grapes were splendidly healthy. Acidities were good, but not *very* high. Must weights were highly satisfactory, and it should not have been necessary to chaptalise. Only if you over-produced do you have wines without the depth and structure, or the grip, to last at least some years in bottle. Overall we have feminine wines - I apologise for the sexist expression, but it does describe the character of the 1992s - fragrant, gentle, complex and appealing. Some required bottling earlier than usual, in order to entrap the youthful fruit and freshness. Malos presented no problems. The wines showed well when I visited in June 1993.

I last made an in-depth survey of the 1992 whites in May 1996. By that time I had formed the impression, despite some inconsistency at certain village levels, where some growers were caught by the rain or had over-cropped, of an easy to drink and enjoy, charming vintage, at its best with very lovely fruit-salad type fruit. The parallels with the past are with the 1973s, the 1979s and the 1982s: not wines for the very long term, but supple and complex. There is less structure than in the wines of 1990 and 1989, and less depth too. But there is more fruit and intensity than in the 1991s, the 1988s and the 1987s. The vintage is now more or less ready, except for the tightest of the *grands* and *premiers crus*, and is soft-centred, plump and very enjoyable. But it is not a great year: merely better than some. Only rarely do you come across a wine with depth.

RED WINES

The great Fernand Point, master chef of the twentieth century, was once asked what was his secret. 'The finest ingredients, the finest butter, and lots of time,' was his reply. Without the finest grapes you will never produce the finest wine. This means, even in an abundant harvest like 1992, a low yield, staying within the *rendement annuel*, not having to ask for the PLC. It entails, inevitably it seems these days, a green harvest, thinning out surplus fruit in July before the *véraison*. It requires a severe *triage*, eliminating sub-standard fruit in the vineyard and in the winery. In 1992 it may well have been essential to perform a *saignée*, a bleeding off of juice before fermentation in order to produce a better ratio of liquid to solid. Unlike in 1990, when even the *verjus* could be picked to make good wine, 1992 is a vintage where the yield was vital, and the fruit which was not ripe enough, not concentrated enough, *had* to be laid aside. Or preferably not allowed to progress as far as the harvest in the first place.

The wines, said Jacques Lardière of Maison Jadot in November 1993, were slow to evolve but were showing better than anticipated at the outset. At least the grapes were ripe and healthy, so growers could macerate as long as they wished. Because of the relatively low acidities it was not an easy vintage to vinify, said Madame Georges Mugneret. There was always a danger of excessive volatile acidity. She too offered the opinion that the wines were only just beginning to come round when I sampled them first some fourteen months after the vintage.

It was, said Lardière, a disaster to have had a too rapid malo-lactic (Pascal Marchand of Domaine Comte Armand also substantiated this). Lardière deliberately sulphured his wines to delay the malos. Marchand says the longer the wines could enrich themselves on their lees before the first racking the better. Thereafter the wines in general seem to have taken longer than usual to recover, to fall bright, and to show themselves respectably. This is always the case with a more fragile vintage.

The 1992s have an attack which is perfumed and often classy, sometimes even intense, but the backbone, grip and puissance of the 1991, 1990, even the 1989, is not there. They can be fat and charming, but are nevertheless soft and supple, and will evolve soon.

It is in a wine's structure and tannin that its origins are truly expressed. And so here too the 1992s can be faulted. They can be attractively plump, but they are somewhat neutral. Many lack real personality, and hence *terroir* definition.

But, as Jacques Seysses of Domaine Dujac said, 'It's better than 1986 and 1987; it's like a cross between 1982 and 1985. The wines have the same aromas as the latter vintage; fat and lots of fruit but not the same weight.' Patrice Rion found the wines similar to 1989. They have the same structure and fruit, he said, but in 1989 the fruit was more cooked, more concentrated. The 1992 fruit is more floral. The difference, in his view, was that in 1989 the September weather was warmer and sunnier, in 1992 colder and more cloudy. Bernard Maume said his wines were a cross between 1982 and 1989: more finesse, more structure than 1982, less intensely ripe than the 1989s. Charles Rousseau summed it up: 1982 *amélioré*.

In sum, as bottle tastings have shown, 1992 is a red-wine vintage of heterogeneous and inconsistent quality in the Côte d'Or. At its best the wines are well-coloured, healthy and attractive, with good plump cherry-raspberry fruit, ripe tannins, adequate acidity and medium weight: a vintage which is a cross between 1982 and 1985 or 1989; wines with much charm which will evolve in the medium term and should be broached before those of 1991 and 1990 - and 1993.

But the quality is mixed. There are variations between Côte and Côte, between village and village, between wines at the top levels and those lower down the hierarchy, and, most importantly, between grower and grower. While as always the most perfectionist *vignerons* have made the best wines, one or two famous names proved to be disappointing visits, and in many *caves* the wines were thin, dilute, superficial and even rustic. Burgundy is a cross between a rabbit warren and a minefield. You must tread carefully, and you must explore it to its limits. But if you are diligent, you will find much to enjoy in 1992.

WHERE ARE THE BEST WINES?

To summarise:

★ The white wines are better than the reds, and are at their best in the Genevrières, Perrières, Charmes section of Meursault and those Puligny *climats* just across the commune boundary.

★ The white wines are proportionately better at *grand* and *premier cru* level than at village level.

★ This is not a particularly successful vintage for the lesser known villages or the Hautes-Côtes.

★ Variable but light-bodied reds, ranging from the weak and feeble to the surprisingly charming, fruity and delicious.

★ More homogeneous in the Côte-de-Beaune than the Côte-de-Nuits.

★ And at *premier cru* rather than village level.

★ But many Côte-de-Nuits *grands crus* lack the intensity of a great growth.

STATE OF MATURITY TODAY

White: All but the most concentrated of the village and *premier cru* wines are now ready. The best should still keep well, however, so there should be no rush to drink them, at least not until 2001 or so. At the weaker village level, of course, we are already beginning to say 'drink soon'.

Over the rest of this decade the *grands crus* will come into their own. There are some lovely wines here, and these should last well over the first decade of the new millennium.

Red: At the lower levels a vintage to be drunk now, while the fruit is still fresh. And there is no need to stand on ceremony. These are – or the best are, at least – charming and fruity and a little simple: wines for quaffing, for barbecues and picnics.

As you ride up the scale the wines will have more substance, and the most structured will still improve. But, as always, it is the grower's name on the label, and his/her reputation which counts. I would nevertheless expect to drink almost all the red wines, however illustrious the provenance, by the early 2000s.

TASTING NOTES

BLANC

Auxey-Duresses   Henri Latour

Henri Latour doesn't make much of this. This 1992 is soft, has a little residual sugar, and a touch of SO$_2$. Pleasant, but not up to the standard of his reds. **(12/95)**

Drink soon   13.0

Auxey-Duresses   Claude Maréchal

Rather rustic. A faint hint of straw. A bit driven. **(02/94)**

Now-2001   12.5

Bâtard-Montrachet   Henri Clerc

Richer and more citrussy on the nose than his Bienvenues. On the palate this is opulent but it lacks a bit of acidity. The finish is lumpy and a bit coarse. The Bienvenues is better. Quite good merely. **(05/96)**

2000-2007   14.0

Bâtard-Montrachet   Jean-Noël Gagnard

Very lovely rich, ripe nose. Very succulent fruit. Smooth and very classy. Fullish, very fresh and vigorous. Excellent grip. This is very elegant and very intense. Everything in its correct place. Lovely. Very fine indeed. **(05/96)**

2002-2015   19.5

**Bâtard-Montrachet
Jacques Gagnard-Delagrange**

Slightly fatter and richer than Jean-Noël's. High quality again. This is fine but it doesn't quite have the vigour and intensity of the Jean-Noël. Very ample ripe fruit. Good grip. Very long. **(05/96)**

2001-2012   17.5

Bâtard-Montrachet   Louis Jadot

Good firm nose. Very good fruit. Plenty of depth. Round, rich classy fruit. Good acidity. A touch of the exotic. Yet somehow not the sparkle for fine. Very good indeed. Several notes. Marked fine 10/94. **(05/96)**

2000-2012   17.0

Bâtard-Montrachet   Louis Latour

Rich, explosive, spicy, a little SO$_2$. Opulent. Fullish and not a bit heavy. Creamy and ripe. This is delicious. Is it better than the Corton-Charlemagne? Fine. Several notes. Did not show quite as well at my May 1996 tasting. **(03/96)**

1998-2010   17.5

Bâtard-Montrachet   Leflaive

High-toned nose. Honeysuckle but quite delicate. Plenty of fruit here. And it is classy and reasonably balanced on the attack. But then it tails off. There is little grip and a lack of backbone. Pretty but not serious. **(05/96)**

1999-2008   15.0

Bâtard-Montrachet   Paul Pernot

Lovely clean pure nose. Excellent fruit. Very poised. Medium-full. Very well balanced, very subtle at the end. Not a blockbuster but a lovely wine. And it will keep nevertheless. Very fine finish. Very elegant. **(05/96)**

2000-2012   18.5

Bâtard-Montrachet   Étienne Sauzet

Closed nose. Rich and quite powerful. Good depth here. This is still a little adolescent. Rich and firm and full on the palate, but a little dumb. Excellent drive and intensity at the end. Very classy. Still very youthful. This should be better

than his Bienvenues. Fine plus - could be better
still. **(05/96)**

2002–2015   **18.0**

Bâtard-Montrachet   Verget

Some oak. This is just a little too exotic and
overblown for me. Better on the palate. This is
concentrated and classy, with lovely rich ripe
fruit (but not too over-ripe) and good acidity.
An open slightly exotic wine. Fine. **(05/96)**

2000–2012   **17.5**

Beaune   Clos-des-Mouches   Chanson

Soft nose. Flowery, elegant, quite intense. Ripe
at first but the nose a bit thin on the palate.
Reasonable balance and style but not ample
enough: not enough character. Dull. And quite
forward. **(05/96)**

Now–2000   **13.5**

Beaune   Grèves   Louis Jadot

Rich nutty nose. Body and depth here. Rich
full and exotic on the palate. This is a fat, quite
tropically flavoured wine with good depth and
grip. Still youthful. Very good. Several notes: all
similar. An individual but interesting wine.
(05/96)

Now–2005   **16.0**

Bienvenues-Bâtard-Montrachet
Henri Clerc

Deeper colour than some. Ripe, rich, exotic,
tropical nose. On the palate there is a hint of over-
ripeness but lots of lovely succulent fruit. Good
acidity and plenty of attraction. Real class,
though, it doesn't have. Very good plus. **(05/96)**

2000–2012   **16.5**

Bienvenues-Bâtard-Montrachet
Étienne Sauzet

Fine nose. Lots of depth. Lovely gently oaky
concentrated fruit. Plenty of backbone and very
good grip. Fullish, very complete, very poised.
This will go a long way. Very fine. **(05/96)**

2000–2015   **18.5**

Chassagne-Montrachet
Marquis de Laguiche, Joseph Drouhin

Light colour. Lean still. All in bud but a lot of
potential here. Very fine acidity. This will
explode. Potentially fine. Real intensity. But all
in potential. **(06/94)**

Now–2007   **17.5**

Chassagne-Montrachet
Michel Morey-Coffinet

A bit four-square and unforthcoming on the
nose. Slight touch of built-in sulphur. Balanced
and quite fresh, reasonable fruit and no lack of
follow-through. But a touch vegetal. But finishes
much better than it starts. Very good. **(03/95)**

Now–2005   **16.0**

Chassagne-Montrachet   Blanchots-Dessus
Darviot-Perrin

Very rich and concentrated. A little SO_2 at first.
This is rich and has *grand cru* depth. Lovely fruit
with a gentle lime-melon aspect. Real complexity. Fine. **(06/96)**

1998–2010   **17.5**

Chassagne-Montrachet   Boudriotte
Jacques Gagnard-Delagrange

Generous, abundant ripe nose. Gentle oak.
Medium-full. Complex. Clean. Very elegant.
Not a bit heavy. This is rich and has plenty of
structure. This will keep well. Fine. **(06/96)**

1999–2012   **17.5**

Chassagne-Montrachet   Caillerets
Marc Colin

Quite a rich, meaty wine on the nose. Lacks a
little flair though. On the palate, soft, flowery,
good fruit and grip. No over-ripeness. Indeed
gets better and better. The finish is long and
ample. Good plus. Marked very good indeed
03/96. **(05/96)**

2000–2005   **15.5**

Chassagne-Montrachet   Caillerets
Jean-Noël Gagnard

Very good nose. Supple, honeysuckle flavoured,
ripe and elegant. This is a delicious example:
everything in place. Very good creamy-rich, but
cool fruit. Not a bit over-ripe. Concentrated,
long, very classy. Fine plus. **(05/96)**

1999–2012   **18.0**

Chassagne-Montrachet   Caillerets
Louis Jadot

A little blowsy. Not as racy as any of the
Pulignys. Slight over-ripeness here. Only quite
good. **(10/94)**

Now–2000   **14.0**

Chassagne-Montrachet   Caillerets
Bernard Morey

Nutty and oaky on the nose. Lacks a little zip
and there is a hint of reduction. But this is just
adolescence. There is plenty of fruit. But essentially it lacks dimension, style and richness.
Slightly four-square. Merely good. **(05/96)**

1999–2006   **15.0**

Chassagne-Montrachet   Caillerets
Jean Pillot

Rather too much sulphur on the nose here. A
rich full wine underneath. Reasonable fruit on
the palate. But killed by the sulphur. **(05/96)**

Now–2003   **12.0**

Chassagne-Montrachet   Caillerets
Roland Remoissenet Père et Fils

This is a little forced on the nose and also on the

palate. For R. Remoissenet's 1992 it is very disappointing. Lumpy, coarse. A second purchase perhaps. Remoissenet sold out of his original stock very quickly, and then went back on the market. The worst 1992 white Burgundy I have ever had from Remoissenet. **(01/95)**

Now–2000   **13.0**

Chassagne-Montrachet   Champ-Gain
Michel Niellon
Good colour. Closed, rich and concentrated on nose and palate. This again is a wine for the long term. On the attack firm, very good grip. Splendidly elegant fruit. More expansive at the end. Even rich. But slightly adolescent at present. Fine, surely. **(10/94)**

1998–2008   **17.5**

Chassagne-Montrachet   Champ-Gain
Jean Pillot
Not as sulphury as his Caillerets. Higher toned, less rich. Cleaner but duller. Yet more enjoyable to drink. Quite good. **(05/96)**

Now–2002   **14.0**

Chassagne-Montrachet   Chaumées
Michel Colin-Deléger
Ample, succulent nose. But a little closed. Medium-full on the palate. Nicely concentrated. Plenty of juicy fruit here and plenty of grip. This will still improve. It lacks just a little elegance for really fine though. **(05/96)**

1999–2008   **17.0**

Chassagne-Montrachet   Chenevottes
Jean-Noël Gagnard
Not as stylish on the nose as the Caillerets. Ripe and ample but a hint of *sur-maturité*. Slightly citrussy as well as peachy. Good ripe accessible wine which ends better than it starts. Long, and yet stylish enough. Very good indeed. **(05/96)**

1999–2008   **17.0**

Chassagne-Montrachet   Chenevottes
Jean Pillot
Nose deadened by built-in sulphur. Can't see much fruit underneath. The attack isn't too bad. Fresh and ripe and peachy. But the SO_2 is there on the finish. A pity. **(05/96)**

Now–2003   **14.0**

Chassagne-Montrachet   Clos-de-la-Chapelle
Duc de Magenta, Louis Jadot
Ripe and fat, but as so often, a little four-square. Good merely. Better than the Caillerets. **(10/94)**

Now–2002   **15.0**

Chassagne-Montrachet   Embrazées
Bernard Morey
Stylish, higher toned than his Caillerets. Good zip. The attack is good, ample, slightly nutty, good acidity. But the finish is less so. A bit driven, and a slightly hot baked taste and slightly four-square. Merely good again. **(05/96)**

1999–2005   **15.0**

Chassagne-Montrachet   Grandes-Ruchottes
Paul Pillot
Firmer and oakier than his Romanée. More depth too. This has very good cool fruit, crab apple and peaches and honeysuckle. Understated. Nicely elegant. Good intensity. This is very good plus. **(05/96)**

1999–2009   **16.5**

Chassagne-Montrachet   Macharelles
Hubert Lamy
Soft, gently flowery, elegant nose, if no great weight or power. Pleasant on the palate but a little dilute. Clean but lacks dimension. Forward too. Quite good at best. **(05/96)**

Now–2000   **14.0**

Chassagne-Montrachet   Maltroie
Fontaine-Gagnard
A bit on the light side on the nose. But stylish and succulent. Clean and fruity, but lacks a bit of dimension and depth. Just a little dilute. Yet what there is is long and elegant. Good plus. **(05/96)**

Now–2002   **15.5**

Chassagne-Montrachet   Maltroie
Jean-Noël Gagnard
A bit flat and fruitless on the nose. Is this young vines? I get neither depth, nor definition here; and there is a lack of real flair and style. I prefer the *premier cru tout court*. **(05/96)**

Now–2002   **14.0**

Chassagne-Montrachet   Morgeots
Jean-Noël Gagnard
Good weight here, but solider than his Chenevottes and Caillerets. Less fruit, less zip. Better on the palate but a wine which is essentially a bit heavy. Balanced though, and the fruit is stylish. But good at best. **(05/96)**

1999–2007   **15.0**

Chassagne-Montrachet   Morgeots
Duc de Magenta, Louis Jadot
The wine is corked but the fruit is very elegant and there is very good grip and concentration. Surely fine. A keeper. **(05/96)**

Now–2007   **17.5**

Chassagne-Montrachet Morgeots
René Lamy

Good quite sturdy nose. Typically René Lamy, typically Morgeots. Good structure. Ripe and abundant. Good grip. This is a very good example. Plenty of wine. No lack of style. **(05/96)**

2000-2012   **16.0**

Chassagne-Montrachet Morgeots
Louis Latour

Surprisingly, not solid. Indeed the fruit has good high tones and good grip. Some oak. Ripe and ample. Good balance. Lacks just a little dimension but very good. And plenty of reserves underneath too. **(05/96)**

2000-2010   **16.0**

Chassagne-Montrachet Morgeots
Olivier Leflaive Frères

Ripe, succulent, not heavy, quite exotic. Medium body only. But a wine with balance, complexity and real depth. Not a bit four-square. This is long and concentrated. Very good grip. Very good indeed. **(05/96)**

1999-2010   **17.0**

Chassagne-Montrachet Morgeots
Bernard Moreau

A little bit of sulphur on the nose. But good fat full rich quite substantial wine. Ripe, quite concentrated. Good acidity. Underneath the SO₂ this is a rich meaty satisfying example. Long and positive at the end. Very good. Marked merely good 05/96. **(06/96)**

Now-2003   **16.0**

Chassagne-Montrachet Morgeots
Bernard Morey

Some fruit, but rather four-square on the nose. Not too heavy, but a touch dilute. What there is is fresh and fruity and balanced. So certainly good. The finish isn't hollow. Indeed the follow-through is better than the attack. **(05/96)**

1999-2007   **15.0**

Chassagne-Montrachet Morgeots
Jean Pillot

Nothing but sulphur on the nose. Quite honeyed fruit on the attack. Good grip too. And less SO₂ on the finish than most of his samples. Lacks nuance. Quite good plus. **(05/96)**

1999-2005   **14.5**

Chassagne-Montrachet *Premier Cru*
Jean-Noël Gagnard

A little heavy, lacking definition on the nose. Just a hint of sulphur on the palate. But the fruit is ripe and there is good grip. It just lacks a little flair and depth. Will still improve. Quite good plus. **(05/96)**

1999-2007   **14.5**

Chassagne-Montrachet La Romanée
Paul Pillot

Interesting slightly citrussy fruit on the nose, but without high tones. Good attack, but a touch dilute on the follow-through. This is reasonable but it lacks nuance and real finesse. **(05/96)**

Now-2003   **14.5**

Chassagne-Montrachet Vergers Ramonet

Firm, rich, concentrated, and *sérieux* on the nose. Still youthful. Wonderful grip and intensity. Very pure fruit. Marvellous concentration. This is special. But it is several years away from maturity. **(05/96)**

2002-2015   **18.5**

Chevalier-Montrachet
Bouchard Père et Fils

Good nose. Ripe and succulent. But by no means brilliant. Soft, round and ripe. Quite stylish. But no more to it than a good Meursault, Charmes. Balanced and positive at the end nevertheless. So very good at best. **(05/96)**

2000-2012   **16.0**

Chevalier-Montrachet Louis Jadot

This is very, very serious. Real essence here. Marvellous finesse and balance. Excellent. **(10/94)**

2000-2015   **19.0**

Chevalier-Montrachet Louis Latour

Lush, rich, ripe nose. This is a lot better than his Bâtard. Fine fruit. Backward and structured. But real concentration and power at last. This will go a long way. This has real *grand cru* intensity. Very fine. **(05/96)**

2002-2015   **18.5**

Chevalier-Montrachet Michel Niellon

Backward, concentrated, but very, very classy. Full, rich, very very lovely fruit. Very good grip. Marvellously balanced. This is very fine indeed. Marvellous finish. Real intensity. Super duper. **(10/94)**

1998-2018   **19.0**

Chevalier-Montrachet Jacques Prieur

Elements of *sur-maturité* here on the nose I don't like. Or is it just alcohol? Not the grip and *élan* it should have. Rich and fat but a bit flat and clumsy. The intensity is lacking. Though it isn't short. **(06/94)**

1999-2009   **14.0**

Corton Chandon-de-Briailles

Stylish but without quite the backbone it should have. Round, oaky, nice and ripe. Well balanced and full of charm. Good positive finish. Very attractive. But not *sérieux*. **(05/96)**

2000-2010   **16.5**

Corton-Charlemagne   Pierre André

Thin and sulphury on nose and palate. Nothing here. This is wine-making at its most cynical. Poor. (05/96)

Now-2000   11.5

Corton-Charlemagne   Pierre Bitouzet

Dignified nose but not that concentrated. Subtle, complex, medium-full body. Clean, balanced. Very well made. But does it really have the intensity or size of *grand cru*? Very classy fruit though. But very good indeed at best. (10/94)

Now-2010   17.0

Corton-Charlemagne   Bonneau du Martray

Very Corton-Charlemagne. Nicely austere. Very good concentration and intensity. Lovely fruit and excellent oaky background. A wine which is still youthful and vigorous. Very long. Very fine. (05/96)

2002-2015   18.5

Corton-Charlemagne   Jean-François Coche-Dury

Laid back, intense and very concentrated. Very special fruit here and of course the oak is classy too, if quite obvious. This is very lovely all the way through. But I don't think it will last as well as the Bonneau du Martray. Yet very delicious. (05/96)

2000-2012   19.0

Corton-Charlemagne   Joseph Drouhin

A round, ripe, soft wine for a Corton. It lacks the austerity, and it lacks the vigour on the follow-through. Nice fruit at first, not short, but a bit feeble thereafter. (05/96)

2000-2008   15.0

Corton-Charlemagne   Joseph Faiveley

This is excellent. Full, firm, rich, ample oaky nose and attack. Excellent concentration, low-*rendement* fruit. Very classy. Real intensity here. Youthful. Very fine. (05/96)

2002-2015   19.0

Corton-Charlemagne   Louis Jadot

Fat, rich, meaty wine. This again has good depth and the typical Corton steeliness. It isn't quite as concentrated as Faiveley or as classic as Bonneau du Martray, but it is long and classy and very fine. This confirms several earlier notes. (05/96)

2002-2015   18.5

Corton-Charlemagne   Louis Latour

Full, firm, slightly tough on both nose and palate. This is a little adolescent but has lots of depth and reserve. This is the best of the Latour wines. Fine rich fruit and plenty of grip. Just

give it time. Several similar notes. (05/96)

2002-2015   18.5

Corton-Charlemagne   Jacques Prieur

I like the nose here. Cool, crisp, elegant, not too dominated by the oak. Laid-back. This is stylish and not a bit heavy. Good discreet ripe wine. Long. Complex. Classy. Fine. A very encouraging first result. (06/94)

1999-2012   17.5

Corton-Charlemagne   Rollin Père et Fils

Clean and fruity but a little weak by comparison with the best. It has the style but not the concentration and depth. Fine long finish nevertheless. Very good. (05/96)

2000-2010   16.0

Criots-Bâtard-Montrachet Fontaine-Gagnard

Delicate nose. Perhaps a little too delicate. On the palate a slight whiff of reduction. Not a wine of great backbone or fat. Indeed a little feeble for a *grand cru* and not quite elegant. Quite good only. (05/96)

1999-2006   14.0

Criots-Bâtard-Montrachet   Louis Jadot

Very closed. Very concentrated. Racy, feminine. Very intense. Fine finish. Lovely. Fine plus. (10/94)

1998-2012   18.0

Criots-Bâtard-Montrachet   Hubert Lamy

Good crisp nose. Nicely flowery, good elegance. Good backbone here. Plenty of depth. Rich and nicely austere. This is long complex, discreet and very stylish. Fine plus. (05/96)

2000-2015   18.0

Marsannay   Alain Guyard

Fresh, ripe, good touch of oak. This is very enjoyable. There is a nice nutty aspect. Good for what it is. (02/94)

Now-2001   14.0

Meursault   Château de Meursault

This is really quite strongly oaky. Fat, rich and opulent. A little lack of real elegance, but generous, ripe, flamboyant. And really quite good, especially if you like lots of oak in your wine. (06/94)

Now-2002   14.5

Meursault   Darnat

Bottled March. A little bit of sulphur on the nose. But this has plenty of depth and concentration for a village wine. Good delicate touch of oak. This is plump, stylish and very promising. (06/94)

Now-2004   15.5

Meursault Sylvain Dussort

A little heavy with built-in sulphur. But good ripe fruit and good acidity. Finishes long. Plenty of life ahead of it. Certainly good. **(12/95)**

1998-2005   15.0

Meursault Paul Garaudet

Slightly flat and yeasty on the nose. Some fruit on the palate. But lacks richness. Clean but a little anonymous. Not bad. **(02/94)**

Drink soon   13.0

Meursault Louis Jadot

A neat wine but forward, a bit neutral and not very long. Quite good only. **(10/94)**

Now-2001   14.0

Meursault Matrot

Good fresh colour. Firm, backward nose. A little SO_2 still. Just a touch of oak. Fullish, ripe, balanced and with plenty of depth on the palate. Lovely fruit. Very long. Very good for a village example. But made for the long term. **(10/94)**

Now-2007   15.5

Meursault François Mikulski

Slightly overblown, but good richness. Good acidity though. But a lack of style. Yet has concentration. Better than it seemed when I tasted it in cask. And this note confirmed 06/94. **(02/94)**

Now-2002   14.0

Meursault Pierre Morey

Closed on the nose. Gently oaky. Youthful, indeed adolescent. The best part is the finish. Good intensity. Very long. Complex and classy but only at the end. Got better and better in the glass. Very Meursault. Inherently soft. **(03/95)**

Now-2005   16.0

Meursault Alain et Christine Patriarche

Rather anonymous. Reasonable balance but no character. **(02/94)**

Now-2001   13.0

Meursault Blagny Château de Blagny, Louis Latour

Full, fat, rich nose. Good depth. Fullish on the palate. As usual a little SO_2. As usual a meaty wine, though not too alcoholic. Four-square but rich and balanced. Still youthful. Good plus. **(05/96)**

Now-2005   15.5

Meursault Blagny Matrot

Ripe nose, but really rather too much sulphur (at first - thankfully most of this blew away). Nevertheless too much SO_2 on the palate for comfort. And yet a ripe, fullish fresh, balanced wine. More 'natural' in that than the Latour.

But only quite good plus as a result of the sulphur. **(05/96)**

Now-2005   14.5

Meursault Blagny Gérard Thomas

This is a bit dilute. Not much evidence of oak. Not up to *premier cru* standard. Lacks richness. **(02/94)**

Drink soon   13.5

Meursault Charmes
Vincent Bitouzet-Prieur

Lightish nose with a little sulphur. On the palate a light forward wine with little depth. Quite stylish but rather slight. **(05/96)**

Now-2000   13.5

Meursault Charmes Jean-Marc Boillot

Rich, full, exotic, almost citrussy nose. Some oak. Some residual sugar. This is very Californian. Quite full. Very ripe. Seductive but not very classy. Good plus. **(05/96)**

Now-2005   15.5

Meursault Charmes Pierre Boillot

Very good, clean, poised nutty wine on the nose. Real depth here. Very classic. Concentrated, very gently oaky, lovely ripe rich fruit. Lots of depth. This will still improve. Very good indeed. **(05/96)**

Now-2005   17.0

Meursault Charmes Bouchard Père et Fils

Ripe nose, but a little dull, and a touch of built-in sulphur. Good fruit on the attack but a lack of concentration and grip and plumpness. And too much sulphur on the palate. Unexciting. **(05/96)**

Now-2000   13.0

Meursault Charmes
Michel Bouzereau et Fils

Quite firm and oaky. A good quite backward example with good acidity. This will still improve. Clean, not exactly opulent and rich. But the good acidity is preserving its youth. Very good plus. **(06/96)**

1998-2006   16.5

Meursault Charmes
Hubert Bouzereau-Gruère

This is thin and poor. Very sulphury and not at all pleasant. Barely drinkable. **(06/96)**

Drink soon   11.0

Meursault Charmes Yves Boyer-Martenot

Good oak, good fruit, good depth on the nose. This is a concentrated wine. Fullish, lots of dimension here. Very good fruit. This will still improve. Very long on the palate. Fine plus. **(05/96)**

Now-2005   18.0

Meursault Charmes Alain Coche-Bizouard
Stylish fruit on the nose. Good depth here. Nicely flowery ripeness. Discreet. On the palate this is medium bodied. And the fruit is ripe and quite long and stylish. But it hasn't got the depth and flair of some. Long lingering finish though. Good plus. (05/96)

Now-2002   16.0

Meursault Charmes Jean-Paul Gauffroy
Thin, sulphury, unpleasant. No. (06/96)

Drink soon   10.0

Meursault Charmes Henri Germain
Good oak. Ripe, not adolescent. Nicely fat and rich but good concentration and acidity. No great finesse, but has depth and interest. Good plus. (10/95)

Now-2004   16.0

Meursault Charmes Louis Jadot
Round, ample, ripe nose. Very clean. Very well balanced. On the palate the attack is good, but the nose tails off a bit. There is a slight lack of grip. Stylish though, and not that short. But very good rather than fine. Several notes. (05/96)

Now-2002   16.0

Meursault Charmes Charles et Rémi Jobard
Slightly funky nose. Just a touch of reduction. On the palate the wine is quite full, quite ripe and quite concentrated. It is slightly heavy though, and the reduction aspect continues, giving a coarse finish. Quite good only. (05/96)

Now-2002   14.0

Meursault Charmes Comtes Lafon
Still closed on the nose. Very youthful. Very lovely concentrated fruit with a good oaky background. Fullish, youthful and individual on the palate. I love the grip and gentle oak background here. This has intensity. Fine plus. But not yet ready. (05/96)

1999-2010   18.0

Meursault Charmes Louis Latour
Good depth and a ripe, slightly citrussy fruit on the nose. This is less full, but also less four-square and more stylish than his Château de Blagny. On the palate it lacks a little zip but it is balanced and rich nevertheless. And there is plenty of depth. Very good plus. (05/96)

Now-2005   16.5

Meursault Charmes Matrot
As usual with young Matrot wines a little too much sulphur here for me. But the wine is fresh and concentrated underneath. On the palate the sulphur dominates too much. And the wine,

though not short, lacks a little intensity at the end. Good at best – when the sulphur has been absorbed. (05/96)

1998-2005   15.0

Meursault Charmes Michelot
Round, ripe and ample on the nose. But there is a little sulphur and the whole thing is a bit unstylish. Similar palate but even coarser. Yet good grip. Some reduction. Not for me. (05/96)

Now-2000   13.0

Meursault Charmes François Mikulski
Nicely crisp and ripe. With a better balance than the Genevrières. Slightly less balance. Round, elegant and fruity. Long. Good plus. (06/94)

Now-2002   15.5

**Meursault Charmes
Roland Remoissenet Père et Fils**
Fullish, ripe, concentrated ample nose. There is a lot of depth here. The wine is still youthful. On the palate there is a hint of reduction, and the wine lacks a bit of zip as if it had been bottled a bit later. But stylish, ripe and long on the finish nevertheless. Very good. (05/96)

Now-2003   16.0

Meursault Charmes Virely-Rougeot
Quite rich on the nose, but a little built-in sulphur. On the palate this has reasonable fruit, balance and style. But it lacks a little concentration and flair. Quite good plus. (12/95)

Now-2004   14.5

Meursault Chevalières Matrot
Rich nose. Not as adolescent as the basic Meursault. Good grip. Lovely fruit. Medium-full. Nicely firm. Plenty of character. Very good. (10/94)

Now-2007   16.0

**Meursault Clos-de-Mazeray
Jacques Prieur**
Under the Poruzots. Very rich but slightly heavy on the nose. Very honeyed. *Agrumes* (citrus peel) as well. A little four-square on the palate. Some oak, but not dominating. Finishes quite stylish. Quite good. (06/94)

Now-2004   14.0

Meursault Clos-Richemont Darnat
Monopole. This is from the *premier cru* Cras, a land more for red wines than white. Fat and masculine, rich and concentrated. A little four-. square. This will keep very well though. Average age thirty years here. 20 *ouvrées* (64 ares). (06/94)

Now-2006   14.5

Meursault Genevrières
Michel Bouzereau et Fils

Slightly less firm than the Charmes. More opulent. Again good oak and good acidity. This is richer and is a little more accessible. Not quite as good as their Meursault, Charmes. Less depth but still very good. **(06/96)**

Now–2005   16.0

Meursault Genevrières
Charles et Rémi Jobard

Cleaner than their Charmes on the nose. Ripe and ample on the nose. On the palate though it seems a little tired; already quite evolved. Didn't last very well in the glass. A blowsy wine. Reasonable style though. **(05/96)**

Now–2000   13.0

Meursault Genevrières François Jobard

Laid-back, youthful, very intense nose. Still not yet fully developed. Very splendid on the palate. Excellent concentration and grip. Very lovely clean fruit. Really intense. A classic. Needs time still. Very fine. **(05/96)**

Now–2010   18.5

Meursault Genevrières Comtes Lafon

Rich, oaky nose. Very exotic, fat and citrussy, very good grip as well. Really concentrated. In total contrast to François Jobard's. This is equally good. Rich and concentrated, very lovely oaky-based fruit. Flamboyant and theatrical. Yet not a hint of blowsiness. Fine plus. **(05/96)**

Now–2010   18.0

Meursault Genevrières
Olivier Leflaive Frères

Very clean nose. Lovely fruit. Ripe and honeyed with a touch of orange peel. On the palate medium body. Fully ready. By no means a wine for the long term. Pleasant, balanced, fruity. But a little simple. A lack of real grip. Good plus. **(05/96)**

Now–2002   15.5

Meursault Genevrières Michelot

Ripe, plump, candied-peel nose. But not very stylish. (Better than the Charmes though.) On the palate a little better. Ripe and ample and not unbalanced. Lacks class but quite good plus. **(05/96)**

Now–2003   14.5

Meursault Genevrières François Mikulski

A little closed at first, and the attack seems a bit four-square. The follow-through is rich and ample. It could have had just a little more zip though. But quite good plus. **(06/94)**

Now–2004   14.5

Meursault Genevrières
Roland Remoissenet Père et Fils

Very finely poised on the nose. This is rich and concentrated, even more so than the Charmes I think. Fullish, very well balanced. Very classy. This is classic. Good firmness underneath. It will still improve. Fine plus. **(05/96)**

1999–2010   18.0

Meursault Goutte d'Or
Alain Coche-Bizouard

Fullish, slightly four-square. Good grip here. A slight lack of dimension to the fruit but it is firm, backward, long and has good depth. Will still improve. Very good plus. **(05/96)**

Now–2005   16.5

Meursault Goutte d'Or Darnat

3 *ouvrées*. Eight-year-old vines. This has recovered better. Elegant for a Goutte d'Or. Very good oak integration. Racy but rich and plump. Long. Stylish. Very promising. **(06/94)**

Now–2005   16.0

Meursault Goutte d'Or
Jean-Paul Gauffroy

Thin, quite sulphury. Not very clean. No. **(06/96)**

Drink soon   10.0

Meursault Perrières
Vincent Bitouzet-Prieur

Pleasant but lightweight nose. Forward and without grip. Too burly, too slight, some sulphur. Unexciting. **(05/96)**

Now–2000   13.5

Meursault Perrières
Yves Boyer-Martenot

Firm, rich, concentrated nose. This has a lot of depth. Fullish, good oak. Very good definition. This is a lovely stylish example which goes on and on. Fine plus. **(05/96)**

1999–2010   18.0

Meursault Perrières
Jean-François Coche-Dury

Very pure. Very lovely concentrated fruit on the nose. With just a hint of oak. A very ample wine. Some oak. A lot of very ripe, poised fruit. Very lovely harmony. Really elegant and very very long. Super duper. **(05/96)**

1999–2010   18.5

Meursault Perrières Joseph Drouhin

Lovely fruit. Very persistent. Gently oaky and very stylish on the nose. Medium-full, very good acidity keeping this wine very fresh and pure. Elegant, complex, long, fine. **(05/96)**

Now–2008   17.5

Meursault Perrières Jean-Philippe Fichet

Good grip, good depth, still youthful on the nose. Fullish, youthful, balanced and concentrated on the palate. Very good grip. This is concentrated and still young. I like the nice austere style here. A lot of depth. Will still improve. Fine. (05/96)

1999–2010   17.5

Meursault Perrières Jean-Michel Gaunoux

Some reduction on the nose but good depth and grip here. There is a little reduction here, which is a pity for there is good concentration and drive and balance. Still youthful. Quite full. Certainly very good, perhaps better if the reduction goes. (05/96)

Now–2005   16.0

Meursault Perrières Albert Grivault

Ripe, slightly candied peel, but a bit overblown on the nose. Stylish, fruity attack. Weak follow-through. Not concentrated enough. Too forward. (05/96)

Now–2000   13.5

Meursault Perrières Louis Jadot

Ample, rich, above all fat - in a fondant sense - on the nose. Not over the top though. Medium-full, concentrated, rich, not quite the personality of some but a finely balanced complex example which is still youthful. Fine. Several notes. (05/96)

1999–2010   17.5

Meursault Perrières Comtes Lafon

Very closed, particularly when compared with the Genevrières. But very fine depth. This is very, very lovely. Still very young. Rich and full and profound and classy. Marvellous fruit and grip. Excellent. (05/96)

2001–2015   19.0

Meursault Perrières Louis Latour

Slightly heavy on the nose. But there is depth here. On the palate a little built-in sulphur, a little four-square. But very good depth. Rich, fat, complex and long. Slightly burly but fine. Will last well. (05/96)

1999–2010   17.5

Meursault Perrières Olivier Leflaive Frères

A little lightweight on the nose. Ripe and fruity but forward. A very pleasant wine for drinking now. Balanced and fruity. Elegant even. Not too lightweight nor too blowsy. Much the best of the Olivier Leflaive Meursaults. Very good plus. (05/96)

Now–2005   16.5

Meursault Perrières Matrot

Some SO$_2$, as usual, but good weight and concentration underneath. Less SO$_2$ than in the Charmes. Much more depth and definition. This is rich and concentrated, backward and classy. Very long. Will be fine. (05/96)

2000–2012   17.5

Meursault Perrières Michelot

Gentle, slightly reduced, fruity nose. No great weight, depth or class. Rather thin and boring on the palate. Cleaner than the other Michelots. But lacks definition. Quite good plus. (05/96)

Now–2002   14.5

Meursault Perrières Jacques Prieur

Ripe and rich, full, slightly flamboyant. Very honeyed. But undeniably concentrated and stylish. On the palate there is a curious flatness about the attack. But the wine begins to come out more. At first I thought too much oak. But the finish is vigorous and full of fruit. Very good grip. Very good. Better and better in the glass. (06/94)

1998–2008   16.0

Meursault Perrières Guy Roulot

Not the size of Lafon or Fichet, more that of Drouhin and Jadot, but very cool, elegant balanced fruit on the nose here. Classy and complex. Gentle rather than a blockbuster. Very lovely discreet wine. Impeccable balance. Now ready. Fine. (05/96)

Now–2008   17.5

Meursault Poruzots Jean-Paul Gauffroy

A bit better than his Charmes. Some depth here. But again rather sulphury. Just about acceptable. (06/96)

Drink soon   12.0

Meursault Poruzots Charles et Rémi Jobard

Good slightly four-square nose. Ripe, again like with the other Charles et Rémi Jobards I get a whiff of reduction. Good depth and fruit on the palate. Nicely ripe. It doesn't have the flair of the best, but a good wine. (05/96)

Now–2003   15.0

Meursault Poruzots François Jobard

Very lovely firm, youthful laid-back nose. This is not yet ready for drinking, and there is a little sulphur at the end but very good grip. No oakiness. Lovely pure fruit. Very fresh. This is concentrated and complex. But it lacks the flair - is that the *climat*? - for fine. (05/96)

1999–2008   17.0

Meursault Poruzots François Mikulski
Fat and concentrated. This has style and depth. Rich, old vines. Fullish and balanced. This is nice and backward. Very good. **(02/94)**
1998-2008   16.0

Meursault Poruzots
Alain et Christine Patriarche
Le Poruzots de Dessous it says. Well, it should be better than this. Quite substantial and rich. Good grip. But lumpy. Without style. Not bad plus. **(02/94)**
Now-2003   13.5

Meursault Poruzots Verget
Ripe, oaky, quite exotic nose. Quite some oak here. Rich. A suggestion of residual sugar. This is Californian in style. Medium weight and balanced. Attractive. But only good plus. Lacks a bit of real flair. **(05/96)**
Now-2003   15.5

Meursault Sous-le-Dos-d'Ane Henri Clerc
Quite scented on the nose. Medium weight. Flowery - more Charmes than Blagny - good acidity. Quite tropical in its fruit but neither blowsy nor too exotic. Finishes long. Very good. **(05/96)**
Now-2005   16.0

Montrachet Marquis de Laguiche,
Joseph Drouhin
Very high-class nose. Really lovely. Not a block-buster, and sometimes this is not compensated for by real intensity. It is very stylish. But it doesn't sing. Is this adolescence? I can't see any real drive and intensity. **(05/96)**
2002-2015   17.5

Montrachet Louis Latour
Old-fashioned powerful nose with a little SO$_2$. Similar palate. A real adolescent toughie here. Full, rich, concentrated and ripe. Good grip. Fine I am sure - but I don't think it is great. I gave it 18.5 in March 1996. **(05/96)**
2002-2015   18.0

Montrachet Jacques Prieur
Backward nose. Rich and very concentrated. Still very closed. Lots of depth. Quite clearly superior to the Chevalier. On the palate ample, ripe, oaky, still very young. But this has class and depth. But does it really have the intensity of Le Montrachet? Certainly very fine at the end without a doubt. **(06/94)**
2000-2020   18.0

Nuits-Saint-Georges Clos-de-l'Arlot
Arlot
Delicate oaky nose with just a whiff of sulphur. Stylish on the palate, but a little light. Lacks a bit

of weight and dimension. The balance is good though, and the fruit pretty. Quite good. **(05/96)**
Now-2000   14.0

Pernand-Vergelesses Jacques Germain,
Château de Chorey
Ripe, crisp, fruity. This has good depth. A stylish wine. For early drinking. **(02/94)**
Drink soon   15.0

Pernand-Vergelesses Rollin Père et Fils
This is suppler, rounder and more fruity than the 1993. Less anonymous. Good acidity. Good depth. Nicely firm. Will last well. Good. **(12/95)**
Now-2000   15.0

Puligny-Montrachet Gérard Chavy
Quite closed but a good firm, racy steeliness. Very Puligny. Good fruit. Very good acidity. Ripe, youthful, balanced. Classy. Very good. **(03/95)**
Now-2007   15.5

Puligny-Montrachet Druid
Good, very clean and classy. Gently oaky nose. Good vigour. Good depth. Slightly spicy fruit and residue from the oak. Slightly Californian exotic in style. But very good. Will still improve. **(10/95)**
Now-2005   15.5

Puligny-Montrachet Louis Jadot
A bit light and inconsequential, but adolescent. Will evolve soon. May get attenuated. Not very exciting. Other notes confirm. **(03/94)**
Now-2000   13.5

Puligny-Montrachet Louis Latour
Slightly closed on the nose. Rich, with a hail of reduction. More expansive as it evolved. Not too heavy. Nor a bit sulphury. Peachy fruit. Good acidity. But not a lot of strength and fat. Not the weight I would have expected but certainly very clean and elegant. Good. **(11/95)**
Drink quite soon   15.0

Puligny-Montrachet Chalumeaux Matrot
Not too sulphury on the nose, compared with some Matrot 1992s. Good fruit but no real flair and style. Medium body. More built-in sulphur on the palate. Rather pedestrian. **(05/96)**
Now-2002   13.0

Puligny-Montrachet Le Champ-Gain
Henri Clerc
Quite a deep colour. Citrussy, rich, overblown nose. Good acidity on the palate. Fullish, exotic. Not exactly stylish but not heavy. Quite good plus. **(05/96)**
Now-2002   14.5

**Puligny-Montrachet   Le Champ-Gain
Louis Jadot**

Closed on the nose. Good depth on the palate though. Nutty and persistent at the end. **(10/94)**

1998-2005   16.0

**Puligny-Montrachet   Le Champ-Gain
Olivier Leflaive Frères**

Lightish nose. A little neutral on the nose. Medium body. Gently oaky. Gently fruity. Lacks a bit of depth and definition but a pleasant elegant wine. Ready now. Good. **(05/96)**

Now-2001   15.0

**Puligny-Montrachet   Le Champ-Gain
Roland Maraslovac**

A bit too much sulphur on the nose. Rather four-square. Sulphury and fruitless on the palate. Reasonable balance. Boring! **(05/96)**

Now-2000   13.0

**Puligny-Montrachet   Champs-Canet
Louis Carillon**

Very lovely nose. Good wood. Flowery and peachy. Very elegant. Very well balanced. Medium-full. Very lovely. Very lemony. Good grip. Splendid fruit and harmony. Really intense. Will still develop. Fine plus. Several notes. **(05/96)**

1999-2010   18.0

**Puligny-Montrachet   Champs-Canet
Olivier Leflaive Frères**

Soft flowery nose. Not a lot of backbone though. *À point.* Stylish, gently oaky. It doesn't have the drive and intensity of Carillon but it is balanced and fruity and charming. Very good. **(05/96)**

Now-2005   16.0

**Puligny-Montrachet   Champs-Canet
Étienne Sauzet**

Good, very stylish, balanced nose. This is poised, complex and has very lovely fruit. Just a suggestion of sulphur at first on the palate. But concentrated fruit, very good grip and plenty of style underneath. Slightly firmer than Carillon. Fine plus. **(05/96)**

1999-2012   18.0

**Puligny-Montrachet   Clavoillons
Gérard Chavy**

Quite delicate (? too delicate) stylish nose. This is clean but it lacks a bit of depth and personality. Just a little oak. Reasonable balance. But only quite good plus. **(05/96)**

Now-2000   14.5

Puligny-Montrachet   Clavoillons   Leflaive

Rather flat on the nose. Some fruit, but a little built-in-sulphur on the palate. Ripe, reasonable acidity. But essentially full, and a little four-square. Quite good at best. **(05/96)**

Now-2002   14.0

**Puligny-Montrachet   Clos-de-la-Garenne
Duc de Magenta, Louis Jadot**

This is a classic. Gently oaky. Ripe and nutty, rich and profound. Very classy indeed. This is very impressive on the palate. Rich, opulent yet fresh. Ample and succulent. Yet very stylish and very long on the palate. Will still improve. Fine. Several notes. **(05/96)**

1999-2010   17.5

**Puligny-Montrachet   Clos-de-la-Garenne
Olivier Leflaive Frères**

Soft, elegant and honeyed. Nice fresh peachy fruit, not over-ripe. But a forward, quite delicate example, like most Olivier Leflaive wines. Accessible, stylish, balanced, long. Very good. **(05/96)**

Now-2003   16.0

**Puligny-Montrachet   Clos-de-la-Garenne
Étienne Sauzet**

Good freshly balanced wine. Not the personality of the Folatières. Good standard stuff. Some body, good grip. Good fruit. Will keep well. But there is a lack of definition. Good plus only. **(05/96)**

Now-2005   15.5

**Puligny-Montrachet   Combettes
Jean-Marc Boillot**

Quite scented, quite exotic, ripe and succulent. Fullish, rich, oaky, positive. This has both grip and depth. This is fine. Lovely style in a flamboyant way. Very long. Will still develop. **(05/96)**

1999-2010   17.5

**Puligny-Montrachet   Combettes
Roland Maraslovac**

Rather sulphury on the nose. Insipid and sulphury on the palate. This is even worse than his Champ-Gain. **(05/96)**

Now-2000   12.0

Puligny-Montrachet   Combettes   Matrot

Rather better than the Chalumeaux on the nose. Less sulphury, more personality. Some depth and balance here. Rich but slightly austere. Still youthful. Rather adolescent. But I think it will be good. **(05/96)**

1999-2006   15.0

**Puligny-Montrachet   Combettes
Jacques Prieur**

A quite alcoholic exotic nose. Good base of oak. This is good. A touch of candied peel. A well-made example. Balanced and stylish. Certainly with very good grip and complexity. Just lacks a little concentration and finesse on the attack and zip on the finish. But very good. Long. Nevertheless has intensity. **(06/94)**

1998-2008   **16.0**

Puligny-Montrachet Combettes
Roland Remoissenet Père et Fils

Lovely nose. Ripe and succulent, honeysuckle flavours. Very stylish. This is a lovely example. Very good fruit. Very good grip. Fullish, harmonious. Long, quite intense. It will keep well. Fine plus. **(05/96)**

1999-2012   **18.0**

Puligny-Montrachet Combettes
Étienne Sauzet

Lovely nose. Ripe, a touch of candied peel - but not over-ripeness. Round and honeyed. Elegant and rich. A touch of SO₂ on the palate. And this detracts from its attraction. Underneath ripe, balanced, nicely fresh. Good concentration. Very good indeed. **(05/96)**

1999-2012   **17.0**

Puligny-Montrachet Demoiselles
Guy Amiot

Elegant nose. Very flowery, a little looser-knit than Colin. Some SO₂ on the palate. Interesting individual character. Good acidity. A succulent wine, but without the flair and depth of Colin. Good plus. **(05/96)**

Now-2002   **15.5**

Puligny-Montrachet Demoiselles
Madame Françoise Colin

Very concentrated nose. Real intensity here. Really profound. This has *grand cru* depth. This is really excellent. Marvellous depth and concentration. Real breed and harmony. Backward, full. Brilliant! **(05/96)**

2000-2015   **19.5**

Puligny-Montrachet Folatières
Henri Clerc

Fuller colour than most. Exotic lemon sherbet nose. Good acidity but quite a tropical flavour. Medium weight. Not exactly classy. Fat and succulent, but it tails off at the end. Quite good only. **(05/96)**

Now-2002   **14.0**

Puligny-Montrachet Folatières
Joseph Drouhin

A little light and overblown on the nose. Lacks depth and grip. Slightly better on the palate. Certainly elegant and reasonably balanced. But lacks flair. Finishes long though. Good plus. **(05/96)**

Now-2002   **15.5**

Puligny-Montrachet Folatières
Louis Jadot

Ample, rich, very elegant. A lot of depth here. Lovely fruit and very complex at the end. Fine. **(10/94)**

1998-2007   **17.5**

Puligny-Montrachet Folatières
Louis Latour

Full, firm, very good depth on the nose. Good grip too. Not too heavy. A backward wine for the long term. On the palate a little overblown and sulphury, which doesn't go with the weight of the wine. Unbalanced. Good at best. **(05/96)**

1999-2007   **15.0**

Puligny-Montrachet Folatières Leroy

Full, quite powerful but heavy nose. A bit too solid. A little reduction on the palate. Good grip but a slight absence of flair and elegance. Adolescent at present. But will never be better than good plus. **(05/96)**

1999-2007   **15.5**

Puligny-Montrachet Folatières
Roland Maraslovac

Light, weedy, sulphury nose. Some fruit on the palate. But basically too feeble and far too sulphury. **(05/96)**

Now-2000   **12.5**

Puligny-Montrachet Folatières
Roland Remoissenet Père et Fils

Rich and honeyed on the nose. But more delicate and less intense than his Meursaults - or the Combettes. Just a little over-ripe perhaps. Rich and fat, very ripe indeed. This has a touch of the Clerc style, but has been better handled. Very good. **(05/96)**

Now-2005   **16.0**

Puligny-Montrachet Folatières
Étienne Sauzet

Youthful but very fine. Beautifully poised concentrated fruit here. Real personality. Very elegant. A lot of depth. Very clean, very harmonious, very lovely fruit without a hint of the exotic or the tropical. Splendid balance. Very lovely. Real poise. Fine plus. **(05/96)**

Now-2005   **18.0**

Puligny-Montrachet Hameau-de-Blagny
Jean Pascal

Some sulphur. Generally a lack of real cleanliness. This is a bit coarse. Medium to medium-full body. Reasonable grip. Not over-ripe or overblown. Better in elegance terms than on the nose. And not too sulphury. But pedestrian nonetheless. Quite good at best. **(05/96)**

Now-2000   **14.0**

Puligny-Montrachet Perrières
Louis Carillon

As with all Carillon wines this has beautiful peachy fruit and real poise. This is ample and succulent, with just a hint of over-ripeness. Good grip. Very good fruit. Not as classy as the Champs-Canet at present, but very good indeed. **(05/96)**

1999-2008   14.0

Puligny-Montrachet Perrières
Étienne Sauzet

Just a little SO$_2$ at first on the nose. And rather more built-in than the other wines. This is the least good of the Sauzets (domaine or *négoce*) this year. The vines are young. Lacks succulence and depth. Quite good at best. **(05/96)**

Now-2000   14.0

Puligny-Montrachet Pucelles
Joseph Drouhin

Beautifully poised on the nose. Gentle honey-suckle flowers in the flavour. Very intense on the palate. Honeyed just to the point beyond which it would be over-ripe. Finely balanced. There is depth and drive here. This is very fine. **(05/96)**

1999-2012   18.5

Puligny-Montrachet Pucelles Leflaive

Richer and oakier than Drouhin. More closed on the nose. But less concentrated on the palate. This is certainly very lovely. It is very fresh and very elegant. But in the end it is fine but not great. There is a nuance missing. Will still improve. **(05/96)**

1999-2009   17.5

Puligny-Montrachet Referts
Louis Carillon

Fine peachy nose. Just a hint of over-ripeness. Fat and rich, but without the class and depth of the Champs-Canet or quite the fruit of the Perrières. It is very good nevertheless. But it doesn't have the definition or the fruit for better. **(05/96)**

Now-2005   16.0

Puligny-Montrachet Sous-le-Puits Verget

Oaky, ripe, quite exotic nose. Good flowery ripeness nevertheless on the palate. And certainly succulent. I like this. Medium-full. Quite meaty. Very good. **(05/96)**

1999-2009   16.0

Puligny-Montrachet Truffières
Jean-Marc Boillot

Quite a big rich oaky wine on the nose. Masculine where Carillon (or O. Leflaive) is feminine. Still some way to go here. But lovely fruit, real grip and lots of depth. This has a splendid finish. Fine plus. **(05/96)**

2000-2012   18.0

Puligny-Montrachet Truffières
Louis Latour

Blunter on the nose than the J.M. Boillot. Again needs time. There is good fruit here but it seems drier, less ripe on the attack. The finish is long and ample and elegant though. This will make a fine bottle. **(05/96)**

2000-2012   17.5

Saint-Aubin Thierry Guyot

Clean, fresh, ripe, just a touch of new oak. This is just about ready. Long. Subtle. Good. **(12/95)**

Now-2000   14.5

Saint-Aubin Louis Jadot

Good firm base to this wine. Good grip too. This will keep. Well made. **(10/94)**

Now-2002   14.5

Saint-Aubin Champlots
Jean-Claude Bachelet

This has a touch of SO$_2$. The wine is richer and lusher but has less grip and freshness. A little fuller. Quite good plus. **(12/95)**

Now-2000   14.5

Saint-Aubin Murgers-des-Dents-de-Chien
Gérard Thomas

Rather forward and watery. Lacks richness. Nothing here. **(02/94)**

Drink soon   12.0

Saint-Aubin Perrières Gérard Prudhon

Ripe, but lacks a little bite; a little dilute, like I thought the Saint-Aubins were last year. Pleasant but no great depth. **(06/94)**

Drink soon   13.0

Saint-Romain Sous-la-Velle
Henri et Gilles Buisson

Like the 1993 this has a little SO$_2$ on the nose at first. Round, *tendre*, fully ready. This is ripe and enjoyable. But the 1993 is better. It has more depth. This will evolve sooner. **(12/95)**

Drink soon   14.0

Santenay Clos-des-Forêts
Hervé de Lavoreille

Ripe, balanced, ready for drinking. This is crisp and balanced and has plenty of character. Gentle and full of fruit and charm. Very good for what it is. **(06/96)**

Now-2003   15.0

Savigny-lès-Beaune Louis Jadot

Soft, spicy. Full of fruit. Crab apple and quince. Pinot Blanc spice. Plenty of interest here. Good weight. Long finish. Good. **(10/94)**

Drink soon   14.0

Vougeot Clos-Blanc L'Héritier-Guyot
This is not so stylish. Round, good acidity. But a touch tired in the middle. A bit *pommadé*. Quite good only. Ready now. **(12/95)**
Now-2000   14.0

Aloxe-Corton *Premier Cru*
Michel Mallard et Fils
Valozières, Toppe-au-Vert, Grandes-Lolières. For a 1992 this isn't too bad. It has reasonable volume, fruit and acidity. But it is a bit lumpy. It lacks real elegance. **(12/95)**
Now-2001   13.5

Auxey-Duresses Clos-du-Val
Dominique et Vincent Roy
Very good colour for a 1992. A lovely wine for a 1992. Very good cool Pinot fruit. Ripe, long, complex, indeed really quite full and intense. Very stylish, very good acidity and very elegant. Very good indeed. **(12/95)**
1998-2007   16.5

Auxey-Duresses Les Duresses
Alain Creusefond
Medium colour. Soft and *tendre*. A suspicion of attenuation and coarseness. But fruity. Positive finish. Reasonable substance. Not bad plus. **(12/95)**
Now-2000   13.5

Auxey-Duresses *Premier Cru* Henri Latour
This is soft and forward, a hint attenuated. But it is for now, not later. Fruity, but not special. **(12/95)**
Drink soon   12.5

Beaune Cent-Vignes Bernard Bescancenot
Good colour for the vintage. Plump nose, but not very concentrated. One can smell the stems. On the palate medium weight, no weakness. Soft and round and fruity. Reasonable length. But a bit one-dimensional. Yet quite good plus for the vintage. The wine is fresh and charming. **(12/95)**
Now-2002   14.5

Beaune Chouacheux Louis Jadot
Medium body. Fragrant, stylish, balanced. Better on the finish than on the attack. Good. **(03/94)**
Now-2002   15.0

Beaune Grèves Daniel Largeot
Very good colour. Good plump nose. But a little rustic. Medium to medium-full. Ripe, good grip. But only marginally stylish. **(12/95)**
1998-2002   14.0

Beaune Perrières François Gay
Evolving quite fast. Not as good as the 1994. A bit blowsy. Lacks zip and style. Medium body. **(12/95)**
Now-2000   13.0

Beaune *Premier Cru* Arnoux Père et Fils
Good colour. Soft, not too weak but quite *tendre* on the nose. Reasonable substance and plumpness. Good grip. But not very stylish. Quite good. **(12/95)**
Now-2000   14.0

Beaune Reversées Jean-Claude Rateau
Rather better colour than the 1994. Plump, but a little reduced on the nose. This is what dominates the palate at present too. Difficult to taste. The wine seems ample, medium bodied and well balanced. **(12/95)**
1998-2004   14.5

Beaune Vigne-de-l'Enfant-Jésus
Bouchard Père et Fils
Medium colour. Persistent cherry redcurrant nose with plenty of depth. Still a bit raw and youthful. On the palate there is a certain aggression about the attack. But there is fruit underneath. Medium body. Some tannin. Good grip. A touch hard on the follow-through. Quite good. **(02/95)**
Now-2003   14.0

Blagny Pièce-sous-le-Bois Matrot
Good full, firm, rich colour. Fine plummy nose. Fullish, sturdy, some tannin. Rich, good finesse. The tannins are ripe and not a bit rustic. Very good grip. This is a fine example of a Blagny. Long. Complex. Will still develop. **(11/95)**
Now-2005   16.0

Bonnes-Mares Louis Jadot
Fine colour. Firm, backward, very concentrated. Masculine for a 1992, but the wine comes from vines which are all on the Morey side. **(03/94)**
2000-2010   17.5

Chambolle-Musigny Hubert Lignier
This is a bit blowsy on the nose. On the palate rather light and weedy, slightly artificially sweet, lacks depth. Rather short. Unexciting. **(05/96)**
Now-1999   12.5

Chambolle-Musigny Combe d'Orveau
Henri Perrot-Minot
Very good colour. Really surprisingly concentrated and classy on the nose. Delicious fruit. Good oaky base. Nicely ripe. Very good length. Fine. **(03/95)**
Now-2005   17.5

Charmes-Chambertin   Henri Perrot-Minot
Good colour. This is quite adolescent at present. The structure shows. Rich, fat and balanced. But not quite the individuality of the Perrot-Minot's Combe-d'Orveau. Seems a little shorter on the palate. Ready. **(02/95)**
Now-2004   15.0

**Chassagne-Montrachet   Boudriotte
Jean-Claude Bachelet**
Medium colour. Good fresh, fragrant Pinot Noir nose. Slightly tight – but that is no bad thing. Classy. Lightish, soft, fragrant palate. Good ripe – if a bit slight – wine here. Balanced and stylish. Forward. But there are good elements here. Just about ready. Reasonable length. **(12/95)**
Now-2000   14.0

Chorey-lès-Beaune   René Podechard
The nose here shows some signs of attenuation. Medium body. Not as fresh as the 1994, but ample enough. Nicely plump. No weakness. Certainly good. **(12/95)**
Drink soon   14.0

Clos-de-Vougeot   Joseph Faiveley
Fine colour. No one can fault this aspect. Very classy nose. Lots of fruit here; balanced and elegant. This is a lovely example. Fullish (very full for a 1992). Very good ripe tannins. A splendidly harmonious and elegant wine. Fresh. Very classy indeed. Very fine long finish. Fine quality. **(11/94)**
1998-2006   17.5

Clos-de-Vougeot   Louis Jadot
Fine colour. Good concentration. Backward. Nicely black-fruity. **(03/94)**
1999-2006   16.5

Corton   Michel Mallard et Fils
Good colour for the vintage. Ripe abundant nose. A bit tight at first, the tannins a little rigid. More generous on the follow-through. Has grip and balance. But not much richness and finesse. Good. **(12/95)**
1998-2004   15.0

Corton   Bressandes   Prin
Good colour. Quite full and ample on the nose. But rather coarse, unbalanced and rustic. Edgy. Some substance. But very rustic. **(12/95)**
Drink soon   12.0

Corton   Clos-des-Cortons   Joseph Faiveley
Medium-full, fresh colour. Youthful oaky nose. Ripe, balanced medium-full wine. Very good grip. Plump and with the oak well integrated on the palate. Very elegant. Fine. **(09/94)**
1999-2009   17.5

Corton   Clos-du-Roi   Comte Senard
Very good colour. Rich nose. Spicy. Good intensity on the palate. Medium-full. A touch of oak. But spicier than Faiveley. Ripe, long. Very well balanced. A more mineral, masculine wine than the Faiveley. Fine again. **(09/94)**
1999-2009   17.5

Corton   Pougets   Louis Jadot
Medium to medium-full colour. Elegant, smooth, medium to medium-full body. Perhaps lacks a bit of concentration. Certainly very stylish though. **(03/94)**
1998-2005   16.0

Echézeaux   Fabrice Vigot
Good colour. A bit suave and rustic. Too sweet. Not for me. Will get attenuated. Coarse. **(12/95)**
Now-2001   13.5

Fixin   Crais   Vincent et Denis Berthaut
Good colour. Much better than 1994. And much more fruit and depth and substance on the palate too. Round, rich, succulent and even quite concentrated. A most attractive bottle. **(12/95)**
Now-2003   15.5

Fixin   Hervelets   Bart
Light to medium colour. The nose shows a little of the stems. But it is softer on the palate. Nice plump fruit. No great depth. But a pleasant, charming wine which is not short. Good for the vintage. **(12/95)**
Drink soon   15.0

**Fixin   Hervelets   Charles Bernard,
Domaine du Clos-Saint-Louis**
Again this has more to it than the Olivier. Round and fruity but forward. Not quite as stylish as the 1993 though. Ready. **(12/95)**
Drink soon   13.5

Fixin   Maizières   Gilbert Moniot-Defrance
Rather light in colour and weight. Quite fruity, quite fresh. Not rustic. But a little slight. Not bad. **(12/95)**
Drink soon   13.0

**Fixin   L'Olivier   Charles Bernard,
Domaine du Clos-Saint-Louis**
Clean but really very light. Ready now. Nothing here. **(12/95)**
Drink soon   12.5

Gevrey-Chambertin   Denis Thibault
Lightish in colour. Rather slight on the palate. Yet balanced and stylish. Not short. But a little too soft. **(12/95)**
Drink soon   13.0

Gevrey-Chambertin *Vieilles-Vignes* Alain Burguet

More closed, but, of course, more depth. Rich, fat, structured and meaty, but harmonious and intense. This is very lovely. Very long and complex. As usual of *grand cru* quality. Marvellous finish. Fine. **(06/95)**

2000–2010   **17.5**

Gevrey-Chambertin Clos-Saint-Jacques Louis Jadot

Medium-full colour. Very lovely essence of Pinot Noir. But with a feminine touch which is 1992. Yet a lot more depth and class and individuality than most 1992s. Lovely. **(03/94)**

1999–2009   **18.0**

La Romanée Bouchard Père et Fils

Medium to medium-full colour. Rich, quite structured, but the nose is a bit lean. On the palate the intense perfume of La Romanée comes out. The wine is sweet and ripe and there is quite good grip. Medium body. A little tannin. There is certainly fragrance and quality here, though not a lot of depth or strength. Very good indeed/fine. **(02/95)**

1998–2008   **17.0**

Ladoix Les Joyeuses Michel Mallard et Fils

A bit stemmy, though none here. Better than their Savigny, Serpentières 1992. More succulence. Reasonable freshness. A little lacking concentration but not bad. Ready. **(12/95)**

Now–2000   **13.5**

Marsannay Echézeaux Marc Brocot

Good colour, especially for the vintage. A little reduction on the nose. But ripe, nicely substantial and succulent on the palate. Ripe and rich. Good grip. This is very good for the vintage. Plenty of vigour and life ahead of it. Will still improve. **(12/95)**

Now–2002   **15.0**

Marsannay Echézeaux Jean Fournier

This is quite evolved, and is getting rapidly attenuated. Good freshness at the end. But a lack of succulence in the middle. The same weight as the 1993. **(12/95)**

Drink soon   **13.0**

Marsannay Echézeaux Huguenot Père et Fils

Good colour. Nicely plump nose. Round, fruity, charming. This is just what you should expect. Medium body. Easy to drink. No attempt to make a silk purse out of a sow's ear. Long. Stylish. Just about ready. **(12/95)**

Now–2000   **14.5**

Marsannay Vignes-Marie Derey Frères, Domaine de la Croix-Saint-Germain

Better colour than the 1993, especially for the vintage. Again a little thin and not very stylish. I can't get enthused. Round and soft, but the fruit a bit meagre. **(12/95)**

Drink soon   **12.0**

Monthélie Bernard Boisson

A bit light, a bit thin, a bit too much of the stems. Not for me. Some fruit, perhaps. **(06/94)**

Drink up   **12.0**

Morey-Saint-Denis Robert Gibourg

Good colour. This is a lot better than the 1994. Ripe, succulent nose. Fullish especially for a 1992. Round, no hard edges. But good structure. Good ripe tannins. This is very good. **(12/95)**

1998–2002   **15.0**

Morey-Saint-Denis Chaffots Michel Magnien

Premier cru. 80 per cent Les Chaffots. This has a reasonable colour but is rather too light and insubstantial underneath. As if it had collapsed in the bottle. Fruit here but not backbone. **(12/95)**

Drink soon   **12.5**

Morey-Saint-Denis En la Rue de Vergy Henri Perrot-Minot

Very good colour. There is depth here on the nose. It will still develop. Fullish for 1992. Lovely ripe plump fruit. Very seductive. This is excellent. Lots of *matière* for a 1992. Yet not a bit forced. Long, fat, rich. Fine. **(10/95)**

Now–2005   **16.0**

Nuits-Saint-Georges Les Athées Christian Gavignet-Bethanie et Filles

Soft, perfumed, quite sweet. Rather concocted. The tannins a bit over-extracted in the background. **(12/95)**

Now–2001   **13.0**

Nuits-Saint-Georges Chaignots Joseph Faiveley

Fine colour. No-one can fault this aspect. The nose is rich, opulent and spicy. A touch over-ripe. On the palate there is medium to medium-full body (very good for 1992). Good grip and an attractively balanced ripe fruity structure. Long. No hard edges. Round. Good class. Plenty of depth. Very good. **(11/94)**

Now–2004   **16.0**

Nuits-Saint-Georges Clos-des-Corvées Louis Latour

Good colour. Rich, robust, oaky, firm. Slightly hard still. But there is depth here. Will evolve well. **(03/94)**

1999–2007   **16.0**

Nuits-Saint-Georges
Clos-des-Forêts-Saint-Georges   Arlot

Medium to medium-full colour. The nose is a bit dumb. On the palate good structure, good fresh plump stylish fruit and very good acidity. This is long, succulent and most attractive. Medium body. Just a little tannin. Long positive finish. Very good. **(09/95)**

1998-2006   16.0

Nuits-Saint-Georges   Pruliers
Château de Bligny

Good substance for a 1992. But rather too four-square and over-extracted. Lacks grace, charm and elegance. **(12/95)**

1998-2002   13.0

Nuits-Saint-Georges   Les Saint-Georges
Henri Gouges

Good colour. This is ripe, fragrant and has plenty of depth. Good round even rich wine. Good grip. Elegant, stylish. Long. Fine for the vintage. **(11/94)**

Now-2008   17.5

Pernand-Vergelesses   Dubreuil-Fontaine

Fruity but simple. Charming but short. No better than a pleasant generic. **(02/95)**

Drink soon   12.0

Pernand-Vergelesses   Rollin Père et Fils

A bit weedy/vegetal on the nose. On the palate some depth and some fruit. A perfectly drinkable - if dull - bottle. Not bad. **(12/95)**

Drink soon   13.0

Pernand-Vergelesses   Ile-des-Vergelesses
Roland Rapet

This is fruity, forward and rather short. For a *climat* such as this it lacks depth and concentration: volume indeed. Not much tannin. Not much grip. Pleasant but not really any style. Disappointing. **(02/95)**

Drink soon   13.5

Pernand-Vergelesses   Ile-des-Vergelesses
Denis Roland Père et Fils

Soft, ripe, stylish, succulent nose. Medium body. This is a lot more elegant than most 1992s. Reasonable grip. Good fruit. Shows well. Good long positive finish. Very good. **(12/95)**

Now-2002   15.5

Pommard   Jean-Marie Capron-Charcousset

Good colour. Ripe, fresh, positive nose. Medium to medium-full, elegant for a 1992. Individual. Balanced. Complex. Unexpected depth here. Long. Very good. **(12/95)**

Now-2002   15.0

Pommard   Château de Pommard
Jean-Louis Laplanche

Good colour. Some oak. A touch rustic. Good acidity though. Very Pommard. **(03/94)**

Now-2001   14.0

Pommard   Chaponnières   Raymond Launay

Reasonable colour. Firm nose for the vintage. There is good fruit here but it is fighting against the usual Launay structure. Meaty. Good enough acidity. But it lacks a little finesse. Good for the vintage. **(12/95)**

1998-2004   15.0

Pommard   Charmots   Jacques Frotey-Poifol

This is soft and stylish. Light but not really weak. Forward. Plump and charming. But a bit one-dimensional. Now ready. Not bad. **(12/95)**

Now-2000   13.0

Pommard   Clos-des-Arvelets   Labry

Good colour. Soft, round, plump nose. Lots of *petits fruits rouges*. Medium to medium-full body. This is positive and elegant for a 1992, and has very good length. A very good example. Lovely fruit. **(12/95)**

1998-2006   16.0

Pommard   Clos-des-Arvelets
Lahaye Père et Fils

Medium colour. Soft, plump nose. Light to medium body. This is soft, plump, positive and fruity. A positive wine for the vintage. Good fruit. Not that elegant though. **(12/95)**

Now-2003   14.0

Pommard   Clos-des-Arvelets   Virely-Rougeot

Lightish colour. This is a bit thin and attenuated. Already too evolved. Old tea and *feuilles mortes*. No future. **(12/95)**

Drink soon   12.0

Pommard   Noizons   Jean Garaudet

Reasonable colour. A little diffuse on the nose. The tannins are a little dry and old leafy. Medium body. I think the 1994 is better than this. There is fruit here, and it is not weak. But it is a bit rustic. Quite good only. **(12/95)**

Now-2002   14.0

Pommard   Vignots   Leroy

Youthful colour. Quite oaky on the nose. Rich, vigorous. Voluptuous and vanilla-chocolate-spicy. Full, very oaky, the tannins still not quite resolved. Good richness. Good grip. Almost too oaky but not quite. Fine and concentrated. **(05/96)**

1998-2012   17.0

Saint-Romain Thierry Guyot

This is very good for a Saint-Romain of this vintage (100 per cent destemming, twenty days' *cuvaison*). Plenty of substance. Good tannins. Not exactly very fat, but the fruit is fragrant and there is good acidity. Long. Good. **(12/95)**

Now–2004   15.0

Saint-Romain Sous-le-Château
Germain Père et Fils

Light to medium colour. This is on the light side, and may get a little astringent. But the wine has fruit and reasonable acidity. Doesn't have the style of the 1993 but a quite good example. Ready now. **(12/95)**

Now–2000   14.0

Saint-Romain Sous-les-Roches
Henri et Gilles Buisson

Light to medium colour. A good success for the vintage. Ripe, balanced and stylish. This is soft but is well balanced. Nicely round. Shows well. Not too tired. Will still last. Good. **(12/95)**

Now–2000   15.0

Santenay Clos-de-la-Confrérie
Vincent Girardin

Good colour for the vintage. Soft, oaky and seductive on the nose. Medium body. Little tannin. Good balanced fruit and oak integration. But a little forward. Good for the vintage though. **(10/95)**

Now–2000   14.5

Santenay Clos-Rousseau Bernard Morey

This is very good. Rich, substantial, concentrated. And has very good grip. Round, amply fruity. Fullish. Finishes very well. Very good. **(10/95)**

1998–2004   15.5

Santenay Gravières Hautes-Cornières,
Jean-François Chapelle

Good colour for the vintage. Fruity nose, but a little diffuse, a little rustic. This lacks grip. And it lacks a bit of elegance. Some substance but a bit lumpy. Drink as soon as it softens up. It won't keep well. **(12/95)**

Drink soon   13.5

Santenay Maladière
Lucien Muzard et Fils

Good colour. Ripe, plump balanced nose. This is a good fresh example. Meaty for a 1992. Stylish for a 1992 as well. Nicely ripe. Nicely positive at the end. Good. **(12/95)**

1998–2004   15.0

Savigny-lès-Beaune Bourgeots
Simon Bize et Fils

Good colour for a 1992. Plenty of round, succulent fruit here. Good backbone and depth for a village wine. Still just a touch raw on the attack. Good acidity. Has style and charm. Very good for a village. **(09/95)**

Now–2002   14.0

Savigny-lès-Beaune Dominode Louis Jadot

Old viney. Good oak base. Fullish. Rich, ample, balanced. Very good indeed. **(03/94)**

1999–2005   16.5

Savigny-lès-Beaune Hauts-Jarrons
Jean Guiton

This is a bit slight. Now getting attenuated. **(12/95)**

Drink soon   12.0

Savigny-lès-Beaune Lavières
Claude Maréchal

A bit light. Certainly getting attenuated. What a disappointment after the delights of the 1993. He picked in the rain, and it shows. **(12/95)**

Drink soon   12.5

Savigny-lès-Beaune Narbantons
Dubois d'Orgeval

Good colour. Rather better substance than 1994. Slightly rustic on the nose. But ripe and quite pleasant on the palate. A little suave perhaps. Not bad. **(12/95)**

Now–2000   13.0

Savigny-lès-Beaune Narbantons
Maurice Écard

Some development already on the colour. Sweet, weedy nose. This is light and a bit confected. Will get attenuated. Unexciting. **(10/94)**

Drink up   12.0

Savigny-lès-Beaune Serpentières
Maurice et Jean-Michel Giboulot

Very good colour. This is a bit softer on the nose. But again rather too tannic and astringent on the palate. Good grip, especially for a 1992. Quite long and some fat at the end. Not bad. **(12/95)**

1998–2000   13.0

Savigny-lès-Beaune Serpentières
Pierre et Jean-Pierre Guillemot

Light to medium colour. A little stemmy but like the 1994 soft and fruity. This is a good effort for 1992. Not short. Not weedy. Just about ready. **(12/95)**

Now–2001   13.0

Savigny-lès-Beaune   Serpentières
Michel Mallard et Fils

Some stems. A bit thin and rustic. Light to
medium body. Still fresh. But it won't age well.
(12/95)

Drink soon   13.0

Savigny-lès-Beaune   Serpentières
Jean-Michel Maurice, Domaine du Prieuré

Lightish colour. Rather weedy on the nose. A
little thin and ungenerous, but not bad for its
vintage. There is a bit of SO$_2$ here. Uninspiring
though. **(12/95)**

Drink soon   13.0

Savigny-lès-Beaune   Vergelesses
Simon Bize et Fils

Medium colour. Soft, plump nose. Not a lot of
grip or depth but very stylish. This is a little
weak and forward. Pleasant fruit but no real
dimension. Not a lot better, except more
elegant than his Bourgeots. **(09/95)**

Now–2002   14.5

Volnay   Marquis d'Angerville

Good colour. Soft, ripe nose. Fine fragrant fruit.
Very good acidity. Slightly lean and tough. This
is rich and very elegant and persistent. Fine for
a village wine. Very long. **(11/95)**

Now–2002   15.0

Volnay   Champans   Marquis d'Angerville

Splendid colour. Lovely fragrant nose. Really
quite intense. Very fruity, very classy. A lovely
example. Medium body. Round, complex, ripe,
succulent. Still just a touch raw. Fine long finish.
Very good acidity. **(09/95)**

Now–2005   16.5

Volnay   Clos-des-Ducs
Marquis d'Angerville

Fine colour. Still quite firm and closed on the
nose. Rich and meaty especially for a 1992.
Good oaky base. Very classy. Real Volnay. Good
length. Lovely succulent fruit. Fine. **(09/95)**

1998–2007   17.5

Volnay   Santenots   Louis Jadot

Very good colour. This has depth and
concentration. Classy, exciting. **(03/94)**

1999–2005   17.5

Volnay   Santenots   Matrot

Quite a light evolved colour. Soft, fragrant nose.
A touch of spice to go with the red fruits. This
is echoed on the palate. Round, very Volnay.
Good acidity. Plump, long, classy. Very
seductive. Ready now. Very good for the
vintage. **(11/95)**

Now–2004   16.0

Vosne-Romanée   Robert Arnoux

Medium colour. Lightish nose. A touch of
chocolate and coffee. On the palate this is
stylish, plump and has good persistence at the
end. Long finish. Very good for a village wine,
especially this year. **(10/95)**

Now–2005   15.5

Vosne-Romanée   Petits-Monts
Pascal Chevigny

Very good colour. Full, rich and very lovely
succulent velvety fruit. 100 per cent new wood,
but it doesn't show. Excellent for the vintage.
Real depth and concentration. The *saignée* really
helped here. Fat, rich, long finish. **(12/95)**

Now–2004   17.5

Vosne-Romanée Aux Reignots   Château de
Vosne-Romanée, Bouchard Père et Fils

Lightish colour with a touch of brown already.
Ripe but a shade lean on the nose. Stylish, but
slightly austere. Not a great deal of weight.
Lightish in body. Pleasant but a bit too
lightweight. Slightly lean and hard on the finish.
Quite good at best even for 1992. **(10/95)**

Now–2000   14.0

Vougeot   Cras   L'Héritier-Guyot

Light to medium colour. Some brown. Round
generous nose though without much class. A
little suave. **(12/95)**

Now–2000   13.5

1991

R A T I N G   F O R   T H E   V I N T A G E

Red: 16.0   **White:** 13.5

S I Z E   O F   T H E   C R O P

(Hectolitres, excluding generic wine)

	Red	White
Grands Crus	10,855	3,476
Village and *Premiers Crus*	166,380	45,104
Total	177,235	48,580

Compared with the five-year average 1991 was a normal-sized harvest, though down by some 12.5 per cent on 1990, both in red and in white. The yield was not, however, even. Localised hail damage in Gevrey in June and two months later in Chambolle reduced the crop to the extent that many *premiers crus* in these communes were vinified together, there not being enough fruit to ferment each *climat* separately. At the Domaine Dujac, for example, no Bonnes-Mares was declared. Gabriel Tortochot produced no Charmes-Chambertin. Elsewhere, by hazard or design, yields were reduced: 26 hl/ha overall at Jadot, 20 at the Clos-des-Epeneaux in Pommard, 30 *chez* the Marquis d'Angerville in Volnay. And these yields are reflected in the character of the ensuing wines. Even more so than usual the amount of wine produced in 1991 is a critical contributor to its quality. 'It was impossible, given the weather conditions, to make a wine of depth with excessive *rendements*,' said Jacques Lardière of Maison Louis Jadot.

W E A T H E R   C O N D I T I O N S

It was a year of the three 22s. It froze on 22 April; it hailed on 22 June; and it hailed again on 22 August. Thankfully, however, none of these three depredations affected the standard of the wine; merely, and qualitatively, the quantity of it.

The frost, as it normally does, injured the vines in the plain more than those on the slopes; the generics and the village vines rather than the *premiers* and *grands crus*. Gevrey, Morey and Nuits-Saint-Georges suffered more damage than did Chambolle and Vosne-Romanée, and Chorey-lès-Beaune, Pommard and Meursault were the most affected areas in the southern sector of the Côte d'Or.

Then followed a cold May, delaying and prolonging the flowering into the second half of June. The hail-storm that occurred then was centred in Gevrey-Chambertin, in a swathe that ran the length of the *grands crus* from Charmes to Mazis. But overall the flowering was irregular; and as a result *coulure* and *millerandage* were widespread throughout the Côte. The crop would be reduced: a good thing. But maturity would be uneven and the harvest would be late. The prospects were not auspicious.

But the weather then changed. On 1 July the summer arrived. For the next ten or more weeks, right up to the brink of the harvest, apart from the odd downpour, it was dry and hot. The fruit began to catch up. There was even a fear of prolonged drought blocking the evolution of the ripening process. The Burgundians had shivered in May. In August they had to worry about sunstroke!

The annual Burgundian nightmare is hail after the *véraison*. Inevitably there are storms in August. Few years go by without a (thankfully) isolated blitz somewhere in the Côte d'Or. The grapes are then bruised, and it is rare that the resulting wine does not show a *goût de grêle*, a sort of hard dirtiness, somewhat like a metallic corky taste.

Chambolle-Musigny was the village chosen to bear the brunt in 1991. (Parts of Savigny and Ladoix, as well as the southern Côte-de-Nuits-Villages, were also affected.) All the way from Le Musigny - but not neighbouring Grands-Echézeaux and Clos-de-Vougeot, which shows how localised hail damage can be - right up to Clos-de-la-Roche the vineyards were battered, the line following that of the *grands* and *premiers crus*.

Remembering 1983, the most punctilious growers such as Jacques Seysses and Christophe Roumier got out their tweezers and carefully removed every single bruised berry which remained on their estate - employing seventeen people for three weeks to do this in the case of Domaine Dujac. Others resolved merely to *trier* carefully at the time of the harvest and adjust the maceration times accordingly.

As it happened, the weather following the hail-storm was excellent: dry, bright and hot. The most badly affected berries shrivelled up and dropped off. The rest seem to have recovered. There is no hail taint in any 1991s. There were, however, fears that progress towards maturity would be *bloqué*. Certainly the 1991 Chambolles exhibit unusually high and masculine levels of tannin. But the concentration of fruit is equal to it. Indeed this is the most successful sector of Burgundy in this vintage: some excellent wines.

The *Ban des Vendanges* was declared on Wednesday 24 September. Somewhat unusually, but explained by generally lower yields and therefore greater concentration, the Côte-de-Nuits started at the same time as the Côte-de-Beaune, rather than a week later. Some rain fell in the Côte-de-Nuits on Friday and Saturday, rather more throughout the region on the Sunday, but it was then fine for at least a week, after which there was a general deterioration in the weather as the late summer tumbled into autumn.

Most growers in the Côte d'Or managed to bring their crop in without the fruit being seriously affected by the rain - indeed Jean Mongeard of Vosne-Romanée says that the first spell unblocked the fruit and increased the eventual sugar levels - but those vines which had not been cleared by 5 October were at risk. These can be generalised as follows:

★ Traditional late pickers.
★ Generic wines from vineyards in the plain.
★ Cooler villages up in the valleys away from the mainstream Côte.
★ The Hautes-Côtes.

Moreover the rain on the first Sunday affected the white grapes, especially where yields were on the high side, more than the reds. The resultant humidity - fortunately the weather was cool during the week of 28 September to 5 October - caused the grapes to turn quickly into a state of over-ripeness, diminishing the acidities without adding to the concentration. This fruit needed to be collected fast.

THE STYLE OF THE WINE

WHITE WINES

This is a very good year for red wines, only a not-bad-plus year for whites. The white wines lack concentration, they lack dimension and they have an absence of real ripeness. In short they are a bit lean, a bit uninteresting: the least good vintage in the 1988-1993 period.

The explanation for this lies in the size of the harvest and the weather conditions. The crop in Meursault was 45.6 hl/ha, that in Puligny 47.3, that in Chassagne even higher: too high, in retrospect, for fruit to concentrate as well as ripen in the weather conditions Mother Nature decreed for 1991. Of the three villages, Meursault is the best. Unlike 1989 and 1990, 1991 is not a year for the lesser villages such as Auxey-Duresses or Saint-Romain. Nor can you point to Corton-Charlemagne, as you can sometimes in lesser years, as being significantly superior to the rest of the *grands crus*.

RED WINES

Imagination was in the Burgundian air in 1991. It was not an easy vintage. As François Faiveley put it: 'It gave us a lot of food for thought. At the outset we were anxious. Every *cuvée* had to be treated differently and flexibly.' Some, such as the Gouges cousins, performed a *saignée*, despite the small crop. Others, such as Jadot (except for the Chambolles), prolonged their *cuvaisons* to maximise the extraction of body and extract. The fruit, thankfully, was healthy. And all the top growers were now performing a serious *triage*, either in the vineyard or back in the winery.

The malos, in general, were rather late to finish, but once the wines had settled down after the post-malo racking and could be properly tasted for the first time they could be seen to be better than had been expected at the outset. They had a good colour; the fruit was plump and elegant; the balance correct; and, where the harvest was low, no lack of backbone or guts. The wines continued to improve throughout the summer, appearing to put on weight, yet nevertheless in November 1992, when I made my second visit of the year, principally to taste the red wines, the word *tendre* (soft) was one I heard frequently from growers. As a result, many wines were bottled earlier than usual, 'to preserve the fruit'.

Five years on, the wines do not seem to be too soft at all, and a criticism I have heard from elsewhere in the intervening period, that the tannins were a bit dry and unripe, is also no longer, it would seem, a problem.

True, the tannins are not as ripe or as sophisticated as they are in the 1993s, but the 1991s have the same medium-full-bodied volume, plenty of backbone, good acidities - without being really long on the palate - and plenty of personality. The fruit is not as lush as in the 1990s, nor as elegant as in the 1993s. Nor are the wines as concentrated as in this earlier year, under whose shadow they were born (to their disadvantage, for the wines were at the outset unfairly denigrated and ignored).

But nevertheless there is plenty to applaud in the 1991s. They are, to quote Philippe Engel at the outset, 'very Pinot, very characteristic of their *cépage* and *terroir*' - though I would make an exception to this statement of the Chambolles, which are bigger and denser than usual. Elsewhere, as with some of the Jadot wines, a longer *cuvaison* has produced somewhat sturdy wines, currently rather adolescent, a few which will always be a bit hard, I fear. In the main, though, 1991 is a success: a very good red-wine vintage which will last well. And it was, and continues to be, very good value for money.

WHERE ARE THE BEST WINES?

A summary can be made of the generalisations:

★ The vintage is, even more so than usual in Burgundy, better at the top of the hierarchy than at the village and generic level.
★ The reds of the Côte-de-Nuits are better than those of the Côte-de-Beaune.
★ The reds are better than the whites.
★ But the whites are better than the reds in the southern Côte-de-Beaune.
★ The mainstream villages are better than the villages up in the valleys and the Hautes-Côtes.
★ In the Côte-de-Nuits the best wines will be found in Chambolle-Musigny. There are some fine Gevreys, Vosnes and Nuits (Morey-Saint-Denis and the Clos-de-Vougeot are the most variable), but you must choose your village wines with caution.
★ The same can be said for Savigny-lès-Beaune, Beaune, Pommard and Volnay.

★ Among the white wines the Meursaults are better than the Chassagnes which are better than the Pulignys, contrary to the usual order. This is not a vintage where the Saint-Aubins and lesser whites shine out as good value for money.

But, as usual, the overriding precept, always even more relevant in a difficult vintage, is: go for the top growers. The following pages will outline who they are.

STATE OF MATURITY TODAY

White: The vast majority of the white wines are now as good as they will ever be, and need drinking soon – in the case of the village examples and minor communes – or fairly soon, i.e. between now and their tenth birthday. Only a few exceptional *grands crus* will last much longer than that.

Red: At the bottom levels, the Choreys and Santenays, the lesser village wines of Volnay and Beaune, the reds are now ready. Much of the rest will come on stream progressively from 1998-1999 onwards. All the good wines will last well into the first decade of the next millennium and the very best well into the decade after that. There is no hurry with the reds of 1991. Drink the 1992s and 1989s first.

TASTING NOTES

BLANC

Auxey-Duresses   Prunier-Damy
This is very good for a 1991. Finely ripe. Good touch of wood. Elegant. Long. A very nice bottle. **(12/95)**
Now-2000   15.0

Beaune   Clos-de-la-Maladière
Henri Cauvard et Fils
Monopole. Some colour. Nutty herbal flavour on the nose. Rather coarse, heavy and sulphury, on the palate. Lacks fruit and a bit tired now. **(12/95)**
Drink soon   12.5

Beaune   Cuvée de la Vierge Blanche
Violland
Quite a full colour. Ripe and with good succulence if not a great deal of finesse. Quite fat. This is fresh. Good, but not special. **(11/94)**
Drink soon   13.0

Bienvenues-Bâtard-Montrachet
Roland Remoissenet Père et Fils
Plenty of depth here. Lovely gentle oak. Good concentration. Long, stylish. Fine. **(03/94)**
1998-2014   17.5

Chassagne-Montrachet   Les Chaumées
Michel Colin-Deléger
Round and surprisingly ripe and full of interest for a 1991. Gently oaky. Long, very seductive. Fine for the vintage. **(10/94)**
Now-2006   17.5

Chassagne-Montrachet   Morgeots
Ramonet
Very classy fruit. Full, rich, ripe; not a bit off-vintage. Very classy fruit. This is excellent for a 1991. Bags of vigour. Fine. **(11/94)**
Now-2006   17.5

Chassagne-Montrachet   Les Vergers
Guy Amiot
Good colour. A little lean on the nose but crisp, stylish, not without fruit, depth and definition on the palate. Good finish. **(10/94)**
Now-2004   16.0

Corton   Vergennes, Cuvée Chanson
Hospices de Beaune, Chanson
Soft, gently oaky on the nose. Quite rich. Quite marked by the wood on the palate. This is just about at the limit. But the fruit is there. Better on aeration. Good. **(11/95)**
Now-2005   15.0

Corton-Charlemagne   Pierre Bitouzet
Slightly hard at present. But plenty of depth underneath. Yet the fruit lacks a bit of real ripeness and generosity. Good grip. Perhaps more sex appeal as it rounds off. **(03/94)**
Now-2009   15.5

Meursault   Darnat
This has gone into a bit of an adolescent phase. On the nose it seems a bit tired. But the finish is better. Honeyed concentration. Good certainly. **(06/94)**
Now-2000   15.0

Meursault   Matrot

The nose is a little closed, and with a touch of SO$_2$. Good racy, ripe style underneath. Lacks a touch of fruit and fat. But balanced and quite round and agreeable nevertheless. Slightly neutral but will last well. Quite good plus. **(11/95)**

Now–2000   14.5

Meursault   Virely-Rougeot

This is a little hard and vegetal, and it is slightly hot at the end. But for the vintage it is not too bad. But the nose and attack are better than the finish. **(12/95)**

Now–2001   13.5

Meursault   Blagny   Matrot

The nose has a bit of built-in SO$_2$ still. And as a result the wine is a bit closed and adolescent. On the palate there is good richness and intensity. Mineral and flinty. Good fruit. Really quite concentrated. A wine which needs time. Very good. **(11/95)**

Now–2004   16.0

Meursault   Charmes   Comtes Lafon

This is an example of the very small element of top quality 1991 white Burgundy. Rich, gently oaky, totally desirable. Good grip, obviously, but very succulent fruit. Flowery, honeyed on the finish. Fine for the vintage. **(06/96)**

Now–2003   17.5

Meursault   Clos-du-Cromin
Patrick Javillier

Good very light gold colour. Mature nose. Not a lot of depth, but fresh, clean, fruity and gently oaky. This is now *à point*. A stylish example with surprisingly good level of interest and character for the vintage. Ripe, balanced and complex. Long and positive at the end. Very good. **(04/96)**

Drink soon   16.0

Meursault   Genevrières   Ballot-Millot

Medium colour. Rather light on both nose and palate. Quite fresh, though there is a little built-in sulphur at first. Gently oaky. Gently honeyed. Quite stylish. But it lacks depth and concentration. Quite good. **(04/96)**

Drink soon   14.0

Meursault   Perrières
Château de Puligny-Montrachet

Not as much to it as their Poruzots. Is this young vines? Quite good. **(03/94)**

Now–2001   14.0

Meursault   Perrières   Matrot

Good crisp colour. Mineral nose. On the palate good richness. Nicely austere. Good acidity.

Not a bit too lean. Classy. Long. Very good indeed for a 1991. **(11/95)**

Now–2005   17.0

Meursault   Poruzots
Château de Puligny-Montrachet

A touch hard. Not a lot of fruit and seems to have too much oak. Reasonable acidity but not a lot of grip. Yet finishes better than it starts. Good. **(03/94)**

Now–2005   15.0

Meursault   Les Vireuils   Dupont-Fahn

Quite a yellow colour. Plump and fruity for a 1991, open and attractive. But rather more developed than I would have expected. Slightly scented, slightly sweet, quite full and fleshy but a little heavy. Reasonable length but not a great deal of grip. Fully ready. Lacks a bit of class. Not bad. **(01/94)**

Drink soon   13.5

Musigny   Comte Georges de Vogüé

Youthful colour. On the nose a combination of SO$_2$, a little suspect, slightly attenuated citrus-peel sweetness and a four-square white in red-wine soil flavour. Some oak, a little thin and lean on the palate. It is un-Chardonnay in character. And seriously over-priced for what it is. It is really a bit ungenerous and unstylish. Quite good at best. **(09/95)**

Now–2000   14.0

Pernand-Vergelesses   Rollin Père et Fils

A bit too much SO$_2$ here but it has kept the wine fresh and the fruit - what there is of it - elegant. Not bad at all for the vintage. But without the fat and generosity of the 1992. **(12/95)**

Drink soon   13.0

Puligny-Montrachet   Louis Carillon

Delightful fruit. Ripe, quite opulent. Not a lot of complexity but well made. Good plus. **(03/94)**

Now–2004   15.5

Puligny-Montrachet
Château de Puligny-Montrachet

Good straight Puligny, but one-dimensional in comparison with Sauzet and Carillon. Quite good. **(03/94)**

Now–2001   14.0

Puligny-Montrachet   Étienne Sauzet

Less opulent than Carillon's. More discreet. Yet very good follow-through. Elegant and long. Lovely fruit. Very good. **(03/94)**

Now–2006   16.0

Puligny-Montrachet   Les Chalumeaux
Matrot

Good fragrant nose. More supple than the Blagny. Good fruit. Medium body. Soft, ripe, charming, fragrant. Nice combination of crab-apple and honeysuckle. Very good balance and complexity underneath. Classy, crisp, fresh, attractive. *À point* now. Very good. **(11/95)**

Now-2002   16.0

Puligny-Montrachet   Les Folatières
Jean-Luc Pascal
Slightly deep colour. A bit heavy and tired on the nose. Similar on the palate. More alcohol (13.5° it says on the label) than fruit and depth. So rather overblown. Already beginning to fall to bits. Lumpy and inelegant. Unexciting. **(04/96)**

Drink soon   12.0

Saint-Aubin   Château de Puligny-Montrachet
Barrel fermented and quite obviously - ?dominantly - oaky. Ripe and rich. Quite good. **(03/94)**

Now-2004   14.0

Saint-Aubin   Les Champlots
Jean-Louis Bachelet
A little neutral, by comparison with the 1992 and 1993, but a good soft, fruity example of the vintage. Just a touch hot at the end. Good for the vintage and a Saint-Aubin. **(12/95)**

Drink soon   15.0

ROUGE

Aloxe-Corton   Michel Mallard et Fils
They didn't have any *premier cru* then, or only a little which went into the village wine. Reasonable colour. Some funkiness on the nose. A bit like a 1987 (dry tannins - evolved). Some grip. But it lacks a bit of elegance. Medium body. Not bad. **(12/95)**

Now-2000   13.0

Aloxe-Corton   Les Chaillots   Louis Latour
Medium colour. A little development. Slightly hard and stemmy on the nose. A lack of grace. Slightly sweet on the palate. Spicy. A bit astringent at the end. Lacks style. Medium to medium-full. **(01/96)**

Now-2002   13.5

Auxey-Duresses   *Premier Cru*   Henri Latour
Good colour. This isn't as stylish as the 1993, but it is a lot better than the 1990. Reasonable substance. But the tannins not very sophisticated. Ripe, balanced. But a bit one-dimensional. Good but not great. **(12/95)**

Now-2000   15.0

Auxey-Duresses   Le Val
Dominique et Vincent Roy
Medium to medium-full colour. Good nose. Stylish, plump, balanced. Medium body. Quite

forward. But fresh and succulent. Just about ready. Good ripe Pinot finish. Long. **(12/95)**

Now-2006   15.0

Beaune   Boucherottes   Jean Germain, Château de Chorey
Medium colour. Ample, soft, attractively fruity nose if without any great depth. Medium body. A touch suave on the finish. But a pleasantly balanced wine. Quite good. **(01/96)**

1998-2004   13.5

Beaune   Bressandes   Albert Morot
Medium-full colour. Rich, firm and backward on the nose. Slightly adolescent. Good fruit but it doesn't seem to have the depth of the Toussaints. Good but slightly hollow in the middle. **(01/96)**

1999-2006   13.5

Beaune   Cent-Vignes
Bernard Bescancenot
Good colour. Still youthful. Clean, elegant, Pinot nose. Very good intensity. Very good fruit and *terroir* expression here. On the palate not quite as exciting. There is a slight lack of succulence in the follow-through. But the tannins are ripe, the wine is sophisticated, and it finishes long and complex and full of finesse. Good plus. **(12/95)**

Now-2005   15.5

Beaune   Cent-Vignes   Jean Germain, Château de Chorey
Medium colour. Good concentrated fruit on the nose. Slightly sweet perhaps. Medium body. Ample and attractive, but I prefer his Cras and Vignes-Franches. Lacks a little grip and depth. Quite good. **(01/96)**

Now-2005   14.0

Beaune   Cent-Vignes   Albert Morot
Medium-full colour. Good rich concentrated nose. Plenty of depth and quality here. Firm, medium-full, backward and rich. A wine which needs time. Slightly four-square. **(01/96)**

1999-2012   14.5

Beaune   Clos-des-Fèves   Chanson
Medium colour. Better fruit on the nose than most Chansons, some SO_2, lacks a little austerity and grip. Rather sweet and bland. Yet much the best of the Chansons. Positive finish. **(01/96)**

1999-2008   14.0

Beaune   Clos-des-Marconnets   Chanson
Medium colour. Soft, plump, fruity nose. Better than most of the Chansons. Medium body. Balanced and fruity. Reasonable finish. Quite good. **(01/96)**

1999-2008   13.5

Beaune Clos-des-Mouches Chanson
Medium colour. A bit lean on the nose. A touch of sulphur. On the palate it lacks fat and I don't find it very stylish. Medium body. Dull. **(01/96)**
Now-2004   13.0

Beaune Clos-des-Mouches Joseph Drouhin
Medium colour. Full, rich, concentrated and backward on the nose. Medium-full. Rich, spicy and gamey. Good acidity. But a very distinctive, slightly boiled-sweet character. Good length and fat finish. Good plus. **(01/96)**
1998-2008   15.0

Beaune Clos-des-Perrières François Gay
Good colour. Slightly dry on the nose. The tannins less ripe than the 1993, the fruit less succulent. The whole thing with less class. But there are good things here nevertheless. Balanced ripe fresh fruit. Good length. Positive finish. Certainly good. May get a bit astringent. **(12/95)**
Now-2002   14.5

Beaune Clos-du-Roi Chanson
Medium colour. A bit light and thin on the nose. Rather thin and dull on the palate. And a little short. Boring. **(01/96)**
Now-2002   12.0

Beaune Clos-des-Ursules Louis Jadot
Medium colour. Full and rich, plenty of depth here. Some oak. Fullish, concentrated, rich, very stylish indeed. A stayer. Needs time. Fine. **(01/96)**
2000-2012   16.5

Beaune Les Cras Jean Germain, Château de Chorey
Medium colour. Ample, rich nose. Medium to medium-full body. Good acidity. Stylish, ample. Nicely long. Yet soft and velvety. But in the end no better than the Vignes-Franches. **(01/96)**
1998-2008   15.0

Beaune Grèves Joseph Drouhin
Medium colour. Lovely nose. A lot of depth: more classic than the Clos-des-Mouches. Lovely fruit here. Real finesse. Lovely balance. Silky smooth. Fine. **(01/96)**
1999-2012   16.0

Beaune Grèves Michel Lafarge
Medium-full colour. Backward, concentrated and stylish on the nose. Fullish, ample, firm, rich, quite backward. Still a little tight. But very good at the end. Much more masculine than the Drouhin Grèves. **(01/96)**
2000-2012   15.5

Beaune Grèves Thomas-Moillard
Medium-full colour. Firm nose. Quite dense at present. Fullish, rich and meaty. Good grip. Lots of depth here. But backward. Not the flair of the Morot Teurons though. **(01/96)**
2000-2012   15.5

Beaune Marconnets Albert Morot
Medium-full colour. Lovely ample fruit on the nose. Quite sturdy, quite earthy. Full, tannic, backward. But good depth. Slightly dense but good. **(01/96)**
2000-2012   14.0

**Beaune Marconnets
Roland Remoissenet Père et Fils**
This is very good. Ripe, rich, concentrated nose with a touch of oak. Lush. Fullish, slightly spicy. Very good. **(03/94)**
1998-2012   16.0

Beaune *Premier Cru* Arnoux Père et Fils
Good colour. The tannins stick out a bit coarsely on the nose. But the wine is rich, still a touch hard. Fullish, sturdy, rich. Long. Meaty. Not the greatest elegance but good plus. **(12/95)**
Now-2005   15.5

Beaune Reversées Jean-Marc Bouley
Medium colour. Some fruit but a touch dry on the nose. Medium body. Some depth and balance. But a slight lack of dimension. Just a bit dull. Quite good. **(01/96)**
1998-2005   13.5

Beaune Reversées Jean-Claude Rateau
Medium colour. Real concentration. Splendid fruit on the nose here. Lots of style too. Medium body. Real depth and individuality here, especially for this *climat*. Long. Intense. But collapsed in the glass. Very curious. A bottle a month earlier, *chez* Rateau, was good, and I saw no hint of deterioration on aeration. **(01/96)**
1998-2003   13.5

Beaune Teurons Albert Morot
Medium-full colour. Marvellous nose. Real depth and quality here. Fullish. Very fine fruit. Quite tannic, certainly backward. Rich, complex finish. A lot of depth. Fine. **(01/96)**
2000-2015   16.0

Beaune Teurons Rossignol-Trapet
Medium colour. Quite a lot of development. Blowsy nose. Weedy palate. Gently fruity. But no class. **(01/96)**
Drink soon   11.5

Beaune Toussaints Albert Morot

Medium-full colour. Firm slightly adolescent nose. Smells a bit of Marmite. Medium-full. A bit ungainly at present but all the elements are here. (01/96)

1999-2012   14.0

Beaune Vigne-de-l'Enfant-Jésus Bouchard Père et Fils

Medium-full colour. Rich plummy nose. On the palate rather more composed than the above. It is not a blockbuster but the fruit is fragrant and balanced, the tannins are ripe and there is quite good intensity. It could have done with a bit more - and a bit more richness. Medium to medium-full. Long. Good plus. (02/95)

Now-2007   15.5

Beaune Vignes-Franches Jean Germain, Château de Chorey

Medium-full colour. Good style and richness of fruit here on the nose. Medium-full. This is cleaner and rather better than his Boucherottes: concentrated, balanced, long. Very good. (01/96)

1998-2008   15.0

Beaune Vignes-Franches Louis Latour

Medium colour. Soft fruity nose. Redcurrants and strawberry/cherry elements. Stylish. On the palate a slightly bitter element. Medium to medium-full. A little hot at the end. A suggestion of astringency. Yet the finish is better. Round, mellow, long. Quite good plus. (01/96)

1998-2005   14.5

Bonnes-Mares Robert Groffier

Medium-full colour. Light, oaky-strawberry nose. Rather light. Quite elegant but merely pretty. No depth. Too forward. (01/96)

1998-2004   13.5

Bonnes-Mares Louis Jadot

Very good colour. Lovely rich oaky nose. Plenty of fruit and volume. Big, masculine. Full body, tannic. Rich and firm. Lots of depth. Lovely Pinot fruit. Very long. Very classy. Fine. Several similar notes. But at the 01/96 three-day tasting seemed rather dense. (03/95)

1998-2015   17.5

Bonnes-Mares Jacques-Frédéric Mugnier

Good colour. Closed nose. A refined example, but without the concentration of Roumier. Lovely fruit. A little astringent. Medium to medium-full. This lacks a little grip and richness but it is long and subtle. Certainly very good plus. (03/95)

2000-2010   16.5

Bonnes-Mares Georges Roumier

Very good colour. Firm nose. Solid, rich, backward but real depth. Bigger, richer, more concentrated (than Jadot's). This has real grip and depth. Full, tannic. Enormously rich and ripe fruit. Very fine. Several similar notes. But did not sing at the 01/96 tasting. (03/95)

1999-2020   18.0

Bonnes-Mares Comte Georges de Vogüé

Very good colour. Bit of SO_2 on the nose. But rich, oaky and generous as well. Fullish, closed and masculine. Well balanced. Rich and multi-dimensional. Fine. (01/96)

2000-2010   17.5

Chambertin Bertagna

Medium-full colour. Quite oaky on the nose without being a blockbuster. On the palate the oak dominates because there is a lack of intensity and grip. But what there is is stylish. (01/96)

1999-2008   15.5

Chambertin Philippe Charlopin-Parizot

Very good colour. Firm, full, opulent, quite oaky, sweet nose. On the palate a little bit forced and sweet. So it lacks grace. But the grip is there. It may soften. But a bit unbalanced. (01/96)

2002-2015   15.0

Chambertin Joseph Drouhin

Medium-full colour. Soft, quite subtle nose. Good class. On the palate only medium weight. Quite balanced. Not enough real intensity and concentration. But stylish. (01/96)

2000-2010   16.5

Chambertin Leroy

Good colour. This is a bit too spicy and rustic and evolved on the nose for a Chambertin. Exotically perfumed. Rather astringent on the palate. This is too evolved. Lacks class. (01/96)

1998-2002   14.0

Chambertin Rossignol-Trapet

Medium-full colour. Rather dry and austere on the nose. Where is the fruit? This lacks a bit of fat and freshness of fruit. Slightly sweet and spicy on the palate. Medium-full. No real class. (01/96)

2000-2010   14.0

Chambertin Armand Rousseau

Good colour. Firm, oaky, closed, classy nose. This is quite brilliant. Totally complete. Majestic and lovely. Very concentrated. A very full, rich, impeccably balanced wine. Fabulous. (01/96)

2003-2018   20.0

Chambertin Jean et Jean-Louis Trapet

Good colour. Lush, fat, rich and oaky on the nose. A full, concentrated, voluptuous wine. Not too closed-in. Rich and fat and very well balanced. Long and very very lovely. (01/96)

2003-2018   18.0

Chambertin, Clos-de-Bèze Bruno Clair

Good colour. Good fruit here. Poised and balanced. A fine opulently fruity wine. Fullish. Good tannins. Lovely and rich and very good intensity again. Fat, lush. Very fine. (01/96)

2002-2016   18.5

Chambertin, Clos-de-Bèze Joseph Faiveley

Good colour. Firm, closed, classy nose. A lot of depth here. Full, firm, backward. Excellently put together. Everything in place. This is very very lovely. Aristocratic. Beautiful fruit. Similar note 10/94. (01/96)

2003-2018   19.5

Chambertin, Clos-de-Bèze Louis Jadot

Good colour. Quite rich and over-ripe again on the nose. On the palate full, very lush and succulent. Very good grip. Good touch of oak. This is certainly fine plus. Lovely rich fruit. Very very long. But not quite the concentration of great. (01/96)

2002-2015   16.5

Chambertin, Clos-de-Bèze Armand Rousseau

Medium-full colour. Firm, backward, rich nose. Quite a lot of oak. Fullish. Very lovely fruit. Very lovely balanced and textured wine. Not a blockbuster. But ripe, rich and intense. This is very lovely. (01/96)

2002-2016   19.0

Chambertin, Clos-de-Bèze Thomas-Moillard

Good colour. Rich, succulent, slightly over-ripe nose. A bit over-extracted. Full and rich on the palate. This is balanced. Has good grip and intensity. It lacks just a little class but it is very long and very good. (01/96)

2001-2012   16.0

Chambolle-Musigny Alain Hudelot-Noëllat

Good colour. Still just a touch hard but there is good fruit here, and plenty of depth for a village Chambolle, and on the finish no lack of fruit. Long, elegant. Good. (02/95)

Now-2004   15.0

Chambolle-Musigny Amoureuses Joseph Drouhin

Medium-full colour. Slightly closed, but impeccable on the nose. This is medium-full. Closed-in. A little cool. But very lovely finish. Impressive fruit. Very impressive in general. (01/96)

2000-2010   18.0

Chambolle-Musigny Amoureuses Robert Groffier

Medium to medium-full colour. Gently oaky on the nose, but how much depth and intensity? Lacks a bit of intensity. Gentle but stylish. Only one and a half dimensions. Yet long, lovely and stylish fruit. Very good. (01/96)

1999-2008   16.0

Chambolle-Musigny Amoureuses Daniel Moine-Hudelot

Good colour. Slightly spicy nose. Angelica and ginger. Odd flavours here and slightly oxidised. Medium-full. Some astringency. Will it turn itself around? Unexciting at present. (01/96)

2000-2010   13.0

Chambolle-Musigny Amoureuses Jacques-Frédéric Mugnier

Medium-full colour. Lovely nose. Real class, real harmony. Lovely fruit. Fullish, rich and fat. Real depth here. Good oak. *Grand cru* concentration. Very fine. (01/96)

2001-2015   17.5

Chambolle-Musigny Amoureuses Comte Georges de Vogüé

Very good colour. Very concentrated. Lovely intense fruit. Slightly astringent. Slightly tough. Slightly four-square. This lacks the silkiness I am looking for. Unimpressive. (01/96)

2000-2010   14.0

Chambolle-Musigny Beaux-Bruns Ghislaine Barthod-Noëllat

Medium-full colour. Fat and ripe and ample on the nose. Fullish, good tannins. Lots of plump, stylish fruit. This is very good indeed, if not fine. Long and complex and full of finesse. Lovely finish. (01/96)

2000-2010   17.5

Chambolle-Musigny Charmes Ghislaine Barthod-Noëllat

Good colour. Slightly sweaty on the nose. Better on the palate but it lacks a little class. Slightly pedestrian. But medium-full body and balanced fruit, if a touch dense and four-square. Good. (01/96)

2000-2010   15.0

Chambolle-Musigny Charmes Christian Clerget

Good colour. Firm but succulent nose. Very good grip here. This is youthful, but it has a lot of depth. Slightly corky, but good persistent, concentrated stuff. Good intensity. Fine if in good condition. (01/96)

2000-2010   17.5

Chambolle-Musigny Charmes
Henri Felletig

This, if anything, is even worse than his *premier cru tout court*. Very light and insubstantial. **(11/94)**

Drink soon   **12.0**

Chambolle-Musigny Charmes
Daniel Rion et Fils

Very good colour. Quite a toasted oaky nose. Fullish, sweet and ripe. Good fresh ripe tannins as well. Balanced, succulent, long. Very good indeed. Several notes. **(01/96)**

2000-2010   **17.0**

Chambolle-Musigny Les Châtelots
Bernard Amiot

Good colour. This is very much better than his *premier cru* 1990. Showing the much reduced harvest. Rich, concentrated, new oaky. This has real depth. Very good grip. Fat and ripe. Long. Very good. **(11/93)**

1998-2008   **16.0**

Chambolle-Musigny Combe d'Orveau
Bruno Clavelier

This and the Perrot-Minot are from the (separate) *premier cru* part of this *climat*. Medium colour. Rather reduced on the nose, and this makes it a bit coarse on the palate. But it is fullish, balanced and ample and the finish is very good. When the reduction blows off this will be very good. **(01/96)**

2000-2010   **16.0**

Chambolle-Musigny Combe d'Orveau
Jean Grivot

Medium colour. Light nose. Medium body. This is pretty but it lacks depth. Yet it doesn't lack length or interest. And it is quite stylish. Very good for a village *Appellation Contrôlée*. **(01/96)**

1998-2006   **14.0**

Chambolle-Musigny Combe d'Orveau
Henri Perrot-Minot

Very good colour. Vegetal nose. This is a good example. Good depth and fruit. Good intensity and grip. Finishes long. A bit unfriendly at present. **(01/96)**

2000-2010   **15.0**

Chambolle-Musigny Combe d'Orveau
Daniel Taupenot-Merme

The colour is a bit light, and the wine a little weedy on the nose. On the palate it is a little fresher. But a little too supple and *tendre*. It lacks middle palate. Quite forward. Not bad at best. **(02/95)**

Now-2002   **13.0**

Chambolle-Musigny Cras
Ghislaine Barthod-Noëllat

Medium-full colour. Slightly tough on the nose. Closed-in. Adolescent. A touch reduced. Fullish, quite some tannin. The tannins are a bit hard but the wine underneath has very good fruit. But it is a little dense and clumsy at present. Will it soften up? Certainly very good. **(01/96)**

2000-2012   **16.0**

Chambolle-Musigny Les Fuées
Joseph Faiveley

Medium-full colour. Rich, full, slightly oaky nose. This is fullish, rich and ample. Very good grip. Slightly spicy but not rustic. Firmish for a Chambolle. Long. Very good indeed. Very good grip. Several similar notes. **(01/96)**

1998-2008   **16.0**

Chambolle-Musigny Les Fuées
Jacques-Frédéric Mugnier

Medium to medium-full colour. Slightly closed in on the nose. But plenty of wine here. Full. Good, slightly tough tannins at present but these will soften. Again rich and with plenty of depth. Not quite as good fruit as Barthod's Beaux-Bruns but very good indeed. Long and satisfying. Several notes. **(01/96)**

2000-2010   **17.0**

Chambolle-Musigny Gruenchers Dujac

Very good colour. Slightly smoky, ample nose. Slightly reduced. Fullish, some oakiness. This has very good balanced fruit on the palate and a long positive finish. Very good plus. **(01/96)**

2000-2010   **16.0**

Chambolle-Musigny Hauts-Doix
Robert Groffier

Medium to medium-full colour. High-toned, perfumed nose. Slightly lean on the palate. Soft, cherry-flavoured. Well balanced. Long and intense. But lacks a bit of fat. Very good though. **(01/96)**

2000-2010   **16.0**

Chambolle-Musigny Les Laviottes
Michel Modot et Fils

Good colour. Fresh nose. Good acidity. Nicely structured. The tannins evident but not too hard. Good follow-through. Stylish and long. A touch austere but now beginning to get rounder and more generous. Good plus. **(02/95)**

1998-2005   **15.5**

Chambolle-Musigny *Premier Cru*
Joseph Drouhin

Medium-full colour. Soft nose. Ample and stylish. Very Chambolle. Medium to medium-full. Composed. Slightly lean at present. But it will get more generous as it develops. Good length and class. Slightly closed-in. Good plus. **(01/96)**

2000-2010   15.5

Chambolle-Musigny *Premier Cru*
Henri Felletig

Light colour. Not much nose. Rather sweet and weedy on the palate. Short and forward. Of little consequence. **(11/94)**

Drink soon   12.0

Chambolle-Musigny Sentiers
Robert Groffier

Good colour. Plump, ample, oaky, stylish nose. This is delicious. Lovely intense fragrant fruit. Very Chambolle. Medium-full, oaky, long and harmonious. Fine. **(01/96)**

2000-2010   17.5

Chapelle-Chambertin
Jean et Jean-Louis Trapet

Medium to medium-full colour. Some evolution. Slightly blowsy on the nose. Lacks grip and style. On the palate it is a bit bland and astringent. Plump and fruity but dull and a bit diffuse. **(01/96)**

1999-2007   13.5

Charmes-Chambertin
Philippe Charlopin-Parizot

Good colour. Firm, quite caramelly-high toasted on the nose. Very tannic and astringent on the palate. Yet underneath plenty of substance and fruit. A bit over-macerated which is a pity. May soften to its advantage. **(01/96)**

2002-2015   15.0

Charmes-Chambertin Bernard Dugat-Py

Good colour. Rich, concentrated, old-viney nose. This is rather special. Full. Very concentrated, almost artificially so. The fruit has real depth and intensity. But the net effect is almost over the top. Confected? Yet I love it! **(01/96)**

2001-2015   17.5

Charmes-Chambertin Dujac

Good fullish colour. Rich, concentrated nose. This has very fine fruit. Medium to medium-full, lush, ripe, succulent fruit. By no means a blockbuster. This is round, balanced, harmonious, complex and very seductive. Long and ripe at the end with a good touch of oak. Very good plus. Didn't show so well 01/96. **(03/96)**

1998-2008   17.0

Charmes-Chambertin Joseph Faiveley

Good colour. Very oaky, but lots of lovely fruit on the nose. Very oaky on the palate. But not quite too much. The finish shows good balanced youthful fruit. Fine but only if you love new oak. **(01/96)**

2000-2012   17.5

Charmes-Chambertin Dominique Gallois

Medium-full colour. Quite rich but closed on the nose. Ripe but slightly bitter on the palate. Fullish. Some fruit but a bit clumsy. Improved in the glass. **(01/96)**

2000-2012   15.0

Charmes-Chambertin
Michel Magnien-Morey

Good colour. Smooth oaky nose. Not a lot of depth underneath. But certainly good ripe fruit. Smooth, mellow, clean. Gently oaky. A seductive wine. Fresh and (for me) surprisingly good. Good intensity and grip. Very good indeed. **(03/95)**

Now-2010   17.0

Charmes-Chambertin Bernard Maume

Medium to medium-full colour. Straight, fruity nose. But a bit unforthcoming. Lumpy and a bit astringent on the palate. Medium body. Un-exciting. Reasonable length and finish. **(01/96)**

2000-2010   14.0

Charmes-Chambertin Joseph Roty

Fullish colour. Soft nose. Quite dominated by the oak. Quite closed and backward on the palate. Yet not that full or intense. This is very good but by no means spectacular. Rich and ample, succulent and seductive. Long on the palate. **(01/96)**

2000-2012   16.5

Charmes-Chambertin Armand Rousseau

Medium-full colour. A bit lactic on the nose. Quite sturdy. Some fruit. But a bit unbalanced. Lacking grace. Reasonable grip. A bit lumpy. May improve as it evolves, I wrote at first. But all it did was get weaker. **(01/96)**

2000-2010   14.0

Charmes-Chambertin Christian Serafin

Medium-full colour. Again quite marked new oak here on the nose. Medium-full, ripe and rich. But the oak is a bit overwhelming. Not quite enough wine for the oak. Rich. Tough. Very good. I didn't find it too oaky on the previous occasion (03/95), and marked it 'fine' (17.5). **(01/96)**

1999-2009   16.0

Charmes-Chambertin
Daniel Taupenot-Merme

Medium to medium-full colour. Plump, cherry-flavoured nose. Reasonable attack but a little weak on the follow-through. *Tendre* and reasonably stylish, but it lacks depth and dimension. Fair. **(02/95)**

Now-2003   **13.5**

Charmes-Chambertin   Gabriel Tortochot
Medium colour. Rather weak and thin on the nose. Far too much so for a *grand cru*. Forward, pretty, will get attenuated. **(01/96)**

1998-2003   **13.0**

Charmes-Chambertin   *Vieilles-Vignes* Denis Bachelet
Medium colour. Some development. Reasonably fresh, plump and fruity. But not a lot of depth underneath. Rich, classy but a touch lightweight. For early drinking. **(03/95)**

Now-2002   **16.0**

Chorey-lès-Beaune   René Podechard
A little *tabac* on the nose. The tannins harder than in 1993, but ripe and rich and positive on the follow-through. A little sturdy but balanced and long. Good. **(12/95)**

1998-2003   **14.5**

Clos-de-la-Roche   Philippe Batacchi
Very good colour. Plump, rich slightly hidden nose. But a little tight perhaps. Fullish. Good balance. Ample but a little unbalanced and edgy. Adolescent. Good stuff underneath though. **(01/96)**

2000-2012   **15.0**

Clos-de-la-Roche   Dujac
Medium-full colour. Good oak, rich and intense. This has a lot of depth. Full, rich, generous, backward. This has very lovely fruit. Ample and fat and concentrated and old-viney. Real quality. Fine intensity. Several notes. **(01/96)**

2000-2012   **17.5**

Clos-de-la-Roche   Hubert Lignier
Very good colour. Good backward concentrated nose. This has depth. Full bodied, spicy, some oak, good grip and succulence. Intense and long. This is fine plus. But it lacks just a bit of class. **(01/96)**

2000-2012   **18.0**

Clos-de-la-Roche   Ponsot
Medium to medium-full colour. Slightly lean on the nose. But good oaky fruit. Good depth. On the palate a touch bitter, but the tannins not too dry. Medium-full. Ripe, succulent. Very good. May improve further. **(01/96)**

2000-2012   **16.0**

Clos-de-la-Roche   Louis Remy
Medium to medium-full colour. Attractive fruit on the nose, but not a lot of weight. Similar palate. This is balanced and stylish, but there is a lack of backbone, and it finishes a little short.

Forward. Good at best. Disappointing for a Clos-de-la-Roche. **(02/95)**

Now-2000   **15.0**

Clos-de-la-Roche   Armand Rousseau
Very good colour. Opulent, fat, oaky, rich nose. This is very good. Full, plenty of wine and plenty of depth here. Good tannins. Still very youthful but very good grip and balance and lovely fruit. Potentially fine. **(01/96)**

2000-2012   **17.5**

Clos-Saint-Denis   Dujac
Medium to medium-full colour. A touch lean, but classy on the nose. Good ripe fruit. Good intensity. Very lovely fruit. Medium-full. Very good grip. This is long and has a lot of finesse. Fine. **(01/96)**

2000-2012   **17.5**

Clos-Saint-Denis   Ponsot
Medium to medium-full colour. Rich slightly spicy nose. Fat, some oak. Medium to medium-full. A little coarse and a little bitter. But I think it will improve in the glass. Quite round and succulent. Quite good plus. **(01/96)**

2000-2012   **14.5**

Clos-de-Vougeot   Bertagna
Medium-full colour. Fullish, good tannin on nose and palate. Ripe and balanced. Good intensity. Long but not that exciting. **(01/96)**

2000-2010   **15.0**

Clos-de-Vougeot   Château de la Tour
Good colour. Cool and Accadian. Medium to medium-full. Slightly sweet. Rather bland and a lack of real grip and depth. Quite good at best. **(01/96)**

1999-2009   **14.0**

Clos-de-Vougeot   René Engel
Medium-full colour. This is a touch simple and thin. Quite advanced. Medium body. No real depth or grip. Fair. Four notes since 03/94. One similar: two rather more enthusiastic. **(01/96)**

1998-2007   **13.5**

Clos-de-Vougeot   Joseph Faiveley
Good colour. Backward but concentrated nose. Full, tannic, but the tannins a bit dry and astringent. Good rich fruit but a bit over-extracted. Yet rich and quite intense. **(01/96)**

2001-2015   **15.0**

Clos-de-Vougeot   Jean Grivot
Good colour. The nose is a bit closed and adolescent. Lovely and ripe on the palate. Fullish, very intense and very classy. Impeccably balanced. Fine plus. **(09/94)**

1999-2012   **18.0**

Clos-de-Vougeot   Anne et François Gros

Good colour. Broad-flavoured, ripe, slightly aromatic nose. Some stems? A touch sweet. Some oak. This is good but a little coarse. Lacks style. **(01/96)**

2000-2011   **15.0**

Clos-de-Vougeot   Gros Frère et Soeur

Good colour. Slightly rustic on the nose. Rather dry as well. On the palate a little raw and astringent. Unbalanced. Yet underneath reasonable guts and grip. A pity. **(01/96)**

1999-2008   **13.5**

Clos-de-Vougeot   Alfred Haegelen-Jayer

Good colour. Rich full fat nose. Slightly dense. A little SO$_2$. Full but the tannins are a bit tough. Some grip. May soften and get more stylish. I marked it better (16.5) last time out (11/93). **(01/96)**

2001-2012   **14.5**

Clos-de-Vougeot   Alain Hudelot-Noëllat

Medium-full colour. Open, accessible plump fruity nose. Ripe, medium-full body. Attractive, generous, and balanced. Very good finish. Very good plus but not great. Several notes. **(01/96)**

1999-2012   **16.5**

Clos-de-Vougeot   Louis Jadot

Medium-full colour. Closed nose. Straight. Not dense. On the palate this lacks fruit and is very anonymous. Dull. **(01/96)**

1999-2009   **13.5**

Clos-de-Vougeot   Leroy

Good colour. Perfumed, oaky, slightly artificial fruit. On the palate a lot of oak. Medium-full. Good grip. This is certainly very good. But it is by no means great. Several notes. **(01/96)**

2000-2012   **16.0**

Clos-de-Vougeot   Méo-Camuzet

Medium-full colour. A little four-square on the nose. Is there a bit of SO$_2$? More to it on the palate. But I don't get the class or depth of their Corton or the other Méo-Camuzet wines here. Medium-full. Ample, slightly spicy. Several notes. **(01/96)**

1999-2009   **15.0**

Clos-de-Vougeot   Mongeard-Mugneret

Medium-full colour. Thin, vegetal, stringy nose. Weedy. This is going to get attenuated. Medium body. Forward. Not special. **(01/96)**

1999-2005   **13.0**

Clos-de-Vougeot   Denis Mortet

Medium-full colour. Aromatic, evolved nose. Sweet and oaky. Some oxidation here. Medium body. Rather too sweet. Too much develop-

ment. Now edgy. ⟨01/96⟩

1998-2004   **12.5**

Clos-de-Vougeot   Georges Mugneret

Medium-full colour. Plump, accessible, oaky. Generous and medium-full. Ripe and rich. Good dimension but not that compelling. Good plus. **(01/96)**

1999-2009   **15.5**

Clos-de-Vougeot   Daniel Rion et Fils

Very good colour. Very intense, very oaky, but lovely pure fruit. Too much new oak on the palate. Full, intense and jammy. But dominated. Will it ever survive? **(1/96)**

2000-2010   **14.0**

Clos-de-Vougeot   Georges Roumier

Good colour. Fruity but a little four-square on the nose. Some SO$_2$. Too much so on the palate. Medium-full. Ungainly. Finishes a bit astringent. **(01/96)**

2000-2010   **13.0**

Clos-de-Vougeot   Thomas-Moillard

Good colour. Quite firm on the nose. Slightly four-square. On the palate it lacks grace. Fullish, inflexible and slightly coarse. Chewy tannins. Only fair. **(01/96)**

2001-2010   **13.0**

Corton   Louis Latour

This is the only Corton Latour have produced this year. Medium-full colour. Slightly smoky, stemmy nose. Very strange. Barley-sugar and boiled-sweets behind it. Better on the palate. Not too sweet. Quite rich and with good acidity. Fullish. Positive finish. Good plus. **(01/96)**

1999-2005   **15.5**

Corton   Michel Mallard et Fils

Quite good colour. Slightly rustic on the nose. Ripe enough, but a little rigid. Medium body only and a bit hollow in the middle. Rather common. **(12/95)**

1998-2003   **13.0**

Corton   Bressandes   Chandon-de-Briailles

Good colour. Lovely nose. More intense than the Maréchaudes, more class too. Medium-full, balanced. Open, very good fruit. Classy. Long. Subtle. Fine. **(01/96)**

2000-2013   **17.5**

Corton   Bressandes   Prince de Mérode

Good colour. New oak here. Good depth and definition. Good grip. This has plenty of personality and good concentrated fruit. Very good plus. **(03/94)**

1999-2012   **16.5**

Corton Clos-des-Cortons Joseph Faiveley

Very good colour. Rich, oaky, concentrated. Marvellously poised. Not a bit aggressive. Not a blockbuster. This is very lovely. Fullish, oaky. Really intense. Very ripe tannins but the tannins quite apparent. Marvellous. Long. Complex finish. Really fine. Several notes. **(01/96)**

2002-2018   18.5

Corton Clos-des-Maréchaudes Saier

Medium-full colour. Fat, rich and oaky but not quite the grip of the Chandon-de-Briailles. Medium body. Good fruit but a lack of real individuality and intensity. Yet the finish is more than correct and it is classy. Very good. **(01/96)**

2000-2012   16.0

Corton Clos-Rognet Méo-Camuzet

Very good colour. Rich, concentrated nose. Very oaky. But a lot of wine here. Fine stuff. Full and concentrated, but not quite enough concentration not to be a bit dominated by the oak. Lovely ripe plummy fruit nevertheless. Good grip. Full. Fresh. Long. Very good indeed. **(01/96)**

2000-2012   17.0

Corton Clos-du-Roi Chandon-de-Briailles

Good colour. Not a blockbuster but concentrated and classy on the nose. Lovely fruit here. Medium-full. A little more tannin than the Bressandes but has a lovely subtle finish. Fine plus. **(01/96)**

2002-2015   18.0

Corton Clos-du-Roi Michel Voarick

Good colour. Dense, unforthcoming nose. No flexibility here. Full, sweet, tannic plate. Will it ever soften up? Good background to it so the answer is yes. But it will always be a bit four-square. **(01/96)**

2002-2010   15.5

Corton Maréchaudes
Chandon-de-Briailles

Good colour. Fat, rich, oaky nose. Smoky too. Fullish. Good ripe tannins. Nice touch of oak. An attractive, opulent, easy-to-appreciate wine with good grip and a long satisfactory finish. Very good indeed. **(01/96)**

2000-2012   17.0

Corton Perrières Didier Meneveaux

Good colour. The tannins here are a little rude, but the wine is round, ripe, quite sweet, a touch spicy. The structure is good, though a little rustic. And the wine is quite good without being great. There is a hard, rather burnt edge. **(02/95)**

Now-2004   14.5

Corton Pougets Louis Jadot

Good colour. Firm, full, backward nose. Very good grip. Nicely austere. Fullish, some oak, very well put together. Lovely ripe tannins and very good grip. Long. Youthful still. Fine. **(01/96)**

2002-2015   17.5

Corton Renardes
Jean-Marie et Bruno Colin

Good colour. Nicely ample, rich and substantial. Good tannins. There is a little reduction in here, on the nose particularly, but the finish is velvety smooth and vigorous. Good fruit. Good. **(02/95)**

1998-2008   15.0

Corton Vergennes Chanson

Medium colour. Ripe, cherry-flavoured, but a little SO_2 and not much grip. Attenuated as it evolved. Some fruit and grip on the palate. But a lack of fat, class and concentration. Quite good at best. **(01/96)**

1998-2008   14.0

Echézeaux Christian Clerget

Medium to medium-full colour. Some development. On the nose this is quite fruity but a little lacking zip. Spicy in a mocha sense. Ripe and balanced. Good. **(01/96)**

1999-2010   15.5

Echézeaux Dujac

Full colour. Firm nose. Stems show a bit more than the other Dujac *grands crus*. Medium-full, backward, firm, a bit of tannin. Good acidity. Currently slightly adolescent. Good depth and grip underneath. Lovely finish. But lacks a little richness. Very good indeed. Several notes; but I didn't like it quite so much 01/96, when I gave it 15.0. **(03/96)**

1999-2009   17.0

Echézeaux René Engel

Good colour. Lovely black cherry fruit on the nose. Medium-full. Good vigorous ripe tannins. Good grip. This has splendid fruit and good backbone. The finish is very elegant. Long, rich and complex on the finish. Fine. **(10/94)**

1998-2015   17.5

Echézeaux Joseph Faiveley

Medium-full colour. Good firm, balanced quite oaky nose. This has a lot of flair. Big, tannic, oaky palate. Rich. Good intensity. Perhaps just a bit too much tannin. Finishes well. So I think this will come round. **(01/96)**

2002-2015   17.0

Echézeaux   Jean Grivot

Very good colour. Peony on the nose. Lovely fruit. Very good intensity. Not as oaky as some. Medium-full. Very very long, individual and complex. But didn't show so well 01/96. **(04/94)**

Now-2012   16.5

Echézeaux   Alfred Haegelen-Jayer

Medium-full colour. Plump nose. Again gentle. Ripe and oaky. Fullish on the palate. Lovely fruit here. Real grip and intensity. Long finish. Very good. Several notes. **(01/96)**

2001-2015   16.0

Echézeaux   Henri Jayer

Medium-full colour. Quite firm on the nose. Lovely rich fruit. This is big and tannic. Backward but rich and really concentrated. Sizeable but not dense. Very good grip. Lovely long finish. Just needs time. **(01/96)**

2003-2018   18.0

Echézeaux   Mongeard-Mugneret

Medium to medium-full colour. Elegant nose. Gently oaky. Not a blockbuster. Perhaps a bit lean. On the palate this lacks fat. Will it get attenuated? It doesn't sing. Medium body. **(01/96)**

1998-2006   13.0

Echézeaux   Romanée-Conti

Good colour. Some evolution on the nose. Plump, ripe, slightly aromatic. A touch of oak. Fullish, accessible. Reasonable fruit. Very good intensity. But not great. But no undue stems, as in the Dujac. **(01/96)**

2000-2010   15.5

Echézeaux   Emmanuel Rouget

Medium colour. Soft fruity nose. Good but lacks a little personality. Some oak. An attractive wine, ample and fruity. Nice grip. Quite intense. Just lacks a little bit of real excitement. Very good. **(01/96)**

2000-2012   16.0

Echézeaux   Thomas-Moillard

Good colour. Quite dense on the nose. Just a touch vegetal and four-square. Lacks grip. Full, tannic, rather stewed. Lacks grace. Rather sturdy, but may soften up. **(01/96)**

2001-2012   14.0

Echézeaux   Fabrice Vigot

Very good colour. A little tough and old-fashioned on nose and palate. But old-viney, rich, naturally sweet ripe fruit. Quite tannic. A little dense but a good finish. This is very good. **(12/95)**

1999-2009   16.0

Echézeaux   *Vieilles-Vignes*
Mongeard-Mugneret

Good colour. Chocolat-y nose. This is rich and ripe and quite substantial on the palate. Fat. Plenty of character and depth. Very good indeed. **(03/94)**

1999-2015   17.0

Fixin   Champs-Perdrix
Gilbert Moniot-Defrance

This is just about ready. Medium-full, ripe and fruity if without a lot of style. A succulent healthy wine nevertheless. Finishes long. Now rounding off. **(12/95)**

Now-2000   14.0

Fixin   Les Crais   Vincent et Denis Berthaut

Medium colour. Quite evolved now. I prefer the 1992. This is getting a little attenuated. Thinning on the palate. Never quite enough grip and concentration. The 1994 is going to get like this. **(12/95)**

Drink soon   12.5

Fixin   Les Hervelets   Bart

Very light colour. Evolved nose. This is light and rather thin. Nothing here. A disappointment. **(12/95)**

Drink soon   12.0

Gevrey-Chambertin   Alain Burguet

This is not the *Vieilles-Vignes*. Smooth, succulent, drinkable. Very good plummy fruit. Deliciously drinkable already. **(02/95)**

Now-2004   15.0

Gevrey-Chambertin   Denis Mortet

Medium to medium-full colour. Firm, abundant, classy rich nose. This is very good. Medium weight. Not quite as concentrated as I thought from the nose. But clean, balanced, stylish. Quite forward. Good. **(01/96)**

Now-2002   15.0

Gevrey-Chambertin
Roland Remoissenet Père et Fils

This is a little disappointing. On both nose and palate thin and weedy. Forward. Short. Fruity but one-dimensional. Not bad at best. **(03/94)**

Now-2004   13.0

Gevrey-Chambertin   Philippe Rossignol

Quite a light colour and quite developed already. Soft, ripe, slight *sur-maturité*, forward nose. slightly hard, lacks a little fruit, and what there is is a bit spurious. Slightly astringent at the end. A bit forced. **(01/96)**

Now-2000   13.0

Gevrey-Chambertin   Denis Thibault

Medium to medium-full colour. Fragrant nose. Ripe and succulent. Medium body. This is rounding off. Lovely elegant fruit. Never a blockbuster but balanced, soft and with a stylish positive finish. Good plus. (12/95)

Now-2005   15.0

Gevrey-Chambertin *Vieilles-Vignes*
Denis Bachelet

Good colour. Soft nose. Nutty and ripe but not the greatest concentration. Medium body. A pleasant fruity example. But it lacks intensity. Quite good plus. (03/95)

Now-2002   14.5

Gevrey-Chambertin *Vieilles-Vignes*
Alain Burguet

Medium-full colour. Quite light on the nose. Fullish, tannic, ripe and with plenty of depth. But not I think really top quality as it usually is. It misses a bit of concentration and richness. Good. Better (17.0) on the two previous occasions I saw this wine. (01/96)

1999-2005   15.0

Gevrey-Chambertin *Vieilles-Vignes*
Philippe Charlopin-Parizot

Very good colour. Smells of bacon. Meaty, fullish, some tannin on the palate. Good richness and weight, even concentration, here. But not the style of Dugat. Backward. Good. (01/96)

1999-2005   15.0

Gevrey-Chambertin *Vieilles-Vignes*
Bernard Dugat-Py

Medium-full colour. Rich, fat, brambly nose. This is ample, medium-full, juicy and generous. Approaching maturity now. One of the better examples. Very good finish. Long and full of fruit. (01/96)

Now-2003   16.0

Gevrey-Chambertin *Vieilles-Vignes*
Michel Esmonin et Fille

Quite good colour. Finely poised fruit on the nose. Not a blockbuster but ripe and succulent. Medium-full. Complex. Very well balanced. Velvety. Very good. Charming. Could it have benefited from a bit of new wood? (11/93)

Now-2009   16.0

Gevrey-Chambertin *Vieilles-Vignes*
Christian Serafin

Good colour. Full, rich oaky nose. This is ample, rich, vibrant and oaky. Not too oaky on the finish. Good ripe fruit. Good acidity. Seductive. Very good. But not as concentrated as Burguet's (see above). (03/95)

Now-2004   16.0

Gevrey-Chambertin Cazetiers
Bruno Clair

Medium-full colour. Slightly cooked on the nose. Rather blowsy and coarse. Medium body. Lacks style and depth. Pretty poor. (01/96)

1998-2004   12.0

Gevrey-Chambertin Cazetiers
Joseph Faiveley

Medium-full colour, quite oaky. Ample, quite alcoholic. Full, tough, tannic. Lacks flair. Too tough. But very good fruit. (01/96)

2000-2012   14.0

Gevrey-Chambertin Cazetiers
Philippe Leclerc

Medium-full colour. Some development. Expansive very oaky nose. Soft and quite succulent. But far too oaky. Medium-full. Quite developed. (01/96)

1999-2008   12.0

Gevrey-Chambertin Cazetiers
Henri Magnien

Light colour. Soft and oaky on the nose. This is a little too soft and therefore over-dominated by the oak. But quite elegant. Quite good. (01/96)

1998-2008   14.0

Gevrey-Chambertin Cazetiers
Philippe Naddef

Medium-full colour. Mocha nose. Rich and fat but a bit too spicy. Medium to medium-full. Good grip. This is good but not great. At least it has a positive finish. (01/96)

2000-2010   15.0

Gevrey-Chambertin Cazetiers
Armand Rousseau

Medium to medium-full colour. Soft nose, quite oaky. Medium to medium-full body. Lacks a bit of grip and acidity. Mellow and fruity but rather dull. Yet balanced and good. (01/96)

1999-2009   15.0

Gevrey-Chambertin Cazetiers
Christian Serafin

Good colour. Quite oaky on the nose. Rich and full and fat. Good freshness and concentration. This is very long and lovely. Fine. (01/96)

2001-2012   17.5

Gevrey-Chambertin Champeaux
Joseph Drouhin

Very good colour. Rich, backward, oaky nose. Fullish, ripe and ample. This is intense and classy. Finishes long and positive. Lovely. (01/96)

2001-2012   16.0

Gevrey-Chambertin   Champeaux
Philippe Leclerc

Very good colour. Some development. Rich, succulent nose. On the palate medium-full body. A little astringent. Over-extracted. Badly made. Some oxidised stewed fruit. **(01/96)**

2000-2012   12.0

Gevrey-Chambertin   Champeaux
Denis Mortet

Very good colour. Perfumed nose. Quite dry and evolved. Some oak. On the palate a touch oxidised. Can I mark this? Will the wine right itself? Good fruit. **(01/96)**

1999-2008   13.0

Gevrey-Chambertin
Champeaux, *Vieilles-Vignes*   **Philippe**
Naddef

Very good colour. Some SO$_2$ here. But a lack of real zip. Slightly four-square. This is a bit lumpy and coarse. Medium-full. Some grip but lacks class. Over-extracted. **(01/96)**

1999-2008   12.0

Gevrey-Chambertin   Champonnet
Des Varoilles

Medium colour. Light nose. Some fruit. But weedy and thin. Forward and rapidly attenuated. **(01/96)**

Drink soon   11.0

Gevrey-Chambertin   Champs-Cheny
Joseph Roty

Village *Appellation Contrôlée*. Medium-full colour. Slightly more development than some. Very good nose. Rich and concentrated. Not unduly oaky. Some oak on the palate - indeed quite a lot of vanilla and spice and tannin as a result. Rich, though. Full and concentrated. Very good. **(01/96)**

1999-2005   16.0

Gevrey-Chambertin   Cherbaudes
Lucien Boillot et Fils

Good colour. Touch reduced, but ample and fruity on the nose. Medium-full. A touch astringent. Quite evolved. Good fruit but lacks just a touch of class. Very good though. **(01/96)**

2001-2010   16.0

Gevrey-Chambertin   Clos-du-Fonteny
Bruno Clair

Very good colour. A bit of SO$_2$, some oak. Lacks a bit of class on the nose. Fullish, sturdy, lumpy wine. Rich but ungainly. Yet good grip. Built to last. Quite good. **(01/96)**

2001-2015   14.0

Gevrey-Chambertin   Clos-Prieur
Harmand-Geoffroy

Good colour. Closed-in but very classy fruit on the nose. Real depth here. This is backward and tannic. Fullish, good tannins. Almost sweet. In the end lacks class. **(01/96)**

2000-2010   14.5

Gevrey-Chambertin   Clos-Prieur
Denis Mortet

Good colour. Quite oaky on the nose. Very good fruit underneath. Medium-full. Balanced. Composed. This is very long, complex and very harmonious. Fine. **(01/96)**

2000-2010   17.5

Gevrey-Chambertin   Clos-Saint-Jacques
Bruno Clair

Very good colour. SO$_2$ here, slightly weak, sweet and attenuated. Very curious. This is a bit weak. But the fruit is not too bad. **(01/96)**

1998-2005   13.0

Gevrey-Chambertin   Clos-Saint-Jacques
Michel Esmonin et Fille

Good colour. Mellow and open and oaky on the nose. Medium-full. A wine of very good fruit and balance if not one of great power and size. Good intensity and balance. But the finish lacks the drive for fine. Several notes. **(01/96)**

2000-2012   17.0

Gevrey-Chambertin   Clos-Saint-Jacques
Jean Fourrier

The colour has not come back yet. And on the nose there is a bit of SO$_2$. Ripe fruit and quite spicy, in a nice coffee-chocolate sort of way. Reasonable grip. But it lacks style and intensity and real richness. Quite long though. So far only fair. **(11/94)**

1998-2004   13.5

Gevrey-Chambertin   Clos-Saint-Jacques
Louis Jadot

Very good colour. Closed but classy on the nose. This is slightly dense on the palate. Just a little burly. But spicy and ripe and full and rich. Very good. Several notes. **(01/96)**

2001-2015   16.0

Gevrey-Chambertin   Clos-Saint-Jacques
Armand Rousseau

Very good colour. Firm, closed, concentrated, lovely grip and fruit. This is very super. Full, firm, very good tannin. Marvellous acidity. Great concentration of fruit. Excellent quality here. Several notes. **(01/96)**

2002-2018   19.0

**Gevrey-Chambertin Clos-des-Varoilles
Varoilles**

Medium-full colour. Thin and dirty-vegetally on the nose. Thin, weak and horrid on the palate. Very poor. (01/96)

Drink soon   10.0

**Gevrey-Chambertin Combe-aux-Moines
Philippe Leclerc**

Good colour. Very oaky indeed. Indeed almost nothing but oak. Very astringent. Some grip. But impossibly unbalanced. (01/96)

2000-2010   10.0

Gevrey-Chambertin Combottes Dujac

Very good colour. Firm, fat, oaky, rich and closed on the nose. Fat, rich ample fruit on the palate. Very good grip. Lovely ripe tannins. This is very fine. (01/96)

2001-2016   18.0

**Gevrey-Chambertin Combottes
Hubert Lignier**

Medium-full colour. Rich nose. Quite oaky. Fresh and plump. Not quite as succulent on the palate. Medium to medium-full body. Just a hint hollow in the middle. Better at the end but it lacks a little grip for better than very good. (01/96)

1999-2009   16.0

**Gevrey-Chambertin Corbeaux
Lucien Boillot et Fils**

Good colour. Slightly herbal on the nose. Loose-knit and high-toned. Soft and fruity. Reasonably fresh and balanced. But unexciting. (01/96)

1999-2008   13.5

**Gevrey-Chambertin
Estournelles-Saint-Jacques Henri Magnien**

Medium to medium-full colour. Evolved rather hollow nose. Some reduction. Old farts. Astringent and old tea. No. (01/96)

1998-2002   11.0

**Gevrey-Chambertin Lavaux-Saint-Jacques
Bernard Maume**

Medium-full colour. Rich, succulent and fruity. Good grip. Nicely alive and not too dense. Medium-full, quite oaky. Rich and fat. A touch astringent and not really the class. But good intensity. Very good. (01/96)

2000-2012   16.0

**Gevrey-Chambertin Lavaux-Saint-Jacques
Vachet-Rousseau**

Good colour. Fat, oaky and succulent. But slightly drab nevertheless. Slightly four-square. Fullish, rather too chunky. Dull. (01/96)

2000-2010   13.0

**Gevrey-Chambertin Petite-Chapelle
Rossignol-Trapet**

Good colour. A bit tight and closed on the nose. Slightly raw and spicy on the palate. This is a bit coarse in its fruit. Slightly astringent as well. Good but not great. (01/96)

2000-2010   15.0

**Gevrey-Chambertin *Premier Cru*
Bruno Clair**

Good colour. Good rich oaky nose. This is classy. Fullish, lovely ample, succulent, balanced fruit. Long, highly promising. Complex. (01/96)

2001-2012   17.0

**Gevrey-Chambertin *Premier Cru*
Michel Guillard**

This is rich, old-viney. Very concentrated. Lovely fruit. Fullish. Very, very concentrated. Lovely. (12/95)

2000-2010   16.5

**Gevrey-Chambertin *Premier Cru*
Harmand-Geoffroy**

Good colour. Ample, nicely exotically fruity nose. Fullish, ample, some tannin. Burly. Lacks a little class. But good substance. Quite good. (01/96)

2000-2010   14.0

**Gevrey-Chambertin La Romanée
Des Varoilles**

Medium-full colour. Slightly tough on the nose. Medium-full, rich and meaty, but it lacks a bit of backbone. Good grip but not really very classy. Somewhat a touch lean. Intense though. Good. (01/96)

1998-2008   15.0

Grands-Echézeaux Joseph Drouhin

Good colour. Classy, oaky nose. A lot of concentration. Splendid fruit. Very good grip. Full, balanced, intense and concentrated. This is very fine. Very lovely harmony and really classy fruit. Very long. (01/96)

2002-2018   18.0

Grands-Echézeaux René Engel

Medium-full colour. Open, gently oaky nose. Plump. Firmer on the palate. Fullish. Some tannin. Very good grip. Very lovely intense fruit. Very long. Very classy. Very fine indeed. Equally brilliant on two other occasions. (01/96)

2002-2018   18.5

Grands-Echézeaux Mongeard-Mugneret

Good colour. Ample, oaky nose. Lots of succulent fruit. A little less fat. I can see some stems here. But poised and balanced. Racy and classy. Fullish. Fine. **(01/96)**

2002-2015   17.5

Grands-Echézeaux   Roland Remoissenet Père et Fils

Good colour. Fine rich concentrated oaky nose. Fullish, quite oaky on the palate. Rich and classy. Long and harmonious. Good intensity. Very good indeed. **(03/94)**

1999-2015   17.0

Grands-Echézeaux   Romanée-Conti

Good colour. Lovely fruit on the nose. Rich, ripe and lovely. This is quite solid and backward. But not too dense. Has a lovely follow-through. Firm, fat and concentrated. Fine intensity. **(01/96)**

2002-2018   18.0

Griotte-Chambertin   Joseph Drouhin

Medium-full colour. Good fruit here. Concentrated and succulent. Fullish, very, very lovely fruit. Excellent balance. Real grip. Not a blockbuster but very intense. Very pure. Very, very long. Fine plus. **(01/96)**

2000-2012   18.0

Griotte-Chambertin André et Frédéric Esmonin

Medium-full colour. Funky nose. Tannins a bit edgy. Slight SO_2. Spicy. Yet very rich. Highish acidity. Medium-full body. Strangely sweet/sour. Yet good fruit and balance. Individual. As far as I am concerned lacks a bit of class. Odd but very good. **(01/96)**

2000-2012   16.0

Griotte-Chambertin   Ponsot

Medium to medium-full colour. Less intense, less weight, but very very poised and elegant on the nose. Medium-full. Exotically fruity, almost sweet. Balanced and succulent. This isn't quite classy enough for fine but it is very long and very good indeed. **(01/96)**

2000-2012   17.0

Ladoix   Les Chaillots   Prince de Mérode

Soft, ripe nose. Not too rustic. Plump, pleasant. Good concentration for a Ladoix. Not a bit stringy. Good. **(03/94)**

Now-2007   14.5

Ladoix   Les Joyeuses Michel Maillard et Fils

Even more rustic than the 1992 and 1993. Do these get more and more rustic as they age? More substance. But the tannins a bit dry. Lacks class. Ready. **(12/95)**

Drink soon   12.0

Ladoix   La Micaude   Capitain-Gagnerot

Premier cru. Round, stylish, full of fruit, even generous. Good grip. Medium-full. Fragrant. Good. **(02/95)**

Drink soon   14.5

Latricières-Chambertin   Joseph Faiveley

Good colour. Firm, rich, quite oaky nose. A lot of depth here. This is quite tough, but it is backward. Meaty and spicy. Good grip and intensity. Full. Needs to soften. Very good but not outstanding. Marked 'fine' (17.5) 10/94. **(01/96)**

2001-2011   16.0

Latricières-Chambertin   Ponsot

Light colour. Weedy, attenuated nose. Even slightly dirty on the palate. This is thin and poor. **(01/96)**

1998-2002   12.0

Latricières-Chambertin   Louis Remy

Medium-full colour. Almost over-ripe fruit on the nose. And thereon quite evolved. This will get pruney. Medium-full body. But not a lot of backbone and structure. Ripe and still quite stylish. Certainly not rustic. But it lacks depth. **(02/95)**

Now-2000   13.5

Latricières-Chambertin   Rossignol-Trapet

Medium to medium-full colour. Plump but unexceptional nose. Medium weight, some fruit. Good acidity. But neither real depth nor real richness. Boring. **(01/96)**

1999-2008   14.0

Marsannay   Clos-du-Roy   Régis Bouvier

Good colour. This is a bit more rigid (than the 1993), a little less stylish. There is good fruit and balance here. Good substance too. But the wine is a bit four-square. It lacks suppleness. Not as elegant. **(12/95)**

1998-2003   13.5

Marsannay   Les Echézeaux   Marc Brocot

Medium colour. This again is just a touch coarse on the nose. On the palate it is round, medium body. Quite fruity but a bit one-dimensional. The 1992 has a better style. This has a hard edge to it and fades away a bit. Not bad. **(12/95)**

Now-2000   13.0

Marsannay   Les Echézeaux   Jean Fournier

Medium colour. Now evolved. A bit suave. Quite fresh and pleasant but not very elegant. Medium body. Now ready. **(12/95)**

Now-2000   13.0

Marsannay   Les Echézeaux
Huguenot Père et Fils

Good fresh colour. This is very good. Slightly hard tannins in the middle but these are softening now. Doesn't have the amplitude of the 1993 but similar in weight. Good grip. Positive finish. Long. Very good. **(12/95)**

1998-2003   14.5

Marsannay   Les Vignes-Marie   Derey Frères, Domaine de la Croix-St-Germain

Rather a better colour than the 1992. Again there is a slight hard edge. And a tanky aspect, though kept in *pièce*. This has more to it than the 1992. But it lacks style. And it will get attenuated. **(12/95)**

Drink soon   12.0

Mazis-Chambertin   Joseph Faiveley

Good colour. This is fine. Lovely slightly cool backward Pinot fruit. Fullish, firmish. Good touch of oak. Very good grip. A very classy wine. Lovely fruit. **(01/96)**

2001-2016   18.0

Mazis-Chambertin   Harmand-Geoffroy

Medium colour. Soft nose. Feminine in its fruit. Medium weight. Quite pretty but not the depth it should have. Good length and style though. Only very good. **(01/96)**

1999-2008   15.5

Mazis-Chambertin   Bernard Maume

Good colour. Still a little closed. Full and rich on the nose. Ample but a little dry on the tannins and on the finish. Slightly spicy. This is good but lacks distinction. Reasonable finish. **(01/96)**

2001-2012   15.0

Mazis-Chambertin   Philippe Naddef

Medium to medium-full colour. Quite oaky. A little over-evolved. A touch astringent. But rich and succulent on the palate. Fullish, ample, very generous. Very good plus. **(01/96)**

2000-2010   16.5

Mazis-Chambertin   Armand Rousseau

Light colour. Light nose. Soft and fruity but no depth. Medium weight, stylish but too forward. Too insipid. No backbone here. Disappointing. **(01/96)**

1998-2004   14.0

Monthélie   Monthélie-Douhairet

Good colour. Fresh and still quite youthful. Quite substantial. Good tannins. Not quite ready yet. Stylish and fruity. Really quite classy. Very good. **(12/95)**

Now-2005   15.5

Monthélie   Les Vignes-Rondes
Michel Dupont-Fahn

Rather a brown colour for a wine barely two years old. A bit thin and vegetal. Quite fresh but not much structure. Unexciting. Not a lot of class. **(01/94)**

Drink soon   13.0

Morey-Saint-Denis   Dujac

Medium-full colour. A touch of brown. Just a hint of the stems. Medium weight. A touch of oak. Medium to medium-full. Good acidity. The attack is a little lean but the follow-through richer and more succulent. Positive and classy. Still needs time. Good grip. But no hard edges. Good plus. **(03/96)**

1998-2005   15.5

Morey-Saint-Denis   Clos-de-la-Boussière
Georges Roumier

Good colour. A bit dry and pinched on the nose. Better on the palate. Medium to medium-full. The tannins a bit hard. Reasonable balance but lacks elegance. A bit brutal. Quite good at best. **(01/96)**

2000-2010   14.0

Morey-Saint-Denis   Millandes   Heresztyn

Medium colour. Oaky but a bit thin on the nose. Medium weight. Quite high acidity but lean. Lacks grace, lacks class. **(01/96)**

1999-2007   13.0

Morey-Saint-Denis   Monts-Luisants
Moillard-Grivot

Very good colour. Ample nose. Aromatic. Just a touch overblown. Fullish. Tannins a little dry. Lacks a bit of zip and class. Some fruit. Quite good. **(01/96)**

2000-2010   14.0

Morey-Saint-Denis   *Premier Cru*
Philippe Batacchi

Fine colour. Soft nose. Fruity but a bit lightweight. Fullish. Some tannin. Ample and round, quite fat. Good balance. But slightly bitter. No better than good. **(01/96)**

2000-2010   15.0

Morey-Saint-Denis   *Premier Cru*
Michel Magnien

(Mainly from Les Chaffots.) Quite good colour. A bit rustic on the nose. Thin and vegetal too. This is poor. Cheap and attenuated. Now getting astringent. No merit. **(12/95)**

Drink soon   12.0

Morey-Saint-Denis   *Premier Cru*   Saier

Downgraded *grand cru* (Clos-des-Lambrays). Medium-full colour. Slightly stringy nose.

Lightish. Attenuated. Thin. No future. (01/96)
Drink soon 11.0

Le Musigny Louis Jadot
Very good colour. Marvellous fruit on the nose.
This is simply splendid. More oaky than the
above. Rich, fat, full and succulent. Very
intense. Very lovely and persistent. This is even
better than Mugnier's. (01/96)
2001-2018 19.5

Le Musigny Jacques-Frédéric Mugnier
Very good colour. Velvety fruit on the nose.
Gently oaky. Fullish, perfumed. Intense and
ripe. This has excellent balance and real depth.
Still very very young. Very long and complex at
the end. (01/96)
2001-2018 18.5

Le Musigny Comte Georges de Vogüé
Very good colour. Soft and concentrated.
Almost over-ripe fruit. Very very lovely on the
palate. Rich and balanced. Very cool. Very
youthful. Fullish. Impeccably harmonious and
classy. Excellent. (01/96)
2001-2018 20.0

Nuits-Saint-Georges Pascal Chevigny
Made by his father, with the stems. Good
colour. Good fruit but slightly vegetal. Ripe on
the finish but a little four-square and rustic.
(12/95)
Now-2000 13.0

Nuits-Saint-Georges Henri Gouges
Good colour. Classy on the nose. On the palate
slightly hard on the attack, the structure
showing but balanced ripe and complex at the
end. Very good especially for a village. (03/94)
1998-2012 15.5

Nuits-Saint-Georges Boudots
Jean-Jacques Confuron
Very good colour. Lots of oak. Slightly concocted fruit but very concentrated. A touch of
toffee too. Just a faint hint of oxidation. Full,
rich, ample and tannic. Very concentration and
lovely. Very fine grip. But a little four-square.
(01/96)
2002-2015 16.0

Nuits-Saint-Georges Boudots
Jean Grivot
Medium colour. Better than the rest of the
Grivot Nuits by a long way. Rich fat and concentrated. Yet on the palate it lacks a bit of
succulence. Good grip but no sex appeal. (01/96)
1999-2001 15.0

Nuits-Saint-Georges Boudots Leroy
Fine colour. Backward, splendidly concentrated
nose. Real depth here. Concentrated, very oaky,
very opulent. Full, rich, very good tannins. This
is a very special example. Very elegant as well as
concentrated. Marvellous balance. Very very
long indeed. Similar note 10/95. (01/96)
2002-2015 18.5

Nuits-Saint-Georges Boudots
Mongeard-Mugneret
Very good colour. Rich, balanced, some stems
on the nose. A little thin as it developed. Good
but lacks a little fat and intensity. Fruity but not
rich. Medium-full. (01/96)
1999-2009 15.0

Nuits-Saint-Georges Boudots Jean Tardy
Very good colour. Fairly tannic and sturdy on
the nose. But good grip. Some SO$_2$ here. A bit
astringent on the attack at first. Rich and meaty
underneath. Finishes well. Very good but not
great. (01/96)
2002-2015 15.5

Nuits-Saint-Georges Bousselots
Jean Chauvenet
Very good colour. Slightly suave nose but ripe,
rich, ample and slightly oaky. Once again a little
perfumed and artificial in its fruit. But rich,
balanced and better than the Perrières. (01/96)
2000-2012 15.5

Nuits-Saint-Georges Cailles
Robert Chevillon
Very good colour. Lovely full, rich concentrated
nose. Really classy. Really splendid fruit. This is
fullish, oaky and of fine intensity. Very good
indeed. Perhaps fine. Very lovely finish. (01/96)
2000-2015 17.5

Nuits-Saint-Georges Chaignots
Robert Chevillon
Medium-full colour. Ripe, meaty, slightly
animal nose. On the palate this is concentrated,
fat and oaky, with a great deal of depth. Very
lovely. Very long. (01/96)
2000-2015 18.0

Nuits-Saint-Georges Chaignots
Gérard Mugneret
Fine colour. Rich, meaty nose. Some oak.
Quite sturdy. Full, oaky palate. Good grip.
Rich, quite powerful. Plenty of fruit. Good
depth. A few hard edges at present but this has
good vigour and will round off well. Very good
plus. (02/95)
1998-2008 16.5

Nuits-Saint-Georges   Clos-des-Argillières
Robert Dubois

Medium colour. A bit of SO₂. Fruity, meaty but lacks a bit of class. Some development and a bit tired in the glass. Medium-full. Astringent at the finish. **(01/96)**

Now–2012   13.0

Nuits-Saint-Georges   Clos-des-Argillières
Daniel Rion et Fils

Good colour. Firm, backward, oaky. Good class here on the nose. Quite concentrated. But an element of oxidation. Tannic on the palate. Rich, meaty. Backward. **(01/96)**

2000–2012   14.5

Nuits-Saint-Georges   Clos-de-l'Arlot
Arlot

Good colour. More evolved on the colour than the Clos-des-Forêts. Lighter and spicier on the nose. On the palate there is some built-in SO₂ and a lack of real dimension. A bit boring but good. Several notes. **(01/96)**

2000–2012   15.0

Nuits-Saint-Georges   Clos-des-Corvées
Louis Jadot

Very good colour. Full. Very rich plummy nose. A lot of depth here if quite upfront. Full, fat, ripe and tannic. Plenty of intensity. Lovely fruit. Very good grip. Slightly four-square. Very good quality. **(01/96)**

2001–2015   16.0

Nuits-Saint-Georges   Clos-des-Forêts
Arlot

Good colour. Rich, fat gamey nose. Ripe, slightly raw tannins. Youthful. Good intensity. Very good fruit and grip. Medium to medium-full. Adolescent at present. But good. Several notes. **(01/96)**

2000–2013   15.0

Nuits-Saint-Georges   Clos-de-la-Maréchale
Joseph Faiveley

Very good colour. Rich, flamboyant, not rustic on the nose. Full, slightly spicy. Good concentration. This is a fine example. Long. **(01/96)**

2000–2015   16.0

Nuits-Saint-Georges   Clos-des-Porrets
Henri Gouges

Good colour. Backward. Closed, muscular nose. More tannic than most. A toughie. But splendid fruit and depth underneath. Full. Very good indeed. Several notes. **(01/96)**

2002–2015   17.0

Nuits-Saint-Georges   Clos-Saint-Marc
Bouchard Père et Fils

Medium-full colour. Slightly hard on the nose. Tannic on the palate yet not very full-bodied. Fruity but unexciting. Lacks class and harmony. Yet reasonably long. **(02/95)**

Now–2006   14.0

Nuits-Saint-Georges   Clos-de-Thorey
Thomas-Moillard

Very good colour. Ripe, almost sweet but muscular nose. A full, tannic, meaty wine. A little forced and even stewed. But good richness underneath. Give it time. Good. **(01/96)**

2002–2015   15.0

Nuits-Saint-Georges   Les Damodes
Christian Gavignet-Bethanie et Filles

Fresh and perfumed on the nose. This is quite elegant. But it doesn't have much Nuits-Saint-Georges character or fat and generosity. Yet fresh and fruity and not too coarse. **(12/95)**

Now–2005   14.0

Nuits-Saint-Georges   Grandes-Vignes
Thomas-Moillard

Very good colour. Tannic, concentrated, old-fashioned nose. Full and very tannic. Rich but a little ungainly and dense on the palate. Slightly four-square. Needs time. Good grip. Quite good. **(01/96)**

2000–2012   14.0

Nuits-Saint-Georges   Hauts-Pruliers
Daniel Rion et Fils

Medium-full colour. Rich oaky nose. More so than the Argillières. But classier and more intense too. This is engaging, open, rich and intense. Lots of satisfaction to be had here. Very good. **(01/96)**

1999–2010   16.0

Nuits-Saint-Georges   Les Lavières
Jean Grivot

Medium colour. Somewhat soapy on the nose. A lack of fruit and succulence. Medium to medium-full body. A bit simple and a little sweet and concocted. Unexciting. But it is only a village *Appellation Contrôlée*. **(01/96)**

1998–2005   13.0

Nuits-Saint-Georges   Les Murgers
Alain Hudelot-Noëllat

Very good colour. Pure, vibrant, balanced, concentrated, backward. This is fine. Old-vine concentration here. Slightly spicy, but intense. Fullish. Very fine grip. This is lovely. Very very long. Fine. **(01/96)**

2000–2015   17.0

Nuits-Saint-Georges Les Murgers
Méo-Camuzet

Very good colour. Laid-back, closed, very concentrated and stylish nose. This is lovely and
complex. Round and mellow. Rich, subtle, very
very long. This is fine. (01/96)

1999-2012   17.5

Nuits-Saint-Georges Perrières
Jean Chauvenet

Very good colour. A little forced, which is a pity
after the Vaucrains, on the nose. Ripe, oaky, a
touch sweet. Lacks real class but quite good plus.
(01/96)

1998-2005   14.5

Nuits-Saint-Georges Les Porrets
Robert Dubois

Good colour. Rather ungainly and adolescent
on the nose. Some tannin on the palate. A little
edgy, but ripe and of reasonable quality. Better
than the Argillières. (01/96)

2000-2010   14.0

Nuits-Saint-Georges Les Porrets
Joseph Faiveley

Very good colour. Firm, full, backward but very
stylish on the nose. A lot of depth here. Full,
rich, and of real concentration and style. This is
very lovely. Excellent. A classic Nuits-Saint-
Georges. (01/96)

2002-2015   17.5

Nuits-Saint-Georges Pruliers
Lucien Boillot et Fils

Good colour. Ripe. Good honest Pinot. Not a
lot of depth perhaps. But good harmony. This is
medium-full, ripe, meaty and stylish. Good
finish. But quite forward. Got shittier as it
developed. (01/96)

1999-2012   13.5

Nuits-Saint-Georges Pruliers Henri Gouges

Very good colour. Very youthful, tannic, backward. Lots of depth. Firm, quite tannic. Lovely
fruit. Backward but very good intensity. Very
long. Lovely. (01/96)

2000-2015   16.5

Nuits-Saint-Georges Pruliers Jean Grivot

Medium colour. Cool, poised, concentrated
nose. Lots of depth here. Medium body.
Somewhat bland and nondescript. Plenty of
fruit but slightly one-dimensional. (01/96)

1998-2008   13.5

Nuits-Saint-Georges Richemones
André Pernin-Rossin

Very good colour. Decayed prunes on the nose.
Horrid. Short and thin and artificial and vegetal.
(01/96)

Drink soon   11.0

Nuits-Saint-Georges Roncières
Robert Chevillon

Good colour. Lovely stylish, composed nose.
Not at all aggressive. Soft, round, oaky, bal-
anced. Lovely fruit. But not as concentrated as his
Cailles, for instance. Very good plus. (01/96)

1999-2012   16.5

Nuits-Saint-Georges Roncières
Jean Grivot

Good colour. Fat, slightly soapy nose. This is
adolescent and more so than the Pruliers. But
has some fruit and balance. Again on the palate
a touch simple. Good follow-through. Good
but not great. (01/96)

1998-2008   15.0

Nuits-Saint-Georges Les Saint-Georges
Michel Chevillon

Very good colour. Rich fat nose. A little rustic.
Fat, slightly spicy fruit. Medium-full. Ripe and
with good grip. This is better than I expected
from M. Michel Chevillon. Good plus. (01/96)

2000-2010   15.5

Nuits-Saint-Georges Les Saint-Georges
Robert Chevillon

Very good colour. Marvellous nose. Really rich
and concentrated. Very elegant fruit. Very
lovely. Fullish. Very ripe tannins. Very lovely
ripe fruit. This is excellent for a Nuits. Real
depth and class. Fine oaky base. Very long.
(01/96)

2002-2015   18.5

Nuits-Saint-Georges Les Saint-Georges
Joseph Faiveley

Very good colour. Impressive nose. Really concentrated. Lovely fruit. Still youthful, still
closed. Fullish, rich and fat. Very good concentrated. Lovely oak base. This is vigorous,
exciting, multi-dimensional. Lovely long complex finish. Fine. (10/94)

1998-2015   17.5

Nuits-Saint-Georges Les Saint-Georges
Henri Gouges

Very good colour. Not as brutal as the other
Gouges wines. More definition and concentration. Fullish. Splendid fruit. Full, tannic,
splendid grip. This is very fine. Real quality
here. (01/96)

2002-2018   18.5

Nuits-Saint-Georges Les Saint-Georges
Gilles Remoriquet

Very good colour. Soupy-sweet. Artificial and
rustic. This is pretty dreadful. Medium-full. Still
something to soften. (01/96)

1998-2002   11.0

Nuits-Saint-Georges   Vaucrains
Jean Chauvenet

Very good colour. Fat, mocha nose. Touch of oak. Good. Fullish. Good ripe tannins. This is ample and sturdy, but not too brutal. Plump, sexy. Very good plus. **(01/96)**

2000-2012   16.5

Nuits-Saint-Georges   Vaucrains
Robert Chevillon

Very good colour. Fine, deep, chocolat-y nose. Touch of oak too. A full, rich, meaty wine, with lovely ripe fruit and very fine intensity and finesse. Lovely. **(01/96)**

2000-2015   17.5

Nuits-Saint-Georges   Vaucrains
Henri Gouges

Very good colour. Tough nose. Tannic but rich. More animal than the other Gouges wines. But lusher as well. Very good grip. This is fine. Long. Complex. Very promising. **(01/96)**

2002-2015   17.5

Nuits-Saint-Georges   Vignerondes
Joseph Faiveley

Good colour. Quite tannic. But splendid fruit and grip to support it. A keeper here. Fullish, backward. Very clean Pinot. Good tannins but quite a lot of them. But very fine long intense finish. Fine. **(01/96)**

2002-2015   17.0

Nuits-Saint-Georges   Vignerondes
Daniel Rion et Fils

Very good colour. Fat, plump, seductively fruity and oaky. Medium-full. Plump and round and delicious. Very good grip. This is classy, long. Most attractive. **(01/96)**

2000-2012   16.5

Pernand-Vergelesses   Rollin Père et Fils

Not a very impressive colour. The nose is vegetal and faded and a bit coarse. Better on the palate. Certainly more to it than the 1992. Fresh acidity. Some fruit. Rather pedestrian but balanced and long. Quite good. **(12/95)**

Now-2000 plus   14.0

Pernand-Vergelesses   Ile-des-Vergelesses
Chandon-de-Briailles

Medium-full colour. Very stylish fruit on the nose. Medium to medium-full body. Nicely poised and concentrated. This has good slightly lean fruit and is very well balanced. Good plus. Several notes, ranging from good plus to very good indeed (17.0). **(01/96)**

1998-2009   15.5

Pernand-Vergelesses   Ile-des-Vergelesses
Roland Rapet

Medium colour. Not much class here either. But some fruit and balance - if only a bit. Reasonable finish. Medium body. **(01/96)**

1998-2004   12.5

Pernand-Vergelesses   Ile-des-Vergelesses
Denis Roland et Fils

Good colour. Quite vigorous on the nose. Good plummy fruit. Medium-full. Fresh. Good ripe tannins. Just about ready though it is still a touch raw. Ripe. Complex. Long. Stylish. Very good. **(12/95)**

Now-2005   15.5

Pernand-Vergelesses   Ile-des-Vergelesses
Rollin Père et Fils

Medium colour. Quite fruity but a little lean. Lacks backbone and concentration. But some fruit and balance. Forward. Average at best. **(01/96)**

Now-2002   12.5

Pernand-Vergelesses   Les Vergelesses
Chanson

Medium colour. Not a lot of class or depth on the nose. Thin, weedy and short. Will get attenuated. Poor. **(01/96)**

Drink soon   11.0

Pommard   Jean-Marie Capron-Charcousset

Good colour. Nicely concentrated, nicely stylish, nicely balanced. Now round and succulent. No hard tannins. This has good fruit. Just about ready. Lacks just a little weight. Good plus for the vintage. **(12/95)**

Now-2004   15.0

Pommard   Argillières   Lejeune

Medium-full colour. Boiled sweety cherryade nose. Similar palate. Medium body. Oaky. Abundant. Some tannin. But rather artificial. Yet well made, undeniably. **(01/96)**

1998-2007   14.0

Pommard   Les Arvelets   Lahaye Père et Fils

Medium to medium-full colour. A touch of things like liquorice on the nose. Medium-full body, quite a tannic structure. Some sign of the stems. Ripe. Good grip. Not exactly a block-buster. Quite elegant. This is a feminine sort of Pommard. Good. **(12/95)**

1998-2005   15.0

Pommard   Chaponnières
Philippe Billard-Gonnet

Medium-full colour. Fruity nose. Quite firm. Reasonable fruit and structure but lacks a little class. Medium body. Quite good. **(01/96)**

1999-2000   14.0

Pommard Chaponnières Raymond Launay

Good colour. This is complex and stylish, and proof that the Launay method has merit. Rich, full, and now that it has rounded off a bit, no lack of depth and interest. Not too hard at all. This is still youthful. But it has harmony and is very good. **(12/95)**

1999-2009   16.0

Pommard   Charmots
Philippe Billard-Gonnet

Medium colour. Slightly caramelly on the nose. Oaky, fruity and quite attractive if rather forward and without a lot of grip. **(01/96)**

1998-2007   14.0

Pommard   Charmots   Jacques Frotey-Poifol

First year of harvest (he declassed the 1990). Good colour. Plenty of structure on the attack, rather more than the 1993. There is grip and tannin here. A slight lack of real succulence and intensity. Curiously aloof. But a good example. Finishes positively. **(12/95)**

1998-2004   14.0

Pommard   Clos-des-Arvelets
Daniel Rebourgeon-Mure

Medium-full colour. Good stylish nose. Balanced and with good depth. Fullish, good tannin. Very good fruit and grip. Not a lot of class but long, intense and very good. Similar note *chez* M. Rebourgeon 12/95. **(01/96)**

2000-2012   16.0

Pommard   Clos-des-Arvelets
Virely-Rougeot

Medium colour. The nose shows a bit too much evolution, just like the 1992. But it is rather better than the 1992. Yet it lacks style. Round, sweet, a little artificial. Dry finish. Not bad at best. **(12/95)**

Drink soon   13.0

Pommard   Clos-Blanc   Raymond Launay

Medium to medium-full colour. Reasonable depth and substance on the nose. Fresh plummy fruit. Medium-full body. Good ripe tannins and good grip. This has personality and breeding without being a wine of great size or tannin. Balanced. Good. **(02/95)**

Now-2004   15.0

Pommard   Clos-des-Epeneaux
Comte Armand

Medium-full colour. Fine masculine, rich full nose. Backward and tannic. Super-duper. Real size and depth. Everything in place. Just needs time. Very fine. **(01/96)**

2002-2018   18.0

Pommard   Clos-de-la-Platière
Prince de Mérode

Good colour. A little hard at the end of the palate. But ripe enough in the middle. Balanced. Lacks a little personality at present. But should be good. **(03/94)**

Now-2007   15.0

Pommard   Clos-du-Verger
Philippe Billard-Gonnet

Medium-full colour. Slightly sweet and caramelly on the nose. This is a bit lean and astringent on the palate. Average. **(01/96)**

Now-2002   12.5

Pommard   Epenots   De Courcel

Medium-full colour. Lacks a little strength and depth on the nose. But adolescent. Lacks a bit of grip. But the fruit is very good. Quite soft and forward and feminine. Medium-full. Good plus. **(01/96)**

1998-2008   15.5

Pommard   Epenots   Joseph Drouhin

Medium-full colour. Lovely fruit here on the nose. Similar weight to De Courcel. Better balance and also better class. Long. Very good intensity. Very good plus. **(01/96)**

1999-2012   16.5

Pommard   Epenots
Héritiers Armand Girardin

Medium-full colour. Lots of depth. Slight touch of mint on the nose. Full, fat, rich and tannic. This is very good. Lots of depth and strength. A typical and very good Pommard. **(01/96)**

2002-2015   16.5

Pommard   Epenots   Louis Jadot

Medium-full colour. Lovely fruit here. Lots of depth. Not as massive as Comte Armand's Clos-des-Epeneaux. But a splendid example. Touch of oak. Real grip, intensity, richness and class. Nearly as good. **(01/96)**

2000-2015   17.5

Pommard   Epenots   Hubert de Montille

Medium-full colour. Quite rich and cool on the nose. Classy, but not that concentrated. Medium-full. Lovely elegant cool fruit. This is intense, long and very good indeed. Lovely finish. **(01/96)**

2000-2012   16.5

Pommard   Epenots, Clos-de-Citaux
Jean Monnier

Medium-full colour. A bit sweet, but good fruit and depth. A ripe, meaty wine. Lacks a little class but fullish and balanced. Quite good. **(01/96)**

2000-2009   14.0

Pommard Fremiers Jean-Marc Bouley

Medium colour. Fruity but bland nose. Ditto palate. Open. Slightly astringent at the end. Harmless but dull. (01/96)

Now-2000   13.0

Pommard Jarollières Jean-Marc Boillot

Medium-full colour. Good nose. Some oak. Lots of concentration. Full, firm, tannic and rich. There is plenty of depth and intensity here. Will last well. Very good. (01/96)

2000-2015   16.0

Pommard Jarollières Pousse d'Or

Medium-full colour. Open, evolved nose. The palate is similar. I find this has very nice ripe fruit. But is too mature too early. Not the class of the Pousse d'Or Volnays. (01/96)

Now-2006   15.0

Pommard Les Noizons Jean Garaudet

Good colour. Fat and ripe on the nose. The same weight as the 1993. A little less depth and class, but the benefit of being rounder and more accessible. Fullish. Good tannins. Good grip. Long and positive. Good plus for a village wine. (12/95)

1998-2005   14.5

Pommard Pézerolles Jean-Marc Bouley

Medium-full colour. Thin, lean astringent nose. Thin, astringent, short and fruitless on the palate. Poor. (01/96)

Drink soon   11.5

Pommard Pézerolles Hubert de Montille

Medium-full colour. Rich, open, slightly evolved nose. Touch of oxidisation. Fresher on the palate. Not as bad as the Rugiens. Cool. Very good fruit. Classy. Very good. (01/96)

1999-2009   16.0

Pommard Rugiens
Philippe Billard-Gonnet

Medium-full colour. Some weight and fruit, but lacks class on the nose. Some astringency and a bit bland on the palate. Yet ripe enough. Lacks grip. A pity! Quite good. (01/96)

1998-2006   14.0

Pommard Rugiens Jean-Marc Bouley

Medium-full colour. Full and fruity, but pedestrian on the nose. Rather astringent on the palate. But the wine has some depth and class. Quite good. (01/96)

1999-2009   14.0

Pommard Rugiens Yvon Clerget

Medium colour. Fruity in a chewing-gum sense on the nose. A little lightweight perhaps. But balanced, ripe and quite classy. This is good plus. (01/96)

1999-2010   15.5

Pommard Rugiens De Courcel

Medium-full colour. Laid-back but very lovely elegant fruit on the nose. Marvellous concentration and intensity. Very fine fruit. Lovely balance. Super. But not a blockbuster. Real class. (01/96)

2000-2015   17.5

Pommard Rugiens
Héritiers Armand Girardin

Medium-full colour. Quite tannic, even dense on the nose. Rich though. Not too structured on the palate. Very good clean Pinot fruit. Good balance and class. Long. Backward. Very good. (01/96)

2001-2015   16.0

Pommard Rugiens Lejeune

Medium-full colour. Opulent, sweet and oaky nose. Too astringent on the palate. Rather artificial attack. Yet long and intense afterwards. An acquired taste. Not for me. But good. (01/96)

1999-2000   15.0

Pommard Rugiens Hubert de Montille

Medium-full colour. As with a lot of these 1991 De Montilles, the nose is very odd and the palate a bit oxidised. To be seen again. (01/96)

Pommard Vignots Leroy

Full colour. Quite brutal and tannic on the nose. Very ripe on the palate. Full, firm, masculine but fat. A lot of depth. Very concentrated. (10/95)

2002-2010   16.0

Richebourg Jean Grivot

Good colour. Rather vegetable-soupy and oxidised. Thin and weak. This lacks concentration and is very disappointing. Stalky. A bad bottle? It wasn't like this in cask. (01/96)

1999-2009   11.0

Richebourg Anne et François Gros

Good colour. Rather weak and insipid on the nose. Slightly astringent on the palate. Medium body. A bit metallic. Unexciting. (01/96)

2000-2010   13.0

Richebourg Jean Gros

Very good colour. Rich, quite oaky nose. This is generous and ample. Fat and almost over-ripe. Lacks just a little zip? But improved in the glass. Real intensity at the end. Very fine indeed. (01/96)

2002-2015   18.5

Richebourg Alain Hudelot-Noëllat

Good colour. Fat and oaky on the nose. A wine of real quality and intensity. Big and fat and really very lovely fruit and harmony. Delicious.

Marvellous finish. **(01/96)**

2003–2020   **19.5**

Richebourg   Leroy

Very good colour. Cool, quite refined nose. A
bit of H₂S on the palate but lots of concentration and fruit here. Fullish. Intense. Not a
blockbuster but real intensity. Fine, indeed very
fine. But currently a bit reduced. But 'brilliant'
(19.5) in 10/95. **(01/96)**

2002–2018   **17.5**

Richebourg   Méo-Camuzet

Full colour. Firm, full, backward, closed nose.
But real concentration and substance here. This
is very fine indeed. Full, very very rich. Real
quality of fruit here. Very lovely. Real intensity.
The finish is most impressive but I don't think it
is as good as their Cros-Parentoux. **(01/96)**

2002–2015   **18.0**

Richebourg   Mongeard-Mugneret

Good colour. Bit of SO₂ here on the nose.
Rather hidden. This is a bit artificial and sweet.
Medium weight. Common. **(01/96)**

1999–2009   **13.0**

Richebourg   Romanée-Conti

Good colour. Slightly sweet and too developed
on the nose. Better on the palate. But a little
astringent. Good fruit but a little unbalanced.
There is a lack of zip. A bad bottle? Underneath
class here though. **(01/96)**

1999–2010   **14.0**

Romanée-Conti   Romanée-Conti

Fine colour. This is a little corked on the nose.
More so on the mouth. Lovely intense fruit but
difficult to compare precisely with La Tâche.
Other tastings indicate less full but more intense,
more feminine; and equally splendid, i.e.
19.5/20.0. **(01/96)**

2003–2018   **(see note)**

Romanée-Saint-Vivant   Arlot

Good colour. Really quite oaky on the nose.
But lovely succulent fruit as well. Some stems
here. Less concentrated than Hudelot-Noëllat's
but very well balanced and very very intense.
Fine but not great. **(01/96)**

2002–2015   **17.5**

Romanée-Saint-Vivant   Alain Hudelot-Noëllat

Very good colour. Fat, concentrated, rich, oaky
nose. Backward, very lovely concentration.
Excellent fruit and grip. This is splendid. Multi-
dimensional and intense. Real elegance too.
(01/96)

2002–2018   **19.5**

Romanée-Saint-Vivant   Louis Jadot

Good colour. Slightly lactic on the nose. Better
on the palate. Medium-full, good quite sturdy
tannins. Ripe balanced fruit. The nose cleaned
up after a bit. Very good plus. **(01/96)**

2002–2015   **16.5**

Romanée-Saint-Vivant   Leroy

Good colour. Firm, rich and concentrated. Big,
structured, tannic, backward. Even a bit dense.
This is a bit tough. But it is certainly fine.
Similar note 10/95. **(01/96)**

2003–2015   **18.0**

Romanée-Saint-Vivant   Romanée-Conti

Good colour. Lovely poised concentrated nose.
Real elegance. On the palate tannins a bit dry at
first. The fruit is lovely though. Very intense.
Very long. **(01/96)**

2003–2015   **18.5**

Ruchottes-Chambertin   André et Frédéric Esmonin

Good colour. Corked but nevertheless a wine of
class and depth. Quite sizeable. Certainly very
good indeed at the very least. **(01/96)**

2001–2015   **(see note)**

Ruchottes-Chambertin   Georges Roumier

Medium-full colour. Lovely firm, classic Pinot
nose. Fullish, excellently balanced. This has very
fine tannins, and very good grip. Long, ample,
complex. Very classy. **(01/96)**

2001–2015   **18.5**

Ruchottes-Chambertin   Clos-des-Ruchottes   Armand Rousseau

Medium colour. Lovely fruit. Soft, very classy,
very intense. Medium-full body. Lovely
harmony. Really very lovely fruit. This is long
and delicious. **(01/96)**

2000–2012   **18.0**

Saint-Romain   Thierry Guyot

20 per cent of the stems here. Lightish colour.
Some evolution. Ripe, spicy nose. The wine
lacks a little weight and fat in the middle but it
is fresh and fragrant and not a bit short. Long.
Good. **(12/95)**

Now–2004   **15.0**

Santenay   Comme   Piguet-Girardin

Slightly rustic, as always, but good ripeness and
concentration. Medium to medium-full body.
Shows well. **(03/94)**

Now–2009   **15.0**

Santenay   Les Gravières   Adrien Belland

Slightly raw and tannic. Lacks just a little
richness and ripeness. Medium-full. Slightly
astringent. Riper on the finish. Quite good

plus. **(03/95)**
Now-2002 14.5

Santenay Les Gravières Des Hautes-Cornières, Jean-François Chapelle
Medium colour. Fresh nose. This is quite elegant, but it lacks grip, fat and succulence, as well as substance. Just about ready. The 1991s are unexciting in Santenay, in general, and this is typical. **(12/95)**
Drink soon 13.5

Santenay Les Gravières
Lucien Muzard et Fils
Medium colour. Ripe but quite spicy on the nose. On the attack a little astringent because of the tannins but this was swallowed up by the fruit. But it is just a touch lean at the end. Ripe and stylish and long on the palate though. Good. **(12/95)**
1998-2006 15.0

Santenay La Maladière
Lucien Muzard et Fils
Medium-full colour. Quite a substantial wine - more so than the Gravières - but not quite as elegant. Slightly heavier, more tannic, but not as intense or as individual. This is good for what it is though. **(12/95)**
1998-2005 14.5

Savigny-lès-Beaune Bataillère/Vergelesses
Albert Morot
Medium-full colour. Lovely fruit on the nose. Real richness and concentration. Old vines? Medium-full body. Good balance. Nicely austere. Well balanced. Long finish. **(01/96)**
1998-2010 15.0

Savigny-lès-Beaune Les Bourgeots
Simon Bize et Fils
Medium colour. A little evolution now. Slight touch of H_2S at first on the nose but this soon went. Very good fruit. No hard edges. Medium to medium-full, nicely smooth tannins. An excellent example. Lovely fruit. Stylish finish. **(09/95)**
Now-2005 15.0

Savigny-lès-Beaune Dominodes Chanson
Medium colour. Slightly *sauvage* nose. Lacks a bit of fruit. Medium body. Lacks style. Astringent at the end. Unexciting. **(01/96)**
Drink soon 11.0

Savigny-lès-Beaune Dominodes
Bruno Clair
Medium colour. Rich, fat, concentrated, quite substantial nose. Plenty of depth here. Fullish, rich, slightly *sauvage*. Now meaty. Will be gamey. Very good finish. **(01/96)**
1999-2012 15.0

Savigny-lès-Beaune Dominodes
Jean-Marc Pavelot
Medium colour. Round, ripe nose. Attractive fruit. But on the palate a bit short and one-dimensional. Medium to medium-full body. Average. **(01/96)**
Now-2004 12.5

Savigny-lès-Beaune Fourneaux
Simon Bize et Fils
Medium to medium-full colour. Slightly hidden on the nose. Not as much depth as his Guettes. Medium body. Slightly stringy, lacks a little fat. The finish is the best bit. Not bad plus. Noted 'very good' 04/94. **(01/96)**
1998-2005 13.5

Savigny-lès-Beaune Gravains
Jean-Marc Pavelot
Medium-colour. Very odd nose. Stringy, slightly vegetal. Medium body. Slightly mean. Certainly a bit lean. Not a lot of style. **(01/96)**
Now-2002 12.0

Savigny-lès-Beaune Guettes
Simon Bize et Fils
Medium colour. Good rich nose. Stylish, nicely slightly lean. Good grip. Medium to medium-full. Just a little austere on the attack. But plenty behind it. Long. Good. **(01/96)**
1998-2008 14.0

Savigny-lès-Beaune Guettes
Jean-Marc Pavelot
Medium colour. Soft, *tendre* nose. Slightly suave. Ample and drinkable if without any great depth or finesse. Medium body. Nearly there. Quite good. **(01/96)**
Now-2004 13.0

Savigny-lès-Beaune Les Hauts-Jarrons
Jean Guiton
This is not very good. Too weak, too short. Now attenuated. Got caught by the rain. **(12/95)**
Drink up 11.5

Savigny-lès-Beaune Lavières
Chandon-de-Briailles
Medium colour. Succulent nose. Some oak. Still quite closed. Medium to medium-full body. Good clean stylish Pinot fruit. Good balance. Could have done with a bit more richness but good. Will get more generous. **(01/96)**
1998-2008 14.0

Savigny-lès-Beaune Marconnets
Simon Bize et Fils
Medium-full colour. Nicely firm and austere on the nose. Underneath there is ample fruit. Good depth here. But a slight lack of class. But good stuff. **(01/96)**
1998-2008 14.0

Savigny-lès-Beaune   Les Narbantons
Dubois d'Orgeval

Good colour. Again a little hard at first. And not
much in the way of finesse. But ripe and meaty,
like the 1993. And more generous than that is at
present. Positive finish. Quite good. **(12/95)**

Now–2002   14.0

Savigny-lès-Beaune   Les Serpentières
Maurice et Jean-Michel Giboulot

Good colour. Just beginning to evolve. This is
softer and more harmonious than the 1993. A
little rigid but there is good fruit here. Finishes
well. Quite good. **(12/95)**

Now–2000   14.0

Savigny-lès-Beaune   Les Serpentières
Jean-Michel Maurice, Domaine du Prieuré

This is cheap and thin. **(12/95)**

Drink up   11.0

Savigny-lès-Beaune   Vergelesses
Simon Bize et Fils

Medium-full colour. Animal, gamey nose. But
good depth here. Medium-full. Rich, concentrated, lots of depth here. Long. Very good
indeed. Similar note 09/95. **(01/96)**

1999–2012   16.0

La Tâche   Romanée-Conti

Fine colour but just a little less than Romanée-
Conti. Marvellous intensity. Very very lovely
fruit. This is absolutely lovely. Very very special
on the finish. Several notes. **(01/96)**

2003–2018   20.0

Volnay   Marquis d'Angerville

Fine colour for the vintage. Lovely fruit on the
nose. Depth and class and good dimension here.
Medium body. Still a little unresolved tannin.
This is rich on the follow-through, unexpectedly so. Lovely fruit. Long and even quite fat at
the end. Complex finish. Fine for a village wine.
(09/95)

1998–2008   15.5

Volnay   Les Angles   Lucien Boillot et Fils

Medium-full colour. Nice Volnay fruit on the
nose. But a bit astringent and a bit short. Lacks
depth and concentration. But quite clean. **(01/96)**

1998–2004   13.5

Volnay   Les Aussy   Vincent Bitouzet-Prieur

Medium colour. Slightly hidden on the nose.
Some fruit. On the palate rather empty. A bit
thin. Yet not souped up. Slightly too lean. **(01/94)**

1998–2000   13.5

Volnay   Caillerets   Vincent Bitouzet-Prieur

Medium colour. Good ripe nose. Quite ample
and stylish. Medium-full body. Lacks a little

intensity but quite concentrated and certainly
fruity and harmonious. Good. **(01/96)**

1999–2009   15.0

Volnay   Caillerets   Bouchard Père et Fils

Good colour. Plump fruit on the attack. But a
lack of grip and real style on the follow-through.
Ripe, reasonable length. Quite forward. **(02/95)**

Now–2002   14.0

Volnay   Caillerets   Jean-Marc Bouley

Medium-full colour. Firm rather burnt oak aspect
on the nose but some succulent fruit at least. On
the palate a little one-dimensional. Medium body.
Lacks depth and concentration. Dull. **(01/96)**

1998–2006   13.0

Volnay   Caillerets   Yvon Clerget

Medium-full colour. On nose ripe but a little
funky. Slightly oxidised? Better on the palate. Good
concentration. Ripe and rich. This has very good
depth. And clean and long. Very good. **(01/96)**

2000–2012   15.5

Volnay   Caillerets, Clos des Soixante-Ouvrées
Pousse d'Or

Medium-full colour. Quite evolved on the nose.
Surprisingly so. Medium to medium-full.
Lovely succulent fruit. Rich, fat and concentrated. This is drinkable and lovely, yet curiously
evolved. **(01/96)**

Now–2008   16.0

Volnay   Carelle   Jean-Marc Bouley

Medium colour. Slightly over-evolved nose.
Blowsy. Medium body. Rather bland. Some
astringency. A little oxidised even. **(01/96)**

Drink soon   12.0

Volnay   Carelle-sous-la-Chapelle
Jean-Marc Boillot

Medium-full colour. Firm, backward nose.
Fullish, cool and ripe. De Montille-ish. Very
concentrated. Very long. This is fine. **(01/96)**

2000–2012   16.0

Volnay   Carelle-sous-la-Chapelle
Yvon Clerget

Medium-full colour. Ungainly nose. A bit lumpy.
Medium-full body. Rather rustic but sweet
fruit. Some structure. But inelegant. **(01/96)**

1999–2007   12.5

Volnay   Champans   Marquis d'Angerville

Very good colour. Enormous concentration and
intensity. Very fine, very classy, poised intense
cassis fruit. Quite brilliant. Full, tannic, masculine. Very very ripe and intense. This is of 1990
depth and excitement. Marvellous. Very very
lovely fruit. Real Volnay. Great class. **(03/95)**

Now–2015   18.5

Volnay Champans Comtes Lafon
Medium-full colour. Firm, backward, good grip on the nose. Full, exotic, rich and meaty. Good stuff. But needs time. Several notes. **(01/96)**
2000-2015   16.5

Volnay Champans Hubert de Montille
Medium-full colour. Slightly oxidised on the nose. But good fruit underneath. Now oxidised on the palate as well, which it wasn't at the outset. Good structure and grip though – perhaps 16.5 when on form. **(01/96)**
2000-2010   **(see note)**

Volnay Champans Jacques Prieur
Good colour. Fullish, rich, oaky nose. Ripe but a little simple on the palate. It lacks concentration. Good quite cool fruit but not a lot of grip, nor any real intensity. Slightly suspiciously sweet and alcoholic. Quite good. **(03/95)**
Now-2001   14.0

Volnay Chevret Joseph Drouhin
Medium-full colour. A bit adolescent. But good fruit. But I find this a little less succulent than the Clos-des-Angles. Fruity but a little dull. **(01/96)**
1999-2009   14.5

Volnay Clos-des-Angles Joseph Drouhin
Medium-full colour. Soft nose. Ample and fruity. Very classic. Medium body. Some oak. Ripe and elegant. Very Drouhin. Very Volnay. Not great but very good. Long and intense. **(01/96)**
1999-2009   16.0

Volnay Clos-de-la-Bousse d'Or
Pousse d'Or
Medium-full colour. Less evolved than the Soixante-Ouvrées. Ripe, succulent, elegant, classic. Again on the palate this is soft and drinkable already. Balanced and complex. Very Volnay. Very elegant. Very long. Fine. **(01/96)**
Now-2010   16.5

Volnay Clos-du-Château-des-Ducs
Michel Lafarge
Medium-full colour. Lots of depth here. This has very lovely fruit. This has real depth and class. Lovely ample fruit on the palate. Rich. Lots of dimension. Fine. **(01/96)**
2000-2015   17.0

Volnay Clos-des-Chênes
Vincent Bitouzet-Prieur
Medium-full colour. Good depth on the nose. Rather better than his other Volnays. Yet a bit astringent and lean on the palate. Unexciting. **(01/96)**
1999-2006   13.0

Volnay Clos-des-Chênes Jean-Marc Bouley
Medium-full colour. Good clean fruity nose. Not quite as good on the palate. But quite rich and sturdy and with good grip. Good. **(01/96)**
2000-2010   15.0

Volnay Clos-des-Chênes Michel Lafarge
Medium-full colour. Backward. Real depth here. Excellent fruit. Marvellous concentration. Very youthful. Fullish. Very, very rich. Splendid finish. Several notes. **(01/96)**
2000-2015   17.0

Volnay Clos-des-Chênes René Monnier
Medium-full colour. Ungainly nose. Some SO_2. Slightly astringent and thin on the palate. A bit dilute. Average at best. **(01/96)**
Drink soon   12.5

Volnay Clos-des-Ducs
Marquis d'Angerville
Excellent colour. The nose has gone into its shell. Lovely ripe concentrated fruit. Quite full and firm, some tannin still. Marvellous grip. Good oaky base. Excellent fruit. A lovely example. **(09/95)**
2000-2015   18.0

Volnay Clos-du-Verseuil Yvon Clerget
Medium-full colour. Round, ripe nose. Medium-full, ripe, slightly straightforward. Nice ample fruit though. Good balance. **(01/96)**
1999-2009   14.5

Volnay Mitans Hubert de Montille
Medium-full colour. Firm, very classic, very elegant nose. This has a lovely nose. Fullish, rich, very concentrated. Quietly successful. Very complex. Will last. Very good. **(01/96)**
2000-2015   16.0

Volnay Pitures Vincent Bitouzet-Prieur
Medium colour. Some fruit but a little hollow and over-evolved. Lacks grip. On the palate cool and a little thin and unripe. Reasonable length. Not bad. **(01/96)**
1998-2006   13.5

Volnay Pitures Jean-Marc Boillot
Medium-full colour. Full rich firm nose. Good depth here. Full, tannic, rich, lots of depth. This is a keeper but a wine with a lot of quality. **(01/96)**
2000-2015   16.0

Volnay *Premier Cru*
Régis Rossignol-Changarnier
Medium colour. Rich full and fat on the nose. Good depth if a little artificial. Fullish, meaty, rather ungainly. Some grip. A bit too sturdy. **(01/96)**
2000-2009   13.5

Volnay   Les Roncerets   Paul Garaudet
Medium-full colour. Good rich nose. A little suave? A little inelegant? Slightly astringent. A bit rough and ready. Slightly short too. Dull. (01/96)
Now-2000   12.5

Volnay   Santenots   Leroy
Medium-full colour. Lovely firm very concentrated nose. Real depth and quality here. This is very fine for a Côte-de-Beaune. Full, very very intense. Very lovely indeed. Marvellously long, clean and pure. (01/96)
2000-2015   18.0

Volnay   Santenots   Matrot
Medium-full colour. Fragrant, stylish nose. Ripe and with good definition. Medium to medium-full body. Quite rich. Good grip. Good. (03/94)
Now-2007   15.0

Volnay   Santenots du Milieu   Comtes Lafon
Medium-full colour. Ripe, seductive, rich and full of bountiful fruit on the nose. Full, rich, oaky, tannic. This is very fine. Pure and lovely. Several notes. (01/96)
2000-2015   17.5

Volnay   Taille-Pieds   Hubert de Montille
Medium-full colour. Rich concentrated nose. Lovely style here. Real Volnay fruit. Fullish, very finely balanced. Marvellous fruit. Real length and finesse. Super. (01/96)
1999-2015   17.0

Vosne-Romanée   René Engel
Good colour. Quite a sturdy nose (this is the second shipment). But ripe and rich for a village wine. Medium-full. Just a touch rustic, but good substance, balance and definition. Long. But the earlier shipment is classier. Good plus. Six months later I wrote: 1) Old label: rich, round, fat and velvety. 2) New label: leaner and more astringent, less smooth. (10/94)
Now-2007   15.0/16.0

Vosne-Romanée   Jean Grivot
Medium to medium-full colour. Plump, fruity, attractive nose. A little rustic on the palate. Medium to medium-full. Slightly too spicy. But reasonable balance. Quite good. (01/96)
1999-2008   14.0

Vosne-Romanée   Jean Mongeard-Mugneret
Good colour. Lovely ripe Pinot noir. Medium-full. Slightly hard in the middle but this is no bad thing. Good grip. A good village example. (03/94)
Now-2009   15.0

Vosne-Romanée   Roland Remoissenet Père et Fils
Much better than the Gevrey. Good acidity. Medium to medium-full. Good start. But the finish is a bit one-dimensional. Quite good. (03/94)
Now-2008   14.0

Vosne-Romanée   Beaux-Monts Bruno Clavelier
Medium colour. Light nose. Quite fruity, but not much depth. Medium body. A bit astringent. An absence here of fat, grip and richness. But a little better than Moillard's Beaux-Monts. (01/96)
1998-2005   13.5

Vosne-Romanée   Beaux-Monts   Jean Grivot
Medium-full colour. A little vegetal on the nose. A lack of fat here. A bit reduced even. Slightly thin. Slightly rustic. Lacks style. But reasonable grip. Quite good. (01/96)
1999-2008   14.0

Vosne-Romanée   Beaumonts Alain Hudelot-Noëllat
Medium-full colour. Firm, rich, backward nose. Full, ample, youthful, quite substantial. Seems to have it all here. Lovely concentrated fruit. Closed at present. Similar note 11/94. (01/96)
2001-2012   16.5

Vosne-Romanée   Beaux-Monts   Louis Jadot
Medium-full colour. Rich and full on the nose. Medium-full, ample and fat. Rich and backward. This is very good but it lacks just a little excitement. Slightly dense. But give it time. (01/96)
2001-2012   16.0

Vosne-Romanée   Beaumonts   Leroy
Very full colour. Lovely rich oaky nose. Ample and plump. Fullish, tannic, structured, oaky. Very good grip. A lot of depth. Fine. The sample in 01/96 was less impressive, somewhat concocted in its fruit, I found; yet finishing well. I marked it very good (16.0). (10/95)
1999-2019   17.5

Vosne-Romanée   Beaumonts André Pernin-Rossin
Good colour. On the nose a curious metallic taste. The bad result of the Accad method. A lack of real succulence of fruit. No fat. A touch of reduction and a touch of built-in sulphur. On the palate a wine without much tannins. Indeed a little hollow on the follow-through. No dimension. Quite good at best. (01/96)
Now-2003   14.0

Vosne-Romanée   Beaux-Monts
Daniel Rion et Fils
> Medium-full colour. Good ripe nose. Some oak. Medium-full. Rich and ample on the palate. Not the greatest depth and concentration but well made and very good. **(01/96)**

2000-2012   16.0

Vosne-Romanée   Beaumonts
Emmanuel Rouget
> Medium-full colour. Firm, full, oaky nose. This is big, backward and quite markedly oaky. But it has good grip and intensity, so not over-oaked. Rich, ample complex finish. Fine. **(01/96)**

2001-2015   17.5

Vosne-Romanée   Beaux-Monts
Thomas-Moillard
> Medium colour. Soft nose. A little astringent on the palate. Rather dry. And a bit over-developed and blowsy. Lacks grip. Medium body. Doesn't excite. **(01/96)**

1998-2003   13.0

Vosne-Romanée   Brûlées   René Engel
> Medium-full colour. Lovely succulent nose. Rich and concentrated. This is full and firm with very fine intensity and depth. A delicious example. Lovely. Several notes. **(01/96)**

2001-2018   17.5

Vosne-Romanée   Chaumes
Joseph Faiveley
> Good colour. Soft, rich, concentrated, stylish nose. Very good definition here. Medium-full. This is good but not as exciting as Faiveley's Chambolle Fuées or Engel's Brûlées. Lacks a bit of concentration and definition and depth. Balanced but slightly one-dimensional. Good merely. **(10/94)**

Now-2008   15.0

Vosne-Romanée   Chaumes   Méo-Camuzet
> Good colour. Quite oaky on the nose but good acidity. Rich. Medium-full, slightly bitter at the end and not exactly covered with fat and grip. Very good but not exciting. **(03/94)**

1999-2015   16.0

Vosne-Romanée   Chaumes
Daniel Rion et Fils
> Medium-full colour. Not much nose. Fullish, quite structured, slightly spicy, slightly animal. Plenty of wine here. Good tannins and grip. But it lacks a bit of finesse. And the finish is a bit astringent. Several notes. **(01/96)**

2001-2012   15.0

Vosne-Romanée   Chaumes   Jean Tardy
> Medium-full colour. Soft, ample, oaky nose. Full and oaky on the palate. Good fruit. Good balance. But the oak dominates. Classy, though. Plenty of depth. Good but too much wood. **(01/96)**

2000-2012   15.0

Vosne-Romanée   Clos-des-Réas   Jean Gros
> Medium-full colour. Slightly pinched on the nose at first. Opened up to reveal an ample, generous, oaky example. Medium-full. Youthful. Very good fruit. Long. Complex and elegant. Fine too. **(01/96)**

2001-2015   17.5

Vosne-Romanée   Cros-Parentoux
Henri Jayer
> Medium-full colour. Quite oaky on the nose. Medium-full, rich and with good ample fruit on the palate. Balanced and concentrated. Quite pronounced oak. Long. Intense. Very fine. **(01/96)**

2001-2015   18.5

Vosne-Romanée   Cros-Parentoux
Méo-Camuzet
> Very good colour. Marvellous fruit and concentration here. This is very fine. Real quality of fruit and real dimension. Brilliantly balanced here. Real grip and drive and intensity. Lovely rich fruit. Still backward and a bit light. Fullish. Long. Potentially very super. **(01/96)**

2000-2015   18.5

Vosne-Romanée   Gaudichots
Vigot-Battault
> Medium-full colour. Fruity nose but a little simple. On the palate the wine is a bit loose-knit and a bit astringent. Slightly dilute. Lacks grip. Only fair. **(01/96)**

1998-2004   13.0

Vosne-Romanée   Malconsorts
Sylvain Cathiard
> Medium-full colour. Quite an austere nose. Medium-full. Some tannin. Good grip. This is youthful, but of very good potential. Rich. Nicely austere. Needs time. Very good indeed. **(01/96)**

2001-2015   17.0

Vosne-Romanée   Malconsorts
Alain Hudelot-Noëllat
> Medium to medium-full colour. Ripe nose. But not a lot of depth. Medium to medium-full body. Slightly vegetal. Good acidity. But lacks a bit of generosity and dimension. Quite long and positive at the end. Good at best. I liked it much better 11/94 - very good indeed (17.0). **(01/96)**

2000-2012   15.0

**Vosne-Romanée Malconsorts
Thomas-Moillard**

Medium-full colour. Lean nose. Backward but complex, intense and stylish. This is fullish, has very good tannins and very good grip. Slightly rustic though. **(01/96)**

2001-2015   **16.0**

Vosne-Romanée Orveaux Sylvain Cathiard

Medium-full colour. Lovely ripe succulent nose. Medium to medium-full. Good grip. This is plump and fruity, elegant and harmonious. Quite forward. Good plus. **(01/96)**

1999-2010   **15.5**

**Vosne-Romanée Orveaux
Mongeard-Mugneret**

Medium-full colour. Firm slightly closed nose, but a lot of fruit and depth. Fullish, good oaky base. Concentrated and intense. This is high class. Ample, balanced. Very very long. Real depth here. Fine. **(01/96)**

2001-2018   **17.5**

Vosne-Romanée Rouges Jean Grivot

Medium-full colour. Slightly light on the nose. But good fruit. Medium to medium-full. Slightly bitter in the fruit. Reasonable balance and style though. Lacks a little fat and depth. Some oak. Quite good plus. **(01/96)**

1999-2009   **14.5**

Vosne-Romanée Suchots Robert Arnoux

Medium-full colour. Slightly tight and slightly herbaceous on the nose. Some stems? Good depth and fruit and real intensity. Fine. **(01/96)**

2001-2018   **17.5**

Vosne-Romanée Suchots Jean Grivot

Medium colour. Gentle but stylish and balanced nose. Medium body. Ample, quite fat. An aromatic wine. But without quite enough class for better than quite good. A little thin and blowsy. **(01/96)**

2000-2010   **13.5**

Vougeot Les Cras L'Héritier-Guyot

Good colour. Stylish nose. Interesting spices here. Medium to medium-full weight. Good grip. Nothing hard about the tannins. Ripe, concentrated. This is complex, long and very good plus. **(12/95)**

1999-2008   **16.5**

1990

RATING FOR THE VINTAGE

Red: 18.5   **White:** 16.5

SIZE OF THE CROP

(Hectolitres, excluding generic wine)

	Red	White
Grands Crus	14,117	3,668
Village and *Premiers Crus*	188,573	51,926
Total	202,690	55,594

With a total of nearly 260,000 hl, 1990 was one of the largest crops of recent years, being surpassed only by 1986 and 1982, and a full 10 per cent more plentiful than the previous vintage, 1989, itself regarded as generous.

And yet, as if to prove the exception to the general rule, the red wines are truly magnificent and the white wines are very good. For quality and consistency you have to go back - for reds - to 1959 or 1964 to find any year that was so satisfactory both geographically and hierarchically. I said at the outset that I suspected some of the great wines of the 1988 vintage might be superior in the long run, if different, to the great wines of 1990, and I still hold with this view. But further down the scale the 1990s get the palm. No-one who has them in their cellar is likely to be disappointed.

An early and mild start to the growing season produced a prolific *sortie* of productive buds, marred only on the lower slopes at the junction of Savigny, Pernand and Aloxe-Corton by a little frost. The weather then deteriorated in June, and the flowering was prolonged, producing both *coulure* (failure of the flower to set into fruit) and *millerandage* (shot berry). Volnay was one of the communes most severely affected.

Thenceforth it was hot and very dry. The younger vines suffered, especially those on the slopes where the soils are thinner and less rich than in the plain. The more mature plants with more complex root-systems were better able to cope, but the progress towards maturation was nevertheless slowed down to a standstill. At the end of August and the beginning of September, just when it was most needed, there were several refreshing thunderstorms - in all some 80 mm of rain fell in one week - the vines woke up and rapidly finished their cycle during three weeks of warm but not excessively hot weather. The red-wine harvest began in the Côte-de-Beaune on 20 September, in the Côte-de-Nuits a week or so later. The advent of full maturity, as a result of the prolonged flowering, was irregular, however, and some did not finish their harvest until 10 October.

One effect of the drought was that a high proportion of leaves had already fallen from the vines by mid-August. This exposed the fruit, concentrated and dried out the berries, and, incidentally, helped to fix the colour better. Canopy management is not a science understood by many Burgundian *vignerons*, but this gain in colour had occurred accidentally, for the same reason, in one of Charles Rousseau's *cuvées* a couple of years ago. Puzzling over the explanation, he had bounced a theory off Gérard Jaboulet in Tain, only to have it confirmed. He now deliberately exposes his grape bunches to the sun in the final month before the harvest.

The result, for those who had prudently pruned hard and green harvested the excessive amount of grape bunches towards the end of July (sensibly knocking off the least favoured bunches in order to mitigate the effects of the prolonged flowering), was a quality of fruit that was second to none. This fruit was abundantly healthy, the skins of the grapes were thick and the ratio of juice to solid matter was low. It normally requires, says Charles Rousseau (to quote him once again) 1 kilo of grapes to make one bottle of wine. Or, to put it another way, ten plastic containers of 30 kilos to fill one *pièce*. In 1990 it took twelve. I remember Rousseau pointing out the same fact when I first tasted his 1983s. The result, obviously, is high concentration. For those who did not crop excessively, as Christophe Roumier pointed out, it was necessary neither to chaptalise nor to acidify. Alcohol levels were naturally 12.5° or above, even as high as 14.5° in some exceptional cases.

Nevertheless, for those who harvested at 40 hectolitres per hectare or more, it was necessary to perform a *saignée* to bleed off excess juice before fermentation. *Saignée*, however, is not a cure-all. It is a *faute de mieux*. It is an essential procedure if rain intervenes at the last minute, as it did in 1991. But reducing the harvest of especially the more prolific younger vines to moderate proportions in the first place, is far more important. Many of the finest aromatic elements are lost in the *saignée*-d juice. It may concentrate the solids, but it does not of itself increase the acidity.

Many people *saignée*-d their 1990 vats. Jacques Lardière at Jadot *saignée*-d all his *cuvées* 20 per cent. Drouhin bled only one, but in retrospect felt they could have done more. What is apparent, all the way up and down the Côte, is a willingness to be flexible, an awareness of the need to keep the size of the harvest within reasonable bounds, and a vastly increasing employment of *tables de trie* at the winery, sorting out the good fruit from the bad. Indeed many now attach a device to blow away excess water if the vintage should take place in the rain. There is a particularly up-to-date device at the Domaine de Courcel in Pommard. There are also experiments under way which attempt to concentrate the wine by evaporating the water in the grapes or must, without either freezing or heating. I await the outcome of these tests with interest.

THE STYLE OF THE WINE

WHITE WINES

Sugar levels were high (though not in general as high as in 1989 because of the increased yield), so as a result alcohol levels are high too. (Yet some growers nevertheless persisted in chaptalising. I wish they wouldn't.) Acidity levels are low, but in contrast to 1989 these acidities were almost entirely tartaric, and the consequent drop during the malo-lactic fermentation was minimal. Moreover, during the fine weather of the final days prior to the harvest all the elements in the fruit were able to concentrate, at least to some extent. However, the state of maturity over the *vignoble* was uneven. Some plots were more advanced than others. It was not the case, as it normally is, that the *premiers* and *grands crus* were in advance of the vineyards of the plain. It was necessary, as it was in Bordeaux, as readers may recall, to choose carefully the date of optimum ripeness, and to plan with precision the rotation of the pickers from one plot to another. Nevertheless, when the fruit was in, the fermentations took place without problems. Cool nights and daytime degrees lower than in 1989 made temperature-control easier and vinification uncomplicated.

'Fat, rich, supple and accessible: like 1982 but more concentrated,' said Claude Bouchard of Bouchard Père et Fils. This team reduced the harvest in their large domaine by crop-thinning, and produced, for example, only 28 hectolitres per hectare in their Montrachet. Others were not so wise. Many exceeded the legal limit of 60 hectolitres per hectare and had to send surplus wine to be distilled. Michelot made as much as in 1988. The Château de la Maltroye over-produced. Even the conscientious, such as Lafon, made 50 hectolitres per hectare overall.

Yet nevertheless the analyses were promising. Acidities were in many cases better than in 1989; in most cases no worse. At the Roulot domaine the pH was 10 per cent less. At the Domaine René Monnier, M. Bouillot claimed 1990s which not only had better acidity but were more concentrated than in the previous year. Thierry Matrot, also in Meursault, preferred the balance and character of his 1990s. These, he said, were more elegant and more delicate wines than his 1989s; they would last better. Others continued these laudatory comments. Franck Grux, in charge of wine-making at Olivier Leflaive Frères, had a high opinion of the 1990s. An excellent maturity, with none of the *sur-maturité* of 1986, he pointed out. The wines turned out better than expected. There was a lot of difference in perceived quality after the rackings following the completion of the malos. (Generally, paradoxically in view of the small amount of malic acid to be transformed, these took their time to take place.) Noël Ramonet said the 1990 vintage was a vintage for keeping. It would need time to mature. He likened the vintage to 1978. Vincent Leflaive suggested a cross between 1983 and 1979. The 1990s were not only far better than the 1988s, he said, but they had more power, even at their best more finesse than the 1989s, but were less concentrated. Even Dominique Lafon, who considered his 1989s far superior, averred that his 1990s were much riper and better balanced than his 1988s; and his 1988s are really very good indeed.

RED WINES

For most growers, especially the younger generation, 1990 was the best vintage they had ever produced. The structure of the 1988s together with the fruit of the 1989s or the 1985s, was how many described it. From a purely chemical analysis point of view, Ghislaine Barthod's consultant oenologist told her, 1990 is the best for a generation or more. 'I prefer the 1990s to the 1988s,' said Jacques Seysses, 'it has less austerity, and I don't like my wines to be too austere. 1990 is more my style.' 'I find my 1990s more voluptuous than the 1988s were at the same time,' echoed Christophe Roumier. 'The 1988s are more classic, but the 1990s have more charm and fat; they will appeal more to the popular taste. But I am not sure which vintage is going to be better.' 'Very fine ripe tannins,' said Stéphane Gelin. 'Despite the abundant harvest an exceptional maturity of fruit and richness of sugar.' As Pascal Marchand of the Domaine du Comte Armand put it: 'The 1990s are more concentrated; they have more alcohol, colour, fruit and tannin. But perhaps the 1988s are better balanced. Nevertheless I prefer the 1990s.' 'A marvellous vintage. A year of real *vins de garde*,' said Christian Gouges, 'but atypically full and rich for Pinot Noir.'

Some, however, are unrepentant 1988 fans, despite the delights of the 1990s. At the Domaine de la Romanée-Conti they consider 1990 not as good as 1988, though better than 1985. Jean Tardy described the 1988s as more complete, more long-lasting. Gabriel Tortochot also preferred the earlier vintage.

Jean-Nicolas Méo, on the other hand, was more even-handed. He had a marginal preference for 1990. But where the vintage was too prolific he considered the 1988 the better of the pair. In the Côte-de-Beaune, more so in Volnay than in Pommard, there were fears at the start that the tannins would be too hard and aggressive as a result of the *millerandage* and the drought having affected the progress towards maturity of the younger vines. Jean-Marc Boillot found his Pommards *plus fondus* (the tannins riper and more complete) than his Volnays. I found all his wines very good indeed. But I did find other Volnays, and other Pommards too, which exemplified this apprehension.

Where the 1990 vintage particularly scores, in my view, is in the quality of the generic wines. Never before, except perhaps in 1976, have I sampled Bourgognes *rouges* and Hautes-Côtes with so much rich fruit. Never before have I seen wines at this level with so much style, so little rusticity.

With one or two exceptions - the village wines in Chambolle and Morey-Saint-Denis are irregular - there is a consistency of good colour, ripe fruit and length on the palate throughout the Côte from Marsannay to Santenay and up and down the hierarchy from village wine to *grand cru*. And with one or two exceptions - Volnays more similar to Pommards than usual, as I have said - the wines are very typical of their communes. The 1990s could be macerated for a long time, and the longer the maceration, the more distinctive the thumb-print of the individual *terroir*.

I was particularly impressed, and I have so far not found out why this should be so, with the standard of the 1990 Clos-de-Vougeots when I first sampled in November 1991. Usually this is what I might term a second-division *grand cru* (like most Corton, Echézeaux and Charmes and Chapelle-Chambertin). It lacks, ultimately, the breed of the top *climats*. And, not surprisingly from such a large piece of land, the wines vary in quality from the occasionally fine to the frankly disappointing. Almost all the 1990s Clos-de-Vougeots tasted well, however.

Equally, what struck me was the exoticism of some of the Côte-de-Beaune wines. There was a gamey, flamboyantly individual richness about many of them, particularly among the *premiers crus* of Beaune. Here, and in Pommard, and also in many of the Volnays, you will find wines of great originality of character; much more so than usual.

This is a vintage where village wines taste like *premiers crus* and *premiers crus* like *grands crus*. It is also a vintage marked by a taste of *rôti*, of old vines, even when the vines are not in fact so old, such is the concentration. It is a vintage with more of a flavour of black fruits - cassis, blackberry, *myrtille* - even in the Côte-de-Beaune, than red fruit such as cherry or strawberry. To echo the phrase which was repeated to me time and time again, from cellar to cellar: 1990 is *une grande année*.

WHERE ARE THE BEST WINES?

In place of the usual generalisations of the best it is perhaps simpler to set out some of the cases where 1990 is *not* as good as elsewhere.

★ In many cases the white wines are better in 1989 than 1990. You have to go from grower to grower. There are no ground rules.

★ There are some irregularities among the red wines at village level in Morey-Saint-Denis and Chambolle-Musigny.

★ And among the Cortons, both red and white.

STATE OF MATURITY TODAY

White: The village wines are now *à point*, but the best can still be kept. *Premiers crus* are beginning to open out, and the best will last well into the next decade. Leave the *grands crus* until the year 2000 and drink them – I hope with pleasure! – right up to 2010 and beyond.

Red: Even some village wines, especially those from the better growers of the Côte-de-Nuits, are barely ready. Most 1990s can safely be left until 2000 or more, and the top *premiers crus* and *grands crus* even longer. They will go on getting even more glorious. So it is a pity to uncork them while we have other vintages to drink or finish up.

TASTING NOTES

BLANC

Auxey-Duresses   Les Boutonniers   Leroy
Firm, closed, adolescent. Juicy but slightly heavy. A bit one-dimensional. **(07/92)**
Now-2000   13.5

Bâtard-Montrachet   Pierre Morey
Brilliant nose. Backward. Hugely concentrated and intense. Very closed in. Underlying oak and concentration. At first really difficult to taste. But just went on getting more and more ample and rich and multi-dimensional in the glass. Brilliant. Very very composed. **(03/95)**
1999-2015   19.0

Bâtard-Montrachet   Ramonet
This is very fine. Considerably superior to their Caillerets. Very intense and concentrated. Lovely fruit. Very good oaky base. Youthful. Very fine indeed. **(09/92)**
1999-2015   18.5

Beaune   Clos-de-la-Maladière
Henri Cauvard et Fils
This is better than the 1991. More fruit. Again a bit hard and spicy though. Good balance, even rich. Unusual but good. *À point.* **(12/95)**
Now-2000   14.0

Bienvenues-Bâtard-Montrachet
Louis Carillon
Light golden colour. A very fine stylish wine with lovely intensity and concentration. Not too oaky. Very good grip. And marvellous fruit. Vigorous. Real class and depth. **(02/94)**
2000-2015   18.5

Chassagne-Montrachet   Ramonet
Rich and fat but a little heavy. A bit adolescent. But underneath real depth here. Fine for a village wine. **(09/92)**
Now-2005   16.0

Chassagne-Montrachet   Les Baudines
Bernard Morey
Doesn't really sing. Lacks a bit of concentration. Slightly hard because of the oak. Quite good. **(07/92)**
Now-2000   14.0

Chassagne-Montrachet   La Boudriotte
Jacques Gagnard-Delagrange
A bit of reduction at the beginning. When this blew off, feminine for Chassagne, balanced, charming, plump. But not a great deal more to it than the village Puligny-Montrachet of G. Chavy. Good. **(09/94)**
Now-2000   15.0

Chassagne-Montrachet   Les Caillerets
Jean-Noël Gagnard
Fresh colour. Very tight and unforthcoming at first, despite having been decanted. Slowly evolved into a rich, classy, gently oaky wine which still needs time to mature properly. Plenty of class and depth here. Still a bit austere. Good grip. Potentially very good indeed, perhaps even fine. **(01/96)**

1998-2008   17.0

Chassagne-Montrachet   Les Caillerets
Ramonet
This is also adolescent but the finish is fresh, complex, vigorous and with lovely fruit. Finesse, intensity. Fine. **(09/92)**

Now-2009   17.5

Chassagne-Montrachet   Les Chenevottes
Michel Colin-Deléger
Rich, firm, stylish nose. Typically slightly four-square Chassagne but with very good fruit and grip and depth. Good gentle oak base. Not great but very good plus. Will still improve. **(02/96)**

1998-2008   16.5

Chassagne-Montrachet   Les Embrazées
Bernard Morey
Better than the Baudines. Richer, fatter, more concentrated. Good depth. Good plus. **(07/92)**

Now-2005   15.5

Chassagne-Montrachet   La Maltroie
Bernard Moreau
Some built-in sulphur on the nose. But ripe and rich enough underneath. Good fruit. Good balance. Stylish finish, and that is the best part. Good concentration and complexity. This will still improve. **(10/95)**

Now-2005   16.0

Chassagne-Montrachet   Morgeots
Jean-Marc Boillot
Neat, well made, oaky and fruity. But good rather than great, like the Jadot/Magenta example below. A bit more concentration and dimension was needed. Good plus. **(10/94)**

Now-2002   15.5

Chassagne-Montrachet   Morgeots
René Lamy-Pillot
Fullish, a little rustic. Less SO_2 than the 1993, though there is certainly some. More weight. Less class. Slightly heavy. Only fair. **(06/96)**

Now-2000   13.5

Chassagne-Montrachet
Morgeots, Duc de Magenta   Louis Jadot
Flavoury, oaky, ripe, medium to medium-full body. Well balanced. But good rather than great.

Has style but lacks a bit of intensity and concentration. Good plus. **(10/94)**

Now-2002   15.5

Chevalier-Montrachet   Marc Rougeot
Ripe colour. Fat and oaky. Quite accessible. Round and ripe. But good grip and depth nevertheless. Good oak. But for a Chevalier, while very seductive, perhaps lacks a bit of austerity and backbone. **(10/92)**

Now-2002   16.0

Chevalier-Montrachet   Les Demoiselles
Louis Latour
Quite a developed colour. On the nose sweet, exotic fruits. Fat and rich and very oaky. On the palate a little alcoholic, rather heavy, lacking grace. What it also lacks, after the Jadot, is the depth and dimension of a great wine. There isn't the same complexity at the end. Good acidity though. Oaky and rich and fat again. Will this come? At this stage seems only very good indeed. **(11/94)**

Now-2002   17.0

Corton   Chandon-de-Briailles
Gently oaky. Quite full. Good grip. Lacks a bit of concentration and real style. But good. **(09/92)**

Now-2000   15.0

Corton-Charlemagne   Louis Jadot
Elegant but lacks real concentration and depth. One rather than three dimensions. **(06/92)**

Now-2000   15.0

Corton-Charlemagne   Louis Latour
Good colour. Full, rich, slightly heavyweight nose. But no undue SO_2. Still very youthful though. Full, fat, good oak integration. Quite alcoholic. But good grip. This is made for the long term. Honeyed underneath. Perhaps it lacks a bit of finesse and nuance. But rich, long on the palate. Plenty of dimension. Certainly fine. **(10/95)**

1998-2012   17.5

Corton-Charlemagne   Leroy
This doesn't impress. Not very ripe or concentrated. Young vines. Not the depth of *grand cru*. No great weight or persistence. Unexciting. **(08/92)**

Now-2000   13.5

Maranges   Contat-Grange
Fresh, a little young-viney, hollow, and rather ephemeral but clean. Not bad. **(03/93)**

Drink soon   13.0

Marsannay   Philippe Charlopin-Parizot
A ripe, fullish but essentially *primeur* style wine. A little four-square but slight oak. Balanced and

agreeable. **(05/95)**

Drink soon   **13.5**

Meursault Charles Jobard
Good substance. This is rich and fat and has good grip. Ripe and honeyed and long on the palate. Very good. **(03/93)**

Now-2001   **15.0**

Meursault Comtes Lafon
Ripe, fresh, plump. Stylish and with good depth. Best on the finish. Very good. Very long for a village wine. **(09/92)**

Now-2004   **16.0**

Meursault René Manuel
Fullish colour. Round and sweet on the nose but a bit four-square and pedestrian. Quite fat, plump. Medium-full. Lacks a bit of richness and definition. Quite good. **(06/92)**

Now-2000   **14.0**

Meursault Matrot
Light golden colour. Round, ripe, aromatic nose. A touch of egg custard. Good fruit on the palate. Good depth and grip too. Slightly adolescent at present. But long, complex. Quite classy. A good example. **(11/95)**

Now-2004   **15.0**

Meursault Pierre Morey
Medium colour. Ripe, quite new oaky - perhaps a bit too much. But balanced, and not too sturdy. Finishes well. Quite good plus. **(02/94)**

Now-2003   **14.5**

Meursault Daniel Nicvert
Quite forward. A little lean, but the acidity makes it stylish. Quite good. **(03/93)**

Drink soon   **14.0**

Meursault Blagny Louis Jadot
Good oak on the nose. Ripe fruit, good grip. Not quite enough concentration and depth on the palate but good nevertheless. **(06/92)**

Drink soon   **14.5**

Meursault Blagny Matrot
Crisp, youthful colour. Good rich nose. Composed, not adolescent. Lots of depth. Fullish, still nicely firm. Very good fruit. A nice Puligny-like steeliness. Long. Again it will still improve. Very good. **(11/95)**

Now-2009   **16.0**

Meursault Les Charmes
Vincent Bitouzet-Prieur
A bit tired on the nose with a suggestion of SO$_2$. Better on the palate. Quite mellow and soft

now. Good attack. Fruity and fresh, but there is sulphur on the finish. But it got better in the glass. Quite good. **(06/96)**

Drink soon   **14.0**

Meursault Les Charmes Charles Jobard
The best of his three *premiers crus*. Complex, poised, harmonious. Delicious. Real style here. Very good plus. **(03/93)**

Now-2003   **16.5**

Meursault Les Charmes Comtes Lafon
Round and ripe and gently oaky. Very good harmony. This is a definite step up. Intense, long. Very attractive. Shows very very well. More sensual than intellectual, opposite to the Genevrières. **(09/92)**

Now-2009   **18.0**

Meursault Les Chevalières Charles Jobard
A touch adolescent but good personality and depth here. Balanced, long; promising. **(03/93)**

Now-2001   **15.0**

Meursault Clos-de-la-Barre
Comtes Lafon
Slight 'do not touch me' about this. Fullish. Slightly four-square. Rich underneath. Plenty of depth and individuality. Best on the finish. Long, subtle. Potentially very good. Lovely balance. **(09/92)**

Now-2006   **17.0**

Meursault Clos-du-Cromin
Patrick Javillier
This is very good. Ripe, very clean. Lots of concentrated fruit. A real star. **(08/92)**

Now-2004   **16.0**

Meursault Désirée Comtes Lafon
This is much more accessible than the Clos-de-la-Barre. Finer it seems. Ample and generous. Ripe and sexy. But the Clos-de-la-Barre has more future. **(03/93)**

Now-2004   **16.0**

Meursault Les Genevrières Charles Jobard
Rather hidden. But good concentration here. Balanced, complex. Impressive finish. Very good. **(03/93)**

Now-2003   **16.0**

Meursault Les Genevrières Comtes Lafon
Suffering more from the bottling on the nose. A little more wood. A little rawer. Yet the follow-through is very rich and intense. Better acidity. More depth. Fatter and fuller and more powerful. Very good. I prefer this to the Charmes. **(09/92)**

1998-2010   **18.5**

**Meursault   Les Genevrières
Mestre-Michelot**

Really quite a deep colour. This is a bit oxidised. Underneath a fat, somewhat four-square wine. Good oak but a bit hot. It lacks elegance. A bit over-ripe and heavy. **(10/94)**

Drink soon   13.0

Meursault   Les Narvaux   Patrick Javillier

Delicate. Lovely fruit. Very clean. This is better than the Clos-du-Cromin. Very elegant and complex on the finish. Fine example. **(08/92)**

Now-2006   17.0

Meursault   Les Narvaux   Leroy

Lush, oaky, stylish. Good depth. Ripe and balanced. Promising. Good plus. **(06/94)**

Now-2003   15.5

**Meursault   Perrières   Jean-François
Coche-Dury**

Fresh colour. At first still a little closed on the nose. Youthful, firm, very, very rich and concentrated. This is very lovely. Delicate yet very intense. Excellent grip. Very fresh. Excellent. Opened up to be a splendid, abundant wine. **(07/95)**

2000-2012   18.5

Meursault   Perrières   Comtes Lafon

Very subtle nose. Soft and delicate but intense. Rich and fat without being a blockbuster on the palate. Round, ripe, subtle, complex and very long. Lovely. Complete. Very fine indeed. Less structure than the Genevrières but more finesse and depth and harmony. **(09/92)**

1998-2010   19.0

Meursault   Perrières   Pierre Moret

Rich, good oak, still very youthful. Classy and plentiful. Good grip. This has a lot of depth and dimension. Lovely balance. Not a vestige of the SO_2 which is in the 1993. Will keep really well. There is backbone here. Fine. **(06/96)**

Now-2010   17.5

**Meursault   Le Poruzot-Dessus
Charles Jobard**

Fine nose. Good reserved wine. Quite masculine and structured. Depth here. A little more four-square than his Genevrières. Good plus. **(03/93)**

Now-2002   15.5

Meursault   Les Tillets   Patrick Javillier

Not as good as his Clos-du-Cromin but still good. Ripe and stylish. Good balance but less distinctive. **(08/92)**

Now-2002   15.0

Monthélie   Denis Boussey

A little overblown, or badly stored, on the nose. But ripe and well made. Good for what it is. Gently oaky. **(06/94)**

Drink soon   14.5

Montrachet   Romanée-Conti

Deeper colour than the 1989. Rich, full, voluptuous nose. Just a touch heavy after the 1989. Less concentrated. But firm and balanced. Very ripe. Quite powerful. Very good indeed. **(06/92)**

1998-2007   17.0

Nuits-Saint-Georges   Clos-de-l'Arlot

Soft, oaky, very stylish. Already very drinkable. But not a stayer. **(03/92)**

Now-2000   15.0

**Nuits-Saint-Georges   Perrières
Henri Gouges**

This is in its adolescence. Finely balanced. Lovely fruit. Delicate. Individual. Soft and understated. **(11/94)**

Now-2000   17.0

Puligny-Montrachet   Jean-Marc Boillot

No undue age on the colour. Slightly scented on the nose. Light, slightly loose-knit. A gentle slightly oaky wine. Made for the American market. There is residual sweetness here. Good. But not really a keeper. Nor a classic. **(03/96)**

Now-2000   15.0

Puligny-Montrachet   Gérard Chavy

Clean, subtle, fully ready. Good balance. Nicely cool and crisp. Finishes long. Very good. **(09/94)**

Drink soon   16.0

Puligny-Montrachet   Henri Clerc

Opulent, quite deep in colour. Ripe, rich, gently oaky. But has good acidity. Spicy and aromatic. Very good. **(03/94)**

Drink soon   16.0

Puligny-Montrachet   Louis Latour

Some SO_2 on the nose. Full and rich, plenty of depth. But a little ungainly at present. But I don't think it is really that good. **(10/95)**

Now-2001   14.0

Puligny-Montrachet   Daniel Nicvert

Better than his Meursault, but a forward, ripe wine without a lot of depth. Quite good. **(03/93)**

Drink soon   14.5

**Puligny-Montrachet   Le Champ-Gain
Olivier Leflaive Frères**

This is just what it should be. Minerally, ripe and crisp, but not a bit lacking fruit and ripeness. Medium to medium-full. Balanced. Very stylish. Quite forward but very good. **(02/95)**

Now-2004   16.0

Puligny-Montrachet   Les Folatières   Leroy

Closed but cool and concentrated. Very young. Fine acidity. Very good indeed. Expanded in the glass. Long. Very complex. **(07/92)**

Now-2004   17.0

Puligny-Montrachet   Pucelles
Joseph Drouhin

One bottle a bit evolved. The other had a reasonably deep colour. Ripe, perfumed, quite 1986-ish nose. Some noble rot. A slight lack of freshness. Better on the palate. Medium-full. Ample, ripe, reasonable acidity. Quite ready already. Lacks a bit of real balance and therefore classy. Only good. **(07/92)**

Drink soon   15.0

Saint-Aubin   Thierry Guyot

No new wood here. Nicely rich and individual. All sort of fruit suggestions here: apricot, melon, lime, mango, blackcurrant even. Good grip. This is still youthful. Very good for what it is. **(12/95)**

Now-2000   15.0

Saint-Aubin   Champlots
Jean-Claude Bachelet

This is very much in the Bachelet style. A touch of sulphur. Quite good fruit. But no great concentration. Fruity, *tendre*, reasonably balanced. Quite forward. Fully ready. Lacks the depth and concentration for better. Quite good. **(12/95)**

Now-2000   14.0

Saint-Aubin   Charmois   Bernard Morey

Plenty of interest here. Good oak. Ripe and fat. Good style too. Concentrated and racy. **(08/92)**

Now-2000   15.5

ROUGE

Aloxe-Corton   Franck Follin

Very good colour. A little tough on the nose. Some stems here? Fullish, rich and meaty on the palate. Plenty of wine. Plenty of fruit. Good grip. The finish is much better than the attack. Will still improve. Good. **(12/95)**

Now-2005   15.0

Aloxe-Corton   Tollot-Beaut

Good colour. Ripe, backward, quite sturdy, plummy nose. Good chocolatey background. On the palate a little cooked and alcoholic. The finish is a bit hot. Ripe and succulent though. Quite good. **(05/93)**

Now-2004   14.0

Aloxe-Corton   Les Fournières
Antonin Guyon

Good colour. Ripe and ample but not exactly super-concentrated on the nose. Does it lack a bit of grip? This lacks a bit of style, as far as I am concerned. Some tannin. A bit peppery and edgy. **(06/92)**

Now-2001   13.5

Aloxe-Corton   Les Vercots   Champy

Very good colour. Rich, meaty, old-viney but a little over-ripe and raisiny. **(05/93)**

Now-2000   12.0

Auxey-Duresses   Henri Latour

Fine colour. Powerful nose. Slightly inky and rigid on the nose. Very good fruit though. And on the palate it is this which sings out. Rich, slightly spicy. Quite tannic, but the tannins ripe. Fullish. Better with food. But certainly good. **(12/95)**

1999-2007   15.5

Auxey-Duresses   Le Val
Dominique et Vincent Roy

Medium to medium-full colour. The tannins are a little more rustic on the nose. This has the succulence of the vintage and plenty of substance and fruit. Good grip as well. But the quality of the later wines shows more elegance and flair. Just about ready. Quite good plus for the vintage. **(12/95)**

Now-2007   14.5

Beaune   Louis Latour

Medium-full colour. Ripe, sweet, alcoholic, a bit hot and spicy. Lacks class but commercial. **(03/94)**

Now-2001   13.0

Beaune   Maillard Père et Fils

Good colour. Ripe standard stuff with a good touch of oak. This has fruit and balance. Very good for a village Beaune. Positive finish. **(02/94)**

Now-2006   15.0

Beaune   Les Avaux   Champy

Fragrant, ripe, balanced. Very good follow-through. Elegant. Very good. Lovely fruit at the end. **(05/93)**

Now-2002   15.5

Beaune   Blanche-Fleur   Sylvain Dussort

Much better colour. An ample wine, but again lean, and this time rather stemmy. Good acidity. But not my style. **(12/95)**

Now-2000 plus   13.5

Beaune   Cent-Vignes   Bernard Bescancenot

Good colour. Sturdy, backward nose. Rich and substantial, even robust; more Aloxe than Beaune. There is a touch of reduction here, which would go if you decanted it. Full, meaty, ripe and balanced. Good but not exactly very elegant. Just like the 1993. **(12/95)**

Now–2005 plus   **14.5**

Beaune Cent-Vignes Jacques Germain, Château de Chorey
Good colour. Ample, old-viney nose. Plenty of depth here. Medium-full, concentrated, backward. Rich and oaky. But needs time. Very good. **(02/94)**

1998–2010   **16.0**

Beaune Chouacheux Bouchez-Cretal
Half bottle. Rather four-square. Good colour. Ripe and sturdy but a little lumpy and one-dimensional. Average. **(02/95)**

Drink soon   **13.5**

Beaune Clos-de-la-Maladière Henri Cauvard et Fils
Very good colour. Rich, substantial, chocolatey. Good substance. But lacks a bit of elegance. Only fair. **(12/95)**

Drink soon   **13.5**

Beaune Clos-des-Mouches Joseph Drouhin
Medium-full colour. Lovely rich clean nose. Very fine palate. Rich, fat, complex and concentrated. This is clearly a long way superior to the 1989, good as that is. Full. Lovely balance. Will be really voluptuous. Very good indeed. Very fine lingering finish. Several notes. **(05/93)**

1998–2009   **17.0**

Beaune Clos-des-Perrières François Gay
Good colour. This is more complete than the 1991. More *tendre* too. And rather more together. So *à point* now. Rich and velvety. More red fruit than black. Plump, soft and subtle. Long. Quite stylish. Just a little touch of the rustic. Good plus. **(12/95)**

Now–2003   **15.5**

Beaune Cuvée Maurice Drouhin Hospices de Beaune, Joseph Drouhin
Fine colour. Still very youthful. Less fat than the Volnay, Chevret. Slight vegetal hardness and tannins from the wood. But ripe and succulent. Good plus. **(02/96)**

1998–2008   **15.5**

Beaune Grèves Bouchard Père et Fils
Good colour. Rich ripe, liquorice-chocolate nose. Quite firm. Fullish, spicy but concentrated. A little hard perhaps. Quite good. **(06/92)**

Now–2003   **14.0**

Beaune Grèves Michel Lafarge
Good colour. Just a touch of oak; fruity, stylish and with good intensity on nose and palate. A good fullish meaty wine, but not a bit dense or heavy. Long balanced elegant finish. Very good. **(10/94)**

Now–2009   **16.0**

Beaune Grèves Bernard Morey
Ripe, a bit hard. Very rich underneath. Very good potential, but currently a bit adolescent. **(07/92)**

1999–2009   **16.0**

Beaune Grèves Roland Remoissenet Père et Fils
Fine colour. Lovely ripe rich nose. Full and oaky. Very good tannins. Ample, firm, balanced. Very concentrated. This will last and last. Very good plus. **(05/93)**

Now–2009   **16.5**

Beaune Montrevenots Jean-Marc Boillot
Fine colour. Rich, plummy, very ripe nose. Fullish. Good tannins. Concentrated and very good grip. Nicely sturdy. Needs time. A meaty wine. Best with food. Good. **(02/94)**

1998–2008   **15.0**

Beaune Montrevenots André Mussy
Slightly lean. Good nose. Classy. Not too bad on the palate either. Better than expected. Old-viney. Intense. **(05/93)**

Now–2007   **15.0**

Beaune Reversées Jean-Claude Rateau
Marvellous colour. Super nose. Ultra rich and concentrated. On the palate this is full, quite powerful, very good tannins. Black fruit in abundance. Fat. Very intense. Powerful without being fiery. Fine. **(12/95)**

1998–2008   **17.5**

Beaune Domaine de Saux Jacques Germain, Château de Chorey
Medium colour. Just a little hard on the nose. Less succulent than the Vignes-Franches. And a little lean on the palate. Medium body. A little tannin; balanced but a bit unsophisticated. Quite good. **(02/94)**

Now–2001   **14.0**

Beaune Teurons Camille Giroud
Fat and rich, just a little rigid on the nose. But very good grip. Fullish. Ample, animal. Lovely, naturally sweet finish. **(09/92)**

Now–2005   **16.0**

**Beaune   Vigne-de-l'Enfant-Jésus
Bouchard Père et Fils**

Full colour. Aromatic nose, but not exactly rich.
This is fullish. The tannins are a little lumpy and
astringent on the attack, and the wine lacks a bit
of fat. But there is depth here. But it is by no
means very exciting. Good plus for the vintage.
(02/95)

1998-2008   15.5

**Beaune   Vignes-Franches
Jacques Germain, Château de Chorey**

Good colour. Plump, new oaky nose. Medium-
full, good tannins. Ripe, balanced, long and
satisfying. Plenty of wine here. Very good.
(02/94)

Now-2009   16.0

Blagny   La Pièce-sous-le-Bois   Matrot

Good colour. Rich nose. Now a touch adolescent. Ripe, fullish, gently oaky. This is best at
the end which is ample and warm. Good grip.
Slightly monolithic but long on the palate.
Certainly very good plus. **(02/95)**

Now-2006   16.5

Bonnes-Mares   Drouhin-Laroze

I find this a little hard and stemmy on the nose.
But richer and firmer and more tannic on the
palate. Has now closed in a bit. Full. Very good
grip. Fine finish. A bit brutal at present. **(09/92)**

Now-2003   16.0

Bonnes-Mares   Dujac

Good colour. Ripe, concentrated, old-viney
nose. Good concentration without being a blockbuster. Stylish though. Medium-full. Some oak.
Very good tannins. Old-viney fruit and
intensity. This is fine quality. Really elegant.
Very long. **(05/93)**

1998-2018   17.5

Bonnes-Mares   Georges Roumier

Much more closed and tannic. A bit adolescent.
Firm, full, not nearly as much on form. On the
finish very very intense though, with a hint of
spice. Very very long. Real reserve. Needs time.
Fine plus. **(09/92)**

1999-2015   18.0

Chambertin   Joseph Drouhin

Medium-full colour. Neatly made, balanced,
stylishly fruity Pinot nose. Good. Full and firm
and tannic on the palate. This is brilliant! Very
lovely concentrated fruit and very good grip to
go with it. Excellent. Backward though. **(06/92)**

1999-2012   19.0

Chambertin   Ponsot

Pinot Droit planted in 1961, and so not as good
as could be. Three/four *ouvrées*. Two/three
barrels is their share. Fat and concentrated but
not a blockbuster. Quite old-viney, but doesn't
quite have the flair one might expect and the
Morey *grands crus* have in spades. Intense at the
end. Very good acidity. Lovely fruit. Very good
indeed though. **(09/92)**

Now-2010   17.0

Chambertin   Rossignol-Trapet

Good colour. Rich, fat, ample and concentrated,
though not a wine of great backbone and grip.
Fullish. Good but by no means great. **(09/92)**

Now-2005   15.0

Chambertin   Armand Rousseau

Fine colour. This is even better than his Clos-
de-Bèze. Very very rich and concentrated.
Splendid intensity of fruit. It is difficult to
conceive of young vine being better than this.
Excellently concentrated. Fabulous intensity of
fruit. *Grand vin.* **(05/93)**

2000-2020   20.0

**Chambertin   *Vieilles-Vignes*
Rossignol-Trapet**

Much better colour. Much better wine. This is
concentrated and rich and has real depth. On
the palate a wine of real dimension. Excellent.
(09/92)

2000-2015   18.5

Chambertin   Clos-de-Bèze   Champy

Not an enormous colour. Good oak and intensity but less of a blockbuster than I expected. Yet
very fine follow-through. Complex. Classy.
Fine. **(05/93)**

1998-2015   17.0

Chambertin   Clos-de-Bèze   Bruno Clair

Full colour. This is very fine. Full, firm, old-
viney, concentrated and rich. There is real depth
here. This is a big multi-dimensional wine. Lots
of tannin. Splendid! **(09/92)**

2001-2017   18.5

Chambertin   Clos-de-Bèze   Drouhin-Laroze

Not an enormous colour. Medium-full, ripe,
sweet. But not in the final analysis serious
enough for this *climat* in this vintage. **(09/92)**

Now-2006   15.5

Chambertin   Clos-de-Bèze   Joseph Faiveley

Fine colour. Splendid nose. This is sheer
brilliance! Amazing intensity of fruit. Full, super
concentration, marvellous quality. Absolutely
lovely. Very, very long and complex at the end.
Grand vin. **(05/93)**

2000-2025   20.0

Chambertin Clos-de-Bèze
Armand Rousseau

Fine colour. Very rich concentrated profound nose. Brilliantly perfumed intense fruit. Full, very concentrated, real depth. This has impeccable balance and real intensity. Very lovely. (05/93)

1999-2020   19.5

Chambolle-Musigny   Bernard Amiot

Not a lot of colour. Slightly rustic on the nose. And on the palate too. This is nothing special. Ripe and sweet, but that is about all there is to it. (11/93)

Now-2001   14.0

Chambolle-Musigny
Ghislaine Barthod-Noëllat

Good colour. Ripe cherry fruit. Elegant. Very Chambolle. Plump without being a blockbuster. This has very good grip and substance for a village wine. Medium full. Good intensity. Shows well. (05/93)

Now-2012   16.0

Chambolle-Musigny   Pierre Bertheau

Good colour. Ample, rich and with very good intensity. Plump and balanced. Complex, generous and satisfying. Very good. (09/92)

Now-2004   16.0

Chambolle-Musigny   Champy

Open, fragrant, flowery, slightly scented violets. Medium body. Slightly raw. A lack of real generosity and suppleness. Better as it developed in the glass. (05/93)

Now-2003   14.0

Chambolle-Musigny   Cottin Frères

Medium-full colour. Somewhat bland on the nose. Medium body, ripe but not exactly rich or concentrated. And the grip is lacking. Average. (06/92)

Now-2000   13.0

Chambolle-Musigny   Dujac

Medium-full colour. Youthful nose. A little chunky, but very good depth underneath. Medium-full. Some oak. Very ripe and engaging. This is open, fresh, accessible and most attractive and seductive. Soft, long and complex. Fine. (05/93)

Now-2015   17.5

Chambolle-Musigny   Alfred Haegelen-Jayer

Good colour. Fragrant nose. Medium body. Soft, quite supple. This hasn't got a great deal of grip but it is round and charming. Good but not great. (09/92)

Now-2002   15.0

Chambolle-Musigny   Joël Hudelot-Baillet

This has a good colour. And plenty of depth and grip. Yet seems strangely neutral. Obviously it has gone into its shell. But nevertheless I don't get the lushness of 1990. It is more like a 1988. Good structure. Good acidity. Good breeding. But a little lean. It lacks charm. (11/94)

1998-2006   14.5

Chambolle-Musigny   Olivier Leflaive Frères

Fragrant nose. But like the above a little slight. Lacks intensity. A bit short. Better than their Morey-Saint-Denis. Quite stylish, but a bit short and one-dimensional. (09/92)

Drink soon   14.0

Chambolle-Musigny   Jacques-Frédéric

Mugnier

Good colour. Violets and raspberries on the nose. With a slightly hard dry edge. Nothing adolescent on the palate though. Cool. Clean. Medium body. Good fruity attack. Just a little less elegant and charming on the follow-through. Good. (05/93)

Now-2008   15.0

Chambolle-Musigny   Daniel Rion et Fils

Good colour. Fullish rich oaky nose. Good ripe fruit. Very good for a village example. Fullish on the palate. Fat, rich, oaky. This has a lot of depth. Real style too. Very good grip. Lots of dimension here. Excellent for a village example. Really complex. (05/93)

Now-2015   17.0

Chambolle-Musigny   Georges Roumier

Medium colour for a 1990. Ripe and succulent. Good but not quite as rich and as intense as the Barthod 1990. Some oak. Medium to medium-full. Very Chambolle. Round and spicy and seductive. Good intensity and finish. (05/93)

Now-2012   15.5

Chambolle-Musigny
Comte Georges de Vogüé

Fine colour. A little closed on the nose. But there is good plummy fruit underneath. Some oak here. Quite meaty for a Chambolle. Quite backward. Rich and fat and full and with good grip and tannin. This again is very fine for a village example. Long. Backward. (05/93)

Now-2015   17.0

Chambolle-Musigny   Les Amoureuses
Pierre Bertheau

Good colour. Very lovely concentrated fruit here. Almost sweet in its intensity. Medium-full. Very good grip. Ample. Very elegant. Fine quality. Very seductive. (09/92)

Now-2008   17.5

**Chambolle-Musigny   Les Amoureuses
Joseph Drouhin**

Fullish colour. Hidden nose. Good concentration. Splendid ripe fruit. Firm and rich and opulent. Plenty of depth. Almost sweet. This is fine. **(06/92)**

Now–2007   17.5

**Chambolle-Musigny   Les Amoureuses
Georges Roumier**

Lovely nose. Marvellous, marvellous fruit. Round fat rich and wonderfully ripe and sweet. Very seductive, but at the same time with grip, depth and personality and reserves. Very lovely. Very Chambolle. Very silky. **(09/92)**

1999–2015   18.0

**Chambolle-Musigny   Les Amoureuses
Comte Georges de Vogüé**

Good colour. Lovely nose. Really fine succulent, concentrated gently oaky fruit. Essence of Chambolle. Very seductive. Fullish. Very good grip. Very good intensity. Gently oaky. This is very lovely indeed. When Chambolles are good they are so good! **(05/93)**

1998–2018   18.5

**Chambolle-Musigny   Les Charmes
Georges Clerget**

Good oak but a bit muddled. Ripe and fat but quite sturdy for this *climat*. **(07/92)**

Now–2004   15.0

**Chambolle-Musigny   Les Charmes
Michel Modot et Fils**

Very good colour. Quite sturdy on the nose. But rich and concentrated and not a bit rustic. Fullish, meaty, very good grip. Plenty of depth and indeed complexity and elegance. This is very good, even within a 1990 context. Finishes very well. **(11/93)**

Now–2006   16.0

**Chambolle-Musigny   Les Charmes
Ponsot**

Raspberry flavoured. Intense. Concentrated. Very Chambolle. Balanced and very stylish. Lovely fruit. Very good ripe tannins. Very good. **(09/92)**

1998–2008   16.0

Chapelle-Chambertin   Ponsot

Good colour. Lovely fruit. Raspberries and mulberries and a hint of chocolate and black cherries. Has recovered very well from bottling. Subtle. Fullish. Balanced. Positive finish. Very stylish. Very long. Very good tannins. Very good indeed. **(09/92)**

1998–2010   17.0

Chapelle-Chambertin   Rossignol-Trapet

Fine colour. Good nose. Very rich and concentrated. Heaps of fruit. Round and fat and ample. Good grip. Enormously seductive. Long. Very good indeed. **(09/92)**

2000–2015   17.0

Charmes-Chambertin   Hervé Arlaud

I think I prefer his Gevrey-Chambertin, Combottes. It seems richer. But this has good grip and plenty of concentration nevertheless. **(09/92)**

Now–2009   16.0

Charmes-Chambertin   Bernard Dugat-Py

Full colour. Rich meaty super concentrated nose. Full, powerful. Very good tannins. Good grip. More oaky. A lot of depth here. Old-viney creaminess. Serious. Very fine. **(09/92)**

2000–2015   18.5

**Charmes-Chambertin
Vincent Geantet-Ponsiot**

Very good colour. Lovely nose. Old-vine intensity. Very good tannins. Rich and almost chocolatey in its concentration. Very good grip. Full, ample, potentially voluptuous. He made 40 hl/ha. Fine. **(09/92)**

2000–2015   17.5

Charmes-Chambertin   Henri Perrot-Minot

Slightly extracted. But there is substance here. Good grip. On evolution the wine lacks a little flair but in its solid way is satisfactory enough. **(09/92)**

1998–2008   15.0

Charmes-Chambertin   Jean Raphet

Good colour. Slightly pinched on the nose. Rather artificial on the palate. The fruit seems soupy. Rather a concoction. Even worse than the Clos-de-la-Roche. **(05/93)**

Now–2006   12.5

Charmes-Chambertin   Christian Serafin

Very good colour. Full, rich and oaky on the nose. Not too dominated by the oak on the palate, like the 1989s. Slightly rigid. Medium-full. Ripe. Good grip. Just a little astringent. But fine rich plummy fruit. Very good plus. **(05/93)**

1998–2015   16.5

**Charmes-Chambertin   *Très Vieilles-Vignes*
Joseph Roty**

Good immature colour. Very oaky on the nose. Very much crushed primary fruit still. Less oaky on the palate, certainly at first. Fine grip. Lots of concentration. Full and intense. Tight at first, but rich, generous, succulent, ripe and voluptuous. Very fine tannins. Excellent. **(07/95)**

2000–2020   19.5

Chassagne-Montrachet   Camille Giroud

Firm, meaty, slightly *sauvage*. But balanced and ripe. Good. **(09/92)**

1998-2008   15.0

**Chassagne-Montrachet
Olivier Leflaive Frères**

Soft, ripe, elegant, balanced. But quite forward for a 1990. It has more style but less muscle than the usual Chassagnes. Perhaps just a bit slight. **(09/92)**

Now-2002   14.0

Chassagne-Montrachet   Bernard Morey

Ripe, concentrated, positive, chocolatey. An example of how good the vintage is. **(07/92)**

Now-2008   15.5

**Chassagne-Montrachet   *Vieilles-Vignes*
Bernard Morey**

Quite different in style. Much more flowery honey fruit. Youthful. Very, very rich. **(07/92)**

2000-2012   17.0

**Chassagne-Montrachet
Clos-de-la-Boudriotte   Ramonet**

Structured, ripe, concentrated, old-viney. Good grip. Long. Satisfying. This is very good. Fullish. Long. Subtle. **(09/92)**

1998-2012   16.0

Chorey-lès-Beaune   Michel Maillard et Fils

Good colour. Ripe, fullish; a straight, well-made example. Clean, balanced. Firm. Plenty of depth and life. **(05/93)**

Now-2007   14.0

Chorey-lès-Beaune   René Podechard

Good colour. The nose just a little closed. But on the palate the wine is rich, very well balanced, fullish, with lovely cool Pinot fruit and plenty of depth. Very very long. Just about ready. **(12/95)**

Now-2007   15.5

Chorey-lès-Beaune   Tollot-Beaut

Good colour. Still youthful. Nicely expansive, rich and pure as it expanded in the glass. A very good basic. Long and satisfying. Good. **(02/96)**

Now-2008   15.0

Clos-des-Lambrays   Saier

Medium-full colour. Somewhat raw and closed on the nose and palate. An inflexible wine. Fruity but not concentrated. Fullish but lacking fat. Adolescent? **(06/92)**

Now-2003   14.0

Clos-de-la-Roche   Jean Raphet

Good colour. A touch of filter paper on nose and palate. Ripe, medium-full, good style.

Reasonable balance. But rather overwhelmed by the astringency and dryness. **(05/93)**

Now-2006   13.0

Clos-de-la-Roche   Armand Rousseau

Medium colour. Soft, accessible, plump, a little jammy. Good wine on the palate. Not a blockbuster but lovely stylish balanced Pinot fruit. This is going to evolve soon for a top 1990. Complex finish. Long. Very good indeed but not really serious. **(05/93)**

Now-2012   17.0

Clos-de-la-Roche   *Vieilles-Vignes*   Ponsot

Very good colour - even a bit inky. Odd vegetably-caramelly-chocolate nose. Individual. Certainly old-viney. There is concentration here. Curiously seductive. A fullish fat opulent wine. Very, very ripe. Good balance. Curious, but individual. Very good indeed but not great. **(05/93)**

Now-2012   17.0

Clos-Saint-Denis   *Vieilles-Vignes*   Ponsot

Slightly rounder, slightly sweeter, slightly more feminine and velvety than the Clos-de-la-Roche. Great fruit. Very harmonious. Very very long. Perhaps even better than the Clos-de-la-Roche this year. Fine plus. **(05/93)**

1998-2005   18.0

Clos-de-Tart   Mommessin

Good colour. Hard nose. Slightly lumpy. The stems show. Ripe and luscious and full and concentrated. But it lacks grace. The class of a *grand cru* is absent. Pedestrian. **(05/93)**

1998-2010   14.0

Clos-de-Vougeot   René Arnoux

Medium-full colour. Slightly sweet on the nose. Medium body, wishy-washy, short. Will fall apart. Disappointing. **(06/92)**

Drink soon   14.0

Clos-de-Vougeot   Château de la Tour

Good colour. Fresh nose. But not a lot of real depth and complexity. Ripe and oaky. Supple. Not a lot of structure. Not a great deal of acidity. It is a plump wine. But curiously anonymous. **(05/93)**

Now-2003   14.0

Clos-de-Vougeot   Joseph Drouhin

Splendid colour. Marvellous nose. Very firm, and concentrated, and very classy multi-dimensional Pinot. Full, tannic, rich and backward on the palate. More awkward than adolescent. Best on the finish. Intense, very long and multi-dimensional. Super fruit. Very good acidity. Very long. Fine. **(10/94)**

1998-2020   17.5

Clos-de-Vougeot Drouhin-Laroze

Rich, fat, ample and oaky on the nose. An attractive fleshy seductive wine. Yet another example of how successful the Clos-de-Vougeots are in 1990. Lovely fruit, ample and delicious. Fine. **(09/92)**

2000-2012   17.5

Clos-de-Vougeot Clos-Frantin-Bichot

Good colour. A bit lumpy on the nose. Smells of geraniums. Rather clumsy on the palate. Fullish, some fruit. But no finesse. A bit astringent at the end. Poor. **(05/93)**

Drink soon   12.0

Clos-de-Vougeot Camille Giroud

Ripe and stylish. Cherry-raspberry fruit. Good grip and substance. This is long and complex on the finish. Very good. **(09/92)**

Now-2010   16.0

Clos-de-Vougeot Alfred Haegelen-Jayer

Good. Not that expressive on the nose. Fat and meaty. Not that startling on the palate either. It is a little closed. Best of all on the finish. Fullish. Good tannin. Respectable acidity but not great grip. Ample fruit though. Old-viney. Long and satisfying. Plenty of depth. Very good but not great. **(09/92)**

1998-2008   16.0

Clos-de-Vougeot L'Héritier-Guyot

Full colour. Quite sturdy on the nose, but a touch rustic. Reasonable acidity. Quite full. But a little lumpy, not very stylish. Only fair. **(12/95)**

1998-2005   13.0

Clos-de-Vougeot Alain Hudelot-Noëllat

Very good colour. Really quite marked by the oak on the nose. On the palate this is not too dominated. Medium-full, ripe, stylish, ample and accessible. Rich, opulent. Very good plus. **(05/93)**

1998-2018   16.5

Clos-de-Vougeot Louis Jadot

Good colour. This has a lovely nose. Toasted. Oaky, caramelly, rich and old-vine concentration. Curiously, even honeyed. This is brilliant. Full, rich and very concentrated. Old-viney and with splendid intensity and backbone. Very very long and lovely. Excellent. **(05/93)**

2000-2025   19.0

Clos-de-Vougeot Labouré-Roi

Medium-full colour. Ripe, gentle, pleasantly fruity, quite elegant nose. In a Chambolle way there is depth here. Medium-full. Good concentration. Good structure. This is balanced and has good intensity. Very good plus. **(06/92)**

Now-2007   16.5

Clos-de-Vougeot Chantal Lescure

Medium-full colour. Rich and chocolatey but how much elegance on the nose? An element of raisins here. On the palate a little raw, a little one-dimensional and a little short. **(06/92)**

Now-2000   13.5

Clos-de-Vougeot Méo-Camuzet

Medium-full colour. Good fresh, aromatic, sandalwoody nose. Medium to medium-full. Good youthful intensity and vigour. Good grip. Fine ripe fruit but not quite the power and concentration of a 1990. More 1989-ish in character. **(10/93)**

Now-2007   16.0

Clos-de-Vougeot Jean Raphet

Medium colour. Lightish on nose and a bit weedy on the palate for a 1990. There is little here. And it is short. Poor. **(05/93)**

Now-1998   12.0

**Clos-de-Vougeot Le Grand-Maupertuis
Anne et François Gros**

Good colour. Fat, concentrated, old-viney, opulent nose. An animal wine. Adolescent at present. Fullish. Tannic. This has a lot of depth. Very good finish. Fine. **(06/92)**

Now-2007   17.5

Corton Bouchard Père et Fils

Medium-full colour. Closed, firm, but seemingly a bit four-square on the nose. This lacks a bit of personality and depth on the palate. Slightly raw but nothing very much underneath. Good at best. **(06/92)**

Now-2002   15.0

Corton Champy

Good colour. Ripe nose. Plummy, concentrated and with finesse. No hardness. Ripe and rich on the palate too. Yet the follow-through is multi-dimensional and shows impeccable balance. Excellent. **(05/93)**

Now-2009   15.5

Corton Michel Maillard et Fils

Good colour. Ample nose. But slightly dry. Slightly lacking concentration. This is rather coarse, but it has good grip and intensity. Rather lumpy. Not enough concentration and grip. **(12/95)**

1998-2005   13.0

Corton Bressandes Chandon-de-Briailles

Very good colour. This has a slightly leaner than their Clos du Roi, less *gibier* nose, but has more depth, better class and is better balanced. Rather more closed but better grip and more dimension. This is going to need time. Lovely complex finish. Very good indeed. **(09/92)**

2000-2015   17.0

Corton Bressandes Dubreuil-Fontaine

Good colour. Ripe, plump, stylish nose. Lovely fruit. Impressive. Complex. Very good Pinot. This has balance and length. Very good. **(05/93)**

1998-2015   15.0

Corton Bressandes Antonin Guyon

Medium-full colour. Good new oak here and good stylish, balanced fruit. Medium-full. But soft and round, not a blockbuster. This is fine. Lovely style. Concentrated, ripe, harmonious and complex. Long and lovely. **(06/92)**

Now-2007   17.5

Corton Bressandes Prin

Good colour. Quite ample on the nose. A touch of new wood. It is rather inky and rather coarse, and for the vintage it is a bit of a disgrace. But there is something here. Fat fruit, damson flavours. Good grip. **(12/95)**

1998-2005   12.5

Corton Bressandes Tollot-Beaut

Good colour. A little burnt and alcoholic, even stemmy on the nose. Raw on the palate. This seems rather astringent. There is some good wine here underneath. But it is poorly made. Lumpy. **(05/93)**

Now-2004   12.5

Corton Clos-des-Cortons Joseph Faiveley

Very good colour. Still very youthful. Closed, new oaky nose. A very big wine currently adolescent. Enormous concentration and depth. Very very rich. Splendid grip. Excellent. **(09/94)**

2001-2025   19.0

**Corton Clos-du-Roi
Chandon-de-Briailles**

Very good colour. More closed but more aristocratic. Hidden but on the finish very concentrated, very good intensity. Fullish, rich. Good grip. Persistent finish. Fine. **(09/92)**

2000-2015   17.5

**Corton Clos-du-Roi Roland Remoissenet
Père et Fils**

Slightly closed on the nose. A bit adolescent. Ripe fruit. Medium-full body. This is a little mixed-up and not showing at its best. Slightly hard. But rich underneath. Good backbone. Very good but not great. **(05/93)**

Now-2008   16.0

Corton Clos-du-Roi Comte Senard

Fine colour. Ripe and oaky on the nose. No particular Accad spice any more. Very clean and pure. Fine acidity and intensity. Fullish. Less adolescent than Faiveley's. Fine. **(09/94)**

2000-2015   17.5

Corton Clos-du-Roi Hippolyte Thevenot

Good colour. Ample oaky nose. Medium-full. Good grip. A slight lack of amplitude and fat. But good intensity. Quite long but a little lean. Good. **(10/94)**

Now-2007   15.0

**Corton Maréchaudes
Chandon-de-Briailles**

Very good colour. Rich and concentrated. Good oak elements. This has plenty of depth. Shows well. Lovely fruit. Fullish, fat and concentrated. Finishes well. Very good. **(09/92)**

1999-2009   16.0

Corton Pougets Louis Jadot

Good colour. Slightly raw still on the nose. A bit austere. More depth and generosity as it developed. Medium-full body. Good grip. Slightly caramelly Pinot but fat and rich and concentrated. This is long and succulent. Very good plus. Several other similar notes. **(05/93)**

Now-2010   16.5

Echézeaux Georges Clerget

This is good. Plenty of ripeness, richness, depth and style. Good oak. Good structure. **(07/92)**

Now-2010   15.0

Echézeaux Joseph Drouhin

New oak. Very ripe and rich. Lovely almost Musigny feminine-ness. Very very long. **(05/93)**

Now-2012   17.5

Echézeaux Dujac

Fullish colour. Fat, rich, full-bodied nose. Very ripe almost *coulis*-ed fruit. Full on the palate. Quite a lot of tannin. This is very rich and concentrated and potentially fine - at least - but currently is adolescent. Lovely meaty finish though. **(03/96)**

2000-2015   17.5

Echézeaux René Engel

Very good colour. Just a bit sweeter, fatter and more adolescent than his Vosne-Romanée, Les Brûlées. Less on form. Good grip. Surely at least as good. **(05/93)**

1999-2019   17.0

Echézeaux Joseph Faiveley

Good colour. Closed on the nose. A bit dumb. On the palate this is really quite soft. Ripe and abundant almost in a 1989 sense but with better acidity. Long and subtle. But without the backbone of a typical 1990. Yet certainly classy, certainly very good indeed. **(05/93)**

Now-2012   17.0

Echézeaux   Jean Fournier

Good colour. This is rich and fat and not bad at all. Medium-full. Supple and generous. Good grip. Good finish. Good. **(12/95)**

Now-2012   **15.0**

Echézeaux   Camille Giroud

Cuvée 1: From Thierry Vigot. Rich, fat and substantial. A meaty concentrated wine. Fine quality. **(09/92)**

1999-2012   **17.5**

Echézeaux   Camille Giroud

Cuvée 2: From Georges Clerget. This is a little less substantial (than the Echézeaux from Thierry Vigot) but more finesse. Good style. Very good grip. Long and fine. A mixture of the two was even better. **(09/92)**

1998-2010   **17.5**

Echézeaux   Alfred Haegelen-Jayer

Medium-full colour. Ripe, opulent and fat, new oaky. There is a lot of quality here. Brilliant quality here. Enormous depth and concentration on the palate. Full. Very very rich. Very good grip. Very fine indeed. **(06/92)**

1999-2013   **18.5**

Echézeaux   Olivier Leflaive Frères

Rich, concentrated, a lot of depth. Very good indeed. **(09/93)**

1998-2010   **17.0**

Echézeaux   Mugneret-Gibourg

Very good colour. Soft, plump, oaky. This is very good. Fullish, ample, seductive. But in the last analysis, it doesn't quite have enough grip and therefore complexity at the end for more than very good plus. **(05/93)**

1998-2012   **16.5**

Fixin   Les Chenevrières   Alain Guyard

Good colour. A bit suave. Not much style anyway. The tannins being a little rustic. Reasonable balance. Not bad. **(02/94)**

Now-2002   **13.5**

Fixin   Clos-Napoléon   Pierre Gelin

Good colour. Rich, fat oaky nose. Full, meaty, not too *sauvage*. Fat and voluptuous. Good black fruit. Touch of chocolate and leather. Good grip. Very good. **(10/94)**

1998-2010   **16.0**

Fixin   Les Crais   Vincent et Denis Berthaut

Very good colour. Rich sturdy nose. Lovely rich palate. Not really that elegant (1992 is more stylish) but fullish and concentrated. Now softening up. Slightly ungainly. But the quality of the vintage comes through. Fat and ripe and long on the finish. **(12/95)**

1998-2012   **16.0**

Fixin   Les Hervelets   Bart

Medium colour. A bit hard and rigid on the nose. There is good rich fruit on the palate. And this is succulent and balanced. Medium to medium-full. Lacks a little grace, but the quality of the vintage pulls it through. Give it another year. Quite good. **(12/95)**

Now-2005   **14.0**

Gevrey-Chambertin   Pierre André

New wood, but underneath cheap and thin. Nothing here. **(09/92)**

Now-2005   **11.5**

Gevrey-Chambertin   Denis Bachelet

Good colour. Marvellously concentrated nose. Quite delicate for a Gevrey - as Bachelet's style always is - but really very elegant and complex. Medium-full. Very rounded tannins. Lovely raspberry-blackberry fruit. Slightly bitter at the end but very long and complex. Splendid for a village wine. **(05/93)**

Now-2012   **16.5**

Gevrey-Chambertin   Philippe Battachi, Clos-Noir

Good colour. Plump nose, with a touch of coffee and toffee. No hard edges. A touch rubbery - whole-grape maceration. Medium body. Ample, a little tannin. Good balance and ripe plummy fruit. But somewhat anonymous. Nothing specially Gevrey about it. Nor any real class. Yet clean. Quite good at best. **(02/95)**

Now-2004   **14.0**

Gevrey-Chambertin   Alain Burguet

Good colour. Rich and clean and plump on the nose. It is still full of rich, puppy-fat fruit. Not having gone into its shell yet. Fullish. Very good. **(06/94)**

Now-2010   **16.0**

Gevrey-Chambertin   Champy

Firm, rich and meaty. Finishes well. **(05/93)**

Now-2004   **14.5**

Gevrey-Chambertin   Claude Dugat

Good colour. This has begun to close in a bit. Fresh fruit but a little astringent at the end. The acidity could have been a bit higher. Good but not exceptional. **(09/92)**

Now-2005   **15.0**

Gevrey-Chambertin   Joseph Faiveley

Very good colour. Lovely ripe nose. This has very lovely fruit. Not as chunky as the Clos-de-la-Maréchale but more intensity, more grip. Very, very long indeed. Fullish, very good tannins. Very concentrated. Lovely. **(05/93)**

Now-2009   **17.0**

Gevrey-Chambertin   Dominique Gallois

This is good for a village wine. Medium body. Stylish. Worth investigating. **(09/92)**

Now-2005   15.0

Gevrey-Chambertin   Jean-Pierre Guyard

Good colour. The nose isn't bad but the palate a little stewed and clumsy. Over-extracted. But the fruit is quite nice and the finish quite positive. Not bad plus. **(02/94)**

Now-2003   12.5

Gevrey-Chambertin   Antonin Guyon

Medium to medium-full colour. Somewhat bland on the nose. This can't be a *premier cru*? Sweet and fruity. Pleasant but short. Forward. Uninspiring. **(06/92)**

Drink soon   13.0

Gevrey-Chambertin   Philippe Rossignol

Very good colour. Medium body. Not a lot of tannin. Plump, blackberry fruit. Easy to drink. Clean, stylish, pleasant. But not that much depth. **(03/94)**

Now-2002   14.5

Gevrey-Chambertin   Armand Rousseau

Medium to medium-full colour. A little over-blown on the nose. Curious. Lacks the style of the above. Lacks the grip too. This is medium-bodied. Plump and accessible. But the length and complexity aspect are not better than good. **(05/93)**

Now-2006   15.0

Gevrey-Chambertin   Gérard Seguin

Medium colour. Good use of oak. A little sweet but quite good at the very least for a village. Perhaps a little lightweight. Quite stylish. **(09/92)**

Drink soon   14.0

Gevrey-Chambertin   Christian Serafin

I compared this with his Bourgogne *rouge*. More fruit, more structure, more backbone, more class. A good example. **(05/93)**

Now-2006   15.0

**Gevrey-Chambertin   *Vieilles-Vignes*
Alain Burguet**

Good colour. Ample, rich and succulent on the nose. Very promising. Old-vine fruit here. Medium-full. Some tannin evident. This has depth too. Concentrated and plummy and complex. Ripe. Long. Still backward. Will develop. Lots of finesse. **(05/93)**

1998-2015   17.5

**Gevrey-Chambertin   Les Cazetiers
Bruno Clair**

Medium-full colour. A little SO₂ on the nose. Seems a little flat underneath. The oak is a little toasted. Better on the palate. Medium-full. Good grip. Ripe tannins. This has good fat and intensity. Long. Stylish. Well-made. Very good plus. Several notes. **(05/93)**

Now-2015   16.5

**Gevrey-Chambertin   Les Cazetiers
Joseph Faiveley**

Very good colour. Splendid nose. Masses of fruit. Real concentration. Full, rich and abundant. Firm still. Excellent tannin. Very well balanced. A backward wine but with a splendid follow-through. Very good indeed. **(05/93)**

1998-2015   17.5

**Gevrey-Chambertin   Clos-du-Fonteny
Bruno Clair**

Good colour. Rich, ripe, round, but a little hollow on the follow-through compared with his Gevrey-Chambertin, Cazetiers. Reasonable finish though. **(09/92)**

Now-2010   15.5

**Gevrey-Chambertin   Clos-Saint-Jacques
Bruno Clair**

Fine colour. Richer, more old-viney than the Cazetiers. Fuller and more concentrated but more adolescent. The finish is excellent though. Lots of depth. Gently oaky. Lovely. Several notes. **(09/92)**

2000-2015   18.5

**Gevrey-Chambertin   Clos-Saint-Jacques
Louis Jadot**

Fine colour. Delicious nose: intense Pinot fruit, lots of depth, good touch of oak. Fullish, rich, balanced, very elegant. Lots of dimension. Fine quality. **(10/94)**

Now-2015   17.5

**Gevrey-Chambertin   Clos-Saint-Jacques
Armand Rousseau**

Good colour. Firm, full, voluptuous, oaky, old-viney. Really velvety potentially. Animal and individual and complex. Full, very very intense. Low *rendement* here. Full but brilliant tannins. Very lovely lush opulent example. **(05/93)**

1999-2020   19.0

**Gevrey-Chambertin   Combottes
Pierre Amiot et Fils**

Medium-full and quite rich, with a good structure. Finishes better than it starts. Good plus. **(09/92)**

Now-2005   15.5

**Gevrey-Chambertin   Combottes
Hervé Arlaud**

Good nose. Good new oaky base. Rich, fat. This is ripe, balanced and fat with good underlying thrust. Clean and concentrated. Very good acidity. Very good indeed. **(09/92)**

Now–2015   **17.0**

Gevrey-Chambertin   Les Corbeaux
Denis Bachelet

Medium colour. A little mint-pine-needles on
the nose at first. Odd. Old-viney on the palate.
Medium-full, fat, quite chocolatey. Fullish and
individual. Good grip and intensity. Very good
indeed. **(05/93)**

1998–2015   **17.0**

Gevrey-Chambertin   Les Fontenys
René Jacquesson

Medium-full colour. Awkward nose. Lacks
style. Vegetal. Coarse and artisanal on the palate.
Raw and edgy. Little merit here. **(06/92)**

Drink soon   **11.0**

Gevrey-Chambertin   Les Fontenys
Joseph Roty

Good colour. Rich, slightly cooked fruit on the
nose. Plum tart and prunes. Plump and spicy.
Ample on the palate. Fullish, quite oaky. This is
good, but I wouldn't call it great by any means,
even within the *premier cru* context. Hard and
brûlé on the follow-through. A bit rigid. Ripe
and balanced. Finishes well. But will it satis-
factorily round off? **(11/94)**

Now–2004   **15.5**

Gevrey-Chambertin   Lavaux-Saint-Jacques
Claude Dugat

Here again I have to say I am not struck. There
is plenty of ripe rich fruit here, but a lack of
grip. A bit *figué*. Good but not great. **(09/92)**

Now–2005   **15.0**

Gevrey-Chambertin   Poissenot
Humbert Frères

Thin and raw. This is dreadful. **(09/92)**

Drink up   **10.0**

Grands-Echézeaux   Joseph Drouhin

Very good colour. Marvellous nose. Plump.
Violets, blackcurrants. Very complex, very ripe.
Not a bit sweet. Full, structured, masculine.
Excellent tannins. Marvellous fruit and excellent
acidity. This is very fine indeed. Real intensity.
Real quality and class. Very very long and
complex on the finish. **(05/93)**

1999–2019   **18.5**

Grands-Echézeaux   René Engel

More classy, more ample, more concentrated
and more depth than the Echézeaux. And the
finish is longer and much more positive. This is
very fine. **(05/93)**

1999–2019   **18.0**

Grands-Echézeaux   Roland Remoissenet
Père et Fils

Fine colour. Lovely rich meaty nose. Fullish,
ripe, fat and ample. Lovely opulent style. Very
good grip. Lovely finish. Fine plus. **(05/93)**

Now–2012   **18.0**

Grands-Echézeaux   Romanée-Conti

Fine fullish immature colour. Rich fat oaky
nose. This has a lot of depth. Fullish, mellow
and lovely. Really fine and stylish Pinot fruit.
Beautifully balanced. Fine. **(03/93)**

1998–2015   **17.5**

Griotte-Chambertin   Joseph Drouhin

Fullish colour. Ripe, youthful, blackfruity nose.
This has good concentration and an element of
sur-maturité. Fullish. Backward. A bit awkward at
present but a lot of quality here. Fine. **(06/92)**

1998–2010   **17.5**

Griotte-Chambertin   Ponsot

This is very good indeed. Much better than the
Latricières. Fullish, quite structured. Cherry-
flavoured like the Clos-de-la-Roche. Backward.
Very good acidity. Fine. **(09/93)**

1999–2010   **17.5**

La Romanée   Bouchard Père et Fils

Not an enormous colour. For a 1990 this is really
a bit ungenerous on the nose. At first an atypical
1990. The fruit is less *coulis*-ed. Yet certainly ripe,
perfumed and ample. On the palate some tannin
and a slight lack of amplitude. But long, definitive,
individual and undeniably classy. Fine finish. Fine
quality. **(02/95)**

2000–2015   **17.5**

Latricières-Chambertin   Joseph Faiveley

Fine colour. Lovely nose. Marvellous complex
concentrated fruit. Not a blockbuster. Very rich.
Chocolatey and gently oaky. Fine grip. Very long.
Real class. Fine quality. Lovely finish. **(05/93)**

1998–2018   **18.0**

Latricières-Chambertin   Ponsot

Medium colour. Quite intense on the nose. But
something lightweight about it at the same time.
Enough acidity? Lovely soft fruit. *Tendre*. Not
quite the grip that it could have after the
Chapelle-Chambertin, perhaps. Very good but
not better. **(09/93)**

Now–2006   **16.0**

Latricières-Chambertin   Rossignol-Trapet

Good full colour. Very closed nose. Oaky,
austere, full but concentrated on the palate.
Backward but very good intensity. A lot of
depth here. Lovely finish. Fine. **(09/93)**

1998–2015   **17.5**

Marsannay   Clos-du-Roy   Régis Bouvier

Good colour. Ample, rich nose. But a slight lack of style. This is rich and fruity and very well balanced on the palate. Fullish. Still with some unresolved tannins. Good but lacks the finesse it should have. Finishes positively. Slightly solid. Quite good. **(12/95)**

1998-2006   14.0

Marsannay   Echézeaux   Marc Brocot

Good colour. Fragrant. Stylish, round, new oaky nose. Attractive. Medium to medium-full, balanced, ripe and charming. This has depth and elegance. A lovely example. Not too big for its boots. **(12/95)**

Now-2002   15.5

Marsannay   Les Grosses-Têtes   Bruno Clair

This is more adolescent than his Langerois, but seems to have less fat, but the finish is very good. This is more austere. More in the style of the 1988s. But very promising. **(09/92)**

Now-2005   14.5

Marsannay   Les Langerois   Bruno Clair

Fine colour. This is rich, with very good tannin. Lovely ripe fruit and very well balanced. **(09/92)**

Now-2005   14.5

Marsannay   Les Vaudenelles   Bruno Clair

Plus tendre than Les Grosses-Têtes. Less to it. Ripe and stylish and balanced. Finishes well. But the less good of the three (Langerois, Grosses-Têtes, Vaudenelles). **(09/92)**

Now-2000   13.5

Mazis-Chambertin   Hubert Camus

This is rich and succulent and most appealing. Lovely blackberry fruit. Very good acidity. This will hold up. 100 per cent wood doesn't show too much. Very good quality. **(09/92)**

Now-2008   16.0

Mazis-Chambertin   Joseph Drouhin

Good colour. Oaky, rich, lush nose. Ample, rich, fat and fullish. Very lovely Pinot here. This is lush and succulent. Plenty of depth. Expansive, even voluptuous. Fine plus. **(05/93)**

1999-2015   18.0

Mazis-Chambertin   André Esmonin

Fine colour again. Quite closed on the nose. Firm, rich and concentrated. Very fine grip. This is splendid. Excellent fruit and real depth. **(09/92)**

2000-2015   18.5

Mazis-Chambertin   Harmand-Geoffroy

Good colour. Positive, rich Pinot Noir. Succulent and ripe on the palate. Blackberries

and raspberries. Real summer-pudding flavours. Medium-full. Good acidity. But in the final analysis it lacks breed and flair. **(05/93)**

Now-2010   16.0

Monthélie   Bernard Boisson

Good colour. (No stems.) Rich, full, sturdy and quite tannic but very good fruit on the follow-through. Good style as well. Shows how good 1990 is even in the lesser corners. **(06/94)**

Now-2005   14.0

Monthélie   Paul Garaudet

Very good colour. Rich, fat, black-cherry and chocolate nose, with a good base of new oak underneath. This is very stylish. On the palate medium-full. Good ripe tannins. Good grip. Plenty of dimension and depth. Fresh. Elegant. Long. Not a bit rustic. Very good. Especially for a Monthélie. **(02/94)**

Now-2010   15.5

Monthélie   Pierre Morey

Rather thin. Not a patch on his Meursault *rouge*. Yet the fruit is quite balanced and stylish. Not bad but not exciting. **(02/94)**

Drink soon   13.0

Morey-Saint-Denis   Hervé Arlaud

Medium colour but youthful-looking. Black-berry and black-cherry nose and palate. Engaging and fruity. Medium body. Very ripe. This is very good for a village wine. Slightly suave perhaps. **(10/94)**

Now-2006   15.0

Morey-Saint-Denis   Dujac

Medium body. Ripe, open, slightly caramelly nose. Doesn't seem to be a lot of depth here. Better on the palate. Medium body. Not a lot of depth or tannin. Indeed more Chambolle than Morey, but ripe and fruity, fresh and clean and charming. Good but not great. But very good for a village example. **(05/93)**

Now-2004   15.0

Morey-Saint-Denis   Jean-Pierre Duprey

Reasonable colour. Quite fresh. A little sweaty on the nose. Medium body. Spicy. Plump. A little artisanal. Balanced but not a lot of depth. Nor much in the way of elegance. Pedestrian. Quite advanced. **(11/94)**

Now-1999   13.5

Morey-Saint-Denis   Olivier Leflaive Frères

This is a little slight. A bit empty. Pretty but forward at best. **(09/92)**

Now-2000   13.5

Morey-Saint-Denis   Henri Perrot-Minot

Medium body. Gently oaky. A touch slight and

a touch lacking grip, but attractive and pleasant. Will evolve quite soon. **(09/92)**

Now-2000   **14.0**

Morey-Saint-Denis   Ponsot
Young Clos-de-la-Roche vines. Medium body. Classy nose. But a little lightweight at the end. Slightly tails off. Good fruit. Balanced but lacks a little intensity. Classier than their Gevrey-Chambertin but more forward. **(09/93)**

Now-2002   **14.0**

Morey-Saint-Denis   Jean Raphet
Good colour. Round, plump, ripe, stylish. Good concentration for a village wine. Good grip too. This shows well. Very good. **(09/92)**

Now-2005   **16.0**

Morey-Saint-Denis   La Riotte
Henri Perrot-Minot
Fine colour. Rich, plump, fat nose. Well-covered tannins. Just a hint of oak. Good grip. Fullish, very velvety. Long. Very good plus. **(03/95)**

Now-2007   **16.5**

Morey-Saint-Denis   En la Rue de Vergy
Rossignol-Trapet
Good colour. Some pepper here on the nose. But there is quite concentrated ripe fruit and good structure underneath. Medium-full, fat, oaky, very ripe, even a bit sweet. The finish is quite long and shows good style and complexity. Very good plus. **(05/93)**

Now-2011   **16.5**

Le Musigny   Joseph Drouhin
Fullish colour. Rich and concentrated on the nose. Breed and depth here. There is an element of oxidisation here but I think it is merely adolescent. Firm, full, concentrated. Very lovely finish. Fine plus. **(06/92)**

Now-2010   **18.0**

Le Musigny   Georges Roumier
Beautiful intensity here. Rather less structured. Round, marvellously concentrated and persistent fruit. Full. Much more accessible. Really quite tannic for a Musigny. But not a bit dense. This is just a very concentrated wine. Very very long and multi-dimensional. Lovely. **(09/92)**

2000-2015   **18.5**

Le Musigny   Comte Georges de Vogüé
Excellent colour. Brilliant nose! This is super concentrated. Very good oak integration. Great intensity. Multi-dimensional. Essence of raspberry. Full, some tannin. You don't see the oak at all, such is the concentration of the wine. Needs time. Excellent. *Grand vin* indeed. Four

notes: all agree this is one of the wines of the vintage. **(05/93)**

2000-2030   **20.0**

Nuits-Saint-Georges   Champy
Ripe, rich, with a spicy cedary caramelly background. Attractive. But not quite as long as I would have liked. **(05/93)**

Now-2001   **14.5**

Nuits-Saint-Georges   Robert Chevillon
Good colour. Rich, fat and caramelly on the nose. Quite soft for a Nuits-Saint-Georges 1990. A bit of new oak and butterscotch here. Quite full. Good grip. A touch raw and astringent. The finish isn't as elegant or as ample as the attack. Good. **(05/93)**

Now-2004   **15.0**

Nuits-Saint-Georges   Henri Gouges
Good colour. Backward, ripe, concentrated nose. Stylish for a Nuits-Saint-Georges. Fullish, rich and meaty. Good fat, good grip. This has depth and a typically Nuits-Saint-Georges ample gaminess. Finishes well. Very good. **(05/93)**

Now-2007   **16.0**

Nuits-Saint-Georges   Henri Jayer
Medium-full colour. Soft nose. But a little anaemic. Where is the 1990 backbone? Soft, a little lactic. Reasonable acidity but no backbone, no grip, no richness. Unexciting. A little oaky. **(05/93)**

Now-2001   **13.5**

Nuits-Saint-Georges   Méo-Camuzet
Good colour. Very strongly oaky on the nose. Does this dominate? Difficult to see the *terroir* here. Medium-full, new oaky, good grip. Quite a soft wine really. Open and attractive. But lacks real depth and complexity. **(05/93)**

Now-2003   **15.0**

Nuits-Saint-Georges   Au-Bas-de-Combe
Jean Tardy
Very good colour. Classy for a village Nuits-Saint-Georges. Good oak. Fat and ripe. Plenty of elegance. Plenty of depth. Very Vosne in character. Lovely fruit. Medium-full. Very good. **(03/94)**

Now-2009   **15.5**

Nuits-Saint-Georges   Aux Boudots
Jean Grivot
Very good colour. Slightly hidden nose. Very rich and succulent. Ripe and fullish but without the noticeable sturdiness of the Gouges. Intense, velvety. Very rich. Good oak. Lovely fruit. Very good indeed. **(09/93)**

Now-2012   **17.0**

Nuits-Saint-Georges   Aux Boudots
Méo-Camuzet

Good colour. Very oaky. Rather a rigid wine at present. Fullish, meaty. Four-square. There is backbone and depth here. Good tannin and fruit. Good but not great. (05/93)

Now-2010   15.0

Nuits-Saint-Georges   Les Chaignots
Dr Georges Mugneret

Good colour. Rich, firm, fat, full, slightly spicy nose with a touch of oak. Fullish on the palate. Very stylish. Lovely concentrated fruit. This is very fine for a Nuits. Not a bit lumpy. Lovely. And very very long and complex at the end. (05/93)

1998-2018   17.5

Nuits-Saint-Georges   Clos-des-Argillières
Daniel Rion et Fils

Good colour. Firm, full, still a little brutal. But certainly with plenty of ripe fruit underneath. This has a lot more depth and class than the Grandes-Vignes but it is more adolescent. Very good. (05/93)

1999-2015   16.0

Nuits-Saint-Georges   Clos-de-l'Arlot
Arlot

Medium colour. Soft, fruity and seductive, but for a 1990 it lacks a bit of real richness and substance. Good but not great. Several notes. (09/92)

Now-2004   15.0

Nuits-Saint-Georges   Clos-des-Corvées
Champy

Fragrant nose. Ripe, quite firm. Medium-full. Good follow-through. Stylish and balanced. Very good. (05/93)

Now-2010   15.5

Nuits-Saint-Georges   Clos-des-Corvées
Louis Jadot

Medium-full colour. Firm nose. Good depth and backbone here. A little evidence of the stalks. Some oak. Medium body. Ripe and spicy. The attack is a bit mixed-up but the finish has depth. This will improve. Good plus. (05/93)

Now-2006   15.5

Nuits-Saint-Georges
Clos-des-Forêts-Saint-Georges   Arlot

Good colour. A little evolution. A little raw on the nose. It seems to lack a bit of fat and richness, but it is quite spicy. A touch of new oak in evidence. It seemed to improve with aeration. Good succulence on the palate. Fullish. Rich. Good but not exactly elegant. Several notes. (09/92)

Now-2007   15.0

Nuits-Saint-Georges   Clos-de-la-Maréchale
Joseph Faiveley

Very good colour. Very rich, concentrated backward nose. Adolescent at present. Ripe and rich and slightly earthy on the attack. Quite structured. Fullish and tannic. Very good follow-through. Super finish. Very good. (05/93)

1998-2008   16.0

Nuits-Saint-Georges   Clos-des-Porrets
Henri Gouges

Very good colour. Lovely nose. Very concentrated fruit. Definitive Nuits-Saint-Georges. Quite a lot of backbone, even sturdy. Backward. Slightly adolescent. Fullish. Some tannin. Slightly rude but with marvellous rich fruit underneath. Very good grip. Lots of potential. Very long. Very rich. Very good indeed. (09/93)

1998-2015   17.0

Nuits-Saint-Georges   Les Damodess
Christian Gavignet-Bethanie et Filles

Cool, violet-cachou nose. Good colour. This is better than his 1991 but it is not very concentrated. Slightly hard in the middle. Lacks distinction. (12/95)

Now-2003   13.0

Nuits-Saint-Georges   Les Damodes
Chantal Lescure

Good colour. Plump, somewhat· four-square nose. Ripe, balanced new oaky palate. Not a wine of great elegance but rich and substantial and satisfying enough. Good plus. (06/92)

Now-2004   15.5

Nuits-Saint-Georges   Les Didiers
Hospices de Nuits, Champy

Quite oaky. Firm, rich, meaty. Some tannin. A touch burly. Quite a high toast. Difficult to see the finesse. (05/93)

Now-2007   14.5

Nuits-Saint-Georges   Grandes-Vignes
Daniel Rion et Fils

Good colour. A rich, almost sweet, sturdy sort of wine. Fullish. Perhaps not the greatest of elegance but ripe and attractive. Meaty. Good. (05/93)

1998-2010   15.0

Nuits-Saint-Georges   Les Hauts-Poirets
Jayer-Gilles

Very good colour. Oaky nose. But a lot of concentration as well. Medium-full. Fat, ripe and spicy. Good blackberry fruit. Quite a firm solid wine. Does it lack a bit of fat and zip at the end? (05/93)

1998-2012   15.0

Nuits-Saint-Georges Aux Murgers
Yves et André Chopin

Good colour. Rich oaky nose. This is a lot more sophisticated than the 1993. A little extracted though. Full, structured, plenty of concentrated fruit. Very good cassis-blackberry flavours. Very good grip. This has plenty going for it. Still youthful. Good plus. **(12/95)**

2000-2012   15.5

Nuits-Saint-Georges Aux Murgers
Méo-Camuzet

Good colour. Rich, ripe, round and oaky on the nose. Rather dominated by the oak, but not too much and not as much as the 1989. On the palate rich fullish and round and concentrated. Succulent. But just a little top heavy. Good plus. **(05/93)**

Now-2012   15.5

Nuits-Saint-Georges Les Pruliers
Château de Bligny

Magnum. Good colour. Full chocolatey, rich nose. Rather hard and with a burnt taste on the palate. There is quite a lot of tannin here but the tannins are rather coarse. Over-extracted. Spoiling the good fruit that was inevitable in this vintage. **(12/95)**

1999-2012   13.5

Nuits-Saint-Georges Les Pruliers
Henri Gouges

Good colour. Ripe, plump, blackberry nose. Good backbone and depth here. Medium-full. Good tannin. Some oak. Spice here, brown sugar in the aftertaste. Good grip though. Long. Very good. **(05/93)**

Now-2009   16.0

Nuits-Saint-Georges Les Roncières
Robert Chevillon

Good colour. Very good nose. Closed, rich, concentrated, very elegant expression of Pinot Noir. A touch of oak. Full body. Good tannins. This is a real 1990. Rich and concentrated, fat and succulence. Fine. Real depth. **(05/93)**

1998-2012   17.0

Nuits-Saint-Georges Les Roncières
Jean Grivot

Soft and spicy. Round and aromatic. But I prefer his Vosne-Romanée, Les Suchots. **(09/93)**

Now-2008   15.5

Nuits-Saint-Georges Les Saint-Georges
Joseph Faiveley

Hand-bottled without filtration. Very good colour. Splendid nose. Real intensity and marked by more new oak than the Maréchale. Full body. Very good tannins. Marvellous fruit.

Real concentration and dimension. This is one of the best Nuits-Saint-Georges I have seen for years. Fine plus. **(05/93)**

1999-2020   18.0

Nuits-Saint-Georges Les Saint-Georges
Henri Gouges

Good colour. Soft but balanced, fat but feminine for a 1990 on the nose. Good grip. Stylish. Fullish, backward, firm on the palate. But poised and definitive. This is fine. Lovely fruit. Long complex finish. **(05/93)**

Now-2012   17.5

Nuits-Saint-Georges Les Vaucrains
Henri Gouges

Medium-full colour. Still youthful. Rich, fat, concentrated, slight touch of caramel. Plenty of depth here. Medium-full. This has a slight austerity still but is very well balanced, concentrated and intense. Very long. It has the slight obvious structure, in a sinewy sense of Nuits-Saint-Georges. But is marvellously complex on the finish. Fine. **(10/95)**

1998-2012   17.5

Nuits-Saint-Georges Vignes-Rondes
Daniel Rion et Fils

Very good colour. Quite oaky. Soft and succulent for a Nuits-Saint-Georges 1990 on the nose. Good fruit, balance and depth though. Ripe and oaky on the palate. Fat and rich. Fullish. Succulent and voluptuous. This has a lot of appeal. Long complex and lovely. **(05/93)**

Now-2012   17.0

Pernand-Vergelesses Rollin Père et Fils

A sample opened the previous evening. *Tenue à l'air* not special. Fat and rich but a whiff of oxidisation. Rich and chunky but rather coarse. Full. Good grip. Lacks finesse and real depth. **(12/95)**

Now-2000   13.5

Pernand-Vergelesses Ile-des-Vergelesses
Chandon-de-Briailles

Good colour. Quite a sturdy nose. More closed than the above. But a lot of substance on the palate. A concentrated wine with a lot of depth. Fullish, very good grip. Ripe tannins. Fine future here. **(09/92)**

1998-2012   17.5

Pommard Jean-Marc Boillot

Very good colour. Slightly rustic and earthy on the nose. Better on the palate. Plump. Good structure and balance. But not a lot of depth or style. Not bad plus. **(02/94)**

Now-2004   13.5

Pommard Jean-Marie Capron-Charcousset

Good colour. Good meaty nose. This is still a little
closed. Quite firm. But rich, fullish and meaty.
The nose shows good fruit. This is echoed at the
end. Good weight. Good grip. Long. Lacks a little
richness for a 1990. Good. **(12/95)**

Now–2005   15.0

Pommard Château de Puligny-Montrachet

Medium colour. Round, attractive fruit.
Medium body. Not a great deal of depth or
class. Pleasant. Quite good. **(10/94)**

Now–2003   14.0

Pommard Olivier Leflaive Frères

This, as one might expect, is a more substantial,
animal wine. Medium to medium-full. Ripe
and meaty and fat. Good grip and style. Good
plus. **(09/92)**

Now–2000   15.5

Pommard Château de Pommard
Jean-Louis Laplanche

Good colour. Old-viney. Concentrated but
closed on the nose. Raw but lacks real concentration and richness on the palate. Good
length but lacks class and dimension. Quite
good. **(10/94)**

Now–2001   14.0

Pommard Argillières Lejeune

Medium-full colour. Some development
already. Perfumed, cherry-like nose. Sweet
berry fruit. Medium body. A little astringency
of tannin on the palate. Ripe but without the
proper structure of Burgundy. Curious. For a
1990 a bit lacking fat and concentration and
grip. Not much new oak noticeable and no real
richness and dimension. **(10/94)**

Now–2004   14.0

Pommard Les Bertins Chantal Lescure

Good colour. Fat and opulent, slightly barnyardy on the nose. Slightly raw. Medium-full
body. This is neat and full of fruit without being
exactly concentrated. Lacks a bit of personality
but well balanced. Good. **(06/92)**

Now–2001   15.0

Pommard Charmots Jean Garaudet

Full colour. Firm, gamey nose. Rich, sweet,
oaky, meaty. Fullish, good structure and balance.
The attack is rich and promising, the finish a
little closed. But good plus. **(09/93)**

Now–2009   15.5

Pommard Charmots Olivier Leflaive
Frères

This is good. There is fat here as well as
substance. Not a blockbuster, but the wine has
interest and balance. Good oaky base. Reason-

able thrust and length. **(09/92)**

Now–2004   16.0

Pommard Clos-des-Arvelets
Virely-Rougeot

Good colour. Fat nose but a little coarse and
farmyardy. This is a little astringent, more than a
little ungainly. It doesn't sing at all. There is a
lack of weight and concentration in the
background. Disappointing. Will dry out from
now on. **(12/95)**

Drink soon   12.0

Pommard Epenots Joseph Drouhin

Good colour. Rich nose. Plenty of spice and
concentration here. A touch of new oak. Better
than Chantal Lescure's Pommard, Les Bertins.
Medium to medium-full. A certain hardness on
the palate. Ripe. Good plus but not great. **(06/92)**

Now–2002   15.5

Pommard Epenots Olivier Leflaive Frères

This has less grip than their Charmots. Less
interest. A pretty wine but not a serious one.
Reasonable follow-through, but I prefer the
Charmots. **(09/92)**

Now–2002   15.5

Pommard Epenots Jacques Parent

Good colour. Firm, masculine, concentrated,
rich. More black fruits than red. Fat, opulent,
but does it lack just a little grip? Ample and full
anyway. Just a shade vegetal on the finish. Good
plus. **(06/92)**

Now–2003   15.5

Pommard Epenots
Daniel Rebourgeon-Mure

Good colour. This is quite full, lush and rich,
and it has a lot of depth. Full, opulent, very ripe
tannins. An abundant wine. Very good. But it
lacks a little finesse to make it great. The tannins
are a little unsophisticated. **(12/95)**

1999–2012   16.0

Pommard Fremiets De Courcel

Fullish colour. Fat and oaky, rich, full and concentrated. This is impressive. Lovely fruit, very
intense, real depth. Fullish and ripe. Very good
tannins. Fine quality. Surprisingly good.
(10/93)

Now–2005   16.5

Pommard Les Noizons Jean Garaudet

Good colour. This is a typical meaty village
Pommard. Structured, rich. Good acidity. The
tannins are just a little rude, but there is plenty
of ripeness of fruit. Not a great bottle but a very
good example. Long, fat and satisfying. Still
needs time. **(12/95)**

1999–2015   15.5

Pommard   Les Rugiens   Jacques Parent

Good colour. Slightly dry on the nose. Recently bottled? Better on the palate. This has concentration and very good grip. Full, positive, multi-dimensional. Satisfyingly rich. Very good finish. Very good quality. **(06/92)**

Now-2005   16.0

Pommard   Les Vignots   Lahaye Père et Fils

Good colour. Fat, plump and rich. This is a satisfying vintage. Typically Pommard-ish example. No great elegance but meaty, spicy and rich as a Christmas pudding in its flavours. Good. **(12/95)**

1998-2006   15.0

Richebourg   Anne et François Gros

Very good colour. This is fine. Concentrated and oaky and with lovely fat fruit. Fullish. Very good tannins and old-vine concentration here. This is fine quality. Rich, balanced, ripe and seductive. Restrained and quietly brilliant. **(05/93)**

1999-2015   19.0

Richebourg   Gros Frère et Soeur

Very good colour. Full, fat, very concentrated nose. Blackberries and blackcurrants with a touch of spice as well as oak. On the palate full and generous, oaky and very lush and con-centrated. Very good grip. A lot of depth and dimension. Long and potentially voluptuous. Very fine. **(05/93)**

1999-2015   18.5

Richebourg   Alain Hudelot-Noëllat

Like the 1989 this is not quite as fine as the Romanée-Saint-Vivant. A slightly bigger wine. But not as subtle. Ripe, opulent. Slightly spicy. Fullish, concentrated. Fine but not great. **(05/93)**

1999-2020   18.0

Romanée-Saint-Vivant   Arnoux Père et Fils

Good colour. Old-viney, rich, substantial nose. This is splendid. Marvellous fruit and depth. Very, very concentrated. Full. Very good tannins. Very long. Very lovely. **(12/95)**

1999-2009   18.5

Romanée-Saint-Vivant
Alain Hudelot-Noëllat

Very good colour. This has a really very lovely nose. Immaculately composed. Very very rich and concentrated. Yet soft and silky, within the context of the 1990 vintage. This is very subtle, really very very long. Intense. Concentrated. Great breed. Magnificent fruit. Great wine. The 1989 is excellent. This is brilliant. **(05/93)**

1999-2020   20.0

Romanée-Saint-Vivant   Marc Rougeot

Quite oaky on both nose and palate. Very good Pinot fruit. But seductive as it is, does it really have the backbone and depth for *grand cru*? **(10/92)**

Now-2006   16.0

Ruchottes-Chambertin
André et Frédéric Esmonin

Fine colour. This is even better, because it is more intense and the tannins are even better covered. Full, ample, concentrated. Real depth and length here. Very fine indeed. **(09/92)**

2000-2015   18.5

Ruchottes-Chambertin
Clos-des-Ruchottes   Armand Rousseau

Very good colour. Splendidly concentrated nose. Real class and intensity. Black cherry. Good acidity. Medium-full. Very ripe tannins. Not very markedly oaky, yet rich and cedary. Very complex. Fine. **(03/94)**

1999-2015   17.5

Saint-Aubin   Les Casses-Têtes
Hubert Lamy

Premier cru. Medium body. Stylish, round, nicely ripe. A touch lightweight but fragrant and intense. Now ready. Good grip. Ripe finish. Quite long. Quite good plus. **(03/95)**

Now-2002   14.5

Saint-Romain   Camille Giroud

This just shows how good the vintage is after the 1991s. A ripe, fat, substantial wine. Very good fruit. Good grip. **(09/92)**

Drink soon   14.0

Saint-Romain   Sous-le-Château
Jean Germain

Good colour. Slightly rigid on the nose. Fullish, meaty, slightly muscular. Good grip. This is a bit more old-fashioned than the wines he makes today. Good grip. A touch of spice. There were some stems here (20 per cent) and this gives it a herbaceous touch. Just about ready. Nicely fat and ripe, even rich at the end. Good plus. **(12/95)**

Now-2005   15.5

Santenay   Gravières   Hautes-Cornières
Jean-François Chapelle

Medium to medium-full colour. A little closed on the nose. This is a bit more old-fashioned. More stems (made by father) and no *macération à froid*. Firm, tannic, rich, but a bit artisanal. Good warmth on the finish. Needs food. Quite good. **(12/95)**

1998-2005   14.0

Savigny-lès-Beaune   Chandon-de-Briailles

Good colour. Ripe, rich, cherry-flavoured nose. Good fruit, good grip, good structure. Balanced and quite sturdy. This has substance and depth. Good for a village wine. Positive finish. **(09/92)**

Now-2005   14.0

Savigny-lès-Beaune   Jean-Michel Giboulot

Full, slightly rustic. Ripe, some tannin now mellowing. But a little sturdy. An earthy spicy flavour. Very Savigny. Quite good. **(03/95)**

Now-2002   14.0

Savigny-lès-Beaune   Camille Giroud

Good colour. Rich, fat and chocolatey. Ripe tannins. Good grip. An animal wine. Needs a bit of aeration but very good for a simple appellation. **(09/92)**

Now-2005   15.0

Savigny-lès-Beaune   Jean-Marc Pavelot

Good colour. Ripe, round, succulent nose. On the palate medium body, a touch rustic, but accessible, gently oaky. Good depth and balance. Very good for a village Savigny. Will still improve. **(02/94)**

Now-2004   15.0

Savigny-lès-Beaune   Les Dominodes
Champy

Good colour. Firm and quite solid, but not *sauvage*. Rich but meaty. Good. **(05/93)**

Now-2002   14.5

Savigny-lès-Beaune   Les Fourneaux
Chandon-de-Briailles

Good colour. On the nose a little less expressive than the Lavières. Lighter in structure, and perhaps in a 1990 context a little slight. **(09/92)**

Now-2005   14.5

Savigny-lès-Beaune   Les Guettes
Simon Bize et Fils

This has finished malo; others haven't. Rich, liquorice. Concentrated. Balanced. A lot of style and depth. Better than 1988? More substance. **(09/93)**

Now-2009   16.0

Savigny-lès-Beaune   Les Hauts-Jarrons
Jean Guiton

Quite full and ripe. But not really very special for a 1990. Sweet but not really any more depth - or not enough. **(12/95)**

Drink soon   13.5

Savigny-lès-Beaune   Les Lavières
Chandon-de-Briailles

Good colour. Meatier and fatter on the nose. This shows a lot better. Medium-full. Good ripe

fruit. Depth and class here. Finely balanced. Subtle. Long. Very good. **(09/95)**

Now-2007   15.5

Savigny-lès-Beaune   Narbantons
Maurice Ecard

Round, well coloured. Elegant. Not quite as concentrated as I expected and has a strange spice. **(05/93)**

Now-2002   14.0

Savigny-lès-Beaune   Les Pimentiers
Dubois d'Orval

Village Appellation Contrôlée. Good colour. Earthy nose. Somewhat lumpy and rustic. Rather rude tannins and not enough fruit. Unexciting. **(02/94)**

Now-2004   12.0

Savigny-lès-Beaune   Les Serpentières
Jean-Michel Giboulot

Medium to medium-full colour. Still youthful. Rich nose if without much finesse. All the fruit of the year. Really very, very ripe. Almost sweet. Less chunky. Less extraction in those days, obviously. A bit ungainly but quite good. **(12/95)**

Now-2004   14.0

Savigny-lès-Beaune   Les Serpentières
Pierre Guillemot

Good colour. Just a little stemmy on the nose but there is good rich fruit underneath. Fullish, rich and spicy, even gamey. Good balance. Opulent. Finishes well. Good plus. **(12/95)**

Now-2002   15.5

Volnay   Jean-Philippe Fichet

Good colour. Rich, ripe and slightly spicy. There is a firm edge here and also quite a lot of alcohol. A little adolescent. Good though. **(05/96)**

1999-2008   15.0

Volnay   Bernard et Louis Glantenay

Good colour. Farmyardy nose. Clumsy and rustic. Rather astringent. **(02/94)**

Now-2000   12.5

Volnay   Olivier Leflaive Frères

This is rather better than their Chassagne-Montrachet. Good nose. But soft nevertheless, and quite forward. Yet there is some substance here. Good tannins and grip. Elegant. Good. **(09/92)**

Now-2002   15.0

Volnay   Brouillards
Bernard et Louis Glantenay

Good colour. Better than his village wine, but there is no grace and style here either. A bit lumpy. Quite prominent acidity. A little stewed. **(02/94)**

Now-2002   12.5

Volnay   Caillerets   Yvon Clerget

Good colour. Closed nose. Slightly medicinal at first but it blew away. Medium to medium-full. Good oak. Very Volnay. Fragrant and ripe. Good plus but not the complexity and finesse for better. Balanced and more-ish though. Better after ten minutes, definitely very good plus. Seemed fatter and more classy and persistent. (09/93)

Now-2009   16.5

Volnay   Caillerets   Pousse d'Or

Medium-full colour. Some development. Clean Pinot on the nose. But slightly attenuated and vegetal. This lacks a bit of style and a bit of real concentration. The attack is reasonable but then it tails off a bit. For a 1990 this is a bit weak and wimpy. No better than quite good plus. (07/95)

Now-2001   14.5

Volnay   Champans   Jean-Philippe Fichet

Good colour. Still youthful. Good, laid-back, cherry-raspberry fruit on the nose. Very ripe. On the palate medium-full body, a little tannin. This will still develop. There is plenty of grip and intensity, and the balance is very good. Complex, profound and long on the palate. Very good plus. (05/96)

2000-2015   16.5

Volnay   Champans   Comtes Lafon

Fine colour. Strange odours at first but these blew off. Closed nose. Nicely concentrated. Oaky. This is fine. Full, rich and concentrated. Lovely ripe fruit. Real depth here. Quite a powerful wine for a Volnay. Long and intense. Several notes. (07/95)

1999-2012   17.5

Volnay   Chevret   Jean-Marc Boillot

Good colour. Vigorous nose. Fresh and new oaky. Plump clean ripe fruit. Medium-full. At first balanced and even quite rich but as time went on the wood began to dominate. Very good but slightly rigid. (06/96)

Now-2000 plus   16.0

Volnay   Chevret   Joseph Drouhin

Very good colour. Little development. Full, fat, gently oaky. Rich and ripe. Fullish, still quite a lot of tannin. Lovely fruit. This is really quite concentrated. Yet has all the breed of Volnay. Lovely finish. Very good indeed. (02/96)

1998-2010   17.0

Volnay   Clos-des-Chênes   Champy

Full colour. Full, rich, concentrated. This has a lot of depth. Very fine. Tannic though. Like other 1990 Volnays. Not typical. But ample if firm at the end. Very good indeed. (05/93)

1998-2012   16.5

**Volnay   Clos-des-Chênes
Fontaine-Gagnard**

Fontaine has 8 *ouvrées* here. Very full and rich. Animal at present. Lovely fruit. Very good acidity and grip. Heaps of fruit and richness here. Full. Balanced, meaty, substantial. Fine. (09/92)

1999-2012   17.5

Volnay   Clos-des-Chênes   Michel Lafarge

Good colour, but a little muddy and developed. Firm, full, rich oaky nose. This is a backward example. Good tannins. Rather adolescent at present. And a bit clumsy. But good grip. Meaty but it lacks a bit of style. Yet it developed well in the glass. Good finish. Several notes: this is a big mouthful. I am sure it will be fine in the end. (07/95)

1998-2010   16.5

Volnay   Clos-des-Chênes   Comtes Lafon

Good colour. Rich ripe and fat. Good base of oak. Very good chocolatey and black-cherry fruit. Perhaps not a great deal of finesse, but a lot of concentration. Quite a lot of tannin and the tannins well covered. Youthful. Good grip. Very good. Several notes. (09/92)

1999-2012   16.0

Volnay   Clos-des-Chênes   René Monnier

Fullish colour. Quite an oaky nose. A little adolescent currently. Reasonable intensity and class but not a lot of concentration. Good merely. (10/94)

Now-2008   15.0

**Volnay   Clos-de-la-Rougeotte
Bouchard Père et Fils**

Good colour. Very good concentration on the nose. This is almost exotic: certainly animal. New oaky, fullish, rich. This has a lot of depth. Lovely finish. Very concentrated. Very good. (06/92)

Now-2004   16.0

Volnay   Clos-de-Verseuil   Yvon Clerget

Lightish colour. Some development. Clean and fruity on the nose but not much depth. Quite a good, rich attack. Not quite the follow-through I had hoped for but this is fat and succulent and nicely long and complex. Very good plus. (07/95)

Now-2009   16.5

Volnay   Fremiets   Olivier Leflaive Frères

Good colour. Fat and ample on the attack. Plump on the palate. Stylish. But it lacks a bit of intensity at the end. It is a more aromatic wine, with more concentration than both the Pommard Charmots and Pommard Epenots. And a better future. But it lacks a bit of real grip at the end. **(09/92)**

Now–2004   15.5

Volnay   Les Santenots   Labouré-Roi

Medium-full colour. A touch dry on the nose. ?Recently racked/bottled. Better on the palate. Finely tuned. Very Volnay. Balanced and intensely flavoured without being a blockbuster. Very good. **(06/92)**

Now–2003   16.0

Volnay   Santenots   Matrot

Very good colour. Rich, warm, sweet, generous. Spicy in a caramel sense. A full, meaty, quite tannic wine. But with very good grip and depth. This has lost its puppy fat but not quite developed its secondary flavours. But plenty of wine here. The finish is very good. **(02/95)**

Now–2005   16.0

Volnay   Santenots-du-Milieu
Comtes Lafon

Fine colour. Much more intense on the nose than the Champans 1990. Yet the harvest was higher here. Real essence of wine. More powerful. Lovely rich wine. Very good balance. Long, long, long on the palate. Sturdy for a Volnay nevertheless. But this is not in any way a criticism. Fine plus. Several notes. **(05/93)**

2000–2015 plus   18.0

Vosne-Romanée   Roland Remoissenet
Père et Fils

Ripe, correct, accessible stylish Pinot Noir fruit. Medium body. Ample, seductive. Good oaky base. Very good for a village example. **(05/93)**

Now–2002   15.0

Vosne-Romanée   Beaumonts
Joseph Drouhin

Fine colour. Fine, classy but essentially soft nose. Could be a Chambolle. Medium-full. Balanced and intense. Just a touch of wood. Long. Complex. Classy. Fine. **(12/95)**

1998–2012   17.5

Vosne-Romanée   Beaux-Monts
Daniel Rion et Fils

Good colour. Slightly rigid on the nose. Full, oaky, a touch dense. But low-*rendement* old-viney follow-through. This is a bit closed and adolescent. But could be very good indeed. Good grip. Fine finish. Needs time. **(05/93)**

1998–2015   16.5

Vosne-Romanée   Les Brûlées   René Engel

Good colour. Full, firm, rich and blackcurrant on nose and palate. Some tannin. Very ripe.

Very good intensity. A touch adolescent but very good indeed. Fine positive concentrated finish. Needs time. **(05/93)**

1999–2019   16.5

Vosne-Romanée   Champs-Perdrix
Bruno Clair

Medium-full colour. Soft nose. Plump but is it a little weak? On the palate though, the wine is balanced and stylish and has fine Pinot fruit. It is not a blockbuster by any means. Elegant. Complex. Long. Very good. **(05/93)**

Now–2008   16.0

Vosne-Romanée   Chaumes   Jean Tardy

This is very good indeed. Rich, full, concentrated, classy, oaky. Very concentrated. Poised, fullish. Backward. Very good grip. Potentially opulent. Very good indeed. **(03/94)**

1998–2012   17.0

Vosne-Romanée   Clos-des-Réas
Jean Gros

Medium-full colour. Curious nose at first. Slight reduction smells. Some oak on the palate. Rich fat concentrated and succulent. It is a bit adolescent at present but there is a lot of complexity here and elegance as well – I think. Fine finish. Very long. Potentially fine plus. **(05/93)**

Now–2012   17.5

Vosne-Romanée   Les Hautes-Maizières
Robert Arnoux

Medium colour. Good ripe slightly nutty nose. Chocolate chips. Good ripe tannin. A good oaky attack but then it tails off a bit. Slightly hollow at the end. For a 1990, and a superior village wine a little disappointing. Yet not too short. **(03/95)**

Now–2002   14.5

Vosne-Romanée   Les Malconsorts
Clos-Frantin/Bichot

Very good colour. Not much nose. Rather astringent on the palate over quite stylish, ripe fruit. This is medium to medium-full. And has plumpness and real class. But it lacks excitement. Quite good plus at best. **(05/93)**

Now–2005   14.5

Vosne-Romanée   L'Orveau
Sylvain Cathiard

Good colour. Lovely rich blackcurrant nose. Firm underneath. Oaky (more new oak than in his 1991). Rich, full, some tannin. Fat and opulent. Naturally sweet. Very good indeed. Lovely finish. **(11/93)**

1999–2012   17.0

Vosne-Romanée   Aux Réas
Anne et François Gros

Medium colour. Light and fruity, some grip but no fat on the nose. Pretty fruit, ripe and balanced. Quite stylish. This is good but not great. **(06/92)**

Now-2003   15.0

Vosne-Romanée   Les Suchots
Robert Arnoux

Good full colour. Closed nose, quite sturdy. Better on the palate. Full, tannic and backward, but rich and succulent and fruity. Good grip and dimension. Not quite the flair for fine but very good plus. **(09/93)**

1998-2015   16.5

Vosne-Romanée   Les Suchots
Labouré-Roi

Medium-full colour. Closed on the nose. Good concentration. Fullish, meaty, masculine. A little raw and tannic at present but there is potential here. Finishes well. Very good plus. **(06/92)**

1998-2006   16.5

Vosne-Romanée   Les Suchots
Chantal Lescure

Good colour. Firm nose. Closed but fat and old-viney, I think. Fullish, concentrated, meaty. Very good fruit. Fine grip. Youthful but of fine potential. Very promising. **(06/92)**

1998-2008   17.5

Vougeot   Les Cras   Mongeard-Mugneret

Good colour. Fat round, oaky, easy to drink. Just a little obvious. But a good example. No lack of substance. Very good. **(02/95)**

Now-2005   16.0

Vougeot   Les Petits-Vougeots   Bertagna

Medium-full colour. Light, feminine, inconsequential nose. Slightly dry filter paper. Better on the palate. Fullish. New oak here. Ripe fruit. Currently adolescent and difficult to judge but ? very good. **(06/92)**

Now-2007   16.0

1989

RATING FOR THE VINTAGE

Red: 16.0   **White:** 16.5

SIZE OF THE CROP

(Hectolitres, excluding generic wine)

	Red	White
Grands Crus	12,673	3,238
Village and *Premiers Crus*	178,971	41,573
Total	191,644	44,811

The red-wine crop in the Côte-de-Beaune, except in Corton where there was hail damage, was almost identical to that of 1988. In the Côte-de-Nuits it was 5 per cent higher, probably as a consequence of rains just before the harvest was due to commence.

The white-wine harvest, however, was much lower; down by 17 per cent in Meursault and 12 per cent in Puligny, though only 2 per cent in Chassagne. But here there was much more of a difference between one grower and another. In parts of Meursault it was as low as 20 hectolitres per hectare. In parts of Chassagne it was 60. Not surprisingly, you can taste the difference!

WEATHER CONDITIONS

A mild winter was followed by a more than clement early spring. Growers had to rush to complete the pruning before the sap began to rise again as the vines woke up after their annual dormancy. The cycle began some fifteen days ahead of schedule and remained this fortnight ahead of the norm throughout the summer: bud-break at the beginning of April being followed by blooming at the beginning of June, *véraison* at the end of July and a harvest which started on 13 September, the earliest date since 1976. The summer was warmer than average, though not as much so as it was in Bordeaux. It was also significantly drier, particularly in July and August.

There were, however, a number of depredations to the potential crop. There was frost in Meursault in the spring, particularly on the lower lying land on the Puligny side, though not in Puligny itself nor in Chassagne. And while the last week of May was fine, the first week of June was indifferent, thus causing some *coulure*. The frost damage plus this bad week produced *millerandage*, and this seems to have affected the white-wine crop more than the *coulure*. And then, as usual, there was hail. There was hail in Meursault early in July on the Monthélie/Volnay side of the commune and in the *climats* of Tessons, Grand-Charron and Sous-la-Velle above and below the village itself. On a separate occasion hail also damaged much of Corton-Charlemagne. The weeks of drought which followed these attacks further diminished the crop by reducing the size of the grapes. This aridity was not so extreme that it affected the quality and retarded the maturation process, however. Only one grower, with vines in the Chassagne-Montrachet *premier cru* of Vergers, where the soil is particularly thin, admitted to any inconvenience. Most just gloated as the calories soaked into their fruit.

The Chardonnay progressed to maturity very quickly. It was necessary to be very exact about the date of collection. By the beginning of September it began to be apparent that rather than a lack of sugar, a deficiency of acidity was going to be a potential problem. Meanwhile the irregularity in the state of ripeness between one *climat* and another, as a result of the difference in the size of the crop, was posing an additional headache. Nevertheless, the fruit was healthy, reasonably plentiful without being excessive, and confidence was high. The week of 11 September, when I was in the region with a group from World Wine Tours, was generally grey and cloudy with occasional showers, though not sustained periods of rain. It was also quite humid. I hoped it was not going to continue. Rot would have posed a major threat to the Pinot Noir if it did. Thankfully the following weekend was fine and sunny. It was a lot warmer and much less humid than earlier in the week, and the harvest passed off without any interruption for bad weather, save for a storm on the weekend of the 22nd.

The Domaine Leflaive began collecting on Friday 15th, on which day Bouchard Père et Fils were collecting their Montrachet. Chartron et Trébuchet picked some of their fruit as early as the 11th, in order to preserve the acidities. By Monday, 18 September, almost everybody had started the harvest, and, as usual, it was the best sites which were cleared first.

In the red-wine areas Gevrey-Chambertin was affected by frost at the end of April, and there were hail showers which at various times during the summer fell on Volnay, Savigny-lès-Beaune, Pernand-Vergelesses, Aloxe-Corton and Gevrey again. Despite this the fruit-set was successful and the potential crop of a plentiful size.

It was warm in Burgundy in September 1989, and the red grapes were arriving at high temperatures. If not cooled immediately there was a danger that fermentations would develop too quickly. One can see the result of this: short *cuvaisons* and a consequent lack of extraction. Pretty wines which lack guts. Those who had the temperature control and could therefore macerate for, say, twenty days rather than ten, gained an advantage.

In 1989 there was a further complication. The skins of the grapes were thin. The ratio of juice to solid was high; and it was consequently difficult to extract the maximum of colour, glycerol and the right sort of tannins. Again those who could precisely control the temperatures of their fermentations and macerations benefited. Additionally, many performed a *saignée*, particularly for their village wine.

It was also necessary not to pick too late. As the harvest was large the fruit merely became over-ripe, it did not concentrate. Moreover with the acidity levels already on the low side, there was a risk that they would fall even more. This, I feel, is one of the explanations - size of the crop is the other - why the *grands* and *premiers crus* are proportionately better than the wines at village level. The village wines, generally from less well-exposed sites, are picked later.

THE STYLE OF THE WINE

WHITE WINES

Overall 1989 is a vintage which is as good as, if quite different from 1990 - and both are better than 1987 and 1988 on the one side, and 1991 on the other. The 1989s are full and fat and ample, with naturally high alcohol levels and acidity levels which range from very good indeed to the less than adequate, depending on the size of the harvest.

The grapes were very ripe indeed; almost at the limit of *sur-maturité*, but not over it (like many 1986s), giving fruit flavours which are very exotic: elements of pineapple, mango and passion fruit, as one grower put it.

The results are varied - and more variable than 1990. Some are supple, some are concentrated. Most have plenty of finesse, but there are those where the acidity is low which have not aged gracefully. There are some splendid wines, and these will last well. Prices at the time, however, were very high.

RED WINES

Nineteen eighty-nine was a large expensive vintage. But there is much enjoyment to be had. In cask the wines were plump and seductive, showing abundant ripe, healthy fruit, if not *that* much structure: less backbone than 1985, but lusher than the 1991s would demonstrate, though perhaps with less grip. When I thought about how they would show in bottle I feared that some wines would be dilute, some would lack acidity, some would turn out over-oaked, some would have been bottled too late. Recent tastings of the wines in bottle have demonstrated the progress in wine-making since as recently as 1985. The marvellous fruit of the 1989s has been preserved, but there is harmony and elegance too. Most of the wines *do* have sufficient grip. And this gives them the class and the balance I feared they would not show at this stage when I sampled them at the outset. I have revised my opinion upwards.

WHERE ARE THE BEST WINES?

★ In general, at village level, there are better wines in the more substantial communes: Pommard rather than Beaune or Volnay, Nuits-Saint-Georges and Vosne-Romanée rather than Chambolle-Musigny.

★ But this variation is less marked as one climbs up the hierarchy, and in the wines of the top growers.

★ Savigny-lès-Beaune and Pernand-Vergelesses produced good wines, but the Cortons are patchy, both in red and in white.

★ Gevrey-Chambertin is variable. In some cases the crop of young vines, planted after the 1985 frost, has not been excluded; in other cases, it has.

★ Among the white wines, Meursault is in general better than Puligny-Montrachet, and Puligny is better than Chassagne-Montrachet. The average *rendements* explain all: Meursault produced least, Chassagne most.

White: In general both village and *premier cru* wines are now ready, though there are exceptions in Meursault where the best Perrières and Genevrières will still improve. As indicated above, the quality is variable. Some wines will not last much longer, others will outlive the 1990s. The *grands crus* should still be kept, to 2000 or beyond.

Red: All but the very top, very concentrated and tannic *grands crus* are now ready. They are ripe and generous and will not disappoint. Obviously the best will continue to drink well for as much as a decade. But the vintage is now *à point* and there is no reason to delay pulling the corks any longer. Drink the 1989s before the 1988s and 1990s.

TASTING NOTES

BLANC

Auxey-Duresses   Olivier Leflaive Frères
Still youthful on the nose. A touch of sulphur? On the palate it lacks a bit of fruit and it already seems a bit old. Four-square. Dull. Hard at the end. **(02/92)**

Drink soon   13.5

Auxey-Duresses   Leroy
A little adolescent. Ripe but a little tarty. Soft but lacks finesse. **(07/92)**

Now-2000   13.5

Bâtard-Montrachet   Blain-Gagnard
On the nose a little slight for a Bâtard. On the palate slightly more evolved than I would have expected. Delicate, steely but not firm. Strange smells of melon and strawberries. Very slight element of botrytis. Lacks a little real *grand cru* concentration. Very good indeed at best. **(07/95)**

Now-2004   17.0

Bâtard-Montrachet   Henri Clerc
Full and fat on the nose. Not as exotic as his Bienvenues. Better fruit, better acidity. This is fine. Rich and full and backward. Finishes well, better than his Chevalier. **(01/91)**

Now-2005   17.5

Bâtard-Montrachet   Louis Latour
Closed nose. Difficult to penetrate. It seems a bit heavy. Fullish, quite muscular. No undue sulphur, but I miss a bit of real zip and excitement. Yet full of fruit and not without concentration. This comment echoed six months later. **(02/92)**

Now-2004   16.0

Bâtard-Montrachet   Ramonet
Heather, juniper, sage, even mint on the nose. Curious. But not unattractive. High tones here on the palate. Medium-full, balanced and elegant and with good zip. Long. Very good but not exceptional. Doesn't quite have the weight of a *grand cru*. **(02/92)**

Now-2001   16.0

Bâtard-Montrachet   Étienne Sauzet
Odd nose; a bit of sulphur, a bit loose, a bit sweaty. Rich but alcoholic. Full but a lot of built-in sulphur. I think it will always be a bit unbalanced and ungainly. Alcoholic finish. Disappointing. **(02/92)**

Now-2002   13.0

**Beaune   Clos-de-la-Maladière
Henri Cauvard et Fils**
Just a touch of reduction, but no hint of *sur-maturité*. Spicy. Rich. Individual. A little more evolved than the 1990. **(12/95)**

Drink soon   13.0

**Beaune   Clos-des-Mouches
Joseph Drouhin**
Fine nose. Concentrated, gently oaky. Intense. Individual. This is very good indeed. Spicy, as always from this *climat*. Fat, rich. Very promising. Fine. **(03/94)**

Now-2005   17.5

Beaune   Les Perrières   Guillemard-Clerc
Good substance and fragrant. Just a little hard on the follow-through. Good grip and length. Stylish. **(07/95)**

Drink soon   15.0

**Bienvenues-Bâtard-Montrachet
Bachelet-Ramonet**
A bit of SO$_2$ on the nose here. Really far too much. On the palate there is a good oaky base and the fruit seems fresh, full, concentrated enough and balanced. Indeed what is underneath is commendable. Plenty of depth there nevertheless, and there is quality. But it is really far too masked by the sulphur. If you have got it, decant it. Just about ready. **(12/95)**

Now-2007   15.0

Bienvenues-Bâtard-Montrachet
Henri Clerc

Honeyed, round, ripe and concentrated on the nose. Elements of citrus and *sur-maturité*. Full, rich, concentrated, alcoholic, quite powerful. This is spicy. It is youthful. It needs time. Plenty of wine here. How much breed? A bit too oaky? **(01/91)**

Now-2002   **16.0**

Bienvenues-Bâtard-Montrachet   Jaffelin

Ripe, youthful nose. Stylish fruit but as the Criots-Bâtard-Montrachet, 1988, no real concentration either. The oak dominates a little. Lacks a bit of depth and concentration, especially for a 1989. **(01/91)**

Drink soon   **15.0**

Bienvenues-Bâtard-Montrachet   Ramonet

Pronounced mint, vervain nose; very curious. Ripe, distinctive, individual. Slightly herbaceous touch on the palate. Slightly hard still. But good grip. Yet I don't find it has the fat and the depth and concentration for great. **(02/92)**

Now-2008   **17.0**

Chassagne-Montrachet   Blain-Gagnard

Firm, rich nose. Ripe. Seems to have some depth. A certain lack of grace here at present. But at least some concentration. Balanced and clean. Will improve. **(02/92)**

Now-1999   **15.0**

Chassagne-Montrachet
Bouchard Père et Fils

Round fruity nose. Reasonable structure. Not a lot of depth but clean and balanced. Lacks a bit of real richness though. **(02/92)**

Drink soon   **14.5**

Chassagne-Montrachet
Chartron et Trébuchet

High-toned, ripe nose. But lacks a bit of grip underneath. Some oak. Some SO$_2$. But a lack of fruit and concentration. Dull and unstylish. **(02/92)**

Drink soon   **13.0**

Chassagne-Montrachet
Marquis de Laguiche, Joseph Drouhin

Fat and rich. Stylish and balanced, but quite masculine. Firm. Intense. An element of over-ripe fruit. Very good. **(06/92)**

Now-2000 plus   **16.0**

Chassagne-Montrachet
Jacques Gagnard-Delagrange

Good ripe concentrated wine here. A touch of oak. This is good for a village example. It lacks a little real charm and richness but it is balanced

and vigorous. **(02/92)**

Now-2000   **15.5**

Chassagne-Montrachet   Henri Laroche

Ripe and fruity on the nose. But does it lack a bit of grip? Good oak base. Flowery and ripe. It doesn't have quite enough acidity but it has fat. And it finishes well nevertheless. **(02/92)**

Drink soon   **15.0**

Chassagne-Montrachet   Louis Latour

Quite clean on the nose but not a lot of depth here. Yet on the palate plenty of fruit. Medium body. Ripe, lean. Well made. Good length, even interest. **(02/92)**

Now-2000   **15.0**

Chassagne-Montrachet   Olivier Leflaive
Frères

Quite full and firm on the nose. Some structure. Just a touch of SO$_2$. On the palate there is some fruit and not too much SO$_2$. But a lack of real life and depth. **(02/92)**

Drink soon   **14.0**

Chassagne-Montrachet   Michel Niellon

Some H$_2$S on the nose. Heavy. Four-square. Slightly scented. Nothing much on the palate. Weedy. Short. **(02/92)**

Drink soon   **12.5**

Chassagne-Montrachet   Ramonet

Ripe nose. Quite firm. Medium to medium-full. Good richness and concentration. This has structure and will still improve. Fat. There is depth here. But a lack of elegance. **(02/92)**

Now-2000   **15.0**

Chassagne-Montrachet   La Boudriotte
Jacques Gagnard-Delagrange

Good fat, gently oaky nose. This has a ripe but satisfyingly lean, austere background. Fullish, youthful. Long on the palate and very stylish and complex. Very good plus. **(09/91)**

Now-2004   **16.5**

Chassagne-Montrachet   Caillerets
Blain-Gagnard

Fresh colour. Nicely crisp, but round and succulent nose. Fullish, ample, well balanced. Absolutely *à point* now. Good fruit. Fine quality. **(06/96)**

Now-2005 plus   **17.5**

Chassagne-Montrachet   Les Chaumées
Michel Colin-Deléger

Good depth here on the nose. Will still evolve. On the palate it lacks a little concentration. Medium body. Reasonable balance. Clean. Good but a bit one-dimensional. **(02/92)**

Now-1998   **15.0**

Chassagne-Montrachet   Les Chaumées
Olivier Leflaive Frères

Rich and honeyed on the nose. Fat. This doesn't quite have the definition of the above but it is not far short. Fullish, ripe, balanced, rich. Very good length. Will still improve. (02/92)

Now-2004   16.5

Chassagne-Montrachet   Morgeots
Blain-Gagnard

Old farts and slightly artificial acidity on the nose. Yet good fruit on the palate. It doesn't quite have the grip and concentration but a good wine with a reasonable finish. (02/92)

Drink soon   15.0

Chassagne-Montrachet   Morgeots
Henri Germain

Rich, fat, oaky nose. A suspicion of H_2S at first. Slightly overblown perhaps. Yet good grip. This has plenty of depth. Youthful and concentrated. A little adolescent. Lacks a little finesse and grace but good. (03/95)

Now-2006   15.0

Chassagne-Montrachet   Morgeots
Ramonet

Some depth here on the nose. Even concentration. Fullish, rich, fat, still young. This has depth. Honeyed. A little four-square like Morgeot often is but very good nevertheless. (02/92)

Now-2000   16.0

Chassagne-Montrachet   Les Ruchottes
Ramonet

Gently oaky. Full. A touch of peppermint. Depth here. Medium-full. Ripe. Good grip. Good oak. This has style and individuality. Good stuff. Finishes long. (02/92)

Now-2002   16.5

Chevalier-Montrachet
Bouchard Père et Fils

Gently oaky but a little dry on the nose. Slightly marmaladey on the palate. Over-ripe and lacks grip. Unexciting. (06/92)

Drink soon   14.0

Chevalier-Montrachet   Jean Chartron

Here there is depth and quality, but it is closed and backward. There is a bit of sulphur here. This is full but although closed and a bit adolescent, it does have the depth. Rich, quite alcoholic. Firm. Long. Fine. (02/92)

Now-2004   17.0

Chevalier-Montrachet   Henri Clerc

This has the same spicy citrus plus oak of Clerc's Bienvenues. The fruit seems a little dominated. But not as much. Yet the impression on the follow-through is more of the barrel than the grape. A firm wine, quite powerful. Best on the nose which is ripe. (01/91)

Now-2000   16.0

Chevalier-Montrachet   Michel Niellon

Dumb closed nose. Very gentle oak. Plump on the palate. It has a good attack but it tails off a bit on the finish. Rich but lacks a bit of concentration and intensity. Unexciting for a Chevalier. (02/92)

Now-2002   15.5

Chevalier-Montrachet   Les Demoiselles
Louis Jadot

Closed nose but a lot of depth behind it. This is lovely! A touch adolescent on the attack but splendid intensity of ripe fruit on the follow-through. Very complex. Very long. Very special. (02/92)

1999-2010   19.0

Chevalier-Montrachet   Les Demoiselles
Louis Latour

Fragrant and oaky, delicate but profound. Very distinctive and lovely fruit on the nose. Quite oaky. Less closed-in. Refined and classy. This has lovely fruit and concentration. Long. Subtle. Harmonious. Fine. (02/92)

Now-2008   18.0

Corton-Charlemagne   Bonneau du Martray

Austere, crisp and classy. Very excellent depth and fruit. This is concentrated, almond-blossomy, firm and profound. With really fine underlying richness. Excellent quality. Very complex. Beautifully balanced. Several subsequent confirmatory notes. (02/92)

Now-2008   18.5

Corton-Charlemagne
Bouchard Père et Fils

Nicely steely at first, but a bit too much on the vegetal side. Quite full and intense but lacks class and grace. (06/92)

Now-2000   15.0

Corton-Charlemagne   Joseph Drouhin

Quite a strong toast to the barrel. Full and firm. Backward. A little alcohol shows. On the palate it lacks a bit of bite. It is rich and ample, but the zip and concentration and dimension are not there. Good but not great. Clean though. (02/92)

Now-2000   15.5

Corton-Charlemagne   Joseph Faiveley

Full, closed, oaky nose. Just a touch of reduction. More personality, grip and definition than Latour. Rich but not heavy. Very good concentration. Still very young. Fine. Needs time. Very long and complex on the finish. (02/92)

Now-2010   17.5

Corton-Charlemagne   Antonin Guyon

Pleasant nose but light and young-viney on the palate. Short and inconsequential. **(6/92)**

Drink up   **11.0**

Corton-Charlemagne   Louis Jadot

Very closed. But rich and concentrated underneath. A lot of vigour at the end. This is going to be fine. **(06/92)**

Now-2005   **17.5**

Corton-Charlemagne   Michel Juillot

A bit of sulphur. But there is ripeness if not great finesse. A little ungainly but there is depth. It seemed to evolve fast in the glass. On the palate it is quite full, quite alcoholic. Not without fruit or grip. But the net effect is a bit lumpy. **(02/92)**

Now-2004   **15.5**

Corton-Charlemagne   Labouré-Roi

Ripe and pleasant but no real depth - or grip - or length. **(06/92)**

Drink soon   **14.0**

Corton-Charlemagne   Louis Latour

Magnum. This is still very young. On the nose it is still unforthcoming. Full on the palate. Good acidity and grip. Rich and ripe and concentrated. Indeed certainly fine. Good oak. Plenty of depth. Slightly sweet. But no botrytis. Several notes. **(03/94)**

Now-2005   **17.5**

Corton-Charlemagne   Louis Voilland

Very forward and short. Nothing here. **(06/92)**

Drink up   **11.0**

Criots-Bâtard-Montrachet   Louis Latour

Full nose. A bit blunt. Rich and quite alcoholic. Can't really get much out of it on the palate. Rather raw and unformed. But the finish is good. **(06/92)**

Now-2005   **16.5**

Meursault   Bouchard Père et Fils

Fresh nose. Quite stylish. Not a lot of depth. Honeyed but lacks real grip. Medium weight. A little hard. It has fruit and balance though, but not enough concentration and style. **(2/92)**

Drink soon   **14.5**

Meursault   Chartron et Trébuchet

Stylish but delicate nose. Slightly oaky. Not a blockbuster by any means. Gentle, balanced. Touch of oak. Long, even complex. Good intensity. **(02/92)**

Drink soon   **15.5**

Meursault   Joseph Drouhin

Delicate nose. Quite stylish, but lacks real grip. Sweet. Better on the palate. Medium weight. Good oak and good grip. Honeyed and fragrant. Very good. Finishes well. **(02/92)**

Drink soon   **16.0**

Meursault   Sylvain Dussort

Raw, fat, spicy but ripe and stylish. Good fruit. Good acidity. À point now. Will still keep well. Good. **(12/95)**

Now-2000 plus   **15.0**

Meursault   François Jobard

Expansive but lovely nose. Really classy. Now à point and without a great deal of drive. Yet subtle and balanced. Good plus. **(03/93)**

Drink soon   **15.5**

Meursault   Comtes Lafon

Oh, if all village Meursaults could be like this! Honeyed, citronelle. Fat and concentrated. Ripe. But plenty of depth. Fine for a village example. **(09/92)**

Now-2000 plus   **16.0**

Meursault   Louis Latour

Full, quite alcoholic. Rich but a bit four-square. Somewhat heavy. A touch of sulphur. Needs time. Underneath the SO_2 quite a good wine. Reasonable grip. **(02/92)**

Now-2000   **14.5**

Meursault   Olivier Leflaive Frères

Quite rich, fat, oaky nose. This is better. Good structure and concentration. Good base of oak. This has ripeness and grip. Even complexity. Good plus. **(02/92)**

Now-2000   **15.5**

Meursault   Matrot

Nothing much on the nose except a bit of wet wool. Nothing on the palate either. Fruitless. Charmless. Poor. **(02/92)**

Drink soon   **12.0**

Meursault   Blagny   Louis Jadot

Round, gently oaky. Good fruit. Honeyed. This has reasonable structure. It is a bit four-square. But it has depth and grip and even concentration. Good. **(02/92)**

Drink soon   **15.0**

Meursault   Blagny   Louis Latour

A little built-in SO_2 and H_2S as well on the nose. The fruit is a little too evolved and the wine lacks style. Heavy footed. **(02/92)**

Drink soon   **13.0**

Meursault   Blagny   Matrot

Old farts on the nose. Heavy, ungainly. Fat and a bit alcoholic hiding an essential lack of real fruit and concentration. **(02/92)**

Drink soon   **13.5**

Meursault Charmes
Vincent Bitouzet-Prieur

This is fresher and purer than his 1990, and altogether cleaner. No undue SO$_2$ here! Slight element of oxidation or *sur-maturité* on the nose. Yet more vigorous and more stylish on the palate. Medium body. Round, *tendre* in style. Good positive finish. Very good. **(06/96)**

Now–2000   16.0

Meursault Charmes
Hubert Bouzereau-Gruère

Quite a deep colour. Some built-in sulphur on the nose. Ripe and succulent underneath. Fullish. Plenty of depth but not a lot of class. Still vigorous. Good grip. Good. **(02/96)**

Now–2000   15.0

Meursault Charmes Henri Germain

A lot of oak, but too much SO$_2$ and H$_2$S on the nose. Too much oak and too much SO$_2$ on the palate. A masculine wine. Too rigid. The oak dominates the fruit. Quite good at best. **(02/92)**

Drink soon   14.0

Meursault Charmes Louis Jadot

Light, flowery nose, but a lack of grip and depth. A gentle wine with a touch of Condrieu. Quite fruity. Reasonable balance. Will not make old bones. **(02/92)**

Drink soon   14.5

Meursault Charmes Comtes Lafon

This is really very serious. Subtle, honeyed and lovely. Complete. Rich and concentrated. Very stylish fruit. Very good grip. Medium-full. Long, complex, intense. Very fine. Extra special. **(09/92)**

Now–2008   18.5

Meursault Charmes Michelot

Quite nutty on the nose. Reasonable depth and style. Quite rich, oaky. Slightly overblown again. On the palate it lacks a bit of concentration. Round and buttery at first but then it collapses. A lack of real grip. **(03/95)**

Now–2000   14.0

Meursault Charmes Pierre Morey

Medium colour. Plump, soft, gently oaky on the nose. Medium body. Not a lot of weight or depth. But balanced. Clean and fresh. Pleasant but not special. Fully ready. **(09/92)**

Now–2000   15.0

Meursault Les Chevalières
François Jobard

More structure and definition than his straight Meursault. And with the extra. Good concentration and balance. Long and positive on the finish. Very good. **(03/93)**

Now–2000   16.0

Meursault Clos-de-la-Barre Comtes Lafon

Very good ripe acidity here. Stylish, complex, fresh. Flowery fruit but with the Clos-de-la-Barre structure underneath. Long. Fullish. Very good indeed. **(09/92)**

Now–2003   17.0

Meursault Les Criots Ballot-Millot

Gentle gold colour. Crisp and nutty on the nose. Quite evolved on the palate. It lacks a bit of concentration and grip. Yet it is not heavy. Round, fruity and quite stylish. But at its best now. **(10/95)**

Drink soon   15.0

Meursault Désirée Comtes Lafon

As always this is lighter and softer than the Clos-de-la-Barre. More feminine perhaps. Also good balance and length. But I prefer the virility of the Clos-de-la-Barre. This has less grip. **(09/92)**

Now–2000   16.0

Meursault Genevrières Comtes Lafon

Firmer, richer, more backward than the Charmes. More structure. Today it is a bit adolescent, but the after-taste is very long and intense. This needs time. Could be just as good. We'll just have to wait and see. **(09/92)**

1998–2008   18.0

Meursault Limouzin Henri Germain

Delicate nose, but harmonious and stylish. This has balance and elegance. Good intensity. Good oak. Ripe and quite concentrated. Everything it should be. **(02/92)**

Now–2000   16.5

Meursault Cuvée Maurice Chevalier
Roland Remoissenet Père et Fils

This is very good. Lovely fruit. Very good balance. Ripe, complex, fresh. Very stylish indeed. A flowery Meursault with zip and peachy fruit. Very good plus. **(08/92)**

Now–2000   16.5

Meursault Perrières Comtes Lafon

Quite lovely nose. Flowery, honeyed, aristocratic, rich. Brilliant fruit. This has the structure of the above and the finesse and aromatic amplitude of the Charmes. The complete Meursault. Great depth. Brilliant. Knocks the others into the sidelines. **(09/92)**

1999–2010 plus   19.0

Meursault Perrières Louis Latour

Light colour. Rich, concentrated nose. This is very classy and it has a lot of depth. No undue sulphur either. On the palate not quite as exciting. Ripe, balanced, gently oaky, stylish. But lacks a little intensity. Very good plus. **(10/95)**

Now–2000 plus   16.5

Meursault Perrières
Olivier Leflaive Frères

Again a good nose. The structure is there.
Fullish, good depth and concentration. Closed
still. Balanced. There is depth and dimension
here. Fine. (02/92)

Now-2000   17.0

Meursault Perrières Matrot

A little SO₂ on the nose. A little hard on the
palate. The fruit – such as it is – is a bit lifeless.
Medium body. No dimension. (02/92)

Drink soon   14.0

Meursault Perrières Guy Roulot

Subtle, youthful, mineral. Fine fruit. Very good
acidity. Only just ready. Rich underneath. Long.
Very stylish. Fine. (11/95)

Now-2007   17.5

Meursault Pré-de-Manche Leroy

Quite evolved. Rich but lacks a bit of class.
Ripe, lush. But I prefer the Narvaux 1990.
Quite oaky. (07/92)

Now-2000   14.0

Montrachet Bouchard Père et Fils

Rich and vanilla-y and over-ripe on the nose.
Concentrated and fat, but it lacks real grip and
class. One-dimensional and lacks a bit of freshness. (06/92)

Now-2005   15.0

Montrachet Louis Jadot

Closed, austere. On the palate I get a bit of burn
of alcohol. Rich and fat and good intensity and
grip, but rather adolescent. (06/92)

1998-2010   17.5

Montrachet Marquis de Laguiche
Joseph Drouhin

Rich, very gently oaky, concentrated and very
ample on the nose. This is absurdly young, yet
nevertheless quite delicious. On the palate full
and ripe and potentially glorious. Marvellous
harmony, intensity and refinement. *Grand vin*.
(11/93)

1998-2018   20.0

Montrachet Louis Latour

Closed but concentrated. After the disappointments of some of the Latour 1989s this is
promising. Not too heavy. Very intense. Very rich
and concentrated. Fine at the very least. (06/92)

1998-2012   18.0

Montrachet Romanée-Conti

Mid-gold colour. Lovely nose. Discreetly ripe
and concentrated fruit, beautifully balanced on
the nose. On the palate a reserved but
concentrated wine of great depth and power of

flavour. A lot of potential here. Best of all on the
finish. Very fine indeed. (06/92)

1998-2010   19.0

Pernand-Vergelesses Ile-des-Vergelesses
Chandon-de-Briailles

For young vines – second year of harvest – this
is very good. Gentle, stylish, oaky and ripe. No
lack of depth and complexity. Finishes well.
(09/92)

Drink soon   16.0

Puligny-Montrachet Louis Carillon

Gentle, honeyed nose. Quite stylish, but more
Meursault in character than Puligny. Good grip.
Quite forward. A touch oaky. Good fruit and
balance. But a little too opulent. Not the
greatest but an elegant wine. Good plus. Several
other tasting notes confirm. (02/92)

Drink soon   15.5

Puligny-Montrachet Joseph Drouhin

Magnum. This is still very youthful. Almost
infanticide. Fat and rich. Quite substantial.
Plenty of reserves. But adolescent. Yet good grip.
Will be very good for a village example. (08/92)

Now-2000   15.5

Puligny-Montrachet Louis Latour

Quite a lot of SO₂ on the nose. It deadens the
fruit. Slightly better on the palate. A little
leaden-footed though. It lacks grace and
complexity. Medium to medium-full. Quite
good. (02/92)

Drink soon   14.0

Puligny-Montrachet Leflaive

Weak on the nose. Lacks grip. Too much SO₂.
Some fruit but no dimension and no grip. Too
much built-in sulphur on the palate. Weedy
finish. Too old already. No future. (02/92)

Drink up   12.0

Puligny-Montrachet Olivier Leflaive Frères

Good oaky nose. This has depth and
concentration. Promising. A fine example.
Good fruit. Good style. Good balance. Typically
steely. Good oak base. Very classic. For a village
example this is very good indeed. (02/92)

Now-2000 plus   16.0

Puligny-Montrachet Étienne Sauzet

A bit four-square on the nose. A lack of real
personality. On the palate a little better.
Reasonable grip. Medium body. A bit dull but
quite good. (02/92)

Drink soon   14.0

Puligny-Montrachet Champ-Gain
Olivier Leflaive Frères

Slightly lean on the nose but better acidity than
their Garennes. Slightly more crab-appley and

less honeyed than their Garennes, but more austere and potentially better. Very good acidity. Round. Masculine. Good structure. Very good indeed. **(09/92)**

Now-2004   17.0

Puligny-Montrachet   Champs-Canet
Louis Carillon

Good subtle oak. Fragrant flowery fruit. There is depth here. Fullish, some alcohol again but fat and concentration and grip. This has plenty of potential. Very good indeed. Finishes very well. Other notes confirm how good this and the other Carillon 1989s are. **(02/92)**

Now-2002   17.0

Puligny-Montrachet   Champs-Canet
Étienne Sauzet

Fullish golden colour. Very fine, stylish, rich nose. Gently oaky. Finely balanced. Very concentrated. This is high class. Fullish, rich on the palate. Very good grip. Fat and mellow yet fresh and vigorous as well. Long and very satisfying at the end. Really elegant. Impeccable harmony. Plenty of drive and intensity. A classic example. Still very youthful. Fine plus. **(07/95)**

Now-2008   18.0

Puligny-Montrachet   Clavoillons   Leflaive

A bit feeble on the nose. Lacks grip. Superficial. Forward. Pleasant fruit originally but some sulphur and a lack of grip. No future. **(02/92)**

Drink soon   12.5

Puligny-Montrachet   Les Combettes
Étienne Sauzet

Slightly fatter, but again no real concentration and fruit here on the nose. Better on the palate. Medium-full. Quite ripe and rich, but a lack of real class. Good at best. Finishes reasonably. Showed better after a few more years in bottle (see Profile). **(02/92)**

Drink soon   14.5

Puligny-Montrachet   Les Enseignières
Chavy-Chouet

Nutty, ripe, ample nose. Round now. Soft and a little one-dimensional but stylish nevertheless. Fully ready. Quite good plus. Clean. **(03/93)**

Drink soon   14.5

Puligny-Montrachet   Les Folatières
Jean Chartron

Ripe, round nose. Good style and depth. Quite a subtle oaky honeyed wine. Balanced. Good dimension. Attractive ripe fruit. This gets better and better. Long. Very good indeed. **(02/92)**

Now-2003   17.0

Puligny-Montrachet   Les Folatières
Joseph Drouhin

This is stylish, and has plenty of depth. Good oak and intensity on the follow-through. Very good indeed. **(06/92)**

Now-2002   17.0

Puligny-Montrachet   Les Folatières
Louis Jadot

This is a fine example. Fresh, gently oaky, round, ripe and profound. Only just ready. Long complex and very elegant at the end. Lovely. Bags of life ahead of it. **(12/95)**

Now-2005   17.0

Puligny-Montrachet   Les Folatières
Louis Latour

Closed on the nose but good depth here. Good oak and fruit base. Medium-full. Ripe, round, oaky. Not great but good concentration. Will still improve. Good grip. But not that long and complex. **(02/92)**

Now-2002   15.5

Puligny-Montrachet   La Garenne
Olivier Leflaive Frères

Rich, opulent, honeyed nose. This has fat but no lack of class or grip at first. Some alcohol here. But structure and depth. But a bit lean. Very good indeed. Very concentrated long finish. **(02/92)**

Now-2004   17.0

Puligny-Montrachet   La Garenne
André Moingeon

This is better than his Puligny-Montrachet but not that inspiring. Lacks real class and concentration. **(03/93)**

Drink up   12.0

Puligny-Montrachet   La Garenne
Gérard Thomas

Cool, slightly lean, but stylish colour. Good balanced, complex fruit. On the palate not as exciting as the nose. Good attack but then it tails off a bit. Balanced though but the follow-through lacks class. Quite good. **(03/95)**

Now-2002   14.0

Puligny-Montrachet   Perrières
Étienne Sauzet

Resinny nose without the toast of the oak. I get a bit more structure than fruit, yet the grip is there and the fruit really quite ripe. This lacks a little grace but it is also worthy of attention and will improve. Very good. Best on the finish. **(02/92)**

Now-2000   16.0

Puligny-Montrachet Les Pucelles Leflaive

Closed nose. A bit of sulphur but there is depth here. Opulent and spicy on the palate. Fullish. Good depth and concentration. Backward. Rich. Closed. Fine. Very good finish. A lot here. Very fine. Very lovely at the end. (02/92)

Now-2006   18.0

Puligny-Montrachet Les Referts
Louis Carillon

Ripe, apricoty, honeyed nose. Soft. Good concentration though. Gentle oak. Opulent and round and rich. Oaky and honeyed and spicy on the palate. Good concentration. Good grip. It lacks a little zip but there is depth here. Finishes well. (02/92)

Now-2002   16.5

Puligny-Montrachet Les Referts
Chartron et Trébuchet

A bit closed on the nose. A touch of SO$_2$. Seems to lack opulence of fruit after the above. Rather tired because of the built-in sulphur. Dead on the finish. Getting astringent. (02/92)

Drink up   11.0

Puligny-Montrachet Les Referts
Louis Jadot

Strange acetone, geranium nose. Sorbic acid. Very old flavour. Reasonable fruit but essentially weak and too advanced. I wouldn't touch this. (02/92)

Drink up if at all   10.0

Puligny-Montrachet Les Referts
Étienne Sauzet

Not much on the nose here. On the palate quite a closed wine. Reasonable fruit and grip but a little four-square. It lacks zip and dimension. It will improve. (02/92)

Now-2002   14.5

Puligny-Montrachet La Truffière
Étienne Sauzet

Closed nose. Perhaps a touch heavy, but there is depth here. Medium-full. Quite ripe. A little four-square. Quite good but lacks real excitement and concentration. Will still improve though. (02/92)

Now-2000   14.0

Saint-Aubin Joseph Drouhin

This has youth on its side. It will still improve. It is a bit hard on the nose but I think it has depth. Medium body. It could do with a bit more class and richness but there is some concentration here. A bit four-square but quite good. (02/92)

Drink soon   14.0

Saint-Aubin Louis Latour

Clean but a little rigid and tanky. Closed but I don't find much depth underneath. A little four-square on the palate. With a rather green herbal spicy touch. Lacks grace. Reasonable grip though. (02/92)

Drink soon   13.5

Saint-Aubin La Châtenière
Gérard Thomas

Good nose. This has depth and the correct sort of structure. Good oak. A nice little wine with good flair. Medium body. Quite concentrated. Ripe. This is good. Good future. (02/92)

Now-2001   15.5

Saint-Aubin Les Frionnes
André Moingeon

A little reduction on the nose. Even discounting this I find the wine a bit common. (03/93)

Drink soon   12.0

Saint-Aubin Les Frionnes Henri Prudhon

A little too oaky, but the fruit is crisp if a little under-concentrated for the wood. À point now. Clean. Reasonable length. Quite good. (10/95)

Drink soon   14.0

Saint-Romain Joseph Drouhin

This has depth, grip and very good oak. Medium to medium-full. Youthful. Ripe, stylish. It has dimension and fruit and will still develop. Very good. Long. Rich. Complex. (02/92)

Now-2002   16.0

Saint-Romain Gras-Boisson

Slightly lean, but ripe and fresh. Ready now. Good for a simple village wine. (03/93)

Drink soon   14.0

Saint-Romain Olivier Leflaive Frères

Soft fruity nose. Quite supple but not a lot of weight. A quite pleasant wine for drinking now but lacks depth and elegance. Already getting a bit old. (02/92)

Drink up   14.0

Saint-Romain Clos-sous-le-Château
Jean Germain

This is surprisingly full, rich and concentrated for what it is. Ripe. Quite backward and intense. Good grip. Closed. Balanced. Long. Good. (09/91)

Drink soon   15.0

ROUGE

Aloxe-Corton Tollot-Beaut

Medium colour. More flowery nose than the 1990, but not as much intensity. Inherently softer but a bit more elegant. Lighter but quite stylish. Good grip. Good length. I prefer it to the 1990. (05/93)

Now-2003   15.0

Auxey-Duresses   Les Duresses
Alain Creusefond
Reasonable colour. Tobacco and mocha nose. Not entirely elegant. Medium body. Good acidity but a little pinched. Some fruit but it lacks fat and succulence. Not bad. But rather coarse really. (12/95)

Drink soon   **13.0**

Auxey-Duresses   Le Val
Dominique et Vincent Roy
Good colour. Plump, ripe, balanced, ready. Full of fruit. But again the tannins less sophisticated than in the vintages today. Yet medium-full, good grip. Positive at the end. Quite good plus. (12/95)

Now-2003   **14.5**

Beaune   Cent-Vignes
Bernard Bescancenot
Good fresh colour for the vintage. An elegant, fragrant example with good acidity for the vintage. Medium to medium-full, balanced, ripe, nicely cool. Good style here. Lacks just a little succulence at the end - I wonder if bottling six months earlier would have kept this. Yet long enough, positive enough. Good. (12/95)

Now-2002   **15.0**

Beaune   Clos-de-la-Maladière
Henri Cauvard et Fils
Supple, round, soft and fragrant. This is attractive and generous. Balanced and still fresh and lively. Ready but will last well. Good. (12/95)

Now-2000   **14.0**

Beaune   Clos-des-Mouches   Joseph Drouhin
Good colour. Slightly gamey nose. Touch of toffee, touch of spice. But still a bit rigid. Still quite fresh. Ample, rich, fullish, good intensity. Plenty of wine here. Very good. (05/95)

Now-2002   **16.0**

Beaune   Clos-des-Ursules   Louis Jadot
This is delicious. Spicy, ripe, lush. But very good grip. (06/92)

Now-2000   **15.5**

Beaune   Grèves   Joseph Drouhin
Good fullish mature colour. Round, rich, ample slightly spicy nose. Good grip. Medium body. Slightly sweet, and a touch of burnt toffee. But succulent and charming. Slight suggestion of astringency on the finish. Good plus. (02/96)

Now-2003   **15.5**

Beaune   Grèves   Michel Lafarge
This is very good. Oaky and rich. One-third new oak. But this is a vintage like Bordeaux which has taken up the wood very much. (09/93)

Now-2003   **15.5**

Beaune   Marconnets
Roland Remoissenet Père et Fils
Soft and seductive, rampant with fruit. But more or less à point now. Medium-full, round, complex. But will it really last? Fine long finish though. Very good. (05/93)

Now-2008   **16.0**

Beaune   Les Mariages   Rossignol-Trapet
Light. A little rustic. (09/93)

Drink up   **12.0**

Beaune   Vigne-de-l'Enfant-Jésus
Bouchard Père et Fils
Medium colour. This has not yet been bottled. There is a slight touch of rubber and digestive biscuit about it. Cleaner on the palate. A ripe wine with good acidity but not a lot of tannin and structure. Will come forward soon. Reasonable finish if a bit raw. Not bad. (09/90)

Drink soon   **14.0**

Bonnes-Mares   Dujac
Medium-full colour. Good complex Pinot fruit on the nose. Not a blockbuster, but a wine of real intensity here. Fullish nevertheless, quite oaky, splendid weight and concentration, and lovely mulberry, raspberry fruit. Fine plus. (05/93)

1998-2015   **17.5**

Bonnes-Mares   Robert Groffier
Good colour. Lovely lush fruit here, and no hard edges - the influence both of the vintage and the Groffier style. Ample, rich, just a touch of oak. Balanced and intense. Fine plus. (05/96)

Now-2007   **18.0**

Bonnes-Mares   Jacques-Frédéric Mugnier
Meaty, masculine. But not the greatest of class perhaps. Yet better on the finish than the attack. Long. Concentrated. Complex. (09/93)

Now-2005   **17.0**

Chambertin   Joseph Drouhin
Fine colour. Still immature. Rather more oaky on the nose than the other top Drouhins. Lovely plummy nose. Ripe and rich but cool and very well balanced. Still quite a lot of tannin. Very good grip. Excellent finish. (10/95)

2000-2015   **18.5**

Chambertin   Rossignol-Trapet
Better colour than their Latricières-Chambertin. Lacks real intensity. Very good but not great. (09/93)

1998-2005   **16.0**

Chambertin   *Vieilles-Vignes*   Louis Trapet
Good colour. Slightly more evolved on the nose than the above wines. Ripe and succulent. Fullish, but rather more evolved, less stylish, less

intensity. Ordinary by comparison with the Rousseau and Drouhin wines above. **(05/93)**

Now-2017   **16.0**

Chambertin Clos-de-Bèze Bruno Clair

Good colour. Full, quite firm, ripe fruit on the nose. But has the essential soft tannins of the vintage. Lovely rich fruit. Very concentrated. Real class. Real depth. This is very fine. Several notes. **(05/93)**

1999-2019   **18.5**

Chambertin Clos-de-Bèze Damoy

Good colour. This is weak and evolved for a Clos-de-Bèze on the nose. No strength or intensity. Short, empty. Dilute. A disgrace. Forward. Yet some style underneath. Similar six months later. **(05/93)**

Now-2001   **14.0**

Chambertin Clos-de-Bèze Armand Rousseau

Good colour. More adolescent than the Ruchottes. Just a whiff of H_2S. Full, rich, concentrated, closed. Not really on form. Splendid fruit. Very good grip. Lovely depth. Surely very fine as well. Perhaps even better. **(05/93)**

1999-2020   **19.5**

Chambolle-Musigny Ghislaine Barthod-Noëllat

Medium colour. Soft but quite evolved. Slightly adolescent but a balanced wine with good fruit and depth. Shows well for a 1989. Plump positive finish. Good plus. **(05/93)**

Now-2004   **15.5**

Chambolle-Musigny Jacques-Frédéric Mugnier

Gentle and oaky. Ripe. Medium body. Not a lot of grip but elegant if forward. **(09/93)**

Now-2000   **15.0**

Chambolle-Musigny Comte Georges de Vogüé

Lightish colour even for a 1989, but not too evolved. This is pretty but at first a little empty on the nose. Better on the palate. Medium to medium-full body. Some concentration. Good depth for a 1989. Nicely austere too. Not as good as the 1990 but a very good example of a village 1989. **(05/93)**

Now-2005   **16.0**

Chambolle-Musigny Les Amoureuses Daniel Moine-Hudelot

Medium-full colour, some development. Quite evolved on the nose. Was this bottled too late? Medium to medium-full, ripe, good grip and

quite intense. But it lacks style. It is a little blowsy. Quite good. **(05/93)**

Now-2006   **14.0**

Chambolle-Musigny Les Amoureuses Jacques-Frédéric Mugnier

Good colour. Lovely nose. This is really stylish and has super-ripe complex fruit. Medium to medium-full. Slight bitterness on the follow-through, but this is no bad thing. Ripe, balanced, subtle. Elegant. Very very long. Very good indeed. **(05/93)**

Now-2012   **17.0**

Chambolle-Musigny Les Amoureuses Comte Georges de Vogüé

Medium-full colour. This too has a lovely nose. It is softer and rounder than the 1990, but has lovely concentrated fruit. A very lovely plump wine. Medium body. Beautifully balanced. Complex, gentle. Very long and intense at the end. Fine. **(05/93)**

Now-2013   **17.0**

Chambolle-Musigny Les Charmes Georges Clerget

Very good colour. A rather robust, clumsy example. Rich and fruity but four-square and tannic. Good acidity nevertheless. But only average. **(11/94)**

Now-2000   **13.5**

Chambolle-Musigny Les Charmes Ponsot

Good colour. Ripe nose. But not a lot of style and complexity. Medium body. Finishes better than it starts. At first seems a little hard, but is riper and more generous on the follow-through. And the finish is long. This needs time. Good. **(05/93)**

Now-2005   **15.0**

Chambolle-Musigny Les Cras Ghislaine Barthod-Noëllat

Good colour. Very fine subtle, poised, elegant nose. Really very lovely Pinot fruit. Medium to medium-full. On the palate not quite as intense as I would have wished, but balanced, full of finesse and very Chambolle, all silk and lace. **(05/93)**

Now-2005   **16.5**

Chambolle-Musigny Les Gruenchers Dujac

Lightish colour even for a 1989. Soft nose. A little SO_2 but there is fruit and style here. Medium to medium-full. Good balance. More seductive soft Chambolle fruit underpinned by a judicious touch of oak. Ripe. Long. Classy. Complex. Very good plus. **(05/93)**

Now-2010   **16.5**

Chambolle-Musigny *Premier Cru*
Joseph Drouhin

Good colour. This is soft and succulent but quite evolved now. I wouldn't hold it too long. Lacks a little grip. But the fruit is ample and stylish. Good. **(02/96)**

Now-2000   15.0

Chambolle-Musigny   Les Véroilles
Ghislaine Barthod-Noëllat

Medium to medium-full colour. A little clumsy on the nose. Some stems evident. Lacks a bit of generosity. Medium body. It seems to be as much astringent as tannic. Ripe but not exactly very long. Nor very complex. One and a half dimensions only. Slightly raw. **(05/93)**

Now-2008   14.5

Chapelle-Chambertin   Pierre Damoy

Medium colour. Soft, sweet, rather artificially fruity. Ripe but one-dimensional. Quite good at best. Not coarse. But not exciting. Forward and artisanal. **(05/93)**

Now-2001   14.0

Charmes-Chambertin   Bernard Dugat-Py

Fullish colour. Good rich, gently oaky nose. Balanced and stylish. Fullish, totally un-souped-up. Good structure. Well made. This has class and potential. Fine. **(05/93)**

1998-2018   17.5

Charmes-Chambertin   Dujac

Fine colour. Quite strongly new oaky nose. Ripe, rich and concentrated. Above all very good acidity. Fullish, good tannin. This has a 1988 austerity. Fine. **(08/92)**

2000-2012   17.5

Charmes-Chambertin
Roland Remoissenet   Père et Fils

Good colour. Round and very ripe, good grip. Very rich. All the *petits fruits rouges* here. This is long and complex and has plenty of personality. Medium-full body. **(05/93)**

Now-2011   17.5

Charmes-Chambertin   Armand Rousseau

Very ripe, gently oaky. Excellent acidity and really complex. This is better than the Mazis. Very good dimension. Medium-full. Really long. **(05/93)**

1998-2012   17.0

Charmes-Chambertin   Christian Serafin

Medium colour. Firm nose. Rather hard and astringent as a result of the new oak. Kept too long in it, which has spoiled what in fact was rather a good wine. Rigid and four-square again. **(05/93)**

Now-2007   14.5

Chassagne-Montrachet
Jacques Gagnard-Delagrange

Soft, quite evolved. A little rustic. But reasonable grip. **(09/93)**

Now-2000   14.0

Clos-de-la-Roche   Dujac

Fine colour. Opulent and rich. Fatter than the Charmes-Chambertin but more concentrated. Very good backbone. Good tannin. Needs time. A lot of depth. **(08/92)**

2000-2015   18.5

Clos-de-la-Roche   Armand Rousseau

Good colour. Rich, opulent meaty nose. Ripe and with very good grip and structure on the palate. Complex. Long. Very stylish. Fine plus. **(05/93)**

1998-2015   17.5

Clos-de-la-Roche   *Vieilles-Vignes*   Ponsot

Good colour for a 1989. Ripe but lacks a bit of intensity on the nose. On the palate the wine is medium to medium-full, has quite good grip, and is similarly opulent and spicy. But lacks a bit of elegance and freshness for better than a good plus. **(05/93)**

Now-2008   15.5

Clos-Saint-Denis   Bertagna

Medium-full. Soft, blackberry fruit with a touch of chocolate. The stems obtrude a bit and give the wine an aspect of astringency and coarseness. Not that exciting, especially for a *grand cru*. **(05/93)**

Now-2002   14.5

Clos-Saint-Denis   Dujac

Medium-full colour. Some development. Firmer than the Combottes, richer, more chocolate, more mocha. Fatter too. Fullish, quite rich, but it lacks a little grip. This is quite accessible. Good acidity. Lots of charm. Round, open, ripe. Long and fragrant. Very good indeed. **(03/96)**

Now-2005   17.0

Clos-de-Tart   Mommessin

Good colour. Somewhat clumsy, solid nose. But it lacks style. On the palate it is also a bit lumpy. Fullish, some tannin. The fruit is a bit one-dimensional and artificial. This is unexciting. **(05/93)**

Now-2007   14.5

Clos-de-Vougeot   Joseph Drouhin

Full colour. Broader than the 1990. More evolved: a bit more vegetal. But even a suggestion of oxidation. Medium-full. A slight astringency on the palate. This is a little flat. It doesn't sing. Least good of the 1990, 1989, 1988 trio. **(10/94)**

Now-2005   15.0

Clos-de-Vougeot   René Engel

This is fat, rich and concentrated. Very good grip. Full and flamboyant fruit with a touch of the exotic. Still young. Plenty of future. Long. **(05/93)**

1998-2015   17.5

Clos-de-Vougeot   Jean Grivot

Medium-full colour. Now some sign of maturity. Slightly confused on the nose. Was a bit reductive at first. Later a little muddy. On the palate spicy and astringent. I prefer the 1991. Lacks a bit of real concentration and intensity. Merely very good. **(09/94)**

Now-2007   16.0

Clos-de-Vougeot   Alfred Haegelen-Jayer

Very good colour. Impressive nose. Full, rich, concentrated, ample and old-viney. Full, structured. Very good tannins. Very fine concentrated fruit. This has real depth. Very fine. A masculine wine which needs time. **(05/93)**

1999-2019   18.5

Clos-de-Vougeot   Louis Jadot

Good colour. Less voluptuous than the 1990. Less sweet and honeyed too, which surprises me. Very elegant and lovely fruit. Cool, balanced, very good grip. This has individuality, complexity and real elegance. Fine long finish. Not a blockbuster but needs time. Very fine. **(05/93)**

1998-2018   18.5

Clos-de-Vougeot   Méo-Camuzet

Good colour. Just a touch of sulphur on the nose at first. Medium-full, round, fat, fruity. A complex wine with a surprisingly good follow-through, because at first it seems to lack a bit of grip. **(05/93)**

Now-2010   17.0

Clos-de-Vougeot   Mongeard-Mugneret

Good colour. A little muddled on the nose. I don't see the class here. On the palate there is a lack of fruit and the wine is a bit weak. Not much structure and no depth or concentration. Disappointing. Forward. **(05/93)**

Now-2000   13.0

Clos-de-Vougeot   Dr Georges Mugneret

Good colour. Firm, backward nose. Very fine, completely unadulterated Pinot fruit. Rich and ripe, but austere and with very fine acidity. Fullish. Very long, very complex. Very classy. This is very fine again. **(05/93)**

1999-2019   18.5

Clos-de-Vougeot   Jean Raphet

Good colour. Fruity nose. But there is a faint lack of grip here - or is it a bit of SO$_2$? Medium body. Some tannin, some fruit, but not the

complexity, depth or class of the above. This is humdrum as Clos-de-Vougeot often is. Slightly blowsy. Quite good at best. **(05/93)**

Now-2007   14.0

Clos-de-Vougeot   Georges Roumier

Fullish colour. Still quite youthful. This is better than his 1991. Full, balanced, ripe and generous. Very good grip. Fine. Still needs time. **(09/94)**

1998-2012   17.5

Corton   Joseph Drouhin

Good colour. Slightly lean on the nose. And an absence of fat on the attack. Good acidity. Medium-full, intense, stylish. Very long. But it lacks a little weight. Will still improve. Good but not great. **(05/95)**

Now-2003   15.0

Corton   Michel Maillard et Fils

Medium colour. Mature. Ripe, soft nose. Round and succulent but it lacks real concentration and breed. Ready. Not for the long term. Not bad at best. **(12/95)**

Now-2000   13.0

Corton   Roland Rapet

Medium colour. Stylish, cool, plummy nose. Medium-full, balanced, quite complex. This is unexpectedly elegant, and, if not a blockbuster, very subtle and well balanced. Long. Very good plus. **(05/93)**

Now-2009   16.5

Corton   Bressandes   Chandon-de-Briailles

Ripe cherry fruit. Medium-full. Good fat. This is essentially soft but quite rich. Good depth. Very good. Finishes long. **(05/93)**

Now-2009   16.0

Corton   Bressandes   Tollot-Beaut

Medium colour. The nose seems a bit fat and sweet. This is just as undistinguished as the 1990. It is less rigid, and a bit more elegant. And it has reasonable balance. But there is a lack of style. **(05/93)**

Now-2004   13.5

Corton   Pougets   Louis Jadot

Medium to medium-full colour. Soft raspberry-flavoured Pinot on the nose. Medium to medium-full body. Clean, stylish, deceptive; because the attack seems plump and soft, though balanced, and the follow-through is complex and intense. Very good plus for a 1989. **(05/93)**

Now-2008   16.5

Corton   Renardes   François Gay

Full colour. Rich, really quite oaky. Full and very ample. This is almost exotic in its character. Lush, but quite structured and tannic for all that.

Good grip. Still youthful. Very good. **(12/95)**
Now–2004   16.0

Echézeaux   René Engel
Fine nose. A lot of depth here. Rich, firm, full, meaty. Very good grip. Rather better than the Brûlées. Fine. **(05/93)**
1998–2012   17.5

Echézeaux   Joseph Faiveley
Good colour. Very lovely intense nose. High quality here. Full, rich, aromatic. Good grip. Opulent and spicy. Gamey even. Plenty of volume. Still a little unfinished. Very good indeed. **(05/95)**
Now–2007   17.0

Echézeaux   G. et H. Jayer
Good colour. Full fat succulent nose. This has a lot of style, and a lot of depth for a 1989. Fine quality. High-class wine here. Medium-full. Good grip if not a great deal of power and backbone. Lovely fruit. Real style, intensity and complexity. **(05/93)**
Now–2018   18.5

Fixin   Les Hervelets   Bart
Good colour. A little rustic on the nose. This was partly kept in *foudre*. Ample, ripe, good grip. A little more animal than the 1990. Quite full for the vintage. This is good. Certainly a success. Even if it could be a bit more stylish. Ready now. **(12/95)**
Now–2000   14.5

Gevrey-Chambertin   Jean Raphet
Medium colour. Light nose. Forward. This is clean and clear, stylish and fruity. Balanced and with plenty of personality for a simple village wine. Forward but good. Pity about the Clos-de-Vougeot. **(05/93)**
Now–2002   14.5

Gevrey-Chambertin   Philippe Rossignol
Medium colour. Soft and fruity on the nose. Clean and well made. Not a lot of depth though. A competent village 1989. Stylish. Medium body. Lacks a little grip. But classy fruit here. **(05/93)**
Now–2004   14.0

Gevrey-Chambertin   Armand Rousseau
Medium to medium-full colour. The nose is a bit odd. Seems a little overblown as well. Lacks style. A little better acidity than it appeared to have at first. Medium body. But I find it no better than competent. Better than the above. **(05/93)**
Now–2004   15.0

Gevrey-Chambertin   Christian Serafin
Good colour. Good fragrant nose. On the palate a soft wine for early drinking. It lacks a little backbone. Not over-oaked, thankfully, but just a little astringent on the attack. Though it finishes better. Could have done with a bit more weight. **(05/93)**
Now–2000   14.0

Gevrey-Chambertin   *Vieilles-Vignes*   Alain Burguet
Good colour for a 1989. At first just a little sulphur and reduction on the nose. Like so many of these 1989 Gevreys a good plump fruity attack and then it dies away a bit. Ripe and stylish even complex though. Good plus. **(05/93)**
Now–2003   15.5

Gevrey-Chambertin   *Vieilles-Vignes*   Christian Serafin
This is rather better than Serafin's basic village wine. More colour. More depth on the nose and rich and satisfying on the palate. Ripe, balanced, subtle. Long on the finish. Not by any means a blockbuster. **(05/93)**
Now–2006   15.5

Gevrey-Chambertin   Cazetiers   Bruno Clair
Good colour. Much fatter and richer than his Fonteny. Plumper and older-viney on the palate. Has the structure of the Fonteny with extra fat and dimension. Long, classy. Fine. **(05/93)**
1998–2012   17.5

Gevrey-Chambertin   Cazetiers   Joseph Drouhin
Medium to medium-full colour. Fragrant, soft, fruity nose. Good class, good intensity. Medium-full body. This has elegance and balance and shows very well. Lovely fruit. Good harmony. Long. Very good. **(10/94)**
Now–2006   16.0

Gevrey-Chambertin   Cazetiers   Christian Serafin
Medium colour. Full nose. A bit H_2S. Rather lumpy. A little rigid on the palate. Edgy acidity. Medium-full but unstylish. Four-square. Slightly astringent. Too much new oak. Has already dried out. (This was a bottle of the 'American *cuvée*' that Serafin gave me: entirely matured in new oak. The rest of the Serafin wines in this tasting were from British sources.) **(05/93)**
Now–2004   12.5

Gevrey-Chambertin   Clos-du-Fonteny
Bruno Clair

Good colour. Firm, rich, classy Pinot. This has depth. But a slightly lean edge nevertheless. Fullish. Concentrated. Poised and balanced. This is very good plus. Long and stylish. Impressive. **(05/93)**

1998-2015   **16.5**

Gevrey-Chambertin   Clos-Prieur
Harmand-Geoffroy

Very good colour. Quite structured and backward for a 1989. Good fresh but ample, full colour. There is a touch of almost burnt caramel here. Fullish, nicely ripe tannins. Good grip of acidity. A sizeable but not over-macerated wine for the vintage. Rich, ripe, and with plenty of depth. Not the greatest of elegance but generous, balanced and very good plus. **(09/95)**

Now-2007   **16.5**

Gevrey-Chambertin   Clos-Prieur
Rossignol-Trapet

Just a touch rustic. But rich and fat. Medium-full, but a lack of grip and intensity. Quite good; but ultimately it lacks flair. **(09/93)**

Now-2000   **14.0**

Gevrey-Chambertin   Clos-Saint-Jacques
Bartet, Bruno Clair

Good colour. Rather closed on the nose. Very rich and concentrated though. This is full and firm and old-viney. It needs time. It doesn't quite sing yet. But the follow-through is long and promising. Long and very complex and showing real finesse. Certainly fine plus. **(05/93)**

1999-2019   **18.0**

Gevrey-Chambertin   Clos-Saint-Jacques
Armand Rousseau

Good colour. Quite a lot of oak, but the concentration of the wine can take it. Very elegant. Fullish, beautifully balanced. Very ripe indeed, essence of fruit. Subtle. Long. Lovely. Very very complex. **(05/93)**

1999-2009   **19.0**

Gevrey-Chambertin   Aux Combottes   Dujac

Fullish colour. Soft, ripe nose. A touch of the stems. Medium-full. Good slightly lean but ripe, chocolate and black-cherry flavours. Good acidity. Nicely cool but also opulent. Long. Very good plus. **(03/96)**

Now-2005   **16.5**

Gevrey-Chambertin   Les Corbeaux
Denis Bachelet

Medium to medium-full colour. Similarly to his 1990, just a touch herbaceous. Stylish attack. Plump and full of fruit. Medium body. But lacks a little grip on the follow-through. Good. One and a half dimensions only. **(05/93)**

Now-2000   **15.0**

Gevrey-Chambertin   Fonteny
Christian Serafin

A little more oak on the nose than the *Vieilles-Vignes*. More colour too. Medium-full, good grip and structure. Nicely austere in the sense that it is not too jammy, but none of these Serafin wines are. Quite fat and rich. Very good. Complex finish. **(05/93)**

Now-2008   **16.5**

Gevrey-Chambertin   Lavaux-Saint-Jacques
Joseph Drouhin

Good colour. Lovely rich succulent nose. On the palate it doesn't have the class of a 1990 but it is ripe and rich and very well balanced. Really fat and abundant. Lovely fruit. Very good indeed. **(02/96)**

Now-2005   **17.0**

Gevrey-Chambertin   Les Levrées
Fougeray de Beauclair

Medium colour. Simple, somewhat sweet and unstylish nose. Cheap stuff! A weak wine on the palate. No fruit, no depth. No class. Poor. **(05/93)**

Now-2000   **12.0**

Grands-Echézeaux   Joseph Drouhin

Good colour. Sweeter nose than the 1990. Less firm, less depth. Strawberries and raspberries. Plenty of interest. Medium-full, plump, fresh, generous and seductive. Balanced and very elegant. Long and lovely. **(05/93)**

Now-2012   **17.0**

Grands-Echézeaux   René Engel

Marvellous fruit. Really full and rich and fat. Bramble and raspberry in flavour. Splendid acidity. Full, young but impressive. **(05/93)**

1999-2018   **18.5**

Griotte-Chambertin   Joseph Drouhin

Medium to medium-full colour. Not very intense and deep, but still youthful. The nose is very intense but still very youthful. There is almost a *coulis* of fruit: raspberry, cassis and cherry backed up with a very fine acidity. Medium body. Concentrated nevertheless. Ripe, very subtly oaky, rich and very very well balanced. Very young still potentially. Very lovely. Fine plus. Tasted again two years later: 'a Musigny of Chambertins' (18.5). **(11/93)**

Now-2012   **18.0**

Griotte-Chambertin   Ponsot

Good colour. Fat concentrated nose. Still backward. Depth and quality here but currently adolescent. Good new wood addition. Fat, plummy and concentrated. This has good grip. Finishes well. Very good indeed. (05/93)

1998-2008   17.0

Latricières-Chambertin   Joseph Drouhin

Fullish, vigorous colour. Barely mature. Ripe, ample nose. A touch of toffee and spice here. Fullish, rich, still a little tight. Not as open as the Griotte. But rich, fat, voluptuous. Very well balanced. Not quite the nuance or elegance as their Griotte 1989 but certainly fine, and with plenty of vigour. (10/95)

Now-2016   18.0

Latricières-Chambertin   Rossignol-Trapet

This lacks a bit of depth. Medium-full. Pedestrian on the nose. One-dimensional on the palate. Disappointing. (09/93)

Now-2000   14.0

Maranges   Joseph Drouhin

Lightish colour. Good strawberry fruit. No hard edges. Light to medium body. A little thin. But ripe and à point. Not bad. (05/95)

Drink soon   13.0

Marsannay   Les Echézeaux   Marc Brocot

Good colour. This is a little lighter than the 1990, has less freshness and grip. But it also has good fruit and style. Medium body. Good long finish. À point. (12/95)

Drink soon   15.0

Mazis-Chambertin   Joseph Drouhin

Fullish, vigorous colour. Barely mature. Fine plummy nose. Nicely elegant and cool. Rather better style and complexity than the Latricières. Still youthful. Fullish, rich, very classy. Very fine tannins. Nicely ripe. Even fat. This is as good as the Griotte. Still youthful. Still not yet ready by any means. Very fine. (10/95)

1998-2020   18.5

Mazis-Chambertin   Bernard Maume

Good colour. Rich, opulent, voluptuous nose. Plenty of intensity here. This is animal and exotic. I don't exactly find it elegant, but it has depth, fat and concentration. Very good indeed. But very individual. Spicy. (05/93)

1998-2018   17.0

Mazis-Chambertin   Roland Remoissenet Père et Fils

Firm, rich and substantial on the nose. Good depth. Oaky, fat and concentrated. Lovely fruit here. Fullish, very good tannins. Complex. Excellent. (05/93)

Now-2015   18.5

Mazis-Chambertin   Armand Rousseau

Surprisingly advanced on colour and nose. Ripe, soft, not as intense as the Charmes. Very good rather than great. (05/93)

Now-2008   16.0

Morey-Saint-Denis   Dujac

Medium body only, even for a 1989. Some development. A similarly soft fruity wine to the 1990. But evolving fast. Again better on the palate. But only a little. Medium body. It lacks real grip. On the finish it is a bit mawkish. (05/93)

Drink soon   13.5

Morey-Saint-Denis   Joseph Faiveley

Good colour. Attractive nose. Caramel and *coulis*-ed plums. Fullish, meaty, balanced. Rich and fruity. Very good indeed for a village wine. À point. (05/95)

Now-2000 plus   15.5

Morey-Saint-Denis   Clos-de-la-Bussière Georges Roumier

Medium to medium-full mature colour. Rich, firm nose. No stemminess, as in his 1985. Medium-full. Finely balanced. Lovely warm rich attack. Very good grip. I prefer this to the 1985. It is classier and more complete. Fine fruit. Long, complex, lovely. Just about ready. (10/95)

Now-2005 plus   17.5

Morey-Saint-Denis   Cuvée des Grives Ponsot

Medium colour. Like the 1990 but rather vacant on the nose behind the stems. This is weak and short and is going nowhere. Somewhat astringent already. Lightish. A bit sweet. Drink soon. (05/93)

Now-1998   13.0

Morey-Saint-Denis   Cuvée Jean Paul II Edouard Bryczek

Medium colour. The nose lacks distinction. Fruity but without much dimension or class. Medium body. Ripe, slightly sweet. Quite forward. Soft and pleasant but nothing special about it. Diffuse. Not bad at best. (05/93)

Now-2004   13.0

Morey-Saint-Denis   En la Rue de Vergy Bruno Clair

Good colour. Quite a firm nose for a 1989 village wine. Good fruity attack. A little solid. Medium-full. Good grip. All it lacks is a little nuance. Finishes well though. Good, especially for a village *appellation*. (05/93)

Now-2008   15.0

Morey-Saint-Denis   En la Rue de Vergy
Rossignol-Trapet

Oaky. Good grip. But not a lot of depth. A competent wine but it lacks a little flair. **(09/93)**

Now-2000   **14.0**

Le Musigny   Jacques-Frédéric Mugnier

Subtle. Gentle. Rich. Complex. Finely balanced. Lovely. A wine of silky-smooth elegance, fullish, very intense. Packed with fruit. Glorious finish. **(09/93)**

1999-2012   **18.5**

Le Musigny   Comte Georges de Vogüé

Splendid colour. Very rich, marvellously elegant and concentrated nose. Splendid fruit. Very lovely balance. This is really classy, warm complex wine. Just about drinkable. But very vigorous. Very Chambolle. Very high class. Several notes. **(11/95)**

Now-2012   **19.0**

Nuits-Saint-Georges   Robert Chevillon

Light to medium colour. This seems a bit weak and feeble on the nose. Rather lightweight. Lacks grip. A bit suspiciously sweet on the follow-through. Will get attenuated. **(05/93)**

Drink soon   **11.0**

Nuits-Saint-Georges   Henri Gouges

Medium to medium-full colour. Soft nose. Lacks just a little succulence perhaps. Medium body. A little astringency. Lacks a bit of zip and flesh. A bit disappointing after the 1990. **(05/93)**

Now-2000   **13.5**

Nuits-Saint-Georges   G. et H. Jayer

Medium colour. Plump and fruity on the nose. Quite accessible. But lacks style. Like the 1990 this seems a bit forced. Reasonable acidity again - indeed good for a 1989. But a lack of succulence and style. Slightly better than the 1990. **(05/93)**

Now-2003   **14.0**

Nuits-Saint-Georges   Les Boudots
Mongeard-Mugneret

Good fullish colour. Slightly robust nose. Fullish. Round, ripe, rich, slightly hot. But good depth and character if not a lot of class. Good at best. **(02/96)**

Now-2005   **15.0**

Nuits-Saint-Georges   Clos-des-Argillières
Daniel Rion et Fils

Full and meaty for a 1989. A little hard, even, perhaps. The succulent fruit of the Grandes-Vignes is not there. But there is a lot more depth at the end. Very good. **(05/93)**

Now-2010   **16.0**

Nuits-Saint-Georges   Clos-des-Corvées
Louis Jadot

Good colour for a 1989, some evolution. Slight reduction on the nose. Sturdy for a 1989. A hint of the stems too. Firm for 1989. A little adolescent. But good complexity and interest. Good backbone and grip for a 1989. Like the 1990 a very good wine. Indeed even better. **(05/93)**

Now-2006   **16.0**

Nuits-Saint-Georges
Clos-des-Forêts-Saint-Georges   Arlot

Medium to medium-full colour. Still fresh. Youthful. Puppy fat. Very young Pinot fruit. Not a wine of great power or concentration by any means but intense and in its own way opulent. But it lacks a bit of grip and drive on the follow-through. It is not exactly short. Just a bit one-dimensional on the finish. Good but not great. **(05/92)**

Now-2000   **15.0**

Nuits-Saint-Georges   Clos-de-la-Maréchale
Joseph Faiveley

Very good colour. Abundant, fat, luscious nose, but with a good grip of fruit. A bit earthy and adolescent on the palate. The tannins show and the background is typically Nuits. But ripe and satisfying. **(05/93)**

Now-2009   **15.5**

Nuits-Saint-Georges   *Grandes-Vignes*
Daniel Rion et Fils

Good colour. Ripe, strawberry-raspberry fruit on nose and palate. This is softer, rounder, less sturdy but more elegant than the 1990. More accessible of course. Shows well. **(05/93)**

Now-2005   **15.0**

Nuits-Saint-Georges   Hauts-Pruliers
Daniel Rion et Fils

Good colour for 1989. Soft, fresh, ripe nose. Good backbone and reserves for a 1989. Raspberry fruit. This is a very good example of 1989. Balanced. Good grip. Not a blockbuster but good intensity. **(05/93)**

Now-2010   **16.0**

Nuits-Saint-Georges   Aux Murgers
Bertagna

Ripe but a touch of astringency. A little jammy. Reasonable acidity but lacks definition. **(05/93)**

Now-2001   **14.0**

Nuits-Saint-Georges   Aux Murgers
Méo-Camuzet

Very good colour for a 1989. Similar nose to the 1990 but a little more oak in evidence because the acidity is less and the wine softer. Here the oak has given the wine a bit of astringency. A pity, because the fruit is ripe and the wine stylish. A little over-oaked. Good length. **(05/93)**

Now-2008   **16.0**

Nuits-Saint-Georges
Les Porrets-Saint-Georges   Roland Dubois

Good colour. At first a bit tough and reductive. But underneath there is reasonable richness and depth. And certainly the balance if very typically robust Nuits-Saint-Georges is actually not bad at all. Meaty, vigorous. Good. Only just about ready. **(11/94)**

Now-2004   15.0

Nuits-Saint-Georges
Les Porrets-Saint-Georges   Joseph Faiveley

Medium to medium-full colour. Intense fragrant nose. Medium to medium-full. Good grip. Full of fruit. Very ripe tannins. Soft but intense, and still to improve. Long. Fine. **(11/94)**

1998-2012   17.5

Nuits-Saint-Georges   Les Pruliers
Lucien Boillot et Fils

Good structure. Very good acidity. Fresh, ripe, ample, stylish. This is fresh, balanced and very very good. **(09/92)**

Now-2005   16.5

Nuits-Saint-Georges   Les Pruliers
Henri Gouges

Medium to medium-full colour. Good for 1989. Fragrant, stylish nose. This has balance and depth for a 1989. Oaky again. Pleasant but it lacks a bit of concentration on the attack. More grip on the follow-through but only good. **(05/93)**

Now-2002   15.0

Nuits-Saint-Georges   Les Roncières
Robert Chevillon

Reasonable colour. Pretty fruit on the nose. Lacks a little personality and depth perhaps. On the palate medium body. Stylish and well made with good, neatly balanced fruit. Fresh for a 1989. Very good. **(05/93)**

Now-2005   16.0

Nuits-Saint-Georges   En Rue de Chaux
Bertrand Ambroise

Good colour. Good sturdy nose. Not too much new wood. Medium-full, ripe, chunky and chocolatey. Good acidity. Lacks a little real concentration and dimension on the follow-through but good stuff. **(05/93)**

Now-2001   15.0

Nuits-Saint-Georges   Les Saint-Georges
Henri Gouges

Good colour for 1989. Elegant nose. Good intensity and grip and lovely fruit. Medium-full. Good acidity. Perfumed raspberry fruit. Long. Cool. Very elegant. Fine especially for a 1989. **(05/93)**

Now-2010   17.0

Pernand-Vergelesses   Ile-des-Vergelesse
Chandon-de-Briailles

Good colour. This is not a wine with a lot of drive. Indeed it is ready now. Medium body. Elegant. Ripe. Good finish. But a little weak for a 1989. Quite good. Several notes. **(11/94)**

Now-2000   14.0

Pernand-Vergelesses   Ile-des-Vergelesses
Roland Rapet

Medium colour. A little development. Fresh, plump, pleasant but with not great intensity on the nose. Medium body. A ripe wine but with the slightly lean touch of Pernand behind it. Good chewy fruit. Good acidity. Finishes stylishly. Quite good plus. **(05/93)**

Now-2005   14.5

Pommard   Capron-Charcousset

The stems show a bit on the nose. Reasonable colour. Medium body. Good fruit. Good balance. Quite intense. A slight absence of real fat and richness. But quite long and succulent. Ready now. Good. **(12/95)**

Now-2000   15.0

Pommard   Joseph Faiveley

Medium, mature colour. Broad, slightly spicy, mature nose. Some of the usual Pommard sturdiness. Black cherries and quite evolved on the palate. This has a little evidence of sulphur on the aftertaste. *Élevage* not as sound as it could be. Fair only. **(05/95)**

Drink soon   13.5

Pommard   Chaponnières
Raymond Launay

Very good colour. Full and still very vigorous. This is a muscular 1989, and the tannins aren't as sophisticated as the 1991. Slightly bitter. Good fruit here. But a little lumpy. The wines here are better today. Quite good. **(12/95)**

Now-2004   14.0

Pommard   Clos-des-Epeneaux
Comte Armand

Very good colour. Very fine full, rich, concentrated nose. Lots of depth here. Full, structured, very tannic for an 1989. The attack is dense and backward. The follow-through shows real depth, dimension and class. Excellent. Needs time. Very lovely long finish. **(05/93)**

1999-2018   18.5

Pommard   Epenots   Pierre Morey

Medium-full colour now brown at the rim. This is fully ready, soft and fragrant. Ripe and mellow. Not a wine of great concentration and depth. But balanced and elegant. Good. **(06/96)**

Now-2005   15.0

**Pommard Grand-Clos-des-Epenots
De Courcel**

Medium colour. Less than the Rugiens. The
nose is a little drier and not as intense as the
Rugiens. Medium-full, softer, plumper, but less
interest, less depth. Certainly good. But it is
eclipsed by the above. **(05/93)**

Now–2004   **15.0**

Pommard Jarollières Jean-Marc Boillot

Medium to medium-full colour. ripe and rich
on the nose but it has not really opened out yet.
On the palate medium to medium-full. Gentle
for a Pommard even in 1989. Good tannins.
Elegant and balanced. This is already very good.
Will get even better. But round rather than full
and muscular. Plenty of dimension and grip at
the end. Very good plus. **(02/94)**

Now–2008   **16.5**

Pommard Jarollières Pousse d'Or

This, like Lafarge's Clos-du-Château-des-Ducs
has gone into its shell. Currently a bit tannic and
hard. Good acidity but adolescent. Lacking
generosity. Waiting to mellow. But good
potential. **(06/94)**

Now–2010   **15.0**

Pommard Les Noizons Paul Garaudet

Good colour. The wood comes out a bit more
here, because the wine is more evolved. Lovely
fruit. Very good structure. Fullish for a 1989.
Good acidity for the vintage too. Ripe, elegant,
long, even complex - even classy. Very good
indeed. **(12/95)**

1998–2008   **16.0**

Pommard Rugiens Billard-Gonnet

Medium-full, fresh colour. Good style and
depth on the nose. Mellow but youthful. Quite
an earthy wine, but now fully soft on the palate.
Medium to medium-full. Good acidity. Fragrant,
balanced, plenty of depth. Just about ready. This
has plenty of character and complexity. Long on
the finish. Very good. **(02/96)**

Now–2005 plus   **16.0**

Pommard Rugiens De Courcel

Good colour. Rich plummy nose. Lovely ample
ripe fruit. Fullish, firm, quite structured. But
balanced, complex. Lots of depth. This is very
good indeed. Very long. **(05/93)**

Now–2012   **17.0**

Pommard Rugiens Lejeune

Good colour. Caramel, gingerbread and boiled
sweets on the nose. Medium-full. The tannins
stick out a bit, and the wine has a very curious
spice. Slightly astringent. Unbalanced. **(05/93)**

Now–2002   **13.0**

Richebourg Anne et François Gros

Good colour. This lacks just a little zip on the
nose, though it is plump and fruity. Medium to
medium-full. Quite fresh on the palate. Stylish
and very good. But lacks a bit of concentration
and intensity. Very long though. **(05/93)**

1998–2010   **16.5**

Richebourg Jean Gros

Very good colour. Rich, oaky nose. Fullish,
ample, subtle, but curiously supple as well. This
is ripe and concentrated. Reasonably good
acidity. And has breeding. But it lacks just a little
intensity. A little better than the above. Fine
plus. Seductive. **(05/93)**

1998–2019   **17.5**

Richebourg Alain Hudelot-Noëllat

Very good colour. Firm nose. Much more closed.
But on the palate not quite as interesting. There
is plenty of fruit. Good grip and plenty of
depth, but not quite the definition, the complexity or the class. Fine at best. **(05/93)**

1999–2019   **17.5**

**Richebourg Roland Remoissenet
Père et Fils**

Gamey, gypsy-like. Rich. Fine. Sexy. Full, very
good grip. Fine. But very individual. **(09/92)**

1999–2015   **17.5**

La Romanée Bouchard Père et Fils

Similar colour to the 1990 (i.e. not enormous).
A little lighter. Softer on the nose than the 1990,
and a little more attractive. Opulent, fat and rich
on the palate. I like this very much. There is
generosity as well as aristocracy. Fullish, ripe
tannins. Long, ample. Intense. Very fine. The
best of these three (1992, 1991, 1990). **(02/95)**

1999–2015   **18.5**

**Romanée-Saint-Vivant
Alain Hudelot-Noëllat**

Very good colour. Splendid nose. Marvellous
concentrated velvety fruit. Very ripe and rich.
Real class. Fullish, very ripe and concentrated.
Old-viney. Crammed with fruit. Very good grip.
Long. Lovely. And it has the feminine touch of a
true Romanée-Saint-Vivant. Very elegant at the
end. Marvellous finesse. A great 1989. **(05/93)**

1998–2015   **19.5**

**Ruchottes-Chambertin
Dr Georges Mugneret**

Good colour. Firm, rich, oaky nose. Good
depth. Very good style. Nicely austere. Full,
firm, rich, gently oaky on the palate. Lovely
fruit. Structured, balanced. Classy. Quite a
different style from Rousseau. But even better.
More intense. **(05/93)**

1999–2020   **18.5**

Ruchottes-Chambertin
Clos-des-Ruchottes   Armand Rousseau

Good colour. Ripe, succulent nose. Velvety and seductive. Classy and rich. Medium-full. Balanced. Intense. Oaky but not overpowered. This is once again a fine Rousseau wine. (05/93)

1998-2018   18.0

Santenay   Les Gravières   J.F. Chapelle

Evolved colour. Slightly rustic and evolved on the nose. Light, has dried up a bit. Lacks acidity. Now a bit astringent. (12/95)

Drink up   13.0

Savigny-lès-Beaune   Chandon-de-Briailles

Ripe nose. This is not a blockbuster but has good acidity and reasonable structure. A little dry in the middle but better at the end. Quite good. (05/93)

Now-2003   14.0

Savigny-lès-Beaune   La Dominode
Bruno Clair

Medium colour. Ample, plump, rich and old-viney - and quite structured - on the nose. Fullish for the vintage. Good grip. Plenty of depth. This is going to need time. Firm and even a bit *sauvage* at present. But the finish is long and ample. Very good. (05/93)

Now-2009   16.0

Savigny-lès-Beaune   Les Fourneaux
Chandon-de-Briailles

A little bit more *sauvage* than the village wine. A little more intensity. Good. Finishes well. (05/93)

Now-2005   14.5

Savigny-lès-Beaune   Les Hauts-Jarrons
Jean Guiton

This is better than the 1990. Ripe and succulent. Not a lot of dimension or depth. But has fruit and charm and some substance. Quite good plus. (12/95)

Now-2002   14.5

Savigny-lès-Beaune   Les Lavières
Chandon-de-Briailles

This is really a little dry, because it doesn't quite have the acidity of the Fourneaux. Less grip and less drive. (05/93)

Now-2002   14.0

Savigny-lès-Beaune   Les Lavières
Claude Maréchal

This is not as fine as the 1993 is. There has been a learning curve here. (This was Maréchal's first vintage.) But it is ripe and succulent. But there is something a bit coarse about the tannins. Ready now. (12/95)

Now-2000   13.5

Volnay   Gilles Lafarge

Not bad. A touch raw perhaps. Good acidity. (09/93)

Now-2000   13.5

Volnay   Caillerets
Vincent Bitouzet-Prieur

Good colour. Soft nose. Forward, fragrant. A nice touch of violets here. Medium body. Has charm and plump ripe fruit. But not a wine for the long term. Yet the finish is long. An elegant wine. Very Volnay. Good. (05/93)

Now-2005   15.0

Volnay   Caillerets   Yvon Clerget

Medium-full colour. Quite rustic on the nose. A little reduction here. Better on the palate. Nicely fragrant. Fullish. Harmonious. Long. A classic example if a little farmyardy. Very good. (07/95)

Now-2008   16.0

Volnay   Champans   Marquis d'Angerville

Medium colour. Some development. Rich, round, ripe and fragrant. Very berry-like, almost sweet. Quite oaky, in a sandalwoody way. On the palate it is a bit heavy and a bit edgy. The acidity seems a bit artificial. Medium-full. Unbalanced. Will this get itself together as it ages? (07/95)

Now-2006   14.0

Volnay   Champans   Comtes Lafon

This is bigger, fatter and more concentrated than the Clos-des-Chênes 1989. Lovely in fact. Delicious fruit. Fullish but already velvety. Harmonious and subtle and very elegant. Lovely. Very good oak base. Very fine fruit. (09/92)

1998-2010   17.0

Volnay   Champans   Joseph Voillot

Classically generous and fruity. Very representative of the vintage. Medium to medium-full body. Fragrant, ripe and stylish. A good, well-made example. (06/94)

Now-2005   15.0

Volnay   Clos-de-la-Barre
Olivier Leflaive Frères

Slightly rigid, but ripe and stylish. Reasonable depth. Medium body. Slight hardness here. (09/92)

Now-2004   15.0

Volnay   Clos-du-Château-des-Ducs
Michel Lafarge

Fine colour. This has closed in, and tasted more like a 1988 and a 1989. Very good acidity. Austere. fullish. Classic Pinot fruit. But it is going to need time. Very good quality indeed though. (06/94)

1998-2012   17.0

Volnay Clos-des-Chênes Joseph Drouhin

Good colour. Lovely nose. A touch of chocolate as well as violets and raspberry. Still fresh. Medium body. Fragrant, good acidity, plenty of length and complexity. Real Volnay style and finesse here. Very good indeed. (05/95)

Now-2001   17.0

Volnay Clos-des-Chênes Michel Lafarge

Fuller, richer, more backward. More profound than the Château-des-Ducs. Fine plus. (09/93)

2000-2015   18.0

Volnay Clos-des-Chênes Comtes Lafon

Ripe, fresh, soft fruity nose and palate. Very good grip. Ample and lush. Soft and silky. This seems more elegant than the 1990. (09/92)

Now-2007   17.0

Volnay Fremiers Lucien Boillot et Fils

Very fine colour. Still closed on the nose. Rich and black-cherry fruit on nose and palate. Just possibly a little suave. But clean and classy. Fat and concentrated and plump. Can be drunk now but better still in two to three years. Very good plus. (02/94)

Now-2010   16.5

Volnay Fremiets Olivier Leflaive Frères

Rich and fat and with good acidity. This is stylish. Good balance. Medium body. Good length. Shows well. (09/92)

Now-2004   16.0

Volnay Santenots Matrot

Medium-full colour. Some development. A touch vegetal on the nose, which is curious for this vintage. Quite a spicy example. Richer than it appeared on the nose. Medium-full. Slightly tails off at the end. Lacks a little intensity. Good. (07/95)

Now-2005   15.0

Volnay Santenots-du-Milieu Comtes Lafon

Full colour. Full and immature. Closed, full, quite tannic nose. Good fruit though. Fullish, fat, rich and meaty – in the best sense – not as concentrated or as much depth as the 1990, but a fine, straight, nicely harmonious and fresh 1989. This is much less adolescent than the 1990. Very pure. (07/95)

Now-2009   17.5

Vosne-Romanée René Engel

Good colour. Slight reduction taint on the nose. Better on the palate. Quite structured for a village 1989. Good intensity. Plenty of depth here. Very good indeed for a village wine. (05/93)

1998-2009   15.0

Vosne-Romanée Daniel Rion et Fils

Medium-full colour. Ripe, concentrated fragrant nose. A lot of depth for a village wine. Tannins just about absorbed but still a little raw. Very good grip. Slightly rigid perhaps but this will go. Good. (10/95)

1999-2009   15.0

Vosne-Romanée Emmanuel Rouget

Henri Jayer by another name . . . and at half the price. Good colour. Very good *petits fruits rouges* and oak nose. Very good concentration and grip. Almost on the verge of being too oaky. Two glasses was fine. I am not sure I would have really wanted the whole bottle to myself. Just about ready. Finely made. 18.0 or 15.0 according to taste. (06/96)

Now-2005 plus   16.5

Vosne-Romanée Les Beaux-Monts Bertagna

Medium to medium-full. Good acidity. This is a little raw but has good depth. Slightly adolescent. But stylish and fruity. (05/93)

Now-2004   15.5

Vosne-Romanée Les Beaumonts Jean Grivot

Good full fresh colour. Quite firm and closed. Very concentrated and fresh on the palate. Full, aromatic, very ripe. This is concentrated, very good grip. Still very young. Still slightly lumpy and aggressive. But the finish is rich, balanced, intense and classy. Lush fruit underneath. Will still improve. Very good indeed. (11/95)

Now-2010   17.0

Vosne-Romanée Les Brûlées René Engel

Fullish, meaty, rich. Very good tannins. Enough acidity. Slightly tails away at the end but not short. Lovely bramble fruit. Very good. (05/93)

1998-2010   16.0

Vosne-Romanée Champs-Perdrix Bruno Clair

Medium-full colour. Good for 1989 but really surprisingly developed. No undue development on the nose and palate though. Soft, round, quite forward. A plump attractive wine but without the elegance and complexity of the 1990. Good. (05/93)

Now-2003   15.0

Vosne-Romanée Clos-des-Réas Jean Gros

Medium-full colour. Fine poised elegant gently oaky nose. This is very stylish. Not a blockbuster but very good intensity for a 1989. Lovely fruit. Much more together than the 1990. This shows very well indeed. Super succulent finish. Very well balanced. Fine plus. (05/93)

Now-2000   17.5

Vosne-Romanée L'Orveau
Sylvain Cathiard

Good colour. Quite firm, even slightly hard on the nose, without the opulent fruit of most 1989s, but certainly with no lack of substance. This is a touch astringent. A little over-extracted. But good grip. Perhaps it will round out. **(11/93)**

Now–2005   **15.5**

Vosne-Romanée Suchots
Alain Hudelot-Noëllat

Good colour. This has good depth and structure for a 1989. Rich, not apparently very oaky. Good grip. What it lacks is a little finesse and real personality. Medium full. Good plus. **(06/96)**

Now–2005   **15.5**

Vougeot Les Perrières Bertagna

Ripe attack and with reasonable acidity. But on the follow-through a slightly earthy taste and a lack of fat. Lacks a bit of style. **(05/93)**

Now–2002   **14.0**

1988

RATING FOR THE VINTAGE

Red: 17.0   **White:** 14.5

SIZE OF THE CROP

(Hectolitres, excluding generic wine)

	Red	White
Grands Crus	12,797	3,533
Village and Premiers Crus	170,056	46,434
Total	182,853	49,967

A large white-wine crop: 27 per cent above that of 1987 and 11.5 per cent more than what 1989 would produce, though smaller than 1986 and more than 10 per cent less than 1990. The red-wine harvest was 5 per cent less than what the next year would bring, and only 7 per cent up on the previous vintage.

It was a late harvest, and one where the weather improved as September progressed. As a consequence it is a much better vintage in red wine than in white: only average to good for the latter, very good indeed – even fine – for the former.

WEATHER CONDITIONS

A mild wet winter was followed by a mild wet spring. It was warm in April, though there was frost in some of the Meursault vineyards towards the end of the month, and the first half of May was really quite hot. Then the rain returned and the temperatures dropped, but as the growth of the vines was already a week or more in advance of the norm this did not cause any anxiety. In June the weather improved, and four days of fine sunny weather between the 10th and 15th saw the flowering take place without mishap. Again the cool wet weather returned, winding up to a final thunderstorm on 29 June, and finally blowing itself out. From 1 July onwards the climate improved. The latter half of the month was exceptionally warm – reaching 33 degrees on the 23rd – though interrupted by brief thundershowers, one of which brought hail to parts of Volnay, Monthélie and Meursault, though as far as the latter village was concerned, not in the *premier cru* vineyards. August was dry and warm, as was the beginning of September. So we come to the vital month, the four or five critical weeks which precede the start of the vintage and during which the grapes are collected. It began badly. The week prior to 18 September was cloudy and cool; there was rain. Thereafter the weather improved. There were a few showers in the first and second weeks of October, but by this time, as far as the Côte-de-Beaune was concerned, the harvest was safely in the cellar.

The date of the harvest was as critical as the size of the yield. Some growers commenced on September 22nd and had finished by the 29th. These producers picked fruit which was not only barely ripe but also still diluted by the rains which had fallen earlier in the month. I need hardly add that the results are indifferent. Those who waited until the end of the month fared better. The grapes gained a degree if not a degree and a half of potential alcohol in the fortnight after 20 September. At the end of the harvest the old vines in the *grands crus* were coming in at 14 degrees, and the few showers in October, I was told, did little harm.

THE STYLE OF THE WINE

WHITE WINES

Though there was no rot, the September rains caused problems for the white-wine growers. 'It was not that there was such a large quantity of bunches,' said Gérard Boudot of Domaine Étienne Sauzet, 'but that the berries were very large. It would have been better to have produced the same quantity with a third more bunches. We would have had a better ratio of juice to grape-skins, under which is all the flavour.'

The result was wines which were clean and healthy, but at the start somewhat neutral, and a wide variation between the quality - the depth and interest - of the village wines and the best of the *premiers* and *grands crus*.

But they have kept well, because the acidity levels are good. Despite the mediocre overall mark above, there are plenty of pleasant surprises.

RED WINES

The word for the vintage is consistency. It is consistent from Bourgogne *rouge* to *grand cru* and consistent from Marsannay in the north to Santenay in the south. I find it particularly exciting in Gevrey-Chambertin. I have also tasted some fine Volnays and Pommards. The Cortons and the Nuits-Saint-Georges, though, are patchy.

It is a vintage of classically balanced, slightly austere but ripe wines with delicious fresh fruit. The fruit flavours run across the spectrum from cherries and redcurrants to raspberries, blackberries, damson and blackcurrant. Some wines, particularly those vinified with a prior *macération à froid* show additional aromatic elements which suggest liquorice, hot tea, bitter chocolate, resin, and molasses. Some, and this I always recognise as a good sign in a young Burgundy, indicate freshly ground coffee. What I like about the 1988 wines is their vigour and personality and their potential ability to last and age well. The wines are fullish, the tannins mature, the grip sound. It is a fine vintage. It will also keep exceptionally well.

WHERE ARE THE BEST WINES?

★ Much better in red than in white: and more consistent too.

★ The whites are proportionately better as one climbs up the hierarchy from village to *premier cru* and *grand cru*.

★ A good year for the out-of-the-way white wine villages which pick later.

★ A fine year for Corton-Charlemagne.

★ Consistent red wines, in general proportionately better in the Côte-de-Nuits than in the Côte-de-Beaune.

State of Maturity Today

White: All but the very, very best *grands crus* are now fully ready. In the case of some of the village wines it would be best to drink them soon, before they lose their freshness. As for the better wines, the 'pleasant surprises' (see above) will last well, but the rest again need drinking fairly soon. They have got as far as ever they were going to.

Red: Even some simple village wines still need keeping. They will continue to round off to their advantage. Most of the *premiers crus*, let alone the *grands crus*, are several years from their peak, still rather lean and austere, though they are beginning to soften up. In general 1988 is a vintage which need give no-one any qualms about continuing to cellar. The longer the better! This vintage will last and last, the wines becoming increasingly more elegant and complex as they age. They will never have the lush generosity of the 1990s, but what they will offer, in their somewhat stand-offish way, is purity and finesse.

Tasting Notes

Blanc

Bâtard-Montrachet   Blain-Gagnard

A little four-square on the nose. But closed as well. Yet I don't think this has the richness and concentration it should have. Quite full, but a bit heavy. It lacks zip and depth. Ripe but pedestrian and one-dimensional. **(02/92)**

Now–2002   14.5

Bâtard-Montrachet   Jacques Gagnard-Delagrange

Seems a little weak on the nose. Already very evolved. This is fluid and insipid. Grossly over-produced, I would guess. Will turn up its toes soon. **(01/91)**

Drink soon   13.5

Bâtard-Montrachet   Louis Latour

Quite closed but ripe and opulent and honeyed on the nose. Good reserves underneath. On the palate it is a bit too evolved, even a touch oxidised. It lacks acidity. This is a disappointment. Yet the fruit is/was quite classy. A pity. **(02/92)**

Drink soon   14.0

Bâtard-Montrachet   Leflaive

Corked but seems fat, concentrated and fruity, but not as concentrated as Sauzet's. Suggest very good indeed. **(01/91)**

Now–2005   17.0

Bâtard-Montrachet   Ramonet

Strongly oaky, good depth, backward nose. This is high quality. A full, classic, concentrated wine which needs time. Closed-in at present. **(01/91)**

1998–2010   18.0

Bâtard-Montrachet   Étienne Sauzet

A lot better on the nose than his Bienvenues. Stylish, subtle, even concentrated. There is breed and quality here. Very Sauzet, all in delicacy and finesse. Good concentration. Long. Subtle. Fine. **(01/91)**

Now–2007   17.5

**Bienvenues-Bâtard-Montrachet
Louis Carillon**

Delicate nose, almost to the point of being watery. Stylish though. Pretty but lacks depth. The follow-through is a bit dilute but the finish comes back. A subtle wine, but not a great one by any means. **(01/91)**

Now–2002   16.0

**Bienvenues-Bâtard-Montrachet
Étienne Sauzet**

Something a little rancid about the nose. The oak is a bit forced. Underneath there is stylish fruit and good acidity, but not enough concentration. The whole thing is a little fluid and one-dimensional for a *grand cru*. **(01/91)**

Now–2002   14.5

Chassagne-Montrachet   Chartron et Trébuchet

High-toned, ripe nose. But lacks a bit of grip underneath. Some oak. Some SO_2. But a lack of fruit and concentration. Dull and unstylish. **(02/92)**

Drink soon   13.0

**Chassagne-Montrachet
Michel Colin-Deléger**

Gentle, fragrant nose. Bit of H_2S. Lightish, lacks a bit of grip. Pretty but too forward to be

serious. **(02/92)**
Drink soon   13.5

Chassagne-Montrachet Joseph Drouhin
This seems a bit too evolved already. Thin and weak. Far too old already. Poor. **(02/92)**
Drink up   11.0

Chassagne-Montrachet Henri Laroche
Fresh and balanced on the nose, but not a lot of structure. Lightish. A little empty and fruitless. But quite clean. Boring essentially. Not bad plus. **(02/92)**
Drink soon   13.5

Chassagne-Montrachet Ponsot-Morey
Youthful nose but lacks real depth. Superficial. Honeyed but lacks substance on the palate as well as grip. Evolving fast. **(02/92)**
Drink soon   13.0

Chassagne-Montrachet Étienne Sauzet
Ripe, quite forward Chardonnay with just a vestige of SO_2. A little four-square. Lacks a little zip and dimension. Better as it evolved in the glass. Stylish, nutty, attractive. Good acidity. Not a great deal of concentration. **(02/91)**
Drink soon   14.0

Chassagne-Montrachet Caillerets
Jean-Noël Gagnard
Very good gentle oak, but a little austere on the nose; but in a stylish, ripe enough way. On the palate this is clean and very elegant. But two rather than three dimensions. Lacks a bit of concentration. **(06/92)**
Drink soon   15.5

Chassagne-Montrachet Caillerets
Jean-Marc Morey
Just a little weak on the nose. Medium body. Quite pretty and reasonably balanced. But a lack of real depth. Quite good only. **(02/92)**
Drink soon   14.0

Chassagne-Montrachet Les Embrazées
Bernard Morey
Over-evolved, scented, slightly oxidised nose. A disgrace. Already tired. **(02/92)**
Drink up   11.0

Chassagne-Montrachet Morgeots
Jean-Noël Gagnard
Ripe, balanced, full of interest. Quite fat, a little four-square. Good length. Good vigour. Very good. **(10/92)**
Drink soon   16.0

Chassagne-Montrachet Morgeots
Bernard Morey
Slightly heavy on the nose. A bit of H_2S. On the

palate there isn't too much SO_2. Full. Good grip. This is youthful, fresh and balanced. Quite a masculine example. **(02/92)**
Now-2000   16.0

Chassagne-Montrachet Morgeots
Roland Remoissenet Père et Fils
This is a little flat, some built-in sulphur. Rather boring. Quite youthful still, but no life, no fruit, no personality. **(06/96)**
Drink soon   14.0

Chassagne-Montrachet Morgeots, Clos-de-la-Chapelle Duc de Magenta, Louis Jadot
Ripe and clean, slightly hard, now just about mature. Not a lot of fat and concentration but stylish and balanced. **(08/93)**
Drink soon   15.0

Chassagne-Montrachet Vide-Bourse
Gabriel Jouard
Slightly overblown, but ripe enough and with reasonable acidity. But tastes older than it is. **(03/93)**
Drink soon   14.0

Chevalier-Montrachet Jean Chartron
Oak and fat but evolved, lacks zip. Both on nose and palate. This doesn't have much of a future. **(01/91)**
Drink soon   14.0

Chevalier-Montrachet Leflaive
Not a blockbuster. Nor a wine of powerful intensity of fruit, but that is the vintage. Yet balanced and stylish and subtle. Very good indeed but not great. Sauzet's Bâtard is better. **(01/91)**
Drink soon   15.5

Chevalier-Montrachet Les Demoiselles
Louis Latour
Good oak, but a little sulphur. A little of a lack of grip on the nose. An opulent wine. Rich, gently oaky. Subtle. This has splendid elegance and definition. Very fine. **(02/92)**
Now-2010   19.0

Corton Blanc Chandon-de-Briailles
This is still very youthful. Fresh, fullish. Very good oaky elements. Good acidity. Nicely ripe without being very rich. Delicious. Plenty of life. Fine. **(11/95)**
Now-2000 plus   17.5

Corton-Charlemagne
Bonneau du Martray
Round, soft and almost gentle - it certainly will be in a couple of years. Good grip. Plenty of depth. Very classy oaky support. It is not as concentrated as the above but it has breed and

complexity and very good fruit. Long and lovely on the finish. Fine. **(02/92)**

Now–2004   **17.5**

Corton-Charlemagne   Louis Latour

Quite firm. Oaky, with almost a hazelnut aspect. Plenty of ripe fruit. This is good. Yet on the palate, though more obviously oaky and more accessible, it doesn't have the depth of the Bonneau du Martray. **(02/92)**

Now–2004   **17.0**

Corton-Charlemagne
Olivier Leflaive Frères

Fragrant nose. Quite full, but fleshy, even a touch scented as well. Good oak. On the palate the oak is evident and there is good fresh fragrant fruit. Like the above that extra element of real depth is missing. Very good though. **(02/92)**

Now–2002   **16.0**

Corton-Charlemagne   Roland Rapet

Rather a lot of sulphur on the nose. Difficult to see what, if anything, lies under the wet wool. The answer on the palate is 'nothing much'. **(02/92)**

Drink soon   **13.5**

Corton-Charlemagne   Roland Remoissenet
Père et Fils

This is quite delicious. Soft and gently oaky. Ripe and round. Stylish. Long. Very classy. Lovely fruit. Fine. **(01/91)**

Now–2005   **17.5**

Criots-Bâtard-Montrachet
Olivier Leflaive Frères

Backward nose but subtle, oaky, balanced and stylish. This is fine. Balanced and complex. Fullish. All elements in place and in harmony. Ripe and concentrated. This has breed. Several notes since confirm this as an excellent 1988. **(02/92)**

Now–2010   **18.5**

Meursault   Henri Germain

Ripe and honeyed on the nose, though it lacks a bit of structure and grip. Good oak. A harmonious wine. Good for a village example. Long. Very good fruit. Complex. Very good. **(02/92)**

Now–2000   **16.0**

Meursault   Louis Jadot

Good oak. Not a blockbuster though. Already quite evolved. Yes, there isn't much fruit here. And it already shows a bit of age. Quite good at best. **(02/92)**

Drink soon   **14.0**

Meursault   Charles et Rémi Jobard

Nose a bit awkward but ripe, balanced and concentrated on the palate. Long, plenty of character. Very good for a village 1988. **(03/93)**

Now–2005   **16.0**

Meursault   Comtes Lafon

Ripe, restrained Chardonnay. Oak, Granny Smith, butter nose, with a touch of mint. This has good fresh acidity, balance, style and interest. Still crisp. A lot more personality than most. Good for a village example. **(08/91)**

Now–2002   **15.0**

Meursault   Louis Latour

Quite stylish on the nose. But a bit delicate. Reasonable acidity but lacks a bit of fruit and succulence. Essentially boring. **(02/92)**

Drink soon   **14.0**

Meursault   Matrot

Slightly overblown on the nose. Sweet, lacks grip. On the palate rather hard and charmless, though some fruit and not too short. But essentially dull. **(02/92)**

Now–2000   **13.5**

Meursault   Michelot

A lot of sulphur here on the nose also. A bit fresher than the above. A little more oak and fruit. This is at least drinkable - just! **(02/92)**

Drink soon   **12.5**

Meursault   Blagny   Louis Latour

Light nose. High-toned. Lacks structure and depth. Too superficial. Thin on the palate. Now showing age. Little here. Except that it is reasonably clean, I suppose. **(02/92)**

Drink soon   **13.0**

Meursault   Blagny   Matrot

SO_2 on the nose. A lack of depth underneath. This is a bit rigid. There is more structure than fruit. Yet it is better than the above. It may improve. **(02/92)**

Now–2000   **14.0**

Meursault   Bouchères   Joseph Faiveley

Crisp colour. Rich nutty oaky nose. Smoky oak. Soft on the palate. Good acidity. This is delicate and stylish. **(06/92)**

Drink soon   **15.0**

Meursault   Charmes   Henri Germain

Firm, backward nose. A little four-square but there is depth here. This is in the same mode but the balance and extract is better and the oak doesn't dominate too much. Good grip. Quite rich. **(02/92)**

Now–2000   **16.0**

Meursault Charmes Louis Jadot

Round, flowery nose. Some fat. Good depth here. Concentrated. Backward. Masculine. This has structure and grip. Plenty of fruit. Long. Very good plus. (02/92)

Now-2000   16.5

Meursault Charmes Comtes Lafon

Fatter, richer nose, more hidden. More concentrated. There is plenty of depth here. Good grip. Quite full, plenty of character. This will still improve. Satisfying mixture of oak and fruit on the palate. More opulent than the village Meursault. A significant step up. Several notes. (08/91)

Now-2005   16.5

Meursault Charmes Matrot

Fresh colour. Good nutty nose. Fresh, classy and nicely austere on the palate. Medium body. Good acidity. Clean flowery fruit. Long, stylish, complex at the end. Very good. (11/95)

Now-2003   16.0

Meursault Clos-de-la-Barre Comtes Lafon

Quite marked acidity at the end. Yet slightly evolved on the nose. Spicy. All these are much more elegant on the palate than on the nose. Medium body. A little lean. But the finish is fresh if a bit one-dimensional. Yet good for the vintage. (06/94)

Now-2002   16.0

Meursault Genevrières Comtes Lafon

A bit tarty. Slight touch of astringency. More to it than the Charmes. Reasonable depth. Long. Very good. Will still develop. Four-square. But it lacks real elegance, especially on the nose. (06/94)

Now-2005   17.0

Meursault Genevrières Louis Latour

Good nose. Still a little closed. Fragrant. Has depth. Round. Gently oaky. Full. Concentrated, backward palate. Rich, slightly hidden. Fine finish. This is a serious wine. Fine. (02/92)

Now-2000   17.0

Meursault Goutte d'Or Comtes Lafon

Original nose. A quite four-square wine with a crab-apple flavour. Good acidity. But in comparison with the 1989 *premiers crus* a touch rustic. Slightly hard. Medium-full. What it lacks is a bit of fat. But no lack of thrust and substance. Good plus, but one and a half dimensions only. (09/92)

Now-2003   15.5

Meursault Les Narvaux Chavy-Chouet

A touch of SO$_2$ on the attack but not on the finish. Like many 1988s it lacks a little

personality, but it is fresh and balanced. (03/93)

Drink soon   14.0

Meursault Perrières Joseph Drouhin

Rich, fat, good fruit and good depth. This is succulent and balanced. Seems ready now but it will last well. (02/92)

Now-2002   17.0

Meursault Perrières Comtes Lafon

Much the best. Fresh, plump. Even fat. Flowery. Peachy. This is very enjoyable. Long. Stylish. Oaky. Plummy. A little blowsy on the nose but fine on the palate. (06/94)

Now-2004   17.5

Meursault Rougeots
Jean-François Coche-Dury

Good colour. The acidity and the oak - very good oak - show a bit at the beginning. But the wine is very well made and very classy and it gets rounder and rounder as it develops. Very good indeed and plenty of life. Classy, complex finish. (02/94)

Now-2000   17.0

Meursault Les Tessons Pierre Morey

Fine fresh nose. This is stylish. Slightly austere. Slightly almost bitter aftertaste. Plenty of fat and depth underneath. Subtle. Very good acidity. Real depth here. Fine for a village wine. Several notes. (02/96)

Now-2002   16.0

Le Montrachet Marquis de Laguiche, Joseph Drouhin

This is very stylish on the nose. Plump, discreet, concentrated on the palate. This has a lot of depth and style. Lovely fruit. Long, subtle. Delicious. (01/91)

Now-2015   18.5

Le Montrachet Ramonet

Fine, concentrated, oaky nose. Fine acidity, concentrated and closed. This is a brilliant wine. Finely balanced. Sensational quality. Real depth and breed. Very long. Multi-dimensional. Really lovely. (01/91)

1999-2020   20.0

Le Montrachet
Roland Remoissenet Père et Fils

Still very young. The nose is still closed. On the palate fullish rather than very full. Very good grip. Very stylish oaky base. But at first not the strength of Le Montrachet. It developed considerably in the glass though. This is a lot richer than most 1988s. Got fatter and fatter and richer and richer. After half an hour one had a wine with real depth and concentration. Very long. Very complex. Very fine indeed. Several notes. (03/94)

1998-2018   19.5

Le Montrachet Romanée-Conti

Closed, rich, a little dumb at present. But plenty of depth here. Certainly fine quality. Needs time. Best of all on the finish which is oaky and fat. **(11/91)**

Now-2005   **18.5**

Musigny Blanc Comte Georges de Vogüé

Medium gold colour. Delicate, honeyed, oaky nose. Rich, fullish, aromatic, apricotty. Good acidity. Fresh and quite alcoholic. Much more impressive than older vintages I have had. This will keep. For a 1988 it is complex and has enough fruit to keep for ten years at least. Essentially subtle and delicate. **(07/91)**

Now-2003   **17.0**

Puligny-Montrachet Louis Jadot

Rather heavy and four-square on the nose. Alcohol and sulphur. Some richness underneath. This will get better, but it lacks real depth and class. The fruit is essentially one-dimensional. **(02/92)**

Drink soon   **14.0**

Puligny-Montrachet Leflaive

Pretty nose but lacks intensity and depth. A little weak as well. A gentle wine, quite pretty, but lacks real grip. Pleasant for now but not for the long term. **(02/92)**

Drink soon   **13.5**

Puligny-Montrachet Étienne Sauzet

Quite closed on the nose. Good fruit. This has subtlety. It is young at the moment and there is a little sulphur but there is richness and depth too. Good plus. Finishes very well. **(02/92)**

Now-2000   **15.5**

Puligny-Montrachet Champs-Canet Joseph Drouhin

Closed nose. Quite full and rich though. Yet a touch heavy, it seems. On the palate not too bad. Medium-full. Ripe. Quite stylish and balanced. Quite fat and rich even. Will improve. **(02/92)**

Now-2000   **15.5**

Puligny-Montrachet Clavoillons Leflaive

A bit of sulphur over a four-square wine with a lack of real fruit. Rather a dull wine. Rich but a bit heavy. There is something here but it lacks class. And I don't think it will really improve with age. **(02/92)**

Drink soon   **13.5**

Puligny-Montrachet Clos-de-la-Garenne Joseph Drouhin

A bit overblown on the nose. Lacks grip. A bit of weakness here. Weedy on the palate. Pretty but coarse. No future. **(02/92)**

Drink soon   **13.0**

Puligny-Montrachet Clos-de-la-Mouchère Jean Boillot

This is good, but it is by no means brilliant. For what it lacks is real concentration and finesse. Medium body. Crisp and balanced. Gently oaky. Quite ripe and honeyed. But there is a touch of built-in SO_2 and it is quite evolved. Yet it is not inelegant. **(02/95)**

Drink soon   **15.0**

Puligny-Montrachet Les Combettes Leflaive

Quite strong toasted oak on the nose but how much depth is there underneath? Certainly quite ripe and concentrated at the very least. Ripe, rich, good grip and freshness. This is still young. But potential here. Fine. **(02/92)**

Now-2004   **17.5**

Puligny-Montrachet Les Combettes Étienne Sauzet

Backward nose but it doesn't really excite. On the palate there is fruit, grip and oak. Even concentration and ripeness on the finish. It finishes better than it starts. Medium-full. **(02/92)**

Now-2001   **15.0**

Puligny-Montrachet Les Enseignières Chavy-Chouet

Better than their Narvaux. More personality, more depth. Good structure and balance. Good. **(03/93)**

Drink soon   **15.0**

Puligny-Montrachet Les Folatières Boisson-Vadot

Quite oaky, some fruit but not a lot of depth on the nose. Medium body. Ripe and pleasant but it lacks real depth and grip. Starts and finishes reasonably but no real dimension. **(02/92)**

Drink soon   **14.5**

Puligny-Montrachet Les Folatières Henri Clerc

Rich, fat, good fruit and good depth. This is succulent and balanced. Seems ready now but it will last well. **(02/92)**

Now-2000   **16.0**

Puligny-Montrachet Les Folatières Joseph Drouhin

Fullish, a little hard and ungenerous. High acidity. Will get better as it rounds off. But it lacks a little ripeness and fruit. Good plus. **(02/92)**

Now-2000   **15.5**

Puligny-Montrachet Les Folatières Louis Latour

A little austere but stylish, balanced nose. Not a lot of richness and dimension. But what there is is fresh and balanced. Medium body. Good finish. Will keep well. Good but not great. **(02/92)**

Now–2000   **15.0**

Puligny-Montrachet   Les Garennes
Olivier Leflaive Frères

A shade austere, if not four-square on the nose. It lacks a little richness. Rather short and dilute on the palate. Lacks fruit. **(02/92)**

Drink soon   **13.5**

Puligny-Montrachet   Les Pucelles   Leflaive

More austere nose than their Combettes. Less richness. A bit more obvious sulphur. Nevertheless good on the palate. Fullish, a bit four-square but for a 1988 this has depth and quality. Very good. Finishes well. **(02/92)**

Now–2000   **15.5**

Puligny-Montrachet   Les Pucelles
Olivier Leflaive Frères

Soft, scented, creamy nose. Medium-full, fragrant, round and flowery. Good complexity, class and harmony. Essentially feminine. Just about ready. Very good. **(02/92)**

Drink soon   **16.0**

Puligny-Montrachet   Les Referts
Étienne Sauzet

Seems a bit weak and vegetal on the nose. Weedy and insipid on the palate. Lacks depth. Now getting old. **(02/92)**

Drink up   **12.0**

Saint-Aubin   Louis Jadot

Soft but quite stylish nose. Yet a bit hard and fruitless on the palate. Lacks real fat and richness. Medium body. Good acidity but a bit anonymous and four-square. **(02/92)**

Drink soon   **14.0**

Saint-Aubin   Les Champlots
Jean-Claude Bachelet

Still some SO_2 here, indeed far too much. It is masking the fruit. Reasonable fruit underneath. Now soft. But too much – and too much in-built. Hot finish. It is getting rigid. **(12/95)**

Drink soon   **13.0**

Saint-Aubin   Les Frionnes
André Moingeon

A bit watery. Dull. **(03/93)**

Drink up   **12.0**

Vougeot   L'Héritier-Guyot

Good style. Good depth. Crisp. Not too alien in flavour – q.v. Musigny *Blanc*. Stylish. Ready. **(03/93)**

Drink soon   **15.0**

ROUGE

Auxey-Duresses   *Premier Cru*   Henri Latour

Good colour. Lovely fresh, complex, damson fruity nose. This is fine. Fullish, marvellous balance. Rich, firm and succulent. Quite a lot of tannin but these are ripe, and the whole thing is nicely austere and 'cool'. Will last well. **(12/95)**

2000–2012 plus   **15.5**

Auxey-Duresses   Le Val   Vincent Roy

Very good colour. This is fine. Lovely fruit. Good substance. Good tannins. Really quite full. Very fine stylish, balanced, youthful wine. Nicely austere. Long, elegant. Very good. **(12/95)**

1998–2009   **16.0**

Beaune   Blanche-Fleur   Sylvain Dussort

I prefer this to the Blanche-Fleur 1990. This is fresher and fruitier, less spicy. Fullish, good acidity. Stylish and not as stemmy. Finishes well. **(12/95)**

Now–2000 plus   **14.0**

Beaune   Boucherottes   Jean Joliot

Good vigorous colour. Rich nose. Quite sturdy. Good grip. A little robust. Ample, meaty and sweet but a little rustic. Lacks a bit of style. Quite good. **(01/95)**

Now–2002   **14.0**

Beaune   Boucherottes   Pothier-Rieusset

Medium-full colour. Rich and quite oaky on the nose. Medium body. Good acidity and quite pronounced new oak – though not excessively – but not a lot of dimension on the palate. I miss a little depth. **(01/91)**

Drink soon   **14.0**

Beaune   Bressandes   Henri Germain

Medium colour. Rather more forward on the nose than some. Soft, fruity, elegant. Light to medium body. As much astringent as tannic. Pretty but a bit one-dimensional. Lacks both length and depth. A shade disappointing. Forward. **(01/91)**

Drink up   **13.0**

Beaune   Bressandes   Albert Morot

Medium-full colour. Good, firm fruit but somewhat closed on the nose. This is fat, succulent and gently oaky. Medium body. Rich and firm. Good grip. At present a shade adolescent but there is depth here. Finishes well. **(01/91)**

Now–2003   **15.0**

Beaune   Cent-Vignes   Bernard Bescancenot

Very good colour. Medium-full, still fresh. This is ripe, balanced and medium-full, with good freshness and harmony, good complexity even. But it lacks a little finesse, like some of the other Bescancenot Cent-Vignes. Long enough. But not exciting enough at the end for better than quite good plus. **(12/95)**

Now–2004   **14.5**

Beaune   Cent-Vignes   Albert Morot

Good colour. Nicely cool, austere, laid-back, yet rich and ripe. Medium-full, balanced. Very elegant. A lot of depth. Very classy. Very good grip. Very intense and persistent on the finish. Very good indeed. **(03/94)**

Now-2005   **17.0**

Beaune   Clos-des-Avaux
Hospices de Beaune, Louis Jadot

Good colour. Ripe, fragrant, cool, stylish nose. Medium-full. Not a bit too oaky. Rich and even quite opulent - for a 1988. Very good grip. This is very elegant. Long and complex. Very good indeed. **(12/94)**

Now-2006   **17.0**

Beaune   Clos-des-Avaux   Louis Jadot

Medium colour. Good plummy nose. Touch of new oak. Accessible. Medium body, a little tannin. Good grip and good stylish Pinot. Finishes well. This is not a wine of great weight and concentration but has interest and dimension. A good example. **(01/91)**

Now-2000   **14.5**

Beaune   Clos-de-la-Maladière
Henri Cauvard et Fils

Rather a lot of SO$_2$ here. This is a bit coarse. Beginning to dry out. Bottled too late? **(12/95)**

Drink soon   **12.5**

Beaune   Clos-des-Mouches
Joseph Drouhin

Medium-full colour. Firm, backward nose. Good depth. Elegant Pinot. Very classic. Medium body. Not a lot of tannin. Lovely fruit but not a blockbuster. Stylish and balanced. Good but not as interesting as the Ursules. Finishes well though. **(01/91)**

Now-2000   **15.0**

Beaune   Clos-de-la-Mousse
Bouchard Père et Fils

Medium-full colour. Round, fat, spicy nose. Less elegant but perhaps a bit hidden, compared with the Clos-des-Ursules. On the palate medium body but lacks a little personality. Good balance but a shade dull. **(01/91)**

Drink soon   **14.0**

Beaune   Clos-du-Roi   Gabriel Bouchard

Good colour. Succulent, quite fat, straight, stylish nose. Medium-full, good ripe tannins. This has depth and quality. Long and elegant and complex on the finish. Very good. **(01/91)**

Now-2004   **16.0**

Beaune   Clos-du-Roi   Tollot-Beaut

Medium colour. Plump, fruity nose. Ripe and seductive. Medium body. Good grip. Not a

great deal of depth or richness but the finish is long. A soft, oaky wine. Quite good. **(01/91)**

Now-2002   **14.0**

Beaune   Clos-des-Ursules
Vignes-Franches   Louis Jadot

Medium colour. Youthful still. Succulent nose. Fruity, elegant. Plump and gently oaky. Medium body. Round and ripe, oaky and stylish. A wine with more depth and personality than the Clos-des-Avaux. Good concentration. Finishes long. Very good. Several notes. **(01/91)**

Now-2003   **15.5**

Beaune   Coucherais   François Labet

Fullish colour. Exotic nose, not exactly Pinot, possibly even slightly oxidised. Plenty of fruit though. A wine of somewhat stewed concentration. Spicy and closed in. Presently not a lot of style. This is an Accad wine. **(01/91)**

Drink soon   **13.0**

Beaune   Grèves   Moillard

Full colour. Firm, earthy nose. An element of solidity detracts from the elegance. Medium to medium-full body. Some tannin. Slightly more macerated than most, evidently, but doesn't have any more succulence. In fact has less fruit. A bit dense. **(01/91)**

Drink soon   **13.5**

Beaune   Grèves   Jean-Marc Morey

Medium colour. Rather clumsy on the nose, even as far as being not entirely clean. Medium body. Burly, somewhat artisanal character, with an underlying bitterness from the stalks. Lacks style. **(01/91)**

Drink soon   **12.5**

Beaune   Marconnets
Bouchard Père et Fils

Good colour. Ripe, new oaky nose. Fat, generous and succulent. This is an attractive wine. Medium body. Good grip. With a touch of spice - sandalwood, cinnamon - and a positive follow-through. Good. **(01/91)**

Now-2002   **15.0**

Beaune   Marconnets
Roland Remoissenet Père et Fils

Medium-full colour. Stylish nose, but not one of great weight and concentration. A bit hidden. Fat and ripe on the palate. Slightly sweeter than most of the above. Medium body. Gently spicy, old-viney Pinot depth, well balanced with acidity. Good. Individual. **(01/91)**

Now-2002   **15.0**

Beaune   Montremenets   André Mussy

Medium colour. Still youthful. Slightly rustic nose but quite good richness and fat as well.

Slightly hard on the nose. Lacks a little richness and ripeness but will get rounder. Not bad. **(01/91)**

Drink soon   **13.0**

Beaune Reversées Jean-Marc Bouley

Good vigorous colour. Mellow, quite new oaky nose. Medium-full body. The oak tends to dominate the fruit, and now it sticks out. Otherwise now mellow. Ripe. But the finish is a little one-dimensional. Good (plus). **(01/96)**

Now-2003   **15.0**

Beaune Teurons Bouchard Père et Fils

Medium-full colour. Less concentration than the above. Good austere, plummy fruit though. A fat wine with an element of spice. Medium body. A little tannin. This has good depth, and is rather better than the Clos-de-la-Mousse. Finishes well. Opens up at the end to show interest and ripeness. **(01/91)**

Now-2002   **15.0**

Beaune Vigne-de-l'Enfant-Jésus Bouchard Père et Fils

Medium-full colour. Backward nose. Stylish, but more hidden than the Teurons. A little more body and texture. Less evolved but more depth. Best on the finish. Rich, quite sturdy. Ripe. Long. Good plus. **(01/91)**

Now-2004   **15.5**

Bonnes-Mares Joseph Drouhin

Good colour. This is beginning to open out now. Nicely ripe and a suggestion of sweetness at the end. Medium-full. Good grip. Good tannins. An elegant wine with plenty of depth. Fine. Still needs time. Several notes. **(11/94)**

1998-2015   **17.5**

Bonnes-Mares Robert Groffier

Medium-full colour. Rich, full and firm and new oaky. A lot of depth here. Medium-full, gentle - very Chambolle - ripe. Elegant. A wine of subtlety and finesse. But it doesn't have the intensity of great. **(01/91)**

Now-2003   **16.5**

Bonnes-Mares Louis Jadot

Medium-full colour. Rich and plump but slightly jammy on the nose. Quite full, ripe and with good tannins. This has depth and concentration. Good oak. Not uninspiring but very good nevertheless. A little adolescent and peppery at present. **(01/91)**

Now-2007   **14.0**

Bonnes-Mares Jacques-Frédéric Mugnier

Medium to medium-full colour. A touch insipid on the nose. Lacks concentration. Soft, medium to medium-full body. But lacks depth.

Unexciting, especially compared with his Musigny. **(01/91)**

Now-2007   **14.0**

Bonnes-Mares Newman

Medium to medium-full colour. Not exactly fat on the nose but good, slightly lean fruit and balance. Medium body. Some oak. Not as stylish or as concentrated as the Vogüé, Bonnes-Mares but good grip. Good length. Good. **(01/91)**

Now-2003   **14.5**

Bonnes-Mares Georges Roumier

Medium-full colour. Firm, rich and oaky on the nose. This is still closed. A structured wine with a lot of depth. Fat, rich, tannic. Backward. Very fine. Very good length and concentration. The best of the Bonnes-Mares. Several notes since then confirm this. **(01/91)**

Now-2009   **18.0**

Bonnes-Mares Thomas-Moillard

Medium-full colour. A shade structured and four-square on the nose. A shade dense. Rich, firm and oaky on the palate. This has good potential. Quite concentrated. Finishes well. **(01/91)**

Now-2005   **17.0**

Bonnes-Mares Comte Georges de Vogüé

Medium-full colour. Very good nose. Still quite closed. On the palate the wine is fullish. Quite structured. Very elegant and very intense. A bigger wine than the Leroy's Musigny. Several notes. **(10/94)**

Now-2018   **17.5**

Chambertin Rossignol-Trapet

Fullish colour. Less oaky, more closed, not as concentrated. This is good but lacks real intensity of fruit here. This is the same wine as the Jean Trapet. **(01/91)**

Now-2002   **15.0**

Chambertin Armand Rousseau

Medium-full colour. Rich, concentrated, oaky nose. A lot of merit here. This is excellent. Backward, concentrated. Intense. Youthful. *Grand vin!* **(01/91)**

Now-2012   **20.0**

Chambertin Jean Trapet

Medium-full colour. Closed and rich but not that concentrated. This is disappointing. Rather forward. A bit hollow. Merely pretty. **(01/91)**

Now-2002   **15.0**

Chambertin *Vieilles-Vignes* Rossignol-Trapet

Medium-full colour. Gentle, aromatic, concentrated but quite accessible. Very stylish though. Ripe and rich and fat. This has more to it. **(01/91)**

Now-2004   **17.0**

Chambertin *Vieilles-Vignes* **Jean Trapet**
Medium-full colour. Rich, backward, concentrated fruit. Seems more closed than the Rossignol-Trapet's. This, again, is the same wine. **(01/91)**
Now-2004   17.0

Chambertin   Clos-de-Bèze   Bruno Clair
Medium-full colour. Ample, plump, rich nose. This has very good fruit. But on the palate it lacks a bit of grip. Full, but a little suave. Fat, slightly spicy. **(01/91)**
Now-2002   15.0

Chambertin   Clos-de-Bèze   Joseph Faiveley
Medium-full colour. This is also very fine (tasted alongside the Rousseau). Rather more closed. Oak and breed also very evident. This is better still. It has more concentration. Rich, powerful. Fullish. Serious wine. **(01/91)**
Now-2010   19.5

Chambertin   Clos-de-Bèze   Louis Jadot
Medium-full colour. Rather more closed on the nose. Does it have the depth of the Faiveley? Quite stylish and oaky. Ripe and rich but does it really have *grand cru* intensity? No better than very good. **(01/91)**
Now-2008   16.0

**Chambertin   Clos-de-Bèze
Armand Rousseau**
Medium-full colour. Lovely nose. Ample, rich, concentrated and oaky. Quite accessible. Round and stylish. This is a very charming example. Good grip. Seductive. **(01/91)**
Now-2008   19.0

**Chambertin   Clos-de-Bèze
Thomas-Moillard**
Very good full youthful colour. The nose is still close. Full and tannic, austere and adolescent on the palate. Currently just a little dense and firm. Will get more generous as it mellows. The finish is long and fine and multi-dimensional. Needs time. Several notes. **(12/93)**
1999-2015   17.5

**Chambolle-Musigny
Comte Georges de Vogüé**
Medium colour. Fragrant, stylish Pinot nose. Good austerity and acidity on the palate. Medium body. Some tannin. A very typical elegant Chambolle. Good for a village *Appellation Contrôlée*. Complex, long. **(07/91)**
Now-2002   16.0

**Amoureuses   Chambolle-Musigny
Joseph Drouhin**
Medium-full colour. A rawer wine than the Charmes. Less developed. Good acidity but lacks a bit of generosity at present. This is strangely adolescent. The elements are there, it seems, but it lacks consistency. Finishes better than it starts. I shall give it the benefit of the doubt. But today it is the Charmes which sings. **(01/91)**
Now-2004   16.0

**Chambolle-Musigny   Amoureuses
Robert Groffier**
Medium-full colour. Quite strongly oaky on the nose but ripe and intensely flavoured to balance it. This is a more concentrated wine than the Sentiers. Very lovely fruit. Medium-full body. Finely balanced. Very stylish. Very long and complex. **(01/91)**
Now-2006   17.5

**Chambolle-Musigny   Amoureuses
Jacques-Frédéric Mugnier**
Medium-full colour. Like his Fuées, this I fear is a little fluid. Gentle but elegant though. A spicy wine. Round, medium body. It lacks a little zip. A shade disappointing. Marginally better than his Fuées. **(01/91)**
Now-2000   15.0

**Chambolle-Musigny   Amoureuses
Comte Georges de Vogüé**
Better colour. More depth on the nose. Rich and fullish on the palate. This is rather more spicy, more meaty, more profound than the village wine. There is quite a bit more tannin too. Very long and complex. Very good indeed. **(07/91)**
Now-2012   17.0

**Chambolle-Musigny   Beaux-Bruns
Ghislaine Barthod-Noëllat**
Medium-full colour. Fruit, balance and style here. Even concentration. This has promise. It also has a lot of depth. Medium to medium-full. Ripe, with a touch of spice. The attack is a bit adolescent but the follow-through is quite rich and ample. **(01/91)**
Now-2004   15.5

**Chambolle-Musigny   Charmes
Joseph Drouhin**
Good colour. This has lovely fruit and real concentration and fat on the nose. Fine. This is concentrated and complex. A lot of depth. Very lovely Pinot. Fine. **(01/91)**
Now-2006   17.0

**Chambolle-Musigny   Charmes
Henri Felletig**
Medium-full colour. Reasonable fruit but it seems to lack a bit of depth and concentration on the nose. But round, ripe and succulent on the palate. This has charm and even sex appeal. No great weight but long and balanced. Good. More to it than appears on the nose. **(01/91)**
Now-2002   15.0

Chambolle-Musigny Combe d'Orveau
Jean Grivot

Good colour. Slightly austere nose. A bit austere on the palate. It is a lean wine. Lacks a bit of generosity. But the follow-through is fatter and riper. This has good depth. Just give it time. Quite good. **(02/95)**

Now-2004   14.0

Chambolle-Musigny Feusselottes
Dr Georges Mugneret

Medium-full colour. Good oak. This has style and substance. Ripe and complex. A medium to medium-full bodied wine with very good fruit. Some oak but poised and stylish. Not dominating. Good acidity. This has depth. Very good. **(01/91)**

Now-2004   16.0

Chambolle-Musigny Fuées Joseph Faiveley

Medium-full colour. Good new oak. Complex, succulent and stylish. Medium to medium-full. This is very Chambolle. Ripe, stylish and complex on the palate. Long. Lovely. **(01/91)**

Now-2005   16.5

Chambolle-Musigny Fuées
Jacques-Frédéric Mugnier

Medium-full colour. Ripe, forward, fruity. Just a touch ephemeral, I think. Medium body. Not much tannin. A plump, fruity, elegant wine but lacks a bit of structure. Yet quite persistent on the finish. **(01/91)**

Now-2000   14.5

Chambolle-Musigny Gruenchers
Armelle et Bernard Rion

Medium-full colour. Lumpy and unstylish on the nose. A bit stewed. A bit stalky and astringent on the palate. This is raw and a bit coarse. Yet good grip. But lacks real succulence. **(01/91)**

Now-2002   13.0

Chambolle-Musigny Hauts-Doix
Joseph Drouhin

Good colour. Not as intense or as concentrated on the nose as Drouhin's Sentiers. But stylish nevertheless. Medium body. Quite elegant but lacks just a bit of depth. **(01/91)**

Now-2001   14.5

Chambolle-Musigny *Premier Cru*
Daniel Moine-Hudelot

Medium colour. Delicate but stylish nose. Medium body. Not a lot of structure. But the fruit is balanced and pretty, the wine is not weak. The extraction is perhaps just a shade forced. But this is at least verging on good. Good grip. **(01/91)**

Now-2002   14.5

Chambolle-Musigny Sentiers
Joseph Drouhin

Medium-full colour. Good oak, a gentle stylish wine with complexity and fruit. Medium body. Quite accessible. Good grip. Quite long and complex. This has a lot of charm and it finishes well. **(01/91)**

Now-2003   15.5

Chambolle-Musigny Sentiers
Robert Groffier

Medium-full colour. Good fruit. New oaky like the Drouhin. Is this the same wine? It is certainly very similar, but a little higher toned. More new oaky, and this dominates just a shade. But there is lovely fruit. Good, long, complex finish. **(01/91)**

Now-2003   15.5

Chambolle-Musigny Sentiers
Jean-Philippe Marchand

Medium-full colour. A bit closed on the nose, but a lot more style than his Clos-des-Ormes. Quite full, ample and rich. It lacks a little elegance but the fruit is good - if not very concentrated - and the wine is certainly balanced. Needs time. Finishes well. **(01/91)**

Now-2004   15.0

Chambolle-Musigny Sentiers
Jacky Truchot-Martin

Medium colour. This is a bit wishy-washy on the nose. The wine lacks structure. Medium body. A bit blowsy. A touch sweet/sour. Lacks style. Finishes insipidly. **(01/91)**

Drink soon   13.5

Chapelle-Chambertin Rossignol-Trapet

Medium-full colour. Slightly unclean on the nose but not, I think, corky. Lots of SO_2. The wine seems a bit astringent on the palate as a result. Adolescent. Difficult to taste. Medium-full. Finishes reasonably. Good but not great. **(01/91)**

Now-2000   15.0

Charmes-Chambertin Denis Bachelet

Medium-full colour. Rich and firm and oaky on the nose. Quite closed. This is a wine with a lot of charm and a lot of depth. But it is feminine for a Chambertin. Concentrated fruit. Long and complex. Very long. Very fine. **(01/91)**

Now-2008   17.5

Charmes-Chambertin
Philippe Charlopin-Parizot

Fullish colour. More delicate. Gently oaky. The tannins obtrude a little more. This is medium-full, concentrated and balanced. The attack is more closed, the finish almost equally long and complex, if not as charming at present. **(01/91)**

Now-2007   17.0

Charmes-Chambertin   Joseph Drouhin

Medium-full colour. I don't find a lot of concentration or style here on the nose. Good fruit but lacks a bit of depth for a *grand cru*. Medium-full. Yet very stylish, undeniably. A subtle wine. (01/91)

Now-2002   15.0

Charmes-Chambertin   Dujac

Medium-full colour. Quite jammy-oaky on the nose. Essentially round. Fat, plump, oaky and rich. Fullish, ample. Ripe and opulent. This is very seductive. Very long and complex on the finish. Several subsequent notes. (01/91)

Now-2008   17.5

Charmes-Chambertin   Christian Serafin

Fullish colour. Strange nose. A touch of the Accads? (No. This is not an Accad wine.) Slightly tannic and oxidised. Good new oak. Old-vine concentration. A bizarre wine but I think it has merit. Certainly individual. (01/91)

Now-2008   17.0

Charmes-Chambertin   *Très Vieilles-Vignes* Joseph Roty

Fine colour. Full, rich, oaky nose. Very ripe and exotic indeed. Even a whiff of the Accads on the nose. A more backward, more closed, more concentrated wine than Roty's Griotte. This has a lot of depth and concentration. It is less exuberant but all the more serious and potentially satisfying for all that. (01/91)

Now-2016   18.5

Charmes-Chambertin   Morgeots, Clos-de-la-Chapelle   Duc de Magenta, Louis Jadot

Lightish colour. Good nose. Very stylish. Lush and ripe. Fresh. Medium body. A little tannin. This is quite a reserved wine. A little closed. Very good follow-through. Long, interesting. Balanced. Very elegant. Good. (01/91)

Now-2004   15.0

Clos-des-Lambrays   Saier

Medium-full colour. Rather vegetal on the nose. There is a lack of concentration here. Pleasant fruit. Good acidity but a little assisted, an absence of fat and concentration. Doesn't sing. (01/91)

Drink soon   14.0

Clos-de-la-Roche   Guy Castagnier

Full colour. Not a lot of development. Full and rich but animal and not exactly elegant. A little four-square. Good acidity. Underneath there is good fruit. And it is reasonably balanced. Good length. But it lacks nuance and flair. Good but not great. (02/95)

Now-2005   15.0

Clos-de-la-Roche   Joseph Drouhin

Medium-full colour. Fine oak. Delicate Drouhin concentration. This has depth, but it is feminine and subtle for a Clos-de-la-Roche. Ripe, medium-full. Good tannins. Oaky and subtle. Generous and stylish. Fine. (01/91)

Now-2006   17.5

Clos-de-la-Roche   Dujac

Medium-full colour. Concentrated, oaky, mellow, lovely. Real depth and complexity on both the nose and the palate. Quite marked by the oak. Full, firm, excellent, old-vine, creamy fruit. Quite lovely. Very fine. (01/91)

Now-2012   18.5

Clos-de-la-Roche   Joseph Faiveley

Medium-full colour. Full and oaky but a shade minty as well. Yet rich and backward. Quite dominated by the oak. A little rigid as a result. Yet stylish Pinot. Certainly very good but not great I fear. (01/91)

Now-2005   16.0

Clos-de-la-Roche   Georges Lignier

Medium colour. Just a little sign of maturity. Soft, Chambolle-ish. Intensely fruity. Very stylish. Quite developed for a 1988. Good new oak. On the palate slightly diffuse but ripe and generous. Good grip on the follow-through and certainly very classy. Fine. (01/95)

Now-2008   17.5

Clos-de-la-Roche   Armand Rousseau

Good colour. Very ample, concentrated, old-viney nose, not as new oaky as Rousseau's Ruchottes, but perhaps even more depth. Less structure. Tasting the two alongside each other one can perceive the difference between Morey and Gevrey. Great intensity of flavour though. Excellent balance. Very long. Very lovely. (01/91)

Now-2015   18.5

Clos-de-la-Roche   Jacky Truchot-Martin

Good colour. A bit four-square on the nose. Fullish, fruity. Ripe. Yet behind a certain lack of real style and a bit obviously sweet. Pedestrian. A little edgy. (01/91)

Now-2000   14.0

Clos-de-la-Roche   Cuvée William   Ponsot

Medium-full colour. Less to it than the Clos-Saint-Denis. Almost an element of gas on the nose. This is disappointing. Weak and insipid. Poor. One-dimensional. Forward. (01/91)

Drink soon   13.5

Clos-Saint-Denis   Dujac

Fullish colour. Some development. Very fine classy nose. Deliciously complex. Full, rich, fat, and concentrated. Quite developed. Marvellous balance and depth. Ready soon. Very fine indeed. Several notes. (03/96)

Now-2012   18.5

Clos-Saint-Denis   Georges Lignier

Medium-full colour. An ample, fat, plump wine, but is the fruit a shade oxidised - or at least overblown? Similar on the palate. Quite rich but a certain absence of style. Good concentration though. (01/91)

Now-2006   15.5

Clos-Saint-Denis
Philippe Charlopin-Parizot

Fullish colour. Slight touch of Accads. Exotic but ripe. Good raspberry fruit. Good acidity. Fullish, good tannin. Plump and ample. A touch four-square. Good acidity. It lacks a bit of charm at present. (01/91)

Now-2008   16.5

Clos-Saint-Denis   *Vieilles-Vignes*   Ponsot

Fullish colour. Open, ripe but a little blowsy and obvious on the nose. Soft, ripe and spicy but lacks a bit of concentration and grip. A fat wine. Good length, it must be said and certainly better than the Clos-de-la-Roche. (01/91)

Now-2006   15.5

Clos-de-Tart   Mommessin

Medium-full colour. A little four-square but quite good fruit. Fullish, plump, tannic, ripe. This has got good depth but the tannins are a bit peppery. It lacks nuance. Needs time. (01/91)

Now-2004   15.5

Clos-de-Vougeot   Charles Mortet

Medium-full colour. Not a blockbuster but elegant Pinot on the nose. An accessible example, elegant, medium-full, oaky, but lacks a bit of real concentration. Good to very good. (01/91)

Now-2003   15.5

Clos-de-Vougeot   Château de la Tour

Full colour. Plump, ripe fruit in abundance on the nose. In total contrast to Grivot (this is also an Accad wine), this is clearly a concentrated, ample wine. Fullish, good ripe tannins. Good intensity of flavour. Very good. But slightly bizarre in flavour. (01/91)

Now-2006   16.0

Clos-de-Vougeot   Daniel Chopin-Groffier

Good colour. Fat, slightly raw, oaky nose. On the palate medium-full, good tannin. Good depth and oak. This has charm, balance and style. Even complexity. Not a blockbuster, but fine and long. Subtle. (01/91)

Now-2007   17.0

Clos-de-Vougeot   Drouhin

Full colour. Just a hint of maturity. Lovely nose. Really classy fruit. Firm, ripe and complex. Still youthful. Quite a lean wine on the attack. Medium-full. Still a bit of unresolved tannin. Warmer and more generous on the follow-through. Best with food. Lacks a little generosity still and the tannins are not as ripe as in the 1990. Very good, especially at the end which is long and ample. But needs time. Classy though. (10/94)

Now-2018   16.5

Clos-de-Vougeot   René Engel

Good colour. Plump, voluptuous nose. Medium-full, rich, a little abrupt, the tannins and new oak evident on the follow-through. Good stuff though, but it lacks just a little style for great. (01/91)

Now-2004   16.5

Clos-de-Vougeot   Joseph Faiveley

Medium-full colour. Noticeable toasted oak on the nose but by no means a blockbuster. Round, rich, complex and intensely flavoured on the palate. This is fine and long and has a lot of dimension. (01/91)

Now-2008   17.5

Clos-de-Vougeot   Jean Grivot

Fullish colour. Bizarre nose, a touch vegetal, even a shade oxidised. I can't enthuse about this on the palate. The Pinot elegance and succulence is missing. The wine is balanced but not really stylish at all. I wouldn't buy this myself! (01/91)

Now-2003   14.0

Clos-de-Vougeot   Alain Hudelot-Noëllat

Medium colour. Some development. Elegant fragrant nose but not a great deal of weight. So is the wine on the palate. It is only medium bodied, and it has neither the power nor the concentration for *grand cru*. Pretty, and attractive, but good rather than great. Not short though. (08/93)

Drink soon   15.0

Clos-de-Vougeot   Louis Jadot

Fullish colour. Round, ripe, concentrated and succulent on the nose. Like the Drouhin wine I find this though good - indeed better - a touch bland on the attack. Yet the follow-through is ample and concentrated. Good oak. Rich and balanced and vigorous and complex. (01/91)

Now-2009   17.0

Clos-de-Vougeot   Leroy

Fullish colour. There is plenty of fruit here but the wine lacks a bit of zip, as if the topping up wasn't regular enough. It is a bit dead. Better as it evolved. There is a lot of concentration here. But the wine is a little four-square, I find, compared with some. Backward certainly. **(01/91)**

Now-2008   16.0

Clos-de-Vougeot   Dr Georges Mugneret
Medium-full colour. Classic concentrated Pinot on the nose. More closed than the above. Good depth on the palate but it lacks a little depth and excitement. Very good but not great. The concentration is missing. **(01/91)**

Now-2007   16.0

Clos-de-Vougeot   Roland Remoissenet Père et Fils
Good colour. Fine, youthful coffee-chocolate flavours on the nose. Fullish, balanced with very good acidity. Lovely Pinot fruit again. A backward wine. Another fine example. **(01/91)**

Now-2010   17.5

Clos-de-Vougeot   Armelle et Bernard Rion
Fullish colour. This is concentrated, a little closed, but fine and stylish. Even better than the Mugneret on the nose. Fullish, good tannins, lovely Pinot fruit. Not the concentration of the Faiveley but certainly fine. The zip is missing on the finish. Yet the wine is not a bit short. **(01/91)**

Now-2008   17.0

Clos-de-Vougeot   Daniel Rion et Fils
Full colour. Still immature. Full and ample, but it lacks a little definition and class (and a bit of new oak). Slight tannin. Meaty. Good richness. Better on the palate and finish than on the nose. Very good plus. **(01/95)**

Now-2007   16.5

Clos-de-Vougeot   Georges Roumier
Medium-full colour. Firm, rich, backward and concentrated. The bottle is corked but nevertheless one can see a fine, if quite muscular wine here. I think this can be rated highly. Needs time. **(01/91)**

Now-2005   17.0

Clos-de-Vougeot   Thomas-Moillard
Fullish colour. Rich, closed, a touch dense, but chocolatey. Good raspberry fruit. Quite a big, tannic wine. Ripe, spicy and extracted but there is good grip and depth. Not the most enormous elegance. **(01/91)**

Now-2007   16.0

Corton   Bouchard Père et Fils
Good colour. Firm, a touch rigid, but basically good Pinot on the nose. Not a lot of breed though. Improved on aeration. This has style

and substance though it is a touch four-square. Good grip. Finishes well. Fullish. **(01/91)**

Now-2004   16.0

Corton   Claude Cornu
Good colour. Still youthful. Oaky, backward, rich, stylish. This is the best - of the 'simple' Cortons - fullish, succulent, stylish, harmonious. This has depth and style. Very good. Long. Classic. **(01/91)**

Now-2008   16.5

Corton   Joseph Drouhin
Fullish colour. Great Pinot elegance. But a delicate wine for a Corton. On the palate, medium to medium-full body only but very good style and fruit. Not a blockbuster. Not the intensity of *grand cru* perhaps. Good though. Long. **(01/91)**

Now-2003   15.5

Corton   Roland Rapet
Medium-full colour. Very elegant Pinot fruit on the nose if no enormous concentration. Not a wine of great dimension or succulence but one of good fruit. But a bit lacking in depth for a *grand cru*. Medium-full body. **(01/91)**

Now-2002   14.5

Corton   Comte Senard
Good colour. Rather more hidden on the nose than his Clos-des-Meix. On the palate it lacks real depth though, and the flavours are alien. Disappointing. **(01/91)**

Now-1999   14.0

Corton   Tollot-Beaut
Good colour. Good Pinot nose but not really with the depth and richness of a *grand cru*. Youthful. Medium to medium-full bodied wine with good acidity. Lacks just a bit of concentration. Merely good. **(01/91)**

Now-2004   14.5

Corton   Bressandes   Chandon-de-Briailles
Medium-full colour. Fat and succulent. Rich but closed on the nose. Medium-full. Plenty of style and concentration here. Good straight fruit. Good grip and good balance. Lacks a little concentration but certainly very good. Will keep well. **(01/91)**

Now-2006   16.0

Corton   Bressandes   Comte Senard
Very fine colour. Slightly spicy sweet on the nose. Doesn't have the dimension or depth of Faiveley. But ripe and round. Still needing a few years. Very good. **(09/94)**

Now-2007   16.0

Corton Clos-des-Cortons Joseph Faiveley

Very good colour. A backward wine still. Lovely pure Pinot Noir. Fullish, rich and concentrated. Slightly more austere and not the richness and concentration of the 1990 but a lovely example all the same. Still very young. Several notes. **(09/94)**

2000-2020   17.5

Corton Clos-des-Meix Comte Senard

Good colour. Fat, rich, succulent, exotic nose. Lacks a bit of style perhaps. A little reduction. A little more stewed than it should be. Quite ripe and with reasonable acidity. But it doesn't sing. Medium-full body. An Accad wine. **(01/91)**

Now-2002   15.0

Corton Clos-du-Roi
Chandon-de-Briailles

Fullish colour. Richer, fatter and more concentrated than the Briailles Bressandes. This is very promising indeed. Not quite the depth and concentration on the attack to be graded 'great' but there is breed and complexity here on the follow-through. Long and complex. Very fine. Lovely. **(01/91)**

Now-2010   17.5

Corton Clos-du-Roi Dubreuil-Fontaine

Medium-full colour. A shade vegetal on the nose. Even a touch oxidised. On the palate it is only medium bodied. And there is nowhere near the intensity of the Chandon-de-Briailles example. Lacks style. **(01/91)**

Now-1999   14.5

Corton Clos-du-Roi Thomas-Moillard

Medium-full colour. Full, closed, austere but rich on the nose. Full, but a bit rigid on the palate. Yet there is good depth underneath. Closed-in but plenty of depth. This is very good. Could even be better still. Firm. Needs time. **(01/91)**

Now-2009   16.5

Corton Clos-du-Roi Michel Voarick

Full immature colour. Firm nose. Ripe but slightly austere and masculine. Old-fashioned. Tannic. Dense. Fullish, almost an Italianate astringency and acidity. Slightly inky. Good at best. **(01/95)**

Now-2006   15.0

Corton Clos-des-Vergennes
Thomas-Moillard

Medium to medium-full colour. Stylish Pinot on the nose. Medium to medium-full. Good class; if not the weight of *grand cru*, it has at least the intensity. Ripe, long, succulent, but possibly a little facile. Good length but lacks a bit of muscle. **(01/91)**

Now-2004   16.0

Corton Maréchaudes
Jean-Pierre Maldant

Medium colour. Fine, ripe nose. Good succulence, an attractive touch of oak as well. But not a very firm wine. On the palate this has plenty of style and has good classic Pinot fruit. But it doesn't have the depth and intensity of a *grand cru*. Very good but no better. **(01/91)**

Now-2003   16.0

Corton Pougets Louis Jadot

Good, fat, rich stylish but closed on the nose. Starts well, finishes less excitingly. Stylish, balanced. Medium to medium-full on the attack but then it falls away. Slightly dilute at the end. Good but no better. Other notes more encouraging. (06/92: 'better than 1987 and 1989, rich, very long.') **(01/91)**

Now-2005   15.0

Corton Renardes Marius Delarche

Medium-full colour. A touch stalky on the nose. Rather raw and souped-up and unstylish on the palate. Medium body. As much astringent as tannic. No depth. Ordinary. Disappointing for a *grand cru*. **(01/91)**

Now-1999   14.0

Echézeaux Daniel Bocquenet

Medium-full colour. Quite a lot of new oak on the nose. By no means a blockbuster but succulent, balanced and stylish. This is long and complex, with good grip and fine Pinot fruit. Very good but not great. **(01/91)**

Now-2005   16.0

Echézeaux Jacques Cacheux

Good colour. Ripe, ample nose. Richer than the Vosne. Fatter and more accessible. Medium-full body. Good ripe tannins. This is not a blockbuster but it is balanced and elegant. Good grip. Good definition. Fine finish. **(01/91)**

Now-2005   17.0

Echézeaux René Engel

Good colour. Firm, rich, concentrated and backward. Not too oaky. There is depth here. Plump, fat, oaky and concentrated. This is a structured wine with a lot of depth. Still a touch adolescent. The tannin obtrudes. Needs time. Ripe and succulent underneath. But not the elegance of the Groffier Amoureuses. **(01/91)**

Now-2004   16.0

Echézeaux Joseph Faiveley

Medium-full colour. Less fat, good oak, very stylish on the nose. Medium-full. Not too tough. This has succulent fruit, very good harmony and a lot of elegance. Long. Fine. **(01/91)**

Now-2008   17.0

Echézeaux   A.F. Gros

Medium-full colour. This is corked on the nose. It seems a softer wine than the Engel. Elegant certainly, and not without depth. **(01/91)**

Now-2003   **16.0**

Echézeaux   Henri Jayer

Good colour. Impressive concentration. Splendid fruit. No excess oak on the nose. Full, intense, enormous fruit. Marvellous concentration. Very backward. Disarmingly brilliant. Excellent. **(01/91)**

Now-2015   **19.0**

Echézeaux   Mongeard-Mugneret

Medium-full colour. Rich, oaky, raspberry-flavoured wine on the nose. Good style here. As it evolved, a vegetal aspect appeared, as if some stems had been dunked in the wine. Reserved. Good fruit and acidity. Quite concentrated. But it doesn't sing. Adolescent. Give it time. Good but not great. **(01/91)**

Now-2004   **15.0**

Echézeaux   Romanée-Conti

Medium-full colour. Markedly oaky nose, of course, but quite accessible, without the usual pepperiness of young DRC Echézeaux. Medium-full, good tannins, good acidity. A touch of bitterness on the follow-through - which is not a bad thing. Quite concentrated. Good intensity of fruit. Very good. Complex finish. **(01/91)**

Now-2009   **16.5**

Echézeaux   *Vieilles-Vignes*
Mongeard-Mugneret

Medium to medium-full colour. Ripe, oaky, almost an exotically spicy nose. A bit 1985-ish. Firm, full, old-fashioned. Rich and mellow and oaky on the follow-through. This is very good. **(01/91)**

Now-2006   **16.5**

Fixin   Clos-du-Chapitre   Pierre Gelin

Medium-full colour. Open nose. A little more oxidised than most. Slightly less fresh than I would have liked. Slight vegetal element. Medium-full. A little *sauvage*. Slightly bitter and adolescent. Lacks a bit of concentration. **(01/91)**

Now-2000   **14.0**

Fixin   Les Hervelets   Charles Bernard, Clos-Saint-Denis

A little reduction on the nose. Quite light in colour and structure but round, elegant and fruity. Positive finish. Fully ready now. Quite good. **(12/95)**

Drink soon   **13.5**

Gevrey-Chambertin   *Vieilles-Vignes*
Alain Burguet

Full colour. Excellent fruit, gently balanced with oak. Very concentrated. Very lovely nose. Full, closed, masculine. Rich. Intense. Very good grip. Very good indeed. **(01/91)**

Now-2006   **16.5**

Gevrey-Chambertin   *Vieilles-Vignes*
Philippe Charlopin-Parizot

Fullish colour. Plump, fruity, quite elegant nose. Not a blockbuster. Accessible. Medium body. A little raw at present. Quite good richness of fruit but a bit hard on the follow-through. **(01/91)**

Now-2001   **14.0**

Gevrey-Chambertin   Cazetiers
Bruno Clair

Medium-full colour. Corked on the nose. A pity because the wine is stylish, concentrated, spicy and oaky. Shows promise. **(01/91)**

Now-2006   **16.0**

Gevrey-Chambertin   Cazetiers
Joseph Faiveley

Medium-full colour. Elegant, oaky nose. Medium-full, balanced, stylish and concentrated. This has lovely Pinot fruit and complexity on the follow-through. Finishes ample and long. A generous wine. **(01/91)**

Now-2003   **16.5**

Gevrey-Chambertin   Cazetiers
Philippe Leclerc

Fullish colour. Elements of volatile acidity on the nose. Even metallic. On the palate the wine is fullish, quite tannic, rich and oaky, but it lacks a bit of zip. Lumpy, essentially. **(01/91)**

Now-2002   **14.5**

Gevrey-Chambertin   Cazetiers
Armand Rousseau

Good colour. Fine, ripe, plummy nose. Not too obviously oaky. Finely poised, not a bit sweet. Very stylish. Medium-full body. A very good, austere wine with chocolate and coffee undertones. Very well balanced. Long and complex. Fine. **(01/91)**

Now-2008   **16.5**

Gevrey-Chambertin   Cazetiers
Christian Serafin

Fullish colour. Good concentration on the nose. Quite austere. Backward. Firm, rich, concentrated. This shows well. A fat wine - old-viney - with good depth and plenty of *matière*. Finishes well. Very good plus. Needs time. **(01/91)**

Now-2007   **16.5**

Gevrey-Chambertin   Champeaux
Charles Mortet

Medium-full colour. Soft, fruity nose. Black-berries. Not a blockbuster but a well-made, harmonious wine. Consistent. Quite classy. Good fruit and length. **(01/91)**

Now-2002   15.0

Gevrey-Chambertin   Champonets
Des Varoilles

Medium to medium-full colour. Soft, gentle, stylish, oaky nose. Accessible. Medium body. Ripe, good fruit and good grip. Not exactly very concentrated but the wine is elegant and it finishes well. Good oak. **(01/91)**

Now-2000   15.0

Gevrey-Chambertin   Clos-du-Fonteny
Bruno Clair

Medium-full colour. Plummy nose, the tannins are a little peppery. Medium body. This is pretty but a bit too straightforward. It lacks depth and concentration. May get astringent. **(01/91)**

Now-1999   14.0

Gevrey-Chambertin   Clos-Saint-Jacques
Bruno Clair

Medium to medium-full colour. Good concentrated nose. The fruit is slightly jammy and the wine has just slightly more volatile acidity than most. Oaky. Fullish, rich, good tannins. This has depth and concentration. Good grip and style. **(01/91)**

Now-2004   16.0

Gevrey-Chambertin   Clos-Saint-Jacques
Louis Jadot

Medium-full colour. This is very good. Rich, concentrated, lovely fruit. Depth and class here. Fine. Full and rich and meaty. Good depth of oak. A lot of concentration. Lovely finish. Very complex. **(01/91)**

Now-2008   17.5

Gevrey-Chambertin   Clos-Saint-Jacques
Armand Rousseau

Medium-full colour. This is also fine. Old-vine concentration. Lovely, rich fruit. More backward than the above. Even better. This is really fat and concentrated. Also a fine oak base. Full. Firm and multi-dimensional. *Grand cru* quality. **(01/91)**

Now-2010   18.5

Gevrey-Chambertin   Clos-des-Varoilles
Varoilles

Medium-full colour. Lean but quality on the nose. Good fruit. Not a blockbuster. Medium to medium-full. Round, just about ready. Good stylish. Quite ample. Long. Not quite as intense or as rich as it could be but very good plus. **(01/95)**

Now-2010   16.5

Gevrey-Chambertin   Combe-aux-Moines
Joseph Faiveley

Medium to medium-full colour. A bit blunt on the nose. More structure than fruit. Somewhat astringent on the palate. It lacks fruit. **(01/91)**

Now-2000   13.5

Gevrey-Chambertin   Combe-aux-Moines
Philippe Leclerc

Medium-full colour. Quite a backward nose. Closed, austere, plummy fruit. Oaky. A backward wine. This has some tannin. The attack is firm, the finish rich. Good length and black-fruit flavour. Finishes well. **(01/91)**

Now-2002   16.5

Gevrey-Chambertin   Combottes
Hervé Arlaud

Magnum. Medium to medium-full colour. A little maturity on the nose. Soft, a little sweet, but plump and fruity on nose and palate. Quite sophisticated. Medium to medium-full body. Good acidity. The start is good. Then it tails off a bit. Lacks a little fat, concentration and real distinction at the end. Good but should have been better. **(02/96)**

Now-2005   15.0

Gevrey-Chambertin   Combottes
Jean-Philippe Marchand

Medium-full colour. A bit ungainly on the nose. A little adolescent. Medium-full, some tannin. A bit closed at present. Good, but doesn't have a great deal of depth. **(01/91)**

Now-2004   15.0

Gevrey-Chambertin
Estournelles-Saint-Jacques   Louis Jadot

Fullish colour. Accessible Pinot fruit on the nose. Medium body, a bit of tannin. But lacks a bit of depth. Yet pleasant. Not unbalanced. Not lacking style. Just a shade dull perhaps. **(01/91)**

Now-2007   14.5

Gevrey-Chambertin   Les Fontenys
Joseph Roty

Fine colour. Rich, exotic, very ripe, very new oaky nose. There is a high toast here, making the flavours very aromatic. Medium-full, concentrated, oaky palate. Good grip. This is very seductive. Good ripe tannins. Fine quality. Long finish. Impressive. **(01/91)**

Now-2008   16.5

Gevrey-Chambertin   Lavaux-Saint-Jacques
Joseph Drouhin

Medium-full colour. Attractive nose. Not a blockbuster. A gentle, aromatic, oaky wine. Has charm and balance. Long, harmonious and stylish. Very good. **(01/91)**

Now-2003   16.0

Gevrey-Chambertin Lavaux-Saint-Jacques
Bernard Maume

Medium-full colour. Oaky, stylish nose. Good Pinot fruit. A bit firm on the palate. There is depth here, good oak. Black-fruits flavour. Finishes fat. More closed than most. **(01/91)**

Now-2004   **15.5**

Gevrey-Chambertin Les Marchais
Joseph Faiveley

Medium-full colour. Good Pinot on the nose and palate though not a lot of depth or richness. Balanced though, very pretty fruit. A forward wine. Stylish. **(01/91)**

Now-2000   **14.5**

Gevrey-Chambertin Perrières
Lucien Geoffroy

Fullish colour. Plump nose, but lacks a little grip and depth perhaps. Some structure though. This is a little sweeter and spicier, but it also lacks concentration. Not very stylish either. **(01/91)**

Now-1999   **14.0**

Gevrey-Chambertin Platières
Philippe Leclerc

Medium-full colour. A little four-square on the nose. Lacks style. Quite a chunky, toasty, oaky wine. Rich and fat and meaty. Starts off a bit lumpy but the follow-through is better. Adolescent. But not exactly very elegant. **(01/91)**

Now-2004   **14.0**

Gevrey-Chambertin La Romanée
Varoilles

Medium colour. Quite an austere nose. The acidity shows. Better on the palate. There is good balanced fruit here. Even quite concentrated. This has more dimension than most. Finishes long. **(01/91)**

Now-2002   **15.5**

Grands-Echézeaux René Engel

Good colour. Compared with the Echézeaux there is a bit of oxidation on the nose. Fullish, closed-in. On the palate a bit more structure but quite a bit richer. This has depth. Fine. But backward. If this will recover the oxidised aspects it will be fine. **(01/91)**

Now-2009   **17.0**

Grands-Echézeaux Roland Remoissenet
Père et Fils

Good colour. Feminine, intense, good grip. Splendid expression of Pinot fruit. Cedary, fragrant, very definitive. Quite lovely. Brilliant fruit. Excellent balance. Medium body. Real length and complexity. More Musigny than Bonnes-Mares. Excellent. **(01/91)**

Now-2009   **18.0**

Grands-Echézeaux Romanée-Conti

Fullish colour. Firmer, fuller and richer on the nose than the DRC Echézeaux. Quite a bit more closed. Quite a step up, as always. This is a fullish, tannic backward wine. Still raw and hard. Good depth though but the muscle shows at present. Good grip. Very good potential. Rich finish. **(01/91)**

Now-2012   **17.0**

Griotte-Chambertin Joseph Drouhin

Medium-full colour. Gentle, stylish, concentrated nose. There is a lot of depth here. This is classic. Very good fruit. Lovely balance. Good oak. Rich, complex. Lovely. But not a blockbuster. **(01/91)**

Now-2005   **18.0**

Griotte-Chambertin Ponsot

Medium-full colour. Very jammy, even sweet. High-toned on the nose but doesn't seem to have much depth behind it. Balanced, pretty, medium to medium-full. Charming. Certainly quite long. A feminine example. But it doesn't really have the intensity. **(01/91)**

Now-2003   **15.5**

Griotte-Chambertin Joseph Roty

Not as intensely coloured as Roty's Charmes, nor as intensely flavoured. Ripe, oaky nose. Fullish. Good structure and ripe tannins. This has fat and grip. It is more austere than the Fontenys and has significantly more depth. Fine, but doesn't quite have the depth of his Charmes. **(01/91)**

Now-2012   **17.5**

Ladoix Bois-Roussot
Gaston et Pierre Ravaut

Good, medium to medium-full, mature colour. Round, ripe and stylish on the nose. Medium body. This is now soft. Good acidity. Not a bit rustic. Nor too austere. Long. Elegant. Still with plenty of vigour. Very good for what it is. **(12/95)**

Now-2000   **15.0**

Latricières-Chambertin Joseph Faiveley

Medium-full colour. Quite pronounced new oak on the nose. Accessible, charming. Plump. I don't think this has quite the concentration of Faiveley's Mazis but it is a fine example nonetheless. Long and classy. **(01/91)**

Now-2009   **17.5**

Latricières-Chambertin Ponsot

Fullish colour. There is something a little stalky and pruney on the nose. Spicy on the palate. Fullish. Lacks a bit of class. **(01/91)**

Now-2002   **14.0**

Latricières-Chambertin Rossignol-Trapet

Medium-full colour. Not enormous concentration or class on the nose here, I fear, but the fruit is agreeable. Medium-full, balanced and quite elegant, but it doesn't have the power and intensity it should have. Stylish though. **(01/91)**

Now-2012   **16.0**

Maranges Clos-des-Loyères, *Vieilles-Vignes* Vincent Girardin

Medium colour. This is almost too synthetically jammy on the palate, which is not to say it is too sweet. Touch of oak. Medium body. Perfumed. Curious. Not really my taste. **(01/91)**

Drink soon   **13.5**

Marsannay Clos-du-Roy Régis Bouvier

Good colour. Still alive and fresh. This is more stylish than the 1990. Lovely fruit. Very fragrant. Long, balanced, warm and generous. Very good indeed. **(12/95)**

Now-2005   **15.0**

Mazis-Chambertin Joseph Faiveley

Medium-full colour. Ripe, stylish, gently oaky on the nose. Fullish, fat, concentrated on the palate. The oak doesn't dominate. This has good intensity and plenty of breed. Very fine. Lovely long finish. **(01/91)**

Now-2009   **18.0**

Mazis-Chambertin Lucien Geoffroy

Fullish colour. Full, concentrated, backward nose. Rich, closed, full, tannic and still very youthful. The follow-through is very concentrated. There is a lot of wine here. Excellent. **(01/91)**

Now-2012   **18.0**

Mazis-Chambertin Louis Jadot

Fullish colour. Very rich and concentrated. Closed. Excellent. Really fine black fruit here. A wine in the same mould as the Faiveley which is even better still. Marvellous fruit and concentration. Really lovely. Very, very long. Powerful and concentrated on the finish. **(01/91)**

Now-2012   **19.0**

Mazis-Chambertin Bernard Maume

Fullish colour. Does this have the intensity or the class of the Jadot or Faiveley? I don't think so. Fat, opulent and exotic. Rich and toasted. Yet gentle, stylish, even feminine. A pretty example, but it lacks a bit of real intensity. **(01/91)**

Now-2002   **15.5**

Mazis-Chambertin Armand Rousseau

Good colour. Fine nose. Concentrated 'cool' Pinot fruit. Lovely intense ripeness and richness but not a bit sweet. Full body, good structure,

good grip. This has fine concentration and a lot of depth. A lovely wine. **(01/91)**

Now-2012   **18.0**

Morey-Saint-Denis Clos-de-la-Boussière Georges Roumier

Medium-full colour. Very fine nose. Lovely, rich, succulent fruit. Good old-vine concentration. This has class and a good oaky background. A little stalky and austere on the attack. Firm, youthful, a bit adolescent. Good grip. Plenty of future here. Very good. **(01/91)**

Now-2005   **16.0**

Morey-Saint-Denis Clos-des-Ormes Jean-Philippe Marchand

Fullish colour. Rather a lumpy wine on the nose. There is a lack of style here. It got better as it evolved in the glass. Medium-full body. A bit of tannin. Finishes better than it starts, which is a good thing. But lacks a bit of class. **(01/91)**

Now-2002   **14.0**

Morey-Saint-Denis Clos-Sorbe Joseph Drouhin

Medium-full colour. Much better concentration than the Monts-Luisants. Good style. A touch of oak. Medium-full. Good, ripe tannins. Has a touch of spice. This detracts a little from the elegance but balanced and long. Very good. **(01/91)**

Now-2005   **16.0**

Morey-Saint-Denis Millandes Pierre Amiot

Medium-full colour. A soft nose, a little too ephemeral perhaps. But quite stylish. A pretty wine but a bit forward. Ripe and balanced but lacks depth. Yet the fruit is elegant. **(01/91)**

Now-1998   **14.5**

Morey-Saint-Denis Monts-Luisants Joseph Drouhin

Medium colour. Aromatic, stylish but delicate nose. Good fruit. Very Chambolle rather than Morey. Medium body. Not a lot of structure. The wine has elegance and good acidity but lacks a bit of fat and concentration. **(01/91)**

Now-2000   **14.5**

Musigny Joseph Drouhin

Good colour. Oaky nose. Similarly toasted. But seems to have more depth underneath. A wine of really ravishing charm and extract and concentration. Long, subtle, complex. Very Musigny. Very lovely. **(01/91)**

Now-2012   **19.0**

Musigny Leroy

Splendid colour. Very lovely, sweet, fragrant. Very Musigny. Not too backward. Oak. Medium-full, beautiful fruit and great acidity.

Very classy, very complex. Splendidly multi-dimensional follow-through and finish. **(10/94)**

Now-2027   19.5

Musigny   Jacques-Frédéric Mugnier

Good colour. Ripe, fragrant, elegant, oaky nose. This has a lot of style, but it is very feminine and typically Musigny. A very subtle, ripe, lovely wine. This has real breed. Good length. **(01/91)**

Now-2008   17.5

Musigny   *Vieilles-Vignes*
Comte Georges de Vogüé

Good colour. Rather more toasted, spicy oak. The vanilla shows. But otherwise similar to the above. It is not quite as complex - or as accessible - on the attack. But the follow-through is very good indeed. Long, subtle. Very fine. Several notes. **(01/91)**

Now-2009   18.0

Nuits-Saint-Georges   Château Gris
Lupé-Cholet

Good colour. A little soupy and four-square on the nose. Medium body, as much astringent as tannic. A bit rustic as well. Lacks style. **(01/91)**

Drink soon   12.5

Nuits-Saint-Georges   Boudots
Joseph Drouhin

Medium-full colour. Raw and malic on the nose. This is rather disagreeable. Medium body. As much astringent as tannic. Lacks real succulence. **(01/91)**

Now-1999   13.5

Nuits-Saint-Georges   Boudots   Jean Grivot

Good colour. Exotic nose. Medium-full. Some tannin. Good acidity. Bizarre though. Very good grip and concentration and length, it has to be said. **(01/91)**

Now-2003   16.0

Nuits-Saint-Georges   Boudots   Leroy

Medium-full colour. Firm, slightly earthy nose with a suggestion of bonfires. Medium to medium-full body. Complex, balanced fruit. This has depth and interest, style and personality. Very good. **(01/91)**

Now-2003   16.0

Nuits-Saint-Georges   Boudots
Méo-Camuzet

Medium-full colour. Stylish nose. Good oak. Not a wine of great power. Medium to medium-full. Round and oaky on the palate. I find the oak just a little too obvious. Has merit though. The fruit is ripe and stylish. **(01/91)**

Now-2002   15.0

Nuits-Saint-Georges   Boudots
Mongeard-Mugneret

Medium-full colour. Slightly raw and unformed on the nose but there is fruit and depth here, and a suggestion of oak. On the palate this is a bit jammy and peppery, but not without style. Adolescent at present. **(01/91)**

Now-2001   15.0

Nuits-Saint-Georges   Boudots   Jean Tardy

Medium to medium-full colour. Round and fruity but a bit bland on the nose. Medium body. A bit peppery, but better grip than the nose would indicate. Finishes better than it starts. Not exciting, but not bad. Indeed better still when I went back to it. **(01/91)**

Now-2003   15.0

Nuits-Saint-Georges   Les Cailles
Alain Michelot

Medium colour. Not a very concentrated nose but ripe, stylish and oaky. Accessible and generous. Reasonable body but just a shade lacking intensity. Quite good at best. **(01/91)**

Now-2001   14.5

Nuits-Saint-Georges   Chaignots
Robert Chevillon

Very good colour. Lovely, rich, old-viney nose. Full and rich with real concentration. Good underlying oak. Good grip. This is youthful, tannic and of very high potential. Excellent example of a Nuits. **(01/91)**

Now-2003   17.5

Nuits-Saint-Georges   Chaignots
Daniel Chopin-Groffier

Medium colour. Round, ample, succulent nose with a touch of spice, but with the usual element of Nuits solidity. Good element of new oak. Fullish, fat and rich on the palate. This has good depth. Rather closed but shows promise. Good to very good. Finishes well. **(01/91)**

Now-2006   15.5

Nuits-Saint-Georges   Chaignots
Alain Michelot

Medium colour. A little firmer on the nose than Michelot's Cailles. A little more depth and concentration. Rather better. Medium to medium-full. Just a little tannin. Good follow-through. Ripe and complex. Yet even here just a bit more concentration would have made an enormous difference. **(01/91)**

Now-2004   15.5

Nuits-Saint-Georges   Champs-Perdrix
Michel Chevillon

Medium-full colour. Somewhat insipid on the nose. Rather evolved and a touch oxidised. An edgy wine, with a bitter after-taste. Medium

body. As much astringent as tannic. Undistinguished. **(01/91)**
Drink soon   **12.0**

Nuits-Saint-Georges   Les Charmois
Jean Grivot
Good colour. This has reasonable substance and is certainly ripe and elegant. A little tannin, but the tannins ripe. Medium-full. Good fruit and depth. Slightly austere at present but the finish is long. Good plus. **(02/95)**
1998-2005   **15.5**

Nuits-Saint-Georges   Clos-des-Argillières
Daniel Rion et Fils
Medium-full colour. Firm, solid, earthy nose. This is a fullish, quite closed-in wine still. Good fruit in a very Nuits-Saint-Georges way, and it has depth and even concentration. Good finish. Even quite complex. **(01/91)**
Now-2004   **16.0**

Nuits-Saint-Georges   Clos-de-l'Arlot
Arlot
Light colour. Stylish oaky nose but not a great deal of weight. This is rather more forward than I had expected. Light to medium body. Reasonable intensity on the palate. Ripe and oaky and with good grip. Not a lot of structure or fat though. Good but not great. Several notes. **(01/91)**
Now-2000   **15.0**

Nuits-Saint-Georges   Clos-des-Corvées
Louis Jadot
Medium colour. Lightish nose. Slight but undistinguished. Medium body. A touch of oak. Good, fresh fruit but it lacks a bit of depth. Finishes better than it starts though. Not bad. **(01/91)**
Now-2001   **14.0**

Nuits-Saint-Georges
Clos-des-Forêts-Saint-Georges   Arlot
Similar colour and nose. Just a shade fresher. This is marginally better than the Clos-de-l'Arlot, with a little more grip and intensity. Good to very good. Several notes. **(01/91)**
Now-2003   **15.5**

Nuits-Saint-Georges   Clos-de-la-Maréchale
Joseph Faiveley
Medium-full colour. Firm nose. A little more rigid and less oaky and opulent than Faiveley's Les Porrets. Rather more closed. Less fat. Less breed. Certainly good though. A fullish, backward wine. Several notes. **(01/91)**
Now-2008   **15.5**

Nuits-Saint-Georges   Clos-des-Porrets
Henri Gouges
Medium-full colour. Slightly raw on the nose. Lacks depth and concentration. As much astringent as tannic. A light, gentle, quite stylish wine, but it lacks the dimension for a *premier cru*. Quite forward. **(01/91)**
Drink soon   **14.0**

Nuits-Saint-Georges   Clos Saint-Marc
Bouchard Père et Fils
Medium-full colour. A little tough on the nose. Quite solid. Lacks a bit of elegance. Medium to medium-full. Good balance and fruit. Not exactly very stylish but this is adolescence rather than an inherent fault. Not bad. **(01/91)**
Now-2002   **14.0**

Nuits-Saint-Georges   Clos-de-Thorey
Thomas-Moillard
Medium-full colour. Round, soft nose. Gentle. Quite stylish but without a great deal of depth. Medium body. Ripe, round and quite oaky. Quite forward. This has charm and succulence. Finishes well. An elegant example. Good. **(01/91)**
Now-2002   **15.5**

Nuits-Saint-Georges   Les Corvées-Pagets
Robert Arnoux
Medium-full colour. Open nose. Medium weight and depth. Okay but not exciting. Medium body. Ripe, gentle, quite forward. Good oak. Stylish. Finishes well. This is quite good but for a *premier cru* it lacks a bit of complexity. **(01/91)**
Now-2001   **14.0**

Nuits-Saint-Georges   Damodes
Jayer-Gilles
Fullish colour. Quite pronounced oak on the nose. Quite an accessible wine underneath. Soft, gentle and stylish. Medium to medium-full, oaky and tannic. The oak is just a little too pronounced. Seductive, undeniably, because the fruit is elegant. But the wine lacks concentration. **(01/91)**
Now-2000   **14.5**

Nuits-Saint-Georges   Damodes
Chantal Lescure
Medium-full colour. Spicy nose. Quite dense. Lacks style. Rather a coarse example. Medium body. Quite fat. But no elegance. Undistinguished. **(01/91)**
Drink soon   **13.0**

Nuits-Saint-Georges   Damodes
Machard de Gramont

Medium to medium-full colour. Light nose. Lacks a bit of concentration. Medium body. Not much tannin. Good acidity but an absence of succulence of fruit. Lacks depth. (01/91)

Drink soon   13.5

Nuits-Saint-Georges   Grandes-Vignes
Thomas-Moillard

Medium-full colour. Good oaky nose. Quite rich, plummy fruit. Accessible. Medium-full body. Ripe and stylish, with the unusual Nuits-Saint-Georges earthiness. Good follow-through. Finishes well. (01/91)

Now-2004   15.0

Nuits-Saint-Georges   Hauts-Pruliers
DANIEL RION ET FILS

Medium-full colour. The fruit is ripe and stylish on the nose. Round, ripe, fullish, oaky. This has depth and ripeness and no lack of concentration. Breed and quality here. Good long finish. (01/91)

Now-2004   16.5

Nuits-Saint-Georges   Hospices de Nuits,
Cuvée Soeurs Hospitalières
Thomas-Moillard

Medium-full colour. A full, muscular, spicy nose, a touch oxidised perhaps. Ripe and plump, but without real breed. Yet the balance is correct. Bad *élevage*? A bit. This could have been good. (01/91)

Now-2000   13.0

Nuits-Saint-Georges   Murgers
André Chopin et Fils

Medium to medium-full colour. This has a good nose. Just a little austere. But fragrant and stylish. Good depth and interest. Getting cedary underneath. Medium-full, good intensity. This is stylish and harmonious. Not a bit rustic. Nice and fresh. Vosne-ish. Complex. Long and most attractive. Nearly ready. But a year won't do it any harm. Very good plus. (12/95)

Now-2010   16.5

Nuits-Saint-Georges   Murgers
Armelle et Bernard Rion

Fullish colour. Round and spicy. A touch blowsy. Lacks a little style on the nose. Medium body. Not much tannin. Not much depth and interest either. A bit coarse. Certainly rather dull. Lacks concentration. (01/91)

Drink soon   13.0

Nuits-Saint-Georges   Murgers
Thomas-Moillard

Medium-full colour. A ripe, fat nose, but somewhat clumsy. This is adolescent. Medium to medium-full body. Good grip. The finish is the best bit. Quite stylish. I think this will be good. (01/91)

Now-2002   15.0

Nuits-Saint-Georges   Porrets
Bouchard Père et Fils

Fullish colour. Curious nose. A touch sweaty; a touch sweet/sour. Medium body. Some oak. Not enough fruit and not enough concentration. Reasonable finish. Not bad. (01/91)

Drink soon   13.5

Nuits-Saint-Georges   Porrets
Michel Chevillon

Medium-full colour. Coarse, dirty, oxidised nose. Light, stewed, disagreeable palate. Astringent. No merit. (01/91)

Drink up   11.0

Nuits-Saint-Georges   Porrets
Thomas-Moillard

Medium-full colour. Oaky, plummy-blackberry, fruity nose. But does it have much depth underneath? Yet there is undeniable style and charm here. On the palate the tannin from the oak is quite evident. There is depth here though. Good grip. Quite closed. Good. (01/91)

Now-2004   15.5

Nuits-Saint-Georges
Les Porrets-Saint-Georges   Joseph Faiveley

Medium to medium-full colour. Ripe, rich, stylish, new oaky nose. Good concentration and depth here, and not as sturdy as most of the commune. Fullish and with very good grip on the palate. Rich underneath. This needs time. Very good indeed. (01/91)

Now-2008   17.0

Nuits-Saint-Georges   *Premier Cru*
Michel Chevillon

Medium-full colour. Round, solid, earthy nose. Not very stylish. Even a shade oxidised. Quite high acidity. Medium to medium-full body. Peppery. Lacks style on the palate, and also doesn't have much depth. (01/91)

Drink soon   13.0

Nuits-Saint-Georges   Pruliers
Château de Bligny

Quite evolved now. Medium body. Not the quantities of rude tannin in the 1990. This is rather an anonymous not very stylish Pinot. Rather ordinary. Ready but not special. (12/95)

Now-2000   13.0

Nuits-Saint-Georges   Pruliers
Lucien Boillot et Fils

Medium-full colour. Somewhat edgy on the nose. Fullish but a bit stewed. Reasonable grip but no style. **(01/91)**

Drink soon   13.0

Nuits-Saint-Georges   Pruliers
Henri Gouges

Medium-full colour. A touch oxidised on the nose. A bit raw and unshapely on the palate. Medium-full, lumpy. Lacks grace and style. **(01/91)**

Now-2000   13.0

Nuits-Saint-Georges   Pruliers
Jean Grivot

Good colour. Fat and rich with 1988 austerity on the nose. A touch of the stems here on the attack. Not quite as concentrated as I might have hoped but ripe and long and stylish. Good grip. Quite good for a *premier cru*. **(02/95)**

1998-2005   14.0

Nuits-Saint-Georges   Les Roncières
Jean Grivot

Very good colour. Rich and tannic on nose and attack. Good fruit here. I prefer this to the Pruliers. Quite concentrated. Ripe and balanced with a good grip and a nice chocolatey background. Very good. **(02/95)**

1998-2005   16.0

Nuits-Saint-Georges   Rue de Chaux
Dupasquier/Ambroise

Medium-full colour. A firm nose. This is backward. Good depth and richness though. Fullish, firm, closed. This has potential. Rich fruit on the follow-through. Even concentration. But needs some time. Very good. **(01/91)**

Now-2004   16.0

Nuits-Saint-Georges   Les Saint-Georges
Michel Chevillon

Medium-full colour. Smells of old compost heaps or soup that has gone off. Oxidised and maderised. This is very artificial and disagreeable. Medium-full. Astringent. **(01/91)**

Now-1999   12.5

Nuits-Saint-Georges   Les Saint-Georges
Joseph Faiveley

Medium to medium-full colour. Firm, backward, oaky nose. Round, stylish, not a wine of great structure but all the better for not having the usual Nuits solidity. Balanced and charming and stylish. This is long and complex. Fine. **(01/91)**

Now-2006   17.5

Nuits-Saint-Georges   Les Saint-Georgess
Henri Gouges

Very good colour. Closed nose but very good depth. Fullish, rich and concentrated. Closed. Very good grip but lacks a little dimension. Masculine. This improved considerably in bottle. Subsequently I rate it at least as high as the Vaucrains. **(01/91)**

Now-2003   16.0

Nuits-Saint-Georges   Les Vaucrains
Henri Gouges

The colour is still very fresh. Fullish. On the nose this has begun to soften up. Fragrant, plummy, rich. Not as burly as one might have expected for Vaucrains. No aggressive tannins. Fine fruit. Very fine acidity. Approaching maturity. Long, distinguished. Fine. **(11/95)**

Now-2015   17.5

Nuits-Saint-Georges   Vignes-Rondes
Daniel Rion et Fils

Fullish colour. A little raw and even a shade malic on the nose. Pronounced acidity. A cool wine. Not without style. Medium to medium-full. A little stewed, as much astringent as tannic. Lacks a bit of generosity. Lacks fat as well. **(01/91)**

Drink soon   13.5

Pernand-Vergelesses   Rollin Père et Fils

Evolved colour. Old tea on the nose. A bit thin and attenuated. Good acidity. Quite fresh fruit. But rigid and unharmonious. Unexciting. Coarse. Will get worse as it evolves. **(12/95)**

Drink up   11.0

Pernand-Vergelesses
Clos-de-la-Croix-de-Pierre   Louis Jadot

Medium to medium-full colour. Still very purple. Plump, ripe, plummy nose. Slightly lean and austere. Well made. Reserved wine. Lacks a little generosity at present. Medium body. Has good length. Will get more seductive as it mellows. Quite good. **(01/91)**

Now-2004   13.5

Pernand-Vergelesses   Ile-des-Vergelesses
Chandon-de-Briailles

Good colour. Quite firm but certainly rich and very ripe on the nose. Medium-full. Stylish, balanced. Good cherry-raspberry fruit. Touch of underlying oak. This has depth though it could do with a bit more concentration. Lovely Pinot. **(01/91)**

Now-2004   15.5

Pommard   Jean Joliot

Good full colour. Robust, meaty, animal nose. A little tannin on the palate. Slightly rustic. But good for a village wine. The finish shows balance and plenty of dimension. Long. Quite good plus. **(01/95)**

Now-2007   14.5

Pommard Bertins Chantal Lescure
Medium-full colour. Firm, straight, austere nose. Rather closed at present. A bit raw and rigid on the palate, with a lack of depth and length - and interest. A bit stewed on the finish. **(01/91)**

Drink soon   13.5

**Pommard Chaponnières
Philippe Billard-Gonnet**
Medium to medium-full colour. Ripe, rich, classic Pinot-Pommard nose. Rather more concentration than his Clos-Verger. Good oak. Good depth. This has the flexibility that most of the above lack. Medium to medium-full. Ripe. Balanced. Good depth. Fine Pinot fruit. Very straight. **(01/91)**

Now-2004   15.5

**Pommard Charmots
Philippe Billard-Gonnet**
Medium-full colour. Ripe, opulent nose. Good Pinot. A firm wine on the palate. A touch four-square but there is good straight fruit here, if a bit peppery at present. **(01/91)**

Now-2000   14.5

**Pommard Clos-Blanc
Machard de Gramont**
Medium-full colour. Good smoky nose. Meaty. Proper Pommard. Rich and full. Quite sturdy. Good ripe plummy fruit. Some tannin. Good grip. Good plus. **(01/95)**

Now-2009   15.5

**Pommard Clos-des-Epeneaux
Comte Armand**
Medium-full colour. Full, firm, concentrated classic nose. This has real merit. Full, firm, rich and with the masculinity of Pommard and the depth of a good wine. This needs time. Austere and quite tannic at present. A classic example. Fine. Many subsequent notes. **(01/91)**

Now-2005   17.5

**Pommard Clos-Verger
Philippe Billard-Gonnet**
Medium-full colour. Good, straight Pinot, if a little raw on the nose. On the palate an accessible, pleasant wine but rather one-dimensional, and a bit short. Medium body. Not bad. Forward. **(01/91)**

Now-2004   14.0

Pommard Clos-Verger Pothier-Rieusset
Medium-full colour. Round, oaky, slightly sweet and spicy nose. A touch vegetal but quite a succulent, interesting wine nonetheless. Good grip. Medium to medium-full. Lacks a bit of style. Reasonable finish. **(01/91)**

Now-2002   14.5

**Pommard Grand-Clos-des-Epenots
De Courcel**
Medium colour. Less firm but lovely succulence. Breed and intensity here. Medium to medium-full body. Balanced, gently oaky. Very stylish and delicious. Equally good as Comte Armand. More sexy at present. Very good indeed. **(01/91)**

Now-2005   17.0

Pommard Epenots André Mussy
Light to medium colour. Not much to it on the nose. Lightish body. No tannin. Slightly malic on the palate. No richness or depth. Disappointing. **(01/91)**

Drink soon   12.0

Pommard Epenots Pothier-Rieusset
Fullish. An oaky nose but a touch overblown. Faintly oxidised? Medium to medium-full body. Rather a rigid wine. It lacks a bit of depth and succulence. Dull. **(01/91)**

Drink soon   14.0

Pommard Fremiets Jean-Marc Bouley
Fullish. Firm nose. Oaky, a touch stewed. Firm and full on the palate. Good fruit underneath. A little raw. Lacks charm and succulence. **(01/91)**

Now-2000   14.0

Pommard Fremiets Coste-Caumartin
Medium-full colour. Closed nose again, also austere, but ripe Pinot underneath, even a touch more volatile acidity than most. This is sturdy and old-fashioned, with good acidity. A little more astringent than tannic. Lacks bit of style. **(01/91)**

Now-2000   14.0

**Pommard Pezerolles
Philippe Billard-Gonnet**
Medium to medium-full colour. Also ripe, but not as stylish as his Chaponnières. Less concentration. Less interest. Medium body. More forward. **(01/91)**

Now-1999   14.0

Pommard Pezerolles Jean-Marc Bouley
Fullish colour. Rich and fat on the nose. Not as stewed as his Fremiets. Fat and succulent on the attack but lacks a bit of zip and dimension on the follow-through. Quite good only. **(01/91)**

Now-2000   14.5

Pommard *Premier Cru*
Bouchard Père et Fils

Fullish colour. Round, ripe nose but a touch of reduction, like the other Bouchard Père samples. An oaky wine. On the palate there is plenty of fruit here. The wine is a bit raw but there is good depth. Medium-full. Good grip. Good potential. **(01/91)**

Now–2004   15.0

Pommard *Premier Cru* **André Mussy**

A little less colour than Mussy's Montremenots. Stylish, ripe, fat nose. Good richness, rather better than the Montremenots. More covered. Good grip but not enough substance. Quite good. **(01/91)**

Drink soon   13.5

Pommard Rugiens
Philippe Billard-Gonnet

Medium-full colour. A firm nose. Not a touch over-chaptalised. But rather closed at present. The best of the Billard-Gonnet wines. Fine Pinot. Medium-full. Not too sturdy. Good, balanced fruit. This has depth. A bit closed at present but very persistent on the finish. **(01/91)**

Now–2004   16.0

Pommard Rugiens Jean-Marc Bouley

Medium-full colour. Full but a touch rigid on the nose. An oaky wine. Sturdy but a touch dense. It lacks fat and succulence underneath. A bit one-dimensional. **(01/91)**

Now–2000   14.5

Pommard Rugiens Yvon Clerget

Fullish colour. Firm, closed nose. A touch rigid and impenetrable on the nose. Good stuff on the palate. Quite structured, but there is depth here. Needs time. Finishes very well. **(01/91)**

Now–2004   16.0

Pommard Rugiens De Courcel

Medium to medium-full colour. Richer and fuller than De Courcel's Epenots. Similarly concentrated and stylish. Yet better on the palate. Oaky but not rigidly so. Long. Succulent. Intense. Very fine. Very long. Lovely. **(01/91)**

Now–2010   17.5

Pommard Rugiens Lejeune

Fullish colour. Exotic, oaky, opulent and sexy on the nose. How much style, I wonder? Medium body. Sweet, bizarre. A little stewed. Curiously sweet. Very strange but not dis-agreeable. But not a bit classic. Tastes like a summer pudding. **(01/91)**

Now–2000   14.0

Pommard Rugiens Pothier-Rieusset

Fullish colour. Like his Epenots I get a touch of oxidisation on the nose here. Riper than the above. Medium-full, quite fat, but there seems to be a lack of real style at present. **(01/91)**

Now–2000   14.5

Pommard Saucilles Jean-Marc Boillot

Good colour. Rich, fat, oaky nose. Good black cherry and blackberry flavour. Quite full, quite firm. Good grip. This is a closed-in wine with good concentration and stylish fruit. Long on the palate. **(01/91)**

Now–2004   16.0

Richebourg Jean Grivot

Fullish colour. Bizarre nose. A little vegetal, certainly exotic. I am very puzzled by this. I can't get enthused. But it is an Accad wine. Medium-full. Ripe, good extraction. But an absence of breed. Long though. **(01/91)**

Now–2005   15.0

Richebourg Anne et François Gros

Medium-full colour. Fine nose. Delicate - more Musigny than Richebourg - but stylish and concentrated nose. Good Pinot fruit. A subtle wine. Good grip. This is very good but doesn't quite have the extra for fine. Yet has a lovely complex finish. Very long. **(01/91)**

Now–2005   17.0

Richebourg Jean Gros

Fullish colour. Very strongly oaky on the nose. This dominates the fruit a bit, but the fruit is certainly stylish. A gentle wine for a Richebourg. It is very stylish but it doesn't have the concentration of Leroy. Long though, and complex. **(01/91)**

Now–2005   17.5

Richebourg Leroy

Fullish colour. This has real depth and concentration. Very much an infant but real potential here. More austere than the Leroy, Romanée-Saint-Vivant. More backward. But great intensity of flavour and class. Excellent. **(01/91)**

Now–2010   19.5

Richebourg Romanée-Conti

Medium-full colour. A bigger, rawer, more backward wine than the Romanée-Saint-Vivant. More muscular but less classy. This is closed-in and grumpy. The finish is the best bit. It will be a fatter more aromatic wine. Fine but today I prefer the more feminine character of the other. **(01/91)**

Now–2012   17.5

La Romanée Bouchard Père et Fils
Fullish colour. Pronounced oak, but a little raw, lacks succulence. Fullish but not that much concentration. A touch rigid. Good fruit but an absence of real length or complexity. Merely good. **(01/91)**
Now-2004   15.0

Romanée-Conti Romanée-Conti
Fullish colour. A less opulent nose than the La Tâche. More refined, more discreet, more subtle. This is a wine of great breed. Silk rather than velvet. It is the La Tâche which sings today. This appears a little lighter, a little less lush. It has a greater intensity of flavour however, and the finish is longer and more complex. The finish, in fact, is disarmingly brilliant. *Grand vin!* **(01/91)**
Now-2016   20.0

Romanée-Saint-Vivant Leroy
Fullish colour. Firm, full and oaky. Backward. This also has depth. This is even better. Real breed and concentration here. A lovely wine with a fine future. Great harmony and splendid fruit. **(01/91)**
Now-2010   19.0

Romanée-Saint-Vivant Romanée-Conti
Medium-full colour. Soft, oaky nose, plump and accessible. Lovely complex, fragrant fruit here if not a great deal of power. Plenty of class and intensity though. More reserved on the palate. A youthful wine with lovely subtle flavours, very good grip and delicious fruit. Very fine. Very long. **(01/91)**
Now-2012   18.0

Romanée-Saint-Vivant Thomas-Moillard
Fullish colour. Closed nose. Concentrated and fat and with a lot of depth. Full, concentrated, stylish wine on the palate. Lovely fruit. This is very fine. **(01/91)**
Now-2010   18.0

Ruchottes-Chambertin Louis Jadot
Full colour. Very fine. Good oak and old-vine fruit here. Very concentrated. Lovely. Fullish. Good tannins. Backward and concentration. This is another very fine example. Fine fruit. Quite powerful and intense. Still closed. **(01/91)**
Now-2012   18.0

Ruchottes-Chambertin Armand Rousseau
Good colour. Rather more oaky than the Rousseau Mazis. More structure on the palate. More concentration and depth, fuller and more backward. This is even better. Excellent. A really splendid Burgundy. Old-vine concentration here! **(01/91)**
Now-2015   18.5

Santenay Clos-de-la-Confrérie
Vincent Girardin
Good colour. Quite a firm nose. Fresh. Good fruit. This is rather more stylish and balanced. A good basic example. Well made. Medium body. Finishes well. **(01/91)**
Drink soon   13.5

Santenay Clos-Tavannes Denis Clair
Medium colour. A broad nose, quite boiled sweet-y. Medium body. A little tannin. This is better on the palate than on the nose. Good acidity. But lacks a bit of style and richness. **(01/91)**
Drink soon   12.0

Santenay La Comme Naigeon-Chauveau
Medium-colour. Mature. A bit dumb on the nose. Ripe on the palate. Good acidity. Good grip. This is mellow and stylish. Good depth. But lacks a little generosity. Long though. **(01/95)**
Now-2005   14.5

Santenay Les Gravières
Hautes Cornières, Jean-François Chapelle
Medium to medium-full colour. This has a good fresh, firm nose. Medium to medium-full. Good grip. This is good. Plenty of depth. Nicely fresh on the palate. Not too artisanal. Lovely fruit. Rounding off well. Good. **(12/95)**
Now-2005   15.0

Santenay Les Gravières Vincent Girardin
Good colour. Fresh, positive nose. Good straight Pinot. This has style. Medium body. Ripe. Quite concentrated. Good depth. Well balanced. A fine example for what it is. **(01/91)**
Now-2000   14.5

Santenay Les Gravières
Roland Remoissenet Père et Fils
Good colour. No marked new oak on the nose, but good, fat, plump fruit. Medium body. Ripe, lush, succulent. Most attractive. A very good example. **(01/91)**
Now-2000   16.0

Savigny-lès-Beaune Les Hauts-Jarrons
Jean Guiton
This is also ready, like the 1989. A little firmer than the 1989. But good acidity. Round, ripe in a slightly aloof way. Quite good plus. **(12/95)**
Now-2001   14.5

Savigny-lès-Beaune Les Liards
Gabriel Bouchard
Good straight fruit. Meaty and ripe and stylish. Not hard. The fruit is very good. So is the grip. This is rather good. Has depth. **(01/91)**
Now-2002   14.5

Savigny-lès-Beaune Les Serpentières
Maurice et Jean-Michel Giboulot

Sulphured highly to prolong *macération à froid*.
But then had difficulties with the malos. So gave
it up. This is a little raw at first and hard and
astringent after. Lacks fat and generosity. **(12/95)**

Drink soon   12.0

Savigny-lès-Beaune Aux Vergelesses
Simon Bize et Fils

Medium colour. An element of the Savigny
sauvage quality. Slight element of the stems as
well. A spicy wine. Seems to lack lushness on
the attack but the finish is richer. Long.
Medium body. Good. **(01/91)**

Now–2004   14.5

La Tâche Romanée-Conti

Fullish colour. Marvellous nose. Deep, rich,
old-viney, chocolatey almost. Fat, aromatic and
crammed with ripe fruit. Fullish, oaky,
potentially very velvety: an ample wine with
splendid lush fruit, beautifully balanced by ripe
acidity. Very concentrated. Very lovely.
Excellent finish. **(01/91)**

Now–2016   19.5

Volnay Jean-Marc Bouley

Fullish colour. Fresh, woody, almost spearminty
nose. New oak here. Good depth. Fullish for a
Volnay. Quite substantial. Rich, ripe, balanced.
Good concentration. This has depth if not real
Volnay style. Very good grip and length. **(01/91)**

Now–2004   15.5

Volnay Joseph Drouhin

Medium to medium-full body. Lovely, soft,
aromatic nose. Great charm. Medium body. Not
a wine of great depth but lovely fruit. Round,
soft, plump. **(10/94)**

Drink soon   15.5

Volnay Caillerets Marquis d'Angerville

Medium-full colour. This seems to have a
sweeter, more toasted oak than the Champans.
A touch more overtone. While it doesn't have
the class of the Pousse d'Or this is the best of the
Angervilles. A bit of oak and structure sticks out
on the attack but good fruit and concentration
on the follow-through. Very good. **(01/91)**

Now–2004   16.0

Volnay Caillerets Bouchard Père et Fils

Medium colour. Quite an evolved nose. A
touch sweet. Like the Taille-Pieds there is a
touch of reduction here which detracts from the
elegance. Medium-full. Some tannins. Good
extract. Like the Taille-Pieds I shall give this the
benefit of the doubt. **(01/91)**

Drink soon   15.0

Volnay Caillerets Yvon Clerget

Good colour. Fat, rich, succulent nose. Full,
expansive. Still closed but very fine quality. Real
concentration, real intensity. Very fine. Several
notes. **(07/95)**

Now–2015   18.0

Volnay Caillerets Pousse d'Or

Medium colour. Very elegant, lush Pinot fruit on
the nose. Classic Volnay. Lovely, balanced, delicate, elegant, complex fruit. Medium to medium-
full. Long, complex. Very good indeed. **(01/91)**

Now–2005   17.0

Volnay Caillerets, Clos-des-Soixante-
Ouvrées Pousse d'Or

Medium-full colour. Very fine nose. This is
even better than the Bousse d'Or. The fruit is
very stylish and complex, the balance lovely. A
poised, very classic example. Medium to
medium-full and with great intensity of flavour.
Very long and complex. **(01/91)**

Now–2005   17.5

Volnay Carelle-sous-la-Chapelle
Jean-Marc Bouley

Medium-full colour. Quite oaky but a touch
four-square on the nose. Solid and with some
tannin. Medium-full. Reasonable grip but a
lack of nuance on the attack. Better on the
finish but it doesn't have the nuance of Clerget's
example. **(01/91)**

Now–2002   14.5

Volnay Carelle-sous-la-Chapelle
Yvon Clerget

Medium to medium-full colour. Very straight,
classic Pinot on the nose, and rather more stylish
than Clerget's Santenots. Medium to medium-
full body. Good style, good balance. Good
depth. There is the concentration of old vines
here. Very good. **(01/91)**

Now–2004   16.0

Volnay Champans Marquis d'Angerville

Medium-full colour. Fat and opulent on the
nose, though there is something a touch rigid
about it at present. Medium-full body. Quite
sturdy and a touch of the stalks. But ripe and
backward. This has neither the fruit nor the grip
of the Clos-des-Ducs. It is a firmer, more closed
wine. Best on the finish. But it doesn't sing at
present. **(01/91)**

Now–2003   15.0

Volnay Champans Monthélie-Douhairet

Medium-full colour. Sweet nose but something
a little rustic as well. Bitter on the palate. This
lacks a little style and a little fruit, and the finish
is a bit astringent. **(01/91)**

Drink soon   13.0

Volnay   Clos-de-la-Barre
Olivier Leflaive Frères

Full colour. Lovely nose. Very good, subtle oak base and elegant fruit to accompany it. This has style. This is balanced and positive, like Matrot's example the wine is oaky but the oak is well assimilated. Lovely fruit. Very long. Very good. **(01/91)**

Now-2005   16.5

Volnay   Clos-de-la-Bousse-d'Or
Pousse d'Or

Medium-full colour. An open nose. Quite fat and ripe, but it seems to have less acidity than the above. Medium body. Ripe and classic. No lack of acidity on the palate. This is very stylish and very complex - and very Volnay. A super example of Volnay. Subtle and distinguished. **(01/91)**

Now-2005   17.0

Volnay   Clos-des-Chênes
Jean-Marc Bouley

Fullish colour. Full, fat, rich, spicy and oaky on the nose. Rather better than his Carelle. An oaky wine, quite macerated on the palate, almost to the extreme of being a little stewed. Good fruit and acidity underneath, but lacks a little style and succulence. **(01/91)**

Now-2003   15.0

Volnay   Clos-des-Chênes   Michel Lafarge

Very good colour. Some development on the nose. Ripe and fragrant. A little oak. Fullish. Very lovely fruit. Balanced. Concentrated. Rich and ripe. Really fine again. Very very long and complex. Even more intensity. Several notes. **(07/95)**

Now-2012   18.5

Volnay   Clos-des-Ducs
Marquis d'Angerville

Fullish colour. Very definitely oaky on the nose. Closed. A bit hidden at present. Evolved in the glass. This has class and depth. Ripe, oaky and spicy - also slightly stalky - on the palate. It doesn't have the grip of Matrot's Santenots but has good length and no lack of interest. Best on the finish. Seen several times. I am tending to note very good plus (16.5) now. **(01/91)**

Now-2002   15.5

Volnay   Clos-du Verseuil   Yvon Clerget

Medium-full colour. Good Pinot on the nose, but I don't find it as interesting as his Carelle. Less dimension, less plentitude of fruit. Medium to medium-full. Good Pinot. Reasonable balance and style but lacks a little interest. Very correct though. **(01/91)**

Now-2000   14.5

Volnay   Santenots   Pierre Boillot

Medium-full colour. Quite an opulent, ripe nose. A touch exotic. Quite firm on the palate. Closed. Noticeable tannins. A shade raw at present but there is depth here, as well as concentration. Needs time. Finishes very well. Old vines? **(01/91)**

Now-2004   15.5

Volnay   Santenots   Yvon Clerget

Medium to medium-full colour. Stylish Pinot on the nose but with a touch of the Meursault clumsiness compared with the wine of Matrot. Medium body. Quite accessible. Good fruit and good grip. Not short of elegance on the palate, though it lacks a little depth. Finishes well. **(01/91)**

Now-2000   14.5

Volnay   Santenots   Comtes Lafon

Good purple colour. Very impressive fruit. Just a touch cooked, raspberry and black cherry with a hint of the kernel within. Fullish, backward, even a shade harsh and raw still. Some tannin. Even a touch of bitterness. Firm. High acidity. But a meaty example, even adolescent at present. You can see the Meursault influence. But very good indeed. **(08/91)**

Now-2005   17.0

Volnay   Santenots   Matrot

Very good colour. Nicely sweet and ripe on the nose. Is there a slight lack of zip? Medium body. This is a bit more developed and rather less exciting. Reasonable intensity. But not quite as rich and fat and voluminous on the finish. Very good. **(07/95)**

Now-2009   16.0

Volnay   Taille-Pieds
Bouchard Père et Fils

Fullish colour. Firm and oaky, opulent and spicy, with a touch of H_2S on the nose. A full, quite succulent and muscular wine. Somewhat unsubtle in character. Medium-full. A shade raw. This is adolescent, but there is depth and balance here. I shall give it the benefit of the doubt. **(01/91)**

Now-2003   15.0

Vosne-Romanée   Beaux-Monts
Joseph Drouhin

Medium to medium-full colour. Not a blockbuster. Quite a lot of oak on the nose. Stylish, sweetly ripe Pinot. Quite a delicate wine for a Vosne. Balanced, long and elegant. Finishes well. More accessible than most. **(01/91)**

Now-2003   15.5

Vosne-Romanée Beaux-Monts Leroy

Medium-full colour. Rich, fullish, oaky nose. Possibly a bit over-extracted. On the palate I find this lacks depth. It is ripe and stylish but a bit dense. And it lacks a bit of zip. Good but not great. **(01/91)**

Now-2000   15.0

Vosne-Romanée Beaux-Monts Daniel Rion et Fils

Fine colour. Lovely, lush, oaky, ripe nose. An opulent wine. Medium-full. Very classic. Good grip. Good intensity. Ripe tannins. This is very good. **(01/91)**

Now-2005   16.5

Vosne-Romanée Beaux-Monts Thomas-Moillard

Medium-full colour. Rather a lot of oak on the nose. A little sweet/sour and dense. This is also not on form. Raw and peppery and a bit vegetal on the palate. **(01/91)**

Now-2000   13.0

Vosne-Romanée Brûlées René Engel

Medium-full colour. Just a touch overblown on the nose. On the palate as much astringent as tannic. Lacks depth. Merely pretty. **(01/91)**

Now-1999   14.0

Vosne-Romanée Chaumes Daniel Rion et Fils

Fullish colour. Rather stewed on the nose. Lacks style. A solid, rather dense wine. The tannins are not entirely ripe on the attack, which is a bit raw. Finishes better than it starts though. **(01/91)**

Now-2000   13.5

Vosne-Romanée Chaumes Jean Tardy

Very good colour. Fine blackcurrant fruit. Very good acidity, yet ripe and intense. Potentially fat and velvety. Medium-full. Not as opulent or as oaky as the 1990. But very impressive intense complex finish. This is a fine example. Better than his 1990 perhaps. **(03/94)**

Now-2012   17.5

Vosne-Romanée Clos-des-Réas Jean Gros

Medium-full colour. Gentle, oaky, stylish nose. Not a blockbuster though. Medium to medium-full body. Aromatic, lush and seductive. Long and complex. Very good. **(01/91)**

Now-2004   16.5

Vosne-Romanée Gaudichots Thierry Vigot

Fullish colour. A bit stewed on the nose. Over-extracted. A fullish, dense, solid wine. Lacks

charm. Four-square. Tasted three subsequent times. Marks up to 15.0. Not as exciting as it appeared in cask, sadly. **(01/91)**

Now-2000   13.0

Vosne-Romanée Malconsorts Thomas-Moillard

Fullish colour. Ripeness and oak here on the nose, but a shade blunt at present. Good oak but not a great deal of dimension underneath. Medium body. Quite good. Reasonably positive finish. **(01/91)**

Now-1999   14.0

Vosne-Romanée Suchots Jacques Cacheux

Medium-full colour. Cool, slightly resinny nose. Good straight fruit. Not a bit sweet. Ripe, quite structured. A touch of new oak. Good grip. Quite an austere example. But long and classy. Very good. **(01/91)**

Now-2004   16.5

Vosne-Romanée Suchots Jacky Confuron-Cotetidot

Good colour. Vigorous. Rich, fat, full, ample nose. Lovely blackberry fruit. Really intense and stylish. Just a touch of new oak. Ample, round, good acidity. Interesting fruit. Long. Slightly austere still. Will improve. Very good indeed. **(01/95)**

Now-2010   17.0

Vosne-Romanée Suchots Joseph Drouhin

Medium-full colour. Slightly dense but there is good fruit here on the nose. Medium-full, ripe, quite classy fruit. There is dimension here. Needs time. Finishes well. **(01/91)**

Now-2003   15.5

Vosne-Romanée Suchots Alain Hudelot-Noëllat

Fullish colour. Closed but concentrated nose. Good fruit and depth here. On the palate this is not a wine of great muscle. There is dimension here though. Stylish Pinot. Long. Very good. **(01/91)**

Now-2002   16.0

Vosne-Romanée Suchots Louis Jadot

Fullish colour. Not a blockbuster but good stylish fruit here on the nose. On the palate medium to medium-full. Has charm and style but no real depth and concentration. Good merely. Lacks a bit of dimension. **(01/91)**

Now-2002   15.0

1987

Red: 14.5   **White:** 13.5

SIZE OF THE CROP

(Hectolitres, excluding generic wine)

	Red	White
Grands Crus	11,018	2,785
Village and *Premiers Crus*	159,322	36,593
Total	170,340	39,378

Though 1987 would prove to be a small crop by comparison with later vintages - we have not had a shorter year since - and was a full 25 per cent less than the voluminous 1986 vintage, it was nevertheless larger than the trio of 1983, 1984 and 1985 in both red wine and overall terms. The white wines were somewhat light and lacking fruit, but the red wines were at least satisfactory, in the Côte-de-Beaune much better than the 1986s; and both were cheap by comparison with the high prices of 1985. This is a vintage which except at *grand cru rouge* level is nearing the end of its useful life, if not past it. Those with 1987s in their cellar should now make plans to drink them up.

WEATHER CONDITIONS

It was not a very auspicious summer. As one grower said to me, 'We only had six weeks of fine weather in 1987: three in March and three in September.' After a cold January, the early spring was dry. April was miserable, and May not much better, though there was an improvement towards the end of the month. The *sortie*, though large, was a fortnight late, and indifferent weather in June retarded the flowering until the end of the month.

The climate continued to be disappointing. Though there was not much *coulure* there was widespread *millerandage* - albeit less in the Chardonnays than in the Pinots, which had flowered earlier when the weather was poorer still. Moreover hail in parts of Meursault further reduced the size of the eventual crop; fortuitously as it turned out, for in those cooler corners further up in the hills where the flowering took place even later and in slightly better conditions, the crop was larger, but consequently more dilute.

It was not until the beginning of September, with growers already anticipating the worst, that the weather improved. Three weeks of sun saved the crop. After 20 September the weather broke, diluting the concentration which had been building up. There were several days of rain but at the same time there was a cool north wind. This dried the fruit and prevented the formation of rot. Indeed because of the *millerandage* the mature berries in each bunch were separated from each other and so there was less incidence of *pourriture grise* than in 1986 and 1985. The harvest was generally under way by the 27th and at first took place under clear skies. From 3 or 4 October onwards it was intermittently wet, not just during the rest of the harvesting period but right through the winter.

THE STYLE OF THE WINE

WHITE WINES

The sugar reading of the musts was average, neither encouragingly high nor disappointingly low, but acidity levels were higher than normal, and this gave rise to fears of rather charmless wines, lacking fruit. We have something which is closer to the 1984 than to 1986, a grower said to me in November 1987. The malo-lactic fermentations took place without causing any problems, unlike in 1986, and helped by a mild winter. It was not until these were finished that the true character of the 1987 white Burgundies began to emerge: crisp but *tendre*, light but racy, forward but fragrant.

What the wines generally lacked was fat and concentration, depth and richness. There was a general leanness which meant that keeping them at least a few years to round off would do them no harm, but then they should be consumed quickly before they got tired. This consumption period is now.

RED WINES

A feature of the 1987s at the beginning was their good colour. This was due not only to the absence of rot, to the low yield, to the thickness of the skins and to the small amount of juice relative to pulp, but also to the fact that it was the younger, higher-yielding vines which suffered most as a result of the poor weather during the flowering. The wines also had a good level of acidity. This helped keep the colour fresh at first, but after 1992 or so they rapidly took on quite a distinct brown tinge at the rim and then began to lighten up.

At the outset many growers expected the wines to be somewhat harder, less generous than they in fact turned out. The malos took a long time to complete – except where artificially assisted – but this was no bad thing, for it gave the chance to the young wines to feed off the lees of dead yeast cells and the rest, so absorbing more depth and richness, before the first racking in barrel.

As I have said, the 1987s in the Côte-de-Beaune are noticeably more impressive than the 1986s. For reasons of the size of harvest and the climatic conditions at the beginning of October, many 1986 Côte-de-Beaunes are a little hollow, lacking definition and concentration. This is particularly true at the village level. In 1987, right from the very first serious wine I sampled in November (a Volnay *chez* Lafarge – but then he can always be trusted!), I found a more regular consistency between the village wines and the *premiers crus*. The wines would, I decided, evolve in the medium term, from four to six years. They had elegance, freshness and fruit. The best had substance and no lack of concentration.

In the Côte-de-Nuits the position was more complicated. There was rain before the harvest on 19 September. Then again intermittent showers at the beginning of the week of 3 October, by which time most of the Côte-de-Beaune had completed their collection but just as the Côte-de-Nuits was due to commence, and then five days of dry weather after the 7th. It largely depended on when the vineyards were cleared.

In the Côte-de-Nuits it is impossible to generalise about which – 1986 or 1987 – is better. Opinions were divided then, they are divided now. The 1987s were usually fuller and more tannic, but the tannins rather ungainly, and many now have dried up, leaving a dead leaf undergrowth flavour which seems as if it is submerging whatever fruit is left. That is one-half of the vintage. These need drinking up. The better wines, on the other hand, are still ripe and succulent, and can be kept, though not for much longer.

I will report on a ten-year-on tasting of this vintage in *The Vine*, November 1997.

WHERE ARE THE BEST WINES?
AND STATE OF MATURITY TODAY

★ Most white wines, never very exciting in the first place, are now nearing their end, if not past it.

★ The Côte-de-Beaunes are better in 1987 than 1986.

★ As far as the Côte-de-Nuits is concerned it is impossible to generalise: it depends on the domaine.

★ Neither vintage approaches either 1985 or 1988 in quality.

★ Most red wines now need drinking up or soon.

TASTING NOTES

BLANC

Bâtard-Montrachet   Leflaive
Slightly faded on the nose. Gentle, oaky, light but stylish. *À point*. Not great. But complex and delicate if a bit slight. **(10/92)**
Drink soon   16.0

Bâtard-Montrachet   Étienne Sauzet
Full, ripe, new oaky, lanolin and vanilla nose. This has a lot of concentration. Much superior to the Combettes. Full, very good grip. Classy. A lot of dimension. Fine character. Very long. High class. **(02/91)**
Now-2000   17.5

Bienvenues-Bâtard-Montrachet   Ramonet
Very classy and very delicious. Good grip and depth. Lovely oaky base. Nicely austere but not really off-vintage at all. Plenty of vigour. Very fine. **(12/94)**
Now-2000 plus   18.0

Chassagne-Montrachet   Morgeot, Clos-de-la-Chapelle   Louis Jadot, Duc de Magenta
Ripe, concentrated, surprisingly good intensity. A shade lean but the high acidity keeps it fresh and elegant. Very good. **(06/92)**
Now-2000   16.0

Chassagne-Montrachet   *Premier Cru*
Jean-Noël Gagnard
A fresh, gentle, lightly oaked wine which is more elegant than I expected, because I have found some of his wines a bit sulphury. Still vigorous. But not a lot of fruit here so drink soon. Good plus for the vintage. **(09/91)**
Drink soon   15.5

Chassagne-Montrachet   La Romanée
Paul Pillot
Quite a deep colour. This is rich and oaky, full and ample with very good fruit. Much more

depth and quality than I expected. Very good. Drink soon but no hurry. Slightly four-square perhaps. Slightly alcoholic. **(11/94)**
Drink soon   14.5

Chassagne-Montrachet   Les Ruchottes
René Monnier
Full, fat, firm, rich and holding up well. A very good example indeed of a 1987. No weakness. Plenty of class and depth. Nice touch of oak. Not a bit off-vintage. **(03/96)**
Now-2000   17.0

Chevalier-Montrachet   Jacques Prieur
Oak but no fruit. Poor. Already evolved. **(01/91)**
Drink up   11.0

Corton-Charlemagne   Camille Giroud
Slightly herbal, a touch of new oak. Ripe but not rich. This is a wine to admire rather than to get seduced by. It is a little austere, though not astringent, and never had much sex appeal. As it evolved it got fatter and more interesting. Good. **(11/95)**
Now-2000   15.0

Corton-Charlemagne   Louis Jadot
Light colour. Slightly austere nose. A little one-dimensional but good fruit. Gently oaky. Very stylish. Good. **(09/91)**
Now-2000   16.0

Corton-Charlemagne   Roland Rapet
This is a bit meagre. A lack of oak. A lack of elegance. Little interest. Hard. Quite youthful on the nose but getting attenuated at the end. **(11/95)**
Drink up   12.0

Meursault   Charmes   Comtes Lafon
Quite an evolved colour. Rich oaky nose. Not a bit weak or lean. Ample, balanced, youthful.

Very delicious. Remarkably good for a small year. Very good fruit. Round, ripe, rich. Plenty of vigour. Very fine. Several notes. **(02/95)**

Now–2000 plus 18.0

Meursault Désirée Comtes Lafon

Ripe, gently oaky, *à point* but vigorous. Fruity and balanced. Plenty of depth and concentration and class. Really very good for a 1987. **(09/92)**

Now–2000 16.0

Le Montrachet Guy Amiot

A rather evolved, somewhat faded but alcoholic wine. No style. Horrid. **(01/91)**

Drink up 10.5

Le Montrachet Marquis de Laguiche

Medium-gold colour. Ripe, elegant, just slightly lean on the nose. A touch of sweetness on the palate. Very ripe. Nothing lean or off-vintagey about this. Plump, vigorous, balanced. Round. Unexpectedly delicious. Very fine. Bags of life. Yet not a completely satisfactory *tenue à l'air*. Less elegant after 30 minutes. **(11/93)**

Now–2000 18.0

Le Montrachet Jacques Prieur

Round and oaky but disagreable. Quite high acidity. Better than his Chevalier, but that is not saying much. **(01/91)**

Drink up 12.0

Le Montrachet Romanée–Conti

This is unexpectedly good for a 1987. Round, oaky, ripe and complex. Slightly austere but not lean. Good vigour. Will still keep well. Classy too. Very good indeed. **(02/95)**

Now–2003 17.0

Musigny Comte Georges de Vogüé

Odd apricot, plum, herb nose. Not typical of Côte-de-Beaune Chardonnays. A touch lean but nevertheless ripe. Perhaps a bit of an acquired taste, but I like it. Individual. Rich. Long. As it evolved almost a petrolly hint. *À point.* **(05/92)**

Drink soon 16.0

Nuits-Saint-Georges Clos-de-l'Arlot Arlot

A good vigorous and nicely oaky and individual wine. Not a bit off-vintage. Fully ready but no hurry to drink. Round, ripe and lean in the best sense, i.e. with good grip and drive on the finish. Very stylish. Very good. Several notes. **(01/95)**

Now–2000 16.0

Puligny-Montrachet Étienne Sauzet

A more evolved nose than his Chassagne-Montrachet, 1988. Again just a touch of SO_2. A little obviously chaptalised. A good basic

though. Elegant, ripe, balanced. On the palate a little one-dimensional. As good as it will ever be. Good for a basic 1987 but lacks excitement. Clean and stylish though. **(02/91)**

Drink soon 15.0

Puligny-Montrachet Clavoillons Leflaive

Slightly dumb on the nose. But very good on the palate. Gently oaky, rich, good fruit and good acidity. Plenty of life, plenty of depth. Less four-square than some Clavoillons. Elegant at the end. Improved in the glass. Best of all on the finish. Very good. **(05/95)**

Drink soon 16.0

Puligny-Montrachet Les Combettes Étienne Sauzet

A little more colour. Much more obviously oaky. Quality and depth here. Delicious Chardonnay. Very elegant. The oak gives it structure, bite and personality. Very much better than the simple village wine. Very good. **(02/91)**

Now–2000 16.0

Puligny-Montrachet Les Pucelles Leflaive

Fresh nose with plenty of interest. Good grip as well as acidity. This is surprisingly good (especially when I remember the 1986). Medium body. Good depth. Nicely ripe fruit, and if not rich at least with a consistency from start to finish, and all the elegance you expect. *À point.* Very good. **(01/95)**

Now–2000 16.0

ROUGE

Aloxe-Corton Roland Rapet

Good colour. Slightly lumpy but fruity nose and palate. Slightly rigid. Good acidity but a lack of succulence and smoothness and class. Acidity shows on the finish. Not bad plus. **(11/95)**

Drink soon 13.5

Aloxe-Corton Comte Senard

Medium colour. Light, sweet, spurious. No merit. Now getting thin. **(11/95)**

Drink soon 11.0

Aloxe-Corton Les Valozières Comte Senard

Medium colour. Rather sweet on the nose. Light and wimpy on the palate. Thin and sweet and undistinguished. **(11/95)**

Drink soon 11.5

Beaune Bressandes Chanson Père et Fils

Slightly more evolved on the colour than the Clos-des-Mouches. Rather more so on the palate as well. This is beginning to shorten a little at the end. Nicely plump and balanced, but without quite the grip perhaps of the Clos-des-Mouches. Not quite as stylish either now. But good. **(11/95)**

Drink soon   **15.0**

Beaune   Bressandes   Albert Morot

Good colour. Quite evolved on the nose but not dry or rustic. Fresh on the palate but a touch lean. Medium body. Not a lot of complexity. This is pleasant but not exciting. Quite good. **(11/95)**

Now-2000   **14.0**

Beaune   Cent-Vignes   René Monnier

This is an attractive, consistent example. Medium to medium-full. Ripe, cherry-flavoured fruit. The nose is fresh and plump, the palate round and quite rich. Balanced and with no hard edges. Easy to drink. Very good. **(11/95)**

Now-2000   **16.0**

Beaune   Clos-des-Couchereaux   Louis Jadot

Good mature colour. Quite sturdy on the nose. A suggestion of the stems. Ripe and generous on the palate. Still quite fresh. But a slight lack of real class. Good plus. **(11/95)**

Now-2000   **15.5**

Beaune   Clos-des-Mouches
Chanson Père et Fils

Medium to medium-full colour. Still vigorous. Interesting cedary-oaky nose. Nicely fresh. Medium to medium-full. No great depth but plump, agreeable, balanced. Attractive. Finishes well. Good plus. **(11/95)**

Now-2000   **15.5**

Beaune   Clos-des-Mouches
Joseph Drouhin

Good fresh but mature colour. Quite evolved on the nose with that dry touch of stems touch. Ripe, mellow. Medium to medium-full. Fully mature. This is plump and agreeable, though with a slightly hard touch to it. Lacks a bit of generosity and now has suspicions of astringency. Good. **(11/95)**

Drink soon   **15.0**

Beaune   Grèves   Michel Lafarge

Medium to medium-full colour. Very clean supple fresh nose. Lovely raspberry fruit. Really stylish. Medium-full body. Ripe, complex, Volnay-ish. Very long and elegant and fragrant. Much fresher than most 1987s. Good concentration. Long. Fine. **(11/95)**

Now-2005   **17.5**

Beaune   Grèves
Roland Remoissenet Père et Fils

Good, fullish, vigorous colour. Fresh, plump, stylish nose. Medium-full body. Round, balanced, will still improve. The tannins are ripe and there is good grip. Nice and ripe and abundant. Good style. Plenty of vigour. Very good plus. **(11/95)**

Now-2007   **16.5**

Beaune   Grèves, Vigne-de-l'Enfant-Jésus
Bouchard Père et Fils

Good colour. The nose is a bit evolved and a bit coarse. Elements of dry, not very sophisticated tannins, and the stems. On the nose it is a lot more pleasant. Reasonable grip. Plump fruit. No undue astringency. Quite vigorous. Even stylish. Good plus. **(11/95)**

Now-2000   **15.5**

Beaune   Marconnets   Albert Morot

Vigorous colour. Quite a rich nose. Clean. Good fruit. A little closed. Medium to medium-full body. Nicely complex fruit. Good *matière*. Good grip. This is fresh, long, generous and very good. **(11/95)**

Now-2002   **16.0**

Beaune   Montées-Rouge   Leroy

Medium colour. Round and rich and soft. A little hard at first but more generous on aeration. Long. Nicely elegant. Good plus. **(11/95)**

Now-2000   **15.5**

Beaune   Montrevenots   Jean-Marc Boillot

Good fresh colour. Just a little funky on the nose. Medium body. Quite ripe, but an underlying slightly rustic astringency. This is pleasant but not special. Quite fresh still. Quite good plus. **(11/95)**

Now-2000   **14.5**

Beaune   Les Perrières   Camille Giroud

Very good colour. Full and youthful. Firm, full, fleshy slightly rustic nose. This is concentrated and rich. A meaty example. Old-viney. Very good fruit. There is a certain astringency as well as the richness here (the bottling after two years) but this would not be evident with food. Expansive. Very good. **(11/95)**

Now-2000   **16.0**

Beaune   *Premier Cru*   Labouré-Roi

Very good colour. Still very vigorous. Nicely full. A little dry tannin on the nose but no evolution on the nose. Medium full. Slightly hard and coarse, quite sweet. A bit hot. Lacks nuance. Fair at best. **(11/95)**

Now-2000 plus   **12.5**

Beaune   Teurons
Jacques Germain, Château de Chorey

Good youthful colour. Clean, fruity nose. Good depth and elegance. This is crisp and fresh. Ample and fruity. Medium to medium-full body. Ripe and elegant. Harmonious. Long and persistent. Very good. **(11/95)**

Now-2003   16.0

Beaune   Teurons   Albert Morot

Very good colour. Rich, chocolate/coffee nose. Plenty of depth on the palate. Fullish, rich and ripe. Good tannin. This is fresh and vigorous. Still young. Lots of life here. Very good rich follow-through. Ample. Very good indeed. **(11/95)**

Now-2005   17.0

Beaune   Vignes-Franches
Château de Chorey

Good youthful colour. Slightly lean, cherry-fruity nose. Ripe, stylish. Medium body. This is fresh if not very rich. Very elegant. Slightly less than the Teurons but good plus. **(11/95)**

Now-2000   15.5

Blagny   La Pièce-sous-le-Bois
René Lamy-Pillot

Medium colour. Slightly fading but not too rustic a nose. Getting a little old now on the palate. Yet the fruit is quite plump and was elegant once. But now rather lean. **(11/95)**

Drink up   12.5

Blagny   La Pièce-sous-le-Bois   Matrot

Quite an evolved colour. And nose as well. A bit too much dead leaves. Light and fruit, fresher than the nose would suggest. But nearing the end nevertheless. Better follow-through. A bit 'hot'. Some richness. But only quite good. No great finesse. Getting a bit hollow at the end. **(11/95)**

Drink soon   14.0

Bonnes-Mares   Comte Georges de Vogüé

Medium colour. Somewhat diffuse on nose and palate. A bit light. A bit coarse by comparison with today. Quite good sweet fruit. No lack of grip. The finish is fresh. But not really that impressive. Good merely. **(11/95)**

Drink soon   15.0

Chambertin   Clos-de-Bèze   Louis Jadot

Fine colour. This is still not really ready. Marvellous finesse and concentration and aristocracy. Fullish. Very very classy. Very good grip as well. It is all there. And it got better and better in the glass. Excellent. **(11/95)**

Now-2020   19.5

Chambolle-Musigny   Leroy

This is more evolved than the Nuits-Saint-Georges. But the nose is lovely, not a bit coarse, and on the palate the wine is soft, fruity, plump, fresh and elegant. Very good. **(11/95)**

Now-2000 plus   16.0

Chambolle-Musigny   Les Charmes
Ghislaine Barthod-Noëllat

This is just a bit lighter than the Barthod Cras, and then is more rustic and more evolved. On the palate too this is less exciting. The wine isn't as fresh or as succulent. Good acidity but less grip, less ripe. Quite good only. **(11/95)**

Drink soon   14.0

Chambolle-Musigny   Les Cras
Ghislaine Barthod-Noëllat

Good colour. Slightly funky nose. Suggestions of old tea. Medium weight. Good acidity and general freshness. And as with many, the wine is better on the palate than the nose. Round, ripe, quite stylish. Still plenty of vigour. Good plus. **(11/95)**

Now-2003   15.5

Charmes-Chambertin   Joseph Drouhin

Good vigorous mature colour. Fragrant, mature nose. Good freshness here. Medium-full. A classy wine. Fresh and well balanced. Long and complex. Still has plenty of life. This is long, positive and complex. Fine. **(11/95)**

Now-2005   17.5

Charmes-Chambertin   Bernard Dugat-Py

Bernard's first vintage after taking over from his father Pierre; seven-year-old vines. Medium colour. Fully mature. Slightly diffuse on the nose. No astringency. Some depth. Medium to medium-full. This has good fruit and even intensity, with concentration and fat as well. A little unsophisticated but long enough. Good plus. **(11/95)**

Drink soon   15.5

Charmes-Chambertin   Christian Serafin

Fine colour. Very youthful still. Firm, fresh concentrated nose. Rather riper than the Cazetiers. Full. Still quite a lot of unresolved tannin. Rich, fresh, very stylish. Lots of depth. Unexpected finesse. Fine plus. **(11/95)**

Now-2005 plus   18.0

Chassagne-Montrachet   René Lamy-Pillot

Medium colour. Quite fresh. Quite rich and gamey on the nose. Fullish, quite fresh but a little hard and rustic on the palate. Not much charm here. **(11/95)**

Drink soon   13.0

Chassagne-Montrachet Fernand et Laurent Pillot

Good colour. Nothing diffuse or spicy on the nose. Slightly hard at first. Underneath ripe, if not classy. Fullish. Good depth. Good vigour here. Ample. Attractive. Very good. **(11/95)**

Now-2000   16.0

Chassagne-Montrachet Clos-de-la-Boudriotte Ramonet

A little more colour than the Morgeots. The nose is similar but slightly firmer. More *gibier*, less *faisandé*. Richer, fresher, fuller. This is ample and satisfying. Good grip. Vigorous. Again no real elegance but a thoroughly enjoyable bottle with plenty of life ahead of it. Very good. **(11/95)**

Now-2005   16.0

Chassagne-Montrachet Clos-Saint-Jean Guy Amiot

Good colour. Slightly rustic on the nose. Reasonable depth. Good balance and vigour. Rich and fat and meaty on the palate, much less rustic. This has personality and dimension. Good sturdy stuff. Very good. **(11/95)**

Now-2005   16.0

Chassagne-Montrachet Morgeots Ramonet

Medium colour. This is gamey on the nose, with good ripe fruit. On the palate it is medium to medium-full body. Ripe and spicy. There is good acidity. *À point* now. Not that elegant but an attractive bottle. **(11/95)**

Now-2000   15.0

Clos-de-la-Roche Dujac

Very good colour. This is riper, richer, more substantial and above all more classy on the nose than the Clos-Saint-Denis. Full, rich, ample, still youthful. Still a little unresolved tannin. Much more class and depth. Lovely fruit. Real complexity. Very very long. Delicious. Very fine. **(11/95)**

Now-2010   18.5

Clos-de-la-Roche Roland Remoissenet Père et Fils

Good full colour. Rich, expansive, meaty nose. Now just about ready. Full, fat, ripe and rich. Quite some tannin here but the tannins nicely ripe and now properly rounded just about. This is only just ready. Lovely rich finish. Classy too. Very fine. **(11/95)**

Now-2012   18.0

Clos-Saint-Denis Joseph Drouhin

Good vigorous mature colour. rich, quite gamey nose. Fullish, ripe, even sweet. Not exactly very classy but a vigorous plump example with good weight and grip. Finishes well. Still has life. Very good. **(11/95)**

Now-2000   16.0

Clos-Saint-Denis Dujac

Very good colour. Barely mature. Slightly diffuse on the nose. On the palate this is rich and succulent, but it doesn't at first have a lot of depth and finesse. This is misleading, for the follow-through is very intense and vigorous. The wine is ripe and the finish very elegant, very fresh and even very intense. Very lovely still. Fine. **(11/95)**

Now-2005   17.5

Clos-de-Tart Mommessin

Good fresh colour. On the nose the stems are evident. On the palate it is richer, if a bit astringent on the edges. But sweet, vigorous. Slight cigar flavours. Quite powerful. Fullish. Lacks a bit of fat and elegance and velvetiness. Good plus. **(11/95)**

Now-2000 plus   15.5

Clos-de-Vougeot Louis Jadot

Good vigorous colour. Plump and rich and aromatic on both nose and attack. Vigorous, it seems. Perhaps a little astringent at the end. This is a curious animal. A touch dense and tannic. Yet I like the fruit. Very good plus. **(11/95)**

Now-2002   16.5

Clos-de-Vougeot Roland Remoissenet Père et Fils

Good colour. Still very vigorous. Just a little closed and dry on the nose. This is rich and fat and spicy. Full but lacks a little fragrance and elegance for better than fine. But it will still develop. There is a good grip and plenty of backbone. Finishes long, fat and concentrated. **(11/95)**

Now-2013   17.5

Corton Clos-des-Meix Comte Senard

Medium colour. Thin nose. Nothing much behind it. A soft, rather obviously sweet wine. Medium body. Boiled sweet type fruit. Unexciting. **(11/95)**

Drink soon   12.0

Corton Maréchaudes Prince de Mérode

A bit light-weight, but clean and stylish. Medium colour. Good acidity. Quite plump fruit. Not the distinction of a Corton though. Good merely. **(11/95)**

Drink soon   15.0

Corton Pougets Louis Jadot

Good colour. This is quite evolved now. A little gamey and rustic on both nose and palate. Quite smooth still. Fullish. Not astringent. But now is the time, while it is still fresh and fruity. Very good at best. (11/95)

Now–2000   16.0

Echézeaux   René Engel

Good colour. Fine nose. Fresh and concentrated and elegant. Plenty of depth here. Lovely blackcurrant fruit. Fat and rich. Plump and generous. Medium to medium-full body. Very elegant. Very accessible. Absolutely *à point*. Good long positive finish but slightly dense as it developed. Fine nevertheless. (11/95)

Now–2002 plus   17.5

Echézeaux   Jean Grivot

Fine colour. Very lovely nose. This is very classy. Rich and fat and intense without a touch of the rustic from start to finish. Medium-full. Balanced. Really classy, real depth. Very fine indeed. (11/95)

Now–2005   19.0

Echézeaux   Roland Remoissenet Père et Fils

Fullish colour. Now accessible on the nose. Plump, cherry-plummy fruit. Round and balanced. Rich, fullish, *à point*. Not the greatest concentration but an attractive and fresh wine. Very good plus. (11/95)

Now–2007   16.5

Gevrey-Chambertin   Lucien Boillot

Good colour. No undue age. The nose shows good depth and structure if a slight lack of finesse. On the palate the wine is quite full, nice and ripe and plump, and has good grip. At the end it is a little sharp and astringent at first. But this disappears on aeration. Will keep well. Nice long finish. Very good. (11/95)

Now–2000   16.0

Gevrey-Chambertin
Claude et Maurice Dugat

Medium colour. A little evolved and not very stylish on the nose. Twiggy and burnt-sugar elements. Bitter on the palate. Some substance, some richness, some finesse. Not too dry. Quite fat and concentrated in fact. Fully evolved. Quite good. (11/95)

Now–2000   14.0

Gevrey-Chambertin   Bernard Dugat-Py

Light to medium, quite evolved colour. This is not astringent, but it lacks a bit of finesse. A fully mature, medium-weight wine. Fruity and spicy. Not bad, but not up to today's standard (in those days Bernard and his father sold everything except a little for home consumption to the *négoce*). Easy to drink. (11/95)

Drink soon   13.5

Gevrey-Chambertin   Camille Giroud

This is a fine example. Rich in colour. Rich and cassis/redcurranty on the nose. The tannins very ripe. Excellent acidity. Round, concentrated, velvety, very long. Very complex. Very good indeed. (11/95)

Now–2005   17.0

Gevrey-Chambertin   Denis Mortet

Good colour. Ripe, ample nose and palate. This is clean, plump and easy to drink. But it is fullish and still vigorous. And it lacks no element of grip and style. Slightly spicy. But long and satisfying. Very good. (11/95)

Now–2000   16.0

Gevrey-Chambertin   *Vieilles-Vignes*
Philippe Charlopin-Parizot

Very good colour. Rich, succulent, slightly animal but not diffuse or coarsely astringent on the nose. Good fullish fresh wine. This was made with some stems. But it is not a bit rustic. Fresh, meaty, vigorous. Good length. Very good plus. (11/95)

Now–2002   16.5

Gevrey-Chambertin   Les Cazetiers
Christian Serafin

Very good colour. Still vigorous. Very stylish, rich, balanced nose. Very fresh. A lot of depth. Fullish, concentrated, still some unresolved tannins. Black-fruit flavours. Good grip. Fresh. Long. Not exactly very rich or generous but very stylish. Very good plus. (11/95)

Now–2005   16.5

Gevrey-Chambertin   Champeaux
Pierre Dugat

This is today exploited by Bernard Dugat's sister, Madame Seguin, who sells in bulk to Bourée. Medium colour. Some depth but essentially a fully evolved pleasantly balanced fruity wine. No undue astringency. Easy to drink. Unexceptional. (11/95)

Drink soon   14.0

Gevrey-Chambertin   Champeaux
Denis Mortet

Good full mature colour. Good full slightly gamey nose. Ample, ripe. Medium body. Fresh but accessible. Not a lot more body than the village. But slightly longer and more complex. A little younger. Very good plus. (11/95)

Now–2002   16.5

Gevrey-Chambertin   Clos-Prieur
André et Frédéric Esmonin

This was just about the beginning of large-scale bottling here. Good colour. Fresh, ripe, ample and stylish on the nose. Good fat and grip.

Medium-full. More vigorous and less evolved on the palate than the nose. This is *à point*. Succulent, fresh and very good plus. (11/95)

Now-2000   16.5

Gevrey-Chambertin   Clos-Saint-Jacques
Michel Esmonin et Fille

Good colour. A little funky on the nose. But ripe and generous and fullish. (Michel made, Sylvie matured, the first vintage they bottled.) Good meaty fullish wine on the palate. Quite rich. Now ready. Good vigour and balance. Long and satisfying. Very good plus but not the class or length and concentration for better. (11/95)

Now-2000 plus   16.5

Gevrey-Chambertin   Clos-Saint-Jacques
Louis Jadot

Very good colour. The nose suggests a little astringency but the palate is silky smooth, very concentrated and elegant and quite delicious. Very long. Fullish, intense, very classy finish. Fine. (11/95)

Now-2005   17.5

Gevrey-Chambertin   Les Combottes
Roland Remoissenet Père et Fils

Good full vigorous colour. Fine nose. Rich and fragrant. This is a most attractive lush example. Now just about ready. Fullish, rich, round. Very good tannins. Well balanced and nicely abundant fruit. Just a touch of oak. Long. Volnay touches for a Chambertin. Fine. (11/95)

Now-2009   17.5

Gevrey-Chambertin   Les Corbeaux
Lucien Boillot

Very good colour. Quite elegant on the nose. But a little lightweight on the palate. It is fresh but it is a bit short. Pleasant, indeed stylishly fruity. But now a little frail. A feminine wine. I prefer the vigour of the village wine to the elegance of this. Good plus. (11/95)

Drink soon   15.5

Gevrey-Chambertin   Lavaux-Saint-Jacques
Bernard Maume

Medium-full colour. Fully mature. Round, amply fruity nose with a touch of spice. Not that elegant, but no undue age either. On the palate this is a little rustic but is fresh and vigorous, ample and succulent. And the finish is long and positive. Still very vigorous. Good plus. (11/95)

Now-2002 plus   15.5

Gevrey-Chambertin   Lavaux-Saint-Jacques
Vachet-Rousseau

Good fresh, fullish colour. Good nose. Still quite firm. On the palate this has good meaty fruit. Well balanced. Ample and rich. Positive and classy. And still has lots of life left. This is very good indeed. (11/95)

Now-2005   17.0

Grands-Echézeaux   Romanée-Conti

Good colour. No undue maturity at all. Still fresh. Quite tough and robust on the nose. Firm, slightly stemmy, a bit *sauvage*. Fullish, still very vigorous. Good acidity. Quite muscular tannins. Good richness. Sweet finish. Plenty of depth and quality here. Long. Fine. Got rounder in the glass. (11/95)

Now-2005   17.5

Monthélie   Les Duresses   Paul Garaudet

Good fresh colour. Plump, slightly assisted on the nose. Fresh on the palate. This is pleasant and is still vigorous. But it lacks a certain generosity and personality. Quite good though. (11/95)

Now-2000   14.0

Le Musigny   Louis Jadot

Good colour. Round and rich and voluptuous. Aromatic and slightly spicy. But nothing coarse here. Fat and quite structured. Very rich. Very long. Very fine indeed. (11/95)

Now-2005   18.5

Le Musigny   Comte Georges de Vogüé

Medium colour. Clean nose. Soft and fragrant, a bit too soft, perhaps. This has good fruit and persistence, though there is an element in the background I find a bit attenuated, which detracts from the finesse. But quite long. Not weak. Very good plus. (11/95)

Now-1999   16.5

Nuits-Saint-Georges   Labouré-Roi

Good colour. This has an attractive chocolatey nose. Plump, fruity, ripe and attractive on the palate. Even stylish. Still vigorous. Finishes positively. Holding up well. Good plus. (11/95)

Now-2000 plus   15.5

Nuits-Saint-Georges   Leroy

A nice meaty example, easy to drink. Fat, fullish and quite masculine. Very Nuits-Saint-Georges. Good substance and depth. Plenty of fruit if no great nuance. Good plus. (11/95)

Now-2002   15.5

Nuits-Saint-Georges Les Boudots
Jean Grivot

Very good colour. This is all of a piece and quite evolved. Round. Quite spicy. Some elements of old wine here. A little sweet. No hard edges. The tannins less rigid. But this is curious. Are other bottles fresher? Certainly most enjoyable. But not fine. **(11/95)**

Now-2000   16.5

Nuits-Saint-Georges Les Boudots
Jean Tardy

Fine, fullish, mature nose. Closed nose. Smelling of its stems. Much better on aeration. Ripe, fat, vigorous. Ample and meaty. All with good acidity. Ripe, but the tannins are a bit hidden. Very good plus/fine. The finish is less elegant. **(11/95)**

Now-2002   17.5

Nuits-Saint-Georges Les Chaumes
Jean Grivot

Good colour. The nose is a little burnt and spicy. Autumn leaves, old coffee grains. On the palate, rich, ample, medium body, fresh and with good class, warmth and intensity. Very attractive. Long on the finish. Very good plus. **(11/95)**

Now-2000 plus   16.5

Nuits-Saint-Georges Clos-des-Corvées
Louis Jadot

Good mature colour. This is fresh, fullish, concentrated and has very good grip. Cool, not a bit too clumsy. Fullish, vigorous. Very good fruit. Complex. Long. Bags of life. Very good indeed. **(11/95)**

Now-2005   17.0

Nuits-Saint-Georges Clos-des-Grandes-
Vignes Thomas-Moillard

Mature colour. Quite evolved on the nose. And without much class either, but it is not too dry. This is a little artificially sweet, with some astringency and rather a rustic character. Even a little volatile. Unexciting. **(11/95)**

Drink up   13.5

Nuits-Saint-Georges Clos-Saint-Marc
Bouchard Père et Fils

Good colour. Vigorous nose. Nice and rich and not too *sauvage*. Full, rich, structured. Typically Nuits-Saint-Georges but vigorous and rich and with very good grip. Finishes long and satisfying. Plenty of life left. Very good indeed. **(11/95)**

Now-2005   17.0

Nuits-Saint-Georges Hauts-Pruliers
Daniel Rion et Fils

Very good colour. Bonfires on the nose. Rich but smoky. Fullish on the palate. Quite sturdy. But slightly more evolved than the Chaumes. Quite rich. But slightly less elegant. Good. **(11/95)**

Now-2000   15.0

Nuits-Saint-Georges Les Porrets
Thomas-Moillard

This is quite a lot better than the Grandes-Vignes. Fullish, meaty, fresher, plumper. Medium-full. No undue astringency. Ripe and generous. Very good. **(11/95)**

Now-2000   16.0

Nuits-Saint-Georges *Premier Cru*
Jean Chauvenet

Because of hail damage, a single *cuvée* from his first growths. The wine is 50 per cent Bousselots. This was made with some of the stems, which he doesn't do today. Good quite fresh sturdy nose. Rich, full, masculine. Quite solid. The tannins are not that sophisticated but the wine is vigorous and enjoyable. Very good. **(11/95)**

Now-2003   16.0

Nuits-Saint-Georges Les Vaucrains
Camille Giroud

Full mature colour. On the nose a touch of coffee, chocolate and caramel. Rich, meaty, fresh. Fullish on the palate. Good intensity. Good grip. Nicely fleshy and animal, plenty of depth. As well as the size and the fruit. There is a touch of astringency which would be less apparent with fruit. Very good indeed. **(11/95)**

Now-2003   17.0

Pernand-Vergelesses Ile-des-Vergelesses
Roland Rapet

Good colour. Rich fullish vigorous nose. Quite concentrated, quite fresh. This has good genuine Pinot fruit and is not too rigid. Quite stylish, even complex. Good vigour. Very good. **(11/95)**

Now-2000   16.0

Pommard Paul Garaudet

Good fresh colour. Some structure, but a bit vacant on the nose. Light, suave. Finished. **(11/95)**

Past its best   10.0

Pommard Chaponnières Jacques Parent

Good mature colour. Slightly soupy but not dry on the nose. A bit coarse though. Soft, not astringent, not diffuse. Better on the palate.

Richer, more elegant. Good grip. Slightly four-square and slightly hard and dense. But ample and ripe. Good. **(11/95)**

Now-2003   15.0

Pommard   Clos-des-Epeneaux Comte Armand

Medium-full colour. Quite burly on the nose, but rich inside. A little austere and one-dimensional on the palate. Medium to medium-full body. Lacks a bit of richness and fat. But cool and quite classy. Quite good. **(11/95)**

Now-2000   14.0

Pommard   Clos-de-la-Platière Prince de Mérode

Good colour. Slightly sweet on the nose. No great finesse but medium body. Round, ripe, a little astringent. Quite pleasant. Slightly lumpy. **(11/95)**

Drink soon   13.0

Pommard   Les Croix-Noires Lucien Boillot et Fils

Good colour. Rich, fat, slightly spicy. But fresh on the nose. On the palate this has good size and opulence. Nicely ripe and balanced. Long and positive. Vigorous and rich. Meaty. Plenty of life ahead of it. Well balanced. This is very good indeed. **(11/95)**

Now-2003 plus   17.0

Pommard   Epenots   Pierre Morey

Medium-light colour. Quite evolved now. Similar on the nose. Not rustic but lightening up certainly. Medium body. Stylish and balanced but it is now getting a bit fluid. Still enjoyment to be had. Ripe on the finish. But drink soon. Quite good plus. **(11/95)**

Drink soon   14.5

Pommard   Epenots   Jacques Parent

Very good colour. Much better nose than the Chaponnières. Lush, full, rich, meaty. Fullish, quite structured. Good but slightly four-square tannins and fruit. Round. Long. Good plus. **(11/95)**

Now-2002   15.5

Pommard   Rugiens   Jean-Marc Bouley

Good colour. Nothing diffuse here. Rich nose. Just a touch of reduction giving it a gamey animal touch. Full, opulent. Quite rich. The tannins are a little hard and unsophisticated but this is a very good meaty wine. Good grip. Slightly astringent at the end. **(11/95)**

Now-2002   16.0

Rugiens   Pommard   De Courcel

Medium-full colour. Good nose. Nicely rich and balanced. Good grip. Good class. Fullish,

ample, ripe and long. This is a very satisfactory example. Long. Very stylish. Very good indeed. **(11/95)**

Now-2005   17.0

Pommard   Rugiens   Hubert de Montille

Good colour. Fat, ripe, substantial on the nose. Quite rich on the palate. Medium to medium-full. But not quite enough fat underneath. This is balanced but a little ungainly. Fruity but a bit four-square. Very good. **(11/95)**

Now-2000   16.0

Pommard   Saussilles   Jean-Marc Boillot

Good fresh colour. Not too funky at all on the nose. Nice and rich. Slight spicy touch. Good freshness. On the palate this is consistent, attractive, ripe and caramelly. Even rich. Medium-full. Still fresh and vigorous. Very good. **(11/95)**

Now-2005   16.0

Pommard   Les Vignots   Leroy

Very 1987-ish on the nose. Slight dead leaves and diffuse. A little astringent on the palate. Medium-full, ripe and quite vigorous. Lacks a bit of class. **(11/95)**

Drink soon   14.0

Puligny-Montrachet   Clos-des-Caillerets Jean Chartron

Reasonable colour. Fully mature. Fully mature on the nose too. Rather diffuse. Like many it is better on the palate. But it lacks class. Plump fruit but a little lumpy and coarse. But it still has some vigour. Quite good. **(11/95)**

Now-2000   14.0

Richebourg   Jean Grivot

Excellent colour. Marvellous rich classy nose. This is very excellent. Full, very fine tannins. Very very lovely fruit. Balanced. Still very very vigorous. Bags of life. Indeed it will even get better. Quite brilliant. **(11/95)**

Now-2010 plus   20.0

Richebourg   Jean Gros

Full, vigorous colour. Splendidly full, rich aristocratic nose. This is still youthful. Full, very fine ripe tannins. Very good acidity. Marvellous plentiful rich vigorous fruit. Still a bit of unresolved tannin. Opulent. Very classy. Very lovely indeed. Very fine indeed. **(11/95)**

1998-2015   19.5

Santenay   Clos-Rousseau   Camille Giroud

Good colour. No undue brown. Medium to medium-full weight. Plump, spicy nose. A little diffuse. Medium body. Nicely ripe, but it lacks a little grip at the end. Still fresh. Attractive. *À point.* Quite good. **(11/95)**

Now-1998   14.0

Savigny-lès-Beaune Les Dominodes
Jean-Marc Pavelot

Very good colour. Quite solid on the nose. A touch rustic. Rather better on the palate. Full, fat, slightly spicy. Opulent. Rich. Old-viney concentration. This is very good indeed. A lovely generous example. **(11/95)**

Now-2005   17.0

Savigny-lès-Beaune Les Guettes
Jean-Marc Pavelot

Good colour. Quite a firm nose. Sturdy tannins apparent at first but this blew off. On the palate nice mature, lush, complex fresh fruit. No hard edges. Good depth. Mellow and sophisticated. Very good. **(11/95)**

Now-2000   16.0

Savigny-lès-Beaune Les Narbantons
Lucien Camus-Brochon

Good colour. This is a little rustic, and the acidity shows at the end. But in the middle it is fresh and ample, with no dry tannins, if without real class. But it is clean and fresh. Quite good. **(11/95)**

Now-2000   14.0

La Tâche Romanée-Conti

Good colour. Just a little brown. This is very sophisticated on the nose. Very lovely velvety texture. Rich, smooth, very classy. This is fragrant. Good acidity. Concentrated, classy. No hard edges now but plenty of depth. Very high class, silky smooth wine. Only just ready. Very fine indeed. **(11/95)**

Now-2010   19.0

Volnay Paul Garaudet

Last vintage of old vines here. Good fresh colour. Soft, fruity nose. Still quite fresh. But on the palate drying up. A bit astringent. Nothing special. **(11/95)**

Drink up   13.0

Volnay Caillerets Jean-Marc Bouley

Good colour. A little burly and reduced on the nose at first. Smoother, more civilised later. Medium to medium-full body. Ripe, spicy, balanced. Plenty of depth if not a lot of class, but meaty and vigorous. Good plus. **(11/95)**

Now-2002   15.5

Volnay Caillerets, Clos-des-Soixante-
Ouvrées Pousse d'Or

Very good colour. A little dry and coarse on the nose. Yet rich enough underneath. On the palate nice and fruity. Still young. Good acidity, and sophisticated tannin and fruit. Good grip. Long, ample. Slightly hard at the end. Still very youthful. Very good plus. **(11/95)**

Now-2007   16.5

Volnay Champans Monthélie-Douhairet

Medium colour. The nose is fresh. The palate is rustic, even a bit dirty. Not too chaptalised at least. But lacks finesse. **(11/95)**

Drink soon   13.0

Volnay Clos-de-la-Bousse-d'Or
Pousse d'Or

Good colour. Similar to the Soixante-Ouvrées. Slightly lighter and less ample on the palate, but on the follow-through shows good grip and intensity and very stylish fruit. In fact this seems more ample and rich and seductive. A little more evolved. Slightly less hard. Very good indeed. **(11/95)**

Now-2007   17.0

Volnay Clos-des-Chênes Michel Lafarge

Very good colour. Lovely nose. Really rich. Impressively concentrated. Still not quite ready. Full, still some unresolved tannin. Splendid fruit. Good grip. Fat, rich, a lot of depth and above all a lot of class. Still needs time. Very fine. **(11/95)**

Now-2012   18.5

Volnay Clos-des-Chênes Leroy

Very good colour. Slightly diffuse and evolved on the nose but rich, fat, seductive and with lovely warm fruit on the palate. This is very good plus. **(11/95)**

Now-2000 plus   16.5

Volnay Clos-des-Ducs
Marquis d'Angerville

Good colour. Lovely nose. Clean, elegant, fragrant, now getting soft and round. Medium to medium-full. No hard tannins. *À point.* This is above all stylish and very well balanced. Fresh, round, sweet and velvety. Very distinguished for a 1987. Still vigorous. A fine bottle. **(11/95)**

Now-2005   17.5

Volnay Santenots Matrot

Evolved colour. This is light, thin and rather weedy. Nothing left, but I don't think there was much to start with. Disappointing. **(11/95)**

Drink up   12.0

Volnay Taille-Pieds Hubert de Montille

Good colour. This is totally harmonious from start to finish. Round, rich medium body. A little neutral on the nose. Round, balanced and stylish on the palate. Long. Complex. Still vigorous. Not a lot of structure. Very good plus. **(11/95)**

Now-2000   16.5

Vosne-Romanée   Régis Forey

Good fresh colour. No undue brown. Open, slightly spicy nose. No lack of grip or style here. Good acidity. Bramble fruit. No aggressive tannins. Accessible. Plump. This has good style. Very good plus. **(11/95)**

Now-2003   16.0

Vosne-Romanée   Les Brûlées   René Engel

Good colour. No undue maturity. Slightly funky on the nose. Dry and astringent. Quite evolved. Not very elegant. On the palate succulent and fresh. No great depth and class but very pleasant. Reasonable length. Good plus. **(11/95)**

Now-2000   15.5

Vosne-Romanée   Les Chaumes Daniel Rion et Fils

Good colour. Full and rich with good sweet fruit and good grip on the palate. Plenty of vigour. Only on the nose a little rustic. Ripe. Long. Will keep well. Very good. **(11/95)**

Now-2003   16.0

Vosne-Romanée   Clos-des-Réas   Jean Gros

Very good colour. Still vigorous. Good rich plummy-raspberry nose. Fresh, stylish and concentrated. This is medium-full, *à point* now. Plump and generous. Not great grip and volume but most attractive. And long and elegant, even complex. Good ripe tannins, even sweet. Very good plus. **(11/95)**

Now-2005   16.5

1986

RATING FOR THE VINTAGE

Red: 14.5-12.0   **White:** 16.5-13.5
(variable)   (variable)

SIZE OF THE CROP

(Hectolitres, excluding generic wine)

	Red	White
Grands Crus	14,877	2,957
Village and *Premiers Crus*	197,856	48,302
Total	212,733	51,259

A very large crop: the biggest in recent years after the 1982. But larger in retrospect in *rouge* than in *blanc*. It was a vintage which was variable from the outset. Vintage rain separated the quality of the Côte d'Or reds into good Côte-de-Nuits (though not exceptional) and disappointing Côte-de-Beaunes. The white wines, though, seemed very much better, and there were many at the outset who opted for 1986 over 1985. As these wines have evolved these rosy expectations have proved hollow. Too many white wines were made with over-ripe grapes and rapidly coarsened up, even dried up in bottle. One of the wines I have always collected is the Domaine Leflaive's Puligny-Montrachet, Les Pucelles. Today I would rather drink my 1987 than my 1986, while the 1985 is magnificent and will still repay keeping.

WEATHER CONDITIONS

The winter of 1985-86 was cold but the excesses of 1985 were avoided. There was no frost damage. Spring was cool, wet and miserable, retarding the development of the viticultural cycle, but June was warm and sunny. More importantly, it was exceptionally dry, enabling the flowering to take place successfully thus ensuring a crop which, barring disaster, would be large. July was a little hotter and a little drier than the norm and August was, at first, also dry and fine. From the middle of the month onwards however, the weather was patchy, and as the climate deteriorated further, fears of the quality of the harvest began to mount. September was somewhat cooler and considerably wetter than the average: 115 mm of rain fell compared with under 10 mm in 1985. It was also humid, particularly between two important downpours of 12-15 September and 24 and 25 September. This humidity, arriving when the grapes were already almost at maturity, encouraged the spread of rot and, for the most part, as far as the Pinot Noir was concerned, it was *pourriture grise*, though in the case of the whites, at least partially noble rot. What the onset of this did, in its turn, was to encourage some growers to start their harvest as early as 20 September. Those who did, or who started as soon as the rain stopped on the 25th, have made weak watery wine in huge quantity: wine of no merit.

Thankfully, after the clouds had blown away on the 25th the barometer rose, the humidity was rapidly chased off by a cool, drying wind from the north and there was no further rain until the third week of October by which time all the white grapes had been gathered in safely.

The best growers delayed starting their harvest until the beginning of October by which time both the Chardonnay and the Pinot Noir grapes had benefited from the drying wind, and if not really very concentrated, were fully ripe - indeed, some even had the beginnings of *pourriture noble* which gave the wines some extra fatness, but at the expense of reducing the acidity. The grapes gained as much as half a degree of potential alcohol per day in maturity during the vital week after the rain had ceased. The size of the white-wine harvest was as large as anticipated but in those *climats* not affected by frost in the previous vintage, no larger than in 1985. That of the red-wine harvest, though, despite a great deal of *triage*, was much greater.

THE STYLE OF THE WINE

WHITE WINES

Plump, ripe and very aromatic, the white wines were very seductive at the outset. While they didn't have a great deal of backbone - indeed were what the French call *tendre* - they seemed to have the elegance and the balance. Nineteen eighty-five had the volume, 1986 the finesse, was how one grower put it. It was accepted that they were more delicate, and so many growers bottled them early, but it was thought that they would last well, at least in the medium term. Many growers (Jean-François Coche was an exception) when pushed, stated a preference for 1986 over 1985 and drew parallels between the latter and 1979 and 1973, white wines from prolific vintages which nevertheless eventually proved to have both breeding and staying power.

Too many wines, however, were made from over-ripe fruit: fruit that 'was on the turn': browny-purple rather than green-lemon-gold in colour. These wines lacked acidity then; they lack grip and interest now. As a result they are blowsy, heavy and rather coarse. Today they possess rather a jaded tropical flavour: pineapple, lychees and mango but beyond their sell-by date. They can only get worse.

There are, thankfully, growers who abhor white wines with a suggestion of *pourriture*. And their 1986s have lasted. Even these are not as good as the 1985s though. In retrospect it seems curious that so many should have got it so wrong at the time.

RED WINES

The Côte-de-Beaune could hardly escape the vintage rain, especially as the weather forecast was more pessimistic than in fact would be the case. The Côte-de-Nuits, vintaging later, had the best of it. Here there are many pleasant wines, whose style resembles somewhat the 1982s: round, fruity, but rather loose-knit; wines with no complications nor hard edges. These are the best. There are others which are more similar to the Côte-de-Beaunes, wines which never had enough structure, and are now falling apart.

The fact that there *are*, despite the weather conditions, some worthy Côte-de-Beaune red wines, as you will note in the ensuing pages, deserve our unrestrained applause. As always in Burgundy - or nearly always - there are some who can pull the cat out of the bag.

Where Are the Best Wines? and State of Maturity Today

★ The 1986 vintage is better for whites than for reds.

★ But in both cases it is variable.

★ The Côte-de-Nuits reds are better than the Côte-de-Beaune reds.

★ All but the very best wines, red and white, now need drinking soon. Some Côte-de-Beaune reds and lesser whites are already past their best.

Tasting Notes

BLANC

Bâtard-Montrachet Albert Morey
Good rich colour. Slight touch of reduction on the nose. But youthful, rich and fat. On the palate fullish, a little four-square. But certainly has depth. Masculine. Austere. Still a bit closed. Good grip. Got better and better in the glass. Best of all on the finish. Youthful. Long. Impressive for a 1986. Fine but not great. **(05/94)**

Now-2010   17.5

Bâtard-Montrachet Ramonet
Quite full colour. A core of iron. Still youthful. Marvellous palate. Rich and concentrated. Very lovely balance. Peachy. Real depth. One of the best 1986s I have had for ages. Will still improve. Very fine indeed. **(10/94)**

Now-2010   19.0

Chassagne-Montrachet Château de la Maltroye
Youthful colour. Sauerkraut nose. Some sulphur. This has begun to fall apart. Lacks grip. Lightening up in the middle. This still has some enjoyment to offer. There is style if not balance. **(03/96)**

Past its best   13.0

Chassagne-Montrachet Les Boudriottes Jacques Gagnard-Delagrange
Light-medium colour. Ripe, stylish nose with plenty of depth. Good acidity on the palate. Honeyed and peachy. Not heavy. Shows well. Good plus - but not the individuality and class for great. **(06/92)**

Drink soon   15.5

Chevalier-Montrachet Leflaive
Fine nose. Good touch of oak. Ample, rich, ripe and profound. This has good backbone - rather more than the Pucelles I sampled a few months ago. **(01/92)**

Now-2004   17.5

Chevalier-Montrachet Michel Niellon
Quality here. Very fine ripe concentrated stylish fruit. Fruit-salady. Balanced, gently oaky. Fresh, ready but vigorous. Fine. **(08/92)**

Now-2002   17.5

Chevalier-Montrachet Les Demoiselles Louis Jadot
Good colour. Rich, full, fat, oaky nose. Good grip. Still youthful. This is a splendid wine. Now just about ready. Ample and ripe, but closed and concentrated. Not a bit overblown. Very elegant. Will still keep well. Fine plus. **(11/94)**

Now-2000   18.0

Chevalier-Montrachet Les Demoiselles Louis Latour
Evolved colour. Honeyed, rich, fat nose. Full, lovely and rich without being over-ripe or over-alcoholic. Very good grip for the vintage. Especially at the end. This is very fine for the vintage. Still youthful. Very lovely. Lots of life left. Great intensity. **(11/95)**

Now-2005   18.5

Corton-Charlemagne Louis Latour
Light, fresh colour. A touch overblown on the nose. But less evolved than many 1986 whites. Rich, fat, stylish. Good grip. Nice round ripe stylish fruit. Good positive finish. Slight touch of honey and botrytis. Fine. **(03/93)**

Now-2000   17.5

Corton-Charlemagne   Tollot-Beaut

Magnum. Round, rich, ripe, balanced, fresh and stylish. A very harmonious wine. But very good indeed not fine. **(06/96)**

Now-2000   17.0

Meursault   Blagny   Louis Jadot

This is vigorous and fruity at first. The finish is less good but the wine has grip and even class. Very good. **(06/96)**

Now-2000   16.0

**Meursault   Charmes
Vincent Bitouzet-Prieur**

He picked quite early and didn't get any *pourriture noble*. The wine has a surprisingly good acidity. Not a lot of style: there is some SO$_2$ here, especially at the end. But it improved in the glass. Gently oaky. Holding up well. Good. But sulphur on the finish. **(06/96)**

Now-2000   15.0

Meursault   Charmes   Camille Giroud

Round, ripe, soft and without a hint of over-ripeness. Very good acidity. Even slightly lean. But very good indeed. **(06/96)**

Now-2000 plus   17.0

Meursault   Charmes   Louis Jadot

This is still very young. Surprising grip of acidity for a 1986 at the start, even a touch austere. As it warmed up and developed one could see an excellent wine, with the ample ripeness of the 1986 but none of the blowsiness. And a very good backbone. Fine. And it will keep. **(10/95)**

Now-2004   17.5

Meursault   Charmes   Comtes Lafon

Seems to have quite a lot of alcohol on the nose. But only 13.0°. Quite full and even heavy. This is rich but a touch blowsy, and I'm not sure whether it will hold up its elegance. But this, says Jasper Morris M.W. (one of Lafon's major UK customers), is more elegant than at the outset. Perhaps this slightly heavy, spicy style is just not my taste. Others liked it better than me. Fat, rich, good acidity. But essentially a burly wine. **(09/92)**

Now-2003   16.0

Meursault   Charmes   Matrot

No over-ripeness but some SO$_2$. Fresh but lacks depth and style. Only fair. **(06/96)**

Now-2000   14.0

**Meursault   Genevrières
Bouchard Père et Fils**

Good colour. This is a very good result indeed. Plump and rich but without a trace of over-ripeness or noble rot. Crisp, ripe. Long. Stylish. Very good indeed. **(02/95)**

Now-2000 plus   17.0

Meursault   Genevrières   Comtes Lafon

Some colour here. Ample and rich and voluptuous, but not over-ripe. Plenty of depth. Medium-full, ripe, sweet, nutty. An abundant voluptuous example. Gently oaky. Fruit-salady and for a 1986 very well balanced. The best of Lafon's 1986s. Fat. Long. Plenty of life still. Fine quality. Several notes. **(10/94)**

Now-2000 plus   17.5

Meursault   Goutte d'Or   Comtes Lafon

Deep colour. The nose is almost sweet. Exotic, rich, ample, not a bit too over-ripe. Gently soft, harmonious and with good acidity. This is like a fine 1982. Very good intensity at the end. Even class. **(10/95)**

Now-2000   16.0

Meursault   Narvaux   Patrick Javillier

A little tired but reasonable depth. Good acidity. Not over-ripe. **(06/96)**

Drink soon   15.0

Meursault   Perrières   Comtes Lafon

Golden colour. Old, fat, exotic nose. Some oxidation. This is ripe - even over-ripe - almost too evolved. Medium-full. Good but not exactly elegant. And it missed a bit of intensity and thrust at the end. Voluptuous. Slightly over the top. Curious. Very good. Several notes. **(10/94)**

Drink soon   16.0

Meursault   Perrières   Leroy

Good colour. Firm, full, concentrated, rich. Almond and hazelnutty. Typically structured Leroy wine. This is big, very concentrated, still very young. Fresh for a 1986. Fat, rich, substantial and plenty of grip. Fine. **(10/95)**

Now-2005   17.5

Meursault   Perrières   Matrot

Potentially delicious when it throws off its SO$_2$. Cool. Composed, plump, rich, balanced. Concentrated. Fine. **(06/96)**

Now-2000 plus   17.0

Meursault   Perrières   Pierre Morey

Fat and rich on the nose. Quality here but quite alcoholic, even a little oily and heavy. Yet classy fruit and good acidity. Oaky, ripe, peachy, balanced. Very good but it lacks just a little class at the end. **(04/92)**

Now-2000   16.0

Pernand-Vergelesses   Dubreuil-Fontaine

Well matured, but not a bit blowsy. Lean, soft, apple-y, interesting. Better than I expected. Even a bit of class. **(06/92)**

Drink up   14.0

Puligny-Montrachet Jean-Marc Boillot

Magnum. At the end of its life but very good. Soft, not too over-ripe. Plump. Stylish. Very good. **(06/96)**

Drink up 16.0

Puligny-Montrachet Étienne Sauzet

The nose seems a little four-square. Some built-in SO_2. Not a patch on the 1985. Rather better on the palate. Fullish, rich, good concentration, with a spicy element. Has grip but not a lot of finesse. Rather better than the 1987 though, but a little disappointing. **(02/91)**

Drink up 15.0

Puligny-Montrachet Clavoillons Leflaive

Very youthful colour. Some sulphur on the nose. After this blew off one could see a much fresher 1986 than the Pucelles. But again not one with a great deal of class. There is a slight noble-rot-caused *sur-maturité* coarseness. Yet at the same time a firm acidity. Only medium body. No concentration or depth. The whole is unspectacular. Merely good. If that. **(10/94)**

Now-2000 14.0

Puligny-Montrachet Les Champs-Canet Louis Carillon

Quite a developed colour. Ample, ripe, but - in a 1986 way - delicate nose. Clean, no botrytis. Good acidity. Medium to medium-full body. Plump, ripe and stylish. An elegant example with plenty of depth. Firm and long on the finish. Still very vigorous. Very good. **(10/94)**

Now-2000 16.0

Puligny-Montrachet Les Combettes Matrot

Rich colour. Rich nose. Just the faintest touch of the usual 1986 character. Fat, spicy. Not any trace of botrytis. Aromatic, very ripe but not too over-ripe. A full meaty wine. Fine. **(11/95)**

Now-2003 17.5

Puligny-Montrachet Les Demoiselles Madame Françoise Colin

Medium colour. Aromatic nose. Individual, quite full, well balanced, quite concentrated. There is a certain hardness and dryness on the follow-through and it is still quite firm but this has class and depth. Finishes fat and ripe. Very good. **(06/92)**

Drink soon 16.0

Puligny-Montrachet Les Demoiselles Olivier Leflaive Frères

Magnum. A little over-evolved. But very good concentration, style and individuality. This has depth. Very good indeed but drink soon. **(06/96)**

Drink soon 17.0

Puligny-Montrachet Les Pucelles Bouchard Père et Fils

Still a little hard, but beginning to come out now. A little SO_2 still. This diminishes the class. Rich though. **(11/91)**

Drink soon 15.0

Puligny-Montrachet Les Pucelles Leflaive

Light colour. Closed nose. Lemony. On the palate a little SO_2, not a lot of strength. Nor a lot of oak. Slightly soft and citrussy. Not a lot of grip. Yet some acidity and intensity at the end. Very good but not great. Lacks focus. Several notes. This wine is declining fast. By 1996 I was noting only 14.0. **(12/93)**

Drink soon 16.0

ROUGE

Beaune Bressandes Jacques Prieur, Antonin Rodet

This is a good effort for the vintage. Reasonable fruit and some acidity. Still quite fresh. But a bit slight and thin. **(09/90)**

Drink soon 13.0

Beaune Clos-des-Couchereaux Louis Jadot

Light colour. Elegant but light on the nose. A bit soft and evolved on the palate. Quite fresh though. Elegant. Good fruit. Good length. Good plus. **(06/96)**

Now-2000 15.5

Beaune Grèves Michel Lafarge

Splendid colour for the vintage. Full rich oaky and substantial and concentrated. Very good indeed for a Beaune 1986. Fullish, meaty, a super example. Real length and depth. Surprisingly fine. Very good indeed. **(06/96)**

Now-2005 17.0

Beaune Montrevenots Jean-Marc Boillot

Magnum. Good fresh colour. Round slightly sweet nose. Good substance underneath. Quite full, meaty, a little rigid. But not a bit weak. Good grip. Some tannin. Slightly ungainly but quite good plus. **(06/96)**

Now-2000 plus 14.5

Bonnes-Mares Georges Roumier

Very good colour. Still vigorous. Round and rich, even sweet. Full, meaty, fresh. I thought this was a 1989. Full. Plenty of depth. Good concentration for 1986. Slightly muscular and dense. Slightly rigid. No sign of life. But good stuff. Very good indeed. Similar note 06/96 when from magnum. **(11/95)**

Now-2000 plus 17.0

Chambertin   Denis Mortet

Good colour. Full, substantial nose. Ample, rich, plump and vigorous. Not the greatest of style. But a fine wine nevertheless. **(06/96)**

Now-2005   **17.5**

Chambertin   Ponsot, Domaine des Chézeaux

Light to medium colour. Curious vegetable-pruney nose. Rather light and short on the palate. This is getting astringent. Unexciting. **(12/93)**

Drink up   **12.0**

Chambertin   Armand Rousseau

Medium-full colour. Stylish. Slightly roasted nose. This is oaky, subtle, quite developed. I am not sure the Ruchottes is not as good. Because this has acidity but not really the extra grip and finesse. Perhaps slightly better. Only 17.0 in 12/93 when sampled against the Clos-de-Bèze. **(06/96)**

Now-2000   **18.5**

Chambertin   Clos-de-Bèze   Joseph Faiveley

Reasonable but not a brilliant colour. Still quite fresh. On the nose the wine has good strength if not the greatest amount of class and depth. A little evidence of chaptalisation. Good acidity. Good guts. Good vigour. Just a touch of astringency. Fresh and fruity. Will still improve. Finishes long and positive. It has the volume and the depth of *grand cru*. But it lacks the fragrance of really classy Burgundy. Very good indeed for the vintage. **(05/95)**

Now-2005   **17.0**

Chambertin   Clos-de-Bèze   Louis Jadot

Full, vigorous colour. Plenty of depth, even concentration on the nose. Medium-full. Rich. Old-viney. This is classy and has a lot of depth. Fat and concentrated. Lovely elegant Pinot fruit. Long, complex and distinguished. Fine plus. **(03/94)**

Now-2010   **18.0**

Chambertin   Clos-de-Bèze
Armand Rousseau

Medium-full colour. Mature. Slightly more diffuse nose than the Chambertin. On the palate though very similar. A little drier perhaps on the attack but a bit more grip and backbone on the finish. A bit more definition. Very good plus for the vintage. **(12/93)**

Drink soon   **16.0**

Chambolle-Musigny   Georges Roumier

Magnum. Good colour. Nice vigorous nose. Quite substantial but good vigorous fruit. Ripe, and plenty of life. Rich and balanced and stylish. This is really very good indeed for a village wine. Very good. **(06/96)**

Now-2000 plus   **16.0**

Chambolle-Musigny
Comte Georges de Vogüé

This is good for a village 1986. Fresh, fragrant, long, stylish. Full of fruit. Rather better in its context than I had expected. **(07/91)**

Drink soon   **15.0**

Chambolle-Musigny   Les Amoureuses
Robert Groffier

Good colour for a 1986, full mature. Soft and fragrant, mellow and elegant on the nose. Good fresh raspberry fruit. Ripe, medium body, slight lack of sweetness on the palate but good acidity. Certainly elegant. Long. Good dimension. Complex. Very good. **(03/93)**

Drink soon   **16.0**

Chambolle-Musigny   Les Amoureuses
Jacques-Frédéric Mugnier

Medium-full colour. Mature. Very lovely soft elegant nose. This is a bit less concentrated and less vigorous than Roumier. Better on the nose, not quite as good on the palate. Yet long and very stylish. Really classy. Very good indeed. **(06/96)**

Now-2000   **17.0**

Chambolle-Musigny   Les Amoureuses
Georges Roumier

Medium-full colour. Mature. Quite tough on the nose compared with Mugnier. But lovely fruit underneath. Concentrated and slightly chocolatey. Very good depth. Still very young. Lovely. Ripe. Vigorous. Long. Fine. **(06/96)**

Now-2005   **17.5**

Chambolle-Musigny   Les Beaux-Bruns
Ghislaine Barthod-Noëllat

Good colour. Fullish ample nose. Slightly more muscle than finesse. Chunky and ripe. Possibly slightly assisted. A little astringent. Lacks class. Fair only. **(06/96)**

Drink soon   **13.0**

Chambolle-Musigny   Les Sentiers
Robert Groffier

Medium colour. A little browner than the 1987 but alive enough. Gently plump, fresh aromatic nose. Light but classy. Not a touch diffuse or astringent. Soft, a little lacking real depth and dimension but fresh, stylish, long and satisfying. No hurry to drink. Very good plus for 1986. **(10/95)**

Now-2003   **17.0**

Chapelle-Chambertin   Louis Jadot

Medium-full colour. No undue brown. Ripe, fresh nose. Good depth here. Elegant Pinot. Medium to medium-full. Good acidity. A touch of oak. A shade lean but very stylish. Complex at the end. This will still improve. Very good indeed. Not a bit dilute. Very positive and complex. A bottle tasted on 06/96 was old and tired. **(03/94)**

Now-2006   **17.0**

Chapelle-Chambertin   Jean Trapet
Magnum. Good colour. Gentle but slightly weak on the nose. Better on the palate. Stylish, ripe, good balance. This has grip and depth. Very good plus. **(06/96)**

Now-2000 plus   **16.5**

Charmes-Chambertin
Philippe Charlopin-Parizot
Magnum. Medium-full colour. A little lumpy on the nose. Slightly assisted. Ungainly. Acidity and astringency beginning to show. This is only average. Lumpy. **(06/96)**

Drink up   **13.5**

Charmes-Chambertin   Bernard Dugat-Py
Medium-full colour. Some age. A bit old and rustic on the nose. Got more and more reductive. Not for me. **(06/96)**

Past its best   **12.0**

Charmes-Chambertin   Armand Rousseau
Good colour. Fine fresh Pinot nose. Fragrant and stylish. Round and quite rich. A little cool. It lacks a little real concentration but clean and elegant. Ready now. Good balance. Finishes long. Very good plus for the vintage. **(12/91)**

Drink soon   **16.5**

Charmes-Chambertin   Thomas-Moillard
Good colour. Ripe nose, but on the palate a bit dried out. Astringent. Good structure. But now past it. **(06/96)**

Past its best   **12.0**

Chassagne-Montrachet   Guy Amiot
Reasonable colour. Rather pruney on the nose. Plus rather weedy and tired despite the colour being quite vigorous. On the palate this is still quite fresh. Not short. Reasonably alive at the end. Plump and fruity if not that much class. But good for the vintage in the Côte-de-Beaune. **(11/95)**

Drink soon   **14.5**

Chassagne-Montrachet   Morgeots
Louis Jadot
Medium colour. Rich fat nose. Good depth. Fullish, nice ripe tannins. Plenty of depth and very good grip. Stylish. Long. Very good. **(01/96)**

1998-2008   **15.5**

Clos-de-Tart   Mommessin
Reasonable colour. A ripe, mellow wine. Slightly hard and twiggy/stemmy on the nose. But round, sweet - if a bit suave - on the palate.

Fresh. Not that classy. But an attractive example. Really, for a 1986, reasonably fresh and very good. Very similar note 06/96. **(02/95)**

Now-2000   **16.0**

Clos-de-Vougeot   Jean-Jacques Confuron
Good colour. Good substance, has begun to lose its fruit a bit. A little light but balanced and quite stylish on the palate. Quite good. **(06/96)**

Now-2000   **14.0**

Clos-de-Vougeot   François Gros
Medium colour. Light, developed. Some residual elegance but has now lost its fruit. Over the hill. **(06/96)**

Past its best   **12.0**

Clos-de-Vougeot   Méo-Camuzet
Medium-full colour. Not a lot of brown. Smells like uncooked bacon. No new wood on the nose but more on the palate (100 per cent). Quite a structured wine. Some age but a certain leanness. Slightly rigid. Slightly four-square. Lacks a bit of charm. Odd bacon flavours. Quite good. **(02/93)**

Drink soon   **14.0**

Clos-de-Vougeot   Georges Roumier
Magnum. Good colour. Good substance, has begun to lose its fruit a bit. A little light but balanced and quite stylish on the palate. Quite good. **(06/96)**

Now-2000   **14.0**

Clos-de-Vougeot   Musigni
Gros Frère et Soeur
Good colour. Firm oaky nose. Rich, slight aspect of reduction. Fullish, good grip. Reduction on the palate. Vigorous but not stylish. Tried two bottles. **(06/96)**

Now-2000   **13.5**

Corton   Bressandes
Olivier Leflaive Frères
Magnum. Medium-full, fully mature. Round, ripe, stylish. Medium-full, succulent and ripe on the palate. Very good indeed. **(06/96)**

Now-2000 plus   **17.0**

Corton   Clos-des-Cortons   Joseph Faiveley
Magnum. Good colour. Really classy on the nose. Rich and complex. This has real depth and class. Lovely fruit. Good freshness. Not a blockbuster but long and complex and fine plus. **(06/96)**

Now-2005   **18.0**

Corton   Clos-du-Roi   Thomas-Moillard
Good colour. Rich, masculine, chunky. Youthful. Quite solid and masculine. Rich. Quite tannic. Good grip. This has plenty of life ahead

of it. But it lacks a bit of nuance. **(06/96)**

Now–2000   **16.0**

Echézeaux   Romanée-Conti

Good vigorous colour. Soft and stylish. Round and succulent without being a bit over-extracted. Slightly lean but fine and very classy. *À point.* Not for the long term. Clean. Long. Very stylish. Fine. **(06/96)**

Now–2005   **17.5**

Gevrey-Chambertin
Philippe Charlopin-Parizot

Magnum. Medium colour. Mature. The nose is a bit aged (astringent) and ordinary (lacking class) and the wine is now on the descent. Not exciting. **(06/96)**

Past its best   **12.5**

Gevrey-Chambertin   *Vieilles-Vignes*
Alain Burguet

Magnum. Medium-full colour. Rich, vigorous, plummy nose. Fullish and fat and rich. Not much style but has plenty of life. Good. **(06/96)**

Now–2000 plus   **15.0**

Gevrey-Chambertin   *Vieilles-Vignes*
Bernard Dugat-Py

Medium colour. Quite developed. A bit farmyardy on the nose. Ripe but not very stylish. Has acidity but has now lost a bit of its elegance. Not bad. **(06/96)**

Drink soon   **13.5**

Gevrey-Chambertin   Cazetiers Bruno Clair

Magnum. Good colour. Splendid class here on nose and palate. Cool and clean and positive. This is really good. Great balance and finesse. Lovely finish. Very long. Fine. **(06/96)**

Now–2005   **17.5**

Gevrey-Chambertin   Les Champeaux
Denis Mortet

Good vigorous colour. Meaty nose. Smells of bacon. A little tough and rigid on the palate. Slightly lacks succulence and generosity. I prefer the Clos-Prieur. **(06/96)**

Drink soon   **14.0**

Gevrey-Chambertin   Clos-des-Fontenys
Bruno Clair

Magnum. Medium-full mature colour. Fresh, vigorous, elegant nose. On the palate similar. Only at the end a suspicion of attenuation. Something hollow here. Good but not great. **(06/96)**

Drink up   **15.0**

Gevrey-Chambertin   Clos-Prieur
Denis Mortet

Good vigorous colour. A rich, meaty wine on both nose and palate. Good acidity. This has class and vigour. Good grip. Long. Meaty. Slightly tough but very good. **(06/96)**

Now–2000 plus   **16.0**

Gevrey-Chambertin   Clos-Saint Jacques
Bruno Clair

Magnum. Medium colour, fully mature. Today it is the Cazetiers which sings. This is a bit "hot" and a bit astringent. Good fruit but slightly rigid. Very good at best. **(06/96)**

Now–2000   **16.0**

Gevrey-Chambertin   Clos-Saint Jacques
Michel Esmonin et Fille

Medium colour. Fully mature. Classy nose. But a bit light. A little astringent on the palate. A little obvious assistance. But round and ripe and not bad at all. **(06/96)**

Drink soon   **13.5**

Gevrey-Chambertin   Les Combottes
Jean Raphet

Medium colour. Still fresh looking. Still fresh on the nose. Pure but lightish Pinot, but certainly elegant, and also ripe. Not a wine of richness or weight but a wine of generosity and complexity. Ready now. Should last well because the acidity is very good. Very good. **(12/91)**

Now–2000   **16.0**

Grands-Echézeaux   Romanée-Conti

Good colour. The nose is fresh, balanced and concentrated. Still quite youthful and firm. A little austere. Oaky. But fine. **(03/92)**

Now–2005   **17.5**

Marsannay   Les Longeroies   Bruno Clair

Fully matured colour. The nose and the palate show rather a weak, over the top wine, but once this was neat and stylish. **(06/96)**

Past its best   **11.0**

Mazis-Chambertin   Joseph Faiveley

Good colour. Plum and raspberry jam on the nose. Quite oaky. Soft, slightly loose, aromatic. Good attack and reasonable length and style but a touch one dimensional compared with the Ruchottes 1987 of Mugneret. Dried out a bit in the glass. **(11/93)**

Drink soon   **16.0**

Mazis-Chambertin   Philippe Naddef

Medium to medium-full colour. Now mature. Slightly diffuse on the nose. But rich and for 1986 concentrated and fat. Medium body. Good acidity. A little one-dimensional and short but pleasant fruit, if not very stylish with it. Quite good plus. **(10/95)**

Drink soon   **14.5**

Monthélie Monthélie-Douhairet

Full, rich colour. Somewhat rustic on the nose but surprisingly full and succulent - if in a rather robust way - on the palate. No dilution. Ripe. Plenty of *matière*. Good extraction and plenty of vigour. Shame about the rusticity. **(02/94)**

Now-2003   14.0

Monthélie Les Duresses Paul Garaudet

Magnum. Medium mature colour. Well-matured nose. Succulent and fruity. Light but not weak. No great class but not rustic or dead leaves-ish. Medium to medium-full. Surprisingly vigorous. Good acidity. Quite elegant. Quite good. **(06/96)**

Now-2000   11.0

Morey-Saint-Denis Joseph Faiveley

Good colour. Vigorous, full, only just mature. This is a medium-full, ripe, round wine with plenty of grip and fruit. Very good tannins. *À point* and with plenty of vigour. Most attractive. Very good. **(01/93)**

Drink soon   16.0

Le Musigny Joseph Drouhin

Medium-full colour. Fully mature. Touch of Marmite on the nose. Succulent and rich on nose and palate. The colour is deceptive. This is soft but vigorous. Very clean pure Pinot fruit. Very lovely. Very fine. **(06/96)**

Now-2005   18.0

Le Musigny Louis Jadot

Fullish colour. No undue brown. Youthful, classy and fragrant on the nose. This still has a little unresolved tannin. Medium-full. Slightly hard. But there is depth here, though it lacks a little generosity at present. But for Musigny not that special. But best on the finish. Very good nevertheless. **(03/94)**

Now-2003   16.0

Le Musigny Jacques-Frédéric Mugnier

Fine vigorous colour. Splendid fat, rich, concentrated. This really is very lovely. Generous, ripe, exciting flavours on the palate. Very complex and lovely. This is splendid. Better even than Gros' Richebourg. Very brilliant finish. **(06/96)**

Now-2005   19.5

Nuits-Saint-Georges Boudots Jean Grivot

Slightly weak colour. Diffuse nose. Slightly sweet on the palate. But rather developed. Not too short. Just a little weak and feeble. Yet elegant underneath, undeniably. Quite good plus. **(06/96)**

Drink soon   14.5

Nuits-Saint-Georges Boudots Jean Tardy

Reasonable colour. Nice old-viney rich but slightly austere fruit on the nose. Good grip. Good structure. The tannins lack a little ripeness but this is long and classy. Very good indeed. **(06/96)**

Now-2003   16.5

**Nuits-Saint-Georges Chaignots
Alain Michelot**

Good well-matured colour. Much fatter and richer than his Vaucrains. Fresher too. This is full and fat and succulent and has good chocolatey fruit. Holding up well. Very good. **(06/96)**

Now-2000   16.0

**Nuits-Saint-Georges Champs-Perdrix
Alain Michelot**

Medium-full colour. Mature colour. Stylish nose. Some development. Good grip. Fullish. Ample. Good plus. **(06/96)**

Now-2000   15.5

**Nuits-Saint-Georges Clos-des-Argillières
Daniel Rion et Fils**

Good colour. Plump and succulent. Vigorous and oaky. But on the palate rather more fruit and vigour than the Lavières. This is well made, plump and attractive. Good plus. A certain rigidity prevents it from being very good. **(06/96)**

Now-2000   15.5

**Nuits-Saint-Georges
Clos-des-Forêts-Saint-Georges Arlot**

Made by the previous *régime*. Good fullish colour. Full, chaptalised and rustic on the nose. Clumsy and coarse. Full, soupy and beneath one's dignity. No. Still vigorous. **(06/96)**

Drink soon   11.0

**Nuits-Saint-Georges Hauts-Pruliers
Daniel Rion et Fils**

Good colour. As usual rich and oaky. Nicely plump fresh acidity here. Fullish. Youthful. Good grip. Slightly austere but very good. **(06/96)**

Now-2000   16.0

**Nuits-Saint-Georges Les Lavières
Daniel Rion et Fils**

Good colour. Still vigorous. Fat and succulent and a little new oak on the nose. Not a lot of fat and sweetness on the palate but good acidity. Now perhaps beginning to lose its fruit. Lacks a bit of charm. Quite good. **(06/96)**

Drink soon   14.0

Nuits-Saint-Georges   Pruliers
Lucien Boillot et Fils

Medium-full colour. Good plump slightly sweet
nose. A bit light and rustic on the palate.
Medium body. Slightly astringent. Not bad at
best. **(06/96)**

Drink up   **13.0**

Nuits-Saint-Georges   Richemones
Thomas-Moillard

Good colour. Big and succulent. Slightly tannic.
Fat. Plenty of wine here. Spicy. Rich and long
on the palate. And grip. But only a vestige of
real elegance. Good plus. **(06/96)**

Now-2005   **15.5**

Nuits-Saint-Georges   Les Saint-Georges
Henri Gouges

Developed colour and quite developed nose.
Not the greatest definition. On the palate the
fruit has dried out, the acidity shows and there
is a lack of fat and elegance. Only fair. **(06/96)**

Drink soon   **13.5**

Nuits-Saint-Georges   Vaucrains
Alain Michelot

Well-matured colour. Slightly dried up and
diffuse on the nose. A little astringent on the
palate. Quite elegant residue though. Quite
good plus. **(06/96)**

Drink soon   **14.5**

Pernand-Vergelesses   Ile-des-Vergelesses
Chandon-de-Briailles

Medium colour. Soft, elegant but persistent
nose. This is surprisingly stylish. Round, good
vigour. Long and gentle. Very good. **(06/96)**

Now-2000   **16.0**

Pommard   Labouré-Roi

Reasonable colour. A little dry and diffuse on
the nose. Better on the palate. Medium body.
Still fresh. No great length, depth or style. But
not short. Quite plump. Indeed it finishes well.
(11/95)

Now-2000   **14.0**

Pommard   Clos-des-Epeneaux
Comte Armand

Magnum. Good colour. Slight touch of rustic
on the nose. A bit dried out on the palate. Not
special. **(06/96)**

Drink soon   **12.5**

Pommard   Epenots   Jacques Parent

Magnum. Medium to medium-full colour.
Mature. Nutty, spicy, sweet and soupy on the
nose. A touch aged on the palate. Not enough
succulence. A bit rigid. Only fair. **(06/96)**

Drink soon   **13.5**

Pommard   Pezerolles   Hubert de Montille

Very good colour. Still fresh. Quite substantial
and meaty on the nose. Cool on the palate. A
certain austerity. The tannins with a suggestion
of astringency. But classy and vigorous. Just lacks
a bit of charm. Will keep. Good plus. **(06/96)**

Now-2000   **15.5**

Pommard   Rugiens   Hubert de Montille

Very good colour. Rich and fat and substantial
for a 1986. On the palate a little austere but
more succulence than the Pezerolles. Good
follow-through. Good substance. Lovely fruit.
Good tannin. Not a bit of a 1986 character.
Very good indeed. **(06/96)**

Now-2000   **17.0**

Pommard   Saucilles   Jean-Marc Boillot

Good colour. Nicely fat and vigorous on the
nose. Plummy, meaty, a little residual tannin.
There is plenty of wine here and it is now *à
point*. Good plus. **(06/96)**

Now-2000   **15.5**

Richebourg   Gros Frère et Soeur

Good fullish vigorous colour. Ample raspberry-
strawberry jam on the nose. Not over-oaked.
Fullish, fresh, gently oaky. Clean, ample, very
attractive. Good dimension. Medium-full.
Ready but will keep. Not the greatest of depth
or class, but that is 1986. A super example of the
vintage though. **(10/94)**

Now-2004   **18.5**

Richebourg   Jean Gros

Fine colour. As you might expect this is very
fine. But it is not great. Rich, succulent. Good
touch of oak. Real *grand cru* finesse. Good
vigour. Finely balanced. Lovely finish. Really
classy. Very fine indeed. **(06/96)**

Now-2005 plus   **19.0**

Romanée-Saint-Vivant   Romanée-Conti

Good mature colour. Slightly cool and austere.
Yet a lot of class both on the nose and on the
palate. Medium body. A certain dryness as it
developed, and the stems showed. But this is
only in the middle. The finish was long and
complex, and fresh. Very good indeed. **(11/93)**

Now-2002   **17.0**

Ruchottes-Chambertin   Clos-des-Ruchottes
Armand Rousseau

Mature colour but good vigorous nose. On the
palate this is laid back, gently together and
stylish. Long and rather more subtle and classy
than the nose indicated. In fact this is very fine.
(06/96)

Now-2000   **18.0**

Savigny-lès-Beaune Les Dominodes Bruno Clair

Good colour. Firm, full and chunky on nose and palate. Rather classy and very vigorous. This is a splendid example. Quite sturdy. Plenty of vigour. Very good. **(06/96)**

Now–2005   16.0

Volnay Clos-des-Chênes Michel Lafarge

Magnum. Medium to medium-full colour. Mellow, elegant nose. Quite fat. Good substance on the palate. The usual elegance and intensity. Splendidly so for a 1986. Long, classy. Fine. **(06/96)**

Now–2000 plus   17.5

Vosne-Romanée Les Beaumonts Jean Grivot

Medium colour. Fresh, ripe and stylish. Not a great deal of backbone but very respectable. Good fruit. Quite long. À point. Very good for the vintage. **(09/92)**

Drink soon   16.0

Vosne-Romanée Les Chaumes Daniel Rion et Fils

Good colour. Now mature. As always quite oaky on the nose. Medium body. Lacks a little succulence on the palate. Not as ripe and as concentrated as the best Nuits of Rion. Quite stylish. Slightly astringent at the end. Quite good. **(06/96)**

Drink soon   14.0

Vosne-Romanée Clos-des-Réas Jean Gros

Magnum. Good colour. Fat. Succulent, round and delicious on the nose. À point. Medium-full. Round and soft, ripe, very elegant. Long. Fine. **(06/96)**

Now–2000 plus   17.5

Vosne-Romanée Malconsorts Thomas-Moillard

Good colour. Still vigorous. Smells a little of bonfires. Good acidity but a bit ungenerous. Quite chocolatey. But the structure shows a bit. Meaty. Very good but not great. Too chunky. **(06/96)**

Now–2000 plus   16.0

Vosne-Romanée Suchots Champy

Very good colour. Slightly chunky but rich and full and vigorous on the nose. Slightly solid on the palate. The tannins show. Good grip. Not exactly elegant but good wine here. Will get a bit astringent soon. **(06/96)**

Now–2000   15.0

Vosne-Romanée Suchots Camille Giroud

Good colour. Now à point. Very classy. Old-viney and profound on the nose. Good elegant attack. Rich and full. Slightly tannic astringency at the end. But long and stylish. Very good indeed. **(06/96)**

Now–2000 plus   17.0

1985

RATING FOR THE VINTAGE

Red: 16.5   **White:** 17.5

SIZE OF THE CROP

(Hectolitres, excluding generic wine)

	Red	White
Grands Crus	9,699	2,506
Village and Premiers Crus	129,445	44,066
Total	139,144	46,572

A small crop in retrospect, looking at the quantities being regularly produced in the 1990s, but, despite serious winter frosts, well over the ten-year average at the time, and if anything quite plentiful in white-wine terms.

After the controversial and inconsistent 1983 vintage and the lean, somewhat ungenerous 1984s, one turns almost with a sense of relief to the 1985s. This is an excellent vintage for white wine, the best of the decade, and so far unsurpassed in the 1990s. It is also, if not quite great, at least a very good vintage for red wine.

WEATHER CONDITIONS

The key to the answer, as so often, lies in the weather. The 1985 season commenced with a bout of really savage frost – the temperature descending to -28°C in Chablis, a level at which even the vine is vulnerable. Although the thermometer did not fall quite so low in the Côte d'Or, much damage was done in plots where there were young vines, where there was a hollow in which the frost could collect, or just where for one reason or another there were plants which were particularly susceptible. Some vines were killed outright. Others did not produce in 1985. A few suddenly gave up the ghost in the years to come. Not since 1956 had there been such arctic weather in Burgundy.

In the Côte d'Or the overall effect of the frost, though over-played at the time, was important but not serious, both in terms of the 1985 crop and the long term. Much of the damage was in AC. Bourgogne *rouge* vineyards, not in the village wines, though a little pocket of *premiers crus* in Gevrey, where the land dips between the *grand cru* of Mazis and the main road, suffered badly, as did part of the low-lying ground behind the walls of Clos-de-Vougeot, and also parts of Aloxe and Chorey. In these areas large-scale replanting was necessary. Estimates of the total losses added up to 250 hectares in the Côte d'Or. This represents just under 3 per cent of the area under vines.

Following the cold winter, the spring and early summer progressed without mishap. The flowering was a little late, but on those vines not affected by the frost a perfectly satisfactory amount of flowers set into fruit. Up to the beginning of August the climate was neither exceptionally good nor worryingly bad, but then a perfect *fin de saison* set in. August and September were extremely dry, with barely 10 millimetres of rain being precipitated during the two months, an unprecedented drought, and, though August was not particularly warm, September was really quite hot. This transformed the crop from something uneven, behindhand and unpromising at the beginning of the month to something ripe, uniform, healthy and concentrated by the last week when the harvest began to get under way.

The harvest progressed swiftly and safely. There was no rot; there had been no hail. It was hardly necessary to pick over the bunches either in the vineyard or in the *chai* to eliminate anything rotten. All the fruit was ripe, all of it was healthy. At the Domaine Rousseau in Gevrey-Chambertin, twenty-five pickers were employed for six days. In 1986 it would require fifty for twelve. It was an easy harvest: no rain, no vinification problems despite the fine weather, and no lack, it seemed, of either bunches of fruit or juice.

THE STYLE OF THE WINE

WHITE WINES

The white wines were firm, understated and classic in their youth, perhaps not very forthcoming but with plenty of depth for those who went in search for it. They have developed beautifully. Many are still youthful and vigorous. Their balance is impeccable, the fruit discreet and elegant, and the best will continue for a number of years. There has not been a better white-wine vintage since.

RED WINES

This is what I wrote at the time: 'The 1985s can be warmly welcomed and are easy to welcome. Rarely have I seen a young Burgundy vintage which is so *flatteur*. The wines are well coloured, abundantly rich and fruity, medium- to full-bodied and with round ripe tannins.

These are plump, ample, seductive wines which have none of the hard edges of the 1983s. They will, I believe, always show their charm - and hence may encourage infanticide. And they may well prove to be considerably more popular with the consumer than the earlier vintage. Consistently from Fixin to Santenay, grower after grower will present you with attractive samples, crammed with ripe fruit. Unlike in 1983, there was no hail, nor was there any rot. Few growers seem to have had problems with the vinification. And the crop was satisfactory in size.

'And yet . . . nagging at the back of my mind, increasingly so the more growers I visited, was a doubt. Is the vintage just a little *too* appealing at this early stage? Should there be a bit more reserve, a bit more strength? Do the wines have enough backbone? Do they have enough acidity? Delicious as they undeniably are now, how will they keep? How many of them are *grands vins*?'

'I think the worst cracked up years ago and the best are not yet ready,' was the opinion of one serious Burgundy importer when I invited him to a tasting I organised in London in February 1995. 'Some lack staying power and concentration, but many made brilliant youthful drinking, and others will age well,' echoes Anthony Hanson in his *Burgundy* (Faber and Faber, 1995), adding, 'The best white wines were initially dumb and four-square, but are ageing magnificently.'

So in reds (I agree absolutely with Hanson's assessment of the whites) we appear to have two sorts of wine: on the one hand those which were all charm and fresh fruit, but ephemeral, and those with the intensity and concentration to last. It all boils down, I believe, to the question of acidity. Where the 1985 offers disappointments it is in the wines which were made for keeping, but lacked the correct ingredients. Where it differs by comparison with the identical wine made today is that a whole host of the present generation had only recently been in charge and responsible for large-scale domaine-bottling in 1985. There are wines with too much extract, wines - even those of the great Henri Jayer - which are over-oaked, others which are clumsy.

But despite the disappointments, there are lots which are delicious, and will still keep very well indeed. And not all of these are Côte d'Or *grands crus*. Indeed some of the best wines come from Volnay, from those such as Lafarge, de Montille and the Domaine de la Pousse d'Or.

TASTING NOTES

BLANC

Bâtard-Montrachet   Fontaine-Gagnard
Light, evolved nose. No depth. No *grand cru* quality. This is thin and short. Poor. **(06/95)**
Drink soon   12.0

Bâtard-Montrachet   Louis Jadot
Firmer, more discreet than the Sauzet Bâtard. Marvellously rich, firm and complete. Real depth and class. Still very youthful. Excellent. Will last for ages. Indeed will still improve. **(06/95)**
Now-2010   19.0

Bâtard-Montrachet   Gabriel Jouard
Quite an evolved colour and nose. Old, ordinary. Reasonable style but not the depth of a *grand cru*. **(06/95)**
Drink soon   13.0

Bâtard-Montrachet   Louis Latour
Fine, full, rich, masculine and meaty nose. Similar palate. Good oaky base. Very good grip. Firm, very vigorous. Splendid depth. Very high quality. Lovely balance. Not a bit heavy or four square. Bags of life. High class. **(07/94)**
Now-2005 plus   18.5

Bâtard-Montrachet   Leflaive
Rich firm, backward nose. A touch of built-in sulphur. Rich and full-bodied. A little four-square. I prefer both the Pucelles and the Chevalier. **(06/95)**
Now-2010   17.0

Bâtard-Montrachet   Étienne Sauzet
Good colour. The nose is still very backward, with just a touch of SO_2, but good richness and concentration and a touch of oak. Clean and pure after a few minutes. Full, rich, nutty,

backward. Even firm. But very good grip. A quite powerful wine. Lots of depth and quality. Still very young. Not a bit heavy. Fine. **(10/95)**
1998-2012 **17.5**

Chassagne-Montrachet   Baudines
Gabriel Jouard
Too old. Already a touch of oxidation. **(03/93)**
Past its best **12.0**

Chassagne-Montrachet   Caillerets
Jean-Noël Gagnard-Delagrange
Better than the Morgeots. Flowery nose. Quite crisp. But on the palate not that exciting. Reasonable fruit. Reasonable freshness and balance. **(06/95)**
Now-2002 **15.5**

Chassagne-Montrachet   Champ-Gain
Jean-Marc Morey
This seems quite evolved for a 1985. And less fat and concentrated and fresh than I would have expected. More like a good 1987. **(07/94)**
Drink soon **13.0**

Chassagne-Montrachet   Maltroie
Fontaine-Gagnard
Strangely vegetal nose. Rather watery on the palate. Fresh but no depth. Disappointing. **(06/95)**
Drink soon **13.0**

Chassagne-Montrachet   Morgeots
Jean-Noël Gagnard-Delagrange
Slightly four-square on the nose. A touch of sulphur. Ripe but a little ordinary. Fullish, rich and balanced, but lacks flair. **(06/95)**
Now-2000 **15.0**

Chassagne-Montrachet *Premier Cru*
Château de la Maltroye
A little reduction on the nose. Some built-in sulphur. Rather coarse. A bit better on the palate. Ripe and fullish. The fruit indeed is quite impressive. But essentially it lacks class. Yet balanced and still quite vigorous. Quite good. **(07/94)**
Drink soon **14.0**

Chassagne-Montrachet   Vergers
Jean Germain
A little SO$_2$, a little reduction, and a little old-on-the-fruit-side on the nose. A little old. But good class originally. Medium-full. Some concentration. But the finish is a bit coarse now. Quite good plus. Losing its fruit and drying out. **(07/94)**
Drink soon **14.5**

Chevalier-Montrachet   Leflaive
This is very brilliant on the nose. Full, rich, very very concentrated. Excellent grip. Marvellous intensity. Still far from its peak. Brilliant complexity and depth of flavour. **(06/95)**
2000-2020 **20.0**

Chevalier-Montrachet   Michel Niellon
Good colour. Still very youthful and closed on the nose. This is a brilliant example. Lovely fruit. This is still a way away from its peak. Very intense. Excellently balanced. Very fine indeed. **(10/94)**
1998-2015 **18.5**

Corton-Charlemagne   Pierre André
This is even worse than Chartron et Trébuchet's Le Montrachet. Very cheap wine. A poor Ladoix at best. No ripeness. Very common. **(06/95)**
Drink soon **11.0**

Corton-Charlemagne   Louis Jadot
Some development in the colour. Quite cool on both nose and palate. It doesn't exactly sing great wine but it needed to develop in the glass. This is quite developed: rich, not exactly fat or concentrated. Good acidity. Got better in the glass. Very good plus but should have been more spectacular than this. **(03/96)**
Drink soon **16.5**

Corton-Charlemagne   Louis Latour
This is high quality. Light golden colour. Ripe, concentrated, stylish, oaky. Ample, even a touch sweet. A lot of depth. Good grip. Will still develop. **(10/95)**
Now-2009 **17.5**

Corton-Charlemagne   Roland Rapet
Firm nose. A little SO$_2$. But there is depth here. Fresh, ripe, a little four-square. Still youthful. But lacks a little flair. **(06/95)**
Now-2005 **15.5**

Corton-Charlemagne
Roland Remoissenet Pére et Fils
This is still a very young wine. A lot of concentration but still rather dumb on the nose. Fullish, quite alcoholic. Good acidity. Quite powerful. It needs time, and it is difficult to see quite how much class there is here. But I think it will certainly last, and probably will show its finesse in due course. Yet it doesn't sing as much as I would have liked even as it evolved. **(09/91)**
Now-2000 **16.0**

Corton-Charlemagne   Rollin Père et Fils
Elegant concentrated nose. Not a lot of oak. Nicely lean and vigorous. Not brilliant but very good plus. Ripe fruit and good style on the attack, a slight lack of dimension on the follow-through. But balanced and long and quite complex. Fresh. Lacks a bit of oak taste too. **(07/94)**
Now-1999 **16.5**

Criots-Bâtard-Montrachet
Blain-Gagnard

Youthful colour. Crisp, lemony, very young on the nose. Fullish, not quite as much grip and intensity and concentration at the end for fine. But very good indeed. At the end, more developed than it appeared at first. (04/95)

Now–2000 plus   17.0

Criots-Bâtard-Montrachet   Louis Latour

Quite a golden colour. Fat, rich, concentrated youthful nose. Quite oaky. Full, ample, very classy. Very well balanced. Powerful for a Criots, but it is 1985 and Louis Latour. But it is not too alcoholic. Long. Very good grip. Still an infant. Very fine. (10/95)

Now–2005 plus   18.5

Fixin   La Croix-Blanche   Bruno Clair

Good colour. Nicely fresh on the nose. Really quite good depth. Nothing rustic or *sauvage* about this. A little lean and with not much depth but enjoyment to be had. Quite good. (06/95)

Drink soon   14.0

Meursault   Château de Meursault

Rich colour. Very oaky. Almost sweet. Certainly popular but far too exotic and perfumed. Fullish. But tarty. Fresh for a ten-year-old wine though. (10/95)

Now–2000   14.0

Meursault   Labouré-Roi

A little built-in sulphur on the nose. Fat but rather blowsy. Ripe but rather heavy and unstylish. Finishes coarse. (07/94)

Drink soon   13.0

Meursault   Matrot

A little heavy, a bit of dead sulphur showing. The fruit has dried out a bit. Full and firm. Not bad at best. (06/95)

Drink soon   13.0

Meursault   Prosper Maufoux

Not much nose. Quite ripe and stylish. But a little lacking real depth and dimension, and now beginning to show a little age. Reasonable follow-through. Quite good. (07/94)

Drink soon   14.0

Meursault   Charmes   Louis Jadot

Fine nose. Very firm and classy. A lot of depth here. Lovely fruit. This is still very youthful. Best, it would appear, with food. Rich, concentrated, very complex. Very long. Several notes. (06/95)

Now–2005 plus   17.0

Meursault   Charmes   Comtes Lafon

This is very, very rich and ample on the nose. Almost exotic. Almost over-ripe but just not quite. Underneath there is very good grip. Very ripe, very lovely, good oaky base. This is now *à point*. Succulent. Lovely. Several notes. (06/95)

Now–2005 plus   17.5

Meursault   Charmes
Olivier Leflaive Frères

Lovely nose. Ripe and abundant. Still fresh, nicely peachy still. There is substance and depth here. Good acidity. Very good plus. (06/95)

Now–2000 plus   16.5

Meursault   Charmes   Matrot

Slightly heavy, quite evolved on the nose. A little sulphur. The fruit has dried out somewhat. Obviously it is richer than his basic but again there isn't much enjoyment any more. (06/95)

Drink soon   14.0

Meursault   Clos-de-la-Barre
Comtes Lafon

Quite an old colour. Aspects of 1978 if not 1972. Touch of oak at the start. Ripe, fragrant, very stylish. Long and complex. But just slightly hard at the end. Very good fruit. Fine with food. Several notes. (06/96)

Now–2005   16.0

Meursault   Genevrières   Comtes Lafon

Even more exotic, but with less acidity than the Charmes. Abundant and *farouche*. Almost over-ripe, not quite the grip of the Charmes. A little too spicy for comfort. Very good but not fine. Almost approaching blowsiness. Several notes. (06/95)

Now–2003   16.0

Meursault   Genevrières   Leroy

A certain amount of reduction at the beginning but this soon blew off to reveal a very youthful, firm, nutty, gently oaky, rich wine. Excellent grip. Barely drinkable. Very complex. Very concentrated. Real *grand cru* intensity here. Fine plus. (04/95)

Now–2005   18.0

Meursault   Genevrières   Michelot-Buisson

Good colour. A little too much built-in sulphur on the nose. And not enough concentration and intensity on the palate. Quite fresh. But lacks real class. Flat at the end. A disappointment. (04/96)

Drink soon   13.0

Meursault   Genevrières   Pitozet-Urena

Ripe nose. A little diffuse perhaps. Lacks grip and class. Medium body. This has a little too much built-in sulphur. Now a bit short. (06/95)

Drink soon   13.0

**Meursault   Les Grands-Charrons
Claude et Hubert Chavy-Chouet**

Ripe but a little one-dimensional. Reasonable style but now losing its vigour. There is good acidity and the wine is still quite fresh. But an absence of depth and flair and concentration. Quite good plus. **(02/94)**

Drink soon   **14.5**

Meursault   Perrières   Comtes Lafon

Firm, rich, very concentrated nose indeed. And very concentrated fruit. Real depth, really complex. Very fine. A really lovely wine. Several notes. **(02/95)**

Now-2008 plus   **18.5**

Meursault   Perrières   Matrot

Cooler than Lafon. Firmer. Rich, plenty of depth. There is a little built-in sulphur here. Less satisfactory on the palate as a result. Yet the background is very good. A pity. Will this blow away? An unlucky bottle? **(06/95)**

Now-2005   **16.0**

Meursault   Perrières   Guy Roulot

Fullish, fresh, minerally, very classy fruit. This is gently oaky, finely balanced, beautifully poised. Discreet and lovely. Fine. **(06/95)**

Now-2003 plus   **17.5**

**Meursault   Rougeots
Jean-Françoise Coche-Dury**

Rich oaky nose. Mature and quality here. Delicate complex and balanced. On the palate this is fine. A lot of depth here. Classy and harmonious. Lovely. Long and multi-dimensional. Vigorous. Bags of life. Excellent for a village wine. **(10/92)**

Now-2005   **16.5**

**Meursault   Santenots
Monthélie-Douhairet**

Light colour. Smells a little of straw, and a touch of built-in sulphur. Medium-full, good grip. Ripe but a little rustic. But became less rustic as it developed in the glass. Fresh. Not bad. Youthful. Plenty of guts. A white wine made on red soil. **(11/94)**

Now-1999   **13.0**

Meursault   Tessons   Guy Roulot

Quite an evolved colour. Ripe, fully evolved nose. This now needs drinking but is a most attractive example. Balanced. Losing a little of its grip. Good. **(06/95)**

Drink soon   **15.0**

Meursault   Tillets   Patrick Javillier

Ample rich fruit. Finishes rich and ripe. Good oaky depth. This is complex, stylish, fullish. Bags of life. Long. Very good plus. **(06/95)**

Now-2000 plus   **16.5**

Meursault   Tillets   Guy Roulot

Plump on the nose. Fruit-salady ripe. Very stylish. Touch of oak. Very fresh. Lovely fruit. This is even better than Javillier's Tillets. Very good indeed. **(06/95)**

Now-2000 plus   **17.0**

Le Montrachet   Chartron et Trébuchet

Very evolved sweetish but thin sulphury nose. A total disgrace! Some oak, a thin, pretty, little ripe wine. But that is it. **(06/95)**

Drink soon   **13.0**

Le Montrachet   Romanée-Conti

Opulent, oaky, voluptuous, some alcohol. This is less rigid than the Thénard. Seems even riper and more succulent. Good oak. A lot of style and depth but not great. Certainly fine. Will keep. **(01/91)**

Now-2005   **19.0**

Le Montrachet   Baron Thénard

Rich, firm nose. Oaky and concentrated. A little rigid, but there is good acidity here, and although this is a bit clumsy it is certainly very good. Will develop. **(01/91)**

Now-2005   **18.5**

**Le Montrachet   Marquis de Laguiche
Joseph Drouhin**

Fine, oaky, full, rich, concentrated, excellent. Unfortunately rather corky. Still infanticide until the year 2000. **(01/91)**

2000-2020   **19.5**

**Nuits-Saint-Georges   Perrières
Henri Gouges**

Ripe, round, mature but vigorous. Individual, stylish and full of fruit. Complex. Very good. **(10/94)**

Now-2000 plus   **16.0**

Puligny-Montrachet   Jean-Marc Boillot

Lean, slightly aged nose. The fruit was crisp but seems to have dried up a little. Still good on the palate. Needs drinking soon but ripe and stylish. Quite good plus. **(06/95)**

Drink soon   **14.5**

Puligny-Montrachet   Leflaive

Fresh, slightly closed at the outset. Ripe but understated. Not exactly rich or powerful. Medium body. Balanced. Elegant. Came out more and more in the glass as it evolved. A delicate wine. Very good indeed for a village *Appellation Contrôlée.* **(03/95)**

Now-2005   **17.0**

Puligny-Montrachet   Étienne Sauzet

Firm nose, but with depth and concentration. Classic Chardonnay. Lovely fruit. A very good example of a village wine. Still youthful. Good acidity. Long. Even complex. Lovely finish for a village wine. (02/91)

Now–2000   16.5

Puligny-Montrachet   Les Combettes
Louis Jadot

The colour is now quite deep but the wine is still very young. Indeed still a little light. Suspicions of reduction. On aeration this blew away, and on decanting the wine began to flower: full, rich, very concentrated - indeed *grand cru* concentration. Pure, ripe, quality Chardonnay. Rich and fat, profound and delicious. Lovely. Will keep for ages. (03/95)

Now–2010   18.5

Puligny-Montrachet   Les Combettes
Leflaive

Youthful colour. Still firm and slightly undeveloped on the nose. Still very young. Rather more expansive on the palate, especially on the follow-through. Fullish, very lovely concentrated oaky fruit. Very good grip. Rich, complex and very very classy. This is a super wine. Fine at the very least. Bags of life. (10/94)

Now–2010   17.5

Puligny-Montrachet   Les Combettes
Étienne Sauzet

Discreet nose. This has plenty of drive on the palate though. Good intensity. Good richness. Gently oaky. Yet the class you would expect is not here. For once this is not Sauzet's best *premier cru*. (06/95)

Now–2000   15.5

Puligny-Montrachet   Folatières
Chartron et Trébuchet

Closed, hollow, a bit short. Unexciting. A little SO$_2$. A second bottle very much better, fruity, concentrated, but lacks real grip nevertheless. Only good. (05/90)

Drink soon   15.0

Puligny-Montrachet   Folatières
Louis Latour

This is good, but it lacks a little concentration compared with some. A little built-in sulphur. But underneath the wine is a bit light and insignificant for a top *premier cru*. Disappointing. (06/95)

Drink soon   13.5

Puligny-Montrachet   Perrières
Louis Carillon

Classic. Discreet, youthful, understated. Very ripe. Lovely nose. Not quite as intense as Sauzet but nevertheless very ample. Very well balanced. Very long. Very classy. (06/95)

Now–2005   17.5

Puligny-Montrachet   Perrières
Étienne Sauzet

Pure, cool, balanced, crisp and youthful. Complex and delicate. Lovely fruit, lovely concentration. Very intense. This is delicious. A very fine, and very, very elegant example. (06/95)

Now–2005 plus   19.0

Puligny-Montrachet   Pucelles   Leflaive

Firm nose. Still very youthful. Still hidden. Very concentrated and ripe underneath. This is closed and fine on the palate. Best of all on the finish. Very ripe. Very good grip. Very long. Several notes. (06/95)

Now–2010   18.5

Saint-Romain   Alain Gras

This is very good for what it is. No undue age. Clean and crisp. Good ripe appley-peachy fruit. Good grip. Not much oak if any. Plus depth and personality. Very good for a Saint-Romain. (07/94)

Drink soon   14.5

ROUGE

Aloxe-Corton   Rollin Père et Fils

Medium colour. Quite an evolved nose. Lacking style. Sweet palate. Over the top. Horrid. (06/95)

Drink soon   11.0

Aloxe-Corton   Valozières   Comte Senard

Good colour. Plenty of depth and vigour here. The nose is still a little hidden, but has good style and balance. Nicely cool. On the palate the wine is ripe, quite structured, only just ready. Very Corton. Fine acidity. Very long. Shows well. Very good plus. (10/93)

Now–2008   16.5

Beaune   Cent-Vignes   Bernard Bescancenot

Colour beginning to lighten up it seems. Now fully mature. I get more stems on the nose than in recent vintages. But the same amount then as now. Medium body. Soft, fragrant and quite complex. Round and elegant. This is balanced and really quite stylish. Good. (12/95)

Now–2002   15.0

Beaune   Chouacheux   Chantal Lescure

Medium, mature colour. Not much style on either the nose or the palate. A bit sweet. Reasonable grip. But all rather artificial. Common. (12/94)

Drink soon   13.0

Beaune   Clos-de la-Féguine   Jacques Prieur

Good colour. A little hard on the nose - more tannin than fruit. Because it lacks a little grip it also lacks elegance. Rather over-extracted. A bit too chaptalised and alcoholic as well. A clumsy wine. Fullish. Undistinguished. **(09/90)**

Now-2000   **13.0**

Beaune   Clos-des-Marconnets   Chanson

Medium colour but youthful and vibrant. Slightly lean on the nose. What it lacks is substance and generosity. But it is undeniably stylish. Medium body. Even quite intense. Still youthful. But, as on the nose a lack of fat and succulence. Good plus at best. Will keep well. **(02/94)**

Now-2000 plus   **15.5**

Beaune   Clos-de-la-Mousse
Bouchard Père et Fils

This is a little faded, never having had much grip. The fruit has died and there is a certain amount of astringency. A pity, as there was some elegance here. **(12/94)**

Drink soon   **14.5**

Beaune   Clos-des-Ursules   Louis Jadot

Good colour. Still youthful. Lovely ripe cherry, raspberry, strawberry nose. Round and mellow and stylish. Medium to medium-full. Ample, balanced, elegant, long and intense. Very complex at the end. Long. A lovely example. **(10/93)**

Now-2005   **17.0**

Beaune   Grèves   Michel Lafarge

Good colour. Still youthful. On the nose also very fresh, with very lovely fruit. Complete, classy. Fullish, rich, ample. Ripe long finish. Very good indeed. Bags of life. Just about *à point*. **(06/95)**

Now-2010 plus   **17.0**

Beaune   Grèves   Tollot-Beaut

Good colour. Very lead-pencilly on the nose. Attractive fresh fruit as well though. Fullish, vigorous. Quite oaky. Good grip. Succulent. This is good plus and has plenty of life. **(06/95)**

Now-2005   **15.5**

Beaune   Marconnets
Bouchard Père et Fils

Medium-full mature colour. Quite fresh on the nose. Sturdy. Quite rich. Reasonable fruit. Good vigour. This is good. If not spectacular. **(12/94)**

Now-2000   **15.0**

Beaune   Montrevenots   Jean-Marc Boillot

Good mature colour. Quite animal on the nose. Not exactly classy. Better on the palate. Lots of red fruit. Good balance. Plenty of intensity. Long. Very pleasant if not very serious. Good plus. **(06/95)**

Now-2005   **15.5**

Beaune   Les Teurons   Albert Morot

Medium colour. Fully mature. Delicious *tendre*, fragrant nose. Medium-full. Very good intensity. Lovely fruit. Very classy. Soft and long and delicately intense on the finish. Delicious. Not a stayer though. Very good plus. **(10/95)**

Now-2000   **16.5**

Blagny   La Pièce-sous-le-Bois   Matrot

Medium colour. Ripe but with some sulphur on the nose. And the sulphur dominates the palate. This could have been good. **(06/95)**

Drink soon   **14.0**

Bonnes-Mares   Louis Jadot

Very good colour. Closed nose. Youthful, a little dumb. Splendid palate though. Fullish, ample, ripe and concentrated. Very good acidity. Still needs time. Still just a little adolescent. Fine quality. Several notes. **(10/92)**

Now-2012   **17.5**

Bonnes-Mares   Georges Roumier

Good colour. Quite firm and meaty on the nose. Slightly tough. This is still youthful. On the palate full, rich, vigorous and with real depth. This is masculine. Not yet ready. But very fine. Several notes: one in 04/95, from a tasting in London more developed, and given only 17.0. **(06/95)**

1999-2020   **18.5**

Bonnes-Mares   *Vieilles-Vignes*   Varoilles

Good colour. Rich oaky nose. Still youthful. Good raspberry and cream fruit here. But quite solid. Fullish. Good acidity. A little austere on the attack but long, subtle, oaky and of high quality on the finish. Similar note twelve months later. **(11/92)**

Now-2008   **17.0**

Chambertin   Héritiers-Latour

Good fresh youthful colour. Cherry, plummy nose. Quite soft. Especially for a Chambertin. Sweet and perfumed (violet cachous). More spicy as it developed. Medium to medium-full. Not that rich or concentrated. But not cooked or over-alcoholic. But for Chambertin a bit disappointing. Lacks intensity and real class. Good plus. **(10/94)**

Now-2004   **15.5**

Chambertin   Armand Rousseau

Fine colour. Unforthcoming nose. Marvellous rich fruit on the palate. Full bodied, excellently put together. Real breed. Very, very lovely classy fruit. Very good grip. Classic. But still infanticide. A more evolved bottle (18.5) at Restaurant Pic in Valence twelve months later. Several other notes recently, all very enthusiastic. **(06/95)**

1998-2020   **20.0**

Chambertin   Louis Trapet

Good colour. Like the Chapelle the nose is toasted and biscuity but this has more concentration. On the palate too this has richness and depth. But it lacks the class for great. This is no better than very good plus. **(06/95)**

Now-2003   16.5

Chambertin   *Vieilles-Vignes*   Louis Trapet

Medium-full colour. Rich and fat on the nose. Concentrated on the palate. Fine quality plummy fruit. This is serious. Quite sweet and rich. Good grip. Fine plus. **(06/95)**

Now-2015   18.0

Chambertin   Clos-de-Bèze   Dr Marion

Good colour. Fullish and vigorous. Rich, fat, oaky nose. Lovely concentrated fruit. Medium-full. Open. Oaky. Ripe and fruity, even concentrated. Good grip. But not quite the intensity and class on the finish for this 5-star *climat*. Very good indeed. **(10/93)**

Now-2010   17.0

Chambertin   Clos-de-Bèze   Louis Jadot

Full colour. Still youthful. Concentrated but still a bit dumb on the nose. Rich, fat and opulent. But not the greatest class. There is something slightly rustic here. Fullish. Very good indeed (but just). By no means great. **(03/96)**

1998-2012   17.0

Chambertin   Clos-de-Bèze
Armand Rousseau

Very good colour. Lovely rich oaky nose. Seems more evolved than his Chambertin. On the palate very delicious. This is certainly very fine indeed if not quite great. Marvellously rich, balanced and poised. Very very good grip. This is long, complex and very lovely. Quite delicious. Several notes: not quite as good as Rousseau's Chambertin at its best. **(06/95)**

Now-2005   19.0

Chambolle-Musigny   Guy Vadey-Castagnier

Good colour. Good oaky nose. Soft and cedary and aromatic. Quite spicy on the palate, and a little dry and hard. Medium-full. Lacks a little succulence and grip. Quite good. **(11/92)**

Drink soon   14.0

Chambolle-Musigny   Les Amoureuses
Jacques-Frédéric Mugnier

Good colour. Ample, succulent, ripe, and stylish. Less vigour than Roumier. Less strength and concentration. But the class of the *climat* comes shining through. Very complex at the end. Essentially gentle. Fine. **(06/95)**

Now-2000 plus   17.5

Chambolle-Musigny   Les Amoureuses
George Roumier

Good colour. Firm, youthful nose. This has very classy fruit indeed. Very ripe, beautifully balanced. Really classy. Fullish, very harmonious. Very long. Lovely. Very vigorous still. Very fine. Several notes. **(06/95)**

Now-2010   18.5

Chambolle-Musigny   Les Charmes
Gaston Barthod-Noëllat

Good fresh colour. Quite full. Slightly papery on the nose. Not a lot of succulence. I get a taste of stems on the palate. And the wine, though ripe and fruity, lacks richness. The wines are better today. **(06/95)**

Now-2004   14.0

Chambolle-Musigny   Les Cras
Gaston Barthod-Noëllat

Medium colour. Ample, succulent fruit. Not as poised as the wines today but attractive, ripe and stylish. Fully ready, fully ripe, smooth, most seductive fruit. Subtle, lovely. *À point*. Not a wine for a very long future, but lovely. Very good indeed. **(06/95)**

Now-2000 plus   17.0

Chambolle-Musigny   Les Feusselottes
Dr Georges Mugneret

Double magnum. Fine vigorous colour. Rich plummy nose. This has good size, concentration and vigour, but underneath the velvetiness and fragrance of quality Chambolle. Good grip. Plenty of fruit depth. Not fine, but very good indeed, and, in this size at least, bags of life left. Lovely example. **(06/95)**

Now-2005 plus   17.0

Chambolle-Musigny   *Premier Cru*
André Pernin-Rossin

Half bottle. Medium colour. Quite evolved, and on the nose too. The tannins are a bit dry and unsophisticated and the wine is quite diffuse. I would have taken it more for a good 1986. As a 1985 it is a bit disappointing. Spicy, lacking grip. Rather blowsy. **(02/95)**

Drink soon   13.5

Chapelle-Chambertin   Louis Trapet

Good colour. Open accessible, biscuity nose. On the palate a slight lack of class and intensity. This has nowhere near as much finesse as most of the rest of the *grands crus*. Good plus at best. Yet balanced and fruity. Several notes. **(06/95)**

Now-2000 plus   15.5

Charmes-Chambertin   Denis Bachelet

Very good colour. Marvellous nose. Very lovely rich, ripe fruit. Very harmonious and very classy. This is excellent. Marvellous balance and finesse. Very very concentrated. Real intensity. Exciting quality. This is brilliant. Will still improve. How I wish I had bought some of this for myself! (06/95)

Now-2015   19.5

Charmes-Chambertin Philippe Charlopin-Parizot

Splendid colour. Very youthful nose. Oaky, rich, plummy fruit. But not yet, it seems, totally integrated. Slightly tough, slightly four-square. But there is good quality here. Will still improve. Very good indeed. (06/95)

Now-2015   17.0

Charmes-Chambertin   Joseph Drouhin

This is fullish on the colour, with no sign of age. The nose is very classy. Fragrant and rich, and complex. Soft, fullish, mellow, fully ready. This is delicious and complex. Long and lovely. Fine but not great. (03/96)

Now-2005 plus   17.5

Charmes-Chambertin   Bernard Dugat-Py

Five-year-old vines here. Good colour. The nose is fruity, classy and clean and attractive, and so is the wine on the palate. Only at the end is it a little simple. But for vines of this age surprisingly good. (06/95)

Now-2000   16.0

Charmes-Chambertin   Dujac

Medium-full mature colour. Slightly dry on the nose. A little stemmy, oaky-sweet. Well made, fresh. Very good fruit, very harmonious on the palate. This is delicious. But it is not as spectacular as Denis Bachelet's. Several similar notes. (06/95)

Now-2015   18.0

Charmes-Chambertin Roland Remoissenet Pére et Fils

Good immature colour. Surprisingly fresh. A youthful, stylish Pinot. Very good acidity for 1985. Lovely fruit. Not a bit suave. Long, complex, vigorous. Lingering fragrant finish. Very good indeed. (08/92)

Now-2008   17.0

Charmes-Chambertin   Joseph Roty

Fine, very full, immature purple colour. This is very splendid - Roty thinks it is the best vintage/wine he has ever made, better than 1990 - oaky, enormously concentrated. Very very rich. This still needs a couple of years. Almost sweet and over-ripe. Yet good grip. Huge concentration and intensity. Very fine. Similar note 10/95. (04/95)

Now-2017   18.5

Charmes-Chambertin   Armand Rousseau

Medium-full colour, just about ready. Soft, gently oaky, feminine and fragrant nose. Medium to medium-full. Composed, ripe, charming but with good intensity on the nose. Fine. (06/95)

Now-2012   17.0

Clos-de-la-Roche   Pierre Amiot

Medium-full colour. Mature. Quite evolved ripe nose. Allspice and cinnamon. Medium-full, ample, voluptuous, very well balanced. Lovely fruit. But what it lacks is a little class. Good intensity though. Nicely concentrated. Just about ready. Very good plus. (10/95)

Now-2005 plus   16.5

Clos-de-la-Roche   Dujac

Medium colour. Lean nose. The stems show a bit. Yet ripe and stylish. Quite powerful. A wine of intensity and depth, class and succulence. Very good acidity. Very good indeed. Two other similar notes a few months later. (06/95)

Now-2012   17.0

Clos-de-la-Roche   Armand Rousseau

Very good colour. Ample, plump, rich nose. Nicely caramelly and spicy. This is more old *gibier* Pinot than the Dujac. It is richer and more voluptuous. Fat, rich, full. Good acidity. This is generous and flamboyant. Sweeter with a lovely long finish. Still very young. Very fine. Confirmed a tasting earlier in the year. (11/95)

Now-2005   18.0

Clos-de-la-Roche   Guy Vadey-Castagnier

Good full colour. Animal, exotic nose. Perfumed and funky. Fullish. Good acidity and balance. Very good quality but perhaps not the greatest of class. Long. Very good. (11/95)

Now-2008   16.0

Clos-Saint-Denis   Georges Lignier

Medium to medium-full colour, mature. Not a lot of strength on either nose or palate. Medium body. Not a great deal of concentration either. The fruit is pretty but the wine lacks intensity and real class. Quite good plus at best. (06/95)

Now-2002   14.5

Clos-de-Vougeot   Château de la Tour

This is ripe but it is not as concentrated or as vigorous as I would have liked. Medium body. Soft. Round. Balanced. But one-dimensional rather than three. Good but not great. Similar note 10/94. (08/93)

Drink soon   15.0

Clos-de-Vougeot   Joseph Drouhin

Medium-full colour. Mature. Open, accessible,

spicy nose. A little diffuse. Medium body. Soft, good acidity. Plump and Chambolle-ish. For Clos-de-Vougeot it lacks a little richness and weight. It is more like a Chambolle, Charmes. Elegant, long, fresh. Not too diffuse on the palate. Very good plus. **(10/95)**

Now-2007   16.5

Clos-de-Vougeot   René Engel

Fine colour. Very classy nose. Better than Gros Frère et Soeur. Cooler. But ample and rich on the palate. Very good acidity. This is old-viney, very concentrated and very classy. Fine plus. **(06/95)**

Now-2015   18.0

Clos-de-Vougeot   Lescure

Thin, brown colour. This is not very inspiring. Not much nose. Weak and astringent on the palate. No fruit. Rather disappointing. **(10/93)**

Drink soon   13.0

Clos-de-Vougeot   Méo-Camuzet

Medium-full colour, mature. Rich, fat, quite oaky. As it evolved rather herbaceous and diffuse. Fullish. Slight spicy touch. Lush and open. Just a little obvious. This is very good but not the greatest Clos-de-Vougeot. It lacks class. Balanced, lush. Attractive but a little diffuse. Just about ready. Very good. Similarly in 10/94. **(10/95)**

Now-2007   16.0

Clos-de-Vougeot   Dr Georges Mugneret

Very pure delicious fruit on the nose. Various cherries as well as cassis. Medium weight. Chambolle-ish. But very classy. Very well balanced. Very lovely tannins. This is high class and will last well. Not a blockbuster though. **(02/96)**

Now-2009   17.5

Clos-de-Vougeot   Musigni
Gros Frère et Soeur

Fine colour. Fine nose. Concentrated. Abundant, slightly spicy. Very good but quite toasted oak. This is a masculine, firm, youthful, vigorous Clos-de-Vougeot. Lots of depth. Lots of wine here. Not great but with bags of life and fine. **(06/95)**

Now-2010   17.5

Corton   Bonneau du Martray

Reasonable colour. Some brown. Plump nose, but not a great deal of vigour and intensity - or class. Medium body. Pleasant but a bit one-dimensional. Good acidity but a little lean. Lacks structure and concentration. Quite good only. **(10/93)**

Now-2000   14.0

Corton   Claude Cornu

Medium-full colour. Now mature. A little bit stringy and attenuated on the nose, as well as farmyardy. Rather lacking class here. Medium body. A bit astringent on the palate. Lean and a bit late bottled. Unexciting. **(11/92)**

Drink soon   13.0

Corton   Joseph Drouhin

Very good colour. Finely balanced, very pure Pinot. Very elegant nose. Youthful. Slightly austere. A typically masculine Corton. Just a little four-square. A little tannin still. Still needs time. Very fine. **(06/95)**

1998-2015   18.0

Corton   Bressandes   Chandon-de-Briailles

Very good colour. Evidence of the stems on the nose. Ripe and pleasantly rustic but a bit loose-knit. Similar on the palate. Fully ready. Quite fruity but a bit diffuse. Several notes. **(06/95)**

Now-2000   15.0

Corton   Bressandes   Comte Senard

Medium colour. Fresh fruit on the nose, but not a lot of depth or concentration. Medium to medium-full. This is quite stylish, nicely fruity and has good length. But it doesn't have the concentration of *grand cru*. Very good but not fine. **(06/95)**

Now-2003   16.0

Corton   Bressandes   Tollot-Beaut

Good colour. Good fresh fruit on the nose. Very raspberry. Medium-full. Ample, classy, concentrated and ripe. This is very good indeed. Lovely stylish wine. Very positive at the end. **(06/95)**

Now-2005 plus   17.0

Corton   Château Corton-Grancey
Louis Latour

Medium-full colour. Mature. The nose is a little dry but riper and more succulent than some vintages of this wine. Medium-full, good grip. Slightly rustic and raisinny, but has complexity and dimension. Not too alcoholic either. Ripe. Lacks a little class. Very good though. Just about ready. **(10/95)**

Now-2005   16.0

Corton   Clos-du-Roi
Chandon-de-Briailles

Very good colour. This is a lot better than the Ile and the Bressandes. More volume, more definition, more class, more life. Good fruit. Slightly rough on the tannic department. But long and stylish. Will still improve. **(06/95)**

Now-2007   16.5

Corton   Clos-du-Roi   Thomas-Moillard

Medium-full colour. Barely mature. Firm nose,

slightly austere. Nice cassis flavours, still youthful but with very good grip. Slightly old-fashioned. Full, tannic, some oak, slightly earthy. Not rustic. But there is a lot of structure here. Slightly over-macerated perhaps. Very good fruit behind it though. Give it another two years. Very good plus. **(10/95)**

1998-2008   **17.0**

Corton   Clos-de-la-Vigne-au-Saint
Louis Latour

Lightish colour. Quite developed. Rather a weak nose. And not very inspiring on the palate either. Thin, stemmy. No richness. No class. Vegetal finish. Disappointing. **(06/95)**

Drink soon   **12.0**

Corton   Pougets   Louis Jadot

Medium to medium-full colour. Still immature. The nose, too, is still firm and closed, though there is plenty of depth and even richness, in an austere way, behind it. Medium-full body, a little tannin. Good grip. As usual with a Corton, rather reserved. It lacks the fat of a great wine, but has the grip and length. Very good but misses sex appeal. Confirmed in 09/93 and again in 04/95. **(09/91)**

Now-2003   **16.5**

Corton   Renardes   Pierre André

Good colour. Sweet but a bit loose-knit on the nose. Nothing here on the palate. Weak. **(06/95)**

Drink soon   **13.0**

Corton   Rognets   Méo-Camuzet

Made by Christian Faurois. Good colour. Rich, youthful, classy, meaty and concentrated. This is slightly austere still but a wine of real class and depth. Fine. **(06/95)**

Now-2010   **17.5**

Echézeaux   Clos-Frantin

Full colour. Quite meaty, ample chocolatey nose. On the palate the wine is fullish but the fruit is a little artificial. But round and mellow, plump and ample. Very pleasant if not great. Very good plus. **(03/96)**

Now-2005   **16.5**

Echézeaux   Dujac

Good fullish, vigorous, mature colour. An ample, plump nose with a suggestion of the stems, but no obvious new oak. Not a lot of depth and distinction, but classy enough. On the palate the fruit is ripe and the acidity very good. Lots of elegance. But a touch lean, even austere. It is long and subtle and has plenty of dimension. But it lacks a little weight and fat. Very good but not great. **(10/94)**

Now-2009   **16.0**

Echézeaux   Mongeard-Mugneret

Good colour. Fully mature. Good plump ripe nose. Just a touch of the stems. Ample, sweet, ripe, fullish on the palate. It lacks a bit of grip and real class, but there is a classy example of Echézeaux here: nicely rich and substantial, plenty of *matière*, but only marginally of *grand cru* quality. **(10/95)**

Now-2002   **15.5**

Echézeaux   Romanée-Conti

Medium-full colour. Just about mature. Firm and slightly rustic on the nose. The stems evident. But ample and rich enough. But still closed. Fullish. Still has some tannin. Ripe but a slight robustness I always associate with this wine. Firm, vigorous, very well balanced. Just about ready. Very good plus. **(10/95)**

Now-2010   **16.5**

Gevrey-Chambertin   Pierre Bourée

Why does it smell like a bubble-bath? Is it the glass? Good vigorous colour. Quite spicy, but fresh and plump and with plenty of depth. Fullish, meaty, vigorous. The nose is less fat than the palate. Not a lot of finesse but a good bottle. **(11/94)**

Now-2000   **15.0**

Gevrey-Chambertin   Philippe Charlopin-Parizot

Good colour. Plump, ample but not exactly very classy nose. This is *à point*. It is ripe and it is balanced. A very good basic. **(06/95)**

Now-2008   **15.0**

Gevrey-Chambertin   Michel Guillard

Medium colour. Youthful. On the nose I get quite high acidity and a little spirit. On the palate a certain lack of generosity and fat, though it seems correct. But it lacks charm. Medium body. Good acidity, a lack of structure. Quite long. May round off. Good but not special for a village. **(11/94)**

Now-2000   **17.0**

Gevrey-Chambertin   *Vieilles-Vignes*
Denis Bachelet

Very good colour. Lovely nose. Rich, fat, very concentrated, very stylish. This is of fine *premier cru* quality. Full, rich, very finely poised fruit. Harmonious, ripe. Very delicious. Will still improve. Very classy. Fine plus. **(06/95)**

Now-2015   **18.0**

Gevrey-Chambertin   *Vieilles-Vignes*
Alain Burguet

Very good colour. Full, rich, masculine, meaty. As usual, a lot of depth, very lovely concentrated fruit. Fullish, good tannins but quite a lot of them. Plenty of vigour. Slightly more robust than Bachelet, marginally less exciting. Very good indeed. **(06/95)**

Now–2015   17.0

Gevrey-Chambertin   *Vieilles-Vignes*
Bernard Dugat-Py

Fine colour. Rich, ample fat nose. Fullish, ripe and plump. Lovely fruit. Vigorous, classy. An aromatic wine. Very well balanced. Delicious. Just about ready. **(11/94)**

Now–2005   16.5

Gevrey-Chambertin   Cazetiers
Joseph Faiveley

Medium-full colour. Mature. Splendidly rich oaky nose. Voluptuously rich and ample. Lush. Fullish, very well balanced. Rich and very, very ripe. This is a fine youthful example with real elegance. Long complex finish. **(10/95)**

Now–2010   17.5

Gevrey-Chambertin   Cazetiers
Camille Giroud

Good but mature colour. Ample nose. Evolved and slightly animal. Slightly astringent on the palate. Full and rich but a lack of real style. Slightly burnt and hot at the end. Good merely. Lacks velvet and class. **(06/95)**

Now–2000   15.0

Gevrey-Chambertin   Champeaux
Denis Mortet

Good colour. Lovely plump, meaty, rich nose. Very good grip. Fullish, not really that different from his Clos-Prieur. A little more distinction, a little less earthy. But lots of fat, richness and definition. Fine. **(06/95)**

Now–2015   17.5

Gevrey-Chambertin   Clos-Prieur
Denis Mortet

Very good colour. Ample, rich and plump on the nose. This is a most attractive sexy example. Full, balanced. Very good tannin. This is fine quality. Classy, meaty, vigorous. **(06/95)**

Now–2015   17.5

Gevrey-Chambertin   Clos-Saint-Jacques
Michel Esmonin et Fille

Good colour. Lovely rich nose. Ample, ripe and fat. Still very youthful. A touch of oak. Very concentrated, vigorous, stylish fruit. This is much better than Jadot. Still young. Lovely. Nicely clean and austere yet ripe and rich. Fine. **(06/95)**

Now–2015   17.5

Gevrey-Chambertin   Clos-Saint-Jacques
Louis Jadot

Very fine colour. Good but not as brilliant as I would have liked. There is a touch of sulphur here. This blew away after a bit. But the wine didn't really sing out with its class. Full. Rich. Good acidity. Very good. But not great. This was a bottle direct from Jadot's stocks. Four months later in London, I marked another example fine plus (18.0) and for drinking 1998-2015. **(06/95)**

Now–2005   16.0

Gevrey-Chambertin   Clos-Saint-Jacques
Armand Rousseau

Good colour. Biscuity and oaky on the nose. Rich and fat and plump and classy. Fine on the palate. Nicely evolved. Not as much grip as the Esmonin. But rather more class. Yet it is not mind-blowing. Very fine but not great. Lovely though. Several similar notes. **(06/95)**

Now–2012 plus   18.0

Gevrey-Chambertin   Clos-des-Varoilles
Varoilles

Good colour. A little development now. Elegant nose. Soft and ripe and stylish. Lacks a little drive and intensity. Medium-full. Good austerity though the tannins now resolved. Still a little firm. Good grip. But the finish is long, classy, nicely good, complex and generous. Very good. **(10/93)**

Now–2008   16.0

Gevrey-Chambertin   La Combe-aux-Moines
Philippe Leclerc

Medium colour. Plump, slightly sweet, aromatic nose. Good vigour. Lots of fruit. Quite full, with a good touch of the rustic. Good meaty concentration, ripe. Good acidity. This is of very good quality. Better than I expected. Nicely fat. Good vigour. Ripe. Similar note 02/96. **(11/95)**

Now–2010   16.0

Gevrey-Chambertin   Les Corbeaux
Lucien Boillot et Fils

Very good colour. Rich ample nose again. But not quite the class of some. There is a rustic, earthy quality here. On the palate just a little weak. It lacks grip. Ripe but it tails off. Merely quite good. **(06/95)**

Drink soon   14.0

Gevrey-Chambertin   En Pallud
Bernard Maume

Good fresh colour. Solid meaty nose. Fullish, nicely ample and rich. Good grip. This is an ample, satisfying and very fruity wine. Very good plus. **(06/95)**

Now–2012   16.5

Gevrey-Chambertin   Le Fonteny
Christian Serafin

Good colour. Rich, plump, good old-vine concentration. Very good grip. Not a bit too oaky. Fresh. Full and meaty. Slightly animal.

Very ripe. Delicious. Very good plus. **(06/95)**
Now-2015   16.5

Grands-Echézeaux   Henri Lamarche
Empty colour. Watery, insipid. Not too rustic.
But no concentration here. And now astringent.
(06/95)
Drink up   12.0

Grands-Echézeaux   Mongeard-Mugneret
Full colour. A little weak on the nose. This is
rather too watery for what it is. Rather short. And
it now lacks class. Very disappointing. **(06/95)**
Drink soon   13.0

Grands-Echézeaux
Roland Remoissenet Père et Fils
This is closed-in on the nose. More open on the
palate. Fine, especially as it developed in the
glass. Very complex. **(09/92)**
Now-2010   18.0

Grands-Echézeaux   Romanée-Conti
Good colour. Fat, very ripe mulberry fruit on
the nose. Still a little reserve on the palate. Good
acidity. Medium-full. Long and satisfyingly
plump and generous. Fine complex finish.
(10/93)
Now-2009   17.0

Griotte-Chambertin   De Chézeaux
Good colour. Fullish and vigorous. Slightly
animal nose. Fleshy and exotic. Fat and plumpy
fruity. On the palate gamey, slightly higher
volatile acidity than most. Fullish. A little
tannin. Voluptuous and generous. But lacks a
touch of class. Yet very ripe. Very good indeed.
(10/93)
Now-2009   17.0

Griotte-Chambertin   Joseph Drouhin
Very good colour. Lovely nose. A touch of
vanilla, a touch of *crème brûlée* and lots of *petits
fruits rouges*. Ample, balanced, poised, classy.
Medium-full. Not as great as Bachelet's
Charmes but fine plus. Just a touch sweet.
(06/95)
Now-2009   18.0

Griotte-Chambertin   *Vieilles-Vignes*
Ponsot
Very fine rich full colour. Very young.
Marvellous nose. This is rich, complex, con-
centrated and crammed with fruit. Real breed
and depth. Still very fresh. Very ample.
Marvellous wild cherry fruit. This has real
intensity and dimension. Excellent balance.
Brilliant. Individual. Very fine quality. **(10/95)**
Now-2010 plus   18.5

Marsannay   Bruno Clair
Medium colour but still quite fresh. Holding up
really quite well. It is light and simple, but is
quite stylish and fruity. **(06/95)**
Drink soon   14.5

Mazis-Chambertin   Bouchard Père et Fils
Fine colour. Rich, masculine, oaky. Firmer in
one bottle than the other. This is a little over-
ripe. And it lacks the style of the Faiveley. But it
is concentrated and rich and very good indeed
nonetheless. **(06/95)**
Now-2010   17.0

Mazis-Chambertin   Joseph Faiveley
Very good colour. Ample, rich, concentrated,
oaky, classy nose. Very straight. This is crisp and
nicely clean and un-souped up. It is also very
concentrated and classy. Very very lovely. One
of the best wines of all. Marvellous finish. Very
fine indeed. **(06/95)**
Now-2020   19.5

Mazis-Chambertin   Leroy
Full colour. Barely mature. Amazingly rich, even
powerful. Full body, still tannic. Still very youthful.
Rich concentrated fat and fabulous. Quite oaky.
Marvellous fruit. Old-fashioned in size and
intensity but excellent. Several notes. **(10/95)**
1998-2020   19.5

Mazis-Chambertin   Bernard Maume
Good fullish colour. Rich, plump, nicely exotic.
But still very vigorous. Fullish, plump, lush.
This is very good indeed but it doesn't quite
have the class and concentration of great. Very
pure blackberry/currant fruit. Good acidity. Just
a little tannin. Long. Rich finish. Fine. **(04/95)**
Now-2009   17.5

Mazis-Chambertin   Armand Rousseau
Medium-full colour, just a little brown. Nose a
little hidden at present but on the palate this
wine is rich, ample, complex and classy - and
very well balanced. Very good indeed. **(03/92)**
1998-2008   17.0

Monthélie   Paul Garaudet
Good colour. Frank, ripe, fruity on nose and
palate. Clean and clear. This is well made.
Medium to medium-full. Stylish, ripe and long.
Good plus. **(06/95)**
Now-2004   15.5

Monthélie   Monthélie-Douhairet
Good colour. Old-fashioned nose. Ripe and full
but a touch rustic. Yet underneath reasonably
balanced. The fruit is attractive and balanced. It
would be better with food. Quite good. **(06/95)**
Drink soon   14.0

Monthélie   Les Duresses   Paul Garaudet

Richer and more concentrated. More vigour and more style. This again is well made. The fruit is very well balanced and stylish. Very good. **(06/95)**

Now-2007   16.0

Morey-Saint-Denis   Clos-de-la-Bussière
Georges Roumier

Medium-full mature colour. Firm, full but a little stemmy on the nose. This detracts from the finesse. Better on the palate. Full, rich, intense, quite classy, very harmonious. Very good grip. I don't find it has quite the class on the finish, but it has plenty of dimension and length. Very good for 1985. Will keep well. **(10/95)**

Now-2005   16.0

Le Musigny   Louis Jadot

Very good colour. Lovely class and great intensity on the nose. Still reserved. This has splendid fruit. But it is currently still a little adolescent. Fullish. Harmonious. Very, very long. Very individual. Very lovely. But great? **(06/95)**

Now-2012   17.5

Le Musigny   Jacques-Frédéric Mugnier

Good colour. Very very lovely nose. Fresh, gentle, assured, pure Pinot. This is very lovely. It is not quite as classy or as poised all the way through to the end as it possibly could be. But almost. This has very lovely fruit and real class and balance. Excellent. **(06/95)**

Now-2005   19.0

Le Musigny   Comte Georges de Vogüé

Medium-full colour. Mature. Soft fragrant, elegant nose if without the real class and intensity of today's wines. On the palate a touch pinched but the fruit is classy and it expanded in the glass. Fine but not as concentrated or as elegant for great. Fully ready. Another note, at the 06/95 tasting not so enthusiastic: only 16.0. **(11/95)**

Now-2003   17.5

Nuits-Saint-Georges   Jean Gros

Good mature colour. Abundant nose with a little reduction. Medium body. A good straightforward village example. Ripe, balanced, seductive. But only one and a half dimensions. Good. **(06/95)**

Now-2000 plus   15.0

Nuits-Saint-Georges   Les Boudots
Jean Grivot

Good colour. Fat, rich, vigorous nose. Plenty of depth here. But a little too rude to have much class. Full, meaty, ample. But a suggestion of the sweet-sour. Good but not great. Plenty of vigour. **(06/95)**

Now-2005   15.0

Nuits-Saint-Georges   Les Boudots
Méo-Camuzet

Splendid colour. And altogether a splendid bottle. Vigorous, rich, opulent and very pure and elegant. Very (of course) Vosne-ish. No excessive new oak. Full, complex, ample and classy. It has excellent grip for a 1985. And is only just ready. Very fine. **(02/95)**

Now-2012   18.0

Nuits-Saint-Georges   Les Boudots
Gérard Mugneret

Good colour. Ripe, rich, but quite sturdy nose. Perhaps a little over-extracted. Slightly green tannins. Still youthful. A little austere. But good elements, the fruit is classy. One wishes for a bit more warmth and succulence. Good nevertheless. But he makes better wine now. **(02/95)**

Now-2000 plus   15.0

Nuits-Saint-Georges   Les Boudots
Jean Tardy

Very good colour. Much classier on the nose than Grivot. Full, ample, rich, very beautifully together. Long, very ripe and complex. Fine. **(06/95)**

Now-2010   17.5

Nuits-Saint-Georges   Les Cailles
Robert Chevillon

Medium to medium-full colour. Mature. Nicely ample and rich on the nose, but a slight touch of the rustic. Good fruit. Nice and ripe. Not at all rustic on the palate. Fullish. Good grip. Nice raspberry-blackberry fruit. Very stylish, very complex. Barely mature. Very good indeed. **(10/95)**

Now-2005 plus   17.0

Nuits-Saint-Georges   Les Chaignots
Alain Michelot

Medium to medium-full colour. Soft, sweet, fully mature nose. Pleasantly fruity but a bit light and one-dimensional. Quite fresh. But basically a bit dull. **(06/95)**

Drink soon   13.5

Nuits-Saint-Georges   Clos-des-Corvées
Louis Jadot

Medium-full colour. A bit tough on the nose. Muscular, some H_2S. Meaty, tannic. Rich and ripe but it lacks a bit of style. Rather lumpy. Quite good. **(06/95)**

Now-2005   14.0

Nuits-Saint-Georges   Clos-de-la-Maréchale
Joseph Faiveley

Medium to medium-full colour. Rich, full nose. Plenty of *matière* and not too lumpy and aggressive. Fullish, ripe and rich on the palate. Good structure. Good grip. This is very good. Just about ready. **(06/95)**

Now-2007   16.0

Nuits-Saint-Georges   Clos-des-Porrets
Henri Gouges

This is clean and quite stylish, but a bit lightweight. Good acidity. But it lacks richness and depth. Had been re-corked. (They had a weevil problem.) Quite good plus. **(06/95)**

Drink soon   **14.5**

Nuits-Saint-Georges   Clos-de-Thorey
Thomas-Moillard

Very fine colour. Barely mature. Very fine concentrated fruit on the nose. Rich, chocolatey. This is fine. Full, backward, concentrated. Very good grip. The tannins full but not too aggressive. Very youthful still. Fine. **(11/95)**

Now-2010   **17.5**

Nuits-Saint-Georges   Les Damodes
Robert Jayer-Gilles

Medium-full colour. Oaky nose. Rich and fat but not fat enough to absorb the oak. This is too dominant. A pity: the wine has balance and the fruit has complexity otherwise. Even long on the palate. **(06/95)**

Now-2005   **15.5**

Nuits-Saint-Georges   Les Damodes
Machard de Gramont

Full colour. Sturdy nose. Gamey, fat, slightly four-square wine. A little hard. Lacks a little fruit. Lacks a little nuance and finesse. Good but not great. **(10/92)**

Drink soon   **15.0**

Nuits-Saint-Georges   Grandes-Vignes
Daniel Rion et Fils

Good colour. Ripe nose. Very good depth - this is only a village wine, though very well placed - ample, rich, nicely concentrated, very stylish. This is long. A splendid result. Very velvety. Very well balanced. Very good. **(06/95)**

Now-2005 plus   **16.0**

Nuits-Saint-Georges   Les Murgers
Daniel Rion et Fils

Medium-full colour, fully mature. Rather a rustic nose. On the palate some astringency. The fruit has lightened up and the wine is rather coarse. Nothing special. **(06/95)**

Drink soon   **13.0**

Nuits-Saint-Georges   Les Perrières
Machard de Gramont

Good colour. Firm, earthy, molasses nose. Cigar box and coffee. Leather. But rich. Fullish, meaty, still a little tannin. But plenty of grip and depth. Good positive even concentrated follow-through. Very good. **(11/92)**

Now-2004   **16.0**

Nuits-Saint-Georges   Les Pruliers
Jean Grivot

Medium-full colour. A touch of stems on the nose. Slightly austere on the palate. The tannins still marked. The wine is ripe but not really rich or generous. A bit four-square. Will it improve as it develops further? **(06/95)**

Now-2005   **14.0**

Nuits-Saint-Georges   Les Richemones
Leroy

Full colour. Very youthful. Firm, earthy nose. Backward and tannic. A little fiery. This is barely ready. Full, quite chunky. Good acidity. Slightly hard. But though it will round off will it have the class and charm to mark it better than very good? **(10/95)**

1998-2010   **16.0**

Nuits-Saint-Georges   Les Roncières
Joseph Drouhin

Good fullish colour. Barely mature. Good fat rich nose. Elegant for a Nuits-Saint-Georges. Medium body. Good acidity. Indeed a little lean. It lacks the muscle and fat of a Nuits. Not short. A bit one-dimensional at the end. Quite ready. Quite good. **(02/94)**

Drink soon   **14.0**

Nuits-Saint-Georges   Les Saint-Georges
Joseph Faiveley

Good colour. Little sign of maturity. Profound, classy nose. Hint of coffee and chocolate. This is fullish, meaty and ample. A little tannin still. Very good grip. Fat underneath, will still develop. A vigorous, lovely wine. Long and with a hint of caramelly spice on the finish. **(02/92)**

Now-2005   **18.0**

Nuits-Saint-Georges   Les Saint-Georges
Henri Gouges

Medium-full colour, fully mature. Rather weak on the nose. The Pinot fruit is very pure, which is commendable, but the wine lacks intensity and concentration. Delicate, which is curious. But quite long. Good at best. **(06/95)**

Now-2000   **15.0**

Nuits-Saint-Georges   Les Saint-Georges,
Cuvée des Sires de Vergy   Hospices de Nuits

Fullish colour. Oaky nose. Rich and fat and opulent. Slightly oxidised and with H_2S on the palate. But also very oaky. Unbalanced. Ugly at the end. **(06/95)**

Now-2000   **13.0**

Nuits-Saint-Georges   Les Vaucrains
Jean Chauvenet

Medium-full colour. Slightly artificial fruit. Curiously sweet-sour. A bit thin. This is rather coarse and uninteresting. **(06/95)**

Drink soon   **12.0**

Nuits-Saint-Georges   Les Vaucrains
Henri Gouges

Medium colour. Well matured. A little weak and thin on the nose. A lack of richness and concentration. On the palate not too bad. Quite ripe and fruity. Sweet at the end. But for a 1985 a lack of real concentration, dimension and class. Quite good. **(10/95)**

Now-1999   **14.0**

Nuits-Saint-Georges   Vignes-Rondes
Daniel Rion et Fils

Good colour. Rich nose. Meaty and fullish. A bit more depth than the Grandes-Vignes but perhaps not so much vigour. Ripe, youthful, stylish and very good (? plus) all the same. **(06/95)**

Now-2005   **16.0**

Pernand-Vergelesses   Ile-des-Vergelesses
Chandon-de-Briailles

Medium colour. Now mature. Medium weight on the nose. Slightly sweet on the palate. A lack of class and real definition. And it is a little simple, a little sweet. Quite good. **(06/95)**

Now-2000   **14.0**

Pernand-Vergelesses   Ile-des-Vergelesses
Roland Rapet

Good colour. Attractive, stylish fruit on the nose. This is plump, generous and nicely poised. On the palate it is ripe but there is a slightly lean, slightly sulphury, almost bitter flavour which I don't enjoy. Reasonable length. **(06/95)**

Now-2002   **14.0**

Pernand-Vergelesses   Ile-des-Vergelesses
Rollin Père et Fils

Good colour. Pleasant fruity nose, round and fragrant. Slightly sweaty. On the palate this is medium body. Slightly astringent. A bit pedestrian. A bit soupy. Unexciting. **(06/95)**

Now-2000   **14.0**

Pommard   Capron-Charcousset

This is the proof that these wines do soften up and become more generous. Very good grip and depth. Lovely ripe fruit. Delicious. **(12/95)**

Now-2000 plus   **15.5**

Pommard   André Mussy

Good colour. Only a little mature. Full and slightly funky on the nose. But quite clean. It just lacks a little new oak definition. Fullish, ripe Pinot, balanced. Old-viney. Good but not the class for better. **(11/92)**

Drink soon   **14.5**

Pommard   Chanlins   Virely-Rougeot

Medium to medium-full colour. No undue brown. Rather light and rustic. Losing its fruit.

Tastes slightly bitter and of old tea. Not very exciting at all. **(12/95)**

Drink soon   **12.5**

Pommard   Clos-des-Epeneaux
Comte Armand

Very good colour. Rather a tough nose. Typical slightly rustic Pommard. Good but not a patch on what he makes today. Full, ample, rich, plenty of body. But not a lot of class. Best with food. Good plus. **(06/95)**

Now-2000 plus   **15.5**

Pommard   Clos-de-la-Platière
Prince de Mérode

Medium-full fresh colour. Good fruit and style for a Pommard. Ripe, medium-full body, balanced. Gently oaky. Complex, stylish. Very good. **(10/94)**

Now-2005   **15.5**

Pommard   Epenots   Jacques Parent

Very good colour. Ripe nose with a touch of animal-gaminess. Full, a bit too sweet, a bit coarse, and rather hot at the end. Lacks grace. Average. **(06/95)**

Drink soon   **13.0**

Pommard   Pézerolles   Michel Lafarge

Good colour. Somewhat lumpy on the nose. On the palate this is a little rigid. It is all correct but there is a lack of generosity. A bit four-square. May get rounder as it develops further. It is still young. **(06/95)**

Now-2008   **14.5**

Pommard   Rugiens   De Courcel

Fine colour. Ripe, rich, abundant fruit. This is fullish and if not really classy is certainly full of attraction. But on the follow-through, though ample, it lacks style. Good plus at best. But like the Clos-des-Epeneaux, rather disappointing compared with the top Volnays. **(06/95)**

Now-2000 plus   **15.5**

Pommard   Rugiens   Hubert de Montille

Fine colour. Firm, slightly austere but fragrant nose. This is still very young. Rich and cool and plummy. Very good acidity. The tannins still need to soften a bit. But very good indeed. Could it be a bit more generous and fat? Will it get more so as it develops? **(11/95)**

Now-2012   **17.0**

Pommard   Saucilles   Jean-Marc Boillot

Good colour. Seems a little pinched on the nose. Medium body. Medium interest. Not a lot of concentration. It is quite fruity. But it is a bit short now. A bit one-dimensional. Quite good. Certainly perfectly correct. **(06/95)**

Drink soon   **14.0**

Pommard Vignots Leroy

Good colour. Vigorous. Rich. Substantial. More weight than elegance. But balanced and ripe and with plenty of life ahead of it. Very good finish. Very good. **(05/95)**

Now-2005 plus   16.0

Richebourg Jean Gros

Very good colour. Splendid nose. High quality very concentrated fruit. Beautifully balanced. Marvellous, concentrated, classy fruit on the palate. Really poised and complete. This is very fine indeed. And it could still do with a year or two. **(06/95)**

Now-2010   19.0

Richebourg Henri Jayer

Fine colour. Still very youthful. Really quite oaky nose. Almost cloves. Fullish, still youthful. Lovely fruit. Slight touch of tannin. Slightly rigid. Is this going to mellow properly? Class though, undeniably. But though full of fruit a little tough. Yet intense and concentrated. Very fine. **(10/94)**

Now-2015   18.0

Richebourg Méo-Camuzet

Full, mature colour. Splendidly ripe, classy, concentrated nose. Not yet quite smooth enough to be fully ready for drinking. Yet exotic. Fullish, laid-back, oaky but not aggressively so. Excellent acidity. Marvellous fruit. Still very very young. Real class. Fat and succulent. This is potentially very very fine. The *grand cru terroir* finesse and complexity come roaring out. **(10/95)**

Now-2015   18.0

Richebourg Romanée-Conti

Good full colour. No undue brown. Just a faint touch of hail here on the nose. Much less on the palate. A long way from the Tâche, but fullish, meaty, rich and quite concentrated. Good acidity. No astringency. Very good indeed. **(10/94)**

Now-2005   17.0

Romanée-Saint-Vivant Robert Arnoux

Medium to medium-full colour. Fully mature. Quite an old nose. Elements of old tea. This is very curious. On the palate this has good acidity but is weak and thin. Almost 1984-ish rather than 1985. No fat. Strange vegetal finish. **(10/95)**

Drink soon   12.5

Romanée-Saint-Vivant Romanée-Conti

Medium-full colour. Barely mature. Closed nose. Rich ample and concentrated. Splendid balance. This is very classy. Fullish, rich, concentrated, a touch of oak, a lot of very youthful intense fruit. No undue element of the stems. Still very young. Very good acidity. Needs time. Marvellous finish. This is very fine. Echoing a note taken 10/94; and in 11/92. **(10/95)**

Now-2018   18.5

Romanée-Saint-Vivant Les Quatre-Journeaux Louis Latour

Medium-full fully mature colour. Good fresh nose. Ripe, meaty, blackberry-cherry fruit. Soft. This hasn't the depth of the best Romanée-Saint-Vivants but has succulence, class and length. Fully ready. **(06/95)**

Now-2008   17.0

Ruchottes-Chambertin Clos-des-Ruchottes Armand Rousseau

Fine colour. Adolescent on the nose. But intense, ripe, concentrated and very classy on the palate. Lovely fruit. Very, very well balanced. This is very fine. **(06/95)**

Now-2015   18.5

Santenay Charmes Vincent Girardin

Medium colour. Mature. Round, very ripe, succulent charming nose. Not a bit tough. An attractive very fruity wine. Medium bodied. Balanced. Easy to drink. Very good for a village example. **(06/95)**

Now-2004   14.0

Santenay Maladière Vincent Girardin

Medium colour. Mature. Good meaty, ripe nose. Medium to medium-full on the palate. The tannins are a little lumpy, but the wine is balanced and the finish is clean and cherry-redcurrant fruity. Quite good plus. **(06/95)**

Now-2005   14.5

Savigny-lès-Beaune Dominodes Bruno Clair

Very good colour. Fine rich concentrated nose. This is fullish, very pure, very well balanced. Rich, black fruity flavours. Fatter and more concentrated and ample on the follow-through than it seems at first. Very, very long. Very, very classy too. Fine. Similarly at the vintage celebration the following June. **(02/95)**

Now-2010   17.5

Savigny-lès-Beaune Dominodes Jean-Marc Pavelot

Very good colour. Lovely rich nose. Ample, plump and vigorous. This is a quite different style of wine to that of Bize. Still youthful. A plummy wine. Very good. **(06/95)**

Now-2005 plus   16.0

Savigny-lès-Beaune   Aux Grands-Liards
Simon Bize et Fils

Medium colour. Mature. Ripe, slightly sinewy, mature nose. A little ungenerous on the palate. There is a lack of succulence. But the balance is correct and it finishes better than it starts. A little tight but quite good. Long. **(06/95)**

Now-2005   **14.0**

Savigny-lès-Beaune   Guettes
Simon Bize et Fils

Medium to medium-full colour. Very stylish fruit here on the nose. Round, plenty of depth. An ample if slightly austere example. A little reduction. Cool and slightly austere. Medium-full. Finishes well though. Ample at the end. Good. **(06/95)**

Now-2007   **15.0**

Savigny-lès-Beaune   Hospices de Beaune,
Cuvée Fouquérand   Arthur Barolet

Good full colour. Quite rich on the palate. A bit alcoholic. Fullish on the palate. Quite rich and fruity if no great subtlety or nuance. Fresh. Quite good plus. **(10/95)**

Now-2002 plus   **14.5**

Savigny-lès-Beaune   Lavières
Lucien Camus-Bruchon

Medium-full colour. Rich full nose. A little pedestrian but ripe enough not to be too affected by a slight lumpiness. A bit old-fashioned on the palate. Fullish and robust, some astringency. Not bad. **(06/95)**

Now-2001   **13.5**

Savigny-lès-Beaune   Marconnets
Simon Bize et Fils

Good rich colour. Fat, ripe nose. Plenty of depth. Fullish, ample, ripe and earthy. A typical Marconnets and a fine example. Rich and meaty. Very good. **(06/95)**

Now-2007   **16.0**

Savigny-lès-Beaune   Peuillets
Capron-Manieux

Medium colour. On the nose quite evolved, a little untidy and unstylish. A little simple and a little short. Getting a bit astringent at the end. Average. **(06/95)**

Drink soon   **13.0**

Savigny-lès-Beaune   Les Serpentières   Leroy

Deep colour. Very youthful. A full, intense, firm wine with a lot of concentrated fruit and very good acidity. This has lots to it. Fine for a 1985 Savigny. Luscious, very fresh fruit. Hardly mature. Very good plus. **(02/96)**

Now-2010 plus   **16.5**

Savigny-lès-Beaune   Les Vergelesses
Robert Ampeau

Medium colour. Nice youthful fragrant nose. Medium body. Nicely intense. Ripe and mature but vigorous. Good acidity. There is a slightly lean background here but no lack of quality. Good. Will still improve. **(11/05)**

Now-2005   **15.0**

Savigny-lès-Beaune   Aux Vergelesses
Simon Bize et Fils

Typical Bize Savigny. Slightly tough on the nose. Animal but ripe underneath. On the palate it is a little astringent and aggressive on the attack but the fruit is balanced and classy underneath. Better with food. Fine finish. But a little lacking charm at the start. Very good plus. Several notes. **(06/95)**

Now-2005   **16.5**

Volnay   Caillerets   Marquis d'Angerville

The colour and the attack a little more evolved than I had expected. But if a touch less vigour certainly all the charm, elegance and depth you could ask for. A true, lingering, subtle Volnay. *À point.* Very good indeed. **(06/96)**

Now-2000   **17.0**

Volnay   Caillerets   Yvon Clerget

Good colour. A little more brown than his Santenots. An ampler, richer wine though. Fine fruit but it doesn't quite have the intensity of the above. Yet it is very good plus all the same. Softer, more delicate. **(06/95)**

Now-2004   **16.5**

Volnay   Caillerets   Pousse d'Or

Fullish colour now mature. Fine fragrant nose. Medium body. Just a touch of astringency compared with the above. Medium to medium-full. Lacks a bit of extra dimension at the end. Very good at best. But getting attenuated. Yet plump and elegant enough. **(01/96)**

Now-2000   **16.0**

Volnay   Caillerets   Vaudoisey-Mutin

Very good colour. Good ripe Pinot on the nose. Not too bad on the palate. It is balanced and correct. But slightly one-dimensional. Good plus though. Finishes long and stylishly. **(06/95)**

Now-2006   **15.5**

Volnay   Champans   Monthélie-Douhairet

Good colour. Only a little mature. A little unforthcoming and barnyardy on the nose. But better on the palate. Medium-full. Good intensity and class. Very Volnay. Very good long complex finish. Very good. **(11/92)**

Drink soon   **16.0**

Volnay   Champans   Hubert de Montille

Very good colour. Very youthful. Ample, full and full of fruit on the nose. This will still improve. Fullish, plenty of depth and substance. Abundant and with very good grip. Even better than the Taille-Pieds? Fine plus. (06/95)

Now-2010   18.0

Volnay   Clos-de-la-Barre
Olivier Leflaive Frères

Good fresh colour. Just a little light on the nose. A medium-bodied, intense, quite classy wine on the attack, but the fruit is a little one-dimensional and the follow-through also doesn't add much. Good style though. Reasonable finish. Quite good plus. (06/95)

Now-2002   14.5

Volnay   Clos-de-la-Bousse-d'Or
Pousse d'Or

Good colour. Classy nose. On the palate fully evolved. Round, ripe, slightly spicy. An ample, ripe wine. Good depth. Nicely positive classy finish. Very good indeed. Several notes. (06/95)

Now-2005   17.0

Volnay   Clos-des-Chênes   Joseph Drouhin

Medium-full, mature colour. Good nose. Still has depth and vigour as well as richness and fruit. Elegant, medium to medium-full. Good intensity. Long. Very good indeed. Other bottles have been better. (11/95)

Now-2005   17.0

Volnay   Clos-des-Chênes   Michel Lafarge

Full colour. Rich ample nose. A lot of depth here. This is very ripe and very seductive. Yet at the same time very classy. Fullish, round, very well balanced. Super fruit. Very fresh. It is fatter than the De Montille examples. And richer than those of Pousse d'Or. Impressive quality as usual. Fine. Several notes. (06/95)

Now-2010   17.5

Volnay   Clos-des-Chênes   René Monnier

Medium colour. Quite some brown now. Ripe, slightly sweet, broad nose with a hint of ginger biscuits. This has got good structure and fat though it lacks a little of the usual Volnay finesse. Yet good intensity. Long. (10/93)

Now-2003   16.5

Volnay   Clos-des-Ducs
Marquis d'Angerville

Good medium colour. Firm, fragrant, very stylish nose. Rich and complex. Very lovely fruit. Very ripe, almost sweet. Delicate but fullish. Composed. Intense. Fine. Several notes. (06/95)

Now-2007   17.5

Volnay   Fremiets   Bouchard Père et Fils

Medium to medium-full colour. Mature. Quite an earthy wine. More Savigny than Volnay. Reasonable balance but it lacks fruit. Dull. (12/94)

Now-2000   14.0

Volnay   Santenots   Robert Ampeau

Good mature colour. Soft, elegant nose. Less austere than the 1988s, but a wine of impeccable style and balance. Medium to medium-full body. Still very very fresh. Very elegant. Very very long and silky. Only just ready. (07/95)

Now-2008   18.5

Volnay   Santenots   Yvon Clerget

Good colour. Pleasant fruit on the nose. But a little light. Better on the palate. Cool. Classy, rich, complex. Very Volnay. Very good indeed. Lovely finish. (06/95)

Now-2009   17.0

Volnay   Santenots   Matrot

Good colour. Nicely backward - without being tough - cool, stylish, very pure Pinot. A touch of built-in sulphur on the palate. But rich and fat. Ample and delicious all the same. Very good long finish. Very good. (06/95)

Now-2005   16.0

Volnay   Santenots-du-Milieu
Comtes Lafon

Good colour. Smells of roast beef. Quite tough. Very odd on the palate. The acidity is edgy and the fruit evolved. The second bottle was smoother but didn't have much class. (06/95)

Now-2000   15.0

Volnay   Taille-Pieds   Hubert de Montille

Splendid colour. Full and youthful. Ripe but cool and austere on nose and palate. Very classy. Very pure Pinot. This is concentrated and rich. Poised and beautiful. Lovely balance. Will last for years. Fine. (06/95)

Now-2008   17.5

Vosne-Romanée   René Engel

Fine colour. Rich, meaty, muscular nose. Not quite as exciting as the Rion on the palate. A little *fatigué*. But a good wine nevertheless. Plump and ripe. (06/95)

Now-2000   15.0

Vosne-Romanée   Camille Giroud

Good colour. Slightly tough and rustic on the nose. Plenty of wine on the palate in a slightly old-fashioned way. Full, tannic, very good grip. Needs food. Lots of vigour. Very ripe. Very good. (06/95)

Now-2005 plus   16.0

Vosne-Romanée   Mongeard-Mugneret

Quite a developed colour. Light to medium. Stems on the nose a little dry and smoky. Better on the palate. Good grip and fruit. No new oak. But it doesn't really excite. Slightly lumpy. Quite good. **(02/93)**

Drink up   14.0

Vosne-Romanée   Daniel Rion et Fils

Good colour. Nicely ripe and abundant nose. Fat, rich, ripe and ample on the palate. This is a very good example of a village wine. Stylish. Quite *à point*. Good. **(06/95)**

Now–2000   15.0

**Vosne-Romanée   Les Beaux-Monts
Daniel Rion et Fils**

Very good colour. Rich, ample, full, concentrated nose. A lot of style and depth here. Very complete – rather more so than Tardy's Chaumes – rich, fullish, very well balanced. Very classy. This is fine. **(06/95)**

Now–2005 plus   18.0

Vosne-Romanée   Les Brûlées   René Engel

Good full mature colour. Fat, plump, rich nose. Full body. Nicely concentrated, nicely austere. Lots of depth. Very good acidity. Considerably better than his village example. Lots of life. Fine. **(06/95)**

Now–2009   17.5

Vosne-Romanée   Les Brûlées   Henri Jayer

Fullish colour, fuller than the Cros-Parentoux. Very lovely concentrated, fat, intense nose. Very oaky of course. But very pure Pinot. Very rich. Is it too oaky? If so then it is a great pity. For there is plenty of wine here. And the fruit has real class. On evolution not a bit too oaky – but that was the next day. With food after the tasting the oak still seemed excessive. Was 18.5. Now only 17.5. **(06/95)**

Now–2012   17.5

Vosne-Romanée   Les Chaumes   Jean Tardy

Good colour. Stylish nose with the aspect of sweetness one finds in the Chaumes. A certain leanness too. On the palate this is medium to medium-full, balanced, ripe and stylish. I don't find it quite as seductive as his Boudots, but it is long, complex and very good plus. **(06/95)**

Now–2005   16.5

Vosne-Romanée   Clos-des-Réas   Jean Gros

Good colour. On the nose velvety-smooth, rich, subtly oaky. Very seductive. Good depth. Medium-full. Good acidity. This is most enjoyable. Very classy. Fine. **(06/95)**

Now–2005 plus   17.5

**Vosne-Romanée   Cros-Parentoux
Henri Jayer**

Fullish colour. Fatter, richer, more spicy than the Brûlées. But the oak is more dominant. Similar palate. Slightly more acidity. Juicier, less fat. Less spicy. But fabulous fruit. Yet I prefer the above. It is classier. But on evolution not too oaky but that was the next day. But with food after the tasting the oak still seemed excessive. **(06/95)**

Now–2012   17.0

**Vosne-Romanée   Les Petits-Monts
Mongeard-Mugneret**

Medium-full colour. Plump nose. But a little four-square. On the palate this is unbalanced and rather coarse. Sweet but artificially so. Medium body. Not very nice. **(06/95)**

Drink up   12.5

**Vosne-Romanée   Aux Reignots
Bouchard Père et Fils**

Good youthful colour. Rich and ample on the nose. This is very good indeed. Very good ripe, nicely balanced, plummy cassis fruit. Still a little reserved, still a little austere. But very good grip. Very ripe. Very elegant. Fine. **(02/95)**

Now–2009   17.5

1984

RATING FOR THE VINTAGE

Red: 13.0   **White:** 12.0

(past their best)

SIZE OF THE CROP

(Hectolitres, excluding generic wine)

	Red	White
Grands Crus	8,939	1,902
Village and *Premiers Crus*	123,492	31,815
Total	132,431	33,717

Nineteen eighty-four was said to be a small harvest. It was indeed smaller than 1983, let alone 1982, and was to turn out smaller than 1985 and 1986. Nevertheless the size was still 10 per cent above the ten-year running average, and double what this average was as little as fifteen years ago. 'Small' is relative these days.

Three things combined to warp the future of this misbegotten vintage. Firstly, despite the best endeavours of people such as I, the world *does* look at vintages in black and white terms: all 1984 bad, all 1985 good. Secondly it was not cheap enough, and thirdly it was followed by 1985 and the run of good to great vintages which has continued to this day.

WEATHER CONDITIONS

We begin, as always, with the climatic conditions in the vineyard. It was a late spring, delaying the flowering until early July. Progress was further retarded by July and August which were rather dry. This led to widespread *millerandage* (when the embryonic berries fail to develop), which, added to a certain amount of *coulure* (failure of the flower to set into fruit) had the effect of reducing the potential crop. As a balancing factor, however, the fact that the bunches were not entirely full did ensure a certain amount of protection against eventual rot in the bad weather that was to come, and the size of the harvest not being as prodigious as 1982 or as large as 1983 did at least mean that what fruit there was was able to take most benefit of the meagre amount of sun that was to follow.

For it was a depressing end to the season. Sunless and chilly, it rained for most of September and even when it wasn't raining it continued cold. Towards the end of the month the rain stopped, and then from 2 to 5 October it rained again. After the 7th it began to brighten up and the fruit was able to dry out. In retrospect the growers were lucky it continued cold. As one grower told me: if it had suddenly warmed up after all that rain in September the harvest would have been as rotten as 1965 or 1968. It was only the cool weather which reduced the humidity and kept the fruit healthy.

In the Côte d'Or the harvest had generally begun by 1 October. Some growers persisted during the downpours which followed (and probably made an 8 degree *rosé*). Others stopped. By 15 October they were able to pick fruit which would make a respectable wine. Those who allowed a certain amount of the most dilute free-run juice to be tapped off before fermenting the remainder - at the time a new process known as *saignée* (literally 'bleeding') - made more concentrated wine as a result.

The Style of the Wine

White Wines

The whites had reasonable structure – more so than the 1987s would have – but less fruit and more, lean acidity. Some growers – Lafon, Roulot in Meursault, for example – managed to make wine with a bit more richness and ripeness than others, and these were still alive and kicking in 1994 when I made a ten-years-on tasting. The rest are best forgotten. One fine wine is the Domaine de la Romanée-Conti's Montrachet. Yet another example of the classic Burgundian equation: fine *terroir* plus fine domaine equals good wine (at the very least), however hopeless the climatic conditions – provided there is no rot, that is.

Red Wines

One's first sight of the vintage was on the weekend of the Hospices de Beaune. Indisputably poor at the Hospices tasting itself, mixed at the Hôtel de Ville – as far as one could judge in the crush and the cigarette smoke (the average Burgundian can taste wine without having to remove his *Gauloise* from his mouth) – and *sérieux* at the Salle des Jeunes Professionnels, exhibiting for the first time.

Overall the Côte-de-Nuits seemed better than the Côte-de-Beaune, except in areas when the rot had seriously taken hold, for more growers to the north had waited until mid-October before commencing their harvest. Quality was very variable.

Lean they might have been, but at least they were healthy, and, Burgundy not being a wine of great structure, at least without the great shaft of green tannin which marred the 1984 Bordeaux.

After a few years the 1984s began to soften up. The good acidity preserved the fruit, and, in the best *climats* and from the top growers, wines of elegance, even, in a few cases, of generosity, began to emerge.

Today many need drinking soon, but a surprising number are still holding up well and will keep four or five years more. And there are many commendable wines.

Tasting Notes

Blanc

Bâtard-Montrachet   Leflaive
Fresh colour. A little lean on the nose but undeniably stylish. A bit light and one-dimensional on the palate. Gentle. Good oak integration as usual. Not a bit heavy. Very good. **(03/93)**
Drink soon   16.0

**Chassagne-Montrachet   Morgeots
Louis Jadot**
Fullish, firm, vigorous nose. Oaky, rich and with good depth on the palate. This has substance and grip. And good style, though it is beginning to lose its style now. **(06/94)**
Drink up   15.0

Corton   Chandon-de-Briailles
A bit dry and neutral on the nose. Rather four-square, unusually sweet (in parts), but coarse and petrolly on the palate. Unexciting. **(06/94)**
Past its best   10.0

Corton-Charlemagne   Dubreuil-Fontaine
Rather coarse and old on the nose. Reasonable fruit but a bit of built-in sulphur on the palate. Fresh but a little astringent. **(06/94)**
Drink up   13.5

Meursault   Leroy
Slightly hard lean nose. Not entirely clean. Drying up now. Sharp harsh finish. **(07/92)**
Past its best   12.0

Meursault   Charmes   Matrot
Evolved nose. A touch of oxidisation, a touch lactic even. Yet rich. On the palate it has lightened up and dried off. A bit astringent even. Has seen better days. **(06/94)**
Past its best   10.0

Meursault   Désirée   Comtes Lafon
Good vigour. A touch of oak. Rich, fat nose. This has plenty of fruit and is round and attractive. Surprisingly good. Still has life. Very good. **(06/94)**
Drink soon   16.0

Meursault   Perrières
Robert Ampeau et Fils
Slightly chaptalised on the nose. But quite classy. Fruity and ample. Crisp and well made. No leanness. This is surprisingly good. Has depth and complexity. **(01/94)**
Drink soon   16.0

Meursault   Perrières   Louis Jadot
Quite firm and oaky and rich on the nose. Yet, of course, not a lot of fruit. On the palate this is getting a little old now. A lack of zip. And the finish is weak. Not bad though. **(06/94)**
Drink up   13.0

Meursault   Perrières   Guy Roulot
Some age on the nose. But not without substance and depth. On the palate it is soft, but it is plump and elegant. Discreet. Well made. Good length. Very good. **(06/94)**
Drink soon   16.0

Montrachet   Romanée-Conti
Very good, gently rich and gently oaky nose. Concentrated. Substantial. Vigorous. This is a lovely wine and an excellent example. Plenty of dimension and follow-through. Plenty of vigour. Cool, classy, flowery, gently ripe and honeyed. Fine plus. **(06/94)**
Now-2000   18.0

Morey-Saint-Denis   Bruno Clair
Good crisp nose, fruity and nutty. Less good on the palate. A little weak and neutral. But not a bit too aged. Just rather one-dimensional. **(06/94)**
Drink soon   12.5

Puligny-Montrachet   Jean-Marc Boillot
The nose is plump, though it is getting a bit aged. On the palate the same thing is evident. Not bad. But it was better five years ago. **(06/94)**
Past its best   12.5

Puligny-Montrachet   Les Pucelles   Leflaive
I find this more elegant than the 1987 and with more vigour too, though a little less fat. Good depth. Nice fruit. Good style. **(12/94)**
Drink soon   15.0

ROUGE

Beaune   Boucherottes   Louis Jadot
Good fresh colour. Round nose. A touch of spice. Still fresh. Not exactly elegant but round and with plenty of interest. On the palate losing a bit of its vigour and substance. But not bad. The acidity beginning to come through on the finish. Drink soon. **(06/94)**
Drink soon   13.0

Beaune   Bressandes   Henri Germain
Surprisingly good colour. Fresh nose. Not fruitless, though inevitably a little one-dimensional. But very much better than expected. On the palate the same. Surprisingly agreeable. Some weight, even quite plump and rich. Fresh, attractive, finishing positively. Very good indeed for a 1984. **(02/94)**
Drink soon   16.0

Beaune   Grèves   Michel Lafarge
Light medium colour. Mature. Fully mature nose. Quite evolved even. Spicy, quite ripe, but now needing drinking. There is interest here, but not for long. A little dry at the end. Quite good. **(06/94)**
Drink soon   14.0

Beaune   Marconnets   Château de Beaune
Medium colour. Old tea and faded fruitless nose on the nose. Mean on the palate. Little pleasure here. **(09/90)**
Past its best   11.0

Bonnes-Mares   Georges Roumier
Medium colour. A touch vegetal on the nose. A little dilute on the palate. This has style but lacks the depth and concentration for a *grand cru*. Getting a bit astringent at the end. Quite good. **(06/94)**
Drink soon   14.0

Chambertin   Denis Mortet
Good colour. Rich concentrated nose. On the palate plump but getting a little too soft and dilute. Yet not astringent. Certainly classy. Certainly good plus. Lacks dimension though. **(06/94)**
Drink soon   15.5

Chambertin   Armand Rousseau
Good colour. Full, plump, rich. Vigorous and substantial. Fullish on the palate. A little rigid compared with the Gros Richebourg. But fine and complex and classy nevertheless. Plenty of life. Best with food. **(06/94)**
Now-1999   18.5

Chambolle-Musigny   Champy
Very good colour. Fat nose. Warm. A little souped-up perhaps. A meaty example on the palate. Some oak. Even rich. Though a bit astringent at the end. Slightly solid. Not exactly pure 1984 Pinot. But a good commercial example. **(06/94)**
Now-1999   14.0

Chambolle-Musigny   Jean Tardy
Reasonable colour. Spicy nose. A touch of caramel. Soft, getting a little astringent. But plump and agreeable. A good result for a village

wine. But a little one-dimensional. **(06/94)**

Drink soon 14.0

Chambolle-Musigny   Les Amoureuses
Jacques-Frédéric Mugnier

Light to medium colour. Fully evolved. The nose is light and elegant but now lightening up. Soft and light but getting rather astringent on the palate. Yet the finish is fat and not too short or dry. Finesse here. Quite good plus. **(06/94)**

Drink soon 14.5

Charmes-Chambertin
Philippe Charlopin-Parizot

Good colour. A bit of reduction at first on the nose. Yet cleaner later. But on the palate a little dried out now. Has seen better days. **(06/94)**

Past its best 12.5

Clos-de-la-Roche   Dujac

Evolved colour. Rather watery nose and palate. Sweet, pleasant. Not astringent. But short. Not much here. Disappointing. **(06/94)**

Drink soon 13.0

Clos-de-la-Roche   Hubert Lignier

Good colour. Fresh and fruity. This is surprisingly good. Not a bit hard or lean. A shade one-dimensional, the acidity shows a bit but the class is there also. **(09/91)**

Drink soon 16.0

Clos-de-Vougeot   Champy

Good colour. Very vigorous looking. Toffee on the nose. A bit dry, thin and dried out on the palate. Short but not acid. Souped up a bit. Rather neutral. **(06/94)**

Drink soon 12.5

Clos-de-Vougeot   Jean Gros

Very good colour. No undue age. Stylish, but a touch lean on the nose. Yet there is no lack of fruit here. Not as full as the 1981 Gros Richebourg but ripe and balanced, cool and very elegant and subtle. Medium body. Gentle, balanced, fruity and even abundant. Great style and length and complexity. Long and lovely. Excellent for the vintage. **(05/92)**

Now-2000 18.5

Clos-de-Vougeot   Denis Mortet

Good colour. A bit of a reduction on the nose. Rather astringent on the palate. This is a little dilute. It is not too bad, not mean at the end. But a bit short. Dull. **(06/94)**

Drink soon 13.5

Corton   Bressandes   Tollot-Beaut

Medium colour. Mature. Quite an evolved nose. Slightly weak and stringy, but with a residual oaky, slightly sweet base. Attractive but not serious. Now getting a little astringent. Yet has elegance and good positive finish. Good. **(06/94)**

Drink soon 15.0

Corton   Clos-du-Roi   Dubreuil-Fontaine

Reasonable colour. A bit chunky on the nose. Not a lot of style. Rather dried out and fruitless on the palate. And a bit artisanal too. Not bad. **(06/94)**

Drink up 13.0

Corton   Pougets   Louis Jadot

Good colour. Ripe, positive, plummy nose. This has good dimension. On the palate it is rich and substantial. Gently oaky. Fresh and plump. There is a sort of masculine austerity behind it. But no lack of depth. Good with food. Very good plus. **(06/94)**

Now-2000 plus 16.5

Echézeaux   Jean Grivot

Very good colour. Fine nose. This has depth, class and vigour. Even real concentration. Not a bit of an off-vintage aspect here. Full, concentrated, ripe and substantial on the palate. This has a lot of depth and vigour. Fine plus. **(06/94)**

Now-2000 plus 18.0

Gevrey-Chambertin
Philippe Charlopin-Parizot

Reasonable colour. Slightly meaty but a little artisanal on the nose. And showing a bit of age. Quite astringent on the palate. Some fruit. Not bad. **(06/94)**

Drink up 13.0

Gevrey-Chambertin   Denis Mortet

Fully mature colour. Fully evolved nose too. Soft, quite plump and fruit but not a lot of elegance. Better on the palate. Attractive and not too old. A plump wine. Medium weight and depth. Quite good. **(06/94)**

Drink soon 14.0

Gevrey-Chambertin   *Vieilles-Vignes*
Bernard Dugat-Py

Good colour. Still vigorous. Certainly old-viney on the nose. Depth and concentration here and a nice spicy/oaky background. Fullish, plump attack. The acidity shows a little on the follow-through but this has dimension and style. Very good. **(06/94)**

Drink soon 16.0

Gevrey-Chambertin   Champeaux
Denis Mortet

Reasonable colour and freshness on the nose. But not a lot of style. On the palate it is beginning to get a bit astringent. The astringency is showing. And it lacks grace. **(06/94)**

Drink soon 13.0

Gevrey-Chambertin   Clos-Saint-Jacques   Armand Rousseau

Magnum. Good colour. Lots of vigour on the nose. Plump, ripe and concentrated. Very good style too. Plenty of life left here. And a lot of depth. Good oaky base. Medium-full. Rich and very attractive. This is lovely. **(06/94)**

Now-2000   **17.5**

Grands-Echézeaux   Joseph Drouhin

Good mature colour. Ripe nose. Attractive fruit. Round and fruity on the palate with good ripe acidity. Not a bit lean. Good style. Good substance. Surprisingly attractive. Long. Very elegant. Fine plus. **(06/94)**

Now-2000   **18.0**

Grands-Echézeaux   Romanée-Conti

Brown colour. Rather austere and stemmy on the nose. Rather fruitless on the palate. A little dilute. But nevertheless the wine is not astringent. And is fruity at the end. Good, it has to be said. **(06/94)**

Now-2000   **15.5**

Griotte-Chambertin   Joseph Drouhin

Fresh mature colour. Medium weight - indeed surprisingly full and vigorous for a 1984. The nose is a little dry but the palate plump and complex, intense enough. Very fresh. Not very fat, full or concentrated, but very well balanced. Got more ample as it developed. Complex, classy and not a bit off-vintage. Fine plus for 1984. Will still hold up very well. Similar note 06/94. **(11/93)**

Now-2000   **18.0**

Monthélie   Paul Garaudet

Light medium colour. Mature. Soft nose. A little rustic, but fresh and quite round. Not without depth and substance. This is a very pleasant glass of wine. Stylish and fruity enough. Good length. Shows well. **(06/94)**

Drink soon   **14.0**

Morey-Saint-Denis   Bruno Clair

Really quite brown on the colour. And a bit faded on the nose. Rather dried out on the palate. Was quite respectable once. Not rustic. But has seen better days. **(06/94)**

Drink up   **13.0**

Le Musigny   Jacques-Frédéric Mugnier

Medium colour. Not too old. Soft nose. Gentle - even too much so, some might say - yet though a light wine one with very lovely style and intensity, and no lack of fruit, nor any astringency. Long. Complex. Really elegant. Very fine indeed. **(06/94)**

Now-2000   **18.5**

Nuits-Saint-Georges   Daniel Rion et Fils

Reasonable colour. But a bit of the stems on the nose. Yet quite vigorous. Some acidity and a bit of astringency on the palate. Dry at the end. Not bad. **(06/94)**

Drink up   **13.0**

Nuits-Saint-Georges   Les Argillières   Daniel Rion et Fils

Good colour. Ripe and plump on the nose. Good depth and vigour. Some oak. It lacks a little concentration and fat on the follow-through but it has got style and vigour. **(06/94)**

Now-2000   **15.0**

Nuits-Saint-Georges   Les Saint-Georges   Henri Gouges

Light to medium colour. Fully mature. Light nose. Fully evolved, even getting a little dilute. On the palate rather light and some astringency. A little weak and simple but not without elegance. Yet not that exciting. **(06/94)**

Drink up   **14.0**

Pommard   Jarollières   Pousse d'Or

Good colour. Plump, ripe but spicy funky nose. This is better than the Bousse d'Or. There is good freshness and an underlying oak on the palate and the wine is consistent from start to finish. Nicely plump and rich (for a 1984) on the finish. Very good plus. **(06/94)**

Now-2000   **16.5**

Pommard   Pézerolles   Hubert de Montille

Very good colour. Rich nose. Good depth. But it is more evolved than the Taille-Pieds and has less interest. On the palate, it lacks a little fruit and has a bit of astringency, by comparison with the Volnay. But the wine has substance and the finish is positive. Good plus. **(06/94)**

Now-2000   **15.5**

Richebourg   Jean Gros

Good colour. Very fine rich plump nose. This is excellent. Concentrated, plump, fruity and even rich. Good oak. Lots of depth here. Above all vigorous. Lovely. Bags of life. **(06/94)**

Now-2000 plus   **19.0**

Ruchottes-Chambertin   Clos-des-Ruchottes   Armand Rousseau

Medium to medium-full colour. Mature. This has a certain acidity and austerity, but has reasonable class. But *au fond* what it lacks is real fruit. One-dimensional but not too much of a taste of old tea. Very good for the vintage. **(01/92)**

Drink soon   **16.0**

**Savigny-lès-Beaune Dominodes
Bruno Clair**

Good colour. Still very fresh. Very good nose. Rich, gently oaky, really quite a lot of concentration and fat, especially for a 1984. Fullish, ripe, slightly solid. A touch dense at the end with the acidity showing and a bit of astringency. Better with food. Quite good plus. **(06/94)**

Now-2000   **14.5**

**Savigny-lès-Beaune Vergelesses
Simon Bize et Fils**

Light to medium colour. Mature. Just a little dry on the nose. But round and fruity underneath. More substance on the palate. Elegant and even rich. Balanced and positive. Long. Good. But a bit dry at the end. Now 1998. **(06/94)**

Drink soon   **14.5**

Volnay Les Angles Lucien Boillot

Light to medium colour. The nose has softened and diluted, but it hasn't dried out or coarsened up. This is a bit dilute on the palate though, and never had much fruit or interest. Unexciting. **(06/94)**

Drink soon   **12.5**

**Volnay Clos-de-la-Bousse-d'Or
Pousse d'Or**

Good colour. Fine fresh plump nose. A touch of astringency on the palate but good stylish fruit nevertheless and no lack of weight. A wine for food. Ripe, balanced. Really very good. **(06/94)**

Drink soon   **15.5**

Volnay Clos-des-Chênes Michel Lafarge

Good. Good weight on the nose, if a little pinched. Medium to medium-full. Some fruit. But a little tough, a little astringent. Yet underneath quite vigorous and positive. Quite good plus. **(06/94)**

Now-2000   **14.5**

Volnay Santenots Matrot

Light to medium colour. This is fully evolved and beginning to crack up. A bit funky, a bit astringent, though quite sizeable. A plumpish wine but now a bit past its best. Good once. **(06/94)**

Drink up   **13.0**

**Volnay Santenots-du-Milieu
Comtes Lafon**

Medium colour. Not too developed. Good plump nose. No weakness here. Fullish, ripe. Good substance and plenty of fruit. This is very good. It has a fine silky finish and could even be said to be generous. **(06/94)**

Now-2000   **16.0**

Volnay Taille-Pieds Hubert de Montille

Very good colour. Lovely stylish, ripe nose. Real depth and elegance here. Even concentration. A rich wine for a 1984 with a lot of dimension. Fullish. Generous. Fat. Gently oaky. Very long. A lovely example. Bags of life still. **(06/94)**

Now-2000 plus   **17.0**

Vosne-Romanée Daniel Rion et Fils

A plumper example than his village Nuits. Riper, richer and more vigorous. A touch lean. But positive and vigorous. Good. **(06/94)**

Drink soon   **15.0**

**Vosne-Romanée Les Beaumonts
Daniel Rion et Fils**

Good colour. Quite a meaty, fat nose for a 1984. Fullish on the palate. Quite rich. Not too lean at all. This even has complexity. Good style. Good length. Good plus. **(06/94)**

Now-2000   **15.5**

Vosne-Romanée Clos-des-Réas Jean Gros

Quite an evolved colour. Plump but now evolved nose. A little old perhaps, getting mushroomy. Better on the palate. Fresher, and more stylish than on the nose. Good plump fruit. Style here. But drink up. **(06/94)**

Drink up   **15.0**

1983

Red: 17.0-12.0 **White:** (13.5)
(variable) (past their best)

SIZE OF THE CROP

(Hectolitres, excluding generic wine)

	Red	White
Grands Crus	11,955	3,038
Village and Premiers Crus	143,435	36,527
Total	155,390	39,565

At nearly 200,000 hectolitres overall, the biggest vintage (apart from the previous one) since 1979 and 1973, 1983 was regarded as a plentiful crop at the time. Today 1991, 16 per cent more plentiful, is regarded as a short crop.

Since the outset, opinions have been divided about the 1983 vintage. 'Garbage,' said an American magazine about the Domaine de la Romanée-Conti 1983s. These and other wines certainly were atypical. The tannins were solid and rather dry; and the wines, once the puppy-fat had disappeared, were unwieldy in their youth. Burgundy, we used to tell ourselves, is not the full-bodied, warm-hearted wine the old books told us about. It is a wine of fragrance and delicacy, intensity but not muscle. And just as we were getting the message across, along came the 1983s to refute us. Many who wrote about the 1983s were confused. Some lambasted the whole vintage because they found a few big-name wines in Gevrey-Chambertin with rot, and others of equal standing in Vosne-Romanée demonstrating a taint of hail, and overall they couldn't understand the atypical volumes of dry tannin. Then the 1985s came along and everybody jumped overboard in pursuit of its bubbly, charming fruit: a no-problem vintage we could all enjoy relatively young. And so we could forget about the 1983s.

And I began to feel like an Old Testament prophet. But I have stuck to my guns. The best 1983s, I have always felt, would exceed - in concentration, in intensity and in complexity, not to mention, in the long-term, in finesse - the best of the 1985s. I waited until the vintage was ten years old, and I have since sampled and re-sampled a wide range. It is now clear that there *are* some great wines in this vintage. The rotten and the hail-tainted should not prevent us from acknowledging this fact. But they are not typical Burgundies.

WEATHER CONDITIONS

The start was not auspicious. The early spring was late, very cold and particularly wet. Budding was normal but humidity was high and there were fears that rot might develop prematurely in the vineyards. However, the end of May saw a marked improvement. June brought the sun and dry weather and the flowering took place in the middle of the month in excellent conditions. It looked as if it was going to be a good-sized crop and, numbering the usual 100 days between the onset of the flowering and the date of picking, a harvest which would not be too late.

The weather continued fine except for a particularly bad hail-storm in Vosne, Vougeot and Chambolle in July (of which more later) right up until the end of August. It was particularly hot and dry and, as will be seen, this was the salvation, or at least one of them, of the 1983 harvest.

September, however, brought rain. Not just a little much-needed moisture but almost continual downpours for two whole weeks. The growers began to fear for the worst. Luckily, just in time, the rain stopped. Because of the heat during July and August, the grapes had built up very thick skins and did not seem to be too affected by the early September inundation. Moreover, with the fine weather came great heat. The fortnight prior to the start of the harvest (25 September) saw temperatures in the upper 20s Celsius. The fruit was therefore able to become super-ripe and super-concentrated with extract, sugar and acidity levels all increasing as the water evaporated in the grapes.

This is the secret of both the success and the atypicality of the 1983 vintage. The grapes were very concentrated, with very thick skins, but, like the 1975 Bordeaux, some of the 'fat' of the tannins - not being a scientist I speak unscientifically - had been washed away by the rains of the first two weeks of September. Thereafter the hot weather concentrated everything. But it left a tannic structure Burgundy had not seen since the early 1950s, with the exception of 1976. In some of the wines the tannins were too dominant full stop. In others too dominant for many tastes. In many of the best wines though, the fruit is so rich that the tannins, though obvious, do not present a problem, especially if the wines, as they should be, are consumed with food.

So the 1983 fruit was super-ripe and super-concentrated. As one grower pointed out: in 1983 the grapes ripened in 90 days and not 100. Most people picked after 100 days so the fruit had an element of *sur-maturité* not seen in Burgundy for more than twenty years. Who would need to chaptalise the 1983s?

Yet there were problems. Not all the 1983s are quite as marvellous as the above might indicate. The first problem was that of the hail. Hail is particularly tragic. It is isolated, attacking one vineyard or village but not the next. As a result, it is more capricious, the action of mean and spiteful gods. A good *vigneron* may suffer, his neighbour, a rogue, may be spared. A year's hard toil in the vineyards may be rendered totally in vain within a matter of minutes.

As I have said, the communes most affected by hail were Vosne-Romanée, Vougeot and Chambolle-Musigny, though in the latter much more in the southern end (Le Musigny) than in the northern (Bonnes-Mares). It is a tribute to the art of wine-making now prevalent in Burgundy that so few wines seem to be seriously affected and at many estates such as at the Domaine de la Romanée-Conti, whose vineyards were in the heart of the storm, the top wines show no trace whatsoever of any taint.

Rot was another problem. It will be remembered that the first half of September had brought two weeks of almost continual rain. Despite the hot dry weather afterwards, some damage was inevitably done to the quality of the fruit. Some grapes, those perhaps already slightly damaged, served as incubators for rot and this would spread quickly to neighbouring berries. *Triage*, the picking out and removal of anything not up to standard, was absolutely vital. As one grower said to me: '*Il a fallu trier, trier et encore trier*,' to produce a healthy vat of grapes. As another pointed out, some grapes were only minutely affected at the point where the stalk finds its entrance to the grape and this was missed by some. The result: wine with a taste of *moisi* - rot.

THE STYLE OF THE WINE

WHITE WINES

The whites were clumsy, big, beefy and alcoholic. Some with genuine *pourriture noble* - Dominique Lafon made a 'Meursaulternes' as these were dubbed - were fine with something larger than life such as a shrimp curry or *bouillabaisse* with plenty of *rouille* when young, but the older they became the less attractive they were. And elegance was an attribute they could never aspire to. There is little pleasure to be had from them today.

RED WINES

When I first tasted the 1983 red Burgundies from cask, originally in the spring of 1984 and again in March 1985, I formed the impression that despite certain problems - rot here, hail damage there and hard tannins overall - the vintage was a very worthy one. The yield was not of high quantity but it was at least satisfactory, not disastrously short. The wines were irregular, but the best were not only full, firm, tannic and rich; they had a concentration of ripe fruit which I found exciting. They had depth, character, complexity and length. Above all, they were real *vins de garde*.

In travelling up and down the Côte d'Or and tasting the wines in the growers' cellars, particularly in early 1985 when the malos had completely finished and the wines had already been racked a couple of times, I found some wines - or, more exactly, some casks of some wines - which had taints which were clearly unacceptable. Commenting on these met with no hostile response. 'We'll see how they progress,' said some. 'We think these will disappear,' said others. And one was given the impression that anything untoward, anything not up to standard, would be eliminated, not bottled under the domaine label or at least not under the name of an illustrious *cru*. Moreover, the vast majority of the samples I was given to taste had no problems to offer. Such wines as were marred by undue *goût de grêle* or were definitely rotten formed only a tiny minority.

Since then I have participated in a number of tastings of the 1983s in bottle, some of which were subsequently written up in *The Vine*. On each occasion I have noticed wines which had an aspect of hail taint but as time has gone on I have become less and less worried about this. Luckily, as I explained earlier, the hail-storm in Vosne-Romanée and the surrounding vineyards took place in July before the *véraison*. The more I have seen of these wines, the more I have been convinced that, in the majority of cases, any taste of hail damage that there might have been originally would eventually be submerged and would disappear. Luckily the 1983 vintage has had the power and concentration to last. And today we can see that the hail, though still a problem in some cases, is not as much of a defect as we thought at first.

Once a wine is rotten, however, it is always rotten. There is little you can do about it except dilute that *cuvée* with another which is healthy and hope no-one will notice. The rot affects the core of the wine, the taste and quantity of the fruit. What now seems apparent to me is that some growers who had both untainted and tainted *cuvées* - and who only offered the former for tasting - have *not* eliminated the bad. In some cases, I have seen both healthy and unacceptable bottles of what purports to be the same wine, indicating that bottling of different casks, both good and bad, took place separately. In others, whilst what I was given to taste in cask was delicious, what I have seen subsequently in bottle has been less exciting.

So the vintage is irregular. At the Domaine de la Romanée-Conti, while I have nothing but the greatest enthusiasm for the Romanée-Conti itself and La Tâche, I have problems with a hail taste in the lesser wines. Some bottles on some occasions have been acceptable, others in other circumstances not. It depends on the richness and vigour of the bottles. It depends whether you drink them with food or sample them in more ascetic conditions.

Those of Charles Rousseau are also variable - and not for a reason of hail: this time because of rot. Not the three top wines, the Chambertin, the Clos-de-Bèze and the Clos-Saint-Jacques, but the rest. Again the bottles are irregular. The Clos-de-la-Roche is an example. My question to both domaines is, was there a complete *égalisage* before bottling? And if not, why not?

Elsewhere there is a difference between bottles and magnums. And between notes on samples direct from the grower's cellar and those from sources in Britain and the USA. Is this solely due to bottle-size and storage conditions?

In case all the above sounds unduly discouraging, let me reiterate that there is much to enjoy and a lot to get really enthusiastic about in the 1983 vintage, as the following notes will show.

BLANC

Auxey-Duresses   Leroy

Alcoholic, blowsy. Very 1983. Lacks grip. Some SO$_2$. Unexciting. **(07/92)**

Drink soon   12.5

**Bienvenues-Bâtard-Montrachet
Henri Clerc**

This is a very good 1983. Fullish colour. The nose shows the alcohol, but it is ripe, fullish and rich - even nutty - on the palate, with a touch of spice. Certainly fat and opulent. Very good plus. **(06/93)**

Drink soon   16.5

Chevalier-Montrachet   Leflaive

This is a typically rich 1983. Slightly hot but aromatic and honeyed. Slight smokiness of alcohol. Rich, oaky, fat, ripe and balanced. A lot of depth and length. Lovely long ripe fruity finish. Not a bit smoky or coarse. Fine. Several notes on this but none recently on the domaine's Bâtard. **(06/93)**

Now–2000 plus   17.5

Corton-Charlemagne   Joseph Drouhin

Quite a deep colour. Aromatic, rich coffee/butterscotch flavoured nose. A little alcohol, just a little heavy. A full, rich wine with a suspicion of sweetness and a slight oiliness. Good acidity but lacks a bit of elegance. **(06/93)**

Drink soon   14.0

Corton-Charlemagne   Dubreuil-Fontaine

Fresh, camomile and citronella, good depth on the nose. This has weight and is very clean and stylish. Classy and complex on the palate. Honeyed, without a trace of blowsiness. Fine quality. Plenty of life. Lovely finish. **(06/93)**

Now–2000 plus   17.5

Fixin   La Croix-Blanche   Bruno Clair

Fuller nose, aromatic, more animal. Medium-full. Ripe, fresh. Good backbone. This has good depth and concentration. Slightly hard but not blowsy. Finishes very positively. **(06/93)**

Now–2000   14.5

Meursault   Leroy

Rich nose. Good balance and succulence for a 1983. Fat and ripe attack but lacks a bit of grip on the finish. Not bad. **(07/92)**

Drink soon   13.5

Meursault   Joseph Matrot

Ripe, rich, mellow but quite fresh on the nose. Good fruit and good grip on the palate. This

shows well. Plenty of life ahead of it. Good plus. **(06/93)**

Drink soon   15.5

Meursault   Charmes   Comtes Lafon

Just a little deeper in colour than the 1985. Very ripe, almost raisiny nose. There is a touch of botrytis here, even a hint of petrol on the nose. Rather more grapey, but not exactly sweet. Almost a hint of sherry, both on the nose and on the palate. It was four years in barrel. An illusion of sweetness. Slightly rigid. Very curious. Very individual. Full. Plenty of fruit. A wine for food. An abnormal flavour. Quite alcoholic. **(08/91)**

Drink soon   (see note)

Meursault   Charmes   Joseph Matrot

Aromatic nose. Good depth. This has excellent concentrated fruit and no trace of blowsiness. Rich and still youthful on the palate. Plenty of character and even finesse here. Long. Full of fruit. Complex. Very good plus. **(06/93)**

Now–2000   16.5

**Meursault   Clos-de-la-Barre
Comtes Lafon**

Domaine bottled. Extraordinary nose. More Rhône than Burgundy with a touch of botrytis. Quite alcoholic. Rich, fat, but balanced. Exotically fruity - mango and pineapple. Abnormal. Yet not a bit too heavy on the palate or without interest. **(03/92)**

Drink soon   17.0

**Meursault   Clos-des-Perrières
Albert Grivault**

Has the aggressive dry, slight botrytis, high alcohol smell of the vintage. Full and rich and fat. But not very elegant. Rather aggressive. Better with food. Slightly bitter at the end. **(10/95)**

Drink soon   14.0

Meursault   Les Cras   Joseph Voillot

This is extremely fresh, without a bit of *surmaturité* or clumsiness. Fullish, with the slightly four-square element of the wine grown on red-wine soil. But a very good example. Still good for several years. Interesting. **(06/94)**

Drink soon   16.0

Meursault   Désirée   Comtes Lafon

Broad nose. Fat and spicy. Good acidity though. On the palate it is fresher. Quite complex. Good depth. Will still keep well. Long and really quite stylish. Very good. **(06/93)**

Now–2000   16.0

Meursault   Les Luchets   Guy Roulot

Light golden colour. Nutty, suggestions of sweetness. A little like a dry Sauternes on the nose but much fresher on the palate. Ripe, honeyed in the best sense. Good acidity. Ample and spicy but still very crisp and vigorous. Medium-full. Lots of interest, even elegance. Plenty of life ahead of it. Very good. **(07/94)**

Now-2000   16.0

Meursault   Perrières   Jean-Philippe Fichet

Good colour. This is ripe and stylish, without any of the usual diffuse, slightly *pourriture* astringent taste of some 1983s. Not heavy either. Balanced. Fresh. Plump and fruity. A fine example. Could have said it was a 1985. Long, succulent. **(02/95)**

Now-2000   17.0

Le Montrachet   Joseph Drouhin

Rich nose. A lot of depth and concentration. Quite well matured. Lovely on the palate. Full, very concentrated. Very good acidity. Marvellous fruit. This is splendid. Not a bit blowsy. Very long and complex. Very fine indeed. **(06/93)**

Now-2005   18.5

Le Montrachet   Romanée-Conti

Matured nose. A little more alcohol than the Laguiche. Ripe but aromatic. A full, rich wine, but it doesn't have quite the style or the grace and complexity of the Laguiche. Good grip. Quite powerful. Fine. **(06/93)**

Now-2005   17.5

Puligny-Montrachet   Jean-Marc Boillot

Ripe and fruity and with good - or at least reasonable - vigour. If not a lot of grace or complexity, it has plumpness and no lack of length. Very good. **(06/93)**

Drink soon   16.0

Puligny-Montrachet   Labouré-Roi

Mature colour. Quite a spicy, honeyed, evolved nose. Slightly heavy, slightly evolved palate. Never a great deal of class. And on top the slightly alcoholic character of 1983. Clumsy. **(10/94)**

Drink soon   13.0

ROUGE

Beaune   Boucherottes   Louis Jadot

Good colour. Fresh, plump, fruity nose. This is a very good example. Rich, plump and not a bit dry. Fullish, ample and long. Complex and succulent and with plenty of life ahead of it. Long, complex and stylish at the end. Very good plus. **(06/93)**

Now-2000   16.5

Beaune   Clos-des-Ursules   Louis Jadot

Good colour. Fully matured. Gamey, pruney old Burgundy on the nose. But fat and fruity and still vigorous. Medium-full. Good grip. Not astringent. A meaty wine with plenty of depth. Finishes well. Will last. Very good. **(06/93)**

Drink soon   16.0

Beaune   Cuvée Maurice Drouhin
Hospices de Beaune, Joseph Drouhin

Very good colour. No undue brown. This is a fine example of a Côte-de-Beaune 1983. Rich, spicy nose and palate. Medium-full, concentrated, ripe, balanced. Lovely naturally sweet. Long. Fine. **(03/94)**

Now-2000 plus   17.5

Beaune   Grèves   Camille Giroud

Very good colour. Animal, rich, fat nose. Full, tannic, chunky. Good acidity but a bit rigid. Fresh and vigorous but a bit four-square. Yet may still mellow with time. Good. **(06/93)**

Drink soon   15.0

Beaune   Grèves   Michel Lafarge

Very good colour. Lovely rich, concentrated, ample nose. Not a bit 1983-y. Full, ripe, complex, elegant and lovely on the palate. Naturally sweet. Very concentrated, very subtle. A lovely wine. Marvellous finish. **(06/93)**

Now-2000   17.0

Beaune   Grèves   Tollot-Beaut

Medium-full, mature colour. Round but meaty on the nose. Good robust and slightly *rôti* Pinot fruit. Quite fresh and vigorous though. Fullish, fat and attractive, though without a lot of elegance. Good plump gamey attack. Not quite so much dimension on the finish though. There is a hint of astringency. Yet still quite vigorous. Good plus. **(06/93)**

Drink soon   15.5

Beaune   Teurons   Bouchard Père et Fils

Medium-full colour. A little brown. Quite a roasted nose. The rather dry and hard tannins still out. Rather better on the palate. This is still a bit solid and raw but the finish shows good fruit and richness with a touch of *crème brûlée*. **(09/90)**

Now-2000   14.0

Blagny   La Pièce-sous-le-Bois   Matrot

Fine colour. Rich aromatic, slightly gamey nose. Sweet and succulent. Medium to medium-full, still very fresh and vigorous. Allspice flavours. Not a touch of astringency. Good grip. Slightly over-ripe. Long, vigorous, ample. Just the wine for a Boeuf Bourguignon. Very good. **(11/95)**

Now-2003   16.0

Bonnes-Mares   Clair-Daü

Good colour. Round, ripe, rich concentrated nose. No suggestion of dry tannins. Quite full on the palate. Ample lush Chambolle style. Complex, subtle. Getting soft now. Very fine. **(06/93)**

Now–2000   18.0

Bonnes-Mares   Georges Roumier

Magnum. Full colour. Rich and fat and concentrated on the nose. Not a vestige of taint. Full chunky, fat and quite solid on the palate. This has a lot of vigour and depth. Structured but very fine. Very good acidity. Several notes. **(06/93)**

Now–2005 plus   18.5

Chambertin   Joseph Drouhin

Full. Excellent nose. Old-viney. Very very concentrated again. Even better than the Clos-de-la-Roche. Full, very rich, very velvety. None of the toughness, but all the intensity of the vintage. Splendidly structured. Great vigour. Splendid! **(06/93)**

Now–2008   19.5

Chambertin   Charles Rousseau

Fullish colour. Still youthful. Restrained, but very fresh raspberry Pinot on the nose. Good grip. Profound and concentrated. Slight touch of paper. Still young. Full, the tannins a little unresolved. Oaky. Very fresh indeed. More 1988 than 1983 in character. Lovely cool, uncooked fruit flavours. Very very young. Most impressive. Real class here. Several notes. **(06/93)**

Now–2015   19.5

Chambertin   Jean Trapet

Medium to medium-full mature colour. Odd nose. Dry. A little vegetabley, yet with a sweet touch. Slight decay here. Some overlying sulphur. Thin on the palate, rather astringent, rather sulphury. Some acidity but lacks real concentration, and style as well. Not bad at best. Rather coarse. **(06/93)**

Drink soon   13.0

Chambertin   Cuvée Héritiers-Latour
Louis Latour

Fullish colour but well matured. Typically 1983: full, spicy, tannic. Slightly robust on the nose yet quite rich on the palate. Slightly jammy though. A little artificial and cooked. Lacks a little freshness. Good finish though. Not short. Nor astringent at the end. Good plus. **(12/93)**

Drink soon   15.5

Chambertin   *Vieilles-Vignes*   Jean Trapet

Medium-full colour. Fully mature. Cedar, sandalwood and caramel on the nose at first. Just

a slight lack of real concentration underneath. A very stylish wine, not a blockbuster, but persistent, slightly on the austere side. Good grip. Really very long and complex. Will get mellow and more generous as it ages. Fine but not quite the weight and concentration for great. **(06/93)**

Now–2008   17.5

Chambertin, Clos-de-Bèze
Bouchard Père et Fils

Medium-full colour. Mature. Rather too astringent on both nose and palate. Not mouldy. Just very dry. Little charm or merit. **(12/94)**

Drink soon   13.5

Chambertin, Clos-de-Bèze
Charles Rousseau

Fine colour. Fine nose. Completely clean and rich and lovely. Full, old-viney, quite structured, but very ripe tannins and no astringency at all. A lovely wine. Indeed a great wine. The finish is multi-dimensional, very classy, very long and quite superb. **(06/93)**

Now–2015   19.5

Chambolle-Musigny   Antonin Guyon

Medium-full colour. A little brown. Good firm rich slightly 'hot' cooked/burnt black-fruity nose. No undue dry tannins. Good straight Pinot. Quite full, good grip. Ripe meaty ample wine. Lacks a bit of nuance and finesse but a surprisingly good example. **(06/93)**

Now–2000   14.5

Chambolle-Musigny   Les Amoureuses
Georges Roumier

Fullish colour. Still vigorous. Old-vine concentration. Meaty, animal, voluptuous. Real depth here. There is a little of a taint here, but such an abundance of ripe fruit it hardly seems to matter. A soft, voluptuous but nevertheless fullish wine. Fat, animal. Very long. Very ripe. **(06/93)**

Now–2010   18.0

Chambolle-Musigny   Les Charmes
Gaston Barthod-Noëllat

Medium colour. Quite well matured. But fresh and round and elegant on the nose. On the palate ripe and clean and not a bit astringent. This is fresh, ample, genuinely sweet and surprisingly elegant. A lovely example. Fine. **(06/93)**

Now–2000   17.5

Chapelle-Chambertin   Clair-Daü

Medium-full colour. Fully mature. A bit dry on the nose. But not rotten. Still plenty of fruit on the palate. Good acidity. Lacks a little fat and succulence. Subtle on the finish. Good plus. **(03/94)**

Drink soon   15.5

Charmes-Chambertin   Denis Bachelet

There is a bit of a taint in this wine. Lovely fruit nonetheless. It is not so apparent on the nose, but at the end of the palate. A pity. Merely good. Second bottle, sampled in London a month later: good colour. No undue age. Animal-gamey nose. Even with a hint of reduction. No toughness though. Medium-full, ripe and spicy and exotic, fat and voluptuous. Not much refinement but plenty of succulence and concentration and a long finish without a hint of astringency. Fine, even a bit of class here. Plenty of life. **(06/93)**

Now–2000 plus   18.0

Charmes-Chambertin   Bernard Dugat-Py

Good. Soft and plump, elegant concentrated and old-viney, with a feminine touch as is appropriate for this *climat*. Lovely concentration. Very good depth. Fine plus. Really complex. **(06/93)**

Now–2000   18.0

Charmes-Chambertin   Joseph Roty

Medium to medium-full mature colour. Clean, fresh, plump nose. Not that full or strongly flavoured. Medium to medium-full body. Ripe, tannins a touch rigid as a result of new oak. Good intensity of fruit on the follow-through. But the tannins dominate a bit in the end. Clean and stylish though. Very good. **(06/93)**

Now–2000   16.0

**Chassagne-Montrachet   Morgeots
Bernard Morey**

Deep colour. Quite rich nose but not too alcoholic, not too chunky. Good acidity. Fat and grapey. This is very good both for 1983 and Morgeots. Not a bit too heavy. **(06/93)**

Now–2000   15.5

**Chassagne-Montrachet   *Premier Cru*
Jacques Gagnard-Delagrange**

Slightly rustic on the nose. Splendid vibrant colour. No brown. Very lovely fresh concentrated fruit. Not a bit *figué*. Fresh, succulent. This is rather special. Fine. Has lots and lots of life. Not a bit rustic or *sauvage* or shitty on the finish. Very good. **(06/96)**

Now–2005 plus   16.0

Clos-des-Lambrays   Saier

Medium colour. A bit old. The nose and the attack on the palate are a bit dried out, though not tainted. The finish is a little better. But nothing special. Reasonable fruit but light. No depth, no complexity. Quite good. **(06/93)**

Drink soon   14.0

Clos-de-la-Roche   Joseph Drouhin

Good colour. Lovely nose. Rich, concentrated, very fine. Old-vine concentration here. Excel-lent tannins. Very very rich fruit. Multi-dimensional. Splendid wine. Only just ready. **(06/93)**

Now–2005   19.0

Clos-de-la-Roche   Dujac

Medium colour. Quite a fresh nose. Not a lot of concentration or depth, but less tainted than the Rousseau. On the palate this is more tainted, and it is a bit dry and rigid. Fruity but a little lean and not very generous or charming. Good at best. **(06/93)**

Drink soon   15.0

Clos-de-la-Roche   Armand Rousseau

Medium-full colour. Still very fresh. Odd nose. Not entirely clean. A little vegetable-soupy. Medium body. Astringent. Dry. Rather short and more than a bit musty. This is not good at all. A bottle at the Studley Priory Wine Weekend in November 1991 was also tainted but less so, but fatter, richer and much more vigorous; and enjoyable. I gave it 16.5 out of 20. Two different *cuvées*/bottlings? **(06/93)**

Drink up   13.5

Clos-de-la-Roche   *Vieilles-Vignes*   Ponsot

Full colour. Vigorous. Rich, fat, concentrated oaky nose. A big wine and quite powerful. Still some tannins. But not 1983-ish at all. Very fresh. A masculine wine. Vigorous. Very good grip. Totally clean. This is very fine. I have had less good bottles of this. **(12/93)**

Now–2010   18.5

Clos-Saint-Denis   Dujac

Fullish colour. Still youthful. This has a pronounced taint on the nose. Less so on the palate. It is medium-full, slightly rigid, but has good acidity and plenty of fruit. It will still round off, and there is good grip here. The finish shows plenty of complexity and soft, ripe fruit if not a lot of weight. Very good. **(03/93)**

Now–2005   16.0

Clos-de-Vougeot   Bouchard Père et Fils

Medium-full colour. Mature. A little astringent on the attack, but not hail-tainted or mouldy. Quite rich underneath. Good fruit. Some vigour. Good if not exceptional. **(12/94)**

Now–2000   15.0

Clos-de-Vougeot   Champy

Good colour. A touch of the vegetal sweet-sour on the nose. But fresh, vigorous, stylish and fruity nevertheless. Very good. Slightly caramelly on the palate. Quite fresh. Good complexity. Good depth. No astringency here. Very good. **(06/93)**

Now–2000   16.0

Clos-de-Vougeot Jean Grivot

Good colour. Fullish, rich and plump on the nose. Meaty and concentrated and old-viney on the palate. This again is concentrated and ripe and rich. The finish is long and ample. There is plenty of wine here. Long. Fine. **(06/93)**

Now-2000 plus   18.0

Clos-de-Vougeot Jean Gros

Good colour. This is more smoky than the Champy on the nose, but it is more stylish. On the palate there is a little astringency on the attack, but none on the finish. Old-viney, concentrated, very elegant, very complex, very long. Very fine. **(06/93)**

Now-2000 plus   18.0

Clos-de-Vougeot Alain Hudelot-Noëllat

Full, mature but vigorous colour. Rich and fat and voluptuous. This has low yield, old-viney concentration. A profound wine on the nose. Once again a slight touch of hail, but enormous depth and concentration. This is fat and concentrated and very lovely. Marvellous complexity. Still young. Very fine. **(06/93)**

Now-2005 plus   18.5

Clos-de-Vougeot Henri Lamarche

Medium colour. Rather light and weedy on the nose. Reasonable fruit, surprisingly on the palate, and quite fresh. Indeed this is better than I expected from the nose. Not too dry, though there is some astringency. Good. **(06/93)**

Drink soon   15.0

Clos-de-Vougeot Mongeard-Mugneret

Medium colour but fresh-looking. Slightly 'hot' and alcoholic on the nose. Yet rich and concentrated as well, but the alcohol makes it a bit rigid. On the attack the wine is a little hard and dry, and there is a touch of evidence of hail. Yet plenty of rich concentrated fruit here as well. The follow-through is cleaner. This is not too tainted. The wine is still young. Good grip. **(06/93)**

Now-2005 plus   16.5

Clos-de-Vougeot Mugneret-Gibourg

Medium-full colour. Slightly brown. Again slightly vegetable-soupy on the nose. I find a rather hard aspect of hail taint on the palate. The wine has not the amplitude of the Hudelot wine, the tannins producing an astringency. Another bottle was quite different. Softer, richer, riper. Very nice. No problem. Very good. **(06/93)**

Drink soon   16.0

Clos-de-Vougeot Daniel Rion et Fils

Very good colour. Still immature looking. Just a little four-square on the nose, but good grip. Very fresh and youthful, a touch of oak, a hint of the stems. Just a little hard perhaps. Slight hint of mint. Medium-full, very rich, but the tannins a little separate, not integrated into the wine. Slightly rigid. Lacks a bit of style. Ripe but solid. Will a couple more years in bottle help? There is plenty of acidity and good length. Good plus. **(06/93)**

Now-2003   15.5

Corton Jaffelin

Good full colour. Rather an un-Burgundian nose, though not astringent. Just clumsy. Well, there is no finesse here, nor anything much except fairly full juicy artificial Pinot fruit. But it is still quite fresh. No style though. Spurious. This tastes as if it has some southern Rhône in it. **(06/93)**

Drink soon   13.5

Corton Protheau

Good colour. Slightly hard on the nose. Firm, slightly exotic in flavour (Mercurey). Medium body. Some development now. This is quite rich and has good grip. But lacks a little nuance and elegance. Good at best. **(10/95)**

Now-2002   14.5

Corton Bressandes Chandon-de-Briailles

Mature colour. Medium-full, just a touch less than star bright. Well matured, quite sweet Pinot on the nose. Just a little chunky and astringent. Fullish on the palate. Sweet and a little spicy. Chunky but not astringent at the end. Vigorous. Not that stylish but very good. Will keep well. **(06/93)**

Drink soon   16.0

Corton Bressandes Tollot-Beaut

Good fullish mature colour. Quite light at the rim. A broad nose. Quite ripe and round but not very concentrated, nor that much grip. The fruit is drying out. Essentially an elegant wine, but it lacks a bit of real concentration. Medium-full. Good attack but the finish shows a little age and astringency. Yet there is style and enjoyment here. Good. A magnum, direct from the domaine cellars, was rated 17.5 in France a few weeks later. **(06/93)**

Drink soon   15.0

**Corton Château Corton-Grancey
Louis Latour**

Medium-full colour. Some brown. Slightly diffuse, roasted, lumpy on the nose. Some alcohol. Full but inelegant, with a weak attenuated middle, though not exactly short. Medium body. **(06/93)**

Drink up   13.0

Corton Clos-des-Cortons Joseph Faiveley
Medium colour. No undue brown though.
Gamey, fleshy, animal nose. Fat and rich. There
is a little dryness from the tannins underneath.
But on the palate nothing rude about it. Fullish,
rich, slightly cooked black-cherry fruit. Good
grip and concentration. This is still vigorous.
Very good indeed. **(05/92)**
Now–2000 plus   17.0

Corton Clos-du-Roi
Chandon-de-Briailles
Mature colour. Fullish. Lightening at the rim.
Well-matured nose. Round and soft, but
lightening and drying now. Medium weight,
rather one-dimensional now. Reasonable attack
but no depth, and the finish is a bit astringent.
Yet soft and pleasant. Quite good at best. **(06/93)**
Drink soon   14.0

Corton Clos-du-Roi Dubreuil-Fontaine
Very good colour. Firm nose. Sturdy, but no
trace of astringency. On the palate it is a bit dry,
and it is not as exciting as the Tollot-Beaut. But
there is good rich concentrated fruit on the
follow-through and the finish is long and stylish.
Very good plus. **(06/93)**
Now–2000   16.5

Corton Cuvée Dr Peste Hospices de
Beaune Jeanne Marie de Champs
Medium-full colour. Some maturity. Soft, ripe
Pinot nose. Not a great deal of intensity but no
hard tannins and no lack of elegance. Good
raspberry flavour. Full, good tannin, meaty, some
new oak. Depth and complexity. Fine. **(06/93)**
Now–2000   17.0

Corton Pougets Louis Jadot
Good colour. Classy nose. Rich, profound,
complex, distinguished. Full, velvety-rich.
Lovely fruit. This has a lot of depth. Not a
touch of astringency. Fine. Lovely long complex
finish. Very elegant. **(06/93)**
Now–2000 plus   17.5

Echézeaux Romanée-Conti
Medium colour. Quite brown. The nose shows
a little of the hail-taint hardness. Medium body.
Ripe, fresh and quite vigorous, if not very
concentrated. But the wine is a little hollow and
dry and tainted on the follow-through. It
finishes a bit short. This has not lived up to its
early promise. Quite good at best. **(06/93)**
Drink soon   14.0

Fixin Leroy
Dry tannins on the nose. But quite rich and
opulent and spicy on the attack. Not bad finish
but lacks a little fruit. **(07/92)**
Drink soon   13.5

Gevrey-Chambertin Joseph Faiveley
Good medium-full colour. No undue age. A
little hard on the nose. No rot though. Better on
the palate. Some astringency on the attack. But
medium body. Clean and with good acidity.
The finish is not very rich, but fresh and fruity
and not cooked, surprisingly. **(06/93)**
Drink soon   14.5

Gevrey-Chambertin Henri Magnien
Good colour. Soft plump nose. But not a lot of
depth. On the palate a little chunky. Quite high
acidity and the astringency from this lacks grace.
But very fresh. No real 1983 character. Good.
(06/93)
Now–2000   16.0

Gevrey-Chambertin Vachet-Rousseau
Fullish colour. Little sign of maturity. Fine firm
nose, not 'hot'; closed but not overly tannic.
Fine austere fruit, very straight, tannic,
masculine. Plenty of depth. Even finesse.
Slightly earthy but good plus. **(06/93)**
Now–2005   15.5

Gevrey-Chambertin *Vieilles-Vignes*
Denis Bachelet
Good. Lovely supple – for a 1983 – plump fruity
nose. Real elegance, as always with Bachelet.
Medium-full. Ripe, complex, old-viney, rich.
This is better than Burguet's *Vieilles-Vignes*. It
has more elegance and insistency of fruit. Very
lovely indeed. Several notes. **(06/93)**
Now–2000   17.5

Gevrey-Chambertin *Vielles-Vignes*
Alain Burguet
Fullish colour. Just about mature. Fullish nose.
Firm, fresh, rich, balanced. This has a lot of
depth. Firm, full and tannic on the palate.
Ample, rich and almost chocolatey-cassis. Very
good grip. A bit astringent on the attack but
quite powerful and structured on the follow-
through. Good concentration. Very good.
Several notes. **(06/93)**
Now–2000 plus   16.0

Gevrey-Chambertin *Vieilles-Vignes*
Bernard Dugat-Py
Good colour. Aromatic nose. Round, quite
evolved. Medium body, plump, clean, stylish.
This is especially fine for a village example. Not
a trace of rot here. Very good indeed. **(06/93)**
Now–2000   17.0

Gevrey-Chambertin Cazetiers
Camille Giroud
Good colour. Big and chunky, no rot, but rather
too structured for me. Yet the finish is ripe and
old-viney, concentrated and it is clean. Full.
Better with food. Long. Good plus. **(06/93)**
Now–2000   15.5

Gevrey-Chambertin Cazetiers
Henri Magnien
Good colour. Ripe nose. A little astringent on the palate. A little dull on the palate. This lacks a bit of character. It is not spoiled, but it is a little astringent at the end. Quite good. **(06/93)**

Drink soon   14.0

Gevrey-Chambertin Champeaux
Denis Mortet
A little more to it than the Clos-Prieur, but in the same style. Better colour. More substance. Fruity and quite fresh at first, but a little astringent on the finish. Lacks real style and complexity. Quite good plus. **(06/93)**

Drink soon   14.5

Gevrey-Chambertin Les Cherbaudes
Lucien Boillot et Fils
Good colour. Fresh nose. Plenty of fruit. A bit astringent on the palate. A little old. Not rotten, just needs food. A little chunky. Yet the finish is long and clean and concentrated. Very good. **(06/93)**

Drink soon   16.0

Gevrey-Chambertin Clos-Prieur
Denis Mortet
Medium colour. Quite some age. Quite evolved on the nose. And a bit light on the palate. This is a little slight for the vintage. Not astringent. Balanced and fruity but one-dimensional and dull. Quite good at best. **(06/93)**

Drink soon   14.0

Gevrey-Chambertin Clos-Saint-Jacques
Charles Rousseau
Good colour. Fine, succulent, concentrated, oaky nose. Marvellous rich concentrated old-viney wine on the palate. This is full, vigorous, clean and delicious. Great depth, concentration and intensity. Excellent. Marvellous finish. Very high class. Several notes. **(06/93)**

Now-2005   18.5

Grands-Echézeaux Mongeard-Mugneret
Medium-full colour. No undue brown. Ripe, voluptuous, fruit-cakey spicy nose, with an element of caramel. Plenty of depth. As it developed, a suggestion of a hail taint. Good acidity and plenty of fruit on the attack. Medium-full. The hail taint is just a little obtrusive at first. This makes it rather hard and dry on the palate. The wine lacks a bit of generosity at first but developed quite considerably in the glass. Structured and rich. Very good. **(06/93)**

Now-2005   16.0

Latricières-Chambertin Newman
Brown, old, finished. Not tainted. But too old. **(06/93)**

Past its best   10.0

Latricières-Chambertin Jean Trapet
Medium-full colour, not too brown. Slightly astringent on the nose. Ripe and rich and spicy. Plenty of substance. Nothing weak or attenuated about this. Quite fat. Good plus but not exactly very elegant. Yet long and meaty. Got cleaner as it evolved. Very good with food. **(10/94)**

Now-2003   16.0

Marsannay Bruno Clair
Good colour. Crisp nose. Surprisingly fresh. While there isn't any great depth, this is youthful, fruity and charming and will still keep. Ripe, accessible and long on the palate. Unexpectedly good. **(06/93)**

Drink soon   14.0

Mazis-Chambertin Joseph Faiveley
Full colour. Rich, old-viney nose, just a little astringent. But clean on the palate. Full and rich and gently oaky. Ripe, profound. Very good grip. This has real length. Classy. Very fine. **(06/93)**

Now-2000   18.0

Mazis-Chambertin Gabriel Tortochot
Good colour. Slightly tough nose. Totally clean but a little late bottling, a little dry. Yet enough concentration to overcome this. Fullish. Gamey. No less than very good. **(06/93)**

Drink soon   16.0

Mazis-Chambertin Cuvée Madeleine
Collignon Hospices de Beaune
Coron Père et Fils
Fullish colour. Still youthful. Gamey, animal nose. Good acidity, perhaps a slight absence of real fat. Yet plenty of new oak. This is quite brilliant. Huge concentration of fruit. Marvellous depth of character. Full-bodied and awe-inspiring. Great wine here. Several notes. **(06/93)**

1998-2020   20.0

Morey-Saint-Denis Champy
Good fresh colour. Ripe nose. Good depth for a village wine. Good fruit and freshness. More chunky on the palate. Fullish. Good ripe fruit. Clean and quite stylish. Finishes positively. No astringency. Good. **(06/93)**

Drink soon   15.0

Nuits-Saint-Georges Jean Gros
Good colour. Slightly smoky on the nose. Lacking a bit of freshness. On the palate much better, round, soft, clean, gently oaky, stylish. Good grip. Medium body. Finishes very well. Very good, especially for a village example. Good length. **(06/93)**

Now-2000   16.0

Nuits-Saint-Georges
Jacqueline Jayer-Grivot

Good fullish, mature colour. Rich, quite sturdy, masculine nose. Ample but quite evolved now. Lacks a little style. Fullish, still some tannin. Ripe, plump, balanced. Plenty of depth. Good. **(06/93)**

Now-2000   15.0

Nuits-Saint-Georges   Les Damodes
Machard de Gramont

Lightish colour. Quite brown now. Clean, fragrant, refined nose. There is ripe plump fruit here and no astringency. On the palate it is medium body, a little pinched, and beginning to dry out. Yet still has length. Good. **(06/93)**

Drink soon   15.0

Nuits-Saint-Georges   Lavièress
Daniel Rion et Fils

Good colour. Full, rich and ample on the nose. This is better than Gros. Fullish, sturdy, quite structured. But plenty of fruit and plenty of depth. A wine for food. Slight dryness but not on the finish. Very good. **(06/93)**

Now-2000   16.0

Nuits-Saint-Georges   Porrets
Alain Michelot

Light to medium colour but still quite vigorous. Soft nose. Fully mature. Ripe cherry-strawberry fruit. Not a lot of depth, but quite elegant. Medium body. Clean, fresh, gently oaky. Not a blockbuster by any means. Indeed more Côte-887de-Beaune than Côte-de-Nuits. Yet round, fragrant and long. *À point* but good acidity and potential, despite being a bit slight. **(06/93)**

Drink soon   15.5

Nuits-Saint-Georges   *Premier Cru*
Robert Chevillon

Medium-full colour. Slightly brown at the edge. A little lumpy on the nose. Here is a certain astringency. Though the wine has, essentially, very good fruit and complexity and no lack of breeding. Yet not the grip of the best. Chocolate and cooked plums. As it evolved the nose got worse, the acidity a bit raw. **(06/93)**

Drink soon   14.0

Nuits-Saint-Georges   Roncières
Jean Grivot

Medium to medium-full, mature colour. Ripe, opulent, but slightly hard and masculine nose at first. Liquorice, even peppermint aspects as it developed. Fullish, quite chunky at first on the attack. But plenty of fruit, plenty of depth, plenty of complexity and plenty of grip. This is very good indeed. Lovely finish. Bags of life. **(06/93)**

Now-2005   17.0

Nuits-Saint-Georges   Les Saint-Georges
Henri Gouges

Very good colour. Lovely nose. Not a touch unclean. Splendid concentrated fruit from start to finish. Fullish, rich, fat and *rôti*. Very 1983 in character. The follow-through is ample, slightly solid, but has depth and length. Very good indeed. Plenty of vigour. **(06/93)**

Now-2000 plus   17.0

Nuits-Saint-Georges   Les Vaucrains
Henri Gouges

Good colour. Not too brown. A bit dry on the nose. The fruit has faded. On the palate it is medium-bodied, a little astringent. The attack lacks succulence and charm. But the follow-through is better, indeed even quite ripe and positive. No taints. **(06/93)**

Drink soon   14.5

Nuits-Saint-Georges   Vignes-Rondes
Daniel Rion et Fils

Good colour. The nose is a little tight, but fruity enough, and not tainted though perhaps the volatile acidity is a little high. On the palate it is a little solid and clumsy, and it would be better with food. **(06/93)**

Drink soon   15.0

Pommard   Leroy

Slight oxidisation here. Very good colour. Lumpy, tannic and dense. Alcoholic but coarse. **(07/92)**

Drink soon   13.0

Pommard   Jean Michelot

Good full colour. No undue maturity. Rich, plummy nose. No hardness. Slightly artisanal. Plump, fullish, slightly sturdy, slightly dense. Good acidity though. Good with food. A good village example but not the finesse or depth of better. Slightly lumpy at the end. Quite good. **(10/94)**

Now-2000   14.0

Pommard   Clos-des-Epeneaux
Comte Armand

Magnum. Good colour. Artisanal nose. Chunky and farmyardy. Rather undistinguished wine but there is nothing wrong with the *matière première*. Rich but rather clumsy and now astringent. Not bad. **(06/93)**

Drink soon   13.0

Pommard   Epenots   B. et J.M. Delaunay

Good rich, mature colour. Ripe, mature but vigorous nose. Round and rich enough and still fresh. Fullish, good grip. No undue astringency. Slightly gamey. But essentially cherry flavoured. Good fruit. Soft at the end but holding up well. Good plus. **(04/94)**

Drink soon   15.5

Pommard Epenots Joseph Drouhin

Medium colour. Some brown. Slight lack of grip on the nose, a little diffuse at first. More definition after a little while. More Volnay than Pommard. Better on palate than nose. Ripe, gentle (in a 1983 sense) Pinot. Again slightly hard on the finish. But has good depth. Some, but not undue, tannins. Quite good grip. **(06/93)**

Now–2002   15.5

Pommard Epenots Jacques Parent

Magnum. Good colour. Fullish, slightly sweet, aromatic nose with a touch of caramel. A sturdy wine. A bit sweet and alcoholic with a fiery finish. But vigorous and not astringent. Plenty of fruit. No great finesse but will keep. Good. **(06/93)**

Now–2005   15.0

Pommard Grands-Epenots
Hubert de Montille

Magnum. Good colour. Fine rich nose which puts Armand to shame. Lots of depth. This starts well but doesn't quite have the depth on the palate of his Volnay Taille-Pieds. Rich, fresh, vigorous. Very good indeed. Still young. **(06/93)**

Now–2005   17.0

Pommard Rugiens Hubert de Montille

Magnum. This is better than his Grands-Epenots. Richer, plump, full and delicious. Fat and concentrated. Full on the palate. This is lovely. Lots of life. A true Pommard, with not a bit of solidity. Fine. **(06/93)**

Now–2005   17.5

Richebourg Clos-Frantin Bichot

Medium to medium-full mature colour. Ripe, pruney nose. Not a lot of finesse but not too evolved, nor too dry. This is still quite fresh. But the fruit is a bit over-ripe. Fullish palate. Some tannin. Quite rich, but rather rampant acidity. The net effect is rather Italian. Dense, solid even. Meaty. Better with food. Good plus, but it lacks both Pinot elegance which perhaps you don't expect with 1983s, but also real richness. Yet vigorous. Plenty of life. But as it evolved got a little sour. No sweetness. Only quite good. **(10/93)**

Now–2000   14.0

Richebourg Jean Gros

Fine colour, mature. Rich, concentrated, quite austere nose. And I thought at first a little solid. But as it developed it expanded and rounded. On the palate again a touch chunky, but the finish is clean and very very rich and concentrated. Old-viney depth and class. Very fine indeed. **(06/93)**

Now–2000   18.5

Richebourg Romanée-Conti

Very fine colour. Slight hard vegetal aspects on the nose. Certainly doesn't sing. Better on the palate but quite tannic and certainly a *goût de grêle* on the attack. Yet the finish richer, more concentrated, not as tainted. Will it completely clean up? Several notes. **(06/93)**

Now–2000 plus   16.0

Romanée-Saint-Vivant
Les Quatre-Journeaux Louis Latour

Good colour. Still fresh-looking. No hail-taint here. Mellow, sweet cedar-woody nose. Good concentration. But lightened and got a little vegetal as it evolved. Fullish, meaty, caramelly and a little sweet-sour. It lacks refinement, but the finish is rich and fat and long. Very good indeed. **(06/93)**

Now–2000 plus   17.0

Ruchottes-Chambertin Clos-des-Ruchottes
Armand Rousseau

Full colour. Fine nose. Suspicion of rot here. Yet a lovely wine underneath but slightly astringent. I haven't seen this for some time. It is a bit of a curate's egg. With food I suspect there would be plenty of enjoyment to be had. Medium-full. I wouldn't kick it out of bed. Several notes. **(06/93)**

Drink soon   16.0

Savigny-lès-Beaune Dominodes
Bruno Clair

Good colour. Full, rich, concentrated nose. Ripe and meaty. A plummy wine. Slightly solid but not a bit blowsy. Fresh, rich, cool and long and lovely and complex on the finish. Not a bit 1983 in character. Very good grip. Very good plus. **(06/93)**

Now–2000   16.5

Savigny-lès-Beaune Aux Guettes
Simon Bize et Fils

Good colour. A little tight and dry on the nose. A sturdy wine. Fullish and a little structured on the attack, but the follow-through is ample enough. A wine for food. Good richness in fact. Finishes positively. Good plus. **(06/93)**

Drink soon   15.5

Savigny-lès-Beaune Lavières
Chandon-de-Briailles

Quite a brown colour. This is just a little blowsy on the nose but is fresher than I expected; and not too loose. Medium-full, aromatic. Good fruit. No more than a touch of astringency. Fresh, indeed. Shows well. Good plus. **(06/93)**

Drink soon   15.5

La Tâche   Romanée-Conti

Fine colour. Still vigorous. Marvellous nose and not a touch of hail or any other taint. An austere wine still, but marvellously rich concentrated fruit. Better with food. But undeniably great. Real intensity. Very very long on the palate. Brilliant. Several notes. This wine is getting better and better, and shows no trace of any hail-taint now. **(06/93)**

Now-2010   **19.0**

Volnay   Les Caillerets   Pousse d'Or

Good fresh medium-full colour. Soft and cherry-like on the nose. A little tough on the attack but ripe, vigorous, good grip and good depth. This is certainly very good plus in a 1983 context. Plenty of vigour. **(10/93)**

Now-2000   **16.5**

Volnay   Caillerets, Clos des Soixante-Ouvrées   Pousse d'Or

Magnum. Medium-full colour. Fresh colour. Medium weight, but no astringency. Complex, but just a little dry. This is fresh, fragrant, elegant and complex. There is plenty of style and dimension and it is not dry on the palate. Very good indeed in fact. Lovely finish. Very long. **(06/93)**

Now-2000   **17.0**

Volnay   Clos-de-la-Bousse-d'Or Pousse d'Or

Magnum. Slightly fuller, fresher colour than the Soixante-Ouvrées. Riper, more ample on the nose. Very good. Slightly full, slightly more meaty. A little richer. But less fragrant, less elegant, less complex than the Soixante-Ouvrées. Still long and fresh and lovely. Very good. Cool finish. From a bottle, in London a month earlier, I was less impressed (14.5). **(06/93)**

Now-2000   **16.0**

Volnay   Clos-des-Chênes   Antonin Guyon

Fine colour. Fine nose, lovely Pinot fruit, intense, complex, concentrated. Quite full, good ripe tannins. Very good grip. Slightly austere on the attack. More ample on the follow-through. Will still develop. Ample and meaty. De Montille style. A lot of depth. Very good. **(06/93)**

Now-2000   **16.5**

Volnay   Clos-des-Chênes   Michel Lafarge

Splendid colour. Marvellous ripe nose. Rich, substantial and concentrated. Fullish, a lot of depth and concentration. Full body, rich, ample, old-viney. This is a very serious wine. Marvellous dimension. Really concentrated. Very well balanced. Excellent. **(06/93)**

Now-2000 plus   **17.5**

Volnay   Clos-des-Ducs Marquis d'Angerville

Fullish, fresh colour. Refined, raspberry nose. Medium-full, vigorous, plump, gently oaky. This has very good grip and is still just a little austere. But the fruit is rich and ample. Structured. Long. Firm. But not a bit brutal. Just about ready. **(06/93)**

Now-2000 plus   **16.0**

Volnay   Mitans   Hubert de Montille

Magnum. Fine colour. This is a bit more chunky and solid than the Taille-Pieds. It has good freshness and fruit but less grace. Full, vigorous, tannic. Very good. **(06/93)**

Now-2005   **16.0**

Volnay   Taille-Pieds   Hubert de Montille

Magnum. Fine colour. Rich plump vigorous nose. Good structure, there is tannin here but no astringency. The wine is simply very young and still has time to go. Rich, fat and concentrated on the palate. Lovely fruit. Still needs time. Fine. **(06/93)**

Now-2005 plus   **17.5**

Vosne-Romanée   Daniel Rion et Fils

Good colour. Ripe, aromatic, surprisingly supple on the nose. Fullish, good grip. Quite complex. A little chunkiness, and not much dimension but a good example. Lacks a little grace. Good. **(06/93)**

Drink soon   **15.0**

Vosne-Romanée   Les Beaumonts Camille Giroud

Excellent colour. Old-fashioned, tough nose. A bit smoky and chunky. This blew off after a while, but nevertheless on the palate something which is really far too dry and blowsy. Not much enjoyment here. **(06/93)**

Drink up   **12.0**

Vosne-Romanée   Les Beaumonts Henri Jayer

Medium colour. Some age. Not much on the nose. This is a little old now. Medium to medium-full. The astringency is taking over. Sweet though. Stylish, oaky. No 1983 character except that the finish is a little vegetal. **(10/94)**

Drink soon   **14.0**

Vosne-Romanée   Les Beaumonts Louis Latour

Good colour. No undue brown. Ripe nose, sultanas and prunes and fruit-cake flavours. Just a little dry. On the palate the wine is fullish, creamy and oaky and quite concentrated. Slightly sweet but certainly with plenty of fruit. Good grip. Positive finish. Very good. **(06/93)**

Now-2000   **16.0**

Vosne-Romanée   Les Chaumées
Daniel Rion et Fils

Medium colour. No undue brown. Fragrant nose, a little suave, and a hint of mint. But no hail-taint. Medium to medium-full. Fresh and vigorous. Quite sturdy but ripe and fleshy and not a bit dry. Lacks a little elegance but good plus and will keep well. **(06/93)**

Drink soon   15.5

Vosne-Romanée   Clos-des-Réas   Jean Gros

Medium-full colour. Not a lot of brown. Good oak here. Very stylish. Ripe and complex on the nose. Lots of depth. Fullish, rich, very sweet and concentrated on the palate. Just a suspicion of a hail-taint. But not enough to worry one again. Very good acidity. Long, complex and clean (or cleaner) on the palate. This is very vigorous. But round and soft and lovely. Fine. **(06/93)**

Now-2005   17.5

Vosne-Romanée   La Grande-Rue
Henri Lamarche

Good colour. Only just mature looking. Evolved, slightly dried out nose. A little astringency. Some old tea. Medium-full, good richness and concentration, and indeed grip, if not a load of class. But at the same time quite a lot of astringency. With food really rather good, surprisingly. Finishes long and rich and vigorous, despite the astringency. **(06/93)**

Drink soon   15.5

Vosne-Romanée   Malconsorts
Alain Hudelot-Noëllat

Good full rich mature colour. Old at edge but vigorous in the middle. Splendid nose. Rich and concentrated. Very good grip. Youthful and plummy. Old-vine depth. Full, rich, quite muscular and rigid. A little hail-taint which wasn't evident on the nose. Not enough to worry me. A wine of real concentration and marvellous dimension. Fine plus. **(06/93)**

Now-2005 plus   18.0

Vosne-Romanée   Les Suchots
Alain Hudelot-Noëllat

Fullish mature colour. Old at the rim but good vigour in the middle. This is a profound, old-viney wine. Not a bit solid, just very very rich and concentrated. High-toned nose. There is something decadent here. On the palate a full, muscular, somewhat rigid wine, with a little hail-taint and some astringency. Is it enough to put one off? It is a question of taste. I like the kinkiness of this wine. Very good indeed. Still holding up well 01/96. **(06/93)**

Now-2005   17.0

1982

RATING FOR THE VINTAGE

Red: 14.5   **White:** 15.5

SIZE OF THE CROP

(Hectolitres, excluding generic wine)

	Red	White
Grands Crus	17,933	4,002
Village and *Premiers Crus*	233,894	53,397
Total	251,827	57,399

A huge vintage. Even today, fifteen years on, a total of 309,000 hl seems large. Only twice has 250,000 hl been exceeded. And yet the vintage had, and continues to have, a lot of merit. True, the reds are not *that* concentrated, but where not cropped to excess, are ripe and generous, healthy and succulent, and the best are still vigorous. The whites are plump and stylish, surprisingly well balanced, with more than enough definition. They are by no means past it either.

WEATHER CONDITIONS

Burgundy, like Bordeaux, enjoyed a marvellous summer in 1982. Indeed it could be argued that it was too good. The spring was warm and sunny, allowing the vines to develop from bud to flower without mishap - no frost, no hail - and to begin the flowering very early indeed, for it was complete by 1 June.

A large amount of buds set into a very large amount of bunches of grapes: again no mishaps, neither *coulure* nor *millerandage*, though during July, as the weather continued dry, there were some fears of drought. The crop, barring accident, would be prolific, at least as big as that of 1973, probably the biggest ever.

Like 1973, there was rain in the run-up to the vintage, but unlike in 1973, this occurred in August rather than in September. Yet the result was similar; there was a further inflation of the size of the harvest, and, inevitably, some dilution of the concentration and extract within the grape.

September brought a return to marvellous weather, indeed to heat-wave conditions. This had a number of far-reaching effects. On the one hand it helped to concentrate the grapes at least partially, mitigating to some extent the dilution caused by the August rains. This would have had a great impact on the final quality had the harvest not been quite so large. If the harvest had been the size, say, of that of 1983, or had the Pinot Noir vine like the Cabernet Sauvignon been able to bear such a prolific quantity of grapes, the result might have been similar to the 1982 vintage in Bordeaux. Equally, if growers had had the courage at the time of the *véraison* at the end of July to prune off some of the bunches, the rest might have been able to concentrate to a satisfactory level of extract and depth of character. This sadly was not the case.

However, what the hot weather did ensure was that the grapes were healthy as well as ripe when the harvest began in the Côte d'Or on 17 September. There was not a trace of rot. What French oenologists call the *matière première* was in first-rate condition, and neither hail nor rain would intervene to alter this.

The problems however were firstly the sheer quantity of wine, and secondly the torrid conditions, producing fruit which arrived in the winery at a temperature which made control of the fermentation without suitable equipment a hard task indeed. Moreover, because of this heat, the level of acidity of much of the crop was low.

Some growers then were overwhelmed with the quantity of must they were required to ferment. Some of those who had young, vigorous, and over-prolific (in 1982 terms) plants were unable to cope. Space was at a premium and some vats could not be allowed sufficient time to macerate with skins and pulp, thereby gaining backbone and extract, before they had to be run off to make way for the next batch. Others received fruit at a dangerously high temperature and without adequate cooling mechanisms fermentations took place at levels which in retrospect can be seen to have been too high, even if, in most cases, the danger of infection by volatile acidity was avoided.

THE STYLE OF THE WINE

WHITE WINES

The 1982 white wines are similar in style to those from vintages such as 1979 and 1973, and to those produced a decade later in 1992. They are soft rather than firm, round and accessible from the outset, and despite no apparently marked acidity have remained fresh despite now being fifteen years of age. Above all they have plenty of elegance. In the fact that despite the size of the harvest there was no rot, either noble or ignoble, lies much of the explanation for this. But no-one at the outset expected them to last quite this well. That *has* been a surprise. Drink them up now, though. Don't push your luck too far!

RED WINES

It is a variable vintage. There is the good, and there is what Remington Norman (*The Great Domaines of Burgundy*) calls corsetless pap. Thankfully what was uninspiring has long since been consumed and cast into oblivion. That which is left has much to commend it. Few wines are great, but the best are more enjoyable than their equivalent 1980s and 1979s, and are more attractive than the 1981s. There have been one or two occasions in vertical tastings where I have preferred the more austere, tight-knit fragrance of this earlier year to the more open and fleshy but somewhat bland 1982s. But in general I prefer the 1982s. My conclusion after my ten-year-on tasting was that the vintage was both more interesting, and holding up better, than I had expected, and four years on I still find much to admire and enjoy, though most wines now need drinking soon.

TASTING NOTES

BLANC

Bâtard-Montrachet   Leflaive
Magnum. Good colour. Fat, rich, very good oak. Good grip. This is very rich and opulent. A wine of real depth and concentration. Fine quality. Not a bit of undue age. Long, ripe, fresh. **(05/92)**
Now-2000   17.5

Corton-Charlemagne   Bonneau du Martray
Excellent fruit. Very, very ripe and concentrated. Youthful and laid-back. Very high concentration. Marvellous class. Very stylish oak. Intense high quality. Just about ready but still very youthful. Excellent grip. Not a trace of over-ripeness or blowsiness. **(03/95)**
Now-2005   18.5

Corton-Charlemagne   Dubreuil-Fontaine
Crisp, ripe nose. Good depth here. Fullish, fresh, positive. Good oaky base. This is very good for the vintage. Concentrated and complex. Long. **(06/92)**
Drink soon   16.0

Corton-Charlemagne   Louis Latour
Quite a deep colour. Aromatic nose with a touch of vegetal fade. It is loosening up. Medium body. A fat, opulent, almost glyceriney

wine. Quite high acidity. Good freshness but the finish is a little heavy, even astringent. Lacks elegance and freshness. Good but not great. Quite oaky. Luscious. **(09/91)**

Drink soon   **16.0**

Le Montrachet   Comtes Lafon

Fat, rich, opulent and concentrated. Quite strongly and even rigidly oaky but good acidity. There is depth here. Ripe, stylish and balanced. This is lovely Chardonnay. Fat and fruity. Very good depth. Long, succulent. A lovely wine for a 1982. Will still improve. **(01/91)**

Now–2000 plus   **19.0**

Le Montrachet   Ramonet

Good colour. Splendid masculine concentration on the nose. Real volume here. Just a faint touch of H_2S. Medium-full. Ripe. But on the palate does it really have the grip and intensity of a Montrachet? Slightly disappointing for Ramonet, Montrachet and 1982. Yet long. Subtle, fully ready. I have had better bottles. This has not lived up to its original promise. Fine. H_2S noticed in another bottle sampled 01/91. **(10/94)**

Now–2000   **17.0**

Meursault   Bème

Nicely green. Good old wine. Low *rendement* concentration. Nice and ripe. Good substance and depth. Shows very well. **(06/96)**

Now–2000   **16.0**

Meursault   Charmes, Cuvée Albert Grivault Hospices de Beaune, Joseph Drouhin

Good colour. Delicate, luscious nose. But getting a little tired now perhaps. Much better on the palate. Lovely, gentle ripe fruit. Complex. Very elegant. Soft and honeyed and long and flowery-fresh. Good finish. Will still keep. Fine. **(10/95)**

Now–2000   **17.5**

Meursault   Charmes, Cuvée Bahèzre de Lanlay   Hospices de Beaune, Lupé-Cholet

Good colour. Quite an evolved nose. A bit of built-in sulphur and now the fruit has dried up a little. Better on the palate. This is rich and full and quite masculine. Not as stylish as the Drouhin Cuvée Albert Grivault but fuller, more grip. Very good plus. **(10/95)**

Now–2000   **16.5**

Meursault   Genevrières   Comtes Lafon

Light golden colour. Rich, fat, concentrated. This is very superior. Fullish, oaky. Very concentrated. This is very fine indeed. Real dimension and depth here. Fat. Remarkably

vigorous. Absolutely delicious. Several notes. Better than the Perrières when sampled together. **(10/94)**

Now–2005   **19.0**

Meursault   Perrières   Jean-Philippe Fichet

Youthful colour. Mature, quite fat nose with a hint of built-in sulphur. Just beginning to get a bit diffuse. On the palate this is quite full and it has good fruit. But it lacks a bit of flair and definition. Good at best. **(01/96)**

Drink soon   **15.0**

Meursault   Perrières   Comtes Lafon

Last vintage of René Lafon. Bottled January 1985 (by Dominique). This has a fine, ample, aromatic nose. Violets and raspberries; Pinot Noir-ish. Beeswax and hazelnuts also. Soft, vigorous, quite rich, round nevertheless. Intense and very harmonious. Very good acidity. Very fine. Complex. Bags of life. Several notes, before and since. **(09/92)**

Now–2002   **18.5**

Meursault   Perrières   Matrot

Flowery nose. A touch tired and sulphury. Quite ripe but the fruit has begun to dry out a bit. Yet good grip. Not bad. **(06/92)**

Drink soon   **14.0**

Morey-Saint-Denis   Monts-Luisants   Ponsot

Fresh colour. The usual curious, slightly vegetal nose of this wine. But round, stylish, delicately oaky. Fresh on the palate. Medium-full. Balanced, complex, individual. Full of interest. Crab apple, mango aspects. *À point.* No hurry to drink. Very good plus. **(10/94)**

Now–2000   **16.5**

Puligny-Montrachet   Les Combettes   Étienne Sauzet

Fine, mature gently oaky Chardonnay on the nose. Fully mature on the palate. Ripe, honeyed, raspberry elements to the flavour. Not the greatest of zip but balanced. Long and classy. Gently ripe. **(02/91)**

Drink soon   **16.5**

ROUGE

Beaune   Clos-des-Ursules   Héritiers Louis Jadot

Medium fully mature colour. Not enormous concentration on the nose but attractive and plump and quite elegant. Medium to medium-full. Now ready but has good structure and vigour and balance. Ample fruit. Still fresh. Very good for the vintage. **(09/90)**

Drink soon   **16.0**

Beaune   Grèves   Camille Giroud

Very good colour. Full and alive. Fresh. Concentrated. Plenty of depth. This is very vigorous for a 1982. Old-viney, aromatic flavour with a good base of oak. Full, old-fashioned in the best sense. A certain hardness but good fruit and grip. Still quite firm. Plenty of life. Good. **(06/92)**

Drink soon   15.0

Beaune   Grèves   Michel Lafarge

Good colour. Good, vigorous, fragrant nose. Plenty of depth and vigour. A touch of astringency and bitterness on the palate though. Fullish, good grip nevertheless. Ripe. A little sturdy. Better with food. Plenty of ripe fruit. Good. **(06/92)**

Drink soon   15.0

Beaune   Montremenots   André Mussy

Very good colour. Still quite purple. Plump, ripe and old-viney; good acidity. Medium-full, a touch rustic but enjoyably fruity. Good grip. Spicy, fresh and still with life. Quite good. **(06/92)**

Drink soon   14.0

Bonnes-Mares   Robert Groffier

Medium colour, but no undue brown. Fragrant, rich, fresh nose. Not a lot of body and intensity. Very Chambolle, very Groffier. But has balance and style. Plenty of life left. Very good. **(10/92)**

Drink soon   16.0

Bonnes-Mares   Georges Lignier

Medium colour. Fully mature. Good richness on the nose. Soft and mellow but not empty or old. Nicely ripe and vigorous. Medium to medium-full. Good plump fruit. Round. In the background quite sturdy and plummy. Finishes long and well. Very good. **(12/95)**

Now-2000   16.0

Bonnes-Mares   Georges Roumier

Very good colour. Firm, a little chunky. Rich, full, ripe. A little over-extracted perhaps. A touch of rigidity and astringency at the end. Good grip though. Very good but not great. **(06/92)**

Drink soon   16.0

Chambertin   Armand Rousseau

Good colour. Firm, very concentrated, youthful nose. Marvellous depth and finesse here. Multi-dimensional. On the palate full, oaky, rich and concentrated. Very good grip. Splendid quality. Very very long and complex on the finish. Excellent. **(06/92)**

Now-2000 plus   19.0

Chambertin   Jean Trapet et Fils

Good colour. Round. Slightly sweet, ripe, concentrated nose. A fat wine with a hint of allspice, vanilla and cedarwood. Fullish, a little open-knit for a wine of this provenance. It is certainly not great. But it is balanced and stylish, plump and vigorous. Very good plus. **(06/92)**

Drink soon   16.5

Chambertin, Clos-de-Bèze
Armand Rousseau

Very good colour. Barely mature. Full, rich concentrated nose with a very good oaky base. Concentrated intense and classy. This is very lovely. Rich and blackfruity as well as raspberry. Very fine. Lots of vigour. Mocha flavours. Still some tannin. Plenty of backbone. A lovely long complex, classy finish. Very fine indeed for a 1982. **(01/94)**

Now-2000   19.0

Chambolle-Musigny
Gaston Barthod-Noëllat

Good colour. Lovely fresh nose. Fragrant and full of violets; for a simple village wine this is lovely. Good concentration, grip and finesse on the palate. Harmonious and velvety. Very good indeed. Plenty of life still. **(06/92)**

Drink soon   16.5

Charmes-Chambertin   Dujac

Medium colour. Fully mature. Very fragrant on the nose. Sweet and exotic. Ditto palate. Definitely oaky, especially on the aftertaste. Medium body. Very good acidity, especially for 1982. Complex. Seductive. Fine for the vintage. Plenty of life. **(10/92)**

Now-2000   17.5

Clos-de-la-Roche   Dujac

Light to medium colour. Lovely nose. Plenty of vigour and great complexity and finesse. Medium body. Good grip. As usual with Dujac's wines both intense and a touch lean at the same time. Fine multi-dimensional finish. Plenty of life. Fine but a touch austere. **(06/92)**

Now-2000   17.5

Clos-de-la-Roche   Ponsot

Medium colour. No undue age. A little blowsy on the nose. Soft on the attack. But good acidity. Fresh, stylish fruit. Complex. Long. Very drinkable. Very good indeed. **(09/92)**

Drink soon   17.0

Clos-de-Vougeot   Joseph Drouhin

Medium-full colour. Ripe. Slightly shitty/gamey nose. Soft and fat and succulent. Medium-full. A mature, complex, round example. Plenty of depth. Very well balanced. Very good indeed but not quite the finesse or intensity for great. (06/92)

Drink soon   17.0

Clos-de-Vougeot   Jean Grivot

Good colour. Fine nose. Rich and fat and succulent. Still young. On the palate fullish, just a little raw still, remarkably. It will still improve. Very good concentrated fruit. Very good grip. Very fine indeed. A real classic. (06/92)

Now-2000 plus   18.5

Clos-de-Vougeot   Alain Hudelot-Noëllat

Good colour. Rich, fat and succulent, with a gamey touch. Medium-full. Ripe and fleshy. Good grip, but not the finesse of his Romanée-Saint-Vivant. Soft but fragrant. Lovely finish. Fine. (06/92)

Drink soon   17.5

Clos-de-Vougeot   Daniel Rion et Fils

Medium colour. Is this young vines? It seems a touch green and artificial. There is a touch of oak which isn't quite integrated. Medium-full. Ripe, good grip. The elements are here but they are not completely harmonious. Very good but not great. (06/92)

Drink soon   16.0

Corton   Bressandes   Dubreuil-Fontaine

Medium-full colour. Fragrant nose. Good fruit, but less substantial and vigorous than the Jadot's Corton-Pougets. Good but not great. It is ripe but not that stylish, and there is a certain vegetal aspect lurking underneath. Good, merely. (06/92)

Drink soon   15.0

Corton   Clos-des-Cortons   Joseph Faiveley

Very good colour for a 1982. No undue maturity. Ripe nose, but lacks a little concentration. Yet certainly stylish. Fullish for 1982. Good fruit on the attack. Balanced and elegant but lacks a little depth. Yet very good. Finishes long. Plenty of life still. (10/93)

Drink soon   16.0

Corton   Pougets   Louis Jadot

Medium-full colour. Rich, quite concentrated, gently oaky nose. Plenty of vigour. Fullish, youthful, good grip, plenty of concentration. This shows very well indeed. Fine. (06/92)

Now-2000 plus   17.5

Echézeaux   Jaffelin

Good colour. Fullish, slightly spicy, round, robust even, nose. Rich though, quite sturdy. It is a touch rigid but there is good fruit and good grip. Very good plus but not fine. (06/92)

Drink soon   16.5

Echézeaux   Manière-Noirot

Medium colour. Soft, fragrant nose. Medium-full. This is quite well evolved but good concentration. Very good unmessed-up Pinot fruit. Indeed it has balance and finesse. Fine quality. (06/92)

Drink soon   17.5

Gevrey-Chambertin   Lucien Boillot et Fils

Medium-full colour. A little bit woody/dirty - not exactly corked. On the palate not too bad. Medium-full, ripe, balanced. Reasonably concentrated. But not completely clean. (06/92)

Drink soon   14.0

Gevrey-Chambertin   Bernard Dugat-Py

Good colour. Fine ripe, concentrated vigorous Pinot Noir for a village 1982. Fullish. Well extracted. Good grip. No real finesse or complexity but a very honourable example. Good fruit. Still vigorous. Good. (06/92)

Drink soon   15.0

Gevrey-Chambertin   *Vieilles-Vignes* Alain Burguet

Good colour. Fine fresh concentrated Pinot Noir. Sturdy, rich, fullish. Still very vigorous. This has a lot of depth and style. Lovely austere Pinot Noir fruit. Fine. (06/92)

Now-2000 plus   17.5

Gevrey-Chambertin   Les Champeaux Denis Mortet

Very good colour. Full, rich, concentrated, oaky, old-viney. This is fine. Yet on the palate a little lumpy and rigid. The acidity was not quite what it could have been and the fruit, though still sweet and not astringent is a touch coarse. Good plus though. (06/92)

Drink soon   15.5

Gevrey-Chambertin   Clos-Prieur Denis Mortet

Very good colour. Something a little strange here on the nose. I think it is built-in sulphur. It also seems a bit attenuated. Medium-full. This is a bit rustic and sweet-sour. Yet not short. But it lacks style. (06/92)

Drink soon   14.0

Gevrey-Chambertin   Clos-Prieur Louis Trapet Père et Fils

Medium colour. A little shitty on the nose. Medium body. Sweet, not without vigour and fruit, nor grip, but just a little simple and one-dimensional. Just about 'good'. (06/92)

Drink soon   15.0

Gevrey-Chambertin   Clos-Saint-Jacques Armand Rousseau

Medium colour. Lovely complex nose. Not perhaps as full as I had expected but a lot of concentration and finesse here. Ripe, oaky, harmonious and fragrant. Real *grand cru* quality. Perfectly *à point*. Lovely plump Pinot. Very, very long on the palate. Fine. **(06/92)**

Drink soon   **17.5**

Mazis-Chambertin   Joseph Faiveley

Full colour. Still very vigorous. Lovely rich nose. Plenty of concentration and grip. This is a very fine 1982, with bags of life left. Fullish, ample, meaty. Structured for a 1982. Lovely fruit. Very fine. **(01/94)**

Now-2000 plus   **18.0**

Mazis-Chambertin   Camille Giroud

Medium-full colour. Well-matured, stylish, fat and concentrated nose. Good ripe Pinot here. On the palate a touch of astringency, a touch loosening of grip. A touch of a vegetal stalky aspect behind it. Yet very good and complex on the finish. **(06/92)**

Drink soon   **16.0**

Musigny   *Vieilles-Vignes*
Comte Georges de Vogüé

Good fullish mature colour. Good round soft nose. Good round soft spicy attack. Then it appears to tail off a bit, but the finish is more vigorous than the aftertaste suggests. Plump, fruity. Not unstylish and still plenty of vigour. Very good. **(07/91)**

Drink soon   **16.0**

Nuits-Saint-Georges   Les Boudots
Jean Grivot

Medium colour. Fine vigorous concentrated Pinot Noir. This shows very well indeed. Fragrant, complex and surprisingly well balanced. This has a lot of depth and plenty of life still. Firm. Fullish, rich, masculine. Fine. **(06/92)**

Now-2000   **17.5**

Nuits-Saint-Georges   Les Porrets-Saint-Georges   Joseph Faiveley

Good colour. Vigorous as well. Rich, concentrated old-viney. Low harvest year. Quite chunky, typically Nuits - more so than Grivot's Boudots, not surprisingly. Fullish, vigorous. Sturdy. Better with food. Very good indeed. **(06/92)**

Drink soon   **17.0**

Nuits-Saint-Georges   Les Saint-Georges
Henri Gouges

Good colour. Ripe and fragrant on the nose, but not that much intensity. Medium-full. Riper, sweeter and more vigorous on the palate than the nose would indicate. Good style. Rich and long on the finish. Very good. **(06/92)**

Drink soon   **16.0**

Nuits-Saint-Georges   Les Vignes-Rondes
Daniel Rion et Fils

Medium colour. Round and fresh and very oaky on the nose. This has cast a certain bitter astringency on to the wine, but medium-full, ripe, balanced and fresh, if a little rigid. Very good. **(06/92)**

Drink soon   **16.0**

Pommard   Clos-des-Epeneaux
Comte Armand

Good colour. Ripe and rich and supple and balanced. Charmingly full of fruit. No great power, but plenty of depth. Lots of charm. Long. Very good for the vintage. Not marked so well at the 06/92 tasting, but seems to have improved as it has softened further. **(02/95)**

Now-2000   **16.0**

Pommard   Les Jarollières   Pousse d'Or

Good colour. Rich, ripe nose. Good depth and complexity. This is rather better than the Bousse d'Or, as well as more alive. The fruit has begun to lose its sweetness, but there is a good grip of acidity. Finishes better than it starts. Good plus. **(06/92)**

Drink soon   **15.5**

Pommard   Les Rugiens   Jacques Parent

Very good colour. Still vigorous. Plump, rich, oaky nose. Good depth here. Fullish; evidently a vintage which suits the Parent sturdy style. Rich, succulent, satisfactory. Very good. Plenty of life still. **(06/92)**

Drink soon   **16.0**

Puligny-Montrachet   Les Houillères
Duc de Magenta

Lightish colour. Soft, gentle but fragrant Pinot Noir. This is ripe and stylish. Still fresh. Medium body. Nothing solid or rustic about it. Balanced, long. Not exactly complex or concentrated but a nice little wine. Holding up surprisingly well. **(06/92)**

Drink soon   **14.0**

Richebourg   Jean Gros

Very good colour. Full, concentrated, rich, oaky nose. Still youthful. A very fine very concentrated wine. Lovely old-viney fruit. Great class and depth. Intense, persistent. Excellent. **(06/92)**

Now-2000 plus   **19.5**

Richebourg
Roland Remoissenet Père et Fils

A little inevitable dilution because of the vintage. Not really rich or concentrated, but fresh nevertheless, no age or attenuation. Good class of fruit. Reasonable balance and positive finish. Very good for 1982. But by no means great. **(06/96)**

Drink soon   **16.0**

Richebourg   Romanée-Conti

Medium-full colour. Mature but not unduly so. Sturdy nose. Dry tannins. This is sturdy but rich and fat and with good acidity touch but not without merit. Yet hard and slightly unforthcoming. Yet the finish is clean and long and fine. **(07/92)**

Now-2000   **17.0**

Romanée-Saint-Vivant
Alain Hudelot-Noëllat

Good colour. Aromatic nose. There is a certain well-evolved aspect on the nose. On the verge of oxidation. But this is lacking on the palate. Full, rich, concentrated. Complete. A lovely harmonious, complex wine with really good style. Long, fragrant. Delicious. Very fine. **(06/92)**

Now-2000   **18.0**

Romanée-Saint-Vivant   Romanée-Conti

Good colour. Fragrant, concentrated, oaky nose. On the palate youthful, full, concentrated. Very good grip. This has class but it is still very young. Fine but not great. What it lacks is a little real class and succulence. **(06/92)**

Now-2000 plus   **17.5**

Romanée-Saint-Vivant   Michel Voarick

Medium-full colour. A bit rigid on the nose but good acidity. Somewhat souped-up, over-macerated and ungainly on the palate. Fullish but four-square and slightly coarse. Will get astringent. **(06/92)**

Drink soon   **14.0**

Ruchottes-Chambertin   Clos-des-Ruchottes
Armand Rousseau

Mature medium colour. Nice and ripe on the nose and on the attack but it lacks fat and it shows a bit of a lack of concentration and too much acidity at the end. It has lost its fruit. A bit thin and mean. Quite good. **(02/94)**

Drink soon   **14.0**

Savigny-lès-Beaune   La Dominode
Bruno Clair

Good colour. Rich, concentrated nose. Not a bit Côte-de-Beaune. More Nuits in flavour. Firm and full, just a little hard. Perhaps the fruit needs a little more aeration. Because it finishes better than it starts. Plenty of depth here but a little austere. Yet plenty of life. Good plus. **(06/92)**

Drink soon   **15.5**

Savigny-lès-Beaune   Les Guettes
Simon Bize et Fils

Good colour. Good ripe, spicy, gently oaky Pinot Noir. Depth and vigour here. Ripe cherries. Fat on the attack, quite full. A touch of astringency at the end but a wine of complexity and style. Good concentration even. Surprisingly good. **(06/92)**

Drink soon   **15.0**

Savigny-lès-Beaune   Les Lavières
Chandon-de-Briailles

Good colour. A touch vegetal on the nose. But quite full and ripe and pleasant on the palate. Good depth and vigour. Fat and fruity. Good grip. Not exactly very stylish but good nevertheless. **(06/92)**

Drink soon   **14.5**

Savigny-lès-Beaune   Les Vergelesses   Leroy

A bit of oxidisation. Old-fashioned. Slightly over-macerated. Ripe but not graceful. Quite good. **(07/92)**

Drink soon   **14.0**

La Tâche   Romanée-Conti

Good colour. No undue maturity. Fresh, sturdy and rich on the nose. But slightly hard as a result of the stems. Fuller, richer and more generous on the palate. Full, vigorous, very very ripe. Gamey. But slightly lean at the end. Very good but not great for a La Tâche. Vigorous. Bags of life. **(10/92)**

Now-2000   **17.0**

Volnay   Clos-de-la-Bousse-d'Or
Pousse d'Or

Medium colour. Fully mature. This is fresh and delicious on the nose. This is very stylish indeed. Very good grip. This is drying a little but I love the style. Really complex. Very pure and totally unadulterated. Very fine for the vintage. **(07/95)**

Drink soon   **18.0**

Volnay   Caillerets   Pousse d'Or

Medium to medium-full, vigorous colour. Soft and fragrant, plump and stylish and attractive on nose and palate. Holding up well. Clean and sweet, balanced and elegant. Lots of character. Long, subtle, even had depth. Plenty of life ahead of it. Very good indeed for a 1982. **(09/94)**

Drink soon   **17.0**

Volnay   Champans   Hubert de Montille

Reasonable colour. Mature. Fat, fragrant and gamey nose. This shows good style and vigour. On the palate this is medium body. Showing a little sign of astringency. No point in pushing one's luck. Nice fruit. Good freshness still. Very good. **(07/95)**

Drink soon   **16.0**

Volnay   Clos-des-Chênes   Michel Lafarge

Good colour. Lovely nose. This is rich, creamy, complex and beautifully balanced. And a great deal more elegant than the Lafarge Beaune, Grèves. Fullish, à point. Long, very stylish. Excellent finish. Fine quality. **(06/92)**

Now-2000   **17.5**

Volnay   Santenots   Robert Ampeau

Fine colour. Still vigorous. Round, ripe, surprisingly youthful on the nose. Delicious fruit. Lots of complexity and depth. This is riper and more vigorous than most 1982s. Classy. Harmonious. Long. Will still keep well. Complex positive finish. **(07/95)**

Now–2000   17.5

Volnay   Santenots   Matrot

Fullish, fully mature colour. Smooth, soft and elegant. Very good grip. Silky, fragrant. Long and complex. This is *à point* and delicious. Naturally sweet at the end. Not that concentrated but very good indeed for the vintage. **(11/95)**

Now–2000   17.0

**Volnay   Santenots-du-Milieu
Comtes Lafon**

Reasonable colour. Mature. Beginning to get attenuated on the nose. But ripe and quite pleasant. Round. Elegant, ripe, complex, fully developed. Medium body. Good freshness still. Drink soon. Very good plus. Several notes. **(07/95)**

Drink soon   16.5

Vosne-Romanée   Jean Gros

Very good colour. Toasted oaky nose. Ripe and rich and fresh. Fullish, succulent, ample and oaky on the palate. Alive and balanced. Very good style. Like the Barthod-Noëllat Chambolle a remarkably good example of a simple village wine. Very good indeed. **(06/92)**

Drink soon   16.5

Vosne-Romanée   Leroy

Ripe, complex, balanced and succulent. A little one-dimensional but good for a village *Appellation Contrôlée*. Still fresh. **(07/92)**

Drink soon   15.0

**Vosne-Romanée   Cros-Parentoux
Henri Jayer**

This is a very impressive bottle. Good colour. No undue age. Rich, mature complex, concentrated nose. A lot of depth. Fullish for a 1982, very vigorous. Rich and subtle and persistent on the palate. Very fine and very elegant. A very lovely example. Multi-dimensional. **(06/96)**

Now–2005   18.5

Vougeot   Les Cras   Bertagna

Medium colour. Fresher and more stylish than the Petits-Vougeots. A little more depth and substance as well as vigour. Yet also getting towards the end of its life. Yet reasonable fruit and style. Quite good plus. **(06/92)**

Drink soon   14.0

Vougeot   Les Petits-Vougeots   Bertagna

Medium colour. Quite a fragrant nose but showing a little age now. A touch of oak. Medium body. Ripe but lacks a little dimension and now losing whatever style it had. Quite good. **(06/92)**

Drink up   14.5

1981

Red: (12.0)   **White:** (11.0)
(both now past their best)

SIZE OF THE CROP

(Hectolitres, excluding generic wine)

	Red	White
Grands Crus	7,115	1,859
Village and Premiers Crus	83,685	25,036
Total	90,800	26,895

At less than half of what would today be an average harvest and only 38 per cent of what would be produced in 1982, 1981 is indeed tiny. It ranks with 1971 and 1975 as the smallest Burgundy has produced in modern times.

Sadly the quality too was miserable. Despite some unexpectedly good wines the overall standard was disappointingly poor. God did not smile on Burgundy in 1981.

WEATHER CONDITIONS

Nineteen eighty-one gives us a demonstration of yet another adage. Irrespective of the weather in May or June or July, or indeed August, the quality of any year is decided by what happens in September. Prior to the heavy thunderstorms which set in about ten days before the harvest was due to commence on 1 October, and which continued all the way through the picking, it had in fact been exceptionally dry and hot. May was cold, and there was considerable frost damage, so it was a very small crop. But the flowering was reasonably successful, and the weather thereafter gave rise to a cautious optimism and finger-crossing hopes for an outcome such as 1961 (in Bordeaux) or 1971 (in Burgundy), vintages of scarcity but high quality.

Sadly it was not to be. Not only was the harvest tiny but the quality was indifferent. Moreover many Côte-de-Nuits villages had suffered hail damage in August.

THE STYLE OF THE WINE

WHITE WINES

Beyond the occasional surprise the vast majority of 1981s were lean and sour at the outset and never matured into anything better than 'just about palatable'. They are now tired.

RED WINES

Despite the bedraggled conditions, the Pinot Noir fruit, protected by the thick skins which had been created by the earlier dry weather, was not too diluted by the rain. Nor was rot too widespread, though, as always with the Pinot Noir, conscientious growers performed a *triage* to eliminate the worst. The wines were lean rather than watery, lacking that extra ripeness, concentration and generosity that another fortnight's dry warm weather would have brought. Acidities, obviously, were quite high, but this was not necessarily a bad thing. As they have evolved one can see that if there was not much in the way of charm or sex-appeal, there was at least elegance in the wines of the best-exposed sites and the most perfectionist growers. But this is now history.

TASTING NOTES

BLANC

Chevalier-Montrachet Leflaive

An evolved wine which now lacks a bit of fruit. Yet there is breed and balance here. Still alive but drink soon. **(02/92)**

Drink up   15.0

Corton-Charlemagne Bonneau du Martray

Elegant nose. No built-in sulphur. Slightly lean but certainly has depth and class. Medium body. Quite ripe. Has depth. This has length and complexity too. Good. **(06/91)**

Drink up   15.0

Meursault Genevrières Comtes Lafon

Very fresh colour. A little lean on the nose but much more opulent on the palate. Classy, more so than the Perrières. Ripe, balanced, gently oaky. Fine for the vintage. Will still last. More complete than the Perrières. Long on the palate. **(01/94)**

Drink soon   17.5

Meursault Perrières Comtes Lafon

Fresh colour. A slightly fatter wine than the Genevrières on the nose. But less alive and fruity on the palate. A little flatter. Just a little dull. Less dimension. Very good but not fine. **(01/94)**

Drink soon   16.0

Meursault Perrières Matrot

Leanish wine, with a touch of SO_2. No oak. Not a lot of fruit or vigour. Pleasant but not a lot of enjoyment, let alone sex-appeal here. **(02/95)**

Drink soon   14.0

Le Montrachet Comtes Lafon

Golden colour. Opulent, spicy, gently oaky nose. On the palate, though classy, lacks the real breed and concentration of Montrachet. I prefer the Genevrières. It has more life and complexity. Yet this is fat, aromatic and ripe. Very good indeed. **(01/94)**

Drink soon   17.0

Puligny-Montrachet Les Pucelles Leflaive

Good subtle oak but a little lean, a little obviously chaptalised and a touch of sulphur. Yet there is stylish if somewhat one-dimensional fruit here. Good for the vintage. Got better and better in the glass. Good less lumpy, more elegant. Very good. **(02/92)**

Drink soon   16.0

Puligny-Montrachet Les Truffières
Étienne Sauzet

Quite an old colour. An interesting nose. Classy

but slightly vegetal and with an element of old vegetable soup to this aspect. This is not as good as the 1982 Combettes. A little overblown. Lacking real classy fruit and ripeness. A bit old now. Yet has interest. **(02/91)**

Drink up   13.0

ROUGE

Beaune Boucherottes Louis Jadot

Medium colour. Not much nose but what there is is pleasant. Medium body. The acidity and the structure show a bit, but there is a good base of oak here. Some fruit. Quite stylish. Reasonable length. Good. **(06/91)**

Drink soon   15.0

Beaune Grèves Michel Lafarge

Good colour. Plump nose. Surprisingly good fruit. A meaty example, not a bit lean. Ample and even rich. This has substance and depth and good grip. Plummy fruit. Finishes positively. Very good. **(06/91)**

Drink soon   15.5

Beaune Les Sizies Antonin Rodet

Reasonable colour. Still fresh. Not much fruit on the nose though. Yet not nearly as bad, or as old as the 1984. This is better than I expected. Medium body. Reasonable fruit. If a bit one-dimensional. Good acidity. Still alive. Not bad. **(09/90)**

Drink up   13.0

Chambertin Armand Rousseau

Good colour. Full, rich, oaky concentrated nose. This is excellent. A really classy wine with depth, fruit, dimension and vigour. A lot of depth. Long and complex. Bags of life. **(06/91)**

Drink soon   19.0

Chambolle-Musigny
Gaston Barthod-Noëllat

Medium colour. Elegant nose. Still fresh. Good fruit. Medium body. This is a supple, plump attractive wine with plenty of depth and complexity. Medium body. Surprisingly good. **(06/91)**

Drink soon   16.5

Chambolle-Musigny Les Amoureuses
Jacques-Frédéric Mugnier

Medium colour. A little pongy on the nose. Slightly faded and dry. Getting a shade coarse. Lightish. This is a shade astringent and the acidity shows. **(06/91)**

Past its best   13.0

Clos-de-la-Roche   Dujac

Medium body. Round, slightly sandalwoody, fragrant nose with a touch of spice like cinnamon. This is a medium to medium-full, round, ripe, oaky wine. It hasn't a great deal of vigour but it is subtle and still fresh and long. Fine. **(06/91)**

Drink soon   17.0

Clos-de-Vougeot   Alain Hudelot-Noëllat

Magnum. Good colour. Fat, ripe nose. This has freshness and depth. Good new oak and plenty of concentration. Ripe, vigorous. Not a bit off-vintage. This is excellent. Lovely long ripe succulent finish. **(06/91)**

Drink soon   18.0

Corton   Bonneau du Martray

Medium colour. Light but fresh. Not a great deal of substance but has fruit and reasonable style and complexity. A bit lightweight and now fading a bit. Quite good. **(06/91)**

Drink up   14.5

Corton   Bressandes
Pierre Dubreuil-Fontaine

Better colour. Fuller spicier nose. Slightly gamey. Medium-full. A touch of astringency and rusticity but there is substance and vigour here if not a great deal of style. Fat, meaty. Good plus. **(06/91)**

Drink soon   15.5

Echézeaux   Romanée-Conti

Medium to medium-full colour. Surprisingly voluptuous. Strawberry, black cherry nose. No lack of ripeness and quality here. Fullish, structured. Very good grip. This is fine, multi-dimensional. Surprisingly good. Bags of life. Lacks just a little distinction at the end. Lost a little fruit as it developed. **(10/93)**

Drink soon   17.5

Gevrey-Chambertin   Lucien Boillot et Fils

Good colour. Good fresh nose. Medium body. Fresh and fruity but a touch one-dimensional, and now nearing the end of its useful life. Ripe fruit. Clean and classy. But not a lot behind it. Good though. **(06/91)**

Drink up   15.0

Gevrey-Chambertin   Denis Mortet

Medium colour. This is getting a little gamey and over-evolved on the nose, but there is still fruit here. On the palate a wine with a little less intensity and freshness than the above. Quite good. **(06/91)**

Drink up   14.0

Gevrey-Chambertin   *Vieilles-Vignes*
Denis Bachelet

Good colour. Ripe, fat, spicy nose. This is still fresh. Excellent palate. Rich, ripe, concentrated. Balanced and elegant and long. Fine. **(06/91)**

Drink soon   17.0

Gevrey-Chambertin   *Vieilles-Vignes*
Alain Burguet

Magnum. Good colour. Firmer, slightly spicier, slightly fuller on the nose. A medium-full ample example. But not as fresh and as concentrated as the Bachelet *Vieilles Vignes*. Ripe, quite complex. Certainly quite classy. I've had this wine before and it showed better. **(06/91)**

Drink soon   15.5

Gevrey-Chambertin   Clos-Saint-Jacques
Armand Rousseau

Good colour. Very classy nose. Soft but complex. Plump and even rich. Above all has breed. Touch of oak. Medium-full body. Elegant. Round. Still long and fresh. Fine. **(06/91)**

Drink soon   17.5

Ladoix   Chevalier Père et Fils

Medium colour. Still fresh. A little lean on the nose. But not rustic. On the palate not at all bad. Lightish, soft. Not a lot of concentration or succulence. A little lean as the nose suggests. But quite elegant. And certainly pleasant. Positive finish. **(02/94)**

Drink soon   14.0

Mazis-Chambertin   Joseph Faiveley

Because of the frost 7 hl/ha here. Fine colour. Still very youthful. Austere, firm, but very elegant nose. This is a little lean on the palate but not unconcentrated. Nor unstylish. Very good. Still has life. **(11/93)**

Drink soon   16.0

Mazis-Chambertin   Gérard Vachet-Rousseau

Good fresh mature colour. Not a bit weedy. On the palate it is only medium body. But plump, fruity and stylish. Even round. *À point*. Fresh. Not a bit lean. Surprisingly good. Most enjoyable. **(11/95)**

Now-2000   17.5

Nuits-Saint-Georges   Les Saint-Georges
Robert Chevillon

Medium colour. A bit faded and rustic on the nose. And rather astringent on the palate. Wasn't too bad once. There was fresh fruit if a bit of a lack of dimension. **(06/91)**

Past its best   13.0

**Nuits-Saint-Georges Les Vaucrains
Alain Michelot**

Medium colour. Has faded a little on the nose. Lightened a bit. Now a touch astringent and even coarse on the palate. **(06/91)**

Past its best   13.0

Pommard Epenots André Mussy

Good colour. Fat plump nose. Not as rustic as I feared. This still has fruit though the acidity is beginning to show. Medium body. Slightly spicy. Getting a shade coarse at the end. Good though. **(06/91)**

Drink soon   15.0

Richebourg Jean Gros

Medium-full colour. Mature but no undue age. This is more satisfactory on the nose than the Clos-de-Vougeot 1984 from Jean Gros. Rich, fat, concentrated and stylish. This is brilliant evidence that even in the poor vintages the quality of old vines and *grands crus climats* will out. On the palate classic Pinot, concentrated, even rich. Very lovely fruit. Finely balanced. Lively. Very long. It even improved as it evolved. Above all, great class. Very good indeed. **(05/92)**

Drink soon   17.0

Richebourg Romanée-Conti

Good colour. A little stemmy on the nose. Slightly hard and austere. Rounder and riper on the palate. Still youthful. Good grip. Still a little hard and austere on the follow-through though. Yet classy and long. **(06/91)**

Drink soon   16.0

**Savigny-lès-Beaune Vergelesses
Simon Bize et Fils**

Medium colour. Ripe, gamey nose. Not too faded, nor too rustic. A bit linear on the palate but not too lean. Fresh. Some fruit. Not inelegant nor short. Quite good. **(06/91)**

Drink soon   14.0

Volnay Lucien Boillot et Fils

Good colour. Not a wine of great style but has balanced fruit and depth, though it is lightening up now. Fresh though, not astringent. But a little coarse at the end. Quite good. **(06/91)**

Drink up   14.0

Volnay Clos-des-Chênes Michel Lafarge

Good colour. Very good nose. Touch of oak, ample, elegant, complex fruit. There is nothing a bit off-vintage about this. Not quite as fat on the palate as it appeared on the nose but has length and depth. More elegance but less fat compared with the Beaune, Grèves. Very good. **(06/91)**

Drink soon   16.0

Vosne-Romanée Jean Gros

Good colour. Ripe, fresh, complex, oaky nose. This has plenty of grip and plenty of style. Medium body. A shade lacking richness but a finely balanced example. Very good plus. **(06/91)**

Drink soon   16.5

1980

RATING FOR THE VINTAGE

Red: 16.0-13.0   **White:** (12.0)
(variable)   (past their best)

SIZE OF THE CROP

(Hectolitres, excluding generic wine)

	Red	White
Grands Crus	9,959	2,518
Village and *Premiers Crus*	141,410	35,023
Total	151,369	37,541

Apart from 1979, 1980 was the largest crop between 1973 and 1982. From the start it was steeped in controversy.

Many Beaune *négociants*, those who have land of their own in the Côte-de-Beaune, but not in the Côte-de-Nuits, tend to view Burgundy through Beaune-tinted spectacles. As it tends to be the Beaunois to whom wine writers and journalists, domestic and foreign, address themselves when they want to hear what a vintage is like, rather than for example, a grower in Gevrey or merchant in Nuits, and as it is Beaune which is the focus of the Hospices de Beaune weekend, when many descend to make their own assessment of the new vintage, there is a danger, should the quality be quite different in one Côte from another, that what will be taken away - and promulgated to the world at large - will be a distorted picture. Couple this with the superficiality and generality of much wine journalism - things have to be cut and dried, black and white - and it is not surprising that the consumer, even the merchant, tends to be given a misleading picture.

Where this is particularly unfair is when the vintage is indifferent in the Côte-de-Beaune but rather better in the Côte-de-Nuits. The Beaunois will condemn it; the poor Gevrey or Vosne grower, having done his best and produced perfectly respectable - indeed very good - wine will find it hard to sell. Few merchants will take the trouble to go and find out for themselves, or have the courage to contradict the received view.

Nineteen eighty-six was one of these vintages. Poor in the Côte-de-Beaune because of rain, rather better in the Côte-de-Nuits. Here the message of the variation did seem to get across. It was different for the 1980s. The situation was parallel. But in 1980 the injustice was compounded. One important *personnage*, the proprietor of one of Beaune's senior *négociant* companies, and owner of a large domaine in Corton - yes, Louis Latour himself - publicly expressed his disfavour with the quality of the crop. The 1980s have lived under a cloud ever since. That M. Latour made an unfortunate error will be seen in the tasting notes which follow.

WEATHER CONDITIONS

The 1980 vintage followed those of 1978 and 1979. All three were late harvests, the first part of the year being generally cold and wet. In all three the late summer produced better climatic conditions; an excellent *fin de saison* and a short crop in 1978 making for a fine vintage with good firm acidities; the very large crop in 1979 generally succeeding better in the Côte-de-

Beaune than in the Côte-de-Nuits (as my notes on this vintage in the next chapter will show); but the weather pattern in 1980 producing the reverse effect.

In 1980 August and September were more than satisfactory. The size of the crop was above average. The Hospices de Beaune auctioned 643 casks as against 712 in 1979 and 361 in 1978, and would sell off 429 *pièces* in 1981 and 712 again in 1982. There was rain during the vintage, however, and it was also humid. Not only was some of the fruit not altogether ripe, there was also rot.

Nineteen eighty was a vintage where the skill of the wine-maker was paramount. The spread of quality was wide, as you might expect. On the one hand, I remember from my journeys in the region in 1981, there were decidedly weak and fruitless wines - though they were not excessively acid, merely charmless. On the other, for instance from the firm of Bourée in Gevrey, the wines had a lot more definition and grip than the 1979s. I formed the impression that in the Côte-de-Nuits it was the 1980 in general which was the better vintage.

THE STYLE OF THE WINE

WHITE WINES

Nineteen eighty was one of those just-about-all-right vintages, like 1984, like 1987, where with careful selection of the very best growers you could find something decent amid a sea of rather lean dross. The vast majority of wines are now past it.

RED WINES

The reds are a different matter. There are some perfectly respectable Côte-de-Beaunes. These started off, like the whites, rather lean and unfriendly. The best had sufficient weight, if not the roundness of the 1979s, to mature into something quite a lot better than merely good. They were a little obviously 'assisted' though, and elegance was at a premium. Most of these should be drunk soon.

Move into the Côte-de-Nuits and you are presented with a quite different picture. The vigour is much in evidence, as is the finesse and the concentration. Overall it is significantly better, and there are a handful of domaines - the Domaine de la Romanée-Conti, Henri Jayer, Jean Gros, Hudelot-Noëllat, Roumier, Rousseau, Faiveley and Dujac, to pick those that come to mind immediately - whose top wines are outstanding: very much better than the equivalents in 1979. And they will still keep.

TASTING NOTES

BLANC

Chevalier-Montrachet   Leflaive

Deepish colour, especially compared with the Clavoillon 1979. Not a lot on the nose. Very good wood-fruit integration. High-class oak as always. Good fruit without great concentration but lovely style. Still bags of life. Very good indeed. **(03/93)**

Now-2000   **17.0**

Meursault   Perrières
Robert Ampeau et Fils

Very fresh colour. Fresh nose. Slight touch of reduction. On the palate a touch tired and attenuated. Less good than the 1984. Some sulphur here. **(01/95)**

Drink up   **12.5**

Montrachet   Louis Jadot

Golden but not aged colour. A soft wine with a good base of oak. No undue age. Mellow. Complex, classy, no lack of fruit. Surprisingly fine - not great, but undeniably fine. Will still last. **(06/96)**

Now-2000 plus   **18.5**

ROUGE

Beaune   Clos-des-Coucherias   Louis Jadot

Medium body. Hard, vegetabley nose, not much fruit, rather green and stalky. The fruit has dried out and the wine has got a bit coarse. Just a touch more fruit on the palate. Quite high acidity so it is not too rustic. Uninspiring though and past its best. **(06/90)**

Past its best   **13.5**

Beaune Clos-des-Ursules
Héritiers Louis Jadot

Medium colour. Mature. Soft nose. Fully mature. The fruit is beginning to dry up and coarsen. On the palate this is reasonably plump and attractive. Some dimension. Quite good for the vintage. (09/90)

Drink up   **14.0**

Beaune Grèves Michel Lafarge

Good colour. A little assisted and a little attenuated now. Quite ripe and rich. Medium-full body. Not bad but past its best. (06/90)

Past its best   **14.0**

Bonnes-Mares Georges Roumier

Medium body. Fully mature. A ripe nose but more gamey and vegetal than the above. Soft and round and fat and concentrated on the palate. Finishes long. Slightly more vigour and complexity than the above. But one can see the resemblance. Very good indeed. A similar note in March 1993. (06/90)

Now-2000   **17.0**

Chambertin Armand Rousseau

Fine colour. Still very young. Marked new oak on the nose. Full, ripe and concentrated on the palate. Not quite as intensely concentrated as the above. Not quite as fat but very classy. Very fine indeed. (06/90)

Now-2000 plus   **18.5**

Chambolle-Musigny Les Amoureuses
Jacques-Frédéric Mugnier

Medium colour. Not very intense but still quite youthful. Ripe, blackberry nose. On the palate this is medium-full, vigorous, ripe and very straight. It is even a little austere. Good balance. Long. Stylish. Very good. (06/90)

Now-2000   **16.0**

Clos-de-la-Roche Dujac

Good youthful-looking colour. Nose still a bit closed. Quite firm on the palate. Full, rich, intense. Very good grip. A lot of class. This is excellent. Ripe and concentrated and voluptuous. Two similar notes since. (06/90)

Now-2000   **18.5**

Gevrey-Chambertin *Vieilles-Vignes*
Alain Burguet

Good mature colour. Firmer nose and a little more rigid than the above. There is a touch of astringency about it on the attack. Full. Finishes better than it starts. Rich, vigorous. But not as generous and attractive as the above. A second bottle was rounder, more ample, much more positive. Very good indeed. (06/90)

Now-2000   **17.0**

Gevrey-Chambertin *Vieilles-Vignes*
Philippe Charlopin-Parizot

Good colour. A little age and lack of intensity on the nose. On the palate it has also lost a little of its fruit. Medium body. The acidity shows a little bit. Yet not too bad. Medium to medium-full body. (06/90)

Drink soon   **13.5**

Gevrey-Chambertin Les Champeaux
Charles Mortet

Good fullish, mature colour. Soft, ripe and gamey on the nose. No lack of fruit and class. Fullish on the palate. More vigorous than I would have expected. Round and generous with good fresh, stylish fruit. Shows well. Very good plus. (06/90)

Now-2000   **16.5**

Gevrey-Chambertin Clos-Saint-Jacques
Armand Rousseau

Fine colour. Vigorous but mature. Rich and round and vigorous on nose and palate. Lots of class. *À point.* This is ripe, reasonably structured, with very good grip. A lovely example. Proof again how good this vintage is. Fine fruit. Fresh and complex. Very fine indeed. (11/94)

Now-2000   **18.5**

Mazis-Chambertin Joseph Faiveley

Good colour. Excellent nose. Real concentration and depth. Fullish, fine old-vine complexity and intensity of flavour. Rich. Vigorous. Long. This is excellent. Quite lovely. (06/90)

Now-2000 plus   **19.0**

Morey-Saint-Denis Dujac

Magnum. Good fresh colour. Ripe nose, but now showing a little age. Medium body. Good class, good intensity. Better on the palate. Good fruit and grip. But now approaching the end of its life. Very good for a village wine. (03/94)

Drink soon   **16.0**

Musigny *Vieilles-Vignes*
Comte Georges de Vogüé

Good fresh, fullish colour. Delicious fragrant silky nose. This is high quality. Ripe and full of lovely soft raspberry fruit. Medium to medium-full body. Balanced. Very classy. Vigorous, surprisingly so. Silky, round and seductive. (10/92)

Drink soon   **18.0**

Nuits-Saint-Georges Les Hauts-Pruliers
Daniel Rion et Fils

Good colour. A softer, plumper, more fragrant, more stylish nose. Medium-full. Lovely fruit. Finely balanced. Rich, plump and generous. Very good indeed. Raspberry, mulberry and blackberries with good acidity. Still plenty of life. Very good indeed. **(06/90)**

Now-2000   17.0

Nuits-Saint-Georges   Les Pruliers
Henri Gouges

Medium colour, fully mature. On the nose there is a little attenuation. More stylish on the palate but a wine which now needs drinking, is beginning to fall apart. Essentially ripe, quite stylish, with good acidity. Was better a few years ago. Still enjoyable though. The finish is still reasonably fresh. Good. **(06/90)**

Drink soon   15.0

Nuits-Saint-Georges   Les Vignes-Rondes
Daniel Rion et Fils

Good colour. Ripe, meaty, fullish, ample. Plenty of depth here and even some class. Good rich fruit, quite concentrated. Medium-full. Ripe and balanced. Shows very well. Long. Vigorous. Very good. **(06/90)**

Now-2000   16.0

Pommard   Clos-des-Epeneaux
Comte Armand

Full, vigorous colour. Rich, ripe, old-vine, small *rendement* nose. But both gamey and farmyardy as well. Full, ripe and rich, plenty of extract and depth. Basically a fine wine to some extent diminished by bad wine making. Still enjoyable. Good. **(06/90)**

Drink soon   15.0

Pommard   Epenots   André Mussy

Medium colour, reasonable vigour. Slightly attenuated on the nose. This was a good wine but it is a little over the hill. The fruit has lost its richness, the style is getting a touch coarse. Medium-full. A touch astringent. Yet good depth. Quite good. Was better a few years ago. **(06/90)**

Drink up   14.0

Pommard   Jarollières   Pousse d'Or

Medium colour. Quite a vigorous nose and attack, but like his Volnay a little age on the follow-through. Ripe, stylish fruit but a touch of astringency and on the finish a slight lack of class and cleanliness. Not bad. **(06/90)**

Past its best   13.0

Romanée-Saint-Vivant
Alain Hudelot-Noëllat

Good colour. Lovely, concentrated, vigorous, generous nose. Nothing a bit non-vintage about this. Very stylish, ripe Pinot. On the palate fullish, round and velvety. Ripe. Very complex. Long. Vigorous. Excellent. **(06/90)**

Now-2000 plus   19.0

Ruchottes-Chambertin   Louis Jadot

Medium colour. Quite an evolved nose but not old. Plump, soft, round, velvety. Generous. A very ripe wine. Good fruit. Good acidity. Most attractive. But not, essentially, enough breed or complexity. Very good rather than very fine. **(06/90)**

Now-2000 plus   16.0

Santenay   Louis Clair

Light to medium colour. Quite brown. Rustic, somewhat attenuated nose. Rather blowsy. Better on the palate than the nose. Reasonable acidity. Some fruit. Medium body, not very stylish though. A little over-assisted. Drink soon. **(06/90)**

Past its best   13.5

Savigny-lès-Beaune   La Dominode
Bruno Clair

Good colour. Fresh, firm nose with a slightly burnt, liquorice flavour to it. A little rigid on the palate. A bit hard. Quite high acidity but not lacking fruit or even richness. Has depth. Good. **(06/90)**

Drink soon   15.0

Savigny-lès-Beaune   Les Lavières
Chandon-de-Briailles

Lightish colour but not too brown. Yet on the nose rather old, tired and blowsy. Lightish body. The fruit has dried up – whatever there was – and the acidity shows. Not special. Past its best. **(06/90)**

Past its best   13.0

Savigny-lès-Beaune   Les Marconnets
Simon Bize et Fils

Reasonable colour, not too much brown. A little blowsy and assisted on the nose. Better on the palate. Quite stylish Pinot; fresh acidity. Ripe and rather more generous than the Chandon-de-Briailles' Lavières. But doesn't have quite as much depth. Quite good. **(06/90)**

Drink soon   14.0

La Tâche   Romanée-Conti

Full colour. Just about mature. Animal, concentrated, gamey, exotic nose. Fullish, sweet, rich, vigorous and concentrated. Good grip. Just a touch of the stems, but only when you know to look for it. Faded just a little in the glass. But smooth, very elegant, very lovely indeed. Very very long. Very fine indeed. **(03/95)**

Now-2000   19.5

Volnay   Caillerets, Clos-des-Soixante-
Ouvrées   Pousse d'Or

Medium colour. Good soft nose. Stylish Pinot. Not too old. On the palate there is a touch of astringency. Medium body. Slightly less exciting on the finish than I had anticipated on the nose. Quite good. **(06/90)**

Drink up   **14.0**

Volnay   Champans   Marquis d'Angerville
Lightish mature colour. Light on the nose. But pleasantly soft and stylish and slightly vegetabley. On the palate a little astringent. Acidity beginning to show. Quite good but on the descent now. **(07/95)**

Drink up   **14.0**

Volnay   Clos-des-Chênes   Michel Lafarge
Good colour. A great deal more vigour and style than the Beaune, Grèves. Good rich wine on the palate. Fullish, meaty. Perhaps just a touch assisted. Perhaps not enormous finesse but very good all the same. **(06/90)**

Now-2000   **16.0**

Volnay   Santenots   Robert Ampeau et Fils
Good vigorous colour for a 1980. Good nose. But a little H$_2$S. Lacks a bit of class. Slightly soupy. This is still attractive and vigorous, if not with a lot of elegance. More structure than the above. But again at the end it is falling apart a bit. **(07/95)**

Drink soon   **15.0**

Volnay   Santenots-du-Milieu
Comtes Lafon
Good colour. Still youthful. Rich, firm but somewhat austere nose. Fullish, fine plummy fruit on the nose. More generous on the palate. This has plenty of depth and bags of life. Long, complex, balanced. Very good. **(06/90)**

Now-2000   **16.0**

Vosne-Romanée   Jean Gros
Medium-full, mature colour. Plump, fruity nose, but now showing just a little age. Certainly a bit gamey. Medium-full, ripe. Very good old-vine concentrated Pinot for a village wine. **(06/90)**

Drink soon   **15.0**

Vosne-Romanée   Les Beaumonts
Alain Hudelot-Noëllat
Medium to full body. Fully mature. Not that intense or luscious on the nose but there is good fruit here if not a lot of vigour now. A little sweet, a little inelegant. Medium-full but quite soft. Not bad at best. **(06/90)**

Drink up   **13.0**

Vosne-Romanée   Les Chaumes
Daniel Rion et Fils
Good colour. Still vigorous. Quite a sturdy nose. But has good richness, even depth. Medium body. I don't find this quite as alive or as interesting as the other two Rion wines. The acidity is beginning to show just a little. Medium-full. Ripe. Good fruit nevertheless. Good. **(06/90)**

Drink soon   **15.0**

Vosne-Romanée   Cros-Parentoux
Henri Jayer
Very good colour. Plenty of fruit here if not a lot of richness. Good firm acidity. A slightly stemmy, rustic aspect and very much less oak than today. Fullish. Still vigorous. Very good but not great. **(10/93)**

Now-1999   **16.0**

Vosne-Romanée   Clos-des-Réas   Jean Gros
Good colour, still fresh. Ample, fruity nose with good vigour and depth. A ripe wine. Medium-full, a little gamey but ample, vigorous, balanced and complex and sensual. Good depth. Fine. Long. **(06/90)**

Drink soon   **17.5**

1979

Red: 14.5   **White:** 16.0

SIZE OF THE CROP

(Hectolitres, excluding generic wine)

	Red	White
Grands Crus	10,630	2,796
Village and *Premiers Crus*	148,905	45,007
Total	159,535	47,803

Overall a full third larger than 1978 (50 per cent up in white, 28.5 up in red), but only 13 per cent more than 1976 and 10 per cent greater than what 1980 would bring. A very large vintage for the time nevertheless.

WEATHER CONDITIONS

The start to the season was slow. It was a cold winter. After a glorious autumn at the end of 1978 the first few months of 1979 were wet and generally inclement, and this cool period continued into May. Though there were spring frosts the *sortie* was large and the flowering successful. Hail during the nights of 11 and 13 June reduced the crop in Nuits-Saint-Georges, Vosne-Romanée and Chambolle-Musigny but thereafter, though it was not exactly hot, the fruit was able to progress towards maturity without mishap, and the vintage began in the last week of September.

THE STYLE OF THE WINE

WHITE WINES

This is one of those large vintages, like 1973 and 1982, where for some reason the white wines were not only rather more concentrated and elegant than one was led to expect, but have lasted very much better. They have a better acidity than the 1982s, but otherwise are as accessible, as friendly, as plump and transparently 'honest' as in this later vintage. They have held up well in bottle. All but the very best now need drinking.

RED WINES

Commentators love to generalise. Of the 1979s it was said that the Côte-de-Beaune was better than the Côte-de-Nuits (the reverse was said about the 1980s). The wines were elegant and fruity but they lacked backbone and concentration. They would come forward soon. Prices dropped by some 18 per cent at the Hospices de Beaune auction, but remained at 1978 levels on growers' and *négociants'* tariffs. But there was plenty of wine, and these prices would remain stable for a number of years.

It is in fact impossible to generalise about Burgundy. I have had a number of excellent bottles (and my share of the watery, the attenuated and the inferior), and I only repeat that in Burgundy, especially in a prolific vintage, you must pick and choose and go to a name with an honourable reputation.

In the best 1979s - to contrast them with the 1978s - there is a feminine touch and a spicy element. The wines are less firm; acidity levels are lower. Yet, if there is no power or real concentration, there is balance, length and no lack of depth and attraction. There may well be many 1979s which are now nearing the end of their useful life. But the best, as the following tasting notes will show, are still vigorous and mouth-watering.

TASTING NOTES

BLANC

Beaune   Clos-des-Mouches   Joseph Drouhin
Ripe, slightly spicy. Gently oaky. Rather more on the palate than on the nose. Quite rich. Soft and stylish. Finishing long. Holding up well. Good. **(06/89)**
Drink soon   15.0

**Chassagne-Montrachet   Morgeots
Roland Remoissenet Père et Fils**
A little heavy and even sulphury. Typically Morgeots in its four-square aspect. Yet very young for a 1979. Rich, fat, opulent. Plenty of fruit. Quite full. But it lacks a bit of grace and bite. Improved in the glass. Gained elegance. Good plus. **(09/91)**
Drink soon   15.5

Chevalier-Montrachet   Georges Deléger
This is very classy indeed. Very fresh, excellently balanced. Cool and complex and intense. This is fullish but quite delicate, very long, very concentrated and very lovely. Super fruit, not a bit over-ripe. Very fine indeed. Proof again what a fine vintage 1979 is for white. **(10/95)**
Now-2000 plus   18.5

Chevalier-Montrachet   Leflaive
Now *à point*. Very elegant. Very harmonious. Great depth. Lovely. Will keep still very well. Medium-full. Real concentration and intensity. Brilliant. Several notes since. All ecstatic. **(03/92)**
Now-2000 plus   19.0

Corton-Charlemagne   Bonneau du Martray
Good fresh colour. Old nose but a very good acidity keeps it crisp and fresh. Intriguing floral flavours. Lime blossom and angelica, green hazelnuts. On the palate the wine is fully mature. Not a lot of evidence of oak. Delicate and fine. But not as rich and intense as I remember. Seems to be ageing faster than I thought in wood. Two other notes confirm this. **(05/94)**
Drink soon   17.5

Corton-Charlemagne   Louis Latour
Oldish colour. Quite fat on the nose. A slight lack of zip. On the palate the fruit has dried out

a little. Quite stylish, but a little lean. This is a little pedestrian. Rather four-square and a bit hard. Disappointing. Has it been well stored? **(01/95)**
Drink up   (see note)

Meursault   René Thevenin
This is delicious. Completely fresh. Balanced and elegant and clean. Good acidity. Now ripe, round, fresh and complex. Still will keep. Very good. **(12/95)**
Now-2000   16.0

Meursault   Blagny   François Jobard
Fresh colour. Fine nose. Full and concentrated. Lovely fruit. Good structure. Very Blagny. On the palate a beautifully made restrained example, like the man himself. Medium-full. Real concentration and intensity. Fresh. Very stylish fruit. Excellent grip. Lovely. Fine quality. And plenty of life ahead of it. **(10/94)**
Now-2000 plus   17.5

**Meursault   Charmes, Cuvée Albert Grivault
Prosper Maufoux, Hospices de Beaune**
Rich, quite oaky. Full and fat on the nose. On the palate youthful but now fully mature. Good acidity. Fresh and peachy. Lovely fruit. Complex and vigorous. Very good indeed. **(10/95)**
Now-2000 plus   17.0

Meursault   Goutte d'Or   Comtes Lafon
Intriguing smoky nose. There is a slight herbal, vegetal aspect - the mark of Goutte d'Or. Good acidity. Slightly four-square. Lacks a little *rondeur*. Best with food. Good vigour. Quite full. Mineral. Good but not great. **(09/92)**
Now-2000   15.0

**Meursault   Perrières
Robert Ampeau et Fils**
Very fresh colour. Round, nutty nose. Very good. This is *à point* and very good. But getting to the end. Plump and ample. Long and composed. Now soft. Complex and gentle. Still very fresh. Classy. Fine. **(01/95)**
Drink soon   17.5

Meursault   Perrières   Comtes Lafon
This is a sensual wine. Full and rich and quite powerful on the palate. Very concentrated. Very

lovely. Still has plenty of life. Indeed really vigorous for a wine of this age. Really quite masculine. **(10/95)**

Now-2005   **18.5**

Meursault Perrières Guy Roulot

This is quite firm and full. Good depth. Good acidity with a touch of greenness and hardness underneath. I thought it was 1978. Got fatter as it evolved. Youthful. Ripe. Rich. Vigorous. Fine. **(11/95)**

Now-2000 plus   **17.5**

Montrachet Comtes Lafon

Quite a deep colour. But a fresh, very very ripe, concentrated nose. Lovely. This is balanced, subtle and fragrant. Very *petits fruits rouges* as well as Chardonnay. Fine acidity. Great breed. The complete wine. *Grand vin*. Bags of life. **(09/92)**

Now-2005 plus   **20.0**

Morey-Saint-Denis Les Monts-Luisants Ponsot

Quite a deep colour. Full, oaky nose. Broad, highish acidity. Mature, ripe, medium-full, slightly austere. Gently oaky. Slightly vegetal and not classic Burgundy. Yet good (if not great) quality. Interesting. Still fresh. *À point*. **(05/92)**

Drink soon   **15.0**

Puligny-Montrachet Clavoillon Leflaive

Good colour. Little sign of age. Firm nose. Still very youthful, a lot of depth here. Fullish, broad, just a touch four-square but this has fine quality. Lovely fruit. High class. Real nuance and dimension. Bags of life. Fine. **(03/93)**

Now-2000   **17.5**

Puligny-Montrachet Les Combettes Étienne Sauzet

Now has lost a little of its vigour. Fat and rich but not quite the zip that it had five years ago. Fullish. Ample. Better on the finish than the nose which is a little petrolly. Very good. **(03/93)**

Drink up   **16.0**

Puligny-Montrachet Les Folatières Roland Remoissenet Pére et Fils

Fine mature wine here. Full, still very fresh. Very good grip. This is rich and classy, with plenty of depth. Now nutty as well as peachy. Holding up very well. Long, rich, complex, satisfying. Fine. **(06/96)**

Now-2000 plus   **17.5**

Puligny-Montrachet Les Pucelles Leflaive

Ripe, rich, profound and oaky, with lovely peach fruit - even a touch of redcurrants and raspberries. Medium-full. Vigorous. Long and complex. Very fine and very delicious. Very

lovely. Very fine lingering finish. **(03/93)**

Now-2000   **18.5**

Beaune Cent-Vignes Albert Morot

Medium colour. No undue age. Ripe, fragrant, gentle, fresh nose. Fully mature but still vigorous. Medium body. Good grip and good intensity. Now soft and not for the very long term. But it is elegant and stylish and plump and complex, if a little delicate. And good plus, even very good. For the end is long and subtle with plenty of finesse. **(07/94)**

Drink soon   **16.0**

Beaune Clos-des-Mouches Joseph Drouhin

Good colour. Fine, very elegant nose. An excellent expression of Pinot Noir fruit. Soft and fragrant. Still very fresh. Medium-full. Balanced and femininely soft. Good ripe fruit and if no great power or richness, certainly has length and depth. Very good. **(06/89)**

Drink soon   **16.0**

Beaune Clos-des-Ursules Héritiers Louis Jadot

A little more colour than the 1980 but a touch browner. Much better, more ample fruit than the 1980. Elegant. Pleasant and balanced. This has a lot more to it than most 1979s. Good concentration, no lack of grip. Medium body. Very good. **(09/90)**

Now-2000   **16.0**

Beaune Grèves Michel Lafarge

Good colour. Fine nose. Fatter and more concentrated than the Clos-des-Mouches. A lot of depth here. Fullish, ripe, stylish. A good gingerbread and cinnamon touch to add to the fruit. Still vigorous. A lovely example which will still keep well. Fine. **(6/89)**

Now-2000   **17.5**

Bonnes-Mares Georges Roumier

Good colour. Firm, rich, substantial nose. A fullish wine, spicy as well as sweet. Meaty but lacking a little dimension and elegance. Will still keep though. Certainly very good. **(06/89)**

Drink soon   **16.0**

Chambertin Louis Latour

Magnum. Medium-full mature colour. Fine, rich, ripe nutty nose. Very good oaky base. Fullish, very good grip. Classy. Very good depth. This is rich and concentrated. This is elegant, harmonious, long and complex. Just at the end it is a little 'hot'. But a fine example. **(03/94)**

Now-2000   **17.5**

Chambolle-Musigny   Les Amoureuses
Jacques-Frédéric Mugnier

Good colour. Quite solid on the nose. An element of rusticity and even a touch of volatile acidity. A bit solid and the fruit has lightened up and lost its elegance. Needs drinking soon. Not special. **(06/89)**

Drink up   **13.0**

Chambolle-Musigny   Les Charmes
Louis Jadot

Good colour. Curiously light and neutral, a little lacking vigour on the nose. Medium body. Quite fruity in a simple, pretty, slightly sweet way, but a lack of depth, power and concentration, not even compensated for by a Chambolle finesse. **(06/89)**

Drink soon   **15.0**

Chambolle-Musigny   Les Cras
Ghislaine Barthod-Noëllat

Good mature colour. Soft, elegant, stylish nose. This has good plump fruit and plenty of generosity and elegance. Complex. A lovely example of the vintage. Medium to medium-full. Plenty of vigour. Very good indeed. **(11/93)**

Now-2000   **17.0**

Clos-de-la-Roche   Dujac

Fullish colour. Lovely nose; stylish fruit, complex, persistent, still vigorous. Quite full, ripe and with a touch of spice, but like so many of these Côte-de-Nuits a little lack of real class and depth. Rather better than most though. Fine. Will still last. **(06/89)**

Now-2000   **17.5**

Clos-de-Vougeot   Château de la Tour

Good full colour. Slightly jammy on the nose: strawberries, raspberries and cherries. Medium-full; this has been a little over-assisted, there is a brown sugar element on the follow-through. Also a touch of astringency on the finish. Quite good. **(06/89)**

Drink soon   **14.0**

Clos-de-Vougeot   René Engel

Magnum. Medium-full colour. Fine ripe, opulent nose with a touch of spice; very seductive. On the palate this is not as vigorous as some, indeed, it needs drinking soon. The attack is better than the follow-through. Medium-full, ripe raspberry-flavoured wine. Finishes long nevertheless. Very good. **(06/89)**

Drink soon   **16.0**

Clos-de-Vougeot   Daniel Rion et Fils

Medium-full colour. Slightly pinched on the nose, and on the palate there is a certain filter-papery dryness. Medium body. Lacks a bit of richness and dimension. Good but not great. **(06/89)**

Drink soon   **15.0**

Corton   Château Corton-Grancey
Louis Latour

Medium-full colour. Good vigour. Mature nose, not a lot of concentration or depth or style. Medium body. Quite fresh. But a bit simple. Slightly boiled-sweety. Reasonable acidity. Good but not great. **(10/94)**

Drink soon   **15.0**

Corton   Clos-des-Meix   Comte Senard

Medium colour. Less vigorous on the nose; there is even a little fade here. Medium body. Ripe and fragrant and soft on the attack, getting a little thin on the finish. No astringency though. Just has lost a little of its vigour. Good but not great. **(06/89)**

Drink up   **15.0**

Corton   Clos-des-Cortons   Joseph Faiveley

Fine full colour. Splendid nose. Rich and fat and concentrated. A lot of depth and interest here. Fullish and again rich, fat and concentrated on the palate. A vigorous meaty wine. *À point* now and will keep very well. Lovely fruit. Excellent balance. Very fine. **(06/89)**

Now-2000 plus   **18.0**

Corton   Pougets   Louis Jadot

Good colour. Still youthful on the nose. Fine slightly firm Pinot, typically Corton. Quite full on the palate. A fine ripe, balanced wine but with a certain cold steeliness to it in the middle. Yet the finish is certainly warm, as well as vigorous. Will still keep very well. Fine. **(06/89)**

Now-2000   **17.5**

Gevrey-Chambertin   *Vieilles-Vignes*
Alain Burguet

Splendid colour. Lovely nose, very fine, rich, concentrated vigorous fruit. This is excellent. Full, rich and ripe, mult-dimensional, beautifully balanced. There is a great deal of depth, even power, here. High class. **(06/89)**

Now-2000   **17.0**

Gevrey-Chambertin   La Combe-aux-Moines
René Leclerc

Good vigorous colour for the age and vintage. Soft, animal, slightly exotic, slightly shitty. But lacks real elegance. Medium to medium-full body. Good grip. Mature but healthy. No real class but round and warm and generous. Good. A second bottle was fresher, less animal. **(11/92)**

Drink soon   **15.0**

Grands-Echézeaux   Romanée-Conti

Medium-full colour. Still vigorous. Fresh, open ripe nose. Quite a lot of stems. Fullish. Good structure. Ample, rich balanced fruit. Soft, quite well matured at the end. Mellow. No austerity. Long and balanced. This is ripe and very good, but not brilliant. It doesn't have the complexity, concentration and intensity. The 1979s were bottled without a single racking, fining or filtering. They spent all their life in the same cask. Some bottles have a lot of CO_2 in them still. Wines bottled barrel by barrel. Other bottles have been 'fine'. **(10/94)**

Now-2000   16.0

Morey-Saint-Denis *Vieilles-Vignes*
Hubert Lignier

Premier cru. Fragrant, medium weight. Good fruit but not super concentrated. But quite new oaky, just about at, if not over, the limit. Not enough substance in the wine to match this. Quite stylish though. Good. **(10/93)**

Now-2002   15.0

Nuits-Saint-Georges   Clos-des-Corvées
Louis Jadot

Medium colour. This is getting just a touch lean on the finish. There is a slight vegetal touch. But the grip is there, and at the same time it is youthful. I would think that this has a somewhat 1972 aspect in its youth. Yet a good mature fruit. Rather better with Epoisses. The acidity cut into the cheese. The fat of the cheese added to the roundness of the wine. Developed in the glass. Got more generous. Will still keep very well. **(6/94)**

Now-2000   15.5

Nuits-Saint-Georges   Les Hauts-Pruliers
Daniel Rion et Fils

Good colour. Fragrant, very youthful indeed. Even a touch raw Pinot on the nose. Medium-full, ripe, young, lacking a little richness and fat. Quite pronounced acidity. Still will keep well. Good but not great. **(06/89)**

Now-2000   15.0

Nuits-Saint-Georges   Les Perdrix   Leroy

Very fine full colour. Full, concentrated nose, very splendid rich, concentrated, meaty fruit. Black cherries and plums. A fullish very young wine with very ripe creamy fruit. Still a little tannin. Very fine. A typically masculine meaty, four-square Nuits-Saint-Georges in the best sense of the expression. **(06/89)**

Now-2000 plus   18.0

Nuits-Saint-Georges   Les Vaucrains
Henri Gouges

Good full colour. A strong smell of lees and reduction on the nose. Medium body, round and fat with a strong *goût de terroir*. A touch of astringency on the finish. Good but not great. **(06/89)**

Drink up   15.0

Pommard   Clos-des-Epeneaux
Comte Armand

Magnum. Good full colour. Fullish, concentrated, fresh, very ripe and very youthful on the nose. Both power and depth here. Excellent. A fullish meaty wine. Ripe and succulent on the attack, warm and opulent on the finish. Vigorous if not an enormous amount of style. Very good. **(06/89)**

Now-2000   16.0

Pommard   Pézerolles   Hubert de Montille

Very good colour. Still very fresh looking. Lovely nose. Rich, succulent, pure fruit. Very pure indeed. Classy. Balanced. Medium-full. Ripe and round. Smooth, velvety but very vigorous. A lovely example. I haven't had a 1979 as good as this for ages. Bags of life. **(10/94)**

Now-2000 plus   15.0

Pommard   Rugiens   Lejeune

Fresh, deep, ruby colour. This is plump, youthful and vigorous for a 1979. It is a little souped-up, and it lacks the fat and concentration and backbone of a Rugiens. And essentially it lacks class. But it is a generous, seductive, attractive bottle with plenty of life left. Good. **(07/95)**

Now-2000 plus   15.0

Romanée-Saint-Vivant   Romanée-Conti

Really quite an evolved colour for a 1979 of this class. Yet fragrant and ripe enough on the nose. On the palate medium to medium-full. Sweet if a bit simple. Not a great deal of class but certainly very good. Not a great deal of vigour but certainly will last until 1999, but just. At the 'ten year on' tasting in 1989 was very classy, and marked 18, but that was a bottle direct from the domaine. **(11/93)**

Drink soon   16.0

Savigny-lès-Beaune   Les Guettes
Simon Bize et Fils

Magnum. Good colour. A meaty nose with a touch of the Savigny firmness and rustic farmyardness. Ripe, with a slight element of cooked fruit. Fullish, rich, fat, slightly spicy. Black cherry fruit with a touch of molasses. Still very youthful for a ten-year-old 1979. Will last well. Good. **(06/89)**

Now-2000   15.0

**Volnay Clos-de-la-Bousse-d'or
Pousse d'Or**

Magnum. Fullish colour. Excellent nose again. Ripe, spicy, subtle, slightly more gingerbready than the Clos-des-Chênes. On the palate just a little more evolved, despite being in magnum, but good concentration and depth. Not quite as creamy and exciting but fine nonetheless. **(06/89)**

Drink soon   17.5

Volnay Clos-des-Chênes Michel Lafarge

Good colour. Lovely nose. Real elegance and complexity here. A lovely expression of fruit. Medium-full. Ripe and rich, subtle and multi-dimensional. Very long. Once again this will keep very well. A really lovely example. Very fine. **(06/89)**

Now-2000 plus   18.0

Volnay Santenots Robert Ampeau et Fils

Good colour. No undue brown. Quite pure on the nose. Less sweet than the Remoissenet. Good acidity. Very good style and length. This is excellent. A lovely touch of oak. Very complex. Very pure. Very long. Very classy. Volnays don't come much better than this! **(07/95)**

Now-2000 plus   18.0

Volnay Santenots Comtes Lafon

Good colour. No undue brown. Very fragrant on the nose. Again ripe and sweet, but not soupy. Gentle, complex and classy. This is showing a bit of age now. Slightly astringent. Medium to medium-full body. Long. Not as good as the nose at first. **(07/95)**

Drink soon   16.0

**Volnay Santenots Roland Remoissenet
Pére et Fils**

Very good colour for a 1979. Nicely sweet and chocolatey on the nose. Ripe raspberries. Still vigorous. Round and smooth. Fullish, very silky. Ripe and rich and attractively fruity. Long. Very good indeed. **(07/95)**

Now-2000 plus   17.0

Vosne-Romanée Daniel Rion et Fils

Good colour. Fresh, ripe Pinot on the nose. Very straight. Good for a village wine. This is by no means outclassed. Medium-full, ripe and meaty and masculine. Has size, depth and balance. Fine. Very good indeed. **(06/89)**

Now-2000   17.0

**Vosne-Romanée Les Beaumonts
Jean Grivot**

Good colour. Quite fat on the nose with a slight earthy, vegetal touch. This is rapidly losing what fruit it had. There is a slightly sour vegetal element on the palate. Medium-body. Not exciting. **(06/89)**

Drink up   13.0

1978

RATING FOR THE VINTAGE

Red: 16.5   **White:** 15.5

SIZE OF THE CROP

(Hectolitres, excluding generic wine)

	Red	White
Grands Crus	8,546	2,103
Village and *Premiers Crus*	115,606	29,670
Total	124,152	31,773

One of the smaller crops of the decade. Only 1981, 1975 and 1971 are significantly lower. Nineteen seventy-four, however, is almost identical in size.

WEATHER CONDITIONS

The 1978 weather pattern followed that of 1977, and was echoed by both 1979 and 1980 – though not by 1981. The resulting wines were different, but one important factor links these four successive harvests. In each the progress of the vine was severely delayed by poor weather in the spring. Where 1978 differs from the other years was in the quality of the weather in late summer and early autumn. From the very lip of disaster the vintage, miraculously, was not just rescued into the realms of the acceptable, but promoted into the ranks of the successful. From the first week of August, when the vine was almost a month behind schedule, the sun shone and the grapes were enabled to swell and ripen without interference. The fine weather continued until mid-October, when, more than a fortnight late, the vintage was finally ready to begin.

At the beginning, it hardly seemed possible that the miracle had happened. As late as the first of October, sugar readings in the vineyard indicated below 10 (alcoholic) degree wines, suggesting that a lot of chaptalisation would be required – the legal limit is the amount of sugar which will increase the alcoholic degree by 2 degrees. My supplier of Bourgogne Aligoté and Montagny - for I was a wine-merchant in those days - Roger Rageot, the Director of the Buxy Cooperative in the Côte Chalonnaise, told me that the grapes gained 2 degrees in the last fortnight.

Initially, also, though the colour was adequate, it was by no means as full as the 1976 vintage had been at the outset, and the wines, though fruity and elegant, seemed to lack a bit of guts; they appeared a little hollow in the middle. Red Burgundy, however, takes on both colour and body during the winter, partly from the oak casks - though few growers are as insistent as their Bordeaux peers on new oak - and partly from the lees. I do remember, though, being disappointed by the Hospices wines, which I found light, even thin, with the exception of the new addition, the Hospices' only Nuits holding, a splendid Mazis-Chambertin. Wines tasted elsewhere, however, on the *Trois Glorieuses* weekend, seemed more ripe, more concentrated, and one was reminded to make allowance for their youth, for they were barely three weeks old, half the age the 1976s had been on the same weekend.

THE STYLE OF THE WINE

WHITE WINES

The whites were blessed by good acidity. They were quite full, had good structure, and were ripe, racy, balanced and stylish. As they evolved - and were compared with the 1979s - it became a question of individual taste which one preferred: the charm and instant appeal of the one, or the sometimes rather austere rigidity - but certainly depth - of the other. In the long run the 1979s won, in my view, but there are plenty of equally as good if not better 1978s. Today, not unexpectedly, after nearly twenty years, they are nearing the end of their active life.

RED WINES

The reds too had good acidity. At first they were clean, richly fruity and had a lot of style. They were clearly better, if not as big as the 1976s, but they did not quite have the refinement of the 1971s. On the other hand they were more even and lasted better.

Today the mark of the 1978 vintage is a finesse and consistency throughout the Côte; this is not one of those vintages (both 1979 and 1980 spring to mind) where one can single out a section of the *vignoble* as being superior to the rest. The wines have a vigour and a harmony which have given them structure to last. Pleasant as they were in their youth, they now have the extra dimension and character of maturity. The best will last safely until the year 2000 or more. While in the final analysis few wines have the richness, the succulence and the generosity to make them really fine, 1978 is a very good vintage.

TASTING NOTES

BLANC

Bâtard-Montrachet Leflaive

This is very lovely. Rich and oaky. Profound and with heaps of ripe complex succulent fruit. Good acidity. Still very fresh. Very fine. Not perfect - but very fine. Didn't quite hold up in the glass as well as the initial attack would indicate. (09/91)

Drink soon   18.5

Bâtard-Montrâchet Ramonet

Quite a deep colour. Rich, round, fat very oaky nose. Despite the colour still very fresh. Because of the oak quite structured. Fullish, rich and balanced. An open ample, seductive wine. Still has life. A little rigid at the end. Very good though. (03/94)

Drink soon   16.0

Chevalier-Montrachet Louis Latour

Rich, full, a lot of concentration. This is a fine example. Vigorous, ample, very good oak, very good grip. Not alcoholic nor sulphury. Youthful, very rich on the follow-through. Very classy. Very fine. Plenty of life. (03/94)

Now-2000 plus   18.0

Corton-Charlemagne Bonneau du Martray

Ripe, delicate, cool, gently oaky. Not, perhaps as fine or as complex as the 1979, but plenty of dimension here. Good acidity. Long. Peachy. Fresh. Very good indeed. (03/94)

Drink soon   17.0

Corton-Charlemagne Louis Latour

Evolved colour. Old slightly vegetal but rich mellow, complex classy nose. Splendid depth. A lot of class. Still very, very fresh. Not a bit heavy. This has very, very good grip. Nicely austere. Long. Classy. Fine. Eighteen months earlier a bottle tasted alongside the Bonneau du Martray was less good: a little sweet and a little pedestrian. (11/95)

Now-2000   17.5

Meursault Charmes Comtes Lafon

Rich, firm nose. A lot of individuality. Full, fleshy, old-vine concentrated. Good oak. All sorts of fruit from crab apple to peach to quince. Long. Complex. Intense. Fine. (03/94)

Now-2000 plus   17.5

Meursault Les Chevalières Leroy

Good colour. Vigorous, gently oaky nose. This is gentle, very stylish, subtle, ripe and delicious. Medium body. Fragrant, fresh, long and lovely. Bags of life. (03/94)

Now-2000   16.0

Meursault Clos-des-Perrières
Albert Grivault

An ample wine. Very good plump nose. Rich, fullish, just a little four-square, but ripe, gently oaky. Good class. Still fresh. Still plenty of vigour. Good length. Very good plus. (03/94)

Drink soon   16.5

Puligny-Montrachet Louis Latour

Fresh colour. Smells like a wine which has always been rather dominated by its sulphur and has now lost a bit of its fruit. On the palate now a touch astringent and rigid, the acidity beginning to show. Not very exciting. (03/94)

Drink up   13.0

Puligny-Montrachet Combettes
Robert Ampeau et Fils

Good fresh colour. Rich, fresh, nutty nose. This is a lovely example, very vigorous. Medium to medium-full, good acidity. Delicate, intense, finely balanced. Very good indeed. Not exactly fat though. À point. (09/95)

Now-2000 plus   17.0

Puligny-Montrachet Clavoillons Leflaive

Ripe, vigorous, fat. A little built-in sulphur. On the palate while elegant, a little attenuated. Not dried out. Was better ten years ago. Not bad. (03/94)

Past its best   13.0

ROUGE

Beaune Cuvée Bétault
Hospices de Beaune, Louis Latour

Very good colour. Plenty of life. Classy nose. A lot of depth and dimension here. Fine fruit, lots of vigour. Evolved fast in the glass though. While essentially the fruit is more complex and more elegant than the Clos-des-Avaux of Ponelle it became a touch astringent. Long and lovely nevertheless. Fine. (03/94)

Drink soon   17.5

Beaune Cuvée Brunet
Hospices de Beaune, Lupé-Cholet

Very good colour. Plenty of life. Good nose, ripe and succulent, plenty of grip and vigour. But not as much distinction or dimension as the Cuvée Betault or the Clos-des-Avaux (Ponelle). Medium body. Slightly caramelly and very grapey on the palate but slightly funky. Only reasonable length. Good plus. (03/94)

Drink soon   15.5

Beaune Chouacheux Louis Jadot

Fresh medium to medium-full colour. This, as with so many 1978s, is a touch lean and austere. Mineral. Lacking a little fat and generosity. Yet it has class and balance and plenty of dimensions at the end. Medium to medium-full body. Soft, elegant and long. Good finish. It needed, says Jacques Lardière, another half a degree of ripeness. This, say I, would have given it the glycerol it lacks. Good plus though. **(11/94)**

Now-2000   15.5

Beaune Clos-des-Avaux Champy

Medium colour. Fully mature. Light, soft, fragrant nose. This is a ripe but quite lean wine. With elegance but without real depth and richness. Medium body. Good acidity. Good plus. **(07/94)**

Drink soon   15.5

Beaune Clos-des-Avaux
Hospices de Beaune, Pierre Ponnelle

Very good colour. Rich full meaty nose. Full and fat, plump and plummy. Ripe and substantial. This is a fine example. Generous, round and vigorous. Velvety at the end. Long. Fine plus. Confirmation of a note taken two years previously. **(03/94)**

Now-2000 plus   18.0

Beaune Clos-de-la-Féguine Jacques Prieur

Medium-full colour. Mature. Sweetish, but, with a slightly spicy nose. Quite fat but lacks elegance. Quite full, structure and alcohol show. I prefer the Jadot 1979. **(09/90)**

Drink soon   14.0

Beaune Clos-des-Mouches Chanson

Fullish, mature colour. Ripe sweet nose, just a little hint of vegetal astringency though. Medium-full. Has lost a little of its fruit and vigour, so the acidity shows and the wine is rather dry at the end. Yet the fruit is still reasonably enjoyable and the wine is not short. Has class. Good. **(03/94)**

Drink soon   15.0

Beaune Clos-des-Mouches Joseph Drouhin

Fullish, mature colour. Rather more evolved on the nose than Chanson's Clos-des-Mouches. A little astringency. Classy though, nevertheless, as well as ripe. Medium-full, on the palate a little fresher than the Chanson. Cool raspberry fruit. Stylish, long, very good. Much better than the nose would suggest. **(03/94)**

Drink soon   16.0

Beaune Sizies Leroy

Colour and nose show a bit of age. Lacks a little style on the palate. Fruit beginning to dry out. **(07/92)**

Drink up   13.0

Beaune Vignes-Franches Louis Latour

Full colour. Good vigour. Rich fat, meaty nose. Quite fat, quite sweet, quite structured but a little heavy really. Lacks style. I prefer it to the 1979 Corton-Grancey though. Slightly alcoholic at the end. Good plus. **(10/94)**

Now-2000 plus   15.5

Bonnes-Mares Clair-Daü

Lightish colour. Not too aged. Soft, ripe, oaky and silky on the nose. Sweet and cedary. On the palate it shows a bit of age but is delicate, persistent, mellow and rich. Fragrant, complex and plenty of depth. Lovely. Yet more Musigny than Bonnes-Mares in character. Very soft and feminine. Very elegant and complex. Fine. Three recent notes, one less exciting. **(03/94)**

Drink soon   17.5

Bonnes-Mares Robert Groffier

Medium-full mature colour. Good vigour. A little dried out on the nose. Hard and a bit fruitless. Similar on the palate. Medium body. Not exciting. Yet still has interest. **(03/94)**

Past its best   13.0

Bonnes-Mares Georges Lignier

Good medium-full colour. Good vigour. Rich, ripe, plump nose. Still fresh. On the palate it shows a little age. The fruit is just a little dried out. Medium-full body. But good harmonious ripeness and depth underneath. Good substance too. The finish is ripe and positive and sweet and classy. Very good indeed. **(03/94)**

Drink soon   17.0

Bonnes-Mares Comte Georges de Vogüé

Medium colour. Fully mature. Soft nose. Elegant but not very intense. This is a feminine Bonnes-Mares. Well matured. Fresh but very mellow now and getting a little bitter at the end. Elegant though. Very good but drink soon. **(03/93)**

Drink soon   16.0

Chambertin Pierre Bourée

Fine full vigorous colour. Firm, slightly roasted nose. Full, rich and meaty. A succulent, aromatic wine here. Full, structured. Good tannins. This is a bit old-fashioned, but mellow, rich, subtle, long. Fine. But lacks the class of great. Plenty of life ahead of it. A year earlier, a bottle was less impressive . . . 'not the nuance and concentration of a true Chambertin'. **(03/94)**

Now-2000 plus   17.5

Chambertin Hubert Camus

Fine full mature colour. Vigorous for its age. Put on weight as it was exposed to air in the glass. Fine nose. Rich, fat and concentrated. Quite oaky. This has plenty of depth. Fullish, generous, balanced and vigorous. Very good style. Very fine finish. Unexpectedly good. Fine. **(01/95)**

Now–2000   17.5

Chambertin   Pierre Damoy

Fullish colour. Mature. Slightly toasted nose. A little lean and vegetal nevertheless. Medium to medium-full. Ripe, aromatic. A little diffuse, a little astringent. Yet reasonable grip and length. Quite good plus. But lacks distinction. **(03/94)**

Drink soon   14.5

Chambertin
Roland Remoissenet Père et Fils

Fine full vigorous colour. Fat, rich, ample nose. Very good Pinot fruit. Lots of depth. Still youthful. Quite tough still. A bit adolescent. Ripe. Full, plenty of depth. A bit four-square though. Lacks velvet. Lacks a little real class. But very good. **(03/94)**

Now–2000   16.0

Chambertin   Philippe Remy

Fullish colour. Mature. Curious apple touch to the nose. This blew off after a while. Good ripe fruit but a little weak and a little astringent. Yet underneath there is intensity and class and an old-viney touch. A fine wine somewhat ruined by bad *élevage*. **(03/94)**

Drink soon   15.0

Chambertin   Armand Rousseau

Rather a light colour here. Fully mature. A bit thin on the nose. A bit attenuated and thin on the palate. Lightish. The acidity shows a bit. The wine has had cancer, been eaten away from the inside. Lean finish. (This was from the period when Rousseau had a bug in his cellar.) **(10/94)**

Drink soon   14.0

Chambertin   Louis Trapet et Fils

Medium-full colour. No undue brown. Ripe, aromatic nose. Medium to medium-full weight. Round, mellow, quite classy, certainly balanced. But lacks a little strength. Yet long, subtle. Ripe. Very good indeed. **(03/94)**

Drink soon   17.0

Chambertin   Clos-de-Bèze   Clair-Daü

Medium colour. Well matured. The nose, though, is rich, fat, ripe and concentrated. Cedary background. Medium to medium-full. Oaky. Balanced. This is not the usual Clos-de-Bèze blockbuster. But it is subtle and complex. Long. Fine. But is it better than the Clos- Saint-Jacques? Seems a bit more evolved. And to have less weight. **(03/94)**

Drink soon   17.0

Chambertin   Clos-de-Bèze   Pierre Damoy

Old-looking colour. Soft nose, not decrepit, but certainly more 1960s than 1970s. No great depth. No great class or concentration. No more than a pleasant bottle. But not too coarse or astringent. **(11/92)**

Drink soon   14.0

Chambertin   Clos-de-Bèze   Drouhin-Laroze

Mature colour. Fullish. Slightly stemmy but ripe, if a touch jammy. Concentrated. Quite vegetal, animal as it evolved. Good balance. Still vigorous. Very good indeed. In March 1994 a bottle was rather less good: 13.5 at best. **(08/92)**

Drink soon   17.0

Chambertin   Clos-de-Bèze   Pierre Gelin

Good full, vigorous colour. Full, oaky, rich and vigorous. Plenty of depth and concentration. Impressive. Full body, meaty, aromatic. This has real substance. But a touch four-square and over-macerated. Lacks a little real class. Very good plus. **(03/94)**

Now–2000   16.5

Chambertin   Clos-de-Bèze   Robert Groffier

Rather a light colour. Well matured. Old. High volatile acidity. Underneath not a blockbuster. Old-vine concentration. But this bottle is spoiled. **(03/94)**

Past its best   **(see note)**

Chambolle-Musigny   Joseph Faiveley

Medium-full colour. Mature. Silky smooth, very ripe, old-vine concentrated nose. This is richer and more generous than Leroy; but again needs drinking. Medium to medium-full body. Good oaky base. Stylish and harmonious. Nicely fat. Very good. **(03/94)**

Drink soon   16.0

Chambolle-Musigny   Leroy

Medium to medium-full colour. Mature. Rich and ripe, gently oaky, stylish, vigorous, all spice, cinnamon touches, like a freshly baked fruit cake. On the palate a little drier than on the nose, and a little leaner too. The acidity is beginning to show. It has lost a bit of generosity. No astringency though. Medium body. Persistent. Quite good and stylish nevertheless. Three recent notes. **(03/94)**

Drink soon   14.0

Chambolle-Musigny   Les Amoureuses
Robert Groffier

Medium-full colour. Good vigour. Yet on the nose a slightly thin and vegetal touch. Not too bad on the palate though. Medium to medium-full body. Ripe. Has lost a bit of its generosity but has plenty of depth. The finish is the best part. **(03/94)**

Drink soon   16.5

Chapelle-Chambertin   Pierre Damoy

Lightish, well-matured colour. Light nose, a bit
shitty, a bit diffuse, now a bit dried out. Some
fruit on the palate but a bit sweet. Now a bit
astringent. Loose knit. Unexciting. But not
undrinkable. Not bad plus. Quite plump and
balanced. **(03/94)**

Drink soon   13.5

Charmes-Chambertin   Armand Rousseau

Fullish mature colour. Rich, firm, full, gently
oaky nose. Plenty of depth. A ripe, vigorous
wine, now in its prime. Full, meaty. Balanced
and rich. Really quite concentrated. Very good
grip. Totally unsouped up. Not great but very
good indeed. Holding up very well. Long,
vivacious, plump, most attractive. Two years
later another bottle was elegant, but somewhat
lean: only 'good'. **(03/94)**

Now-2000   17.0

Clos-de-la-Roche   Jaboulet-Vercherre

Good full vigorous colour. A little old on the
nose. Quite substantial though. Rich and fat.
On the palate it lacks distinction and is now
even rather coarse. The fruit has dried out.
Fullish. Reasonable grip. But I don't think it
ever had depth and class. **(03/94)**

Past its best   11.0

Clos-de-la-Roche   Georges Lignier

Fullish colour. Good vigour. Good rich full
vigorous nose. Plenty of concentration and
depth here. More vigour than his Clos-Saint-
Denis. Fullish, round, rich, fresh. This is
profound and has plenty of dimension.
Concentrated and fat and very fine on the
follow-through. Very fine. **(03/94)**

Now-2000   18.5

Clos-de-la-Roche   Ponsot

Good medium-full mature colour. Ripe, meaty
nose. A touch of the stems. Fullish on the palate.
Ample, fresh and ripe. A touch of the 1978
austerity. Beautifully fresh, excellently balanced.
Real intensity and concentration. Classic fine
Burgundy. **(10/94)**

Now-2008   18.0

Clos-Saint-Denis   Dujac

Medium-full, fully mature colour. Vinified with
all the stems, slightly lean and vegetal nose.
Quite old now. Medium to medium-full. Good
intensity and grip, quite high acidity. Good
class. But lacks charm and generosity. Older and
less succulent and attractive than I would have
expected. Good at best. **(03/96)**

Drink soon   15.0

Clos-Saint-Denis   Georges Lignier

Medium-full colour. Good vigour. Ripe nose.
A touch gamey, a little robust, perhaps begin-
ning to lose just a little of its fruit. Got fatter as
it developed. Medium-full. Plenty of depth.
Good grip. This is complex and animal. Long.
Fine plus. **(03/94)**

Now-2000   17.5

Clos-de-Tart   Mommessin

Medium to medium-full colour. Fully mature.
Ripe nose, not dried out, but it has lost a little
of its vigour. Got plumper as it developed
though. Medium-full body. Rich, meaty, touch
of oak. Good grip. A wine of good depth and
substance but a certain lack of class. Yet very
good nevertheless. Bigger than it looks. **(03/94)**

Now-2000   16.0

Clos-de-Vougeot   Robert Arnoux

Medium-full colour. Good vigour still. Nice
and rich and old-viney on the nose. Not a
blockbuster. Lost a bit of class and freshness as it
developed. Medium-full. Ripe, a touch sweet.
This has more vigour than the Machard de
Gramont and is more complex at the end. Long,
classy. Very good. Improved in the glass.
(03/94)

Drink soon   16.5

Clos-de-Vougeot   Joseph Drouhin

Medium colour, still youthful. Fresh cherry,
raspberry nose but an absence of real richness
and concentration. On the palate there is a
slightly vegetal, mint and sage element. Good
balance. Good style. Good length. Medium
body. Fresh. Lacks a bit of generosity and
dimension. Yet very stylish. Good. Second
bottle had more sugar and richness, was fatter.
(05/90)

Drink soon   15.5

Clos-de-Vougeot   Louis Gouroux

Full rich colour, but fully mature. Full, very rich
old-viney and concentrated on the nose. Highly
promising. Full, rich, coffee damsonny. Not as
good as his Grands-Echézeaux. Fat. Old-viney
and very vigorous still. A little sweet but very
good indeed. **(03/94)**

Now-2000   17.0

Clos-de-Vougeot   Jaboulet-Vercherre

Medium-full colour. No undue age. Rather
rigid nose, but quite chocolatey, cigar boxy and
gamey. On the palate not too sweet. Nor too
spurious. Nor too rigid. Medium to medium-
full. Balanced. Rich. Good fruit. Good acidity.
Quite complex. Very good. And still has life.
Lacks a bit of fat and concentration though.
(03/94)

Now-2000   16.0

Clos-de-Vougeot   Louis Latour

Good, full, vigorous colour. Chocolate and caramel on the nose. Good richness. Quite sweet. Medium-full, good acidity. Ripe but not exactly very fat or concentrated. And rather sweet. It is good but it lacks real dimension and intensity. Balanced though. Not short. But a little astringent on the finish. It lacks personality. (03/94)

Drink soon   **15.0**

Clos-de-Vougeot   Leroy

Full, rich, youthful colour. Firm nose. Full, slightly austere, even a touch dense. After a while it softened up. Ample and fullish, raspberry flavoured. Classy. But nevertheless slightly austere, slightly four-square. Doesn't quite sing. Yet very good plus. Will it ever round up? (10/94)

Now-2000   **16.5**

Clos-de-Vougeot   Machard de Gramont

Medium-full colour, fully mature. This smells a bit tough and dried out. Medium-full, a bit astringent. Has lost a bit of its grip and intensity. Ripe but now a bit past its best. Still has pleasure to give. The acidity is beginning to show. (03/94)

Drink up   **14.0**

Corton   Bonneau du Martray

Medium colour. Fully matured. Plump and still sweet on the nose with a strong whiff of cloves. But a lack of backbone. Yet not dried out. Medium body. Cherry-raspberry flavoured. Quite high acidity. Lacks velvetiness. Less structure. And on the finish a little 'hot'; not very elegant. Quite good only. Still quite fresh though. Several notes. (03/94)

Drink soon   **14.0**

Corton   Labouré-Roi

Medium-full, well-matured colour. Vegetal, slightly sweet, evolved nose. This has lightened up. A bit coarse. Medium body. Vegetal palate. A bit astringent. Past its best. (03/94)

Past its best   **12.0**

Corton   Roland Rapet

Fullish colour. Still good vigour. Some fruit but a little astringent on the nose. Lacks class. This is a little faded now. The fruit has lost its vigour, and there is a little astringency. Not much elegance. Unexciting. (03/94)

Past its best   **12.0**

Corton   Clos-du-Roi   Dubreuil-Fontaine

Medium to medium-full colour. A little mature now, but still vigorous. Slightly austere but ripe nose. Medium weight, cherry fruit, but fragrant. Classy indeed. On the palate a soft quite well-matured wine. Medium body. Delicate. The acidity beginning to show a little. Not exactly fat and voluptuous and sweet but fragrant and classy. Very good indeed. (10/94)

Drink soon   **17.0**

Corton   Cuvée Dr Peste
Hospices de Beaune, *éleveur* unknown

Good medium-full, vigorous colour. Rich, classy nose. Very good concentrated fruit. This has distinction. Still very vigorous. Medium-full, balanced, very elegant. Ripe and rich, plump and velvety. Lovely. Very complex finish. Very fine indeed. (03/94)

Now-2000   **18.5**

Echézeaux   Mongeard-Mugneret

Good, full, well-matured colour. Structured nose, a little four-square. Has the fruit lightened up a bit? Fullish, gamey, nicely but quite markedly sweet. A hint of the stems. But good grip. It isn't quite as fat as the Thomas example. Very good plus. Good meaty finish. (03/94)

Drink soon   **16.5**

Echézeaux   Thomas Frères

Good, full, vigorous colour. Full, meaty, rich, concentrated and vigorous on the nose. Full, ripe mature Burgundy. Very good grip. A gutsy wine. Plenty of life still. Quite spicy. A wine for game or some other rich, full-flavoured dish. This is fine. It makes up in size for what it lacks (just a little) in real elegance. Long. (03/94)

Now-2000 plus   **17.5**

Gevrey-Chambertin   Pierre Ponnelle

Fullish colour. Still vigorous. Ripe, plump and round, if with no real depth. But no sign of age. Fullish, good substance. Nicely rich and oaky. This is very good for a village wine. And still has complexity on the follow-through. Persistent finish. Elegant. (03/94)

Now-1999   **15.5**

Gevrey-Chambertin   Clos-Saint-Jacques
Clair-Daü

Medium-full colour. No undue age. Rich, complex nose. Plenty of depth here. This seems a little pinched at first but got better and better in the glass. Full, still quite firm. Profound and classy. Good reserves. Very good grip. Oaky. Fine quality. (03/94)

Now-2000   **17.5**

Gevrey-Chambertin   Clos-des-Varoilles
(Tastevin)   Varoilles

Good vigorous mature colour. A little dry on the nose. On the palate a wine of medium interest. Medium body. The fruit a little one-dimensional. But quite fresh still. Lacks a bit of class and complexity. Good but not great. (09/92)

Drink soon   15.5

Gevrey-Chambertin
Estournelles-Saint-Jacques   Clair-Daü

Good mature colour. A little thin and vegetal on the nose. Similar on the palate. Medium body. Fully ready and not unduly aged. But it lacks fat, richness and generosity. A bit too lean. Unexciting. (07/95)

Drink soon   13.0

Grands-Echézeaux   Louis Gouroux

Good, full, vigorous colour. Rich, damson fruit, old-vine concentration on the nose. This is excellent. Full, oaky, very concentrated. Coffee flavours. Fat and very very rich. Splendid fruit. Real essence of wine. Very good grip. Long. Very lovely. Bags of life. (03/94)

Now–2000 plus   18.5

Grands-Echézeaux   Romanée-Conti

Good, full, vigorous colour. Rich nose, but the usual robustness and stemmy character of DRC Grands-Echézeaux. Fullish, ripe, quite sweet. Well balanced. Not quite rich or classy enough for great. But certainly very good plus. Good length. Fresh and clean. Plenty of life ahead of it. (03/94)

Now–2000 plus   16.5

Clos-des-Lambrays   Lambrays

Magnum. Full, rich, vigorous colour. Good concentration on the nose. Old-viney, aromatic and a little animal, fat and rich. This promises well. An old-fashioned wine. Long macerated, full, fat, rich and concentrated. Very good grip. Very good vigour. A bit artisanal but a very good example indeed. (03/94)

Now–2000 plus   17.0

Latricières-Chambertin   Hubert Camus

Good full mature colour. Vigorous. Mature nose, a touch of the stems, but plump and ripe. Excellent acidity. Well-covered tannins. Nicely generous and succulent. Just a little austere but not a bit lean. Long, complex. Elegant. Fine. (02/95)

Now–2005   17.5

Mazis-Chambertin
Cuvée Madeleine Collignon
Hospices de Beaune, Pierre Ponnelle

Fine, full, vigorous colour. Full, rich, youthful very oaky nose. Lots of depth here. Fullish, very oaky on the palate. Lovely ripe rich old-viney fruit. This is one of the best of all these 1978s. Very, very young still. Bags of life. Splendid. (03/94)

Now–2000 plus   19.0

Musigny   Clair-Daü

Medium-full colour. Mature but still vigorous. Lovely nose. Round, marvellous depth, very fragrant elegant fruit. Medium-full. A wine of poise, harmony, complexity and persistence. Still very long; very well balanced. Very fine. Got better and better in the glass. (03/94)

Now–2000   18.0

Musigny   Joseph Drouhin

Medium to medium-full mature colour. Mature, silky-smooth, very ripe and intense nose with all the feminine delicacy and subtlety of Musigny. Very lovely. Dreamy on the palate. Medium-full, very very fresh and vigorous. Marvellous fruit. Very ripe and very intense. Excellent grip. Real vigour and concentration on the finish. Great wine. Indisputably so. Bags of life. Impeccable condition. (10/94)

Now–2015   20.0

Musigny   Jacques Prieur

Medium-full colour. No undue maturity. Soft, mellow, oaky, a little sweet on the nose. Not over-acid. But the fruit is less vigorous than it was once. And it lacks intensity. Soft and enjoyable and clean at the end. But will get a bit astringent soon. (03/94)

Drink soon   15.5

Musigny   Roland Remoissenet Père et Fils

Fullish mature colour. Slightly animal on the nose. Slightly suave. Fragrant, ripe, not the greatest class or depth but reasonable balance and good acidity. Not really top *grand cru* here but certainly ripe and rich. Very good but not great. (09/95)

Now–2000 plus   16.0

Musigny   Comte Georges de Vogüé

Medium-full colour. Mature. Real quality on the nose here. Mellow, rich and really profound. Lovely. Medium-full, quite oaky. Rich and very very well balanced. Very persistent on the follow-through. Lovely fruit. Really aristocratic. Very fine indeed. Will still keep. Three notes since then, all similar. (03/94)

Now–2000   18.5

Nuits-Saint-Georges   Château Gris
Lupé-Cholet

Fullish colour. Reasonable vigour. Full, ample but gamey nose, but showing some age now. Better on the palate but not a wine of great elegance. Reasonable grip. Quite fresh. Medium to medium-full. A typical Nuits-Saint-Georges in that there isn't much class. But still has life. Good fruit. Quite good. (03/94)

Drink soon   14.0

Nuits-Saint-Georges Les Chaillots
Robert Dubois et Fils

Full colour. Fully mature. Ripe nose but a little coarse. Medium body. A touch sweet-sour. The acidity shows now; especially at the end. And the wine is a bit astringent. Not bad at best. A little over the hill. **(03/94)**

Drink up 13.0

Nuits-Saint-Georges Clos-des-Porrets
Henri Gouges

Medium to medium-full colour. Fully mature. Soft nose. Somewhat shitty. Medium body. A bit weedy and attenuated. Lacks substance, fat and depth. Young-viney. Unexciting. Not astringent though. **(03/94)**

Drink up 12.0

Nuits-Saint-Georges Les Perdrix Leroy

Very good full mature colour. Nicely rich, structured, gamey but still quite austere and youthful nose. Full, meaty and ripe. Very good grip and generosity. Fat and spicy. Lots of depth. This is very fine. Lovely finish. **(11/94)**

Now-2000 plus 18.0

Nuits-Saint-Georges Les Saint-Georges
Henri Gouges

Medium to medium-full colour. Well matured. On the nose the fruit seems a little dry. Medium body. Rather dilute and weedy. Less attenuated than the Clos-des-Porrets. But lacks fat and structure. The acidity shows on the follow-through. Unexciting again. **(03/94)**

Drink up 12.0

Pommard Bertins Machard de Gramont

Medium-full colour. Fully mature. Typically Pommard. Full, tannic, dense nose. On the palate not too tough, nor astringent either. Medium-full, a little firm but now mature. Good acidity. Vigorous. Good plummy fruit. Balanced and long. But not exactly very classy. Very good though. **(03/94)**

Now-2000 16.0

Pommard Grand-Clos-des-Epenots
De Courcel

Fullish colour, still vigorous. Full, rich, ripe nose. Velvety and harmonious; an intriguing whiff of baked potatoes and bonfires. Fullish, balanced; rich, fat fruit. Succulent, generally, long and elegant. This is mellow, complex and fine. A lovely example. Very elegant. **(03/94)**

Drink soon 17.5

Richebourg Gros Frère et Soeur

Medium to medium-full colour. Mature but not unduly so. On the nose a touch attenuated though now. Medium body. Slightly astringent.

Ripe and sweet but it is cracking up. It lacks a bit of class as well. **(03/94)**

Drink up 13.5

Richebourg Jean Gros

Good full, rich colour. Lovely rich concentrated nose. Fresh, old-viney. Marvellous blackberry-cassis fruit. Real essence. Fullish on the palate. Ample and rich and fat and concentrated. Good grip. But not a trace of 1978 leanness. Very vigorous still. Very classy. Very lovely. Very fine indeed. **(10/94)**

Now-2010 19.0

Richebourg Henri Jayer

Very full, vigorous colour. Marvellous nose. Very very concentrated Accad type nose. Quite oaky. Real depth. This is still very, very young. Super concentrated. Low *rendement*. Oaky. Seems to be still improving. Full. Very good grip. Excellent. Yet as it developed never really achieved any great generosity. Curious. But undeniably impressive. **(03/94)**

Now-2005 plus 19.0

Richebourg
Roland Remoissenet Père et Fils

Full rich vigorous colour. Full, firm, rich and youthful on the nose. A bit muscular though. This is still young. Full and rich but a little hot, a little ungainly. Yet very good grip. Fine fruit. Got better in the glass. Concentrated. But a little four-square. Very good indeed but not great. **(03/94)**

Now-2000 plus 17.0

Richebourg Romanée-Conti

Very full mature colour. More developed than Jayer or Remoissenet. Rich, lush and succulent, but now slightly animal fruit. Fullish. A little stemmy. Gamey. Very good grip and fruit but not up to the quality of Jayer. Fine but not great. **(03/94)**

Now-2000 plus 17.5

Romanée-Saint-Vivant Robert Arnoux

Fullish, rich, vigorous nose. Fragrant, fresh, old-viney concentration on the nose. A lot of class here. A lot of complexity too. Nice and fat. Fullish, lovely fruit. Round and smooth. Beautifully balanced. Long and complex. Very lovely indeed. Great stuff. Plenty of life. **(03/94)**

Now-2000 plus 19.0

Romanée-Saint-Vivant Joseph Drouhin

Full mature colour. But amazingly youthful on the nose. Fresh, blackcurrant plummy nose. This has marvellous depth and real breed. Very lovely fruit of real complexity. Fullish. Excellent acidity. Plump and ample. Fat for a 1978. This is a great wine. Still young. Only just ready. Very very elegant. Intense. Concentrated. Brilliant. Multi-dimensional. Marvellously balanced and complex. Very fine indeed. **(05/93)**

Now–2010   **19.5**

Romanée-Saint-Vivant   Louis Latour

Good fresh, fullish colour. This is very classy. Good acidity. Fragrant, with the feminine aspects of this climat. Fullish, vigorous, complex, fine plus. More 1978 than Latour. Long and subtle at the end. **(07/94)**

Now–2000   **18.0**

Romanée-Saint-Vivant   Marey-Monge
Romanée-Conti

Fullish, rich, very vigorous colour. Fresh nose. Full, velvety, classy, complex. Quite structured, but the stems show a little. But lovely fruit underneath. Good grip. Balanced. Long. Plenty of life. Fine but not great. I prefer the Arnoux. A little hot at the end. **(03/94)**

Now–2000 plus   **17.5**

Santenay   Clos-des-Tavannes   Louis Clair,
Domaine de l'Abbaye

Medium colour. No undue age. Rich, concentrated and old-viney. Very good fruit. On the nose you can tell the wine was vinified with all the stems. On the palate this has flair, complexity, elegance and balance. No sign of age. Indeed very vigorous. Very good. **(12/95)**

Now–2000 plus   **16.0**

Santenay   Les Gravières
Roland Remoissenet Père et Fils

Good fullish, vigorous, mature colour. A little restrained on the nose. Just a little animal but basically fresh. Rich and fat and meaty on the palate. Plenty of fruit. Nicely ripe and succulent. With good thrust and vigour. Fullish. Stylish for a Santenay. Will still last well. Good plus. **(01/95)**

Now–2000   **15.5**

Savigny-lès-Beaune   Narbantons   Leroy

Fine colour. Lovely nose. Refined, spicy-sweet, fragrant. Not a touch *sauvage*. This has a volume and an amplitude which most 1978s lack. Good structure. Very good grip. Just beginning to get a little gamey. But still very fresh. Fullish. Lovely finish. A very good example indeed. **(11/94)**

Now–2000 plus   **17.0**

Savigny-lès-Beaune   Les Serpentières
Maurice et Jean-Michel Giboulot

Good fullish fresh colour. On the nose this shows good fruit if not much elegance, and the palate is like that too. Still fresh. Good balance. A little artisanal but long and positive. Not bad. **(12/95)**

Now–2000 plus   **13.0**

La Tâche   Romanée-Conti

Very full vigorous colour. Firm, full and aristocratic on the nose. Rather more refined and more vigorous than the Richebourg. Full, fat, very concentrated and old-viney. This is a significant step-up as always. Marvellously intense fruit. Truffles as well. Very fine indeed. Very very long. **(03/94)**

Now–2005   **19.0**

Volnay   Caillerets   Henri Boillot

Medium colour. Fully mature. Smells like a pub latrine: piss and chlorine. Dry and hard and slightly vegetal (or straw) behind. Better on the palate. Quite fresh and fruity. Good but not brilliant. **(07/95)**

Drink soon   **15.0**

Volnay   Caillerets   Pousse d'Or

Very good colour. Fullish and still vigorous. Classy and fragrant and soft and complex on the nose. Very lovely. This is plump, ripe, poised and classy. It needs drinking quite soon. But it still has intensity and length. Lovely. **(07/95)**

Drink soon   **18.0**

Volnay   Clos-des-Chênes   Comtes Lafon

Medium to medium-full colour. No undue maturity. Interesting nose. Getting a little dry but there is interest and class here. Medium to medium-full body. Ripe, complex and pure and delicious. Very smooth. Very complex. Lovely finish. (Five-year-old vines! Remarkable.) Fine. **(07/95)**

Now–2000   **17.5**

Volnay   Clos-des-Chênes
Roland Remoissenet Père et Fils

Medium-full mature colour. Interesting nose. Silky smooth, coffee and caramel and chocolate. But dried up and lost its class rather quickly. The attack is good and fragrant. But the follow-through a bit lumpy. Past its best. Quite good plus. **(07/95)**

Drink up   **14.5**

Volnay   Clos-des-Ducs
Marquis d'Angerville

Full, mature colour. Rich, stylish nose. Plenty of depth here. Nicely animal now but very good grip and complexity. Fullish, classy. Fragrant, long. This is fine. The finish is splendidly intense and multi-dimensional. Will still keep well. Chocolate and raspberry elements on the palate as it developed. **(03/94)**

Now–2000   **17.5**

Volnay   Clos-des-Verseuils   Yvon Clerget

This is complex and stylish, but both a little lean and very slightly rustic. With a hint of reduction. Balanced and fresh, but it lacks a bit of real velvet and generosity. **(11/91)**

Drink soon   **14.0**

Volnay Santenots Robert Ampeau et Fils

Fullish colour. But quite developed. Vegetal nose in a real vegetable-soup sense. Bovril. Smooth - not astringent - but getting a little lean and sour on the palate. Quite good. Lacks generosity. **(07/95)**

Drink soon 14.0

Volnay Santenots-du-Milieu Comtes Lafon

Fullish, mature colour. Lovely nose, plums and apple, mango, quince. Chocolate and caramel. A lot of vigour still here. Full body, still very young. Complex fruit. Very good acidity. Very interesting, slightly sweet/sour flavour. A touch vegetal. A little bit more four-square than D'Angerville's Clos-des-Ducs. Long, classy. Very good. Plenty of life. Several notes.

Volnay Taille-Pieds Hubert de Montille

Medium-full, youthful colour. Rich, slightly austere nose. But more and more generous as it evolved. On the palate, balanced, ripe, complex, fresh. Vigorous and stylish. Very good indeed. Two similar notes. **(09/92)**

Now-2000 plus 17.0

Vosne-Romanée Robert Arnoux

Round and ripe and vigorous. Plump, slightly sweet, slightly jammy. Good but not exactly stylish. Not lean though, and plenty of life still. Two similar notes. **(06/92)**

Drink soon 15.0

Vosne-Romanée
Château de Vosne-Romanée

Medium-full colour. A touch of age. Oldish but sweet gamey nose. But a touch of fade. Medium body. Ripe but now beginning to break up. Wasn't too bad once. Reasonable balance. Even quite elegant. **(03/94)**

Past its best 12.0

Vosne-Romanée Les Beaumonts
Prosper Maufoux

Medium-full colour. Good vigour still. A little rigid and four-square on the nose. But good plump, vigorous fruit. Fullish, good grip and structure. Plummy, even quite concentrated. Good follow-through. Quite creamy. Ample, balanced, long. Good. **(03/94)**

Drink soon 15.0

Vosne-Romanée Les Brûlées Jean Grivot

Magnum. Good fullish colour, but quite well-matured at the rim. Soft, fragrant, plump Pinot nose. A lot of elegance. Medium-full body, good acidity. Not a lot of fat but good depth, if not that much concentration. But long on the palate. Very good but not great. **(11/92)**

Drink soon 16.0

Vosne-Romanée Les Chaumes
Robert Arnoux

Medium-full colour. Mature but not unduly so. Quite a sturdy nose, but ripe and rich underneath. Medium-full, a touch of oak. Good grip, ripe and plump. This has depth and vigour and length. Really quite concentrated. Just a little sweet and suave. Good plus. **(03/94)**

Drink soon 15.5

Vosne-Romanée Clos-des-Réas Jean

Gros

Medium-full colour. Mature but not unduly so. A little rigid at first on the nose. Better on the palate. Fullish, firm, slightly hard and rigid. Yet this improved in the glass. Eventually rounded off. And good grip and style. Long. Very good. **(03/94)**

Drink soon 16.0

Vosne-Romanée Cros-Parentoux
Henri Jayer

Excellent colour. Full, vigorous. Very young, could be a 1988. Marvellous nose. Fat and rich and concentrated. Slightly oaky still. Full, remarkably vigorous and fresh. Still quite structured. Very good acidity. This is still very very young, even slightly rigid. Will still improve and round out. Potentially super. **(10/94)**

Now-2010 18.5

Vosne-Romanée Les Suchots
Robert Arnoux

Medium-full colour. Mature but not unduly so. More developed than his Chaumes. A bit astringent. A little herbaceous. Some of the fruit has gone. Yet better on the palate. Some fruit. But a little past its best. Only fair. **(03/94)**

Drink up 13.5

Vosne-Romanée Les Suchots Louis

Latour

Fullish colour. No undue age. Ripe, plump, rich, quite sweet nose. Still fresh though. Good raspberry fruit. Got a little vegetal as it developed. On the palate a little dense, the stems showing. A lack of succulence and sex appeal. Yet the finish is still rich and positive. Good. **(03/94)**

Drink soon 15.0

1976

Rating for the Vintage

Red: 14.5   **White:** (13.0)
(past their best)

Size of the Crop

(Hectolitres, excluding generic wine)

	Red	White
Grands Crus	11,146	2,012
Village and *Premiers Crus*	142,613	28,077
Total	153,759	30,089

Nineteen-seventy six was a sizeable crop, as large as 1970, though down on both 1972 and 1973, and, as it would turn out, 1977.

After a string of poor years 1976 was almost bound to be over-written, especially as it was the product of an absolutely gorgeous hot summer and an early harvest. And so it was. But we must beware of now reacting in an opposite direction. There are a lot of parallels between 1976 and 1983.

Weather Conditions

The summer, as I have indicated, was hot and dry. The harvest was abundant, but in these conditions the very last grape was able to get to full ripeness and concentration, even as early as the second week of September. Moreover the fruit was very healthy, and collected in good conditions (much better than in Bordeaux) well before the weather began to deteriorate towards the end of the month.

The Style of the Wine

White Wines

The white wines were big, spicy, alcoholic and unbalanced. They lacked that *sine qua non*, good acidity. Controls were not what they are today, and more than one wine, in cask, was oxidised. Most were far too blowsy. They did not last.

Red Wines

As in other very concentrated years more fruit was required to yield a barrel's-worth of must than usual: not 300 kilos, but more like 400. The wines had good colour, plenty of ripe if rather 'cooked' fruit, were high in alcohol, lowish in acidity, and of course were unduly high in tannin.

At the outset they were hard, but had plenty of flavour and extract. The Côte-de-Beaune seemed less unbalanced than the Côte-de-Nuits. But the wines looked like *vins de garde* with richness and substance.

In general, twenty years on, the vintage is uneven. Some wines are past it. Others are too tannic and the tannins too unsophisticated. They will never get there. But, search hard and you will find plenty of good, if rather tough, wines. Few, sadly, are really elegant, and it is this which marks the vintage down.

TASTING NOTES

BLANC

Bienvenues–Bâtard–Montrachet
Bachelet–Ramonet

Quite a deep colour. Somewhat maderised on the nose but not undrinkable. Rich and oaky underneath. But the fruit beginning to dry out now. (03/96)

Past its best   13.5

Chassagne–Montrachet
Jacques Gagnard–Delagrange

This is elegant and delicate for a 1976. Very ripe but soft and not at all heavy and alcoholic. Still fresh but drink soon. Almost red fruit (raspberry) in flavour. Very good indeed. (03/92)

Drink soon   17.0

Chassagne–Montrachet   Les Chaumées
Gabriel Jouard

Quite a lot of H$_2$S. Ripe and round and not too old underneath. (03/93)

Drink up   13.5

Corton–Charlemagne
Bonneau du Martray

Ripe nose. Rich and slightly spicy but still fresh. On the palate it has lost a bit too much of its fruit though. Yet the finish is more positive than the above. Quite good. (06/91)

Past its best   14.0

Corton–Charlemagne   Louis Latour

Extremely fresh colour for a 1976. Rich, oaky, complex nose. This is fresh and has a lot of depth. Honeyed but not blowsy. Profound and still with grip. This is very fine - particularly so for a 1976. Against his 1986 it was heaps better, much more classy and complex. Splendid acidity. Rich. Very profound. Will still last very well. This must be one of the few 1976s with balance and real class and depth. Excellent. (03/96)

Now–2005   19.0

Corton   Vergennes, Cuvée Paul Chanson
Hospices de Beaune

Second year after the donation. Rich, oaky, fat, opulent. But balanced with good acidity. There is a voluptuous spice here. But the structure is given by the grip. Long. Vigorous. Fine. (01/96)

Now–2000 plus   17.5

Meursault   Désirée   Comtes Lafon

Three and a half years in cask, because the malo occurred so late. Honeyed, with a herbal,

camomile, *tilleul* aspect. No undue acidity. Most attractive. No sign of age. Fullish, vigorous. Round and ample. Very good acidity. Plump, slightly crab-appley. Complex. Quite structured still. A substantial, very slightly four-square wine. A red wine in white-wine clothes. Held up very well in the glass. Nose got more and more interesting. A great surprise. (03/96)

Drink soon   16.0

Meursault   Perrières   Joseph Drouhin

Past its best. (03/96)

Past its best   (see note)

Le Montrachet   Pierre Olivier

Light golden colour. Either it has loosened up or it never was very concentrated in the first place. The nose is a bit pinched as is the attack. The follow-through is more expansive but nevertheless it isn't very special. (03/96)

Past its best   13.0

Le Montrachet   Baron Thénard,
Roland Remoissenet Pére et Fils

Sweet, ripe. There is a sweet/sour element here. Full and oaky and spicy. But rather blowsy. Lacks acidity. (01/91)

Drink soon   15.0

Puligny–Montrachet   Jean–Marc Boillot

A bit too evolved on the nose. Ripe and plump and spicy on the palate but lacks a bit of zip. Yet was very good for the vintage. Better on the palate than on the nose. Not astringent but now past its best. (06/91)

Past its best   (see note)

Puligny–Montrachet   Les Combettes
Jacques Prieur

Astonishingly fresh colour. Slightly tight on the nose. Not exactly expansive. Rather rigid on the palate. Fresh but a lack of charm and real class. Slightly bitter at the end. Curious. (03/96)

Drink up   12.0

Puligny–Montrachet   Les Referts
Louis Latour

Past its best. (03/96)

Past its best   (see note)

ROUGE

Beaune   Boucherottes   Louis Jadot

Full, vigorous mature colour. Very alive, rich, chocolatey nose. Delicious. Fullish, plump, cooler and better balanced than most. Lovely classy damson fruit. Very long on the palate. Complex. Plenty of life. Very good indeed. **(03/96)**

Now-2000 plus   17.0

Beaune   Clos-des-Mouches   J.L. Darviot

Medium, fully mature colour. Rich, mature, mellow spicy nose. Good depth and quality. Medium-full body. Good richness and grip, especially on the follow-through. Quite structured. Still has life. Good. **(03/96)**

Now-2000   15.0

Beaune   Clos-des-Mouches   Joseph Drouhin

Magnum. Good colour. Rich, ripe, *rôti*, spicy, meaty nose. This is fat and sensual. Not exactly stylish, but attractive, inviting and vigorous. Good finish. **(06/91)**

Drink soon   15.0

Beaune   Marconnets   Bouchard Père et Fils

Full, mature colour. Rich, plump, plummy, vigorous nose. Good depth and quality. Fullish, quite tannic still. Good classy fruit. Quite structured. Plenty of grip. Some signs that it is beginning to dry out. But good plus. **(03/96)**

Drink soon   15.5

Beaune   Marconnets
Roland Remoissenet Pére et Fils

Good vibrant colour. Youthful for a 1976 and a wine nearly twenty years old. Meaty, spicy nose. Definite sweet, caramelly touches. No dry tannins though. But some slightly over-ripe pruney aspects. Fullish, just a touch of tannin. No undue bulk though. An ample fleshy wine. Good vigour and reasonable balance. But not exactly elegant or fragrant. Good though. **(01/95)**

Now-2000   15.0

Beaune   Vignes-Franches   Louis Latour

Medium-full mature colour. Some development, indeed age on the nose. Lacks a little succulence. Slightly vegetal/compost heap aspects. Has now dried up a little. Residue of quite classy fruit. But not what it was. Good though. **(03/96)**

Drink up   15.0

Bonnes-Mares   Thomas-Moillard

Fullish, fully mature colour. Fine rich slightly dense nose. Still vigorous. A full-bodied, tannic wine. Nice and rich. Sturdy and meaty. Not too dense. Still vigorous and definitely a wine for food. But good concentrated stuff. Naturally sweet and not hot at the end. Plenty of life. Fine. **(03/96)**

Now-2000   17.5

Bonnes-Mares   Comte Georges de Vogüé

Fine full, vigorous colour. Fine, fragrant nose. This is very lovely. Not a bit hot. Medium-full. Rich, very cool, very complex, very very long. A wine with real grip and dimension at the end. Very classy. Lots of life ahead of it. Very fine. Another bottle (10/94) was rather less impressive: 'good at best; drink to 2000'. **(03/96)**

Now-2005   18.5

Chambertin   Héritiers-Latour
Louis Latour

Full mature colour. Rich nose, quite sizeable. But not too tough. Fullish, good grip. This is beginning to lose its grip now, which is a pity, for the wine is very classy and well balanced, if not that fat and concentrated. But it is not too hot or alcoholic. Very good indeed. **(03/96)**

Drink soon   17.0

Chambertin   Louis Trapet et Fils

Lightish, not very concentrated or backward - indeed fully ready - but very clean Pinot on the nose and palate. Not dilute. Good acidity and quite intense. Stylish too. Good but not great. **(09/92)**

Now-2000   15.0

Chambertin   Clos-de-Bèze   Louis Jadot

Full rich vigorous colour. Splendid nose. Youthful, rich, concentrated, real depth and class. Not a touch tough or sturdy. This is fresh, plump and very complex. A wine of real subtlety, length and class. Still very young, and not a bit hot or tannic or alcoholic. Very fine indeed. **(03/96)**

Now-2005   19.0

Chambertin   Clos-de-Bèze
Roland Remoissenet Pére et Fils

Full rich vigorous colour. Rich, chocolatey, mocha nose. Soft and mellow not tough. Fat and fullish, but a little artificial somehow. Lacks a little austerity. Yet the grip is good and the wine still fresh. Fine but not great. **(03/96)**

Now-2000   17.5

Chambolle-Musigny   Jean Hudelot,
Alexis Lichine

Medium to medium-full colour. Fully mature. Ripe, succulent, but a little hint of maderisation. Medium body, lightening and drying up as well as getting oxidised and maderised. A very good example once though. But now over the hill. **(03/96)**

Past its best   13.0

Chambolle-Musigny Louis Latour

Medium-full colour. Fully mature. Pleasant, fragrant nose. No undue age. But a bit tight as usual. On the palate the fruit has dried up a bit and so it is now a bit lumpy. But quite good plus still. (03/96)

Drink soon   14.5

Chambolle-Musigny
Roland Remoissenet Pére et Fils

Fullish colour. Good vigour. Fragrant and stylish but the muscle of 1976 nonetheless. Medium-full body. Very Chambolle. Good intensity. Long. Good plus. (07/92)

Drink soon   15.5

Charmes-Chambertin Louis Latour

Fullish mature colour. Nose seems to be losing its grip and whatever class it had. Medium body. Rather astringent. Not a full wine, and not too hot. But fading now. (03/96)

Past its best   13.5

Charmes-Chambertin Christian Serafin

Medium-full colour. An older nose but has plenty of depth and class. Lovely ripe blackcurranty fruit. Medium-full. This has a bit of astringency now on the palate but has a lot of complexity. (06/91)

Drink up   16.0

Chorey-lès-Beaune Leroy

Very good colour. Still very youthful. Ripe, *rôti*, chunky. Good depth and grip though. Long. Very good for what it is. (07/92)

Now-2000   15.0

Clos-de-la-Roche Bourée

Full, vigorous colour. Rich full, rather too sturdy. A bit old. On the palate this is thin, dry and unclean. The fruit has lightened up. But this was never a wine of flair and balance. Inky now. (03/96)

Drink up   12.0

Clos-de-la-Roche Philippe Remy

Good full mature colour. Rich, concentrated and old-viney, but a bit inky. Dried out on the palate. Not exactly very clean either. This is a disappointment. (03/96)

Drink up   13.0

Clos-Saint-Denis Georges Lignier

Very full mature colour. Succulent but not really very concentrated or very classy. Medium-full. Nice plump fruit. Not too sturdy. Quite ripe and rich. This is very good and still has life. But it lacks flair. (03/96)

Now-2000   16.0

Clos-de-Tart Mommessin

Fullish mature colour. Full, bramble-berry, sturdy, tannic nose. A little bit too sturdy. Nice full sweet start but then too astringent and burly. No elegance. Good at best. Better with food. (03/96)

Drink soon   14.5

Clos-de-Vougeot Drouhin-Laroze

Fullish, still a little tannin. But not hard. Nor without fruit or grip. Fat, indeed. Ripe. This is very good. (06/92)

Now-2000   16.0

Clos-de-Vougeot Jean Grivot

Fine full mature colour. Fine, rich, fat, stylish, concentrated nose. This is splendid. Full, composed, profound, rich, concentrated and vigorous. Quite sturdy on the attack. Mellow and multi-dimensional and with very good grip at the end. Real class and complexity here. Bags of life. This is very fine indeed. (03/96)

Now-2005   18.5

Clos-de-Vougeot Grand-Maupertuis
Jean Gros

Good colour. Fat, rich, vigorous and complex on the nose. Very fine. Lovely gently oaky mature wine. Fullish, above all really classy. This has a lot of dimension. A really seductive complex wine. Excellent. Beautiful balance. (06/91)

Now-2000   18.5

Clos-de-Vougeot Alain Hudelot-Noëllat

Magnum. Full colour. Rich and meaty on nose and palate. Ripe, complex, vigorous and gamey. With an opulent cooked plump flavour and a touch of both coffee and chocolate. Fine. Long. Complex. (06/91)

Drink soon   17.0

Clos-de-Vougeot Jacques Prieur

Magnum. Full vigorous colour. Rich, fat, meaty nose. Fullish, but getting a little astringent now. Is losing its class and has lost its fruit and sweetness. Just about enjoyable still. But has seen better days. (03/96)

Drink up   14.5

Clos-de-Vougeot Georges Roumier

Good colour. This tastes more like a 1988 than a 1976. Slightly lean on the nose and palate. Medium-full. Good structure. Just a touch of oak. Not exactly fat and generous - or not yet - but rich enough, and balanced. Very good certainly. Satisfying at the end. Bags of life. (11/94)

Now-2010   16.0

Clos-de-Vougeot   Varoilles

Full mature colour. Nicely rich, stylish colour. Not as concentrated or as ripe as Grivot's though. Medium-full, no undue muscularity. Balanced, smooth, cool, harmonious, laid-back. Long and complex at the end. Fine. **(03/96)**

Now-2000   **17.5**

Corton   Bonneau du Martray

Quite good colour. Ripe quite stylish nose. Soft, lacks a bit of concentration. Medium body, still fresh. But a bit one-dimensional. Quite good. **(06/91)**

Drink up   **14.0**

Corton   Bressandes   Chandon-de-Briailles

Good colour. Slightly dense on the nose. A little astringent on the palate. Ripe but lacks a bit of flexibility. This tastes older than some. Quite good. **(06/91)**

Drink up   **14.0**

Corton   Clos-des-Corton-Faiveley   Joseph Faiveley

Full mature colour. A little pinched on the nose. A little vegetal too. This has not held up as well as I had hoped. There is elegance here, but it has lightened up a bit. Fruity and balanced. Not inharmonious or inelegant. But lacks a little richness, concentration and vigour. Merely good. **(03/96)**

Drink soon   **15.0**

Corton   Clos-de-la-Vigne-au-Saint   Louis Latour

Very good colour. Rich and full, mature. Vigorous, full black-cherry, blackberry nose. Full, rich and tannic on the palate. This is an expansive wine, better with food, with good acidity and classy fruit. Still has plenty of life. Fine. **(03/96)**

Now-2000 plus   **17.5**

Corton   Pougets   Louis Jadot

Good colour. A little fading and farmyardy. Yet still quite substantial on the nose. Better on the palate. Fat and quite rich. Quite vigorous still. Meaty. A touch astringent and not exactly elegant. Good though. **(03/96)**

Drink up   **15.0**

Echézeaux   Mongeard-Mugneret

Fullish mature colour. Quite robust, slightly tobacco-y nose. Fat and rich. Good depth. A little sturdy and tough on the palate. Better with food. Good cherry, cassis-chocolate flavour. Good acidity. A bit aggressive at the end. Very good. Not the class or smoothness for fine. **(03/96)**

Drink soon   **16.0**

Gevrey-Chambertin   Denis Mortet

Good colour. Fresh plump nose. A little burnt, like a cooked plum tart. Fresh. Plump. Meaty and succulent. Full. Good. **(06/91)**

Drink soon   **15.0**

Gevrey-Chambertin   Les Champeaux   Denis Mortet

Very good colour. Chocolatey, concentrated nose. Full, fine, rich and concentrated. This has plenty of depth and plenty of vigour. More life than the above. **(06/91)**

Drink soon   **16.5**

Gevrey-Chambertin   Clos-Saint-Jacques   Roland Remoissenet Pére et Fils

Medium-full mature colour. Ripe, succulent nose. Fullish, rich, opulent, a touch of spice. Not unbalanced. Now beginning to lose its grip at the end. But plump and full of fruit. Fine. **(03/96)**

Drink soon   **17.5**

Gevrey-Chambertin   Les Combottes   Roland Remoissenet Pére et Fils

Fullish colour. Youthful. Good depth. A touch of H$_2$S. Morey style. Round, fat, complex. Long. Fullish. Very good plus. Bags of life. **(07/92)**

Now-2000   **16.5**

Gevrey-Chambertin   Estournelles-Saint-Jacques   Clair-Daü

Medium-full colour. Mature. A little old and mixed-up on the nose. And somehow a touch lean and vegetal underneath as well. Curious. On the palate the wine is cracking up. Sweet at first, then dirty and astringent. **(03/96)**

Past its best   **12.0**

Grands-Echézeaux   Romanée-Conti

Medium to medium-full fully mature colour. The usual slightly lean and vegetal/stemmy nose of old Domaine de la Romanée-Conti at this level. Very composed on the palate. Medium-full, balanced, intense. Long and complex and mellow on the palate. Bags of life. Very good indeed. **(03/96)**

Now-2000 plus   **17.0**

Latricières-Chambertin   Hubert Camus

Full, vigorous colour. No brown. Tar and roses and a little structure showing on the nose. Full, tannic, *rôti*, a little clumsy. But rich and fat on the follow-through. No astringency. Good grip. Vigorous. Better with food. A meaty, somewhat chunky wine. Very good. **(10/93)**

Drink soon   **16.0**

Latricières-Chambertin   Camille Giroud

Fine colour. Fat, rich, plump nose. Still vigorous. Full and meaty, fat and tannic. Still heaps of life left. Splendid rich flavour of cooked plum tart. No new oak. Not a wine of enormous class but plenty of depth. (06/91)

Now-2000   16.0

Mazis-Chambertin   Joseph Faiveley

Medium-full, well-matured colour. On the nose this is ripe and succulent, but the stems show, and the wine is fading now. This is a bit of a disappointment. Medium-full. Still positive at the end - just. But should have been better. Two notes from 1994 were 'very good': more vigorous. (03/96)

Drink up   15.0

Morey-Saint-Denis   Clos-des-Ormes
Georges Lignier

Medium-full colour. Mature. Quite vigorous, clean and classy on the nose. This is medium-full. Quite clean, still alive. Slightly concocted in its fruit. The finish is a bit confected. But good. (03/96)

Drink soon   15.0

Le Musigny   Joseph Drouhin

Very youthful colour for this vintage but not that full. Sturdy, chunky and though soft and fruity, a little four-square on the nose and palate. There is muscle but a lack of grace. Better on nose than palate. There is, surprisingly, a little acidity on the finish. Lacks generosity and fat and lusciousness. Good but by no means spectacular. Indeed for Drouhin and Le Musigny it is disappointing. (09/93)

Drink soon   15.0

Le Musigny   Louis Jadot

Rich full mature colour. Rich nose, youthful, a touch of oak. Opulent. A big, full, youthful wine. Slightly rigid. A touch of unresolved tannin. Doesn't quite make it into the fine class. And it is not really what you expect from Musigny. Slightly tough and masculine. Yet vigorous. Very good indeed. (03/96)

Now-2000   17.0

Le Musigny   Louis Latour

Rich, full mature colour. Full, rich but slightly sturdy nose. Good vigour though. A fullish, slightly astringent wine on the palate. It lacks concentration and grip underneath. Is it drying out? Acidity getting dominant. Lacks succulence. Disappointing. (03/96)

Drink soon   15.0

Le Musigny   Comte Georges de Vogüé

Less colour than the Bonnes-Mares. Fully mature. Soft, fragrant nose. This is quite evolved now, and a bit astringent at the end. The Bonnes-Mares is much better. There is class here, but not enough grip and vigour. Very good plus at best. (03/96)

Drink soon   16.5

Nuits-Saint-Georges   Louis Latour

Good fullish mature colour. Ripe nose. Frank statement of good mature fruit. Full but ample, not too sturdy. Rich, balanced, even classy. Plenty of life ahead of it. Very good. (03/96)

Now-2000   16.0

Nuits-Saint-Georges   Leroy

Good colour. Chunky and four-square. Very Nuits-Saint-Georges. On the palate a bit lumpy but spicy and quite rich and with good grip and depth. Yet not much class. Good though. Still young. Held up well in the glass. (07/92)

Now-2000   15.0

Nuits-Saint-Georges   Les Chaignots
Alain Michelot

Quite good colour. A touch vegetal on the nose. A bit astringent on the palate. This doesn't have much style. And has now also a bit over the top. (06/91)

Past its best   12.0

Nuits-Saint-Georges   Clos-de-la-Maréchale
Joseph Faiveley

Fullish, well-matured colour. Evolved, slightly animal nose. Fat and rich. This has begun to collapse and decay. Fullish. Not what it was. (03/96)

Past its best   11.0

Nuits-Saint-Georges   Les Saint-Georges
Michel Chevillon

Good colour. A touch overblown and astringent on the nose. Lacks a bit of class. Medium body. Similar palate. This is a bit old now, and never had much class. (06/91)

Past its best   12.0

Nuits-Saint-Georges   Les Saint-Georges
Henri Gouges

Good colour. Interesting, indeed curious, spicy nose. Quite evolved now. This has thinned out a bit. Had some style once but now a bit past it. (06/91)

Past its best   13.0

Nuits-Saint-Georges   Les Vaucrains
Alain Michelot

This is rather better. Richer, riper, fatter. Still has life. Good meaty example with plenty of blackberry fruit. Very good. (06/91)

Drink soon   16.0

**Pernand-Vergelesses Ile-des-Vergelesses
Denis Roland Père et Fils**

This is round and rich and mature, but not a bit
funky. Good freshness. This is very good. Fat,
succulent and fresh. Most attractive. No
aggressive tannins. (12/95)

Now-2000 plus   16.0

**Pernand-Vergelesses Les Vergelesses
Laleure-Piot**

Medium colour. Quite old-looking now. Fragrant
on the nose though. No undue age. On the
palate it has lost its fruit. Not astringent but
rather sour. (03/96)

Past its best   12.0

Pommard Bitouzet-Prieur

Medium colour. Fully mature. Ripe, meaty, not
without style on the nose. But getting a touch
dry now. Fullish, a little animal, a little spice. A
bit mixed up and sweet-sour. Not too bad, but
beginning to lighten up. Was better five years
ago. (03/96)

Drink up   13.5

**Pommard Clos-des-Epenots
Comte Armand**

Magnum. Good colour. Rustic. Artisanal. Well
past it. (06/91)

Past its best   (see note)

**Pommard Clos-des-Epenots
Roland Remoissenet Pére et Fils**

Full colour. Youthful. Rich. Concentrated,
chocolatey. Masculine. Very Pommard. Good
depth. Plenty of dimension. Very good indeed.
(07/92)

Now-2000 plus   17.0

**Pommard Clos-de-la-Platière
Prince de Mérode**

Good colour. Slightly pruney on the nose.
Slightly dense, with a bit of astringency and
rather dominant tannins. Good fruit, but it lacks
grace and vigour. (03/96)

Drink soon   13.5

Pommard Epenots Louis Latour

Medium-full colour. Fully mature. Rich nose.
Full, nicely substantial. Fat and full of fruit. Full-
bodied, rich but earthy, and a little astringent
and loose-knit now on the follow-through. But
still good. (03/96)

Drink up   15.0

Pommard Epenots André Mussy

Very good colour. Rich, spicy, concentrated nose.
This has a lot of old-vine depth. Full, tannic,
meaty and gamey. A rich almost dense wine.
Rustic in the best sense. Very good. (06/91)

Drink soon   16.0

Pommard Epenots Jacques Parent

Fine colour. Rather robust, dense nose. Slightly
dry. On the palate full and rich, a little rigid but
no astringency. A bit of a lumpy wine but one
which is not without richness and interest.
Quite good. (11/95)

Now-2000   14.0

Pommard Rugiens Jean-Marc Boillot

Good colour. A little faded on the nose. Rather
astringent on the palate. This has lost its grip
and is past its best. (06/91)

Past its best   13.0

Pommard Rugiens De Courcel

Very good colour. Full, firm, rich nose. A bit
old-fashioned, a bit astringent, but ripe and fat
and meaty. Full and if slightly dense, certainly
plenty of depth and enjoyment. (06/91)

Drink soon   15.5

Richebourg Jean Gros

Good colour. A less full but more stylish,
fresher, more complex wine than the Clos-de-
Vougeot. This is long, ripe, very subtle and
marvellously balanced. Quite lovely. Will keep
for ages. *Grand vin* without a doubt. (06/91)

Now-2000 plus   20.0

Richebourg Henri Jayer

Splendid rich full vigorous colour. Marvellous
rich concentrated oaky nose. Opulent. The
residue of a very oaky wine. Very intense but a
little dominated. Super-duper fruit. Still very
very young. Very good grip. Could have been
great. The palate doesn't live up to the nose.
(03/96)

Now-2000 plus   18.0

Richebourg Prosper-Maufoux

Fullish mature colour. Slightly inky, fruity, dense
nose. Unbalanced. Fullish, quite oaky. Underneath there is fine quality here. But the handling
was a bit inept. Good richness, concentration, fat
and depth. But a lumpy element. Very good but
should have been very fine. Hot finish. (03/96)

Drink soon   16.0

Richebourg Romanée-Conti

Medium-full mature colour. Rich, more
opulent and more vigorous than the Domaine
de la Romanée-Conti's Romanée-Saint-Vivant.
But with the same leanness (compared with
Henri Jayer). Fullish, rich, very intense, very
youthful. This is very lovely. Very long and very
fine. (03/96)

Now-2005   18.5

Romanée-Saint-Vivant Romanée-Conti

Medium to medium-full, fully mature colour. Mellow, laid-back nose. Less stemmy than the Grands-Echézeaux. Ripe and fragrant. Not a bit hot. Much superior to the Grands-Echézeaux. Very mellow, very lovely fruit. Real intensity, complexity and depth. Very, very long and lovely. This is very fine. 'Very good at best' (10/94). **(03/96)**

Now-2005   **18.0**

Romanée-Saint-Vivant
Les Quatre-Journeaux Louis Latour

Full, vigorous, rich colour. This is very fine indeed on the nose. Marvellously rich, full, fat and composed. Really ripe still. Still sweet at the end. Full, rich, fat and oaky on the palate. Concentrated and intense. Real depth. Long. Once again even better with food. Very fine. 'Good at best' (07/94). **(03/96)**

Now-2005   **18.0**

Santenay Louis Latour

Medium, fully mature colour. Spicy nose, with just a very faint hint of maderisation. But ripe, plump and full of fruit. On the palate a little sweet-sour. Some astringency. Would be better with food. Medium-full, a little ungainly but quite good. **(03/96)**

Drink soon   **14.0**

Savigny-lès-Beaune Les Vergelesses
Simon Bize et Fils

Magnum. Lightish colour, but not old looking. Not a wine of great weight but soft, plump and fresh. This is fully à *point*, and surprisingly good for the vintage. There is good acidity here and plenty of fruit. Clean, positive and very good. **(05/94)**

Drink soon   **16.0**

La Tâche Romanée-Conti

Medium to medium-full mature colour. Compared with the Domaine de la Romanée-Conti's Richebourg this is richer, fatter and much more concentrated and complex. Naturally sweeter and more generous. This is really excellent. A big step up - as usual - from the Richebourg. Long. **(03/96)**

Now-2005 plus   **19.5**

Volnay Clos-de-la-Bousse-d'Or
Pousse d'Or

Full mature colour. Round, rich, quite tannic nose. A little tough but not too dense. Lots of bonfire smells. Quite good fruit here. This is balanced and stylish in its rough and ready way. Fullish. Ripe but a bit four-square at the end. Good plus. **(07/95)**

Now-2000   **15.5**

Volnay Caillerets Pousse d'Or

Very fine full colour. Still vigorous. Tar, camphor and rich cooked fruit on the nose. Not a bad wine. Fullish but now a bit astringent. Good style. Better with food. Reasonable finish. Very 1976. Quite fresh. Got drier and drier in the glass. **(07/95)**

Drink soon   **15.0**

Volnay Champans Hubert de Montille

Medium-full colour. Mature. Fragrant, old roses and raspberries on the nose. Lovely natural sweet, ripe fruit. Subtle, not a bit hot and alcoholic. Balanced complex medium-full-bodied wine. Long. Classy. Very good indeed. **(03/96)**

Drink soon   **17.0**

Volnay Clos-des-Chênes Michel Lafarge

Good colour. Fine, vigorous, concentrated nose. Good oaky base. This is classy, gently oaky, ripe even voluptuous. Most seductive. Very good. Bags of life. **(03/96)**

Now-2000 plus   **16.5**

Volnay Mitans Louis Latour

Medium-full colour. Mature. Just a little tight and lactic on the nose. But good classy fruit as well. Slight vegetal twiggy-ness from the stems. A touch astringent. Fullish. Caramelly in the background. Good but was better a few years ago. Finishes a little hot. **(03/96)**

Drink up   **15.0**

Volnay Santenots Robert Ampeau et Fils

Full colour. Still vigorous. Less dense than most, but yet an odd element of the vegetal, of toffee and other spices. This is better mannered than most 1976s. Quite smooth and velvety. Rich, plump, complex finish. And long too. But it is a lot smoother than most. This is a very good example indeed. **(07/95)**

Now-2003   **17.0**

Volnay Santenots Roland Remoissenet
Pére et Fils

Medium-full well-matured colour. Smells of old-style Barolo. There is structure and tannin. And there is some sweetness here. Rather dense. Acidity shows. Clumsy. Full. But coarse and 'hot'. Fell away in the glass. **(07/95)**

Drink soon   **13.5**

Volnay Taille-Pieds Hubert de Montille

Fine colour. Full and youthful. Some tannin still on the nose in a slightly dry sense. Full and rich. A little musty/corky. Ample, slightly astringent at first but despite the dry full body this has good grip. Got fatter as it evolved in the glass. Pity about the corkiness. **(09/92)**

Drink soon   **?16.0**

Vosne-Romanée   Louis Latour

Medium to medium-full colour. Fully mature. Ripe but a little dry on the nose. Better on the palate but just about at the end of its useful life. Balanced, not hot. Still positive at the end. Good. **(03/96)**

Drink soon   15.0

Vosne-Romanée
Roland Remoissenet Pére et Fils

Medium-full colour. Good vigour. Sturdy nose. Fullish, round, ripe and vigorous. Slight spice. Good grip and interest. Good if not the style or dimension for great. **(07/92)**

Now-2000   15.0

Vosne-Romanée   Beaumonts
Antonin Rodet

Medium-full colour. Fully mature. Sweet nose. Almost some honey and botrytis. Very curious. Has lightened up on the palate. Diffuse. Dirty barley sugar. **(03/96)**

Past its best   12.0

Vosne-Romanée   Les Chaumes
Jean Grivot

Magnum. Fine colour. Rich, full, fat and meaty. Slightly rigid at first but expanded considerably in the glass. Spicy. Plenty of depth. Good acidity. Not too *figué* or pruney. Concentrated. Long. Vigorous. Fine. **(09/92)**

Now-2000 plus   17.5

Vosne-Romanée   Clos-des-Réas   Jean Gros

Fullish mature colour. Full, rich, concentrated, vigorous. This is fine and alive. Full body. Clean, classy and concentrated. Fine old Burgundy. Low yield intensity. Not hot. Long. Complex and delicious. Bags of life. Very fine. **(03/96)**

Now-2000 plus   18.0

Vosne-Romanée   Les Malconsorts
Clos-Frantin

Fullish colour. Still vigorous. Full gamey nose. Soft but earthy tannins. Medium-full. Rich and ripe and complete. This has life and depth. It is quite chunky but the fruit finishes sweet and the wine is not too solid. Plenty of life. Finishes well. Very good indeed. **(10/93)**

Now-2000   17.0

Vosne-Romanée   Les Suchots
Robert Arnoux

Good full, fresh colour. Rich, meaty nose, not too aggressively tannic. This has plenty of fruit and is not a bit astringent. Very clean. Stylish. Long. Very good plus. **(03/95)**

Now-2000   16.5

Vougeot   Les Cras   Mongeard-Mugneret

Medium-full colour. Fully mature. Slightly sweaty on the nose. But ripe and meaty and not too aged. A sturdy example. Quite spicy. Not exactly elegant. But quite substantial. Slightly hot. Slightly astringent at the end. Quite good. **(03/96)**

Drink soon   14.0

1972

Red: 15.0   **White:** (12.0)
(past their best)

SIZE OF THE CROP

(Hectolitres, excluding generic wine)

	Red	White
Grands Crus	12,273	2,216
Village and *Premiers Crus*	147,956	28,292
Total	160,229	30,508

In contrast to Bordeaux, where 1972 was only of average size - and of miserable quality - Burgundy produced a large crop, and one which, at least in Pinot Noir, would eventually be recognised as of good quality.

WEATHER CONDITIONS

This was one of the longest growing seasons on record. There was an early bud-break, with thankfully no frost, but the spring was cold and damp, and the vines late to flower. By that time it was less wet, though not much warmer, and the flowering took place successfully, intimating an abundant harvest. It continued cool - indeed it was the coldest summer for many a year - but thankfully it remained dry, and, rarely in Burgundy, there was no hail-damage anywhere in the region.

You need sun, however, to produce concentrated grapes, and the sun obstinately refused to appear until 10 September. Finally the weather got warmer, and belatedly the fruit began to ripen. The harvest did not begin until well into October, but the conditions remained favourable, the grapes were healthy, and the crop, as anticipated, was very large.

THE STYLE OF THE WINE

Ignored at the outset, for they arrived in the middle of the 1973/1974 *crise*, appeared green, unripe and austere, and came from a vintage which was singularly unattractive in Bordeaux, the 1972s took time to win any friends.

About the end of the 1970s, however, I remember being offered various bin-ends of Remoissenet wine from the London merchants Saccone and Speed. These included a Chambolle-Musigny, Les Amoureuses, Gevrey-Chambertin (Lavaux-Saint-Jacques, as I remember), Nuits-Saint-Georges, Boudots, and Vosne-Romanée, either Malconsorts or Beaumonts: as good a quartet of *premiers crus* as you would wish. The colours were very good, the wines were pure and had finesse, and they were agreeably mellow in their somewhat unfleshy way. They may have lacked charm, but they had quality. They drank well with food. I bought them. My customers liked them. But this was more or less my first encounter with the 1972s in bottle.

After that I began to see more of the 1972s. I remember a series of Dujacs at a wine weekend at Studley Priory near Oxford. I recall the Musigny *Vieilles-Vignes*, either with an Avery's label, or with a Remoissenet label, and indeed with the De Vogüé label. But all the same wine originally. This was an excellent example. Indeed the last of the great De Vogüé wines until recent years.

Today the 1972s are still vigorous, still well coloured, and sometimes vegetal or gamey. They will never be exactly fat or really generous, but they have depth and finesse and the best have plenty of character. They have much more vigour than the majority of the 1971s, and are not marred by the hail taste which you will find in many wines of this earlier vintage. The vintage is clearly at its best in the Côte-de-Nuits rather than the Côte-de-Beaune.

TASTING NOTES

BLANC

Chassagne-Montrachet   Les Vergers
Michel Niellon

Deep but greeny gold colour. Lean but not aged, mature nose. Good class. No lack of fruit. And really quite elegant and dimensional. A bit lean on the palate but not vegetal. Complex, has finesse. Good clean finish. Surprisingly vigorous. Surprisingly good. No hurry to drink. **(10/94)**

Drink soon   **15.5**

Meursault   Genevrières, Cuvée Baudot
Hospices de Beaune, Louis Latour

This smells delicious but is a disappointment on the palate. Buttery - even butterscotchy - on the nose but a little mean on the palate. Not too excessively acidic but a bit linear. Still fresh though. **(08/91)**

Drink soon   **13.5**

Montrachet
Roland Remoissenet Père et Fils

Fresh but mature colour. Rich, profound, gently oaky nose. Still very youthful. This is a lot more alive than a whole load of 1984s tasted recently. Fullish, round and nutty. No enormous depth. But plenty of finesse. High quality. Remarkable for the vintage. And plenty of life. A bottle three months later was equally fine. **(07/94)**

Now-2000   **18.0**

ROUGE

Beaune   Cuvée Maurice Drouhin
Hospices de Beaune, Joseph Drouhin

Good fullish, well-matured colour. Soft nose. Ripe and sweet; certainly very elegant; but delicate now. This is a sturdier and better wine than the Volnay, Clos-des-Chênes. Ripe and meaty. Slightly vegetal and lean on the follow-through. Reasonable substance. Good complexity on the aftertaste. Good. **(10/94)**

Drink soon   **15.0**

Bonnes-Mares   Bouchard Père et Fils

Full mature colour. Round, rich, plump nose. Ample and with no undue austerity. Good blackberry fruit. Medium-full. Balanced. Good acidity. Quite rich. Certainly still vigorous. Yet in the end with only a bit of real class. Very good plus. **(10/94)**

Now-2000   **16.5**

Bonnes-Mares   Robert Groffier

Full mature colour. Elegant nose. Good depth and grip. Nicely cool and natural. A delicious example. Medium-full, balanced, spicy-sweet but not souped up. Quite a delicate example for a Bonnes-Mares but nicely vigorous still. Long, subtle. Just a bit more age than the Varoilles. Fine. **(10/94)**

Now-2000   **17.5**

Bonnes-Mares   Varoilles

Full mature colour. Nicely mature, round, almost sweet nose. Good residual oak. Very elegant. Medium-full, lovely concentration. Lots of definition. This is a lovely example. Not souped up. Complex. Elegant. Very fine. Long multi-dimensional finish. **(10/94)**

Now-2000 plus   **18.0**

Bonnes-Mares   Comte Georges de Vogüé

Fullish colour. No undue maturity. Delicious nose. Fragrant. Definitive, poised lovely fruit. Real class. Fullish, fat, round, very plump, good oaky background. Very beautifully balanced. Really classy. Very very long and lovely. Multi-dimensional. Quite a lot more structured than the Amoureuses. **(10/94)**

Now-2005   **19.0**

Chambertin   Jaffelin

Medium-full, well-matured colour. Smells of black coffee. A slight lack of fruit, slightly hard. But has depth. This has lost a little of its fruit. The palate shows medium to medium-full body, a certain astringency; a lack of generosity, and a little meanness. Not much charm here. Good at best. **(10/94)**

Drink soon   **15.0**

Chambertin Jacques Prieur

Very good mature colour. Ample, rich nose. Slightly vegetal-animal flavour of old Burgundy. Supple. Not a bit hard. Medium-full, nicely soft and plump. Good oaky background. This has plenty of class and dimension. Typical 1972 acidity but softer and easier to drink than most. But good depth and fine quality. Will still keep well. **(10/94)**

Now–2000 plus   **17.5**

Chambertin Armand Rousseau

Full vigorous but mature colour. Fresh and ripe if slightly vegetal on the nose. Lean but vigorous on the nose. Rich and full, if not exactly fat. A slight hard edge to the finish and a certain austerity. Very good. Certainly has depth and also equally plenty of vigour. But lacks a bit of generosity and class. Very fine indeed for a 1972, at the very least. But the finish is hard. **(11/94)**

Now–2000   **18.0**

Chambertin Clos-de-Bèze Pierre Gelin

Medium-full, well-matured colour. Soft and vegetally in the best sense. But not entirely clean on the nose. Got more unclean as it developed. Underneath a very good wine indeed. Medium-full, nicely ripe, nicely balanced. Neither too hard, nor too acidic. Finishes very well. Could be fine, if not tainted. Are all the bottles like this? **(10/94)**

Now–2000   **17.0**

Chambolle-Musigny Leroy

Good colour for the age. Vigorous but slightly vegetal nose. Sweet, concentrated, mellow. Perhaps a little suave but a very attractive generous wine and with plenty of vigour. Very good. **(03/93)**

Now–2000   **16.0**

Chambolle-Musigny
Comte Georges de Vogüé

Medium colour. No undue maturity. Soft, fresh, pure, elegant nose. Medium body. Very fresh. Mellow. Long, complex. Very good intensity. A beautiful example. Not a bit lean. Excellent for a village wine. **(10/94)**

Now–2000   **17.0**

Chambolle-Musigny Les Amoureuses
Comte Georges de Vogüé

Medium-full colour. Fully mature. Very delicious, ample nose. Marvellously intense ripe fruit. Remarkable for this vintage. Very fine palate. Medium-full, very good oak base. Lovely intense fruit. A splendid wine. Very very long and complex sweet finish. **(10/94)**

Now–2000 plus   **18.5**

Clos-de-la-Roche Bouchard Père et Fils

Good, full, vigorous colour. Interesting nose. Caramelly sweet, almost butterscotch. Fullish, plenty of substance. A touch rigid. Fruity but in a slightly spurious way. Yet though it has dried up a little, and is a little hard at the end, a wine which still offers pleasure. Slightly coarse on the finish. Good plus. **(10/94)**

Drink soon   **15.5**

Clos-de-la-Roche Dujac

This is fresh but quite well advanced. Medium intensity and depth. Balanced and stylish. I might have expected a bit more backbone. Good but not special. **(09/92)**

Drink soon   **15.0**

Clos-de-Vougeot Jean Grivot

Good full, mature colour. Ample, spicy-animal nose, no lack of suppleness, depth and class. Fullish, good grip. Ripe and supple but with plenty of depth and character. Lovely complexity especially on the finish. Long. Plenty of vigour. Fine. **(10/94)**

Now–2000 plus   **17.5**

Corton Bressandes Joseph Drouhin

Fullish, mature colour. Slightly unclean on the nose. Pinched and vegetal. On the palate quite full, quite fresh. Not too much acidity. But quite stylish and elegant. Good length. Subtle and complex and long at the end. Soft but vigorous. Lovely finish. **(10/94)**

Drink soon   **16.5**

Corton Château Corton-Grancey
Louis Latour

Full, well-matured colour. Soft, supple, even quite sweet on the nose. This has good depth. Medium-full, quite generous, animal flavours. Good vigour. Good complexity. Slightly vegetal (and getting very soft as it evolved) at the end but very good. Will keep. **(10/94)**

Now–2000   **16.0**

Gevrey-Chambertin Cazetiers Leroy

Good fresh colour. Round, slightly lean and vegetal on nose and palate. Slightly less substance than the Lavaux-Saint-Jacques. But good style. Good richness. Got warmer in the glass. Medium to medium-full. Good acidity of course. Quite classy. Good plus. **(10/94)**

Drink soon   **15.5**

Gevrey-Chambertin Combottes
Roland Remoissenet Père et Fils

Double magnum. Very good colour. Round and rich, not austere on the nose. Good grip but sufficiently supple to be most enjoyable, even seductive. Fullish, round, ample, vigorous. This is very good indeed. Better than the Lavaux-Saint-Jacques from Leroy sampled two weeks ago. **(01/95)**

Now–2000   17.0

Gevrey-Chambertin   Lavaux-Saint-Jacques Leroy

Very good full vigorous colour. Lovely nose. Blackcurrants and blackberries. Velvety. Firm. Vigorous. Full on the palate, very fresh, austere. This is still very youthful. High acidity. A slightly rigid wine, but with very good fruit. Yet a touch ungenerous on the finish. Very good plus. Several notes. **(10/94)**

Now–2000 plus   16.5

Grands-Echézeaux   Romanée-Conti

Mature but vigorous colour. Medium to medium-full. Nice soft classy nose. Not too vegetal. Not too structured. Good grip. Very clean ripe fruit. This is in lovely condition. Clean and totally un-souped up. Good vigour. Long. Very good indeed. **(10/94)**

Now–2000 plus   17.0

Mazis-Chambertin   Pierre Gelin

Good full colour. No undue maturity. Firm, rich nose. The usual quite high acidity of the 1972s. Medium-full. Nicely attractive, ripe and fruity. No great concentration or depth but a good ripe example if not perhaps with real *grand cru* depth. Very good. **(03/96)**

Now–2000 plus   16.0

Morey-Saint-Denis   Joseph Faiveley

Medium-full mature colour. Rich nose. Quite evolved. Not too lean. Not a bit coarse either. Ripe, mellow, complex. This is really very fine for a 1972 village. Sweet, gentle, mellow. **(11/95)**

Now–2005   16.5

Musigny   Clair-Daü

Good colour. No undue maturity. Quite austere on the nose. Slightly vegetal too. It lacks a bit of succulence. Medium-full body. It shows a little acidity and a little ungenerosity. Perhaps it has lost a little fruit. Rather hard going. I would only give it a 'good' today. **(01/95)**

Drink soon   15.0

Musigny   Louis Latour

Full mature colour. Some structure and a little astringency evident on the nose. Not that elegant. A bit souped up. Vegetally on the nose. Just a touch oxidised on the palate. Is drying up now. A little skeletal and stemmy at the end and now a bit hard and ungenerous. Lacks real class. Merely good if that. **(10/94)**

Drink soon   15.0

Musigny   Comte Georges de Vogüé

Fullish, vigorous colour. Very concentrated. Very fine nose. Splendidly classy concentrated fruit. The same weight, it seems, of the Bonnes-Mares. But even more intensity and class. Still very youthful. Brilliant fruit. Marvellous balance. This is excellent. Very very long, multi-dimensional finish. **(10/94)**

Now–2005   19.5

Nuits-Saint-Georges   Leroy

Mature, fullish colour. Good bead. Rich, aromatic nose. Fragrant, classy. A little thin on the palate. Not as fat or as rich as the nose would suggest. Yet quite long and intense. Some class. Needs drinking. **(03/96)**

Drink soon   14.0

Nuits-Saint-Georges   Les Pruliers Henri Gouges

Magnum. Medium-full colour. Good vigour. On the nose a touch lean but clean and un-souped up. On the palate medium to medium-full, round, rich and stylish. A smooth wine. No undue acidity. Very elegant. Not exactly fat. But has plenty of character. Very good. **(10/94)**

Now–1999   16.0

Nuits-Saint-Georges   Roncières   Avery's

Medium colour. No undue maturity. Slightly astringent on the nose. Sweet and animal. On the palate medium body. A little coarse. A little old. But quite pleasant at the end. Spicy. Not too lean. Perhaps a little spurious. **(10/94)**

Drink soon   14.0

Richebourg   Romanée-Conti

Medium-full colour. Mature. Plump nose. But quite firm. Certainly vigorous. Very good fruit. Fullish, good backbone, good grip. Just a touch vegetal at the finish. This is very good indeed, but it doesn't quite have the class for fine. **(10/94)**

Now–2000   17.0

Romanée-Conti   Romanée-Conti

Full, very vigorous colour. Very rich, much more intense than the Tâche on the nose. Broad, ample, lovely texture, very velvety. Rich. Full, concentrated, very good grip. Real intensity here. Multi-dimensional. Again a lot of structure. Self-evidently a wine for food. Extra dimension to the Tâche. Brilliant. But the De Vogüé Musigny is better. **(10/94)**

Now–2005 plus   18.5

La Tâche   Romanée-Conti

Full mature colour. Considerably superior to the Richebourg in terms of intensity. Good structure. Still very fresh. Round, rich and fullish. Slightly hard. But this has vigour still, and improves on aeration. Meaty. A lot of depth. A structured wine. Very fine indeed. Bags of life. But compared with the top De Vogüé wines it lacks the finesse. **(10/94)**

Now–2005 plus   18.0

Volnay   Chevret
Roland Remoissenet Père et Fils
Good colour. No undue maturity. Fragrant, classy and vigorous on the nose. This is very delicious. Fullish, vigorous, ripe and even generous. Plenty of depth and intensity. Will still keep well. Fine. **(07/95)**

Now–2000 plus   17.5

Volnay   Clos-des-Chênes   Joseph Drouhin
Medium to medium-full colour. Well matured. Soft, ripe, elegant nose which held up well: a touch of cloves. Quite a high level of acidity on the palate. Medium body. A little lean and ungenerous. But not unstylish. Not a lot of dimension though. Quite good. **(10/94)**

Drink soon   14.0

Volnay   Cuvée Général Muteau
Hospices de Beaune, Henri de Villamont
Good fullish mature colour. Full, meaty nose. Good depth. Nutty. Medium-full body, good grip. Plenty of fruit and interest here. But not exactly really stylish. Animal as well as vegetal. Good follow-through. Good plus. **(10/94)**

Drink soon   15.5

Volnay   Santenots   Robert Ampeau et Fils
Good fresh vigorous colour. Ripe, mellow nose. Classy and sweetly fragrant. Not a bit lacking in generosity. Ripe, harmonious, long. Medium to medium-full. Very lovely on the finish. Fine. **(07/95)**

Now–2000   17.5

Volnay   Taille-Pieds   Hubert de Montille
Not a bit too austere. Very elegant. Very complex. Lovely fruit in its cool way, and no lack of flesh to the structure. Pure Pinot. Long. Slightly animal as it developed. Still has life. Ripe finish. Delicious. **(02/95)**

Now–2000 plus   17.5

Vosne-Romanée   Leroy
Medium colour. Serious nose. Good slightly appley fruit. Plenty of depth and vigour. Very good for a village wine. Medium-full. Ripe. Good grip. Like many 1972s slightly austere but stylish and long. Sweet. Yet dried out in the glass. **(07/92)**

Drink soon   15.0

Vosne-Romanée   Les Champs-Perdrix
Clair-Daü
Good full, vigorous colour. Rich, plump, firm nose. Plenty of depth and vigour. Fullish, good acidity, good backbone, good fruit. This is a wine with plenty of dimension and quality, especially for a village wine. No undue austerity. Even rich on the finish. Very good plus. **(10/94)**

Now–2000 plus   16.5

1971

R A T I N G   F O R   T H E   V I N T A G E

Red: 16.0   **White:** (18.0)
(past their best)

S I Z E   O F   T H E   C R O P

(Hectolitres, excluding generic wine)

	Red	White
Grands Crus	7,533	1,527
Village and *Premiers Crus*	83,926	17,674
Total	91,459	19,201

This was the smallest vintage of the 1970s decade: 60 per cent lower than the ten-year average. Nineteen seventy-three would produce almost twice as much, 1982 almost three times the meagre 1971 crop.

Nineteen seventy-one was one of the first vintages that I was responsible for buying as a merchant. The choice was fraught with danger. For while the vintage was generally fine there was a lot of hail-damage - and *goût de grêle* in the wines - in the Côte-de-Beaune, particularly in Volnay and Pommard; and similar problems in Nuits-Saint-Georges and Vosne-Romanée. There were also, it seemed to me, though none of the reports commented on it - and it was a small, essentially concentrated vintage - one or two wines which, while they were well-coloured and seemed ripe and fruity enough, did not have the length and grip I would have expected. To explain all this, with hindsight, we need to go back to the weather.

WEATHER CONDITIONS

The spring was generally mild, and the buds burst early, but it was a small *sortie* and the subsequent crop was further reduced by a cold and wet June, causing widespread *coulure* and *millerandage*. July was hot and dry; August, as so often, was unsettled, with a period of storms and cool weather in the middle of the month when much of the Côte was affected by hail: three successive waves in the afternoon of the 19th. But then there was a return to fine weather in September. The harvest began early, on around 15 September, and a small harvest of grapes was gathered in excellent conditions.

THE STYLE OF THE WINE

WHITE WINES

The whites were exceptional, and, of course, there was no problem with a hail taste. They were full, balanced and concentrated. They had real *terroir* definition, and were very classy indeed. They lasted very well, but now over twenty-five years later, can hardly be expected still to be vigorous. I am still tempted, after all this time, to rate this vintage above all others in recent years - for its white wines.

RED WINES

At the start the wines had a good colour, plenty of concentrated ripe fruit and seemed to have good acidity. There were flaws in much of the Côte-de-Beaune reds and you had to pick and choose in Nuits-Saint-Georges and Vosne-Romanée. Two domaines which were affected - two of the few which offered wine in bottle then - were Henri Gouges and the Domaine de la Romanée-Conti. Yet the latter are brilliant. And of the rest, if carefully chosen, there was much to excite.

While everyone seemed determined to rate the 1971s as *vins de longue garde* I was a little hesitant. They had more breed, certainly, than the 1969s. They were less lush and spicy. But they were less tannic and less alcoholic. Did they really have the grip and the volume? At the top levels, yes. But lower down the scale - perhaps a little surplus 1970 had been added to compensate for the short crop - I thought not, or not always.

As the 1971s have evolved we have been able to separate the pleasantly ripe, but best-at-eight-to-ten-years sheep from the firmer, more concentrated and long-lasting goats. Now at over twenty-five years old, no wine should be criticised for needing drinking soon. And there are still some magnificently vigorous examples (the top Rousseaus, for instance). There are some very fine 1971s, and these have real breed.

BLANC

Corton-Charlemagne Louis Latour

Fresh colour. Delicate on the nose. Cool, gently oaky, but intense. Ripe, concentrated. Very well balanced. Very elegant. A very fine wine. Very good grip. Long. Super. **(03/95)**

Now–2000   18.0

Meursault Charmes Comtes Lafon

Quite a mature colour. Pinot Noir nose. Raspberry as well as peach and hazelnuts and butter. Some maturity. Full, fat, meaty. This is fine, complex, concentrated. Very good acidity. A very rich classy wine. Lovely. Improved in the glass and held up very well. Very very long. **(09/92)**

Now–2000 plus   17.5

**Meursault Clos-du-Cromin
Raymond Javillier**

Fresh colour. Quite an evolved nose. On the palate the fruit has lost a bit of its sweetness but the wine is fresh and balanced. Just a touch bitter. Medium body. Not totally over the hill. Has depth and class and is still positive at the end. Good. **(10/95)**

Drink up   15.0

**Le Montrachet Marquis de Laguiche,
Joseph Drouhin**

Golden colour. Old nose, at first, but fresh, curiously grapey as well as a touch of oxidisation. Fresher on the palate. Not oxidised, but slightly tropically fruity. This has lightened up more than I would have expected. Who knows where it has been? Should have been better. Lacks real concentration and fat. **(10/94)**

Drink up   14.0

ROUGE

Beaune Bressandes Albert Morot

Good vigorous colour. Rich, tannic, touch of the stalks. Good acidity. Ripe and vigorous. Animal and old but complex and balanced and with plenty of life. I am quite surprised by the level of acidity here. Very good. Got a touch astringent as it evolved in the glass. Did the malo finish before this wine was bottled? **(06/92)**

Drink soon   15.5

Beaune Cent-Vignes Duchet

Quite an old colour. A sturdy nose. Fresh and ripe, a little lumpy but fresh enough, nicely plump. Not a hint of age. Not as fragrant as the

Morot, but more life ahead of it. Very good. **(03/95)**

Drink soon   16.0

Beaune Cent-Vignes Albert Morot

Good fullish colour. Fragrant nose. Classy, rich, complex, very smooth, very well balanced. This is a well-made, typical Beaune. *À point* now. Long finish. Very good plus. Similar note (09/94). **(03/95)**

Drink soon   16.5

Beaune Clos-des-Ursules Louis Jadot

Good fresh colour for a 1971. Classy nose. Slightly lightening up. Slightly leafy and peppermint. Much better on the palate. Ripe, complex, slight caramel and prune-raisin spice. Very good fruit. Plenty of vigour. This is long and surprisingly good. Long. Very good indeed/fine. Several notes. **(10/94)**

Now–2000   17.0

**Beaune Cuvée Dames Hospitalières
Hospices de Beaune, Bouchard Aîné**

Full, but quite old colour. Fine nose, a little hint of the stems. Old and sweet on the palate. Delicate and fragrant. Residual fat. High class here. Ripe and succulent. Beautifully balanced. Good vigour. One of the best 1971s I have had for ages. Very complex long finish. Fine. **(09/94)**

Now–2000 plus   17.5

**Beaune Cuvée Rousseau Deslandes
Hospices de Beaune, *éleveur* unknown**

Fully mature colour. Medium-full. Soft slightly mocha nose. Fragrant, soft, very stylish. Medium to medium-full, not that substantial but good intensity. Quite old now. Not great but very good indeed. **(03/96)**

Drink soon   17.0

Beaune Grèves Joseph Drouhin

Mature colour but not unduly so. Now both animal and vegetal on the nose. Medium body. It has dried up a little on the palate and it is past its best now. Was certainly elegant. But now a little sour. **(10/94)**

Past its best

**Beaune Vigne-de-l'Enfant-Jésus
Bouchard Père et Fils**

Fullish, mature colour. Silky-smooth, sweet, fragrant, oaky nose. A very round gentle wine, but disarmingly soft and seductive. On the palate this is getting towards the end. For there is a touch of astringency in the middle and acidic hardness on the aftertaste. But it is very stylish nevertheless, and still long and complex. Very good. **(01/95)**

Drink soon   **16.0**

Bonnes–Mares   Louis Latour

Medium–full mature colour. Some reduction on the nose. A little astringent on the palate. Medium–full body, a bit rigid. Lacks class and velvetiness. Dry finish. Uninspiring. **(03/95)**

Drink soon   **13.5**

Bonnes–Mares   Georges Lignier

The colour looks a little old. But the nose is fresh and plump. Good blueberry fruit. On the palate plump and fresh. Quite delicate for a Bonnes–Mares. This is beginning to lose its vigour but still very good plus nevertheless. The Clos-de-la-Roche is holding up better. **(03/95)**

Drink soon   **16.5**

Bonnes–Mares   Georges Roumier

Fullish mature colour but still has vigour. Very fine rich vigorous nose. Rich, some stems apparent. This is really concentrated. Splendid classy fruit. Full, rich, masculine. A wine for food. Good intensity and vigour especially at the end. Fine plus. **(03/95)**

Now-2000   **18.0**

Bonnes–Mares   Sichel Frères et Fils

Medium–full, well-matured colour. Very similar to the Romanée-Saint-Vivant of Sichel on the nose. Ample, strangely sweet, lumpy and four-square. Drying out at the end. Cheap and spurious. **(03/95)**

Drink up   **12.0**

Chambertin   Camille Giroud

Good full vigorous colour. Full vigorous slightly reductive nose. A bit burly. Full, tannic, meaty, plenty of drive and grip. This is a little too obviously structured, but would be fine with food. Lovely fruit. Lots of depth here. Plenty of concentration. **(03/95)**

Now-2000 plus   **17.5**

Chambertin   Jaffelin

Medium–full colour. Fully mature. This is now quite evolved and loose-knit on the nose. It has lost its grip. Diffuse. This has lost whatever quality and vigour it ever had. Lean finish. **(03/95)**

Drink up   **13.5**

Chambertin   Héritiers-Latour

Good full colour. No undue maturity. Rich, full and vigorous. This has a lot of depth. Masculine and full and gamey. This is less vigorous on the palate than the nose would indicate. Sweet. Getting diffuse. Lacks a bit of class. But nevertheless very good. **(03/95)**

Drink soon   **16.0**

Chambertin   Jacques Prieur

Medium–full colour. Fully mature. Rich, full, ripe and oaky. A bit rigid and sweet. Fullish, slightly rigid oakiness. Good freshness. Good grip. Very good but not exactly great. Rich fruit. Plenty of life ahead of it. **(03/95)**

Now-2000   **16.0**

Chambertin   Philippe Remy

Medium–full colour. Mature. Plump, fragrant, slight boiled-sweet – but in a good sense – nose. A bit diffuse on the palate. Good fruit. Reasonable acidity. But not a great wine. Still reasonably fresh. **(03/95)**

Drink soon   **15.0**

Chambertin   Armand Rousseau

Medium–full colour. Fully mature. Fresh, round, full, very classy fruit on the nose. This is a bigger wine than his Clos-de-Bèze; richer, fuller and more vigorous. Lovely fruit. Very fine grip. Very classic. Very clean. Very complex. Very classy. Excellent. **(03/95)**

Now-2000 plus   **20.0**

Chambertin   Louis Trapet Père et Fils

Fine, rich, mature but vigorous colour. Delicious, elegant, complex, fragrant nose. Almost sweet. Fullish but mellow, still intense. Very good concentration and grip. This has the depth and personality and still, after 22 years, the vigour that many younger wines do not. And the result is a multi-dimensionality of flavour which is subtle, complex and very fine indeed. Very very long and lingering on the finish. A bottle 03/95 was corked but otherwise equally impressive. **(11/93)**

Now-2000   **19.0**

Chambertin   Clos-de-Bèze
Armand Rousseau

Medium–full colour. Fully mature. Older, less vigorous than the Chambertin on the nose. Softer, but less grip. This is very fine. Now *à point*. Balanced, plump, classy fruit. Fullish. Slightly gamey and animal. Slightly less vigorous than the Chambertin. Very fine. **(03/95)**

Now-2000   **19.0**

Chambolle-Musigny   Les Amoureuses
Pierre Bertheau

Fine colour. Good concentrated nose. At present just a little closed. On the palate full, good ripe tannins, very rich, old-vine concentration, very elegant. This is a very good example indeed. Lovely ripe fruit. Very good harmony and structure, and a lush rich, long finish. **(11/93)**

Now-2000   **17.0**

Chambolle-Musigny   Les Amoureuses
Georges Roumier

Fully mature colour. Fullish. Classy nose. Showing a little age. But the fruit is lovely. It is beginning to dry up on the palate, and there may be a hint of hail. But it is very pure, intense and classy still. Quite distinctive. Quite structured. Very long. Very Roumier. Fine. (03/95)

Drink soon   **17.5**

Chapelle-Chambertin   Louis Trapet et Fils

Lightish colour. Fully mature. Light and perfumed nose, getting astringent. This has lightened up a bit. This has aged fast but there is very good elegant plump concentrated plummy fruit underneath. Good plus. (03/95)

Drink soon   **15.5**

Charmes-Chambertin   Louis Latour

Good vigorous mature colour. Some fruit on the nose. But a little tight and dry and astringent. Sweet on the palate. A little rigid. But not coarse. Still enjoyment to be had and a good positive follow-through. Needs food. But rather hard, really. (03/95)

Drink soon   **16.0**

Clos-des-Lambrays   Cossin

Fine colour. Full, very vigorous for a 1971. Ample, old-viney, spicy nose. Now mature. Ripe and sweet. Medium to medium-full. Very intense, concentrated and laid back. Chambolle rather than Gevrey. Fully *à point*. Quite delicious. *Grand vin*. Very, very long. Very, very complex. Naturally sweet and exciting. (10/94)

Now-2000   **19.5**

Clos-de-la-Roche   Georges Lignier

Good vigorous colour. Lovely nose. Rich, meaty, fleshy, classy fruit. No sign of age here. An ample bottle. Fullish, sweet, rich and complex on the palate. Fullish, good fresh acidity. Long, ripe and elegant. Plenty of depth. More Chambolle than Gevrey. Didn't hold up too well in the glass. Fine. (03/95)

Drink soon   **17.0**

Clos-de-Vougeot   Camille Giroud

Good full mature colour. Full, vigorous, even firm nose. Slightly rustic, certainly solid. Plenty of depth. Plenty of grip. Fullish. A little astringent as it developed. Sturdy. Plenty of life left but not exactly very elegant. Good plus. (03/95)

Now-2000   **15.5**

Clos-de-Vougeot   Louis Jadot

Good full mature colour. Vigorous, rich plump. Very classy. Full, very complex, subtle and complex. This has real intensity. Very fine. A delicate wine. Lots of finesse. But drink quite soon. (10/94)

Now-2000   **18.0**

Clos-de-Vougeot   Jacques Prieur

Good full mature colour. Full, ripe, rich, oaky nose. Good depth here. Fullish and mellow on the palate. Smooth, complex, balanced. Very long. This is nicely fresh and very elegant. Lots of depth. Very good. But how much real *grand cru* class? (Had been 'very good indeed' in 10/94 and 'fine' in 03/94. (03/95)

Now-2000 plus   **16.0**

Clos-de-Vougeot   Georges Roumier

Good full mature colour. This is a little dry and sour on the nose. And has possibly even a hail taste as well. Medium-full. Good acidity. But has lost a little fruit. Yet still has some vigour, and still very classy. Still sweet and fresh on the finish. (03/95)

Drink soon   **16.0**

Clos-de-Vougeot   Varoilles

Good full mature colour. Nice ripe fragrant nose. Lovely cherry, raspberry fruit, plus complex spice, and a touch of mocha and chocolate. On the attack it is showing a little fade but the follow-through is more positive. Intense old-viney concentrated fruit. Good balance. A lot of depth here. Very good indeed. (03/95)

Now-2000   **17.0**

Corton   Mommessin   *(Tasteviné)*

Good colour for age. Fragrant fat and sumptuous on the nose. Still sweet. Certainly very elegant. On the palate ripe and stylish and balanced. Fat and fullish. An ample wine for a 1971 and still vigorous, if showing a little suggestion of age at the end. Very good indeed. (09/94)

Drink soon   **17.0**

Corton   Château Corton-Grancey
Louis Latour

Light to medium, fully mature colour. Ripe and fruity but a little bland on the nose. Sweet and slightly alcoholic on the palate. Heavy, clumsy. Unexciting. A bottle from the same batch in 10/94 was 'holding up well': 15.5. (03/95)

Drink soon   **14.0**

Corton   Clos-des-Cortons   Joseph Faiveley

Fresh, medium-full colour. Good full firm nose. Plenty of depth. Quality here. Full, rich, meaty, still very fresh and vigorous. A lovely example. Very good grip. Long. Very pure. Nicely austere. Bags of life. This is fine plus. But I had a less good bottle 07/94: 'not as good as the Clos-des-Cortons these days; good plus.' (03/95)

Now-2000 plus   **18.0**

Corton   Perrières   Louis Chapuis

Lightish, mature colour. Soft nose. A bit diffuse, but quite elegant and no lack of fruit. Ripe and sweet. Fresh. Good acidity. Not a lot of fat and weight. But fruity and elegant. Very good. (03/95)

Now-2000   16.0

Gevrey-Chambertin   Dugat-Humbert

Very good colour. Still very vigorous. Ripe, youthful, gently oaky, slightly sandalwoody. This is very good indeed. Lovely ripe, old-viney fruit. For a village wine a lot of depth. Splendid quality. Really classy. Bags of life. Very good indeed. (03/94)

Now-2000   17.0

Gevrey-Chambertin   Clos-Saint-Jacques
Fernand Pernot

Medium to medium-full, fully mature colour. A lighter, loose-knit wine than the Seguin, but high-toned and classy. Medium body. Balanced, stylish fruit. This has good intensity if never any great structure. Good grip. Long, complex, elegant. Very good plus. (03/95)

Drink soon   16.5

Gevrey-Chambertin   Clos-Saint-Jacques
André Seguin

Good vigorous mature colour. Plump, rich nose. Quite an animal flavour, and so not exactly elegant. Fullish, round, good ripeness and grip. This has good softness but it is a bit coarse. Didn't hold up very well in the glass. (03/95)

Drink soon   15.0

Grands-Echézeaux   Mongeard-Mugneret

Good full mature colour. A bit dense and dried out on the nose. Some fruit on the palate. But this is really a bit too inky, and the after-taste is lean and bitter. Full bodied. But past its best. (03/95)

Past its best   12.0

Mazoyères-Chambertin   Hubert Camus

Medium colour. Soft stylish Pinot Noir. Lightish but elegant. Mature and round and soft but not very vigorous. Yet long. Classy but lacks a little definition. A bit lightweight. Very good. (12/93)

Drink soon   16.0

Mazis-Chambertin   Lichine-Newman

Fine fullish colour. Still vigorous. This is corked. Good rich vigorous stylish fruit nevertheless. Another bottle could be fine. (03/95)

Now-2000   ?17.0

Morey-Saint-Denis   Clos-de-la-Bussière
Georges Roumier

Good fully mature colour. Rich nose, good grip. Fat, ripe, raspberry fruit. Round, rich, meaty and vigorous. Fullish. Quite sturdy, as

usual. Plenty of vigour here. Ripe and rich. Balanced. Good intensity on the finish. Very good plus. Similar note 10/94. (03/95)

Now-2000   16.5

Morey-Saint-Denis   Clos-des-Ormes
Georges Lignier

Medium, fully mature colour. The fruit has lost its sweetness and vigour on the nose. This is a little faded now. But on the palate it is not astringent and the fruit is ripe and full of interest. Good sweetish finish. Better than the nose would suggest. Not past it. Certainly elegant. Very Chambolle in character. Very good. (03/95)

Drink soon   16.0

Musigny   Bouchard Père et Fils

Fullish mature colour. Stylish, fragrant, clean nose. Good vigour. Very good class. Very Musigny. This is gentle but fading on the palate but once was very fine. And it is totally genuine. Soft, fruity, elegant. Still positive at the end. Still very good indeed. (03/95)

Drink soon   17.0

Musigny   Chemardin

Medium to medium-full colour. Soft, gentle, losing a little of its vigour. Some oak but now drying up a bit. Still soft. Still ripe. Now has lost a little fruit. But certainly elegant. Medium body. The acidity beginning to show. (03/94)

Drink soon   16.0

Musigny   Joseph Faiveley

Fullish mature colour. This is just quietly triumphant. A brilliantly fruity, poised, classy, complete and harmonious wine with a good base of oak. This is splendid. Real class, real intensity, real depth, and very very harmonious. *Grand vin*! (03/95)

Now-2000   20.0

Musigny   Prosper Maufoux

Fullish, well-matured colour. Good fullish fruity wine on the nose. Just a hint of maderisation. Quite genuine though. A bit alcoholic and soupy on the palate. Now rather old and coarse at the end. (03/95)

Drink up   13.5

Musigny   Daniel Moine-Hudelot

Very good colour. Still vigorous. Very rich and concentrated on the nose. Lovely cassis, raspberry nose. On the palate this is still amazingly fresh. Smooth, clean, abundantly fruity. A lovely example. What it lacks is a little real Musigny class. But a fine positive finish. (03/95)

Now-2000   18.0

Musigny   Jacques Prieur

Fullish, mature colour. Sweet, oaky, slightly rigid nose. On the palate a little too sweet. Some oak. Reasonable grip. I find it a bit commercial, but certainly attractive. Plump, fat, ripe finish. What it lacks is real Musigny definition. Very good at best. **(03/95)**

Now-2000   **16.0**

Musigny   Georges Roumier

Fullish, mature colour. Sadly very corky and dirty. Yet very good fruit and texture underneath. What a pity! **(03/95)**

Now-2000   **?18.0 plus**

Nuits-Saint-Georges   Les Chaignots Henri Gouges

Fullish, rich, well-matured colour. Rich, slightly gamey nose. Good grip. Opulent and concentrated but quite evolved. Full and fat and meaty. Good structure. Fine quality. Essentially has the Nuits sturdiness, which is now evolved into a spicy, animal sort of wine. Rich and classy and with plenty of depth. Good depth and complexity. Very good grip. Very long. Very good plus. **(10/93)**

Now-2000   **16.5**

Nuits-Saint-Georges   Clos-des-Porrets-Saint-Georges   Henri Gouges

Medium-full colour. Quite some brown now. Definitely an old Burgundy on the nose but mellow and ripe and complex. Not too animal or mushroomy, but beginning to fade a bit. Medium body. Still sweet and classy on the palate. Complex. Not as faded as I thought from the nose. Fine quality, but drink soon. **(10/93)**

Drink soon   **17.5**

Nuits-Saint-Georges   Les Lavières Henri de Villamont

Good full colour. Fully mature. Fat, ripe and rich on the nose, mellow, sweet and caramelly. Good depth here. Fullish on the palate. Fragrant. Still alive, still stylish. Still fresh. This is a very good example. Long. Very much a wine from the Vosne side of Nuits. **(03/95)**

Now-2000   **16.0**

Pommard   Leroy

Mature colour. A lot of concentration here. Chocolatey. Stylish, vigorous. Complex and long. Very good. **(07/92)**

Now-2000   **16.0**

Pommard   Clos-de-Citeaux   Jean Monnier

Medium colour. Fully mature. Fragrant nose. A touch of the stems. Ripe. Fresh on the palate. Plump. Vigorous, rich and fruity. Very well balanced. This is very good. Still has life. Long

finish. Echoes a note from 06/92. **(03/95)**

Now-2000   **16.0**

Richebourg   Joseph Drouhin

Full colour. No undue maturity. Quality fruit and real class here. Plus an exciting opulence. This is a lovely example. Fragrant. Intense. Fullish. Very elegant indeed. Beautiful fruit. Ample, round, very complete, very harmonious. Very fine indeed. **(03/95)**

Now-2000   **18.5**

Richebourg   Romanée-Conti

Vigorous full colour. Splendid nose. Raspberries, redcurrants and oak. Still youthful. Concentrated and profound. Very high quality. On the palate full, very good grip. Rich but slightly muscular and sinewy. Yet fat and multidimensional. This is very fine. And still has bags of life. **(05/94)**

Now-2005   **18.0**

Romanée-Saint-Vivant Les Quatre-Journeaux   Louis Latour

Fullish, mature colour. Interesting slightly burnt, slightly caramelly, slightly echo of bonfires nose. Sweet, oaky. Fullish, classy on the palate. Genuine and fresh. Good length and complexity at the end. Now beginning to lose its vigour. Fine though. But by no means great. **(03/95)**

Drink soon   **17.5**

Romanée-Saint-Vivant   Marey-Monge Romanée-Conti

Fullish, mature colour. Very lovely concentration, nice, intense and stylish nose. There is coffee, chocolate and plums in brandy here. This is still very fresh. Delicious fragrance. Very fine. Fullish. Very good grip. Marvellous fruit. Hugely intense and concentrated high quality Pinot fruit. And in this bottle's showing has bags of life left. Very very subtle. Very very long and complex at the end. **(03/95)**

Now-2005   **18.5**

Romanée-Saint-Vivant   Sichel Frères et Fils

Full, mature colour. Fat, rich, chocolatey nose. Somewhat bolstered? Certainly vigorous. Full and rich. Good structure. Just a hint of maderisation. Rather four-square. Disappointing for a Romanée-Saint-Vivant and without any of this *grand cru* character. Lumpy. No flair. **(03/95)**

Drink soon   **14.0**

La Tâche   Romanée-Conti

Magnum. Fine colour. Mature but no age. Mellow, rich, classy, velvety and concentrated on the nose. On the palate this is well matured and now soft, with good acidity. It is intense, balanced and stylish. Plenty of grip. Plenty of vigour. But I wouldn't keep it too long. I detect on the finish - and NB it is a magnum - a hint of coarseness. But lovely. **(10/95)**

Drink soon 18.5

Vosne-Romanée   Les Beaux-Monts
Sichel Frères et Fils

Full mature colour. Good rich meaty nose. Fat, full and slightly robust. Sweet, chocolatey palate. Good grip. Good concentration. A little souped up but the base wine was good. Rather a burnt after-taste. Yet ample and quite vigorous. **(03/95)**

Drink soon 14.5

Vosne-Romanée   Les Champs-Perdrix
Clair-Daü

Fully mature colour. Good fresh, stylish nose. A little lean but not unripe. Good acidity. Medium body. Not astringent but now a little old perhaps. Yet still ripe and reasonably succulent.

Just a touch ungenerous. Slight hail taste? Quite good. Several notes. **(03/95)**

Drink soon 14.0

Vosne-Romanée   La Grande-Rue
Henri Lamarche

Medium to medium-full colour. Very well matured, almost green at the rim. Quite a faded nose. Very faded on the palate. It is not astringent. But it has lost all of its fruit. Probably always rather loose-knit. But there might have been some elegance once. **(03/95)**

Past its best 10.0

Vosne-Romanée   Les Suchots   Louis Latour

Fully mature colour. Broad nose. A little dried out. On the palate this is a bit astringent, yet has some fruit, grip and style still. Good structure, reasonable fruit and acidity. Not blowsy. But not really ever much concentration or fat. Good at best. **(03/95)**

Drink soon 15.0

1970

RATING FOR THE VINTAGE

Red: (14.5)   **White:** (14.5)
(most wines, red and white, now old)

SIZE OF THE CROP

(Hectolitres, excluding generic wine)

	Red	White
Grands Crus	12,756	2,356
Village and *Premiers Crus*	141,018	27,985
Total	153,774	30,341

At the time 1970 was a record crop (though it would soon be eclipsed by 1972 and 1973): half as much again as 1967, 1969 and 1971. Superficially both the climatic conditions and the size of the crop paralleled that of Bordeaux. Yet while the Gironde produced a splendid vintage, 1970 in Burgundy left much to be desired.

WEATHER CONDITIONS

The spring was wet, cool and miserable, but not so much so as to cause any damage to the vines, and from the end of May it began to warm up to a very fine June, ensuring a successful flowering and a large potential crop. Thereafter, apart from a week in August, the summer was warm and sunny, right through the vintage, which began in the last week of September, and beyond.

THE STYLE OF THE WINE

From the start it was clear that neither the red wines nor the whites had the concentration and backbone of the 1969s, even the 1966s. Here was the proof that while you could produce record quantities without losing intensity in Bordeaux, in Burgundy the diminishing returns set in at much lower levels of *rendement*. Alcoholic degrees were low, the wines fruity and pleasant, but they arrived at their peak relatively soon. In retrospect it was a pity the practice of *saignée* had not yet arrived in Burgundy cellars.

TASTING NOTES

BLANC

Meursault Perrières Joseph Drouhin

Medium colour but showing age. Faintly oxidised on the nose, though fresher on the palate. This is just about at the end. Not astringent. Indeed mellow, quite fat, still nutty. But in the end has lost some of its fruit. Was a very good, even fine, elegant wine in its prime. **(10/94)**

Past its best (see note)

Puligny-Montrachet Henri Boillot

Very good colour for a wine of this age. The fruit is a touch lean and vegetal on the nose but the wine isn't old. More fruity on the palate. Stylish. Good vigour. Medium-full. Good classy long finish. Has held up very well, though at first fell away in the glass. Very good. **(10/94)**

Drink soon 16.0

ROUGE

Bonnes-Mares Dujac

Magnum. Mature, medium to medium-full colour. Fragrant, subtle, mellow nose. Some of the stems evident. But rich and vigorous as well as good acidity. Medium body. Soft. It lacks a bit of succulence but classy and long on the palate. Sweet on the finish. Fine. **(10/95)**

Now-1999 17.5

Charmes-Chambertin Noblet-Giroy, Mommessin

Good colour. Fullish. No undue age. Getting a little lean on the nose. Has lost a bit of generosity. Medium-full. Slightly lumpy and rigid. Has lost a bit of its fruit. Good but not great. **(03/94)**

Drink soon 15.0

Clos-de-Vougeot Lamarche

Lightish colour. Fragrant, mellow, soft, succulent, very ripe nose and palate. Though on the nose some stems. Good fresh acidity. This is soft and luscious, but lightening up now. Fresh. Very good indeed. Drink soon though. **(02/96)**

Drink soon 17.0

Corton Clos-du-Roi Prince de Mérode

Good colour. Rich plump vigorous nose and palate. Mellow but with more body and fat than I would have expected for a 1970. Rich fruit. Medium-full. Good grip. Classy. Long. Fragrant and complex. Plenty of life. Very good indeed. **(10/93)**

Now-2000 17.0

Echézeaux Lamarche

Fullish colour. This is a ripe sturdy wine, beginning to fade a little. A chewier, richer wine, with more depth and class than the Clos-de-Vougeot. But a little older. Was fine. Now good plus. **(10/93)**

Drink up 15.5

Nuits-Saint-Georges Les Saint-Georges Joseph Faiveley

Fullish, but quite old colour. This is quite old on the nose. Delicate, fragrant but a little past its best. On the palate a little astringent. A touch perhaps of the *goût de grêle*. Good acidity. But still has fruit if not fat. Expanded in the glass. Certainly succulent. Got solider and meatier in the glass. Fragrant, classy. Fine. **(09/94)**

Drink soon 17.5

Nuits-Saint-Georges Les Saint-Georges Henri Gouges

Medium to medium-full colour. Fully mature. Plump, fruity, round and stylish on both nose and palate. Good acidity. Really quite concentrated and intense for a 1970. Still vigorous. Very classy. Fresh cherry-like. Good long finish - cinnamony, as it developed. Shows very well indeed. Another bottle, a month previously, was less alive. **(09/93)**

Drink soon 17.5

Pommard Clos-de-Citeaux Jean Monnier

This is getting a bit tired and coarse. Browning. A little maderised. A little bitter at the end. It is also a little sweet. Got cleaner as it developed in the glass. **(12/92)**

Drink up 13.0

Volnay   Santenots   Robert Ampeau et Fils
Well-matured colour. This is showing a bit of age on the nose. Good fruit though. Slightly four-square, but reasonable class and character. Medium-full body. Good but lacks complexity. **(07/95)**
Drink soon   **15.0**

**Volnay   Santenots-du-Milieu
Comtes Lafon**
Fullish, not too well-matured colour. This is, though quite old and soft, fresh and rather elegant. Even fresher on the palate, round, stylish, good concentrated very complex fruit for a 1970. Medium-full, good intensity still. This will still keep well. Lovely, especially on the finish. **(08/91)**
Now–2000   **18.0**

1969

RATING FOR THE VINTAGE

Red: 16.0   **White:** (17.0)
(now likely to be a bit old)

SIZE OF THE CROP
(Hectolitres, excluding generic wine)

	Red	White
Grands Crus	8,084	1,499
Village and *Premiers Crus*	92,673	19,759
Total	100,757	21,258

In total contrast to Bordeaux, 1969 was a very successful harvest in Burgundy, though a small one, and is much to be preferred to 1970 (and more consistent than 1971). Indeed one could well argue that, with 1966, this was the best vintage of the decade after 1964.

WEATHER CONDITIONS

The climate, however, was not all that auspicious. Spring was late, the flowering delayed and protracted, leading to wide-spread *millerandage*, reducing the crop, and it wasn't until July that the summer really began. Thereafter, though September was uneven, the weather in general was fine and hot, enabling the maturation to catch up a little. The vintage was nevertheless a little late, but the harvest was collected in good weather.

THE STYLE OF THE WINE

The white wines were very good indeed: firm, rich, concentrated and intense, really classic examples that lasted very well indeed, the best since 1959. Sadly they are now old.

The red wines are a different matter. Full and rich and ripe, yes. But balanced and elegant? Not quite so high on the scale. There is a robust quality about many 1969 Burgundies, and in some cases the tannins obtrude. The 1964s are more complete. The 1966s, though a little less structured, can show finer Pinot Noir fruit. Yet there is much enjoyment still to be found in this vintage, and the best wines are still vigorous.

TASTING NOTES

BLANC

Chassagne-Montrachet Caillerets
Jacques Gagnard-Delagrange

Deliciously fresh. Complex. Gently oaky. Very elegant. Quite delicious. Very velvety-smooth. Long. Subtle. Excellent. Plenty of life here still. **(02/95)**

Drink soon   18.5

Chassagne-Montrachet Morgeots
Marquis de Laguiche, Joseph Drouhin

Light golden colour. Evolved nose. A little oxidised. Yet plenty of peachy fruit. As it evolved, really quite drinkable. Much better on the palate than on the nose. Not a bit short. But a little too soft at the end. **(10/94)**

Drink up   14.0

Chevalier-Montrachet Louis Latour

Quite a rich colour; evolved too. Big, nutty, alcoholic nose. At first a bit heavy but got better as it evolved. Full, rich, quite structured. A bit fat concentrated wine. Good acidity. Plenty of depth. It lacks a little delicacy and finesse but there is a lot of size here. A bit H$_2$S as it developed. Very good indeed. **(10/94)**

Drink soon   17.0

Meursault Roland Remoissenet Père et Fils

Avery's label. Old gold colour. The nose is sweet but faded but on the palate it is fresher, even rich and luscious. A ripe vintage, and an old, but still delicious wine. Fullish. Good backbone. High quality. Lots of enjoyment to be had. **(05/94)**

Drink up   17.0

Le Montrachet Romanée-Conti

Good fresh fullish colour. Aromatic. Slight *surmaturité* on the nose. Spicy. No hint of botrytis though. Full, rich, fat and generous. Good grip. Quite well matured now though. But not a bit blowsy. Fine. Similar 11/94. **(02/95)**

Now-2000   17.5

ROUGE

Aloxe-Corton Roland
Remoissenet Père et Fils

Good mature colour. Fragrant, stylish, meaty nose. No undue sweetness. Still very vigorous. A very classy nose. Fullish, intense, well balanced. A splendid example of a village wine. Lots of life ahead of it. Very good. **(10/94)**

Now-2000   16.0

Aloxe-Corton *Premier Cru*
Roland Remoissenet Père et Fils

Full but mature colour. Definite brown at the edge. Aromatic nose. Full, ripe - almost overripe - old and lush. Full and roasted. Almost Rhônish. **(09/91)**

Drink soon   15.0

Auxey-Duresses Les Duresses Bernard Roy

Fresh colour. Youthful for age and provenance. Slightly attenuated on the nose. But still sweet and fruity. A little sturdy but a little rigid. Surprisingly fresh and elegant on the nose. Medium body. No undue age. Sweet finish. Elegant. Very good. **(10/94)**

Drink soon   16.0

Beaune Cent-Vignes
Roland Remoissenet Père et Fils

Very good full, vigorous, glowing colour. Full, very vigorous nose. Ripe and rich. Just a little chunky but plenty of fruit. Balanced though, nonetheless. And stylish too. Fullish, ample, surprisingly young. Yet with all the gamey complexity and sensuality of fully mature Burgundy. Good follow-through. A lovely example. Still has plenty of life. Very good. **(01/95)**

Now-2000   16.0

Beaune Clos-des-Ursules Louis Jadot

Very lively colour. Hardly any brown. Fragrant, spicy, nutty and caramelly, almost cooked jam on the nose. On the palate fresh, stylish, complex. This is very good. Will still last. **(08/92)**

Now-2000   16.0

Bonnes-Mares Clair-Daü

Magnum. Fullish but quite well-matured colour. Dried out somewhat on the nose as it developed. There is an element of the compost heap and the vegetal but good acidity so not as astringent on the palate. Yet past its best. **(10/89)**

Past its best   (see note)

Bonnes-Mares Georges Roumier

Medium-full mature colour. Rich succulent nose. Riper than the Amoureuses. Better covered tannins. Good depth. Plummy raspberry fruit. Youthful and vigorous. Full, still a little tannic. This is a fine meaty wine, with concentration and richness. Fine but not the finesse at the end for great. **(10/89)**

Now-2000   17.5

Bonnes-Mares Comte Georges de Vogüé

Medium-full mature colour. A softer more delicate, more aromatic nose than the Roumier. Elegant. Fine fruit. Medium-full, round, soft, ripe and generous. Good oak. Perhaps just a little spuriously sweet. Yet elegant. Very fine. **(10/89)**

Now-2000   18.0

Chambertin　Pierre Bourée

Good medium-full mature colour. Fat, rich, substantial nose. A masculine wine with real depth. Quality here. This is a fine wine. Young, full, rich, complex. Less new oak than the Charmes. The Charmes is the more seductive. Very fine but not the concentration, complexity and sheer breed for great. Ultimately there is something a bit four-square. **(10/89)**

Now-2000   **18.0**

Chambertin　Louis Latour

Magnum. Very full vigorous colour. Rich, sweet - almost too sweet - concentrated nose. Very, very ripe and rich indeed. Similar on the palate. Alcoholic. Almost spirity. Yet very good. But almost cough-mixturey on the finish. **(10/89)**

Now-2000   **16.0**

Chambertin　Ponsot

Medium to medium-full colour. Less vigorous than Clos-de-Vougeot 1971 (Jadot). Very complex lovely ripe fruit. On the palate fullish. Very good intensity and real class. Lovely. Very long. Lots of dimension. Lots of life ahead of it still. Real intensity at the end. Very fine. **(03/96)**

Now-2000 plus   **18.0**

Chambertin　Jacques Prieur

Good fullish mature colour. Interesting high-toned oaky nose but a touch of the sweet-sour about it. Slightly stewed. Something curious on the palate. Edgy. Medium-full body. Yet underneath there is quality here. **(10/89)**

Drink soon   **14.0**

Chambertin　Louis Trapet et Fils

Marvellous colour. Real intensity. This is very fine. Full but balanced, classy and laid-back. Very very concentrated on the palate. Rich, fat, complete. Very vigorous. Lovely. Very complex. **(09/92)**

Now-2000   **19.0**

Chambolle-Musigny
Roland Remoissenet Père et Fils

Good colour. Soft, fragrant, velvety nose. Medium body. Good grip still. Round. Fat cherry-raspberry flavours. Long. Fresh. Very good for a village wine. Similar note 09/91. **(07/92)**

Drink soon   **15.5**

Chambolle-Musigny　Les Amoureuses
Georges Roumier

Good full colour. No undue maturity. Fuller than the Roumier, Bonnes-Mares. Full, vigorous nose but seems to be not only a bit chunky which you might expect from Roumier, but

lacking real richness. Riper on the palate. A wine of strength and alcohol. It has a hot slightly coarse finish. But full, rich and meaty on the palate. Very good. **(10/89)**

Now-2000   **16.0**

Chambolle-Musigny　Les Amoureuses
Sichel

Magnum. Good colour. Broad, fat, earthy but genuine and stylish nose. Good depth. Warm and slightly sweet. Fullish, good evidence of a hot vintage. Rich and vigorous. Very good. The same wine, from bottle, was only quite good. **(10/89)**

Now-2000   **16.0**

Charmes-Chambertin　Pierre Bourée

Good full mature colour. Rather solid and stewed on the nose. Rich and meaty underneath. Good quality. Much better as it evolved. Rich, oaky and gamey. Full and succulent. A lot of wine here. Still fine and vigorous. Has the coffee taste of good Burgundy with depth. Very fine indeed. A masculine wine. **(10/89)**

Now-2000   **18.5**

Charmes-Chambertin　Louis Latour

Good fullish mature colour. Solid, sturdy meaty nose, but not without depth. Fullish, the usual sturdy-solid Latour aspect. Not sweet and rich like the Latour, Le Chambertin. Again a slight burn of alcohol on the finish. Slightly tough but vigorous. Very good. **(10/89)**

Now-2000   **16.0**

Clos-de-la-Roche　Dujac

Fine colour. Vigorous and full. This is lovely. Rich, meaty, complex and concentrated. Very good grip. Lovely long lingering finish. **(09/92)**

Now-2000   **17.5**

Clos-de-la-Roche　Louis Remy

Medium-full, vigorous but mature colour. Plenty of depth and *matière* here. Rich, concentrated, intense and classy. It is beginning to show a little age now. But soft, well matured, sweet, mellow, classy and old-viney. This is a delicious example. Very fine fruit. Delicate. Very long. Real *grand cru*. Marvellous finish. **(10/94)**

Drink soon   **18.0**

Clos-de-la-Roche　Armand Rousseau

Medium-full, fully mature colour. Fine fragrant classy nose. Breed and harmony here. Sweet coffee. Not as vigorous as some. Getting towards the end of its useful life but round, ripe and very stylish. A lovely wine, medium-full body. Long and harmonious. **(10/89)**

Drink soon   **17.0**

Clos-Saint-Denis   Dujac

Good mature but very vigorous colour. Delicious fragrant complex nose. Nicely fat, not too robust, gently sweet. Very finely balanced. Long, fragrant, subtle and very fine. **(11/94)**

Drink soon   18.0

Clos-de-Tart   Mommessin

Very full, vigorous colour. Vegetabley and dank on the nose. Meaty but solid and stalky. Dense, soupy and tannic. Rather four-square. May be beginning to get astringent. Full bodied. No finesse. **(10/89)**

Drink soon   13.5

Clos-de-Vougeot   Gros Frère et Soeur

Full colour. Earthy and very cassis, showing a little sign of astringency but meaty and with a good grip. Curiously perfumed. There is a certain metallic leanness underneath. An old-fashioned wine. **(06/89)**

Drink soon   15.0

Clos-de-Vougeot   L'Héritier-Guyot

Medium colour. Mature. Fine coffee and cocoa powder nose. Elegant. Fragrant. Classy and balanced. Sweet. Old roses. Soft. Fine. **(05/90)**

Drink soon   17.5

Clos-de-Vougeot   Jacques Prieur

Medium-full mature colour. Round, sweet, vanilla-y oaky nose, some butterscotch. Curious on the palate as well. A soft, oaky, certainly predominantly Pinot wine - and good complex Pinot at that - yet overlaid by this curious chaptalised flavour. A butterscotch-flavoured, instant whip made with 'off' milk. **(10/89)**

Drink soon   14.0

Clos-de-Vougeot   Clos-du-Frantin   Bichot

Good full colour. No undue maturity. Rich, full, vigorous, chocolatey nose: as much Rhône as Burgundy. Full on the palate, warm, still has some tannin. There is a lot of heat here. A ripe rich vigorous wine. Not exactly very genuine Burgundy, but good stuff. **(10/89)**

Drink soon   14.0

Corton   Bressandes   Prince de Mérode

Fullish mature colour. Meaty, gamey nose, some sweetness, slightly burnt and smoky. Robust wine but with good meaty fruit, even concentration. This has depth and at least some finesse. Still very youthful. Vigorous on the finish. Very good plus. **(10/89)**

Now-2000   16.5

Corton   Château Corton-Grancey
Louis Latour

Good colour. Hot, alcoholic, ripe but slightly sweet nose. Fullish. Nutty, brown sugar and *crème brûlée*. Not a wine of great style. Slightly smoky-dry as it developed. **(12/92)**

Drink soon   14.0

Corton   Les Vignes-au-Saint   Louis Latour

Good colour. Medium-full; not too brown. Complex, fragrant nose. Ripe, vigorous. On the palate a more sturdy wine with a firm, slightly alcoholic Latour burn. Not a lot of finesse but no undue age. Yet more body than fruit. Good but not great. **(10/89)**

Drink soon   15.0

Echézeaux   Veuve A. Clerget

Good full, fully mature colour. Voluptuous, rich, ample nose with a touch of toffee and a touch of spice. Not the greatest of elegance, but fat and generous, and it has good acidity. Fullish on the palate. Nice and ripe. Still fresh. Not too gamey. Indeed it has plenty of style, and it is long and complex. Very good plus. **(07/94)**

Now-2000   16.5

Gevrey-Chambertin   Clos-Saint-Jacques
Roland Remoissenet Père et Fils

Fine full colour. Very little sign of maturity. Fat, rich, concentrated and super. Very young. Very lively and lots of fresh fruit. Very youthful. Fine quality. **(08/92)**

Now-2000   17.5

Gevrey-Chambertin   Les Combottes
Roland Remoissenet Père et Fils

Very good colour. Lovely ripe nose. Delicious fruit. Good full body, balanced, complex, vigorous. Long. Very good but not as good as the 1964. **(07/92)**

Now-2000   16.0

Grands-Echézeaux   René Engel

Good mature colour. Delicate nose. Soft, but perhaps a little light. Certainly elegant and fragrant. Ripe but neither too gamey nor too *rôti*. On the palate medium-full, mellow and very, very smooth, without a touch of astringency. Rich, sweet, nutty. Very clean. Very classy. Not quite the intensity for great, nor the concentration. But very good. (Was 'very good indeed' 09/93). **(05/94)**

Drink soon   16.0

Grands-Echézeaux   Louis Gros

Good full colour; no undue maturity. Fine old concentrated Pinot nose, gamey and vegetabley. Fragrant. High toned. Perhaps fading a little.

On the palate it has lost a little of its fruit, so there is a lean touch. Medium-full, genuine Pinot. A little past its best but a noble echo of what was once a very fine wine. Getting a bit acid on the finish. **(10/89)**

Past its best   15.0

Grands-Echézeaux Romanée-Conti

Well-matured, lightish colour. Lean, *tabac*, stemmy nose. Medium to medium-full. A slight lack of fat. Good acidity. Lacks a little richness but has depth and complexity, even class. Good plus. **(05/96)**

Drink soon   15.5

Musigny Jacques Prieur

Fully mature colour. Deeper than Vogüé. Good nose. This has plenty of depth. Full and fat and youthful. Good attack but after that seems to tail off. A statement without supplementaries. Fresh and youthful without being a blockbuster. Yet curiously short and one-dimensional. Quite chunky at the end as it evolved. Fine certainly. But not great. **(10/89)**

Drink soon   17.5

Musigny *Vieilles-Vignes*
Comte Georges de Vogüé

Medium colour, fully mature; less colour than the Vogüé, Bonnes-Mares. On the nose rather more evolved. Yet more complex. Delicate and feminine. Fragrant fruit. Fine ripe acidity. Fresh and flowery. Very subtle. A lovely wine. Several notes since. Still very delicious in 10/94. **(10/89)**

Drink soon   19.0

Nuits-Saint-Georges Clos-des-Porrets
Henri Gouges

Medium mature colour. A touch of vegetal reduction on the nose at first. Concentration and quality underneath. Ripe, medium to medium-full. Good freshness. Complex. Concentrated. Elegant. Good intensity. Lovely finish. Lots of life ahead of it. Very good indeed, even fine. **(10/94)**

Drink soon   17.0

Nuits-Saint-Georges Les Porrets
Joseph Faiveley

Good colour. No undue maturity. Soft, ripe, round raspberry-Pinot nose. Not too animal, nor too *rôti*. Balanced, fresh and stylish. Medium-full, complex, silky-velvety. Very harmonious. This has a lot of elegance for a Nuits and a 1969. Best drunk quite soon. Good vigour still, and good length. Very good. **(09/92)**

Drink soon   16.0

Pommard Daniel Rebourgeon-Mure

Mature colour. Fragrant nose. There is a touch of the rustic about the tannins. Medium-full,

soft, sweet, fully mature. Doesn't seem to be a blockbuster, but it has good intensity and elegance. This is a lovely - unexpectedly lovely for a village - example. Still holding up very well. **(12/95)**

Now-2000   16.5

Pommard Clos-des-Epenots
Château de Meursault

Medium colour. Still very fresh. On the nose a little pinched. But not a bit too oaky. The palate is better: plump, soft, but it doesn't really have the depth of a great *premier cru*. **(11/94)**

Drink soon   14.0

Richebourg Jean Gros

Very good colour. Mellow, classy nose. Very good Pinot, not too hot, as it often is in this vintage. Complex, fragrant. Vigorous and soft on the palate. Complex. Long. Improved in the glass. This is very lovely. Not quite *grand vin* but not far short. Abundant but refined, harmonious subtle fruit. Multi-dimensional. Very fine indeed. Several notes. **(12/92)**

Now-2000   19.0

Richebourg Romanée-Conti

Very good vigorous fullish colour. Concentrated nose. Rich and fat and with a touch of herbs: thyme and peppermint. Very classy. Fullish, vigorous, round and fat. Lots of flavour, very well balanced. Plenty of life ahead of it. Very long. Complex, satisfying. Fine. **(10/94)**

Drink soon   17.5

Richebourg Charles Vienot

Full colour. Rich, fat, meaty, slightly earthy nose. A vigorous wine. Sturdy and dense. Lacks the breed of a Richebourg. Got a little oxidised as it developed. Has life but coarse and boring. **(10/94)**

Now-2000   14.0

La Romanée Bichot

Fullish mature colour. Fat, rich, coffee and chocolate and mocha nose. Plump, vigorous. Classy. This has a lot of depth. Fullish, lovely ample fruit. This is better and more vigorous than a La Tâche sampled alongside it. Ripe, balanced, long. Fine finish. Excellent. **(10/89)**

Drink soon   19.0

Romanée-Conti Romanée-Conti

If anything, a lighter colour than the above. Delicious nose. Very, very complex. Delicacy rather than power. Great finesse. Medium-full, finely balanced, very stylish mature Burgundy. Delicious complex wine but like the above getting towards the end of its life. By 04/94 was definitely showing a bit of age. **(10/89)**

Drink soon   19.0

Romanée-Saint-Vivant   Marey-Monge
Romanée-Conti

Mature colour. Fine, classy, complex, fragrant nose. Both delicate and subtle. Medium-full, freshly balanced. Lovely rarefied fruit. Long and multi-dimensional. A lovely wine. Beautifully constructed. All in finesse. Sweet and complex. But perhaps beginning to lighten up now. Last sampled 10/94: classy but lightening up. (10/89)

Drink soon   18.0

Santenay   Camille Giroud

Very good colour. A chunky, rich old-fashioned wine. Ripe and meaty, even quite solid. No oakiness. Very good acidity. This is a wine built to last. Still needs time. Good. (10/94)

Now-2007   15.0

Santenay   La Comme   Lequin-Roussot

Medium colour. But no undue age. The nose is not very expressive. A touch of astringency on the palate. But ripe and plump, raspberry flavoured. Good old-vine character. Sweet, quite sturdy. Good. Still has life. (10/93)

Drink soon   15.0

Savigny-lès-Beaune   Cuvée Fouquerand
Hospices de Beaune, *éleveur* unknown

Fullish, mature colour. Fullish nose. Sweet and with a touch of chocolate blancmange. Medium-full, still ripe and succulent, but a bit beginning to lose its vigour and grip. Attractive Pinot, balanced and quite classy. Still sweet. Good. (01/95)

Drink soon   15.0

La Tâche   Romanée-Conti

Compared with Richebourg this is a bit more evolved. But it is still fresh. The nose is complex, rich, classy, and even if a little less vigorous today than the Richebourg, has more depth and intensity. On the palate, full and complex, richer and longer on the palate than the Richebourg if slightly more evolved. Very classy. Very lovely. But I have had less vigorous bottles. (10/94)

Drink soon   18.5

Volnay   Caillerets, Clos-des-Soixante-
Ouvrées   Pousse d'Or

Fine mature colour. This is very fine indeed. Fresh, elegant, ripe, naturally sweet. Still vigorous. Medium-full, splendidly mellow and silky. Impeccably balanced. Very classy. Very intense. Very fine. Bags of life ahead of it. Brilliant. Beautifully delicate. But not as good as the 1964? (07/95)

Now-2000 plus   18.5

Volnay   Champans   Marquis d'Angerville

This still has plenty of vigour. Medium to medium-full colour. No undue age. Full, spicy, ripe and succulent. Balanced, intense and complete. Fine quality. Long and complex. Bags of life. Still rich and fat. (12/93)

Now-2000   17.5

Volnay   Clos-des-Chênes
Roland Remoissenet Père et Fils

Fine vigorous colour. This is a bit of a vigorous wine. A touch of volatile acidity on the nose. Full, plump, fruity but a touch lumpy and four-square. Compared with the Soixante-Ouvrées of the Pousse d'Or, it is good but totally outclassed. It lacks the Volnay delicacy and fragrance. (07/95)

Now-2000   15.5

Volnay   Santenots   Berry Bros & Rudd

Good full mature colour. Nothing very Pinot about the nose. It is sweet, but not fragrant, and it is full and earthy. Slightly better on the palate. At least some Pinot here. Good balance, some fragrance. And the finish is quite soft and sweet. Reasonable vigour. But some acidity lurks underneath. Fair. (01/95)

Drink soon   14.0

Volnay   Les Taille-Pieds
Hubert de Montille

Fine vigorous colour – would have said it was a decade younger. Fine ripe nose. Lovely fresh Pinot fruit, only just beginning to acquire the flavour of maturity, it seems. Fullish, more evolved on the palate than the nose would indicate. Rich, fat and, as often with this domaine, more Pommard than Volnay. Very good. (10/89)

Drink soon   16.0

Vosne-Romanée   Les Beaumonts
Jean Grivot

Good fullish mature colour. Slight touch of the stems on the nose. A bit thin. Ripe and fragrant underneath. Medium-full, very well balanced. Lovely stylish complex fruit. Less robust, more stylish than many 1969s. On the lightish side for 1969. But long and elegant. Very good but not great. Lacks real concentration, fat and richness. (03/96)

Drink soon   16.0

Vosne-Romanée   R. Nize   (*Tasteviné*)

Medium colour. Fully mature. Fresh, fragrant, soft and mature on the nose. This is most attractive. Still silky and smooth and plump and vigorous. Medium body. Long, sweet, stylish. Very nice. (10/95)

Now-1999   15.0

Vosne-Romanée   Les Beaumonts
Thomas Frères

(Distributed by Pierre Olivier, *négociant* in Nuits-Saint-Georges.) Fullish colour. Still youthful. Fat, rich, full, vigorous but a little dense on the nose. On the palate this is very concentrated, and has lovely rich ripe fruit. Very very good grip. Powerful, intense. Very vigorous. This is fine. Long, really not a bit robust. Nicely cool. Even sweet. Tastes like a very ripe 1978. **(03/96)**

Now–2005   17.5

1967

RATING FOR THE VINTAGE

Red: (14.5)   **White:** (15.0)
(both wines, red and white, now past their best)

SIZE OF THE CROP

(Hectolitres, excluding generic wine)

	Red	White
Grands Crus	9,931	11,548
Village and *Premiers Crus*	102,061	117,778
Total	111,992	129,326

Unlike in Bordeaux, where 1967 was a huge harvest, 1967 was a small year in the Côte d'Or. It was also irregular. There were widespread frosts in May, affecting particularly the white-wine villages of the Côte-de-Beaune and Beaune itself. After that it was warm and sunny, but there was hail in August and ten days of rain in September which encouraged the onset of rot. Nevertheless the skies cleared, and the vintage took place in early October in fine conditions.

THE STYLE OF THE WINE

Today's growers are more meticulous, and a better general result would have been obtained. Back then it was only the conscientious who made good wine. Most 1967 reds (the whites were rather better) were loose-knit, light in colour and evolved fast. The best wines, however, were and are quite another matter: serious, if now after thirty years quite naturally getting to the end of their collective lives. There is elegance and concentration here, and no lack of character.

TASTING NOTES

ROUGE

Bonnes–Mares   Comte Georges de Vogüé

Good, fullish mature colour. Nicely nutty, fragrant Pinot Noir. Good class and depth. Fullish, just something not quite clean. Is it rot or decay? But otherwise rich, balanced and vigorous. Long positive finish. Very good plus. (03/96)

Drink soon   16.5

Chambertin   Pierre Damoy

Medium-full, well-matured colour. Coffee, milk-chocolate elements on the nose. Fullish, vigorous, classy. Very fine fruit and a very good grip. This is long, masculine, virile. Fine plus. (03/96)

Now–2000 plus   17.5

Chambertin
Roland Remoissenet Père et Fils

Fresh, ripe nose. Good acidity but fragrant and aromatic, indeed fat. An intriguing mixture of richness and almost 1972-ish grip. Best of all on the palate which is concentrated and old-viney with a great deal of depth. Coffee, toffee, molasses and black cherry fruit. This is splendid. (09/91)

Now–2000   18.5

Chambertin   Armand Rousseau

Medium-full, well-matured colour. Mellow, concentrated, classy nose. Lovely fruit. Aromatic. Complex. Real finesse. Well matured but no undue age. Medium-full but soft on the palate. No hard edges. Long and very lovely and intense at the end. Will still keep well. Very fine. Similar note 03/94. (03/96)

Now–2000 plus   18.5

Chambertin   Louis Trapet et Fils

Fullish, well-matured if not old colour. Yet it is not maderised or oxidised on the palate. Fullish, rich, firm, slightly robust and bitter. A little tight. But there is quality here. Good grip. Definitely a masculine wine. Still sweet. Very good indeed. (03/96)

Drink soon   17.0

Chambertin   Cuvée Héritiers-Latour
Louis Latour

Full, mature colour. Very ripe and rich, slightly confected perhaps on the nose. This is full and masculine, quite alcoholic, and a touch hot at the end. Not quite as classy as his Romanée-Saint-Vivant, but a more substantial wine, and certainly fine. (03/96)

Now–2000 plus   17.0

Charmes–Chambertin   Pierre Bourée

Fullish mature colour. Quite a chunky wine. Hot and spicy. On the palate this is sweet and sturdy. And enjoyable. But it doesn't taste like Burgundy, especially a 1967. Dense and getting a bit four-square at the end. (10/94)

Drink soon   13.5

Echézeaux   Leroy

This is very fine indeed. Fine colour. Still impressively vigorous all the way through. Full, rich, succulent, classy. A bit of new wood I would suggest. Most of the stems, I would judge. Very clean and pure and without a suggestion of age. Fine plus.

Now–2000 plus   18.0

Echézeaux   Romanée-Conti

Full mature colour. No undue age. Lovely nose. Rich and full, sweetly ripe. Vigorous. No obvious stems. Lush and generous. On the palate full and rich, complex and vigorous. Plenty of depth. Long and very classy. Plenty of vigour. Fine. (03/96)

Now–2000 plus   17.5

Le Musigny   Jean Hudelot, Lichine

Medium to medium-full well-matured colour. Ripe, soft, fragrant, classy nose. This is still fresh on the palate, long and complex. A delicate wine, but still harmonious. Very Musigny. Very lovely. But beginning to fade now. (03/96)

Drink soon   18.0

Le Musigny   Comte Georges de Vogüé

Old fullish colour. Now very oxidised/maderised on the nose. Too old. (03/96)

Past its best   (see note)

Richebourg   Romanée-Conti

Full mature colour. Impressive nose. Rich and full. No sign of age. Fresh, balanced, composed. Underneath very concentrated fruit. Complex and profound. Marvellous ripeness and richness. Fullish, opulent. Not quite as vigorous as the Romanée-Saint-Vivant (Marey-Monge) but more profound, more dimension. Very fine. A bottle 10/94 was more developed: only 'very good indeed'.(03/96)

Now–2000   18.5

Romanée-Saint-Vivant   Marey-Monge
Romanée-Conti

Medium colour. Fully mature. Softer, gentler than the Latour. A little more stems. Not as much as the Echézeaux. Just as vigorous though. This developed in the glass to give a wine of more vigour than Latour's Romanée-Saint-Vivant. Real class and splendidly harmonious. Real intensity and depth. Very fine. **(03/96)**

Now-2000 plus   **18.5**

Romanée-Saint-Vivant
Les Quatre-Journeaux   **Louis Latour**

Medium-full, mature colour. Clean, ripe, sweet but gentle. Classy on the nose. Slightly caramelly. Medium-full. Very good grip. Fine fruit. This has freshness and a lot of depth. Long and positive and classy at the end. Gently sweet. Fine. **(03/96)**

Now-2000 plus   **17.5**

La Tâche   **Romanée-Conti**

Full mature colour. A bit more age than the Richebourg. Just a hint of oxidation. Very ripe fruit. Slightly astringent on the palate. A pity that this doesn't show as well as it should, because the other Domaine de la Romanée-Conti wines are showing extremely well. A bottle in 03/94 was also not entirely satisfactory: vigorous but only 'very good': 16.0. **(03/96)**

Drink soon   **15.0**

1966

RATING FOR THE VINTAGE

Red: 16.0   **White:** (15.0)
(past their best)

SIZE OF THE CROP
(Hectolitres, excluding generic wine)

	Red	White
Grands Crus	10,682	2,146
Village and Premiers Crus	115,134	27,070
Total	125,816	29,216

Nineteen sixty-six ranks in my view just ahead of 1969 in being after 1964 the best of the decade's red-wine vintages in Burgundy and, judging by a tasting thirty years on, the wines seem to be holding up well. The Domaine de la Romanée-Conti wines, in fact, seem to be even better than they were in the earlier vintage.

WEATHER CONDITIONS

The weather pattern was mixed, with clement conditions in June, leading to a larger than normal harvest, and then rather poorer weather throughout July and most of August. September, however, was splendid, with enough short showers of rain to keep the progress towards maturity on an even keel. The harvest commenced in the last week of the month and took place under sunny blue skies.

The Style of the Wine

There is much that is highly satisfactory about the 1966s. They have balance and elegance; they are clean, pure and intense; most have plenty of character; and the best have no lack of vigour. Best of all they have a poise lacking in the 1969s and sometimes overwhelmed by the richness and substance in the 1964s.

Tasting Notes

Blanc

Bâtard-Montrachet   Edmond Delagrange, Lichine

Quite a deep gold colour. Just about at the end of its life. Not oxidised. Still quite fresh in its acidity but it has lost a bit of its fruit. Yet the finish is very long, complex and classy. Was a splendid bottle once. **(03/96)**

Drink up   16.0

Meursault   Les Chevalières René Monnier, Lichine

Mature golden colour. Opulent rich nose. Barley sugar and butterscotch. This is full and ample and ripe. Still quite fresh. Shows well. **(03/96)**

Drink soon   14.5

Meursault   Goutte d'Or   Comtes Lafon

Fresh colour. Lovely healthy round, ripe nose. Very clean and fresh. Delicate and complex with none of the usual Goutte d'Or four-square character. Gentle, velvety. Very good acidity. Really peachy in flavour. Very subtle. Long. Medium to medium-full body. Very good indeed. **(09/92)**

Now–2000   17.0

Puligny-Montrachet   Combettes Henri Clerc

Youthful colour for a wine of this age. Very fresh nose. Not very expressive at first. It has lost a little fruit but the acidity is fine and the wine still has a lot of fruit. Just a little rigid at the end. Very good. **(10/94)**

Drink soon   16.0

Rouge

Beaune   Bressandes   Duchet

Well-matured colour. Fading but caramelly nose, which became oxidised quickly in the glass. A little astringent as well. But there was class and balance once. Medium body. Now over the hill. **(03/96)**

Past its best   11.0

Beaune   Clos-des-Marconnets   Chanson

Fullish but well-matured colour. Good fullish meaty nose. No undue age. Slight mocha elements. Fullish on the palate. Good grip. Ripe and plump. Balanced and stylish. Nice and positive at the end. Good plus. **(03/96)**

Drink soon   15.5

Beaune   Cuvée Guigone de Salins Hospices de Beaune, Ropiteau

Full but well-matured colour. Rich, mocha/spice nose. Medium body. This is still fresh and balanced, but it has lightened up a bit and lost some of its concentration and grip. Was very good. Now merely pleasant. **(03/96)**

Drink soon   14.5

Bonnes-Mares   Comte Georges de Vogüé

Medium-full colour. A little old-looking compared with his Chambolle-Musigny, Les Amoureuses. Good, fat, firm nose, though. No lack of vigour. Classy fruit. Some alcohol but not as 'hot' as the Amoureuses. Fullish, ample, weighty. Very good grip. Still very fresh. Fine. **(03/96)**

Now–2000 plus   17.5

Chambertin   IEC Wine Society

Bottled in England. Full, rich, mature colour. This is from Remoissenet. This is high class. Fresh, balanced, full, very rich, very old-viney. Full but very concentrated and velvety on the palate. A lovely example. Very splendid. Surprisingly so. And vigorous. Several notes. **(03/96)**

Now–2005   19.0

Chambertin   Cuvée Héritiers-Latour Louis Latour

Fullish colour. Fully mature. Aromatic, cedary, cigar-box spice. On the palate this is full, quite sweet, just a touch oxidised – merely a hint. Slightly rigid. Is this any better than the Charmes? Certainly fine. **(03/96)**

Now–2000   17.5

Chambertin   Jean Trapet et Fils

Full, but well-matured colour. Rich, high
quality, ripe nose but a little diffuse. Not unduly
aged on the palate, but getting towards the end.
Fullish, ripe, a little 'hot'. A plump wine. Just a
little rigid in parts. Very good indeed though.
(03/96)

Now-2000   **17.0**

Chambertin   Clos-de-Bèze   Avery's

French bottled. Good full colour. Soft, plump
nose. Classy on the palate. Balanced, fullish.
Good intensity. Good fruit and acidity. This is
long and fragrant and has good class and vigour.
Will still keep. **(03/96)**

Now-2000 plus   **17.5**

Chambertin   Clos-de-Bèze   Clair-Daü

Good fullish mature colour. Rich toffee mocha
nose. Full-bloodied fruit. Got better and better
in the glass. Fullish, ripe and spicy. Not the
greatest of class perhaps but vigorous and ample.
Plump and rich. Very good indeed. Was even
better 01/94 and 12/93. **(05/96)**

Now-2000   **17.0**

Chambertin   Clos-de-Bèze   Joseph Drouhin

Full colour. Fully mature. Cool, classy, very
concentrated, very laid-back on the nose.
Lovely fruit. Fullish on the palate. Very
harmonious. Not a blockbuster. Subtle and
fragrant. Still vigorous and intense. Delicious.
(03/96)

Now-2000 plus   **18.5**

Chambertin   Clos-de-Bèze   Pierre Gelin

Very full mature colour. A bit inky on the nose.
Sizeable but dense and ungraceful. Sturdy, a
little astringent. This has grip and concentration. Much better with food. A meaty, full
wine. Bramble fruit. A little short and one-
dimensional. It was better ten years ago. **(10/94)**

Drink soon   **13.0**

Chambolle-Musigny
Comte Georges de Vogüé

Full, serious, mature colour. Splendid nose. Full,
rich, concentrated, aromatic, vigorous. Lovely
fruit. Great complexity. Round, mellow, a lot of
depth and dimension. Very good balance. This
has surprising class. Surely declassified *premier cru*
or *grand cru*! Still lots of life. Got better and better
in the glass. Fine. **(07/92)**

Now-2000   **16.5**

Chambolle-Musigny   Les Amoureuses
Comte Georges de Vogüé

Medium-full colour. Mature. Fragrant nose but
a little too much tobacco and a little reduction.
Quite a sizeable, indeed 'hot' wine. But very
good plump fruit and good grip. Vigorous and

very good but it lacks a little grace. **(03/96)**

Now-2000 plus   **16.0**

Chambolle-Musigny   Les Charmes   Grivelet

Good fullish well-matured colour. Soft and ripe
on the nose, but not that much definition and
class. Medium to medium-full body. Quite
sweet. 'Hot' on the follow-through. Undistinguished but still has vigour. **(03/96)**

Now-2000   **13.5**

Charmes-Chambertin   Louis Latour

Full colour. Fine nose. Lovely fruit. Plump and
fresh and ripe. This is one of the best Latour
wines: rich, concentrated, classy and cool. Very
ripe. Very old-viney. Long. Not too 'hot'. Very
good indeed. **(03/96)**

Now-2000 plus   **17.0**

Charmes-Chambertin   Misserey

Good full colour. No undue maturity. Fat, rich,
plummy nose. This has good freshness and
concentration. Medium-full, fresh, blackberry,
black cherry, plump. Really rather good fruit.
Balanced. Stylish. Very more-ish. Almost sweet.
Very good finish. Very good indeed. **(10/94)**

Now-1999 plus   **17.0**

Clos-de-la-Roche   Bertagna

Full but very well-matured colour. This is just
on the turn. A hint of maderisation. Medium-
full, plump, balanced. A little diffuse at the end
- and too maderised on the palate. **(03/96)**

Drink up   **16.0**

Clos-de-Vougeot   Joseph Faiveley

Fullish, mature colour. Profound, rich,
balanced, concentrated nose. Good class here.
Full, fat, voluptuously rich wine with a touch of
spice. Very good grip. Long. Opulent. Fine
plus. **(03/96)**

Now-2000 plus   **18.0**

Clos-de-Vougeot   Méo-Camuzet, Lichine

Fullish colour. Well matured. Rich, full nose.
Lots of depth. No undue age. On the palate a
little astringent and a little decay. The fruit is
beginning to dry up. Slightly past its best. Was at
least very good indeed. Now only good.
(03/96)

Drink up   **15.0**

Clos-de-Vougeot   Christian Noëllat

Fullish colour. Fully mature. Somewhat spurious
but still quite vigorous. An earthy spicy wine.
Not bad. Not unbalanced. **(09/93)**

Drink soon   **13.0**

Corton   Bouchard Père et Fils

Medium-full, mature colour. Refined nose.
Subtle, but perhaps gently fading now. Lovely

old Burgundy on the palate. Cool, fresh, balanced and with good intensity. Medium-full. Very long. Fine and complex. **(03/96)**

Now–2000 plus   17.5

Corton   Leroy

Two bottles, out of the same box. One with a slight ullage, the other fine. Not a lot of difference between the two, though, strangely, the fuller bottle showed the least colour. Rich, ripe, intense nose; the second wine cleaner but blander, the first more evolved but more intense. On the palate less difference. Sweet, ripe and classy. But good rather than great. **(10/94)**

Now–2000 plus   15.0

Corton   Château Corton-Grancey
Louis Latour

Fullish, mature colour. Rich, full, opulent, fat nose. The fruit is quite cooked and there are elements of mocha. Fullish, quite hot and alcoholic. Firm and vigorous though. Plenty of fruit. Better with food. Very good but it lacks a little class and grace. **(03/96)**

Now–2000 plus   16.0

Corton   Clos-du-Roi   Joseph Drouhin

Fullish, mature colour. Ample nose. Quite evolved. Medium-full, ample and plump. Very stylish balanced fruit. This is still long, fine, subtle and multi-dimensional. But is nearing the point at which it will begin to decline fast. Fine. **(03/96)**

Drink soon   17.5

Corton   Cuvée Dr Peste
Hospices de Beaune, Moillard-Grivot

Full, mature colour. Firm, rich, full nose. Opulent and very spicy. Fullish, quite a lot of alcohol. A meaty, even robust wine, but with good grip underneath. Lacks a bit of elegance but very good plus. Still very vigorous. **(03/96)**

Now–2000 plus   16.5

Echézeaux   Romanée-Conti

Said to be a bit over-evolved (drunk at the DRC) and not as it should be. Quite evolved, a touch attenuated, especially as it developed. Ripe but lacks a little class. Medium-full. Sweet. Certainly not at all bad. But not special. **(11/93)**

Drink up   15.0

Gevrey-Chambertin   Les Combottes
Roland Remoissenet Père et Fils

Very good colour. Fresh nose. Not quite as good as 1964 or 1969. A little more linear and less generous. But still life and fruit. **(07/92)**

Drink soon   15.0

Gevrey-Chambertin   Lavaux-Saint-Jacques
Roland Remoissenet Père et Fils

Fine colour. Rich and plummy on both nose and palate. Really very very young. Opulent but very well balanced. Full, mature. Round and rich, yet in the background a certain austerity. Smooth and cedary. Yet still vigorous on the finish. Very good; indeed, lovely. **(09/91)**

Now–2000   17.0

Grands-Echézeaux   Joseph Drouhin

Medium-full, well-matured colour. Touch of oak, lovely fruit. Very classy ripe nose. Not aggressive. Medium-full. Very lovely composed, fragrant wine. Lovely fruit. Long, complex. Very fine. Still holding up well, it seems. **(03/96)**

Now–2000   18.0

Grands-Echézeaux   Romanée-Conti

Slightly ageing colour. A strange spicy flavour. Quite high acidity. A little stewed. A little sturdy. A little lumpy in fact. Lacks grace. I can't say this enthrals me. **(03/92)**

Drink soon   14.0

Latricières-Chambertin   Joseph Faiveley

Good fresh colour. Slightly lean but elegant on the nose. A little one-dimensional in the sense that it lacks richness and concentration, but very classy. Complex. Medium body. Long. Very good but not great. I prefer this to the 1964. Got fatter as it developed. **(12/91)**

Now–1999   16.0

Mazis-Chambertin
Roland Remoissenet Père et Fils

Full, vigorous colour. Concentrated, chocolatey nose, but rather muddy, evolved and individual. Slightly lactic. Full and very rich. Old-viney. Some residual oak. Some tannin too. Long on the palate and still agreeable. But not what it should be. **(03/96)**

Drink up   14.0

Morey-Saint-Denis   Chanson

Fullish, well-matured colour. Some sweetness on the nose. A touch of butterscotch. On the palate medium body. Lacks a bit of concentration and class but fruity and pleasant. Slightly diffuse at the end. **(03/96)**

Drink soon   14.0

Morey-Saint-Denis   Les Chézeaux
Louis Remy

Old colour. Past it by some way. **(03/96)**

Past its best   **(see note)**

Le Musigny   Joseph Drouhin

Good full colour, no undue signs of maturity. Soft, fragrant nose, with a little gingerbread and a touch of sweetness. Complex, classy. Multi-dimensional and still vigorous. On the palate the acidity shows a little more than in the Faiveley example, but the wine is nevertheless ripe, fat and concentrated. And delicious. This has class. Medium to medium-full. It showed no signs of fading. If anything, it got a little four-square as it evolved. And began to lose a little of its elegance as it developed. Nevertheless still long and lovely after half an hour. Fine plus. **(11/93)**

Drink soon   **18.0**

Le Musigny   Joseph Faiveley

Fine colour. No undue signs of maturity. Very delicious fragrant nose. Mature, elegant, silky, complex and fresh. This is like the entrance to a very sophisticated harem: there is something sweet, exotic and magical, very faintly animal. A lot of depth and intensity and plenty of vigour. On the palate round and mellow and soft, sweet, yet with plenty of vigour. Multi-dimensional. Beautifully balanced, with all the delicacy Musigny should have. Very lovely long, complex, lingering finish. A very silky wine. *Grand vin.* Equally good 03/94. **(11/93)**

Now-2000   **20.0**

Le Musigny   *Vieilles-Vignes*
Comte Georges de Vogüé

Full mature colour. Fragrant, quite delicate, very classy. Very *typé*. But quite some alcohol, a little more apparent than the Bonnes-Mares. I have had better bottles. This is a little old, drying up now. Losing fat. The acidity dominates on the finish. This bottle merely good. 'Excellent' in 10/94: 19.0. **(03/96)**

Now-2000   **15.0**

Nuits-Saint-Georges   Clos-de-la-Maréchale
Joseph Faiveley

Very full mature colour. Full, rich, vigorous nose. This is substantial and ripe, but not too burly. Full bodied, rich and chocolatey. The residues of quite a lot of tannin. Now mellow but virile and structured. Very good indeed. **(03/96)**

Now-2000   **17.0**

Nuits-Saint-Georges   Les Saint-Georges
Lionel J. Bruck

Full, mature colour. Rich, meaty nose, with a whiff of oxidation. On the palate the wine is not unduly aged. It is plump and ripe and enjoyable. But it lacks a little class. Good plus though. **(03/96)**

Now-2000   **15.5**

Nuits-Saint-Georges   Les Saint-Georges
Joseph Faiveley

Good vigorous colour. This has a lot of depth and class on the nose. A wine of richness and

natural sweetness. Full, not unduly sturdy. Ripe and balanced. Unusually stylish for a Nuits. Long and warm and vigorous and satisfying. Bags of life still. Fine. Several notes. **(07/95)**

Now-2000 plus   **17.5**

Pommard   Les Argillières   Lejeune

Fullish, mature colour. Rather too much volatile acidity on the nose for comfort. On the palate medium to medium-full body. Some fruit. But the volatile acidity spoils it. Otherwise certainly quite good. Not too robust, and with good fruit. **(03/96)**

Drink up   **14.0**

Pommard   Epenots   Louis Latour

Fullish, mature colour. Fullish, caramelly-rich, fat nose. Good full vigorous wine. Fat and rich and very Pommard in size and structure. Good depth. Good class. Good vigour. Very good. **(03/96)**

Now-2000   **16.0**

Pommard   Grands-Epenots
Michel Gaunoux

Fullish, well-matured colour. Fat and rich and spicy - slightly robust - on the nose. This is rich and fat and structured. It shows a faint touch of astringency, which would be less noticeable with food. Fullish, balanced, just a little lumpy, but good. Will still keep. Marked 'very good' 09/94. **(07/94)**

Now-1999   **16.0**

Richebourg   Bouchard Père et Fils

Full mature colour. Rich, fat, voluptuously fruity nose. Old-viney. A touch of oxidation. On the palate a touch of astringency, a little age. But nevertheless a wine of high quality, good intensity, and fine balance. Now soft. Fine plus. **(03/96)**

Drink soon   **18.0**

Richebourg   Joseph Drouhin

Fullish well-matured colour. Fat, velvety, fragrant nose. Just a touch sweaty. Fullish, balanced, fragrant. Cleaner than the nose (the sweaty nose disappeared too after a while). Laid-back, delicate but intense. Lovely. Very very long and complex. **(03/96)**

Now-2000 plus   **19.0**

Richebourg   Jean Gros, Lichine

Medium-full, well-matured colour. Full, rich nose. Fat and old-viney. This has real depth and quality. Fullish on the palate. Fatter and more velvety than the Marey-Monge Romanée-Saint-Vivant. Very good intensity, very lovely concentrated fruit. Long. Vigorous. Really profound and multi-dimensional. Excellent. **(03/96)**

Now-2005   **19.0**

Richebourg   Romanée-Conti

Fullish, mature colour. Youthful, rich, concentrated nose. Rather more vigorous than the Romanée-Saint-Vivant. Fullish, very good acidity. This, incredibly, still has a youthful rigidity. It improved on aeration. Very, very concentrated. Very good grip. Bigger and burlier than Gros or Drouhin. Fuller than Romanée-Saint-Vivant (Marey-Monge). Excellent. **(03/96)**

Now-2005   **19.5**

Romanée-Conti   Romanée-Conti

Very full mature colour. Brilliant as the Tâche is, this is yet better. Vigorous and very pure. The ripest and most complex expression of classy fruit that you could imagine. Fabulous. This is not as obvious a wine as the Domaine de la Romanée-Conti Richebourg but something of real depth and profundity and subtlety. Fabulous fruit. Perfect harmony. Brilliant. Will keep for ages. Similar note 03/94. **(03/96)**

Now-2005 plus   **20.0**

Romanée-Saint-Vivant   Marey-Monge
Romanée-Conti

Fullish, well-matured colour. Fine, rich, vigorous nose. The usual Domaine de la Romanée-Conti leanness. But the usual DRC class. Fullish on the palate. Very fresh. Very ripe, very classy. Lovely fragrant pure Pinot. Very fine. Bags of life. **(03/96)**

Now-2005   **18.5**

La Tâche   Romanée-Conti

Full mature colour. Brilliant nose. This is very aristocratic and very fresh. Marvellous fruit. But then it collapsed in the glass. Musty. The level was quite low and the cork very moist. A bad bottle? **(03/96)**

Now-2000   **(see note)**

Volnay   Caillerets
Roland Remoissenet Père et Fils

Full vigorous colour. Round, fat, vigorous, stylish. Fullish, youthful. Good fruit, nicely fresh. Long and complex. Lovely raspberry flavour. Good pure Pinot. Fine. **(07/95)**

Now-2000 plus   **17.5**

Volnay   Champans   Comtes Lafon

Beginning to decay slightly. And also to thin out. But ripe and balanced. Yet a slight absence of fat. **(03/92)**

Drink up   **14.0**

Volnay   Clos-des-Chênes   Joseph Drouhin

Well-matured colour. Still some intensity on the nose, but a little reduction. Medium body. Classy, still has vigour. This is balanced, intense and very Volnay in character. Clean, ripe fruit. Long and complex. Very good. **(03/96)**

Drink soon   **16.0**

Volnay   Clos-du-Verseuil   Jean Clerget

Well-matured colour. Almost a deepish amontillado. Fading gently but there was class here once on the nose. And it is not astringent. On the palate medium body. Still sweet. This is very pleasant but the acidity is beginning to dominate - or will soon. **(03/96)**

Drink soon   **14.5**

Volnay   Cuvée Général Muteau
Hospices de Beaune, *éleveur* unknown

Good mature colour. Soft, ripe, delicately sweet nose. Fragrant and stylish. Fullish, ample, round, plump, ripe and fruity. Just a touch of oak. At the end there is a little touch of bitterness. But essentially this is still an elegant, fragrant, very Volnay example of Pinot Noir. Very good. **(01/95)**

Drink soon   **16.0**

1964

RATING FOR THE VINTAGE

Red: 17.5   **White:** (16.0)
(past their best)

SIZE OF THE CROP

(Hectolitres, excluding generic wine)

	Red	White
Grands Crus	12,168	2,047
Village and *Premiers Crus*	117,095	24,900
Total	129,263	26,947

I did not buy the 1964 vintage – I was a student travelling the vineyards of France at the time – but I am sure I would have enjoyed doing so. My first encounter with them was when they were first offered *en primeur* in late 1966 or early 1967, after they had been bottled and shipped. From the start I loved the vintage. To this day I rate it with 1949 and 1952 as the best of what I call 'old-fashioned' Burgundy.

I mean old-fashioned in the best sense: low yields, concentrated wines, genuine Pinot, and Pinot *fin*. I do not mean Rhône or Algeria-bolstered soupy stuff, *ersatz* Châteauneuf-du-Pape with a little Beaune or Nuits-Saint-Georges added: what used to be enjoyed in Britain and other northern European countries, but which had no more relation to good De Vogüé or Rousseau than a MacDonald's has to a fillet of beef.

For Burgundy was old-fashioned then. Tractors had hardly begun to appear in the vineyards. Horses and oxen were still more commonplace. There was electric light in the cellar but otherwise little had changed for 100, even 200 years. Fermentation took place in wood, not stainless-steel; ice or cold water were the only methods of controlling the temperature; and the *pigeage* was performed by the proprietor and his children, naked in the vats. Ladies were not admitted. Empiricism was the order of the day. The new wine would begin to ferment again in the spring. We thought this was in sympathy with the evolution of the vines for next year's crop. No-one had heard about malo-lactic.

WEATHER CONDITIONS

Nineteen sixty-four was the best vintage of the decade, and an almost perfect summer. The spring was cool, but the flowering swift and untroubled. June was warm, July very hot, and there was just enough rain in August to keep the evolution of the vines on an even keel. There were some showers in September, which enabled the tannins to ripen properly, and a large-sized vintage of small berries with thick skins – a splendid ratio of solid to liquid – was gathered from 18 September onwards in fine weather. When it did begin to rain, as it did in Bordeaux from 8 October onwards, the Burgundy harvest was safely evolving into wine in the growers' cellars.

THE STYLE OF THE WINE

'Rich, ample and concentrated' said a review at the time. Aromatic, nicely (but not excessively) alcoholic, with a good touch of spice, I would add. And the wines had good acidity. The quality of the red wines was even throughout the Côte, from Santenay to Gevrey-Chambertin. Some of the whites were a little heavy. They are and were at their best on the hill of Corton.

The red wines showed every promise of a long and successful life, and this is how they have turned out. Today the 1964s remain a splendid and consistent vintage, and many still have a future, even at more than thirty years of age. For those who like sensual wine (and who does not, of those who love ripe Burgundy?), this is a marvellous vintage. I still buy it where I can, and I am rarely disappointed.

TASTING NOTES

BLANC

Bâtard-Montrachet   Camille Giroud
Lime-gold colour. Slightly restrained nose at first, camomile and daffodils rather than nuts. As it developed in the glass became absolutely delicious. Fullish, fat, concentrated, nutty and oaky. Still very fresh. Velvety, rich, subtle, long. A fine wine. Amazingly fresh. (09/91)
Drink soon   17.5

Chevalier-Montrachet   Jean Chartron
Quite an old colour. Somewhat old, even slightly sherry-like on the nose. Ripe, sweetish, a little over-the-top on the palate. Rather too old but concentrated and with good acidity and elegance. A curiosity but not at all disagreeable. Class here. (03/95)
Drink up   14.0

Le Montrachet   Comtes Lafon
Good fresh colour. Quite old-fashioned. Vigorous and chunky. Splendidly rich. Quite alcoholic. Still quite a lot of oak. Full, masculine, splendid vigour. Splendid quality. Excellent. Better and better in the glass. Bags of life. (07/94)
Now-2000 plus   19.0

Le Montrachet   Jean Milon-Mathey
Quite an old colour. Old and faded and fino-sherry-like on the palate. This is well past its best. Difficult to tell whatever it was like in the first place. (03/95)
Past its best   10.0

ROUGE

Beaune   Clos-des-Mouches   Joseph

Drouhin
Finished. Volatile acidity. But something here. Fat and meaty. Rich and sweet. Could have been still very vigorous. (10/94)
Now-2000   15.0

Beaune   Cuvée Nicolas Rolin
Hospices de Beaune, Boutet-Coudroy
Good colour: full and fresh and no undue sign of age. Quite sweet and spicy on the nose. A little souped-up at first but better mannered later. The fruit is getting a little strained now. There is bitterness on the finish. But the wine is still essentially sweet and enjoyable. Good but lacks the real style for great. (03/93)
Drink soon   15.0

Beaune   Teurons   Bouchard Père et Fils
Good mature colour. Good concentration on the nose. Curate's eggy. Just a touch over-ripe. Voluptuous and sensual. Well matured now. Concentrated, caramelly, quite full. There is a satisfactory velvety, old-viney essence of wine aspect here. Yet slightly sweet. Just a little cooked and soupy. Reasonable length only and reasonable elegance only. But good. (01/95)
Drink soon   15.0

Beaune   Vigne-de-l'Enfant-Jésus
Bouchard Père et Fils
Magnum. Fine colour. Still very youthful. Very lovely nose. Rich and ample and slightly spicy. A touch of mocha. Very good grip and vigour still. Fullish, smooth, fresh with strawberries and fruit. A gentle, balanced, very composed wine. Lots of vigour. (02/95)
Now-2000   16.0

Bonnes-Mares   Chanson
Very good mature colour. A little evolved. A touch of oxidation and maderisation. But ripe and stylish and meaty underneath. On the palate quite full and solid. But now rather astringent and light. The finesse has gone. Yet certainly very good in its time. Good grip. (03/95)
Past its best   16.0

Bonnes-Mares   Joseph Faiveley

Good mature colour. Firm, vigorous nose. Lots of depth here. Vigorous fruit. Fine. Excellent for a Bonnes-Mares. Stylish youthful. Good quite structured tannic wine. Meaty. Very 1964. Good grip. A fine long follow-through. This is very stylish. Very fine positive long finish. **(03/95)**

Now–2000   18.0

Bonnes-Mares   Jean Hudelot

Good mature colour. Good soft fragrant nose here. Fresh but a little four-square. Quite tannic and possibly a bit over-macerated. It finishes a little astringent, a little inflexible. Good plus but not great. **(03/95)**

Now–2000   15.5

Bonnes-Mares   Georges Roumier

Good mature colour. Firm, vigorous, rich, very good grip on the nose. Fine quality. Plenty of wine here. Plenty of depth. Full, masculine, austere. Classic. Very good Pinot fruit. A very fine classic example. Very vigorous at the end. Still very fresh. Splendidly complex finish. Very very long. Bags of life. Very fine plus. **(03/95)**

Now–2005   18.5

Bonnes-Mares   Comte Georges de Vogüé

Good mature colour. Round, very ripe, sensual nose. But it is beginning to lose its grip. Lovely smoky flavours. Very elegant. Very complex. Not as firm as Roumier. But lovely. Fragrant on the palate. Not quite the class it must have had five to ten years ago but fine nonetheless. Still long and positive. **(03/95)**

Now–2000   17.5

Chambertin   Pierre Bourée

Fullish mature colour. Old dead bonfires on the nose. Slight reduction. A bit sweet-sour. Lumpy. Fullish. Unstylish. Rather too sweet. Fair at best. **(03/95)**

Drink soon   13.0

Chambertin   Cuvée Héritiers-Latour
Louis Latour

Fullish, but fully mature colour. Coffee-toffee nose. Soft now. Quite sweet. Ripe but showing age. Rather spicy and concocted. Sweet finish. Fullish. Mellow. Unpleasant. **(03/95)**

Drink soon   12.5

Chambertin   Jacques Prieur

Full, vigorous colour. Dense, astringent nose. Rather unpleasant. Sweet on the palate. Full, rather unbalanced. Getting astringent at the end. Fullish. Unexciting. **(03/95)**

Drink soon   13.0

Chambertin   Ropiteau Frères

Fullish, but fully mature colour. Full, quite sturdy, even a little brutal, but now oxidised on the nose. Slightly over-ripe. Fullish. Mellow. Oxidised. A little astringent at the end. Pruney. Apart from the oxidation, not bad. **(03/95)**

Drink up   13.5

Chambertin   Armand Rousseau

Fullish mature colour. Rich, concentrated, mellow, ripe, elegant nose. This is fullish, oaky, balanced, rich and profound. It is not great, but it is at least commendable (the rest of the Chambertins in this line-up weren't). Quite gamey. Good grip. Still fresh. Yet it lacks real class and concentration. **(03/95)**

Now–2000   16.5

Chambolle-Musigny   Les Amoureuses
Veuve Jean Bertheau

Very good mature colour. Attractive, stylish, lovely Pinot fruit here on the nose. This is a fine example. Intense and with very good grip. Good vigour. Balanced. Very good acidity. Long and complex. Most seductive. Sweet finish. Fine. **(03/95)**

Now–2000   17.5

Chambolle-Musigny   Charmes
Roland Remoissenet Père et Fils

Fine vigorous full colour. Rich, fresh fullish nose. Plenty of depth and class here. Yet inherently soft. Intense, plump, medium-full. Lovely silky sweet, violet, raspberry fruit. Bags of life. Very good indeed. **(10/94)**

Now–2000 plus   17.0

Chambolle-Musigny   Fremières
Louis Remy

Medium mature colour. Indeed well-matured nose. Not old on the nose. Earthy, a little shitty (in the best sense), nutty, but full of interest. Fragrant Chambolle flavours. Round, ripe, very 1964. Very rich and succulent. Very good indeed. **(10/94)**

Drink soon   17.0

Chambolle-Musigny   *Premier Cru*
Henri de Villamont

Good mature colour. Rhônish sort of nose. Ripe, alcoholic, sweet. A touch of oxidation. Fullish on the palate. A bit rigid and hot, a bit sweet-sour. Rather spurious. Certainly un-stylish. **(03/95)**

Drink soon   13.0

Charmes-Chambertin Patriarche

Fullish, fully mature colour. Stemmy nose. A little dried out and clumsy. Getting loose now as well. The fruit has collapsed and the acidity shows. Quite substantial. Rather astringent at the end. Unattractive. **(03/95)**

Drink up   **12.5**

Clos-de-la-Roche Joseph Drouhin

Good fullish, mature colour. Fragrant nose. Very stylish. Just a touch faded. Still fresh on the palate, though perhaps it has lightened up. Ripe, pure, intense Pinot nevertheless. Complex. Long. Fine. Held up well in the glass. **(03/95)**

Drink soon   **17.5**

Clos-de-la-Roche Leroy

Medium to medium-full colour. Mature. Lightish nose for a 1964. This is a bit of a disappointment. Round and ripe on the palate, but a bit one-dimensional and anaemic. Acidity beginning to show. Getting a little old. Some elegance, but a lack of richness and structure. Uninspiring. Especially for Leroy. **(10/94)**

Drink up   **14.0**

Clos-de-Tart Mommessin

Medium-full, mature colour. Vigorous, meaty, spicy nose. A touch of stems. Fullish, mellow, good vigour on the palate. Quite rich. Nicely ripe and aromatic. Plenty of life ahead of it. Good substance. This is much more enjoyable than the Clos-de-Tarts of today. Very good indeed. Several notes. **(03/95)**

Now-2000   **17.0**

Clos-de-Vougeot Chanson

Medium-full mature colour. Ripe, fragrant, elegant fruit on the nose. Soft on the palate. But still fresh. Nicely aromatic. A little astringent at the end and a little coarseness too. But certainly very good. And still long and positive. **(03/95)**

Now-1999   **16.0**

Clos-de-Vougeot René Engel

Full mature colour. Good, vigorous, quite sturdy, ripe nose. Sweet and spicy. This is ripe and opulent. Nicely concentrated and old-viney. Not a bit dry. Mellow, classy, long. Very plump and round. Long positive finish. Very good indeed. **(03/95)**

Now-2000   **17.0**

Clos-de-Vougeot Joseph Faiveley

Good mature colour. Full, rich, classy nose. Lovely Pinot fruit here. Fullish, fragrant, complex; now gentle but harmonious and profound. Delicious ripe fruit on the palate. Very long. Very classy. Very fine. Somewhat less good: 'could be a bit more concentrated'; 16.0 in 10/94. **(03/95)**

Now-2000 plus   **18.0**

Clos-de-Vougeot Jean Faurois

Lichine label. Fullish colour. Fully mature though. Good full, old-viney concentration here on the nose. Quite full and sturdy. Rich, some tannin. Quite spicy. Good grip though. Good old Pinot flavours. Long and fragrant. Very good plus. **(03/95)**

Now-2000   **16.5**

Clos-de-Vougeot Jean Grivot

Half bottle. Fine fullish mature colour. Lovely nose. Real breed here. Vigorous but mature, and multi-dimensional. This is very fine indeed. Full, ample, rich and very well balanced. Marvellous intensity on the follow-through. Vigorous too. Very fine indeed. And very real mature Pinot fragrance without being too animal. I had two of these half bottles: the other was equally delicious in 10/93. **(07/94)**

Now-2000   **18.0**

Clos-de-Vougeot Jean Gros

Good full colour. No undue age. Fullish, mellow, aromatic, quite intense on the nose. Nicely spicy. This is rich, full and complex. Getting towards the end of its life but fat, meaty and satisfying. Better on the nose - which is brilliant - than on the palate. But good grip. No hurry to drink. Good concentration and very fine indeed. **(10/95)**

Now-2000   **18.5**

Clos-de-Vougeot Jacques Prieur

Good fullish vigorous colour. Rich, sweet and oaky/caramelly. Slightly sweet-sour. Fullish. A little ungainly. A little tight. Ripe though. Balanced. Positive finish. Quite good plus. No hurry to drink up. **(03/95)**

Drink soon   **14.5**

Clos-de-Vougeot Roland Remoissenet Père et Fils

Very good colour. A little shittiness on the nose at first. Slightly four-square after a bit. On the palate full and rich but a little solid. Needed time to come out. Then if a little chunky certainly rich, balanced and very good - but not great. **(03/94)**

Now-1999   **15.0**

Clos-de-Vougeot Veuve Clément Tachot

Medium colour. Well matured. Fragrant nose, gently fading but stylish nevertheless. A little astringency here on the palate, and it has lost a little of its finesse. Good grip though. A medium-full, balanced wine which is still positive. Was originally at least very good. **(03/95)**

Drink soon   **15.0**

Corton   IEC Wine Society

Bottled in England. Very good colour. Rich, plummy nose, an abundant wine, fat and slightly gamey, but certainly voluptuous. This is oaky, full bodied and very concentrated on the palate. A very lovely wine. Real *grand cru* quality at a very high level. Good mellow tannins and backbone. Still bags of life. Very long. Multi-dimensional. Fine plus. **(10/95)**

Now-2000 plus   **18.0**

Corton   Bressandes   Prince de Mérode

Light to medium colour. Fully mature. Rather light and loose-knit on the nose. A bit faded. Better on the palate. Medium body. Balanced. Classy. Needs drinking. But good length and good harmony and elegance. Very good. **(03/95)**

Drink soon   **16.0**

Corton   Château Corton-Grancey
Louis Latour

Medium-full colour. Still quite youthful. This is quite different from the 1971. Fresh, full, plummy. Good ripeness and concentrated. On the palate full and vigorous. Long and nicely cool. For once not too alcoholic. Fine. Several notes: better than the wine is today. **(03/95)**

Now-2000   **17.5**

Corton   Clos-des-Cortons   Joseph Faiveley

Very good colour. Still vigorous. Lovely rich fat concentrated nose. No undue age. Full, very lovely fruit. Still youthful. Lovely ripe classy fruit. Harmonious. Long, complex, impressive. Excellent. **(03/95)**

Now-2000 plus   **18.5**

Corton   Cuvée Charlotte Dumay
Hospices de Beaune, Caves de Bousserolles

Good medium-full colour. No undue age. Elegant but slightly cool, austere nose. Lovely fruit on the palate. Fullish, ripe, vigorous and velvety. This is a lovely bottle. Beautifully poised. Fine plus. **(03/95)**

Now-2000   **18.0**

Echézeaux   Leroy

Good fullish mature colour. Lovely nose. Rich and full and concentrated. Splendid cassis fruit. Very distinguished. Real *grand cru* quality on the palate. Full, very youthful still. Fresh. Very good acidity. Lovely. Nicely austere. Tastes like a wine half its age. **(03/95)**

Now-2005 plus   **18.0**

Gevrey-Chambertin   Les Combottes
Roland Remoissenet Père et Fils

Fine colour. Lovely concentrated nose. Better than the 1966 or 1969. Fullish. Complex, concentrated fruit. Breed here and a lot of depth. Very good balance. Lovely finish. Excellent. **(07/92)**

Now-2000   **17.5**

Grands-Echézeaux   Mongeard-Mugneret

Good fullish mature colour. Good rich classy vigorous nose. Mellow and spicy. This has lightened up a little. There is a round vegetal/animal softness on the palate. Still has good length and style. But it needs drinking soon. Good. **(03/95)**

Drink soon   **14.5**

Latricières-Chambertin   Joseph Faiveley

Very good. Vigorous colour. Fat, rich, full and classy on the nose. Good vigour. On the palate this is fullish, cool, fresh. Not a bit too sweet. Quite sturdy. Ripe, very fresh and youthful. Very good indeed. **(03/95)**

Now-2000 plus   **17.0**

Mazis-Chambertin   Pierre Gelin

Medium, fully mature colour. Rich and sturdy on the nose. Not a lot of finesse though. Good oak. Sweet. Fullish. A bit earthy. Getting a bit coarse at the end. **(03/95)**

Drink soon   **13.5**

Musigny   Joseph Faiveley

Very good colour. Lovely vigorous, rich, classy, mellow nose. Very fine indeed. Fullish, very harmonious, very mellow, very complete. Fresh, very classy fruit. This is excellently pure and intense. Profound and very elegant. Super. **(03/95)**

Now-2000 plus   **19.5**

Musigny   Jean Hudelot

Fine full vigorous colour. Lovely nose. Very classy and complex. Aristocratic fruit, ripe, velvety and very intense. On the palate a rich, fullish wine of great depth and finesse and real dimension and intensity. Naturally sweet finish. A great wine. Multi-faceted, especially super at the end. Beautiful. **(10/94)**

Now-2000   **19.5**

Musigny   Jacques Prieur

Good vigorous colour. A bit sweet and a bit tight on the nose. This is rather a rigid wine. Fullish. But not very classy. Not very Musigny at all. Rather tough. Rather sweet-sour. Disappointing. **(03/95)**

Drink up   **14.0**

Musigny   Georges Roumier

Medium-full mature colour. There is a little age here. And a little rigidity on the nose. Touch of oxidation as it developed. Fullish. Evolved fast. A pity. Because good class and lovely fruit here. A bottle in 03/95 was well past its best. **(10/94)**

Drink up   **18.0**

Musigny *Vieilles-Vignes*
Comte Georges de Vogüé

Good vigorous colour. Quite sweet on the nose. Classy, but it is beginning to lose a bit of its vigour. On the nose lightish, fragrant, curiously un-Pinot, yet not inelegant. But now a little bit past its best. **(03/95)**

Past its best   **16.0**

Nuits-Saint-Georges Leroy

Medium to medium-full colour. Not too old but a little cloudy. Rather light and diffuse on the palate. Yet not old and astringent. Curious. A bad bottle. **(03/94)**

(see note)

Nuits-Saint-Georges Les Saint-Georges
Henri Gouges

Very good colour. Round, rich, good acidity. Very fragrant on the nose. On the palate plump and ripe, and generous. Quite virile. Good grip. Sweet and vigorous on the finish. Very classy. Very fine. **(01/94)**

Now-2000   **18.0**

Pommard Epenots Parent

Good mature colour. Fine roasted gamey nose. This is rich and sweet on the palate if without being very fat and generous. An oddball. Still vigorous. Good. **(11/95)**

Now-2000   **15.0**

Richebourg Avery's

From Remoissenet, bottled in France. Very fine full vigorous colour. This is very similar on the nose to the Remoissenet example, not surprisingly. Big, rich, chocolatey, ample and lush. On the palate rich, nutty. Very good grip. Very good vigour. **(03/95)**

Now-2000 plus   **18.5**

Richebourg Gros Frère et Soeur

Good vigorous colour. A very, very sensual nose here. This is less vigorous than the Avery's or the Remoissenet bottle. Very good, indeed fine originally, but faded in the glass. Real class still on the finish. Still very long. Still a lot of enjoyment. **(03/95)**

Drink up   **17.0**

Richebourg
Roland Remoissenet Père et Fils

Very fine full vigorous colour. Very like the Avery's bottle. Full, velvety, opulent, classy. Not quite as spicy and as animal on the palate. It seems to have more class. But essentially the same wine. This is the fresher but less sensual of the two. Plenty of life. Very lovely. **(03/95)**

Now-2000 plus   **19.0**

Richebourg Romanée-Conti

Good vigorous colour. Intense, poised, flavourful. This is very delicious and still remarkably youthful. Rich but sturdy on the nose. Very complex. Very classy. Not exactly lush or fat though. Full, mellow, remarkably fresh. But it lacks a bit of real grip and intensity. Fine plus but not great. **(03/95)**

Now-2005 plus   **18.0**

Romanée-Conti Romanée-Conti

A firmer nose than the Tâche. Not as rich. This is very individual, beautifully intense, poised and concentrated. Full and vigorous but with excellently ripe tannins. Pure Pinot. Multi-dimensional. Marvellously balanced. Real thrust, and persistence at the end. Very brilliant. But the Tâche is even better. **(03/95)**

Now-2000 plus   **19.5**

Romanée-Saint-Vivant Pierre Bourée

Full colour. No undue age. Rich and sturdy, somewhat bolstered up. It is also corked. Fullish, rather soupy, but now a bit sour at the finish. Never very genuine, never very stylish. **(03/95)**

Now-2000   **13.5**

Romanée-Saint-Vivant Joseph Drouhin

The colour has, I feel, begun to lighten up a bit now. And on the nose there is a little fade. On the palate it is soft and fragrant, gentle and stylish. But it is now past its best. Was fine once though. **(03/95)**

Past its best   **(17.5)**

Romanée-Saint-Vivant Charles Noëllat

Old fully mature but not aged colour. Fragrant, soft, delicate nose. No undue age. No fade or decay. Sweet, classy, really quite vigorous fruit. Medium-full. Good intensity. Good grip. This is very long and lovely, very elegant and complex at the end. But drink soon. **(03/94)**

Drink soon   **18.0**

Romanée-Saint-Vivant
Roland Remoissenet Père et Fils

Youthful full colour. Rather four-square, fullish, high acidity, structured. What it lacks is real breed, succulence, mellowness. Not *grand cru* really. And a bit of a disappointment. Has aspects of a 1964 Médoc. *Bloqué.* Certainly very good indeed. But not fine. **(02/94)**

Now-2000 plus   **17.0**

Romanée-Saint-Vivant Marey-Monge
Romanée-Conti

Very good vigorous fresh colour. Full, sturdy, rich, plenty of depth. Plenty of vigour. Quite a substantial wine, and, while rich and opulent, it is the structure that hits you at first. Slightly tough. Plenty of wine here but a slight lack of real concentration and generosity. Very good indeed but not great. Plenty of vigour. **(03/95)**

Now–2005 plus   17.0

Santenay Graviéres Joseph Drouhin

Good colour. A little old and slightly maderised on the nose. But ripe, sweet and vigorous on the nose. Rich and meaty. Still quite vigorous. Residual elegance. But beginning to lose its fruit and get slightly astringent. **(10/95)**

Drink up   16.5

La Tâche Romanée-Conti

Fine vigorous colour. Marvellous nose. Yards ahead of the Richebourg. Very fat, very rich, very concentrated, very complete. This is a great wine. Marvellous fruit. Superb vigour and intensity. Full. Very, very concentrated. Totally brilliant in all respects. Essence of Pinot. Incredibly youthful. Very very long indeed. *Grand vin!* **(03/95)**

Now–2005 plus   20.0

Volnay Caillerets, Ancienne Cuvée Carnot Bouchard Père et Fils

Round, gamey, exotic, rich, still vigorous. Ripe. Sweet. Medium-full, ample, a touch of the usual Burgundian undergrowth and barnyard, so not that elegant. Very pleasant though. Still plenty of life. Good grip. Long and fat. Very good indeed. **(11/91)**

Now–2000   17.0

Volnay Taille-Pieds Roger Clerget

Roger Clerget in Pommard. Quite an old colour. Fragrant, complex old Pinot on the nose. A delicate wine. Naturally sweet. Getting a little diffuse but still has intensity and plenty of length. Fine. **(07/95)**

Drink soon   17.0

Vosne-Romanée Beaumonts Jean Grivot

Very good, virile colour. Fine rich, fat, 'complete' nose. This is delicious, complex, round and has a lot more style than the 1969.

Fresh on the palate. Full, rich, nicely succulent, sweet and spicy. Very good grip. This is a lovely fine elegant example. Long, harmonious. Will still last well. Fine. **(03/96)**

Now–2000 plus   17.5

Vosne-Romanée Clos-des-Réas Jean Gros

Fine full colour. No undue maturity. A little hard on the nose. Ample and rich on the palate, but not an enormous amount of depth. Young vines? Very fresh. But not the amplitude and intensity, or fat of a real 1964. Very good but not the dimension of great. **(10/94)**

Drink soon   16.0

Vosne-Romanée Malconsorts Avery's

Shipped from Remoissenet. Good vigorous colour. Rich and sweet on the nose. Roasted nut flavour. On the palate fullish, ample, vigorous, balanced. A meaty example with plenty of life ahead of it. Plenty of class too. Very long on the finish. Fine quality. **(10/94)**

Now–2000   17.5

Vosne-Romanée Malconsorts Roland Remoissenet Père et Fils

Very good colour. As so often with Remoissenet wines, this is seemingly ageless. Not a bit of fade here. Ample, vigorous, balanced stylish nose. Medium-full body. Lovely mature Pinot. Good grip. Earthy in the best sense. Good intensity. Rich and ripe. Very good indeed. Similar 03/95. **(11/94)**

Now–2000   17.0

Vosne-Romanée Suchots Camille Giroud

Good fullish mature colour. Full, sturdy, rich nose. Nicely spicy. Plenty of vigour. Fat, rich and still quite firm on the palate. Good grip. Youthful. Slightly earthy, slightly volatile, but that is no bad thing. Good length. Good. **(03/95)**

Now–2000   15.0

1962

Red: 15.5   **White:** (17.0)
(past their best)

SIZE OF THE CROP

(Hectolitres, excluding generic wine)

	Red	White
Grands Crus	9,870	1,592
Village and Premiers Crus	100,089	20,197
Total	109,959	21,789

WEATHER CONDITIONS

Nineteen sixty-two, by contrast with 1964, was a late developer right from the beginning. The bud-break was late, April and May were cold and sunless, though dry, and as a result the flowering - though it was successful - was late, not until the second half of June. From then on the weather improved, progressively warming up through July until August, which was hot and sunny, with some welcome rain at the end of the month. September was good, if not brilliant, but the harvest did not begin until 8 October. Again it was a large crop. And the quality was very good.

THE STYLE OF THE WINE

Right from the very beginning the 1962 Burgundy vintage - rather like the 1972s in the end - resisted being put into a Bordeaux straitjacket. Here was a vintage which in many respects, especially in white, was every bit as good as 1961, and of course much more abundant. But it was over-shadowed by 1959 and would be by 1964. For the 1962s the word generous is extremely apt. Ample, plump, fruity, with a coming-out-to-embrace-you immediate charm: these were other attributes showered on it at the time. Unsaid was the implication that for all its appeal, the 1962s would not be real stayers. A parallel would be the 1985s today. Balance, ripeness and finesse, they were all there. But what about the backbone?

As it turned out there are plenty of 1962s at the top level which even after thirty years have plenty of vigour. On the basis of the wines below I would still be prepared to have a punt at any 1962 of reasonable *provenance* and appearance. The vintage is holding up very well indeed. Dare I suggest it's out-lasting the 1962 Bordeaux? And these have lasted rather better than expected.

TASTING NOTES

BLANC

Meursault Charmes Ropiteau Frères
Half bottle. Quite a developed colour. Getting a bit old now. Buttery and toffee residual flavours. Certainly concentrated. Certainly classy. This was very good indeed, even fine. There is still intensity and class on the finish. (10/94)

Drink up   17.0

Meursault Perrières Comtes Lafon
Quite a well-matured colour. Absolutely lovely nose. Fresh, fragrant, complex. Honey and delicate multi-dimensional fruit, flowers and herbs. Medium-full. Concentrated but gentle. Very good grip. Amazing vigour and real harmony. Everything from start to finish in place. (09/92)

Now-2000   18.5

ROUGE

Bonnes-Mares Langlais-Cotte
Medium colour. Very well matured. Long in wood on the nose. Quite old, a little dried out. Medium-body, somewhat thin, certainly lean, the fruit having leached out. Acidity shows at the end. Never had much class. Now too old. Difficult to see how genuine this is. (10/94)

Past its best   10.0

Bonnes-Mares Comte Georges de Vogüé
Medium-full mature colour. Lovely fragrant stylish nose. Ripe mellow classy fruit. Real elegance on the palate. Delicate for Bonnes-Mares. Medium-full, alive and complex and lovely. This is very delicious. Sweet and superbly elegant. Very lovely. (05/94)

Now-2000   18.5

Chambertin Pierre Bourée
Full, vigorous colour. Rich, full, fat, aromatic, toffee-caramel nose. Fullish, rich, sweet, ample palate. Good acidity. Plenty of enjoyment here, despite the fact that this wine doesn't really have Chambertin class and definition. Plump at the end. Still fresh. (10/94)

Now-2000   16.0

Chambertin, Clos-de-Bèze Clair-Daü
Full, vigorous colour. Very classy nose. Real breed; real complexity; splendid fruit. Fullish, beautifully balanced. A mellow, gently oaky yet vigorous wine with real dimension; very long and stylish at the end. True *grand cru* quality. Perhaps just beginning to lose its grip. But still very long, very lovely. Held up better than the Faiveley. (10/94)

Now-2000   19.0

Chambertin, Clos-de-Bèze Joseph Faiveley
Full, vigorous colour. Full, rich, more 'old-fashioned' than Faiveley today, but none the worse for that. Plenty of finesse, plenty of depth. Full, ample, rich, surprisingly youthful. Quite a structured example. Splendid fruit. A wine of size, vigour and dimension. And real breed. Excellent. (10/94)

Now-2000   19.0

Chambolle-Musigny *Premier Cru* Henri de Villamont
Very full colour. Vigorous. Spurious. Youthfully fresh, oaky, smooth, sweet nose. Medium-full, some tannin. As a wine it is fruity and quite structured, not unpleasant. But as a Burgundy, especially a Chambolle, this is a fraud. Dense acidity on the finish. (10/94)

Drink soon   12.0

Charmes-Chambertin Joseph Drouhin
Fullish, mature colour. Plump nose. Good vigour. Good class and depth too. As it evolved a bit pinched. And on the palate just a hint of astringency. Yet the finish is warm and not unduly aged. Good class, but not a great wine. And it was probably better a few years ago. (10/94)

Drink soon   16.0

Corton Château Corton-Grancey Louis Latour
Good full colour. Well matured. Ample, sweet, nutty nose. A little age now. Fullish, sweet and alcoholic. Not a great deal of class. Good grip though. Shows some sign of getting lighter and more vegetal soon. Still long. Still fresh. Very good but by no means great. (10/94)

Drink soon   15.5

Corton Clos-des-Cortons Joseph Faiveley
Very good vigorous colour. Fine, full, ample, rich nose. Full body. A firm, sturdy, but rich and concentrated example. Good grip. Plenty of depth. Meaty but with good fruit and class. Still very vigorous. The finish is long, fat and complex. Very good indeed, even fine. (10/94)

Now-2000   17.5

Echézeaux Romanée-Conti
Mid shoulder or slightly less fill. Good fresh colour. Clear, clean, slightly vegetal nose. Round, sweet, medium body. Good intensity. But somehow a little artificial (after a series of 1964s), and simple, alongside the Grands-Echézeaux. Good depth and vigour though. Plenty of life. Very good plus. (10/94)

Now-2000   16.5

Gevrey-Chambertin   Clos-Saint-Jacques   Clair-Daü

Medium-full mature colour. Round, classy, well-matured nose. But it held up well. No undue age here. Fullish body, plenty of depth. This is a classy wine. Well balanced. Ripe. Complex. Long. A lot of finesse. Lovely fruit. Very fine quality. Plenty of life still. **(10/94)**

Now-2000   **18.0**

Grands-Echézeaux   Mongeard-Mugneret

Medium to medium-full. Mature colour. Plump nose, ripe, still fresh. Quite aromatic. But fading a bit now. More vigorous on the palate. Fullish. Good intensity. Very good grip. This is ripe and complex. Long and meaty. Very good. Can still be kept. **(10/94)**

Drink soon   **16.0**

Grands-Echézeaux   Romanée-Conti

Medium-full, vigorous mature colour. You can certainly smell the stems here. But there is undeniably classy concentrated fruit. This aspect is much more apparent on the palate. Fullish, intense, multi-dimensional. Very ripe, very well balanced. And real concentration. Very long. A fine example. Bags of life. Tasted twice in 10/94: similar notes. **(10/94)**

Now-2000 plus   **17.5**

Musigny   Comte Georges de Vogüé

Medium-full colour. Mature but not unduly so. Delicate but very stylish on the nose. Lovely fruit. Medium-full, balanced, intense, quite well matured now. Good grip. Indeed the acidity threatening to dominate the fruit. The finish is long and certainly classy, but this is a little past its best. Very good. Was it ever 'very fine'? **(10/94)**

Drink soon   **16.5**

Pommard   Langeac

Good medium-full colour. Well matured. Slightly inky, slightly volatile, but a fat ample nose underneath. No astringency though. On the palate this is fullish, quite alcoholic, ample, sweet and not really too bad at all. But a little past whatever best it had. Slightly hard and coarse at the end. **(10/94)**

Drink up   **13.0**

Romanée-Saint-Vivant   Pierre Bourée

Full, vigorous colour. Sweet, oaky nose. Fat and rich and aromatic. Very ripe. This is like a more structured version of Louis Latour's Romanée-Saint-Vivant. Full. Oaky. Tannic. And sweet. A bit chunky now. **(10/94)**

Now-2000   **15.0**

Romanée-Saint-Vivant   Les Quatre-Journeaux   Louis Latour

Fullish, mature colour. Ripe, balanced, classy complex fruit on the nose, with a touch of sweetness. Mellow and with a touch of oak. Fullish, rich, good intensity and grip. A wine which would make a lot of friends. But why does it have to be so sweet? It destroys the *terroir* definition and the class. **(10/94)**

Now-2000   **16.5**

La Tâche   Romanée-Conti

Full, mature colour. Firm, rich, meaty nose. Fresh still, vigorous. The stems show on nose and palate. Fullish, slightly hard, rich fruit in a vegetal stemmy way. Good grip. Very vigorous. A touch sweet. Very classy but not great. What it lacks for me is a bit of fat, plump generosity. **(10/94)**

Now-2000 plus   **18.5**

1961

RATING FOR THE VINTAGE

Red: 15.5   **White:** (16.5)
(past their best)

SIZE OF THE CROP

(Hectolitres, excluding generic wine)

	Red	White
Grands Crus	7,496	1,365
Village and Premiers Crus	76,182	16,943
Total	83,678	18,303

The reputation of the vintage in Burgundy was much helped by the excellence of the wines in Bordeaux. In reality the wines are good, but they are by no means great. Both 1959 and 1964 were clearly superior vintages. Even 1962 is better.

WEATHER CONDITIONS

An irregular growing season. The spring was unnaturally warm, leading to an early development of the buds. The flowering conditions, however, were cool, reducing the crop through *coulure*, and it was then not really hot until August, and even then only patchily. September was fine though, right through until the end of the harvest, but the ripeness and concentration of the fruit was uneven.

THE STYLE OF THE WINE

This is a vintage about which it is difficult to generalise. There are some extremely good wines, as a glance here and in the Domaine Profile section will show. But in general I prefer the 1962s. They are not as uneven. Some 1961s lack succulence and generosity.

TASTING NOTES

BLANC

Le Montrachet   Comtes Lafon
Quite a powerful nose. After a while - improving in the glass all the time - rich, fat, concentrated, even alcoholic. Yet not very high. A little evolved now. Spicy aspects. The fruit loosening its persistence and elegance. Very good but not great. Slightly four-square. **(09/92)**

Drink soon   **16.0**

ROUGE

Aloxe-Corton   Les Boutières   Christophers
Bottled in England. Full mature colour. Rich, full, fat. Rather maderised. **(10/95)**

Past its best   **(see note)**

CHAMBERTIN   VINCENT LAVRENTIN-CARAVACHE
Full vigorous mature colour. I have never heard of this merchant (not, it would appear from the label, a grower), but the wine is rich, fat, full and concentrated - and classy too; both sweetly ripe and old-viney. Low *rendement*. Vigorous. Long. Very good indeed. Sampled again 09/95. **(03/94)**

Now-2000   **17.0**

Chambertin   Clos-de-Bèze   Charles Vienot
Medium-full, quite mature colour. Evolved nose. A little age, indeed. On the palate a bit of age - or even more - but I don't think it ever had a lot of class. Medium-full. Balanced. But undistinguished. **(10/94)**

Drink up   **13.0**

Chambolle-Musigny Jean Hudelot

Excellent colour. No undue brown at all. A delicious example. Very rich and sweet and fresh, but totally un-souped-up. This is classy, surprisingly youthful, very very concentrated for a village wine. Real intensity. Delicious. Complex. Very very long lingering finish. Fine. (03/94)

Now-2000   17.0

Clos-de-Vougeot Poulet Père et Fils

Good fresh colour. Good old nose, though lacks a little elegance and fragrance. Round, vigorous, quite alcoholic. Fullish, aromatic, quite sweet on the finish. Still fresh. Good but not special. Lacks class. (03/96)

Now-2000 plus   14.0

Gevrey-Chambertin Combe-aux-Moines
Jules Regnier

French bottled. Magnum. Very good colour. This is a lovely concentrated sweet wine with a touch of spice on both nose and palate. Velvety, multi-dimensional, succulent. Delicious. Fine wine. Very classy. Lovely nose. Lingering finish. (12/91)

Now-2000 plus   17.5

Gevrey-Chambertin *Premier Cru*
Louis Trapet et Fils

Old but vigorous colour. Good acidity. Very good depth. Tasted younger than it is. Stylish, vigorous and concentrated. Plenty of life left. Fine. (09/92)

Now-2000   17.5

Grands-Echézeaux
Roland Remoissenet Père et Fils

Good colour. Still very fresh. Still a faint touch of CO_2 on the tongue. That's what has preserved it for thirty-five years. Malo definitely took place in bottle. Plump, black cherry flavours and warm brick flavours. Slightly earthy aspect of Grands-Echézeaux. Not fine but very good indeed. Will still last. (06/96)

Now-2000 plus   17.0

Le Musigny Jean Hudelot

Very good colour. Fine raspberry nose. Rich, plummy, very fresh, very delicious. At first very fine. Developed quite fast in the glass. Great intensity and fruit. Very ripe and concentrated. Long. Very lovely indeed. But not as fine as it once was. (10/94)

Drink soon   18.0

Nuits-Saint-Georges Les Vaucrains
Henri Gouges

Good colour. Now mature. Fragrant, soft, silky, almost sweet on the nose. Very refined. This is old but vigorous. Still fresh. Complex. Very long. Naturally sweet finish. Distinguished. Lovely. Fine plus. (09/95)

Now-2000 plus   18.0

Pommard Grands-Epenots
Michel Gaunoux

Good very deep vigorous mature nose. Eucalyptus, slightly minty nose. Rich and substantial and fat. Opulent and sweet. Full and ample and tannic on the palate. Rich and sweet and spicy. Very good grip. Lovely velvety structure. Vigorous. Very long and subtle. Bags of life. Fine. Similar in 09/95. (07/94)

Now-2000 plus   17.5

Richebourg Romanée-Conti

Splendid colour. Mature but still vigorous. Splendidly rich, chocolatey-coffee, oaky nose. A lot of depth here. Very very concentrated. This is voluptuous and fat, underneath old-viney, sturdy - almost muscular. Very ripe. Still vigorous. Marvellous complexity. Naturally sweet. Great wine. (07/95)

Now-2000   19.0

La Romanée   Leroy

Medium colour. Some brown. Rather oxidised. But sweet and concentrated and intense nonetheless. Not astringent at all. I am sure other bottles in good condition are brilliant. (03/94)

Past its best   (see note)

Romanée-Saint-Vivant Bouchard Aîné

Half bottle. Splendid colour. Full, no undue maturity. Vibrant. Just a whiff of volatile acidity on the nose. But rich and fat and concentrated if a touch inky. The volatile acidity impinges much less on the palate. Full, oaky, plenty of ripe tannin, fat and structured. Old-viney concentration. Very black fruits. The texture of a Richebourg more than a Romanée-Saint-Vivant. Meaty. Vigorous. Almost fine - if it wasn't for the nose. Long but structured finish. Very good indeed. (10/94)

Drink soon   17.0

1959

RATING FOR THE VINTAGE

Red: 18.0   **White:** (17.5)
(past their best)

SIZE OF THE CROP

(Hectolitres, excluding generic wine)

	Red	White
Grands Crus	7,255	1,836
Village and *Premiers Crus*	108,722	23,321
Total	115,977	25,157

A large, glorious and early vintage. You have to go back to 1949 and forward as far as 1990 for something as successful as this, though 1964 was not far behind. The whites lasted very well, though at more than thirty-five years on it is no surprise they are now old. The best of the reds, even at this age, are still vigorous - virile indeed.

WEATHER CONDITIONS

Fine weather in early June, following a mild spring, enabled the vines to flower swiftly and successfully, ensuring not only a large and early harvest, but one of even maturity. July and August were very hot and dry. Early September brought just enough rain to keep the maturation process on an even keel. And the harvest took place in ideal conditions, beginning two weeks earlier than usual on 14 September.

THE STYLE OF THE WINE

The whites were full, concentrated and rich: right at the verge of *sur-maturité* without being over the top. Acidities were nevertheless enough, and the flavours were opulent without being heavy or too exotic.

The red wines are full, ample, rich and generous. There is structure and backbone, acidity and grip, and much that is both complex and classy. You can taste the heat of the summer, for there is plenty of warmth in the wines. But there is no lack of fresh fruit and elegance either. A classic vintage of depth and concentration.

TASTING NOTES

ROUGE

Beaune   Clos-des-Fèves   Chanson
Medium-full colour. Well matured. Fine nose. Raisiny fruit. Complex. Still fresh. This is excellent. Medium-full. Fresh fruit. No undue age or astringency. Finely balanced. Very good indeed. **(10/89)**
Drink soon   17.0

Beaune   Clos-du-Roi   Louis Latour
Medium-full colour. Not as old looking as the Clos-des-Fèves. Fresh and plump. Slightly four-square on the nose. This is less sweet and spicy, a bit more chunky. Some astringency. The fruit has dried out more. **(10/89)**
Drink up   14.0

Beaune   Cuvée Brunet
Hospices de Beaune, Chevillet

Lightish colour. Similar nose. But a little more vigour. Slightly sturdier. Quite sweet. A bit chunky at the end. Very good. **(10/89)**

Drink soon   16.0

Beaune   Cuvée Guigogne de Salins
Hospices de Beaune, F. Schoonmaker

Good fullish colour. Fine rich nose. Very good fruit and an aspect of nuts. There is a little fade but essentially there is good ripe fruit here with a touch of fruit cake. Classy. Balanced. **(10/89)**

Drink soon   17.5

Beaune   Cuvée Nicolas Rolin
Hospices de Beaune, Drapier et Fils

Full but well-matured colour. Fat and rich and plump, with a touch of maderisation. Full, ripe, spicy. A rather more masculine wine. Still enjoyable. Though there is this touch of maderisation the wine is otherwise still vigorous. Long. Fine. **(10/89)**

Drink up   17.5

Beaune   Vignes-Franches   Louis Latour

Good fullish colour. Good rich nose. Still fresh, an aspect of digestive biscuits. Vigorous, fat, meaty wine on the attack. Good fresh acidity. Quite sturdy as Latour often is. Beginning to shorten up and showing a little astringency. Very good. Held up well in the glass. **(10/89)**

Drink soon   16.0

Bonnes-Mares   Clair-Daü

Magnum. Good full vigorous colour and fine ripe nose. Fullish, meaty, oaky, stylish. Sweet. This is still vigorous and complex. It seems as if it will still improve. Fine. **(06/90)**

Now-2000   17.5

Bonnes-Mares   Joseph Drouhin

Good colour. Very toffee/barley sugar and butter-scotch on the nose. Sweet and burnt. Quite full and vigorous but for Drouhin lacking style and not enough grip and purity of Pinot. **(06/90)**

Now-2000   15.0

Bonnes-Mares   Olivier

Full, rich mature colour. Splendid vigorous nose. Rich, concentrated, plummy and meaty. Old vines. Slightly earthy but high quality. A little old-fashioned but very high quality. A lot of concentration. Full and rich. Masculine. Very fine indeed. Still bags of life. Very straight. **(10/89)**

Now-2000   17.0

Chambertin   Pierre Bourée

Very full vigorous colour. Fine, rich, creamy nose. Good concentration. Full, vigorous. A meaty, slightly old-fashioned wine, possibly a bit assisted with wine from further south. The alcohol is evident. Rich and fat. A bit burnt; some astringence at the end. **(10/89)**

Now-2000   15.0

Chambertin   Reine Pédauque

Full colour. Fullish, sturdy, somewhat inky nose. Some volatile acidity. Similar palate. A bit sweet. Ungainly, coarse. A bit astringent. **(10/89)**

Past its best   13.0

Chambertin   Louis Remy

Full mature colour. No undue maturity. Very classy nose. Good new oak. Real complexity. Lovely depth of fruit. This is excellent. Fullish. Lovely fragrant, classic concentrated Pinot on the palate. Harmonious, long. Complex. Excellent. *Grand vin.* **(10/89)**

Now-2000   19.5

Chambertin   Clos-de-Bèze   Louis Jadot

Good colour. Rich fat caramelly nose. Luscious and exotic. Very long and full of finesse as it developed. Full, masculine, slightly earthy. Vigorous. Excellent fruit. Bags of life left. Complex, sweet. Long. Lovely. Very fine indeed. **(10/94)**

Now-2000   19.0

Chambertin   Clos-de-Bèze   J. Thorin

Good colour. Still vigorous. Evidence of new oak on the nose but now a touch high-toned, even a shade maderised. Better than most but uninspiring. Quite good at best. **(06/90)**

Past its best   14.0

Chambolle-Musigny   Antoine Clavelier

Good colour. No undue age. Rich, plump, slightly dense and four-square nose but concentrated and fat, particularly as it developed. Very good Pinot fruit. Succulent. Sweet on the finish. Very good plus. **(03/94)**

Drink soon   16.5

Clos-des-Lambrays   Saier

Medium colour but no undue maturity. Slightly fading on the nose. Medium body. Good quality. Genuine Pinot. Good balance and fragrance. Good elegance. A little past its best but still enjoyable. A fine wine. **(10/89)**

Past its best   17.5

Clos-de-Vougeot   Roland Remoissenet
Père et Fils

Good fullish colour. Still looks vigorous. On the nose it has lightened up a little. But there is nevertheless quality here. Good oak. Now a little attenuated. **(10/89)**

Past its best   15.0

Corton Avery's

Bottled in England. Full mature colour. Chocolate, coffee, leather and liquorice. Rich, some alcohol. Very good but how genuine? Full, roasted, a shade Rhônish and sweet. Yet vigorous, with depth, and long and positive on the finish. Certainly a good wine but not a good Burgundy wine. Will still last. **(10/89)**

Now-2000   **15.0**

Corton Bouchard Père et Fils

Concentrated, full, spicy-earthy-liquoricy. *Gibier*, animal, nutty, *sauvage*. This is masculinity of Corton now soft. Fine. But obviously a wine marked by the heat. Doesn't have the class of the Romanée-Saint-Vivant 1959 of Louis Jadot. **(09/90)**

Drink soon   **17.5**

Corton Sichel

Bottled in France. Medium-full colour. Some maderisation on the nose but still enjoyable. New oak here. Fullish. Meaty, rich, sweet and a shade maderised but balanced. Still with something to offer. And very fine and classy once. Lightening up a little now. **(10/89)**

Drink soon   **16.0**

Corton Bressandes Chandon-de-Briailles

Fine colour. Still very youthful. Funky nose but much better on the palate. Fullish, rich, complex. Certainly a hot year. Very very ripe fruit. Good grip. This is fine plus and still youthful. Lovely. **(09/92)**

Drink soon   **17.5**

Corton Clos-du-Roi Chandon-de-Briailles

Good full colour. Fragrant, soft nose. Complex. A wine of great delicacy and finesse. Naturally sweet. Very classy. Beautifully balanced. Medium to medium-full. Finesse rather than power. Long, balanced. Subtle, lovely. Not gamey. Not hot. Atypical of a 1959. **(12/93)**

Drink soon   **17.5**

Corton Clos-du-Roi Olivier

Good colour. Full, no undue maturity. Fullish nose. Something slightly sweet and vegetal, yet with the acidity showing. Better on the palate. Full. Quite sturdy but rich and meaty. Intriguing. Good old-vine concentration. Not too sweet. Ripe and with good acidity. Long. Complex. Fine. Real depth and finesse. **(10/89)**

Now-2000   **17.5**

Corton Les Vignes-au-Saint Louis Latour

Fullish mature colour. The nose is a bit dumb at first. More forthcoming on the palate. Fullish, new oaky. Ripe, good mellow, sweet plummy-pruny fruit. Good. Quite full. Quite classy. Fragrant. Still plenty of life. But perhaps a little too sweet. **(10/89)**

Drink soon   **15.0**

Gevrey-Chambertin Tête de Cuvée Bernard Dugat-Py

This was a mixture of Gevrey and Charmes; what he kept after selling the rest to the *négoce*. Fine colour. Very deep. Very vigorous. The nose took a bit of time to come out. Old-viney. Mature but very much alive. Rich and complex and multi-dimensional. Quite brutal in its youth. I would have said old-fashioned in the best sense. Lovely finish. A splendid old (but still hale and hearty) wine. **(11/93)**

Now-2000   **17.5**

Grands-Echézeaux Bousserolle

Fullish mature colour. Ripe and spicy on the nose. Quite meaty and vigorous. Fullish and chunky but slightly sweet fruit. Holding up well. A sturdy wine, typical of the *climat*. Reasonable breed. Good acidity. **(10/89)**

Drink soon   **16.0**

Grands-Echézeaux Roland Remoissenet Père et Fils

Medium-full colour. Slightly lactic on the nose. Oaky and ripe on the palate. But has lightened a little now. Yet good fragrant Pinot. Good acidity. This is elegant and has dimension. Very good. **(10/89)**

Drink soon   **16.0**

Grands-Echézeaux Romanée-Conti

Fullish nose. Still very fresh. Fine, rich classy nose. Rich yet a touch of the stems is apparent. Medium-full. Ripe, now softening a little. But the wine is really quite silky and complex. Still long. Very good indeed. **(10/94)**

Now-2000   **17.0**

Mazis-Chambertin Joseph Faiveley

Medium-full vigorous colour. Fine ripe masculine nose. A lot of depth here. Full, old-vine concentration. Fruit still fresh. Very cool and straight. Lovely Pinot. Very great finesse and complexity. Lovely wine. Still bags of life. Great wine. **(10/89)**

Now-2000   **19.0**

Musigny Joseph Drouhin

Medium colour. A little H_2S at first on the nose. Good soft but almost too delicate fruit on the nose later. Medium-full. Lovely fruit. Really complex. Delicious fragrant finish. Very very long. **(06/90)**

Now-2000   **19.0**

Musigny   Jacques Prieur

Fullish mature colour. Rich, oaky, mellow, high quality nose. Youthful and very stylish indeed on the palate. Fullish, mellow, fragrant and balanced; lots of dimension. A lovely bottle. Will still keep well. **(10/89)**

Now-2000   18.5

Musigny   *Vieilles-Vignes*
Comte Georges de Vogüé

Full vigorous colour. This has an extra element of breed and complexity and distinction. Fullish, ripe, complete wine. Still young. Exciting. Lovely fruit and great charm. But substance and depth. A château Palmer 1961 of a wine. *Grand vin.* Bags of life. Brilliant wine. **(10/89)**

Now-2000   20.0

Nuits-Saint-Georges   Morin

Good colour. Slight volatile acidity on the nose. Sweet, somewhat spurious on the palate. Vegetal on the finish. Unexciting. **(06/90)**

Drink up   12.5

Nuits-Saint-Georges   Les Roncières   Avery's

Medium-full colour. Mature. Fat, rich, vigorous, earthy, *sauvage* nose. Youthful. Very Nuits-Saint-Georges. Full body, sweet, quite alcoholic, even a touch spirity. Warm follow-through (typical 1959). Concentrated, meaty. Still vigorous. Very good plus. **(10/94)**

Now-2000   16.5

Nuits-Saint-Georges   Les Saint-Georges
Pierre Ponnelle

Good vigorous colour. Plenty of intensity on the nose. Nicely rich and robust, typically Nuits-Saint-Georges and 1959. Rich, full and fat. Spicy. Good rich follow-through. Concentrated. Classy. Old-viney. Perfumed for a Nuits. Vigorous. Fine. **(10/94)**

Now-2000   17.5

Nuits-Saint-Georges   Les Saint-Georges,
Cuvée des Sires de Vergy
Hospices de Nuits, Pierre Ponnelle

Full vigorous colour. Just a touch papery on the nose. Fullish, rich and sweet on the palate. Slight evidence of alcohol. Very good but it lacks a little nuance and complexity at the end. **(10/89)**

Drink soon   16.0

Pernand-Vergelesses   Pierre Ponnelle

Medium colour. One bottle a little dried out and watery with a touch of seaweed on the nose. The other simply a little astringent. The latter medium bodied, a bit aged. Lacking class. Uninspiring. **(06/90)**

Past its best   12.0

Pommard   Barolet

Very full colour. Full, a bit stewed and inky on the nose. Solid and tannic, good acidity but a bit chunky and astringent. Lacks style. **(10/89)**

Drink soon   12.5

Pommard   Cuvée Billardet
Hospices de Beaune, Guichard Potheret

Medium-full, fully mature colour. Lovely nose. Silky, sensual, soft and mellow, slightly vegetal. Ample and ripe and balanced on the palate. Very classy. Medium-full, very fresh. Very good grip. There is plenty of life here, and plenty of intensity too. Fine complex finish. Fine plus. **(03/95)**

Now-2000   18.0

Pommard   Epenots   Parent

Fine colour. Full, ripe, sweet, concentrated and vigorous at first. This is very good. A typical slightly sturdy Pommard with plenty of depth and even style. Full. Old-viney. Fullish, round, good grip. Just a little vegetal at the end as it developed. **(12/92)**

Drink soon   16.0

Pommard   Grands-Epenots
Michel Gaunoux

Medium to medium-full colour. Mature. Well-matured nose. Just a touch of volatile acidity. Has it lost a little of its fruit? On the palate medium to medium-full, plump, succulent and ripe. Slight touch of decay at the end. This needs drinking. But it has class and depth and a good meatiness which it should have being a Pommard and the warmth of 1959 is still there. Good (was very good). **(10/94)**

Drink soon   15.0

Richebourg   Bichot

Good colour. Somewhat maderised on the nose. Full, rich, ripe and fat but spurious. Slightly rigid. Still vigorous. Clumsy. **(06/90)**

Past its best   12.0

Richebourg   Charles Noëllat

Good medium-full mature colour. A little assisted perhaps but good ripe fruit. Still fresh. Plump and vigorous. Full and meaty. Good wine here. Will still keep. Good balance of acidity. Finishes long. A wine of fine quality. **(10/89)**

Now-2000   17.5

Richebourg   Prosper Maufoux

Full vigorous colour. Fine strongly oaky nose. High quality. Full, rich, meaty and ample. Very concentrated. Old-vine wine. A lot of quality and depth. Splendid. Still vigorous. High class. **(10/89)**

Now-2000   18.5

Richebourg   Romanée-Conti

Very full, barely mature colour. A lot of breed
and concentration on the nose. Very high quality
here. This is a marvellous wine. Full, rich and
very concentrated. Real breed and multi-
dimensional. Real length. *Grand vin!* (10/89)

Now–2000   19.5

Romanée-Saint-Vivant   Joseph Drouhin

Medium colour. Fine nose. Good new oak.
Fragrant, medium body, balanced but I would
have expected a bit more muscle and vigour.
Second bottle better. Fine lovely long stylish Pinot.
Very good finish. Lovely but not as concentrated as
the 1945 or 1952 La Tâche. (06/90)

Now–2000   18.0

Romanée-Saint-Vivant   Louis Jadot

This is brilliant. Really lovely mature Burgundy.
Not a trace of age. This has class and lovely fruit.
Sensual but with the femininity of Romanée-
Saint-Vivant. Still very fresh. Not marked by the
heat. (09/90)

Now–2000   18.0

Savigny-lès-Beaune   Louis Latour

Fraudulent label. The label and cork say '*Grand
Cru Exceptionnel*'. Lightish mature colour. Light,
somewhat faded and attenuated nose. Similar on
the palate. Definitely Pinot Noir and not
without style. Now fading. (10/89)

Past its best   13.0

La Tâche   Romanée-Conti

Full colour. Rich, vigorous, youthful nose. A
real blockbuster. Still has a way to go. Very
raspberry fruit. Tannic. Full, rich, the flavours
still disparate. Potentially fine. But perhaps a
little too obvious for great. (06/90)

Now–2000   19.5

Volnay   Quancard

Good full mature colour. No undue age. Quite
high volatile acidity on the nose. After this and
a certain bottle stink had disappeared one had
something round and mellow. Shows a bit of age
on the palate now. Has lost its vigour and there
are dirty edges. Medium body. Not bad; indeed
quite pleasant. (10/89)

Past its best   13.5

Vosne-Romanée   Grivelet, Clos-du-Frantin

Medium-full mature colour. Mature fragrant
nose. No great muscle. Soft and round.
Medium-full as much spicy and fruity. Some
alcohol. Quite vigorous but not a lot of breed.
Good finish. Yet getting a little short as it
developed. (10/89)

Drink soon   14.0

Vosne-Romanée   La Grande-Rue
Henri Lamarche

Good full mature colour. Full, chunky, sturdy
nose. Seems a little astringent. Has it lost its
fruit? On the palate rather better. Good oak.
Full, ripe and rich. This is a bit old-fashioned
but very fine. Still plenty of life. Earthy finish.
(10/89)

Drink soon   15.0

1957

RATING FOR THE VINTAGE

Red: 16.0   **White:** (15.0)
(past their best)

SIZE OF THE CROP

(Hectolitres, excluding generic wine)

	Red	White
Grands Crus	6,379	914
Village and *Premiers Crus*	54,225	9,118
Total	60,604	10,032

Nineteen fifty-seven produced some surprisingly good wines, both in white and in red. They were not hard, as were the clarets, nor were they lean, as would be the 1972s. But a firmness of acidity was a keynote nonetheless. The whites are good, but now past it. The reds, though, can still give much pleasure.

WEATHER CONDITIONS

The spring was warm, ensuring a good flowering; and it was very hot at the end of June. July and August were cool and wet, but the weather improved in September. The harvest was late, picking not commencing until the first week of October, but the fine weather continued. As in 1978, those who picked latest of all made the best wines.

THE STYLE OF THE WINE

The vintage is best in the Côte-de-Nuits. Without the hard tannins of their Bordeaux equivalents the wines are mellow with a good grip and backbone, and long on the palate: nicely austere, but with plenty of class. The vintage is holding up surprisingly well.

TASTING NOTES

ROUGE

Chambertin   Berry Bros & Rudd
Quite an old colour now. Rich, spicy, even caramelly on the nose and palate. Getting a touch stringy. Certainly more than a little sweet. Fullish, meaty, 'old-fashioned'. Slightly spurious Burgundy. But not at all bad. **(12/93)**
Drink soon   14.0

Chambolle-Musigny   Clair-Daü
Low neck. Good colour. Liquorice and meaty. Ripe, oaky. Distinctive. Impressive, especially for a village wine. Second bottle less vigorous. **(06/90)**
Drink soon   16.0

Chambolle-Musigny   Les Charmes   Avery's
Good colour. No undue age. Fine mature quality Burgundy. Quite full, fresh, plenty of stylish fruit. Not a bit hard. This is a very good wine which is holding up well. Fragrant, spicy, nicely ripe, but nicely cool. Not a bit vegetabley or gamey. Very good indeed. **(05/96)**
Now-2000   17.0

Clos-de-la-Roche   Joseph Drouhin
Good colour. Now fully mature. Ripe nose, not too rigid. Medium-full, spicy, complex, full-flavoured wine. Not that graceful but meaty and with depth. Very good. Second bottle not as good. **(06/90)**
Drink soon   16.0

Corton   Clos-du-Roi   Paul Bouchard
Fresh colour still. Medium-full. Quite a classy nose. Fragrant, mellow, full, mature. Nicely gamey. Medium-full body, good acidity. Ripe

and meaty. A certain austerity but this is no bad thing. This has depth and grip and style. Very good. **(01/95)**
Now-2000   16.0

Latricières-Chambertin   Joseph Drouhin
One bottle better than the other. Lowish fills. Good fresh colour. Slightly earthy nose. Ripe and quite structured. A meaty wine with less finesse but more vigour than their Charmes-Chambertin 1955. Good to very good. The other bottle more elegant, more stylish fruit. Less farmyardy. **(06/90)**
Now-2000   16.0

Latricières-Chambertin
Roland Remoissenet Père et Fils
Fullish mature colour. No undue age. Lovely ample, rich and structured nose. Lots of depth, slight spice, aromatic. Has the power and depth of a 1959, but never moved from the Remoissenet cellar. Rich. Long. Complex. Fine plus. **(06/96)**
Now-2000 plus   18.0

Pommard   Clos-de-la-Commaraine
Jaboulet-Vercherre
Medium colour. Not much nose. Medium-full body. Lacks style. Quite plump. Both bottles similar. Boring. Coarse finish. **(06/90)**
Past its best   12.0

Richebourg   Jean Gros
Good full mature colour with no undue age. Ripe and fragrant on the nose, sweet, slightly vegetal - rather than *gibier* - but with good freshness and finesse. On the palate the attack is firm and quite full, with good richness. At first

the follow-through was a little lean but it fattened up, became more generous, as it evolved in the glass. Not a great wine, but a very good one. Still with plenty of vigour. **(12/92)**

Now-2000 17.5

La Tâche   Romanée-Conti
One bottle lighter, very curious scented-dilute-lanolin nose. Soapy. Second better colour. Rude, lumpy vegetal nose. Somewhat earthy, acidity shows. Astringent. **(06/90)**

Drink soon 13.0

Vosne-Romanée   La Grande-Rue
Henri Lamarche
Very good colour. Not a bit hard. Just a touch stringy. Mellowed in the glass. Good fresh acidity. A little tannin obvious. But very good intensity. Long. Still very fresh and youthful. Lovely. Very elegant. **(10/94)**

Now-2000 17.5

1952

RATING FOR THE VINTAGE

Red: 16.5   **White:** (16.5)
(past their best)

SIZE OF THE CROP
(Hectolitres, excluding generic wine)

	Red	White
Grands Crus	6,845	1,184
Village and *Premiers Crus*	61,509	12,991
Total	68,354	14,175

WEATHER CONDITIONS

In total contrast to 1951, which was about as bad as you could imagine in your worst nightmares, and 1950, which was very abundant, indeed a record crop, 1952 was small and beautiful. It could have been great. There was a small *sortie*. The spring was warm and the flowering swift and even. June was fine and very dry. July and August very hot, interspersed by storms, especially in the later half of the month. At the beginning of September the weather cooled. It had promised to be a vintage on a par with the magnificent 1949 crop. But that final extra push to super-concentration never arrived. The vintage began in the first week of October, and a small amount of thick-skinned, very healthy grapes was gathered in good weather.

THE STYLE OF THE WINE

The 1952s are - or were - structured wines: sturdy, tannic, and old-fashioned. But in few cases, unlike some Bordeaux, too big for their own good. Together with the size there was a splendid concentration of fruit. And there was no lack of grip. In Burgundy this was the best vintage between 1949 and 1959.

Only the top wines, not unreasonably, are still vigorous, and these do not include Romanée-Conti itself, the first vintage of the new grafted vines, planted in 1946. But I have excellent examples from Faiveley, Gros, Leroy and others. These are still worth looking out for.

Tasting Notes

ROUGE

Clos-de-Vougeot   Charles Noëllat

Good full vigorous colour. Plump nose. Reasonable style and vigour. Full, ripe, quite structured in an old-fashioned way on the palate. Good grip. Chocolatey. Good depth. Good freshness. Ample fruit. Nice and fat at the end. Very vigorous. Fine. (10/94)

Now-2000   **17.5**

Corton   Château Corton-Grancey
Louis Latour

Full mature colour. No undue age. Rather tired and dried out on the nose. On the palate dead, sweet and astringent. Sweet-sour finish. Undrinkable. Nasty. (10/94)

Past its best   **(see note)**

Echézeaux   Romanée-Conti

Good fullish colour. No undue maturity. Medium-full, fragrant, round and delicious. No fade or coarseness, nor maderisation - surprisingly so. This has sweet ripe fruit, was hot and powerful once. Most enjoyable. A bottle in 03/93, however, was far too sweet and alcoholic. (10/89)

Now-2000   **17.0**

Grands-Echézeaux   Romanée-Conti

Quite an important ullage: a good 3 inches from the base of the cork. Good mature full colour. Fresh nose. A slight lack of generosity and fat, but no undue age. Just a little lean and stemmy. Ripe, quite sweet, fullish on the palate. A touch of astringency at the end. It lacks a bit of finesse, and the finish doesn't add anything. Quite alcoholic. Very good but not great. (10/94)

Drink soon   **16.0**

Richebourg   Prosper Maufoux

Very good very full vigorous colour. Ample, rich, concentrated, vigorous nose. Breed and depth here. This is serious stuff. Full, concentrated and vigorous on the palate. Old-viney essence of fruit. Very classy. This is a lovely rich wine, very complex, multi-dimensional. Really intense and fat. A beautiful wine. And still very vigorous. *Grand vin!* (10/94)

Now-2000 plus   **19.5**

Richebourg   Romanée-Conti

Fine old colour. Fragrant mature nose. Obviously a rich and hot vintage - yet there was a goodly percentage of youngish vines in the wine - complex, well matured. Classy but not great. (11/91)

Drink soon   **17.5**

Romanée-Conti   Romanée-Conti

Good colour. Somewhat tough and rigid on the nose. Quality here, indisputably, despite young vines. Slightly sweet. A little alcohol burn. A bit four-square. Good though. Still fresh. (06/92)

Drink up   **15.0**

Romanée-Saint-Vivant
Roland Remoissenet Père et Fils

Fine fresh colour. Fragrant, complex, very very classy nose. Soft, naturally genuinely sweet. Very lovely. Did this come from Marey-Monge? On the palate not quite as fine at first. But more vigorous later. Medium-full. Ripe, as it evolved. Slightly spicy. This is very fine indeed. (06/90)

Drink soon   **18.5**

La Tâche   Romanée-Conti

Good full mature colour. Rich nose but there is evidence of the stems. Not as ample as Maufoux's Richebourg. But a wine of breed, intensity and vigour. Lovely complex fruit on the palate. Full, smooth and mellow. Very long and harmonious. Very lovely. Very fine indeed. Bags of life ahead of it. Lovely in 06/90 as well. (10/94)

Now-2000 plus   **18.5**

Vosne-Romanée   Chevillot

Very good colour. Extraordinary vigour for the age. Fat, rich and meaty, touch of boot polish. A bit larger than life. Holding up well. Not really genuine Pinot but a good wine. (06/90)

Drink soon   **15.0**

Vosne-Romanée   Quancard

Good full vigorous colour. Some delicate fruit on the nose. Medium body. Has lightened up but there is still a little residual sweetness. Yet the finish is a little lean and astringent. (10/94)

Past its best   **12.0**

1949

Red: 19.0   **White:** (18.0)
(past their best)

SIZE OF THE CROP

(Hectolitres, excluding generic wine)

	Red	White
Grands Crus	5,620	759
Village and Premiers Crus	47,567	8,196
Total	53,187	8,955

This is the best vintage of them all, equal to 1945 or 1961 in Bordeaux. It contains some wines of such perfect beauty and purity, that I have had to control myself not to weep with pleasure when I have tasted them. I count myself privileged to have been able to consume so many great wines in their prime.

WEATHER CONDITIONS

The growing season paralleled 1961 - but 1961 in Bordeaux rather than in Burgundy. Warm weather in the early spring produced an early bud-break. But then atrocious weather - prolonged rain rather than frost - wiped out much of the crop during the flowering. Thereafter, as if to compensate, the summer was warm, without being very, very hot, and noticeably dry until just before the harvest, when there was just the right amount of rain to swell the grapes and enable the tannins to mature. The harvest began on 27 September and took place in fine weather.

THE STYLE OF THE WINE

The red 1949s are the epitome of the Pinot Noir. Good structure, perfect harmony, generously fruity and of real intensity and breed. Everything is in place: glorious wines.

Such whites as I can remember are very fine too.

TASTING NOTES

BLANC

Chassagne-Montrachet   Clos-de-la-Maltroye   Château de la Maltroye
Mature colour. Buttered toast nose. Full and rich. Old but high quality. Ripe. Good richness. Nice peachy fruit. A fat wine, fullish. Long. Honeyed. Now quite old, but delicious nevertheless. **(01/95)**
Drink soon   **16.0**

ROUGE

Bonnes-Mares   Sichel
Quite fragrant on the nose. Medium body. On palate good oak. This is round, ripe, genuine and stylish. Creamy rich. Smooth and elegant. Long and complex. Very good plus. **(06/90)**
Drink soon   **16.5**

Chambertin Chevillot

Good colour. Lacks class and varietal flavour on the nose. Rigid, bolstered-up. Sweet on the palate. Acidity shows. A bit stewed. Now clumsy and drying out. (06/90)

Past its best   12.0

Chambertin Joseph Faiveley

Fine full colour. Rich full concentrated nose. A lot of quality and depth here. This is excellent. *Grand vin* indisputably. Marvellous fruit. Masculine. Tannic originally. Austere. Long and multi-dimensional. Similar note 10/94. (10/89)

Now-2000   20.0

Chambertin Leroy

Well-matured colour and nose. Quality, breed, depth and complexity on the palate. Rather better than the nose would suggest. Vigorous. Long, succulent. Medium-full body. Long and lovely. Excellent. More finesse as it evolved than Faiveley. A beautiful wine. *Grand vin.* (10/89)

Now-2000   20.0

Chambertin Marion

Similar colour. Good honest Pinot on the nose but some signs of drying out. Yet fragrant. Medium-full body. This has plump fruit and good balance. Fresher than the nose might suggest. Fine but not the real dimension of *grand vin.* Reasonable length. (10/89)

Drink soon   17.5

Chambertin Savin

Medium-full mature colour. No undue age. Delicious, fragrant, nutty nose. Perhaps not entirely Pinot. Some oak. Medium-full. Ripe, fruity and sweet but a lack of length, subtlety and genuiness. Somewhat chunky. May get astringent. (10/89)

Past its best   15.0

Chambertin Clos-de-Bèze Bichot

Similar colour to Chevillot's Chambertin 1949. Sweet nose. Soupy, round and sweet on the palate. Fullish. Fresher than Chevillot's but no more genuine. Not bad at best. Yet still finishes vigorously. (06/90)

Drink soon   13.0

Chambolle-Musigny Bouchard Père et Fils

Good vigorous colour. Still bags of life. Old nose but still has interest. Sweet but oxidised nose. Quite high in alcohol. A little hot. I can't really enjoy this. (03/94)

Past its best   (see note)

Chambolle-Musigny Bousserolle

Good colour. Slightly jammy nose but still very fresh. Falling away a bit as it developed. Slightly edgy. Full and chunky. Perhaps a little assisted. (10/89)

Past its best   12.0

Clos-de-Vougeot Joseph Drouhin

Good mature colour. Fine full succulent nose. But has it lost a little of its vigour? More vigorous than Leroy's on the palate. Full, concentrated, spicy, meaty. Ripe. A full concentrated wine. Chocolatey and caramelly. Excellent. Will still last. A similar bottle 06/90, but also one a little oxidised. (10/89)

Now-2000   18.0

Clos-de-Vougeot Leroy

Fine colour. Full rich nose, slightly chunky but ripe and vigorous. Yet on the palate it is beginning to lose a little of its vigour. Fine and full but without the beauty of Drouhin's Clos-de-Vougeot. (10/89)

Drink soon   17.5

Corton Château Corton-Grancey
Louis Latour

Medium-full colour. Mature but not unduly so. Smells a little like a 1983. Slightly astringent. Pruney. Sweet and alcoholic on the palate. A little lumpy. Ripe and plummy. Lacks a little grace. But fullish and still vigorous. Merely good. (04/94)

Drink soon   15.0

Gevrey-Chambertin Pierre Ponnelle

Splendid colour for this age. Still clear and vigorous. Fine nose. Old-viney, clean and classic. Very good Pinot fruit. Good persistence. Medium-full. Long and elegant and very complex. A fine example of a village wine. (03/94)

Drink soon   16.0

Latricières-Chambertin Louis Remy

Good fullish colour. Smoky bacon nose. Vigorous, full, perhaps not entirely Pinot Noir. Beefy, some alcohol. Quite sweet. Not genuine Burgundy. Certainly has a Châteauneuf-du-Pape aspect. (10/89)

Drink up   13.0

Mazis-Chambertin Leroy

Good mature colour. A little maderised on the nose at the start and it got worse as it developed. Pity. (10/89)

Past its best   (see note)

Musigny Bichot

Quite good colour. A little oxidised and faded on the nose. But quite genuine and meaty on the palate. Soft, elegant, long. Very good. (06/90)

Past its best   16.0

Musigny Camille Giroud

Fine old colour. But not a bit too old. Lovely elegant nose. Rich and soft and silky. Fullish and vigorous still. This is very lovely. Honeyed and fat and hugely fruity. Still bags of life. **(09/92)**

Now–2000   18.5

Musigny   Lebègue-Bichot

Good colour. Fat, ripe, slightly overblown nose. Fresh nose. Slightly chunky but fat and ripe. Fullish, meaty. No undue age. This has a lot of quality, though the De Vogüé's Musigny, *Vieilles-Vignes* is better yet. Good succulent fat and quite masculine for Musigny. **(10/89)**

Drink soon   18.5

Musigny   Leroy

Full but well-matured colour. A little dry on the nose. Slightly four-square and chunky. On the palate a little dried out compared with the Vogüé. Yet fragrant and classy. Much more feminine. Long and delicious on the palate nevertheless. Probably this had the most finesse, but for current drinking I prefer the Vogüé. Yet it held up very well. Excellent! Indeed *grand vin*. Quite marvellous again in 06/90. **(10/89)**

Now–2000   19.5

Musigny   *Vieilles-Vignes*
Comte Georges de Vogüé

Good colour. Similar nose but riper and more satisfying. A lot of rich fruit. Full and delicious oaky depth. Slightly less chunky but a lot more breed and concentrated. Velvety (rather than silky). Chocolate on the finish. Lovely. Very well balanced. High class. Long on the finish. Not as vigorous in 06/90 but also lovely: 'better than the 1945 and 1947'. **(10/89)**

Drink soon   19.5

Nuits-Saint-Georges   Les Boudots
Jean Grivot

Fine, vigorous old colour. Ripe, fragrant, rich, old, concentrated, fat. This is very fine and sweet and vigorous. Rugged background. Medium-full. Elegant, delicious. Very very lovely indeed. Seriously good. Still has life. Delicious. **(09/94)**

Drink soon   18.5

Richebourg   Leroy

Fine colour. Amazingly lovely nose. New oaky, cedary, complex and totally brilliant. Superb. On the palate equally fabulous. This is one of the best Burgundies I have ever had in my life. Timeless balance and vigour. Sheer beauty. Fresh as a daisy. Has everything: concentration, depth, subtlety and distinction. Aristocratic wine. *Très grand vin*. Equally splendid 06/90.

Now–2000   20.0

Richebourg   Roland Remoissenet
Père et Fils

Very good vigorous colour. Very fine. Gros provenance. This is brilliant. Full, very rich and fat and concentrated, even structured. But soft and sweet. Incredibly youthful and fresh. Magnificent. Marvellous class. Brilliant fruit. Excellent. **(10/94)**

Now–2005 plus   19.5

Romanée-Saint-Vivant   Avery's

Quite an old colour. Getting a little faded on the nose. But fragrant and classy on the palate. Genuine Pinot – and in its prime, five to ten years ago, really rather fine. Still intensely flavoured but a little awkward on the finish. Losing a little fruit. **(09/92)**

Past its best   17.0

Romanée-Saint-Vivant   Marey-Monge
Romanée-Conti

Well-matured colour. Has lightened up a bit on the nose but high quality nevertheless. Medium-full, coffee and mocha aspects. Balanced and fragrant. Not the vigour or delight of the Latour, Romanée-Saint-Vivant but fine nevertheless. **(10/89)**

Drink soon   17.5

Romanée-Saint-Vivant
Les Quatres-Journeaux   Louis Latour

Fine colour. Still youthful looking. Lovely nose. Fragrant and complex and vigorous. Fullish, ripe, plump, succulent and lovely. Beautiful wine. Still fresh, subtle and complex. Round and with ethereal fragrant fruit. Delicious. Coffee and toffee elements. *Grand vin*. **(10/89)**

Now–2000   19.5

Volnay   Clos-des-Chênes   Jacques Arnoul

Bigger colour. Fullish, ripe, vigorous nose. Ripe, spicy with a touch of caramel on the palate. Quite big for a Volnay. But the most youthful of all in this flight. Ripe finish. The second bottle less good. Very good plus. **(06/90)**

Drink soon   16.5

Volnay   Clos-des-Chênes   Charles Giraud

A little H$_2$S on the nose in one of these bottles. Soft, fragrant, elegant. Typically Volnay in the better bottle, a little drying out in the other. Yet a wine of style here which is consistent through to the finish. Very good. **(06/90)**

Drink soon   16.0

Vosne-Romanée   Grivelet, Clos-Frantin

(Le Domaine du Général Legrand, Maréchal de Camp de L'Empereur.) Good colour. This is quality old Pinot Noir. Fullish, sweet, fragrant. Good vigour. A bit suave perhaps but there is quality here. Still plenty of life. **(09/93)**

Now–2000   16.0

Vosne-Romanée   Clos-des-Réas
Roland Remoissenet Père et Fils

Mature colour nose. Clean and ripe on the nose but lacks a little zip now. I have had better bottles. But though a little bland at first, soft and elegant at the end. But very good rather than startling. Better notes in 1991 and 1992, when I marked it up to 18.0. **(04/94)**

Drink soon   16.0

1947

R A T I N G   F O R   T H E   V I N T A G E

Red: 16.5   **White:** (15.0)
(past their best)

S I Z E   O F   T H E   C R O P

NB Production figures 'not available' according to the local INAO.

T H E   W I N E S

Like Bordeaux, this is a larger than life vintage. The summer was splendidly hot and dry, the harvest early (16 September), and the vintage took place in great heat. Growers in those days lacked temperature control. The only way to cool things down was to add ice in sacks to the fermenting vats, or, as Pierre Boillot of Meursault remembers, to hose down the baskets of fruit in the evening and leave them outside overnight.

Nevertheless there are some splendid red wines. They are naturally rich, the stable acidities are very low but the volatile acidities high, and yet they still seem to be holding up. Inevitably, however, there is much irregularity: lumpy, stewed tannins, for instance, and a lack of velvet and breed. Many whites were blowsy and prematurely oxidised, as they would be in 1976. I would not expect the red wines of this vintage to be holding up as well as 1945, 1949 or 1952.

T A S T I N G   N O T E S

BLANC

Puligny-Montrachet   Gauthier, *négociant*

Quite sweet. A touch oxidised. Almost an element of botrytis. Fat and with a touch of oak. A curiosity but by no means over the hill. Didn't collapse in the glass. **(09/91)**

Past its best   (see note)

ROUGE

Beaune   Les Avaux   Marey-Liger-Belair

One bottle corked. Cherry, high-toned nose. On the palate medium body. Ripe, soft and with interest but it is getting a bit mean. Not bad. **(06/90)**

Drink up   13.0

Beaune   Clos-du-Roi   Marey-Liger-Belair

Medium colour. Soft, elegant, fragrant nose. Medium body. Ripe, balanced, supple, almost sweet. Still alive, though the acidity shows a bit. Good plus. **(06/90)**

Drink up   15.5

Beaune   Marconnets   Bouchard
Père et Fils

Very good colour. Full, still vigorous. Rich, full, earthy, oaky nose. Robust, a little bit suspiciously sweet on the palate but good Pinot nevertheless and it was a hot vintage. Rich, meaty, fleshy. No great elegance but very good. **(06/90)**

Drink up   16.0

Bonnes-Mares   Marey-Liger-Belair
Tasteviné

Very good full colour. No undue age. Very fine classy wine; cedary and sandalwoody aspects. Lovely ripe, laid-back fruit. On the palate very smooth. Very well balanced. Delicate and fragrant. Sweet and complex. Very Chambolle. Long, lingering finish. Delicious. **(03/96)**

Now-2000   18.0

Chambertin   Pierre Ponnelle

Very full mature colour. No undue maturity. This is another old-fashioned wine. Very concentrated and rich. Meaty, masculine. Full, concentrated. High quality. Still fresh. Shows how magnificent and powerful this vintage can be. **(10/89)**

Now-2000 plus   18.5

Chambertin   Clos-de-Bèze
Drouhin-Larose

Mature medium to medium-full colour. Gently fading nose, marked by the new wood. Lightening up now, with a suspicion of maderisation as it evolved. Soft on the palate, certainly. Sweet and rich. A bit sweet and sour. Quite long. Quite classy. But needs drinking soon. Very good. **(03/96)**

Drink soon   16.0

Chambolle-Musigny   Les Amoureuses
Pierre Ponnelle

Medium colour. Still vigorous. Stylish oaky nose and palate. Soft typical Chambolle raspberry and violets style. Complex. Sweet, lots of lovely ripe fruit. Balanced, graceful, long. Fine. **(06/90)**

Drink soon   17.5

Charmes-Chambertin   Chevillot

Two bottles very similar. Good colour, but quite old. My bottle somewhat oxidised on the nose. Ripe and sweet on the palate. Medium body. Acidity shows a bit. Cracking up. A bit dry on the palate though not astringent. **(06/90)**

Past its best   14.0

Clos-des-Lambrays   Cosson

Magnum. Very good colour. No undue maturity, indeed very fresh. Excellent fresh fruit on the nose - raspberries, currants, but at the same time slightly chunky. Some volatile acidity. Very youthful. Fullish. Slightly four-square. A bit old-fashioned. But certainly very good. Long. Complex. But the fruit has dried out a bit. What it lacks is a bit of fat. **(08/92)**

Drink soon   16.0

Corton   Joseph Faiveley   *Tasteviné*

Medium-full colour. No undue age. Firm, even slightly hard on the nose at first. But good

quality fruit underneath. Full, fat meaty palate. Lacks a little distinction but an ample, spicy example. Still alive and vigorous. Fine but not great. **(03/96)**

Now-2000   17.5

Corton   Bressandes   Sichel

Good colour. Strange nose. Smells a bit grassy and old tea (both bottles). A lot of *vin de presse*. Fullish, somewhat stewed. A bit hot and alcoholic. A little rigid again. Not bad. **(06/90)**

Past its best   13.0

Gevrey-Chambertin   Yves Ambal, *négociant*

Very good full vigorous colour. Bitter chocolate and cherries on the nose. Very fresh. Firm, fat, vigorous. Naturally sweet and rich. Just what Gevrey should be. Full, quite muscular and sturdy. Quite 'hot'. Good vigour. Good natural sweet finish. Very good again, especially for a village wine. **(06/90)**

Now-2000   16.0

Grands-Echézeaux   Lupé-Cholet

Estate bottled. Marvellous colour. A fine glass of wine. Very ripe, opulent, sweet and concentrated. Obviously a firm rich classy wine, both originally and still now. Full, masculine, concentrated. Still genuinely sweet. Lovely. Bags of life. Very fine. **(02/94)**

Drink soon   18.0

Musigny   Pierre Ponnelle

Very full mature colour. No undue maturity. This is an old-fashioned rich meaty wine with no concession to the idea that Musigny should be somewhat feminine. Concentrated and fruity with quite high acidity. Fullish. Good but lacks a bit of real finesse. **(10/89)**

Drink soon   15.0

Musigny   *Vieilles-Vignes*
Comte Georges de Vogüé

Low shoulder. This like the 1945 is also past it. Again the acidity is lacking. **(06/90)**

Past its best   (see note)

Nuits-Saint-Georges   Patriarche

Rich, Rhôney sweet nose. Alcoholic. Ripe. Fat full and exotic. Old-fashioned Burgundy in the best sense. Still very fresh and long. But hot and south of France-ish without a doubt. **(09/91)**

Drink up   13.0

Richebourg   Rodet

Good appearance. Delicate, fragrant nose. This has a slight touch of volatile acidity as it developed. Soft, sweet, not a bit faded. Very lovely indeed. More Romanée-Saint-Vivant than Richebourg. A feminine aspect. **(10/94)**

Drink up   18.5

Romanée-Saint-Vivant   Bichot
Good colour. Still vigorous. Ripe nose but lacks
Pinot elegance. On the palate this is a little
faded but quite full and rich. Lacks class.
(06/90)
Drink up   14.0

Volnay   Clos-des-Chênes
Pierre Latour-Giroud, Charles Giroud
Good colour. Still very much alive. Soft, very
ripe indeed. Plump and succulent. Medium to
medium-full. Fresh, complex. Very Volnay.
Delicious. Will still hold up. **(03/94)**
Drink soon   17.5

1945

Rating for the Vintage

Red: 18.5   **White:** (16.0)
(past their best)

Size of the Crop

NB Production figures 'not available' according to the local INAO.

The Wines

Not quite as great a vintage as 1949 but nevertheless one of splendid quality. As in Bordeaux
a tiny crop owing to bad weather in the spring but then, to make up for the frost, a glorious
summer and an early harvest.

Very concentrated wines, very structured too, most with noticeable tannins, some with too
much solidity. But inside there is the most impressive quantity of fruit, very well balanced with
acidity. The best are holding up remarkably well, not having the innate astringency of their
equivalents in Bordeaux.

Tasting Notes

ROUGE

Bonnes-Mares   Joseph Drouhin
Somewhat unbalanced. Sweet and with built-in
SO_2. Medium colour. Curious wet wood nose.
A little vegetal (the other bottle very vegetable
soup). Disappointing. **(06/90)**
Past its best   **(see note)**

Clos-de-Lambrays   Cosson
Excellent colour. Still very full and very
youthful. Marvellous perfumed nose. Very rich,
cedary-spice, and cinnamon-like complexity.
Full, intense. Subtle, ripe. Very concentrated,
but not a bit too over-structured. Fat, velvety,
very fine grip and excellent length and vigour.
A great wine. **(10/94)**
Now–2000   19.5

Clos-de-Lambrays   Leroy
Two bottles circulating: one nearly gone -
pungent, sweet-sour but thin; the other old-
fashioned and dense but rich and fat and

concentrated. Porty elements. A little clenched.
Better with food. Very good but lacks a little
grace and refinement. **(10/95)**
Drink up   16.0

Musigny   Vieilles-Vignes
Comte Georges de Vogüé
Quite marked ullage. Both the colour and the
nose are a bit faded. Sweet but now faded. The
acidity seems a bit feeble. This is past it, but was
good once. **(06/90)**
Drink up   15.0

Pommard   Epenots   Jacques Parent
Fully mature colour. Splendidly rich nose. No
hard edges here. Very very concentrated. This is
very pure and gently sweet. Marvellously
balanced. Lingering but not fragile. Long and
fine. Delicious. **(11/95)**
Drink soon   17.5

Richebourg   Grivelet
My bottle finished. The other a bit dried out on
the nose. Some sweetness on the palate. Not too

astringent. Not that bad but a bit mean on the finish now. Medium to medium-full. For a 1945 Richebourg a disappointment. **(06/90)**

Drink up 14.0

Richebourg   Jean Gros

Huge colour. On the nose rich, slightly dense, in the best sense. Chocolatey, very black fruits. Very full, still some tannin. Very very structured. High acidity. At first a bit solid. Not as silky smooth and sweet as a 1949. But a great wine. Enormous depth and class. Great concentration. Real distinction. Very very fine. Essence of wine here. Still very young. Marvellous. **(06/95)**

Now–2000 plus 20.0

Richebourg   Lebégue-Bichot

Three inches of ullage. Splendid colour. Could be a 1985. Marvellously rich, ripe, concentrated nose. On the palate very ample and full and intensely sweet. Genuine. Very classy. Very plump and velvety, fat, balanced. Old-vine fruit. This is great wine. Bags of life. **(10/94)**

Now–2000 plus 19.5

La Tâche   Romanée-Conti

Reasonably full colour. One bottle better than the other. The better rich, full and concentrated and sturdy on the palate. Will still develop – and did so in the glass. Very fine quality. The second a bit older but more elegant. Long. Complex. Very fine. **(06/90)**

Now–2000 plus 18.5

BIBLIOGRAPHY

ABRIC, Loïc
Le Vin de Bourgogne au XIXème Siècle; Editions de l'Armançon, Dijon, 1993.

ANDRIEU, Pierre
Petite Histoire de la Bourgogne et de son Vignoble; La Journée Vinicole, Montpellier, 1955.

ARLOT, John and FIELDEN, Christopher
Burgundy, Vines and Wines; Davis-Poynter, London, 1976.

ARNOUX, Claude
Dissertation sur la Situation de Bourgogne; London 1728 (Facsimile edition published by Daniel Marcrette, Luzarches, 1978).

BAZIN, Jean-François
Le Clos-de-Vougeot, 1987.
Le Montrachet, 1988.
Chambertin, La Côte de Nuits de Dijon à Chambolle-Musigny, 1991.
La Romanée-Conti, La Côte de Nuits de Vosne-Romanée à Corgolin, 1994.
All in the series *Le Grand Bernard des Vins de France*, published by Jacques Legrand, Paris.

BEESTON, Fiona
The Wine Men; Sinclair, Stevenson, London 1991 (Bruno Clair and Jacky Confuron-Cotetidot).

BERTALL
La Vigne; Plon, Paris, 1878.

BLANCHET, Suzanne
Les Vins de Bourgogne; Editions Jéma, Marmonde, 1985.

BOURGUIGNON, Claude
Le Sol, La Terre et Les Champs; Editions Sang de la Terre, Paris, 1989.

BROADBENT, Michael
The Great Vintage Wine Book II; Mitchell Beazley, London, 1991.

CANNARD, Henri
Balades en Bourgogne; Dijon, 1988.

CHAPUIS, Claude
Corton, in the series *Le Grand Bernard des Vins de France*; Jacques Legrand, Paris, 1989.

COATES, Clive
The Wines of France; Century, 1991.

COURTÉPÉE, M. and BÉGUILLET, M.
Description Générale et Particulière du Duché de Bourgogne, 7 vols 1775–85; second edition in 4 vols, Dijon, 1848.

DANGUY, M. R. and AUBERTIN, M. Ch.
Les Grands Vins de Bourgogne: La Côte D'Or; H. Armand, Dijon, 1892.

DION, Prof. Roger
Histoire de la Vigne et du Vin en France des Origines au XIXème Siècle; Paris, 1959.

DROUOT, Henri
La Côte D'Or. (Publisher and date unknown.)

DUCOURNEAU, Alix and MONTEIL, Armand-Alexis
Bourgogne, Histoires des Abbayes, Communes et Châteaux; Paris, 1844. Reprint Belna Editions, Beaune, 1992.

DUIJKER, Hubrecht
Wijnwijzer Bourgogne; Het Spectrum, Utrecht, 1986.

DURAND, E. and GUICHARD, J.
La Culture de la Vigne en Côte D'Or; Arthur Batault, Beaune, 1896.

EYRES, Harry
Wine Dynasties of Europe; Lennard, 1990 (Jean Grivot).

FIELDEN, Christopher
White Burgundy; Christopher Helm, London, 1988.

FOURGEOT, Pierre
Origines du Vignoble Bourguignon; Presse Universitaire de France, Paris, 1972.

FRIED, Eunice
Burgundy, the Country, the Wines, the People; Harper and Row, New York, 1986.

GADILLE, Rolande
Le Vignoble de la Côte Bourguignonne; University of Dijon, 1967.

GWYNN, Stephen
Burgundy; Constable, London, 1934.

HALLIDAY, James and JOHNSON, Hugh
The Art and Science of Wine; Mitchell Beazley, London, 1992.

HANSON, Anthony
Burgundy; Faber and Faber, London, 1995.

HYAMS, Edward
Dionysus: a Social History of the Wine Vine; Thames and Hudson, London, 1965.

JEFFERSON, Thomas
Jefferson and Wine; E. R. de Treville Lawrence Sr, Vinifera Wine Growers Association, The Plains, VA, 1976.

JEUNET-HENRY, François (M. et Mme)
L'Historique de la Vigne et du Vin de Bourgogne Par la Chronologie et l'Anecdotique; La Pensée Universelle, Paris, 1994.

JOHNSON, Hugh
The World Atlas of Wine, 4th Edition; Mitchell Beazley, London, 1994.

JOHNSON, Hugh
Wine Companion, 3rd Edition; Mitchell Beazley, London, 1991.

JOHNSON, Hugh
The Story of Wine; Mitchell Beazley, London, 1989.

JULLIEN, A.
Topographie de Tous les Vignobles Connus; Paris, various editions from 1816 onwards.

KRAMER, Jane
Letter from Europe (article on Mme Monthélie-Douhairet); *The New Yorker*, 1 Jan. 1990.

KRAMER, Matt
Making Sense of Burgundy; William Morrow, New York, 1990.

LACHIVER, Marcel
Vins, Vignes et Vignerons: Histoire du Vignoble Français; Fayard, France, 1988.

LANDRIEU-LUSSIGNY, Marie-Hélène
Le Vignoble Bourguignon, Ses Lieux-Dits; Jeanne Laffitte, Marseille, 1983.

LAURENT, Robert
Les Vignerons de la Côte D'Or au XIX Siècle (2 vols); University of Dijon, 1958.

LAUTEL, Dr Robert
Terroirs des Bourgognes; Revue des Oenologues (date unknown).

LAVALLE, Dr Jean
Histoire et Statistique de la Vigne et des Grands Vins de la Côte D'Or; Dusacq, Paris, 1855.

LENEUF, Noël, MERIAUX S., CHRÉTIEN J. and VERNIN P.
La Côte Viticole, Ses Sols et Ses Crus; Extract from (?) Bourg (photocopy indistinct!), Tome 34 pp. 17-40, 1981.

LENEUF, Noël, LAUTET Robert and RAT, Pierre, in *Terroirs et Vins de France*, ed Charles Pomerol, Total-Editions-Presse, Paris, 1984.

LÉON-GAUTHIER, Pierre
Les Clos de Bourgogne; Librairie de la Renaissance, Beaune, 1931.

LOFTUS, Simon
Puligny-Montrachet: Journal of a Village in Burgundy; Ebury Press, London, 1992.

LUCHET, Auguste
La Côte D'Or; Levy, Paris, 1858.

LYNCH, Kermit
Adventures on the Wine Route; Farrer, Strauss and Giroux, New York, 1988.

MORELOT, Dr
Statistique de la Vigne dans le Département de la Côte d'Or; Dijon, Paris, 1831.

MOUCHERON, E. de,
Grands Crus de Bourgogne, Histoires et Traditions Vineuses; Dupin, Beaune, 1955.

NORMAN, Dr Remington
The Great Domaines of Burgundy; Kyle Cathie, London, 1992.

OLNEY, Richard
Romanée-Conti; Flammarion, Paris, 1991.

PARKER, Robert M. Jnr
Burgundy; Simon and Schuster, New York, 1990.

PEYNAUD, Emile (trans. Schuster, Michael)
The Taste of Wine; MacDonald Orbis, London, 1987.

PEYNAUD, Emile
Connaissance et Travail du Vin; Dunod, Paris, 1981.

PITIOT, Sylvain and POUGON, Pierre
Atlas des Grands Vignobles de Bourgogne (2 vols); Jacques Legrand, Paris, 1985.

REDDING, Cyrus
A History and Description of Modern Wines; London, 1833 and many editions thereafter.

ROBINSON, Jancis (ed)
The Oxford Companion to Wine; OUP, Oxford, 1994 (esp. contributions by Jasper Morris and Mark Savage on Burgundy, Mel Knox on barrels).

ROBINSON, Jancis
Vines, Grapes and Wines; Mitchell Beazley, London, 1986.

ROBINSON, Jancis
The Great Wine Book; Sidgwick and Jackson, London, 1982 (articles on Laguiche, Domaine de la Romanée-Conti, de Vogüé).

RODIER, Camille
Le Vin de Bourgogne; Dijon, various editions from 1921 onwards.

RODIER, Camille
Le Clos-de-Vougeot; Venot, Dijon, 1948.

ROUPNEL, Gaston
La Bourgogne; Paris, 1923.

ROZET, Georges
La Confrèrie des Chevaliers du Tastevin; Editions EPIC, Paris, 1950.

ROZET, Georges
La Bourgogne, Tastevin en Main; Horizons de France, Paris, 1949.

SADRIN, Paul and Anny
Meursault.
In the series *Le Grand Bernard des Vins de France*, Jacques Legrand, Paris, 1994.

SEWARD, Desmond
Monks and Wine; Mitchell Beazley, London, 1979.

SIMON, Joanna (ed)
Harrods Book of Fine Wine; Mitchell Beazley, London, 1990 (article on Drouhin by Serena Sutcliffe).

SUTCLIFFE, Serena with SCHUSTER, Michael
Guide to the Wines of Burgundy; Mitchell Beazley, 1992.

SUTCLIFFE, Serena (ed)
Great Vineyards and Wine Makers; MacDonald, London, 1982 (articles on Ampeau, Comte Armand, Bouchard Père et Fils, Clair-Daü, Dujac, Gouges, Louis Latour, Leflaive, Rousseau, Varoilles and de Vogüé).

VERGNELLE-LAMOTTE, A.
Mémoires sur la Viticulture et l'Oenologie de la Côte D'Or; Dijon, 1846.

VIENNE, H.
Essai Historique Sur la Ville de Nuits; Dijon, 1845. Reprint, Laffitte Reprints, Marseille, 1976.

WALLERAND, Jean-Claude and COULAIS, Christian
Bourgogne, Guide des Vins; Gilbert et Gaillard, Solar, France, 1992.

YOUNGER, William
Gods, Men and Wine; The International Wine and Food Society/Michael Joseph, London, 1966.

YOXALL, H. W.
The Wines of Burgundy; The International Wine and Food Society/Michael Joseph, London, 1968.

Appendix One

Rating the Vintages
(Out of 20)

	Red	White
1995	17.5	16.0
1994	14.5–13.0	13.5
1993	17.5	15.0
1992	14.0	15.5
1991	16.0	13.5
1990	18.5	16.5
1989	16.0	16.5
1988	17.0	14.5
1987	14.5	13.5
1986	14.5–12.0	16.5–13.5
1985	16.5	17.5
1984	13.0	(12.0)
1983	17.0–12.0	(13.5)
1982	14.5	16.0
1981	(12.0)	(11.0)
1980	16.0–13.0	(12.0)
1979	14.5	16.0
1978	15.5	15.5
1977	–	–
1976	14.5	(13.0)
1975	–	–
1974	–	–
1973	(14.0)	(15.5)
1972	15.0	(12.0)
1971	16.0	(18.0)
1970	(14.5)	(14.5)
1969	16.0	(17.0)
1968	–	–
1967	(14.5)	(15.0)
1966	16.0	(15.0)
1965	–	–
1964	17.5	(16.0)
1963	–	–
1962	16.0	(17.0)
1961	15.5	(16.0)
1960	–	–
1959	18.5	(17.5)
1957	16.0	(15.0)
1952	17.0	(16.5)
1949	19.0	(18.0)
1947	16.5	(15.0)
1945	18.5	(16.0)

–   Never of much consequence: now dead and buried

( ) Now old

Where alternative marks are given, this indicates a variation, either between the wines themselves or between one end of the Côte and the other. See the individual vintage assessments for further explanation.

Marks given out of 20

13.0 = Not bad
14.0 = Quite good
15.0 = Good
16.0 = Very good
17.0 = Very good indeed
18.0 = Fine plus
19.0 = Very fine indeed

Please note: In every vintage, however bad, the very best growers make surprisingly good wine. The reverse, sadly, is also true.

APPENDIX TWO

RATING THE VINEYARDS

THREE STAR

Red

Romanée-Conti
La Tâche
Richebourg
Romanée-Saint-Vivant
Grands-Echézeaux
Clos-de-Vougeot (top)
Le Musigny
Clos-de-la-Roche
Chambertin
Chambertin, Clos-de-Bèze
Mazis-Chambertin (*haut*)
Ruchottes-Chambertin (*bas*)
Corton, Clos-du-Roi

White

Le Montrachet
Chevalier-Montrachet
Corton-Charlemagne
(the *lieu-dit* Le Charlemagne
and the southerly part of
En Charlemagne)

TWO STAR

La Romanée
La Grande-Rue
Echézeaux
Clos-de-Vougeot (lower parts)
Bonnes-Mares
Clos-des-Lambrays
Clos-Saint-Denis
Chapelle-Chambertin
Charmes-Chambertin
Corton (except Clos-du-Roi)
Griottes-Chambertin
Latricières-Chambertin
Mazis-Chambertin (*bas*)
Mazoyères-Chambertin
Ruchottes-Chambertin (*haut*)
Gevrey-Chambertin, Clos-Saint-Jacques
Chambolle-Musigny, Les Amoureuses

Corton-Charlemagne (the rest)
Bâtard-Montrachet
Bienvenues-Bâtard-Montrachet
Criots-Bâtard-Montrachet
Clos-de-Tart
Meursault, Les Perrières (*dessous*)
Puligny-Montrachet, Les Caillerets

Gevrey-Chambertin:
   Les Cazetiers
   Estournelles-Saint-Jacques
   Lavaux–Saint-Jacques
   Les Combottes

Chambolle-Musigny:
   Les Fuées
   Les Cras
   La Combe-d'Orveau

Vosne-Romanée:
   Les Beaumonts (*bas*)
   Les Brûlées (north side)
   Les Suchots (upper section)
   Cros-Parentoux
   Les Malconsorts

Nuits-Saint-Georges:
   Aux Boudots
   Les Saint-Georges
   Les Vaucrains
   Les Cailles
   Les Porrets/Clos-des-Porrets

Pernand-Vergelesses:
   Ile-des-Vergelesses

Pommard:
   Les Petits-Epenots
   Les Rugiens (*bas*)

Volnay:
   Les Caillerets (*dessus*)
   Clos-des-Chênes
   Taille-Pieds
   Les Santenots-du-Milieu

Meursault:
   Les Genevrières (*dessous*)
   Les Charmes (*dessous*)
   Les Perrières (the rest)

Puligny-Montrachet:
   Les Combettes
   Les Perrières
   Les Pucelles
   Les Folatières (lower section)
   Clos-de-la-Garenne

Chassagne-Montrachet:
   Blanchot (*dessus*)
   En Remilly
   Les Caillerets
   La Grande-Montagne
   Les Grandes-Ruchottes
   La Romanée

APPENDIX THREE

RATING THE DOMAINES AND THE *NÉGOCIANTS*

★★★ THREE STAR

Comtes Lafon, Meursault
Leroy, Vosne-Romanée
Romanée-Conti, Vosne-Romanée
Armand Rousseau, Gevrey-Chambertin
De Vogüé, Chambolle-Musigny

★★ TWO STAR

D'Angerville, Volnay
Comte Armand, Pommard
Auvenay, Auxey-Duresses
Coche-Dury, Meursault
J. J. Confuron, Nuits-Saint-Georges, Prémeaux
Drouhin, Beaune
Dujac, Morey-Saint-Denis
Engel, Vosne-Romanée
Faiveley, Nuits-Saint-Georges
Gouges, Nuits-Saint-Georges
Grivot, Vosne-Romanée
Jadot, Beaune
Henri Jayer, Vosne-Romanée
(for the wines made up to his retirement) and Emmanuel Rouget, Flagey-Echézeaux
Lafarge, Volnay
Maison Leroy, Auxey-Duresses (up to 1988 – since superseded by the Domaine – see above)
Méo-Camuzet, Vosne-Romanée
H. de Montille, Volnay
Denis Mortet, Gevrey-Chambertin
Georges Mugneret/Mugneret-Gibourg, Vosne-Romanée
J. Frédéric Mugnier, Chambolle-Musigny
Ramonet, Chassagne-Montrachet
Georges Roumier, Chambolle-Musigny

★ ONE STAR

Côte-de-Nuits
Arlot, Nuits-Saint-Georges, Prémeaux
Robert Arnoux, Vosne-Romanée
Denis Bachelet, Gevrey-Chambertin
Ghislaine Barthod-Noëllat, Chambolle-Musigny
Alain Burguet, Gevrey-Chambertin
Sylvain Cathiard, Vosne-Romanée
Jean Chauvenet, Nuits-Saint-Georges

Robert Chevillon, Nuits-Saint-Georges
Bruno Clair, Marsannay
Bruno Clavelier, Vosne-Romanée
Jacky Confuron-Cotétidot, Vosne-Romanée
Claude Dugat, Gevrey-Chambertin
Bernard Dugat-Py, Gevrey-Chambertin
André Esmonin, Gevrey-Chambertin
Michel Esmonin et Fille, Gevrey-Chambertin
Régis Forey, Vosne-Romanée
Robert Groffier, Morey-St-Denis
Anne (and François) Gros, Vosne-Romanée
Jean and Michel Gros, Vosne-Romanée
Alain Hudelot-Noëllat, Vougeot
Gérard Mugneret, Vosne-Romanée
Philippe Naddef, Couchey
Henri Perrot-Minot, Morey-Saint-Denis
Ponsot, Morey-Saint-Denis
Daniel Rion et Fils, Nuits-Saint-Georges, Prémeaux
Joseph Roty, Gevrey-Chambertin
Christian Serafin, Gevrey-Chambertin
Thomas-Moillard, Nuits-Saint-Georges

Côte-de-Beaune
Robert Ampeau et Fils, Meursault
Simon Bize et Fils, Savigny-lès-Beaune
Jean-Marc Boillot, Pommard
Bonneau du Martray, Pernand-Vergelesses
Michel Bouzereau et Fils, Meursault
Yves Boyer-Martenot, Meursault
Louis Carillon et Fils, Puligny-Montrachet
Chandon de Briailles, Savigny-lès-Beaune
Château de Chorey-lès-Beaune, Chorey-lès-Beaune
Colin-Deléger, Chassagne-Montrachet
Courcel, Pommard
Didier Darviot-Perrin, Monthélie
Jean-Noël Gagnard, Chassagne-Montrachet
Gagnard-Delagrange, Chassagne-Montrachet
Vincent Girardin, Santenay
Patrick Javillier, Meursault
François Jobard, Meursault
Leflaive, Puligny-Montrachet
Olivier Leflaive Frères, Puligny-Montrachet
Matrot, Meursault
Prince Florent de Mérode, Serrigny
Pierre Morey, Meursault
Albert Morot, Beaune
Michel Niellon, Chassagne-Montrachet
Paul Pernot et Fils, Puligny-Montrachet
Jean and Jean-Marc Pillot, Chassagne-Montrachet

Pousse d'Or, Volnay
Remoissenet Père et Fils, Beaune
Guy Roulot, Meursault
Étienne Sauzet, Puligny-Montrachet
Comte Senard, Aloxe-Corton

Outside the Côte d'Or

Michel Juillot, Mercurey
Rodet, Mercurey
Maison Verget, Sologny, Mâconnais

APPENDIX FOUR

CÔTE D'OR

THE SIZE OF THE CROP

Hectolitres, excluding generic wine

		Red	White	Total
1995	*Grands Crus*	11,720	3,286	15,006
	Village and *Premiers Crus*	173,727	46,575	220,302
	TOTAL	**185,447**	**49,861**	**235,308**
1994	*Grands Crus*	12,605	3,504	16,109
	Village and *Premiers Crus*	183,337	50,549	233,886
	TOTAL	**195,942**	**54,053**	**249,995**
1993	*Grands Crus*	11,895	3,577	15,472
	Village and *Premiers Crus*	181,477	49,681	231,158
	TOTAL	**193,372**	**53,258**	**246,630**
1992	*Grands Crus*	13,278	3,600	16,878
	Village and *Premiers Crus*	182,261	48,606	230,867
	TOTAL	**195,539**	**52,206**	**247,745**
1991	*Grands Crus*	10,855	3,476	14,331
	Village and *Premiers Crus*	166,380	45,104	211,484
	TOTAL	**177,235**	**48,580**	**225,815**
1990	*Grands Crus*	14,117	3,668	17,785
	Village and *Premiers Crus*	188,573	51,926	240,499
	TOTAL	**202,690**	**55,594**	**258,284**

		Red	White	Total
1989	*Grands Crus*	12,673	3,238	15,911
	Village and *Premiers Crus*	17,8971	41,573	220,544
	TOTAL	**191,644**	**44,811**	**236,455**
1988	*Grands Crus*	12,797	3,533	16,330
	Village and *Premiers Crus*	170,056	46,434	216,490
	TOTAL	**182,853**	**49,967**	**232,820**
1987	*Grands Crus*	11,018	2,785	13,803
	Village and *Premiers Crus*	159,322	36,593	195,915
	TOTAL	**170,340**	**39,378**	**209,718**
1986	*Grands Crus*	14,877	2,957	17,834
	Village and *Premiers Crus*	19,7856	48,302	246,158
	TOTAL	**212,733**	**51,259**	**263,992**
1985	*Grands Crus*	9,699	2,506	12,205
	Village and *Premiers Crus*	129,445	44,066	173,511
	TOTAL	**139,144**	**46,572**	**185,716**
1984	*Grands Crus*	8,939	1,902	10,841
	Village and *Premiers Crus*	123,492	31,815	155,307
	TOTAL	**132,431**	**33,717**	**166,148**
1983	*Grands Crus*	11,955	3,038	14,993
	Village and *Premiers Crus*	143,435	36,527	179,962
	TOTAL	**155,390**	**39,565**	**194,955**
1982	*Grands Crus*	17,933	4,002	21,935
	Village and *Premiers Crus*	233,894	53,397	287,291
	TOTAL	**251,827**	**57,399**	**309,226**

		Red	White	Total
1981	*Grands Crus*	7,115	1,859	8,974
	Village and *Premiers Crus*	83,685	25,036	108,721
	TOTAL	**90,800**	**26,895**	**117,695**
1980	*Grands Crus*	9,959	2,518	12,477
	Village and *Premiers Crus*	141,410	35,023	176,433
	TOTAL	**151,369**	**37,541**	**188,910**
1979	*Grands Crus*	10,630	2,796	13,426
	Village and *Premiers Crus*	148,905	45,007	193,912
	TOTAL	**159,535**	**47,803**	**207,338**
1978	*Grands Crus*	8,546	2,103	10,649
	Village and *Premiers Crus*	115,606	29,670	145,276
	TOTAL	**124,152**	**31,773**	**155,925**
1977	*Grands Crus*	11,413	2,191	13,604
	Village and *Premiers Crus*	138,156	35,375	173,531
	TOTAL	**149,569**	**37,566**	**187,135**
1976	*Grands Crus*	11,146	2,012	13,158
	Village and *Premiers Crus*	142,613	28,077	170,690
	TOTAL	**153,759**	**30,089**	**183,848**
1975	*Grands Crus*	7,451	1,680	9,131
	Village and *Premiers Crus*	87,971	18,354	106,325
	TOTAL	**95,422**	**20,034**	**115,456**
1974	*Grands Crus*	10,090	2,064	12,154
	Village and *Premiers Crus*	115,498	22,590	138,088
	TOTAL	**125,588**	**24,654**	**150,242**

		Red	White	Total
1973	*Grands Crus*	12,758	2,801	15,559
	Village and *Premiers Crus*	156,857	33,404	190,261
	TOTAL	**169,615**	**36,205**	**205,820**
1972	*Grands Crus*	12,273	2,216	14,489
	Village and *Premiers Crus*	147,956	28,292	176,248
	TOTAL	**160,229**	**30,508**	**190,737**
1971	*Grands Crus*	7,533	1,527	9,060
	Village and *Premiers Crus*	83,926	17,674	101,600
	TOTAL	**91,459**	**19,201**	**110,660**
1970	*Grands Crus*	12,756	2,356	15,112
	Village and *Premiers Crus*	141,018	27,985	169,003
	TOTAL	**153,774**	**30,341**	**184,115**
1969	*Grands Crus*	8,084	1,499	9,583
	Village and *Premiers Crus*	92,673	19,759	112,432
	TOTAL	**100,757**	**21,258**	**122,015**
1967	*Grands Crus*	9,931	1,617	11,548
	Village and *Premiers Crus*	102,061	15,717	117,778
	TOTAL	**111,992**	**17,334**	**129,326**
1966	*Grands Crus*	10,682	2,146	12,828
	Village and *Premiers Crus*	115,134	27,070	142,204
	TOTAL	**125,816**	**29,216**	**155,032**
1964	*Grands Crus*	12,168	2,047	14,215
	Village and *Premiers Crus*	117,095	24,900	141,995
	TOTAL	**129,263**	**26,947**	**156,210**

		Red	White	Total
1962	*Grands Crus*	9,870	1,592	11,462
	Village and *Premiers Crus*	100,089	20,197	120,286
	TOTAL	**109,959**	**21,789**	**131,748**
1961	*Grands Crus*	7,496	1,365	8,861
	Village and *Premiers Crus*	76,182	16,943	93,125
	TOTAL	**83,678**	**18,308**	**101,986**
1959	*Grands Crus*	7,255	1,836	9,091
	Village and *Premiers Crus*	108,722	23,321	132,043
	TOTAL	**115,977**	**25,157**	**141,134**
1957	*Grands Crus*	6,374	914	7,288
	Village and *Premiers Crus*	54,225	9,118	63,343
	TOTAL	**60,599**	**10,032**	**70,631**
1952	*Grands Crus*	6,845	1,184	8,029
	Village and *Premiers Crus*	61,509	12,991	74,500
	TOTAL	**68,354**	**14,175**	**82,529**
1949	*Grands Crus*	5,620	759	6,379
	Village and *Premiers Crus*	47,567	8,196	55,763
	TOTAL	**53,187**	**8,955**	**62,142**

NB These figures do not include the yields from Maranges, which is outside the Côte d'Or in the Saône et Loire *département*. Statistics prior to 1949 are not available.

Sadly the statistics I have been able to obtain for the older vintages do not allow me to parallel these production figures with surface areas. The areas producing generic and non-generic wine are not separated. However in 1949 a total of 8,980 ha was under production in the Côte d'Or. This is uncannily close to the area in 1995: 8,970 ha of which 5,531 ha produced village, *premier* and *grand cru*, and 3,439 ha produced generic wine. (See appendix 5.)

APPENDIX FIVE

CÔTE D'OR

SURFACE AREAS – A SUMMARY

(Hectares, excluding generic wines)

CÔTE-DE-BEAUNE	**1995**
VILLAGE A.C. ROUGE	1520
VILLAGE A.C. BLANC	639
PREMIER CRU ROUGE	967
PREMIER CRU BLANC	391
GRAND CRU ROUGE	99
GRAND CRU BLANC	84
TOTAL CÔTE-DE-BEAUNE	**3700**
CÔTE-DE-NUITS	
VILLAGE A.C. ROUGE	1089
VILLAGE A.C. ROSE	57
VILLAGE A.C. BLANC	32
PREMIER CRU ROUGE	381
PREMIER CRU BLANC	7
GRAND CRU ROUGE	264
GRAND CRU BLANC	1
TOTAL CÔTE-DE-NUITS	**1831**
TOTAL	
VILLAGE A.C. ROUGE	2610
VILLAGE A.C. ROSE	57
VILLAGE A.C. BLANC	670
TOTAL VILLAGE A.C.	**3337**
PREMIER CRU ROUGE	1347
PREMIER CRU BLANC	397
TOTAL PREMIER CRU	**1744**

(divided by 476 *premiers crus* equals 3.66ha per *climat*)

GRAND CRU ROUGE	363
GRAND CRU BLANC	84
TOTAL GRAND CRU	**447**

(divided by 32 *grands crus* equals 13.97ha per *climat*)

TOTAL ROUGE	**4320**
TOTAL ROSE	**57**
TOTAL BLANC	**1154**
TOTAL SURFACE AREA	**5531**

APPENDIX SIX

MEASUREMENTS AND CONVERSION TABLES

SURFACE AREA

1 hectare = 100 ares = 10,000 sq metres = 2.471 acres.

One *ouvrée* corresponds to the amount of land one worker can cultivate by hand in one day. It measures 4.285 ares.

One *journal* (plural *journeaux*) is the equivalent of the area one worker can cultivate per day with the help of a horse and plough. A *journal* equals 8 *ouvrées*. There are 2.92 *journeaux* per hectare.

CAPACITY

1 hectolitre = 100 litres = 22 gallons = 133.3 bottles = 11.1 cases.

1 Burgundian *pièce* = 228 litres = 304 bottles = 25.33 cases.

A *feuillette* is a half-size cask; a *quartaut* a quarter-size cask. A *queue* is two *pièces*, a *tonneau* four.

YIELD

In general one vine will yield one bottle of wine.

In most vintages 10 plastic containers of 30 kilos each (300kg) will produce one *pièce* (228 litres) of wine. Sometimes the fruit contains less juice, in which instance 12 or 13 containers (360–390kg) are required.

Most of the best growers aim to produce a maximum of three-quarters of a *pièce* per *ouvrée* (18 *pièces* per hectare) for village wine (39.91 hl/ha) and proportionately less for their better wines. One *pièce* per *ouvrée* (53.22 hl/ha) is considered excessive.

The law normally allows (*rendement de base* plus 20 per cent PLC) a maximum of 42 hl/ha for *grand cru rouge*, 48 hl/ha for *grand cru blanc*, and 48 hl/ha (*rouge*) and 54 hl/ha (*blanc*) respectively for village and *premier cru*, red and white.

Given a yield of one *pièce* per 300 kilos of fruit, one ton per acre is equivalent to 19.08 hl/ha.

INDEX

French articles and prepositions preceding names or within names (such as the many entries under *Clos*) are printed in the normal way but are ignored for purposes of alphabeticization. Thus, Les Charmes is indexed under C.

Page references in **bold type** indicate the entry's principal reference or references. Abbreviations: Dom. = Domaine; fam. = family.

Trapet, François, 69, **85**

Trapet, Jean and Jean-Louis, 65, 67, 68, **85**

Les Travers-de-Marinot, 297

triage, 31-2

Truchot-Martin fam., 67

La Truffière, 273, 276

Les Tuvilains, 201, 203

Union Générale de Syndicats, 48

Vachet-Rousseau Père et Fils, 69, 70, **85-6**

Vadey-Castagnier fam., 68, 69

Vadey-Rameau, Gilbert, 95-6

Val Vergy, Dom. du, 163

Les Vallerots, 144, 147

Les Valozières, 176, 178

Les Varoilles, 67

Varoilles fam., 86, 105

Les Vaucrains, 144, 147-8, 458-9

Vaudoisey, Christophe, 233

Vaudoisey-Martin, Bernard, 218, **233**

Les Vercots, 176, 178

Aux Vergelesses, 189, 344-5

Les Vergelesses, 181, 183, 189

Vergelesses, Dom. des, 180

Les Vergers, 286-7, 401-2, 443-6

Verget Sarl, Dom. *(Sologny, Mâconnais)*, 312

Les Véroilles, 107

En Verseuil, 227, 228-9

Vide-Bourse, 286

Vieilles-Vignes, 571-2, 576-7

Vigne-Blanche; Chassagne-Montrachet, 286, 288; Le Clos-Blanc, 114, 117

Vigne-Derrière, 286

La Vigne-de-l'Enfant-Jésus, 17, 201, 354-6

Les Vignes-Blanches, 227

Les Vignes-Franches, 201, 204

Vignes-Moingeon, 297

Les (Aux) Vignes-Rondes, 143, 145-6, 236, 237

Les Vignots, 532

Vigot, Fabrice, 137-9

Vigot-Battault, Thierry, 125, 127, **164**

Le Village; Monthélie, 236; Morey-Saint-Denis, 94; Pommard, 216; Saint-Auban, 297; Volnay, 227

De Villaine, Aubert, 599-600

De Villamont, Henri, 125

vineyards; rating, 984; spelling names, 46

viniculture, *see* élevage; red wine-making: triage; white wine-making

vintages, 41-2, 43, 983-4

Virely-Rougeot fam., 222-3

En Virondot, 286

viticulture, 26-33; bio-dynamism, 27, 134, 529-30; clonal selection, 27-8; diseases, 31; erosion, 28; leaf canopy, 29; machine harvesting, 31-2; pruning and training, 29-30; rootstock, 28; soil

preparation, 26-7; spacing of vines, 28

Voarick, Michel, 171, **180-81**

Voegeli, Alain, 86

De Vogüé, Comte George, Dom. *(Chambolle-Musigny)*, 104, 105, 106, **110-11**, **651-6**

Voillot, Joseph, **233**

En-Vollon-à-l'Est, 297

Volnay, 18, **224-33**, 320, 321-5, 504-9, 525-6, 531-2, 545-9, 578-84

Volpato, Léni, 111

Vosne-Romanée, **119-40**, 423-9, 477, 483, 495-9, 527-34, 540-44, 563-7, 594-5, 596-608, 638-40

Vougeot, 35, **112-18**, 480-83, 646-50, *see also* Clos-de-Vougeot

white wine-making; fermentation, 37; premier cru, 58; pressing, 37; skin contact, 36-7

wine-writers, 20-22

yeasts, 35